The Christmas Encyclopedia

Second Edition

The Christmas Encyclopedia

Second Edition

William D. Crump

McFarland & Company, Inc., Publishers
Jefferson, North Carolina, and London

Frontispiece: Engraving from the 1880s after a work by an artist identified as "Minthrop." From Charles Wesley, *Hark! The Herald Angels Sing* (New York: Dutton, 1889).

Illustration research and selection by Linda Campbell Franklin

Library of Congress Cataloguing-in-Publication Data

Crump, William D., 1949–
    The Christmas encyclopedia / by William D. Crump.— 2nd ed.
        p.   cm.
    Includes bibliographical references and index.

    ISBN 0-7864-2293-9 (illustrated case binding : 50# alkaline paper) ∞

    1. Christmas— Encyclopedias.   I. Title.
GT4985.C74   2006
394.2663'03 — dc22   2005025349

British Library cataloguing data are available

Cover image ©2005 BananaStock

Manufactured in the United States of America

McFarland & Company, Inc., Publishers
    Box 611, Jefferson, North Carolina 28640
        www.mcfarlandpub.com

Contents

Acknowledgments   vii
Preface   ix

The Encyclopedia   1

References   447
Index   455

This volume is dedicated to the
Lord of Christmas
and to all who keep Christmas in their hearts
the year round

Acknowledgments

The Second Edition

In addition to those who made valuable contributions to the first edition, grateful appreciation is extended to the following for their equally valuable assistance with the second edition: the George Bush Presidential Library, College Station, Texas (Mary Finch, audiovisual archivist); Manfred W.K. Fischer of the *Stille Nacht Gesellschaft* in Austria and Christmas historian Bill Egan, who provided helpful comments about the entry **Silent Night**; the Library of Congress Photoduplication Service, Washington, D.C.; Archbishop Gabriel Montalvo, Apostolic Nuncio, Apostolic Nunciature of the United States of America, Washington, D.C.; Press Office of the Holy See, the Vatican (Joy Stellato Gabrielli); the Ronald Reagan Presidential Library, Simi Valley, California (Josh Tenenbaum, audiovisual archivist); the White House, Washington, D.C. (William G. Allman, curator); and the White House Historical Association, Washington, D.C. (William Bushong, historian and webmaster).

I give special thanks to the following for donating photographs from their collections with permission to reproduce them in this edition: Diane Burt D'Amico of Variety Artists for donating a photograph of her father, Alfred S. Burt; Steve Cooper, Chrismons secretary at Ascension Lutheran Church, Danville, Virginia (who also provided helpful comments about the entry **Chrismons Tree**), and photographer Hugh Preston Leonard of Winston-Salem, North Carolina, for donating a photograph of a Chrismons tree; Gil Frank and the Candle Tea, sponsored by the Women's Fellowship of Home Moravian Church, Winston-Salem, North Carolina, for donating a photograph of the Manger Scene from the 2001 Candle Tea Nativity *Putz*.

Grateful appreciation is also extended to the following institutions and organizations, which granted permission to reproduce photographs or copyrighted material from their collections: the American Society of Composers, Authors and Publishers (ASCAP) (Phil Crosland, vice-president, marketing), for "Top 25 Holiday Songs of the [20th] Century" and "Top 25 Holiday Songs List"; the Andover-Harvard Theological Library of Harvard Divinity School, Harvard University, Cambridge, Massachusetts (Frances O'Donnell, curator of archives and manuscripts), for a photograph of the Rev. Edmund Hamilton Sears; the Boston Public Library Print Department (Aaron Schmidt, photo collection), for a photograph of the Rev. Phillips Brooks; the Georgia Historical Society, Savannah, Georgia (Susan Dick Hoffius, director of library and archives, and Mandi D. Johnson, visual materials archivist), for a photograph of James Lord Pierpont; the Newberry Library, Chicago (John Powell, permissions officer), for a photograph of an 1804 manuscript of "Adeste Fideles"; the Vermont Historical Society, Barre, Vermont (Paul Carnahan, librarian), for a photograph of the Rev. John Henry Hopkins, Jr.; and the Tourist Association of Oberndorf, Austria (Christine Deutinger), for a postcard portrait of Franz Xaver Gruber.

I also give special thanks to my sister, Julie Crump Pugh, for assistance in preparing the manuscript.

The First Edition

I extend grateful appreciation to the following individuals and institutions for contributing valuable information or assistance in the preparation of this manuscript: American Society of Composers, Authors and Publishers (ASCAP), for granting permission to reproduce its list of the "Top 25 Holiday Songs of the [20th] Century"; Jennifer Anthony, visiting assistant professor, Music Library, University of Illinois at Urbana-Champaign; Josip Barlek, professor and higher curator, Ethnographic Museum, Zagreb, Croatia; John Whit Curtis, for his assistance with the entry **Beautiful Star of Bethlehem**; Diane deBlois, Public Affairs Office, Canadian Consulate General, Atlanta, Georgia; Father Krikor Maksoudian, director, Krikor and Clara Zohrab Information Center, Diocese of the Armenian Church of America, New York City; the Institute of Ethnology and Folklore, Zagreb, Croatia, which provided the hardcover book *Christmas in Croatia*; Peter McInally, British Information Services, New York City; Linet Mavesere, curator of Ethnography, Zimbabwe Museum of Human Sciences, Zimbabwe, Africa; Creighton Pencheon, Ag Director of Culture in the Ministry of Culture, Youth and Sports, Basseterre, St. Kitts, West Indies; Julie Crump Pugh; Ronnie Pugh, Country Music Foundation, Nashville, Tennessee; Richard Starbuck, director, Archives of the Moravian Church in America, Southern Province, Winston-Salem, North Carolina.

Grateful appreciation is also extended to Linda Campbell Franklin for illustration research.

I also would like to thank the following foreign embassies in Washington, D.C., for providing summaries of Christmas traditions and customs in their respective countries: Austria, Barbados, Brazil (Philip Dimitrov, ambassador), Colombia (Assad Jater, cultural attaché), Czech Republic, Denmark (Sarah L. Rothmann, information officer), Ecuador (Jorge Saade-Scaff, cultural and press attaché), Ethiopia, Fiji (Lele Vosailagi), Finland, France, Greece, Guyana (Annette Carter-Harris, executive officer), Iceland, Indonesia (Puspita Sariwati), Ireland, Italy, Japan, Latvia (Sandija Macane), Lebanon (Wajdi Najjar), Lithuania, Netherlands, Norway, Poland, Sierra Leone (J.G. Caulker, first secretary), Sweden, Switzerland (C. Cadem), Ukraine (Irene Datsenko, librarian), Venezuela (Karl Krispin, cultural attaché).

Preface

The Second Edition

Continuing in the format of its predecessor, the second edition adds 120 new entries, thus expanding *The Christmas Encyclopedia* to more than 480 entries. All of the original entries have been retained. A number of historic photographs have been added to complement the original drawings. Although various portions of text from the first edition have been rewritten to enhance clarity, nearly 60 of the original entries have been updated as new information surfaced. Several entries from the first edition have been divided into smaller entries to facilitate easier location of subject matter. For example, whereas the history of the song "Rudolph, the Red-Nosed Reindeer" formerly resided within a larger entry dealing with the origins of the Rudolph character and his creator Robert May, the song and the character are now discussed as two separate entries. Some subjects have been moved to more appropriate locations. For example, whereas the National Christmas Tree and the Nation's Christmas Tree were formerly discussed as two subheadings within the larger, generic entry **Christmas Tree**, they are now subheadings within the entry **United States**.

Video information for motion pictures, television specials, and animated cartoons has been updated to reflect the availability on DVD or alternatively on VHS if not on DVD. Unless otherwise indicated, all film titles originate in the United States and are photographed in color; the designation "B & W" notes photography in black and white.

Most of the references to books and periodicals from the first edition have been retained because of the unchanging information inherent with long-established traditions and literary works. New references include those that pertain to the new entries, and updates of reference texts reflect the latest editions as applicable. Internet references have been extensively updated. Although web sites may disappear from the Internet without warning, as of mid–2005, all references to the Internet reflect active web sites; those no longer online that were listed in the previous edition have been removed and suitable replacements found.

The First Edition

The search for "Christmas Past and Present" began in 1994, when my family made a three-hour audio cassette tape as a holiday project. We collected the best renditions of sacred and secular carols that we could find, recited carol poems, and attempted to sing a few ourselves. We also wanted to include short background sketches about the carols, while the finale would include a segment that detailed the origins of popular Christmas symbols and traditions. Of course, we, like so many other families, had blindly carried on these traditions without knowing exactly why we did, and it was time to change that. So off I headed to the library.

I managed to compile sufficient facts to complete the family project. Gleaning them, however, was an education in itself.

To say that the subject of Christmas is vast is a gross understatement. It is astronomical. After all, from the manger to the space age, we have 2,000 years of holiday history, music, traditions, personages, stories, legends, and symbols with which to contend, and all on an international level. Out of all this subject matter, most Christmas books concentrate on just a few facts or themes, requiring persons with more than a passing interest, or Christmas "addicts" like myself, to peruse scores of volumes and other media in order to receive a comprehensive Christmas education. A similar scenario exists when one enters the world of Christmas on the Internet.

It is not difficult to imagine that the average reader (with a passing interest but with no desire to wade through multiple tomes) would most likely shy away from such a formidable holiday arsenal. How, then, could readers become better acquainted with the complete "who, what, when, where, why, and how" of Christmas, and have it all wrapped up in a single, convenient package?

This volume was conceived with just this goal in mind. From a multitude of Christmas sources (reference texts, novels, children's books, poems, anecdotes, short stories, magazine reprints, songbooks, record and compact disc liner notes, videocassettes, and the Internet), this book concisely compiles and reviews essential and fanciful subjects that provide a solid foundation for understanding and appreciating the holiday from every aspect. However, had I attempted to include every facet of Christmas that has ever appeared in print or in the entertainment media since the foundation of Christmas itself, there would have been no end to this book. Therefore, the entries herein are those that have remained Christmas treasures through popular association and usage over decades and sometimes centuries.

This volume contains more than 340 entries, the bulk of which place strong emphasis on Christmas as depicted in the popular media. Among the subjects of the entries are individual carols and songs, motion pictures, nonanimated television specials, animated cartoons, Christmas episodes of television series, literary subjects, and celebrations around the world. Also covered are familiar aspects of the holiday

such as biblical and secular events that have shaped Christmas in history; St. Nicholas, Santa Claus, and other mythical spirits who bring gifts; and symbols such as the Yule log, Christmas tree, holly, ivy, and mistletoe.

Because not every country celebrates Christmas, I have included entries for those nations and regions in which Christianity has been most influential. Some foreign countries stand as individual entries, whereas others are grouped together under larger headings (including, for example, "Africa," "Baltic States," "Central America," and "South America") because of their geographic proximity or their similar customs. I also include the phrase for "Merry Christmas" in the official or principal language of each country.

In a few instances, the principal text for a custom common to a group of countries may appear as a separate entry with appropriate cross-referencing. For example, the entry Las Posadas ("The Lodgings") discusses a popular custom found in many Latin American countries.

Whereas traditions may evolve over the centuries, the discussions concentrate on customs currently in vogue. It is not the purpose of this book to render detailed accounts and histories of archaic customs long abandoned, except where they have significantly affected current practices.

Entries appear alphabetically throughout with extensive cross-referencing. Terms not found as cross-references may be accessible through the index. In general, foreign words appear as principal headings or cross-references only when they name a major custom, event, or item. When incidental foreign words appear within the body of an entry but do not form a part of the heading itself, they are listed only in the index.

Entries for motion pictures, television specials, and cartoons include production credits (principal actors, year released, writers, producers, directors, production companies, video companies, color format, and running times) if such are available. Not all film titles appear on video, titles may appear on alternate or additional video labels than those cited herein, and studios may withdraw previously released titles from the video market at any time. Therefore the designation "Video N/A" means either that a video version does not yet exist or that specific video information was simply unavailable at this writing. All videos cited are in VHS format, and the designation "B & W" indicates that a film is photographed in black and white.

References are listed at the end of this work and include books, periodicals, sound recordings, and Internet sources.

I received considerable information from foreign embassies in Washington, D.C., and directly from some sources overseas regarding international Christmas customs. Most of these sources provided either photocopied material or firsthand accounts that had been written by embassy staff, an ambassador, or some other authority. All identifiable media sources from this collection are listed with the references.

All biblical quotations are taken from the King James Version.

A

Account of a Visit from St. Nicholas
See **A Visit from St. Nicholas**

Adeste Fideles
See **O Come, All Ye Faithful**

Advent

Derived from the Latin *adventus* ("coming"), the four-week period prior to Christmas Day observed chiefly by the Roman Catholic, Lutheran, Anglican, and Episcopal churches. Advent commences on the Sunday nearest November 30 (St. Andrew the Apostle's Day) and terminates on Christmas Eve. It is a time in which believers are to undergo spiritual cleansing and sometimes fasting in preparation for the Feast of the Nativity, or Christmas.

Although legend holds that an Advent season originated with the Apostle Peter in the first century, the exact time when Advent was first introduced into the Church remains obscure. Early evidence vaguely referring to an Advent period includes the Acts of the Synod of Saragossa (year 380); the writings of St. Maximus, bishop of Turin (415–466), and those of St. Caesarius, bishop of Arles (502–542); and documents of the Synod of Lerida, Spain (542), and the Council of Tours, France (567). The Synod of Mâcon in Gaul (581) specified the period from November 11 to Christmas Day, while homilies of Pope St. Gregory the Great (590–604) only included a sermon for a second Advent Sunday. By 650 in Spain, Advent spanned the five Sundays before Christmas Day, but Pope St. Gregory VII (1073–1085) reduced these to four Sundays instead, and this number has remained constant since then.

While Advent probably was well established by the sixth century in the Western Church, no evidence for its observance in the Orthodox, or Eastern, Church appeared until the eighth century. Even then, instead of joyous anticipation, a mood similar to Easter Lent prevailed, for the Orthodox pre–Christmas period consisted of fasting and abstinence for 40 days, from November 15 to Christmas Day, which commemorated Christ's fast of 40 days in the wilderness. Today, except for the fast, there is no special Advent liturgy in the Orthodox Church. Advent begins the ecclesiastical year in the Eastern and Western churches.

Advent focuses on the four great "comings" of Christ: His coming in the flesh, His coming into the hearts of all who believe in Him, His coming at the hour of death to the faithful, and His coming at the final judgment. Advent colors are blue, symbolic of the Virgin Mary's robe, and purple, symbolic of the penance and spiritual cleansing of the season. In the Roman Catholic and Anglican churches, the color scheme changes to rose on the third Advent Sunday, termed "*Gaudete* Sunday" from the first word of the Introit of the Mass, *Gaudete* (Latin imperative, "Rejoice!"). Hence, this Sunday introduces the theme of joy in Christ and at His coming. The church, previously unadorned in this season, may be decked with flowers on this day and the organ, previously silent, may be played.

Advent wreaths and candles adorn churches and homes alike. Attributed to Martin Luther (1483–1546), a German priest who initiated the Protestant Reformation, Advent wreaths are fashioned from various species of evergreen branches and are either hung from the ceiling or used as table centerpieces. Affixed to the wreath are four candles, each one representing an Advent Sunday. Three candles are purple (for penance) and one is pink (for the coming joy), although some wreaths sport all red candles (symbolic of Christ's blood) or all white candles (symbolic of Christ's purity). The evergreen wreath itself, forming a never-ending circle, symbolizes the promise of eternal life through Christ.

Churches and families successively light one candle on the first Advent Sunday, two the following Sunday, and so on, starting with the purple candles and ending with the pink candle on the fourth Sunday, when all the candles burn. Each lighting provides families with an opportunity to convene for quiet devotions. On Christmas Day, a large red candle can be added, representing Christ.

A variation on this theme is the single Advent candle with the numbers 1 through 25 stamped into the wax. The candle is lit on December 1, allowed to burn down to the number 1, then extinguished. The process is repeated daily, allowing the candle to burn to the corresponding day until Christmas Day.

In some areas of Europe, it is customary for someone named John or Joan to light the Advent wreath, for the Gospel of John describes Christ as the Light of the World, symbolized by the burning candles. The custom may also stem from a legend stating that John the Baptist first beheld a halo around Christ following His baptism.

Designed especially for children, Advent calendars and Advent houses portray behind little flaps sacred or secular holiday themes for each day from December 1 through December 25. On opening each flap, children may find a Bible verse or character, a winter scene, or a small toy or money. On Christmas Day, the final flap reveals either the Nativity scene with the Holy Family or Santa and his reindeer.

During the Advent season, churches additionally observe the feast days of certain saints or other religious events as described below. Although a nation's opening date for its "Christmas season" may not always coincide with the commencement of Advent, the date is usually found among the following:

• ST. ANDREW'S DAY (November 30). One of Christ's 12 apostles, St. Andrew by tradition received martyrdom through crucifixion on an X-shaped cross (now known as St. Andrew's cross) on the island of Patmos. He is a patron saint of Scotland and Russia.

• ST. BARBARA'S DAY (December 4). Legend holds that the third-century martyr St. Barbara converted to Christianity after her father, de-

siring to protect her from the world, confined her to a tower in what is now Ismit (formerly Nicomedia), Turkey. Subsequently beheading her for her faith, the father was struck and killed by lightning, for which St. Barbara became associated with storms. She is the patron saint of artillery. Although the Roman Catholic Church dropped St. Barbara from the church calendar in 1969, there remains a tradition throughout Europe wherein girls place cherry tree branches ("Barbara branches") in water indoors on this day. If buds bloom by Christmas Eve, the girls will wed within the new year.

• ST. NICHOLAS'S DAY (December 6). This holiday honoring the fourth-century archbishop of Myra (now Demre), Turkey, is celebrated widely throughout Europe. It is probably the most popular of Advent feast days and is detailed further in a separate entry. *See also* **Saint Nicholas's Day.**

• FEAST OF THE IMMACULATE CONCEPTION (December 8). This feast, commemorating the belief that the Virgin Mary was born without original sin, opens the Christmas season in many Latin American countries and is detailed in a separate entry. *See also* **Feast of the Immaculate Conception.**

• ST. LUCIA'S DAY (December 13). Legend states that St. Lucia, a native of Syracuse on the island of Sicily, was martyred in 304 for her Christian faith, having been stabbed in the throat. By the fifth century, she is said to have saved Syracuse from famine and to have brought food to Christians hiding in catacombs to escape persecution. To avoid a suitor, she plucked out her eyes and gave them to him, after which the Virgin restored her eyesight; thus artists have rendered her as a maiden wounded in the throat and carrying a knife with two eyes on a tray. St. Lucia is particularly noted for brilliant light radiating from her face, which stems from *lux* (light), the Latin derivative of her name.

Prior to the adoption of the Gregorian calendar in the sixteenth century, St. Lucia's Day fell on the winter solstice, which poses a factor in her association with light, and her day Christianized a day formerly associated with the pagan Germanic goddess Berchta (also variously known as Perchta, Bertha, Hertha, Holda, and others). While some ethnologists identify her as a goddess of the home, spinning, and children, others equate her with death. Thus, in various regions of the Balkans, the child-eating witch *Lutzelfrau* ironically appears on St. Lucia's Eve with gifts for children. Other pre–Christian witches bearing gifts have included "Black Lucia" and "Grandma Luca" (from "Lucia"), the latter a Croatian being who scorched the fingers of naughty children and punished girls who had not learned to crochet.

An old superstition also stated that sitting on a stool, the construction of which commenced on St. Lucia's Day and ended on Christmas Eve, enabled one to see witches. Other traditions forbade women to conduct some household chores on this day, and girls practiced divination rituals regarding future marriage. Elsewhere, St. Lucia brings gifts to children on the eve of her feast day.

"Lucia Day" (without the designation "saint") is especially noted for opening the Christmas season in Sweden, and Lucia is the patron saint of Syracuse, Milan, sight, tailors, and blacksmiths. *See also* **Sweden.**

• ST. THOMAS'S DAY (December 21). The Anglican Church still observes this date, the Roman Catholics having moved the date to July 3. According to legend, after the three Wise Men left Bethlehem, their journeys took them to India, where many years later St. Thomas the Apostle, having established himself as an evangelist in that region, converted them to Christianity. In another story from India, St. Thomas took a large sum of money, for which he was to have erected a king's palace, and distributed it among the poor. This latter legend led to the old British custom of "Thomasing" or begging from door to door on December 21, a custom that prevailed from the eighteenth to the early twentieth centuries. *See also* **Great Britain.**

Africa

Because vast areas of this continent remain unsettled, Christmas customs are observed chiefly in a few countries where Christianity has been introduced (as opposed to Islam), principally by European missionaries. Hence, the customs reflect those of the missionaries' home countries as well as native culture. Several traditions are common among the Christians on this continent: attendance at Christ-mas church services (even if these are the only services attended during the year), which may continue for several hours; the acquisition of new clothes, which parents and children wear at Christmas services; the giving of simple gifts; and feasting with family and fellow members of one's village. The following paragraphs summarize more specific customs for several countries:

• EGYPT. About 10 percent of the people in this predominantly Muslim nation embrace Christianity; most of these belong to the Coptic Orthodox Church, a body that dates to the fifth century. This church observes Christmas on January 7, which corresponds to the Coptic month of *Khiahk*, or December 25 on the Julian calendar ("Christmas Old Style"). To commemorate Christ's suffering in the wilderness for 40 days after His baptism, Christmas is preceded by a 40-day fast with abstinence from meat and dairy products. Christmas Eve includes Midnight Masses, the chief of which is celebrated in Alexandria by the Coptic pope. Following services, people usually observe an early morning breakfast of bread, rice, garlic, and boiled meat. On Christmas Day, the wealthy distribute *zalabya* (doughnuts), *bouri* (mullet fish), and candles to the poor, the latter gift symbolizing the light that illuminated the scene of the Nativity. Christmas is a time for visiting relatives and friends, with the serving of *kahk* (sweet biscuits marked with a cross).

In January 2003, President Hosni Mubarak issued a presidential decree authorizing the celebration of Christmas as a national holiday. It was the first time that the Egyptian government recognized a Christian holy day.

"Merry Christmas" in Egypt is: *Idah Saidan Wa Sanah Jadidah* (Arabic). *See also* **Christmas Old Style, Christmas New Style.**

• ETHIOPIA. St. Frumentius brought Christianity to what formerly was known as the Kingdom of Aksum early in the fourth century. Some 50 percent of the population remains Christian, primarily in the north, and belongs to the Ethiopian Orthodox Church. Closely related to the Coptic Church of Egypt (see above), the Ethiopian Church also observes *Genna* (Christmas) on January 7 and *Timkat* ("Baptism," Epiphany) on January 19. Because *Genna* actually refers to a national game similar to field hockey that is played only on Christmas Day, the name has become synonymous with Christmas itself. Christmas dinner may consist of *injera* (flat, sourdough bread) and *dorowat* (chicken stew).

The most elaborate religious rites occur on the eve of *Timkat*, as a procession of worshippers follows priests bearing a *tabot* (ark), a replica of the biblical Ark of the Covenant, to a nearby body of water where celebrations take place all night amid feasting and dancing. On *Timkat* morning, priests bless the water by immersing a cross, after which celebrants often wash themselves to receive the blessing. The ark replica derives from legends stating that the St. Mary of Zion Church in the city of Aksum presently enshrines the actual Ark of the Covenant, presumed to have been lost when the ancient Israelites were taken into Babylonian captivity. The shrine is well guarded, and entry is prohibited. At this time, people make pilgrimages to 12 monolithic churches hewn from solid, volcanic rock in the city of Lalibela. Legends contend that King Lalibela in the twelfth century enlisted the help of angels to build these structures, which stand in two groups on either side of a gorge called the River Jordan.

Children traditionally receive simple gifts such as clothing only on *Timkat*, and a favorite sport is *feres gugs*, which resembles the jousting matches of medieval Europe. "Merry Christmas" in Ethiopia is: *Melkam Yelidet Beaal* (Amharic, the official language). *See also* **Epiphany.**

• GHANA. Some 60 percent of Ghana's people are Christian, 16 percent are Muslim, and over 20 percent follow traditional beliefs. Christmas dinner often consists of fowl, pork, goat, or sheep, along with rice, *fufu* (yam paste), fruits, and soup consisting of eggs and meat, okra, or beans. Festivities continue for eight days with processions of street bands and dancers; groups of children carol from house to house and traditionally receive gifts from the residents. Families usually decorate a fruit tree with colored paper ornaments, and folklore holds that Father Christmas, a variant of Santa Claus, emerges from the jungles with gifts for the children. "Merry Christmas" is said in English, the official language; also *Afishapa* (Akan language).

• KENYA. About 66 percent of the population is Christian, 6 percent Muslim, and the remainder of the people follow traditional African religions. Christmas dinner includes *nyama choma* (roasted meat), often goat, along with *chapatis* (flat bread). Carolers make their rounds from house to house on Christmas Eve, and the monetary gifts received are donated to local churches. "Merry Christmas" in Kenya is: *Krismas njema na heri za mwaka mpya* (Swahili, a principal language of many.)

• REPUBLIC OF SOUTH AFRICA. South Africans are principally (about 80 percent) Christian Protestants. Falling during the summer, Christmas is celebrated with outdoor activities, including "Carols by Candlelight," a custom originating in Australia. Other customs reflect those of Dutch (now termed Afrikaners or Boers) and English settlers, such as children hanging up their stockings in anticipation of a visit by Father Christmas, pantomimes, and Boxing Day. Many native Africans observe a week-long carnival in costumes with gifts, singing, dancing, and feasting. "Merry Christmas" is said in the two official languages, English and *Geseende Kerfees* (Afrikaans), and in a number of other African tongues, such as *Sinifesela ukhisimusi omuhle nonyaka omusha onempumelelo* (Zulu). *See also* **Australia; Boxing Day; Great Britain; The Low Countries (The Netherlands).**

• SIERRA LEONE. Some 10 percent of the people are Christian, 30 percent follow traditional African beliefs, and 30 percent are Muslim. Christmas traditions merge with those of traditional religions. In Freetown, the capital, festivities commence two or three weeks prior to Christmas, during which time bands tour the streets, collecting donations. Children accompany adults who are masked as devils, the latter performing dances for profit. Popular devils consist of the *Fairy*, which resembles a fairy; the *Jobai*, noted for its small head and flamboyant spinning; and the *Congoli* or *Gogoli* with its large head. Sending Christmas cards is also popular, and festivities continue into the New Year. "Merry Christmas" is said in English, the official language.

• UGANDA. About 75 percent of the population is Christian, 16 percent Muslim. Because the usual diet consists of a starch with stewed vegetables, meat is important for Christmas.

Therefore Christmas dinner consists of beef or chicken with *matoke* (mashed and cooked banana, served with groundnut sauce). Although no gifts are exchanged as such, men customarily purchase new dresses for their wives at this time. "Merry Christmas" is said in English, the official language; also as *Webale Krismasi* (Rutooro language).

• ZIMBABWE. The population of this former British colony of Rhodesia consists of 25 percent Christians; the majority of the remainder are Synchretics, with a minority following traditional African religions. A key feature of the latter is the worship of family ancestors. Regardless of religious affiliation, families come together at Christmastime, and urban dwellers return to their ancestral homes as well as paying visits to rural relatives. Making such travel convenient, most businesses close for three weeks during the Christmas–New Year season.

Synchretics, who mix Christianity with traditional religions, combine elements of both beliefs into Christmas celebrations, which include Christian sermons, followed by dancing and singing to drums and horns, slaughtering cattle to appease the ancestors, and feasting upon the beef. There is much carousing and visiting between Synchretic households and villages, where drinking and brawling constitute the principal festivities.

Non-Christians choose Christmas Day as a special time to give thanks to, and seek guidance from, the spirits of their ancestors, while the Christian minority celebrates in typical British fashion with roast turkey and Father Christmas, who leaves gifts in a stocking or under the Christmas tree (*see* **Great Britain**).

Soliciting gifts from one's relatives on Christmas Day is a most proper and universal custom, which expresses kinship and family ties. A related custom states that, should two people meet, the first to ask for "Christmas" (implying a gift) will be the recipient of a gift from the other; a person may seek gifts in this manner from as many people as possible, but not twice from the same person. Such a custom is virtually identical to the "Christmas gif'!" custom that slaves commonly practiced in America's Old South (*see* **United States**). Because the government stresses that people's resources should be shared especially during the holidays, each city hosts a "Mayor's Christmas Cheer Fund" in which the rich are urged to give to the poor. "Merry Christmas" is said in English, the official language.

Ah, Bleak and Chill the Wintry Wind
See **Alfred Burt Carols**

Alabaster's Song: Christmas Through the Eyes of an Angel

Inspirational children's picture book written by American author Max Lucado, published in 1996.

As a six-year-old boy admires the little angel atop his Christmas tree, he addresses it with a series of seemingly mundane questions. But his inquiry about the angel's experience in Bethlehem is a different matter, for the angel, whom the boy has named Alabaster, suddenly appears beside him as a child about his own age. With halo, white feathery wings, and a lisp because his two front teeth are missing, Alabaster sings a most heavenly song on Christmas Eve, just as he had done with the angel chorus at the first Nativity. By Christmas morning, the angel is still singing, yet none of the older members of the boy's family hear the melody.

For several years afterwards, the boy continues to hear Alabaster's song each Christmas, until he becomes a man and fails to listen. Then the music ceases. Alabaster and his special song are all but forgotten, until one Christmas, when the man's own little boy asks if his daddy can hear the song. Here the book closes and allows the reader to ponder the question. (See Matthew 18:2–4.)

An animated cartoon adaptation of the story is included as a bonus DVD with the live-action video adaptation of Lucado's Christmas book, *Jacob's Gift*.

Max Lucado is a minister and the daily speaker for the radio program *UpWords*. His other Christmas books include *The Crippled Lamb* (1994), *The Christmas Cross* (1998), *Cosmic Christmas* (1997), and *Jacob's Gift* (1998), all of which are discussed as separate entries.

The Alan Brady Show Presents
See **The Dick Van Dyke Show**

Alfred Burt Carols

Designation applied to 15 carols, the music for which was composed by the American jazz trumpeter Alfred Shaddick Burt (1920–1954), from 1942 to 1954. They were published collectively and posthumously in 1954.

In 1922, the Rev. Bates G. Burt, Alfred's father and an Episcopal minister, began the annual tradition of composing an original carol and sending copies with specially created Christmas cards to family and friends. After Alfred graduated from college with a music degree in 1942, he assumed the role of music composer at his father's request, while the Rev. Bates Burt remained as lyricist until his death in 1948. Thereafter, the Burt family asked Wihla Hutson, a close family friend and church organist, to provide the lyrics. Thus the carol tradition continued until Alfred's untimely death from lung cancer in 1954 at the age of 33.

The following lists the Alfred Burt Carols in chronological order of their composition: "Christmas Cometh Caroling" (1942 — the Rev.

Alfred S. Burt (1920–1954), American jazz trumpeter who composed the music to 15 carols collectively known as the Alfred Burt Carols. Photograph c. 1943. Used by permission of the Burt family.

Bates Burt took the text from "O, Christmas Cometh Caroling," a carol by Father Andrew, an English Roman Catholic priest); "Jesu Parvule" ("Poor Little Jesus," 1943); "What Are the Signs" (1944, originally written under the title "Carol in War-Time" and subsequently changed to "What Are the Signs," based on the first line of the lyrics, "What are the signs of the morning?"); "Ah, Bleak and Chill the Wintry Wind" (1945); "All on a Christmas Morning" (1946); "Nigh Bethlehem" (1947); "Christ in the Stranger's Guise" (1948, lyrics based on an Old English rune); "Sleep, Baby Mine" (1949, also known as "Carol of the Mother"); "This Is Christmas" (1950, also known as "Bright, Bright the Holly Berries"); "Some Children See Him" (1951); "Come, Dear Children" (1952); "O Hearken Ye" (1953); "Caroling, Caroling" (1954); "We'll Dress the House" (1954); and "The Star Carol" (1954).

Originally composed for *a cappella* voices, the Alfred Burt Carols manifest a deep, simple reverence and often a quick-spirited, medieval flair.

Of the three carols composed in 1954, "The Star Carol" was selected for the Christmas card list, which had grown from 50 to 450. This was Alfred Burt's last carol, completed shortly before his death in February of that same year.

Although Alfred Burt was relatively obscure as a composer at the time of his death, carol authority William Studwell (*The Christmas Carol Reader*) believes that his carols "comprise one of the most significant bodies of holiday songs ever produced by one artist." They have enjoyed performances and recordings by a host of noted artists over the years. Columbia Records first recorded 12 of the carols in an album entitled *The Christmas Mood* (1954), featuring the Columbia Choir. A compact disc version of this album, available from Collegium Records, also includes the Ralph Carmichael Brass Ensemble. A later album, *This Is Christmas* (produced by Alfred's wife, Anne S. Burt, and released by Warner Bros., 1963), featured the complete set of carols with renditions by the Voices of Jimmy Joyce, a 16-voice *a cappella* choir. This latter album, now available on compact disc from Collegium Records, was nominated for a Grammy Award in 1964. Another early recording of note was by country artist Tennessee Ernie

Ford, who included "The Star Carol," "O Hearken Ye," and "Some Children See Him" in his 1958 Gold Record-winning Capitol album, *The Star Carol*, which made the *Billboard* charts in 1958, 1959, and during most of the 1960s. Today the most popular of the Alfred Burt Carols are "Caroling, Caroling"; "Some Children See Him"; "This Is Christmas"; "We'll Dress the House"; and "The Star Carol."

Born in Marquette, Michigan, Alfred Burt studied music at the University of Michigan School of Music in Ann Arbor and served in the Army Air Corps Band during World War II. Subsequently, he was an arranger and trumpeter for the Alvino Rey Orchestra in California.

The carols are further detailed at the "Official Burt Carols Website": www.alfredburtcarols.com.

An All Dogs Christmas Carol

See **A Christmas Carol** (Film and Television Versions)

All I Want for Christmas

(1991). Motion picture comedy/drama.

For seven-year-old Hallie O'Hallon (Thora Birch) and her older brother Ethan (Ethan Randall), the first Christmas in New York City since their parents' divorce will be a trying experience. Wishing that her family could be reunited, Hallie takes her Christmas request to the one person most likely to make miracles happen at this season — the Santa Claus at Macy's Department Store (Leslie Nielsen). But when their mother Catherine (Harley Jane Kozak) would remarry during the holidays, Hallie and Ethan conclude that Santa requires some assistance. Therefore, they concoct a scheme to get their parents back together by Christmas, and Ethan's girlfriend Stephanie (Amy Oberer) joins the crusade.

First, they purchase white mice from a pet shop and plant them in Catherine's house on Christmas Eve, which forces her to evacuate the premises overnight. Hallie and Ethan are to spend the night with their restaurateur-father, Michael (Jamey Sheridan), whose apartment lies above his diner. To separate Catherine from her fiancé Tony (Kevin Nealon), the children persuade him to drive them to the diner, where they lure him out of the car on pretense of searching for Hallie's pet mouse Snowball, then lock him in the back of an ice cream truck. Tony's frantic calls for help are futile, and the driver, blissfully deaf, speeds away. While Ethan arranges to have Tony's car towed, Stephanie telephones Catherine with a phony message that Tony is otherwise detained and cannot keep their date. Meanwhile at the diner, Hallie feigns an illness, which brings Catherine to her side right on time. Soon, Catherine and Michael pleasantly reminisce over their former marriage, then fall asleep together on a couch as the conspirators, their mission tentatively accomplished, romp outdoors in the season's gift of snow.

Christmas morning brings confession and reconciliation — Ethan takes full responsibility for orchestrating the events of the previous evening, all for the sake of family stability; Catherine ends her engagement when an enraged Tony, returning from having escaped his chilly "prison," threatens violent discipline on her children; and Michael and Catherine, realizing that they never stopped loving each other, decide to begin anew. And dropping by to return Snowball, Hallie's pet mouse that was presumed lost, is Santa himself. Lauren Bacall appears as Lillian, the grandmother.

In 1993, this picture was nominated for two Young Artist Awards for Best Young Actor and Young Actress Starring in a Motion Picture (Ethan Randall and Thora Birch).

Written by Thom Eberhardt and Richard Kramer. Produced by Marykay Powell. Directed by Robert Lieberman. Paramount Pictures. VHS: Paramount Studios. 92 min.

All I Want for Christmas Is My Two Front Teeth

American novelty song composed by Pennsylvania native Don Gardner in 1946. Although the song was first introduced on Perry Como's radio show by an obscure singing group, "The Satisfiers," it did not achieve national fame until 1948, when a zany recording by Spike Jones and His City Slickers on the RCA Victor label made it the top Christmas song that year. There, George Rock portrayed a child longing for his lost teeth so that he could wish everyone "Merry Christmas" without lisping. Don Gardner produced no other pieces that remain familiar today.

All My Heart This Night Rejoices

("Fröhlich soll mein Herze springen"). German carol, the lyrics of which are considered to be the most familiar work of Lutheran minister Paul Gerhardt (1607–1676). A popular hymn writer, Gerhardt produced 132 hymns, publishing "All My Heart" in 1653. His poem has enjoyed several musical settings, most notably that of 1666 by composer and compatriot Johann Ebeling, who contributed scores to 120 of Gerhardt's lyrics. Horatio Parker, chairman of Yale University's music department in the United States, provided another setting (1894). Great Britain's Catherine Winkworth (1827–1878), a respected translation specialist, contributed the most widely sung English version of the lyrics.

Consisting of 15 verses, "All My Heart" is a joyful proclamation of the Gospel of Christ with references to the Nativity interspersed. It rings a message of hope for the weary and wretched of spirit that Christ removes all sin, and that in Him, death is only the beginning of a far better life.

All on a Christmas Morning

See **Alfred Burt Carols**

Alvin's Christmas Carol

See **A Christmas Carol** (Film and Television Versions)

Amahl and the Night Visitors

Opera in one act, the first opera written for television, with music and libretto by Italian-born composer and conductor Gian Carlo Menotti. The NBC Opera Company presented the premiere performance from New York City on Christmas Eve, 1951, starring Chet Allen as Amahl and Rosemary Kuhlman as his mother. Other cast members included Andrew McKinley (Kaspar), David Aiken (Melchior), Leon Lishner (Balthazar), Frank Monachino (the Page), and the Chorus of Shepherds and Villagers. Thomas Schippers conducted the orchestra and chorus.

Amahl, a poverty-stricken, crippled boy who hobbles on a crutch, lives with his widowed mother in the mountains of Italy. Traveling to Bethlehem, the "Visitors" — the three Wise Men and their page — stop by, seeking shelter for the night, and are welcomed into the house.

As the Wise Men unveil the importance of their mission, Amahl desperately wishes that he could also give as precious a gift to the Christ Child as the Wise Men's gold, frankincense, and myrrh. His mother, on the other hand, covets the gold and steals a portion later that night, but the page apprehends her in the act. Though she pleads that she desperately needs the gold to feed her child, she repents and returns it, and the Wise Men forgive her. She wishes that she could also send a gift to the Christ Child, whereupon Amahl offers to the Wise Men his only possession, his little crutch. In so doing, he is miraculously healed and is able to run like other children. He then accompanies the Wise Men to Bethlehem.

After 1951, Bill McIver played Amahl for a number of seasons on the air, while Kuhlman continued as the mother. *Amahl* received its first stage performances in 1952 at Indiana University, Bloomington, and simultaneously in New York City. In 1953, the *Hallmark Hall of Fame* presented *Amahl* as the first sponsored television show in color. NBC Television remade the opera in 1978, with Robert Sapolsky as Amahl, Teresa Stratas as the mother, and Giorgio Tozzi, Nico Castel, and Willard White as the Wise Men. VHS: Republic Studios. 60 min.

An American Christmas Carol

See **A Christmas Carol** (Film and Television Versions)

The Andy Griffith Show

Popular television situation comedy series that aired on the CBS network from 1960 to 1968, set in the town of Mayberry, North Carolina. Principal cast members included Andy Griffith as Sheriff Andy Taylor, Ronny Howard as son Opie Taylor, Frances Bavier as Aunt Bee Taylor, and Don Knotts as Deputy Barney Fife.

Of the series' 249 episodes, only one featured a Christmas theme. Titled simply "Christmas Story," it aired on December 19, 1960, during the series' first year.

The scene is Christmas Eve at the Mayberry courthouse. Reviewing the mail, Andy and Barney enjoy a Christmas card from the

Hubacher brothers, which reads, "Merry Christmas from state prison." Barney also receives a card from an old flame, Hilda Mae, which reads, "Merry Christmas, Barney Parney Poo." Operating on a penal honor system, Andy releases his stock of prisoners for the holidays on their word that they will return to finish their sentences on the day after Christmas. Suddenly in bursts the old, cantankerous merchant, Ben Weaver (Will Wright), dragging in Sam Muggins (Sam Edwards) on a charge of selling bootleg whiskey. Andy certainly has no desire to arrest anyone on Christmas Eve, of all times, and tries to delay everything until the holidays are over. "Christmas? Ha!" is Ben's Scrooge-like reply to Andy's plea for clemency.

Although Andy has no choice but to lock up Sam, he decides that Sam will have a Christmas party despite the circumstances. Together with Aunt Bee and druggist Ellie Walker (Elinor Donahue), the lawmen and Opie all throw a Christmas party at the jail for Sam, his wife Bess (Margaret Kerry), and their two children, Effie and Billy. The festivities include Christmas trees for the office and Sam's cell, courtesy of Barney, who dons a Santa suit; an Andy-Ellie duet of "Away in a Manger" with Andy accompanying on guitar; and a turkey dinner with eggnog, courtesy of Aunt Bee. When Ben returns to see the merriment at hand and denounces the scene, Andy cleverly replies that not only was it necessary to arrest the remainder of Sam's family as "accessories" in crime, but that he was also compelled to deputize Aunt Bee, Ellie, and Opie to guard the "desperate" prisoners.

Foiled at every turn, Ben strangely commits a series of misdemeanors himself, but Andy remains compassionate, letting Ben go unpunished. When Ben hauls off a sidewalk bench, Andy lets him keep it as a Christmas present, and Ellie even pays Ben's two-dollar fine in another mishap. Only when he discovers that Ben has fallen off a crate while peering into the jail does Andy realize Ben's utter loneliness and desire to spend Christmas with others. "Arrested" for disturbing the peace, Ben returns with a large suitcase, which Barney immediately searches. To Ben's "incredulity," it contains roller skates, which he gives to Opie; a baseball mitt for Billy; a doll for Effie; perfume

for Ellie; a sewing basket for Aunt Bee; and wrapped gifts for the others. As the episode closes, everyone sings "Deck the Halls," and Aunt Bee serves Ben a hearty Christmas dinner.

Written by David Adler. Directed by Bob Sweeney. This episode is available in the DVD box set *The Andy Griffith Show — The Complete First Season* from Paramount Home Video. B & W. Episode 30 min.

The Andy Williams Christmas Show

Popular, annual telecast and seasonal highlight of the Emmy Award–winning television comedy-variety series, *The Andy Williams Show*, which aired weekly on the NBC network from 1962 to 1971.

Contrary to the weekly telecasts, which usually included a host of celebrity guest performers, the importance of family and togetherness prompted Andy to focus the Christmas shows around his own family in a down-home setting of merriment and nostalgia. Among those featured were his wife, French singer Claudine Longet; his three young children, Noelle, Christian, and Bobby; his parents, Jay and Louise; and his three brothers with their families, vocalists Bob, Don, and Dick, who, together with Andy, composed the Williams Brothers. Although the brothers had disbanded as a professional quartet in 1951, Andy persuaded them to make an annual appearance on his Christmas show for the sake of their parents, who had organized a Presbyterian church choir in their home town of Wall Lake, Iowa, and had first encouraged their sons to sing there. Also joining Andy were the Osmond Brothers (Alan, Wayne, Jay, Merrill, and later Donnie), who often appeared on the weekly shows.

Amid festive sets, backup singers and dancers clad in colorful, vintage costumes, and performances that often included ice skating, flying sleighs, and antique automobiles, the musical numbers primarily consisted of popular, secular standards composed during the twentieth century. Even though songs like "White Christmas," "I'll Be Home for Christmas," and "Silver Bells" reigned, Andy always paused for spiritual reflection and included a few older, sacred numbers. Among the best remembered were his solo renditions of "Silent Night," "O Holy Night," and "Ave Maria."

Andy often opened the Christmas shows with a lilting version of "It's the Most Wonderful Time of the Year," a song especially written for the show that has since become a holiday standard (*see* **It's the Most Wonderful Time of the Year**). In addition to musical numbers, family members participated in assorted skits, and one particular diversion, "Cookie Bear," was carried over from the weekly series. Portrayed by Janos Prohaska, Cookie Bear would appear unexpectedly in holiday attire and solicit cookies. Then Andy would bristle and exclaim, "No cookie — not now — not ever — NEVER"! According to legend, the Cookie Bear sketch inspired computer pranks that involved the word "cookies" in the 1970s and further led to the Internet term "cookies."

• LATER CHRISTMAS SPECIALS. After the weekly telecast left the air in July, 1971, Andy returned with Christmas specials on NBC in 1971 (with the Lennon Sisters), 1973, and 1974, which continued the family reunions. *Andy Williams' Early New England Christmas* (1982, CBS) featured guest celebrities James Galway, Dorothy Hamill, Aileen Quinn, and Dick Van Patten. *Andy Williams and the NBC Kids Search for Santa* (1985) showcased child stars Tempestt Bledsoe, Keshia Knight Pulliam, Malcolm-Jamal Warner, and Lisa Bonet (all from *The Cosby Show*); Mindy Cohn (*The Facts of Life*); Ami Foster, Casey Ellison, Soleil Moon Frye, and Cherie Johnson (all from *Punky Brewster*); and Joey and Matthew Lawrence (both from *Gimme a Break!*). In November and December of each year since 1992, Andy has performed his Christmas show to live audiences from his 2,000-seat Moon River Theater in Branson, Missouri (see below).

• VIDEO HIGHLIGHTS. Memorable clips from *The Andy Williams Christmas Show* have been compiled in several video recordings:

The Best of Andy Williams Christmas Shows (2001). Andy sings "It's the Most Wonderful Time of the Year," "White Christmas," "Happy Holiday"/"It's the Holiday Season" (Williams Brothers and Osmonds), "My Favorite Things" (with Claudine Longet), "You Meet the Nicest People," "What Are You Doing New Year's Eve,"

"Skater's Waltz" (Andy skates on ice with backup singers), "Some Children See Him," "Silver Bells" (with the Osmonds), "I'll Be Home for Christmas" (Williams Brothers), "Jingle Bells" (Williams Brothers), "The Christmas Song," "Ave Maria" (Bach/Gounod setting), "Moonlight in Vermont," "Sleigh Ride," "Mary's Boy Child," "Village of St. Bernadette," "It's Christmas," "Silent Night," "O Holy Night," and "May Each Day." Also featured is a Cookie Bear sketch in the first hour. The second hour includes additional clips from the Christmas shows in segments titled "Andy and the Osmond Brothers," "Andy's Most Wonderful Time of the Year" (a brief history of the song), and "Up Close and Personal." Here, Andy intercuts the numbers with brief comments and reflections about the Christmas shows, his own family, and his guests. The Williams Brothers recreate one of their early radio commercials by singing "A Time to Shine," while clips showcase the Osmonds' harmony with "Side by Side," "The Frivolous Four Plus One," "Heigh-Ho," "Whistle While You Work," and "It's the Most Wonderful Time of the Year" (the latter while skating on ice). Lastly, Andy emphasizes that the traditional music of Christmas lives on, because it brings back wonderful memories of the past and the time spent with family and friends at home. Produced by Andy Williams and Bobby Williams. Blue Field Entertainment and Moon River Enterprises. DVD: Questar. 120 min.

A 60-minute VHS tape of the same title is also available from Questar.

Happy Holidays: The Best of the Andy Williams Christmas Shows (2001). This collection, available only through various fund-raising drives of the Public Broadcasting System (PBS), reproduces many of the same numbers with Andy's intercutting commentary as in the DVD collection above. Differences include special appearances by Donnie Osmond and Andy's son Bobby as adults, while Claudine Longet is shown only as a bystander on the set. According to Donnie, "It never ceases to amaze me, to this day people come up to me and say, 'Oh I wish *The Andy Williams Christmas Shows* were back on the air.'" At the same time, Donnie believes that it would be difficult to recreate the feeling of those shows today, because they had a heart, soul, and simplicity that are now gone from television programming. And Bobby Williams assures viewers that the portrayal of a happy and warm, loving family on the set was indeed genuine, for such was life in the Williams household. In a most sentimental moment, Andy remarks that the memory of his parents dancing on the show to "White Christmas" always makes him "misty," because he still misses them. Numbers included here but not on the DVD above are "Caroling, Caroling," "Christmas Is Here," "Santa Claus Is Coming to Town" (all by the Williams Brothers), and a caroling medley by the Osmonds: "Here We Come A-Caroling," "Joy to the World," "Deck the Halls," and "We Wish You a Merry Christmas." Written, produced, and directed by David Leaf and John Scheinfeld. Moon River Enterprises. VHS: PBS Network. 60 min.

The Andy Williams Christmas Show (Live from Branson) (1993). This live recording of Andy's Christmas show from Branson, Missouri, again features the Osmond Brothers (minus Donnie) along with country singer Lorrie Morgan. Although it recreates in part the atmosphere of his earlier television specials with holiday standards, his surviving family members do not participate. Among the 26 numbers presented are "Christmas Needs Love to Be Christmas"; Andy tap dancing to "I Saw Mommy Kissing Santa Claus" along with four reindeer dancers; "My Favorite Things" (Lorrie Morgan); "Little Snow Girl" (Andy and Lorrie, from her album *Merry Christmas from London*); "White Christmas" (Andy, Lorrie, Osmonds); and a backup choir of young teens attired in colorful sweaters. The Osmonds further accompany Andy on "Happy Holiday"/ "It's the Holiday Season" and sing three familiar tunes *a cappella*: "Here We Come A-Caroling," "Christmas Is Coming," and "We Wish You a Merry Christmas." Andy then bids the audience to join him in singing "Angels We Have Heard on High," "Joy to the World," "O Come, All Ye Faithful," "The Bells of St. Mary's," and "Silent Night." Before closing the show with "O Holy Night," Andy waxes philosophical about the true meaning of Christmas and delivers an adaptation of "One Solitary Life," a short essay about the life of Christ. That adaptation ends with, "All the armies that have ever marched, all the navies that were ever built, all the parliaments that ever sat, all of the kings that ever reigned, put together, have not affected the life of man upon the earth as this one solitary life." Although Andy mentions Jim Bishop (1907–1987), a nationally known newspaper columnist, in connection with the essay, the author is Dr. James Allan Francis (1864–1928), former pastor of First Baptist Church in Los Angeles. Francis's essay was part of "Arise, Sir Knight!" a sermon which he delivered to the National Baptist Young Peoples' Union Convention in 1926. Produced for the stage by Tennyson Flowers and for television by John L. Meek. Directed by Phillip Byrd. Ozarks Public Telecommunications and Moon River Enterprises. DVD: Kultur Video. 78 min.

The Angel of Pennsylvania Avenue

(1996). American/Canadian made-for-television drama set during the Depression in 1931.

Because work is scarce, Angus Feagan (Robert Urich) leaves his home in Detroit, Michigan, at Christmastime to seek work in Kansas City, Missouri, while his family remains behind. When a riot erupts, he is jailed for a crime he did not commit.

Believing that President Herbert Hoover can work miracles, Angus's three children, Bernice (Tegan Moss), Lilly (Brittney Irvin), and six-year-old Jack (Alexander Pollock), set out for Washington, D.C., hoping to see the president on behalf of their father. They hop trains, hitch rides, and meet several interesting people along the way, including Box Car Louie (Tom Heaton), a pleasant hobo who provides shelter and guidance in the wild, and Andy Handy (Matthew Walker), a traveling puppeteer. When the children need bus fare for the final stage of their journey, Lilly stands on a park bench and sings Christmas carols, while the other two pass the hat. Meanwhile, Annie Feagan (Diana Scarwid) pursues her children, hitching rides from kind-hearted strangers like Ray Needles (Alfred Humphreys) and others.

With help from a crowd loitering outside the White House, who create a diversion, the children manage to slip into the mansion and, after dodging the guards, Bernice plunges into Hoover's quarters and pleads dearly for her father. With assurance that Hoover (Thomas

Peacocke) will do all that he can for Angus, Annie and her children happily return home to prepare for Christmas. Angus's call, however, with news that he will probably remain for another year in prison, shatters their dreams, and Bernice finds it most difficult to attend Christmas Eve services a few days later. But as the children's choir sings "O Come, All Ye Faithful," in walks Angus, a free man, to a splendid Christmas reunion.

In 1997, this picture received Young Artist Award nominations for Best Family Cable Television Movie and Best Young Actress (Tegan Moss).

With Frank Turner, Don S. Davis, and Camille Mitchell. Written by Michael DeGuzman and Rider McDowell. Produced by Tom Rowe and Lisa Towers. Directed by Robert Ellis Miller. Video N/A.

Angel Tree

A ministry of Prison Fellowship, the largest prison outreach and criminal justice reform organization in the world. Angel Tree mobilizes churches and other organizations throughout the United States to supply Christmas gifts and practical, emotional, and spiritual support to the more than two million children, one or both of whose parents are currently incarcerated. The only nationwide program that ministers to children of prisoners, Angel Tree in addition provides year-round programs of mentoring and summer camps.

Angel Tree was founded in Birmingham, Alabama, in 1982 by Mary Kay Beard. Convicted of burglary, grand larceny, and robbery, Beard had witnessed female inmates wrapping as Christmas gifts for their children the various toiletries that they had received in charity packages and the joy their children expressed at receiving such simple gifts. She was released in 1976 and subsequently joined Prison Fellowship in 1981 as an area director for Alabama. To induce shoppers to provide gifts for prisoners' children, Beard first erected two Christmas trees in shopping malls and hung thereon the names of the children written on paper angels; hence, Angel Trees. In that first year, 556 Alabama children received gifts.

Since the inception of Angel Tree, hundreds of thousands of volunteers through churches and various organizations have distributed nearly 13 million gifts to more than six million children across the nation. About 32 percent of all children of incarcerated parents currently receive gifts from Angel Tree, and in 2003 alone, more than one-half million children received gifts through 14,000 churches.

Prison Fellowship itself was founded in 1976 by Chuck Colson (former special counsel to Richard Nixon and who served a prison term for Watergate-related crimes) and led by former Virginia attorney general Mark Earley. The organization has programs in prisons in all 50 states and in 110 foreign countries.

See also **Salvation Army; Toys for Tots.**

Angels and Other Strangers: Family Christmas Stories

Young adult fiction, collection of nine contemporary short stories with inspirational messages of hope and peace, written by American author Katherine Paterson, published in 1979. She wrote them throughout the course of her husband's ministry at the Takoma Park (Maryland) Presbyterian Church, and the Rev. John B. Paterson read them to his congregation each Christmas Eve. The following paragraphs briefly summarize these stories:

"Angels and Other Strangers." En route to pick up her cantankerous Aunt Patty on Christmas Eve, Julia's car runs out of gas on a remote highway. Suddenly, as the figure of Jacob, a large, elderly black man, approaches the car, Julia seriously doubts that his intentions are appropriate for the holiday. Instead, Jacob walks two miles out of his way for gas, then refuses any compensation for his trouble. Though the idea is "ridiculous" to Aunt Patty, to Julia's little boy Kevin, Jacob is their Christmas angel, because Jacob had told them not to be afraid. And as everybody knows, that's what *angels* say.

"Guests." Despite the loss of his wife and children in war-torn Japan and the fact that the police forbid open Christian services, Pastor Nagai holds to his faith. His congregation has virtually vanished, yet with Christmas Eve upon him, Pastor Nagai prepares for the service as if thousands will attend. Only one little seven-year-old girl appears, attracted by the carols that he sings, and the pastor teaches her all about Christ. After the service, a policeman — the girl's uncle — steps forth, for he had been spying on the service. Bidding this enemy of Christianity to hear the Christmas message, Pastor Nagai begins anew, and for the first time in years, he heeds the angel's command: "Fear not."

"Many Happy Reruns." Little Elizabeth feels angry, jealous, and neglected, now that baby brother Joshua has arrived at Christmastime. She overreacts first by destroying a stuffed toy. Next, her good intentions of decorating the Christmas tree all by herself only succeed in damaging her aunt's prized Nativity set. Finally in a fit of rage, Elizabeth slaps Joshua. Childishly believing that her tiny blow could be fatal and that she is doomed to hell, Elizabeth rushes to her church nearby to find Jesus, her only hope. That hope comes in the form of Miss Violet, her elderly Sunday school teacher, who weeps compassionately with her, then tenderly sets her mind at ease. As Elizabeth is reconciled with her family, she can truly wish Jesus a happy birthday with "many happy reruns of the day."

"Tidings of Joy." After losing her baby girl Joy at birth, Carol first blamed herself, then God. Where was God when she really needed Him? Why hadn't God comforted her? Six months later, as Christmas approaches, nothing has changed, and Christmas will come even without Joy — an ironic pun indeed. Posters on a church wall arrest her attention and shout a distinct message: posters of a man in prison, an old woman in a nursing-home bed, the swollen belly of a Biafran child (see Matthew 25:34–40). At last, Carol realizes that no one, not even she, is immune from suffering and death, and neither was Christ on earth, as a garish figure of the cross attests, in contrast to the empty manger of a Nativity scene.

"Maggie's Gift." Mr. McGee, a poor, lonely widower who wishes to give Christmas to the underprivileged, is elated at the prospect of taking in two foster children, a sister and brother, ages eight and five, respectively. Unfortunately, time initially spent with the children is anything but peace on earth. Although the boy is shy and uncommunicative, the girl is a fount of unspeakable insults and curses, which she heaps upon Mr. McGee at every turn. At first, he ignores her taunts, but when she

repeatedly addresses him as "Maggie," Mr. McGee provides much-needed discipline. More docile, the girl departs from the Christmas Eve service much impressed that, as she and her brother were born in a charity hospital, so was Jesus born into poverty. The boy, however, departs with the Baby Jesus figure from the crèche. To Mr. McGee, however, the boy just didn't want Jesus spending Christmas in an institution.

"Star of Night." For five years, Carl has been seeking Jimmy, his runaway son. Although multiple leads have been false, some even alleging that the boy is dead, Carl has never abandoned his search. Finally, another lead brings Carl from Chicago to Washington, D.C., on Christmas Eve. With the assistance of a local church and two young street children, Carl discovers Jimmy living an abandoned, unheated, rat-infested house, together with his paramour and infant child. After Carl saves the baby from an aggressive rat, Jimmy is confident of his father's undying love, and the reunion is sealed. Carl would have Jimmy and family return with him to Chicago, but Jimmy promises to return only in the spring.

"He Came Down." In order for Dolores Mendez to portray Mary in the church Christmas play, Lydia Paxton, an unhappy widow, finds herself baby-sitting not only the girl's infant brother but Mrs. Mendez as well. The latter, poverty stricken and recently widowed, lies in bed with severe depression. When Mrs. Mendez seems oblivious to her baby's cries, Lydia takes over. Rocking the little boy, she recalls the lyrics to the carol "Once, in Royal David's City": Jesus came down to be with "the poor, and mean, and lowly." Suddenly Mrs. Mendez, enraged that another woman holds her baby, screams obscenities in Spanish and hurls a crucifix at Lydia. The incident forces Lydia to realize that, cultural and financial differences aside, both women have allowed their unhappiness to turn them against God, instead of turning them *to* God. See also **Once, in Royal David's City.**

"Woodrow Kennington Works Practically a Miracle." Believing that her family hates her now that baby Daniel has arrived, five-year-old Sara Jane Kennington reasons that a pious demeanor will surely turn the tide. Her long prayers and false sincerity—imitations of her favorite televangelist—irritate older brother Woodrow to the point that he covertly sabotages the television set to quiet her. Instead, Sara Jane fervently prays that God heal the television, then rejects Him and even Christmas when results are not forthcoming. Feeling guilty that he has turned his sister against God, Woodrow stages an ethereal setting on Christmas Eve by placing "Jesus" (Daniel) in a "manger" (bureau drawer) beneath their Christmas tree. Disguised as an angel, he bids Sara Jane to go and see the miracle. The trick convinces her that Baby Jesus actually lies before her; that is, until Woodrow stumbles, exposes himself, and confesses the ruse. Sara Jane is delighted nonetheless, especially when big brother provides assurance that God and her family will always love her just for being herself.

"Broken Windows." A baseball accidentally thrown through the church window and a ragged teddy bear deposited in the manger of the crèche lead the Rev. Philip to Mrs. Slaytor, a poverty stricken single mother with two little boys, Bobby and Wayne. Philip learns that Mr. Slaytor had deserted his family, and that it was Wayne who left the bear in the manger, not by accident, but as a gift to God. This is Wayne's way of asking God to find his daddy and bring him home for Christmas. Deeply moved, Philip makes many calls, then descends into the slums and byways of the city on Christmas Eve, armed only with a picture of Slaytor. For his efforts, Philip is mugged and awakens in jail with a concussion, his mission unsuccessful. Yet Philip gains new insight into his Christmas text, Psalms 51:17—God born as man, Who accepts the sacrifices of a broken and contrite heart; Jesus, friend to the friendless.

Katherine Paterson has won multiple awards for her children's books, including the Newbery Medal and the National Book Award. Another collection of her Christmas stories is entitled *A Midnight Clear: Stories for the Christmas Season* (1995).

See also **A Midnight Clear: Stories for the Christmas Season.**

Angels and Shepherds
Traditional carol, the music of which arose during the seventeenth or eighteenth century from the Bohemian region of the former Czechoslovakia. Although the original text, beginning as "Nesem vám noviny," reflected a nonpastoral theme, the carol achieved popularity when the German composer Karl Riedel (1827–1888) coupled the original melody with text adapted from Bohemian shepherd songs that comprised Nativity folk dramas of that region. Riedel published his version as "Kommet, ihr Hirten" ("Come, You Shepherds") in the collection *Altböhmische Gesänge* (Leipzig, 1870). Other English translations include "Come, All Ye Shepherds," "From Bethl'em's City," and "Hear What Great News We Bring."

The title "Angels and Shepherds" is derived from Riedel's text, in which the angelic host first bid the shepherds and others to follow them to the manger. The shepherds then joyfully respond with a desire to hurry to Bethlehem to publish abroad all that they witness there, and the carol concludes with the glad tidings of "Peace on earth" to all.

Angels, from the Realms of Glory
English carol, lyrics composed by James Montgomery (1771–1854). Initially a social activist, Montgomery edited the *Sheffield Iris* (formerly the *Sheffield Register*) for 31 years, during which time he published antigovernment sentiments for which he was occasionally jailed. He left the *Iris* in 1825 and devoted his latter days to composing some 400 hymns and adapting many others.

Inspired by the older, familiar French carol, "Les anges dans nos campagnes" ("Angels We Have Heard on High"), Montgomery published one of his most famous hymns, "Angels, from the Realms of Glory," in the *Iris* on Christmas Eve, 1816. Well received throughout England, it appeared in hymnals and broadsheets from 1819 onward and was sung exclusively, and not surprisingly, to the tune of "Les anges" for some 50 years following its initial publication.

The most prominent of several other musical settings arrived with the publication in 1866 of "Regent Square," which the blind London organist Henry Smart composed for *Psalms and Hymns for Divine Worship*, a Presbyterian hymnal. Today the "Regent Square" tune has found a more compatible match with Montgomery's

lyrics in the United States. The English, still preferring the tune of "Les anges," reserve Smart's
melody for the hymn "Light's Abode, Celestial
Salem."

See also **Angels We Have Heard on High**.

Angels' Mass
See **Christmas Masses**

An Angel's Story
See **Cosmic Christmas**

Angels We Have Heard on High
("Les anges dans nos campagnes"). French
traditional carol thought to have arisen during
the eighteenth century in Lorraine or Provence. The complete obscurity of its origins has
prompted several speculations, particularly
regarding the Latin refrain, "Gloria in excelsis
Deo" ("Glory to God in the Highest"). According to one, in the year 129, Telesphorus, bishop
of Rome, commissioned a Christmas carol, a
line of which became the refrain for "Angels."
Another states that French shepherds, calling
the "Gloria" to each other from hilltops on
Christmas Eve, supposedly used a traditional
tune (possibly from a late medieval Latin
chorale) that was identical to the refrain of
"Angels." These speculations imply that, because the text consists of two languages, the
carol must be derived from two sources. This
reasoning does not always apply, as "The Boar's
Head Carol" illustrates: of unquestionably
English origin throughout, it is peppered with
Latin phrases (see **The Boar's Head Carol**).

Whatever the source, music authorities
feel that the style of the original text and music
dates "Angels" to more modern times. Its earliest known printing lies in Louis Lambillotte's
collection *Choix de antiques sur des airs nouveaux*, published in Paris, 1842. Prior to that
time, "Angels" was known in England, at least
in 1816, for it was the basis for James Montgomery's "Angels, from the Realms of Glory,"
published that year (see **Angels, from the Realms
of Glory**).

Many different English-language translations exist, the first by James Chadwick, Catholic
bishop of Newcastle and Hexam, which appeared in *The Holy Family Hymns* of London,
1860. The text most often sung today was

*Beautifully chromolithographed, embossed diecut
"scraps" mostly made in Germany were sold by the
billions in America, Canada and England in the
1870s and 1880s. This one is 2¼" high and shows
baby Jesus holding a Christmas rose, while the
angels' banner proclaims, "Gloria in excelsis Deo"
(Glory to God in the highest)— a refrain popularized by the Christmas carol "Angels We Have Heard
on High."*

adapted from Chadwick by Newcastle composer Henri Hémy, who included it in *The
Crown of Jesus Music* of 1864.

The Animal Carol
See **The Friendly Beasts**

Annabelle's Wish
(1997). Made-for-video animated cartoon,
based on a short story by Dan Henderson.
Wishes and miracles fill the holidays in this tale
of Annabelle, a calf born on Christmas Eve at
Charles Baker's farm in the rural community of
Twobridge, Tennessee. Charles, a widower, is
also raising Billy, his grandson, an orphan who
suddenly went mute after Charles rescued him
from a barn fire some years ago.

As midnight approaches, the farm animals anticipate the arrival of Santa, who annually bestows upon them the secret gift of speech for Christmas Day only. It's Annabelle's first encounter with Santa and his flying reindeer, and the latter impress her so much that she is determined to fly some day as they do. Annabelle, Billy's Christmas gift that year, reveals the animals' secret when she automatically says, "Bless you!" after Billy sneezes, but he gladly keeps the secret under his hat. When she expresses her fondest wish to be a reindeer and fly, Billy ties two small branches to her head to simulate antlers. She and Billy become quite close, and joining them in their winter capers is Billy's good friend Emily.

Into such wholesome surroundings, trouble and heartache must inevitably fall. While the three are out sledding on Christmas Day, Billy and Annabelle lose control and crash through neighbor Gus Holder's fence. Holder and his boys, Bucky and Buster, Scrooges of sorts, loathe Christmas and seize every opportunity to tease Billy about his handicap. To cover the damages, Holder lays claim to Annabelle, since Charles has no ready cash. But rather than see Billy without his calf, Charles sells a beautiful music box that had belonged to Billy's late mother, and Annabelle is returned.

Life is again peaceful until Christmas Eve of the following year, when Billy's rich, lonely, and spiteful Aunt Agnes arrives with a court order granting her guardianship over Billy until such time as he can speak. While Billy prepares his belongings, the animals tow Agnes's car into a pond, forcing her to spend the night on the farm. Once again Santa greets the animals at midnight, but this time Annabelle whispers a special request, since she's been a good little calf all year. On Christmas morning, Billy opens a small box from Santa containing dust. Spilling it on himself, he is able to speak (nullifying the court order), for it is the magic dust of speech that Santa sprinkles on the animals. Annabelle's wish was to give Billy her gift of speech forever, and by so doing, she will never speak again. Holder, learning the sacrifice Charles made to pay for his fence, pops over with his boys, apologizes for being a poor neighbor, and returns the music box.

Years pass. Billy and Emily are now married and still live on the farm. Late one Christmas Eve, Billy follows an aged Annabelle out into a pasture, where she collapses. Suddenly Santa appears and transforms Annabelle into a lovely, talking reindeer that leads the team into the Christmas sky. Annabelle receives her fondest wish at last.

In 1998, this picture received a Golden Reel Award nomination for Best Sound Editing. Nominated for Young Artist Award, Best Young Actress Voiceover (Aria Noelle Curzon).

Narrated by Randy Travis. Principal voices: Jay Johnson, Jerry Van Dyke, Jim Varney, Rue McClanahan, Cloris Leachman, Aria Noelle Curzon, James Lafferty, Charlie Cronin, Jennifer Darling, Clancy Brown, Stu Rosen, Jerry Houser, Brian Cummings, Kaye E. Kuter, Kath Soucie, and Hari Oziol. Musical score by Steve Dorff. Lyrics by Steve Dorff, John Bettis, and Randy Travis. Vocals by Randy Travis, Alison Kraus, Beth Nielson Chapman, and Michael McGinnis. Written by John Bettis, Ken Blackwell, John Couch, *et al.* Story by Dan Henderson. Produced by Barbara Dunn-Leonard. Directed by Roy Wilson. A Ralph Edwards Films Production. DVD: Sony Wonder Video. 54 min.

Ralph Edwards Films dedicated this picture to the Make-a-Wish Foundation, an organization that seeks to fulfill wishes of terminally ill children, and vowed to grant the wishes of 100 children through the Foundation's 82 organizations across the country at that time.

Argentina
See **South America**

Armenia
The person or persons who introduced Christianity into Armenia remain unknown. Two of Christ's apostles, Bartholomew and Thaddeus, are said to have first preached there, whereas St. Gregory the Illuminator (257?–337?), the patron saint of Armenia, is also credited with establishing Christianity there in the year 301. In any event, Armenia became the first nation to embrace Christianity, which led to the Armenian Orthodox Church, the principal faith in that country. Most Armenian churches observe Christ's Theophany (Epiphany in the Western Church), which includes His

Nativity and Baptism, all on January 6 by the Gregorian calendar, the exception being the church in Jerusalem, which still adheres to the older, Julian calendar. January 6 on that calendar corresponds to January 19 on the Gregorian calendar.

• HISNAK ("Fifty Days"), the Advent season, extends for a period of 50 days prior to January 6, with one week of strict fasting prior to the commencement of Advent. Strict fasting includes abstinence not only from milk and all animal products, but also from liturgical commemoration of saints. The Saturday of that week, however, commemorates St. Nicholas along with St. Gregory the Wonderworker and Bishop Myron of Crete, and the Saturday preceding the third Sunday of Advent again commemorates St. Nicholas. Another week of fasting follows the third Advent Sunday, and the Saturday of that week commemorates St. James of Nisibis, said to be the nephew of St. Gregory the Illuminator. The following saints' days, all movable, follow the fourth Advent Sunday: King David; St. James, brother of Jesus; St. Stephen; St. Peter the Apostle; and the "Sons of Thunder" (St. James the Apostle and St. John the Evangelist, sons of Zebedee).

Considered a holiday period during which no work is done, the final week of strict fasting from December 31 to January 6 closes Advent and precedes the Feast of Theophany, during which time *Kaghand* (New Year's) is observed on January 1 with gift exchanges, feasting within the limitations of the fast, and visitations. In some regions, children receive their gifts by gathering on rooftops and letting down handkerchiefs into which parents place treats. Although a strict fast is in force, one of these last seven days is a floating day that commemorates all of the following saints: St. Basil, St. Gregory of Nyssa, Pope St. Sylvester I of Rome, and St. Ephrem the Syrian.

Strictly a religious observation, the Feast of Theophany begins late in the afternoon of January 5, a day termed *Chragaloyts* ("Lighting the Lamps"), for the church lamps are filled with wax and new wicks. Following Vespers, numerous readings from the Old Testament, and celebration of a solemn Mass, the clergy form a procession around the church and line up in the nave to sing "Great Mystery," a Nativity hymn about the Incarnation, based on a homily by St. Gregory the Wonderworker. Following a reading from Luke 2:8–14, the congregation is blessed and dismissed. The Feast continues on January 6 with the Holy Offices of the Night Vigil, Matins, and another solemn Mass. Following this is the ritual of "Blessing the Water," wherein the priest places a cross and pours Holy Crism (consecrated oil, symbolic of the Holy Spirit) into a large basin of water. Members of the congregation then take small quantities of the water home with them to anoint the sick. Most Armenians receive Holy Communion either on January 5 or 6. The Feast of Theophany extends for eight days until January 13, during which period there is neither fasting nor commemoration of saints, and people engage in family reunions and greet one another with the salutation, "Christ is born and is revealed." The expected response is, "These are great tidings to you and to us." The eighth day is dedicated to the Circumcision of the Lord.

Because of the political and social upheavals in the last two centuries, the customs and cuisine once specific to various Armenian cities have largely disappeared.

"Merry Christmas" in Armenia is *Shenoraavor Nor Dari*.

See also **Advent; Christmas Old Style, Christmas New Style; Epiphany**.

As I Sat on a Sunny Bank
See **I Saw Three Ships**

As Joseph Was A-Walking
See **The Cherry Tree Carol**

As with Gladness Men of Old

English carol, the lyrics of which were written on January 6 (Epiphany), 1859, by William Chatterton Dix (1837–1898), a poet, hymn writer, and manager of a marine insurance company in Bristol. The day was significant, for Dix, ill in bed at the time, was reading the Gospel of Matthew's account of the Wise Men's visit to the Christ Child, which inspired the lyrics about their mission and journey. Dix also wrote the lyrics to another well known carol, "What Child Is This?"

The musical setting for "As with Gladness" is an adaptation of a selection from "Treuer

Heiland," a German chorale of uncertain authorship that was published in 1838 in a collection edited by organist Conrad Kocher, also perhaps the composer. William H. Monk undertook the adaptation and paired Dix's lyrics with this melody and published them together in *Hymns Ancient and Modern*, edited by William Clowes (London, 1861). Perhaps better known as the setting for the hymn "For the Beauty of the Earth," the Kocher tune ultimately acquired the alternate name of "Dix"; ironically, Dix was never fond of the music.

See also **Epiphany; What Child Is This?**

ASCAP List of Christmas Songs

The repertory of certain music, the rights of which are held by the American Society of Composers, Authors and Publishers (ASCAP), includes a number of popular Christmas songs that were composed during the twentieth century. In December of 1998, the society published a list of its 25 most frequently performed holiday numbers of that century. Early into the twenty-first century, however, public preferences had changed, which was reflected in an updated list, published in December 2004. The following two lists of songs and their composers, ranked in descending order, illustrate those changes and are respectively reproduced with the permission of the American Society of Composers, Authors and Publishers (ASCAP), (c) 2000 and 2004 ASCAP:

• TWENTIETH CENTURY—1. "White Christmas" (Irving Berlin). 2. "Santa Claus Is Coming to Town" (J. Fred Coots, Haven Gillespie). 3. "The Christmas Song (Chestnuts Roasting on an Open Fire)" (Mel Tormé, Robert Wells). 4. "Winter Wonderland" (Felix Bernard, Richard B. Smith). 5. "Rudolph, the Red-Nosed Reindeer" (Johnny Marks). 6. "Sleigh Ride" (Leroy Anderson, Mitchell Parish). 7. "Have Yourself a Merry Little Christmas" (Ralph Blane, Hugh Martin). 8. "Silver Bells" (Jay Livingston, Ray Evans). 9. "Let It Snow! Let It Snow! Let It Snow!" (Sammy Cahn, Jule Styne). 10. "Little Drummer Boy" (Katherine K. Davis, Henry V. Onorati, Harry Simeone). 11. "Jingle Bell Rock" (Joseph Carleton Beal, James Ross Boothe). 12. "I'll Be Home for Christmas" (Walter Kent, Kim Gannon, Buck Ram). 13. "Frosty the Snow Man" (Steve Nelson, Walter E. Rollins). 14. "Blue Christmas" (Billy Hayes, Jay W. Johnson). 15. "Carol of the Bells" (Peter J. Wilhousky, Mykola Leontovich). 16. "It's Beginning to Look a Lot Like Christmas" (Meredith Willson). 17. "Here Comes Santa Claus (Right Down Santa Claus Lane)" (Gene Autry, Oakley Haldeman). 18. "(There's No Place Like) Home for the Holidays" (Bob Allen, Al Stillman). 19. "Rockin' Around the Christmas Tree" (Johnny Marks). 20. "I Saw Mommy Kissing Santa Claus" (Tommie Connor). 21. "We Need a Little Christmas" (Jerry Herman). 22. "The Christmas Waltz" (Sammy Cahn, Jule Styne). 23. "The Chipmunk Song (Christmas Don't Be Late)" (Ross Bagdasarian [David Seville]). 24. "Feliz Navidad" (José Feliciano). 25. "A Holly Jolly Christmas" (Johnny Marks).

• DECEMBER 2004—1. "The Christmas Song." 2. "Have Yourself a Merry Little Christmas." 3. "Winter Wonderland." 4. "Santa Claus Is Coming to Town." 5. "White Christmas." 6. "Let It Snow! Let It Snow! Let It Snow!" 7. "I'll Be Home for Christmas." 8. "Rudolph, the Red-Nosed Reindeer." 9. "Little Drummer Boy." 10. "Jingle Bell Rock." 11. "Silver Bells." 12. "Sleigh Ride." 13. "Feliz Navidad." 14. "It's the Most Wonderful Time of the Year" (Edward Pola, George Wyle). 15. "Blue Christmas." 16. "Rockin' Around the Christmas Tree." 17. "Frosty the Snow Man." 18. "A Holly Jolly Christmas." 19. "I Saw Mommy Kissing Santa Claus." 20. "It's Beginning to Look a Lot Like Christmas." 21. "Here Comes Santa Claus." 22. "Wonderful Christmastime" (Paul McCartney). 23. "Carol of the Bells." 24. "Santa Baby" (Joan Ellen Javits, Philip Springer, Tony Springer). 25. "This Christmas" (Donny Hathaway, Nadine McKinnor).

"We Need a Little Christmas," "The Christmas Waltz," "The Chipmunk Song," and "Home for the Holidays" had fallen from the updated list in December 2004. Added to this new list were "It's the Most Wonderful Time of the Year," "Santa Baby," "This Christmas," and "Wonderful Christmastime."

Each of these songs is discussed further as a separate entry.

Asia and the South Pacific

With the exception of the Philippines, where Roman Catholicism predominates, most of the countries in this part of the world are non–Christian, and Christmas as a religious holiday is not widely observed. Rather, it is more commonly a secular season occupied with gift exchanges, family reunions, and Westernized customs (Christmas trees, Christmas cards, pageants and plays, and the like); despite the secular bent of the holiday, Western religious customs are also in evidence (Nativity scenes, carols, Midnight Mass). The following paragraphs describe those Christmas customs that can be identified in several countries. Christmas in the Philippines is discussed as a separate entry.

• CHINA. For *Sheng Dan Jieh* ("Holy Birth Festival"), homes are decorated with paper lanterns, and fireworks greet the Nativity. Christmas trees (known as "Trees of Light," decorated with paper ornaments) and Santa Claus (known as *Dun Che Lao Ren*, "Christmas Old Man," or *Lan Khoong-Khoong*, "Nice Old Father") are familiar to the nation's approximately 12 million Christians. Hong Kong celebrates *Ta Chiu*, a festival of peace, in which Taoists invoke their gods and Christians pay homage to patron saints. This festival closes with the burning of a paper horse to which the names of all villagers are attached. It is believed that in this burning, their names will arise to heaven. The principal festival is Chinese New Year, termed "Spring Festival," which is held near the end of January. There, amid fireworks displays, children receive new clothes and toys, and ancestors are worshipped. "Merry Christmas" in China may be heard as *Seng Dan Fai Lok, Sang Nian Fai Lok* (Cantonese) or *Kung His Hsin Nien Bing Chu Shen Tan* (Mandarin).

• FIJI ISLANDS. The population of this former British colony consists of approximately 50 percent Fijians, 45 percent Eastern Indians, and the remainder Europeans and other Asians. About 56 percent of the population are Christians (Methodists and Roman Catholics), Hindus 33 percent, and Muslims 7 percent. People of all regions, including those living in urban areas, return to their native villages and extended families for the holidays. Numerous cows and pigs are slaughtered and roasted in an earthen oven known as a *lovo* for the Christmas feasting, which is held after early morning church services on Christmas Day. Boxing Day (December 26), paralleled after the British practice, is a day for relaxing and visiting friends and family. Gift-giving and a mythical being who brings gifts to children are not traditional. "Merry Christmas" in Fijian is: *Me Nomuni na marau ni sega ni sucu dei na yabaki vou. See also* **Boxing Day.**

• INDIA. Seventy-five percent of the population are Hindus, with 12 percent Muslims and 6 percent Christians. Christmas customs parallel those of Great Britain, which formerly occupied the country. Festivities include children dancing to the music of drums, tambourines, cymbals, and colored sticks. Servants accept *baksheesh* (money tips) from their employers. A unique symbol of esteem is the lemon, offered to convey wishes of long life and prosperity. For those living in the plains, Christmas trees are constructed of straw, twigs, and mud, with paper decorations and candles. People in the mountainous regions may cut real evergreen trees. Banana and mango trees often receive decorations, and homes may be decorated with mango leaves. In the North, the aboriginal Bhils engage in all-night caroling during Christmas week, and in the South, citizens often place lighted clay oil lamps on their rooftops and along the walls outside. Christmas services often extend up to three hours. One way of saying "Merry Christmas" in India is *Shubh Naya Baras* (Hindi, one of 1,600 dialects in India).

• JAPAN. The prevailing religions are Shintoism and Buddhism, with only four percent of the population professing Christianity. Yet since the end of World War II, with the influx of Western customs, Japan has adopted *Kurisumasu* (Christmas) strictly as a festive work day. Families send Christmas cards and erect plastic Christmas trees decorated with origami figures, particularly swans, while children exchange origami "birds of peace." Christmas Eve parties, held either in hotels, restaurants, or at home, are fashionable, with chicken as a popular dish. A popular dessert provided on a large scale by confectioners is *Kurisumasu Keiki* (Christmas cake), which is similar to a Western birthday cake. Bearing candles, a Santa figure, and a Christmas greeting, such cakes are served only on Christmas Eve and are deemed worthless thereafter; hence, the term

"Christmas cake" is an alternate reference to any woman unwed by the age of 25. Other sites for Christmas Eve entertainment include Tokyo Disneyland, any of the urban leisure parks, and overnight cruises.

Children receive gifts from Santa, known either as *Santa Kurosu* or *Hoteiosho*. Because he always knows children's behavior, he is believed to have eyes in the back of his head.

Sometime during December, most organizations provide year-end bonuses and sponsor a *bonenkai* ("forget-the-year party") as an expression of thanks to employees for their services. In the custom of *seibo* ("year's end"), people present gifts to their social superiors and to those from whom they have received favors during the year (an identical custom, *chugen*, is observed at midyear). Polite etiquette requires personal delivery of the gifts.

Shogatsu (term for the first month of the year as well as the New Year holidays, December 31 through January 3) constitutes the most important of Japan's national holidays. Near year's end, houses are thoroughly cleaned, and a *shimenawa* (sacred straw rope) with *shide* (dangling white paper strips) is hung over the front door to greet the *toshigami* (harvest god of the new year) and to repel evil. This god is said to reside in a *kadomatsu* (arrangement of pine boughs [symbol of longevity] and bamboo), one of which is placed on each side of the entrance. The main room of the house features a *toshidana* ("year shelf"), an altar on which is placed a *kagamimochi* (offering to the gods consisting of *mochi* [rice cakes], *sake* [rice wine], and fruit). On *Omisoka* (New Year's Eve), rural families may still practice *mochitsuki* ("rice cake pounding"), the ancient art of forming rice cakes by pounding glutinous rice. Rice cakes, along with *toshikoshi soba* ("year-crossing noodles"), *zoni* (rice cake soup with vegetables), and *toso* (spiced rice wine), are traditional New Year's dishes; the long noodles symbolize hope for a lengthy family fortune. Because Buddhists believe that 108 earthly desires plague mankind, temple bells ring 108 times at midnight, a custom known as *joya no kane*, to encourage people to purge themselves of these evils in the new year.

On *Ganjitsu* (New Year's Day), families congregate, and the emperor offers prayers for the nation. On January 2 and 3, the visitation extends to friends and business associates. During this season, parents and relatives present children with *otoshidama* (spending money), and families observe *hatsumode* (first visit of the year to shrines and temples) to pray for a rich harvest in the new year. One is expected to send *nengajo* (New Year's cards, government-issued postcards with lottery numbers) to all relatives, friends, and business customers. The Japanese postal service collects and holds all cards that were mailed by Christmas and delivers them *en masse* on New Year's Day.

Traditional New Year's games include *sugoroku* (variant of Parcheesi), *karuta* (card games), *hanetsuki* (badminton with shuttlecock and battledore), and *takoage* (kite flying). In rural areas, costumed dancers repel evil by performing a *harukoma mai* (pony dance) or a *shishi mai* (lion dance).

"Merry Christmas" in Japanese is: *Kurisumasu Omedeto*.

• PAKISTAN. Ninety-seven percent of the population are Muslims. The Christian minority observes *Bara Din* ("Big Day," Christmas) in typical Westernized fashion. In addition, December 25 is the birthday anniversary of the founder of Pakistan, Quaid-I-Azam Mohammed Ali Jinnah, and is a national holiday. "Merry Christmas" in Pakistan is: *Nave sal di mubaraka* (Punjabi) or *Naya Saal Mubarak Ho* (Urdu).

• REPUBLIC OF INDONESIA. About 87 percent of the population are Muslims with 9 percent Christians (primarily Protestants). The Christmas season extends from Christmas Eve until the second week of January, and customs reflect 350 years of Dutch occupation (since the early seventeenth century). Traditions also are not markedly different from those in the United States, except that Santa Claus (Dutch *Sinterklaas*) in many areas still brings the Christmas gifts on December 5, the eve of St. Nicholas's Day. During the second week of December, many of the shopping malls and hotels sponsor events in which children may have lunch with Santa and be photographed with him. The Christmas dinner often features a blend of Indonesian, European, and Chinese foods, including assorted soups, stir-fry vegetables, chicken, beef, seafood, and pork (Muslims abstain from pork). "Merry Christmas" is *Selamat Hari Natal* (Bahasa Indonesia, the official language and the most widely spoken of more than 300 languages in Indonesia). *See also* **Saint Nicholas's Day.**

• SRI LANKA. Seventy percent of the population are Buddhists, with 11 percent Hindus and 8 percent each Christians and Muslims. Christmas Eve combines Christian and pagan observances, with bonfires, drums, and devil dances. The Christmas tree is known as the Tree of Life and is decorated with colored paper ornaments. "Merry Christmas" is: *Suba nath thalak Vewa* (Sinhalese).

Auld Lang Syne

("Old Long Ago"). Scottish folk tune of dismissal, the sentiments of which are now popularly associated with the celebration of the New Year. It was brought to prominence by Robert Burns (1759–1796), considered to be the national poet of Scotland, who claimed that he discovered "Auld Lang Syne" from an old man's singing and that it had never been in print. To the original three verses, Burns added two of his own in similar Scottish dialect, one beginning with "We twa hae run about the braes," the other with "We twa hae paidl'd in the burn," and sent them to a colleague, James Johnson, a music engraver in Edinburgh and a collector of Scottish folk songs. Having solicited Burns's assistance in acquiring such pieces, Johnson published *The Scots Musical Museum* between 1787 and 1803, a collection of six volumes for which Burns acted as editor until his death in 1796, and to which he contributed some 160 songs of his own. Burns's version of "Auld Lang Syne" first appeared in the fifth volume of the *Museum* some six months after his death. Johnson initially hesitated to publish it because the melody (not the melody familiar today) had appeared previously in the same collection to lyrics written by another poet, Allan Ramsay (1686–1758), beginning with "Should auld acquaintance be forgot, / Tho' they return with scars?" That same melody originally used for Ramsay's and Burns's lyrics had first been published in a separate collection, *Original Scotch Tunes* (1700).

The lyrics for "Auld Lang Syne" derive from several sources. One is a folk ballad of 1568, "Auld Kyndnes Foryett." Another is a poem by Sir Robert Ayton (1570–1638), published in *Choice Collection of Scots Poems* (1711), which begins, "Should auld acquaintance be forgot, / And never thought upon." A third possibility is a late seventeenth century street song containing the following refrain: "On old long syne. / On old long syne, my jo, / On old long syne: / That thou canst never once reflect / On old long syne." There are others in like vein.

The familiar tune paired with "Auld Lang Syne" today was selected by George Thomson, a music enthusiast and Burns contemporary, who occupied himself in finding suitable musical settings for Scots folk verses. Considered to be a common Scots country dance, this tune was variously named "The Miller's Wedding" in *Scots Reels* (1759) or "The Miller's Daughter" in *Strathspey Reels* (1780), among other versions and titles. Thomson published Burns's lyrics (by then, Burns had substituted "my dear" for "my jo" in the refrain) with the present tune in *Select Scottish Airs* (1799).

On the American scene, the band of Guy Lombardo and His Royal Canadians popularized "Auld Lang Syne" when they first played it on their New Year's Eve radio broadcast of 1929. It established the work not only as Lombardo's signature song but also as the theme for rejoicing in the coming new year.

Using the same melody but fashioning lyrics that combined Christmas with the New Year sentiment, Frank Military and Mann Curtis produced "Christmas Auld Lang Syne" in 1960, which teen idol Bobby Darin successfully introduced in a recording for the Atco label that year. Formerly associated with Dean Martin and Frank Sinatra, Military is not known for any other major hits. Curtis's other contributions, however, include lyrics for "The Story of a Starry Night" (1941) and "Let It Be Me" (1955), among others.

Australia

Christmas traditions on this continent stem principally from British occupation (beginning with the continent's use as a penal colony) dating to the eighteenth century. Australia observed its first Christmas in 1788 in Sydney, its first settlement, with Arthur Phillip as governor. Because of the season, Phillip commuted the flogging sentence of one Michael Dennison, convicted of having stolen a pound of flour, from the customary 200 lashes to only 150. Today, an Australian Christmas includes a variety of traditions from the influx of immigrants from Northern Europe, Italy, Greece, Spain, France, the Middle East, Asia, and North and South America.

Christmas arrives at the beginning of summer vacation, and, amid figures of Santa and Father Christmas clad in shorts and T-shirts, a picnic atmosphere with water sports activities at the beaches prevails, for the majority of Australia's citizens reside along the coast. According to local tradition, Swag Man, a figure akin to Santa and probably derived from a personage in the aboriginal folklore, lives under Uluru in the Northern Territory (Ayers Rock, the largest monolith in the world) and emerges at Christmastime with his dingoes to deliver gifts. Children, however, write letters to Santa or Father Christmas, and gifts are exchanged as in Great Britain.

Although Christmas trees may consist of cuttings from the native eucalyptus or gum trees, many Australians prefer artificial trees decorated either with Western ornaments or natural elements such as seed pods, gum nuts, or berries. As in the West, decorated Christmas trees are found in all public places, and Sydney's Queen Victoria Shopping Center boasts the largest artificial tree in the Southern Hemisphere, standing at a height of three stories. Other holiday decorations include native flowers such as the Christmas bell or Christmas bush (*see* **Christmas Plants**).

Initially, the Christmas dinner was a formal affair held indoors (where temperatures often exceeded 100 degrees Fahrenheit) and consisted of the traditional British fare of roast turkey with dressing, plum pudding, and other heavy dishes. By the end of the nineteenth century, however, Australians along the coast abandoned this tradition for Christmas at the seaside, or at least outdoors with a buffet and a menu of cold meats or seafood, salads, fruit, ice cream, fruit cake, chocolates, and perhaps even the traditional mince pie or plum pudding. The latter is still served with items such as a coin, ring, or thimble inside, and folklore holds that whoever finds these items will come into, re-

spectively, wealth, marriage, or spinsterhood in the coming year. Australia also holds the world's record (1987) for the largest plum pudding, weighing some 3,000 pounds and commercially cooked in Kensington, Victoria. Another favorite dessert is *pavlova*, a dish of whipped cream and fruit served in a meringue shell. Christmas meals also include the British "crackers," "poppers," or "bonbons," identical terms for party favors wrapped in hollow tubes that make a popping sound when opened.

Traditions unique to Australia include "Carols by Candlelight," large, community-wide singing festivals held in public parks, such as the one held on Christmas Eve at Melbourne's Myer Music Bowl. Although the custom is said to have originated in 1865, when Cornish miners from Moonta in Southern Australia gathered on Christmas Eve to sing carols by the light of candles attached to their hats, the modern "Carols by Candlelight" premiered in 1937 at Melbourne's Alexandria Gardens. Norman Banks, a local radio personality at the time, organized the event because he was touched by those who suffered loneliness at Christmastime, especially the elderly. The largest of these events, "Carols in the Domain," is always held on the last Saturday before Christmas at Sydney's Royal Botanic Gardens. The event is broadcast on radio and television throughout Southeast Asia and New Zealand, and the proceeds of the broadcasts are donated to charity. Other notable festivities in coastal cities include Queensland's "Christmas Lantern Festival," a week-long carnival before Christmas with parades, fireworks, and ornate lantern displays; and Sydney's "Twelve Days of Christmas at Darling Harbor," held 12 days before Christmas and featuring a number of cultural events.

An isolated life exists for those living on ranches in Australia's interior ("bush" or "outback"), where hundreds of miles may lie between them and the nearest village. Yet family members strive to return home for Christmas, and Santa manages to appear via small aircraft or railroad car. For some 40 years, the "Tea and Sugar Train" ran a 1,050-mile course in the Nullarbor Plain between Adelaide, South Australia, and Kalgoorlie in Western Australia. The train serviced the railroad camps along the route, and at Christmastime, Santa, decked out in red, brought gifts to some 1,000 children in the 1960s. Today most of those camps are closed.

Boxing Day, December 26, is a national holiday given almost entirely to sporting events or games of skill around the country. The most famous of these is the 630-mile yacht race from Sydney to Holbart, the capital of the island of Tasmania, which features entries from not only Australia and New Zealand, but also Great Britain, Japan, and the United States.

See also **Boxing Day; Great Britain**.

Austria

French missionaries first brought Christianity to Austria in the sixth century when they established the first monastery at Passau on the Danube River. Principally a Roman Catholic nation, Austria observes many Christmas customs quite similar to those of neighboring Germany.

The Christmas season begins with Advent, which features Christmas markets and multiple displays of *Krippen* (Nativity scenes) in church and public places. A noted *Krippe* resides at Steyr in Upper Austria, extant since 1579. The crypt at St. Peter's, Vienna, also hosts an exhibit of Nativity scenes, where the Society of the Friends of the Nativity Scene encourages new designs.

Households cut branches from cherry trees and place them in water on December 4, St. Barbara's Day. Termed "Barbara branches," these sprigs honor St. Barbara, a third-century Turkish martyr. According to legend, a single person whose Barbara branch blooms by Christmas Day will marry in the coming year. To celebrate St. Barbara's Day, miners from Matzen in Lower Austria have organized an *Erdölpfarre* ("Petroleum Parish") on the first Sunday of Advent since 1950 with a Mass, band concerts, and other ceremonies.

On December 5, the eve of St. Nicholas's Day, a hideous, fur-clad personification of Satan, known variously by the names of *Krampus*, *Knecht Ruprecht*, *Pelznickel*, and others, accompanies St. Nicholas for the ecclesiastical quizzing of children, distribution of gifts, and administration of punishment to the naughty. Village squares may sport one or more people dressed as this devil, at whom children delight in throwing snowballs. Another tradition is

Nicholas plays, often known by the name of the demon who accompanies St. Nicholas, such as *Klaubaufgehen* (after *Klaubauf*) at Matrei in Tyrol and *Bartel-Lauf* (from *Bartel*) at Oberdrauberg in Carinthia. Another masked figure, *Thomasnikolo* ("Tom Nicholas"), is peculiar to Gams of Styria and appears only on December 21, the former feast day of St. Thomas.

The second Thursday of Advent is devoted to *Wildes Gjaid* ("Wild Hunt") in Salzburg, in which men don masks portraying creatures of folk legends. This custom recalls the belief, prevalent throughout Europe from the ninth to the fourteenth centuries, that spirits of the dead flew about in midwinter, especially during the 12 days of Christmas, to increase the fertility of the fields. Other Advent customs include the "Walk Through Advent," an attraction presented on each of the four Advent Sundays in Salzburg, featuring music, recitations, and Nativity plays. Another featured Nativity folk play is the one held every four years at Bad Ischl in Upper Austria.

Christmas carols are not usually heard as such until Christmas Eve, when groups "showing the Christ Child" may carry a manger from house to house while singing carols. The Christmas tree, sporting real candles, is usually not erected and decorated until this time, after which a bell rings in the home to signal that the *Christkindl* ("little Christ Child")— or more specifically His winged messenger, depicted as a small, winged girl — has deposited the gifts under the tree. It is she to whom children write letters outlining their Christmas wishes. They place these letters on windowsills, hoping that the letters will vanish overnight, for then the Christ Child will grant their wishes. Since 1950, the town of Christkindl has sponsored the official *Posant Christkindl* (Christmas Post Office), where children may receive a reply postmarked with the traditional stamp showing the Holy Family under the Star of the East.

Other Christmas Eve customs include *Turmblasen* (brass ensembles playing Christmas chorales from church towers) and the *Herbergsuchen* ("Searching for Shelter"), a custom similar to the Latin American *Las Posadas*, in which groups reenact the Holy Couple's search for shelter in Bethlehem and which terminates with *Mitternachtsmette* (Midnight Mass). (*See* **Las Posadas.**)

The Christmas dinner usually features carp, and holiday baked items often include *Hetzen-brot* (fruit bread), *Lebkuchen* (gingerbread), *Hussarenkraperl* (Hussar jam-and-almond cookies), *Vanillekipferl* (vanilla crescents), *Kokobusserl* (coconut kisses), and *Zimtsterne* (cinnamon stars), among others.

On St. Stephen's Day (December 26, "Second Christmas Day"), families make traditional visits to friends and relatives. Holy Innocents Day (December 28) is marked with children "beating" their comrades and relatives with sticks to bring luck for the coming year, a custom known in Carinthia, Styria, and Burgenland as *Frish- und G'Sundschlagen* ("Beating to Wellness and Good Health").

On New Year's Eve (St. Sylvester's Day), men dress as an old, hideous creature of pagan origin, the mistletoe-clad "Sylvester" (renamed after the fourth century Pope St. Sylvester I), and seek to kiss maidens who chance to walk under evergreen sprigs. At midnight, Sylvester is driven out with the new year. Vienna traditionally stages a production of Johann Strauss's operetta *Die Fledermaus* on New Year's Eve, and instead of singing "Auld Lang Syne" at midnight, the Viennese dance to Strauss's "Blue Danube Waltz." Since the eighteenth century, the Vienna Philharmonic Orchestra has held a performance every New Year's Day, which is broadcast worldwide.

Epiphany features men dressed as the Three Kings who ride about on horseback. *Sternsinger* ("star singers"), bearing illuminated, revolving stars on poles, parade about while singing the traditional "Song of the Three Kings." Masked figures or mummers include *Glöckler* of Upper Austria, groups wearing elaborate, illuminated headdresses, who race down hillsides and deliver good luck by knocking on doors. A similar group, the *Perchten* (after the mythical goddess Perchta), runs near Salzburg. Attired in tall hats, animal masks, and ornate headdresses, they are accompanied by transvestite men who leap and dance about. The quality of their dancing supposedly determines the fate and bounty of the village for the new year. Stilt-dancers also bring good luck, and masked *Tresterer* are dancers whose movements mimic

threshing. These mummings recall the ancient conflicts between the life of summer and the death of winter, of fertility versus impotence.

"Merry Christmas" in Austria is spoken in German: *Fröhliche Weihnachten*.

See also **Advent**; **Germany**; **Mistletoe**; **Silent Night.**

The Autobiography of Santa Claus

Historical novel written by American author Jeff Guinn, first published in 1994 with the subtitle *It's Better to Give* and designated "edited by Jeff Guinn." In 2003, a revised edition modified the subtitle to *As Told to Jeff Guinn*. Written from the perspective of Saint Nicholas, the fourth century archbishop from Asia Minor, the novel spans seventeen centuries, places the jolly saint at the scene of major events in history that have affected the Christmas season, and traces his transformation from cleric to Santa Claus, the immortal distributor of gifts to children.

After writing a column filled with little-known facts about Christmas for his newspaper, *The Fort Worth Star-Telegram*, Guinn is invited to the North Pole to interview Santa Claus, who feels that the world should know the truth about him. Nicholas, as he calls himself, launched a life of year-round, secret philanthropy for the poor at an early age. His mission carried him to distant lands, whereupon he found that he could travel much faster through time than other people, except when in the proximity of wars and battles, and that he would grow no older than 63 years of age; that is, Nicholas's mission had endowed him with immortality. The same fate befell those most dear to Nicholas, including his wife Layla, whom he met in Constantinople, and those whom he solicited to accompany him as his assistants, such as Felix, a runaway slave; Attila the Hun and his wife Dorothea; King Arthur of England; St. Francis of Assisi; and other historical figures. Not serving as assistants, figures such as Charlemagne, crowned emperor of the Holy Roman Empire on Christmas Day in 800 A.D., urged Nicholas to keep December 25 a special day for gift-giving, whereas Queen Isabella of Spain, influenced by St. Francis, financed Christopher Columbus's expedition to the New World and generously supported

Nicholas's European toy enterprise as well. In the New World, Nicholas became a favorite among the Dutch settlers, his popularity increased through the drawings of cartoonist Thomas Nast. His role as Christmas gift-giver was forever established in the poem "A Visit from St. Nicholas," which Nicholas attributed to Clement Moore.

Filled with fantasy and magic, this book of 25 short chapters is designed to be read on each of the 25 December nights leading up to Christmas.

Jeff Guinn is an award-winning journalist and book editor for *The Fort Worth Star-Telegram*. His works include, among others, *Sometimes a Fantasy: Midlife Misadventures with Baseball Heroes* (1994) and *Our Land Before We Die: The Proud Story of the Seminole Negro* (2002).

See also **Saint Nicholas; A Visit from St. Nicholas.**

Ave Maria

("Hail Mary"). Title applied to a number of musical pieces in honor of the Virgin Mary, the two most prominent of which were written by Austrian composer Franz Schubert (1797–1828) and French composer Charles Gounod (1818–1893).

Schubert, who wrote over 600 songs, composed his "Ave Maria" in 1825, originally with verses from "The Lady of the Lake," a poem written in 1810 by English author Sir Walter Scott (1771–1832). In that poem, the heroine is forced into an unwanted marriage and appeals to the Virgin Mary for help. Later, the music was adapted to the Latin text of the Roman Catholic prayer to the Virgin, better known as the "Hail Mary," based on the angel Gabriel's annunciation to Mary that she is to be the mother of Jesus (Luke 1:26–28). The first performance in 1825 featured Schubert with his favorite vocalist, Johann Michael Vogl.

Gounod, also known for his operas *Faust* and *Romeo and Juliet*, among other works, originally published his melody in 1853 as an instrumental piece, "Meditation on the First Prelude of S. Bach." It consisted of an original, counterpoint melody superimposed on the opening C-major prelude of *The Well Tempered Clavier*, a collection that German composer

Johann Sebastian Bach had published in 1722. Gounod treated the Bach prelude as background harmony for his own melody, leaving Bach's subtly changing arpeggios intact, and scored his hybrid piece for violin, piano and organ. Although some verses and a soprano part were added later, the Bach-Gounod setting, as it is now known, was adapted to the Roman Catholic prayer, "Hail Mary," in 1859.

Away in a Manger

American carol, erroneously attributed to Martin Luther, the German priest of the Middle Ages who initiated the Protestant Reformation, and to an obscure Carl Mueller, to whom there is no other connection. The first two of its three anonymous verses appeared in *Little Children's Book for Schools and Families* (Philadelphia, 1885), authorized by the General Council of the Evangelical Lutheran Church of North America. The third verse (sometimes attributed, without substantiation, to a John T. McFarland) was first published in another Lutheran collection, *Gabriel's Vineyard Songs* (edited by Charles H. Gabriel, Louisville, Kentucky, 1892). In between these two publications, the carol's appearance in *Dainty Songs for Little Lads and Lasses, for Use in the Kindergarten, School and Home* (Cincinnati, 1897), edited by James R. Murray (1841–1905), initiated the confusion about Martin Luther. There, Murray included the heading "Luther's Cradle Hymn (Composed by Martin Luther for his children, and still sung by German mothers to their little ones)." He signed this setting with his initials and included "Music by J. R. M." in a subsequent publication a year later. Whether Murray genuinely believed that Luther had written the words or whether he merely used Luther's name for publicity, the carol quickly became popular and perpetuated the Luther myth for some 60 years. According to research published in 1945 by Richard S. Hill from the Library of Congress, however, the words to the first two verses originated as an anonymous poem taken from a series of American Lutheran children's dramatic presentations, which honored the four-hundredth anniversary of Luther's birthday in 1883. This settled the Luther issue.

The carol has been sung to some 40 different musical settings, the most popular of which in America is that composed by James R. Murray. Two other notable settings are those by Americans Jonathan E. Spilman in 1836 (also the setting for Robert Burns's poem "Flow Gently, Sweet Afton") and William J. Kirkpatrick in 1895 (more popular in England), the latter of whom also supplied the music for hymns such as "Tis So Sweet to Trust in Jesus" and "We Have Heard the Joyful Sound."

B

B.C.: A Special Christmas

(1981). Made-for-television animated cartoon, based on the popular comic strip *B.C.*, created by Johnny Hart.

Cavemen Peter and Wiley devise a money-making scheme by creating the legend of a man who delivers presents to everyone once a year. When people accept the legend, they will give gifts, which Peter and Wiley will sell to their friends in the name of this man, who will be called "Santa Claus." A tree will be his symbol, and he will fly in a reindeer sleigh. Since the two cavemen will sell "X" amount of merchandise to the "masses," the holiday will be known as "Xmas."

But during the planning, the true Santa makes his visit on December 24, and the legend becomes a reality.

Principal voices: Bob Elliott, Ray Goulding, Barbara Hamilton, Henry Ramer, Keith Hampshire, John Stocker, and Melleny Brown. Written by Johnny Hart. Produced and directed by Vlad Goetzelman. A Cinera Production in association with Hardlake Animated Pictures and Field Enterprises. VHS: Columbia/Tristar Video. 30 min.

Babar and Father Christmas

Classic children's book by French author Jean De Brunhoff, published posthumously in 1940.

In this tale set in the Elephants' country, Zephir the monkey has discovered that on Christmas Eve, Father Christmas brings toys to all the children in Man's country. Receiving no reply after he and his friends, elephant children Arthur, Pom, Flora, and Alexander, write letters inviting Father Christmas to visit them also, elephant king Babar decides to find Father Christmas and extend a personal invitation.

Babar's trek carries him to Europe, where he learns that Father Christmas lives in Bohemia on a mountain near "Prjmneswe." Accompanied by Duck, a little dog who tracks Father Christmas's scent on a doll, Babar easily overcomes a group of mountain dwarfs bent on preventing their access to Father Christmas's secret cave. A sudden storm forces the two to burrow into what seems to be a snow bank but in reality is a chimney, and they fall into Father Christmas's parlor. When he politely declines Babar's request on the basis of weariness and pressures of schedule, Babar invites Father Christmas to take a vacation in the Elephants' tropical clime, to which he agrees. They all return in Father Christmas's flying machine, which bears the initials "PN 1" for *Père Noël* 1 (Father Christmas 1).

As Christmas Eve approaches and Father Christmas prepares for his rounds, he commissions Babar to deliver the gifts to the residents of the Elephant country and provides Babar not only with a Santa suit that enables him to fly, but also with a magic bag that always remains filled with toys. Thus Babar brings Christmas to his land, and Father Christmas promises to return each year.

Jean De Brunhoff (1899–1937), originally a painter, based a series of children's books on stories told by his mother, who had created an elephant character for her children. Brunhoff later named the elephant Babar. His first book, *The Story of Babar* (1931), included illustrations by the author with text in cursive handwriting. Following Brunhoff's death, his son Laurent supplied the colors to the drawings in his father's unfinished works and eventually published his own *Babar* books, beginning with *Babar and That Rascal Arthur* (1946).

In 1986, *Babar and Father Christmas* was adapted as an animated cartoon for television under the same title, narrated by Laurent De Brunhoff. Principal voices: Jim Bradford, Courtney Caroll, Amie Charlebois, Noel Counsil, Derek Diorio, Kemp Edwards, Kai Engstad, Rick Jones, Roc LaFortune, Les Lye, Bridgitte Robinson, and Louise Villenueve. Vocals: John Brough, Teresa Dunn, Geri Childs, and Craig Kennedy. Written by Gerry Capelle, Laurent De Brunhoff, and Merilyn Read. Produced by Alison Clayton. Directed by Gerry Capelle. An Atkinson Film Arts and MTR Ottawa Production. VHS: Family Home Entertainment. 25 min.

Babes in Toyland

Operetta written in 1903 with musical score by the Irish-American composer Victor Herbert (1859–1924) and lyrics by Brooklyn native Glen MacDonough (1870–1924). The production was principally a musical revue with a minimal story line revolving around Mother Goose nursery rhymes and storybook characters: Two children, Alan and Jane, escaped from their miserly uncle to the fantasy world of Toyland via the garden of Contrary Mary ("Mary, Mary, quite contrary..."). Highlights of the operetta, which saw nearly 200 stage performances, included an elaborate Christmas pageant and the songs "Toyland" (vocal) and "March of the Toys" (instrumental).

Babes in Toyland is now best remembered through its motion picture versions. Although childhood fantasy, and not Christmas as such, is the central theme of these productions, it is this fantasy that makes the story especially appealing at Christmastime, when the season turns most adults into children again for a few days.

In 1934, producer Hal Roach (of the *Our Gang* comedies) created a different and more substantial story line for a film that would feature the renowned comedy team of Stan Laurel and Oliver Hardy. Laurel preferred a more fanciful approach, however, and that is what viewers see today. The Laurel and Hardy film, originally released as *March of the Wooden Sol-*

diers, incorporated a large segment of Herbert's score as background music with several vocal solos, time constraints precluding the other numbers. Two songs, "Go to Sleep, Slumber Deep" and "Castle in Spain," which had been cut from the original operetta, appeared in the 1934 film. Two additional songs from "outside" sources, "Who's Afraid of the Big Bad Wolf?" and "Rock-a-Bye Baby," were the respective creations of Walt Disney Studios (for the *Three Little Pigs*) and Effie I. Canning. In addition to the titles *Babes in Toyland* and *March of the Wooden Soldiers*, this film is known as *Laurel and Hardy in Toyland*, *Wooden Soldiers*, and *Revenge Is Sweet*.

In the film, Mother Goose (Virginia Karns) introduces the principal nursery rhyme and storybook characters depicted in Toyland: "Little Bo-Peep"; "Tom-Tom, the Piper's Son"; "The Little Old Lady Who Lived in a Shoe"; "Hi Diddle Diddle, the Cat and the Fiddle"; "The Three Little Pigs"; "Little Miss Muffet"; "Rock-a-Bye Baby"; "Mary, Mary, Quite Contrary"; "Little Jack Horner"; "Jack and Jill"; and "Little Red Riding Hood."

When Widow Peep (Florence Roberts), proprietor of a boarding shoe-house, defaults on her mortgage payment to Silas Barnaby (Henry Brandon, credited as Henry Kleinbach), this "meanest man in town" offers to cancel the mortgage if her daughter, Little Bo-Peep (Charlotte Henry), will marry him. Knowing that Bo-Peep is engaged to Tom-Tom (Felix Knight), boarders Stannie Dum and Ollie Dee (Laurel and Hardy, their characters parodies of Tweedle Dum and Tweedle Dee) attempt to steal the mortgage. With Ollie hidden in a large gift box, Stannie carts him to Barnaby's house, admonishing Barnaby not to open the box until Christmas, which is five months away. The plan almost works, until Stannie calls out, "Good night, Ollie," and Ollie answers. Charged with burglary, Stannie and Ollie are sentenced by Old King Cole (Kewpie Morgan) to be dunked in a pond and exiled to Bogeyland, but when Bo-Peep intervenes and consents to wed Barnaby, he drops the charges. Determined to foil Barnaby, Ollie gives the bride away and destroys the mortgage papers as Barnaby lifts the veil, only to find that his "bride" is Stannie in drag. With no mortgage and no bride, Barnaby seeks revenge by kidnapping one of the Three Little Pigs and planting the evidence (his fiddle, hat, and some sausage links) in Tom-Tom's house. Framed, Tom-Tom is thrown into Bogeyland for "pignapping." When Ollie discovers that the sausage is beef instead of pork, he and Stannie rescue the pig, kept prisoner in Barnaby's cellar, after which Toyland pursues Barnaby, who escapes through a secret passage into Bogeyland. Summoning all the bogeymen (hideous, half-human monsters), Barnaby and his troupe storm into Toyland, where a battle of good versus evil rages. After Stannie and Ollie rescue Tom-Tom, victory is assured when they activate 100 six-foot mechanical toy soldiers, who rout the villains out of the city forever.

A particularly memorable comedy routine features Stannie and the game of Pee-Wee. Stannie has used up his and Ollie's savings to buy Pee-Wees, short, round, wooden pieces tapered on both ends. Placing a Pee-Wee on the ground and striking one end with a stick pops it into the air; then Stannie bats it like a conventional baseball, and it comes back to him like a boomerang. The game proves most useful for knocking Barnaby in the head. In another routine, Stannie and Ollie, employees at the Toyland Toy Factory, have misinterpreted Santa's order for 600 toy soldiers, each one foot high. Instead, the factory makes 100 mechanical soldiers, each six feet high. A demonstration of their working functions leaves the factory in shambles, and the boys are fired on the spot. Of course, these six-foot soldiers later save the day.

With Marie Wilson and Johnny Downs. Written by Frank Butler and Nick Grinde. Produced by Hal Roach. Directed by Gus Meins and Charles Rogers. Hal Roach Studios and Metro-Goldwyn-Mayer. DVD: Goodtimes Home Video. B & W. 77 min.

• REMAKES OF BABES IN TOYLAND:

(1954). Live NBC television adaptation starring Wally Cox, Dave Garroway, and Jack E. Leonard. Written by Glen MacDonough. Video N/A. B & W.

(1960). Made-for-television version starring Paul Ford, Shirley Temple, and Jonathan Winters. Production and video N/A.

(1961). Disney motion picture starring Ray Bolger, Tommy Sands, Annette Funicello, Ed Wynn, Tommy Kirk, and Kevin Corcoran. In 1962, it received the following honors: Academy Award nominations for Best Costume Design and Best Musical Scoring; Golden Globe Award nomination for Best Motion Picture Musical; Grammy Award nomination for Best Soundtrack Album; won Golden Laurel Award for Top Musical Score and Golden Laurel third place for Top Musical; Writers' Guild of America Award nomination for Best Written American Musical. Written by Lowell S. Hawley, Ward Kimball, and Joe Rinaldi. Produced by Walt Disney. Directed by Jack Donohue. DVD: Walt Disney Home Video. 106 min.

(1986). Made-for-television adaptation starring Drew Barrymore, Richard Mulligan, Eileen Brennan, Keanu Reeves, and Pat Morita. In 1988, it received a Young Artist Award nomination for Best Young Female Superstar in Television (Drew Barrymore). Written by Paul Zindel. Produced by Tony Ford and Neil T. Maffeo. Directed by Clive Donner. Orion Television Entertainment, the Finnegan Company, and the Finnegan-Pinchuk Company. VHS: Metromedia Home Video. 140 min.

(1997). Animated cartoon with principal voices: Charles Nelson Reilly, Lacey Chabert, Joseph Ashton, Raphael Sbarge, Catherine Cavadini, Christopher Plummer, Susan Silo, Bronson Pinchot, James Belushi, and Lindsay Schnebly. Cavadini and Plummer received 1998 Annie Award nominations for Outstanding Achievement in Voice Acting in an Animated Feature. Written by John Loy. Produced by Paul Sabella, Jonathan Dern, Kelly Ward, and Mark Young. Directed by Charles Grosvenor, Toby Bluth, and Paul Sabella. Metro-Goldwyn-Mayer. VHS: MGM/UA Studios. 74 min.

Baboushka
See **Russia**

A Baby in the Cradle
See **He Smiles Within His Cradle**

Baby Jesus, in a Manger
See **Infant Holy, Infant Lowly**

A Baby Lies in the Cradle
See **He Smiles Within His Cradle**

Baby's First Christmas
See **The Smurfs**

Bagpipers' Carol
See **Carol of the Bagpipers**

Bah, Humbug! The Story of Charles Dickens' "A Christmas Carol"
See **A Christmas Carol** (Film and Television Versions)

Bahamas
See **West Indies**

Baltic States (Estonia, Latvia, Lithuania)

These nations have enjoyed Christmas since the thirteenth century, when German Crusaders brought Christianity to this region. While Estonia and Latvia primarily adhere to the Lutheran Church, Lithuania remains predominantly Roman Catholic. Although specific Christmas traditions differ within the three nations, they share a mixture of Christian beliefs with those centering on agrarian rites and superstitions from ancient pagan winter solstice festivals, and they also share typical Advent customs. During the period from 1940 to 1991, Soviet occupation suppressed Christmas celebrations and established a secular season by substituting "Grandfather Frost" for St. Nicholas as the bearer of gifts and by transferring the winter festival to New Year's Day. Once again independent, these three nations have reinstated their former traditions, which the following paragraphs summarize.

• ESTONIA. Although the *Jõulud* (Christmas) season extends from Advent to Epiphany, the principal holidays occur between Christmas Eve and the two days following Christmas. In southern Estonia, Christmas is known as *Talvistepüha* ("Winter Holiday"). Santa Claus and Christmas trees are well known, the latter adopted from local German culture during the mid–nineteenth century. Trees, often fir, are decorated with small toys, sweets, and candles. Other traditions include "Little Christmas" observances borrowed from Scandinavians, which consist of office parties during early Advent; bringing home Christmas straw, symbolic of the manger; making Christmas crowns in the likenesses of church chandeliers

(the custom was brought from Finland through Swedish descendants living on the island of Vormsi); bathing in a sauna on Christmas Eve prior to any festivities; dressing children in new clothes for Christmas Eve services; and the annual Christmas Eve declaration of "Christmas Peace" by the Estonian president, a tradition practiced since the seventeenth century.

Seven to 12 different meals are served on Christmas Eve (abundant food symbolizes bounty for the coming year), and the menu traditionally consists of pork with sauerkraut, "white" and "blood" sausages, Christmas barrow (bread), ale, and mead. Livestock receive portions of the meal, the remainder of which must stand on the table overnight for the benefit of the spirits of family ancestors, and a fire must also burn throughout Christmas Eve night to dispel evil (a custom deriving from ancient pagan winter solstice festivals).

Following Christmas Eve church services, families adorn graves of family members with lighted candles, a custom that also once symbolized a national protest against the Communist regime. Christmas Day is spent with immediate family, while the remaining holidays are given to outside visitations.

"Merry Christmas" in Estonia is: *Rõõmsaid Jõulupühi.*

• LATVIA. *Ziemassvetki* ("Winter Festival," Christmas) extends for four days, symbolized by the Brothers Ziemassvetki, four mythical, celestial beings of undifferentiated form who are believed to bring prosperity and gifts. Tradition also celebrates this time as the birth of *Dievs* (God). In addition to Christmas trees, homes are decorated with sun symbols made from straw, which are hung from the ceiling and corners, along with birds' feathers and dried flowers.

As the festival commences, families pull an oak log around the exterior of the house during the day in the belief that all the year's evil is transferred to the log. Then the log is burned that night amid a chorus of carols to cleanse the house and fields from the evil trapped therein. This ritual also stems from ancient rites that supposedly aided the sun's ascent at the winter solstice. The festival includes much singing and dancing as *kekatnieki*, throngs of people costumed as wolves, bears, or other animals, walk about frightening away evil spirits in rural areas and performing plays and skits. Other groups consist of *kaladnieces*, roving bands of female carolers, who receive treats and gifts from homes serenaded, and *Iekatas*, costumed singers who also set fire to tires and roll them down hills as symbols of the "burning wheel" of the winter solstice. A favorite costume is "Death" (white head scarf, flour on the face, and black circles under the eyes), which wards off its namesake. Urban regions are more likely to sport a Father Christmas figure.

The principal feast occurs on Christmas Eve with a menu often consisting of smoked pig's head and all manner of pork products, gray beans for maturity and strength, peas to shed fewer tears, *piragi* (dumplings stuffed with bacon and ham) for sunny days, breads, baked apples, and beer. The more one eats, it is believed, the healthier one will become, and those men who consume the greatest quantity of sausages are considered to be the strongest.

"Merry Christmas" in Latvia is: *Prieci'gus Ziemsve'tkus.*

• LITHUANIA. The principal season, extending from Advent to Epiphany, is dominated by the rituals of *Kucios* (the same word denotes "Christmas Eve" and "Christmas Eve Supper"), which commences when the first star of the evening is sighted, believed to be the Star of Bethlehem. The meal begins with unleavened communion wafers, variously known as *plotkeles*, *paplotelis*, *plokstainelis*, or *Dievo pyragai* ("God's cakes"), that are stamped with Nativity scenes. As family members exchange portions of wafer with ritual greetings, each person attempts to break off a piece larger than what remains behind, for a larger piece portends a successful new year. In contrast, he whose piece is smaller has his luck broken. Apples on the table also commemorate December 24 as the feast day of Adam and Eve. The lady of the house slices an apple and presents the first piece to her husband, symbolic of Eve offering the forbidden fruit to Adam as detailed in the Book of Genesis, after which she distributes the remaining slices to those at the table. Symbolic of the manger, hay or straw lies beneath the white tablecloth. The table has been decorated with candles and fir boughs, and the commu-

nion wafers, one for each person present, have been arranged on a plate at center table.

Meat is no longer forbidden, yet to observe strict *Kucios* tradition is to serve 12 meatless courses, symbolic of Christ's 12 Apostles. The menu may include herring and other fish, *slizikai* (small, hard biscuits served with poppy seeds and honey sauce or milk), *kisielius* (cranberry pudding), dried fruit compote, mushroom soup, potatoes, assorted dried or pickled vegetables, sauerkraut, bread, and assorted cakes. Drinks include water or juice but never alcohol or other stimulants. Some regions may feature *kucia*, a most traditional dish of bygone days, which consists of a mixture of cooked grains served with honey and boiled water.

Anyone who does not at least taste each course is said to risk death within the coming year; a similar fate awaits the person who does not participate in the breaking of the wafer.

Fir twigs and myrtle adorn the seats at the table, and a vacant place, marked with a chair, a plate with a burning candle, but no eating utensils, is set for any deceased family member. Any food remaining is left on the table overnight for the spirits of deceased family members who are believed to return overnight, and no one leaves the table until all have eaten and the auguries have been read (see subentry below, "Superstitions"), lest death befall him.

Decorating Christmas trees and other secular aspects of Christmas such as gift-giving came into vogue in Lithuania at the turn of the twentieth century; prior to that time, Christmas was observed as a strictly religious holiday. The most distinctively Lithuanian Christmas tree ornaments are fashioned either from real wheat or rye straw or plastic drinking straws into elaborate mobiles of innumerable sizes and shapes. Some ornaments are created from colored eggshells, paper, pastry, apples, pine cones, and nuts, but these are usually omitted when straw ornaments are utilized. If a tree decorated with straw ornaments is to be illuminated, custom dictates using only yellow lights, which enhance the straw shapes in ways not possible with multi-colored lights. Straw may also form the principal element of wayside shrines adorning country roads. The Christmas tree is decorated on Christmas Eve prior to *Kucios*, and gifts are opened after the auguries and a period of caroling around the family tree.

With the coming of independence, Santa Claus has returned to Lithuania in the form of *Kalédu Senelis* ("Grandfather Christmas"), who arrives on Christmas Eve demanding a "price" from children in exchange for gifts. To that end, children sing carols, recite poems, dance, or play instruments for his amusement. Following these festivities, Christmas Eve concludes with *Piemeneliu Misos* ("Shepherd's Mass"), which is held either at midnight or at dawn on Christmas Day. Families attend church services and visit friends on Christmas Day.

New Year's Eve recalls the atmosphere of Christmas Eve with another family dinner and a repetition of auguries, and young people masquerade about in costumes of animals or as the "Old Year" and "New Year." On Epiphany, families write "K.M.B.," the initials of the three Wise Men (Kaspar, Melchior, Balthazar) on their doors along with signs of the cross, and young people masquerade as the Wise Men.

"Merry Christmas" in Lithuania is: *Linksmu Kalédu.*

• SUPERSTITIONS. According to folklore, by no means unique to the Baltic States, the future may be revealed on Christmas Eve and New Year's Day, for whatever transpires on these two days will affect the coming new year. Because the number of superstitions is almost without limit, only a few are cited here. For example, many stars clustered together forecast a good year. If there is snow on Christmas Day, Easter will be green, and vice versa. A clear New Year's Day that brings good news or frost covering the trees predicts a bountiful year; snow, rain, or thick fog on New Year's Day predicts disaster. To become wealthy, carry a black cat around a church, eat as many gray peas as possible, or eat nine times before midnight on Christmas Eve.

A girl may seek glimpses of her future mate through several rituals. If she pours hot lead into a glass of water, the shape of the mass will reveal his occupation. After Christmas Eve supper, if a girl sweeps the floor and tosses the refuse at a crossroads, the next dog that barks determines the direction from which her future husband will come; one variation calls for the girl merely to stand outside and howl like a dog, then listen for the bark. The length and shape of a straw pulled randomly from beneath the tablecloth or a piece of wood pulled from a woodpile predicts a future spouse's physical appearance (fat or thin, short or tall). For one already married, a fat or thin straw or corresponding piece of wood forecasts abundance or poverty, respectively, in the coming year. If a girl tosses her shoe backward toward a door and the toe points to the door, she will wed in the coming year; if the toe points away, she will remain single that year. If a girl can count any batch of items evenly by twos, she will wed in the new year. In one elaborate ritual, a girl writes the name of a different boy on each of 12 slips of paper, folds them in half, then distributes them around the edge of a bowl of water. She places a small, lighted candle in half of a nutshell and floats this on the water. The name at which the "boat" stops reveals the name of her future husband.

If the first person to visit the home on New Year's Day is a man (akin to the British "first footing"), the entire year will be plentiful; the opposite is in store if the visitor is a woman.

See also **Advent**; **Great Britain**; **Epiphany**.

Barbados
See **West Indies**

Barbie in "The Nutcracker"
See **The Nutcracker**

The Bear Who Slept Through Christmas

Children's book published in 1980 by John Barrett, also adapted for television as an animated cartoon.

Ted E. Bear dreams of being the first bear to find Christmas, with all of its gifts and music, said holiday rumored to be supervised by a man wearing a red suit and white beard. When Ted is fired from his job at Organic Honeyworks for daydreaming, he sets out for the city in quest of Christmas. He investigates a toy store with dazzling gifts and surveys a church, the choir of which certainly provides the beautiful music, but, to his dismay, Christmas is not there.

By chance, Ted meets the red-suited, white-bearded man, who advises that Christmas can only be found in the heart and offers an address where Ted can fulfill his wish. The address is an ordinary house, to which Ted easily gains access, and there he finds only a Christmas tree and a few gifts but no music. Falling asleep under the tree, he awakens in the morning to find a happy little girl cuddling him closely to her, overjoyed that Santa brought him as her Christmas gift. Ted has found Christmas, for as Santa said, Christmas is a way of giving, of sharing, and of loving.

The 1983 television animated cartoon featured the voices of Tom Smothers, Barbara Feldon, Arte Johnson, Robert Holt, Kelly Lange, Michael Bell, Casey Kasem, and Caryn Paperny. A Sed-Bar Production in association with De-Patie-Freleng Enterprises. VHS: Lionsgate/Fox. 30 min.

Other books by John Barrett include *Christmas Comes to Monster Island* (1981), *Easter Bear* (1981), *The Great Bear Scare* (1981), and *Ted E. Bear Rescues Santa Claus* (1985).

The Bears' Christmas
See **The Berenstain Bears**

Beautiful Star of Bethlehem
Popular American Southern Gospel carol, the lyrics of which were written by Robert Fisher Boyce (1887–1968), a rural dairy farmer who resided in the Big Springs community south of Murfreesboro, Tennessee. Claiming to have received inspiration from God, Boyce penned the lyrics in his barn during the summer of 1938 and then provided a musical setting with assistance from a daughter, Nannie Lou Taylor. Afterwards, Boyce attended so-called singing schools sponsored by the James D. Vaughan Publishing Company of Lawrenceburg, Tennessee, a firm that promoted the sale of hymnals and gospel music by offering courses in music notation. Aside from the merits of the carol itself, Boyce's subsequent service as an instructor for these courses probably contributed to the publication of "Beautiful Star," which Vaughan first published in their 1940 song book *Beautiful Praise* and later in their *Favorite Radio Songs*. Although Boyce is considered to be the sole lyricist, printed arrangements have included the name of Adger M. Pace, an editor for Vaughan at the time.

Boyce's creation, an allegory in which the

Star of Bethlehem serves to light the path to salvation through Christ, was originally intended as a simple hymn to be sung throughout the year, yet its popular appeal over time through the country, gospel, and bluegrass genres has associated it far more with the Christmas season.

The John Daniel Quartet first recorded "Beautiful Star" in Nashville on their Daniel label with John "Whit" Curtis as arranger and sole accompanist, the latter citing Christmas of 1953 or 1954 as the year of this debut. Two recordings have been proposed as definitive versions: one by the Stanley Brothers in their album *Hymns from the Cross* (King Records, 1964) and one by Ralph Stanley and the Clinch Mountain Boys in their album *Clinch Mountain Gospel* (Rebel Records, 1977). Other notable recordings featuring "Beautiful Star" include the Jimmie Davis album *Highway to Heaven* (Decca, 1964); the Emmylou Harris album *Light of the Stable* (Warner Bros., 1981); and The Judds album *Christmas Time with The Judds* (RCA/Curb, 1987). The Judds also performed "Beautiful Star" at the White House during a Bob Hope television special.

Robert Boyce had been writing songs since the age of 24, yet only one other title is known, "Safe in His Love," his first work, which was published by the A.J. Showalter Company.

Behold a Branch Is Growing
See **Lo, How a Rose E'er Blooming**

Belgium
See **The Low Countries**

Belize
See **Central America**

The Bells of St. Mary's
(1945). Motion picture drama, a sequel to *Going My Way*. Like its predecessor, *Bells* was not originally intended as a Christmas movie. However, its inspirational themes of faith, goodwill, and the occasional plot references to Christmas have brought it into the realm of Christmas classics by popular association.

Bing Crosby reprises his role as the affable and easy-going Father Chuck O'Malley, this time sent to be the pastor of St. Mary's, a dilapidated parochial school, and to determine whether it should be razed and the children sent elsewhere. Next door, greedy land developer Horace P. Bogardus (Henry Travers) is erecting a commercial building and would have St. Mary's property on which to build a parking lot. Sister Mary Benedict (Ingrid Bergman), the sister superior, however, maintains a steadfast faith that Bogardus will miraculously donate his building to be the new St. Mary's School.

Around this scenario, the story pits the easy Father and strong-handed Sister against each other in a good-natured battle of wits and opposing views about running the school. Each has personal charges of sorts: Sister Benedict teaches one small boy to defend himself through boxing, and Father O'Malley, through the song "Aren't You Glad You're You?" imparts insight and wisdom to a troubled student, Patsy Gallagher (Joan Carroll). Furthermore, after the Father locates her long-estranged father for a happy reunion with her mother, there's musical wisdom for the couple through "In the Land of Beginning Again." Another brief diversion, but precious nonetheless, is the first-grade Christmas play, in which the children completely ad-lib their lines among simplistic pops and sing "Happy Birthday" to Jesus instead of "Adeste Fideles," the latter of which the Father rehearses with the older students.

While discussing St. Mary's situation with Father O'Malley, Bogardus is initially annoyed to hear the sisters singing the carol "O Sanctissima," but when the Father joins in, Bogardus suddenly experiences an ethereal vision of school children seated behind desks within his building. This and his doctor's admonition (at the Father's prompting) that benevolence and generosity will strengthen his weak heart serve to make a new man out of Bogardus, who donates his building to St. Mary's after all. Such news is most bittersweet, for it comes at a time when Father O'Malley must transfer Sister Benedict elsewhere. Yet she is made much happier knowing that the reason lies in an early diagnosis of tuberculosis rather than because of any differences of opinion that they may have shared.

Two notes of trivia: As the children recite the Pledge of Allegiance, viewers will note the phrase, "one nation, indivisible" with the absence of "under God." The latter two words (a controversial issue in the twenty-first century) were added in 1954 by an act of Congress. *The Bells of St. Mary's* was the movie playing at the Bedford Falls theater on Christmas Eve in *It's a Wonderful Life.*

In 1946, this picture won an Academy Award for Best Sound Recording. Academy nominations: Best Leading Actor (Bing Crosby), Best Leading Actress (Ingrid Bergman), Best Director, Best Film Editing, Best Original Song ("Aren't You Glad You're You?" by Jimmy Van Heusen and Johnny Burke), Best Music Scoring, and Best Picture. Won Golden Globe Award for Best Actress (Bergman). Won New York Film Critics' Circle Award for Best Actress (Bergman). Won Gold Medal from Photoplay Awards.

With William Gargan, Ruth Donnelly, Martha Sleeper, Rhys Williams, Richard Tyler, and Una O'Connor. Story by Leo McCarey. Screenplay by Dudley Nichols. Produced and directed by Leo McCarey. NTA Pictures and Rainbow Productions. DVD: Lionsgate/Fox. B & W. 126 min.

The Bells of St. Mary's was remade for CBS Television in 1959, starring Claudette Colbert as Sister Benedict and Robert Preston as Father O'Malley. Produced by Jacqueline Babbin. Directed by Tom Donovan. Video N/A. B & W. 90 min.

See also **Going My Way.**

Ben-Hur: A Tale of the Christ

Highly acclaimed American novel and best-known work of Lewis (Lew) Wallace, published in 1880. Although this historical novel, most often remembered for its spectacular chariot race, does not typically fall into the Christmas literary repertoire, its "Book First," designed as an extended prologue, beautifully expands upon the Nativity story as presented in the Gospels of Matthew and Luke. Having received a summons from the Holy Spirit and riding white camels, the three Wise Men, Melchior of India, Gaspar of Greece, and Balthazar of Egypt, rendezvous in the Arabian Desert on December 25 in the year 747 of Rome to commence their search for the Christ. Arriving in Bethlehem 12 days later (Epiphany), they find a cave wherein the Babe lies in a manger fashioned not of wood but of stone.

Read the Book - See the Movie
BEN-HUR

The Story of the Christ
By General Lew Wallace

The tender lilt of a love song mixed with the thundering, clashing cymbals of mad lust re-echo through and through this fascinating story of the time when Rome was arrogant mistress of the world—when old Egypt glowed like a smouldering flame in splendid decline—and the whole is softened and mellowed by the tender touch of the Christ, whose life and final supreme sacrifice is most dramatically told.

Ben-Hur will leave you breathless with its mighty wonder. Long after the book is laid aside you will remember the tense, fierce atmosphere of the arena, the vivid description of the famous chariot race and the soul stirring scene of the crucifixion. You are unfair to yourself unless you read this immortal masterpiece of General Lew Wallace.

This story will be released in the movies very shortly and, in order to properly appreciate the movie, you should read the book first. Bound in cloth, 491 pages. Size, 5½x7½ inches. Shipping weight, 1¼ pounds.
3D101..**68c**

"In order to properly appreciate the movie, you should read the book first," advises this 1915 Sears Roebuck catalog plug for Ben-Hur. *The famed chariot race gets the starring role.*

The novel's epigraph cites lines from *On the Morning of Christ's Nativity*, an ode written by English poet John Milton.

Initially an agnostic, Lew Wallace (1827–1905), a noted American Civil War general and literary genius, set out to write a book that would destroy Christianity. For two years, he conducted research in the best libraries of America and Europe. While writing the second chapter of this book, all his research abruptly ceased when, reviewing all the accumulated evidence, he was overwhelmed with the sudden conviction that Christ is the Son of God. Wallace found himself on his knees pouring forth his faith, a faith which later enabled him to write *Ben-Hur*. His other novels include *The Fair God* (1873) and *The Prince of India* (1893).

See also **Epiphany; On the Morning of Christ's Nativity; Nativity; Wise Men.**

The Berenstain Bears

Large, popular series of books for young children begun in 1962, written and illustrated by the award-winning husband-and-wife team of American cartoonists, Stan and Jan Berenstain. The original characters included Papa, Mama, and Brother Bear. Sister Bear arrived in 1974 and the youngest, Honey Bear, in 2000.

Of the more than 250 titles in which the Berenstain Bears appear, four center around Christmas. Secular themes predominate, yet the basic holiday sentiments of goodwill, caring, and giving are clearly interwoven.

The Bears' Christmas (1970). In this beginners' reader, Papa Bear spends Christmas Day attempting to teach his young son how to use the sled, ice skates, and skis that Santa brought. At every turn, Papa only succeeds in creating disasters for himself, yet bear and son consider this the best Christmas ever. A 1989 animated version of the same title on video includes two additional stories: *Inside, Outside, Upside Down* and *The Bike Lesson*. VHS: Sony Wonder. 24 min.

The Berenstain Bears' Christmas Tree (1980), based on the 1979 animated television special of the same title. Papa Bear takes Brother and Sister Bear on a trek to find and cut down the perfect Christmas tree. At first thinking of his own Christmas interests, Papa soon realizes that many animals have set up housekeeping in the trees. Because he spares them and because Grizzly Gus's Christmas tree lot is sold out, the same forest animals surprise Papa and the cubs by decorating the exterior of their house/tree. Animated version narrated by Ron McLarty. Principal voices: Pat Lysinger, Jonathan Lewis, and Gabriela Glatzer. Teleplay by Stan and Jan Berenstain. Produced by Buzz Potamkin. Directed by Mordicai Gerstein. A Cates Brothers Company Production in association with Perpetual Motion Pictures. VHS: Goodtimes Home Video. 24 min.

The Berenstain Bears Meet Santa Bear (1984). Dazzled over television commercials for Christmas toys, yet not wanting to appear greedy, Sister Bear, at Brother Bear's suggestion, prepares a more respectable wish list worthy of Santa Bear's approval. After buying gifts for Mama and Papa Bear (Santa Bear only visits cubs, not parents) and contributing to the needy, Sister wonders how Santa Bear can visit every cub in the world in one night. Papa sums it all up: Christmas is a magical time, and Santa Bear has the best job in the world, because the joy of giving is what Christmas is all about.

The Berenstain Bears Save Christmas (2003), illustrated by son Mike Berenstain. Through his scanner machine, Santa Bear witnesses such appalling Christmas commercialism in Bear Country that he threatens to cancel the holiday unless the true spirit of Christmas be found. When news of his disappearance from the North Pole is broadcast, Mama Bear convinces her family to set a good example by forsaking their artificial, gaudy displays and long wish lists and return to the simple, old-fashioned traditions of yore. When on Christmas Eve a stranger caught in a blizzard visits the Bear family, he is heartened to find hospitality, simple holiday trimmings, and letters to Santa Bear that convey only special requests for their friends and neighbors, not themselves. The stranger's identity is easily deduced, for, traveling incognito, he has found the spirit of Christmas in the Bear family.

The Berenstain Bears' Christmas Tree
See **The Berenstain Bears**

The Berenstain Bears Meet Santa Bear
See **The Berenstain Bears**

The Berenstain Bears Save Christmas
See **The Berenstain Bears**

The Best Christmas
See **The Waltons**

The Best Christmas Pageant Ever

Children's book written by American author Barbara Robinson, published in 1972. An abbreviated version appeared in *McCall's* magazine as "The Christmas Pageant."

For years, the annual Sunday school Christmas pageant has featured the same songs, the same cast (Alice Wendleken always portrays Mary), and the same script. The children certainly loathe it, and nobody really enjoys attending such an ordeal.

This year, however, everything changes when the Herdmans arrive. Incorrigible school bullies, forever pulling pranks (like blowing up Mr. Shoemaker's tool shed with a chemistry set), and totally unfamiliar with the Christmas story, the abominable Herdman children — Ralph, Imogene, Leroy, Claude, Ollie, and

Gladys—crash the Christmas pageant rehearsal and take over the lead roles by intimidating the other children, including Alice. Latch-key children because their father has deserted them and their mother works double shifts at the shoe factory, the Herdmans develop an interest in Sunday school and thence the pageant through Charlie, a schoolmate who deceives them with notions of receiving delicious refreshments there.

With Mrs. Armstrong out of commission with a broken leg, Charlie's mother assumes the role of pageant director, which includes familiarizing the Herdmans with the Nativity. As she reads from Luke and Matthew, surprisingly they ask innumerable questions about the characters' roles. They are appalled that a pregnant Mary must reside in a "barn," and they take much interest in King Herod, whom Imogene especially wants to punish because he sought to kill Baby Jesus. The Herdmans also decide that more "decent" gifts than gold, frankincense, and myrrh must be sought for the pageant.

On pageant night, the congregation, deliciously anticipating Herdman mayhem, turns out in droves to see Imogene as Mary; Ralph as Joseph; Leroy, Claude, and Ollie as Wise Men; and little Gladys as the Angel of the Lord. The production at first includes the usual minor miscues, but the atmosphere changes as Mary enters, burping a baby doll; the Angel addresses the shepherds with, "Hey! Unto you a child is born!"; and the Wise Men lay a large ham (from the Herdmans' Christmas food basket) before the manger. And as everyone sings a final "Silent Night," the magnitude of Christmas overwhelms Imogene, who begins to weep. This best-ever pageant transforms the ragamuffins and congregation alike: the former are more sedate, docile, and perhaps more considerate of others afterwards; the latter more clearly sees the human side of the Nativity — impoverished parents facing hardships while bringing a new life into the world.

A 1983 American-Canadian adaptation of the story for television starred Loretta Swit, Anthony Holland, Jackson Davies, David Alexander, Fairuza Balk, Ocean Hellman, Teri Dean, Beau Heaton, Megan Hunt, Jason Micus, Shane Punt, and Glen Reid. Written by Barbara Robinson. Produced by George Schaefer. Directed by Richard Crick and George Schaefer. Schaefer-Karpf Productions in association with Comworld Productions. VHS: Television Represent. 48 min.

A native of Portsmouth, Ohio, Barbara Robinson has written a number of children's books, among them *Across from Indian Shore* (1962), *The Fattest Bear in the First Grade* (1969), *Temporary Times, Temporary Places* (1982), and *The Best School Year Ever* (1994). Her stories have appeared in women's magazines.

Bewitched

Popular Emmy Award–winning television situation comedy series of 254 episodes that ran on the ABC network from 1964 to 1972. *Bewitched* revolved around the zany "mixed marriage" of mortal Darrin Stephens (played by Dick York from 1964 to 1969 and Dick Sargent from 1969 to 1972) and his wife Samantha (Elizabeth Montgomery), a beautiful, immortal witch. The Stephenses enjoyed Christmas in four December episodes:

A Vision of Sugar Plums (1964). Visiting the local orphanage on Christmas Eve, the Stephenses have arranged for six-year-old Michael (Billy Mumy), a disturbed little boy who cares nothing for Christmas or Santa, to share the holiday with them in their home. Their neighbors, Abner and Gladys Kravitz (George Tobias and Alice Pearce), take home seven-year-old Tommy (Kevin Tate), a firm believer in Santa. When all else fails to raise Michael's spirits, including Darrin's posing as Santa, Samantha confesses that she is a witch and zaps herself into a black costume with pointed hat. Determined to convince the boy that Santa is real, she whisks him and Darrin as well off to the North Pole on her broomstick to see St. Nick himself, one of Samantha's personal friends. Amid the toys and elves, Michael is more than convinced, and Santa's (Cecil Kellaway) sentimental philosophy that the real happiness of Christmas lies in giving hits home. Encouraged to select a gift, Michael chooses a toy fire truck, which he gives to Tommy the next morning. He also presents a toolbox, a most promising sign, to the Johnsons (Bill Dailey and Gerry Johnson), a couple who had unsatisfactorily adopted him twice before and

who have stopped by with Mrs. Grange (Sara Seegar) from the orphanage to try again. This episode was rerun in December 1965. Written by Herman Groves. Produced by Danny Arnold. Directed by Alan Rafkin. Screen Gems and Columbia Pictures Television. This half-hour, B & W episode is included in the VHS video collection *A Bewitched Christmas* from Columbia/Tristar.

Humbug Not to Be Spoken Here (1967), a parody on the Dickens classic *A Christmas Carol*. Darrin and his boss, Larry Tate (David White), are anxious to have the Mortimer Soup Company as a client of their advertising firm, but Mr. Mortimer (Charles Lane), a Scrooge at heart, tries Darrin's patience by demanding a business meeting on Christmas Eve. Over Mortimer's objections, Darrin leaves by mid-evening to buy a Christmas tree and spend time with Samantha and their young daughter Tabitha (Erin Murphy). Dropping in on the happy Stephens family with Larry, an enraged Mortimer cancels the account. Later that evening, Samantha, dressed in glittering red, surprises a sleeping Mortimer by confessing that she is a witch and transports him to see the real Santa via her red-and-white striped broomstick. After joining Santa (Don Beddoe) on his worldwide rounds, Samantha and Mortimer watch the latter's butler Hawkins (Martin Ashe) making merry with his wife and child at home. When Mortimer wonders why the financially strapped butler is so happy, Samantha asks Mortimer if wealth has really made him happy. On Christmas morning, Mortimer, a changed man, drops by to apologize and brings a gift box of Mortimer Instant Soups. Seeing Samantha plus Tabitha's new "Susie-Bruisie" doll (he had seen the same doll at the North Pole), Mortimer wonders if his trip was real or just a dream, and Samantha invites him to spend Christmas with them. With Rosalyn Burbage. Written by Lila Garrett and Bernie Kahn. Produced and directed by William Asher. Screen Gems and Columbia Pictures Television. This half-hour, color episode is included in the VHS video collection *A Bewitched Christmas* from Columbia/Tristar.

Santa Comes to Visit and Stays and Stays (1969). Two days before Christmas, Samantha enlists Cousin Esmeralda (Alice Ghostley) to baby-sit while she goes shopping. Esmeralda's magic often backfires; in this episode, when she sneezes, creatures appear. Following sneezes that conjure up first a goat and then two seals, a third sneeze zaps up Santa himself (Ronald Long). Ordinarily, the creatures vanish over time, but Santa remains far too long, and now Christmas Eve is at hand. Because he has much work remaining, Samantha twitches up the elves, whom Santa supervises in double-time toy-making in her living room. When she zaps the sleigh and reindeer onto her front lawn, neighbor Abner Kravitz (George Tobias) believes that the Stephenses have done a remarkable job of exterior decorating. Larry Tate (David White), having had a few drinks, arrives just as Santa takes to the skies, but Larry passes off the "hallucination" as a case of mild inebriation. With Dick Sargent, Erin Murphy, and Sandra Gould. Written by Ed Jurist. Produced by William Asher. Directed by Richard Michaels. Screen Gems and Columbia Pictures Television. This half-hour, color episode is included in the VHS video collection *A Bewitched Christmas II* from Columbia/Tristar.

Sisters at Heart (1970). This was Elizabeth Montgomery's favorite episode. The story was written by Marcella Saunders's tenth-grade English class, fifth period, at Thomas Jefferson High School, an inner-city school in Los Angeles, with assistance from *Bewitched* writer Barbara Avedon. Originally the story line centered around true kinship being based on spirit and not skin color, but Avedon took a further step and suggested building that theme around Christmas. The episode won the Governor's Award at the 1971 Emmy Awards ceremony.

Tabitha (Erin Murphy) wishes that she and her African American friend Lisa Wilson (Venetta Rogers) could be real sisters, but feels that their different skin colors prevent that. To make them both look alike, Tabitha zaps white spots on Lisa and black spots on herself, a spell that seemingly cannot be reversed. Meanwhile, Mr. Brockway (Parley Baer), a million-dollar client of the McMann-Tate advertising firm, while checking up on Darrin, arrives at the erroneous conclusion that Tabitha and Lisa are products of an interracial marriage and makes excuses to have Darrin removed from the account. Unaware of Brockway's bigotry, Larry

(David White) feels that if Darrin hosts the office Christmas party at his home and invites Brockway, the account can be saved. Lisa's parents arrive, for her father, Keith (Don Marshall), is a McMann-Tate agent, and Samantha frantically searches for a spell to remove the children's spots. According to Dr. Bombay (Bernard Fox), the supernatural physician, only Tabitha can remove the spots and only if she truly wishes for them to leave. The spell is reversed after Samantha convinces Tabitha that she and Lisa can always be friends in spirit, despite their different races. Seeing Darrin conversing with Lisa's mother Dorothy (Janee Michelle), Brockway assumes that she is Darrin's wife until Samantha appears, to Brockway's relief. The scene reveals his racist reasons for wanting Darrin removed, an irate Larry cancels the account, and Samantha teaches Brockway a lesson by forcing him to see himself and all of his friends as black. On Christmas morning, a more sober-minded Brockway returns to apologize to the Stephenses and the visiting Wilsons, and Samantha invites him to Christmas dinner. Additional dialogue by William Asher. Produced and directed by William Asher. Screen Gems and Columbia Pictures Television. This half-hour, color episode is included in the VHS video collection *A Bewitched Christmas II* from Columbia/Tristar.

Bing Crosby Christmas Specials

Popular, annual broadcasts by the legendary American crooner Harry Lillis ("Bing") Crosby (1903–1977), airing initially as the seasonal highlights of a string of daily or weekly radio variety shows that he hosted from 1936 to 1963, then regularly as television specials from 1961 to 1977.

• RADIO SHOWS. Debuting on radio in 1931, Crosby first hosted the *Kraft Music Hall* (1935–46, NBC), on which he introduced Irving Berlin's "White Christmas" in December 1941, shortly after the Japanese attack on Pearl Harbor. The song would become Crosby's holiday signature song and would hold special significance for veterans of World War II (*see* **White Christmas** [song]). In 1950, the *Chesterfield Show* (1949–52, CBS) featured a holiday broadcast that included the only appearance by

Crosby's first wife, singer Dixie Lee (1911–1952), along with sons Gary, Phillip, Dennis, and Lindsay. Crosby's regular radio series ended with *The Crosby-Clooney Show* (1960–62, CBS), with singer Rosemary Clooney.

During the latter years of his radio career, Crosby hosted annual, one-hour Christmas specials from 1955 to 1963 on CBS titled *A Christmas Sing with Bing* that included such notable guests as, among others, second wife Kathryn (who first appeared in 1960), announcer Ken Carpenter, the Mormon Tabernacle Choir, the St. Louis Carol Association, Les Brown, Maurice Chevalier, Rosemary Clooney, José Ferrer, the Norman Luboff Choir, Johnny Mercer, the St. Michael's Choir, Jo Stafford, Paul Weston and His Orchestra, and Edgar Bergen with Charlie McCarthy reciting "'Twas the Night Before Christmas." The 1955 broadcast featured music from around the world and was released as a best-selling, long-playing album on the Decca label.

• TELEVISION SPECIALS. Prior to the annual holiday specials beginning in 1961, Crosby made occasional television appearances, the first of which was in December 1948, when he sang "Silent Night" with the Mitchell Boys' Choir on the *Philco Television Playhouse*. He also joined Frank Sinatra for a half-hour of carols in *Happy Holidays with Bing and Frank* (December 1957, ABC), which was a special broadcast of *The Frank Sinatra Show* that ran for only one season. The scene portrayed Crosby visiting Sinatra in his bachelor pad amid drinks, gifts, and holiday nostalgia, and closed with their duet rendition of "White Christmas." Filmed in color, broadcast in B & W. In 2001, Sinatra's daughter Nancy discovered a theretofore unknown color print of the show, which is now available on DVD from Hart Sharp Video, running 26 min. The following paragraphs list the titles of the annual, predominantly hour-long Bing Crosby Christmas specials in chronological order:

The Bing Crosby Christmas Show (1961, ABC). As Crosby walks the streets of London in this special filmed on location, he celebrates the season with Terry-Thomas, Marion Ryan, Dave King, Shirley Bassey, Sidney Green, Richard Hills, Miriam Karlin, Miles Malleson, Lennie Mayme, the Buskers (a troupe of street musi-

cians), and Bob Hope in drag. The VHS version from Festival Films includes "Real Estate Venture" (1965), an episode from Crosby's half-hour situation comedy show (*The Bing Crosby Show*, 1964–65, ABC), starring Beverly Garland, Frank McHugh, and Ruth Roman. B & W and color. 85 min.

The Bing Crosby Christmas Show (1962, ABC's first special to be broadcast in color). With Mary Martin, Andrè Previn, and the United Nations Children's Choir.

The Promise (1963, ABC). Centered around Crosby narrating the Christmas story.

The Bing Crosby Christmas Show (1964, ABC). Episode from *The Bing Crosby Show*, with Beverly Garland, Carol Faylen, Diane Sherry, and Frank McHugh. 30 min.

The Hollywood Palace (1965–68, ABC). Four Christmas specials during the years that Crosby hosted *The Hollywood Palace* variety shows (1964–70). Guests included Fred Waring and His Pennsylvanians, Dorothy Collins, Bob Crane and the cast of *Hogan's Heroes*, Kate Smith, Cyd Charisse, Bob Newhart, the King Family, Louis Nye, Adam West, the Lennon Sisters, Glen Campbell, and John Byner. Crosby's wife Kathryn and their children, eight-year-old Harry, five-year-old Nathaniel, and seven-year-old Mary Frances, made their debut appearances on the 1966 special and returned annually thereafter. Though originally broadcast in color, the 1965, 1966, and 1967 specials are available on DVD in B & W from Festival Films.

Bing and Carol Together Again for the First Time (1969, NBC). With Carol Burnett, Roy Clark, and Juliet Prowse.

Bing Crosby's Christmas Show (1970, NBC). With Jack Wild, the Doodletown Pipers, and Melba Moore.

Bing Crosby and the Sounds of Christmas (1971, NBC). With Mary Costa, Robert Goulet, and the Mitchell Boys' Choir.

A Christmas with the Bing Crosbys (1972, NBC). With Sally Struthers and David Hartman.

Bing Crosby's Sun Valley Christmas Show (1973, NBC). Filmed on location at the Sun Valley resort in Idaho, with Michael Landon, Connie Stevens, and John Byner.

Christmas with the Bing Crosbys (1974, NBC). With Mac Davis and Karen Valentine.

Merry Christmas, Fred, from the Crosbys (1975, CBS). With Fred Astaire and the Young Americans.

The Bing Crosby White Christmas Special (1976, CBS). With Jackie Gleason and Bernadette Peters.

Bing Crosby's Merrie Olde Christmas (1977, CBS). With David Bowie, Twiggy, Ron Moody, Stanley Baxter, and the Trinity Boys' Choir. Crosby taped this final special in England in September 1977. Although he passed away in Spain a month later, this special aired posthumously on November 30.

• VIDEO HIGHLIGHTS. Excerpts from 15 specials are provided in the video collection *A Bing Crosby Christmas* (1998), hosted by Gene Kelly and Kathryn Crosby in archive footage. Dates of specific scenes are rarely given, yet the year often can be determined from Crosby's guest roster above.

The collection opens with brief clips of Crosby singing "Winter Wonderland," "Do You Hear What I Hear?" "Let It Snow! Let It Snow! Let It Snow!" and "Hark! The Herald Angels Sing," followed by a song-and-dance routine to "Jing, Jing, Jing of the Jingle Bells" with Crosby and dancers dressed as toy soldiers, then a black-and-white clip of "Doin' the Bing" (1962).

Crosby introduces Kathryn and children on the 1966 special, and clips of the Crosby family in action focus on "Silver Bells," "Talk to the Animals," "Do You Hear What I Hear?" "Jingle Bells," "Sleigh Ride," "The Christmas Song" (Crosby with son Harry on guitar), "We Three Kings," "We Need a Little Christmas," "Home for the Holidays," "Camaraderie" (dressed as hobos), and "Children" (Crosby solo).

Outdoor scenes from Sun Valley (1973) include Crosby in a song-and-dance routine with a snowman to "Style" and a spin in a horse-drawn sleigh as the Crosbys, Michael Landon, Connie Stevens, and John Byner sing "Sleigh Ride."

Several clips feature Crosby in duets or skits with his guests: "Wait Till the Sun Shines, Nellie" (with Mary Martin, 1962); "Have Yourself a Merry Little Christmas" (with Carol Burnett, 1969, and with Twiggy, 1977); a song-and-joke routine with Roy Clark on banjo (1969); a skit with Crosby as a sidewalk Santa and Melba

Moore as a Salvation Army soldier (1970); "Sleigh Ride" (with Fred Astaire, 1975); "A Couple of Loafers" (with Jackie Gleason, 1976); and simultaneous renditions of "The Peace Carol" and "The Little Drummer Boy" (the former by David Bowie, the latter by Crosby, 1977).

In the final moments of the program, Crosby delivers a recitation of the essay "One Solitary Life," a summation of the life of Christ, by Dr. James Allan Francis, followed by a series of sacred carols: "O Holy Night," "The First Nowell," "O Come, All Ye Faithful," "Silent Night," and "Joy to the World." Crosby closes with "White Christmas," presented in a succession of clips that does not break the rhythm or pitch of the song.

Video collection written, produced, and directed by Marshall Flaum. The Konigsberg Company. DVD: University of Georgia Anthropology. 60 min.

The Birds
See **Carol of the Birds**

The Birds' Christmas Carol

Classic, bittersweet children's novel, written by American author Kate Douglas Smith Wiggin, first printed privately in 1886, then published in 1888.

Because she was born on Christmas Day, Carol Bird is a most special child, with cheeks and lips the color of holly berries, hair the color of Christmas candles aglow, eyes as bright as stars, a laugh as merry as Christmas bells, and hands eager to give. Even her name Carol rings of Christmas music, bestowed when her mother heard the church choir sing the hymn "Carol, Brothers, Carol." As a youngster, Carol is an inspiration and joy to all who know her.

Ten years pass, the last three of which have confined Carol to her bed with a chronic, painful illness that is slowly taking her life. Yet Carol has remained the epitome of love, goodness, and generosity. Knowing that only a short time remains for her, Carol plans a most unforgettable Christmas dinner-party for the nine children of the less fortunate Ruggles family next door: Sarah Maud, Peter, Kitty, Susan, Peory, Cornelius, Clement, Eily, and Baby Larry. To help fund the affair, Carol writes an article about her years of confinement and sells it to a magazine for $25. Then she insists that, rather than receive Christmas gifts from her parents, those gifts should go to the Ruggles children instead. Carol needs no other gift, she says, than the abiding love of her family. With the party in readiness, Carol observes several American and European traditions peculiar to Christmas Eve: hanging up stockings, scattering seed over the snow for the birds, stuffing dry grass into the fireplace for Santa's reindeer, arranging the family's shoes in a row to prevent quarrels, and placing a candle in a window to light the Christ Child's path.

To the Ruggles children, Carol's party is pure magic beyond their wildest imaginings: a feast with turkey and chicken, cranberry sauce, six vegetables, mince pie, plum pudding, ice cream, nuts, raisins, and oranges. Then they behold a gloriously lighted Christmas tree sporting gilded walnuts, little silver balloons, and popcorn chains. Lastly, each child receives not only a practical and much-needed article of clothing, but also a special "fun gift." It is an event the children will never forget, and it is the happiest day in Carol's life.

Later on Christmas night, strains of the choir singing "Carol, Brothers, Carol" and "My Ain Countree," two of Carol's favorite hymns, pour from the nearby Church of Our Savior. Several days before Christmas, Carol had requested that the organist play those hymns at this hour, and as they fill her room, Carol quietly slips into the peace of eternity.

The two hymns cited in this novel most befit Carol's character. "Carol, Brothers, Carol" was written by the Rev. William Augustus Muhlenberg (b. 1789, ordained in 1820), an Episcopal priest who founded the Church of the Holy Communion in New York City. Not well known today, the hymn urges that all be thankful for their blessings, to remember the unfortunate, and to put away discord, especially at Christmastime. The other hymn, "My Ain Countree," was written by Scottish poet Allan Cunningham (1784–1842). The lyrics, reproduced in full in the novel, yearn to depart this weary life for the love, peace, and comfort that God the Father will provide in heaven.

In 1917, the novel was adapted to the silent screen under the title *A Bit o' Heaven*, starring Mary Louise as Carol, Donald Watson and Ella Gilbert as Mr. and Mrs. Bird, and Mary Talbot as Mrs. Ruggles. Directed by Lule Warrenton.

Kate Douglas Smith Wiggin (1856–1923) organized the first free kindergarten west of the Rockies and originally published *The Birds' Christmas Carol* to help fund her kindergarten in San Francisco. She is best known for the classic children's novel *Rebecca of Sunnybrook Farm* (1903).

Birth of Christ
See **Christmas Day; Nativity; Wise Men**

The Birthday of a King
American carol written around 1890 by Brooklyn native William Harold Neidlinger (1863–1924). A choral conductor, singing teacher, and organist, Neidlinger principally composed songs for children in such collections as *Earth, Sky and Air in Song* and *Little Folks' Song Book*. His 1896 work *Small Songs for Small Singers* was a popular book for kindergartens. Probably his most famous song is "The Birthday of a King."

Consisting of two verses, the simple lyrics recall that a holy light shone over the place where the Child lay in Bethlehem, and that from a humble manger, a holy way led to God. In the refrain, angels sing a birthday song to Jesus in the form of an "Alleluia."

The Bishop's Wife
(1947). Motion picture comedy/romance, based on the 1928 novel of the same title by Robert Nathan.

Too preoccupied at Christmastime with raising funds for a new cathedral in New York City, Bishop Henry Brougham (David Niven) neglects his wife Julia (Loretta Young), young daughter Debbie (Karolyn Grimes), and even St. Timothy's Church, where he was formerly the rector. The church's wealthiest patron, a demanding Mrs. Agnes Hamilton (Gladys Cooper), has pledged one million dollars toward the cathedral, provided that it be built as a shrine to her late husband. Henry, torn over this ethical and spiritual dilemma, prays for guidance, whereupon the angel Dudley (Cary Grant) appears in answer and poses as Henry's assistant.

Dudley, however, takes more interest in Julia's happiness and well-being, which includes lunching with her at Michele's, buying her a hat she's always wanted, and ice skating with her in the park — in short, being a substitute Henry. A jealous Henry finally confronts Dudley and affirms his love for his wife, at which point Dudley's work is finished. Departing, he leaves no memory of his visit behind.

Dudley's encounter with several other people on Christmas Eve changes their lives for the better. Old Professor Wutheridge (Monty Woolley) receives the inspiration to write a long-overdue history of Rome; the cabby Sylvester (James Gleason) develops more faith in humanity; and Mrs. Hamilton diverts her millions to causes more desperate than the erecting of cathedrals. Leaving, Dudley also touches an unwitting St. Timothy's congregation through Henry's Christmas Eve message, which Dudley has altered. On the subject of Christmas stockings, the message calls for filling Jesus' stocking with loving kindness, warm hearts, and a stretched-out hand of tolerance, all the shining gifts that make "peace on earth."

In 1948, this picture won an Academy Award for Best Sound; Academy nominations for Best Picture, Best Director, Best Film Editing, and Best Music Scoring.

With Elsa Lanchester and the Mitchell Boys' Choir. Written by Robert E. Sherwood and Leonardo Bercovici. Produced by Samuel Goldwyn. Directed by Henry Koster. The Samuel Goldwyn Company and RKO Radio Pictures. DVD: MGM/UA Video. B & W. 109 min.

Several interesting behind-the-scenes anecdotes are notable. Originally, Cary Grant was cast as the bishop and David Niven as Dudley, with William Seiter directing. After several weeks of filming, Goldwyn reversed Grant's and Niven's roles and brought in Henry Koster to replace Seiter as director. Loretta Young was the third choice for Julia after Teresa Wright and Jean Arthur rejected the role. Once, when Grant complained that a wintertime picture should display frost on the windows, a scene was delayed while the stage crew added that extra little touch. Grant's and Young's vain insistence on having only their right profiles filmed prompted a sarcastic Goldwyn to ask if they would be willing to work for half salary.

Child actors Karolyn Grimes (Debbie Brougham here) and Bobby Anderson (boy in the snowball fight here) also starred in another Christmas classic, *It's a Wonderful Life*. There, Karolyn played George Bailey's daughter Zuzu, and Bobby played a young George Bailey.

The Bishop's Wife was the first American film to be selected for a screening by the royal family at England's Royal Command Performances for movies, begun in 1946.

The film was remade in 1996 as *The Preacher's Wife*, featuring a virtually all–African American cast, including Denzel Washington, Whitney Houston, and Courtney B. Vance. It received the following honors in 1997: Academy Award nomination for Best Original Music; won Image Awards for Outstanding Lead Actress (Whitney Houston) and Outstanding Supporting Actress (Loretta Devine); Image Award nominations for Outstanding Motion Picture, Outstanding Supporting Actress (Jennifer Lewis), and Outstanding Youth Actor (Justin Pierre Edmund); Young Star Award nomination for Best Young Actor (Justin Pierre Edmund). Nominated in 1998 for a Blockbuster Entertainment Award for Favorite Soundtrack. Written by Nat Mauldin, Allan Scott, and Todd Graff. Produced by Samuel Goldwyn, Jr. Directed by Penny Marshall. Mundy Lane Entertainment, Parkway Productions, The Samuel Goldwyn Company, and Touchstone Pictures. DVD: Buena Vista Home Entertainment. 124 min.

Blackadder's Christmas Carol

See **A Christmas Carol** (Film and Television Versions)

Blessed Be That Maid Marie

English traditional carol, the modernized lyrics of which are derived from a fifteenth century manuscript of carols that resides in the British Library in London. The Rev. George R. Woodward (1838–1934), the Anglican priest who adapted the text, sought artistic worth in church music over the Victorian styles at the turn of the twentieth century. He also composed original hymn lyrics in the style of the sixteenth or seventeenth century, then selected appropriate melodies from that era to fit his lyrics. In fact, it is thought that, of the five verses that comprise "Blessed Be," verse three is Woodward's alone. He was responsible for many of the reforms in *The English Hymnal* (1906) and compiled three collections, *Songs of Syon* (1904), *An Italian Carol Book* (1920), and *The Cowley Carol Book* (1901 and 1919 [2nd edition], for the Fathers at Cowley, Oxford), the latter three in collaboration with Cambridge musician Charles Wood (1866–1926). "Blessed Be" first appeared in both editions of *The Cowley Carol Book*. Wood provided the musical setting, a folk tune originally titled "Staines Morris," which first appeared in a lute book by a William Ballet (c. 1600).

The macaronic verses (a mixture of Latin and vernacular English) recall that because God, present before time began, was born in time as the Son of Man in a manger, was serenaded by angels, and was visited by kings, we should make merry on this fest. While verses 2–5 each contain one Latin line (the others being English), the refrain is entirely Latin: "Eya! Ihesus hodie / Natus est de Virgine" ("Rejoice! Jesus today is born of a Virgin").

Blessing of the Waters
See **Epiphany**

The Blessings of Mary
See **The Seven Joys of Mary**

Blizzard
(2003). American/Canadian motion picture fantasy that combines live-action with computer-generated reindeer images.

Discovering that her ten-year-old niece Jess (Jennifer Pisana) is dispirited because a good friend has moved away at Christmastime, Aunt Millie (Brenda Blethyn) tells her the story of Blizzard and Katie Andrews, set in the 1940s.

Born to reindeer Blitzen and Delphi at the North Pole, young Blizzard (voice of Whoopi Goldberg) has been blessed with all three reindeer gifts: the ability to fly, the ability to become invisible, and the gift of "empathic navigation" (a strong sense of others' feelings). Yet Archimedes (Kevin Pollak), Santa's (Christopher Plummer) rules-conscious manager, brands her a freak and plots to banish her. Blizzard finds use for all of her gifts (and breaks all of Archimedes' rules) when she befriends young

Katie (Zoë Warner) and encourages her dream of becoming a figure-skater. Although archrival Erin (Brittany Bristow) ruins Katie's skates prior to competition, Blizzard borrows a pair from the North Pole, and together she and Katie later rescue Erin when she later falls into an icy pond. The two girls become friends, and Blizzard's exploits reach the ears of Archimedes, who places her on trial. But when Katie returns the skates to the North Pole and pleads the case before Santa, Blizzard receives another chance. Though she and Katie must forever part, they will always have good memories.

In 2003, this picture won the Heartland Award of Excellence. In 2004, it captured the following honors: won the Directors' Guild of Canada Team Award for Outstanding Team Achievement in a Family Feature Film; Genie Award nominations for Best Achievement in Costume Design, Best Original Song ("Center of My Heart" by LeVar Burton, David Martin, and Pamela Phillips Oland), and Best Supporting Actor (Plummer); Young Artist Award nomination for Best International Feature Film.

Story by Agnes Bristow and Leif Bristow. Written by Murray McRae. Produced by Leif Bristow and J. Miles Dale. Directed by LeVar Burton. Holedigger Films, Knightscove Entertainment, and Ralph Winter Productions. Video N/A. 96 min.

Blowing in the Yule
Christmas Eve tradition found in Germany, Austria, and portions of Scandinavia, whereby brass ensembles herald the coming of Christmas by playing chorales from church towers. The custom derived from the pagan belief that loud noises created during winter solstice festivals dispelled the spirits of darkness.
See also **Winter Solstice; Yule.**

Blue Christmas
Popular American song written in 1948 by Billy Hayes and Jay W. Johnson, the only Christmas piece of the eight tunes upon which the two collaborated. "Blue Christmas" centers on the "blue" or melancholy spirits evoked when one must spend the holidays without the person he loves. Initial recordings by various artists failed to generate a hit, until country singer

Ernest Tubb recorded his version on the Decca label in 1949 with a vocal group, the Beasley Sisters. His record competed for the number one spot on the pop charts of 1949 with two by Gene Autry, "Rudolph, the Red-Nosed Reindeer" and "Here Comes Santa Claus," and together these three hits helped to establish the country Christmas tradition. Other "Blue Christmas" recordings making the charts in 1949 included those by Russ Morgan (Decca) and Hugo Winterhalter and His Orchestra (Columbia). In 1964, Elvis Presley's rendition (RCA), briefly achieving the number one position that year and again in 1973 on the *Billboard Special Christmas Singles* chart, sold over a million copies and continued to make the pop charts each year in between.

Of the 25 most frequently performed Christmas songs of the twentieth century listed by the American Society of Composers, Authors and Publishers (ASCAP), "Blue Christmas" ranked number 14. By December 2004, it ranked number 15.

Other tunes by Hayes and Johnson include "House Warmin,'" "How Now Brown Cow," "Little Wedding Bells," "Peaceful," "Pizza Polka" (with Harry Simeone), "There's a Cute Little Pig," and "Whittlin'" (with Lionel Taylor).

See also **ASCAP List of Christmas Songs.**

The Boar's Head Carol

Title applied to several English carols that accompanied the traditional ceremony of serving a wild boar's head at Christmas feasts during the Middle Ages. This tradition probably derived from pagan Scandinavian winter solstice festivals, at which a wild boar was sacrificed to Freya, Norse goddess of fertility, who was symbolized as riding across the heavens on a golden boar. Another possible derivation is from the annual slaughtering of pigs and other livestock in late fall as an alternative to witnessing their starvation during heavy winter snows.

The custom is still observed annually, most notably at Queen's College, Oxford, where the carol adopted for the ceremony has become the most familiar of the boar's head carols. The

"Be glad, both more and less/For this hath ordained our steward,/To cheer you all this Christmas—/The boar's head, and mustard!" reads a stanza of a verse in "A Boy King's Christmas," a story from Our Young Folks: An Illustrated Magazine for Boys and Girls *(Boston: Ticknor and Fields, 1868).*

anonymous text, thought to date from the fifteenth century, is taken from Jan van Wynkyn de Worde's *Christmasse Carolles* (London, 1521), the oldest surviving collection of printed Christmas carols; its tune, also anonymous, derives from at least the eighteenth century. Its macaronic lyrics (a mixture of Latin with vernacular English) call for all to make merry at the feast with song and praises to the Lord. Latin is used not only for the last line of each of the three verses but the entire refrain as well. Originally the refrain read, "Caput apri defero / Reddens laudes Domino, / laudes Domino, laudes Domino, Domino" ("I bring in the boar's head, / Giving thanks to the Lord, thanks to the Lord, thanks to the Lord, to the Lord"), but in 1901, the music of the refrain was rewritten and its text shortened to eliminate the repeated "laudes Domino."

The circumstances under which Queen's College instituted a boar's head ceremony are a matter of amusing legend. Allegedly, a wild boar threatened a young student of the college as he perused a book containing the works of Aristotle while walking in Shotover Woods on Christmas Day. Exclaiming, "Graecum est!" (Latin, "It is Greek [to me]!"), the boy saved himself by ramming Aristotle down the boar's throat and choking it, then served the animal to the student body with elaborate festivities that evening. The special reference to Aristotle supposedly implied that, even in the Middle Ages, the Greek philosopher was as unpalatable as he is today.

Since the fourteenth century, a trumpet fanfare has announced the ceremony at Queen's, after which the provost and fellows of the College assume their places. Following grace, the procession enters: first the solo singer, then the choir walking backwards, facing three chefs who bear the boar's head (actually that of a suckling pig, for wild boars became extinct in England during the seventeenth century) on a silver platter, which is flanked by torch bearers. Garnished with bay and rosemary, as the carol dictates, the head sports a crown and flags, the mouth an orange. The procession advances only during the refrains and pauses for the verses, at the conclusion of which the provost distributes the garnishments to the choir and the orange to the soloist.

Whereas "The Boar's Head Carol" of Queen's College is actually more convivial than religious, the opposite is true for another and lesser known of these carols, "The Exeter Boar's Head Carol." Written by Richard Smert, rector of Plymtree in Devon from 1435 to 1477 and vicar choral of Exeter Cathedral from 1428 to 1466, this carol is quite unique in that it reveres the boar's head as a symbol of Christ.

Bob Hope Christmas Specials

Popular, annual telecasts by British-born American comedian Leslie Townes (Bob) Hope (1903–2003), legendary star of vaudeville, radio, motion pictures, and television. After making his radio debut in 1932, Hope performed with the USO at American military bases and overseas deployments during World War II, beginning in 1941 with a performance for the airmen at March Field, California. In December 1948, at the request of Stuart Symington, then–Secretary of the Air Force, Hope, with guests Doris Day and Jinx Falkenburg, entertained the troops involved in the Berlin Airlift in Germany, a performance that launched Hope's annual tradition of touring overseas military bases at Christmastime.

From 1954 with his show at Tule Strategic Air Command Base in Greenland (guest-starring William Holden and Anita Ekberg), 90-minute *Bob Hope Christmas Specials* were filmed on location and sold to NBC television for broadcast in the United States every holiday season until his last Vietnam tour in 1972 (guest-starring Lola Falana, Redd Foxx, and Miss World). His 1966 Christmas special from Southeast Asia with Carrol Baker won an Emmy Award for Outstanding Variety Special (the only Emmy Hope ever won), and the 1967 and 1968 Christmas specials also received Emmy nominations. The 1969 tour, considered to be the most ambitious, included a preliminary performance at the White House before President and Mrs. Nixon (the event marked Hope's first USO performance there), followed by shows in then–West Berlin, Italy, Turkey, Vietnam, Thailand, Taiwan, and Guam. Guests on that tour included astronaut Neil Armstrong, Connie Stevens, Teresa Graves, and the Golddiggers. The 1970 Christmas special was the highest-rated program in television history at that time.

From 1973 to 1982, Hope brought his show back home to military bases and veterans hospitals in the United States, but resumed overseas tours in 1983. After entertaining the troops of Operation Desert Storm in Saudi Arabia in 1990, Bob Hope ended a 42-year tradition of morale-boosting Christmas tours. Between 1942 and 1990, he had starred in more than 1,000 USO shows, for which he was dubbed "America's Ambassador of Goodwill."

Hope's format, not only for the Christmas specials but also for his monthly or semi-monthly television comedy specials (he purposefully avoided a weekly series for fear that his form of humor would grow stale), was an opening monologue of jokes and one-liners centering on current events and politics. On the troop tours, Hope, sporting a golf club and often appearing on stage dressed in military khakis with a cap that bore the insignia of the local base, opened each show with, "This is Bob [name of military camp] Hope." Over the years, virtually every celebrity in the entertainment industry appeared on his specials at one time or another, both at home and abroad. Especially for the troops, Hope always brought along a bevy of young, voluptuously beautiful actresses and chorus girls, including the reigning Miss World, who interacted with Hope and selected members from the audience to participate in a series of skits, songs, and dances. Though primarily festive and secular, the Christmas specials nevertheless often closed on a sacred note with "Silent Night" or a similarly suitable carol.

• VIDEO HIGHLIGHTS. Several video collections compile memorable scenes from Hope's Christmas specials both at home and abroad:

A Bob Hope Christmas. Although this is the title on the video container, the program itself, from 1993, is titled *Bob Hope's Bag Full of Christmas Memories.* As Hope, his wife Dolores, and their children and grandchildren host a gala Christmas party at the Hope home, they periodically view nostalgic clips from Hope's earlier Christmas specials: tours in the Persian Gulf, Iceland, Vietnam, and Korea, with Barbara Eden, Brooke Shields, Jayne Mansfield, and Marie Osmond. Clips of skits with guests include Jack Benny as a gangster who robs Hope as Santa at the North Pole (1965); Hope as Santa with Phil Silvers as a traffic cop (1967); Redd Foxx and Hope as two reindeer (1975); Hope as a bum to Red Skelton's Freddie the Freeloader (1978); Loni Anderson portraying a sexy robot Christmas doll, with Phyllis Diller (1982); Hope, Brooke Shields, and Emmanuel Lewis as dolls on a toy shelf (1985); parody on *Steel Magnolias* with the Judds and Hope in drag (1989); Loni Anderson and Joan Van Ark (1990); and Hope as Scrooge to Reba McEntire and Macaulay Culkin (1991).

Following a parade of all–American college athletes who had appeared on Hope's specials over the years, Hope and Dolores deliver a rendition of "Silver Bells," which he had introduced in the motion picture *The Lemon Drop Kid.* Their song provides a voice-over for clips of Hope singing similar duets with other female guests on his specials: Gale Storm, Kathryn Crosby, Shirley Jones, Marie Osmond, Loretta Swit, Gloria Loring, Olivia Newton-John, Dyan Cannon, Barbara Eden, Donna Mills, Dixie Carter, Phylicia Rashad, Reba McEntire, and Loni Anderson.

This collection closes with a series of non-seasonal skits with Bing Crosby (1965), Lee Marvin (1971), and Lucille Ball (1973), followed by John Wayne and Hope singing a duet of "Have Yourself a Merry Little Christmas" (1976).

Written by Martha Bolton. Produced by Linda Hope. Directed by Sid Smith. A Hope Enterprises, Inc., Television Production. VHS: Guthy Renker Video. B & W and color. 60 min.

Bob Hope's Christmas with the Troops. This is the title on the video container, yet the program is titled *The Bob Hope Christmas Special: Around the World with the USO.* It focuses solely on the ambitious 1969 tour mentioned above and compresses it into 65 min.

Written by Mort Lachman, Bill Larkin, Mel Tolkin, Lester White, Charles Lee, Gig Henry Genemoss, and James Thurman. Executive Producer: Bob Hope. Directed by Mort Lachman. A Hope Enterprises, Inc., Film Production. VHS: Guthy Renker Video.

The Ultimate Bob Hope Collection. A three-DVD boxed set comprising highlights from more than 50 years of Hope's television specials. R2 Entertainment. 7 hours.

Cited by *The Guinness Book of Records* as the most honored entertainer in the world, Bob Hope received over 2,000 awards and citations, including 54 honorary doctorates. When Congress made him an Honorary Veteran in 1997, he became the first person to receive this honor in the history of the United States, and in 1998, Queen Elizabeth II bestowed upon him an honorary knighthood: Knight Commander of the Most Excellent Order of the British Empire.

Bolivia

See **South America**

Borrowed Hearts: A Holiday Romance

(1997). American/Canadian made-for-television drama.

In order to close a multimillion-dollar transaction at Christmastime, playboy-bachelor-businessman Sam Field (Eric McCormack) must prove that he is a family man to his client and holiday houseguest from Mexico, the distinguished and cultured Javier Del Campo (Hector Elizondo). To portray his wife and daughter, Sam hires one of his regular employees, single mother Kathleen Russell (Roma Downey), together with her precocious, seven-year-old daughter, Zoe (Sarah Rosen Fruitman). At first, the relationship is quite awkward as the three players stumble over answers to Del Campo's probing questions about their married life, and Kathleen, of high morals, insists that Sam sleep in a dressing closet rather than on the couch in the same bedroom.

Although the three Americans appear as the ideal family, they are racked with emotional unrest: Sam has had virtually no meaningful family life and can only relate to matters of money; Kathleen's ex-husband Jerry (Kevin Hicks) had left her and Zoe for the professional golf circuit; and Zoe, feeling that she is not lovable, just wishes that an angel would bring her daddy back for Christmas, which leads to Del Campo himself. Frequently only Zoe, not the others, is aware of soft, ethereal music in his presence, the same music she has heard when she has been alone. Her baby sitter once said that hearing music with no one visible was indicative of an angel's presence. Given a knowing look and a slight wink from Del Campo, Zoe deduces his real identity and is confident that her Christmas wish will come true. All the while, the magic of Christmas love is providing Sam, Kathleen, and Zoe with a powerful, intangible gift of its own.

On Christmas Day, Del Campo would finalize business with Sam, which would move his company to Mexico and lay off a large number of employees in the United States, many of whom are single mothers. Having learned of the plan beforehand, Kathleen has pleaded with Sam to reconsider; now with reality just a signature away, Sam cancels the deal, and Del Campo leaves with the parting thought that, regarding matters of real importance, it is always better to think with the heart, not with the head, for the heart is wiser. Unfortunately, the day provides Zoe with a hard lesson in reality concerning her father Jerry, who arrives only to bid her a final adieu for the golf circuit. Devastated, she would have lost all faith in humanity, but Sam catches her when she falls from a tree. It is the final link that joins Sam, Kathleen, and Zoe together as a loving family.

In 1998, this picture won the ALMA Award for Outstanding Actor in a Made-for-Television Movie or Mini-Series (Hector Elizondo).

Written by Pamela Wallace and Earl Wallace. Produced by Mary Kahn. Directed by Ted Kotcheff. Atlantis Films Limited and Canadian Television. VHS available through Feature Films for Families (www.familytv.com). 97 min.

Boxing Day

Falling on December 26, Boxing Day is a legal holiday in those countries forming the Commonwealth of Nations, especially Australia, Canada, and Great Britain. It is also known as Second Christmas Day and, in the Roman Catholic Church, as St. Stephen's Day, which honors Stephen, the first Christian martyr.

Boxing Day, which became a public holiday through an act of Parliament in 1871, derives its name from an English tradition dating to the Middle Ages, when churches opened their alms boxes, or Christmas boxes, on this day and distributed funds to the poor. This practice had evolved by the seventeenth century into members of the working class seeking gratuities from those to whom they had rendered services during the year, and the tips received became known as "boxes."

This custom of boxing fell into decline by the nineteenth century, principally because the increasing number of tradespeople soliciting "boxes" had become quite burdensome. This did not prevent generous employers, however, from voluntarily bestowing monetary gifts upon their employees in the spirit of the season, which formed the basis for the Christmas bonuses that were more prevalent during the late nineteenth century. By the end of the twentieth century, Christmas bonuses had also declined but had not completely vanished.

From the eighteenth century or earlier, the British Isles and France observed "Hunting the Wren" on St. Stephen's Day, a custom that survives in modified form in Ireland. Boxing Day currently is a day for recreation, with pageants, plays, pantomimes, and sporting events, for example.

See also **Great Britain; Hunting the Wren; Ireland.**

Boy-Bishop

Ecclesiastical office originating in Europe during the Middle Ages, instituted in 844 by Pope Gregory IV and observed particularly in England. As a tribute to St. Nicholas, the fourth century bishop of Myra and patron saint of children, on St. Nicholas's Day (December 6), one boy from the local church or monastery school was elected by his peers to serve in the full capacity of a bishop until Holy Innocents Day (December 28), a day memorializing those children (innocents) massacred in Bethlehem by King Herod the Great (Matthew 2:1–18). Arrayed in official vestments and miter, the boy-bishop assumed all responsibilities of the Church and toured his parish blessing the people as his comrades followed in priests' robes. Should he die in office, he was buried with full ecclesiastical honors. In England, at the cathedral in Salisbury and at Lulworth Castle, are

A Boy-Bishop, from an unnamed parish, as depicted in William Hone's Ancient Mysteries Described *(London: 1823).*

the remains of two boys, both of whom are believed to have died as boy-bishops.

In other parts of Europe by the eleventh century, Holy Innocents Day had also become a feast for students and choirboys, and the holiday, including the role of boy-bishop, had degenerated to an atmosphere of secular revelry. Because several other riotous holidays were observed between Christmas and Epiphany (January 6), these festivals were collectively termed the Feast of Fools. The Council of Basle finally abolished the office of boy-bishop in 1431 on the European continent, but in England the custom survived until the reign of Elizabeth I.

See also **Feast of Fools; Holy Innocents Day; Nativity; Saint Nicholas's Day.**

A Boy Is Born in Bethlehem

("Puer natus in Bethlehem"). Traditional, medieval Latin carol, one from a host of such carols that has managed to retain some popularity through the centuries. Believed to have originated in Bohemia, its earliest written sources include a processional from a Bohemian Benedictine nunnery that dates to 1320 and a late thirteenth century antiphonary from Bobbio, Italy. Although these earlier settings consisted of only three verses, additional stanzas accumulated over the centuries. *The Hereford Breviary* (1505) shows ten and the *Piae Cantiones* (Greifswald, 1582) 14, four verses of the latter having been contributed by a Hermann Bonn (1504–1548), a hymn translator and pupil of Martin Luther.

From the sixteenth century on, "A Boy Is Born" enjoyed numerous harmonizations, notably by German composers Michael Praetorius (1571–1621) in his 1607 and 1609 volumes of *Musae Sioniae* and J.S. Bach (1685–1750) in his Epiphany Cantata *Sie werden aus Saba alle kommen* (BWV 65). Organ chorale preludes based on the carol were also written by Bach (*Orgelbüchlein*, BWV 603); Bach's cousin, Johann Walther (1684–1748); and the Dane Dietrich Buxtehude (1637–1707).

A Boy's Thanksgiving Day

See **Over the River and Through the Woods**

The Brady Bunch

Popular family television situation comedy series of 117 episodes that aired on the ABC network from 1969 to 1974. The principal characters included Mike and Carol Brady (Robert Reed and Florence Henderson); their children, Greg (Barry Williams), Peter (Christopher Knight), Bobby (Mike Lookinland), Marcia (Maureen McCormick), Jan (Eve Plumb), and Cindy (Susan Olsen); and their housekeeper, Alice Nelson (Ann B. Davis).

The original series featured only one holiday episode, "The Voice of Christmas," which aired during the first season in December 1969. As the Bradys launch into Christmas Eve, Carol develops laryngitis and will be unable to sing a solo in church the next day. Alice soaks a towel in a revolting home remedy of mustard, camphor, vinegar, and pepper and places this around Carol's neck with faith that it will cure her. When Cindy visits a department store Santa (Hal Smith), her only wish is that he restore her mother's voice, and Santa agrees to the cure. Mike cautions Cindy not to expect miracles, but her faith in Santa cannot be shattered. The other children, however, are prepared to postpone Christmas until Carol regains her voice. Later that night, Mike awakens to hear Carol humming "O Come, All Ye Faithful" in her sleep. With her voice restored, she delivers a beautiful rendition of the same carol in church as planned. Cindy writes a note of thanks to Santa, and Mike enjoys renewed faith in Christmas miracles.

The next celebration of Christmas with the Brady family occurred in 1988 with *A Very Brady Christmas*, the third-highest-rated television movie for that year. The movie features the original cast, except for Cindy, played here by Jennifer Runyon. After 20 years, Mike and Carol are now alone, for their children are grown and have moved away. The two independently plan to give each other vacations to Greece and Japan as Christmas presents, but their coincidental meeting at the same travel agency puts this idea on hold. Alice appears on their doorstep, her husband, Sam the butcher, having left her, and the Bradys take her in. As Mike and Carol reminisce about vacations, the scene flashes back to the episode "A-Camping We Will Go" (November 1969), in which the girls

frightened the boys into believing that a bear was outside their tent. This gives Carol the idea to have all the Brady children and their families return home for a Christmas reunion.

The children agree to come, but Mike and Carol are unaware that bits of humbug surround the children's personal lives. Wally Logan (Jerry Houser), Marcia's husband, has just lost his job as salesman for Tyler Toys; Jan, an architect like her father, and her husband Phillip Covington III (Ron Kuhlman), a university professor, are separating; Peter's boss, Valerie Thomas (Carol Huston), is more than romantically interested in him, which disturbs macho Peter; Bobby has dropped out of graduate school to race cars; and Cindy, about to graduate from college and feeling that her parents are ordering her home, would rather have gone on a skiing trip with her friends. The problem for Greg, now a physician, is that his nurse-wife Nora (Caryn Richman) wishes to spend Christmas with her parents while Greg and little son Kevin (Zachary Bostron) go on to the Bradys.

Although Christmas Eve sees the brood arriving amid mirth and joy, Carol senses that all is not well. Soon, however, Jan and Phillip have patched up their differences. On Christmas Day, Mike, tipped off by Wally's boy Mickey (G.W. Lee), introduces Wally to neighbor Leonard Prescott (F.J. O'Neil) of Prescott Toys, who hires him as a new salesman. During Christmas dinner, the other Brady children openly confess their secrets or problems, and Peter and Valerie simultaneously propose to each other. Mike is called away to a construction site on which he was formerly the architect (he resigned because the client had declined his added safety recommendations), where a cave-in has trapped two security guards. Mike goes in to rescue them, but after the guards escape, the site collapses, now trapping Mike.

As the Bradys wait, Cindy exhorts Carol to have faith, and the scene flashes back to the earlier Christmas episode, when Carol lost her voice. First Carol, then Cindy, then all the Bradys begin singing "O Come, All Ye Faithful," after which Mike emerges from the ruins, shaken but unharmed. Back home, Sam the butcher (Lewis Arquette) appears dressed as Santa and begs Alice to take him back.

In 1989, *A Very Brady Christmas* won a Young Artist Award for Best Family Television Special and was nominated for a Young Artist Award for Best Young Actress (Jaclyn Bernstein).

With Jaclyn Bernstein and Phillip Richard Allen. Written by Sherwood Schwartz and Lloyd J. Schwartz. Produced by Lloyd J. Schwartz and Barry Berg. Directed by Peter Baldwin. The Sherwood Schwartz Company in association with Paramount Pictures Television. VHS: Paramount Studios. 94 min.

Brazil
See **South America**

Break Forth, O Beauteous Heavenly Light

("Brich an, o schönes Morgenlicht"). German carol, the lyrics of which were written by Johann Rist (1607–1667), a hymn writer, pastor, and physician in Wedel near Hamburg. With nearly 700 hymns to his credit, of which "Break Forth" remains his most significant and best-known work, Rist received the title of poet laureate from Emperor Ferdinand III in 1645. The carol was first published in Rist's music collection *Himmlische Lieder* (Leipzig, 1641), together with the musical setting entitled "Ermuntre dich, mein schwacher Geist" ("Be of Cheer, My Weak Spirit") by Rist's friend Johann Schop (1590–1664). A composer and violinist, Schop also served as music editor for *Himmlische Lieder*. Further contributing to the carol's longevity has been the harmonization by J.S. Bach (1685–1750), who included it as a chorale in his *Christmas Oratorio* (BWV 248) of 1734.

The lyrics focus on the angels' annunciation to the shepherds and bid those mortals not to shrink in fear of the heavenly beings bathed in brilliant glory. Their message brings confidence that the Christ Child, though weak as a mortal infant, will eventually break the powers of Satan. English clergyman John Troutbeck provided the dominant English translation, c. 1885.

See also **Christmas Oratorio**.

Breaking Up Christmas

Designation applied to an annual series of holiday house parties once prevalent in rural communities throughout the Blue Ridge Mountains of northwestern North Carolina and southwestern Virginia. Depending on the locale, the series of parties commenced before or after Christmas and lasted up to two weeks, with friends and neighbors meeting at a different home on each consecutive night for purposes of feasting, dancing, socializing, and enjoying music from old-time, mountain string bands playing acoustic instruments. It was customary to remove the furniture from as many rooms as was necessary to make room for dancing; in the days of two-room log cabins, the string musicians played in the doorway between the two rooms as guests feverishly danced on both sides. Many of these parties "broke up" or ended on Old Christmas (Epiphany, January 6), a day that traditionally ended the Christmas season in past eras; hence, these parties eventually took on the name "Breaking Up Christmas" (*see* **Christmas Old Style, Christmas New Style**).

Predating the Civil War, what would become the "Breaking Up Christmas" tradition is thought to have arisen from slave communities in the Blue Ridge Mountains, who celebrated the holidays by burning a large Yule log or backlog. According to custom there and on Southern plantations elsewhere, the slaves were given respite from their daily labors as long as the backlog burned, and to prolong the burning, the log was cut from a green gum tree and soaked in water; by so doing, the log often burned for two weeks, during which time the slaves made merry. From these beginnings arose a lively, special folk tune for the occasion, also appropriately titled "Breaking Up Christmas," which originally was played only on January 6 to end the festivities, but which eventually came to be a type of theme song for a fortnight of celebrations. Simple lyrics in couplet verses evolved with the tune:

Hooray, Jake! Hooray, John!
Breaking up Christmas all night long.
Way back yonder, a long time ago,
The old folks danced the do-si-do.
Santy Claus come, done and gone,
Breaking up Christmas right along.

The couplets, individually sung by one of the musicians between instrumental interludes, expressed no specific thread, except for the last couplet, which implied that the tradition was principally observed after Christmas. The tune also carried its own form of the "Breaking Up Christmas" dance, in which men and women faced each other in opposite rows and danced to steps that combined the Virginia Reel with those of the minuet, but executed in faster tempo.

The "Breaking Up Christmas" tradition had its heyday during the early twentieth century, during the Depression era and the years leading up to World War II, with mountain string-band music made popular by such artists as Charlie Lowe, Tommy Jarrell, Kyle Creed, and Fred Cockerham. Following the war, the tradition initially declined as the country music, bluegrass, and rock-and-roll genres gained popularity over string-band music, then experienced a resurgence in the 1970s that paralleled folk-music revivals.

Today the "Breaking Up Christmas" tradition survives in regions such as the Galax, Virginia, area, the Round Peak area on the North Carolina-Virginia border, and in Mt. Airy and Surry County, North Carolina. The celebrations have found principal venues in dance halls and community centers, where string-band music still predominates, yet parties in individual homes have not completely fallen by the wayside.

The "Breaking Up Christmas" song has been recorded by a number of old-time string bands, such as that with Tommy Jarrell, Bobby Patterson, Kyle Creed, and Audine Lineberry on the album *June Apple* (Heritage Records); Fred Cockerham, Paul Sutphin, Verlen Clifton, and Kyle Creed on *The Camp Creek Boys* (County Records); and the Benny Jarrell Band on *Benny Jarrell: Lady of the Lake* (Heritage Records). "Breaking Up Christmas" and other Blue Ridge Mountain tunes were featured on *Breaking Up Christmas: A Blue Ridge Mountain Holiday*, a 1997 National Public Radio (NPR) documentary by Paul Brown, then–program director for NPR station WFDD at Wake Forest University. Comprised of field and commercial recordings, Brown's program won the 1998 Silver Reel Award for Special Entertainment and was issued as a compact disc, *Blue Ridge Mountain Holiday: The Breaking Up Christmas Story* (County Records, 1997).

Br'er Rabbit's Christmas Carol

See **A Christmas Carol** (Film and Television Versions)

Brightest and Best of the Sons of the Morning

English carol for Epiphany, the lyrics of which were first published in the *Christian Observer* (1811) by Reginald Heber (1783–1826), a hymn writer and Anglican vicar of Hodnet, Shropshire, who in 1823 became bishop of Calcutta, India. Also known under the shorter title "Brightest and Best," the carol appeared in William Caldwell's collection *Union Harmony or Family Musician* (Maryville, Tennessee, 1837) under the title "Star in the East," based on a line in the first verse. Heber originally wrote four verses filled with high imagery and repeated the first verse as a fifth. An additional, anonymous verse was added at some point, incongruous with the others because of its reference to Christmas rather than Epiphany. In *The New Oxford Book of Carols*, this altered carol is titled "Hail the Blest Morn!" with the rogue verse shifted to the fore, Heber's first verse as the refrain, and the remaining verses as 2–4.

The lyrics have been paired with some 20 different musical settings, several from the American South, such as those harmonized by William Walker in *The Southern Harmony* (Spartanburg, South Carolina, 1835) and by William Caldwell above. Another setting derives from a tune written in 1892 by James P. Harding (1850–1911), a London civil service clerk and church organist. No particular setting has gained popularity over the others, however.

Other well-known hymns by Heber include "Holy, Holy, Holy" and "From Greenland's Icy Mountains."

Bring a Torch, Jeannette, Isabella

("Un flambeau, Jeannette, Isabelle"). Provençal traditional carol believed to date to the seventeenth century and possibly earlier. Sources vary in descriptions about the carol's origin. According to the Reader's Digest Association, the melody dates at least to the fourteenth century and first appeared with text in the 1553 collection *Cantiques de Première Advenement de Jésus-Christ*. According to *The New Oxford*

Book of Carols, however, the lyrics derive from a Provençal carol titled "Vénès leou vieira la Pieoucelle," which was first published in the collection *Recueil de noëls provençaux* compiled by Nicholas Saboly (1614–1675). From this carol Émile Blémont constructed the modern French translation, beginning as "Un flambeau," which first appeared in Julien Tiersot's *Noëls français* (Paris, 1901). The *Oxford Book* further attributes the tune as the drinking-song creation of French composer Marc-Antoine Charpentier (1645–1704), which was later paired with Blémont's translation. The most popular English translation, beginning as "Bring a torch," was provided by Englishman Edward Cuthbert Nunn (1868–1914).

The reference to torches in the lyrics recalls the custom of torch-lit processions to Midnight Mass on Christmas Eve. Although the specific identities of "Jeannette" and "Isabella" are lacking, their names may have influenced a Nativity painting by the French artist Georges de La Tour, which depicted two maids observing at a distance.

Bugs Bunny's Christmas Carol

See Bugs Bunny's Looney Christmas Tales

Bugs Bunny's Looney Christmas Tales

(1979). Made-for-television collection of three animated, holiday cartoon "shorts" from Friz Freleng and Chuck Jones, who at the time were directors of the animation department at Warner Bros. Studios. These cartoons feature the famous Warner Bros. characters popular since the late 1930s in theatrical shorts, including Bugs Bunny, Elmer Fudd, and Porky Pig.

Bugs Bunny's Christmas Carol. Abbreviated spoof of the Dickens classic, with Yosemite Sam as Scrooge, Porky Pig as Bob Cratchit, and Tweety Bird as Tiny Tim. Trickster Bugs pulls slapstick gags on Scrooge, then poses as the "Ghost of Christmas" and threatens to take him to see the man with the red suit in the nether regions (not Santa), whereupon Scrooge reforms.

Freeze Frame. Wile E. Coyote attempts to nab the Roadrunner by chasing him into the mountains, for, according to *Everything You Ever Wanted to Know About Roadrunners but Were Afraid to Ask*, snow is a roadrunner's nemesis. As usual, every ploy used by Coyote backfires.

Fright Before Christmas. The Tasmanian Devil, escaping from an aircraft over the North Pole on Christmas Eve, parachutes into Santa's suit drying on a clothesline and hijacks the reindeer sleigh. Entering Bugs's home via the chimney, "Taz" wreaks havoc and finally floats into the sky after swallowing a gift from Bugs, a life raft that inflates on consumption.

Principal voices: Mel Blanc and June Foray. Written by Friz Freleng, John Dunn, Chuck Jones, and Tony Benedict. Produced and directed by Friz Freleng and Chuck Jones. A DePatie-Freleng Enterprises and Chuck Jones Enterprises Production in association with Warner Bros. Television. VHS: Warner Studios. 25 min.

Bulgaria

This nation has celebrated Christmas since 865, when Boris I (ruled 852–889), the khan, accepted Christianity upon yielding to pressure from the Byzantine emperor Michael III. He embraced the Eastern Orthodox Church over the Roman Catholic Church when the latter failed to appoint an archbishop for Bulgaria. Thus Bulgarians remained predominantly Orthodox and observed Christmas according to the old Julian calendar until 1916, when they adopted the present Gregorian calendar. The preserved Christmas traditions are largely a blend of Orthodoxy and pagan, agrarian rituals, especially in rural regions.

The principal celebration is *Koleduvane* (Christmas Eve), the Christianization of a winter solstice festival that once heralded the birth of the sun. Often the head of the house cuts a large oak or peach log, which burns through the night, a symbol of Christ Who will be resurrected. Upon entering his home with the log, the man proclaims, "Do you glorify the young God?" whereupon the household responds with, "Yes, we do, welcome!" Christians keep a 40-day fast before Christmas (to commemorate Christ's ordeal of 40 days in the wilderness following His baptism) by abstaining from all animal products. In memory of Christ's 12 Apostles, the Christmas Eve dinner consists of 12 meatless dishes, eaten on a table covered with straw, which honors the manger. When someone sights the first star of the evening, believed to be the Star of Bethlehem, the dinner commences. Just prior to the dinner there are greetings from the host, who proclaims, "Christ is born," after which the family members respond with, "He is born indeed." The host offers grace, then purifies each room of the house with incense. The traditional menu consists of cabbage or vine leaves stuffed with rice, beans, lentils, boiled wheat, stewed fruit, and *saint*, a ritual bread loaf containing a coin. The eldest woman breaks this bread, then distributes the pieces, and whoever finds the coin in his piece will receive good luck.

Earlier in the day, groups of boys eight to 12 years of age tour neighborhoods with cornel sticks. To wish each home a good crop, they rap the thresholds with these sticks, whereupon the hostess anoints the boys with wheat seed. At midnight, groups of single men, or *Koledars*, also visit homes to sing *koledari* (Christmas carols) and to bestow wishes for health, good luck, and fertility. Attired in traditional *kalpaci* (fur hats) decorated with local flowers, *yamurluci* (hooded cloaks), ornate leggings, sandals, embroidered white shirts, and carved wooden staffs, the *Koledars* travel through the streets. Each procession is led by an older man, the *stanenik*, who carries a cask of red wine and a cornel-tree branch decorated with popcorn and pretzels. At each home, the *Koledars* antiphonally serenade the members from a repertoire of scores of traditional songs and dances learned from childhood. Appropriate songs are especially sung to the male head of the household, his wife, senior citizens, unwed girls, soldiers, livestock, the fields, and so forth. Then the *Koledars* receive rewards such as *koledni gevreci* (round buns), *banisa* (cheese-filled pastry), fruit, nuts, popcorn, wine, and *rakia* (plum or grape brandy). A young girl typically presents a *kravai* (large bagel) to the *stanenik*, who raises it and blesses the house.

Christmas Day is celebrated with relatives and friends. The *Koledars* convene to distribute the *kravais* received the night before, and each man seeks to receive the bagel baked by his special girl. Should more than one man desire a particular bagel, it is auctioned. Groups of children again visit homes, this time carrying *survaknitsa* (bunches of willow twigs woven together) with which to tap adults. Performing this act is termed *survakam*, which conveys wishes for good health and prosperity, and the children receive candy and money.

In the more rural areas on Christmas Day, the head of the household sprinkles corn from a stocking on the doorstep with the same greeting and response uttered prior to the Christmas Eve meal. Next he strikes the Yule log, and with each blow pronounces a wish of good health to the land, the livestock, and a bountiful harvest. Then the ashes are placed in trees to assure a good harvest.

Other religious customs are similar to those of Ukraine. "Merry Christmas" in Bulgaria is: *Tchestita Koleda*.

See also **Ukraine**.

The Burgundian Carol

Title applied to a carol from the Burgundy region of France, written around 1700 by the poet Bernard de la Monnoye (1641–1728) and published in his carol collection of 1701 with a traditional melody of the region. Technically, all of Monnoye's carols could be generically titled "Burgundian Carols," but the specific carol here received its title from the Canadian-born folk singer and recording artist Oscar Brand (1920–   ), who provided an English translation and reworked the lyrics and traditional melody into a folk song. Brand introduced his version of the carol on the *Folksong Festival*, a program he had hosted for more than 50 years on New York City's WNYC Radio. The carol was first recorded by a folk-singing group that had formed in 1948, the Weavers (Pete Seeger, Lee Hays, Fred Hellerman, and Ronnie Gilbert), who included it in their Christmas album *We Wish You a Merry Christmas* (Decca, 1952). Seeger had heard the carol when he appeared as a guest on Brand's program.

"The Burgundian Carol" centers around the traditional ox and donkey who, according to legend, were the Christ Child's stablemates after His birth. In the first verse, the animals' presence keeps Him warm; in the second, their vigil is so intense that they fast; in the third, they kneel and kiss His feet. Following each verse is the refrain asking a rhetorical question: How many oxen and donkeys today would pay such homage had they been present at Christ's birth? The carol seems to convey a moral, namely, that if animals feel compelled to worship at Christ's feet, how much more should mankind feel the same.

C

California Holly
See **Christmas Plants**

Call Me Claus

(2001). Made-for-television comedy.

With his 200-year-old contract soon to expire, Santa (Nigel Hawthorne), who calls himself "Nick," must find a suitable replacement by midnight on Christmas Eve, lest the "Or Else" clause be invoked — the entire polar ice cap will melt and flood planet Earth. His choice is Lucy Cullins (Whoopi Goldberg) of Los Angeles, the producer of a home shopping television network, whose father's death at Christmastime years ago has left her a holiday cynic. By accident, Lucy hires Nick to portray a merchandise-pitching Santa on her network's "Kristmas Korner" segment all during December, and his authentic performance boosts sales to an all-time high by Christmas Eve. Yet Lucy finds his claims to be the one-and-only Santa Claus and his persistent interest in her exasperating. To prepare the world for the advent of a black, female Santa, Nick's frequently improvised dialogue includes a passage from "Can Santa Be Black?" a poem by B.J. Wrights, which implies that Santa becomes whatever race and form are suitable for the occasion or region of the world. As the polar ice slowly melts, if a magical trip to the North Pole doesn't convince Lucy of her destiny, her evil boss's comments do: if she would scheme with him, the two of them could *own* Christmas by next year. With the seed of the Christmas spirit having always resided deep within her, Lucy cannot fathom Christmas as another item to be put on the block for sale, and she dons the magical stocking cap that Santa has left for her. Her act creates a snowfall in Los Angeles as well as at the North Pole, a sign that not only has the baton been passed, but that Christmas and the world are saved.

Principal vocal numbers sung by Garth Brooks. Story by Paul Mooney, Sara Bernstein, and Gregory Bernstein. Teleplay by Sara Bernstein, Gregory Bernstein, and Brian Bird. Produced by Tom Leonardis and Jay Benson. Directed by Peter Werner. Columbia/Tristar Television, Floresta Productions, One Ho Productions, and Red Strokes Entertainment. DVD: Columbia/Tristar Studios. 95 min.

Calm on the Listening Ear of Night
See **It Came Upon the Midnight Clear**

Canada

The first Christmas in Canada dates to 1535 in Ste. Croix, a series of forts that the French explorer Jacques Cartier and his crew built at the mouth of the St. Charles River. Although the fare was lean at that time, by 1606, the French observed the first European Christmas setting in Port Royal, Nova Scotia, founded by Sieur de Monts and Samuel de Champlain. Amid Christmas evergreens, the settlers feasted on roast moose and wild duck. Although the crèche (Nativity scene) dates to 1644 in Canada, the Christmas tree did not arrive until 1781 in Quebec, when Major General Friedrich von Riedesel, a German commander of British troops from Sorel to Montreal during the American Revolution, erected one in his home in Sorel.

Today all Canadians share the season's inauguration by witnessing the Christmas Lights across Canada, held on the first Thursday of December. Citizens gather for the simultaneous lighting of government buildings and tree-lighting ceremonies over the whole nation as they enjoy hot cider, shortbread, fruitcake, and other light holiday cuisine.

Winter activities of cross-country skiing, sleigh riding, and ice skating abound at sites such as Montreal's Mount Royal Park and Quebec City's Mont Ste.-Anne. Special Christmas services appeal to Canadians and tourists alike at such world-famous churches as St. Michael's Cathedral and the Church of the Transfiguration, both in Toronto; St. Joseph's Oratory (with its collection of Nativity scenes from around the world) and Notre-Dame Basilica, both in Montreal; and Quebec City's Ste.-Anne-de-Beaupre with its 240 stained-glass windows.

Canada uses some 100,000 acres across its land for the growing of six million Christmas trees annually, most notably the balsam fir. One-third of this land lies in Nova Scotia alone. Most of these trees are marketed nationally and to the United States, with some ten percent exported to the Caribbean and Central and South America. Annually since 1973, Halifax has presented a 70-foot balsam fir to the city of Boston, Massachusetts, in gratitude for assistance received when, in 1917, an ammunition ship exploded in Halifax Harbor, destroying much of the city. Boston annually erects the tree in its Prudential Square.

• A DIVERSE CULTURE. The Canadian population is quite diverse culturally, with people principally of British, French, Acadian, German, Italian, Polish, Dutch, and Ukrainian heritages, in addition to the Indian tribes indigenous to Canada, who prefer the all-encompassing name First Nations. The Christmas traditions of European Canadians closely parallel those of their parent countries, and the following is a summary of those traditions that have arisen in addition to, or have been modified from, those found in Europe.

British traditions are preserved in museums and historical homes around the country. Christmas parades with Santa Claus date back to 1905 and the T. Eaton Department Store of Toronto, which hosted the first parade. On Prince Edward Island, the annual school concert, traditional for over 100 years, has become the social highlight of the season. Two favorite candies of the Maritime Provinces include "Chicken Bones," a hard cinnamon stick filled with chocolate, manufactured in St. Stephen, New Brunswick, since 1885; and "Barley Toys," colored candy molded into the shapes of animals or toys, manufactured in Yarmouth, Nova Scotia, for more than 175 years. Mumming is found almost exclusively in Newfoundland during the 12 days of Christmas, and Boxing Day, December 26, while a national holiday, no longer carries the promise of gratuity to employees as in former times (*see* **Christmas Drama** [**Mumming**] and **Boxing Day**). Dur-

ing the week before Christmas since 1961, Vancouver, British Columbia, has sponsored a "Carol Ship" that is decorated with lights and a Christmas tree and carries bell ringers and children's choirs on board. As this ship sails through Vancouver Harbor during the evenings, a flotilla of private yachts and other ships follows, while crowds on shore build bonfires and sing along with the choirs. A "Santa Ship" distributes toys in mid-December to needy children living on U.S. and Canadian gulf islands.

To the French, *le réveillon*, the traditional meal following Midnight Mass on Christmas Eve, may consist of *tourtières* (meat pies), *ragout de boulettes* (meat ball and pork stew), pork spread, minced pork pie, partridge with cabbage, goose or turkey, oyster or pea soup, cheeses, condiments, cranberry sauce, numerous pastries such as maple syrup tarts, and *bûche de Noël* (Christmas cake shaped like a log). Children ask blessings from their father, older brother, or other patriarch on New Year's Day, a day that has traditionally been the day for gifts, though children often receive gifts at *le réveillon* as well.

For French- and English-speaking peoples (Acadians) of the Maritime Provinces, Christmas includes the major French and some British customs. *Le réveillon* features rabbit pie and *pâté a la rapure* (meat pie with potatoes, onions, bacon, and seasonings). For their parents, children make a *Bouquet Spirituel*, a decorative card containing all the prayers they have said in the weeks prior to Christmas. New Year's Day includes firstfooting, where a young boy arriving first at one's door brings a year's worth of luck, and older boys beat in the new year by rapping the sides of homes with sticks. The Epiphany Kings' Cake includes a ring (predicting the next to marry) and a silver coin (predicting the one who will become rich), along with the bean and pea (*see* **Epiphany** [**Twelfth Night**]).

Though the Mennonites do not subscribe to specific feast days as do their conventional German counterparts, their children set out plates on Christmas Eve, which their parents fill with treats for Christmas Day. For the Hutterites of Saskatchewan, although Christmas is a three-day holiday from labor, it is spent in strict meditation, prayer, and church services.

Ukrainian children usually receive gifts from St. Nicholas on his feast day, December 19 on the Julian calendar, instead of Christmas Day. The ceremonial Blessing of the Waters is observed on the Feast of Jordan (January 19) and is reenacted at the Ukrainian Cultural Heritage Village near Edmonton, Alberta.

• FIRST NATIONS. Winter solstice celebrations center around gift-giving, feasting, dancing, and games of skill and strength. During a festival of eight days, the Iroquois burn tobacco and petition the Creator for blessings upon their crops. The children visit their mother's relatives on New Year's Day and carry bags for the relatives to fill with treats. Cree children observe a similar custom on Christmas Eve, returning the next day for the filled bags. West Coast tribes observe *potlatch* ("giving"), which celebrates any special occasion during the year. Here, the more gifts a chief or tribe lavishes on the guests, the more prestigious the event. Other Christian tribes hold community-wide parties with carols sung in their native tongues and with appearances from Santa.

The Inuit also hold community feasts, which feature Santa and a menu of caribou, seal, and raw fish, along with the traditional Drum Dance, storytelling, harpoon throwing, wrestling, igloo building, rifle shooting, snowmobile racing, and other games of skill. In the unusual game of Throat Singing, Inuit women pair off and compete by imitating the sounds of the North without breaking the rhythm. On Boxing Day or on New Year's Day, the Inuit observe *pallaq* ("charging"), in which family members with anything to celebrate stand on their roofs and throw gifts to their guests below. Snowmobile parades and rifle shooting again welcome the new year.

The Métis (of French-Canadian and First Nations heritage) of the Prairie Provinces also hold Christmas Eve family reunions with feasting on buffalo, moose, deer, potatoes, berries, and wild rice; gifts, music and dancing; and traditional gunfire. Their celebrations may extend for two weeks.

"Merry Christmas" among First Nations peoples might be said as *Mitho Makosi Kesikansi* (Cree); *Jutdlime pivdlurarit ukiortame pivdluaritlo* (Inuit); or *Ojenyunyat sungwiyadeson honungradon nagwutut* (Iroquois). Christmas greetings in the various European languages are heard throughout Canada, depending on the heritage of the area.

See also **France; Germany; Great Britain; The Huron Christmas Carol; Italy; The Low Countries** (The Netherlands); **Poland; Ukraine.**

Candlemas

Observed by the Roman Catholic Church on February 2 and the Armenian Church on February 14, Candlemas marks the purification of the Virgin Mary and presentation of Jesus in the Temple 40 days after His birth. Until the Second Vatican Council (1962–1965), the date also terminated the Christmas season in the Catholic Church.

According to ancient Jewish law, after a woman gave birth, she was considered to be unclean and was required to spend certain days in purification rites before she was accepted back into society. The time was 40 days if the child was male, 80 if the child was female (Leviticus 12:1–5). A first born child was redeemed through animal sacrifice (Numbers 18:15). Candlemas, a date 40 days past Christmas Day, commemorates not only Mary's purification but the presentation of the infant Jesus in the Temple as well. At that time, according to Luke's Gospel, the prophet Simeon referred to Jesus as "a light to lighten the Gentiles, and the glory of thy people Israel" (Luke 2:22–33). To capitalize on this statement, candle ceremonies play a significant role in Candlemas to symbolize Jesus as Light of the World. Worshipers receive blessed beeswax candles, which are lighted, and the congregation participates in a procession.

The Church in Jerusalem first celebrated a feast of purification during the first half of the fourth century, prior to designating December 25 as Christmas Day. At that time, the feast was known only as "the fortieth day after Epiphany," which implied that, in the Eastern Rite, Epiphany was held as the date of Christ's birth. Originally, the feast was held on February 14, a Christianizing of the ancient Roman purification feast of *Februa*. With the declaration of December 25 as Christmas Day during the latter half of the fourth century, the feast was moved to February 2. It is believed that the Byzantine emperor Justinian I instituted the Candlemas feast around 542 in the East and that Pope Sergius I (687–701) introduced it in the West, although the blessing of candles did not become widespread in the Western Church until the eleventh century.

In the Middle Ages, Candlemas was not only the time for families to select next year's Yule log, it was also the time to burn the Christmas plants (they were never thrown out) plus the remnants of the old Yule log as well, while saving a piece of the old log to light the one for the following year.

An old superstition holding that a sunny Candlemas predicts 40 more days of winter weather forms the basis for "Groundhog Day," February 2, in the United States. According to this folklore, if the groundhog sees his shadow on that day, expect six more weeks of cold weather.

See also **Epiphany**; **Yule**.

Candy Canes

Hard, thin, sugar sticks with one end bent to form a crook, generally with red and white stripes or other colors. Originating in Europe during the seventeenth century, candy canes at first consisted only of straight, white sticks, which mothers gave to their babies as pacifiers and which were hung on Christmas trees as decorations, along with other sweets. According to tradition, in 1670 the choirmaster at the cathedral in Cologne, Germany, had a number of the sticks fashioned as small shepherds' crooks and passed them along to children who visited the cathedral's live Nativity scene that year. The treat, a memorial to the Christmas shepherds of long ago, was again designed to keep little ones quiet during those ceremonies. The innovation became quite popular, especially during the holidays, and spread throughout Europe. Later, candy canes were embellished with white sugar roses.

It is reported that candy canes first came to America with August Imgard, a German-Swedish immigrant of Wooster, Ohio, who decorated his Christmas tree with the sweets in 1847.

Around the turn of the twentieth century, candy canes took on red and white stripes plus

This illustration by M.E. Ohrumschalk, from an unidentified children's book ca. 1920s, shows a small elfin being, perhaps a Scandinavian jultomten, *leading a child through the "Peppermint Stick Gate."*

the flavors of peppermint and wintergreen, but the one responsible for these added accouterments remains unknown. Evidence of the change can be observed in old Christmas cards: Those issued before 1900 show the plain, white canes, and those thereafter feature the striped versions.

Assorted religious interpretations have surrounded the candy cane, all inspirational, but all without definitive source of origin. For example, turned upside down, the cane resembles a "J," indicative of Jesus; the red and white stripes are symbolic of the stripes of flogging that Jesus received prior to His crucifixion and the colors, His blood and purity, respectively; the hard texture symbolizes Christ as the Rock, the foundation of the Church; and the peppermint flavor is reminiscent of hyssop, an aromatic plant that ancient Hebrews used for purification rites. The story that persecuted, early Christians used candy canes as secret means of identifying one another is most certainly a myth, given that this form of candy was a creation of the seventeenth century.

These religious interpretations surrounding candy canes are the subjects of several inspirational books, notable of which is *The Legend of the Candy Cane* (1997), written by American author Lori Walburg and illustrated by James Bernardin. Set at the turn of the twentieth century, when candy merchant John Sonneman sets up shop in a small prairie town, simple candy canes take on a new meaning for little Lucy. Not only are they pleasing to behold and delicious to eat at Christmastime, Sonneman teaches Lucy the significance of their "J" shape, their resemblance to shepherds' crooks when turned upside down, and their red and white stripes. The message that each candy cane brings is so powerful that man and child, while delivering the confections as free gifts to each home in town, spread the story abroad until all have heard its message by Christmas Eve. In 2001, the story was adapted for television under the same title, starring Florence Henderson, Tom Bosley, Bruce Marchiano, Ossie Davis, Jay Underwood, and Malcolm-Jamal Warner. Produced by Rick Eldridge. Directed by John Schmidt. Dean River Productions. DVD: Fox Home Entertainment. 60 min.

Other books along the same thread include *The Candymaker's Gift: A Legend of the Candy Cane* (1996) by Helen Haidle, illustrated by David Haidle; *The Candy Cane Story* (1996) by Joy Merchant Nall and Thomas Nall, Jr.; and *The "J" Is for Jesus* (1998) by Alice Joyce Davidson.

Cards
See **Christmas Cards**

Caribbean Islands
See **West Indies**

Carol for Another Christmas
See **A Christmas Carol** (Film and Television Versions)

Carol of the Bagpipers
("Canzone d'i Zampognari"). Italian traditional carol, also known as "Bagpipers' Carol," "Song of the Bagpipers," "On That Most Blessed Night," and "When Christ, the

Calabrian shepherds (pifferari) *playing in Rome at Christmas, reminiscent of the Italian "Carol of the Bagpipers." Wood engraving after an etching by D. Allan, from* Hone's Every-Day Book *(London: 1836).*

Son of Mary." Reputed to be the best known of Italian carols, it originated in Sicily around the seventeenth century, a period in which, some ten days before Christmas, it was customary for the *pifferari* (Calabrian shepherds) to journey to Rome, Naples, and other cities in southern Italy to play their bagpipes before statues of the Virgin. Traditionally the music was believed to ease the Virgin's impending labor discomfort, and the shepherds also would stop by a carpenter's shop out of respect for Joseph. The custom has since fallen into neglect.

The baroque German composer George Frideric Handel, while touring Italy from 1706 to 1709, was much impressed by those enchanting bagpipe melodies and incorporated them into some of his works. The most notable of these is his oratorio *Messiah*, written in 1741, in which such melodies form the basis for the "Pifa" or "Pastoral Symphony." More specifically, the melody for the aria "He Shall Feed

His Flock" is closely based on that of "Carol of the Bagpipers."

Carol of the Bells

Title of two twentieth century songs, both Ukrainian-American hybrids. The far more popular version, also known as "The Ukraine Carol," was adapted from "Shchedryk," an ancient Ukrainian folk song, which is classified as a *shchedrivka* (New Year's carol). The adaptation was created by Ukrainian composer Mykola Leontovich (1877–1921) in his *Shchedryk*, a choral work that was first performed at Kiev University in 1916. The basis for his piece was an ancient Slavic legend which held that, at midnight when Christ was born, all the bells in the world pealed for joy. Indeed, the music simulates rapidly pealing bells. The American composer, lyricist, and conductor Peter Wilhousky (1902–1978) added English lyrics, beginning with "Hark! How the bells," to Leontovich's music in 1936 and titled the match "Carol of the Bells." Today the appeal of this masterpiece still lies in its choral renditions.

A lesser-known variant, also titled "Carol of the Bells," appeared anonymously in 1972. Although it, too, kept Leontovich's melody, its lyrics began with "Hark to the bells." Two additional American songs, "Ring, Christmas Bells" by M.L. Holman (1947) and the anonymous "Come, Dance and Sing" (1957), each borrowed Leontovich's haunting melody as the setting for original lyrics.

Of the 25 most frequently performed Christmas songs of the twentieth century listed by the American Society of Composers, Authors and Publishers (ASCAP), "Carol of the Bells" (Leontovich/Wilhousky) ranked number 15. By December 2004, it ranked number 23.

See also **ASCAP List of Christmas Songs.**

Carol of the Birds

Generic, English-language title applied to several carols from different regions of the world that focus upon birds rejoicing at Christmastime. With the ever-present ox and ass of Nativity scenes, fowls join the repertoire of traditional holiday creatures, yet the biblical account of the Nativity makes no mention of them whatsoever. The best known of these carols include the following:

"El cant dels ocells," a medieval, Spanish traditional carol from Catalonia, features praise from the nightingale, sparrow, finch, and partridge.

"Žežulka z lesa vylítla," a Czech traditional carol also known in English as "The Birds" and "From out of the Forest a Cuckoo Flew," not only includes adoration by a cuckoo and a dove, but imitations of their cries as well.

"Le Noël des oiseaux" and "Noël des ausels" are two traditional, sixteenth century carols from southern France. The latter, also known in English as "Whence Comes This Rush of Wings Afar?" portrays birds following the Star of Bethlehem and worshiping at the manger with angels and shepherds. Specific mention is made of the greenfinch and philomel (nightingale).

Two English-language carols of the twentieth century designated "Carol of the Birds" include the 1943 contribution by the American folk composer John Jacob Niles (1892–1980) and that by Australians John Wheeler (lyrics) and William Garnet James (music). Written as a contrast to the winter scenes in the Northern Hemisphere, the latter carol features six Australian birds in their natural, summer habitat: brolgas (large cranes with silver-gray plumage and a red patch on the head), woodlarks, bellbirds (so named for their bell-like cry), friarbirds (so named for their tonsured heads), currawongs (large, black-and-white passerine birds with bell-like cries), and lorikeets (small, brilliantly colored parrots). All are singing, "Orana! Orana! Orana! To Christmas Day," which incorporates an Aboriginal word for "welcome."

See also **The Friendly Beasts.**

Carol of the Brown King: Nativity Poems

Collection of six brief poems for young children about the Nativity. Five of the poems were written by the African American poet, novelist, playwright, and lyricist Langston Hughes (1902–1967), a key figure in the Harlem Renaissance of the 1920s and sometimes called the Poet Laureate of Harlem. The sixth poem Hughes translated from an anonymous Puerto Rican Christmas card. Ashley Bryan, noted illustrator of African American spirituals and poetry, compiled the poems and published them together with his illustrations in 1998.

"Carol of the Brown King," the title poem and best known of the collection, asserts that one of the three Wise Men or Magi was black, or in Hughes's words, "a brown man" (some traditions hold that one Wise Man came from Ethiopia). "Shepherd's Song at Christmas" poses the rhetorical question of what fitting gifts a shepherd can bring to the manger. The answer is simple: a song from the heart, a gentle lamb, and one's own heart. "On a Christmas Night" and "The Christmas Story" are Nativity narratives. "On a Pallet of Straw" again recalls the Wise Men who found the Christ Child lying on a straw pallet. Hughes's translation of a Puerto Rican Christmas card consists of eight lines about replacing an orange that the Child has lost.

Carol of the Drum

See **The Little Drummer Boy** (song)

Carol of the Mother

See **Alfred Burt Carols**

Caroling, Caroling

See **Alfred Burt Carols**

Carols

See **Christmas Carols**

Casper's First Christmas

(1979). Made-for-television animated cartoon, based on the character Casper the Friendly Ghost, featured in Harvey cartoons.

Their old, abandoned haunt about to be torn down, mischievous ghost Hairy Scary and his little friend Casper receive unexpected guests on Christmas Eve. Hanna-Barbera cartoon characters Quick Draw McGraw, Huckleberry Hound, Augie Doggy, Doggie Daddy, Snagglepuss, Yogi Bear, and Boo Boo, lost en route to a mountain lodge, stop at the house instead and make it festive.

Initially opposed to Christmas, Hairy attempts to drive them away until he discovers Casper's note to Santa, asking that Hairy's house be spared. Touched, Hairy forms a new opinion about Christmas, and the party resumes. As Casper had hoped, Santa arrives and presents Hairy with a deed to the house, which becomes Hairy's Haunting Lodge, and the gang agrees to celebrate Christmas each year thereafter with Hairy and Casper.

Principal voices: Daws Butler, Paul Dekorte, Don Messick, Hal Smith, Ida Sue McCune, Julie McWhirter, John Stephenson, and Michael Redman. Written by Bob Ogle. Produced by Alex Lovy. Directed by Carl Urbana. Hanna-Barbera Productions. VHS: Hanna-Barbera Studios. 25 min.

See also **Casper's Haunted Christmas**; **Hanna-Barbera Christmas Cartoons**.

Casper's Haunted Christmas

(2000). Canadian made-for-video, computer-generated animated cartoon, based on the character Casper the Friendly Ghost of Harvey Cartoons.

Finding that Casper has failed to scare at least one person per year according to Ghost Law, spectral authority Kibosh banishes Casper and his three uncles (the Ghostly Trio) to Kriss, Massachusetts, "the most Christmasy town in the world." There, the Ghostly Trio must persuade Casper to scare someone by Christmas Day, lest all four be cast into "the Dark," the ghost equivalent of hell. Yet the uncles cannot scare anyone themselves, because their "haunting licenses" have been revoked.

Initially failing in their assignment, the uncles summon Spooky, Casper's tough, lookalike cousin from New York City for the task, but when the challenge defeats even him, they reject him as their equal. Now the Ghostly Trio reasons that, since they are all soon to be doomed to the Dark, they will ruin Christmas by stealing all the presents in town, an act that would parallel that of the Grinch in Dr. Seuss's story *How the Grinch Stole Christmas.* Humiliated, Spooky turns against the Ghostly Trio and warns Casper of their imminent plan. Together with Pearl, Spooky's girlfriend, Casper and Spooky create a successful stunt that not only scares the uncles, thwarts their actions, and saves Christmas in Kriss, but also fulfills Ghost Law and avoids an unpleasant final destiny.

In 2001, this video won the Santa Clara International Film Festival Award for Best Foreign Animation and also won First Prize at the Vancouver Effects and Animation Festival for Animated Feature Film.

Theme song sung by Randy Travis. With Brendon Ryan Barrett as the voice of Casper. Written by Ian Boothby and Roger Fredericks. Produced by Byron Vaughns. Directed by Owen Hurley. Harvey Entertainment and Mainframe Entertainment. DVD: Universal Studios. 84 min.

See also **Casper's First Christmas; How the Grinch Stole Christmas.**

Central America

Overwhelmingly Roman Catholic because the countries in this region were originally Spanish colonies dating to the sixteenth century, Central America celebrates Christmas traditions deriving from Spain. The principal customs common to Central American countries include *Nacimientos* or *Pesebres* (respectively, simple or more elaborate Nativity scenes); the Feast of the Immaculate Conception (December 8); the Midnight Mass, termed "Mass of the Rooster" (*Misa del Gallo*), celebrated on *Nochebuena* ("Good Night," Christmas Eve); a large Christmas Eve dinner for family and friends held either before or just after the Midnight Mass; Holy Innocents Day (December 28); New Year's Day (January 1); and *Día de los Reyes* (Kings' Day, Epiphany, January 6).

Through foreign influences (predominantly from the United States), Santa Claus and Christmas trees are well known, but the Nativity scene remains the most important holiday symbol. It is customary for families to visit Nativity scenes of friends and relatives, as well as the scene erected in the local cathedral. Traditionally, the crib or manger within each Nativity scene remains empty until midnight on Christmas Eve, at which time each family or church adds a figure of the Christ Child to symbolize that Christ is born.

Pesebres are usually handmade and occupy a large space in the principal room of the home. Consisting of ornate landscapes with perhaps hills and waterfalls, they include figures of the Holy Family, animals, angels, shepherds, the Three Kings, and figures of local familiarity, such as the mayor, police officer, butcher, carpenter, and so forth, the latter figures bonding the past with the present.

Formerly, children received gifts only on Epiphany from the Three Kings, but it has become customary for children to receive gifts on Christmas Eve as well, brought either by Santa Claus or the Christ Child. More commonly on Epiphany eve, children place their shoes upon a window sill, and the Three Kings fill them with treats by morning.

Religious processions and festive parades with fireworks, music, singing, and dancing abound. Employers in some regions are compelled by law to provide employees with an *aguinaldo* ("gift," Christmas bonus).

The period from December 16 to 24 constitutes a Novena, on each day of which a special Mass is held. The first Mass is dedicated to the Annunciation; the second, the visit between Mary and her cousin Elizabeth; the third, the journey to Bethlehem; the fourth, the Nativity; the fifth, the shepherds; the sixth, the Magi; the seventh, the flight into Egypt; the eighth, the boy Jesus in the Temple with the scholars; the ninth, the boy Jesus' return to Nazareth. The Christmas season generally ends on Epiphany.

The following paragraphs summarize additional customs found in the individual countries. "Merry Christmas" is spoken in Spanish: *Feliz Navidad*.

• BELIZE. Called British Honduras until 1973, Belize has a population of mixed racial descent, consisting of Creoles, Native Americans (Caribs and Mayans), mestizos, black Caribs (Garifuna), and Europeans (English and Spanish). Nearly 60 percent of the population is Roman Catholic. Despite the ethnic diversity, Christmas decorations and carols reflect American and European influences, and Santa Claus brings the children's gifts. Mestizos observe *Las Posadas* ("The Lodgings") as in Mexico, and the Garifuna follow the rituals of Jonkonnu, as principally found in the West Indies. The Christmas menu varies slightly between ethnic groups, but generally consists of beans, rice, potato salad, turkey with stuffing, tortillas, fish, ham, yams, black cake (dark fruitcake), and *rompope* (eggnog with rum). Favorites among those of Mexican descent are *bollos* (ground corn with chicken, rolled into palm leaves and steamed over an open fire). "Merry Christmas" is said in English, the official language. *See also* **Las Posadas; West Indies.**

• Costa Rica. As mandated by law, around December 1, employers must provide annual *aguinaldos* (Christmas bonuses) to employees, equivalent to one year's salary plus that for one month (average annual salaries are quite low, perhaps $300). Beginning on Christmas Eve, churches observe the Prayer of the Rosary of the Holy Child, a celebration that extends until Candlemas (February 2). Families also observe this prayer before their private Nativity scenes, known in Costa Rica as *portals*. Collectively known as the *Paso* (from *Pasch*, "Passover"), the three most important figures in each *portal* are those of Mary, Joseph, and the Christ Child.

Amid fireworks, Costa Rican celebrations include a menu of tamales (corn dough with meat filling and spicy sauce, wrapped in plantain leaves and steamed), *chica* (liquor with ginger spice), *escabeche* (vinegar relish of carrots, peppers, onions, cauliflower, and green beans), rum, eggnog, fruits, wine, and *queque Navideno* (Christmas cake). Children receive gifts from the Christ Child on Christmas Eve.

Although each local community sponsors fairs, plays, and other public events, those held in San Jose are of special interest. The Festival of Lights, resembling the American Mardi Gras, provides a carnival atmosphere with decorative lights, parades with tropical floats, fireworks, clowns, cartoon characters, and goblins, culminating in a grand street carnival held just before New Year's Eve. An equine parade, *El Tope*, fills December 26 (St. Stephen's Day) with displays of horses imported from Peru and Spain. Children ride with their parents, who are most elaborately dressed. Variations on Spain's "Running of the Bulls" are *Las Corridas* (the Bull Fights) of Zapote, a section of San Jose, in which the most daring of men approach bulls in the ring, touch them with the bullfighter's cape, then try to outrun the enraged animals to safety. Those who succeed are awarded small prizes. And from Christmas Day onward, Zapote also sponsors an open-air fair with rides, food booths, loud music, and all the ingredients similarly found in state or county fairs in the United States. *See also* **Candlemas.**

• El Salvador. The Christmas season begins with the Feast of the Immaculate Conception, followed closely by a similar celebration on December 12, the Feast of Our Lady of Guadalupe. This latter event commemorates the appearance of the Virgin to the Indian Juan Diego, believed to have occurred in 1531 in the city of Guadalupe Hidalgo (now known as Gustavo A. Madero), Mexico. These festivities include appearances from *Inditos* (children dressed as Diego), processions carrying statues of the Virgin, fireworks, dances, and soccer tournaments. Christmas trees, poinsettias, and *Pesebres* constitute the most common of decorations, the latter of those focusing upon the *Misterio* ("Mystery"), a collective term for the figures of Mary, Joseph, and the Christ Child.

Unlike Mexico, which celebrates *Las Posadas* ("The Lodgings") for nine days prior to Christmas, El Salvador observes this custom only on Christmas Eve. The menu at this time usually features tamales, turkey, chicken, pork, rice, green vegetables, assorted desserts, and liquors. Children receive gifts from Santa Claus, who places them either under the Christmas tree or under the children's beds. Christmas Day is marked with church services and beach activities. *See also* **Las Posadas.**

• Guatemala. The Christmas season commences simultaneously with the Feast of the Immaculate Conception and *La Quema del Mal* ("The Burning of the Evil"), the latter custom consisting of burning discarded items with fireworks. For the preceding week, people masked as demons chase children through the streets, a vestige of Mayan rituals now blended with those of Christmas. The burning is a symbolic purging of evil prior to Christmas. Other Advent customs include painting and repairing the house, decorating with poinsettias, and, because Guatemalan law forbids the cutting of whole trees, the significant German population fashion Christmas trees from tree branches. The customary *Las Posadas* ("The Lodgings"), similar to that of Mexico, is also observed for nine days prior to Christmas.

Public festivities fill Christmas Eve with costumed parades and numerous fireworks throughout the day and especially at midnight, after which families congregate for the Christmas dinner. The menu often features tamales and *ponche* (liquor with brown sugar and fruits such as raisins, dates, and plums). Although children receive gifts on Christmas Eve from the Christ Child, adults usually exchange gifts on New Year's Day. Fireworks resume on Christmas Day. *See also* **Las Posadas.**

• HONDURAS. Migrating from the West Indies, black Caribs (Garifuna) settled along the northern shore of Honduras, bringing their traditional dances and customs, such as Jonkonnu. During Advent, bands of Garifuna women perform dances at various homes, for which they receive monetary donations and sweet liquors, such as *guaro.* Spanish children perform *Pastorelas* (Nativity plays), employers grant *aguinaldos* (bonuses) to employees, and Christmas parties abound for employees and youths. On Christmas Eve, a masked dancer, the *Warini*, ushers in Christmas by dancing from house to house with an entourage of singers and drummers and din of firecrackers. The Christmas dinner usually features turkey with stuffing, *lechonitos* (suckling pig), and *rompope* (eggnog with liquor). At midnight on New Year's Eve, families burn an effigy of an undesirable person or object, a custom termed *La Quema de los Años Viejos* ("Burning the Old Year"), which symbolizes cleansing for the new year. The *Warini* closes the season with dances on Epiphany.

• NICARAGUA. The Christmas season commences with the Feast of the Immaculate Conception, the night of which is termed *La Noche de Gritería* ("The Night of the Shouting"). Such a name arises from the highly intense, fervent singing of hymns and carols to the Virgin, which bands of singers present at homes so decorated for their reception. The processions bear *La Gigantona* ("The Giant Female" or "The Super Female"), a large figure of the Virgin. Amid fireworks, hosts reward the singers with candy and treats such as *cañas de azúcar* (sugar canes), sweets, fruit, and cookies, among others. Christmas decorations include *Flores de Pastor* ("Shepherd's Flowers," poinsettias), *muérdagos* (aromatic decorations suspended overhead, imitative of mistletoe), colored streamers, and artificial Christmas trees (pine trees are scarce). The Christmas Eve dinner usually features *gallina de patio* (stuffed chicken), Spanish rice, *nacatamal* (tamales), tortillas, and *ponche* (a rum beverage). Gifts are hidden around the home, and children, believing that *El Niño Jesus* (Baby Jesus) brings them, search for them following Midnight Mass. New Year's Eve is filled with parties and fireworks. It is customary to withdraw a few pieces of straw from the *Pesebre* at church to place in children's shoes on the eve of Epiphany as symbolic fodder for the Three Kings' camels. The Kings remove the straw and fill the shoes with treats.

• PANAMA. During the Novena, a *Misa del Aguinaldo* (Mass of the Gift) is held early each morning. Christmas dinner may feature a variety of seafood, rice with beans, *arroz con pollo* (chicken with rice, saffron, and vegetables), *arroz con piña* (rice with pineapple), and *rom ponche* (rum punch). Instead of writing letters to Santa Claus, children address them to Baby Jesus, care of St. Peter in heaven. Gifts are placed either under the Christmas tree or under children's beds.

See also **Epiphany; Feast of the Immaculate Conception; Holy Innocents Day; Mass of the Rooster; Nativity Scene; Spain.**

A Ceremony of Carols

Musical settings of medieval and fifteenth and sixteenth century English or Scottish poems, written in 1942 by English composer Benjamin Britten (1913–1976). Comprising Britten's Opus 28 and the first of his works to be scored for treble (boys') voices and harp, *A Ceremony of Carols* was written along with his *Hymn to St. Cecilia* during a perilous voyage from the United States to England. It was first published in 1943 and first recorded by the Morriston Boys' Choir and Maria Korchinska with Britten conducting. The following paragraphs summarize its 12 movements.

1 and 12. "Processional" and "Recessional." These identical settings consist of "Hodie Christus natus est" ("Today Christ is Born"), the Latin antiphon plainsong from the Christmas Eve Vespers.

2. "Wolcum Yole" ("Welcome Yule"). Anonymous from the fourteenth century, it bids good cheer and welcome to personalities and events recognized during the Christmas season: the feast days of St. Stephen, St. John, and St. Thomas; the Holy Innocents; Twelfth Night; and Candlemas.

3. "There Is No Rose of Such Vertu [Virtue]." Anonymous from the fourteenth or

fifteenth century, it likens the Virgin Mary to a rose, whose young flower is Christ (*see* **There Is No Rose of Such Virtue**).

4. "That Yonge [Young] Child." Anonymous from the fourteenth century, it asserts that the Virgin's lullaby song to the Babe is far sweeter than any music that a minstrel or nightingale could produce.

5. "Balulalow." This sixteenth century Scottish ballad by brothers James, John, and Robert Wedderburn sets forth the Virgin's lullaby, in which she pledges her heart and everlasting devotion to her Son.

6. "As Dew in Aprille." Anonymous from c. 1400, it likens the birth of Christ to the still and gentle "falling" of April dew; that is, without ceremony.

7. "This Little Babe." This piece by the sixteenth century English poet Robert Southwell presents a series of metaphors in which the Babe, seemingly weak and helpless, nevertheless poses as a formidable Warrior, against Whom the powers of Satan are no match. Thus, the Babe's breast serves as a shield; His cries, "battering shot"; His weeping eyes, arrows; cold and need, His ensigns; His flesh, a steed; the stable, a camp; the manger, a trench; the shepherds, the mustered army.

8. "Interlude." A harp solo based on a plainchant.

9. "In Freezing Winter Night." Robert Southwell's metaphorical piece assigns royal significance to humble emblems of the Nativity: the stable, a "Prince's court"; the manger, a "chair of State"; a wooden dish, His plate; His poor attire and base surroundings, prized as royal pomp in heaven.

10. "Spring Carol." This piece by the sixteenth century poet William Cornish looks forward past the harshness of winter to spring, a reminder to mankind that God is the source of all sustenance.

11. "Adam Lay I-Bounden [Bound]." Anonymous from the fifteenth century, it gives thanks to God for the Fall of Man through the sin of Adam, for without the Fall, Christ never would have been born.

Britten, a prolific composer of operas and other works, also wrote the Christmas choral piece *A Boy Was Born* (1933).

Ceremony of Lessons and Carols

See **A Festival of Nine Lessons and Carols**

A Chance of Snow

(1998). Made-for-television drama.

When a Minneapolis snowstorm delays their separate flights on Christmas Eve, Maddie Parker (JoBeth Williams), a recently divorced journalist, and her ex-husband Matt (Michael Ontkean) become reunited at the airport through the assistance of a loving, elderly couple and a young, widowed custodial worker.

Written by Michele Cook. Produced by Nicholas Bratcher. Directed by Tony Bill. Orly Adelson Productions and the Auerbach Company in association with Hearst Entertainment Productions, Inc. Video N/A.

Chanukah

See **Hanukkah**

A Charlie Brown Christmas

(1965). Made-for-television animated cartoon based on the *Peanuts* comic strip characters created by Charles M. Schulz (1922–2000). Receiving both Emmy and Peabody awards for program excellence, it was the first of the *Peanuts* television specials, the first prime-time cartoon without a laugh track, and the first in which children provided all the voices. Grammy Award–winning pianist Vince Guaraldi provided the jazz piano background score for this and other *Peanuts* specials, including the movie *A Boy Named Charlie Brown*. *A Charlie Brown Christmas* featured his tunes "Christmas Time Is Here" (vocal) and "Linus and Lucy" (for group dance sequences).

According to Charlie Brown, commercialism is destroying the true meaning of Christmas. His little sister Sally wants money from Santa, Snoopy decorates his doghouse and wins the neighborhood display contest, and the Christmas pageant is nothing more than a jazz festival. Derided for selecting a scrubby, real tree for the pageant, instead of a shiny, artificial one, Charlie Brown desperately asks if anyone knows what Christmas is all about. Linus steps to center stage and reverently recites the Nativity story from Luke's Gospel, which renews everybody's faith in the season.

A Charlie Brown Christmas remains one of the very few holiday television specials that actually quotes from the Bible. Against the opinions of television executives, a deeply religious Charles Schulz absolutely insisted that this first *Peanuts* special include the biblical account of the birth of Christ.

Principal voices: Peter Robbins, Tracy Stratford, Christopher Shea, Chris Doran, Karen Mendelson, Cathy Steinberg, Ann Altieri, and Sally Dryer-Barker. Written by Charles M. Schulz. Produced and directed by Bill Melendez. A Lee Mendelson–Bill Melendez Production in association with Charles M. Schulz Creative Associates and United Feature Syndicate. DVD: Paramount Studios. 26 min.

In 2001, Whoopi Goldberg hosted an Emmy Award–winning television documentary entitled *The Making of "A Charlie Brown Christmas,"* which provided interviews with some of the voice actors, now grown, who appeared in the cast, as well as archive footage of the late Charles M. Schulz. With Sally Dryer, Vince Guaraldi, Bill Melendez, Lee Mendelson, Peter Robbins, Christopher Shea, and Tracy Stratford. Produced by Jason Mendelson. Directed by Lee Mendelson. United Feature Syndicate. Video N/A. 30 min.

See also **Charlie Brown's Christmas Tales; Happy New Year, Charlie Brown; I Want a Dog for Christmas, Charlie Brown; It's Christmastime Again, Charlie Brown.**

Charlie Brown's Christmas Tales

(2002). Made-for-television animated cartoon based on the *Peanuts* comic strip characters created by Charles M. Schulz (1922–2000). The program was created to "expand" *A Charlie Brown Christmas* so that the latter could run uncut in a one-hour time slot instead of having four of its original 26 minutes sacrificed for commercials. *Christmas Tales* provides five short, independent vignettes devoted to the core characters of Linus, Lucy, Snoopy, Sally, and Charlie Brown, all adapted from holiday subjects previously published in the *Peanuts* comic strips over the years.

Believing that Santa is actually a woman disguised with a beard, Charlie Brown's little sister Sally addresses her Christmas list to "Samantha Claus," only to discover that fallacy later at school. Ever pining for the "little red-haired girl," Charlie Brown prepares a special hand-drawn Christmas card, while Snoopy enjoys ice skating with Lucy and plays "Christmas Time Is Here" on an accordion. When Lucy demands that her brother Linus buy her a Christmas present because the Bible commands it, Linus counters with, "The Bible says nothing about giving Christmas presents." The Wise Men might have a different opinion.

Jazz score written by Vince Guaraldi, performed by David Benoit. Principal voices: Wesley Singerman, Serena Berman, Corey Padnos, Megan Taylor Harvey, Christopher Ryan Johnson, Timmy Deters, Lauren Schaffel, and Bill Melendez. Charles Schulz posthumously credited as the program's writer. Produced by Lee Mendelson and Bill Melendez. A Lee Mendelson–Bill Melendez Production in association with Charles M. Schulz Creative Associates. Video N/A. 30 min.

See also **A Charlie Brown Christmas; Happy New Year, Charlie Brown; I Want a Dog for Christmas, Charlie Brown; It's Christmastime Again, Charlie Brown.**

The Cherry Tree

See **The Cherry Tree Carol**

The Cherry Tree Carol

English traditional carol, thought to have arisen during the fifteenth century. Opinion varies regarding the original form of the carol. Some authorities feel that this title is merely a collective term for three separate, yet closely interrelated carols. Others believe that it names a single carol that comprises three distinct divisions or parts, with part one having been dubbed "Joseph Was an Old Man," part two "Joseph and the Angel" or "As Joseph Was A-Walking," and part three "Mary and Jesus" or "Mary's Question."

Regardless of the form in which the carol initially appeared, its immense popularity over the centuries has generated countless folk versions, both in text and musical settings, such that no two versions are exactly alike. These alternate versions include titles such as "Joseph and Mary," "When Joseph Was an Old Man," "Oh, Joseph Took Mary Up on His Right Knee," and "The Cherry Tree," these latter four having appeared in the United States during the eighteenth or nineteenth century. The earliest and longest printed version of the three-part text, assembled from a number of broadsides, appeared in William Hone's collection *Ancient Mysteries Described* (London, 1823). While that text is felt to be incomplete, it is considered to be the most satisfactory of those that are available.

"The Cherry Tree Carol" possibly evolved from one of the Coventry Plays, a cycle of mystery plays presented in Coventry, England, during the Middle Ages. Certain similarities exist between the play and part one of the carol. The story line of both is apocryphal and derives in part from the Gospel of Pseudo-Matthew, which originally dealt with the Holy Family's flight into Egypt and a miracle whereby the infant Jesus commanded a palm tree to bend and yield its dates to Mary. For purposes of the play and carol, however, a cherry tree (more familiar to the British) and the prenatal journey to Bethlehem are substituted, in which Christ from the womb delivers a similar command to the cherry tree. Joseph, having previously expressed anger over his doubts about the Child's paternity ("Let him pluck thee a cherry that brought thee with child"), immediately repents upon witnessing the miracle. This version derives from the Protevangelium of James, another apocryphal book.

In part two, also based on the Protevangelium, the angel heralds the impending birth of Jesus to Joseph: the Child shall be born in an ox stall, wrapped in "fair white linen," rocked in a wooden cradle, and christened with "fair spring water."

Part three, associated more with Easter, depicts the young Jesus sitting in Mary's lap and predicting the redemption of mankind through His own death, burial, and resurrection.

According to interpretations set forth in *The New Oxford Book of Carols*, the cherry tree represents the Tree of Life as presented in Genesis 2:9, and Mary represents the new Eve, whose immaculate conception Jesus confirms through His prenatal miracle involving the cherries. Thus Jesus predicts that, through His future death, the original sin of Eve in the Garden of Eden will be absolved.

See also **Christmas Drama; The Coventry Carol; Feast of the Immaculate Conception.**

Chestnuts Roasting on an Open Fire
See **The Christmas Song**

Childermas
See **Holy Innocents Day**

Children, Go Where I Send Thee
African American spiritual, also known as "Little Bitty Baby" and "The Holy Baby." As with many spirituals, specific details regarding authorship and date of composition are lacking. Although the song was first discovered in a rural school for black children in Kentucky, where it was probably sung for many generations, an origin from Arkansas has also been suggested but not proven. It received more widespread attention through the Ritchie Family of Kentucky, particularly Jean Ritchie, who has collected, performed, and recorded American folk songs for more than 50 years.

A children's counting song sung in the same manner as the more familiar "The Twelve Days of Christmas," the lyrics for "Children, Go Where I Send Thee" describe one's going forth to preach the Gospel, based on Him Who was "born in Bethlehem." Various sets of lyrics exist, the most frequently appearing counting scheme of which is as follows: "one for the little bitty Baby, two for Paul and Silas, three for the Hebrew children, four for the poor that came knockin' at the door" (alternatively, "four for the four that stood at the door"), "five for the Gospel preachers, six for the six that never got fixed, seven for the seven that went up to heaven" (alternatively, "seven for the seven that never got to heaven"), "eight for the eight that stood at the gate, nine for the nine that got left behind" (alternatively, "nine for the nine all dressed so fine"), "ten for the Ten Commandments." Other versions continue counting to twelve: "eleven for the eleven deriders, twelve for the twelve Apostles."

The Children's Carol
See **The Waltons**

The Children's Friend: Number III. A New Year's Present to the Little Ones from Five to Twelve

Believed to be the first Christmas book printed in the United States. Written and illustrated in 1821 by Arthur Stansbury, a New York Presbyterian minister, the eight-page picture book depicts St. Nicholas sitting in a sleigh pulled by a single reindeer. Whether Stansbury should receive full credit for contributing a reindeer sleigh to the St. Nicholas repertoire is debatable. It is more likely that this concept was already an integral part of the St. Nicholas traditions that Dutch immigrants brought to New Amsterdam (now New York). The book was published by William Gilley.

See also **Saint Nicholas; A Visit from St. Nicholas.**

Children's Mass

See **Holy Innocents Day**

A Child's Christmas in Wales

Nostalgic recollection of enjoying simple Christmases as a boy, written by Welsh poet, short-story writer, and playwright Dylan Thomas (1914–1953), published posthumously in 1954.

Recalling few differences between Christmases from year to year, Thomas presents especially memorable anecdotes. He recalls hurling snowballs at cats with a friend, and the little fire in a neighbor's home, all on Christmas Eve. A Christmas without snow, church bells, or postal deliveries would be unthinkable. Christmas is a time for dining with one's relatives; for partaking of the turkey, goose, pudding, mince pie, and brandy; of uncles falling asleep afterwards and at least one pleasantly inebriated aunt singing weirdly. Then ghost stories fill the afternoon, followed by singing and playing folk tunes in the evening. As a boy, Thomas groups his Christmas gifts into one of two categories. "Useful" gifts are dull and boring: mufflers, mittens, zebra scarves, wool vests, nose bags, and books without pictures. "Useless" gifts are the most appealing: "jelly babies," folded flags, hatchets, celluloid ducks that make unusual noises,

painting books, toffee, fudge, marzipan and other sweets, tin soldiers, games, hobby sets, dog whistles, and cigarettes (not for smoking but for shocking old ladies into scolding about the evils of smoking).

In 1987, the story was adapted for Canadian public television, starring Denholm Elliott as narrator Old Geraint and Mathonwy Reeves as Thomas. Adapted by Jon Glascoe and Peter Kreutzer. Produced by Seaton McLean and Gillian Richardson. Directed by Don McBrearty. Atlantis Films Limited, Cypress Films, Harlech Television, and WTTW-Chicago. VHS: Warner Home Video. 55 min.

Chile

See **South America**

The Chimes

See **Dickens, Charles, Christmas Stories of**

China

See **Asia and the South Pacific**

A Chipmunk Christmas

(1981). Made-for-television animated cartoon, featuring the Chipmunks, Alvin, Simon, and Theodore, with keeper David Seville.

After Alvin makes a Christmas gift of his Golden Echo Harmonica to Tommy, a sick friend, the chipmunks learn that Dave has booked them for a concert at Carnegie Hall. Unable to afford another harmonica for the act, the chipmunks are unsuccessful at raising sufficient funds. A pleasant old woman whom Alvin meets, describing herself as lonely, far from home, and wishing to bestow gifts, surprises Alvin with a new Golden Echo Harmonica for the concert. On the mend, Tommy is Alvin's guest performer, and together they play a harmonica duet. The old woman's identity is withheld until the close, for she is Mrs. Santa Claus.

Featuring "The Chipmunk Song" ("Christmas Don't Be Late"). Voices: Ross Bagdasarian, Jr., and Janice Karman. Written and produced by Janice Karman and Ross Bagdasarian, Jr. Directed by Phil Monroe. Bagdasarian Productions. VHS: Walt Disney Studios. 24 min.

See also **The Chipmunk Song.**

The Chipmunk Song

Also known as "Christmas Don't Be Late," this popular American novelty song was composed by Ross Bagdasarian, Sr., in 1958. A Hollywood actor prior to that time, Bagdasarian created a truly novel Christmas song that featured three "singing" chipmunks, Alvin, Simon, and Theodore, named after three executives at Liberty Records. Recording under the pseudonym David Seville, Bagdasarian achieved the high-pitched, chipmunk-like harmony by speeding up recordings of his own voice. He had previously used the technique for another novelty song of 1958, "The Witch Doctor." The top Christmas song of 1958, "The Chipmunk Song" sold seven million copies, received a Grammy Award for Best Children's Recording that same year, and launched the singing trio into two television cartoon series, *The Alvin Show* (1961–1962), followed by *Alvin and the Chipmunks* (1983–1990). In the latter series, Ross Bagdasarian, Jr., principally provided the chipmunk voices following his father's death in 1972.

Of the 25 most frequently performed Christmas songs of the twentieth century listed by the American Society of Composers, Authors and Publishers (ASCAP), "The Chipmunk Song" ranked number 23. By December 2004, however, it had fallen from the list.

See also **ASCAP List of Christmas Songs**; **A Chipmunk Christmas**.

Chrismons Tree

A display that converts the conventional Christmas tree into a more significantly religious emblem by utilizing "Chrismons" (from "Christ monograms"), ornaments and symbols representing a variety of biblical and theological concepts.

The Chrismons tree is the inspiration of Frances Kipps Spencer (1917–1990), who in 1957 first introduced such a tree at Ascension Lutheran Church in Danville, Virginia. Believing that conventional Christmas trees were too secular for sanctuaries, Mrs. Spencer drew upon the familiar tradition of celebrating one's birthday with a cake inscribed with the honoree's name, wherein the evergreen tree (itself symbolic of eternal life through Christ) became the "cake." But instead of adorning the tree

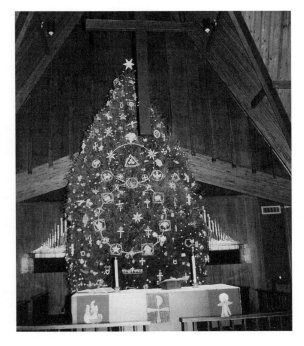

A Chrismons tree decorated with humerous Chrismons, symbols of biblical and theological concepts. Various Chrismons seen here include crosses, lambs, doves, and stars, among others. Photograph by Hugh Preston Leonard. Courtesy Ascension Lutheran Church, Danville, Virginia.

with "Jesus Christ" in English, she used Greek monograms (so used because the New Testament was originally written in Greek), the first two of which were the letters "X" (Chi) and "P" (Rho), the first two letters in "ΧΡΙΣΤΟΣ" (transliterated *Christos*), the Greek word for "Christ." Over time, the popularity of the Chrismons tree grew and spread to other denominations around the world, while Chrismons themselves have become meaningful decorations throughout the year. Chrismons are the trademark of Ascension Lutheran Church and are not commercially manufactured for profit.

At first, Chrismons consisted of only the monograms directly relating to Jesus Christ, accompanied by various styles of crosses, but with time, virtually any Christian symbol was deemed suitable for decorating a Chrismons tree. Examples of other Chrismons, by no means exhaustive, now include Greek letters "A" (Alpha) and "Ω" (Omega), respectively symbolizing Christ as the "Beginning" and the

Chrismons in double loop representing the "Christian Year Series." Top loop represents the Triune God, further represented by a shamrock within a triangle and circle. Counterclockwise, the chief Chrismons include Hand from cloud (Father), Lamb of God (Son), and Descending Dove (Holy Spirit). Counterclockwise, chief Chrismons in lower loop include scroll with prophecy (Advent), gladiolus (Christmas), five-pointed star (Epiphany), pelican-in-her-piety (Lent), rising phoenix (Easter), chariot of fire (Ascension), and seven-tongued flame (Penecost) at junction of loops. Photograph by Hugh Preston Leonard. Courtesy Ascension Lutheran Church, Danville, Virginia.

"End"; lambs, representing Christ as the Lamb of God; angels, who proclaimed the "glad tidings of great joy" to the shepherds; rocks, symbolic of Christ as the Rock of Ages, the Rock of the Church; anchors, symbolic of Christ as the Anchor of Christian faith; doves, symbolic of the Holy Spirit; stars, for the Star of Bethlehem; and fish, the Greek word for which is "ΙΧΘΥΣ" (transliterated *Ichthus*), the latter an acronym for *Iesous Christos Theou Uios Soter* ("Jesus Christ, of God the Son, Savior"). Different Chrismons may be combined to form varied and complex patterns, each new design of which proclaims some truth about God through Christ, as Mrs. Spencer illustrated in five books that she produced on the subject: *Chrismons: Basic Series* (1959); *Chrismons: Christian Year Series* (1961); *Chrismons: Advanced Series* (1965); *Chrismons* (1970); and *Chrismons for Every Day* (1971).

Chrismons may be constructed of virtually any material, but only in combinations of white and gold, which respectively symbolize Christ's purity and majesty. Chrismons trees are illuminated only with white light.

A soft-cover children's book outlining the origins and significance of the Chrismons tree at Ascension Lutheran Church is the subject of *Samuel Sparrow and the Tree of Light*, published in 2003 by Ann Lane Albright.

See also **Christmas Tree; Jesse Tree.**

Christ in the Stranger's Guise
See **Alfred Burt Carols**

Christ Is Born a Child on Earth
See **He Is Born, the Holy Child**

Christians, Awake, Salute the Happy Morn

English carol with lyrics by Dr. John Byrom (1692–1763), music by John Wainwright (1723–1768). A native of Manchester, a non-practicing physician, an inventor of an early form of shorthand, and a Quaker later in life, Byrom wrote this carol in 1749 as a Christmas present for his daughter Dorothy ("Dolly"). In 1750, his friend Wainwright, assistant organist at the Manchester Collegiate Church, provided a musical setting. On Christmas Day, because Byrom had patterned the carol after those sung by the British street minstrels called the "Waits," Wainwright arrived with a group of men and boys and delivered a surprise rendition of "Christians, Awake" at the Byrom residence. The carol's first public performance was said to have occurred that same Christmas at St. Mary's Church in the neighboring village of Stockport, though that event is considered more tradition than fact.

Although "Christians, Awake" had been printed earlier on broadsides, it was included in a posthumous printing of Byrom's works, *Miscellaneous Poems* (1773), and Wainwright also published text and music in his *Collection of Psalm-Tunes, Anthems, Hymns, and Chants* (London, 1767) under the generic title "A Hymn for Christmas Day." The carol in other publications also received some ten alternate titles, such as "Mottram," "Stockport," and "Yorkshire," among others.

Although Byrom's original text consisted of 52 lines without divisions into stanzas, he created a shorter, revised version of 46 lines, which a newspaper, the *Manchester Mercury and General Advertiser*, published in December 1752. Hymnals today present a text based on an adaptation of this revision, which includes divisions into stanzas of six lines. The bulk of the text first elaborates on the angelic "glad tidings of great joy" given to the shepherds, then emphasizes the hope of eternal life, which Christ will provide through His death on the cross.

See also **Waits.**

Christkindl or Christkindlein
See **Germany**

C-H-R-I-S-T-M-A-S
American song written in 1949 by country music songwriter and performer Jenny Lou Carson (given name Lucille Overstake) from Decatur, Illinois, and "Tennessee Plowboy" country and pop music legend Eddy Arnold. In Carson's lyrics, a mother teaches her child the true meaning of Christmas by spelling "Christmas" and associating each letter with a special symbol of the holiday: "C," Christ Child; "H," herald angels; "R," Redeemer; "I," Israel; "S," star; "T," three Wise Men; "M," manger; "A," all that Christmas means; "S," shepherds. Arnold contributed the music and recorded the song on the RCA Victor Label in 1949, where it became a charted single. Independent recordings of the same song by Rosemary Clooney and Al Morgan the following year were not charted.

Arnold also recorded two other songs in 1949 with lyrics by Carson, "Don't Rob Another Man's Castle" and "The Echo of Your Footsteps." Known principally as a lyricist, Carson also penned "Never Trust a Woman" (1942), "Jealous Love" (1945), and "Let Me Go, Lover" (1955), among many others.

Christmas Antiphons
See **"O" Antiphons**

Christmas at Plum Creek
See **Little House on the Prairie**

Christmas Auld Lang Syne
See **Auld Lang Syne**

Christmas Bell
See **Christmas Plants**

Christmas Berry
See **Christmas Plants**

The Christmas Blessing
Inspirational novel written by American author Donna VanLiere, published in 2003. A sequel to *The Christmas Shoes* (2001), it is the second book in VanLiere's Christmas Hope series. The novel poses the premise that God always has a definite purpose for every person's life.

Now in his third year of medical school, Nathan Andrews contemplates dropping out, because he is unable to bear patients' suffering and his own feelings of inadequacy when he cannot alleviate their pain. Having lost his beloved mother to cancer when he was a boy, Nathan now fears that he is about to lose another love, Meghan Sullivan. Meghan, a university student determined to succeed as an athlete despite her congenital heart defect, had laid the groundwork for a charity cross-country run that would provide college scholarships to pediatric heart patients. She had already chosen the first recipient, 12-year-old Charlie Bennett, a beloved friend whose admonition, "Don't ever take your eyes off the goal" had been a constant source of encouragement. But a few days before Christmas, Meghan contracts fulminant hepatitis and is in desperate need of a liver transplant. Although her family members are unsuitable as living donors (only a portion of a liver is donated), Meghan maintains her faith, saying, "There's always a miracle at Christmas."

Throughout the book, Nathan recalls his mother's words of wisdom bestowed years ago to prepare him for her death. Virtually meaningless to him then, he now recalls her assurance that the hurt and pain that he would feel over losing her would help him care for others later in life; that in the valleys of life, love wins, for God always uses those trials for His good. Even Meghan assures Nathan that his love and concern for patients, especially children, is not a weakness but a gift. Patients *must* know that their physicians will give them the emotional and psychological support they need, even unto the end. And what ultimately prevents Nathan from leaving medicine is that he has been *called*— this is his life's purpose, divinely ordained.

At Meghan's insistence, Nathan spends Christmas Day with his family and receives a surprise visit from Robert Layton, the attorney who had paid for the shoes that Nathan had given to his dying mother. Robert had sought Nathan to express his gratitude for that Christmas Eve years ago, for the critical moment had actually saved Robert's failing marriage. Now Nathan realizes that, instead of being with Meghan at the hospital, he was supposed to be with his family to meet Robert. Furthermore, Nathan knows that Meghan could not pass away without his having loved her deeply.

Suddenly on Christmas night, a donor miraculously becomes available, and the liver transplant proceeds immediately. Later Meghan learns that her donor was Charlie Bennett, who had expired that same night, and Nathan, reflecting on the parents' loving gift in time of bitter grief, again recalls his mother's words: "It was Love that came down at Christmas. That is the greatest miracle of all. That is the blessing of Christmas."

Six months later, Meghan's annual scholarship run becomes a reality, held in memory of Charlie, and after Nathan finishes his residency, he and Meghan wed on Christmas Eve to honor his late mother, Maggie Andrews, and Charlie.

Donna VanLiere is an actress and speaker. Her other works include *Sheltering Trees: The Power, Promise, and Refuge of Friendship* (2001), *They Walked with Him: Stories of Those Who Knew Him Best* (2001), and *The Christmas Shoes* (2001).

See also **The Christmas Shoes.**

The Christmas Box

Emotionally packed, best-selling novel published in 1995 by Richard Paul Evans, who based the principal characters and their names on himself, his wife Keri, and their three-year-old daughter Jenna.

Escaping the rat race inherent in a large city, the Evanses move from southern California to Salt Lake City a few weeks before Christmas. In Salt Lake City, workaholic Richard opens a formal-wear store. The family becomes very close to a reclusive, elderly widow, MaryAnne Parkin, in whose expansive home they live as caretakers.

In the course of storing their furniture in Mrs. Parkin's attic, Richard discovers an ornamented walnut Christmas box with brass hinges shaped like holly leaves and with an etching of the Nativity on the lid. The box is worthless to Richard until he experiences a recurring dream, in which an angel descends with outspread wings. As he looks into its face, it turns to stone, and Richard next finds himself in an open field surrounded by indescribably beautiful music. Waking one night, he traces the music to the Christmas box in the attic. Oddly, nothing about it suggests a music box, yet the music ceases at his approach, and a cradle nearby, previously covered, is now bare. Within the box are passionate letters of sorrow addressed simply to "My Beloved," dated December 6 of 1914, 1916, and 1920. (In many parts of the world, December 6 is celebrated as Children's Day and as St. Nicholas's Day, the patron saint of children.)

As Richard ponders this mystery, Mrs. Parkin confides that she is terminally ill and expresses grave concern over Richard's obsession with achieving success to his family's neglect. Adding another mystery, she asks if Richard knows what the first gift of Christmas was. He discerns part of the answer after learning from a neighbor that Mrs. Parkin has grieved for years over the loss of her three-year-old daughter, Andrea, whose gravestone consists of a stone angel identical to the one in Richard's dream. The letters, then, are Mrs. Parkin's expression of unspeakable sorrow.

When Keri discovers Mrs. Parkin's Bible open to John's Gospel, its pages stained with fresh tears, the answer becomes quite clear. The first gift of Christmas was a Child, given and sacrificed for the world by a loving Heavenly Father ("For God so loved the world, that he gave his only begotten son..." [John 3:16]). Richard realizes that, in his quest for success, he had been trading diamonds for stones, so to speak; he was unwittingly parting with his own child at a time in her life that should be most precious for them both.

Richard receives the Christmas box as a gift, the air ringing with its music one last time as Mrs. Parkins joins her little Andrea, who waits for her on Christmas morning.

A 1995 television adaptation of Evans's story, starring Richard Thomas, Maureen O'Hara, Annette O'Toole, and Kelsey Mulrooney, won an Emmy Award for Outstanding Individual Achievement in Costuming. Teleplay by Greg Taylor. Produced by Erica Fox. Directed by Marcus Cole. Bonneville Producers Group and the Polson Company. DVD: Lionsgate/Fox. 92 min.

A former advertising executive, Richard Paul Evans wrote *The Christmas Box* in 1992 as an expression of a father's love for his two daughters, Jenna and Allyson. Initially keeping the story a private endeavor, he made some 20 copies and distributed them to family members as Christmas presents. Their enthusiasm and encouragement eventually led to its publication, following which the book went on to become a number-one *New York Times* bestseller with more than eight million copies in print worldwide. Evans subsequently wrote two prequels to the story, *Timepiece* (1996) and *The Letter* (1997), which revolve around the early lives of David and MaryAnne Parkin and which complete the *Christmas Box* trilogy. Some of his other works include *The First Gift of Christmas* (1996), *The Christmas Candle* (1998), and *The Light of Christmas* (2002); these three are discussed as separate entries.

Christmas Bush
See **Christmas Plants**

Christmas Cactus
See **Christmas Plants**

The Christmas Candle

Inspirational children's picture book written by American author Richard Paul Evans, published in 1998. The book presents a strong moral: that all people of the world belong to one family, and that this timeless truth is best seen in the "joyous illumination of Christmas." This book received the American Mothers 1998 Book of the Year Award.

A man with no time for the less fortunate, Thomas acquires a simple Christmas candle for his lantern from a mysterious old chandler. But the chandler warns that, although the price is a pittance, the man may find it costly indeed. As Thomas walks home on Christmas Eve, one by one he meets three people who at first appear to be members of his own family in the guise of beggars. To his aged mother, he surrenders his cloak. Finding his brother Elin lying in a gutter, Thomas lodges him at a nearby inn, which requires his remaining few pence and his knapsack as payment. For his waif of a little sister, Thomas, now penniless, can do nothing. Yet after each encounter, the magic of the Christmas candle reveals the truth, that these people indeed are strangers.

Thomas arrives home to revelry and a sumptuous banquet with his family, when suddenly the sight of his abundance reminds him of the chandler's words. Leaving the table, Thomas hurries out into the night to find that other little member of his "family."

Best known for his novel *The Christmas Box* (1995), Richard Paul Evans is founder and executive director of the Christmas Box Foundation and the Christmas Box House International, Inc., a nonprofit organization devoted to the building of shelter-assessment facilities for abused children. Evans donated all proceeds from his children's books, including *The Christmas Candle*, to the Christmas Box House International.

See also **The Christmas Box; The First Gift of Christmas; The Light of Christmas.**

Christmas Cards

The custom of exchanging winter holiday greetings can be traced to ancient peoples, such as the Egyptians and Romans, who not only bestowed verbal good wishes for the new year but with them presented gifts to friends, relatives, and persons of authority. Over time, these tokens assumed written form, first on ornamental clay tablets; then on woodblock prints during the Middle Ages in Europe; and, with the invention of lithography in the late

Top: *An English woodcut card of the shepherds by artist C.M. Gere, for 1893.* Middle: *An 1890 woodcut card designed by Frederich Mason, England, of the angel appearing before the shepherds in their field. From "The Story of the Christmas Carol," House & Garden, December 1921.* Bottom: *Christmas post card from Great Britain, Valentine's S series. (Undivided back. Chromolithographed image.) Both the robin and the mistletoe have Christmas connections: The robin supposedly got its red breast by fanning the fire for the Holy Family. The mistletoe has a more varied story with a rich pagan connection.* (See also **Mistletoe.**)

eighteenth century, on colored sheets of paper flanked with biblical scenes or other pleasing designs. The advent of Christianity subsequently saw greetings for the new year combined with those at what was considered to be the more important season of Christmas, especially in England, where the modern Christmas card originated.

The advances in printing during the nineteenth century and the creation of the "penny post" by the British postal system in 1840 set the stage for the mass production of relatively inexpensive Christmas cards. Immediately preceding the advent of conventional, printed Christmas cards, English schoolboys presented their parents with "Christmas pieces," decorative paper on which the boys had written seasonal messages in their best penmanship. In 1844, a W.A. Dobson sent hand-painted cards to his friends, and a Rev. Edward Bradley issued lithographed cards to his acquaintances. As an alternative to cards produced by the rather expensive method of lithography, people sometimes chose to convert their printed calling cards into greeting cards by decorating them with strips of colored cloth or paper and writing an appropriate message.

The English artist John C. Horsley is generally credited with designing the first printed Christmas card around 1843. However, William Egley may have claim to the honor instead, should an obscure date on his card read "1842" rather than the other possibility of "1849"; the date has defied deciphering. Horsley's creation was commissioned by Sir Henry Cole, an English gentleman who, when etiquette dictated that he send seasonal notes to his numerous friends, elected instead to send cards. On the colored, 3-by-5-inch Horsley card, a prominent center panel displayed a large, happy family consuming spirits. Beneath, a caption read, "A Merry Christmas and a Happy New Year to You," and two side panels depicted biblical scenes, titled "Clothing the Naked" and "Feeding the Hungry." Despite the religious panels, some of the more pious citizens strenuously objected to the center panel, claiming that the card encouraged drunkenness. The card was issued as a limited edition of a thousand copies, which sold for a shilling each. After Horsley, various card manufacturers added Christmas cards to their inventory as a sideline, Marcus Ward and Company achieving the forefront with their publication of seasonal greeting cards in 1867. By the 1870s, England was widely exporting Christmas cards to the United States.

R.H. Pease, a printer in Albany, New York, is credited with distributing the first American-made Christmas cards in the 1850s. These depicted a family exulting in the holiday with Santa Claus and his reindeer, presents, and a sumptuous feast. About the same time, German immigrant Louis Prang arrived in America and established himself as a printer in Roxbury, Massachusetts, where he took the Christmas card industry to new heights. Having developed an improved method of color printing, he initially designed a series of cards depicting famous paintings with holiday greetings and exported them to England in 1874. Their immense popularity prompted him to market his cards in America during the following year. Two factors contributed to Prang's success: free mail delivery, newly established in 1863, which became a strong incentive for sending holiday greeting cards; and Prang's sponsorship of annual design contests with considerable cash awards, whereby he acquired the work of the finest artists for his designs. Further, he exhibited the artists' works at the American Art Gallery in New York and captured the public's attention with 7-by-10-inch cards, which sold for one dollar each. By 1890, however, much cheaper cards produced by competitors in Germany succeeded in driving Prang out of the Christmas card market.

Christmas cards today are broadly segregated into the religious and the secular. The former usually focus on Nativity scenes, the Madonna and Child, the Magi, and so forth. The latter cards tend to feature neutral, winter scenes with generic expressions of "Season's Greetings," "Greetings," or "Happy Holidays."

Annually over two billion Christmas cards are sold in the United States. In the early twenty-first century, despite rising costs of first-class postage and the medium of e-mail, 92 percent of American consumers still purchase and send paper Christmas cards, and 76 percent of those consumers send 20 or more cards each.

A Christmas Carol

(Novella). Classic Christmas tale by the celebrated British author Charles John Huffam Dickens (1812–1870). It is also the title of a poem of five stanzas by the same author (see

Top: *Charles Dickens (1812–1870), British author of* A Christmas Carol *and other Christmas books. Engraving by E.G. Williams and Brothers, New York, for* Demorest's Monthly Magazine, *1867. Courtesy Library of Congress.* Bottom: *This is the happy scene of Mr. Fezziwig's Ball as illustrated by John Leech. Scrooge, who as a young man was apprenticed to the jolly Mr. Fezziwig, went to see him with the Ghost of Christmas Past. From Charles Dickens,* Christmas Books. *London: 1876.*

entry below). The novella is considered to be the most popular story ever written about

Famous illustrator John Leech drew this scene of Scrooge facing the second of the Christmas spirits: the Ghost of Christmas Present. From Charles Dickens, Christmas Books, *London: 1876.*

Christmas, second only to the Nativity story in the Bible. This work, written in just six weeks and originally titled *A Christmas Carol in Prose: Being a Ghost Story of Christmas*, was first published in 1843 by Chapman and Hall of London (Dickens financed the project himself) with illustrations by John Leech (four full-color etchings and four black-and-white woodcuts). The story was priced at five shillings (25 cents) and quickly became so immensely popular that it sold about 6,000 copies during the first five days of publication, figures which surpassed sales of the Bible at that time.

Despite this initial success, after the publishers recouped their costs, Dickens had earned 230 pounds (1,000 dollars), a sum that was quickly consumed in litigation over a pirated version of the *Carol*, titled *A Christmas Ghost Story*, which appeared by early January 1844 in *Parley's Illuminated Library*. Although Dickens won his suit, he received nothing from *Parley's* owners, bankrupted defendants Richard

Egan Lee and Henry Hewitt, and instead incurred court costs of 700 pounds. Dickens eventually was able to turn this situation around by giving public readings of the *Carol*, at first for charity and later for profit. The first reading took place in December 1854, and subsequently such readings became annual holiday events. In 1865, Dickens brought the *Carol* and other works to the United States with a reading in Boston. Because the tale was a ghost story, for better effect, Dickens suggested that it be read aloud by candlelight in a cold room.

The plot is well known: Mean-spirited and miserly Ebenezer Scrooge is transformed on Christmas Eve into a kind philanthropist through nocturnal visitations by four ghosts, beginning with the ghost of Scrooge's late partner, Jacob Marley, followed by the ghosts of Christmas Past, Christmas Present, and Christmas Yet to Come. This story line, however, was not original in 1843, for Dickens based *A Christmas Carol* on one of his earlier short stories, titled "The Story of the Goblins Who Stole a Sexton," which had appeared as chapter 29 in his first novel, *The Pickwick Papers* (1836–37). Chapter 28 sets the stage for this story-within-a-story. Mr. Pickwick and his colleagues have arrived at Manor Farm, the estate of their friend, Mr. Wardle, who has invited them to spend the Christmas holidays with his other guests. The ladies and gentlemen present have whiled away Christmas Eve by drinking wassail and playing traditional games, and now midnight approaches. In keeping with the English tradition of telling ghost stories at Christmastime (which derived from the pre-Christian Teutonic and Norse belief that evil spirits prevailed during the winter solstice or Yule festival), Mr. Wardle spins the story about the goblins stealing a sexton:

Like Scrooge, sexton Gabriel Grub is a surly old man who despises Christmas and takes no pleasure in anyone's happiness. While digging a grave on Christmas Eve, he falls asleep and dreams that a troupe of goblins floods the cemetery while playing leapfrog over tombstones. The goblin king whisks Grub into an underground cavern, where he experiences various torments, one of which is the vision of a poverty stricken, simple, loving family, whose youngest boy eventually dies (foreshadowing the Bob Cratchit family with crippled son Tiny Tim). Grub learns that those who snarl at the happiness of others are the "foulest weeds on earth," and he awakens on Christmas Day a changed man.

Dickens experienced an early life of poverty, including working long hours in a factory for a pittance prior to his teenage years. Outraged at the injustices that the rich upper class inflicted on the poor, he often incorporated memories of his unhappy childhood into his fictional works. The *Carol* is no exception, for it condemns greed and those who neglect the less fortunate. Dickens also felt a personal relationship with the characters in the *Carol*, for several of them were based on circumstances and personalities of some of his own relatives. Tiny Tim was a composite, drawn from Dickens's brother, Frederick, and his young nephew, Harry Burnett, the crippled son of Dickens's elder sister, Frances Burnett (nicknamed Fanny). She in turn became the basis for Scrooge's little sister, Fan, and brother Frederick served as the model for Scrooge's nephew, Fred. At first, Dickens had considered using the name Tiny Fred for Bob Cratchit's ailing little boy, because Frederick had acquired that name at the age of two. But Dickens settled on the name Tiny Tim, because it sounded more diminutive and more suitable for a sickly child. Scrooge was partially the embodiment of Dickens himself. Strapped for cash at the time, Dickens wrote *A Christmas Carol* strictly for financial gain. Like Scrooge, he was obsessed with acquiring wealth (an attempt to escape his childhood poverty), but there the similarity between the two men ended. This compulsion to make money actually created feelings of guilt, which clashed with Dickens's strong sense of love for family, community, and simple virtues despite poverty, ideals which he believed should surpass all quest for material gain and which surfaced many times in his literary works.

The present-day tradition of regarding Christmas as a festive occasion owes much to the *Carol*. From the Middle Ages until the mid–seventeenth century, Christmas in much of Europe was an all-too festive occasion that often centered on recklessness and debauchery. The seizure of British Parliament by the

religiously fanatical Puritans in the 1640s, the execution of King Charles I of England in 1649, and the subsequent establishment of a protectorate in 1653 under the direction of Oliver Cromwell essentially abolished all observances of Christmas in England until the ascent of King Charles II in 1660. Even with Christmas restored, the holiday period afterwards was quite subdued and generally consisted of one day of religious devotion and quiet rest at home, nothing more; that is, until *A Christmas Carol*. Despite the somber plot with Scrooge, the story was jam-packed and overflowing with such cheer, feelings of goodwill and kindness toward all, feasting, and the joy of being with family and relatives on the happiest of holidays, that the public gradually became caught up in the sentiment. Thus people sought to recreate the jolly atmosphere of Christmas outlined in the *Carol*, not only for themselves, but for those less fortunate as well. In time, the name of Charles Dickens essentially became synonymous with Christmas itself. To illustrate this point, upon Dickens's death, one saddened little girl was noted to ask if Father Christmas (the British equivalent of Santa Claus) was also going to die.

Probably no other secular story has been adapted for the entertainment media as often as *A Christmas Carol*. Theatrical versions were quite uncommon in the nineteenth century, especially during the Victorian era, however, because many actually considered the *Carol* a sacred work. Nevertheless, three early adaptations appeared on the London stage in February 1844: *A Christmas Carol; or, Past, Present, and Future*, starring an O. Smith as Scrooge, adapted by Edward Stirling (Dickens himself supposedly approved this play); *A Christmas Carol; or, The Miser's Warning*, adapted by C.Z. Barnett; and *Old Scrooge; or, The Miser's Dream*, adapted by Charles Webb. Actor Bransby Williams, who had portrayed a host of Dickens's characters, appeared as Scrooge as early as 1896. Theatrical versions gained greater popularity in the twentieth century, beginning with *Scrooge*, a one-act play by J.C. Blackstone, which debuted in 1901 in London, starring Seymour Hicks. Also noted for his one-man portrayals of the *Carol*, Hicks would recreate the role in motion pictures. As a special tourist attraction, the town of Rochester, County Kent, England, where Dickens lived in his Gad's Hill home, sports a production of the *Carol* each weekend in December. Dressed in period costumes, the citizens recreate the beloved story throughout the town.

Today the original manuscript of *A Christmas Carol* resides in the Pierpont Morgan Library in Manhattan.

• FILM AND TELEVISION VERSIONS. Since the early twentieth century, the immense popularity of the Dickens classic has produced more than 200 motion picture, television, and animated versions, not to mention countless numbers of local theater productions, and the number continues to grow. While many adaptations strive to preserve Dickens's original sentiment, others adulterate the *Carol* with altered story lines and themes in the interest of innovation. The advent of the television situation comedy has especially provided a rich medium for more farcical adaptations and parodies.

The following alphabetical list briefly summarizes many notable *Carol* adaptations but makes no attempt to be exhaustive. The designation "Video N/A" indicates that a version is either not currently available on DVD or VHS, or that specific video information is lacking. Unless otherwise indicated, all versions are in color and originate in the United States. "B & W" indicates "black-and-white." Paul Sammon's *The "Christmas Carol" Trivia Book* also lists several dance adaptations and a compilation of spoken-word versions available on audiocassette and compact disc. Fred Guida's book *"A Christmas Carol" and Its Adaptations* presents a most exhaustive treatment of screen and television versions through the year 1998.

An All Dogs Christmas Carol (1998). Animated cartoon, one of several sequels to the animated motion picture *All Dogs Go to Heaven* (1989). Carface, a mean-spirited bulldog, experiences divine intervention when he plans to ruin Christmas. Principal voices: Steven Weber, Dom DeLuise, Sheena Easton, Ernest Borgnine, Charles Nelson Reilly, and Bebe Neuwirth. Written by Jymn Magon. Produced by Jonathan Dern and Paul Sabella. Directed by Paul Sabella. Metro-Goldwyn-Mayer Animation. DVD: MGM/UA Home Entertainment. 73 min.

Alvin's Christmas Carol (1983). Episode from the television animated series *Alvin and the Chipmunks*. Alvin's lack of concern for others and his obsession over Christmas presents spawns ghostly visits from his brothers, Simon and Theodore, as well as keeper David Seville. Also features "The Chipmunk Song (Christmas Don't Be Late)." Voices: Ross Bagdasarian, Jr., Janice Karman, Thom Watkins, and Dody Goodman. Written by Dianne Dixon. DIC/Bagdasarian Productions. VHS: Buena Vista Home Video. 23 min.

An American Christmas Carol (1979). American-Canadian television movie set in depression-era New Hampshire. Benedict Slade (Henry Winkler), a miserly banker, is haunted by three ghosts resembling people who have defaulted on loans and from whom Slade has seized property as payment. With David Wayne, Chris Wiggins, R.H. Thomson, Kenneth Pogue, Gerard Parkes, Susan Hogan, and Dorian Harewood. Written by Jerome Coopersmith. Produced by Jon Slan and Stanley Chase. Directed by Eric Till. An Edgar J. Scherick/Stanley Chase/Jon Slan Production in association with Smith-Hemion Productions. DVD: Image Entertainment. 98 min.

Bah, Humbug! The Story of Charles Dickens' "A Christmas Carol" (1994). Televised, abridged, dramatic reading of Dickens's story at the Pierpont Morgan Library in New York City where the original manuscript resides. Based on the adaptations that Dickens used for his own public readings. Featuring Robert MacNeil, James Earl Jones, and Martin Sheen. Produced by Richard Somerset-Ward. Directed by Derek Bailey. A MacNeil/Lehrer Production in association with WNET/Thirteen. Video N/A. 60 min.

Blackadder's Christmas Carol (1988). BBC television movie and comedic parody based on a 1980s BBC-TV comedy show, *Blackadder*, which satirized the Middle Ages among other historical periods. The parody features Ebenezer Blackadder (Rowan Atkinson), initially a kind-hearted soul, whom a drunken Christmas ghost converts into a scoundrel. With Tony Robinson, Robbie Coltrane, Miranda Richardson, Hugh Laurie, Stephen Fry, Miriam Margolyes, Jim Broadbent, and Nicola Bryant. Written by Richard Curtis and

Ben Elton. Produced by John Lloyd. Directed by Richard Boden. VHS: BBC Video. 43 min.

Bransby Williams (1953). British television broadcast featuring 83-year-old actor Bransby Williams in a one-man portrayal of the *Carol*. With Kathleen Saintsbury. Produced by Kenneth Milne-Buckley. British Broadcasting Corporation. Video N/A. B & W. 25 min.

Brer Rabbit's Christmas Carol (1992). Animated cartoon featuring *Uncle Remus* characters such as Brer Rabbit, Brer Fox, and Brer Bear. Voices: Ginny Tyler, Christopher Smith, Tom Hill, and David Knell. Written, produced, and directed by Al Guest and Jean Mathieson. Magic Shows, Inc. (Video Treasures). DVD: Delta Entertainment. 60 min.

Bugs Bunny's Christmas Carol. See **Bugs Bunny's Looney Christmas Tales.**

A Carol Christmas (2003). Television movie with gender reversal of Scrooge surrogate. Tori Spelling stars as Carol Cartman, an evil talk show host, whom spirits reform. With William Shatner, Gary Coleman, Barbara Niven, and Dinah Manoff. Written by Tom Amundsen. Produced by Albert T. Dickerson III, Lincoln Lageson, and Randy Pope. Directed by Matthew Irmas. Larry Levinson Productions. Video N/A. 120 min.

Carol for Another Christmas (1964). Television movie that twists the *Carol's* plot into a political crusade against nuclear armament. Written by *Twilight Zone* creator Rod Serling, this contemporary version features Sterling Hayden as a cynical Daniel Grudge who faces a world sliding toward nuclear destruction. With Ben Gazzara, Peter Sellers, Eva Marie Saint, Steve Lawrence, Pat Hingle, Robert Shaw, Britt Ekland, James Shigeta, and Percy Rodriguez. Produced and directed by Joseph L. Mankiewicz. A Telsun Foundations, Inc., Production. Video N/A. B & W. 84 min.

A Christmas Carol (1908). Silent film starring Thomas Ricketts as Scrooge. The Essanay Film Manufacturing Company. Video N/A. B & W. 17 min.

A Christmas Carol (1910). Silent film starring Marc McDermott as Scrooge. With Charles Ogle, William Bechtel, Carey Lee, Shirley Mason, Viola Flugrath, and Leonie Flugrath. Specific director not credited, although J. Searle Dawley, Ashley Miller, and John H. Collins have received credit over the decades (see Guida for further details). Edison Manufacturing Company. On the DVD collection *Christmas Past: Vintage Holiday Films, 1901–1925.* Kino Video. B & W. 17 min.

A Christmas Carol (1914). British silent film, starring Charles Rock as Scrooge. With George Bellamy, Mary Brough, Franklyn Bellamy, Edward O'Neill, Edna Flugrath, Arthur Cullin, Windham Guise, and Asheton Tonge. Written and directed by Harold Shaw. Video N/A. B & W. 22 min.

A Christmas Carol (1938). First sound version of the *Carol* made in the United States, starring British actor Reginald Owen as Scrooge. With Gene Lockhart, Terry Kilburn, Leo G. Carroll, Lionel Braham, Lynne Carver, Ann Rutherford, Barry Macay, D'Arcy Corrigan, Ronald Sinclair, Kathleen Lockhart, and June Lockhart (film debut). Although Lionel Barrymore was originally cast as Scrooge, illness led to the selection of Reginald Owen instead, at Barrymore's suggestion. Written by Hugo Butler. Produced by Joseph L. Mankiewicz. Directed by Edwin L. Marin. Metro-Goldwyn-Mayer. VHS: Warner Home Video. B & W. 69 min.

A Christmas Carol (1940). Reputed to be the first amateur film version of the *Carol*, made by children Gregory, Andrew, and Elaine Markopoulos in Toledo, Ohio. Video N/A. B & W. 5 min.

A Christmas Carol (1943). Experimental television broadcast over the DuMont Network, believed to be the first televised version of the *Carol*. Starring William Podmore as Scrooge. With Don Randolf, Consuela Lembke, Ralph Locke, Noah Julian, Roger DeKoven, and Lon Clark. Written by William Podmore. Directed by George Lowther. Video N/A. B & W. 60 min.

A Christmas Carol (1944). Another DuMont television broadcast, starring Carl Eastman, Helen Jerome, Bobby Hookey, Evelyn Juster, and Beverly Benson. Actor portraying Scrooge not revealed. Video N/A. B & W. 30 min.

A Christmas Carol (1945). Television movie from station WBKB, Chicago. Starring Norman Pellegrini as Scrooge. With Raymond Groya, James Wade, June Schmidt, Dave Koukal, Bruce Fields, Marian Erickson, and Marilyn Fisher, all students from Taft High

School. Written, produced, and directed by Beulah Zachary. Video N/A. B & W. 30 min.

A Christmas Carol (1947). Telecast from station WABD, New York, on the DuMont Network, starring John Carradine as Scrooge. With David Carradine, Bernard Hughes, Eva Marie Saint, Ray Morgan, Somer Adler, Sam Fertig, Helen Stenborg, and Jonathan Marlowe. Director variously listed as James L. Caddigan or David P. Lewis (see Guida for further details). Video N/A. B & W. 60 min.

A Christmas Carol (1948). On *Philco Television Playhouse*, starring Dennis King as Scrooge. With Frank M. Thomas, Harry Sothern, Loring Smith, James MacColl, Judson Rees, and Valerie Cossart. Written by Samuel Taylor. Produced and directed by Fred Coe. Epilogue features Bing Crosby singing "Silent Night" with the Mitchell Boys' Choir. Video N/A. B & W. 60 min.

A Christmas Carol (1949). Television adaptation narrated by Vincent Price, starring Taylor Holmes as Scrooge. With Robert Clarke, Pat White, Nelson Leigh, Bobby Hyatt, George James, and Earl Lee. Opening credits misspell Scrooge's first name as "Ebeneezer." Background carols provided by the Mitchell Boys' Choir. Written and directed by Arthur Pierson. Produced by Mike Stokey and Bernard Ebert. Teltec Company. Video N/A. B & W. 25 min.

A Christmas Carol (1950). British television broadcast starring an 80-year-old Bransby Williams as Scrooge. Narrated by MacDonald Hobley. Adapted and produced by Eric Fawcett from a play by Dominic Roche. British Broadcasting Corporation. Video N/A. B & W. 120 min.

A Christmas Carol (1951). British film also known as *Scrooge*, considered to be the best filmed version, starring Alastair Sim as Scrooge. With Mervyn Johns, Jack Warner, Kathleen Harrison, Michael Hordern, Miles Malleson, Francis DeWolff, and Patrick Macnee. Written by Noel Langley. Produced and directed by Brian Desmond-Hurst. Renown Pictures Corporation. DVD: United Home Video. B & W. 86 min.

A Christmas Carol (1951). Television special on *Fireside Theatre*, starring Sir Ralph Richardson as Scrooge. With Margaret Phillips, Arthur Treacher, Melville Cooper, Malcom Keene, Robert Hay Smith, and Norman Barr. Role of Mrs. Fezziwig played by Charles Dickens's great-granddaughter, Gypsy Raine (uncredited). With introduction and epilogue by "Charles Dickens" (Alan Napier). Written by David Swift. Produced by Fred Coe. Directed by Gordon Duff. NBC Television. Video N/A. B & W. 30 min.

A Christmas Carol (1952). On *Kraft Television Theatre*, starring Malcom Keene as Scrooge. With Harry Townes, Valerie Cossart, Glenn Walken, Richard Purdy, Melville Cooper, and Noel Leslie. Background carols sung by St. Ignatius Boys' Choir. Adapted from Dickens's reading version of the *Carol* by Robert Howard Lindsay. NBC Television. Video N/A. B & W. 60 min.

A Christmas Carol (1953). On *Kraft Television Theatre*, starring Noel Leslie as Scrooge. With Harry Townes, Valerie Cossart, Melville Cooper, Denis Greene, Geoffrey Lumb, Jack Raine, and Naomi Riordan. Background carols sung by the Trinity Boys' Choir of New York. ABC Television. Video N/A. B & W. 60 min.

Christmas Carol (1953). Episode from *Topper*, a television situation comedy series running on various networks from 1953 to 1956 and based on characters created by fantasy novelist Thorne Smith. The series revolved around Cosmo Topper (Leo G. Carroll), a banker haunted by the ghosts of George and Marion Kirby (Robert Sterling and Anne Jeffreys), in whose home Topper lived, and the ghost of Neil, their brandy-guzzling St. Bernard dog. In *Christmas Carol*, Topper falls asleep while reading the *Carol* and dreams that he is Scrooge. This episode is reputed to be the first in a long line of *Carol* parodies that would follow in other situation comedies. Written by George Oppenheimer. Produced by John W. Loveton. Directed by Paul Landres. CBS Television. Video N/A. B & W. 30 min.

A Christmas Carol (1954). Televised, first full musical version of the *Carol* on *Shower of Stars*, hosted by William Lundigan and starring Fredric March as Scrooge. With Basil Rathbone, Bob Sweeney, Ray Middleton, Queenie Leonard, Christopher Cook, and the Roger Wagner Chorale. Unusual in that a mynah bird in a bare tree represents the Ghost of Christmas Yet to Come. Adaptation and lyrics by Maxwell Anderson. Music by Bernard Herrmann. Produced and directed by Ralph Levy. Rebroadcast in 1955 and 1956. CBS Television. Originally broadcast in color. Formerly available on VHS from Viking Video Classics in B & W. 60 min.

A Christmas Carol (1955). Televised broadcast on the *Eye on New York* program, starring Jonathan Harris as Scrooge. With Biff McGuire and Howard Wierum. Significant in that it is the first *Carol* version updated to a twentieth century setting (Scrooge is a corporate president). Written, produced, and hosted by Bill Leonard. CBS Television. Video N/A. B & W. 30 min.

A Christmas Carol (1959). British television film hosted by Fredric March and starring Basil Rathbone as Scrooge. This is an episode from Harry Alan Towers's *Tales from Dickens* series. Produced by Desmond Davis and the Dickens Society of London. A Harry Alan Towers Production. Video N/A. B & W. 25 min.

A Christmas Carol (1960). British film starring John Hayter as Scrooge. With Stewart Brown, Gordon Mulholland, Jimmy Mentis, and Bruce Anderson. Produced and directed by Robert Hartford-Davis. Anglo Amalgamated Film Distributors, Ltd. Video N/A. B & W. 28 min.

A Christmas Carol (1960). Episode from the British television series *The Charlie Drake Show*, which combines the *Carol* story line with characters from Dickens's other novels, such as *Great Expectations, Oliver Twist, David Copperfield,* and *The Pickwick Papers.* Starring Charlie Drake as Bob Cratchit and Philip Locke as Scrooge. Written by Charlie Drake and Richard Waring. Produced by Ronald Marsh. British Broadcasting Corporation. Video N/A. B & W. 30 min.

A Christmas Carol (1962). First operatic version of the carol, produced for BBC Television and starring Stephen Manton as Scrooge. Music by American composer Edwin Coleman. Libretto by Margaret Burns Harris. Produced by Hal Burton. Video N/A. B & W. 60 min.

A Christmas Carol (1969). Animated musical version for Australian television. Music by Richard Bowden. Voices: Ron Haddrick, C. Duncan, John Llewellyn, T. Mangan, Bruce

Montague, and Brenda Senders. Vocals: T. Kaff and C. Bowden. Adaptation by Michael Robinson. Produced by Walter J. Hucker. Directed by Zoran Janjic. Air Programs International. VHS: Rhino Home Video. 46 min.

A Christmas Carol (1970). British television version portrayed through a series of static, watercolor drawings by John Worsley. Produced, adapted, and narrated by Paul Honeyman. Directed by John Salway. Anglia Television. Video N/A. 58 min.

A Christmas Carol (1971). British made-for-television animated special, considered to best animated version and the only *Carol* version to win an Academy Award for Best Short Subject, Animated Film. Principal voices: Alastair Sim, Sir Michael Redgrave, Michael Hordern, and Melvyn Hayes. Produced and directed by Richard Williams. Richard Williams Productions. VHS: Anchor Bay Entertainment. 26 min.

A Christmas Carol (1977). BBC Television production, starring Michael Hordern as Scrooge. Written by Elaine Morgan. Produced by Jonathan Powell. Directed by Moira Armstrong. Video N/A. 58 min.

A Christmas Carol (1978). Operatic version created for Welsh television, starring Sir Geraint Evans as Scrooge. Libretto by John Morgan. Music by Norman Kay. Produced and directed by Michael Hayes. Harlech Television. Video N/A. 55 min.

A Christmas Carol (1981). Televised adaptation from the American Conservatory Theatre in San Francisco, starring William Paterson as Scrooge and Lawrence Hecht as the narrator. Capitalizes on Scrooge's lack of concern for humanity in a futuristic scene from Tiny Tim's funeral. There, the dialogue centers around a paraphrase of Matthew 18:2–6, implying that while innocent little children who perish like Tiny Tim now reside as angels with Jesus, those who harm children by active misconduct or through passive neglect deserve to have millstones hung around them and drowned. Television adaptation by Joshua White. Stage adaptation by Dennis Powers and Laird Williamson. Produced for television by Benjamin Moore. Directed by Laird Williamson. ABC Video Enterprises in cooperation with the American Conservatory Theatre. Video N/A. 110 min.

A Christmas Carol (1982). Australian animated motion picture. Voices: Ron Haddrick, Phillip Hinton, Sean Hinton, Barbara Frawley, Robin Stewart, Liz Horne, Bill Conn, Derani Scarr, and Anne Hardy. Produced by Eddy Graham. Directed by Jean Tych. A Burbank Films Production. VHS: United American Video. 72 min.

A Christmas Carol (1982). Television presentation of an adaptation by the Guthrie Theater, Minneapolis. Opens with a scene in the Dickens home as Dickens puts the finishing touches on the *Carol*. Starring Marshall Borden as narrator Charles Dickens and Richard Hilger as Scrooge. Adapted by Barbara Field. Produced by Bill Siegler. Television direction by Paul Miller. Stage direction by Jon Cranney. The Guthrie Theater in association with Elm Video Theater and the Entertainment Channel. VHS: Video Treasures. 87 min.

A Christmas Carol (1982). Televised, operatic version presented before a live audience by the Royal Opera House, Covent Garden, England, in association with the Virginia Opera Association. Version first staged by the Virginia Opera Association in the United States in 1979. Starring Frederick Burchinal as Scrooge. Libretto and music by Thea Musgrave. Produced by Steve Hawes and David Farrar. Television direction by Dave Heather. Granada Television. Video N/A. 109 min.

A Christmas Carol (1984). British motion picture starring George C. Scott as Scrooge, released in the United States on CBS Television. Considered to be the best television version and the only version of its kind to introduce the character of Scrooge's father Silas (portrayed by Nigel Davenport) into the story line. With Frank Finlay, David Warner, Susannah York, Anthony Walters, Edward Woodward, Angela Pleasence, Lucy Gutteridge, and Roger Rees. Honors: 1985 Emmy nomination, Outstanding Lead Actor in a Special (Scott); won Christopher Award for Distinguished Achievement in Television. Written by Roger O. Hirson. Produced by William F. Storke and Alfred R. Kelman. Directed by Clive Donner. Entertainment Partners, Ltd. DVD: Twentieth Century-Fox Video. 100 min.

A Christmas Carol (1984). French television production starring Michel Bouquet as Scrooge.

Written and directed by Pierre Boutron. TF1 Productions. Video N/A. 90 min.

A Christmas Carol (1990). Animated cartoon. VHS: UAV Corporation. 75 min.

A Christmas Carol (1993). Ballet adaptation made for British television, featuring the Northern Ballet Theatre in performance at the Victoria Theatre, Halifax. Starring Jeremy Kerridge as Scrooge. The story is told almost exclusively through dance and pantomime, and Scrooge does not dance at all until after his reform. Choreography by Massimo Moricone. Music by Carl Davis. Original scenario by Carl Davis, developed with Christopher Gable. BBC Philharmonic Orchestra conducted by John Pryce-Jones. Produced by Christopher Gable. Directed by Kriss Rusmanis. A BBC/Arts and Entertainment Network/RPTA Primetime Co-production. Video N/A. 86 min.

A Christmas Carol (1997). Animated cartoon motion picture, in which the Ghost of Christmas Past is portrayed as a fruits-and-vegetables vendor and the Ghost of Christmas Present is a woman. Principal voices: Tim Curry, Whoopi Goldberg, Michael York, Ed Asner, and Frank Welker. Written by Jymn Magon. Produced and directed by Stan Phillips. DIC Productions and Twentieth Century-Fox Film Corporation. VHS: Twentieth Century-Fox Video. 72 min.

A Christmas Carol (1999). Cable television movie starring Patrick Stewart (famous for his one-man portrayals of the *Carol* on Broadway) as Scrooge. Considered to be highly faithful to the original novella in dialogue and character portrayal, and the only version to open with the burial of Jacob Marley. Honors in 2000: Saturn Award nominations for Best Television Genre Actor (Stewart) and Best Single Genre Television Presentation; Emmy nomination for Best Cinematography; Screen Actors' Guild Award nomination for Outstanding Male Actor (Stewart). With Richard E. Grant, Joel Grey, Ian McNeice, Saskia Reeves, Desmond Barrit, Bernard Lloyd, and Dominic West. Written by Peter Barnes. Produced by Dyson Lovell. Directed by David Jones. Hallmark Entertainment. DVD: Turner Home Video. 93 min.

A Christmas Carol (2000). British television movie, a contemporary portrayal of the *Carol*, in which three spirits reform "Eddie Scrooge"

(Ross Kemp), a mean-spirited loan shark. With Ray Fearon and Angeline Ball. Written by Peter Bowker. Produced by Joshua St. Johnston. Directed by Catherine Morshead. Video N/A. 75 min.

A Christmas Carol (2004). American-Hungarian television musical, starring Kelsey Grammer as Scrooge. With Jason Alexander, Geraldine Chaplin, Patrick David, Emily Deamer, Jennifer Love Hewitt, Jane Krakowski, Jesse L. Martin, Steven Miller, Julian Ovenden, and Joseph Tremain. Original music by Alan Menken. Teleplay by Lynn Ahrens and Mike Ockrent. Produced by Howard Ellis and Steven North. Directed by Arthur Allan Seidelman. Hallmark Entertainment. Video N/A.

A Christmas Carol II: The Sequel (1985). Television episode on *George Burns Comedy Week*. One year after the reform of Scrooge (James Whitmore), all the ghosts return to find that he has become a wimpish philanthropist. With Ed Begley, Jr., and Roddy McDowall. Written by Carl Gottlieb and David Axelrod. Produced by George E. Crosby and Paul Perlove. Directed by Carl Gottlieb. 40 Share Productions, Inc., in association with Universal Studios, Inc. Video N/A. 30 min.

A Christmas Carol at Ford's Theatre (1979). Televised adaptation of the *Carol* from Ford's Theatre in Washington, D.C., starring Ron Bishop as Scrooge. Characters also periodically serve as narrators by directly addressing the live audience in attendance. Emmy nomination in 1980 for Outstanding Achievement in Lighting. Adapted by Rae Allen and Timothy Near. Produced by Christopher Sarson. Directed by Rae Allen and Kirk Browning. Ford's Theatre producer: Frankie Hewitt. A Production of WETA Television. Video N/A. 87 min.

A Christmas Carol: Being a Ghost Story of Christmas (1991). British film directed by Moira Armstrong. Video N/A.

A Christmas Carol in Prose; or, A Ghost Story of Christmas (1960). English title for a West German television production known as *Ein Weihnachtslied in Prosa oder Eine Geistergeschichte zum Christfest*. Starring Peter Arens as Charles Dickens and Carl Wery as Scrooge. Directed by Franz Josef Wild. Video N/A. B & W. 110 min.

Christmas Carol: The Movie (2001). British-German animated cartoon motion picture, also known as *Ein Weihnachtsmärchen*. Live-action introduction and epilogue portray Charles Dickens (Simon Callow) reading the *Carol* to a live audience in Boston (these sequences are shown as a separate track on the DVD version), and two mice characters guide the viewing audience through the animated story. Principal voices: Kate Winslet, Nicholas Cage, Jane Horrocks, Michael Gambon, and Beth Winslet. Song "What If?" sung by Kate Winslet. Written by Piet Kroon and Robert Llewellyn. Produced by Iain Harvey. Directed by Jimmy T. Murakami. Production companies: Film Council, FilmFour, Illuminated Film Company, MBP (Germany), Murakami-Wolf Productions, Scala, and the Film Consortium. DVD: Metro-Goldwyn-Mayer. 81 min.

A Christmas Cruella (1997). Episode from the Disney animated cartoon television series *101 Dalmatians* (1997–98). Dalmatian pups assume the roles of the Christmas ghosts to reform Cruella de Vil, evil neighbor of the Dearly family. This episode appears with another *Dalmatians* tale, "Coup de Vil," in the Disney VHS video *101 Dalmatians Christmas* (1997). Principal voices: Jeff Bennett, Tara Charendorff, David Lander, Michael McKean, Charlotte Rae, Kath Soucie, Frank Welker, and April Winchell. Written by Ken Koonce and Michael Merton. Produced and directed by Victor Cook. 44 min.

Christmas Night (1946). This first presentation of the *Carol* on British television (BBC) is billed as a fantasy that uses mime and ballet. Instead of including the entire story line, a major focus is on Mr. Fezziwig's Christmas ball. Narrated by Hubert Foss. Adapted and produced by Philip Bate. Video N/A. B & W. 60 min.

Christmas Present (1985). Film shown originally at the London Film Festival in 1985 and broadcast on British television. Scrooge-surrogate Nigel Playfayre (Peter Chelsom) must find a deserving member of the poor on whom to bestow a turkey and Christmas cash, lest his own prosperity founder. Written and directed by Tony Bicat. Produced by Barry Hanson. Telekaton International. Video N/A. 75 min.

Dickens' Christmas Carol (1948). Television

special from New York featuring the Rufus Rose Marionettes, under the direction of Rufus and Margo Rose. First live broadcast of a full-length marionette production. Produced by Leonard Steinman. ABC Television. Video N/A. B & W. 60 min.

A Dickens of a Christmas (1983). Episode from the short-lived television animated cartoon series *The Dukes* (20 episodes, CBS), which was a spin-off of the live-action series *The Dukes of Hazzard* (CBS, 1979–85). As the Duke cousins race around the world against Boss Hogg, the competitors arrive in England on Christmas Eve, where spirits haunt Boss Hogg to reform him. Voices: Catherine Bach, John Schneider, Tom Wopat, James Best, Sorrell Booke, and Denver Pyle. Written by David R. Toddman. Produced by Kay Wright. Directed by Ray Patterson. A Hanna-Barbera Production. Video N/A. 30 min.

A Diva's Christmas Carol (2000). Made-for-television comedy/drama, starring Vanessa L. Williams as Ebony Scrooge, an unbearably difficult, cold-hearted pop singer with a nasty attitude in this change-of gender, change-of-race adaptation. With Rozonda "Chilli" Thomas, John Taylor, Brian McNamara, and Kathy Griffin. VH1 Television, Viacom Entertainment, and Viacom Productions, Inc. DVD: Paramount Home Video. 88 min.

The Dream of Old Scrooge (1910). English title for the Italian silent film titled *Il sogno dell' usuraio.* Video N/A. B & W. Approx. 12 min.

Ebbie (1995). Canadian-American production made for cable television. In this contemporary, change-of-gender adaptation, Susan Lucci stars as Ebbie Scrooge, the heartless CEO of a large department store, to whom Christmas is nothing but a season to boost store profits. Two Ghosts of Christmas Past (Jennifer Clement and Nicole Parker) appear as Valley Girls. With Wendy Crewson, Ron Lea, Molly Parker, Lorena Gale, Taran Noah Smith, Jeffrey DeMunn, Adrienne Carter, Bill Croft, and Laura Harris. Written by Paul Redford and Ed Redlich. Produced by Harold Tichenor. Directed by George Kaczender. Crescent Entertainment, Ltd. Video N/A. 100 min.

Ebenezer (1997). Canadian production made for cable television. Jack Palance stars as Ebenezer Scrooge, a ruthless, six-gun-toting, saloon proprietor and card shark in this wild west adaptation, set not in the American West but in Western Canada. To Scrooge, Christmas is not "humbug" but "hogwash." With Rick Schroder, Amy Locane, Daryl Shuttleworth, Richard Comar, Darcy Dunlop, Michelle Thrush, Linden Banks, Susan Coyne, Aaron Pearl, and Albert Schultz. Written by Donald Martin. Produced by Douglas Berquist and Michael Frislev. Directed by Ken Jubenvill. A-Channel Drama Fund and Nomadic Pictures. DVD: Platinum Disc Corporation. 89 min.

The Fat Albert Christmas Special (1977). Episode from Bill Cosby's animated cartoon television series, *Fat Albert and the Cosby Kids* (CBS, 1972–1979). When Tightwad Tyrone, a junkyard owner and Scrooge surrogate, threatens to demolish Fat Albert's clubhouse erected in the junkyard, the Spirit of Christmas provides him with a change of heart. The Cosby Kids also come to the aid of Marshall Franklin, a homeless boy, whose father and pregnant mother are living in their car. Emmy nomination in 1978 for Outstanding Children's Special. Voices: Bill Cosby, Jan Crawford, Gerald Edwards, Eric Suter, Erika Carroll, Eric Greene, Kim Hamilton, Julius Harris, and Ty Henderson. Written by Bill Danch and Jim Ryan. Produced by Norm Prescott and Lou Scheimer. Directed by Hal Sutherland. A Filmation Production in association with Bill Cosby Productions. VHS: Anchor Bay Entertainment. 30 min.

A Flintstones Christmas Carol. See **The Flintstones**.

The Gospel According to Scrooge (1983). Amateur musical stage adaptation televised over the Christian Broadcasting Network, which converts the *Carol* into a Christian evangelical medium. Performed before a live church audience in Minneapolis, this version depicts Scrooge (Robert Buchanan) as a miserable man separated from God. Instead of Marley's Ghost, the Voice of God warns Scrooge that he will be visited, not by three ghosts, but by the angels Peace, Joy, and Hope, their goal being to convert Scrooge to Christianity. Hosted by Dean Jones. With Melanie Burve, Sara Renner, Jim Schumacher, and Robert Whitesel. Music by Tom Elie and John Worre. Written by James P. Schumacher. Television producer: John Worre.

Stage producer: Tom Elie. Directed by Mark S. Vegh. Hope Productions International. VHS: Bridgestone Multimedia. 120 min.

Humbug Not to Be Spoken Here. See **Bewitched.**

The Jetsons Christmas Carol (1985). Episode from the Hanna-Barbera futuristic, animated cartoon television series, *The Jetsons*, which aired in primetime from 1962 to 1963, on Saturday mornings periodically from 1963 to 1983, and again on Saturdays from 1985 to 1986 with new episodes. The principal characters included George Jetson, wife Jane, teenage daughter Judy, young son Elroy, pet dog Astro, robot maid Rosie, and George's boss, Mr. Spacely. In this episode, Scrooge surrogate Mr. Spacely demands that George work on Christmas Eve but allows him to leave at midnight. Falling asleep at his desk, Spacely dreams that his deceased partner, Marsley, announces the coming of three Christmas spirits. They in turn not only reveal that Astro (a Tiny Tim surrogate) has eaten a Spacely product known as a Spacely Sprocket and will likely die, but that George will bring a devastating lawsuit against the company. Spacely, a changed man upon awakening, rushes to George's home with a veterinarian, saves Astro, distributes gifts to all, and avoids the predicted litigation. Voices: George O'Hanlon, Penny Singleton, Janet Waldo, Daws Butler, Don Messick, Jean Vander Pyl, Frank Welker, and Mel Blanc. Written by Marc Paykuss and Barbara Levy. Produced by Bob Hathcock. Directed by Ray Patterson. Hanna-Barbera Productions. VHS: Hanna-Barbera Home Video. 22 min.

John Grin's Christmas (1986). Television special with an all–African American cast, starring Robert Guillaume as John Grin, a Scrooge surrogate toymaker. Also unusual in that it eliminates the visit from the ghost of Grin's former partner as well as the character of Tiny Tim altogether. With Roscoe Lee Browne, Ted Lange, Alfonso Ribeiro, Geoffrey Holder, Candy Ann Brown, Kevin Guillaume, and Melissa Hill-Guillaume. Written by Charles Eric Johnson. Produced by Mark Brull. Directed by Robert Guillaume. Guillaume/Margo Productions. Video N/A. 60 min.

Karroll's Christmas (2004). Television comedy in which the four ghosts mistakenly visit Allen Karroll (Tom Everett Scott), a depressed writer of greeting cards, instead of his truly Scrooge-like neighbor, Zeb Rosecog (Wallace Shawn). The ghosts are also nontraditional: Marley (Dan Joffre) is a Rastafarian; Christmas Past (Larry Miller) is a Jewish comedian; Christmas Present (Alanna Ubach) is an intern; and Christmas Future (Verne Troyer) is a dwarf. Written by Drew Daywalt and David Schneider. Executive Producers: John Cosgrove, Jon Klane, and George Paine. Directed by Dennis Dugan. A & E Channel. Video N/A.

The Legend of Christmas (1947). English title for a motion picture from Spain titled *Leyenda de Navidad*, starring Jesús Tordesillas as "William Scrooge." Significant in that it is the first cinematic adaptation to embrace the strictly religious thread of the story. With Lina Yegros, Manuel Requena, Joaquín Soler Serrano, and Ángel Picazo. Written and directed by Manuel Tamayo. Produced by José María Alvarez. A Varios Production. Video N/A. B & W. 70 min.

The Legend of Christmas (1966). Remake of *Leyenda de Navidad* for Spanish television, starring Luis Prendes as Scrooge. With Nuria Carresí, Joaquin Pamplona, José Luis Coll, José Martín, and Alberto Calvo. Written by Manuel Tamayo. Directed by Alberto Gonzáles Vergel. Televisión Española. Video N/A. B & W. 103 min.

Marcel Marceau Presents a Christmas Carol (1973). BBC Television production featuring Marcel Marceau in a one-man, mime version. Narrated by Michael Hordern. Produced by Tristram Powell. Video N/A. 40 min.

The Merry Christmas (1955). British televised musical adaptation, starring Hugh Griffith as Scrooge. Lyrics and music respectively by Donald Cotton and Brian Burke. Produced by Douglas Hurn. Associated Rediffusion. Video N/A. B & W. 45 min. Rebroadcast in 1958 with different cast, starring Stephen Murray as Scrooge.

Mickey's Christmas Carol (1983). Disney animated cartoon theatrical film, featuring classic Disney characters in the roles of Dickens characters: Scrooge McDuck as Ebenezer Scrooge, Mickey Mouse as Bob Cratchit, Daisy Duck as Belle, Donald Duck as Fred, Goofy as Marley's Ghost, Jiminy Cricket as the Ghost of Christmas Past, Willie the Giant as the Ghost of Christmas Present, and Black Pete the Dog as the Ghost of Christmas Yet to Come. Only in this version does the latter character smoke a cigar. Received Academy Award nomination for Best Short Film, Animated Subjects. Principal voices: Alan Young, Wayne Allwine, Hal Smith, Will Ryan, Eddy Carroll, Patricia Parris, Dick Billingsley, and Clarence Nash. Written by Burny Mattinson, Tony L. Marino, Ed Gombert, Don Griffith, Alan Young, and Alan Dinehart. Produced and directed by Burny Mattinson. Walt Disney Productions. VHS: Disney Home Video. 26 min. The first television release in 1984 included an additional half-hour, behind-the-scenes documentary titled *The Making of Mickey's Christmas Carol*, which has been included in some of the video versions.

Mr. Magoo's Christmas Carol (1962). The first made-for-television animated cartoon special. A myopic old curmudgeon, Magoo became the most popular creation of animators at United Productions of America (UPA) in 1949, particularly Stephen Bosustow, John Hubley, and Ernest Pintoff. This *Carol* features Magoo as Scrooge in a Broadway musical, the lyrics and music of which are provided by Bob Merrill and Jule Styne, respectively. It is considered to be the best musical version, with such songs as "Ringle, Ringle, Ringle, Coins As They Jingle," "It's Cold, It's Cold, It's Cold," "All Alone in the World," "It's Great to Be Back on Broadway," "The Lord's Bright Blessing," "We're Despicable," and "Winter Was Warm." Another UPA character, Gerald McBoing Boing (a little boy who usually communicates through odd sound effects, though he *speaks* here), portrays Tiny Tim. This also is the only version in which the Ghost of Christmas Present appears ahead of the other two Ghosts. In 1970, *Magoo's Carol* was released to theaters, double-billed with the feature-length *Mr. Magoo's Little Snow White. Carol* voices: Jim Backus, Jack Cassidy, Laura Olsher, Joan Gardner, Jane Kean, Royal Dano, Morey Amsterdam, Les Tremayne, Paul Frees, Marie Matthews, and John Hart. Written by Barbara Chain. Produced by Lee Orgel. Directed by Abe Levitow. UPA Pictures. DVD: Sony Music Video. 52 min.

Mr. Scrooge (1964). Musical version, the first *Carol* produced for Canadian television, starring Cyril Ritchard as Scrooge. Unusual for its portrayal of the three ghosts: Christmas Past uses an old-fashioned bicycle to take Scrooge back in time; Christmas Present is a drunken British soldier; and a decapitated Christmas Future talks through his head, carried under his arm (conjuring up images of the headless horseman in Washington Irving's story "The Legend of Sleepy Hollow"). With Tessie O'Shea, Alfie Bass, Eric Christmas, and Gillie Fenwick. Lyrics by Richard Morris, Dolores Claman, and Ted Wood. Music by Dolores Claman. Written by Richard Morris and Ted Wood. Produced and directed by Bob Jarvis. Canadian Broadcasting Corporation. Video N/A. B & W. 60 min.

Ms. Scrooge (1997). Cable television special. Cicely Tyson stars as Ms. Ebenita Scrooge, a miserly African American woman, in this change-of-gender, change-of-race version. Instead of "Humbug!" this Scrooge declaims, "Garbage!" With Katherine Helmond, Michael Beach, John Bourgeois, Rae'ven Kelly, Karen Glave, Ken James, Arsinée Khanjian, William Greenblatt, Michael J. Reynolds, and Julian Richings. Written by John McGreevey. Produced by Julian Marks. Directed by John Korty. Power Pictures and Wilshire Court Productions. VHS: Paramount Home Video. 87 min.

The Muppet Christmas Carol (1992). Motion picture musical comedy, starring Michael Caine as Scrooge with Jim Henson's Muppet characters portraying Dickens characters, such as Kermit the Frog as Bob Cratchit, Miss Piggy as Emily Cratchit, the Great Gonzo as Charles Dickens, and Fozzie Bear as "Mr. Fozziwig." Won Fantafestival Award in 1993 for Best Direction. Songs by Paul Williams. Principal Muppet voices: Dave Goelz, Steve Whitmire, Jerry Nelson, Frank Oz, David Rudman, and Louise Gold. Screenplay by Jerry Juhl. Produced by Brian Henson, son of the late Jim Henson, and Martin G. Baker. Directed by Brian Henson. Jim Henson Productions and Walt Disney Pictures. DVD: Walt Disney Home Video. 89 min.

Music Revue (1955). Episode from the television situation comedy series *Our Miss Brooks* (CBS, 1952–56), starring Eve Arden as schoolteacher Connie Brooks. The episode is significant in that it became the precedent for many televised "plays within plays" involving the *Carol*. Here, Principal Conklin (Gale Gordon) portrays Scrooge in a school play. CBS Television. Video N/A. B & W. 30 min.

Rich Little's Christmas Carol (1978). Canadian television special starring comedian Rich Little in a one-man adaptation of the *Carol*. Little impersonates a number of celebrities portraying Dickens characters: W.C. Fields as Scrooge, Paul Lynde as Bob Cratchit, Johnny Carson as Fred, Laurel and Hardy as charity solicitors, Richard Nixon as Marley's Ghost, Humphrey Bogart as the Ghost of Christmas Past, Groucho Marx as Mr. Fezziwig, Peter Falk as the Ghost of Christmas Present, Jean Stapleton as Mrs. Cratchit, Truman Capote as Tiny Tim, Peter Sellers as the Ghost of Christmas Yet to Come, and others, including James Mason, John Wayne, George Burns, and Jack Benny. Written by Rich Little. Produced by Norman Sedawie and Gale Gibson Sedawie. Directed by Trevor Evans. Canadian Broadcasting Corporation, Dudley Enterprises, Inc., and Tel-Pro Entertainment, Inc. VHS: Columbia Tristar Home Video. 50 min.

The Right to Be Happy (1916). Silent film starring Rupert Julian as Scrooge. It is the only feature-length *Carol* in the silent era. With John Cook, Claire McDowell, Francis Lee, Harry Carter, and Emory Johnson. Written by Elliott J. Clawson. Directed by Rupert Julian. Bluebird Photoplays, Inc. Video N/A. B & W. 60 min.

Scrooge (1901). British silent film and first known film version, also known as *Scrooge, or Marley's Ghost*. Marley's Ghost presents all the visions. Directed by Walter R. Booth. Robert W. Paul Company. Video N/A. B & W. Approx. 11 min.

Scrooge (1913). British silent film, starring Seymour Hicks as Scrooge. With William Lugg, J.C. Buckstone, Dorothy Buckstone, Leedham Bantock, Leonard Calvert, Osborne Adair, and Adela Measor. Written by Seymour Hicks. Directed by Leedham Bantock. Zenith Films. Video N/A. B & W. Approx. 40 min.

Scrooge (1922). British silent film starring Henry V. Esmond as Scrooge. From the *Tense Moments with Great Authors* series. Written by

W. Courtney Rowden. Produced by H.B. Parkinson. Directed by George Wynn. Master Films. Video N/A. B & W. Approx. 23 min.

Scrooge (1923). British silent film starring Russell Thorndike as Scrooge. With Nina Vanna, Jack Denton, and Forbes Dawson. Written by Eliot Stannard. Produced by Edward Godal. Directed by Edwin Greenwood. British and Colonial Kinematograph Company. Video N/A. B & W. 25 min.

Scrooge (1928). British film "short," starring Bransby Williams as Scrooge. This is the first filmed version of the *Carol* to incorporate sound. Written by Bransby Williams. Directed by Hugh Croise. British Sound Film Productions. Video N/A. B & W. 9 min.

Scrooge (1935). British motion picture starring Seymour Hicks as Scrooge. With Donald Calthrop, Barbara Everest, Philip Frost, Mary Glynne, Robert Cochran, Marie Ney, Oscar Asche, and Maurice Evans. Written by H. Fowler Mear (some also credit Seymour Hicks, though he is not listed in the credits). Produced by Julius Hagen. Directed by Henry Edwards. In 1936, Edwards was awarded Special Recommendation at the Venice Film Festival for his work on this picture. Twickenham Film Studios. DVD: Image Entertainment. B & W. 78 min.

Scrooge (1970). Elaborate British motion picture musical, starring Albert Finney as Scrooge. The role of Scrooge originally was offered to Rex Harrison, who declined. This version, the first theatrical release to be filmed in color, contains a scene with Scrooge and Marley in hell. The picture captured the following honors in 1971: Academy Award nominations for Best Art Direction/Set Decoration, Best Costume Design, Best Original Song ("Thank You Very Much"), Best Original Score; BAFTA Film Award nomination for Best Art Direction; won Golden Globe for Best Motion Picture Musical/Comedy Actor (Finney); Golden Globe nominations for Best Musical/Comedy Motion Picture, Best Original Song, Best Original Score, Best Screenplay; Golden Laurel Award nomination, 4th place for Best Male Comedy Performance (Finney). With Alec Guinness, Dame Edith Evans, Kenneth More, Laurence Naismith, Michael Medwin, David Collings, Gordon Jackson, Roy Kinnear, and Kay Walsh. Teleplay, original music, and lyrics by Leslie Bricusse. Produced by Robert H. Solo. Directed by Ronald Neame. Cinema Center Films and Waterbury Films. DVD: Paramount Home Video. 114 min. In 1992, Bricusse adapted this version to the stage under the title *Scrooge: The Musical*, starring Anthony Newley as Scrooge.

Scrooge (1978). Adaptation made for Canadian television, starring Warren Graves as Scrooge. Stage production by Graves originally presented at Theatre Three in Edmonton, Alberta. Unusual in that Marley's Ghost presents all the visions. With Drew Borland, Crystal Fleuty, Colin Graves, Ray Hunt, and Peter Messaline. ITV Television. Video N/A. 70 min.

Scrooge: A Christmas Carol (1989). Television presentation of colorized version of the 1951 film that starred Alastair Sim (see above). Hosted by Patrick Macnee.

Scrooge and Marley (2001). Made-for-television Christian evangelical adaptation, starring Dean Jones as Scrooge. Hating Christmas and outraged at seeing a Nativity scene outside City Hall, Scrooge launches a lawsuit to have the offending display removed. The resulting court case brings on the noted pastor, Dr. D. James Kennedy (portraying himself), president of Coral Ridge Ministries, as an expert witness, who presents crucial evidence for Christ's transformational impact on the world. With Al Quinn, Reg Grant, Greg Wilson, Jason Richards, and Al Arasim. Narrated by Joan Plowright. Written and directed by Fred Holmes. Produced by Cathy King and Fred Holmes. Coral Ridge Ministries. Available on VHS from Coral Ridge Ministries. 48 min.

Scrooged (1988). This dark, comedic parody set in contemporary New York City casts Bill Murray as Scrooge-surrogate Frank Cross, a despicable television network president who sees Christmas only as a means to boost network ratings. He attempts to do so by staging a live broadcast of *A Christmas Carol*, in which he casts Buddy Hackett as Scrooge. Cross is reformed by a Ghost of Christmas Past cabby (David Johansen); a Ghost of Christmas Present fairy (Carol Kane), who administers corporal punishment; and a black-robed, silent Ghost of Christmas Yet to Come, whose face alternately appears as a skull or as a video monitor, which in turn depicts Cross's face as a mutilated mass. With Karen Allen; John Forsythe; John Glover; Bobcat Goldthwait; Robert Mitchum; Alfre Woodard; Mary Lou Retton; John Houseman; Lee Majors; Michael J. Pollard; and Bill Murray's three other brothers, John, Joel, and Brian Doyle Murray. Honors received in 1989: Academy Award nomination for Best Makeup; won BMI Film Music Award for music score by Danny Elfman. Written by Mitch Glazer and Michael O'Donoghue. Produced by Richard Donner and Art Linson. Directed by Richard Donner. Mirage Productions and Paramount Pictures. DVD: Paramount Studios. 100 min.

Scrooge's Rock 'n' Roll Christmas (1984). Syndicated, televised rock music version, in which a nineteenth century Scrooge (Jack Elam) receives the Christmas spirit through holiday standards performed by twentieth century rock musicians: "Rockin' around the Christmas Tree" (Three Dog Night), "White Christmas" (Merrilee Rush), "Jingle Bells" and "The Christmas Song" (Paul Revere and the Raiders), "Some Children See Him" ("Bridget"), "Do You Hear What I Hear?" (Mary MacGregor and Mike Love), "Jingle Bell Rock" (Mike Love and Dean Torrence), "Sleigh Ride" and "Home for the Holidays" (the Association), "Winter Wonderland" (Bobby Goldsboro), and "Have Yourself a Merry Little Christmas" (Mike Love). Written by Rex Sparger. Produced by Bob Franchini. Directed by Lou Tedesco. Formerly available on VHS Sony Video. 44 min.

Skinflint: A Country Christmas Carol (1979). Made-for-television, country/western musical adaptation set in the town of Flint City, Tennessee, featuring a host of country/western music celebrities. Hoyt Axton stars as Cyrus Flint, a Scrooge surrogate and bank president. One of few *Carols* in which the Ghost of Christmas Yet to Come speaks. With Mel Tillis, Lynn Anderson, Larry Gatlin, Tom T. Hall, Martha Raye, Danny Davis and the Nashville Brass, the Statler Brothers, Barbara Mandrell, and Dottie West. 1980 Emmy nomination for Outstanding Individual Achievement in Special Class (Technical Direction and Camera Operation). Lyrics and music by Mel Mandel, Norman Sachs, and Aaron Schroder. Choreography by Scott Salmon. Written by Mel Mandel. Produced by Marc Daniels and Joseph Cates. Directed by Marc Daniels. The Cates Brothers Company. Video N/A. 120 min.

The Stingiest Man in Town (1956). Made-for-television musical first broadcast live on *The Alcoa Hour*, starring Basil Rathbone as Scrooge. With Vic Damone, Patrice Munsel, Martyn Green, Dennis Kohler, Johnny Desmond, and the Four Lads. Screenplay and lyrics by Janice Torre. Music by Fred Spielman. Produced by Joel Spector. Directed by Daniel Petrie. A Theatrical Enterprises Production. Video N/A. 90 min. Remade as an animated cartoon under the same title in 1978 (see below).

The Stingiest Man in Town (1978). Made-for-television cel-animated cartoon, a remake of the 1956 live-action television musical. A cricket, B.A.H. Humbug (voice of Tom Bosley), narrates as Walter Matthau voices for Scrooge (his character is drawn in Matthau's likeness). Songs: "A Christmas Carol," "The Stingiest Man in Town," "An Old-Fashioned Christmas," "Humbug," "I Wear a Chain," "Golden Dreams," "It Might Have Been," "The Christmas Spirit," "Yes, There Is a Santa Claus," "Birthday Party of the King," "One Little Boy," and "Mankind Should Be My Business." Other voices: Robert Morse, Theodore Bikel, Dennis Day, Robert Rolofson, Darlene Conley, Paul Frees, Debra Clinger, Steffani Calli, Eric Hines, Charles Matthau, and Diana Lee. Lyrics and music respectively by Janice Torre and Fred Spielman. Written by Romeo Muller. Produced and directed by Arthur Rankin, Jr., and Jules Bass. Rankin/Bass Productions. VHS: Warner Home Video. 50 min.

The Strange Christmas Dinner (1945). Televised adaptation of a short story by Margaret Cousins, in which Scrooge-surrogate Herman Grubb (John Souther), a New York restaurateur who refuses to grant his employees one day off for Christmas, is reformed by the spirit of Charles Dickens (Grandon Rhodes) instead of the usual ghosts. Narrated by Bill Woodson. Written, produced, and directed by Fred Coe. NBC Television. Video N/A. B & W. 45 min. Remade (60 min.) in 1949 with different cast, starring Melvyn Douglas as Dickens.

The Trail to Christmas (1957). Television Western frontier adaptation on *The General Electric Theatre*, hosted by future president Ronald Reagan. Jimmy Stewart stars as a cowboy who retells the *Carol* to Richard Eyer, a little boy who has run away from home at Christmastime. In Stewart's version, Scrooge (John McIntire) is a miserly ranch owner. With Sam Edwards, Will Wright, Kevin Hagen, Sally Frazier, Mary Lawrence, and Dennis Holmes. Written by Frank Burt and Valentine Davies. Produced by William Frye. Directed by Jimmy Stewart. CBS Television. Video N/A. B & W. 26 min.

The Virtue of Rags (1912). Silent motion picture *Carol* variation, in which a Scrooge-surrogate landlord (Francis X. Bushman) fires his kind-hearted rent collector (Bryant Washburn) for failing to collect the rent from a poor widow (Helen Dunbar). But after the landlord dreams that it is he who becomes destitute, he mends his ways and becomes charitable. Written and directed by Theodore Wharton. The Essanay Film Manufacturing Company. Video N/A. B & W. Approx. 17 min.

See also **Dickens, Charles, Christmas Stories of; Irving, Washington, Christmas Sketches of.**

A Christmas Carol

(Poem). Composition of five stanzas by British novelist Charles Dickens (1812–1870), author of the identically titled novella about the reform of Ebenezer Scrooge. The poem is found in chapter 28 of Dickens's first novel, *The Pickwick Papers* (1836–37). The time is Christmas Eve at Mr. Wardle's estate, Manor Farm, where Mr. Pickwick and his colleagues are spending the holidays with Wardle's other guests. As everyone awaits the midnight hour, Wardle entertains the crowd with this poem as a song, which holds that none of the other seasons can compare with Christmas, "the King of the Seasons all!" Later, the poem itself was set to a popular tune of the time.

Christmas Carols

Sacred or secular songs that celebrate all aspects of Christmas and are considered popular or modern for the era of origin. By strict definition, because carols in general may celebrate religious as well as secular holidays and other special events, they appeal to the public with lyrics and music with which the majority can identify. The word "carol" ultimately

3 Wise Men.

This crude little woodcut of 3 Wise Men was one of several printed on penny sheets of Christmas carols, which were sold by their publisher, T. Batchelar of Moorfields, London, in the early nineteenth century. William Hone, who bought the original printing blocks in 1820, recollected that once a full sheet of carols with eight woodcut sold for a half-penny: "But alas! everything is changed; the present half sheets are raised in price to a whole penny." He also said that people would naturally buy Christmas Carols "as they long for mince pies and eat plum pudding." From William Hone, Ancient Mysteries Described *(London: 1823).*

derives from the Greek *choros* ("chorus"), a circling dance. The latter often appeared in ancient Greek plays, in which performers sang and danced in a circle. Greek also provides *choraules* ("flute player for chorus dancing"); thence derives the Latin *choraula* and the Old French *caroler* to the English "carol."

Although songs celebrating the Nativity have existed since the early Christian era, true carols, Christmas or otherwise, did not arise

English children carolling on Christmas morning as was the custom of the 1870s. According to the book in which the wood engraving appeared, they perhaps were singing "When Christ was born of Mary free,/In Bethlehem, in that fair cite,/Angels sang there with mirth and glee,/In Excelsis Gloria." From Robert Chambers, ed., The Book of Days *(London and Edinburgh: Chambers, 1879).*

until the fourteenth or fifteenth century. Prior to that time, most Christmas music consisted of somber, plainchant hymns originating in the Church, the Latin texts of which appealed little to the public, for only clerics and scholars at that time were proficient in the ecclesiastical language. Indeed, the earliest extant Christmas hymns are those composed by St. Ambrose (340?–397) of Milan, Italy, whose "Veni, redemptor gentium" ("Savior [or Redeemer] of the Nations [or Gentiles], Come") is a more familiar example. His Incarnation themes set a precedent, for the Church subsequently incorporated abstract theology into its Christmas hymns and condemned all forms of jocularity, including dancing, at Christmastime and on other feast days until the appearance of St. Francis of Assisi, Italy.

Considered the parent of the carol, St. Francis (1182–1226) desired that his parishioners acquire a full understanding and appreciation for the Bible, particularly its messages regarding Bethlehem and Calvary. On Christmas Eve of 1223, he attained the first goal by assembling a live Nativity scene in a cave near the village of Greccio, Italy. Amid a reconstructed stable with ox, ass, shepherds, and Wise Men, St. Francis jovially sang the Christmas Mass as spellbound spectators saw the Nativity presented with tender emotion, realism, and humanity theretofore unknown. By interjecting a spirit of joy into religious song, St. Francis revolutionized hymnody and laid the groundwork for changes in the English miracle or mystery plays that would follow, all of which brought Christianity closer in tune with the hearts of the laity and inspired the writing of new religious songs in the vernacular. (*See* **Christmas Drama**.)

Other medieval clerics following in the footsteps of St. Francis included the Italian Jacopone da Todi (1228–1306), a Franciscan mystic whose lyrical Christmas songs pervaded the thirteenth century, and John Audlay, a blind English priest of Haughmond Abbey, Shropshire, whose collection of Christmas carols (1430) bore the following inscription in red: "I pray yow syrs boothe moore and las / syng these caroles in cristemas" ("I pray you sirs both more and less / sing these carols in Christmas"). It is clear that Audlay's goal was to provide spiritual mirth for Christmas.

The fourteenth and fifteenth centuries saw, with the coming of the Renaissance, an upswing in lay patronage of the arts and music, a decline in the plainsongs of the Church, and a rise in vernacular hymns and carols throughout Europe. By the fifteenth century, the word "carol" had become synonymous exclusively with sacred or secular Christmas songs. In England, traditional carols were patterned after ballads or contained refrains, while a macaronic variety (not unique to England and probably the contribution of clergymen) consisted of English verse peppered with familiar phrases from the Latin liturgy. The best-known example of the latter variety, "The Boar's Head Carol," survives in a printed collection of 1521 by Jan van Wynkyn de Worde and is the earliest English carol collection extant.

Christmas carols flourished throughout Europe during the sixteenth century but markedly declined with the advent of the Protestant Reformation. No country saw a greater suppression of carols at this time than did Great Britain, for in 1647 the Puritans, having gained control of Parliament earlier in the decade, completely outlawed all religious feast days and their trappings. Although the ascent of King Charles II in 1660 restored these holidays, Christmas observances never again attained the level of merriment known in former centuries, and the former traditional carols were all but forgotten. From that time into the early nineteenth century, the clergy generated several new hymns, some of which were significant, such as Isaac Watts's "Joy to the World"; others are no longer remembered today. Generally, however, carols superficially survived as folk tunes sung by wandering minstrels, or they sporadically appeared on broadsides.

Fearing a total demise of the English-language carol tradition, a number of prominent nineteenth century scholars individually recovered their country's Christmas heritage in song through a series of carol compilations. *Collection of Christmas Carols* (1822 and 1823) by Davies Gilbert, president of the Royal Society, was considered to be the first modern collection of traditional carols since the Reformation. Other notable collections included *Christmas Carols Ancient and Modern* (1833) and *Christmas Tide* (1852), both by the solicitor-antiquarian William Sandys; *Songs and Carols* (1836) by Thomas Wright, consisting of fifteenth century carols; and *Songs of the Nativity* (1868) by William H. Husk.

Two collections further boosted carols in the eyes of the nineteenth century English clergy. One of these, *Carols for Christmas-Tide* (1853) by the Anglican priest John Mason Neale and musicologist Thomas Helmore, consisted of 12 carols that Neale had translated from *Piae Cantiones (Holy Songs)*, a book of sixteenth century Swedish carols. Among them were the now-familiar "Good King Wenceslas" and "Good Christian Men, Rejoice." Rev. Henry Bramley, Fellow of Magdalen College, Oxford, together with Dr. John Stainer, Magdalen College organist, published the second collection, *Christmas Carols New and Old* (1871). This volume, consisting of a mixture of traditional and contemporary numbers, is reputed to have been the most influential in restoring the English carol tradition.

An interest in carols also blossomed in

nineteenth century America, owing in part to the popularity of such literary works as the poem "A Visit from St. Nicholas" (published 1823) and Charles Dickens's *A Christmas Carol* (1843), as well as to the clergy, who composed some of America's most popular religious carols. For example, "It Came upon the Midnight Clear" (1849), the work of Rev. Edmund Hamilton Sears and Richard Willis, is considered to be America's first prominent carol. Other genres have included African American spirituals such as "Go Tell It on the Mountain" (1800s) and a host of secular carols that especially burgeoned into the twentieth century.

See also entries for individual carols.

The Christmas Child: A Story of Coming Home

See **The Christmas Cross: A Story about Finding Your Way Home for the Holidays**

The Christmas Coal Mine Miracle

(1977). Made-for-television drama, also known as *Christmas Miracle in Caufield, U.S.A.* The story provides a gripping social commentary regarding mine disasters.

On a Christmas Eve in the early 1950s, coal mine workers with no union to support them face a dilemma: continue to work in a mine that they fear is unsafe or hold a wildcat strike and face loss of their jobs. Despite a series of methane gas explosions on previous occasions, the unscrupulous mine owner, Mr. Caufield (Don Porter), has persistently refused to heed the miners' concerns and insists that there is no danger. Reluctantly, they continue working, only to have some 60 of them trapped in a major cave-in. Miners and their families work desperately for a timely rescue, and violent explosions demolish the ill-fated mine just moments after all are safe.

Prefacing the disaster is a subplot depicting turmoil within the family of miner Matthew Sullivan (Mitch Ryan) amid preparations for a frugal Christmas: elder daughter Matilda's (Karen Lamm) initial desire to escape the confines of her small town, younger daughter Kelly's (Melissa Gilbert) crusade against the avarice of Mr. Caufield himself, and the family's concern over the health of their youngest, Timmy (Rossie Harris).

With John Carradine and Kurt Russell. Written by Dalene Young. Produced by Lin Bolen. Directed by Jud Taylor. A Lin Bolen Production in association with Twentieth Century Fox Television. VHS: Twentieth Century-Fox Home Entertainment. 95 min.

Christmas Comes Anew

See **Sing We Now of Christmas**

Christmas Comes to Pac-Land

(1982). Made-for-television animated cartoon, a special Christmas presentation of the Hanna-Barbera *Pac-Man* cartoon series of 16 episodes that aired on the ABC network for one season in 1982. The series was based on a popular video game of the same title at the time from Bally Midway Manufacturing Company/ Namco, Ltd., the principal characters of which were round, colored balls named Pac-Man and wife Pepper, with their nemeses, "ghosts" named Inky, Blinky, Sue, and Clyde.

When Santa takes a wrong route and crashes the reindeer sleigh in the cyberworld of Pac-Land on Christmas Eve, Pac-Man and his colleagues find him an intriguing stranger, for Christmas does not exist in their realm. After Santa explains his mission as gift-giver and that all of his toys must be retrieved, lest there be no Christmas for the children of the world, Pac-Man rises to the task, battling a howling blizzard and the ever-present ghosts to round up the gifts. Despite Pac-Man's efforts, Santa nevertheless decides to cancel Christmas because of reindeer fatigue and the late hour. But all is not lost, for Pac-Man next leads the troupe into the fabled Power Pellet Forest (after persuading the ghosts to let them pass "in the spirit of the holidays"), where the reindeer gain super energy by consuming power pellets. Thus revived, Santa and his team zoom away, but not before stopping at Pac-Man's house to deliver special gifts for them and the ghosts as well.

Principal voices: Peter Cullen, Barry Gordon, Marty Ingels, Chuck McCann, Barbara Minkus, Neilson Ross, Susan Silo, Russi Taylor, and Frank Welker. Produced by Kay Wright. Directed by Ray Patterson. Hanna-Barbera Productions. VHS: Hanna-Barbera Studios. 30 min.

See also **Hanna-Barbera Christmas Cartoons.**

Christmas Comes to Willow Creek

(1987). Made-for-television drama.

With their local cannery closed, the citizens of Willow Creek, Alaska, have little cause for holiday cheer. All is not lost, however, for Al Bensinger (Hoyt Axton), a town native now running a trucking company in Los Angeles, prepares to ship a load of staples and gifts to his friends. When ill health prevents him from making the run personally, Al sends Pete and Ray (Tom Wopat and John Schneider), two employees and rival brothers. Their differences center around Jesse (Kim Delaney), whom Pete had initially met and courted but who had married Ray instead. Now that the two are separated, Ray fears that Pete, a divorced father, will try to win back Jesse, who presently lives in Canada. Complicating the hostilities, Pete brings along his rebellious teenage son Michael (Zachary Ansley), so that they at least will be together for Christmas.

Most of the movie is a running series of heated arguments between the two brothers and between father and son as they travel, with a side trip to Reno for purposes of gambling and brawling. Passing through Vancouver, Ray locates Jesse, now pregnant with his child and living alone, and persuades her to join the group.

Just outside Willow Creek, the show moves into high gear as a nocturnal blizzard forces the rig into a snowbank, and Jesse begins labor. At that moment, they are rescued by the shepherd Domingo (Paul Beckett), who leads them to the shelter of his home and delivers Jesse of a baby boy, while Ray and Pete enjoy one last brawl outside.

Somehow, between that night and the next morning, when the people of Willow Creek find them and dig out their rig, the bickering parties have matured with their differences settled. As for Domingo, no one in Willow Creek has ever heard of him, and no trace of his house exists, which leaves the viewer with images of Christmas spirits and angels.

Story by Michael Norell and Andy Siegel. Teleplay by Michael Norell. Produced by Billie André. Directed by Richard Lang. Blue André Productions in association with ITC Entertainment Group. DVD: Family Home Entertainment. 93 min.

Christmas Cometh Caroling

See **Alfred Burt Carols**

Christmas Crackers

See **Great Britain**

The Christmas Cross: A Story About Finding Your Way Home for the Holidays

Inspirational short story of forgiveness and redemption, written by American author Max Lucado, published in book form in 1998; repackaged and published as *The Christmas Child: A Story of Coming Home* in 2003. The 1998 version uses interactive props within the text, and the 2003 version contains photographs from the motion picture adaptation (see below).

Reluctantly separated from his wife, a Chicago journalist finds himself alone on Christmas Eve in the small Texas town where he was adopted. His mission is not to locate family members but to learn why an anonymous person has sent him the photograph of a church there without any further explanation. The journalist finds the church's outdoor Nativity scene, a handsome set of skillfully hand-carved wooden figures; they are intriguing, especially the Christ Child figure, for its chest bears an indentation that once held a little, scarlet, wooden cross.

According to the elderly caretaker Joe, a Mr. Ottolman had carved and donated the set as penance for causing his pregnant wife's death while driving under the influence; his baby daughter Carmen had survived. Eventually Ottolman had accepted Christ while working on the Nativity figures and received inspiration for the cross motif upon hearing a sermon titled "Born Crucified." The cross had remained with the Christ Child figure until Carmen was 18 years old. At this time she conceived out of wedlock and, late in her pregnancy, suffered mortal injuries in an automobile accident at Christmastime. Again, a drunken Ottolman had been responsible, yet a loving Carmen had forgiven him. As she had lain dying, Carmen had begged to hold a baby on Christmas Eve, and Ottolman had smuggled the church's figure of Baby Jesus to her side, leaving the parishioners to wonder why the manger was suddenly empty for a time. The cross never appeared with the figure again.

To conclude his story, Joe reveals that Carmen's son survived and that Ottolman, who became a church caretaker, had waited many years to pass the little cross on to his grandson, now standing before him. Having discovered his family, the journalist seeks forgiveness and reconciliation from his wife.

In 2003, the story was adapted as a feature film under the title *Christmas Child*, starring Megan Follows, William R. Moses, Vicki Taylor Ross, and Steven Curtis Chapman. Adapted by Andrea Jobe and Eric Newman. Produced by Tom Newman and Penelope Foster. Directed by William Ewing. Impact Productions, LLC. DVD: Goodtimes Home Video. 96 min.

Max Lucado is a minister and the daily speaker for the radio program *UpWords*. His other Christmas books include *Alabaster's Song* (1996), *The Crippled Lamb* (1994), *Cosmic Christmas* (1997), and *Jacob's Gift* (1998), all of which are discussed as separate entries.

A Christmas Cruella

See **A Christmas Carol** (Film and Television Versions)

Christmas Day

Feast commemorating the birth of Jesus Christ. It corresponds to December 25 on the Gregorian calendar in the Roman Catholic, Anglican, Episcopal, and Protestant churches; January 7 in divisions of the Eastern Orthodox Church; and January 6 in the Armenian Church (although its branch in Jerusalem observes January 19). Whereas this entry will focus on December 25, detailed explanations for the other dates will be found under **Armenia; Christmas Old Style, Christmas New Style**; and **Epiphany**.

The word "Christmas" first appeared between the sixteenth and seventeenth centuries as a contraction of "Christ's Mass," based on the three Roman Catholic Masses that composed the liturgy of Christmas Day. "Christ's Mass" further derived from the late Old English *Christes Maesse* (or *Cristes Maesse*) of the early eleventh century, first found in the entry for the year 1038 in *The Anglo-Saxon Chronicle*. The latter was a running compilation of British history originally commissioned by Alfred the Great around 890, which anonymous scribes continuously updated until the mid–twelfth century. Through the centuries, *Cristes Maesse* underwent a series of evolutions, such as *Cristes-messe*, *Kryst-masse*, *Cryst-masse*, *Cristmasse*, *Chrysmas*, *Cristmas*, and so forth (*see* **Christmas Masses**).

The establishment of December 25 evolved not from biblical precedent (indeed, the Bible provides no specific date for the birth of Christ) but from pagan Roman festivals held at year's end, such as the Saturnalia, January kalends, and the combined festivals of two sun gods, the Roman Sol and the Persian Mithra. Roman soldiers, enamored with the cult of Mithra during their campaigns of the first century A.D. in Persia, spread the new religion throughout the Roman Empire, such that Sol and Mithra were regarded as one god. The empire celebrated their birthdays on December 25, the winter solstice according to the Roman (Julian) calendar, with festivities that the emperor Aurelian established in 274 as *Natalis Solis Invicti* ("Birth of the Unconquered Sun").

Early Christian theologians deplored the parallel of celebrating Christ's birth as the pagans did with their gods. As examples, St. Irenaeus (140?–202?) of Asia Minor and the Carthaginian theologian Tertullian (160?–220?) made no mention of a Nativity feast in their era. Clement of Alexandria (150?–215?) criticized his colleagues for attempting to assign a specific date to Christ's birth, and Origen of Alexandria (c. 185–c. 254) cited biblical implications that only sinners celebrated birthdays (Genesis 40:20; Ecclesiastes 7:1; Mark 6:21). Nevertheless, it is believed that early Christians did commemorate the Nativity at year's end, possibly to offset the revelry and unrestraint of those pagan festivals held simultaneously within the Roman Empire.

The earliest evidence that mentions December 25 lies in a church calendar that dates to 336, devised by Furius Dionisius Philocalus of Rome. In the civil portion of the calendar, December 25 is labeled *Natalis Invicti* ("Birth of the Unconquered," implying the solar birthday). In another portion of the calendar known as the *Depositio Martyrum*, a list of universally venerated martyrs, December 25 is labeled with a Latin phrase which translates as, "On the eighth before the Kalends [first day] of January [i.e., December 25], Christ is born in Bethlehem of Judea." Because several dates of other entries in this calendar clash with history and possibility, these and the reference to a December Nativity are felt to be "interpolations," that is, feasts added to the calendar based on popular trends of the time.

During his office, Pope Julius I (reigned 337–352) attempted to calculate the day of the Nativity based on the Scriptures and Jewish holy days. According to Luke 1:5–17, the priest Zacharias was serving in the Temple at the hour of burning incense when he received the angel's annunciation that his wife Elizabeth would bear John the Baptist. All the worshipers were praying outside the Temple and not within, which Julius inferred to mean that this was the Day of Atonement, or Yom Kippur, for only the priest could enter the Temple at this time to conduct the proper rituals. Further deductions, tenuous at best, placed this day in October; since Christ was six months younger than John, Christ was conceived in March and born in December. It is possible that Julius was additionally influenced by the traditional notion that Christ was conceived at the spring equinox, or March 25 on the Julian calendar, and died on that date exactly 33 years later (the so-called astronomical theory). From those deductions, Julius I around 350 declared December 25 as the official date to commemorate the birth of Christ. In so doing, he Christianized the former birthday of the sun (possibly also as an incentive for pagans to convert to Christianity), which drew support from Pope Liberius I around 353 and from St. John Chrysostom (c. 349–407), a theologian from Asia Minor. The latter, drawing a comparison between Christ and *Natalis Invicti*, declared that Christ was the "Sun of Justice," a sentiment that essentially reiterated a Messianic prophecy from Malachi 4:2, which portrayed Christ as the "Sun of righteousness." Although the December feast had been well established

Engraving of a manuscript miniature of the 14th century, showing Charlemagne receiving homage from federal barons. The picture originates in the Chroniqes de Saint-Denis.

by their time, some church leaders, such as St. Augustine (354–430) and Pope St. Leo I (reigned 440–461), remained critical, principally for fear that pagans converting to Christianity had retained the notion that Christ represented the sun.

From Rome, the December feast spread to the churches of the eastern Roman Empire, which had been observing the feast of Christ's Epiphany on January 6 since the second century. Constantinople received the feast of Christmas through St. Gregory of Nazianzus (c. 329–389) in 379, but not until the Synod of Constantinople in 381 did Theodosius I, Roman emperor of the East (ruled 379–395), sanction the December feast in that part of the empire. Cappadocia had received the feast through St. Gregory of Nyssa (c. 335–394) by 380; Antioch, through St. Chrysostom in 386; Alexandria, by 433; Jerusalem, in the latter sixth century. Armenia never accepted the December date.

• CHRISTMAS DAY IN HISTORY. Over the previous two millennia, a number of important historical events have transpired on or about Christmas Day. The following categories list some of the most noteworthy. Unless otherwise specified, all events occurred on Christmas Day:

First Christmas Celebrations
Philocalian calendar first mentions Decem-

ber 25 as a date to celebrate Christ's birth (336).

First official celebration of Christmas after Pope Julius I sanctions December 25 (350).

Christmas is first observed in Cappadocia (380), Constantinople (381, sanctioned by Theodosius I), Antioch (386), and Alexandria (433).

St. Francis of Assisi, Italy, constructs first live Nativity scene in a cave near Greccio, Italy (Christmas Eve, 1223).

Christopher Columbus's flagship *Santa Maria* runs aground off what is now the coast of Haiti in the West Indies. Columbus and his crew become the first Europeans to spend Christmas in the New World; they construct a small settlement from the ship's remains, which they name *Villa de la Navidad* ("Village of the Nativity") (Christmas Eve, 1492).

Explorer Hernando de Soto and party, camping in Spanish Florida (near Tallahassee), are the first to celebrate Christmas in the future continental United States (1539).

First Christmas service on record in St. Augustine, Spanish Florida, is conducted by Father Francisco Lopez de Mendoza Grajales (1565).

First Christmas in Jamestown, Virginia, the first permanent settlement in the English colonies (1620).

First "New Style Christmas" after England adopts Gregorian calendar over Julian calendar. Failure of annual Christmas Eve blooming of Glastonbury Thorn prompts thousands to observe "Old Style Christmas" on January 4 by old Julian calendar, when the Thorn did bloom (1752).

At the first Christmas celebrations in Australia, Governor Arthur Phillip in the penal colony of Sydney commutes the sentence of Michael Dennison from 200 lashes to 150 (1788).

John Adams is the first president to celebrate Christmas in the White House; Queen Charlotte erects the first Christmas tree in Great Britain at Queen's Lodge, Windsor, Berkshire (1800).

Benjamin Harrison is the first president to erect a Christmas tree in the White House (1889) (*see* **United States**).

Christmas Coronations

Charlemagne, as Holy Roman emperor

(800); Photius, as patriarch of Constantinople (857); Charles II (Charles the Bald, grandson of Charlemagne), as Holy Roman emperor (875); Otto II of Germany, as Holy Roman emperor (967); Johannes I Tzimisces, as Byzantine emperor (969); three-year-old Otto III, as king of Germany (983); Heribertus, as bishop of Cologne (999); St. Stephen the Great, as king of Hungary (1001); John Phasanus, as Pope John XVIII (1003); King Henry III of Germany, as Holy Roman emperor (1046); at Parliament of Worms, Emperor Henry III names his cousin, Count Bruno van Egisheim, as Pope Leo IX (1048); consecration of Westminster Abbey, Great Britain (1065); William the Conqueror, as King William I of England (1066); Count Baldwin I of Edessa, Armenia, as king of Jerusalem (1100); Roger II (the Norman), as king of Sicily (1130); Holy Roman emperor Henry VI, as king of Sicily (1194); Giovanni Angelo Medici, as Pope Pius IV (December 26, 1559); Crown Prince Hirohito, as 124th emperor of Japan (1926).

Government, Military, and Political Events of December 25

Roman Empire celebrates *Natalis Solis Invicti* under Emperor Aurelian (274).

St. Rémi baptizes Clovis I, king of the Franks at Rheims in Gaul, bringing Christianity to France (496).

Byzantine emperor Justinian I declares Christmas Day a civic holiday (529).

First observance of the "Twelve Days of Christmas," decreed by Second Council of Tours, France (567).

England adopts the Julian calendar (597).

Hernando Cortez's army marches on the Aztec capital of Tenochtitlan in Mexico (1520).

Scotland under the Puritans outlaws Christmas (1561).

Portions of the Netherlands adopt the Gregorian calendar (1582).

Founding of Natal, Brazil (1599).

Under the Puritans, English Parliament declares Christmas a day of penance (1647).

Puritan suppression of Christmas incites riots in Canterbury, England (1648).

Massachusetts Bay Colony outlaws Christmas and imposes fine of five shillings for observing Christmas (1659, repealed in 1681).

Christmas celebrations resume after ascension of Charles II to British throne and fall of Oliver Cromwell's Puritan Protectorate (1660).

Prussia and Austria sign Treaty of Dresden, giving Silesia to Prussia (1745).

General George Washington and his continental army cross the Delaware River at Trenton, New Jersey, and rout Hessian troops who are otherwise engaged in celebrating Christmas. The victory is a major turning point for the colonists in the American Revolution (1776).

Founding of Nashville, Tennessee (1780).

United States and Great Britain sign Treaty of Ghent, Belgium, which terminates the War of 1812 between these two powers (Christmas Eve, 1814).

Alabama is the first state of the contiguous 48 in the United States to recognize Christmas Day as a legal holiday (1836); Oklahoma is the last of the contiguous 48 to recognize Christmas as a legal holiday (1890).

American troops defeat Seminole Indians at Battle of Okeechobee, Florida (1837).

Parliament through Bank Holiday Act declares Boxing Day, December 26, a legal holiday in the United Kingdom (1871).

United States holds first National Community Christmas Tree lighting ceremony at the Capitol in Washington, D.C. (Christmas Eve, 1913).

Troops during World War I observe unofficial Christmas truces across Europe (1914).

Calvin Coolidge is the first president of the United States to light the National Community Christmas Tree (Christmas Eve, 1923).

Great Britain's King George V delivers first Christmas broadcast via radio (1932).

General Dwight D. Eisehower is appointed supreme commander of Allied Forces in Europe during World War II (Christmas Eve, 1943).

First television broadcast of Christmas message by England's Queen Elizabeth II (1957).

Scotland celebrates Christmas as a legal holiday for the first time since 1561 (1958).

Rev. Jesse Jackson forms Operation PUSH (People United to Save Humanity) (1971).

Meeting of Israeli prime minister Menachem Begin with Egyptian president Anwar Sadat in Egypt (1977).

Execution of Romanian dictator Nicolae Ceausescu and wife Elena (1989).

Mikhail Gorbachev resigns as president of the USSR (1991).

Christmas in Literature, Music and the Performing Arts

Lord Rhys (Rhys ap Gruffydd, prince of Deheubarth) holds elaborate festival with contests between bards and poets and between various musical classes at Cardigan Castle in Wales. It is the forerunner of the Welsh *Eisteddfod* ("A Sitting of Learned Men") (1176).

Premiere of J.S. Bach's *Christmas Oratorio* in Leipzig, Germany (1734).

First full performance of Handel's *Messiah* in the United States (Boston); world debut of "Silent Night" at the Church of St. Nicholas in Oberndorf, Austria, on Christmas Eve (1818).

John Philip Sousa writes "The Stars and Stripes Forever" (1896).

First radio broadcasts: Engelbert Humperdinck's *Hansel and Gretel* is the first opera to be broadcast via radio from New York City's Metropolitan Opera (1931); *A Christmas Carol* debuts on CBS radio, read by actor Lionel Barrymore on *The Campbell Playhouse* (1939); first broadcast of Irving Berlin's "White Christmas," sung by Bing Crosby on *The Kraft Music Hall* (1941).

George Cukor, initial director of *Gone with the Wind* (later replaced by Victor Fleming) announces that Vivien Leigh will play Scarlett O'Hara (1938).

Motion picture debuts: *The Wizard of Oz* (1939); Disney's *Old Yeller* (1957); Disney's *The Sword in the Stone* (1963); *Schindler's List* (1993).

Television debuts: Walt Disney launches into television with *One Hour in Wonderland*, NBC (1950); premiere of Gian Carlo Menotti's opera *Amahl and the Night Visitors*, broadcast from New York City as the first opera written for television (Christmas Eve, 1951).

Christmas in Exploration, Medicine, and Science

Christmas Island in the Indian Ocean is named by Captain William Mynors of the British East India Company (1643).

Swedish astronomer Anders Celsius devises the Centigrade temperature scale and incorporates it into a Delisle thermometer at

Uppsala, initially setting the freezing point of water at 100 degrees and the boiling point at 0 degrees (1741). The scale is reversed after his death.

German farmer and amateur astronomer Johann Georg Palitzsch first sights the returning Halley's comet in 1758. In 1705, English astronomer Edmund Halley had predicted that the comet, first seen in 1682, would be visible from Earth every 75.5 years.

Christmas Island, the largest atoll in the Pacific Ocean, is named by British explorer Captain James Cook on his third voyage to the Pacific (1777).

Biochemist Edward C. Kendall of the Mayo Foundation, Rochester, New York, first isolates thyroxine hormone from human thyroid glands (1914). Thyroxine is used to treat hypothroidism.

American neurosurgeon Dr. Irving S. Cooper of St. Barnabas Hospital, New York City, is inspired to develop the first cryosurgical (freezing) technique to treat various brain disorders after receiving an unusual Christmas present in 1960 — a wine bottle opener that lifted the cork by injecting ice-cold carbon dioxide gas into the bottle. He observed the freezing effects of the gas when applied to living tissue. His technique subsequently used liquid nitrogen.

Apollo 8 astronauts Frank Borman, James Lovell, and William Anders deliver the first televised Christmas message from space while orbiting the moon. Their text is taken from the opening verses of Genesis 1 (Christmas Eve, 1968).

U.S. Skylab III astronauts Gerald P. Carr, William R. Pogue, and Edward C. Gibson take a seven-hour space walk to study comet Kohoutek (1973).

Russian space probe *Venera 11* lands on Venus (1978).

Christmas Births

Jesus Christ in Bethlehem of Judea (?4 BC); Sir Isaac Newton in Woolsthorpe, Lincolnshire, England (1642); English clergyman, chemist, and mineralogist William Gregor in Cornwall, who discovered the element titanium (1761); Clara Barton in Oxford, Massachusetts, nurse and founder of the American Red Cross (1821); Cosmetician Helena Ruben-

stein in Krakow, Poland (1870); Quaid-i-Azam Mohammed Ali Jinnah, founder of Pakistan (1876); Conrad Hilton of Hilton Hotels chain in San Antonio, New Mexico Territory (1887); Robert L. Ripley ("Ripley's Believe It or Not") in Santa Rosa, California (1893); actor Humphrey Bogart in New York City (1899); American physician-turned-researcher Richard E. Shope, who first isolated an influenza virus (1901); German electrical engineer Ernst Ruska in Heidelberg, inventor of the electron microscope (1906); singer-bandleader Cab Calloway in Rochester, New York (1907); Egyptian president Anwar Sadat (1918); television personality Steve Allen in New York City (December 26, 1921); scriptwriter Rod (Edwin Rodman) Serling (*The Twilight Zone*) in Syracuse, New York (1924); Her Royal Highness Princess Alexandra, the Honorable Lady Ogilvy, in London, cousin to Queen Elizabeth II (1936); country singer Barbara Mandrell in Houston, Texas (1948); actress Mary Elizabeth Sissy Spacek in Quitman, Texas (1949).

Christmas Deaths

Pope Hadrian I (795); *The Anglo-Saxon Chronicle* mentions the death of Bishop Brihteh in Worcestershire before *Cristes Maesse* ("Christmas") — it is the first written reference made to the word "Christmas" as such (1038); French explorer Samuel de Champlain in Quebec City, Canada (1635); American inventor Linus Yale, designer of the compact cylinder pin-tumbler lock (1868); film comedian W.C. Fields, aged 67, in Hollywood, California (1946); silent film comedian Sir Charlie Chaplin, aged 88, in Vevey, Switzerland (1977); actress Joan Blondell, aged 73, in Santa Monica, California (1979); actor-singer Dean Martin, aged 78, in Beverly Hills, California (1995); murder of child beauty queen JonBenet Ramsay, aged 6, in Boulder, Colorado (1996); actor Denver Pyle, aged 77, in Burbank, California (1997).

Christmas Don't Be Late
See **The Chipmunk Song**

Christmas Drama
Four principal forms of historical drama were practiced in Europe during the holidays and particularly in Great Britain: masques, mumming, Nativity plays, and pantomime.

• Masques. Taken from the sixteenth century French, "masque" (mask) denotes a formal, masked presentation prevalent at English courts during the seventeenth century, which consisted largely of spectacular pageantry and scenery, along with music and elaborate speeches based on allegorical, mythological, or historical themes. Designed to compliment and entertain the monarchy during holidays and at other special events, English masques derived from early mumming or disguising customs (see **Mumming**, below) as well as from court spectacles practiced in the Renaissance Italy of Lorenzo de' Medici. Passing through France and there giving rise to the *ballet de cour* and the masquerades, masques then appeared in England at the time of the Tudors; King Henry VIII first introduced the formal masque to his court in 1512. There, as in Italy and France, the masquers, whose disguises sometimes included blackened faces, paired with members of the audience as well as the monarch for a grand, central dance called the "revels."

Masques especially flourished during the reign of King James I (ruled 1603–1625). Whereas masques until that time had centered primarily around pageantry and scenic effects with minor emphasis upon text, the celebrated English dramatist Ben Jonson (1572–1637) perfected the masque into a work of lyrical literature, beginning with his appointment as court poet in 1603. Jonson also first applied the word "masque" to his work in this genre, which commenced with *Masque of Blackness* (Twelfth Night, 1605). With this work, he launched a collaboration with the genius of English architect and stage designer Inigo Jones that produced 28 masques until 1634, at which time the two parted because of professional differences. Notable examples of their work include *Oberon, the Fairy Prince* (1611) and *Pleasure Reconciled to Virtue* (1618). Although Jonson's masques frequently were performed at Christmastime, the themes were not necessarily related exclusively to the season. Like most other masques, they generally centered around the resolution of discord or the movement from disorder to order, thus incorporating a moral. In Jonsonian masques were skillfully interwoven elements of comedic satire as well. For example, *Christmas His Masque* (1616),

Jonson's only masque written specifically for the holiday, features a host of allegorical characters that elegantly satirize those secular elements that were commonly associated with Christmas at the time: "Christmas" (the host), "Misrule" (The Lord of Misrule), "Carol," "Minced Pie," "Gambol" (one who frolics), "Post and Pair" (a card game), "New Year's Gift," "Mumming" (see below), "Wassail," "Offering," and "Baby Cake" (Twelfth Night cake with the bean and pea).

Masques virtually disappeared in England following the Puritan rise to Parliament in the 1640s but survived for another century in France and at other European courts. The improvements in changeable scenery and stage machinery later found in other art forms such as the ballet, opera, and pantomime owe much to those innovations developed for the court masque. *See also* **Christmas Pie; Epiphany; Feast of Fools.**

• Mumming. The word derives from the old German *Mumme* and the Greek *mommo* (both indicating "mask") and refers to masked street revels dating at least to the thirteenth century, the amateur participants of which were called "mummers." Their disguises, consisting of outlandish costumes, animal masks, and blacken-

Mummers— masqued revelers who performed folk plays and were often accused of mischief— existed in many countries, including Russia, Great Britain, Austria, and the United States, particularly in Pennsylvania. This engraving depicts a performance of the St. George and the Dragon play which also includes "Old Father Christmas." From Robert Chambers, ed., The Book of Days *(London and Edinburgh: Chambers, 1879).*

ing of the face, led to other folk designations, all corruptions of the word "disguise," such as *guisers* and *guizards*, with further corruptions to "geese-dancing" in Scotland. Providing entertainment from house to house with song and dance, mummers sought money, food, and drink from their hosts. Their cavorting often included rowdy mischief, pranks, and sometimes crimes. Examples of the latter include the failed assassination attempt upon England's King Henry IV in 1400 under the guise of mummers and the rise in murders during the time of King Henry VIII using the same ruse.

It is believed that mumming derived from pre-Christian sources, such as the riotous masquerades of the Roman Saturnalia in December; agrarian ceremonies that symbolized the death of the old year and the rebirth of the new, with perhaps the sacrifice of a mock king; and spring festivals, which celebrated the death of winter and the fertility of spring. As a parallel, the death and resurrection of a central character became prevalent in the so-called mummers' plays of England. These folk plays, performed primarily at Christmastime, arose probably during the seventeenth century, although written documentation about them did not appear until the close of the eighteenth century.

Mummers' plays generally incorporate subjects and characters from mythology or legends, and they can be classed as follows: hero-combat plays (by far the largest group), sword plays, and wooing plays. Of the hero-combat group, "The Play of St. George" remains the most popular, the legend of St. George (d. 303), patron saint of England, having acquired fame through Richard Johnson's *Famous History of the Seven Champions of Christendom* (1596). According to the allegorical legend, St. George thwarts the sacrifice of a Libyan king's daughter (the Church) by slaying her would-be devourer, a dragon (the Devil), then converts the kingdom to Christianity. In keeping with the oral tradition of all mummers' plays, however, there is no definitive St. George play; rather, there are a multitude of variations on dialogue and an odd assortment of characters that accrued over time, all built upon distortions of the St. George legend and interwoven around the pagan ceremonies mentioned

above. Despite the variations, they revolve around the same basic plot: St. George, also known as Sir George, Prince George, or King George, introduces himself as a valiant knight and boasts of his former deeds, particularly having slain the dragon and rescued the "King of Egypt's daughter" whom he married. To this a Turkish knight (also known as "Slasher"), or perhaps even the dragon himself, issues a challenge. A mock battle leaves one combatant "dead" (it matters not which), whereupon a quack doctor arrives and, after boasting of his healing powers, restores the deceased to life. Should similar battles follow between St. George and other heathen challengers, the victim is always resurrected with the doctor's assistance. At the conclusion, the players solicit money or food and drink.

Although the casts consisted overwhelmingly of men, mummers' plays sometimes included a feminine role. In the St. George play, she might be cast as the Presenter, a character who introduced the others; as Sabra, the King of Egypt's daughter; as St. Margaret, to whom Satan appeared in the form of a dragon; or simply as "Maiden." It is thought that the female role paralleled a mother goddess figure from pagan fertility rites. A female presenter might preside at plays on other occasions such as All Souls' Day, Easter, and the Feast of St. George (April 23), but the character of Father Christmas became over time the most suitable presenter for the Christmastime plays. Further analysis of mummers' plays and their variant characters may be found in Chambers's *The English Folk-Play* (1933).

Although mumming declined in England during the mid–nineteenth century, European immigrants had instituted mumming traditions earlier in North America; for example, the English brought mumming to Newfoundland during the seventeenth century, and the Swedes to the city of Philadelphia during the same period. The latter's celebrations centered around the new year, when masked revelers cavorted about, shouting with noisemakers and "shooting in the new year" with firearms. Observed through the American Revolution, this custom merged with the format of English mummers' plays and their trappings. English mumming also merged with the mythical Belsnickel or Pelsnickel, both derived from *Pelz Nicholas* ("Fur Nicholas"), a demon who accompanied St. Nicholas and whom German immigrants ("Pennsylvania Dutch") introduced during the eighteenth century to create the custom of "belsnickeling." Between Christmas and New Year's Day, belsnickelers, clad in disguises or with blackened faces, tramped from house to house committing pranks and seeking treats in return for providing some comic entertainment. When Philadelphia banned Christmastime mumming in 1808 as a public nuisance, members of the working class continued to stage private masquerades on New Year's Day in lesser populated regions outside the city. In 1901, Bart H. McHugh, a Philadelphia theatrical producer and publicity agent, persuaded city officials to sponsor an annual New Year's Day Philadelphia Mummers' Parade. This event has continued to this day and is now a nationally known event consisting of competitions in four divisions: Comic, Fancy, String Band, and Fancy Brigade.

A French scene from a mystery play, "Incarnation et Nativité de nostre saulveur et redempteur Jesuchrist," showing the arrival in Bethlehem. From Harper's New Monthly Magazine, *December 1888.*

• NATIVITY PLAYS. These presentations portrayed the birth of Jesus Christ and varied considerably in complexity. Precursors of these plays included the so-called liturgical dramas or tropes of the medieval Roman Catholic Church across Europe, the earliest of which arose during the tenth century in England as tools for instructing the laity in biblical stories and principles. Brief and initially presented in Latin within the sanctuary, liturgical dramas elaborated upon particular sections of the Mass with the clergy serving as sole actors. The earliest of these dramas focused at first upon the Easter story; later years saw the development of the *Pastores*, Christmas dramas portraying the annunciation to the shepherds. In the latter, a chorister posing as the herald angel sang the "Gloria in Excelsis Deo" aloft as "shepherds" approached the altar. Following a brief dialogue with the attending "midwives," the latter drew back a curtain to reveal a statue of the Virgin and one of the Christ Child lying in a crib. Later dramas incorporated such subjects as the adoration of the Magi, the confrontation with King Herod the Great, Herod's rage, and the Slaughter of the Innocents. In the latter, bruised and "deceased" choirboys were deposited about the altar as "mothers" wailed their laments.

By the twelfth and thirteenth centuries, the Latin dialogue slowly waned in favor of English and Anglo-French vernacular, the latter a remnant of the Norman Conquest of 1066. With their growing complexity, the English liturgical plays gradually moved from the sanctuary to the church grounds, thence away altogether to the market places or other public arenas to be taken up by the trade guilds. In part this migration arose from the interjection of comedy and vulgarity into the dramas. As an example, Christmas dramas had developed prologues in which a series of Old Testament prophets proclaimed the coming Messiah. The sequence of Baalam, whose frightened, talking ass encounters an angel, provided such mirth that additional boisterous and sacrilegious scenes later emerged to amuse the congregation. This, along with the Christmastime revelries surrounding the boy-bishop and the Feast of Fools of the era, contributed to the expulsion of liturgical dramas from the church. (*See* **Boy-Bishop**; **Feast of Fools**.)

With the establishment of the Feast of Corpus Christi (Body of Christ) by Pope Urban IV in 1264 (held on the Thursday after Trinity Sunday), it is generally believed that the liturgical dramas formerly performed in the church probably further evolved into elaborate "mystery plays," which comprehensively encompassed biblical stories from the creation to the final judgment. Along with the pomp and procession of Corpus Christi, trade guilds displayed their crafts through outdoor fairs and further cooperated to produce the cycles of religious plays regularly featured at this summer feast. The mystery play supposedly acquired its designation from the guilds' "mastery" of crafts, and from the local pronunciation of "mastery" as "mystery." Because the guilds were responsible for furnishing appropriate sets and props, it was customary to assign certain segments or pageants from the plays to those guilds, the special crafts of which were most suited to the subjects at hand. Examples of such assignments regarding Nativity pageants can be seen from the York Cycle of England (see below): spicers, "Annunciation and Visitation"; pewterers and founders, "Joseph's Trouble About Mary"; tile thatchers, "Journey to Bethlehem"; chandlers, "Shepherds"; masons, "Coming of the Three Kings to Herod"; goldsmiths, "Adoration of the Magi"; grooms, "Flight into Egypt"; and girdlers and nailers, "Slaughter of the Innocents." The guilds were also responsible for stage construction, and in England particularly, these took the form of wagons for the individual pageants, which could be easily transported to the next station in the cycle. The actors were members of the laity or the guilds.

Probably the best known of the medieval mystery plays are four anonymous and essentially complete English manuscripts surviving from the fifteenth and sixteenth centuries. Named for the place of performance, they include the Wakefield (also known as Towneley, a family that once possessed the manuscript), consisting of 32 plays in the cycle; Chester with 24; York with 48; and "N. Town" or Coventry with 42. Though religious in theme, the plays interjected more comedy, farce, and other worldly sequences that, despite a certain dramatic license not in total compliance with Scripture, nevertheless served to illustrate the interaction of an imperfect human race with the divine. The Nativity pageants were no exception; among the notable examples of these are the two "Shepherds'

Plays" of the Wakefield Cycle. Both cast shepherds as buffoons who rail against the aristocracy (the second play also weaves a stolen sheep into the plot), but the comedy abruptly ceases as the herald angel brings the tidings of good joy. Despite their complexity, some play cycles could be performed completely in one day, but most, not only in England but elsewhere in Europe, required several days. Between the fifteenth and sixteenth centuries in France, for example, mystery plays requiring up to 40 days for a full performance were not uncommon.

Nativity plays elsewhere in Europe are believed to have evolved in much the same manner via early Latin liturgical dramas. The fourteenth century saw the development of two varieties of mystery plays in France: saints' plays, which revolved around the lives of saints, and passion plays. At first, the latter focused only upon the events of Passion Week (the final week of Christ's life); later they incorporated elements such as Christ's Nativity and childhood. Ranking as one of France's best-known passion plays, *Mystère de la Passion* (1450) by Arnoul Gréban incorporates Old Testament scenes as well as those from the life of Christ. In Germany, passion plays were identified from the thirteenth century onward, but vernacular Nativity plays were not as common and dated primarily from the fifteenth and sixteenth centuries. One exception is *St. Galler Kindheit Jesu* (*St. Gaul Childhood of Christ*) of 1330. Scholars believe that drama once thrived within the Eastern Orthodox Church, yet the principal evidence is found in only three extant sources: a group of Byzantine sermon plays from the ninth to eleventh centuries, focusing primarily upon the Annunciation to the Virgin, and two passion plays, both dating to the thirteenth century.

Nativity plays virtually disappeared simultaneously with the mystery plays following the Protestant Reformation and the Roman Catholic Church's opposition to the unsavory dialogue and sequences that occasionally appeared therein. In June of 1998, however, the University of Toronto sponsored a production of the complete York Cycle of mystery plays, the first production since the sixteenth century. Vestiges of mystery plays also survive in the *Herbergsuchen* ("Search for the Inn"), German and Austrian Advent plays that reenact the Holy Couple's search for shelter in Bethlehem with rebuffs from surly innkeepers; in *Las Posadas* ("The Lodgings") of Latin America and the American Southwest, a similar custom that Spanish missionaries instituted in the sixteenth century; and in children's Christmas pageants held annually in churches and schools throughout the world. *See also* **Las Posadas**.

• PANTOMIMES. These art forms can be traced to the *pantomimus* (a solo actor portraying characters via wordless gestures and masks, accompanied by music and a chorus) of ancient Greece and Rome, but the present term refers to traditional Christmastime entertainments developed in English theaters during the eighteenth century.

English pantomimes developed through the efforts of two men connected with London theaters: John Weaver, dancing master at Drury Lane Theatre, and John Rich, manager of Lincoln's Inn Fields Theatre, both of whom separately introduced the "harlequinade," a precursor of the modern pantomime. The harlequinade in turn derived from *commedia dell'arte* ("comedy of the profession"), an improvised comedy that arose in northern Italy during the sixteenth century. Using masks, exaggerated gestures, music, and little dialogue, the *commedia* presented slapstick comedy situations through a series of stock character types, the most notable of which were "Pantalone" (English, "Pantaloon"), an aged suspicious merchant; "Pulcinella," a cruel schemer; "Dottore" (English, "Doctor"), a pedantic physician whose prescriptions could prove fatal; the "Captain," a cowardly braggart; "Columbine," a witty serving-wench; and two lowbrow clowns, the unscrupulous "Brighella" and the virtually amoral, greedy, and womanizing "Arlecchino" (English, "Harlequin").

The latter first appeared in French folk literature around 1100 as Herlekin, Hellequin, and later as Arlequin in the later seventeenth century, when he appeared in the French fairground theaters. Because he had continued to maintain his diabolical reputation, he became the most popular and leading character in the *commedia* repertoire. Harlequin failed to gain popularity with his first appearance in an English play (John Day's *The Travailes of the Three English Brothers*, 1607), yet French *commedia dell'arte* performances in London prompted Rich and Weaver to construct a new entertainment around Harlequin and similar characters, hence the harlequinade.

Weaver first staged the harlequinades in short ballets at Drury Lane in 1716; then Rich (performing under the stage name of Lun) portrayed Harlequin at Lincoln's Inn Fields in his *Harlequin Executed* on December 26, 1717, a piece that Chambers's *The Book of Days* holds to be the first English pantomime. This type of Christmastime entertainment became quite popular, and each production followed the pattern of opening with a serious story in mime taken from classic mythology, between the acts of which was interwoven a comedy segment (the harlequinade), which often consisted of the courtship between Harlequin and Columbine along with a number of special stage effects. This pattern continued until George Colman's *The Genius of Nonsense* (1780) replaced the mythological opening with a fairy tale as standard fare.

The nineteenth century also saw a number of changes: a decline of the harlequinade as the character Joey the Clown, the creation of actor Joseph Grimaldi, shifted the comic emphasis away from Harlequin; the roles of the dame and the hero ("principal boy") were assumed, respectively, by cross-dressed men and women; and extravagant pantomimes featuring dialogue, music, and dance emerged as Christmastime theatrical attractions that focused upon fairy tales or other familiar stories such as *Cinderella* or *Aladdin*. Pantomimes continued into the twentieth century with acrobatics and slapstick humor interwoven around the fantasy story lines. Originally opening on Boxing Day, December 26, today the pantomime season runs a few weeks before Christmas until mid-January. *See also* **Boxing Day**.

Christmas Eve

(1947). Motion picture drama, also known as *Sinner's Holiday*.

Worried that his wealthy, eccentric aunt, Matilda Reed (Ann Harding), will squander her millions on seemingly worthless pursuits, Phillip Hastings (Reginald Denny) schemes to have himself appointed as the executor of her estate. He invites Judge Alston (Clarence Kolb) and Dr. Doremus (Carl Harbord), a psychiatrist, to study Matilda's behavior at tea. Before she enters the room, a bell rings which, she explains, warns people to stop talking about her behind her back. Bird seed sprinkled abundantly on the floor attracts a large flock of birds through an open window for a repast, while a network of electric trains on the table carry condiments to her seated guests. The trains, Matilda adds, are sentimental mementos of three boys whom she adopted years ago, but whom as adults she has not seen for many years. These eccentricities are mild compared to her financial exploits, which include over 1.6 million dollars given to poor children for exterminating rats at the rate of one dollar per rat, a camp for the unhappily married at half that sum, and other strange enterprises.

Distrusting Phillip, Matilda is willing that any of her three sons manage her affairs instead, if only they could be found, for she knows not their whereabouts. Before leaving, they had only promised that if she ever needed them, they would return to New York City. Matilda then bids the judge to return on Christmas Eve, for that's when she will see her sons again, at the time when families come together, and the judge can determine their suitability for himself.

Through a private investigator and worldwide publicity, Matilda learns that son Michael Brooks (George Brent) is financially ruined through gambling and writing bad checks, which debts Phillip has covered on the premise that Michael not approach Matilda. Betrayed by Phillip ten years ago and wanted for a crime he didn't commit, son Mario Volpi (George Raft) is a fugitive living in South America as a nightclub owner, where he has unwittingly become involved with one Gustav Reichman (Konstantin Shayne), a Nazi war criminal wanted in Nuremberg, Germany. And son Jonathan (Randolph Scott) has distinguished himself as a chronic alcoholic and rodeo cowboy. Despite their sordid histories, however, Matilda has faith in her sons.

Upon returning to New York on Christmas Eve, Jonathan unwittingly assists undercover police officer Jean Bradford (Dolores Moran) in exposing an illegal baby adoption racket, and it is he who is the first to appear at Matilda's home with three homeless babies and Jean in tow. The hour is late, and Judge Alston is about to leave, when Michael, wise to Phillip's ulterior motives, arrives with fiancée Ann Nelson (Joan Blondell), and Mario appears with FBI agent Joe Bland (John Litel) close behind. After a happy reunion, in which the sons provide the judge with a series of believable lies about their past, Mario privately confronts Phillip and agrees not to expose him if he will leave town, a discretion for which Matilda is especially thankful. The picture closes as Matilda and her adopted family assemble for Christmas dinner.

Made-for-television movies *The Gathering* (1977) and *Christmas Eve* (1986) present somewhat similar story lines under a different set of circumstances.

Original story by Richard H. Landau and Laurence Stallings. Screenplay by Laurence Stallings. Produced by Benedict Bogeaus. Directed by Edwin L. Marin. Astor Pictures, Miracle Productions, and United Artists. B & W. Video N/A. 90 min.

See also **Christmas Eve** (1986); **The Gathering**.

Christmas Eve

(1986). Made-for-television drama which closely parallels an earlier television special, *The Gathering* (1977).

Suddenly faced with a terminal illness, wealthy New York widow Amanda Kingsley (Loretta Young) hires a private investigator, Morris Huffner (Ron Leibman), to locate her three adult grandchildren, who have been long estranged from their domineering, power-crazed, widower father, Andrew (Arthur Hill), chief executive of Kingsley International. With time uncertain, Amanda's one wish before she dies is that her grandchildren be reunited with their father by Christmas. While Huffner searches, Amanda and her faithful English butler Maitland (Trevor Howard) trek into the slums, distributing coffee, sandwiches, cash, and good cheer to the city's poor and homeless, a nightly mission Amanda has performed for ages. She has come to know many of the destitute personally, and when the police try to haul away her friends, Amanda tries to stop them. She and Maitland are arrested, and she refuses to leave jail until Andrew arranges not only her bail but the others' as well. When bag lady Molly (Kate Reid) is terminally hospitalized in Bellevue, Amanda arranges her transfer to a private hospital, remains with her, then personally handles Molly's funeral arrangements.

A change in Amanda's will, bequeathing all 51 percent of her interest in Kingsley International to the homeless, finally prompts greedy Andrew to petition the courts to have him appointed as his mother's conservator. The court's decision is postponed until after the holidays.

Within a few days of Christmas, Huffner successfully locates the grandchildren: country music devotee Josh (Patrick Cassidy) in San Antonio, actress Melissa (Season Hubley) in Hollywood, and draft-dodger Harley (Wayne Best) in Canada with his wife Nora (Amanda Hancox) and young son Adam (Richard Sole). Through Huffner, Amanda bids them all to return home for Christmas but withholds the principal reason. They make no commitments, but Amanda is not fazed; she has complete faith that her brood will return, and in anticipation for their arrival, she prepares a welcome-home party.

Late into the evening on Christmas Eve, just as she contemplates retiring, her grandchildren arrive en masse, which generates a profoundly emotional scene of tears, hugs, kisses, and profuse apologies on the part of the grandchildren for having neglected their grandmother. Even Andrew has softened. Withdrawing the petition against his mother, he first embraces little Adam, the grandson whom he has never seen, then his own children, and the family becomes one again.

In 1987, this picture captured the following honors: won Golden Globe Award for Best Actress in a Television Motion Picture (Loretta Young); Golden Globe nominations for Best Television Motion Picture and Best Supporting Actors (Rob Leibman and Trevor Howard).

With Charles Frank, Deborah Richter, and Antony Parr. Written by Blanche Hanalis. Directed by Stuart Cooper. National Broadcasting Company. VHS: Burbank Video. 93 min.

See also **Christmas Eve** (1947) and **The Gathering**.

Christmas Eve Lovefeast
See **Moravian Church**

Christmas Every Day
Classic short story by the American author William Dean Howells, first published in 1892.

As Christmas approaches, a little girl wonders what it would be like to experience the joys and fantasies of Christmas every day of the year. When she coaxes a story from her father, the wise gentleman delivers a moral in the form of a story-within-a-story, the subject of which is another little girl whose wish for a full year of Christmas is granted by the Christmas Fairy, and not just for her alone, but for everyone. People open presents each morning, but, because the next day will also be Christmas, they must buy new presents daily. People sing carols and wish neighbors and passers-by "Merry Christmas" without end, all eventually becoming hoarse and losing their voices. Gifts, candy, and other holiday paraphernalia accumulate in homes and overflow into the streets from daily giving and receiving, and rampant poverty ensues as people exhaust their incomes and savings on gifts. In time all people come to despise Christmas, and the child, passionately regretting her wish, begs the Christmas Fairy to abolish the loathsome holiday altogether at the close of the term. Instead of that extreme, the fairy convinces her to accept the once-a-year Christmas that has always pleased humanity ever since Christmas began.

A 1986 made-for-television animated cartoon adaptation of the same title featured the voices of Stacy Q. Michaels, Brian Cummings, Miriam Flynn, Edie McClurg, Marla Frumkin, and Dick Orkin. A CBS Television Production in association with Orkin-Flaum Productions and Calabash Productions. Video N/A.

A 1996 made-for-television comedy adaptation starred Robert Hays, Bess Armstrong, Erik von Detten, Yvonne Zima, Robert Curtis-Brown, Robin Riker, and Julia Whelan. In 1997, the picture received a Young Artist Award nomination for Best Family Cable Television Movie. Eric von Detten received nominations for Young Artist Award and Young Star Award for Best Young Actor in a Television Movie. Written by Stephen Alix and Nancey Silvers. Produced by Gary M. Goodman and Barry Rosen. Directed by Larry Peerce. MTM Enterprises, Inc., and the Family Channel. Video N/A.

William Dean Howells (1837–1920) served as editor for the *Atlantic Monthly* from 1871 to 1881. His works include literary criticisms and some 30 novels. *The Rise of Silas Lapham* (1885) is perhaps his most famous book.

Christmas Fern
See **Christmas Plants**

Christmas Flower
See **Christmas Plants**

Christmas for Cowboys

American country and Western song written in 1975 by Dallas native Steve Weisberg. At the time, Weisberg was a guitarist for singer John Denver, who was recording his Gold Record–winning *Rocky Mountain Christmas* album for RCA. This album comprised a mixture of established traditional and contemporary works as well as some of Denver's original pieces, such as "Aspenglow," "Please, Daddy (Don't Get Drunk on Christmas)," "A Baby Just Like You," "The Music Is You," "Perhaps Love," and "Dreamland Express."

Ordinarily Denver wrote his own material, but when the album was short one song, Weisberg offered "Christmas for Cowboys," which Denver included in the album. The album sold over two million copies, and the song became the top Christmas tune of 1975 (position 58 on the *Billboard Hot 100* chart).

While most people are enjoying traditional presents, football, eggnog, and Christmas parades in the city, according to the nostalgic lyrics, nature offers the cowboy gifts of the sky and the open range, with the stars serving as Christmas lights.

Weisberg's other compositions include "Hitchhiker," "It's Up to You," "Love Is Everywhere," "Our Lady of Santa Fe," and "Pickin' the Sun Down."

The Christmas Gift

(1986). Made-for-television drama.

Having lost his wife a year ago at Christmas, New York City architect George Billings (John Denver) and his young daughter Alex (Gennie James) seek a holiday retreat in Georgetown, Colorado, a remote village in the Rockies, where everyone, regardless of age, truly believes in Santa Claus. George's employer, Thomas Renfield (Edward Winter), a land developer, has ordered him to size up the location for a new recreational development project while posing as a tourist.

George and Alex arrive a few days before Christmas on "Letter Day," a citywide holiday in which everyone convenes at the post office with their letters addressed to Santa. Initially puzzled at such an eccentric community, George, through the hospitality of caring people such as Susan McMillan (Jane Kaczmarek), Georgetown's postmaster, cabby-innkeeper Bud Sawyer (Pat Corley), and his old-maid sister Henrietta (Mary Wickes), soon learns why the town is so devoted to Santa. At the lighting of the community Christmas tree, citizens recall the legend of the Christmas miracle, now 100 years old, that led Georgetown into prosperity:

Caught in a blizzard (says the legend) while crossing the Rockies, their pioneer forefathers faced starvation. On Christmas Eve, when an old, white-bearded stranger begged food from those who had none to spare, a compassionate boy managed to find something for the man. The stranger promised to reward the boy 100-fold, and on Christmas morning, each wagon was found filled with food, blankets, and new toys for the children. To them, the stranger had been Santa Claus himself. Now that a century has passed, the legend will soon repeat itself, for another miracle is about to save Georgetown again.

Charmed by the people's friendliness and warmth, and especially his and Alex's attraction to Susan, George, knowing that Renfield's project will forever disrupt the town, attempts to steer Renfield to alternate locations, but his employer is relentless. The bank having foreclosed on the ranch of Jake Richards (Kurtwood Smith), Renfield desires the property and reveals his plan to bring "progress" at a town meeting. Although George protests and is fired, Susan and Alex initially believe that he has betrayed the town. When Alex runs away, Jake is instrumental in finding her, which prompts George to make a final plea at the church's Christmas Eve pageant. To stop Renfield, at George's suggestion, the citizens pull together and pay off Jake's mortgage, then congregate at his ranch for a candlelight ceremony just as Jake and his children are about to leave. With no property, Renfield is defeated, and the miracle of Christmas again saves Georgetown.

With James Callahan, Anne Haney, and Harvey Vernon. Written by Christopher Grabenstein, David Venable, and Ronald Venable. Produced by David A. Rosemont. Directed by Michael Pressman. VHS: Goodtimes Home Video. 120 min.

Christmas in Bedrock
See **The Flintstones**

Christmas in Calico: An American Fable

Novel by American author Jack Curtis, first published in 1996. Set in the small town of Calico, Nevada, at the turn of the twentieth century, the story more than remotely parallels the sentiment found in Charles Dickens's classic *A Christmas Carol*.

Christmas promises to be lean on the Western plain, especially for Rose Cameron, a widow of eight months and now pregnant at term with her second child. Her thieving hired hand having absconded with most of her stock, Rose can hardly make ends meet with her young son Tommy who, having suffered a rat bite, falls ill with a high fever and racking cough. Compounding her troubles are Max Gotch, Calico's merciless banker, who will seize her ranch by the first of the year, unless the mortgage is paid, and her neighbors, Col. Wayne Damker, a cattle rancher, and Fortunato Fajardo, a Mexican sheep rancher, both of whom desire her land for their own herds and have refused to come to her aid. Topping all this, a deadly winter storm is bearing down on the plains, causing Rose and Tommy to head to town for safety. Before departing, she entrusts her ranch to Joel Reese, a drifter on a black stallion, who also seeks shelter from the storm.

Despite the holiday season, drought and hard financial times have created in Calico "a heart festering from the decline of human pride and common decency," for not only is the town littered with refuse and rats, but the spirit of Scrooge reigns as Calico's "elite" establishments (the hotel, the bank, the mercantile, and even the church) all deny shelter to a pregnant widow and her sick child. And because she cannot pay, Dr. Snarph merely prescribes worthless over-the-counter elixirs for Tommy's cough. In contrast, mother and son find friends in the poor of Shack Town, Calico's "less respectable" district, wherein Rose cheerily waits tables at Ira Armsbury's bar and grill, a generous establishment that neither demands cash in advance nor worries about a patron's credit. And while Rose peddles Christmas cookies in vain through the icy street, a little prostitute, Lena McCoy, helps to nurse Tommy.

Christmas Eve provides a rapid turn of events. Riddled with guilt at this season for having neglected their widowed neighbor, the two ranchers' wives, Nellie Damker and Anaberta Fajardo, find themselves standing vigil over Tommy beside Rose as Joel Reese arrives with his own brand of Christmas gifts. Not only has he defended Rose's ranch against intruders and packaged and frozen her whole flock of turkeys for sale, he has brought the custom saddle for Tommy that his late father had ordered months earlier from Carson, Nevada. Furthermore, he breaks the boy's deadly fever and sternly warns banker Gotch that only by everyone working together and helping one another, instead of keeping to themselves, will they rid Calico of its filth, rats, and disease. Gotch, more interested in developing a personal empire, is skeptical, until he suffers a head concussion and experiences a prophetic vision of rats tormenting him in a hell for unscrupulous bankers. After that, Gotch is a changed man, for he returns Rose's ranch to her as a Christmas gift, buys her flock of frozen Christmas turkeys and distributes them all over town, and sponsors an all-town cleanup. Christmas also changes Damker and Fajardo, who return Rose's remaining horses and cattle, which had wandered onto their property.

With her faith restored in humanity, Rose brings new life to Calico with the birth of a baby girl, born on Christmas night in Ira's abode, which had once been a stable. Now together with her two children and Reese, who accepts her offer of employment, she can begin anew.

In 1999, the novel was dramatized for television under the title *Secret of Giving*, starring Reba McEntire as Rose, Devon Alan as Toby Cameron, and Ronny Cox as Gotch. In 2000, the picture was nominated for a Young Artist Award for Best Family Television Movie. Teleplay by Scott Swanton. Produced by Randi Richmond. Directed by Sam Pillsbury. Jaffe/Braunstein Films, Starstruck Films, and KingWorld. VHS: Paramount Home Video. 87 min.

Christmas in Connecticut

(1945). Motion picture comedy/romance.

Elizabeth Lane (Barbara Stanwyck) is a highly successful writer whose magazine articles about country living, child rearing, and cuisine on her farm in Connecticut are in great demand. Unknown to her publisher, Alexander Yardley (Sydney Greenstreet), are the following facts: Elizabeth is single, lives in New York, receives her recipes from local restaurateur Felix Bassenack (S.Z. Sakall), and doesn't know a toaster from a coffee pot.

A sticky situation arises when Yardley wants Elizabeth to entertain war hero Jefferson Jones (Dennis Morgan) at her farm over the Christmas holidays. Even worse, Yardley plans to come along and see Elizabeth's Christmas decorations, husband, and child for himself. By coincidence, her suitor, John Sloan (Reginald Gardiner), owns a farm in Connecticut, and Elizabeth agrees to marry him at the farm to save her job. With Felix in tow for the cooking, all that's left in the ruse is to find a baby, so Elizabeth commandeers an infant that John's housekeeper Norah (Una O'Connor) keeps for a neighbor during the day.

They maintain the deception with difficulty — a difficulty increased by the attraction between Elizabeth and Jeff — until Christmas night, when everyone attends a dance in honor of Jeff, and Yardley becomes suspicious when Jeff dances too closely with Elizabeth.

Finally the ruse comes apart when Yardley sees the neighbor coming for her baby at the farm later that night. Believing that she is kidnapping Elizabeth's child, Yardley calls the state police and the press. Many explanations are in order, and Elizabeth and Jeff are thrilled to learn that each is neither married nor engaged to anyone else (there was never any time for that farm wedding), for they have fallen in love with each other during Christmas in Connecticut.

With Robert Shayne, Frank Jenks, Joyce Compton, and Dick Elliott. Written by Aileen Hamilton, Lionel Houser, and Adele Commandini. Produced by William Jacobs. Directed by Peter Godfrey. Warner Bros. Pictures. VHS: Warner Studios. B & W. 101 min.

In 1992, the picture was remade for television, starring Dyan Cannon, Kris Kristofferson, and Tony Curtis. In 1993 this version received a Young Artist Award nomination for Best Young Actor in a Cable Movie (Jimmy Workman). Teleplay by Janet Brownell. Produced by Cyrus Yavneh. Directed by Arnold Schwarzenegger. Turner Pictures. VHS: Turner Home Video. 93 min.

Christmas in Killarney

Song written in 1950 by Irish Americans John Redmond, James Cavanaugh, and Frank Weldon. With a melody in the style of an Irish jig, the lyrics claim that there is no happier Christmas on earth than that which is experienced in Killarney, a town in southwestern Ireland, "with all of the folks at home." Irish tenor Dennis Day, noted for his appearances on the hit radio-television program *The Jack Benny Show*, first introduced this song in 1951 with a successful recording on the RCA Victor label.

In addition to their separate contributions on other works, Redmond and Cavanaugh collaborated on such titles as "The Gaucho Serenade" (1940) and "Crosstown" (1940), together with Nat Simon. Cavanaugh and Weldon also paired for "I Like Mountain Music" (1933).

Christmas in My Hometown

(1996). Canadian made-for-television drama, also known as *A Holiday for Love*.

Shortly before Christmas, Jake Peterson (Tim Matheson), a representative from Beane Tractor Company in Chicago, returns to his hometown of Athens, Nebraska, to assess productivity there at the company's factory. Beane is downsizing its work force by 50 percent, and Jake must determine those whose jobs will be terminated after the holidays. To obtain the necessary information, Jake initially poses as a potential client interested in obtaining 80 tractors from the Athens plant. News of such a large contract spreads quickly, and Jake becomes a celebrity overnight as the man who will save the struggling town, for the factory employs a large percentage of local citizens. One of these is the young widow Emma Murphy (Melissa Gilbert), who soon develops a deep affection for Jake as she guides him around town and the plant, while teenage daughter Noelle (Michelle Trachtenberg) envisions him as making a far better stepfather than Emma's fiancé, Sheriff Tom Uhll (Travis Tritt).

Jake's popularity is only short-lived, however, for Cal Marsdon (Gordon Pinsett), Emma's father and the plant manager, quickly deduces Jake's secret, and Emma and Noelle, not to mention the entire town, are crushed at having been deceived. In his report to Chicago, Jake, realizing that a major layoff would destroy Athens, heeds a suggestion from Emma and proposes that, instead of downsizing the work force, Beane downsize its tractors and make them more affordable for the average farmer. Successful, Jake returns to Athens and delivers the good news during the town's annual Christmas dinner at the local home for senior citizens. Not only is Athens saved, but the promise of romance is revived between Jake and Emma.

Written by Darrah Cloud. Produced by Susan Murdoch. Directed by Jerry London. Jaffe/Braunstein Films, Ltd., and Pearson Television International. Video N/A. 96 min.

Christmas in Olden Times
See **Heap on More Wood**

Christmas Is

(Song). American song written in 1966 by Canadian American Percy Faith (music) and Spence Maxwell (lyrics). Recalling certain special items that are necessary for a meaningful Christmas, the song lyrics list sleigh bells, sharing, holly, caring, children with insomnia, fond memories, the warmth of carols, and the brightness of the very holiday when wishes really do come true. The song has been performed by numerous artists. Two of the first vocal recordings were by Johnny Mathis (1971) for Columbia and Tom T. Hall (1979) for RCA.

Faith, a composer, conductor, and arranger, assembled an orchestra that was respected for its renditions of popular favorites, the best known of which was "Theme from *A Summer Place*" (1960). Maxwell collaborated with Faith on a few pieces, such as "Waitin' round the Bend" and "Quiet Day."

Christmas Is

(Television cartoon, 1970). Underwritten by the International Lutheran Layman's League, this animated cartoon stresses the true meaning of Christmas by picturing young Benji and his dog Waldo transported back in time to witness the Nativity. Voices: Richard Susceno, Hans Conried, Don Messick, Colleen Collins, June Foray, Jerry Hausner, and Vic Perrin. A Screen Images Production for Lutheran Television. Video N/A. 30 min.

The Christmas Lamb
See **The Crippled Lamb**

Christmas Lilies of the Field

(1979). Made-for-television sequel to the motion picture *Lilies of the Field* (1963), in which Sidney Poitier starred as Homer Smith, an African American construction worker whom a group of East German nuns persuaded to build a church for them in the American Southwest.

In this sequel, the nuns, led by Mother Maria (Maria Schell), run a makeshift orphanage and persuade Homer (Billy Dee Williams) to build a dormitory for the children by late December. Otherwise, a social worker will place the children in foster homes.

When the government rejects the nuns' request for financial aid and a local charity committee refuses its support because one orphan, Felicia (Julie Delgado), is a pregnant, unwed teenager, the orphans face immediate placement. Miraculously, a group of Pima Indians volunteer their labor, Homer acquires building materials from a dismantled charity bazaar, and the dormitory is finished by Christmastime.

On Christmas Eve, as the children prepare for a Nativity pageant, Felicia delivers her son, whom she names Jesus. Attired as shepherds, angels, and Wise Men, the children gather around Felicia and her child.

Featured songs: "Amen" and the Christmas spiritual "Children, Go Where I Send Thee." With Fay Hauser, Lisa Mann, Hanna Hertelendy, Judith Piquet, Donna Johnson, Bob Hastings, Fred Hart, and Sam DiBello. Written by John McGreevey and Ralph Nelson. Produced by Jack Reddish and Toby Martin. Directed by Ralph Nelson. Rainbow Productions. VHS: MPI. 100 min.

See also **Children, Go Where I Send Thee.**

The Christmas List

(1997). Made-for-television drama.

Whether by coincidence or the hand of Santa, all the wish items on Meloday "Mel" Parris's (Mimi Rogers) Christmas list are being granted. On the light-hearted suggestion of her coworker Naomi (Enuka Okuma), Mel, employed as a perfume salesperson in Seattle, had created her own Christmas list as a small means of adding some spice to her otherwise solitary life. The list included a car; new clothes; her own perfume shop; spending an old-fashioned Christmas with her family; red roses; pink, fuzzy, bedroom slippers; dining at the Skyroom Restaurant; contact lenses; a beauty makeover; Christmas cash; and an engagement ring. Initially conceived as a joke, the list begins to "hatch" soon after Naomi confiscates it and drops it in Santa's mailbox in their department store. As each wish is fulfilled, Mel discovers that true love means far more than good intentions or promises said with vain words, and she gains a new respect for the adage, "Be careful what you wish for."

In 1998, this picture was nominated for two Young Artist Awards: Best Family Television Move and Best Supporting Young Actor (Bill Switzer).

With Stella Stevens, Marla Maples, Rob Stewart, and Jano Frandsen. Written by Marie Weiss. Produced by James Shavick. Directed by Charles Jarrott. A Shavick Entertainment Production. Video N/A. 96 min.

Christmas Masses

Series of three Masses held by the Roman Catholic Church, occurring at midnight on Christmas Eve (Midnight Mass), at dawn on Christmas Day (Dawn Mass), and later that same day (Christmas Day Mass). Respectively, they are also known as the "Angels' Mass," "Shepherds' Mass," and "Mass of the Divine Word," based on the Gospel text used for each service. They also symbolize the "triple birth" of Christ in eternity, in time, and in the soul. Although Christmas is currently the only time when the Catholic Church holds three masses, the Church had conducted a triple Mass formerly on Easter, Whitsun, and the Transfiguration, as documented in the year 845 by Ildefonsus, a Spanish bishop.

The exact year of the inauguration of the triple Christmas Mass is unknown but is believed to have occurred between the fifth and seventh centuries. Rome initially celebrated these Masses in different churches around the city, with the pope conducting Midnight Mass in the chapel of the Church of Santa Maria Maggiore (St. Mary Major). This church on the Esquiline Hill was commissioned by the Virgin Mary, who supposedly appeared to Pope Liberius I in a dream in 352 and commanded that he build the church where he found snow. Liberius noted snow in August of that year, construction commenced, and the basilica, patterned after the Basilica and Grotto of the Nativity in Bethlehem, was completed around 440 under the auspices of Pope Sixtus III. Currently enshrined there are five relics, pieces of boards of sycamore wood believed to have supported Jesus' original stone manger or crib (popular theory holds that not only was Jesus born in a cave that doubled as a stable, but His crib was of stone).

According to *The Catholic Encyclopedia*, Pope Theodore (reigned 640–649) probably acquired these relics, for which St. Mary Major was initially known as *Santa Maria ad Praesepe* (St. Mary to the Crib). These relics are exposed to the public annually on Christmas Eve.

The first of the three Masses was held at midnight on the belief that Christ was born at that hour. Early evidence for this belief dates to a fourth century Latin hymn, "Quando noctis medium" ("When in the Middle of the Night"), and the belief was perpetuated by Saint Elizabeth of Hungary (1207–1231), who allegedly performed a number of miracles.

The Dawn Mass was celebrated in St. Anastasia's Church on the Palatine Hill in Rome. According to legend, Anastasia, a fourth century Sirmian martyr, was beheaded on Christmas Day during the reign of Diocletian, after which her remains were interred in Constantinople in the Anastasis Basilica ("Anastasis," Greek for "Resurrection"). Because the Palatine church was patterned after the Anastasis Basilica in Jerusalem and originally bore the name of "Anastasis" as well, Rome substituted the name of St. Anastasia for Anastasis and initially celebrated this second Mass in honor of the legendary saint. Currently, the Dawn Mass replaces that for St. Anastasia.

The Christmas Day Mass was, and still is, celebrated in St. Peter's Basilica in Rome, as are the other two Masses. Televised broadcasts of the Midnight Mass from St. Peter's have been an annual event since 1948.

Not only do Roman Catholic churches around the world hold the triple Mass today, but many Protestant churches often hold comparable services on Christmas Eve (often terminating at midnight) and on Christmas Day.

See also **Nativity**; **Nativity Scene**; **The Vatican**.

A Christmas Memory

Classic autobiographical short story written in 1956 by American author Truman Capote. First appearing in *Mademoiselle* magazine, the story recalls a special Christmas during the years when Capote lived with a family of distant elderly cousins in rural Alabama until the age of ten. Capote developed a close relationship with one of those cousins, Miss Sook Faulk, who is known only as "my friend" in the story and whom he describes as being "still a child," simple and innocent. She, in turn, refers to young Capote as "Buddy," the name of a childhood friend who died in 1880. This cousin is shy with everyone except strangers, who seem to be not only her truest friends, but Buddy's as well, for the other members of their household have little to do with either of them except to preach and scold.

The story opens late in November, when Buddy's cousin heralds the coming of Christmas by announcing, "It's fruitcake weather!" Having held rummage sales and done odd jobs through the year, she and Buddy scrape together enough cash to buy ingredients for baking 30 fruitcakes, the chief ingredient of which is bootleg whiskey purchased from a giant Indian named HaHa Jones. The cakes are presents for their friends and acquaintances, and one is even mailed to President Franklin D. Roosevelt. Returning from a hike in the woods with their Christmas tree (which is twice as tall as a boy), the two pass a traveler who offers to buy the tree, adding that they can always get another one. The cousin's reply: "There's never two of anything."

Their simple decorations consist of homemade paper drawings of cats, fish, apples, watermelons, and tinfoil angels, hung on the tree with paper clips. Their gifts to each other are homemade kites, which they fly together on Christmas Day in a pasture. Frustrated because she cannot afford a bicycle for Buddy, the cousin states that what's worse than not being able to have something you want is not being able to give somebody something you want them to have.

This is Buddy's happiest Christmas and the last with his friend. Shipped off to military school, he corresponds with her for a few years and receives a fruitcake each November, until that morning when instinct alerts him that she will no longer arise and proclaim that it's fruitcake weather.

Miss Faulk died in 1938 while Capote was attending a military school in New York State.

Truman Capote's "A Christmas Memory" (1966) was an Emmy Award–winning adaptation for television starring Geraldine Page and Donnie Melvin with narration by Capote. Originally broadcast in color. VHS: ABC Television. B & W. 51 min.

A Christmas Memory (1997), another television adaptation, starred Patty Duke and Eric Lloyd, the latter of whom in 1998 received a Young Artist Award nomination for Best Young Actor Age Ten or Under in a Television Movie. Written by Duane Poole. Produced by John Philip Dayton and Glenn Jordan. Directed by Glenn Jordan. Hallmark Entertainment and Holiday Productions. Video N/A.

See also **One Christmas**.

Christmas Miracle in Caufield, U.S.A.

See **The Christmas Coal Mine Miracle**

The Christmas Miracle of Jonathan Toomey

Award-winning, children's inspirational picture book, written by American author Susan Wojciechowski, illustrated in watercolor by P.J. Lynch, and published in 1995. The book is considered to be a modern classic.

Dispirited and bitter after the loss of his wife and child, the lonely woodcarver Jonathan Toomey has been given the nickname "Mr. Gloomy" by the children of the village. To him, Christmas is merely "pish-posh!" But when the widow McDowell and her seven-year-old son Thomas commission him to carve new figures for their Nativity scene, the task changes his life forever.

This book is the recipient of numerous awards, including, among others, the Kate Greenaway Medal, the Christopher Medal for Excellence, and the American Library Association's Notable Book of the Year.

A former school teacher, Susan Wojciechowski writes fiction for children. Among her works are *And the Other Gold*, *Promises to Keep*, and *Don't Call Me Beanhead!*

Christmas New Style

See **Christmas Old Style, Christmas New Style**

Christmas of the Cherry Snow

Inspirational novel set in the 1950s, written by American author Richard Siddoway, published in 2001.

When his father John suffers a near-fatal accident on Christmas Eve and returns home from the hospital in a coma, 12-year-old Rob Henderson is faced with the seemingly overwhelming task of running the family's orchard and coping with mounting household problems. His mother Elizabeth maintains her steadfast faith that someday John will awaken, despite a grim prognosis, and declares that only at that time will they all celebrate Christmas together. Therefore, as the months pass by, the gifts remain unopened beneath a skeletal Christmas tree that has long since shed its needles.

Compounding their tragedy, the Hendersons must contend with their older neighbor Gus, who, initially solicitous and generous, terminates their friendship and becomes a proverbial thorn in the flesh after Elizabeth spurns his improper advances. Yet she and Rob return good for evil and once more befriend their neighbor after Gus suffers a serious injury that permanently blinds him.

All the while, John remains a comatose invalid who shows no sign of improvement, until a miracle in the spring blesses the Hendersons with a belated Christmas as the cherry blossoms in the orchard cast a blizzard of white petals on the wind.

A former bishop in the Church of Jesus Christ of Latter-Day Saints, Richard Siddoway is a Utah State legislator and an educator in the Utah public school system.

See also **The Christmas Quest; The Christmas Wish; Twelve Tales of Christmas.**

Christmas Old Style, Christmas New Style

Terms respectively applied to Christmas observed on the old Julian calendar, authorized by Julius Caesar in 44 BC, as opposed to the holiday observed on the present Gregorian calendar, developed by Pope Gregory XIII in 1582. Because of retrograde inaccuracies in the Julian calendar, which provided for a leap year every fourth year but no other corrections, the year was actually some 11 minutes and 14 seconds longer than the solar year, and important dates such as equinoxes and church feasts gradually fell out of season. By 1582, the vernal equinox occurred on March 11 instead of March 21. The Gregorian calendar corrected this error by dropping ten days from the calendar, retaining every fourth year as a leap year, and establishing every century divisible by 400 also as a leap year. Thus December 25 on the Gregorian or "New Style" calendar was January 4 on the Julian or "Old Style" calendar. Whereas most of central Europe's Roman Catholic nations had adopted the new calendar by the end of the sixteenth century, Protestant nations resisted for some 100 years, the first changes occurring around 1600 as Scotland made the conversion. Most of Eastern Europe converted in the early 1920s with Bulgaria converting in 1916. Turkey converted in 1926.

By 1752, when England adopted the Gregorian calendar, the difference between the two calendars had increased to 11 days, and an event from Glastonbury helped to establish the terms "Christmas Old Style" and "Christmas New Style." For years, that community had traditionally gathered on Christmas Eve to witness the annual blooming of the Glastonbury Thorn, said plant allegedly having sprung from the staff of Joseph of Arimathea. When the thorn failed to bloom on Christmas Eve, 1752, by the new calendar, many citizens refused to observe Christmas until it bloomed 11 days later on January 4 by the old calendar; this latter Christmas was dubbed "Christmas Old Style" or "Old Christmas," with the earlier date termed "Christmas New Style" or "New Christmas." For some 200 years, rural England observed "Christmas Old Style" on January 5 (January 6 after 1800). By the end of the twentieth century, the lapse had increased to 13 days.

Most countries following the Eastern Orthodox faith adhere to the Julian calendar for ecclesiastical events but have adopted the Gregorian calendar for civil purposes. With 13 days' difference in the twentieth century between the two calendars, Eastern Orthodox Christmas is observed on January 7, "Christmas Old Style." Most Armenian Orthodox churches follow the Gregorian calendar but still observe Christmas on January 6. The exception is the Armenian Church in Jerusalem, which adheres to January 6 by the Julian calendar. Accordingly, their Christmas corresponds to January 19 on the Gregorian calendar.

See also **Armenia; Epiphany; Glastonbury Thorn.**

Christmas Oratorio

(*Weihnachtsoratorium*, BWV 248). Musical work for chorus, soloists, and orchestra, written in 1734 by the German composer J.S. Bach (1685–1750). The work actually comprises six independent cantatas corresponding to the six feast days of Christmas observed between Christmas Day and Epiphany. With a total of 64 individual numbers, the *Christmas Oratorio*

premiered during Christmastide, 1734–35, while Bach was cantor of the Thomasschule in Leipzig. Today, the cantatas are more commonly performed together as one work.

Instead of composing entirely new music for the *Christmas Oratorio*, Bach in part employed parodies (new text set to previously composed music) of several of his earlier works. These were primarily derived from three secular cantatas: *Lasst uns sorgen, lasst uns wachen: Herkules auf dem Scheidewege* (*Let Us Tend Him, Let Us Watch Him: Hercules at the Crossroads*, BWV 213), written for the eleventh birthday of Friedrich Christian, prince elector of Saxony (1733); *Tönet, ihr Pauken! Erschallet, Trompeten!* (*Sound, Ye Drums! Resound, Trumpets!* BWV 214), written for the birthday of Maria Josepha, princess elector of Saxony and queen of Poland (1733); and *Preise dein Glücke, gesegnetes Sachsen* (*Praise Now Thy Blessings, O Fortunate Saxon*, BWV 215), written for the first coronation anniversary of King Augustus III of Poland (1734). Bach thus felt that recycling this birthday and anniversary music for royal families was a perfect parallel in celebrating the Nativity of Christ, the King of Heaven. Selected choruses and arias from cantatas BWV 213 and 214 served as models for corresponding numbers in the first five cantatas of *Christmas Oratorio*, with supplementary numbers from cantata BWV 215. It is also believed that one chorus was borrowed from the now-lost *St. Mark Passion*. For the sixth cantata, Bach also adopted much of the music from one of his church cantatas (the original text has been lost), known only as BWV 248a. The chorales for the oratorio included Bach's harmonizations of popular church tunes from the sixteenth and seventeenth centuries by such composers as Martin Luther, Paul Gerhardt, Johann Rist, and others. One of the best known of these chorales today is Luther's "Vom Himmel hoch, da komm' ich her" ("From Heaven Above to Earth I Come"), variations of which appear three times—as the closing chorale of part one and the musical setting for two chorales in part two. Another well known chorale appearing in part two is "Brich an, o schönes Morgenlicht" ("Break Forth, O Beauteous Heavenly Light") by Johann Rist and Johann Schop.

It is generally held that the librettist for the *Christmas Oratorio* was Christian Friedrich Henrici (pseudonym Picander), a poet skilled in parody texts, with whom Bach had frequently collaborated on earlier librettos, including the *St. Matthew Passion* and especially the *Hercules* cantata. The libretto, composed of passages from the Gospels, verses from the chorales, and text in free verse, includes numbers for only three specific characters: an "Evangelist," who principally sings the biblical passages; an "Angel," who sings the biblical annunciation to the shepherds from Luke 2; and "King Herod." The remaining numbers by soloists and chorus are contemplative and emphasize theological concepts.

The first cantata, part one, designated "For the First Day of Christmas" (Christmas Day), is based on Luke 2:1, 3–7 and focuses on the Nativity of Christ.

Part two, designated "For the Second Day of Christmas" (December 26, the Feast of St. Stephen), is based on Luke 2:8–14 and focuses on the Heavenly Host who announce the birth of Christ to the shepherds.

Part three, designated "For the Third Day of Christmas" (December 27, the Feast of St. John the Apostle and Evangelist), is based on Luke 2:15–20 and focuses on the shepherds' visit to the manger.

Part four, designated "For the Feast of the Circumcision" (celebrated at the time on January 1), is based on Luke 2:21 and focuses on the circumcision and naming of Jesus eight days after His birth.

Part five, designated "For the First Sunday in the New Year," is based on Matthew 2:1–6 and focuses on the Wise Men's search for Jesus.

Part six, designated "For the Feast of Epiphany" (January 6), is based on Matthew 2:7–12 and focuses on the meeting of King Herod with the Wise Men followed by the latter's visit to the manger.

See also **Break Forth, O Beauteous Heavenly Light; Epiphany; From Heaven Above to Earth I Come; New Year's Day; The Twelve Days of Christmas** (time period).

Christmas Orchid
See **Christmas Plants**

Christmas Pageant
See **Christmas Drama**

Christmas Pageant of Peace
See **United States** (The National Christmas Tree and the Christmas Pageant of Peace)

The Christmas Path
(1998). Motion picture fantasy/drama. This picture casts Santa in the unorthodox role of a heavenly being with power over angels.

Rebellious and cynical since his father's death, young Cal Banks (Shia LaBeouf) has unwittingly created a gap in the mystical path by which Santa (Bill Lucking) gains access to all people of Earth. Therefore to save Cal and ultimately Christmas itself, Santa hands this assignment to the problematic Christmas angel, Balthazar (Vincent Spano). His task becomes more difficult after he defies Santa and swipes a bag of magic angel dust, for which his powers are revoked until a time when he is deemed worthy to receive them again.

Back on Earth, Cal's adorable little sister Dora (Madylin Sweeten) is the epitome of the Christmas spirit, while their mother Jenny (Dee Wallace-Stone) struggles to make ends meet. At first, Balthazar's interactions with Jenny and her children are offhand and casual, until she receives an eviction notice, and Cal overreacts by breaking into a plush home. Yet it is not Cal whom the police find and arrest, but Balthazar, who had followed Cal to protect him. His powers now restored because of this selfless act, Balthazar makes a believer of Cal when his vision of Dora's imminent danger allows the youth to save his sister from being struck by a car.

The final moments of the picture recall scenes from *Miracle on 34th Street*, for Balthazar must prove that he is a Christmas angel and answer the charges of attempted burglary in a court of law. Now it is Cal's turn to reciprocate, for he confesses his guilt. But when the homeowner realizes that Cal's father had died while saving her own grandson from a car crash, she drops all charges, and the gap in the Christmas path is closed.

Produced by Ami Artzi. Written, produced, and directed by Bernard Salzman. Amco Entertainment in association with

Dream Vision Entertainment III. An Ami Artzi and Darren Leverenz Production. DVD: Good Times Home Video. 95 min.

Christmas Pie

Also known as mince pie and mincemeat pie. This dish originated in medieval England following the Crusades, when returning knights introduced eastern spices into their land. Along with the spices, the ingredients included minced bits of meat from a host of game birds and other hunted animals, apples, raisins, sugar, suet, and molasses.

Mice pies were popular at elaborate court banquets of the Middle Ages, which often featured excessively bountiful tables. Probably the largest mince pie of that era was described as measuring nine feet in diameter, weighing 165 pounds, and containing two bushels of flour, 20 pounds of butter, four geese, two rabbits, four ducks, two woodcocks, six snipes, four partridges, two bovine tongues, two curlews, six pigeons, and seven blackbirds.

It was fashionable at Christmastime to bake a mince pie in the form of a manger topped with an image of the Christ Child fashioned from dough, for the spices and sweetmeats were held as symbols of the Magi's gifts. The Puritans, not only in England but also in the American colonies, strenuously objected to

Illustrator Dan Beard drew "Ghosts from a Christmas Pie" for the December 18, 1888, issue of Harper's Young People. *It warns of the effects of eating too much Christmas pie on a little boy. Nursery rhyme characters, including Bo Peep and Jack and Jill, visit the boy's dream, along with Mother Goose and Santa.*

Printed label for a jar of minced pie meat. Monroe's Patnet, dated October 12, 1869, was for the meat not the container.

these pies and outlawed them under the Commonwealth of Oliver Cromwell, because they considered such images to be idolatrous abominations linked with Roman Catholicism. This sentiment eventually contributed to the modification of mince pies to circular forms divested of any religious ties.

It is said that when anti-Catholic King Henry VIII commenced phasing out England's monasteries in 1532 and seizing their properties, Richard Whiting, the abbot of Glastonbury Abbey, secretly attempted to curb the king's greed by sending him a Christmas pie wherein were hidden the deeds to several of the abbey's choicest estates. Whiting sent his gift via his servant, a Thomas Horner, who allegedly opened the pie and stole one or more of the deeds for himself. Horner's theft was

A collectible Christmas cover mailed from Santa Claus, Indiana, and postmarked December 25, 1948.

immortalized in the well known children's nursery rhyme "Little Jack Horner," which altered Horner's first name and in which the extracted "plum" represented the stolen deed. Despite Whiting's efforts, Henry VIII hanged him in 1539 for treason and added Glastonbury Abbey to his conquests.

Christmas Place Names

A number of cities or regions throughout the United States and its possessions are named for the Christmas season. The most frequently occurring name is "Bethlehem" or a variant thereof, which is found in 20 states: Connecticut, Florida, Georgia, Illinois, Indiana, Iowa, Kentucky, Maryland, Mississippi, Missouri, New Hampshire, New Jersey, New York, North Carolina, Ohio, Pennsylvania, Tennessee, Texas, West Virginia, and Virginia (Bethlehem Fork).

"Christmas" is the second most frequently occurring name, found in ten states: Alabama (Christmas Landing), Arizona, Florida, Maine (Christmas Cove), Michigan, Minnesota (Christmas Lake in Scott County), Mississippi, Oregon (Christmas Valley), Tennessee, and Utah (Christmas City). The citizens of Christmas, Florida, keep a community Christmas tree decorated the year round.

"St. Nicholas" identifies cities in Florida, Michigan, Minnesota, and Pennsylvania; "Santa Claus" is found in Georgia and Indiana; "Santa" is located in Idaho. Santa Claus, Indiana, originally acquired the name of "Santaclause" on Christmas Eve, 1882, but changed it to its present form in 1928. The city sports a Santa Claus theme park with a 23-foot statue of the saint, and children may write to Santa at

his "summer home" there and receive a personal reply.

Only one village in a United States possession bears a Christmas-related name: Bethlehem Old Work, Virgin Islands.

Christmas Plants

There are several plants that either incorporate "Christmas" into their common names, posses legendary holiday significance, or bloom at Christmastime. Major plants such as mistletoe and poinsettia are discussed as separate entries. Holly and ivy are discussed with the carol "The Holly and the Ivy."

• CHRISTMAS BELL. Two species native to Australia. *Blandifordia grandiflora* is a tufted plant with grasslike leaves and flower spikes having some ten bell-like flowers that vary from yellow to red with yellow tips. *Blandifordia nobilis* is similar but smaller; the flowers are cylindrical and always red with yellow tips.

• CHRISTMAS BERRY (*Heteromeles arbutifolia*). Toyon, an evergreen, rosaceous shrub or tree reaching six to eight feet in height, form-

*An engraving of a Christmas Rose (*Helleborus niger*) from a nineteenth century botanical.*

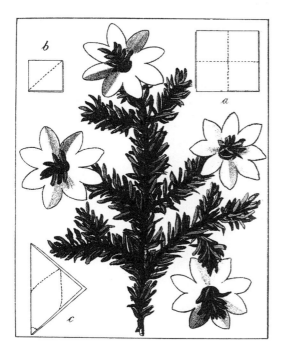

Another type of "Christmas Rose": This 1910 German craft how-to shows "Christrosen" blooms made of cut folded paper, then stuck on a rosemary sprig. From Berta Wegner-Bell, Herzblättchens Beitvertreib *(Berlin: Fleming, 1910).*

The evergreen lavender plant is said to have been used by Mary to scent the Christ Child's clothes. From an unidentified late nineteenth century herbal.

ing a round crown with clusters of small, white flowers in terminal clusters, bright red berries, and elliptical leaves with finely dentate borders. Native to California and northern Mexico. Also known as California Holly.

• CHRISTMAS BUSH. Three species native to Australia. *Prostanthera lasianthos* exists as a shrub or small tree with green, fragrant foliage and small white, pink, or mauve flowers arranged in clusters. *Ceratopetalum gummiferum* is a shrub with light green, trifoliolate leaves and lancelike, tooth leaflets. Terminal sprays of white, stellate flowers yield red, swollen calyces. *Bursaria spinosa* is a thorny shrub with dark green, obovate, shiny leaves and masses of white flowers yielding brown fruits.

• CHRISTMAS CACTUS (*Schlumbergera brigesii*). Also known as crab cactus, a Central American and Brazilian true cactus blooming in December with flat, segmented stems rounded and scalloped at the margins. The flowers at the extremes of the stems are pic-

turesque in shades of red, white, and orange.

• CHRISTMAS FERN (*Polystichum acrostichoides*). A clump-forming evergreen native to North America, growing two to four feet in height with variable spread and with fine leaves.

• CHRISTMAS FLOWER (*Helleborus viridis*). Green hellebore, a Eurasian perennial evergreen, the yellow flowers of which contain five large, petallike sepals and eight to ten inconspicuous, tubular petals, blooming in late winter or early spring.

• CHRISTMAS ORCHID (*Calanthe triplicata*). An evergreen terrestrial orchid with soft, obovate leaves and white flowers on a spike. Native to Australia.

• CHRISTMAS ROSE (*Helleborus niger*). Black hellebore, also a Eurasian perennial evergreen. Bears large, white flowers in midwinter to early spring. Used as an ancient medicinal agent, including purgative, local anesthetic, abortive, and as a treatment for madness and heart ailments (the plant possesses several digitalis-like substances). It is also the subject of Christian and pagan legends. According to a Christmas legend, Madalon, a little shepherd girl, tended her flock as the three Wise Men passed by on their way to Bethlehem with gifts for the Christ Child. Desiring to present a gift but too poor to do so, Madalon wept, whereupon an angel appeared and brushed away the snow from the ground. Revealed was a beautiful white, pink-tipped flower, the Christmas rose, which Madalon carried to Bethlehem. In another version, the angel revealed only solid white flowers. Madalon gathered them for the Christ Child, and where He touched them, there remained small tips of pink. Other legends during the Middle Ages held that a powder made from the plant would make magicians invisible. *See also* **The Legend of the Christmas Rose.**

• DESERT CHRISTMAS CACTUS (*Opuntia leptocaulis*). A bush growing three to six feet high with numerous tangled, reddish, spiny branches and quarter-inch stems. A long spine up to two inches in length grows from each cluster of bristles. Flowers of greenish-yellow bloom up to one inch wide on the stems in the late spring, while bright red, one-half-inch-long rounded fruits remain during the winter. Native to the desert American Southwest and northern Mexico.

• LAUREL (Bay, *Laurus nobilis*, not to be confused with the unrelated mountain laurel). A large evergreen shrub growing to heights of 25 to 60 feet, with small, yellow flowers in clusters and broad, aromatic leaves and black berries, native to the Mediterranean region. Its leaves are primarily used for seasoning in cooking; its oil is an essence of perfumes and a topical medicinal. Its connection to Christmas derives from pre-Christian times, when, as the symbol of victory, crowns and wreaths of laurel were bestowed upon heroes and poets. During winter solstice festivals, such wreaths decorated statues of gods such as Apollo, to whom laurel was sacred. When Christmas Christianized pagan traditions, laurel symbolized the victory of Christ over death and evil.

• LAVENDER (*Lavandula angustifolia*). The common variant is a Mediterranean, evergreen shrub of the mint family with narrow leaves and small, pale purple flowers. Its aromatic oil is used in the manufacture of perfume, toilet water, aromatic vinegar, and clothes sachets. According to legend, the Virgin Mary dried the Christ Child's garments by spreading them on a bed of common lavender, which supposedly thus acquired its sweet scent.

• PENNYROYAL (*Mentha pulegium*). A perennial herb of the mint family, which yields an aromatic oil used in potpourri, cosmetics, and insect repellents. Native to southern Europe and western Asia, it produces clusters of small, purple flowers. According to legend, the manger was lined in part with pennyroyal, which bloomed at the very hour that Christ was born.

• ROSEMARY (*Rosmarinus officinalis*). An aromatic, evergreen shrub of the mint family, the linear leaves of which yield an oil used in seasoning, liniments, and perfumes. The common name derives from the Virgin Mary. Native to the Mediterranean region, rosemary produces small blue flowers in the spring. During the Middle Ages, because rosemary supposedly repelled evil spirits, it was spread on the floor at Christmastime, the aroma pervading the home as people walked on it. According to folklore, anyone breathing its fragrance on Christmas Eve would receive happiness during the coming year. The aroma and blue flowers are the subject of legend, that during the Holy Family's flight into Egypt, when Mary washed the Christ Child's garments and spread them on a rosemary branch to dry, the flowers, initially white, turned blue (the traditional color associated with the Virgin) and became aromatic. A variation states that Mary's blue cloak imparted the color to the flowers when she hung it on a rosemary branch. Another legend holds that on January 5, "Christmas Eve Old Style," rosemary blooms out of season for Christmas. *See also* **Christmas Old Style, Christmas New Style.**

• WESTERN AUSTRALIAN CHRISTMAS TREE (*Nuystia floribunda*). Considered to be both a Christmas tree and a mistletoe, this evergreen tree grows over 30 feet in height with clusters of golden orange flowers blooming in mid-summer. The plant is parasitic, drawing its nourishment from other tree roots. It is native to western Australia.

• WILD THYME (*Thymus serpyllum*). A ubiquitous shrub of the mint family. Its creeping stem produces many tuft-forming branches with low, dense, oval leaves and purple flowers arranged in whorls, united in a head. Now used as a seasoning and to add aroma to potpourri, its pungent oil once was used as an antiseptic and was burned as incense. According to legend, wild thyme formed the Virgin Mary's bedding when she gave birth to Jesus.

Christmas Play
See **Christmas Drama**

Christmas Present
See **A Christmas Carol** (Film and Television Versions)

The Christmas Quest
Novel by American author Richard Siddoway, published in 2002, a sequel to *The Christmas Wish* (1995).

The story continues as real estate executive Will Martin, now living in his home town, has set a goal to adopt his wife Renee's seven-year-old son Justin by Christmas. Although it's early in the year, Will feels compelled to seek the approval of Justin's father, Gary Carr, before he even broaches the subject with Renee and Justin. Yet Gary has supposedly been out of the country for several years, and efforts to locate him have been futile.

Despite the title, a series of subplots consume the vast majority of the book and appear to overshadow Will's original quest: his investment in a speculative land development project that, had it been unsuccessful, would have utterly ruined his firm; his naïve yet victorious battle for a seat in the state House of Representatives against a seasoned, political scoundrel; the frequent conflicts between his family's needs and those of his business; and the abiding love that conquers the initial inabilities of Will and Renee to communicate with each other.

Just before Christmas, Will learns that Gary Carr is deceased, and the predictable adoption of Justin on Christmas Eve adds to a joyous holiday. Yet only Will's attorney, David Jobb, knows the real truth about Gary and his selfless gift to Renee and Justin, which must forever remain bound by attorney-client privilege.

A former bishop in the Church of Jesus Christ of Latter-Day Saints, Richard Siddoway is a Utah State legislator and an educator in the Utah public school system.

See also **Christmas of the Cherry Snow; The Christmas Wish; Twelve Tales of Christmas.**

A Christmas Romance
(1994). Made-for-television drama, based on a novel of the same title by Maggie Davis.

Julia Stonecypher (Olivia Newton-John), a young, beautiful widow and mother of two little girls, faces a bleak Christmas on her mountain farm. Not only has she recently lost her job, but her husband's death two years ago has left her with a sizable mortgage on the property. In response to this and other stressful situations, she frequently utters the seasonal imprecation "Peace on earth, goodwill towards men" as an alternative to swearing. Complicating her holiday is Brian Harding (Gregory Harrison), the debonair vice-president of the bank that holds her mortgage, who recovers at her home from minor injuries sustained in a nearby road accident. Brian had arrived on December 23 to collect back payments from Julia, but his accident, coupled with a heavy blizzard, has forced him to remain as Julia's uninvited houseguest until after Christmas. Although Brian's lack of experience in the rugged outdoors initially irritates Deenie (Chloe Lattanzi), Julia's older child, to little Emily Rose (Stephanie Sawyer), Brian is the "Christmas Stranger" of folklore, for whom families traditionally set a vacant chair at the dinner table on Christmas Eve.

If Brian's arrival was initially an intrusion, his willingness to make an otherwise meager Christmas as bright as possible, his assistance in delivering a dying ewe of its lamb shortly after midnight on Christmas Eve, and his reassuring Deenie and Emily Rose that their father is indeed in heaven, all dispel such a notion. The ensuing days and the close quarters inevitably spawn a tender romance between the

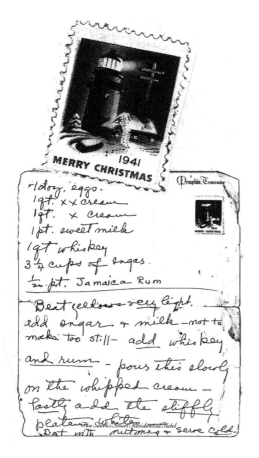

Affixed as decoration to a hastily scribbled recipe for eggnog is a 1941 Christmas Seal, showing a light-house in Maine and the double-barred Cross of Lorraine (not a telegraph pole, as some have supposed). Collection of Mary Mac & Robert D. Franklin.

widow and the banker, for Julia's plight and her simple mountain lifestyle prove to be irresistible circumstances that Brian cannot possibly leave behind.

Olivia Newton-John wrote and sang the picture's opening theme song, "The Way of Love." Teleplay by Darrah Cloud. Produced by Sheldon Larry, Joseph Plager, and Matthew O'Connor. Directed by Sheldon Larry. Dalrymple Productions in association with Steinhardt Baer Pictures Company. VHS: Bonneville Entertainment. 94 min.

Christmas Rose
See **Christmas Plants**

Christmas Seals

Decorative stamps issued each Christmas by various charitable organizations. These stamps encourage donations toward research in the fight against lung diseases.

Christmas Seals originated in Denmark in 1903 when postal worker Einar Holbøll, prompted by large numbers of children dying from tuberculosis (TB), initiated a fund-raising plan for building more TB sanitariums through the sale of special postage stamps, which received support from King Christian IX at the time. Called "Christmas Seals," the first of these stamps, bearing the likeness of King Christian's wife, Queen Louise, was marketed in 1904 at Christmastime. They were designed as added decorations for Christmas cards. The stamps sold at one-half cent each that first year, and over four million were sold.

Christmas Seals came to the United States in 1907 after Dr. Joseph Wales, a physician serving in a small TB sanitarium, appealed to Emily Bissell, his cousin and then–Delaware state secretary of the American Red Cross in Wilmington, for help in raising funds for his struggling institution. Made aware of the success of Christmas Seals in Denmark through an article written by Danish immigrant and New York City journalist Jacob Riis, Ms. Bissell

Left: Denmark issued the world's first Christmas Seals in 1904, shown here inscribed with "Julen" ("Christmas"), a likeness of Queen Louise, wife of King Christian IX, and the year on a purple background. Right: In 1907, the United States issued its first Christmas Seals, shown here inscribed with the American Red Cross emblem between a half-wreath of red holly and the greeting "Merry Christmas / Happy New Year" in red. Another set of the American Christmas Seals that same year simplified the greeting to "Merry Christmas." Collection of William D. Crump.

undertook the campaign by designing the first Christmas Seals in the United States: one set depicted a red cross centered in a half-wreath of red holly above the greeting "Merry Christmas" in red; a second set altered the greeting slightly to "Merry Christmas / Happy New Year." She had 50,000 seals printed on credit, and in December 1907, the first seals went on sale in the Wilmington post office with a notice of explanation that included, "These stamps do not carry any kind of mail, but any kind of mail will carry them." Initial sales were poor, however, whereupon Ms. Bissell convinced Philadelphia newspaperman Leigh Mitchell Hodges of *The North American* to support the campaign by running daily articles titled "Stamp Out Tuberculosis." This generated widespread public support, including an endorsement from President Theodore Roosevelt, and $3,000 was raised that season. By 1908, Christmas Seals were a national entity.

In 1910, the National Association for the Study and Prevention of Tuberculosis (now the American Lung Association) joined the Red Cross in sponsorship of Christmas Seals in the United States, then assumed full sponsorship in 1920. In 1919 the familiar Red Cross emblem coexisted with the double-barred cross, derived from the cross of Godfrey de Bouillon (1058–1100), duke of Lower Lorraine, first king of Jerusalem, and one of the leaders of the First Crusade. From 1920 on, Christmas Seals in the United States bore only the double-barred, Crusaders' cross.

In memory of Holbøll's contribution to mankind, his portrait appeared on the Danish seal in 1927, the year of his death. Currently, scores of countries have adopted the Christmas Seals campaign.

The Christmas Secret

(2000). Made-for-television fantasy, also known as *Flight of the Reindeer*, loosely based on the book *Flight of the Reindeer: The True Story of Santa Claus and His Christmas Mission* (1996) by Robert Sullivan, Glenn Wolff, and J. Porter. An innovative work of science fiction, the book sets out to prove, through "evidence" compiled from scientists, historians, and Arctic explorers, that Santa, his elves, and his team of flying reindeer actually do exist.

Dr. Jerry McNeil (Richard Thomas), a university zoologist intrigued with the concept of flying reindeer, jeopardizes his position and his marriage when he abandons research on flying squirrels to continue the research of one Salomon Andrèe. A nineteenth century scientist, Andrèe had vanished in the Arctic but had left a journal proving that reindeer could fly. Shortly before Christmas, Jerry feels compelled to document the phenomenon himself, whereupon he journeys to Prudhoe Bay, Alaska, and pilots a small aircraft from there toward the North Pole. Elated, Jerry witnesses a reindeer flying ahead of him, but his success is short lived when his plane crashes near the Pole for lack of fuel. He sustains only minor injuries and is reluctantly rescued by the sarcastic Morluv (John Franklin), Santa's chief assistant, who prefers the politically correct title of "Toy Controller" or "Christmas Engineer" over "elf." On the other hand, Santa (Beau Bridges), a youthful appearing man of 1,640 years, prefers to be addressed as "Nick."

Jerry finds himself a prisoner within Nick's gigantic North Pole Village; as one who cannot accept unusual phenomena on faith, he is considered an unbeliever (which explains why Nick has never visited Jerry's family at Christmastime) and will not be permitted to leave. From the beginning, Nick's gift-giving enterprise has operated in isolation for, as Jerry learns from Andrèe himself (now a believing "Helper" residing there), Nick was once a Viking who became the leader of the elfin clan after saving them and their flying reindeer from being captured by his own tribe. Always moving north to escape detection, Nick finally settled at the North Pole on an island of ice, his village completely shrouded in mist from the prying eyes of tourists. Until Nick's village became self-supporting, the elves had flown south on their reindeer and had "borrowed" (stolen) what they needed. To repay the debt, Nick decided to manufacture gifts and distribute them to the world on the most magical night of the year, Christmas Eve.

In addition to learning the North Pole's secrets of Christmas Eve, Jerry establishes a friendly rapport with Nick's two teenage children, who are fascinated with "Grace Tales," a simple game which Jerry had invented for Grace (Taylor-Anne Reid), his seven-year-old daughter. Sensing the togetherness that families might enjoy through such a game, the Claus children convert it into a video format for distribution, and Nick is so impressed that he allows Jerry to enter the forbidden Believers' Room. In this high-tech center that monitors the world's Christmas wishes in real time, Jerry observes Grace's unshakable faith in Santa Claus and her faith that her father is still alive. No longer desiring physical proof, Jerry becomes a true believer and may now depart, whereupon he accompanies Nick on his Christmas Eve rounds, lead by Rudolph. Dropped into a snowbank at Prudhoe Bay, Jerry is reunited with his wife Debbie (Maria Pitillo) and Grace, who had been searching for him.

The final scenes cut to Christmastime a year later. Now tenured and commended for his work on flying squirrels, Jerry teaches his students the lesson he learned from his own daughter: "The most improbable things can happen if you believe with all your heart." And for a surprise gift on Christmas morning, Jerry receives the photograph that he had taken with Nick and Morluv at the North Pole — proof that Nick had visited him after all.

On a historical note, the Salomon Andrèe mentioned in the story was a Norwegian explorer who perished while attempting to reach the North Pole by balloon in 1897.

Teleplay by Bruce Graham. Executive producer, Karen Moore. Directed by Ian Barry. Stratford-Zivic Productions in association with CBS Productions. VHS: Paramount Home Video. 100 min.

The Christmas Shoes

Emotionally packed, inspirational novel by American author Donna VanLiere, published in 2001 and the first book in her Christmas Hope series. Based on a popular song of the same title by Eddie Carswell and Leonard Ahlstrom. The story revolves around two families at opposite ends of the financial spectrum, each of whom must face a crisis during the holidays. The story also poses the premise that if people are receptive, God can use the smallest of items to change their lives, even a pair of shoes.

Robert Layton is a highly ambitious attorney, whose pursuit of wealth and success nearly destroys his marriage. Working 80-hour weeks, he has virtually become a stranger to his wife Kate and their two children, Hannah and Lily. Having felt neglected and abandoned for years, Kate announces shortly before Christmas that she desires a divorce, but for the sake of the girls, she will keep the marriage intact until after the holidays. That course would have been inevitable, had Robert not encountered eight-year-old Nathan Andrews at a department store checkout line on Christmas Eve. Harried with the thoughtless purchase of gifts at the last moment, Robert receives quite a shock when Nathan requests his help in purchasing a pair of silver shoes adorned with red, blue, and green rhinestones with bright sequins. His mother has been sick, says the boy, who further explains, "I want her to look beautiful when she meets Jesus." Robert is unaware that Maggie Andrews is terminally ill from ovarian cancer, yet Nathan's plea instantly alerts the attorney that the boy is about to lose his mother. Although Robert absently fulfills Nathan's request, the little boy's tragedy profoundly shakes Robert into realizing that no one has a greater gift than one's own family, and that no one can give a greater gift than being a loving member of that family.

The story contrasts the material riches of Robert's dysfunctional family with the meager lifestyle of Nathan's closely knit, strongly bonded, and intensely loving family, whose father, Jack, works as a mechanic. One parallel evident with both is that Robert's and Nathan's mothers both adore Christmas and have always strived to instill in their families the true meaning of the season apart from the glitter and presents. Other parallels are the joy evolving from pain and suffering: in one, an attorney becomes a loving husband and father once again to his estranged family; in another, a young mother, dressed in her silver shoes, steps into the waiting arms of her Lord during the wee hours of Christmas morning. She arrives knowing that she has thanked Him every day for her little girl Rachel, and that her greatest joy of her life was being Nathan's mother. She arrives, having prayed that the reason for her passing will always give Nathan peace and hope at Christmas.

In 2002 the novel was dramatized for television, starring Rob Lowe and Maria del Mar as Robert and Kate Layton, Hugh Thompson and Kimberly Williams as Jack and Maggie Andrews, and Max Morrow as Nathan. There, Maggie suffers from congestive heart failure, not cancer. In 2003, this production received Young Artist Award nominations: Best Family Television Movie and Best Leading Young Actor in a Television Movie (Max Morrow). Adapted by Wesley Bishop. Produced by Michael Mahoney. Directed by Andy Wolk. Beth Grossbard Productions and Craig Anderson Productions, Inc. Video N/A. 100 min.

Donna VanLiere is an actress and speaker. Her other works include *Sheltering Trees: The Power, Promise, and Refuge of Friendship* (2001), *They Walked with Him: Stories of Those Who Knew Him Best* (2001), and *The Christmas Blessing* (2003).

See also **The Christmas Blessing**.

The Christmas Song

Popular American song written in 1946 by well known nightclub, radio, and television singer Mel Tormé ("The Velvet Fog") from Chicago and Robert Wells Levinson (known only by his first two names) from Washington State, a producer of nightclub acts, motion picture scores, and television specials.

The song originated when Robert Wells, watching his mother stuff a holiday turkey with chestnuts, was inspired to compile a list of everything that made the season joyful, in addition to roasting chestnuts: Jack Frost's nip, carols sung by a choir, the aroma of holiday cuisine, mistletoe, and wide-eyed children waiting for Santa's visit. Tormé created the melody, and his 1946 recording was successful, although it did not make the pop charts.

The song, also known by its first line, "Chestnuts Roasting on an Open Fire," did not achieve true fame until Nat "King" Cole's recording on the Capitol label was released that same year, selling at least one million copies. Through his rendition, now a perennial classic, Cole became the first African American to introduce an American Christmas standard. Consistently charted into the 1980s, Cole's recording hit the number one spot on the *Billboard Special Christmas Singles* chart in 1963,

1969, and 1972. A later recording by Herb Alpert on the A & M label became the top Christmas song for 1968 (position one on the *Billboard Special Christmas Singles* chart).

Of the 25 most frequently performed Christmas songs of the twentieth century listed by the American Society of Composers, Authors and Publishers (ASCAP), "The Christmas Song" ranked number three. By December 2004 it had risen to number one.

See also **ASCAP List of Christmas Songs**.

Christmas Stamps

In 1898, the British Empire allowed those countries within its realm to opt into an Imperial penny postal rate (two cents) if they so chose, and Canada moved to be effective on Christmas Day. To commemorate the event that season, on December 7, Canada issued the world's first Christmas stamp, which depicted a map of the world as drawn in 1569 by the Flemish cartographer Gerhardus Mercator (1512–1594), inscribed with "Xmas 1898." Canada did not produce a regular run of Christmas stamps until 1964, however.

Since 1898, a number of countries around the world have adopted the custom of printing special postage stamps for the holidays, many with elaborate designs or reproductions of classic works of Christmas art. Austria followed in 1937 with two Christmas stamps, one with a Christmas rose, the other with zodiac signs. Next was Brazil in 1939 with four stamps: Three Kings and the Star, Angel and Child, Southern Cross and Child, and Madonna and Child. Hungary produced a "Soldier's Christ-

A triptych of Greek Christmas stamps from 1974 shows the Holy Family's flight into Egypt in color on a gold background.

mas" stamp in 1941 during World War II. Other countries with early Christmas stamps include Cuba with "Poinsettia" and "Bells" (1951); and Haiti with "Fort Nativity" and "Star of Bethlehem" (1954). The 1950s also saw Christmas issues from Spain, Australia, Korea, Luxembourg, Liechtenstein, and the Vatican. Great Britain first produced Christmas "aerogrammes" in 1965, then followed with a Christmas theme on its postage stamps in 1966. The

Three very colorful British Christmas stamps from 1969. All show a gold silhouette of Queen Elizabeth II. They have stylized depictions of three shepherds, a sheep, and the Star of Bethlehem; the three Magi in richly embroidered robes; and an angel bearing a star disk.

United States Postal Service (USPS) issued its first Christmas stamp in 1962, and from 1966 has issued a "traditional" (often religious) line depicting a classic work of Christmas art with the caption "Christmas." Its "contemporary" (secular) line, often with captions such as "Season's Greetings," "Greetings," "Merry Christmas," and sometimes "Christmas," dates from 1962.

The following list briefly describes the images found on those Christmas stamps issued by the USPS from 1962 to 2004 with their denominations.

1962 (4 cents). Two lighted candles beside an evergreen wreath with red bow. Caption: "Christmas 1962" in white letters on red background.

1963 (5 cents). National Christmas tree with White House in background. Caption: "Christmas 1963" in white letters.

1964 (5 cents). Four stamps, each depicting a different holiday plant in green and red: holly, mistletoe, poinsettia, sprig of conifer. No holiday caption.

1965 (5 cents). Angel in green and gold blowing trumpet. Caption: "Christmas."

1966 (5 cents). First traditional holiday stamp, reproducing the painting *Madonna and Child* by Flemish painter Hans Memling. Caption: "Christmas."

1967 (5 cents). *Madonna and Child* by Hans Memling. Caption: "Christmas."

1968 (6 cents). Detail of the angel Gabriel from *The Annunciation* by Flemish painter Jan Van Eyck. Caption: "Christmas."

1969 (6 cents). Winter Sunday outdoor scene in Norway, Maine. Caption: "Christmas."

1970 (6 cents). Five stamps: *The Nativity* by Italian painter Lorenzo Lotto; the other four each depict a different antique toy: tin and cast-iron locomotive, horse on wheels, mechanical tricycle, doll carriage. Caption on all stamps: "Christmas."

1971 (8 cents). Two stamps: *Adoration of the Shepherds* by Italian painter Giorgione with top caption "Christmas" and bottom caption "Giorgione ca. 1478–1510, National Gallery of Art"; a partridge in a pear tree on green background with caption in red letters: "On the first day of Christmas my true love sent to me."

1972 (8 cents). Two stamps: detail of angels from *Mary, Queen of Heaven* by the Flemish painter known as the Master of the St. Lucy Legend, captioned with "Master of St. Lucy Legend, National Gallery of Art" and "Christmas"; Santa Claus with horn on white background, green border, captioned "'Twas the Night before Christmas."

1973 (8 cents). Two stamps: small *Cowper Madonna and Child* by Italian painter Raphael, captioned with his name, "National Gallery of Art," and "Christmas"; a Christmas tree in colorful needlepoint, captioned "Christmas."

1974 (10 cents). Three stamps: detail of angel from *Perussis Altarpiece*, captioned "Altarpiece, Metropolitan Museum" and "Christmas"; *The Road–Winter* by Currier and Ives, captioned with "Currier and Ives" and "Christmas"; detail of dove weather vane in green atop George Washington's home, Mount Vernon, white background, captioned "Peace on Earth" and "Christmas."

1975 (10 cents). Two stamps: *Madonna and Child* by Italian painter Domenico Ghirlandaio, captioned with his last name, "National Gallery," and "Christmas"; 1878 Christmas card designed by Louis Prang showing a cherub suspended from a holly-clad bell, captioned with "Early Card by Louis Prang" and "Merry Christmas!"

1976 (13 cents). Two stamps: *Nativity* by American painter John Singleton Copley, captioned with his last name and "Christmas"; *Winter Pastime* by Nathaniel Currier, captioned with the painting's title along with "Lithograph by N. Currier" and "Christmas."

1977 (13 cents). Two stamps: George Washington kneeling in prayer on white background, captioned with "Valley Forge" and "Christmas"; open, red rural mailbox stuffed with holiday packages, captioned with "Christmas."

1978 (15 cents). Two stamps: *Madonna and Child with Cherubim* by Italian sculptor Andrea della Robbia, captioned with artist's name, "National Gallery," and "Christmas"; child on white hobby horse with Christmas trees behind on red background, captioned with "Christmas."

1979 (15 cents). Two stamps: *Virgin and Child with Cherubim* by Dutch painter Gerard David, captioned with artist's name, "National Gallery," and "Christmas"; Santa Claus Christmas tree ornament on purple background, captioned with "Christmas."

1980 (15 cents). Two stamps: *Madonna and Child* from the Epiphany window of Washington Cathedral, captioned with "Christmas"; evergreen wreath hung on window with window sill displaying toy top, horn, and drum, captioned with "Season's Greetings."

1981 (20 cents). Two stamps: *Madonna and Child* by Italian painter Botticelli, captioned with his name, "Art Institute of Chicago," and "Christmas"; felt bear on sleigh, orange background, captioned with "Season's Greetings."

1982 (20 cents). Five stamps: *Madonna and Child* by Italian painter Tiepolo, captioned with his name, "National Gallery of Art," and "Christmas"; four different scenes of children sledding, building a snowman, ice skating, and trimming an outdoor Christmas tree (these latter four all captioned with "Season's Greetings"). A sixth, 13-cent stamp depicted a puppy and kitten lying together in the snow without holiday caption.

1983 (20 cents). Three stamps: *Niccolini-Cowper Madonna and Child* by Raphael, captioned with "Raphael, 1483–1983, National Gallery" (marking the 500th anniversary of his birth) and "Christmas"; Santa Claus captioned with "Season's Greetings"; portrait of Martin Luther, German priest and composer of Christmas carols, captioned with "Martin Luther" and "1483–1983" (marking the 500th anniversary of his birth).

1984 (20 cents). Two stamps: *Madonna and Child* by Italian painter Fra Filippo Lippi, captioned with his name, "National Gallery," and "Christmas"; child's drawing of Santa Claus, captioned with "Season's Greetings."

1985 (22 cents). Two stamps: *Genoa Madonna and Child* by Italian sculptor Luca della Robbia, captioned with his name, "Detroit Institute of Arts," and "Christmas"; poinsettias captioned with "Season's Greetings."

1986 (22 cents). Two stamps: *Madonna and Child* by Italian painter Perugino, captioned with his name, "National Gallery," and "Christmas"; drawing of village with falling snow, captioned with "Greetings."

1987 (22 cents). Two stamps: *Madonna and Child* by Italian painter Giovanni Battista Moroni, captioned with his last name, "National Gallery," and "Christmas"; ball Christmas tree ornaments amid fir branches, captioned with "Greetings."

1988 (25 cents). Two stamps: *Madonna and Child* by Botticelli, captioned with his name, "National Gallery," and "Christmas"; one-horse open sleigh with village snow scene, captioned with "Greetings."

1989 (25 cents). Two stamps: *Madonna and Child* by Italian painter Carracci, captioned with his name, "National Gallery," and "Christmas"; sleigh laden with presents on white background, captioned with "Greetings."

1990 (25 cents). Two stamps: *Madonna and Child* by Sicilian painter Antonello, captioned with his name, "National Gallery," and "Christmas"; drawing of white Christmas tree decorated with green garland and colored ornaments on red background, captioned with "Greetings."

1991 (29 cents). Six stamps: *Madonna and Child* by Italian painter Antoniazzo Romano, captioned with "Antoniazzo c. 1480 Houston Museum" and "Christmas 1991"; five figures of Santa: sliding down chimney, checking list, leaving a gift under the tree, going up the chimney, and flying in sleigh, all captioned with "1991 Christmas."

1992 (29 cents). Five stamps: *Madonna and Child* by Italian painter Giovanni Bellini, captioned with "Bellini c. 1490 National Gallery" and "Christmas"; the remaining four stamps each depict an antique toy on white background, all captioned with "Greetings": horse and rider on wheels, steam locomotive, fire engine, and steam boat.

1993 (29 cents). Five stamps: *Madonna and Child in a Landscape* by Italian painter Giovanni Battista Cima da Conegliano, captioned with "Giovanni Battista Cima c. 1497 North Carolina Museum of Art" and "Christmas"; the remaining four stamps consist of cartoon drawings, each captioned with "Greetings": jack-in-the-box, red-nosed reindeer, snowman, and toy soldier.

1994 (29 cents). Four stamps: *Madonna and Child* by Italian painter Elisabetta Sirani, captioned with "Elisabetta Sirani, 1663,

National Museum of Women in the Arts" and "Christmas"; the remaining three stamps consist of cartoon drawings, each captioned with "Greetings": Santa holding a present, stocking filled with gifts, and cardinal in a tree amid falling snow.

1995 (32 cents). Seven stamps: *Madonna and Child* by Italian painter Giotto di Bondone, captioned with "Giotto, National Gallery of Art"; two children on a sled, midnight angel designed by American postcard artist Ellen H. Clapsdale (1865–1934), Santa Claus entering chimney, Santa Claus working on a sled, child holding a jumping jack, and child holding a tiny Christmas tree. No holiday captions on latter six stamps.

1996 (32 cents). Seven stamps: Detail of Madonna and Child from *Adoration of the Shepherds* by Italian painter Paolo de Matteis, captioned with his name, "1996 Va. Mus. of Fine Arts," and "Christmas"; "Hanukkah" stamp showing cartoon drawing of menorah with multicolored candles; cartoon drawing of ice skaters; four stamp cartoons depicting family scenes: sitting before fireplace, mother and daughter carrying wrapped gifts, father lifting child to place star atop Christmas tree, and girl dreaming of Santa's descent into chimney. Secular cards are without holiday captions.

1997 (32 cents). Three stamps: *Madonna and Child with Saints and Angels* by Italian painter Sano di Pietro, captioned with his name, "National Gallery of Art 1997," and "Christmas"; "Kwanzaa" stamp featuring stylized figures in African dress with the symbols of Kwanzaa; sprig of holly, captioned with "1997 American holly."

1998 (32 cents). Five stamps: *Florentine Madonna and Child* terra cotta relief, captioned with "Florentine, 15th C. National Gallery 1998," and "Christmas"; the remaining four stamps depict four different designs of holiday wreaths, each captioned with "Greetings": Victorian, colonial, chili pepper, and tropical.

1999 (33 cents). Four stamps: Detail of *Madonna and Child* by Italian painter Bartolomeo Vivarini, captioned with "B. Vivarini National Gallery of Art 1999" and "Christmas"; stylized antique-gold, prancing deer set against one of four deeply colored backgrounds (red, blue, green, or purple), captioned with "Greetings"; previously issued "Hanukkah" and "Kwanzaa" stamps reprinted in 33-cent denominations.

2000 (33 cents). No new holiday stamps. All 1999 stamps reissued.

2001 (34 cents). Seven stamps: *Madonna and Child* by Italian painter Lorenzo Costa, captioned with "L. Costa Philadelphia Museum of Art 2001" and "Christmas"; four chromolithographic images of Santa Claus holding assorted toys (c. 1880s and c. 1915–1920) without holiday captions; 34-cent versions of the "Hanukkah" and "Kwanzaa" stamps.

2002 (37 cents). Seven stamps: *Madonna and Child* by Flemish painter Jan Gossaert, captioned with "J. Gossaert Art Institute of Chicago 2002" and "Christmas"; four different snowmen on red backgrounds; 37-cent versions of the "Hanukkah" and "Kwanzaa" stamps.

2003 (37 cents). Eleven stamps: Gossaert's *Madonna and Child*, four snowmen, "Hanukkah," and "Kwanzaa" stamps from previous year all reissued; four new Holiday Music Maker stamps without holiday captions depict two deer playing pan pipes and horn and two Santas playing horn and drum.

2004 (37 cents). Seven stamps: *Madonna and Child* by Italian painter Lorenzo Monaco, captioned with his name, "National Gallery of Art 2004," and "Christmas"; new design of "Hanukkah" stamp featuring a dreidel; new design of "Kwanzaa" stamp featuring row of seven stylized figures in flowing African dress; four different stamps depicting painted glass Santa ornaments nestled in tissue paper.

See also **Christmas Seals.**

Christmas Star
See **Star of Bethlehem**

A Christmas Story

(Animated cartoon, 1972). When little boy Timmy forgets to mail his letter to Santa, Gumdrop the mouse discovers it on Christmas Eve and sets out with Goober the family dog to intercept Santa and deliver the letter. Dodging alley cats and other obstacles, the two just manage to miss Santa at every turn. When a neighborhood animal relay also fails to locate Santa, the two dejected searchers return home, fear-

ing that Santa will overlook Timmy. But as they sleep by the Christmas tree, Santa finds the letter nearby and fills Timmy's wish list.

Principal voices: Daws Butler, Don Messick, Hal Smith, John Stephenson, Walter Tetley, Janet Waldo, Paul Winchell, Paul DeKorte, Randy Kemner, Stephen McAndrew, Susie McCune, and Judi Richards. Written by Ken Spears and Joe Ruby. Produced and directed by William Hanna and Joseph Barbera. Hanna-Barbera Productions. VHS: Warner Home Video. 30 min.

See also **Hanna-Barbera Christmas Cartoons.**

The Christmas Story (biblical account)
See **Nativity**

A Christmas Story

(Motion picture comedy, 1983). Popular film based on *In God We Trust, All Others Pay Cash*, a book by novelist and radio-television humorist Jean Shepherd.

Set in fictional Hohman, Indiana, in the mid-1940s, the film, narrated by Shepherd, takes most of its story from the chapter titled "Duel in the Snow, or Red Ryder Nails the Cleveland Street Kid." The story revolves around nine-year-old Ralphie Parker (Peter Billingsley), who has but one wish for Christmas, a "Red Ryder Carbine Action 200-Shot Range Model Air Rifle" (a BB gun). So strong is his wish that Ralphie lapses into daydreams. In the first, armed with the rifle, he rescues his family from Black Bart's gang.

Getting the gun may be a problem, however, because Mother (Melinda Dillon), his teacher Miss Shields (Tedde Moore), and even the demonic Santa (Jeff Gillen) at Higbee's Department Store are of one mind on that subject: "You'll shoot your eye out!" And the odds seem worse when Ralphie, extolling the virtues of owning a Red Ryder in a school theme titled "What I Want for Christmas," earns a miserable C+ (in his second dream, Miss Shields is so pleased with his theme that she writes A+ + + + *ad infinitum* as his class cheers hysterically).

In addition to Ralphie's BB gun obsession, the film presents a number of digressional anecdotes that include his friends, "Flick" (Scott Schwartz) and "Schwartz" (R.D. Robb), the latter of whom persuades Flick via a "triple-dog-dare" to stick his tongue to an icy school flagpole. Together, the three older boys and Ralphie's younger brother Randy (Ian Petrella) endure harassment from the typical schoolyard bully, yellow-eyed Scott Farcus (Zack Ward) and his "little toadie" sidekick Grover Dill (Yano Anaya), noted for his green teeth. But following the seemingly undeserved C+ on his theme, Ralphie is overcome with rage, pulverizes Farcus's face in the snow, and sends Dill scurrying.

Home life is a circus of sorts. Ralphie's father, the "Old Man" (Darren McGavin), frequently pits himself against either a belching furnace, raving and cursing all the while (viewers hear only wild gibberish), or against the foul-smelling hounds of his neighbors, the Bumpuses. His passion, newspaper sweepstakes, nets a "major award" in the "Great Characters in American Literature" contest, a hideous lamp shaped like a stripper's leg. And Randy, never willing to eat, must have maternal encouragement. Other memorable pre–Christmas scenes include Ralphie's bar-of-soap-in-the-mouth punishment for swearing (inducing the final "you'll-be-sorry" daydream of going blind from soap poisoning) and Ralphie's pursuit of a Little Orphan Annie decoder.

When Christmas arrives, although Ralphie looks for a BB gun, at first it seems he will be disappointed. But at last his wish comes true — and Ralphie almost shoots his eye out with the Red Ryder as a pellet ricochets and breaks his glasses.

Events rounding out the Christmas merriment include the Bumpus hounds raiding the kitchen and grabbing the turkey followed by an unsettling dinner at a Chinese restaurant, where waiters stumble over lyrics to "Deck the Halls" and serve roast duck with the head intact.

Shepherd and his wife, Leigh Brown, made cameo appearances in the film as a couple waiting in line to see the department store Santa.

Written by Jean Shepherd, Leigh Brown, and Bob Clark. Produced by René Dupont and Bob Clark. Directed by Bob Clark. Metro-Goldwyn-Mayer. DVD: Warner Home Video. 94 min.

In 1984, *A Christmas Story* won Genie Awards for Best Achievement in Direction and Best Original Screenplay. It received Genie nominations for Best Achievement in Cinematography, Costume Design, Film Editing, Overall Sound, Sound Editing, Best Motion Picture, and Best Performance by an Actress in a Supporting Role (Tedde Moore). The Writers' Guild of America nominated it for Best Comedy Adapted from Another Medium. In 1985, the picture received nominations for three Young Artist Awards: Best Family Motion Picture Musical or Comedy; Best Young Actor in a Motion Picture Musical, Comedy, Adventure or Drama (Peter Billingsley); and Best Supporting Young Actor in a Motion Picture (Ian Petrella).

Jean Shepherd, originally from Hammond, Indiana, appeared on radio for some 30 years as a humorous storyteller, using bits and pieces of his own life as subjects. His stories originally appeared in *Playboy*, where they often won awards for best humor stories of the year. Later he compiled these stories into several novels, including *Wanda Hickey's Night of Golden Memories and Other Disasters* (1971), *The Ferrari in the Bedroom* (1973), and *A Fistful of Fig Newtons* (1981).

Christmas Story (radio episode)
See **Gunsmoke**

Christmas Story (television episode)
See **The Andy Griffith Show**

The Christmas That Almost Wasn't

(1966). American-Italian children's fantasy motion picture.

In this story possessing undertones of *A Christmas Carol* and *It's a Wonderful Life*, mean-spirited, wealthy Phineas T. Prune (Rossano Brazzi) has purchased the North Pole, and Santa (Alberto Rabagliati) is now his tenant. Santa must surrender all of the toys in his workshop to Prune if the rent is not paid by midnight on Christmas Eve. Strapped for cash, Santa turns to an old friend, attorney Sam

Whipple (Paul Tripp), for help. Years before, a much younger Sam had written a letter to Santa, pledging to come to Santa's aid at any time.

Together, Sam and Santa appeal to Prune's memory of his own childhood Christmases, hoping that Prune will relent. Instead, he denies that he ever had a childhood and challenges Santa to prove otherwise. When Prune offers to cancel the rent if Santa promises never again to deliver presents to children on Christmas Eve, Santa opts to raise the cash rather than deprive children of their gifts.

With only a few weeks left before Christmas, Santa takes a job as the "Santa" for Prim's Department Store with Sam serving as custodian. Despite Prune's inept attempts to disrupt Santa's visits with children in the store, all seems well, until closing time on Christmas Eve. Prune strikes again, buying the department store from Prim (Sonny Fox) and firing Santa and Sam.

Seeing the two dejected souls walking the streets, a little boy recognizes Santa and, upon learning of his plight, summons thousands of children to yield their penny banks. The two men arrive back at the North Pole just at the stroke of midnight to foil an awaiting Prune with the rent. As his adversary departs, Santa takes off on his rounds, together with Sam and Mrs. Claus (Lilia Brazzi alternating with Lydia Brazzi), while elf foreman Jonathan (Mischa Auer) tosses on board a last-minute gift. The latter, marked for Prune himself and the last gift to be delivered, consists of a toy sailboat and a note from Jonathan, whom Santa had commissioned to find Prune's name in his record books. Unable to locate the name, Jonathan had found a lost postcard, which Prune as a boy had addressed to Santa, requesting a sailboat for Christmas. Santa's unintentional absence that year had embittered Prune toward children and Christmas ever since.

When Prune receives the sailboat, it melts his malignant feelings completely, and to strengthen Prune's good will, Santa, his wife, and Sam turn Prune's gloomy home into a shining showplace of Christmas cheer.

With John Karlsen, Ruth Enders (wife of Paul Tripp), and David Tripp (son of Paul Tripp). Written by Paul Tripp. Produced by Barry B. Yellen. Directed by Rossano Brazzi. Bambi Productions and Childhood Productions. DVD: Hen's Tooth Video. 94 min.

A Christmas They Never Forgot

See **Little House on the Prairie** (television series)

Christmas Time's A-Coming

American song written by Tex Logan in 1949. Having grown up savoring the sounds of Bill Monroe and the Blue Grass Boys in the 1940s, Tex Logan became proficient on the fiddle and played with various country music groups while working on a Ph.D. degree in electrical engineering at the Massachusetts Institute of Technology. Although he had never met Monroe, Logan wrote "Christmas Time's A-Coming" specifically with Monroe in mind and received his chance to pitch the tune in 1951. Logan's band, together with a number of big-name country artists, including Bill Monroe, had completed a concert in Baltimore during the fall of that year. Backstage, Logan played his song for Monroe, who agreed on the spot to record it (Decca label) in time for the 1951 Christmas sales, although it was not charted. According to liner notes for the Bill Monroe record collection *Bluegrass: 1950–1958*, Logan probably based "Christmas Time's A-Coming" on an earlier tune, "Christmas Time Will Soon Be Over," which an artist known as Fiddlin' John Carson had recorded in 1927. Both songs possessed similar melodies and lyric patterns.

A Christmas Tree

(1972). Cel-animated episode from the syndicated Rankin/Bass television series, *Festival of Family Classics*, which aired from 1972 to 1973. Each episode animated a classic story or folk tale and was introduced by Carl Banas, a Canadian broadcasting personality, with a short clip from the mid-portion of the program.

"A Christmas Tree" is an adaptation of "The Christmas Tree" and other Christmas short stories by Charles Dickens. The celebrated British author in animation takes brother and sister Peter and Mary on a holiday adventure as they relive Christmases of Dickens's youth, which includes a magical Christmas tree that grows up to the sky. The children must climb the tree to rescue the holiday from a giant.

Principal voices: Carl Banas, Len Birman, Bernard Cowan, Peg Dixon, Keith Hampshire, Peggi Loder, Donna Miller, Frank Perry, Henry Raymer, Billie Richards, Alfie Scopp, and Paul Soles. Produced and directed by Arthur Rankin, Jr., and Jules Bass. A Rankin/Bass Production in association with Mushi Studios. Video N/A. 30 min.

See also **Dickens, Charles, Christmas Stories of; Rankin/Bass Christmas Cartoons.**

Christmas Trees

Any one of a variety of genuine or artificial trees erected in homes or public places and decorated for the season. Although known throughout the world, the Christmas tree reigns as the chief physical symbol of Christmas primarily in northern Europe, the United States, Australia, and regions of Canada. In southern Europe, Latin America, and in other Spanish-speaking regions, the Nativity scene predominates.

• ORIGINS AND HISTORY. While the modern Christmas tree is a product of Germany, the origins for the custom are many and varied, taking root first with European pre-Christian

A rough adaptation of a late eighteenth century engraving by Joseph Kellner shows a German scene with a family admiring a Christbaum, *complete with fruit decorations, candles, and some sort of large, probably foil-paper stamped image of the Christ Child. From Clement A. Miles.* Christmas in Ritual and Tradition, Christian and Pagan. *(London: T. Fisher Unwin, 1912).*

conceptions that evergreen trees possessed magical powers because they remained green during the winter, when other trees shed their leaves. Across the Roman Empire at year-end festivals such as the Saturnalia and the January kalends, varieties of evergreen boughs adorned homes, temples, and public statuary. Streamers, ribbons, and images of the god Saturn adorned trees during the Saturnalia. At the winter solstice, pagan Germanic tribes erected fir trees in their homes and burned fir boughs to welcome the annual visit of a domestic goddess variously known as Hertha, Bertha, Berchta, or Perchta, who was believed to appear through the smoke bearing luck and blessings for the household. Regarded as symbols of longevity and eternal life for centuries prior to the Christian age, evergreens acquired a parallel symbolism with the feast of Christmas despite a futile campaign by the early Church to suppress their use as decorations (Tertullian, third century; Second Council of Braga, Portugal, sixth century). During the Middle Ages, evergreen trees factored into certain mystery plays performed on December 24, a day that had originally commemorated Adam and Eve on the early Church calendar. Such plays recalled the Fall of Man in the Garden of Eden; a "Paradise Tree," a fir tree decorated with apples, portrayed the Tree of Forbidden Fruit and served as the only prop for the plays.

Two legends further link the Christmas tree with Germany. The English missionary Winfrid, St. Boniface, while preaching to Germanic tribes in the eighth century, is said to have introduced the fir tree as a symbol of the Christ Child on Christmas Eve. Details and further elaboration upon this legend are found in the entry **The First Christmas: A Story of the Forest**, a classic short story written in 1897 by the American author Henry Van Dyke. According to another legend, a German woodcutter and his wife offered food and shelter for the night to a freezing, starving child, who manifested himself at dawn as the radiantly beautiful Christ Child. To reward their generosity, the Child planted a small fir tree nearby, which grew and bloomed annually at Christmastime. A third legend stated that when Christ was born at midnight in the dead of winter, all the trees of the world bloomed to glorify Him. This

A typical German tabletop tree, with candles and an angel on top, is shown in this vignette from a nineteenth century engraving of a wood-paneled German parlor. Note the little boy's flag with the crossed swords. From the German magazine Fliegende Blätter, *1890.*

legend is believed to have contributed significantly to the decorating of Christmas trees as imitations of those that allegedly bloomed two millennia ago.

The oldest evidence for decorated trees at Christmastime comes from Riga, Latvia (1510), and from Reval, Estonia (1514). Both instances occurred on Christmas Eve, with members of a local guild gathering at the market place, dancing around a fir tree adorned with paper roses, and then burning it. The first reports of German Christmas trees date to 1531 in Alsace, where undecorated trees were erected on tables because a local forest ordinance forbade cutting of firs more than four feet in height. An account from Strasbourg in 1605 first mentioned home-decorated firs adorned with paper roses (symbols of the Virgin), flat wafers (symbols of the Communion Host), apples, gilded candies, sugar candy, and pretzels. In some circles, names such as "sugar tree" or *Christbaum* (Christ Tree) respectively reflected the abundant sugar confections or religious symbols present. Children's gifts of small toys and trinkets were customarily placed among the branches, and the sweets remained on the tree until Epiphany, at which time the tree was dismantled, and the children were afforded the pleasure of devouring the sweets.

German trees were first illuminated with candles. A popular myth attributes the custom to Martin Luther (1483–1546), who supposedly incorporated candles to symbolize the abun-

Christbaumhalters, or stands — one a revolving windup music box — are seen in two ads from the November 29, 1885, issue of Fliegende Blätter, *published in Munich. The tripod stand could have supported a much larger tree.*

E. FERRETT & CO.

PHILADELPHIA:

1845.

The title page of Kriss Kringle's Christmas Tree, *published 1845. Kriss Kringle is hanging a jointed toy on one branch, and he clutches his doll in his other hand.*

dant stars that he had witnessed on a clear Christmas Eve. Before appearing on trees, however, candles adorned the related *Weihnacht-spyramide* (Christmas pyramid), a contemporary structure that featured fir boughs wrapped around a triangular wooden frame containing several shelves increasing in length from top to bottom and decorated with fruits, sweets, and small toys. Also known as a *Lichtstock* (light stick), the pyramid appeared in Germany about the same time as the use of evergreen trees; often the two coexisted in the same home, the pyramid sometimes hanging from the ceiling, the Christmas tree standing on a table. Documented use of candles on trees first appeared in southern Germany around 1660. Over the next two centuries, the German custom gained wide popularity and spread throughout northern Europe, the pyramid having migrated to Italy as the *ceppo* (log) long before it finally disappeared from Germany during the nineteenth century.

The Christmas Tree Book discusses another popular myth, that the Saxon-born Prince Albert, consort to England's Queen Victoria, erected a decorated tree at Windsor Castle in 1841 to celebrate the arrival of his firstborn son, thereby introducing the custom to Great Britain. In reality, the English royal family had been decorating Christmas trees since the beginning of the nineteenth century, Queen Charlotte having erected the first British Christmas tree in 1800 at Queen's Lodge, Windsor, Berkshire. Christmas trees achieved widespread appeal in Great Britain only after the publication in 1848 of a photograph of a tree at Windsor Castle decorated with expensive sweetmeats, candy, gilt gingerbread, and a winged angel for a tree topper. Charles Dickens provided an elaborate description of the British tree in "The Christmas Tree," a short story that appeared in 1850 in his weekly publication, *Household Words*. In addition to myriad candles, virtually every conceivable variety of sweets and toys hung on the branches.

Christmas trees first arrived in America in the form of pyramids brought over by members of the Moravian Church, German immigrants who established their first permanent settlement, Bethlehem, Pennsylvania, in 1747. It is sometimes said that Hessian troops first decorated trees during the American Revolution, but initial evidence documenting the use of decorated fir trees in this country dates only from the 1820s. Examples include a December 1821 entry from the diary of one Matthew Zahm of Lancaster County, Pennsylvania, and the so-called Kris Kringle Tree erected in one Pennsylvania-Dutch community in 1823. The latter was a table-size fir tree decorated with *matzebaum* (cakes of almond paste), *schnitz* (strings of dried apples), marzipan figures, assorted nuts, and other homemade ornaments fashioned from paper and cardboard. Although these trees very probably included candles, there were no reports of them until 1832, when Charles Follen, a German immigrant living in Boston, included candles on a tree decorated with toys and gilded egg half-shells filled with candy. The prohibitive cost of candles, however, prompted others to use simple wicks placed in nut half-shells filled with oil. Decorated trees were so novel that they led to public exhibitions to raise funds for charity and private exhibitions in homes that sold tickets for personal gain.

By the 1840s, the Christmas tree tradition in America had spread from a few principal cities in the Northeast to rural regions and farther west, thanks to German settlers, promotions from newspapers, and children's books such as *Kriss Kringle's Christmas Tree* (Philadelphia, 1845). The title page from the latter clearly depicts a table tree by the fireplace with an elfish, pipe-smoking Kriss Kringle arranging toys on its branches. In rural Pennsylvania, conservation-minded farmers stripped the needles from dried firs and wrapped cotton batting around the skeletons to simulate snow-covered trees that could be reused for several years. The bare branches of non-firs received similar treatment. Rural ornaments were typically simple: pastry, ribbons, candied fruit, nuts, colored paper chains, and strings of popcorn, cranberries, and raisins. In 1851, the Rev. Henry Schwan, a Lutheran pastor and German immigrant living in Cleveland, Ohio, created a furor by erecting the first Christmas tree in an American church; some of his congregation protested this "pagan throwback." By 1860, American Christmas trees had achieved ceiling height and stood on the floor rather than a table, as first depicted in a short story written by Lizzie McIntyre and published that year in *Godey's Lady's Book*, a women's magazine. (When trees were erected on floors, in time the gifts were transferred from the branches and placed beneath the tree.) At the turn of the twentieth century, only one in five families in the United States sported a Christmas tree; by 1930, the custom was almost universal.

• NEW PRODUCTS AND INNOVATIONS. The latter half of the nineteenth century brought a multitude of commercially produced ornaments, accessories, and other innovations, both foreign and domestic, that extended far into the twentieth century. The following chronological list summarizes the most noteworthy of these:

1851. Mark Carr, a logger from the Catskill Mountains with two ox sleds of balsam firs, establishes the first Christmas tree lot in New York City's Washington Market.

1870. First blown-glass balls (*Kugel*) are imported from Lauscha, Germany's chief glass manufacturing city.

1870–1900. Height of popularity for flat tin

These glass tree ornaments were advertised in a 1939 catalog, but they are fashioned to resemble blown glass balls from the 1880s. Though mostly silver, red, green and blue, some were painted in multicolors with floral designs. Some were offered in the shape of fruit or Santa or pine cones. The most unusual shown here is the silver bead biplane with colored wings 4½" × 4½". From the Shure Winner Catalog no. 132 *(Chicago: N. Shure, 1939).*

ornaments, produced in Germany since the eighteenth century.

1870–1910. Height of popularity for wire ornaments imported from Germany.

1875. German wood-carvers first produce a large variety of ornaments shaped like miniature toys; though a fire hazard, celluloid toys become popular.

1876. Philadelphians Hermann Albrecht and Abram Mott receive the first two U.S. patents for a three-legged tree stand.

1878. "Icicles" first produced in Nuremberg, Germany.

1880s. Germany produces "angel hair" composed of spun glass.

1880s–1890s. Prime period when Eastern toy and variety stores import a wide assortment of blown-glass, decorative ornaments (fruit, animals, all imaginable shapes) from Germany. Other imports include silver, gilt paper, and cardboard ornaments; ornate cornucopias, doll-size baskets, and fine net bags for holding candy and nuts; and ornaments of cotton batting glued over a solid frame with chromolithographic images on paper.

1882. Edward Johnson, vice-president of the newly formed Edison Electric Company, demonstrates the first electric lights on a Christmas tree in his New York City home. Eighty blue, red, and white lights were individually wired to the tree by a professional electrician.

1890s. Germany produces rope garlands of tinsel; advent of metal hooks for ornaments (1892); Japan produces ornaments consisting of miniature lanterns, parasols, and fans.

1890s–1910. Prime period for the "Dresden ornaments," a large variety of ornaments from Dresden, Germany, consisting of three-dimensional silver- and gold-embossed cardboard.

1900. Germany produces papier-mâché figures; tree toppers consisting either of foil angels or long glass points; metal caps for glass ornaments with spring clips.

1900s. Outdoor tree lighting ceremonies first introduced in southern California in the early twentieth century.

1901. W. V. McGalliard establishes the first Christmas tree farm in New Jersey with 25,000 Norwegian spruce and markets them six to seven years later at one dollar per tree. (American poet Robert Frost also cites this price in his poem of 1916, "Christmas Trees.")

1903. The Ever-Ready Company of New York City produces the first strings of Christmas light sockets in series (if one light goes out, they all go out), called "festoons." The General Electric Company, having bought out Edison's company in 1890, sells these strings with their own lights (clear, identical to the standard light bulbs of the time with pointed tips) but changes to parallel wiring in 1927.

1908. The Paper Novelty Products Company in New York produces honeycombed, red paper bells as ornaments.

1909. Vienna, Austria, produces the first tree light bulbs in the shape of miniature figures, followed by General Electric with machine-blown glass light bulb figures in 1917. With the onset of World War I, Austria ceases to export bulbs to American retailers, who then import similar bulb figures from the Japanese. Japan exports to the United States until World War II, then resumes exporting in the 1950s.

1910. General Electric changes to colored, ball-shaped lights.

1912. Outdoor tree lighting ceremony on Christmas Eve in Madison Square Park, New York City, encourages citizens of Washington, D.C., to campaign for a similar ceremony at the Capitol.

1913. First National Community Christmas Tree lighting ceremony in Washington, D.C.

1918. United States manufactures its first ornaments, consisting only of round balls.

1920s. United States manufactures "icicles" using lead foil to prevent tarnishing but changes to a silver-mylar base in the 1960s to lessen chances for lead poisoning.

1920s–1930s. United States imports Czech, Japanese, and Polish ornaments.

1930s. The Paper Novelty Products Company produces red and green crushed crepe paper ropes and garlands.

1936. NOMA Lights introduces series-wired lights with colored, plastic lampshades affixed with decals of standard Walt Disney cartoon characters.

1938. The Paper Novelty Products Company produces the first hand-blown glass figures in the United States, consisting of Snow White and the Seven Dwarfs.

1939. Corning Glass turns out the first mass-produced glass ornaments in the United States. Max Eckardt's "Shiney Brite" company, originally in New Jersey, decorates the glass "blanks," which are then distributed by the F.W. Woolworth Company. Following World War II, Shiney Brite becomes the largest ornament company in the world, and Corning becomes the largest supplier of glass ornaments beginning in 1960.

1945. Carl Otis, an accountant for Montgomery Ward, invents "BubbleLights," which incorporate a colored solution of methylene chloride that boils with minimum heat. By the 1960s, only the F.W. Woolworth Company continues to market them.

1950s. Aluminum trees illuminated with floodlamps using a rotating, colored wheel become popular in the United States. Midget light sets imported from Europe and Japan supplant BubbleLights.

1970s. Lifelike artificial trees manufactured from polyvinyl chloride in Asia become popular, and twinkling "mini-lights" are developed, their negligible heat output providing a safer light source.

1973. Hallmark introduces six glass ball ornaments and 12 yarn figures as the first collection of Hallmark Keepsake Ornaments, unique in design and year-dated. Since that time, Hallmark has introduced more than 3,000 different Keepsake Ornaments and over 100 ornament series.

• VARIETIES OF CHRISTMAS TREES. Virtually any tree may be decorated as a Christmas tree, but in North America, the types most commonly chosen are pines, firs, and spruces, all noted for their conical shape. Whereas some people with free access to open timberland may cut their own trees each year, most purchase a tree either from a tree lot or a tree farm. According to the National Christmas Tree Association, the top-selling Christmas trees in the United States include the Scotch pine (number one), balsam fir, Douglas fir, Fraser fir, noble fir, Virginia pine (most popular in the South), and eastern white pine (largest pine in the United States). Other varieties around the world include the Arizona cypress, white fir, eastern red cedar, Canaan fir, grand fir, Leyland cypress (most popular in the Southeast), Colorado blue spruce, Norwegian spruce, and white spruce. Those with larger gaps between their branches, such as the balsam fir, Douglas fir, Fraser fir, and Virginia pine, are probably the easiest trees to decorate. Posing more difficulty is the Norwegian spruce with its drooping branches. Most of these varieties show good needle retention, except for the spruces, which shed their needles easily.

About 30 million real Christmas trees are sold in North America each year. According to industry statistics from the National Christmas Tree Association, Americans purchase 20–25 million real trees each year. In 2003, they purchased over 23 million real trees at a mean price of approximately $34 per tree, compared with nearly 10 million artificial trees purchased at a mean price of nearly $70 per tree. This reflects a 20 percent increase in the purchase of artificial trees since 2001.

Christmas tree farms in the United States currently number about 15,000 and require about one million acres for total production. A third of these farms allow individual buyers to select and cut their trees on site. Although real Christmas trees are grown throughout the United States, those states with the highest yields include Oregon (6.5 million), North Carolina (3 million), Washington, Michigan, Pennsylvania, and Wisconsin.

See also **Chrismons Tree; Jesse Tree.**

Christmas Trees

Poem written in 1916 by American poet Robert Frost. Describing the poem as a "Christmas circular letter," Frost pits nature and the holiday against commercialism. A New England farmer owns a large expanse of land on which grow numerous fir trees. As he admires nature's handiwork, likening his trees to "fir churches" with prominent spires pointing toward heaven, a city buyer offers to purchase all the fir trees on his property for a Christmas enterprise. Estimating a thousand trees, the city dweller offers 30 dollars for the lot (three cents per tree). With Christmas trees selling for one dollar apiece in the city at that time, the farmer, figuring that his trees are worth three cents more to give away than to sell at the offered price, wishes that he could send all his friends a tree enclosed in a letter to wish them a Merry Christmas.

Christmas Vacation

See **National Lampoon's Christmas Vacation**

The Christmas Visitor

(1987). Australian made-for television drama, also known as *Miracle Down Under*.

In 1891, the O'Day family faces Christmas on their sheep ranch in the outback amid poverty and summer drought. Only little Ned

O'Day (Andrew Ferguson) possesses any Christmas spirit, for he is sure that a grizzled stranger with a white beard lurking about is Father Christmas, the British equivalent of Santa Claus. In reality, the man is Max Bell (Charles Tingwell), former partner to now-wealthy landowner Trevor Watson (Bill Kerr). A fugitive from justice for 20 years for illegal horse trading, Bell has returned to claim his share of the profits from Watson. The latter, cynical and bitter following his wife's death years ago, welcomes the holidays by firing his three hired hands and denying water rights to his neighbor, Patrick O'Day (John Waters), Ned's father.

The O'Days' difficulties mount when Patrick, having hired Watson's former hands, strikes a well of salty water on Christmas Day, after which they successfully battle a grass fire, kindled from chimney sparks belched from Watson's Yule log. These disappointments, together with receiving no presents on Christmas morning, smother Ned's faith in Father Christmas. At this point, his mother Elizabeth (Dee Wallace-Stone) reminds him that Christmas is truly a time for giving, not receiving.

In the spirit of the season, Ned presents a bouquet of wild flowers to Watson, and the little boy's simple gift so touches him that not only does Watson restore the water rights, but he and his son Angus (Grant Piro), formerly at odds, are reconciled, and he also gladly restores Bell's share of the profits. Bell, in turn, after making restitution to a store he had robbed, arrives at the O'Day ranch with gifts for all, as would Father Christmas, and secretly plants a gold sovereign in each slice of plum pudding. On Christmas night, as the O'Days are making merry, Bell, having witnessed their happiness through the window, mockingly addresses the sky as he departs, with "Abracadabra!" To his great surprise, the heavens open with a welcome downpour, which ends the drought.

With Francis Bell and Nadine Garner. Written by Jeff Peck. Produced by Peter Beilby and Robert LeTet. Directed by George Miller. Entertainment Media. VHS title *Miracle Down Under* from Walt Disney Studios. 87 min.

The Christmas Waltz

American song written by Sammy Cahn (lyrics) and Jule Styne (music) in 1954 after singer Frank Sinatra asked them to write a Christmas song for him. Styne's habit before writing any music was to run through one particular pair of songs at the piano, a Viennese waltz and a tango. This gave Cahn the idea for Sinatra's song. By slowing down the waltz tempo and tacking on some light lyrics regarding candles, painted candy canes, Santa, and Christmas wishes, the two created "The Christmas Waltz." Sinatra's 1954 recording on the Capitol label failed to make the pop charts, however, and the song never achieved quite the popularity as had an earlier Cahn-Styne seasonal collaboration, "Let It Snow! Let It Snow! Let It Snow!" (1945).

Of the 25 most frequently performed Christmas songs of the twentieth century listed by the American Society of Composers, Authors and Publishers (ASCAP), "The Christmas Waltz" ranked number 22. By December 2004, it had fallen from the list.

Together or separately, Cahn and Styne produced numerous works in the popular music field. Cahn supplied the lyrics for such pieces as "Love and Marriage" (1955), "All the Way" (1957), and "High Hopes" (1959). Styne provided the musical scores for such Broadway productions as *Gentlemen Prefer Blondes* (1949), *Gypsy* (1959), and *Funny Girl* (1964).

See also **ASCAP List of Christmas Songs; Let It Snow! Let It Snow! Let It Snow!**

The Christmas Wife

(1988). Made-for-television drama based on a short story of the same title by Helen Norris.

Having lost his wife earlier in the year, retired architect John Tanner (Jason Robards) faces spending the holidays alone. In past years, he and his family had spent Christmas at their mountain cabin, but now his son Jim (James Eckhouse), daughter-in-law, and grandchildren live across the country in California. When Jim calls his father on Thanksgiving and offers to fly him to the West Coast for Christmas instead, John cannot break with tradition. Desiring to find a suitable female companion with whom to spend Christmas, he investigates a newspaper ad from "Alone Again, Inc.," an agency that arranges social engagements. Although the office is shabby and the "special agent" (Don Francks) is evasive, mysterious, and demands $500 for his services, John allows the agent to draw up a list of candidates for a platonic relationship. But during their second meeting in a hotel lobby, the agent, claiming that suitable choices are virtually nil, has arranged for John to meet only one woman, Iris (Julie Harris), who is just as evasive and mysterious. She and John agree to spend the Christmas weekend together at John's cabin, but Iris insists that John not seek to know anything about her and requests that he meet her at a bus depot on Christmas Eve.

By Christmas Day in the cabin, the two have become well acquainted, considering the circumstances, and John presents Iris with a music box that plays Beethoven's "Für Elise." His gift to himself (he tells Iris that she gave it to him) is a new bow tie. A walk in the woods before Christmas dinner brings them even closer together, and soon he is entertaining her with songs on his ukulele, while she delivers a poem, "One Perfect Rose," by Dorothy Parker.

On the day after Christmas, when John wishes for the relationship to grow, Iris, also most fond of John, breaks down and confesses that not only is she a married woman, but that her husband, the "special agent," put her up to the stunt because they needed the money. Without anger, John asks himself what was he trying to prove by running off with a strange woman. That he was not alone? Iris adds that perhaps he was trying to prove that, even though he had lost his wife, life wasn't over for him yet, and that he was really breaking a spell. Their parting is bittersweet, but they have given each other a beautiful Christmas.

With Patricia Hamilton, Deborah Grover, and David Gardner. Written by Katherine Ann Jones. Produced by Patrick Whitley. Directed by David Hugh Jones. An Edie Landau Production. DVD: UAV Corporation. 72 min.

The Christmas Wish

Inspirational novella with elements of a mystery, written by American author Richard Siddoway, published in 1995.

Following his grandfather's death, Will Martin takes a leave of absence from his Wall Street investment firm to return to his home town. Orphaned at the age of four, Will grew up in the home of his grandparents, Warren and Ruth Martin, and the upcoming holidays bring back cherished memories of beloved Christmas traditions that they shared long ago. The homecoming is bittersweet, however, for not only must Will wrestle with overhauling the family's outdated real estate company, which Warren had run for more than 50 years, but Ruth divulges an item from Warren's private journals that seemingly shatters her husband's pristine image. For 27 years on Christmas Eve, while Ruth and Will were out Christmas shopping, so claim the journals, Warren had visited a woman named Lillian, yet Ruth had known nothing of her until she read the name in the journals. Therefore, Ruth's only Christmas wish is that Will track down Lillian and learn what she had meant to Warren—mistress, child, or other.

With the journals providing leads, Will interviews various people in the area with whom Warren frequently had contact, such as current and former employees, a jeweler, a florist, the owner of a fishing camp two hours away, and the owner of a local Christmas tree farm. Though Will's persistence alienates him from Julia Welsch, his sophisticated, image-conscious girlfriend, he finds a kindred spirit and true love in Renee Carr, a dance instructor and divorced mother, who had once been Warren's secretary. At every turn, Will learns that his grandfather had deeply touched and influenced virtually everyone in town in some way or other with unmeasured kindness and generosity. No one knows this better than Enid Cook, the company's steadfastly loyal accountant. Years ago, when her family had incurred crushing medical bills, Enid, then a secretary, had misappropriated funds from the company, yet Warren had not only forgiven her for the crime, but had cleared her medical debt and promoted her to accountant. Warren had believed more in people than in protocol, which explained the company's unorthodox policies that had been in force.

With such a role model before him, Will becomes a changed man. Instead of implementing drastic changes in company policy, which would have included phenomenal rent hikes and evicting tenants who could not pay, he severs ties with his New York firm and steps into Warren's shoes as the beneficent grandson and new owner of Warren Real Estate.

Eventually Ruth, desiring to remember Warren more for the beautiful marriage they had together rather than for any past transgression, bids Will to abandon his search for Lillian. Yet Will must know the truth. Predictably on Christmas Eve, Will locates Lillian and escorts Ruth into her presence. Lillian's story, a heartwarming blend of love, tears, compassion, and forgiveness, is nothing like Ruth and Will could ever have imagined. It is a powerful Christmas gift that will remain in their hearts forever.

In 1998, the story was adapted for television, starring Neil Patrick Harris as Will, Debbie Reynolds as Ruth, Naomi Watts as Renee, Alexandra Wilson as Julia, and Beverly Archer as Enid. In 1999, the picture was nominated for a Golden Reel Award for Best Sound Editing. Television story by Beth Polson. Teleplay by Greg Taylor. Produced by Erica Fox. Directed by Ian Barry. Bonneville Worldwide Entertainment, Madison Avenue Productions, and the Polson Company. DVD: Fremantle Media. 95 min.

A former bishop in the Church of Jesus Christ of Latter-Day Saints, Richard Siddoway is a Utah State legislator and an educator in the Utah public school system.

See also **Christmas of the Cherry Snow; The Christmas Quest; Twelve Tales of Christmas.**

Christmas with the Kranks
See **Skipping Christmas**

A Christmas without Snow

(1980). Made-for-television drama.

Ms. Michael Learned stars as Zoe Jensen, a recently divorced schoolteacher who moves from Omaha, Nebraska, to San Francisco in the fall to begin a new life. While she settles in, her young son Robbie (Mathew Hautau) remains with her parents in Omaha.

Zoe joins a church choir, the new director of which is a most condescending and exacting Ephraim Adams (John Houseman), whose goal is to whip the ragtag choir into shape to perform Handel's *Messiah* at Christmastime. The story principally revolves around

this central theme, as Adams expertly handles trouble within the ranks, crushing the inflated ego of one new soprano while gently advising an older member that, because she sings off key, she must leave the choir. Several digressions include Zoe's unsuccessful attempt at a relationship with choir member Henry Quist (Ramon Bieri), the choir's Thanksgiving dinner aboard a boat owned by Mr. Wood (William Swetland), Robbie's unexpected arrival in San Francisco after having traveled across the country alone by bus to be with his mother, and the vandalizing of the church's pipe organ. The latter leads to a mistaken accusation by choir member Muriel Moore (Valerie Curtin) that Wendell Curtis (Calvin Levels), a black member, is the culprit, when the guilty party is in fact Terry Lohman (David Knell), the troubled teenage son of the church's pastor, Rev. Lohman (James Cromwell). While the versatile choir pitches in to restore the organ, the church temporarily acquires an electronic model, which frequently broadcasts police calls during services.

One week before the scheduled Christmas performance, Adams suffers a mild stroke. When Rev. Lohman suggests canceling the program, Zoe and the other members override him and persuade organist Seth Rubin (Ed Bogas) to take over for Adams. As Adams proudly watches from a wheelchair, the picture closes with the choir singing lengthy excerpts from the *Messiah*, the last number of which is the "Hallelujah Chorus," as the credits roll.

With Ruth Nelson, Beah Richards, Daisietta Kim, Joy Carlin, Anne Lawder, and Barbara Tarbuck. Written by John Korty, Richard Beban, and Judith Nielsen. Produced by John Korty and Whitney Green. Directed by John Korty. A Korty Films/Frank Konisberg Production. DVD: Diamond Entertainment. 100 min.

See also **Messiah**.

Church of the Nativity

Shrine in Bethlehem, Israel, built over a cave traditionally held to be the site of Christ's birth. It is the oldest church extant in the Holy Land. The construction began in the year 326 at the order of the Roman emperor Constantine the Great (ca. 274–337), whose mother, St.

Helena, had ascertained the particular site on a previous expedition to the Holy Land. The original church, which had replaced the Roman emperor Hadrian's (76–138) temple to the Greek god Adonis, was once rich with mosaics, frescoes, and marbles, and a silver manger had replaced that which had supposedly been fashioned from clay. The cave was encased by an octagonal structure forming the sanctuary of the basilica in the eastern section, and the nave to the west formed five aisles divided by four rows of monolithic columns. The church was destroyed during a Samaritan revolt in 529 but was rebuilt on the same site by the Byzantine emperor Justinian I (483–565). Persians invaded the church in 614 and would have destroyed it, had they not seen a mural depicting the Magi in Persian dress. Crusaders in the twelfth century built a cloister and monastery on the north side of the church, and between 1165 and 1169, further restorations by the Byzantine Empire and the Franks covered many of the walls and floors with marble, mosaics, and mother-of-pearl. The cedar roof was covered with lead. Originally the church had three western entrances. To deter radical and zealous groups from storming the church in the future, two entrances were walled up in the sixteenth century, and the third was reduced to a narrow opening four feet high, which forced all to enter single file and stooping. To capitalize on the emotions of pilgrims visiting the shrine today, local tour guides hold that the entrance was designed to have everyone stoop as an act of reverence. Thus the entrance has been dubbed "The Door of Humility."

Today the church appears as a fortress, encircled by the high walls of three convents: the Franciscan on the north, the Greek Orthodox and Armenian on the south. The rectangular basilica is 180 feet long, the nave 94 feet wide, the transept 120 feet. The nave and its five aisles

Top: *Church of the Nativity in Bethlehem, Palestine, c. 1898–1914, before the founding of the State of Israel. The church itself, rebuilt in the sixth century, is located at the end of the stone pavement and to the left. An Armenian monastery, dating from the Byzantine and Crusader eras, parallels the pavement on the right. Near the right-angle junction of the monastery and church is the tiny entrance to the church, known as the Door of Humility. Whereas the buildings with their fortress-like walls remain virtually unchanged today, the pavement area is now a narrow plaza. Courtesy Library of Congress.* Bottom: *Grotto of the Nativity, the cave beneath the Church of the Nativity in Bethlehem, c. 1898–1914. Featured is the Altar of the Nativity with the 14-pointed silver star in the floor marking the traditional site of Christ's birth. Note the 15 lamps immediately above. Over the altar is a row of icons, and the steps at the left lead up to the high altar. The setting remains virtually unchanged today. Courtesy Library of Congress.*

are divided by four rows of 20-foot columns of red limestone, 11 to a row, the white marble capitals of which are in Corinthian style and bear in the center of the abacus a rosette with an ornate Greek cross. Frescoes of the apostles and saints graced the columns during the Middle Ages and are all but faded now, and the walls show traces of mosaics depicting Christ's ancestors and the first seven Ecumenical Councils. The Armenian altar in the northern transept is known as the Altar of the Kings for there, by tradition, the Magi dismounted when they came to pay homage to the Christ Child. On the eastern end of the nave is the High Altar, over which is suspended a silver and gold chandelier.

From the High Altar on either side, stairs descend into the Grotto of the Nativity beneath, a 10-by-40-foot marbled chamber lighted by 53 lamps, divided among the Greek Orthodox, Roman Catholic, and Armenian churches that principally hold services there. The traditional site of the Nativity, the Altar of the Nativity in the Grotto, is marked with an inlaid, 14-pointed silver star and a Latin inscription, "Hic de Virgine Maria Iesus Christus natus est" ("Here of the Virgin Mary Jesus Christ was born"). Illuminating the star are 15 silver lamps, six of which belong to the Greeks, four to the Catholics, and five to the Armenians. The star and inscription were originally installed by the Catholics in 1717, removed by the Greeks in 1847, and replaced by the Turkish government in 1853. Within the Grotto of the Nativity are two other altars, the Altar of the Manger, where supposedly Christ was laid after His birth, and the Altar of the Adoration of the Magi. The Grotto walls are covered with fire-proof amianthus tapestries belonging to the Catholics, which depict salient facts about Jesus' childhood. From the Grotto, a locked passage leads to three other adjacent grottos or chapels: one commemorates St. Joseph, who by tradition on that site had the dream from God to flee into Egypt; another commemorates the Holy Innocents; the third is the tomb of St. Jerome (Eusebius Heironymus, c. 340–420), who was chiefly responsible for preparing the Latin Vulgate Bible.

Although the main body of the basilica (nave, aisles, choir and sanctuary, south transept, and Altar of the Nativity in the Grotto) is now in the possession of the Greek Orthodox Church, a dispute over its posses-

sion and other holy places in what was once Palestine (dominated at the time by the Turkish Ottoman Empire) began in the sixteenth century between the Orthodox and Roman Catholic churches. In December 1852, the Turkish sultan, responding to pressure from Catholic France, decided in favor of the Roman Catholics. This and other events such as the disappearance of the original star in the Grotto greatly contributed to the Crimean War (1853–1856), which brought Russia against Turkey, France, and Great Britain. In April 1873, armed Greek monks invaded the Grotto, ransacked the cave, and stole the marble slab that had covered the holy crib. Since then, the Grotto has remained under guard.

Today, the remainder of the shrine is divided between the Armenians, who control the north transept and its altar, and the Catholics, who control the Altar of the Adoration of the Magi as well as the silver star. Armenians and Catholics have rights of passage and procession in the nave.

See also **Middle East** (Israel); **Milk Grotto**.

Claymation Christmas Celebration

(1987). Made-for-television, 24-minute animated presentation featuring stop-motion, sculptured clay figures (Claymation) created by Will Vinton.

Dinosaur figures Rex and Herb host a series of carol renditions performed by Claymation characters. "We Three Kings" features a jazz refrain by three camels. In Notre Dame Cathedral, the hunchbacked character Quasimodo conducts a group of bells that knock their own heads with hammers to play "Carol of the Bells." "O Christmas Tree" depicts variously decorated trees in Santa's workshop. To the strains of "Angels We Have Heard on High," walruses and penguins ice skate in the Arctic. "Joy to the World" is performed in African American spiritual style, and the California Raisins swing to "Rudolph, the Red-Nosed Reindeer." Several characters have difficulty with the word "wassailing," pronouncing it "waffling," "waddling," or "wallowing," but eventually everyone sings "Here We Come A-Wassailing" correctly.

In 1988, this program won an Emmy Award for Outstanding Animated Program.

Principal voices: Tim Conner and Johnny Counterfit. Written by Ralph Liddle. Produced by David Altschul. Directed by Will Vinton. Will Vinton Productions. DVD: Hen's Tooth Video. Also contains *Claymation Halloween Celebration* and *Claymation Easter Celebration*. Total time: 71 min.

Columbia
See **South America**

Come, All Ye Shepherds
See **Angels and Shepherds**

Come, Dear Children
See **Alfred Burt Carols**

Come, Redeemer of the Nations
See **Savior of the Nations, Come**

Come, Thou Redeemer of the Earth
See **Savior of the Nations, Come**

Come, Thou Savior of Our Race
See **Savior of the Nations, Come**

Come to the Stable
(1949). Motion picture drama.

Determined to fulfill a vow made to God for saving their children's hospital in France during World War II, two nuns from the Order of Holy Endeavor, Sister Margaret (Loretta Young) and Sister Scholastica (Celeste Holm), arrive in the little village of Bethlehem, Connecticut, with plans to build a children's hospital. They believe that God has led them to this locale because of a picture postcard in their possession that depicts *Come to the Stable*, a Nativity painting by the artist Amelia Potts (Elsa Lanchester), who not only resides in Bethlehem but whose studio was once a stable. Lodging with Amelia, the sisters further determine that a hillside nearby will be the site for their hospital dedicated to St. Jude, the patron saint of hopeless causes.

The sisters manifest such undaunted faith, gentleness, and innocence, that all obstacles barring their goal at first seem to melt away, such that their doubting, practical-minded bishop (Basil Ruysdael) remarks that an irresistible Force has been unleashed in New England. Even New York City racketeer Luigi Rossi (Thomas Gomez), who owns the desired property in Bethlehem but who initially refuses to sell, reconsiders and deeds the land as a gift upon the sisters' heartfelt expression of sympathy over the loss of his son in France.

Adversity strikes when the sisters mistakenly sign a large mortgage for additional property. Given three months to raise the cash lest the bishop order them to return to France, the sisters rally their French cohorts and turn Amelia's studio into a factory for making various crafts to sell. The commotion accompanying these activities upsets Bob Mason (Hugh Marlowe), a reclusive neighbor and songwriter, who opposes building a hospital so close by. Yet it is he who purchases the property when the sisters fail to make payment. Perhaps his reason was simply to prevent the establishment of a foul-smelling fertilizer plant on the site; perhaps instead it eased his feelings of guilt after friends discovered that his latest hit song, conceived on a battlefield in Normandy, closely resembled a Gregorian chant sung by the sisters. Needless to say, Bob now has the key that will seal or break the sisters' plight; but given the cause at hand, Bob eventually yields to that guiding, irresistible Force.

In 1950, the picture received the following Academy Award nominations: Best Actress in a Leading Role (Loretta Young), Best Actress in a Supporting Role (Celeste Holm and Elsa Lanchester), Best Black-and-White Art Direction/Set Decoration, Best Black-and-White Cinematography, Best Original Song ("Through a Long and Sleepless Night" by Alfred Newman and Mack Gordon), and Best Writing of a Motion Picture Story. It received nominations for a Golden Globe Award for Best Motion Picture Drama and from the Writers' Guild of America for Best Written American Comedy.

Story by Clare Booth Luce. Screenplay by Sally Benson and Oscar Millard. Produced by Samuel G. Engel. Directed by Henry Koster. Twentieth Century Fox Film Corporation. VHS: Fox Video. B & W. 95 min.

Come, You Shepherds
See **Angels and Shepherds**

Cosmic Christmas

Inspirational novella written by American author Max Lucado, published in 1997; repackaged and published in 2002 under the title *An Angel's Story*. Going beyond the biblical accounts of the Nativity, the book presents the Christmas story from the perspective of celestial events that transpired when Jesus Christ was born. Two principal factors prompted Lucado to write the book: the concept of war in heaven, as presented in Revelation 12:7–9, and a short story by David Lambert entitled "Earthward, Earthward, Messenger Bright," which appeared in the December 1982 issue of *Moody Monthly*.

Commissioned by God to carry the seed of the Holy Spirit to the maiden Mary on earth, the messenger angel Gabriel and the heavenly host must overcome the dark forces of Lucifer, also known as Satan and the Devil, who will stop at nothing to prevent Gabriel's mission and the birth of Immanuel, "God with us." Once an angel of Light and having rebelled against God, the wily deceiver Lucifer has been reduced to a foul, hideous, skeletal figure shrouded in black.

Four times he and his demons attempt to destroy Gabriel's army, first by ensnaring them in an invisible net in the cosmos. Yet the angels escape by shouting words of praise to God, which break the bonds. Next, they encounter the demon Phlumar, a giant dragon who announces that he and Lucifer will repent and return to God. Knowing the lie, Gabriel bids the dragon first to confess the name of God and worship Him. Because he cannot, the heavenly host cast Phlumar into the Abyss. Twice defeated, Lucifer himself, disguised as a brilliantly handsome angel of Light, confronts Gabriel on earth and claims that the past encounters had just been a test of Gabriel's loyalty, which God had prearranged with Lucifer; therefore, Gabriel's mission is finished. The deceiver is most convincing, and Gabriel and his troops would have yielded, had the angel Sophio not kept his eyes on God and prayed for deliverance. The final battle occurs on the road to Bethlehem as Gabriel, disguised as a Jewish Rabbi, shields Mary from a hoard of demons. But the greatest miracle of all is a command from the unborn Jesus, which prevents the ox

cart in which Mary rides from plunging off a cliff during the demonic assault.

Witnessing the Nativity, the angels ponder the irony of their Master Incarnate as a tiny baby, knowing that within a few years, He will suffer and die for the sins of the world. More ironic still, He has already commanded them not to interfere at that time. "What manner of love is this?" marvels Michael the archangel, who closes the story by leading the heavenly host in praise of, "Glory to God in the highest."

Max Lucado is a minister and the daily speaker for the radio program *UpWords*. His other Christmas books include *Alabaster's Song* (1996), *The Crippled Lamb* (1994), *The Christmas Cross* (1998), and *Jacob's Gift* (1998), all of which are discussed as separate entries.

Costa Rica
See **Central America**

Cotton Bowl
See **New Year's Day**

The Coventry Carol

Name applied to a carol originating from the Pageant of the Shearmen and Tailors (two trade guilds sponsoring the pageant), one in a cycle of medieval mystery plays that was annually performed in Coventry, England, on the Feast of Corpus Christi (originally observed on the Thursday after Trinity Sunday, established in 1264 by Pope Urban IV). In this particular pageant, which depicted the birth of Christ from the angel's annunciation to Mary to the Slaughter of the Innocents by King Herod, three male voices, portraying women bereft of their children in Bethlehem (males commonly assumed female roles in plays at that time), sang what is now known as "The Coventry Carol," a chilling dirge in response to the massacre. It is sometimes known by its opening words in the medieval English vernacular, "Lully, lulla[y], thow littel tyne child" ("Lullaby, lullaby, thou little tiny child").

Where in Coventry the pageant was held is a matter of minor controversy. According to some sources, carts with actors dramatizing various scenes rolled through the streets; other sources say that all the drama transpired on the steps of Coventry Cathedral itself.

The anonymous Coventry Plays are believed to date from 1392, although the oldest known manuscript of dialogue dates from 1534, copied by Robert Croo. Initially the pageant songs were handed down in folk fashion, but in 1591, Thomas Mawdycke added them to Croo's manuscript. In 1879, a fire consumed this manuscript, which had resided in a library in Birmingham, England, but two songs from the manuscript could be salvaged from other engravings: "The Coventry Carol" and "The Coventry Shepherds' Carol," both from the Shearmen-Tailors pageant.

There were two principal parts to the Shearmen-Tailors play: "The Coventry Shepherds' Carol" ended part one, which included the angel's annunciations to Mary and the shepherds plus the Nativity. "The Coventry Carol" was the climax of the second half, which included the Wise Men's visit, the Holy Family's flight into Egypt, and Herod's raid on Bethlehem. In the modern repertoire of best-known Christmas music, few carols address as dark an issue as does "The Coventry Carol."

In 1935, the folk music collector John Jacob Niles, best known for the carol "I Wonder As I Wander," published a carol with wording almost identical to that of "The Coventry Carol" but with a different tune. Titled "Lullay, Thou Tiny Little Child," this carol appeared in his *Ten Christmas Carols from the Southern Appalachian Mountains*. Although Niles claimed to have heard "Lullay" at an Old Timers' Day festival in Gatlinburg, Tennessee, in 1934, it has yet to be identified elsewhere, which leads one to speculate that Niles created the variant carol himself.

See also **Christmas Drama; I Wonder As I Wander.**

The Coventry Shepherds' Carol

See **The Coventry Carol**

Crackers

See **Great Britain**

The Cricket on the Hearth

See **Dickens, Charles, Christmas Stories of**

The Crippled Lamb

Inspirational children's book, written by American author Max Lucado with his three young daughters, Jenna, Andrea, and Sara, published in 1994. More than just a simple Christmas tale, the story carries a clear message of hope and peace.

Joshua the little lamb is different from all the other lambs, not only because is he an orphan, but because he is also spotted black and white and is crippled. Although his inability to run and play with his peers is a source of deep depression, his only friend, old Abigail the cow, assures him time and again that, "God has a special place for those who feel left out." As the flock prepares to move to another pasture, Joshua's shepherd bids him to spend the night in the stable instead, because his gait is too slow, and he reluctantly settles down with Abigail. Awakening to disturbances during the night, Joshua discovers the presence of a mother with her crying baby. Because there are no blankets, he lies beside the child in the hay and offers the warmth of his wool. Through a conversation heard between the mother and her husband, Joshua learns that he has befriended a young King, Jesus, the Son of God. At that moment, the shepherds return to the stable, having received the angelic message of Christ's birth, and then Joshua realizes that, had he been a normal lamb, he would not have been in the stable to serve the Christ Child. Although Joshua had been left out, he rejoices that God had a plan for him.

In 2000, the book was adapted for television as an animated cartoon under the title *The Christmas Lamb*, featuring the voices of Robbie Benson, Jesse Corti, Jeannie Elias, and Mark Hamill. The production was also nominated that same year for a Golden Reel Award for Best Sound Editing. Adapted, produced, and directed by Rob Loos and George Taweel. The Learning Channel. VHS title: *The Crippled Lamb* from Thomas Nelson Publishers. 26 min.

Max Lucado is a minister and the daily speaker for the radio program *UpWords*. His other Christmas books include *Alabaster's Song* (1996), *The Christmas Cross* (1998), *Cosmic Christmas* (1997), and *Jacob's Gift* (1998), all of which are discussed as separate entries.

Croatia

Soviet Communists dominated this former constituent republic of Yugoslavia and other nations in eastern Europe from the end of World War II until 1991, after which Soviet troops withdrew, and Croatia gained her independence from Yugoslavia in 1991. During the approximately 50 years of Communism's atheistic regime, Christmas was repudiated, the midwinter holiday was moved to New Year's Day with a secular agenda, and the St. Nicholas or Baby Jesus figure who had brought children's gifts was replaced by a Soviet "Santa" known as "Grandfather Frost" (*see* **Russia**). Communism nearly extinguished the old holiday customs, yet a number of them still survive, primarily in rural areas; these customs revolve around agrarian rituals and repelling evil. The principal Christian faith in Croatia now is Roman Catholicism.

The Christmas season extends from Advent to Epiphany and officially commences with St. Barbara's Day (December 4). Wheat seeds are traditionally sown in plates either on this day or on St. Lucia's Day (December 13) and should germinate by Christmas Eve, when the green wheat becomes a centerpiece for the Christmas Eve table; alternatively, it is placed beneath the Christmas tree, for the wheat is a symbol of the renewal of life. In the mid–nineteenth century, St. Nicholas's Day (December 6) was observed along with St. Lucia's Day in such northern cities as Osijek, where the saint brought apples and walnuts (denoting plenty and blessing) to deserving children. His accomplices varied among regions, from Luca the Hag (deriving from "Lucia"), to the fur-clad, chain-rattling Krampus, to a devil with an angel. Today, St. Nicholas brings gifts in northern and central Croatia, while it is St. Lucia in the southern and northeastern regions (*see* **Advent** [St. Lucia's Day]; **St. Nicholas's Day**).

Christmas decorations include holly; ivy; branches from an oak, maple, or evergreen tree; and the Christmas tree, the latter having arrived in Croatia around the mid-1800s from central Europe. The evergreen branches are often fashioned into wreaths hung in a cluster above the Christmas table and variously garnished with ornaments, which may include apples, walnuts, flowers, and chains and lanterns made from paper and straw. Depending on the locale, this decoration is known as a *kinč, ojić, vojić, božić*, or *cimer*. Sometimes a simple cluster of red apples (symbols of bounty and plenty, red offering protection against evil) is suspended above the table. Christmas trees, formerly decorated with homemade ornaments, may now include those commercially made. According to strict tradition, these decorations are put up only on Christmas Eve.

A Nativity scene, known as a *Betlehem* or *Jeruzalem*, often resides beneath the Christmas tree at home, certainly in every church, and a group of statutes believed to be remnants of the oldest Croatian Nativity scene (sixteenth century) reside in a Franciscan monastery on the island of Krk (*see* **Nativity Scene**). Reliefs portraying such scenes as the Annunciation to the Virgin, the Nativity, and the Baptism in the River Jordan are found in the Church of the Holy Sunday in Zadar; these date to the eleventh century and are among the earliest renderings of the Christmas story in Croatia. The Advent wreath appeared around the turn of the twentieth century.

Although *Badnjak* ("to be awake"; the word refers to Christmas Vigil or Christmas Eve as well as the virtually extinct Yule log) is still a day devoted to the dead as ancient custom dictates, it is observed perhaps less today as a meatless fasting day steeped in ritual than before the Communist era. Nevertheless, traditionalists still prepare the table by placing straw (symbolic of the manger) beneath it and on it in the shape of a wreath or cross, covering the latter with a tablecloth, sprinkling grains on top, then covering with a second, decorative tablecloth. The centerpiece consists of several items: Christmas bread with a coin hidden inside, its top divided into quadrants by a cross of pastry, the four quadrants containing emblems of the four seasons of the year; a crucifix; a candle; a bowl containing representatives of all seeds sown on the farm; the green wheat sown earlier; and a personal object or a small tool. Farmers may place their plowshares or other tools under the table to receive a blessing.

Badnje jelo (Christmas Eve menu) traditionally consists of foods ordinarily associated with funeral feasts for the dead: hazelnuts, walnuts, almonds, honey, poppy seeds, garlic, apples, legumes, turnips, corn, pasta, cured cod and other fish, potatoes, and pumpkins. Thus, recalling ancient winter solstice customs, Christmas Eve commemorates not only the living but also the spirits of family ancestors and those living who otherwise cannot be present at this dinner, for it is customary for all able family members to attend. For those absent, vacant places are set, a candle or other light is kept burning all Christmas Eve night, and the leftover food remains on the table overnight for visiting spirits. The Christmas bread is displayed throughout the holidays, and it was once traditional for crumbs from the table to be saved and burned as incense for any family member who became ill in the new year.

At midnight, men still shoot firearms to herald Christmas, a throwback to ancient times when noise dispelled evil spirits at the winter solstice. After Midnight Mass, red apples exchanged beforehand between friends or sweethearts are thrown into wells as gifts to the water.

Christmas Day is spent with immediate family at home. The principal cuisine in northern regions usually consists of roasted goose or turkey, whereas the northeastern and southern regions feast upon pork or lamb; cakes and various liquors are universal.

Children no longer receive gifts from Grandfather Frost. Just before Christmas 1992, "Grandfather *Božićnjak*" appeared on the public scene, a weak invention of state television to replace the then-unpopular image of Communism's gift-giver. According to *Christmas in Croatia* by Dunja Rihtman-Auguštin, *Božićnjak* does not describe a specific being but instead refers to a decorated Christmas tree and formerly to a Christmas tax which bonded peasants once paid to landlords. In keeping with Roman Catholic tradition, therefore, the Croatian gift-giver is the Christ Child, Little Jesus, or more specifically His "messenger," depicted as a little girl with wings, crown, and who bears a small fir tree (*see* **Germany**, whence this concept arose). Gift-giving to children and exchanges among adults are more common today than previously.

Families visit relatives on St. Stephen's Day (December 26), and house-cleaning commences on St. John's Day (December 27), on which day the Christmas straw is tied to fruit trees as a talisman for fruitfulness. On Holy Innocents Day (December 28), bands of children parade about with willow branches and "flog" relatives and comrades, the act a symbolic wish for health and well-being.

New Year's Eve is filled with parties and noisemaking as men again shoot firearms at midnight, and this night, as well as Christmas Eve, is devoted to rituals predicting the future. An alternative name for New Year's Day in Croatia is "Little Christmas" or "Second Christmas," which derives from the combined celebrations of Christmas and New Year's Day observed in that part of the world from the fourth to the sixteenth centuries, after which the Gregorian calendar moved New Year's Day to January 1 (*see* **New Year's Day**).

On Epiphany eve, parishioners carry home water and salt blessed in church to be used as talismans against sickness and evil, and on Epiphany, the fields, homes, and other properties are anointed with blessed water. Groups of children may offer carols as they travel about with illuminated stars and mangers. Family members divide the aforementioned Christmas bread among themselves on this day, and the one finding the hidden coin will have good luck in the new year.

Christmastime well-wishers include the *polaznik* ("first guest"), who may appear on St. Barbara's Day, Christmas Day, or St. Stephen's Day. Tradition holds that a young man arriving as the first visitor at one's house on these days brings good luck, and he receives a gift from the household. *Kolede* (carol) processions, more often found in Croatia's Adriatic region, are usually held on Christmas Eve, Christmas Day, St. Stephen's Day, New Year's Eve, New Year's Day, and Epiphany. The *koledari* (carolers) consist of groups of young boys who go from house to house singing wishes for health and bounty with expectations for rewards. Failure to provide the latter invites curses upon the household through song. Related *zvjezdari* ("star processions") run from New Year's to Epiphany and consist of groups of three boys dressed as the Three Kings, one of whom carries an illuminated star on a pole.

Since the Communist era, a renewed air of

nationalism has pervaded the Croatian Christmas. For example, the Christmas candles now sport the red, white, and blue colors of the Croatian flag; Midnight Mass in Zagreb Cathedral has become a gathering of the political elite; and decorations in urban areas reflect not only the Christmas spirit but themes of power and the state.

Yet religious sentiment appears also to prevail. For example, many citizens now prefer to greet one another with more religious phrases such as *Čestit Božić* ("Holy Christmas") or *Blagoslovljen Božić* ("Blessed Christmas") over the former, more secular greeting of *Sretan Božić* ("Happy Christmas").

See also **Advent; Czech Republic; Epiphany; Poland; Slovak Republic; Ukraine.**

Cuba

See **West Indies**

Czech Republic

Czechs and Slovaks united in 1918 after World War I to form Czechoslovakia, which Soviet Communists dominated from the end of World War II until 1991, when Soviet troops withdrew. During the approximately 50 years of Communism's atheistic regime, Christmas was repudiated, the midwinter holiday was moved to New Year's Day with a secular agenda, and St. Nicholas or Baby Jesus, who had brought children's gifts, was replaced by a Soviet "Santa" known as "Grandfather Frost" (*see* **Russia**). Following the cessation of Soviet occupation, Czechoslovakia split into two independent nations, the Czech Republic and the Slovak Republic, on January 1, 1993. Communism had nearly extinguished the old holiday customs, yet a number of them still survive, primarily in rural areas, which revolve around agrarian rituals, romantic matchmaking, repelling evil, and forecasting the future. The principal Christian faith in the Czech Republic now is Roman Catholicism.

During the Advent season, homes and villages display the *Betlem* (Nativity scene), and collections of these may be found in regional museums such as the Museum of Nativities in Karlstejn near Prague. Here, one may view 25 antique wooden Nativities. First introduced in Prague in 1560 by Jesuit priests, the *Betlem* was the chief Christmas symbol until 1812, when the first Czech Christmas tree appeared in Prague. *Betlems*, constructed of paper, wood, or other substances, now consist of elaborate scenes and figures not only of the stable, Holy Family, shepherds, and Wise Men, but also of characters from local surroundings.

Other Advent customs include thoroughly cleaning the house, displaying window decorations of wreaths and lighted stars, mailing out Christmas cards (popular cards feature the work of Czech artist Josef Lada), attending a myriad of Christmas markets and cultural events, and baking a host of Christmas sweets, popular servings of which include Linzer cookies (formed into shapes such as bells, stars, and wheels, pasted together with jam) and vanilla rolls. Instead of writing letters to Santa Claus or St. Nicholas, children address their epistles to *Jezisek* (Baby Jesus), Who brings the Christmas gifts. Television programs feature an assortment of Czech fairy tales and fantasies.

Although Advent observances may include St. Andrew's Day (November 30), St. Barbara's Day (December 4), and St. Lucia's Day (December 13), the only custom still practiced from these three days is the expectation that cherry sprigs cut and placed in vases on December 4 will bloom by Christmas Eve, a positive sign for luck or seeking a mate. The Advent holiday now widely observed is *Mikulas* (St. Nicholas's Day), observed on December 6. Folklore holds that *Svaty Mikulas* (St. Nicholas) descends from heaven on a golden cord at this time and is accompanied by an angel, who distributes gifts to good children, along with the devil, formerly called "Cert," who rattles chains and brings switches or coal to naughty youngsters.

Festivities for *Mikulas* actually commence on St. Nicholas's Eve with parades. Groups of three people dressed as Bishop Nicholas, the angel, and the devil travel from house to house to quiz the children about their behavior and pass out treats, all for the purpose of giving the children a frightening thrill. Before retiring to bed, children place their shoes on the window sill and awaken to find them filled with an assortment of fruits, nuts, and candy.

Principal customs center around *Stedry Vecer* (Christmas Eve), the first of three con-

This frightening masked creature is an image of the devil who accompanies Mikulas, or St. Nicholas, on his day, December 6, seeking out good and bad children. Here, the saint, far right with a bishop's crozier, directs the devil, who is carrying a bag of gifts for good children. In this eighteenth century print, no angel seems to be present. From the journal Český Lid *(published in Prague), 1910.*

Two spicy Yule Dollies from the former Czechoslovakia. On the left is a Baby Cake, the image of the Christ Child in swaddling clothes, with a representation of what would have been a real sprig of rosemary, plain or gilded, stuck in after baking. Such Yule Dollies are common throughout the world for Christmas cakes or cookies; many were iced in brilliant colors. From the journal Český Lid *(published in Prague), 1898.*

secutive Christmas holidays. Because folklore holds that the spirits of one's ancestors are present with the living on Christmas Eve, on that date the oldest child places a lighted candle and a fir sprig on the graves of family members. The Christmas tree is decorated that afternoon. Formerly, the tree was suspended from a central, overhead beam, but most families now adhere to the Western trend of a tree on a floor stand. Although tree decorations in the Communist era usually consisted of glass ornaments and chocolate figures supplied to workers as Christmas "bonuses" by the state, many families today prefer more natural decorations, such as wax candles, red apples, walnuts, ginger-

bread, pine cones, and homemade ornaments of paper, straw, or wood.

Prior to the Communist regime, a host of ancient traditions and superstitions dominated Christmas Eve, especially regarding the Christmas Eve supper. Family members and relatives convened after having fasted all day, and children were told that if they kept the fast, they would see a golden pig on the wall that evening at the supper. Some believe that this fable originated from Freya, Norse goddess of love, beauty, and fertility, who was depicted as riding a golden boar and to whom Norsemen sacrificed a boar at their winter solstice festivals; others held that the golden pig simply symbolized wealth and abundance.

Because the events of Christmas Eve pre-

Two children and an angel carry a small crèche, perhaps to be placed on the table for the Holy Supper on Christmas Eve. From the journal Český Lid *(published in Prague), 1907.*

dicted the type of year to come, past grievances and quarrels were resolved, all objects previously borrowed were returned, and everyone behaved in their most genteel manner. The table was set with a white tablecloth, the legs adorned with garlands (a talisman against theft from the fields) and joined with iron chains (symbolic of family ties and a wish that the table bounty extend into the new year). The floor beneath the table received straw to symbolize the manger. At center table were found various emblems, such as a crucifix, bread (the staff of life), candles (symbolic of Jesus as the Light of the world), and garlic (charm of strength that repelled evil). An additional place was set for any unexpected guests, such as the Holy Family, and a candle placed in a window beckoned the stranger to dine.

All preparations completed, the head of the household dipped shocks of grain into holy water and sprinkled each room to sanctify the house. Children watched for the first star of the evening, believed to be the Star of Bethlehem, for the supper commenced at its appearance. For good luck an even number of diners had to be present. On the foreheads of everyone, the head of the household traced honey in the form of a cross to repel evil and bring a new year of health. Related customs consisted of eating a Christmas waffle laced with honey and garlic, or cutting a loaf of bread and dispensing a slice daubed with honey to each person at the table, beginning with the oldest. Slices remaining portended new birth(s) in the family, whereas insufficient slices signaled death during the coming year.

The menu consisted of 12 meatless courses in honor of Christ's 12 Apostles and featured assorted preparations of fish (symbolic of the Last Supper), *babalki* (small portions of baked dough topped with a mixture of crushed poppy seeds, sugar, and hot water), sauerkraut soup, peas garnished with sugar and gingerbread, dried fruit, *vanocka* (Christmas bread), nuts, candy, strudels, *kuba* (prepared from barley and mushrooms), and *kutia* (boiled wheat with honey, raisins, and nuts). Carp became a traditional dish only during the nineteenth century, and fish scales were placed under each plate to assure health and prosperity.

At some point during the meal, the head of the household tossed a spoonful of *babalki* or *kutia* up to the ceiling. If most of it stuck, the harvest would be bountiful. Reading auguries from such items as cracked walnuts and sliced apples then followed the meal. A rotten walnut portended illness or death; a star pattern seen in one's apple slice forecasted a long life, whereas a cross pattern predicted the opposite. (Other superstitions are discussed below.) During the meal, no one left the table, and at its conclusion, everyone rose in unison, for the first to rise was cursed to die during the coming year.

Today, families may elect to keep such strict traditions or follow a more contemporary menu of carp or breaded fish, potato salad, fish soup, sauerkraut soup, and *vanocka*. Afterwards, the children are escorted out and return only after Baby Jesus has rung a small bell, the signal that He has arranged their presents under the Christmas tree and has now departed the scene. The livestock receive the table leftovers, and the family sing *kolady* (Christmas carols) around the Christmas tree or watch television Christmas programs. Christmas Eve concludes with Midnight Mass, at which churches often feature the *Czech Midnight Mass*, written in 1796 by Czech organist and composer Jakub Jan Ryba (1765–1815). This work has become popular because it replaces the original Latin lyrics of the Roman Catholic Christmas Mass with Ryba's own version of Christ's birth and is patterned after folk Christmas prayers.

Hod Bozi Vanocni (Christmas Day) and *Svateho Stepana* (St. Stephen's Day, December 26), the two remaining Christmas holidays, are spent in feasting, visiting, and receiving guests. On St. Stephen's Day, caroling groups of children parade from house to house and receive treats as rewards.

New Year's Eve, also known as *Silvester* (so named for Sylvester I, the first pope to hold office after the Roman emperor Constantine the Great accepted Christianity in the fourth century), is a rowdy period of family gatherings and parties. To bring good luck, one consumes lentils and avoids poultry on New Year's Day. *Tri kralu* (Three Kings Day, Epiphany) closes the season as groups of boys dressed as the Three Kings again carol in the villages and receive treats.

• OTHER EXAMPLES OF CHRISTMAS EVE SUPERSTITIONS. After a candle is blown out, uprising smoke forecasts health and fortune; falling smoke predicts death.

A small, burning candle is placed in half of a walnut shell and floated in a bowl of water. If the shell remains afloat, long life is in store; if it sinks, the opposite. In another interpretation, the farther the "boat" travels from the side of the bowl, the father one will travel from home.

Three walnuts are split and the meat removed. One of the shells is refilled with dirt, a second with a bit of bread, the third with money. The shells are glued back together and placed in a batch of walnuts. At midnight, each person selects a nut. He who receives the dirt can expect poverty; the bread, a life of comfort; the money, wealth.

An unmarried girl throws her shoes back over her head. Toes pointing toward the door forecast marriage within the coming year; toes pointing back inside indicate another year's wait. If she who must wait ties a strand of her hair to a ring and holds it near a glass, the number of times the ring hits the glass before settling predicts the number of years to wait.

The shape of a piece of wood blindly drawn from a woodpile predicts the physical makeup of a girl's future husband.

A girl receives a clue about her own future or her future husband's appearance by the shape that melted lead attains when poured into cold water. Another variation requires that the lead be poured through a key ring.

If, when a girl taps a henhouse door, a rooster crows, she will wed in the coming year; if a hen clucks, she must wait another year.

By cutting a hole in the ice of a frozen lake or pond and looking therein at midnight, one may see his future.

A girl learns the direction from which her future spouse will come by listening for the first dog bark heard after supper. Another variation requires her to shake a lilac tree beforehand and then listen for the bark.

"Merry Christmas" is *Prejeme Vam Vesele Vanoce.*

See also **Advent; Croatia, Epiphany; Poland; Slovak Republic; Ukraine.**

D

The Day Before Christmas, or Rudolph, the Red-Nosed Reindeer
See **Rudolph, the Red-Nosed Reindeer** (character)

Day of the Innocents
See Holy Innocents Day

December 25
See Christmas Day

Deck the Halls with Boughs of Holly

Welsh traditional dance-carol, believed to date from the sixteenth century or earlier. The tune was originally the setting for a number of different merry-making or romantic texts which had nothing to do with Christmas. It belongs to a tradition in which people, dancing in a ring around a harpist, in turn contributed new verses to a song or were eliminated if they could not. What is now known as the "Fa la la la la," or "answering" section, the harpist originally played alone. Use of these nonsense syllables arose when no harp was present and eventually became a refrain for folk songs throughout the Middle Ages, not only in Wales but elsewhere. In some instances, the "Fa la la" allowed the ring dancer enough time to compose a new verse on the spot. Over time in Wales, the tune became permanently associated with anonymous texts for *Nos Galan* (New Year's Eve) celebrations, with titles such as "Oer yw'r gwr sy'n methu caru" ("Soon the Hoar Old Year Will Leave Us").

The anonymous lyrics to the familiar carol sung in America, "Deck the Halls with Boughs of Holly," first appeared with the traditional Welsh tune in *The Franklin Square Song Collection*, compiled by J.P. McCaskey (New York, 1881). This led to the assumption that these lyrics also arose in nineteenth century America, but documentation to this effect is lacking. The lyrics recall pre-Christian traditions of decorating manor halls with holly and intense merrymaking at Yuletide and the New Year. Variations of these lyrics exist, some of which take considerable interest in holiday imbibing. Line 3 of the first verse has read "Don we now our gay apparel." Line 1 of verse 2 has read "See the blazing Yule before us" and "See the flowing bowl before us!" Line 3 of verse 3 has read "Sing we joyous all together" and "Laughing, quaffing, all together."

Denmark

The Danes have enjoyed Christmas since the tenth century, when Viking King Harald Bluetooth introduced Christianity to his kingdom, and Christmas traditions derive in part from those of the Norse pre-Christian *Jul* (Yule) celebrations. Because Denmark experiences only six hours of daylight at Christmastime, cities and villages throughout the country light thousands of candles during the holidays as a reminder of bygone days when, during the winter solstice, their Viking ancestors set great fires to encourage the return of the sun and to dispel the hordes of spirits that were believed to haunt the long hours of darkness.

Another vestige is the *Julnisse*, shortened to *nisse* (plural *nisser*), a small, mischievous, aged male elf attired in gray homespun, red hood, long red stockings, white clogs, and sporting a long, gray beard. Whereas *nisser* do resemble the American Santa Claus except for size, some have suggested that they also bear a relationship to Satan, an opinion most Danes dismiss. As the Vikings believed that the spirits of their dead returned home annually during the winter solstice (a belief found in the folklore of many cultures), so the modern Danish folklore holds that the *nisser*, the spirits of each family's forefathers, return at the time of Advent as guardians of the home and remain until the end of the Christmas season. Allegedly, they can be seen only by cats, and their favorite haunts are attics or barns. Prone to committing endless pranks, they require a bowl of rice porridge on Christmas Eve to keep them pacified. The *nisser* are Denmark's favorite Christmas characters, and figures of them abound in homes and store displays.

Early in December, families ritually clean their homes and stables in anticipation of the guests that will arrive. Decorations include evergreens in various arrays and, because the state church is Lutheran, Advent wreaths, Advent candles, and Advent calendars, all attributed to Martin Luther himself.

The Swedish custom of observing December 13 as St. Lucia's Day or Lucia Bride became popular in Denmark following World War II. The Danish ritual is similar to that for Sweden (*see* **Sweden**).

Tradition dictates that all holiday guests must receive refreshment, for should they leave otherwise, with them the Christmas spirit departs from the house. Therefore, Danes keep a ready supply of sweets available, which may include *brune kager* (round, brown cookies topped with half an almond), *klejner* (fried cookies twisted into knots), *pebernødder* (peppernuts or spice cookies), marzipan (almond fondant molded into the shapes of fruits, vegetables, or animals), *vanillekranse* (vanilla wreaths), *julekage* (Christmas coffee cake), and *kringle* (a pastry with raisins and almonds).

At least once, but usually several times during Advent, people attend evening parties ironically known as "Christmas lunches." Employers most often sponsor these events at the workplace for their employees, and because spouses are generally not invited (in some areas, family members do attend), these "lunches" have gained a reputation for unrestrained behavior. Along with various Christmas beers and schnapps, the menu may feature herring, curry salad with eggs, ham, sausage, cheese, biscuits, fruits, and sweets.

Two holiday traditions originating in Denmark have gained world renown: collectible Christmas plates and Christmas Seals. In previous centuries, aristocrats annually provided their servants with Christmas gifts of sweets and delicacies served on highly decorative, valuable plates, which the servants collected over the years. Finding that a lucrative market existed in such plates, two porcelain manufacturers introduced limited edition Christmas plates with a different design each year, Bing and Grondahl in 1895 and Royal Copenhagen in 1908. Four years earlier in 1904, Danish postal worker Einar Holbøll had introduced Christmas Seals to his country as a means of raising money to build tuberculosis hospitals (*see* **Christmas Seals**).

Christmas trees have existed in Denmark since 1808, when they were imported from Germany to Holsteinborg on the island of Fyn. For those adhering to tradition, the preferred tree is a fir, which is decorated on *Juleaften* (Christmas Eve) behind closed doors, for children are not allowed to view the tree until it is fully decorated. Danish families generally make their own ornaments, keeping them as heirlooms from year to year. Ornaments may consist of hearts interwoven from red and white paper, the most favored of decorations; garlands of miniature Danish flags; woven heart baskets and colored paper cones, both of which are filled with candy; *nisser*; stars; "crackers" (noise-

makers that pop when both ends are pulled); and sparklers (similar to those used on the American Independence Day), which are placed in the tree and lit on Christmas Eve. A large star usually serves as a tree topper. Whereas Christmas trees in homes are traditionally illuminated by real candles despite the significant fire hazard, Christmas trees in public places are decorated with electric lights, which are illuminated on the first day of December.

On *lille Juleaften* ("little Christmas Eve," December 23), as families prepare the Christmas Eve dinner, they traditionally may invite friends to their homes for *glögg* (spiced red wine with cloves, cinnamon, raisins, and almonds) along with "apple-pieces," small hot cakes which, ironically, contain no apples.

Although most businesses close at noon on *Juleaften*, the ringing of church bells at 4 PM heralds the official commencement of Christmas, and all commerce ceases until December 27 (for many, until January 2). Tradition also dictates that each household hang a *juleneg* (sheaf of grain) for the birds as the Birds' Christmas Tree, and that their livestock receive extra rations of food, for no creature must be neglected at Christmastime. To that end, each house displays a burning candle in a window to welcome the stranger that may pass by.

The traditional *Juleaften* dinner, served after the early evening Lutheran church services (or following Roman Catholic Midnight Mass), usually includes *risengrød* (rice porridge) containing a single almond, and the person finding the almond in his or her serving receives an extra little treat. Alternatively, the almond may be hidden in a cold rice pudding dessert. Other courses include roast goose, turkey, duck, pork, variously prepared potatoes, cucumber salad, *rødkål* (red cabbage), *rombudding* (rum pudding), *æblekage* (apple crumb cake), red wine, and Christmas beers.

A Christmas tree celebration follows the dinner. The tree is finally revealed to the little ones, and, joining hands, everyone in the household walks around the tree while singing traditional carols. Children then open their gifts, which come from the *Julemand* ("Christmas Man"), the Danish equivalent of the American Santa Claus and the British Father

Christmas, who commands a reindeer sleigh with *nisser* for assistants. Often the father or another male will retire and return dressed as the *Julemand*, distributing gifts from a pack and quizzing the youngsters about their behavior over the past year. In Danish folklore, the *Klapparbock* ("Goat with Yule Gifts," derived from two mythical goats, Gnasher and Cracker, which pulled the chariot of the Scandinavian god Thor) also accompanies the *Julemand* and administers punishment to naughty children. Therefore in some locales, a man dressed in goatskins may personify this creature, chasing and frightening children to their delight. Amid coffee, *glögg*, and other confections, the family then opens and reviews all Christmas cards that have been received theretofore.

Christmas Day and the day after, termed Second Christmas Day, are reserved for visiting relatives. Again, a sumptuous table is spread, this time a *kolde bord* (cold table), consisting of cold foods for noonday meals. Following each course, the host offers a *skål* (toast), after which guests reciprocate. In addition to dining, there are outdoor activities such as ice skating and cross-country skiing. On December 26, theaters offer plays and pantomimes, some presenting the same production year after year. For example, Copenhagen's *Folketeatret* has presented *Christmas in Nøddebo Rectory* annually since 1888.

New Year's Eve is filled with parties, fireworks, the committing of numerous pranks, and the monarch's televised address to the nation. The Christmas season ends on Epiphany eve, Twelfth Night, when Christmas trees are dismantled and their sweets eaten, and families light three candles in memory of the traditional three Wise Men.

"Merry Christmas" in Danish is *Glædelig Jul*.

See also **Advent; Epiphany; Greenland; Yule.**

Desert Christmas Cactus
See **Christmas Plants**

Devil's Knell
See **Great Britain**

The Dick Van Dyke Show

Popular, Emmy Award–winning television situation comedy series that aired on the CBS network from 1961 to 1966. The principal cast included Dick Van Dyke as Rob Petrie, a television writer for a fictional variety show, *The Alan Brady Show*; Mary Tyler Moore as Rob's wife, Laura; Larry Mathews as the Petries' young son, Ritchie; Carl Reiner as Alan Brady; Rose Marie and Morey Amsterdam as Sally Rogers and Buddy Sorrell, Rob's assistant writers; and Richard Deacon as producer Mel Cooley.

Of the 158 episodes in the series, only one featured a Christmas theme. That episode, titled "The Alan Brady Show Presents," aired on December 18, 1963. In this show-within-a-show, the staff of *The Alan Brady Show* joins Alan for some holiday merriment on the air. In the most memorable scene, Rob, Laura, Sally, and Buddy dress up as a marching band quartet and sing "We All Are Fine Musicians." Pretending to play different musical instruments and imitating their sounds, Rob mimics a trombone, Laura a piccolo, Sally a trumpet, and Buddy a tuba. As this routine closes, each person "plays" and retreats one by one until Laura is left alone. Unable to face the sudden loneliness, the little piccolo squeaks a final measure and runs off in "tears." Also in this episode, Sally, whom the series portrayed as a man-hungry single woman, appropriately delivers her rendition of an original tune, "Santa, Send a Fella," and Ritchie adds a serious note with "The Little Drummer Boy." Interestingly, the Christmas episode is the only one that ever depicted an actual performance of *The Alan Brady Show*; the other 157 episodes only revolved *around* that show.

The script and most of the musical numbers for this episode originated with Sam Denoff and Bill Persky, both former writers for *The Andy Williams Show*. "We All Are Fine Musicians" had appeared in an earlier *Dick Van Dyke Show* episode titled "The Sam Pomerantz Scandals," which had aired in March 1963. Vacationing in the Catskill Mountains, *The Alan Brady Show* staff performed an identical routine at a local resort as they did for the Christmas show. Dick Van Dyke first became acquainted with "We All Are Fine Musicians" (originally known simply as "The Musicians") from an obscure record in 1953 while hosting a children's television show in Atlanta. He and the children had initially performed the same act that later was incorporated into two episodes of *The Dick Van Dyke Show*.

Creator/producer Carl Reiner at first rejected Denoff's and Persky's idea of making any Christmas episode at all, because he felt that a holiday show would not fit well into the summer rerun schedule. He finally agreed when he realized that he could rerun the same episode every year at Christmastime instead.

With Cornell Chulay and Brendan Freeman. Directed by Jerry Paris. This episode is available on the DVD box set *The Dick Van Dyke Show — Season Three* from Image Entertainment. B & W. Episode 30 min.

Dickens, Charles, Christmas Stories of

In keeping with the British tradition of telling ghost stories at Christmastime, Dickens created five novellas, now collectively termed *Christmas Books*, wherein, with one exception, the supernatural pervades the holiday. The first and best-known example of these is *A Christmas Carol* (1843). But whereas ghosts in that tale transform a basically mean-spirited person into one of compassion and generosity, the spirits in *The Chimes* (1844), *The Cricket on the Hearth* (1845), and *The Haunted Man and the Ghost's Bargain* (1848) serve to reform the flawed attitudes of basically good people. The fifth book, *The Battle of Life* (1846), not only contains no supernatural elements but also is not a Christmas story in the strictest sense of the term and is therefore not discussed in detail here. Although Dickens surely considered its theme of love between two close sisters and the romantic sacrifice that one makes for the other as a tale in keeping with the Christian spirit of the holiday, *The Battle of Life* remains the least known of the collection.

A Christmas Carol is discussed as a separate entry; the following paragraphs summarize the best-known of the remaining novellas.

The Chimes: A Goblin Story of Some Bells That Rang an Old Year Out and a New One In (1844). Toby Veck, a poor ticket porter, initially manifests an optimistic outlook on life,

despite his station, and imagines that the hourly pealing of the church bells signifies good omens. When harsh words from the upper classes suggest that the poor have no rightful place in the upcoming new year, however, Toby's self-esteem falls, and he imagines that even the chimes mock him. Wallowing in self-pity, Toby meets the Goblin of the Great Bell, who upbraids him for actually believing that the working class and the poor are "born bad." The Goblin paints a futuristic scene of a world without Toby's positive influence by showing him the devastating consequences if others, like his dear daughter Meg, abandon all hope of rising above their stations. At the moment when Meg is about to commit suicide rather than remain destitute, Toby awakens from his nightmare at midnight on New Year's Eve. He no longer doubts his capabilities, a lesson he has learned "from the creature dearest to his heart." *The Chimes* was twice adapted in 1914 for the silent screen, once in the United States and once in Great Britain.

The Cricket on the Hearth: A Fairy Tale of Home (1845). The story is based on the legend that a cricket on the hearth is a harbinger of good luck. A series of interconnected doubts and deceptions plagues the characters in this complex New Year's Eve tale. John Peerybingle, a carrier, reasons that his much younger wife, Dot, has deprived herself of a young and active life by marrying him and now only feigns affection for him. Caleb Plummer, a poor toymaker, has deceived his blind daughter, Bertha, from her birth regarding their lifestyle. Believing that she lives in luxury, Bertha falls in love with Mr. Tackleton, her father's sarcastic employer, and Caleb shields her from Tackleton's verbal abuse by explaining that Tackleton is only "joking" with her because his feelings are mutual. Tackleton actually plans to wed Dot's friend, May Fielding, but May still yearns for an old flame, Edward Plummer, Caleb's son, who is presumed dead. Years earlier, Dot's husband John had provided Edward with the means of going abroad; having heard that May would marry, however, Edward returns in the guise of an old man to learn the truth. Dot recognizes him and, meeting him secretly, promises not to reveal his true identity. When John, discovering their meetings and mistaking their intentions, would end his marriage, a fairy emerges from a cricket on the hearth and bids John to reconsider, for Dot has never ceased to love him; her love is genuine. They are reconciled, and Caleb eventually confesses his deception to Bertha, who forgives her father's misplaced intentions. And for a sunny ending, Edward and May wed on New Year's Day.

United States adaptations of *The Cricket on the Hearth* for the silent screen were released in 1909, 1915, and 1923; a United States/Russian version also appeared in 1915.

A musical, animated cartoon adaptation for NBC television, titled *Cricket on the Hearth*, aired December 18, 1967, on *The Danny Thomas Hour*. Voices: Danny Thomas, Marlo Thomas, Roddy McDowall, Ed Ames, Hans Conried, Abbe Lane, and Paul Frees. The special not only marked Marlo Thomas's musical debut but also the first time that she and her father Danny paired for a television musical performance. With the Norman Luboff Choir. Lyrics by Jules Bass. Music by Maury Laws. Written by Romeo Muller and Arthur Rankin, Jr. Produced and directed by Arthur Rankin, Jr., and Jules Bass. A Thomas/Spelling Production in association with Videocraft International, Ltd. VHS: Sony Wonder Video. 50 min. *See also* **Rankin/Bass Christmas Cartoons**.

The Haunted Man and the Ghost's Bargain: A Fancy for Christmas Time (1848). Memories of past sorrows haunt Mr. Redlaw, a kind yet most unhappy chemist. Christmastime is at hand, and whereas a servant remarks that the happiest of his own memories are greatest at this time of year, Redlaw plunges himself into melancholy at this season. When his miserable ego appears as a phantom, Redlaw, seeking relief, petitions the specter to abolish all memories of past injustices. The specter complies but stipulates that those who have any contact with Redlaw henceforth will also lose similar memories. While this request seems merciful, Redlaw rapidly discovers that the inability to recall sorrow or injustice produces a cold, callous behavior devoid of compassion. He revokes his wish, and the phantom reverses the spell. The experience teaches Redlaw that, at Christmastime, the memory of every remediable sorrow and wrong should be especially active, for we remember Christ, Who suffered wrong for us and redeemed us. And as Christ forgave those who wronged Him, it is proper to remember those who wrong us, that we may forgive them.

Other Christmas Stories. In 1850, Dickens founded *Household Words*, a weekly journal in which he expressed his views on current affairs and which, at year's end, included the special feature of a Dickens Christmas short story. This tradition continued when this journal was incorporated in 1859 into *All the Year Round*, which Dickens edited for the remainder of his life. His initial contributions to the 21 tales now collectively known as the *Christmas Stories* consisted of a traditional approach to Yuletide, with recollections of childhood and family festivities. As time passed, Dickens, ever concerned for the neglected poor and alert to social injustice in England, generally dropped Christmas themes as such and used this medium instead as a sounding block for social reform. In four of these stories, Dickens collaborated with Wilkie Collins, who wrote portions of the text.

Dickens's *Christmas Stories* consists of the following titles: "A Christmas Tree" (1850, the only one of his works to mention this decoration); "What Christmas Is As We Grow Older" (1851); "The Poor Relation's Story" (1852); "The Child's Story" (1852); "The Schoolboy's Story" (1853); "Nobody's Story"; "The Seven Poor Travelers" (1854); "The Holly-Tree" (1855); "The Wreck of the Golden Mary," with Wilkie Collins (1856); "The Perils of Certain English Prisoners" (1857); "Going into Society" (1858); "The Haunted House" (1859); "A Message from the Sea," with Wilkie Collins (1860); "Tom Tiddler's Ground" (1861); "Somebody's Luggage" (1862); "Mrs. Lirriper's Lodgings" (1863); "Mrs. Lirriper's Legacy" (1864); "Doctor Marigold" (1865); "Mugby Junction" (1866); "No Thoroughfare," with Wilkie Collins (1867); and "The Lazy Tour of Two Idle Apprentices," with Wilkie Collins.

See also **A Christmas Carol**.

Dickens Christmas Carol

See **A Christmas Carol** (Film and Television Versions)

A Different Kind of Christmas

(1996). Made-for-television drama.

Christmas promises to be a year-round event when "Santa" takes up residence in a California neighborhood in June and bedecks his house inside and out with full trappings, including fake snow, multitudes of lights, and live reindeer on the lawn. Calling his nonprofit enterprise "Santa's Dream World" and driving a bright red Cadillac, this eccentric newcomer is actually Robert George (Bruce Kirby), an elderly barber from Nebraska who retired his razor years ago. Now perpetually attired in a Santa suit and full beard, he devotes the remainder of his life to the happiness of children. But when Robert's neighbors complain about the tourists and commotion that his venture creates, Elizabeth Gates (Shelley Long), the city attorney and candidate for mayor, orders Robert to close down. Her action is not politically wise, for it creates a storm of protest from many citizens, who picket City Hall. Children vilify her as well, especially her ten-year-old son Tommy (Nathan Lawrence), who not only feels neglected by his ambitious mother but believes that the old gent really is Santa. Yet when Robert is later arrested and jailed for violating the ordinance, it is Elizabeth who bails him out.

Reporting Robert's story for the newspaper is Frank Mallory (Barry Bostwick), who feels that such a scoop will advance his career, especially when he concludes from Robert's family photo albums that this "Santa" is really Elizabeth's father. Indeed, Robert's "mission" had embarrassed and alienated Elizabeth all her life, for wherever her father had appeared in public dressed as Santa, the attention had shifted from her to him. Now, Robert's appearance could jeopardize her political career.

To have his daughter in his life again and be near his grandson, Robert temporarily casts Santa aside and returns to being a barber, but not for long. Soon the story breaks that Elizabeth was responsible for his arrest and subsequent release, and Elizabeth has no choice but to confess Santa's real identity to Tommy. Ultimately, Robert decides to leave town for the good of his family, but when Tommy receives the news, he rushes out to prevent the act and is struck down by a truck.

During the anxious hours of waiting while Tommy lies hospitalized in a coma, Elizabeth and her father are reconciled. Miraculously, Tommy recovers, yet Robert, clad once again as Santa, is resigned to return to Nebraska. Two police officers offer him a ride but transport him instead to the city's old historic railroad station, which the city has converted into Santa's Dream World. With daughter and grandson back in his life, Robert remains in town to pursue his true calling, and as everyone sings "Deck the Halls," one final miracle closes the scene — a snowfall in June.

Written by Bart Baker. Produced and directed by Tom McLoughlin. Carroll Newman Productions and Hearst Entertainment Productions, Inc. VHS: Goodtimes Home Video. 93 min.

Ding Dong! Merrily on High

French-English carol. The music is a French folk dance tune, "Branle de l'official" ("Dance of the Official"), which Thoinot Arbeau (1519–1595) included in *Orchesographie* (1588), a collection of sixteenth century music and dance. The Anglican priest George R. Woodward (1838–1934) supplied the text, written in a style commensurate with the music. In fact, Woodward, seeking artistic worth in church music over the Victorian styles of the turn of the twentieth century, preferred to compose hymn lyrics in the style of the sixteenth or seventeenth century, then select appropriate melodies from that era to fit his lyrics. Woodward was responsible for many of the reforms in *The English Hymnal* (1906) and compiled three collections, *Songs of Syon* (1904), *An Italian Carol Book* (1920), and *The Cowley Carol Book* (1901, 1919, for the Fathers at Cowley, Oxford), the latter three in collaboration with Cambridge musician Charles Wood (1866–1926).

The subject of "Ding Dong! Merrily on High," as the title suggests, is the merry ringing of bells both in heaven and on earth at the birth of Christ. Macaronic (having vernacular words mixed with Latin), the carol features a Latin refrain, "Gloria! Hosanna in excelsis!" ("Glory! Hosanna in the highest!"), which is similar in wording and musical phrasing to the refrain of another macaronic carol, "Angels We

Have Heard on High": "Gloria in excelsis Deo!" ("Glory to God in the highest!").

See also **Angels We Have Heard on High**.

A Disney Christmas Gift

(1982). Television presentation of excerpts from classic Disney theatrical cartoons. Included are scenes from four feature films: *Bambi* (1942), *Cinderella* (1950), *Peter Pan* (1953), and *The Sword in the Stone* (1963). Also included are four holiday cartoon "shorts":

The Night before Christmas (1933). Based on the poem "A Visit from St. Nicholas," the story depicts Santa delivering gifts at one house and the merriment that the toys enjoy as they arrange themselves under the tree. Vocals by Donald Novis. Produced by Walt Disney. Directed by Wilfred Jackson.

The Clock Watcher (1945). A frustrated Donald Duck wraps Christmas gifts by the clock in a department store. Voice: Clarence Nash. Produced by Walt Disney. Directed by Jack King.

Once upon a Wintertime (1952). A December valentine featuring the memories of a romantic couple in their courting days. Vocals by Frances Langford. Produced by Walt Disney. Directed by Hamilton Luske.

Pluto's Christmas Tree (1952). When Mickey Mouse and Pluto bring in their Christmas tree, chipmunks Chip and Dale are hidden inside. In vain, Pluto attempts to rid the house of them. With Minnie, Donald Duck, and Goofy. Voices: Dessie Flynn, Clarence Nash, Pinto Colvig, Ruth Clifford, and James MacDonald. Written by Bill Berg and Milt Schaffer. Produced by Walt Disney and John Sutherland. Directed by Jack Hannah.

This program received an Emmy nomination for Outstanding Animated Program (1983–84 season). Prepared by Ed Ropolo, Frank Brandt, Darryl Sutton, and Joan Spollino. Executive producer William Yates.

Walt Disney Company. VHS: Walt Disney Home Video. 47 min.

See also **Jiminy Cricket's Christmas**; **A Walt Disney Christmas**.

Do You Hear What I Hear?

Popular American carol written in 1962 by Noel Regney and Gloria Shayne, the sole work of any significant note from either songwriter. An indirect yet quite unique telling of the Christmas story, this carol personifies Nature, who first learns the good news of Christ's birth, and from there the tidings cascade around the world. More specifically, the night wind, the first informant, asks a lamb if it has seen the bright star overhead. The lamb in turn asks a shepherd boy if he has heard the glorious song that fills the air. The boy then inquires of a king if he knows that a Child shivers from cold and suggests that gifts be brought in homage. Turning to all nations of the world, the king calls for everyone to pray for peace, for the Child is destined to bring goodness and light to an ailing world.

The Harry Simeone Chorale first recorded the carol in 1962 for Mercury Records, but it was not charted. Bing Crosby's recording a year later on the Capitol label was ranked number two on the *Billboard Special Christmas Singles* chart, and Andy Williams's 1965 recording for Columbia placed eighteenth on the same chart.

Dr. Seuss's How the Grinch Stole Christmas
See **How the Grinch Stole Christmas**

Dominican Republic
See **West Indies**

The Dream of Old Scrooge
See **A Christmas Carol** (Film and Television Versions)

E

Ebbie

See **A Christmas Carol** (Film and Television Versions)

Ebenezer

See **A Christmas Carol** (Film and Television Versions)

Echo Carol

See **While by My Sheep**

Ecuador

See **South America**

Eggnog

Thick, rich, holiday drink consisting of beaten eggs, spices, cream, sugar, and some form of alcohol. The name derives from "noggin" or "nog," a strong ale known in Great Britain since the seventeenth century. The British thus are generally credited with creating the drink, which originated from a posset, a hot drink consisting of eggs and milk with nog or wine added. The basic recipe passed to other countries, where variations in the drink were known by names such as *advocaat* (Netherlands), *eggedosis* (Norway), *lait de poule* (nonalcoholic drink of France), and *Biersuppe* (an egg-and-beer soup of Germany). Subsequent to eggnog's arrival in the early American colonies, the alcoholic portion consisted of rum, brandy, bourbon, sherry, and so forth. Despite the variety of liquor added, however, eggnog retains an association with the British "nog."

The eggnog that is sold in grocery stores in the United States is nonalcoholic (leaving the customer to add the potent ingredient), most commonly spiced with nutmeg, and has been cooked to prevent possible contamination from salmonella.

Egypt

See **Africa**

El Salvador

See **Central America**

Elf

(2003). Motion picture comedy.

When Santa (Ed Asner) visits an orphanage on Christmas Eve, an infant boy crawls into Santa's sack of toys and is accidentally taken back to the North Pole. There, Papa Elf (Bob Newhart) names the infant Buddy and raises him as his own elf child. But when Buddy (Will Ferrell) is fully grown, he stands over six feet tall, and it is quite apparent that he will never fit into elf society. Learning that he is adopted and that his real father, Walter Hobbs (James Caan), lives in New York City, Buddy departs from the North Pole at Christmastime to search for his roots, despite knowing that Walter, a workaholic children's book publisher, has landed on Santa's "Naughty" list.

Not only Walter but New York itself initially rebuffs Buddy, who once again finds himself a creature out of his element. Nevertheless, Buddy's naiveté and perennial Christmas spirit work their magic on those around him as well as the remaining members of his family, stepmother Emily (Mary Steenburgen) and ten-year-old half-brother Michael (Daniel Tay).

In 2004, this picture captured the following honors: won ASCAP Award for Top Box Office Film; won Golden Trailer Award for Best Comedy; nominated for MTV Award for Best Comedic Performance (Will Ferrell); nominated for two Teen Choice Awards for Choice Comedy Movie and Choice Comedy Actor (Ferrell).

Written by David Berenbaum. Produced by Jon Berg, Todd Komarnicki, and Shauna Robertson. Directed by Jon Favreau. New Line Cinema, Shawn Danielle Productions Ltd., Gold/Miller Productions, Guy Walks into a Bar Productions, and Mosaic Media Group. DVD: New Line Home Entertainment. 95 min.

Elmo Saves Christmas

(1996). Children's video, a musical parody of William Dean Howells's classic short story, "Christmas Every Day," featuring the Jim Henson Muppets of Sesame Street.

Stuck in Elmo's fireplace because of an oversized bag of toys, Santa (Charles Durning) receives some much-needed assistance from Elmo, who pulls him out. The reason the bag is so large is that Lightning, a curious little reindeer in training, has hidden there. A grateful Santa offers Elmo a special gift, the choice between a pink bear doll or a magical snow globe that grants three wishes. Choosing the globe, Elmo wastes his first wish on a glass of water. His second wish is worse, for he wishes that every day of the year could be Christmas. At Santa's command, Lightning escorts Elmo forward into time to glimpse the future impact of his folly: work piles up because people are on Christmas break, daily carol singing produces hoarse voices, and endless shopping for gifts breeds contempt for the season. Repenting, Elmo accidentally breaks his globe while casting his final wish for all to be restored as it was. The only hope is for Lightning and Elmo to reverse their path and return to that part of time before Elmo received the globe. This time he chooses the bear doll.

With Maya Angelou, Harvey Fierstein, and the singing group "14 Karat Soul." Written by Christine Ferraro and Tony Geiss. Produced by Karin Young Shiel. Directed by Emily Squires. Children's Television Workshop and Jim Henson Productions. DVD: Sony Wonder Video. 60 min.

See also **Christmas Every Day.**

Elves

See **Denmark; Finland; Iceland; Norway; Saint Nicholas; Sweden**

The Elves and the Shoemaker

Modern title applied to "Die Wichtelmänner" ("The Elves"), one of three folk tales with the same title appearing in the German collection *Kinder- und Hausmärchen* (*Children's and Household Tales*), published by brothers Jacob Ludwig Carl Grimm (1785–1863) and Wilhelm Carl Grimm (1786–1859). The collection, better known as *Grimms' Fairy Tales*, was pub-

lished in three volumes from 1812 to 1822 with seven editions, the last in 1857. The final edition contained 200 stories plus ten "Children's Legends."

In "The Elves and the Shoemaker," a poor cobbler awakens on several mornings to find that the materials he had laid out the night before have been transformed into handsomely crafted shoes, which bring a handsome price. Becoming quite rich in this manner by Christmastime, the cobbler and his wife finally decide to hide themselves and see who or what is responsible for making the shoes. At midnight, they witness the appearance of two naked little elves who dance about, then rapidly fashion more shoes from the cobbler's stock material, and just as rapidly disappear. Deeply touched, the cobbler's wife makes Christmas gifts for each elf: a shirt, coat and waistcoat, and a pair of pantaloons, while the cobbler fashions for each a pair of little shoes. Setting these out instead of shoe leather and taking another nocturnal vigil, the couple note the elves' surprise and joy as they don their newfound apparel and, with a final round of dancing about, disappear forever. Yet the cobbler and his wife are set for life, thanks to the elves' initial good turn.

• FILM AND ANIMATED ADAPTATIONS.

Shoemaker and the Elves (1935). Animated cartoon "short" from Screen Gems/Columbia Pictures, produced by Charles Mintz. Video N/A.

Die Heinzelmänchen (1956). West German production starring Rolf Bollmann, Heini Göbel, Elisabeth Goebel, Klaus Havenstein, and Erich Holder. Written by Erich Kobler, Konrad Lustig, and Hubert Schonger. Produced by Hubert Schonger. Directed by Erich Kobler. Schongerfilm GmbH. Video N/A. 78 min. Released in the United States in 1967 as *The Shoemaker and the Elves.*

The Elves and the Shoemaker (1990). Animated cartoon from the Hanna-Barbera video series *Timeless Tales.* Hosted by Olivia Newton-John, who presents an environmental message. VHS: Hanna-Barbera Home Video. 30 min. *See also* **Hanna-Barbera Christmas Cartoons.**

The Elves and the Shoemaker (1994). Segment on the made-for-video title *Muppet Classic Theater,* in which the Muppets provide spoofs of this and five other classic fairy tales. Principal voices: Frank Oz, Dave Goelz, Jerry Nelson, Steve Whitmire, Brian Henson, Bruce Lanoil, Allan Trautman, Bill Barretta, and Julianne Buescher. Written by Jim Lewis and Bill Prady. Produced by Ritamarie Peruggi. Directed by David Grossman. Jim Henson Productions. VHS: Buena Vista Home Video. 68 min.

The Enchanted Nutcracker

See **The Nutcracker**

England

See **Great Britain**

Epiphany

(From the Greek, *Epiphaneia*, "appearance, manifestation"). Feast observed on January 6 by the Roman Catholic, Anglican, and Eastern Orthodox churches. It commemorates the three-part manifestation of Jesus Christ as the Son of God: (1) His physical manifestation to the Gentiles through the Magi at Bethlehem (Matthew 2:1–12); (2) His spiritual manifestation at His baptism in the River Jordan when the Holy Ghost descended as a dove (Luke 3:21–22); (3) His miraculous nature manifested at the marriage in Cana of Galilee when Jesus performed His first miracle by turning water into wine (John 2:1–11). The last day in the period known as the Twelve Days of Christmas, Epiphany ends the Christmas season in many parts of the world and is sometimes called "Little Christmas." In the Roman Catholic Church, however, the Christmas season ends with the Feast of the Baptism of the Lord, observed on the first Sunday after Epiphany (the Monday following if Epiphany falls on a Sunday) (*see* **The Vatican**). Epiphany Eve is often called "Twelfth Night" and Epiphany itself "Twelfth Day," if one considers Christmas Night as the first night and December 26 as the first day in this period. Custom dictates that all Christmas decorations be stored away at this time and that holiday greenery be burned; according to superstition, anyone failing to adhere to this tradition invites bad luck. Other designations include "Feast of Lights," for the early Christians celebrated with lighted torches; "Feast of Jordan"; and "Three Kings Day" or "Day of the Kings" in honor of the Magi.

The fixing of January 6 remains largely traditional in Roman Catholic circles. One theory, however, proposes reckoning backward from April 6, Easter as kept by the Phrygian Montanists, who followed the second century heretical prophet Montanus. Assuming that Jesus lived exactly 33 years, Epiphany would have fallen on January 6. On the other hand, an Internet article about "The Feast of Lights" by the Rev. George Mastrontanis of the Greek Orthodox Archdiocese of America implies that Epiphany Christianized the birthday of Aeon, patron god of Alexandria, Egypt.

Epiphany was first celebrated in the East by the second century, with emphasis placed primarily on Christ's baptism and secondarily on His Nativity. This rationale stemmed from two concepts: one, that Christ's baptism constituted His true, or spiritual, Nativity; two, by tradition, His baptism occurred exactly 30 years from His physical Nativity; thus the two events were celebrated together. Clement of Alexandria (150?–215?), a Greek theologian and church father, wrote that although the followers of Basilides (a second century Alexandrian teacher who founded a gnostic sect) commemorated the baptism and Nativity on January 6, the Church at that time had not embraced Epiphany as an ecclesiastical feast. While Epiphanius (315?–403), a father of the Greek Church and a theologian of Jewish birth, also referred to January 6 as the Epiphany, the Roman historian Ammianus Marcellinus provided the first definite evidence of church involvement by mentioning that in 361, the Roman emperor Julian the Apostate (331?–363) attended an Epiphany feast in Vienne of Gaul. Thus the Western (Roman) Church did not observe Epiphany until the fourth century, when it is believed that the theologian St. Athanasius (c. 293–373) of Alexandria first introduced it to Gaul.

This new feast came to Western knowledge about the same time that the Western Church established December 25 as the Feast of the Nativity, which Christianized the birthday of Mithra, the Persian sun god. With two established dates for the Nativity, the East eventually adopted December 25 as the Nativity of Christ and retained January 6 as the anniversary of Christ's baptism; the West, while also embracing Epiphany, placed far more emphasis on the Magi's visit to Bethlehem on that date. Regarding the miracle at Cana, Epiphanius asserted that water, even rivers and probably the Nile itself, had turned to wine on January 6, a "miracle" that has never been noted in the literature of the Western Church.

Because Epiphany also Christianized certain pagan spring festivals, which honored the gods of running water, rivers, and streams through water purification rituals, it became commonplace to hold baptisms on this date with a special "Blessing [or Sanctification] of the Waters" ceremony. Whereas Epiphany baptisms survived in the African Christian Church, the sanctification of water has remained in the Eastern Orthodox churches, for example, the Greek Orthodox and Russian Orthodox faiths. In some countries, the blessing often involves a priest tossing a cross into a nearby body of water, after which men compete to retrieve it. Believing that the holy water will cure sickness and yield bountiful crops, worshipers return home with some of the water. The priest may also make personal visits to anoint homes and fields with the blessed water.

• TWELFTH NIGHT. Beginning in the Middle Ages, Twelfth Night in Europe was spent in revelry with music, singing, dancing, masques and masquerades, bonfires, pageants portraying the Magi, and feasting, with a mood much akin to that of the Roman Saturnalia. Throughout European courts, it was initially customary to elect a mock king, the Lord of Misrule, to supervise a series of festivities held all during the Christmas season, in which those in attendance were subject to this mock king's ludicrous fancies. By the time of Edward II of England (1284–1327), the mock king had become known as "King of the Bean" from the manner in which he was elected. A large plum cake was served with a bean hidden inside. Each participant took a slice of cake, and whoever found the bean was dubbed King of the Bean. If a woman found the bean, she became Queen and chose a King. Following the festivities, a portion of the cake was donated to the poor. The cake itself, called a "Kings' Cake" in honor of the Three Kings or Magi, originated in France during the twelfth century as a means of choosing the mock king for Christmas court festivities. The hidden object at that time was a bean or perhaps a pea, nut, or a coin, and the one finding the object was either dubbed King for a Day or would receive good luck in the coming year. During the Renaissance, the custom of choosing a King of the Bean had become more associated with Twelfth Night rather than the entire Christmas season as before, and the Kings' Cakes appeared as works of art, often of enormous sizes.

The seventeenth century saw increasing popularity for the innovative custom of drawing slips of paper that contained the names of fictitious, ridiculous characters for revelers to impersonate. This practice gained preference over the King of the Bean game, and by the eighteenth century, the Twelfth Night mock king had become virtually obsolete. The paper slips evolved into sets of professionally printed cards with names and illustrations.

A somewhat related custom, the so-called Urn of Fate, is found in Italy and Spain. On Christmas Day, Italians fill a large urn with wrapped boxes containing either gifts or nothing at all, and each guest has one chance to draw either a prize or a dud. Instead of gifts, the Spanish urn contains paper slips, each with the name of a guest, and the slips are drawn out in pairs. The pairs are encouraged to become good friends during the new year, and "fate" may encourage matrimony for some pairs of unmarried men and women.

By the nineteenth century, the boisterous mood of Twelfth Night had considerably waned, yet a number of countries retain vestiges of this festival. For example, the Kings' Cakes found in the United States today are rounded to symbolize the supposedly circuitous route the Magi took to evade King Herod and are decorated in purple, green, and gold, colors respectively symbolic of justice, faith, and power. These cakes are also fashioned to resembled jeweled crowns of the Magi, and the hidden object often consists of a tiny plastic doll, symbolic of the Christ Child. Twelfth Night initiates the Carnival season in Louisiana, which terminates with Mardi Gras, and the objects once hidden in the Kings' Cakes of England have found a new home in plum puddings.

See also **Christmas Day; Great Britain; Nativity; Saturnalia.**

Ernest Saves Christmas

(1988). Motion picture comedy, one in a series of *Ernest* pictures starring Jim Varney as the wacky, drawling, accident-prone know-it-all Ernest P. Worrell.

For centuries, the role of Santa Claus has been passed from one deserving man to the next, each endowed with that special spirit, a love for children, that makes him worthy of receiving the role. The time has arrived when the present Santa (Douglas Seale), now 150 years of age, must name his successor by 7:00 PM on Christmas Eve, lest the magic of Christmas die forever. Santa's choice is Joe Caruthers (Oliver Clark) in Orlando, Florida, a gentle, highly moral man whose children's television show has been canceled and who now has the opportunity to star in a Christmas movie. With two days remaining, Santa, using no alias and dressed as a businessman, arrives by commercial aircraft with his reindeer and sleigh crated on board. To find Joe, he receives help from Ernest, a cabby filled with the Christmas spirit, and reluctantly from Harmony Starr (Noelle Parker), a cynical runaway teenager in much need of Santa's Christmas spirit.

Adept at trickery, disguise, and deception, Ernest serves Santa well by bailing him out of jail after he is arrested for vagrancy, discovering Joe's whereabouts from a talent agency, and sneaking Santa onto the movie lot where Joe will star. There, Joe declines Santa's proposal, yet he is dissatisfied with the movie and his role, for this "Christmas" film incorporates violence and profanity. As Joe ponders his future, Santa discerns that Harmony has run off with his magic bag but knows that her conscience, longing for a reconciliation at home, will bring her back.

Christmas Eve wanes as Ernest and two of Santa's elves claim the sleigh and eight reindeer at the airport baggage hangar after shocked workmen discover the reindeer attached upside down to the ceiling (they possess a natural affinity for roofs). After Ernest hitches them to the sleigh, they rocket into space and zip wildly through the skies as Ernest, fighting for control, manages to evade two military jets bent on shooting them all down as UFOs.

With minutes to spare, Harmony returns, as does Joe, whom Santa, through a simple handshake, transforms into his successor, complete with all the trappings. As Ernest lands the sleigh in one piece, the new Santa bids him guide his sleigh this one night, and the former Santa resumes his original identity as Seth Applegate.

With Gailard Sartain, Bill Byrge, and Robert Lesser. Written by Bosco Kline and Ed Turner. Produced by Stacy Williams and Doug Claybourne. Directed by John Cherry. Touchstone Pictures in association with Silver Screen Partners IV. DVD: Buena Vista Home Video. 95 min.

Estonia
See **Baltic States**

Ethiopia
See **Africa**

Evergreens
See **Christmas Plants; Christmas Tree; The Holly and the Ivy; Mistletoe**

The Exeter Boar's Head Carol
See **The Boar's Head Carol**

F

A Family Circus Christmas

(1979). Made-for-television animated cartoon, based on the comic strip *The Family Circus*, created by Bill Keane.

As Mommy, Daddy, Billy, Dolly, Jeffy, and PJ decorate the Christmas tree, a sentimental crisis arises when the family cannot find the handmade star fashioned years ago by the children's late grandfather. After dreaming about riding with Santa to the North Pole to see wondrous holiday inventions, Jeffy asks a department store Santa to bring his grandfather back from heaven for Christmas. With faith in such an impossible request, Jeffy does receive a miraculous alternative. On Christmas Eve, the spirits of Santa and his grandfather guide Jeffy to the star, which had been misplaced. Atop the tree and lit, the star symbolizes that Grandfather is still among them.

Principal voices: Anne Costello, Bob Kaliban, Mark McDermott, Missy Hope, Nathan Berg, and Allen Swift. Vocalist: Sarah Vaughan. Written by Joseph C. Cavella. Produced by Edward F. Cullen. Directed by Al Kouzel. A Cullen-Kasdan Production in association with the Register and Tribune Syndicate. VHS: UMVD. 30 min.

Fantasia on Christmas Carols

See **The First Nowell**

Farolitos and Luminarias

Respective Spanish-language designations for "little fires" and "illuminations," two simple holiday lighting decorations found outdoors in the American Southwest and Mexico. *Farolitos*, which line walkways, roofs, buildings, and plazas, consist of waxed brown paper bags filled with several inches of sand and lit by a votive candle wedged into the sand. The tops are cuffed to keep the bags open. Forerunners of *farolitos* were Chinese paper lanterns, which first appeared in Mexico during the sixteenth century as a result of Spanish trade with the Orient. By the nineteenth century, these

lanterns had spread into Spanish territory north of Mexico, where brown wrapping paper subsequently proved to be a more durable medium for construction.

Luminarias, on the other hand, are bonfires of piñon pine logs stacked in squares three feet tall. Most commonly found in rural regions and the pueblos on Christmas Eve, they adorn homes and churches especially in New Mexico. Although *luminarias* are less prevalent now in metropolitan areas, larger cities such as Albuquerque sponsor tours of *luminaria* displays in selected neighborhoods. Where *luminarias* originated is a matter of conjecture. They supposedly derived either from bonfires tended by the Bethlehem shepherds of 2,000 years ago, or from ancient Native American customs that sixteenth century Spanish missionaries Christianized into Christmas celebrations, or from customs these missionaries originally brought to Mexico.

Use of the two terms depends on one's locale. In northern New Mexico, "*farolitos*" implies only the paper bags, but in locales where the bonfire custom is not routinely practiced, *farolitos* are also known as *luminarias*.

The Fat Albert Christmas Special

See **A Christmas Carol** (Film and Television Versions)

Father Christmas

(Book). Classic children's picture book written and illustrated in 1973 by British author Raymond Briggs. It received Great Britain's Kate Greenaway Medal, equivalent to the Caldecott Medal in the United States.

On the morning of Christmas Eve, Father Christmas, the British equivalent of Santa Claus, awakens from dreams of vacations on warm, tropical isles and reluctantly prepares for his annual rounds. With no elves about to help him and knowing that soon he must drive his two-reindeer sleigh through snow, sleet, rain, and fog to deliver his presents, he makes preparations while muttering favorite expressions such as "Blooming snow!" and "Blooming chimneys!" Yet he performs his duties faithfully, arriving at Buckingham Palace, his last stop, at sunrise. He is happiest back home at the North Pole, where he concludes with a turkey dinner and tea. Retiring to bed for another year, he wishes everyone a "Blooming Christmas!"

In 1991, the story was adapted as a motion picture animated cartoon "short," in which Father Christmas fulfilled his dreams by taking a vacation around the world. In the British version, Mel Smith provided the voice of Father Christmas, the only character with dialogue, whereas William Dennis Hunt provided the voice when the picture was released in the United States. Written by Raymond Briggs. Produced by John Coates. Directed by Dave Unwin. Blooming Productions in association with Palace Video, Ltd., and GAGA Communications. DVD: Columbia/Tristar Home Video, which also includes another story by Briggs, *The Snowman.* 25 min.

See also **The Snowman.**

Father Christmas (gift-giver)
See **Great Britain**

Father Knows Best

Emmy Award-winning television situation comedy series of 203 30-minute episodes that aired on the CBS network from 1954 to 1955, on the NBC network from 1955 to 1958, and back on CBS from 1958 to 1960. Created by Ed James and popular for its presentation of wholesome family values, the series featured the following regular cast members: Robert Young as insurance salesman Jim Anderson, Sr.; Jane Wyatt as wife Margaret; Elinor Donahue as teenage daughter Betty ("Princess"); Billy Gray as teenage son Jim, Jr. ("Bud"); and Lauren Chapin as younger daughter Kathy ("Kitten").

Two original episodes were devoted to Christmas with one rebroadcast, as summarized in the following paragraphs:

The Christmas Story (aired December 19, 1954). Desiring to instill the Christmas spirit into his family, Jim takes them on a trek out into the country in search of a Christmas tree on Christmas Eve. Their car runs into a snowbank, whereupon the Andersons seek shelter in a vacant country store. They are not alone, for inhabiting the premises is the lonely old hermit Nick (Wallace Ford), who is overjoyed to have company for Christmas. Although circumstances are certainly less than optimal for Betty and Bud, Kathy finds Nick's enthusiasm so infectious that she gives him her teddy bear as a Christmas present. In turn, Nick selects items from the shelves as presents for the Andersons and, for lack of cash, signs IOUs. Parts of this episode were rebroadcast on December 15, 1958, as flashback sequences while the Andersons decorate their Christmas tree. With William Traylor as Les Turner. Story by Roswell Rogers and Paul West. Teleplay by Roswell Rogers. Produced by Eugene B. Rodney. Directed by William D. Russell. A Rodney/Young Production in association with Screen Gems Television. B & W. Video N/A.

The Angel's Sweater (aired December 19, 1956). Initially, Christmas Eve is less than merry with the arrival of Jim's only sister Neva (Katherine Warren), a lonely spinster who, according to Kathy, "takes a dim view of kids." Tension mounts after she scolds Kathy over a minor mishap, which completely alienates the child, and family morale declines further when a water pipe bursts. As if heaven sent, Jim secures the services of "Mr. Fixit" (Ludwig Stossel), an elderly repairman from the Old World who senses Kathy's unhappiness. While repairing the pipe, he spins a Christmas yarn that changes Kathy's attitude, and while he does, the Andersons portray the story's characters. Following tradition, the little girl Katrina (Kathy) and her mother (Margaret) search for a special gift to bring to church on Christmas Eve that will benefit the poor. As she ponders over what might be the greatest gift, her friend Hans (Bud), a young fisherman, only offers that she must find the answer for herself. Suddenly, a "regulation" angel (Betty) appears to confirm Hans's words. Then Katrina runs to the shop of the benevolent Herr Grosenheimer (Jim) with a most strange request — to buy a sweater for an angel, because the angel's white "nightgown" doesn't appear very warm. Although Katrina's few pennies fall far short of the price, Grosenheimer, seeing that she is in earnest, sells her a "regulation" sweater at a special discount for angels. Outside, an ugly old hag in black (Aunt Neva) covertly steals the sweater, and Katrina believes that it is now in the angel's possession, until she sees the old woman wearing it. Convinced that the angel must have given the sweater to the woman out of love, Katrina decides to love her as well. Suddenly, the woman is transformed into a beautiful matron attired in silver and gold, for Katrina has given her something that no other person had ever given; it is the greatest gift — love. The parable concluded, Kathy softens with love for her aunt, and as the nearby church bells peal glad tidings, the episode closes with the Andersons admiring the evening snowfall. Story and teleplay by Roswell Rogers. Produced by Eugene B. Rodney. Directed by Peter Tewksbury. A Rodney/Young Production in association with Screen Gems Television. B & W. Video N/A.

On December 18, 1977, the original Anderson cast returned to NBC for a reunion special entitled *Father Knows Best: Home for Christmas*. It was one of three pilot films that were planned in an ultimately unsuccessful attempt to revive the series. With Betty, Bud, and Kathy now grown and no longer at home, the holidays promise to be less cheery for Jim and Margaret, who also face the possibility of having to sell their home. But when the children learn of their parents' plight, they all return to support them. Written by Paul West. Produced by Hugh Benson. Directed by Norman Abbott. A Rodney/Young Production in association with Columbia Pictures Television. Video N/A.

Feast of Asses
See Feast of Fools

Feast of Dedication
See Hanukkah

Feast of Fools
Collective term for a series of mock-religious festivals in force by the twelfth century, which divisions of the lower clergy, particularly in France, England, and central Europe, observed between Christmas and Epiphany (January 6). As a release from the solemnity of Christmas itself, deacons observed a feast on St. Stephen's Day (December 26), the priests on St. John the Evangelist's Day (December 27), the choirboys on Holy Innocents Day (December 28), and the subdeacons generally on the Feast of the Circumcision (January 1) or sometimes on Epiphany. The mood of each of these feasts, held within the church, was riotous and often blasphemous, with clowning, buffoonery, obscene songs, the wearing of hideous masks (often depicting wild animals), transvestism, and the reversed roles of superiors and subordinates. Each feast was supervised by an elected Archbishop of Fools, Lord of Misrule, or Abbot of Unreason, the entire affair closely resembling the extravagant license of the ancient Roman Saturnalia, which had included the crowning of a mock king.

Coupled with the Feast of the Circumcision and the revels was the Feast of the Asses, a mock-Christianization of the pagan feast of Epona, Roman goddess of horses, mules, and asses, which had been observed near the new year. On January 1, the local church staged a parody on the biblical flight into Egypt (Gospel of Matthew 2:13–15). In this parody, a young woman holding a baby rode into the sanctuary on an ass (traditionally the Virgin Mary rode an ass into Egypt as well as to Bethlehem). Rituals praised the ass; then, to conclude the service, the priest imitated an ass by braying three times, and the congregation responded in like manner.

The Feast of Asses emerged from a church drama dating to the eleventh century or earlier, which portrayed a series of Old Testament prophets attesting to the birth of Christ. One of these, Baalam, rode upon a wooden ass and reenacted the biblical story about his taking ass and an angel (Numbers 22:22–38). This segment gained wide popularity and, by the thirteenth century, had become an independent play that eventually merged with year-end revels.

Although the Feast of Fools as a whole had existed for centuries, the Church never officially sanctioned the abuses that occurred and largely succeeded in driving the celebrations from its cathedrals by the fifteenth century, although some persisted until the early eighteenth century. The peasantry then took up the merriment by electing a Prince or Pope of Fools, often bestowing upon him a hood with the ears of an ass.

French author Victor Hugo (1802–1885) provides another picture of the Feast of Fools in his historical novel *The Hunchback of Notre Dame* (1831), set in late fifteenth century Paris. Amid bonfires, a maypole, and a mystery play, the hunchbacked bell-ringer Quasimodo, crowned with a tiara and vested with a cloak, is elected Pope of Fools on Epiphany.

See also **Christmas Drama; Epiphany; The Friendly Beasts; Holy Innocents Day; Saturnalia.**

Feast of Jordan
See **Epiphany**

Feast of Lights
See **Epiphany**

Feast of the Circumcision
See **New Year's Day**

Feast of the Holy Family
Festival in the Roman Catholic Church honoring the Holy Family of Jesus, Mary, and Joseph as the virtuous family model for all Christian households, currently observed on the first Sunday after Christmas, or on December 30 if Christmas falls on a Sunday. The feast springs in part from two independent, charitable organizations devoted to their patron saints, the Holy Family: The Association of the Holy Family, founded in Montreal in 1663, and the Daughters of the Holy Family, founded in Paris in 1674. These spawned similar organizations under the same patronage. In 1844, Henri Belletable, an officer in the Engineers' Corp, Liege, Belgium, founded a society for the relief of corpsmen, which the local bishopric erected to the Confraternity of the Holy Family in 1845, and which Pope Pius IX subsequently raised to the Archconfraternity of the Holy Family in 1847.

Desiring that more charitable societies should be founded in honor of the Holy Family, Pope Leo XIII instituted the Feast of the Holy Family in 1893, which was initially

"When Friars, Monks, and Priests of former days,
Apocrypha and Scripture turn'd to Plays,
The Festival of Fools and Asses kept,
Obey'd Boy-Bishops, and to crosses crept,
They made the mumming church the People's rod,
And held the grinning Bauble for a God."

An engraving end verse from William Hone's Ancient Mysteries Described *(1823).*

approved for Canada. Pope Benedict XV extended the feast to the entire Church in 1921 and at first ordered its celebration for the first Sunday following Epiphany (January 6) or on January 12 if Epiphany fell on Sunday; in 1969 the date was moved to the first Sunday after Christmas so that it could become more of a holiday event.

Feast of the Holy Innocents
See **Holy Innocents Day**

Feast of the Immaculate Conception
Festival in the Roman Catholic Church,

observed on December 8. It commemorates the dogma, promulgated by Pope Pius IX in the bull *Ineffabilis Deus* on December 8, 1854, that the Virgin Mary, chosen from the foundation of the world to be the Mother of God, was preserved free from all stain of original sin, as recognized in the Roman Catholic Church. According to that belief, Mary was immaculately conceived by her mother, St. Anne. Coming early in December, the feast often launches Christmas celebrations in Roman Catholic countries, particularly in Spain and Latin America.

The feast arose from a much older celebration, termed the Conception of St. Anne, which the Patriarchate of Jerusalem had observed as early as the fifth century but which the Eastern Church in general did not observe until the eighth and ninth centuries. A similar feast arrived in the Western Church by the eleventh century in England and by the twelfth century in France, Germany, Italy, and Spain.

Early Church fathers who had described the Virgin as "immaculate" included St. Irenaeus of Lyons (140?–202?); St. Ephrem of Syria (306–373), dubbed the Patriarch of Antioch; and St. Ambrose of Milan (340?–397). A significant controversy over the concept of the Immaculate Conception raged between the twelfth and fifteenth centuries, led by such opponents as the French monastic St. Bernard of Clairvaux (1090–1153) and the Italian theologian St. Thomas Aquinas (c. 1225–1274); defenders included the Scottish theologian John Duns Scotus (1266–1308). By the time of Pope Alexander VII (reigned 1655–1667), the Immaculate Conception was universally accepted in the Roman Catholic Church and was officially promulgated by Pope Pius IX. In 1846, the first Council of Baltimore had consecrated the Immaculate Virgin Mary as patron saint of the United States.

Pope Pius IX further memorialized the Immaculate Conception by ordering a column erected in Rome's *Piazza di Spagna* ("Spanish Square") and a statue of the Virgin Mary set thereon. Designed by Luigi Poletti, the *Colonna dell'Immacolata* ("Column of the Immaculate Conception") was dedicated in 1857. From that time as part of the papal traditions of Advent, the Pope has placed a bou-

quet of flowers at the base of the statue annually on December 8.

See also **The Vatican.**

Feliz Navidad

(Spanish, "Merry Christmas"). Popular song written in 1970 by the blind Puerto Rican–American singer-guitarist José Feliciano. His simple lyrics first wish the listener a Merry Christmas and a prosperous New Year in Spanish, followed by a similar sentiment in English. Feliciano first recorded his song on the RCA label that same year, and despite the fact that this recording was not charted, the song has become a Christmas standard.

Of the 25 most frequently performed Christmas songs of the twentieth century listed by the American Society of Composers, Authors and Publishers (ASCAP), "Feliz Navidad" ranked number 24. By December 2004, it had jumped to number 13.

Feliciano remains popular primarily in Spanish-speaking countries, having produced a number of gold and platinum albums, principally outside of the United States.

See also **ASCAP List of Christmas Songs.**

Festival of Lights
See **Hanukkah**

A Festival of Nine Lessons and Carols

An annual musical event held on Christmas Eve in the chapel of King's College, Cambridge, England, since 1918, also known as *A Ceremony of Lessons and Carols*. It should not be confused with *A Ceremony of Carols* by English composer Benjamin Britten.

The format of *A Festival of Nine Lessons and Carols* consists of nine readings of Messianic-related biblical texts (see the lessons below) by members of King's; following each lesson, the King's choir sings at least two carols. Whereas the lesson texts remain constant, the carols may vary from year to year with one exception. Since 1919, the *Festival* has traditionally opened with the carol "Once, in Royal David's City," performed by a single choirboy singing the first verse of the carol *a cappella*. Also by tradition, the choirboy attaining this honor is not selected until a few moments before the *Festival* begins.

The *Festival* evolved from a small Christmas Eve service in 1880 that was built around nine biblical texts and nine carols compiled by the Rev. Edward W. Benson, a pastor in Truro, Cornwall, who later achieved the office of Archbishop of Canterbury. The concept became quite popular, and other churches quickly incorporated the *Festival* for their own Christmas services, the best known of which became that at King's College. The first *Festival* at King's in 1918 was planned by the dean, Eric Milner-White, with organist Arthur Henry Mann directing the music. With the exception of 1930, the *Festival* has enjoyed annual BBC radio broadcasts since 1928 and television broadcasts since 1963. Broadcasts continued through World War II, during which time the chapel glass was removed and the location withheld from broadcasts for security reasons.

Although the order and specificity of the nine lessons may show slight variation from church to church, here listed are the biblical references for, and summaries of, the lessons as observed at King's:

Lesson One: Genesis 3:8–15, 17–19. The Fall of Man and the promise that the seed of woman shall ultimately conquer the seed of the serpent.

Lesson Two: Genesis 22:15–18. God's promise to Abraham that, because of his faith, through his line all nations of the earth will be blessed.

Lesson Three: Isaiah 9:2, 6–7. Prophecy that those who walked in the darkness of sin will see the light of redemption in the Child to be born, Who will also be known as "Wonderful, Counselor, the mighty God, the everlasting Father, the Prince of Peace."

Lesson Four: Isaiah 11:1–4, 6–9. Prophecy that the Messiah will be a descendant of King David (a Branch of Jesse, David's father); also metaphorical prophecy of the coming peace through Christ.

Lesson Five: Luke 1:26–35, 38. The Annunciation to the Virgin Mary.

Lesson Six: Luke 2:1, 3–7. The journey of Mary and Joseph to Bethlehem and the birth of Jesus.

Lesson Seven: Luke 2:8–16. The angelic host appears to the shepherds.

Lesson Eight: Matthew 2:1–12. The account of the Magi.

Lesson Nine: John 1:1–14. Expounds upon Jesus as the Word, the Light, and the Incarnation.

See also **Once, in Royal David's City.**

Fiesta Bowl
See **New Year's Day**

Fiji Islands
See **Asia and the South Pacific**

Finding John Christmas
(2003). Made-for-television drama/fantasy, the second in a series of Daniel H. Blatt Productions to feature Peter Falk as Max, the mischievous angel. This picture is dedicated to all firefighters.

When a holiday photo of a vagrant and his dog appears in the local newspaper, Kathleen McCallister (Valerie Bertinelli), an emergency room nurse struggling to keep her department financially afloat, recognizes him as her older brother Hank (William Russ), a firefighter who has been missing for 25 years. She is determined to find him and enlists the aid of Noah Greeley (David Cubitt), the newspaper's photographer. Considered a town hero for having rescued children in a school fire 25 years ago, Hank becomes the subject of a newspaper publicity campaign to find the vagrant dubbed "John Christmas." Yet the memory of ten children and three fellow firefighters who perished in that fire has left Hank profoundly guilt-ridden and a self-appointed outcast. Mysteriously wealthy, Hank has returned quietly to settle financial debts long overdue and would vanish forthwith; that is, until Max intervenes with a change of plans.

Predictably, Max's little miracles lead to romance, heartwarming reunions with a few surprises, and welcome peace of mind to the poor in spirit — in short, a most happy Christmas for all principal parties involved.

Written by Michael J. Murray. Produced by Ken Gross. Directed by Andy Wolk. A Daniel H. Blatt Production in association with Viacom Productions. Video N/A. 120 min.

See also **A Town without Christmas; When Angels Come to Town.**

A reindeer pulls a Laplander in his sleigh across the icy snow. From the Sunday School Visitor, *1897.*

Finland

From the influences of the Eastern Orthodox Church and the conquest by Roman Catholic Sweden, Finland accepted Christianity over a period of years from 1050 to 1300. When the country broke from Rome in the sixteenth century, the Evangelical Lutheran Church replaced Catholicism and remained as the principal faith.

Joulua (Christmas) commences with the Advent season and citywide bazaars. Since the 1920s, most organizations, businesses, and families have organized social gatherings, called *pikkujoulu* ("Little Christmas"), as typical Christmas parties. Additional lights to combat the long periods of darkness fill the windows of shops and businesses, and decorations include Advent candles, Advent wreaths, Advent calendars, and winter greenery. It is also customary to erect a sheaf of grain on a pole outdoors for the birds ("Birds' Christmas Tree").

Since 1950, Finland has observed December 13 as St. Lucia's Day, a tradition acquired from Sweden in the 1920s and introduced by the Swedish-language newspaper *Hufvudstadsbladet* as well as the Finnish national health organization *Folkhalsan*. Although families select a Lucia among their own kindred, a national fund-raising competition selects one teenage girl annually as Finland's Lucia, who graces various functions, schools, and hospitals. Proceeds fund *Folkhalsan*.

Christmas trees are usually erected a few days before Christmas Eve and decorated with candles, miniatures of the national flag, *himmeli* (straw mobiles) of various sizes and shapes, and paper and wood ornaments.

Christmas Eve officially commences with the "Peace of Christmas," a Scandinavian custom dating to medieval times. An annual ceremony dedicated to this custom is televised throughout Finland and Sweden at noon from Finland's former capital, Turku, which now refers to itself as Finland's "Christmas City." From the balcony of Brinkkala Mansion in the Old Great Square, a public official reads the text of a medieval document that orders all citizens to maintain peace during the Christmas season or suffer criminal penalties. Included in the telecast is a service from Turku Cathedral, in which bishops from the Lutheran, Orthodox, Roman Catholic, and Methodist faiths plead for world peace.

At sundown on Christmas Eve, families adorn the graves of their ancestors with lighted candles and wreaths and visit the sauna prior to the evening's festivities. Whereas manufactured gifts were popular in the early twentieth century, homemade gifts have once again become popular, as they were in the nineteenth century. Children personally receive gifts on Christmas Eve from *Joulupukki* (literally "Yule Buck," Father Christmas), who arrives in the form of a friend or relative dressed similarly to Santa Claus and who traditionally inquires, "Are there any good children here?" Children often dress as *Joulutonttuja* (elves or gnomes) in red suits and caps, while adults entertain the special visitor with carols. According to a tradition established by the Finnish Broadcasting Company in 1927, Father Christmas, who resembles the American Santa Claus with his reindeer and elves, resides with his wife, Mother Christmas, atop Mount Korvatunturi in the eastern region of Lapland belonging to Finland. Children address their Christmas letters to this location, where special postal workers answer each letter in the guise of Father Christmas.

The association of a goat figure with gift-bringer derives from pre-Christian Yule festivals, which paid homage to the gods. At the winter solstice, it was believed that Thor, as he rode through the skies in a chariot pulled by two billy goats named Gnasher and Cracker, distributed gifts to the Vikings while his father and chief of the gods, Odin, riding his white, eight-legged steed Sleipner, escorted the souls of slain heroes into Valhalla. Men costumed as goats portrayed this belief by making surprise entrances at Yule parties, and after dancing about, "died" and then returned to life. During the Middle Ages, the goat figure evolved into the devil in Scandinavian Christmas folk revels, and men costumed in goat skins and masks frolicked about, much to the dismay of the Church, which banned such behavior in the sixteenth century. In more remote regions today, the gift-bearer may be known as Wainamoinen, who arrives on his goat steed, Ukko. The former, depicted as an old man clad in a red coat and sporting a long, white mustache, derives from the principal worker of mighty deeds and hero of the *Kalevala*, a series of anonymous, centuries-old poems that collectively comprise the national epic poem of Finland. In that work, Ukko is the supreme god.

The Christmas Eve meal follows the distribution of gifts and often includes salmon, ham, herring, *lutefisk* (codfish), assorted casseroles, liver pâté, mixed fruit soup with cinnamon, *joululeipä* (Christmas bread), *joulutortut* (Christmas fruit pastry), *piparkakut* (ginger cookies), *korvapuustit* (cinnamon buns), and *glögg* (a warmed, spiced drink composed of red wine, sugar, raisins, cinnamon, cloves, orange peeling, and almonds). A traditional, holiday dish served throughout Scandinavia is rice porridge with one almond in the batch; the person receiving the almond in his serving will have good luck in the coming year. After dinner, there may be readings from the Bible or the singing of carols as family members join hands and walk around the Christmas tree.

Christmas Day is spent with family attending early morning church services and enjoying quiet devotion at home. St. Stephen's Day or "Second Christmas Day" is also a holiday, while traditions of New Year's Eve include fortune-telling games such as interpreting shadows cast from the shapes created after molten lead or tin is cooled in water. The

Christmas season ends on Epiphany, January 6.

"Merry Christmas" is *Hyvää Joulua*.
See also **Advent**; **Epiphany**; **Sweden**.

The Fir Tree

The only fairy tale by the celebrated Danish author Hans Christian Andersen with a Christmas setting. Clearly presenting a strong moral, the story features a young Fir Tree that cannot appreciate its youth or its lovely environment in the forest because it yearns to be taller, older, or somewhere else. When the Tree desires to be a ship's mast, the Sunbeams caution it to rejoice in its youth. When the Sparrow brings news of gorgeous Christmas trees decorated in town, the Fir Tree impatiently wishes to be one. But the elements again caution the Tree to rejoice in the Air, the Wind, and its youth.

At last, the mature Tree is cut down, erected in a grand home, and trimmed exquisitely for Christmas Eve. Now, the Tree believes, it will live in splendor forever. But one of its burning candles scorches a branch, and then children plunder gifts from its branches, leaving its appearance disheveled.

Expecting to be redecorated the next day, the Tree instead is thrown into an isolated garret, where it remains alone for days. Inquisitive mice prompt the Tree to tell them its history, and in doing so, the Tree realizes too late that it really had a good life in the forest. Withered, yellow, and now considered ugly by the children, the Tree is soon burned for firewood.

It is uncertain whether Andersen deliberately incorporated a particular piece of European folklore about Christmas evergreens into the ending, but it is in keeping with the old superstition that, at holidays' end, Christmas evergreens should be burned rather than thrown out. The story also implies that gifts were hung on the tree and not placed beneath, which further implies that the tree was set on a table (*see* **Christmas Tree**).

Hans Christian Andersen (1805–1875) wrote some 150 fairy tales. His life's work as a writer of children's fairy tales and stories commenced with a small volume, *Fairy Tales Told for Children* (1835). Although a number of his tales have winter settings, such as "The Snow

Queen," only two, "The Fir Tree" and "The Little Match Girl," are set amid the holidays. The latter story is a tale of New Year's Eve.

See also **The Little Match Girl.**

The First Christmas: The Story of the First Christmas Snow

(1975). Made-for-television animated story using stop-motion puppets (Animagic).

Three nuns in a French abbey provide care for a little shepherd boy, Lucas, an orphan who is struck and blinded by lightning a few weeks before Christmas. The nuns become fond of Lucas and wish for him to remain, but Father Thomas is set on sending him to an orphanage after the holidays. Lucas's only wish is to have snow for Christmas, though he's never seen it and, barring a miracle, never will. Having nothing with which to buy Christmas presents, Lucas gives Sister Theresa his dog Waggles and his little flock of sheep, his only possessions.

During the Christmas Eve Nativity pageant, as Lucas sings in the angel choir, snow miraculously falls from a cloudless, starlit sky, the first Christmas snow. When flakes touch Lucas's eyes, his sight is restored. In addition to this wonder, Father Thomas grants that Lucas may remain with them always.

Featuring the Irving Berlin classic, "White Christmas." Narrated and sung by Angela Lansbury. Principal voices: Cyril Ritchard, David Kelley, Don Messick, Dina Lynn, Sean Manning, Greg Thomas, Hilary Momberger, Iris Rainer, Joan Gardner, and the Wee Winter Singers. Written by Julian P. Gardner. Produced and directed by Arthur Rankin, Jr., and Jules Bass. A Rankin/Bass Production. VHS: Warner Home Video. 22 min.

This television special is further detailed in Rick Goldschmidt's book, *The Enchanted World of Rankin/Bass.*

See also **Rankin/Bass Christmas Cartoons; White Christmas** (song).

The First Christmas Tree: A Story of the Forest

Classic short story written by the American clergyman and author Henry Van Dyke (1852–1933), who first delivered the story as a sermon to his congregation in 1897. It is based on the legend of Winfried (or Winfrid), the English missionary known as St. Boniface, the "Apostle of Germany," who brought Christianity to Germanic tribes in the eighth century and who supposedly was responsible for the dramatic introduction of the first Christmas tree.

On Christmas Eve in the year 722, Winfried, during a visit to the cloister of Pfalzel in Germany, convinces young Prince Gregor, grandson of King Dagobert, to take up the life of a pilgrim and join him in converting the pagans. On Christmas Eve two years later, Winfried leads his party of 20 to the sacred, giant thunder-oak at Geismar, sacred to the Scandinavian god Thor, where a multitude has gathered to celebrate Yule, to worship Thor, and to appease his wrath with a human sacrifice. The old priest Hunrad chooses Chief Gundhar's young son, Bernhard, who is prepared to enter Valhalla (the domain of the chief god, Odin, into which the souls of slain heroes are received). Staying Hunrad's hand, Winfried announces his intent to deliver them from evil and reads a parchment from the bishop of Rome that summarizes his mission. To prove that Thor is a false god, Winfried and Gregor commence chopping down the great oak, when a sudden, mighty wind, the hand of God, rips the oak from its roots and splits it into four pieces. As Winfried commands the pagans to build a church on the spot with the wood, he notices a little fir tree among the pieces and declares this to be the tree of the Christ Child, the substitute symbol of their new worship. He also commands that they no longer meet secretly in forests but keep their feasts at home with laughter and love. After the fir tree is erected in Gundhar's hall and decorated, the pilgrims chant a Christmas hymn while Winfried shares the Nativity story with everyone.

See also **Christmas Tree; The Other Wise Man; Yule.**

The First Gift of Christmas

Short collection of seasonal thoughts and introspections on love, faith, and parenthood, written by American author Richard Paul Evans, published in 1996. Through poetry, Evans reflects on Christmas from four different aspects, which he terms the "four seasons of Christmas."

First Season — Advent. "What Christmas Asks" recalls the Nativity story as presented in Luke and Matthew, then asks if we are prepared to give Christmas access to our souls, to set aside our daily burdens, and to seek higher spheres.

Second Season — Christmas Eve. "The First Gift of Christmas" romantically muses on the magic of the evening's preparations, the lovely memories of a parent's own childhood, and the first gift of every Christmas, which is a parent's love.

Third Season — Christmas Morning. Aside from the "festive abandon" of presents opened and empty boxes, "Christmas Morning" draws a metaphorical parallel between life and Christmas: both are journeys to be traveled; therefore, may the final destination of each be as sweet and as complete as the journey itself.

Fourth Season — Christmas Night. "Is It Enough?" looks back over the elements of the season — the parties, rituals, music, gifts — with hope that these elements have instilled such awe and magic, faith and values, that they will far outlast childhood.

Richard Paul Evans is best known for his novel, *The Christmas Box* (1995).

See also **The Christmas Box; The Christmas Candle; The Light of Christmas.**

The First Nowell

English traditional carol, a narrative of the Nativity, believed to have arisen during the fifteenth century from the Cornwall region. Often the French word "Noël" ("Christmas") is substituted, resulting in the misconception that the carol is French. Because the English word "Nowell," itself dating at least from the fourteenth century, derives from either "Noël" or "Nouvelle" ("New"), the source for the substitution becomes apparent.

The earliest known publication of the lyrics alone, which had previously surfaced as nine verses on broadsides printed near Cornwall, appeared in the second edition of Davies Gilbert's collection *Some Ancient Christmas Carols* (London, 1823). Ten years later, the tune was first published along with the lyrics in William Sandys's collection *Christmas Carols, Ancient and Modern* (London, 1833). According to Studwell's *The Christmas Carol Reader,*

the notes to the phrase "Born is the King" in the original refrain were subsequently altered to those in common usage today; *The New Oxford Book of Carols* claims that John Stainer modernized the Sandys tune and published it in *Christmas Carols New and Old*, co-edited with Henry Bramley (London, 1871).

Music scholars now believe that Sandys's version derives from several alternate (and earlier) renderings of the carol, the first of which was discovered in 1913 in Cambourne by English carol collector Cecil Sharp. Whereas verse one of Sharp's discovery opens with "Nowell and nowell," the same words also appearing in the refrain instead of "Nowell, nowell," other versions include either "O well and O well" or "Nowell and nowell," which open verse one as well as the refrain.

The English composer Ralph Vaughan Williams (1872–1958) incorporated "The First Nowell" into several of his works: as excerpts in *Fantasia on Christmas Carols* (1912, for baritone, choir, and orchestra); as opening and closing themes in the masque *On Christmas Night* (1925–26); and as the title theme in the Nativity play *The First Nowell* (1958, for soloists, choir, and orchestra).

Firstfooting
See **Great Britain**

Flight of the Reindeer
See **The Christmas Secret**

A Flintstone Christmas
See **The Flintstones**

A Flintstone Family Christmas
See **The Flintstones**

The Flintstones

The first primetime, made-for-television animated cartoon series created by the animation giant Hanna-Barbera Studios. Airing on the ABC network from 1960 to 1966 with 166 episodes, the principal Stone-Age characters included Fred and Wilma Flintstone with daughter Pebbles, pet dinosaur Dino, neighbors Barney and Betty Rubble with son Bamm-Bamm, and Fred's boss at the rock quarry, Mr. Slate. *The Flintstones* revolved around Fred's and Barney's shenanigans in the town of

Bedrock, where every name was derived from some form of stone or prehistoric creature.

The Flintstones and Rubbles enjoyed Christmas in four productions:

How the Flintstones Saved Christmas (1964), an episode from the original series. Needing some extra Christmas cash, Fred takes a part-time job in the Bedrock Department Store. Inept as a gift wrapper and stock boy, he avoids termination by playing the part of the store's Santa Claus, for which he is most qualified. On Christmas Eve, Winkie and Blinkie, two elves sent by the real Santa, offer Fred the opportunity of taking Santa's place that year, because the jolly old elf is sick with a cold. Glad to help, Fred speeds around the world in a sleigh drawn by three little dinosaurs with antlers. As he drops presents from the sleigh, they parachute into the chimneys of homes. But after the elves depart, Fred realizes that he has nothing for his own family, for their gifts were aboard the sleigh. Dejected, he returns home, then rejoices to find that Santa had rallied and had made a special delivery to everyone there, sneezing all the way.

Voices: Alan Reed, Mel Blanc, Jean Vander Pyl, Gerry Johnson, Don Messick, and Harvey Korman. Written by Herbert Finn and Alan Dinehart. Produced and directed by William Hanna and Joseph Barbera. Hanna-Barbera Productions. VHS: Hanna-Barbera Home Video. 30 min.

A Flintstone Christmas (1977). Television special, virtually a remake of the 1964 episode with an additional story line. To keep his job at the rock quarry, Fred agrees to play Santa at a benefit for the Bedrock Orphanage, as requested by Mr. Slate. But when the real Santa slips on Fred's roof and sprains his ankle in addition to catching cold, Fred and Barney must take over Santa's Christmas Eve rounds. With Fred in Santa's own suit and with Barney dressed as an elf, the two bumble their way around the world, losing half of the presents in a snow storm. Forced to return to the North Pole for another load with time drawing nigh for the benefit, Fred kicks the sleigh into high gear, dropping presents like bombs into chimneys. The two arrive back at the orphanage just in the (St.) Nick of time as Mr. Slate is about to fire Fred. Arriving with an empty sack, Fred

quickly takes advantage of Santa's magical suit and conjures up abundant gifts for the children.

Voices: Mel Blanc, Lucille Bliss, Henry Corden, Virginia Gregg, Gay Hartwig, Don Messick, Hal Smith, John Stephenson, and Jean Vander Pyl. Written by Duane Poole and Dick Robbins. Creative producer, Iwao Takamoto. Directed by Charles A. Nichols. Hanna-Barbera Productions. VHS: Hanna-Barbera Home Video. 60 min.

A Flintstone Family Christmas (1993). Television special. On Christmas Eve, Stoney, a "caveless" boy dressed as Santa who cares nothing for Christmas, robs Fred and Barney while they are out shopping. Rather than see him spend the holidays in Juvenile Hall, Wilma persuades a reluctant Fred to bring the boy home to share the season with the Flintstones. In time, Fred and Stoney warm to each other, and the gang heads to a Christmas tree lot, where Stoney sets up a quick game of chance to help raise money for a special tree that Fred cannot afford. The scene further deteriorates when Fred, defending Stoney against a thug who accuses the boy of cheating, is slugged, hospitalized, and unable to play Santa in the Bedrock Christmas Parade as previously planned. Mr. Slate, in charge of Fred's float, must find a replacement, and when he retrieves the Santa suit at Fred's house, Stoney, wishing to do Fred a good turn, locks Slate in the bathroom and rushes the suit to the hospital. Fred's attempt to free Slate lands him and Stoney in jail temporarily on kidnapping charges, but Slate bails them out, and a social worker takes Stoney away. Just making the parade, Fred takes to the skies in his sleigh drawn by six flying pterodactyls, plucks Stoney from the car headed to Juvenile Hall, and takes him home to stay. That evening, after Pebbles with husband Bamm-Bamm and the grandchildren arrive for merriment, Stoney, the newest member of the family, places the star (lit by a firefly) atop the Christmas tree. In 1994, this program received an Emmy nomination for Outstanding Animated Program (One Hour or Less).

Voices: Charlie Adler, Hamilton Camp, Christine Cavanaugh, Didi Cohn, Henry Corden, Nick Jameson, Megan Mullally, Robert Ridgely, Kath Soucie, John Stephenson, Jean

Vander Pyl, B.J. Ward, Frank Welker, and Alan Young. Written by Sean Roche and David Ehrman. Produced by Larry Huber. Directed by Ray Patterson. Hanna-Barbera Productions. This program is included in the video collection *Christmas in Bedrock* (see below).

A Flintstones Christmas Carol (1994). Television special, in which the Flintstones and Rubbles star in the Bedrock Community Theater's production of *A Christmas Carol*, with the usual cast of Charles "Brickens's" characters modified to the Stone Age: Scrooge (Fred); Bob and Mrs. "Cragit," daughter Martha, and Tiny Tim (Barney, Betty, Pebbles, and Bamm-Bamm, respectively); and "Marbley's" Ghost (Mr. Slate). Because the city has been hit with the Bedrock Bug, a nasty 24-hour virus, and many cast members are out ill, Wilma, originally the stage manager and costume designer, also doubles as the Ghost of Christmas Past and as Belle, Scrooge's fiancée. Betty takes over the makeup department, while Dino steps in as a white-hooded Ghost of Christmas Yet to Come. As the play closes and Bamm-Bamm forgets Tiny Tim's famous last line, Pebbles finishes with, "God bless us, every one!" This movie was the recipient of an award from the Film Advisory Board.

Principal voices: Henry Corden, Jean Vander Pyl, Frank Welker, B.J. Ward, Russi Taylor, Don Messick, John Stephenson, Marsha Clark, Will Ryan, Brian Cummings, Rene Levant, and John Rhys-Davies. Written by Glenn Leopold. Produced and directed by Joanna Romersa. Hanna-Barbera Productions. VHS: Hanna-Barbera Home Video. 70 min.

Christmas in Bedrock (1996). Video collection of previously aired *Flintstones* productions: *How the Flintstones Saved Christmas* (1964) and *A Flintstone Family Christmas* (1993), plus two Hanna-Barbera cartoon "shorts": *Breezly and Sneezly in Noodrick of the North* (1965) and *Dino in The Great Egg-Scape* (1995). Hanna-Barbera Productions. Hanna-Barbera Home Video. 60 min.

See also **Hanna-Barbera Christmas Cartoons.**

A Flintstones Christmas Carol
See **The Flintstones**

Football Bowl Games
See **New Year's Day**

The Fourth King
(1997). Made-for-television animated cartoon.

Upon learning that a bright star in the sky heralds Jesus' birth and that three human kings are going to visit Him in Bethlehem, the animal kingdom decides to send a representative of its own. Uno, the lion, feels that he should go, because he is the strongest and wisest. Feathers, the sparrow, insists on accompanying him, and a beaver, rabbit, and turtle join them along the way. Uno, haughty and self-reliant, reluctantly requires his companions' help twice to escape danger, once after he plunges into a river while fleeing Roman soldiers set on capturing him, and again when he is caged after falling into a pit. Following the Star to Bethlehem, a more humble lion and his friends realize that they have no gift for the Christ Child, as do the Three Kings. An inspired Feathers then offers a gift on behalf of all of the animals, a song of love.

Voices: Ted Ross, Laurie Beechman, Arnold Stang, Robert McFadden, and Ed Klein. Written by Alvin Cooperman and Seymour Reit. Produced by Alvin Cooperman and Bruno Caliandro. Directed by Romano Scarpa. A Production of RAI Corporation in association with Fourth King Productions. VHS: Anchor Bay Entertainment. 24 min.

The Fourth Wise Man
See **The Other Wise Man**

France
Predominantly Roman Catholic, this nation has celebrated Christmas since 496, when St. Rémi, bishop of the region formerly known as Gaul, baptized Clovis I (c. 466–511), king of the Franks, along with 3,000 of his army at Rheims on Christmas Day. Clovis's Christian wife, Clotilda of Burgundy, is believed to have had the greatest influence upon his conversion, after which Clovis championed Christianity throughout Gaul.

The Christmas season extends from St. Nicholas's Day (December 6) to Epiphany (January 6). To honor the archbishop of Myra,

While the Miracle Play was going on in a medieval French town, armed guards roamed the streets to watch people's houses, and householders hung many lights from their houses and above the streets to discourage burglaries. From Harper's New Monthly Magazine, *December 1888.*

lollipops, electric lights, and perhaps candles. The Christmas tree was first known in France by 1605, for an account from Strasbourg in eastern France stated that Christmas trees at that time were decorated with apples, paper roses, candy, and other treats. This custom arrived in Paris in 1837 through Princess Helene of Mecklenburg, wife of the Duke of Orléans.

Churches and theaters throughout the country sponsor *pastorales*, miracle plays about the Nativity and French legends surrounding it, many of which date to the Middle Ages. In Provence especially, such plays feature living *crèches* ("cribs") or Nativity scenes (see below), the characters of which form candlelight processions en route to the church on Christmas Eve. Other theatrical events include noted puppet shows in Paris and Lyon, one popular, contemporary example of which is de Marynbourg's "Bethlehem 1933."

By far the most treasured of Christmas symbols is the *crèche*, which decorates every Roman Catholic home and church. Although the family of St. Francis of Assisi first introduced the *crèche* to Avignon during the first half of the fourteenth century, the custom did not become popular until the sixteenth century. Antique *crèches* may be found in the cathedrals at Chartres, Chaource, Nogent-le-Rotrou, Sainte-Marie d'Oloron, and in several museums, such as those in Marseilles and Orléans. *Crèches* are usually erected a week to several days before Christmas Eve, and it is customary to advance the Wise Men closer to the manger with each succeeding day until Epiphany. The figure of the Christ Child is not placed in the manger until Christmas Eve. *Crèches* may be fashioned from wood, paper, porcelain, or from unusual items such as lumps of sugar and bread crumbs. Some may also feature animated figures.

The most famous *crèches* are those from the region of Provence, which traditionally consist of rather expansive scenes depicting not the setting of Bethlehem but the French countryside in elaborate detail, because folklore

most cities host pageants in which men attired as St. Nicholas parade through the streets, followed by St. Nicholas's antithesis, *Père Fouettard* ("Father Whipper"). The latter, a forbidding figure with a long, unkempt beard and a dark robe, carries a basket of switches with which to discipline naughty youngsters. Children customarily receive candy and other treats on this day.

Families prepare their homes with a thorough cleaning and decorate them with fir branches, holly, mistletoe, assorted flowers, poinsettias, and Christmas roses. Candles arranged by the hearth symbolize hope. *Sapins* (Christmas trees) are decorated a few days before Christmas with colored balls, figures of animals and angels, paper fruit and flowers, tinsel, pine cones, walnuts, bags of candy and contends that Jesus was born in France. Amid the miniature figures of the Holy Family, shepherds, ox, donkey, angels, and Wise Men are those portraying people from all modern walks of life, such as the butcher, baker, miller, police officer, and so forth. The Provençal Nativity figures, or *santons* ("little saints"), are just as famous, having been brought to France by Italian artisans who arrived in Marseille in the early 1800s. The figures became popular, and fashioning them became an art that has remained with several French families for succeeding generations. Provence offers two basic varieties of *santons*, those of clay (*santons d'argile*) and those clothed in period costume (*santons habillés*), all of which are displayed at the annual *santon* fair in Marseilles, held since December 1803.

Children receive gifts either from *Le Petit Jésus* ("The Little Jesus") or from *Père Noël* ("Father Christmas"), whom Baby Jesus sends in His place and who, in addition to riding a donkey, closely resembles the white-bearded St. Nicholas clothed in a red cleric's robe, hood, and wooden shoes. Having written their letters to *Père Noël* at the North Pole earlier in the season, children place their shoes near the hearth, near the *crèche*, or under the Christmas tree on Christmas Eve to be filled with presents and treats overnight, and they usually prepare a small snack for *Père Noël* and his donkey. In the spirit of the season, families may welcome children's shoes from homes of lesser means. Traditional receptacles of former days, *sabots* (wooden shoes) now survive as confections molded from chocolate. Before the children retire, parents may treat them to a Christmas story, a favorite of which is "The Three Masses" by Provençal author Alphonse Daudet (1840–1897). In this story, a priest, greedily anticipating the sumptuous meal to follow, receives divine punishment for irreverently rushing through the three Christmas Eve Masses.

With the exception of young children, everyone attends Midnight Mass on Christmas Eve, after which people congregate either in their homes with friends and relatives or in restaurants for *le réveillon* ("the awakening"). This traditional Christmas meal varies considerably from region to region, may feature as many as 15 courses, and often extends until dawn. A broad range of cuisine includes beef, lamb, fowls, venison, assorted seafood, fruits, pastries, pâtés, cheeses, breads, candies, *sotelties* (confections created in the shapes of miniature castles, biblical scenes, or animals), and wines. *Bûche de Noël* ("Christmas log"), a traditional dessert shaped like a Yule log, consists of an elongated sponge cake rolled with chocolate buttercream filling and covered with brown icing. Scoring the latter creates the appearance of tree bark, and the cake is garnished with powdered sugar, nuts, and Christmas images. This dessert symbolizes the Yule log, which was popular in France in previous centuries but largely has been abandoned with the advent of modern heating technology. In the Alpine regions, where torchlight ski processions down mountainsides are common, *le réveillon* may feature beef or an omelet with *escargot* (snails); in Brittany, where it is believed that the angel of the seas guides lost ships on Christmas Eve, there are buckwheat cakes and cream; in Burgundy, turkey with chestnuts. Provence, in addition to lobster, pheasant, and lamb, traditionally serves 13 desserts, symbolic of Christ and His Twelve Apostles. In Paris and the *Ile de France*, oysters on the half shell and *pâté de foie gras* (goose liver pâté) are quite popular.

New Year's Day is devoted to family visitations and a repetition of *le réveillon,* where the principal course is roast chicken. Domestic help customarily receive a seasonal bonus at this time, and adults, not children, exchange *étrennes* (gifts) at this time. This term derives from the Latin *strenae*, which were gifts given to honor the Roman goddess Strenia during the Saturnalia.

On *jour de rois* (Three Kings Day, Epiphany, January 6), the principal custom is to cut a *galette des rois* ("Kings' Cake") in which is hidden a bean or a small porcelain figure. A small child customarily distributes the slices, and whoever finds the object in his becomes "King for a Day," and all guests at such parties are subject to his whims. Instead of receiving gifts on Christmas Day, children in the South of France near Spain receive gifts on Epiphany from the Three Kings.

"Merry Christmas" in France is *Joyeux Noël*.

See also **Epiphany; Nativity Scene; Saturnalia; Yule.**

The Friendly Beasts

Traditional carol of uncertain origin, the music of which derives from an anonymous, twelfth century Latin hymn, "Orientis partibus" ("Song of the Ass" or "Donkey Carol"), although some have credited this music to Pierre de Corbeil, bishop of Sens, France (ruled 1200–1222). The hymn, originating in either England or France, is said to have been used during the medieval Feast of Asses or Donkey Festival, which formed a part of the larger Feast of Fools. More uncertainty surrounds the origin of the lyrics to the carol known today as "The Friendly Beasts." Studwell's *The Christmas Carol Reader* suggests that a Robert Davis, an otherwise obscure American, may have written the lyrics to "The Friendly Beasts," and that they were first printed in 1934 (publisher not listed) but not registered for copyright until 1949. However, until this or any other alleged lyricist for this carol is identified beyond question, this carol must remain "traditional." It is also known as "The Animal Carol" and "The Gift of the Animals."

The subject of the carol is based on legends holding that when Christ was born, the stable animals either presented Him with gifts or performed various services and good deeds for Him, for which He rewarded their kindness with the gift of speech at midnight, not only at the first Christmas, but annually thereafter. In this instance, several animals tell of their gifts to the Babe. A shaggy, brown donkey carried Mary to Bethlehem; a red-and-white cow donates her manger for a cradle and her hay for a pillow; a curly-horned sheep yields its wool for a warm blanket; two doves in the rafters coo the Babe to sleep; and a yellow-and-black camel brings one of the Magi with a gift in his pack. A similar gift theme is found in "The Burgundian Carol."

According to other gift legends, the rooster was the first animal to herald the birth of Christ by crowing at midnight (*see* **Mass of the Rooster**); the robin acquired its red breast by having stood too near the Holy Family's fire while fanning the flames with its wings; the stork donated its feathers to line the manger;

the nightingale, by caroling the "Gloria in excelsis" along with the heavenly host, acquired the sweetest of avian voices. A legend paralleling that of Italy's *La Befana* and Russia's *Baboushka* involves the owl, who decided not to follow the other animals to Bethlehem. Like these two spirits, the owl repented and now forever seeks the Christ Child under the cover of darkness by crying "Whooo," a plea to be led to the Babe.

See also **The Burgundian Carol; Carol of the Birds; Feast of Fools; Italy; Russia.**

From Bethl'em's City

See **Angels and Shepherds**

From Heaven Above to Earth I Come

("Vom Himmel hoch, da komm' ich her"). German carol, the only original Christmas carol, complete with its own music, written by Martin Luther (1483–1546), initiator of the Protestant Reformation. Designed as part of a family ceremony for Christmas Eve 1534, the carol consisted of 15 verses, the first five of which were sung by a man dressed as an angel standing beside a crib to announce that Christ is born. Luther's children took the remaining verses, a running commentary on the Nativity and the divinity of the Babe, with the angel joining them on the last verse, the final praise to God.

Luther initially set his lyrics to a folk tune of the time and published his carol in the *Geistliche Lieder*, printed by a Herr Klug (revised edition, Wittenberg, 1535), then republished the carol with his own superior, original music in *Geistliche Lieder* (Leipzig, 1539), edited by Valentin Schumann. It is this latter setting that established "Vom Himmel hoch" as one of Germany's most popular carols. Great Britain's Catherine Winkworth (1827–1878), a translation specialist, published the best-known English version in 1855.

Not only has Luther's melody been the setting for other hymn texts (for example, Luther's "Vom Himmel kam der Engel Schar" ["From Heaven Came the Angel Host"], 1543), but the German composer J.S. Bach (1685–1750) also used it in his *Christmas Oratorio* (BWV 248) of 1734. In addition, there are a number of organ chorale preludes based on "Vom Himmel hoch," notably those by Bach: *Orgelbüchlein* (BWV 606), BWV 700, BWV 701 fughetta, BWV 738, and BWV 769 canonic variations.

See also **Christmas Oratorio.**

From Out of the Forest a Cuckoo Flew
See **Carol of the Birds**

Frosty Returns
(1993). Made-for-television animated cartoon sequel to *Frosty the Snowman.* Beansboro's annual winter carnival is approaching, but there may be no snow for the occasion because of Summer Wheeze, a snow repellent invented by factory tycoon Mr. Twitchel. Frosty, reincarnated by the magic hat of young Holly DeCarlo, also faces extinction. To save him, Holly presents Frosty at the carnival, where the two expose the evils of Summer Wheeze and the benefits of snow. Twitchel is foiled, and the citizens crown Frosty the king of the carnival.

Featuring the song "Frosty the Snow Man." Narrated by Jonathan Winters. Voices: Jan Hooks, Andrea Martin, Brian Doyle-Murray, Elizabeth Moss, Michael Carter, John Goodman, Steve Stoliar, Philip Glasser, Gail Lynch, and Mindy Martin. Written by Oliver Goldstick. Produced by Eryk Casemiro and Bill Melendez. Directed by Bill Melendez and Evert Brown. Bill Melendez Productions, Broadway Video, and CBS Television. DVD: Sony Music Video. 25 min. Also on the disk is *Frosty the Snowman.*

See also **Frosty the Snow Man** (song); **Frosty the Snowman** (television special); **Frosty's Winter Wonderland; Rudolph and Frosty: Christmas in July.**

Frosty the Snow Man
(Song). Popular American children's song written by New York natives Walter E. "Jack" Rollins and Steve Nelson in 1950. Having almost rejected an earlier children's piece, "Rudolph, the Red-Nosed Reindeer," which he ultimately recorded in 1949, cowboy singing star Gene Autry wisely took the advice of his wife Ina about "Frosty" as well. First recorded by Autry in 1950 on the Columbia label,

"Frosty the Snow Man," a tune about a talking snowman who frolics with children, made the pop charts for the next two years, and the Frosty character was subsequently featured in several animated productions for television.

Of the 25 most frequently performed Christmas songs of the twentieth century listed by the American Society of Composers, Authors and Publishers (ASCAP), "Frosty the Snow Man" ranked number 13. By December 2004, the song ranked number 17.

See also **ASCAP List of Christmas Songs; Frosty Returns; Frosty the Snowman** (television special); **Frosty's Winter Wonderland; Rudolph and Frosty: Christmas in July.**

Frosty the Snowman
(Television special, 1969). Cel-animated cartoon based on the children's song "Frosty the Snow Man" by Walter E. "Jack" Rollins and Steve Nelson.

When second-rate magician Professor Hinkle fails to pull a rabbit out of his hat at a children's school party on Christmas Eve, he discards it. Outside, the children fashion a snowman which they name Frosty, with a corncob pipe, two lumps of coal for eyes, and a button for a nose. The children spy Hinkle's hat lying nearby and place it on Frosty's head, at which the snowman comes to life with the salutation of "Happy Birthday." When the hat is removed, Frosty becomes merely a static snowman; when the hat is replaced, he revives and repeats "Happy Birthday." Frosty frolics with his young friends until rising temperatures threaten his existence. At the suggestion of little Karen, she, Hocus Pocus (Hinkle's rabbit), and Frosty board a refrigerated train bound for the North Pole so that Frosty may stay alive. But Hinkle, seeing what his magic hat did for Frosty and desiring to retrieve it for commercial gain, pursues Frosty along his north-bound trek and ultimately traps him in a greenhouse, where he melts. Santa arrives to restore Frosty and threatens to ignore Hinkle's Christmas list if he harasses Frosty any further. Although Frosty accompanies Santa back to the North Pole, he promises to return to the children with each new Christmas snow.

Narrated and sung by Jimmy Durante. Principal voices: Jackie Vernon, Billy DeWolfe,

June Foray, and Paul Frees. Written by Romeo Muller. Produced and directed by Arthur Rankin, Jr., and Jules Bass. A Rankin/Bass Production. DVD: Sony Music Video. 22 min.

This television special is further detailed in Rick Goldschmidt's book, *The Enchanted World of Rankin/Bass*.

See also **Frosty Returns; Frosty the Snow Man** (song); **Frosty's Winter Wonderland; Rankin/Bass Christmas Cartoons; Rudolph and Frosty: Christmas in July.**

Frosty's Winter Wonderland

(1976). Made-for-television cel-animated cartoon sequel to *Frosty the Snowman*.

Wedding bells ring for Frosty, who takes Crystal as his snow wife. With beads for eyes, a thimble for a nose, pink yarn for a mouth, and a dust mop for hair, Crystal comes to life when Frosty bestows a gift of frost flowers made of snow. Jealous of Frosty's popularity with children, Jack Frost blows a strong blizzard that almost cancels the snow nuptials, until Frosty invites Jack to be his best man. But when Parson Brown refuses to wed a couple made of snow, a snow parson is built, and the wedding proceeds.

Featured songs: "Frosty the Snow Man" and "Winter Wonderland." Narrated and sung by Andy Griffith. Principal voices: Shelley Winters, Dennis Day, Paul Frees, Jackie Vernon, Shelly Hines, Eric Stern, Manfred Olea, Barbara Jo Ewing, and the Wee Winter Singers.

Written by Romeo Muller. Produced and directed by Arthur Rankin, Jr., and Jules Bass. A Rankin/Bass Production. VHS: Warner Home Video. 23 min.

This television special is further detailed in Rick Goldschmidt's book, *The Enchanted World of Rankin/Bass*.

See also **Frosty Returns; Frosty the Snow Man** (song); **Frosty the Snowman** (television special); **Rankin/Bass Christmas Cartoons; Rudolph and Frosty: Christmas in July; Winter Wonderland.**

Fum, Fum, Fum

Spanish traditional carol from the region of Catalonia, thought to have arisen during the sixteenth or seventeenth century. Held as the most popular of carols from Spain, it has received several English translations, the best-known of which begins, "On this joyful Christmas Day sing fum, fum, fum." Another opens with, "On December five-and-twenty, fum, fum, fum." In each of the two or three verses, depending on the translation, the first line is repeated, including the "fum, fum, fum," which also concludes each verse. It is thought that the words "fum, fum, fum" imitate either the beating of a drum or the strumming of a guitar. Whatever the translation, the carol calls for all to be joyful on Christmas Day and to seek the Infant Son of Heaven, Who brings peace and goodwill to earth.

G

A Garfield Christmas

(1987). Made-for-television animated cartoon, based on the comic strip *Garfield*, a lasagna-eating cat created by Jim Davis.

Jon, Garfield's master, packs up Garfield and dog Odie and heads to his parents' farm for Christmas cheer. On Christmas morning, Garfield surprises Jon's lonely grandma with a stack of old love letters written by her late husband, which Garfield discovered in the barn,

and Odie gives Garfield a back scratcher that he built with his own paws. According to Garfield, the giving and receiving are not nearly as important as the loving.

In 1988, this program received an Emmy nomination for Outstanding Animated Program.

Voices: Lorenzo Music, Thom Huge, Gregg Berger, Pat Carroll, Pat Harrington, Jr., David Lander, Julie Payne, and Lou Rawls.

Written by Jim Davis. Produced and directed by Phil Roman. A Phil Roman Production in association with United Media–Mendelson Productions and Paws. VHS: Twentieth Century Fox Video. 24 min.

The Gathering

(1977). Made-for-television drama with one sequel.

Having sacrificed a fulfilling family life for the pursuit of success, Adam Thornton (Edward Asner), president of Thornton Industries, suddenly faces Christmas with the news that he is terminally ill. Though estranged from his four grown children and separated from his wife Kate (Maureen Stapleton) for years, Adam solicits Kate's help to reunite the family one last time at Christmas before he dies. His children, Julie (Rebecca Balding), Tom (Lawrence Pressman), Peggy (Gail Strickland), and Adam "Bud" Jr. (Gregory Harrison), are scattered across the continent. A regretful Adam especially wishes a reconciliation with Bud, his youngest, whose sentiments against the Vietnam War had offended Adam to the point that he had expelled his son from home. Bud had then left the country and fled to Canada under a false identity to escape the draft.

After Kate issues the invitations, taking care only to plead that Adam wishes to see his children again (he would not have them return simply because of his illness), she and Adam make preparations by decorating the family homeplace and the Christmas tree together, as though they had never separated. The holiday spirit overtakes Adam, who, rummaging through the attic for toys to give to his grandchildren, finds and repairs a doll house and an electric train.

On Christmas Eve, the three older children arrive with their families to fellowship, love, carols, and a rendering of "A Visit from St. Nicholas," all of which Adam considers quite a miraculous event, given his neglect of former days. Only Tom suspects his father's motives for calling everyone together when Adam, opening a gift box of fireworks from Dr. John Hodges (John Randolph), refers to him as "my doctor," an unusual phrase for the self-reliant Adam. Yet Tom keeps the secret, and

the two are drawn closer as they light up the Christmas Eve darkness with fireworks.

Bud's arrival on Christmas Day brings the long-expected meeting and forgiveness, along with two new family members whom Adam has never seen: Bud's wife Toni (Stephanie Zimbalist) and infant son, christened Adam Thornton III that same day in a home ceremony. Before everyone departs, Adam's last acts of generosity include offering Bud and Julie's unemployed husband, George (Bruce Davison), positions in his company.

In 1978, this program won an Emmy for Outstanding Drama Special and received Emmy nominations for Outstanding Art Direction, Outstanding Directing, Outstanding Lead Actress (Stapleton), and Outstanding Writing.

With Sarah Cunningham, Veronica Hamel, James Karen, and Edward Winter. Written by James Poe. Produced by Harry R. Sherman. Directed by Randal Kleiser. Hanna-Barbera Productions. VHS: Goodtimes Home Video. 94 min.

A sequel, *The Gathering, Part II*, followed in 1979. Kate assumes control of Thornton Industries and receives amorous advances from a wealthy industrialist (Efrem Zimbalist, Jr.), who wishes to buy the business. The Thornton children are not sure of this suitor's true intentions and rally at Christmastime to protect Kate. Written by Harry Longstreet and Renee Longstreet. Produced by Joel Rogosin. Directed by Charles S. Dubin. Hanna-Barbera Productions. Video N/A. 98 min.

See also **Christmas Eve** (1986), a later television drama which closely parallels *The Gathering*.

Gentle Mary Laid Her Child
See **Good King Wenceslas** (song)

George Balanchine's "The Nutcracker"
See **The Nutcracker**

Germany

This nation has enjoyed Christmas since the eighth century, when the English Benedictine missionary Winfrid, St. Boniface (c. 675–754), brought Christianity to the Germanic tribes of Europe. It is the country from which

Knecht Ruprecht *or* Krampus, *the devilish companion of St. Nicholas who carries the toy bag and helps St. Nick decide who is to get a gift, and who is to be punished. Old engraving reprinted in Phillip Snyder,* The Joys of Christmas Past: A Social History *(New York: Dodd, Mead, 1985).*

On December 5, the eve of St. Nicholas's Day, men dressed as the bishop St. Nicholas in full clerical attire ride about cities on white horses, while children set our their shoes for the saint to fill with toys and treats overnight. A St. Nicholas personage usually visits homes in neighborhoods for the traditional quizzing of children in church doctrine and the assessing of their behavior over the past year. Accompanying St. Nicholas is a personification of Satan, known, depending on the region, by a host of names such as Knecht Ruprecht, Krampus, Grampus, Hans Muff, Hans Trapp, Butz, Klaubauf, Bartel, Budelfrau, Pelznickel, Belsnickel, Habersack, Klaasbuur, Burklaas, Rauklas, Ru-klas, Bullerklaas, Aschenklas, Shaggy Goat, or simply Rider. A hideous, fur-clad figure with blackened face, dark beard, long tail, and red, serpentine tongue, this antithesis of St. Nicholas growls, rattles chains, and sports a whip with which to "beat" naughty children and those ignorant of their catechism. Some characters tote bags or baskets in which they threaten to stuff and whisk away the little offenders. Traditionally, as the Satan figure is

a number of worldwide holiday customs originated (for example, Advent wreaths, Advent candles, Advent calendars, and Christmas trees), richly interwoven with pagan rites of pre-Christian times.

Christmas is preceded by Advent and its associated customs and symbols. Also commencing at this time is the *Christkindlmarkt* (Christ Child market), a large, open-air market hosted in virtually every German city, sporting all manner of Christmas merchandise. The largest and most famous of these markets is that in Nuremberg, an annual tradition of more than 400 years. Roman Catholics erect a *Krippe* (crib), a Nativity scene, in churches and homes. Often these displays are heirlooms featuring wooden figures hundreds of years old, hand-carved by family ancestors.

A German youth, perhaps a baker's boy, carries perhaps a Weihnachtstollen, Stollen, *or fruit loaf under each arm. From the German magazine* Deutscher Kinderfreund, *1910.*

about to spring, St. Nicholas intervenes and saves the children from a fate worse than death. In their shoes on St. Nicholas's Day, naughty children find switches, coal, or dirt, gifts from the Evil One.

St. Nicholas's Day continues with vestiges of pagan rituals. In southern Germany, St. Nicholas personages lead processions to bonfire ceremonies, recalling the bonfires of ancient Yule festivals, which were believed to drive away the spirits of darkness. Donning straw sheaves and wearing grotesque masks, the *Buttenmandelhaut* (Riddle-Raddle Men) of the Bavarian Alps run through valleys creating a din with cow bells and other noisemakers as they symbolically drive away evil, recalling the pagan belief that not only fire, but loud noises, would drive away the evil spirits of winter. Following this commotion and a ceremony honoring St. Nicholas, the Riddle-Raddle Men accompany the saint as he journeys from house to house delivering gifts to children. Finally, in a scene derived from pagan fertility rites, the Riddle-Raddle Men enter homes and simply carry the single women outdoors.

On the three Thursdays before Christmas, Bavarian children observe *Klopfelnachten* (Knocking Nights), a ritual similar to Halloween in the United States. Wearing masks, they go about creating as much noise as possible to banish evil spirits. After reciting rhymes beginning with the work "knock" at each home visited, the children then receive treats from the host.

By Christmas Eve, the seasonal baking is completed, featuring such confections as gingerbread men and gingerbread houses, *Springerle* (cookies with raised designs), *Lebkuchen* (spiced cookies with candied fruit), *Stollen* (candied fruit loaf or fruit cake), *Pfeffernüsse* (pepper nuts), *Aachener Printen* (Aachen almond biscuits), and marzipan (almond confection molded into the shapes of animals or other characters). Families decorate their Christmas trees behind closed doors, and children are not allowed to view the tree until it has been decorated with the traditional gingerbread or marzipan figures, candles, and *Wunderkerzen* (sparklers). A tinkling bell then signals that the children may enter the room and partake of the tree's culinary delights.

Children also receive gifts on Christmas Eve, the traditional gift-bearer being either the Roman Catholic *Christkindl* (Christ Child) or the Protestant *Weihnachtsmann* (Christmas Man). These spirits sprang from the influence of Martin Luther (1483–1546), the German Roman Catholic priest who initiated the Protestant Reformation. Observing that the Church made much ado about honoring St. Nicholas at Christmastime, Luther strongly advocated a Christ-centered season with far less emphasis on the saint. After the Reformation, Catholics adopted the concept of the *Christkindlein* ("little Christ Child," later shortened to *Christkindl*) as the Christmas gift-bearer, yet it was inconceivable to imagine the Son of God in such a role. Therefore, tradition has held that an angelic messenger brings the gifts instead. Also confusingly termed the *Christkindl*, this spirit is depicted as a little girl with golden wings, clad in a white robe and jeweled crown, and who carries a tiny fir tree, a symbol of eternal life. The *Christkindl* supposedly helps to decorate the Christmas tree, and it is she who rings the bell when all the gifts are spread beneath it. The Protestants, on the other hand, rejecting all saints and Church-sanctioned entities as gift-bearers, created the *Weihnachtsmann* as an altered conception of St. Nicholas. His appearance is remarkably similar to that of the American Santa Claus.

In past centuries, parents in northern German villages sent their children's gifts to one man who, attired as *Knecht Ruprecht*, visited all the village homes on Christmas Night in the name of his master Jesus. After hearing an account of the children's behavior, he either distributed the gifts or presented the parents with a rod and urged them to discipline the naughty ones.

In Bavaria on Christmas Eve, the Berchten Runners (named for Berchta, a variant of Hertha, Norse goddess of the home) don grotesques masks and parade about, rhetorically asking what people have done for them during the year. Makers of mischief, they must be placated with gifts. In the city of Berchtesgaden, the minutes before midnight ring with gunfire as shooters attempt to drive away the last remaining evil spirits before Christmas arrives. Around most of the country, it is cus-

The Yule of 1889 is "blown in" by a troupe of musicians with horns, while the householders, their cats, and the postman are surrounded by a sky full of symbolic figures for a happy New Year. From the German magazine Fliegende Blätter, *December 30, 1888.*

tomary to visit the graves of loved ones on Christmas Eve and place lighted candles or small Christmas trees with candles by their tombstones. Another Christmas Eve custom is *Herbergsuchen* ("Searching for Shelter"), a custom similar to the Latin American *Las Posadas*, in which groups reenact the Holy Couple's search for shelter in Bethlehem and which terminates with *Mitternachtsmette* (Midnight Mass) (*see* **Las Posadas**).

Christmas Eve dinner may consist of roast goose with stuffing, turkey, carp, *Spätzle* (dumplings), *Königinpasteten* (meat-filled "kings' pastries"), vegetables, *Bayerisches Kraut* (Bavarian red cabbage), potato salad, spiced cakes, *Stollen*, marzipan, assorted cookies, and wines. Protestant church services are held in the afternoon or evening, Catholics attend Midnight Mass, and *Turmblasen* (brass ensembles) herald the coming of Christmas as they play chorales from church towers. This latter tradition, called "Blowing in the Yule [or Christmas]," is often repeated on New Year's Eve (*see* **Blowing in the Yule**).

Christmas Day is spent in resting and visiting family members. December 26, "Second Christmas Day" (St. Stephen's Day), is a legal holiday. Because St. Stephen is the patron saint of horses, many cities host mounted processions in honor of this saint.

The 12 days of Christmas, from Christmas Day to Epiphany (January 6), are known as *Die Zwölf Rauchnächte* ("The Twelve Smoking Nights"), a vestige of *Jul* (Yule), so named because it is customary during this period to burn incense and build bonfires, the smoke of which was once believed to dispel evil spirits at Yuletide. Additionally, people wear demon masks and make loud noises.

New Year's Eve, St. Sylvester's Day, honors the early fourth century Pope St. Sylvester I. Typically featured are gunfire, fireworks, other forms of noisemaking, and parties. Citizens of Bavaria turn off their lights just prior to midnight, then turn them on to welcome the new year.

Community parties on Epiphany often feature two pastries, each with a single bean baked inside, which derive from medieval Twelfth Night customs. The man and woman finding the beans become the Bean King and Queen of the event and are vested with authority to issue ridiculous commands, which all guests must obey. Should the king and queen both be single, superstition holds that they will eventually marry. Other superstitions include the consecrating of salt and chalk. The salt is fed to the livestock, and with the chalk people write the traditional names of the three Wise Men, Melchior, Gaspar, and Balthazar, on their homes, thus providing protection for their property. In Bavarian Processions of Light, people carry torches and lanterns through the streets and light bonfires on mountains. *Sternsinger* (star singers), groups dressed as the Magi, make rounds singing carols, and one person carries a lighted star on a pole. Pastors bless homes with holy water, by burning incense, and by writing "G+M+B," the Magi's initials, on door posts.

"Merry Christmas" in Germany is *Fröhliche Weihnachten*.

See also **Advent; Christmas Tree; Epiphany; Saint Nicholas; Saint Nicholas's Day; Yule.**

Gesu Bambino

("The Infant Jesus"). Best-known composition of the Italian American organist and composer Pietro A. Yon (1886–1943). Originally written in Italian, with an English version provided by Frederick Martens, "Gesu Bambino" centers around the Nativity, recalling the legend of flowers blooming at Christ's birth ("When blossoms flowered 'mid the snows") and applying other metaphorical attributes such as the "Christmas Rose" and "King of Love and Light" to the Child. Following each verse is the familiar refrain to the carol "Adeste Fideles": "O come, let us adore Him, Christ the Lord." The carol's popularity is attested by the various vocal and instrumental arrangements that have appeared.

Pietro A. Yon served as organist for St. Peter's in Rome (1905–1907), after which he immigrated to the United States. Securing posts as an organist in New York City, first at St. Francis-Xavier's (1907–1919, 1921–1926), then at St. Patrick's Cathedral (a post held for some 17 years until his death), Yon was renowned as an organist, composer, and teacher. In addition to numerous organ compositions, Masses, and religious services, Yon's works include an oratorio, *The Triumph of St. Patrick* (1934).

Ghana
See **Africa**

The Gift of the Animals
See **The Friendly Beasts**

The Gift of the Magi

Classic short story by American author O. Henry (pseudonym for William Sydney Porter, 1862–1910), published in 1905. Contrary to its title, this is not a story of the literal Magi, but of a young, truly loving couple.

With a weekly income of only 20 dollars, eight dollars of which rents a furnished flat in the city, Della Young has been able to save a mere $1.87 with which to buy her husband Jim a gift on Christmas Eve. In desperation, she sells her one prized possession, her own long, gorgeous hair, for 20 dollars to buy a platinum fob for Jim's gold watch. But Jim's gift for Della is a set of jeweled, tortoise-shell hair combs, which he purchased after having sold his most prized possession, his watch. Here the story ends, and the author unveils the hidden moral of the story. Superficially, these two "foolish children" unwisely sacrifice their most precious treasures. But compared to the Magi, who gave wisely to the Babe, those giving gifts in the manner of Jim and Della are truly wisest of all.

One of O. Henry's most popular stories, "The Gift of the Magi" has also appeared in other forms, including a ballet by the American Ballet Theatre and an off-Broadway musical.

• FILM AND TELEVISION ADAPTATIONS:

The Gift of the Magi (1917). Silent motion picture version starring Patsy DeForest, William R. Dunn, and Claire McCormack. Written by Katherine S. Reed. Directed by Brinsley Shaw. Vitagraph Company of America. Video N/A. B & W.

O. Henry's Full House (1952). Motion picture adaptation of five of O. Henry's short stories. Farley Granger and Jeanne Crain star in "The Gift of the Magi" segment (written by Walter Bullock, produced by André Hakim, directed by Henry King). The other stories depicted are "The Cop and the Anthem," "The Clarion Call," "The Last Leaf," and "The Ransom of Red Chief." Narrated by John Steinbeck. Twentieth Century Fox Film Corporation. Video N/A. B & W. 117 min.

The Gift of the Magi (1958). Television adaptation starring Gordon MacRae, Sally Ann Howes, and Tammy Grimes. Video N/A.

The Gift of Love (1978). Television adaptation hosted by Henry Fonda, starring Timothy Bottoms and Marie Ormond. A wealthy orphan is about to enter into an arranged marriage until a Swiss immigrant captures her heart. Written by Caryl Ledner. Produced by Mitchell Brower. Directed by Don Chaffey. Osmond Productions. DVD: Monterey Home Video. 96 min.

The Gift of the Magi (1978). Television musical adaptation starring Jim Backus, Debbie Boone, Peter Graves, John Rubenstein, and Jo Anne Worley. Directed by Marc Daniels. Video N/A.

The Gift of the Magi (1980). Award-winning Canadian adaptation starring George Wendt. Directed by Bert Van Bork. Encyclopaedia Britannica Educational Corporation. DVD: Monterey Home Video. 20 min.

The Gift of the Magi (1997). Finnish production with English subtitles. VHS: Kultur Video. 45 min.

Glastonbury Thorn

Hawthorne tree (*Crataegus mongyna biflora*) found in the town of Glastonbury, Somerset, southwestern England, that blooms at Christmastime. Its association with Christmas further stems from legends surrounding the biblical Joseph of Arimathea, a Jewish leader who donated his own tomb in which to bury the body of Christ following the Crucifixion (Luke 23:50–53). According to one of the numerous legends that also fill the significant hiatus in the Gospel accounts of Jesus' life between the ages of 12 and 30 (the so-called "lost" years of Jesus), the boy Jesus accompanied Joseph of Arimathea on one or more of the latter's voyages to the region of what is now Glastonbury. From a composite of other legends, Joseph, having obtained the Holy Grail following the Crucifixion, returned with it to Glastonbury around Christmastime of A.D. 63

to establish the first English Christian church. After ascending Wearyall Hill, Joseph thrust his staff of hawthorne wood into the ground and slept, then awoke to find that the staff had become a hawthorne tree with blooms. According to the legend, it bloomed annually thereafter at Christmastime.

Although the Thorn's yearly "miracle" attracted thousands over the centuries, the Puritan regime in the latter sixteenth century scorned its association with the supernatural. Some tales hold that one Puritan man, on attempting to destroy the tree, either was blinded or perished for his act of desecration, struck by the hand of divine providence.

Although the Glastonbury Thorn itself had perished by the seventeenth century, cuttings believed to have been taken from the original tree continued to survive in Glastonbury and other locations. By this time, people had anticipated its annual Christmas Eve blooms as a natural sign that Christmas had arrived. When England dropped the old Julian calendar and adopted the present Gregorian calendar in September of 1752, which placed Christmas Eve 11 days earlier, the Glastonbury Thorn failed to bloom on the new date. Instead, it bloomed on January 5, Christmas Eve by the old calendar, for which reason many refused to celebrate Christmas until they witnessed the blooms. The calendar change prompted the terms "Old Christmas Day" or "Christmas Old Style" for Christmas observed on January 6 and "New Christmas Day" or "Christmas New Style" for the holiday observed on December 25.

Descendants of the Glastonbury Thorn survive in England and abroad. Annually on Old Christmas Eve, the mayor and vicar of Glastonbury send a clipping to the reigning English monarch, a custom dating to the Middle Ages. In 1901, the bishop of Washington, D.C., received a clipping from the Glastonbury Thorn to commemorate the building of the National Cathedral there. Planted on Cathedral grounds, the Thorn often blooms on Christmas Day.

Glastonbury was the site of a prominent Celtic abbey, first erected during the fourth century, and was also believed to be the "Island of Avalon" mentioned in the tales of King Arthur. Indeed, during the Middle Ages, monks from Glastonbury Abbey claimed that King Arthur himself was buried in their cemetery. Although the abbey declined around 1539 and ultimately fell into ruins following King Henry VIII's dissolution of British monasteries, the Church of England now controls the estate.

See also **Christmas Old Style, Christmas New Style.**

Gloucestershire Wassail

Eighteenth century folk carol from the Gloucestershire region of England, also known as "Wassail, Wassail All Over the Town" and "Gloucestershire Wassailers' Song." Wassailers from this region reportedly made their rounds carrying a large, decorative wassail bowl while singing this carol, the merry lyrics of which call to mind the revelry and the drinking (wassailing) to the health of not only friends during the holidays but of the hired help and livestock as well. The number of verses varies, usually between five and eight, but in most versions, the carol toasts horses named Cherry and Dobbin; cattle named Broad May, Fillpail, and Colly; the butler and maid; and the wassail leader as well. Other versions permit the carolers to supply the names of those being toasted. Similar English folk carols with like sentiment bear the names of their locales of origin, for example, "The Yorkshire Wassail Song" ("We've Been a While A-Wandering") and "The Somerset Wassail" ("Wassail, O Wassail All Over the Town").

See also **Here We Come A-Caroling; Wassail.**

Gloucestershire Wassailers' Song

See **Gloucestershire Wassail**

Go Tell It on the Mountain

African American spiritual. Sources vary regarding its origin. Whereas some believe that it arose as an anonymous slave song during early 1800s, others attribute it to John Wesley Work, Jr. (1871–1925), a black instructor of Greek and Latin at Fisk University in Nashville, Tennessee (founded in 1865 with the purpose of educating freed slaves). Together with his composer-brother Frederick Jerome Work

(1880–1942), John Work, Jr., collected, harmonized, and published several collections of slave songs and spirituals, the first of which was *New Jubilee Songs as Sung by the Fisk Jubilee Singers* (1901). John Work, Jr., allegedly wrote the lyrics to "Go Tell" and then paired them with the musical setting for an older spiritual titled "When I Was a Seeker" (also the first words to one of the verses to "Go Tell"), for which his son, John W. Work, III (1901–1967), also provided a harmonization. It remains uncertain, however, whether John Work, Jr., wrote the original lyrics to "Go Tell."

According to a source from the Reader's Digest Association, the Jubilee Singers of Fisk University introduced "Go Tell" around 1879 during their fund-raising concert tours in America and in Europe. With the exception of the refrain, which remains constant and from which the title derives, the lyrics vary from source to source. Therefore, it is conceivable that John Work, Jr., his brother, or his son could have contributed additional lyrics after the song became established.

God Rest Ye Merry, Gentlemen

English traditional carol, a narrative of the Nativity, thought to have arisen during the sixteenth century. The "rest" in the title is an archaic term for "keep"; the "merry," a term for "strong" or "well." One of the earliest tangible settings is found in the *Roxburghe Ballads*, a manuscript collection of verses and tunes which resides in the British Library in London. Although the manuscript itself dates to 1770, the pieces contained therein are believed to be much older. Whereas the well known tune is said to have been published initially in 1827 with a variant text, the lyrics commonly sung today appeared in William Sandys's *Christmas Carols, Ancient and Modern* (London, 1833) with a variant tune, while *Christmas Carols New and Old*, edited by Henry Bramley and John Stainer (London, 1871), provided a more reliable source for the present melody.

Needless to say, variant tunes and lyrics exist, developed from the eighteenth century onward. For example, in the first verse, the original lines, "For Jesus Christ, our Savior, / Was born upon this day" have read, "Remember Christ, our Savior, / Was born on Christmas Day." Some versions omit verse two entirely, which begins as, "In Bethlehem in Jewry," or if it is retained, change the first line to the less archaic, "In Bethlehem in Israel." From the original refrain, "O tidings of comfort and joy, comfort and joy, O tidings of comfort and joy," has evolved "O tidings, O tidings of comfort and joy. / For Jesus Christ, our Savior, / Was born on Christmas Day," or simply, "And it's tiding of comfort and joy." Even the original "Ye" in the title is often replaced with a more modern "You." The eighteenth century also saw at least one additional folk tune setting from Cornwall in western England, and in the nineteenth century, Lewis Redner (of "O Little Town of Bethlehem") contributed another melody. The latter two settings are rarely used, however.

A typical wassailing song, "God Rest Ye Merry, Gentlemen" probably was included in the repertoire of songs commonly sung by the Waits of London, licensed bands of holiday singers and town criers. Charles Dickens alluded to this old tradition in *A Christmas Carol*, in which Scrooge threatens to throttle a young boy for singing this carol in the street outside his office.

See also **Waits**; **Wassail**.

Going My Way

(1944). Motion picture drama. Released in May, *Going My Way* was created to support the war effort and was not originally intended as a Christmas movie. However, its inspirational themes of faith, goodwill, and the occasional plot references to Christmas have brought it into the realm of Christmas classics by popular association.

Assigned to instill new life into St. Dominic's Church, a shabby, inner-city Manhattan parish deeply in debt, Father Chuck O'Malley (Bing Crosby) must devise a way to reduce the financial burden and strengthen bonds with the parishioners. His superior, the venerable old Irish curate Father Fitzgibbon (Barry Fitzgerald), at first is most critical of the new priest's youth and informal ways, but the affable, carefree, and nonjudgmental Father O'Malley soon gains the respect and friendship of his elder, as well as of a neighborhood street gang, whose worst crime is stealing turkeys from a butcher. More than a priest, the good Father becomes their father figure by playing baseball with them and taking them to such events as a Brooklyn Dodgers game and the movies. Father O'Malley also finds time for a bit of matchmaking between Carol James (Jean Heather), an attractive runaway who aspires to be a singer, and Ted Haines, Jr. (James Brown), whose father, Haines, Sr. (Gene Lockhart), holds the mortgage on St. Dominic's.

In order to raise the necessary cash, O'Malley transforms the street gang into a boys' choir (he first teaches them to sing "Three Blind Mice" and later "Silent Night"), whom he grooms for a fund-raising tour that includes his friend, opera singer Genevieve Linden (mezzo-soprano Risë Stevens of the Metropolitan Opera). The latter performs the "Habañera" from Bizet's *Carmen*. A songwriter himself, O'Malley composes what he is sure will be a winner, the inspirational piece "Going My Way," yet to his surprise, it is his light-hearted "Swinging on a Star" that gains the attention of his music publisher Max (William Frawley).

Despite the efforts to save St. Dominic's financially, a tragic fire destroys the church, and Father O'Malley is transferred to another parish. Before leaving, he arranges a heart-warming Christmas reunion between Father Fitzgibbon and the latter's 90-something mother from Ireland, Molly (Adeline DeWalt Reynolds), whom Father Fitzgibbon has not seen in decades. Shortly before the credits roll, Bing, Ms. Stevens, and the boys all gather for a rendition of Schubert's "Ave Maria."

Other songs featured: "Too-ral-loo-ral-loo-ral" and "Day after Forever."

In 1945, this picture won the following Academy Awards: Best Leading Actor (Bing Crosby), Best Supporting Actor (Barry Fitzgerald), Best Director, Best Original Song ("Swinging on a Star" by Jimmy Van Heusen and Johnny Burke), Best Picture, Best Original Story, and Best Screenplay. Academy nominations: Best Leading Actor (Fitzgerald), Best Black-and-White Cinematography, and Best Film Editing. Won Golden Globe Awards for Best Director, Best Motion Picture Drama, and Best Supporting Actor (Fitzgerald). Won New York Film Critics Circle Awards for 1944 for Best Actor (Fitzgerald), Best Director, and Best Film. Won 1944 Photoplay Award.

Going My Way is the only film in cinematic history in which the same actor (Fitzgerald) received Academy nominations for Best Leading Actor *and* Best Supporting Actor in the same film. Although Crosby was on the golf course at the time of the 1945 Oscar ceremonies, Paramount Pictures located him and insisted that he make an appearance. Of Crosby, Oscar ceremonies host Bob Hope remarked, "Any man with four children who plays a priest should win an Oscar."

With Frank McHugh, Porter Hall, Fortunio Bonanova, and Carl "Alfalfa" Switzer. Story by Leo McCarey. Screenplay by Frank Butler and Frank Cavett. Produced and directed by Leo McCarey. Paramount Pictures. DVD: Universal Studios. B & W. 130 min.

See also sequel **The Bells of St. Mary's.**

Going on the Wren
See **Hunting the Wren**

Good Christian Men, Rejoice
English title for the German macaronic (a mixture of vernacular German and Latin) carol "In dulci jubilo" ("In Sweet Jubilation"), attributed to the German mystic and Dominican monk Heinrich Suso (1295–1366). In his autobiography of 1328, *Das Büchlein der ewigen Weisheit* (*The Little Book of the Eternal Wisdom*), Suso claimed to have been visited by a company of angels who, to relieve his monastic sufferings, engaged him in ecstatic, heavenly dancing to a tune, the lyrics of which began as "In dulci jubilo." Although this questionable story allegedly inspired Suso to create the carol, it is believed that an anonymous version of this, the oldest of German macaronic carols, existed before the year 1328.

The oldest known manuscript of the carol, currently residing at Leipzig University, dates c. 1400 and consists of a one-verse dance-carol. By the fifteenth century, "In dulci jubilo" had acquired an additional three anonymous verses. Whereas its first printing consisted of only three verses in a Lutheran hymnal in 1533, with one verse expressing Roman Catholic views omitted, Protestant hymnals later adapted and rearranged some of the verses to improve the lyrical sense of the carol.

The best-known English-language version was provided by the Anglican clergyman and hymn translator John Mason Neale (1818–1866), who based his very free translation on a Swedish macaronic version of the carol as found in *Piae Cantiones*, a carol collection published in 1582. Beginning as "Good Christian Men, Rejoice," Neale's version retained none of the Latin phrases. Neal's musical associate, Thomas Helmore, upon transcribing the tune from that same source, mistook two short notes in the middle section for notes of longer duration, which resulted in a score that did not quite fit the lyrics. Rather than alter the tune, Neal simply added a two-word phrase to each verse as a form of exclamation and published his version in *Carols for Christmas-Tide* (London, 1853–54). Thus, in the midst of verse one, there is "News! News!"; in verse two, "Joy! Joy!"; and in verse three, "Peace! Peace!" Some hymnals now omit the extra words. The lyrics simply express joy at the coming of Christ, that He has opened the door to heaven, and that there is no longer any need to fear death.

"In dulci jubilo" has enjoyed numerous musical settings, notably by the German composer J.S. Bach (1685–1750): BWV 368, which his son C.P.E. Bach (1714–1788) published in a collection of his father's vocal chorales (1769); BWV 729 and in *Orgelbüchlein* (BWV 608), the latter two of which are organ chorale preludes. Other organ chorale preludes include those by Johann Michael Bach (1648–1694), Dietrich Buxtehude (1637–1707), Johann G. Walther (1684–1748), and Friedrich Wilhelm Zachau (1663–1712). Michael Praetorius (1571–1621) published several settings in his *Musae Sioniae* (1607, 1609), and the English composer Robert Pearsall (1795–1856) created a popular setting with parts for vocal octet and five-part chorus, published in 1836.

Good King Wenceslas

(Song). English carol, the lyrics of which were written in 1853 by the Anglican clergyman and greatest of English hymn translators, John Mason Neale (1818–1866), as a moral poem for children to illustrate the virtues of charity. Historically Wenceslas (Czech: Vaclav the Good), known for his piety and zeal for spreading Christianity in his country, reigned as duke, not king, of Bohemia from 922 to 929, was murdered by his power-crazed brother Boleslav, and eventually became the patron saint of the former Czechoslovakia. As with St. Nicholas, legends regarding Wenceslas's generosity multiplied, and Neale included one particular legend in his lyrics: As Wenceslas and his page carry food and logs through deep snow to a peasant, the heat radiating from his master's footprints prevents the page from freezing. Another reference to charity (indirectly linking the carol to Christmas) is the "feast of [St.] Stephen," which honors the first Christian martyr on December 26. Also known as Boxing Day in the British Commonwealth, that date was a special time for remembering the poor (*see* **Boxing Day**).

Neal had discovered a thirteenth or fourteenth century Scandinavian spring song, "Tempus ad floridum," within *Piae Cantiones*, a carol collection published in 1582, and wrote the lyrics to "Good King Wenceslas" around this melody. He first published the two together in his own collection, *Carols for Christmas-Tide* (London, 1853–54), co-edited by Thomas Helmore. The spring song has also been matched with lyrics to "Gentle Mary Laid Her Child," a Canadian carol written in 1919 by Joseph S. Cook.

See also **Good King Wenceslas** (television productions).

Good King Wenceslas

(Television productions, 1994). A live-action dramatization of Wenceslas's life of benevolence and political struggle with brother Boleslav starred Jonathan Brandis, Oliver Milburn, Stefanie Powers, Joan Fontaine, and Charlotte Chatton. In 1995, the picture received a Young Artist Award nomination for Best Performance by a Young Actor (Jonathan Brandis). Written by James Andrew Hall. Produced by Adam Clapham and Michael Deakin. Directed by Michael Tuchner. The Griffin Company. Video N/A.

An animated cartoon version of the same title features a voice track of crooner Bing Crosby singing "Good King Wenceslas." Additional voice: Bob Burrows. Directed by Keith

Scoble. VHS: BFS Entertainment and Multimedia Video. 25 min.

Grandfather Frost
See **Russia**

Grandma Got Run Over by a Reindeer

(Song). Highly popular novelty song written by American musician Randy Brooks and popularized by the former husband-and-wife singing group "Elmo & Patsy" (Dr. Elmo Shropshire, a former veterinarian, and Patsy Trigg). The pair were performing at Lake Tahoe, Nevada, in 1979 when Brooks, whose band had rejected "Grandma," persuaded them to record his piece. Although it was first released that same year on Elmo & Patsy's label, Oink Records, no major radio stations or recording studios were interested in promoting "Grandma" until 1983, when a station in San Francisco played it, generating the sale of 10,000 copies in one week. It was the first time in 30 years that a Christmas song had received more time on the air and more sales in one year than Bing Crosby's recording of "White Christmas." Among other examples of its success, a disc jockey in Davenport, Iowa, once played "Grandma" 27 consecutive times on the air (after which he was fired), while another in Godfrey, Illinois, played it 310 consecutive times and made the *Guinness Book of World Records*.

Epic Records released "Grandma" in 1983. The tune, which shot to number one on the Christmas hits charts from 1983 to 1987, has sold over ten million copies since 1979 and has consistently remained a Top Ten Christmas hit each year since 1987. In addition, it has been the most requested holiday song over the radio for more than 20 years.

According to the lyrics, Grandma, tipsy from eggnog, is returning home after visiting relatives on Christmas Eve when she is accidentally run down and killed by Santa's reindeer sleigh racing through town. The lyrics, intending humor, nevertheless created a storm of protest from some, including the Gray Panthers, who once picketed an Elmo & Patsy performance with signs reading "What's so funny about a dead grandma?" The press coverage generated by such controversy only boosted "Grandma" sales even further. To appease those troubled over the tune, however, Elmo & Patsy produced a music video in 1983 in which Grandma survived the accident.

Originally known as "The Homestead Act," Elmo & Patsy adopted their professional title on the advice of the late pianist Liberace. Although they recorded some 50 songs together on five albums during the 1970s and 1980s, "Grandma" was their only hit. One album recorded in 1984 included "Grandma" as the title track, along with humorous songs such as "Percy, the Puny Poinsettia" and "Señor Santa Claus," as well as traditional favorites. After Elmo & Patsy divorced in 1986, Kentucky native Dr. Elmo, as he is now known, moved on to create more "twisted" and wacky music, such as his holiday album, *Dr. Elmo's Twisted Christmas* (Laughing Stock Records, 1992). This not only features "Grandma," but also a series of sequel novelties such as "Grandpa's Gonna Sue the Pants Off of Santa," "Grandma's Spending Christmas with the Superstars," "Grandma's Killer Fruitcake," and "Don't Make Me Play That 'Grandma' Song Again." Dr. Elmo's other holiday albums include *Up Your Chimney* (Laughing Stock Records, 2000) and *Xmas in the USA* (BMG, 2004).

See also **Grandma Got Run Over by a Reindeer** (television special).

Grandma Got Run Over by a Reindeer

(Television special, 2000). Animated cartoon, based on the popular song by Randy Brooks.

Grandma Spankenheimer, an old-fashioned yet universally adored shopkeeper, and her young grandson Jake are virtually the sole residents of Cityville with any spark of Christmas spirit. Operating her shop on a policy of goodwill and fruitcakes instead of cold cash, Grandma refuses to sell out to Austin Bucks, Cityville's wealthiest land developer, who is bent on converting her property into a "sleigh-mobile" enterprise that would deliver the Christmas gifts and make Santa obsolete. Yet Cousin Mel, Grandma's greedy granddaughter, is determined to close the deal and spikes the fruitcakes with a special brew. As Grandma heads out on Christmas Eve to deliver her goodies, the heavy fruitcake aroma overpowers Santa's team flying overhead, and they run her down. Grandma only suffers amnesia, for which Santa carries her back to the North Pole to recuperate, and her family soon reports her as missing.

Despite a citywide search, Grandma is still missing by September of the following year, at which time Mel tricks Grandpa into deeding the shop over to her. With one week remaining until the deal is closed, Jake (the sole witness of Grandma's accident, although no one believes his story) queries Santa via email concerning her whereabouts. In reply, Quincy, the Top Elf, personally escorts Jake to see his grandmother, who, with nothing better to do, agrees to return with him to save the shop, with Quincy and Santa in tow. But while Santa parleys with Bucks about canceling the deal, Mel's devious attorney, Ms. Slime, covertly whisks Grandma away to a remote cabin in the woods, and Santa is jailed on charges of hit-and-run and kidnapping.

Santa's trial drags into December, and the holidays could be cancelled if Santa is convicted. With assistance from his dog Doofus, Jake tracks Grandma to the cabin and there finds incriminating evidence against Mel. While the latter is away, Jake takes Grandma back to her shop, where she regains her memory after sampling some of her fruitcake. Now the two dash into court just as the jury is about to render its verdict, and all charges against Santa are dropped, especially after Mel confesses her misdeeds when confronted with Jake's evidence. Having met Santa and seeing the good that has come from Grandma's shop, Bucks now offers her a nationwide franchise.

Featured songs: "Grandma Got Run Over by a Reindeer," "Grandma's Killer Fruitcake," "Grandma's Spending Christmas with the Superstars," "Grandpa's Gonna Sue the Pants Off of Santa," and "Feels Like Christmas." Narrated by Elmo Shropshire. Principal voices: Elmo Shropshire, Susan Blu, Alex Doduk, Michele Lee, Maggie Blue O'Hara, and Jim Staahl. Vocalist: Gary Chase. Story by Fred A. Rappoport, Elmo Shropshire, Jim Fisher, and Jim Staahl. Screenplay by Jim Fisher and Jim Staahl. Produced by Noel Roman, Jim Fisher, and Jim Staahl. Directed by Phil Roman. Phil Roman/The Fred Rappoport Company, LLC. DVD: Warner Home Video. 51 min.

See also **Grandma Got Run Over by a Reindeer** (song).

Great Antiphons
See "O" Antiphons

Great Britain

Three countries, England, Scotland, and Wales, comprise the island of Great Britain; with Northern Ireland, they form the United Kingdom of Great Britain and Northern Ireland. For purposes of discussion, however, this entry focuses on the countries of Great Britain alone; Irish customs are detailed in a separate entry.

Although there is evidence that Christianity was first introduced with the Roman invasions into Britain for several hundred years after Christ, Saint Columba, an Irish missionary to what is now Scotland, was most influential in spreading Celtic Christianity to the island, beginning in 563. In 596, Pope Gregory I ordered a troupe of missionaries led by St. Augustine (who later became the first archbishop of Canterbury) to Kent, where the baptism of King Ethelbert succeeded in Christianizing the island's southern kingdoms. Although Saint Aidan had established a Celtic branch of the Church by 635 in Northumbria, a northern kingdom of what is now England, its King Oswy embraced the Roman Church in 664 at the Synod of Whitby. Thus the Celtic Church yielded to Rome, and Wales became an English principality following some 200 years of invasions, beginning in the eleventh century. As a result of the Protestant Reformation, the Church of England (Anglican) and the Church of Scotland (Presbyterian) survive as respective state churches. The principal faiths in Wales include the Welsh branch of the Church of England and the Presbyterian Church of Wales (actually a Calvinistic Methodist church).

During the Middle Ages, Christmastime in Great Britain was filled with considerable merriment, revelry, and excesses not unlike those of the Roman Saturnalia. Such feasting and imbibing, gaming and gambling, mumming and masquerading were abominations to the Puritans, a radical, religious group born from the Protestant Reformation. While an exhaustive account of Puritan history is beyond the scope of this text, their actions from the mid–sixteenth century into the seventeenth century had a significant impact upon the future of the British Christmas. After Queen Elizabeth I (reigned 1558–1603) established a compromise in 1559 between Roman Catholicism and Protestant reforms within the Church of England, the Puritans, deploring all Christian feast days for which no biblical precedent existed, further sought a shift to a considerably more fundamental church doctrine. Calling for reforms that included completely abolishing Christmas, in 1642 the Puritans waged a civil war against the reigning monarch, King Charles I. They gained control of Parliament in 1644, executed the king in 1649 for treason, and established a protectorate in 1653 under the direction of Oliver Cromwell, who had played a significant military role in the revolution.

During their regime, the Puritans enacted severe punishments against those who acknowledged Christmas through merry-making, who attended special church services at this time, or who closed their businesses for a holiday. As town criers paraded through the streets with strict admonitions of "No Christmas!" many families covertly celebrated the holiday within their homes, while the citizenry occasionally countered forced compliance with riots and brawls.

Following Cromwell's death in 1658, the protectorate collapsed, and Parliament restored the monarchy when King Charles II ascended the throne in 1660. Although Charles restored Christmas and other religious observances, the Puritan influence had taken its toll, for these celebrations never fully achieved their height of fervent merriment seen in the days of yore. Nowhere in Britain was the impact of Puritanism greater than in Scotland, which had outlawed Christmas in 1561. The holiday remained virtually suppressed despite the British Restoration, and the Scots reserved their winter celebrations for New Year's Day. Indeed, Scotland did not legalize Christmas as a holiday until 1958.

Today the Christmas season extends from Advent until Epiphany. Because of common heritage, the Christmas customs of Great Britain share much with those of the United States, such as Christmas trees, cards, and carols; Nativity scenes, pageants, and plays; decorating with lights and evergreens; church services on Christmas Eve or Christmas Day and a large family meal on either day; wassail; and New Year's celebrations with parties and fireworks.

• FATHER CHRISTMAS. An entity peculiar to Great Britain, Father Christmas not only brings the Christmas gifts today but has also assumed the likeness of the American Santa Claus. Yet Father Christmas once personified only the raucous merry-making and secular pleasures of the holiday. According to Phyllis Siefker's *Santa Claus, Last of the Wild Men*, Father Christmas derived from the "Fool" who choreographed the revelry at year-end festivals. At the Roman Saturnalia, this was the *magister ludi* (master of the games); at the medieval Feast of Fools, this was the Archbishop of Fools, Abbot of Unreason, or Lord of Misrule. Also used to describe the master reveler were terms such as "syre Cristemas" ("sir Christmas") of medieval English carols, "Kyng

A Puritan (left) forbids Father Christmas to enter his town, while a commoner welcomes him in this early woodcut from a cartoon-like broadsheet printed in the late seventeenth or early eighteenth century. Reprinted in J.M. Golby and A.W. Purdue, The Making of the Modern Christmas *(Athens: University of Georgia Press, 1986).*

A favorite English Christmas Eve party game in the nineteenth century and long before that was "Snapdragon." All the lights in a room were extinguished, and a quantity of raisins in a large bowl were covered with brandy and ignited. The party-goers "now endeavor, by turns, to grasp a raisin, by plunging their hands through the flames; … a considerable amount of laughter and merriment is evoked." Part of the rhyme about Snapdragon reads: "But old Christmas makes him come,/Though he looks so fee! fa! fum!/Snip! Snap! Dragon!" From Robert Chambers, ed., The Book of Days *(London and Edinburgh: Chambers, 1879).*

Crestemasse" ("King Christmas") in the revels at Norwich in 1443, and "Yule" in those at York in 1572. At some point, a Father Christmas figure also presided over the mummers' plays, which E.K. Chambers (*The English Folk-Play*) believes occurred around the seventeenth century. A personification of Christmas gained wider popularity through the dramatist Ben Jonson's (1572–1637) court masque, *Christmas His Masque* (1616), the principal character of which is "Christmas," who refers to himself as "old Christmas," "Captain Christmas," and "Christmas of London." Although the term "Father Christmas" was probably in use much earlier, it first appeared in two pamphlets

related to the Puritan decimation of the feast, *The Arraignment, Conviction, and Imprisonment of Christmas* (1645) and *The Examination and Tryal of old Father Christmas* (1678). His appearance also evolved over time. Jonson portrayed him as an elder man attired in round hose, stockings, doublet, high hat with brooch, long thin beard, and white shoes; following his "imprisonment" during the Puritan regime, the once-corpulent, gray-bearded elder shrank to emaciation. On the other hand, Charles Dickens, in his desire to revive the failing customs of the holiday during his era, portrayed a bare-chested, younger, virile, and jolly Father Christmas through the Ghost of Christmas Present in *A Christmas Carol* (1843). Undoubtedly patterned after popular images, Dickens's Ghost, amid the cornucopia symbolic of the "Golden Age" of the Roman god Saturn, sported a cornucopia-like torch, a green robe lined with white fur, and a holly wreath crowning his head (*see* **Saturnalia**).

• FIRSTFOOTING. A custom once widespread throughout Europe, firstfooting has been quite popular in Great Britain since at least the eighteenth century. On Christmas Day or New Year's Eve, according to superstition, the physical characteristics of the first person ("firstfooter") to cross one's threshold after midnight predicts what luck is in store for the year. A strong, dark-haired man is the most desirable firstfooter, who enters bearing the traditional gifts of coal and bread, along with money or salt (respective symbols of warmth, food, and wealth) or a sprig of holly. Women, fair-haired or red-headed men, and people with flat feet, crossed eyes, or other physical deformities are generally considered to bring bad luck, although some regions make exceptions. Hired firstfooters are not uncommon, and some homes may attach a sprig of prickly holly (the so-called "man's plant") to the door to dissuade women from entering after midnight. The household customarily serves the firstfooter with food, drink, and perhaps money. Those taking the custom most seriously are also quite familiar with spells to counter any infractions of the taboos. For example, should a woman become the firstfooter, several little boys must march through each room of the house to restore the luck. Firstfooting similarly applies

A MERRY CHRISTMAS AND A HAPPY NEW YEAR!

Everyone gets in on the Christmas Feast parade in this wood engraving for Punch, *December 1858. A turkey, with the body of a plum pudding, is pulled along on a sleigh, while children and the irascible Punch and some nursery rhyme characters skate alongside.*

to the first person that one encounters on the road; children and oxcarts supposedly bring the best luck.

The following paragraphs summarize additional. customs found in the individual countries.

• ENGLAND. During the German occupation of World War II, Norway's King Håkon found political asylum in England. As an annual token of its appreciation, since 1947 the city of Oslo has shipped one of its best Christmas trees to London, where it decorates Trafalgar Square. Some weeks before Christmas, children write letters to Father Christmas, but instead of mailing them to the North Pole, the children throw them into the fire, for it is believed that Father Christmas will favor those letters that

burn quickly; otherwise they must be rewritten.

Noteworthy Christmas Eve celebrations include *A Festival of Nine Lessons and Carols*, held annually at King's College in Cambridge, and the "Devil's Knell" (or "Old Lad's Passing Bell"), the latter a formerly widespread custom throughout Europe that originated in the Middle Ages. For at least one hour before midnight on Christmas Eve, churches tolled the death of Satan who, according to folklore, perished at the midnight birth of Christ. One bell tolled once for each year that had passed since that time, then bells pealed joyfully upon the stroke of midnight to herald the arrival of Christmas. Although the Protestant Reformation virtually eliminated the custom,

omitted the meat and replaced plums or prunes with raisins. Because the seventeenth century use of the word "plum" broadly implied any form of dried fruit, these recipes were dubbed "plum puddings" (the same reasoning applied to raisins and the term "figgy"). They became popular Christmas dishes by the nineteenth century.

Most puddings were prepared several weeks in advance of Christmas, principally on the Sunday preceding the first Sunday of Advent. Called "Stir-Up Sunday," this day acquired its designation not only from the Anglican prayer offered in church to "stir-up" the faithful for Advent, but also because it was customary on this day for family members to stir the pudding batter for luck while making a wish. In 1819 the village of Paignton in Devon cooked a 900-pound pudding, the largest recorded in history.

Today's plum puddings feature a hidden coin, and the person finding the coin in his slice will receive good luck. Alternatively, some puddings include not only a coin, but other objects such as a ring, a small wishbone, an anchor, or a thimble; the coin signifies wealth; the ring, marriage; the wishbone, luck; the anchor, safety; the thimble, thrift, or spinsterhood to an unmarried woman. Inserting objects in plum pudding is a vestige of the Kings' Cakes of Twelfth Night, the latter virtually extinct in England since the nineteenth century.

At each person's plate is found a Christmas "cracker," a traditional party favor that consists of a small, cardboard tube covered with a twist of colored paper. When both ends are pulled simultaneously, a small pyrotechnic device explodes, producing a loud pop (hence the name "cracker"), and the favor bursts open to reveal a written joke or riddle, a colorful paper hat, a balloon, and a variety of small toys. Crackers, the innovation of Tom Smith, a London confectioner, evolved over a period of seven years, commencing in 1840 with the Christmastime marketing of wrapped bonbons, which Smith had discovered earlier that year in Paris. Later he added bits of love verses or mottos. When a crackling fire inspired him to develop a chemical strip that popped with the application of friction, he abandoned bonbons

A beautiful plum pudding, stuck with almonds and holly, decorates this Christmas postcard, printed in Germany for the English-speaking market. The postmark is 1909. The artist was Ellen H. Clapsaddle, whose cards are avidly collected today.

it survives in the village of Dewsbury in Yorkshire.

The Christmas dinner menu often features roast turkey, goose, or beef, along with potatoes, vegetables, and plum pudding, the latter a traditional dessert also known as Christmas pudding or figgy pudding. "Plum" pudding is a misnomer today because the dessert contains no plums. Instead it consists of dried fruit (particularly raisins), spices, sugar, butter, flour, eggs, and suet, and is usually topped with a brandy syrup. Plum pudding evolved from medieval porridge or pottage dishes, which were concoctions of meat, currants, and spices that, by the sixteenth century, also included plums and dried fruits; hence the early name of "plum porridge." During the seventeenth and eighteenth centuries, the evolving recipes for this new device, which retained the mottos and included surprise gifts. First marketed in 1847, these "cosaques," as Smith initially called them, were Great Britain's first crackers. Following the Victorian age, jokes and riddles supplanted the love poems, and by the turn of the twentieth century, the demand had considerably grown for crackers not only at Christmastime but also for a host of other special occasions, the mottos bearing suitable verses as well. Today the Tom Smith Group Limited, the largest manufacturer of crackers in the world, produces an estimated 38 million crackers annually and ships about 15 percent of these to some 34 countries abroad.

Another postcard printed in Germany about 1910 shows a British Punch-like figure and a Germanic pinecone pulling a Christmas cracker — a party favor that exploded with a "pop," when pulled, revealing tiny toys, printed jokes, and so forth.

In 2001, children and parents from the Ley Hill School, Ley Hill, Chesham, Buckinghamshire, constructed the world's largest cracker, 207 feet long and 13 feet in diameter. The project, which raised funds for local schools and charities, required four days to complete and utilized one-half mile of cardboard, 1,300 bolts, 1,000 nails, 500 screws, one-half mile of plastic tape, and more than 650 feet of timber. Forty-four children and members from the Saracens Rugby Team pulled this giant cracker, which popped open to reveal 300 balloons, presents for the children, a giant hat, and a traditional joke.

On Christmas Day, families often occupy themselves with parlor games, a custom dating to the Middle Ages, and listen to the monarch's annual Christmas message. King George V first broadcast the latter in 1932, and it has been televised since 1956. The traditional fare at Queen's College, Oxford, is to serve the "boar's head" with pomp and ceremony, and some regions observe the ancient custom of "hodening" (from "hobby horse"). The latter, which entails a horse skull or wooden effigy thereof, is much akin to the Welsh *Mari Lwyd* (see below).

Boxing Day, December 26, also known as St.

Stephen's Day, is a legal holiday given to various sporting and theatrical events, such as fox hunting, soccer matches, and pantomimes. On Epiphany Eve or "Christmas Old Style" (January 5), the mayor and vicar of Glastonbury send a clipping from the Glastonbury Thorn to the reigning monarch, having done so for some 400 years. The thorn, said to be a descendant of a tree that sprouted from the staff of Joseph of Arimathea, is also said to have bloomed annually on "Old Christmas Eve" prior to England's adoption of the Gregorian calendar in 1752.

See also **Advent; The Boar's Head Carol; Boxing Day; Boy-Bishop; Christmas Cards; Christmas Drama; Christmas Old Style, Christmas New Style; Christmas Tree; Epiphany; Feast of Fools; A Festival of Nine Lessons and Carols; Glastonbury Thorn; The Holly and the Ivy; Mistletoe; Nativity Scene; Waits; Wassail.**

• SCOTLAND. The principal winter festival is *Hogmanay*, observed on New Year's Day. The term is of obscure origin, thought by some to derive from an old French phrase for Christmas, "*Homme est né*" ("Man is born"), or *aguillaneuf* (French, "New Year's Gift"). Other likely sources include *haleg monath* (Anglo-Saxon, "holy month") and *oge maidne* (Gaelic, "new morning").

The festival commences with the firing of guns at midnight on New Year's Eve, a custom dating to ancient winter solstice festivals, in which loud noises supposedly drove away the spirits of darkness. Men meeting the requirements of "firstfooters" then make their rounds, bearing *handsels*, the customary offerings (see subentry **England**, above). The host accepts the food and drink by sharing it with all present, especially the firstfooter, who adds fuel to the fire (or a token lump of coal for the home without a fireplace) and pronounces wishes for a good new year with many more to come. The stranger then receives the customary rewards of a bottle of whiskey and an oatcake. A gift to the host may include the "black bun" (fruitcake with almonds, spices, and whiskey), a traditional holiday cake deriving from the Kings' Cake of Twelfth Night.

A spectacular New Year's fire ceremony takes place in Stonehaven, south of Aberdeen on the northeast coast. Sixty men march through High Street swinging 20-pound fireballs on five-foot metal poles. The custom dates to pre-Christian winter solstice festivals, in which the fireballs dispelled evil by symbolizing the power of the sun.

Some countries of eastern Europe (for example, Bulgaria and Romania) feature the New Year's custom of children tapping adults with decorated poles to convey good wishes for health and prosperity. A related custom is found on the islands of Lewis and South Uist in the Hebrides of western Scotland. Groups of boys bearing sticks enter homes and chant Gaelic rhymes. The leader, clad in sheepskin, walks clockwise around a chair while his comrades tap the sheepskin with the sticks. Following the ritual, the boys receive oat cakes. The custom recalls ancient fertility rites, in which beating with sticks on certain holidays supposedly aided health and growth.

Hogmanay was once associated with a host of customs and superstitions, most of which have long been abandoned or are no longer widely practiced. For example, *Hogmanay* was the chief day for giving gifts, and children went from door to door requesting a *hogmanay*, a gift of cheese or oat cakes. Today, whether children receive gifts varies from region to region. People were on their best behavior, for whatever happened on New Year's Day would influence the entire year; the old year's bad luck was burned with the *cailleach*, a small wooden effigy of an old woman that represented the Spirit of Winter; and a girl would surely marry that year if she was the first to draw water from the well that day and her beau drank thereof, a custom once known as "creaming the well."

Scotland's Shetland Islands terminate the winter holidays with "Up-Helly-Aa" (the name possibly derives from the old Scots "Uphaliday" or "Epiphany"), a fire festival held most notably in the town of Lerwick on the last Tuesday of January. Believed to postdate the Napoleonic Wars (1799–1815), initial celebrations occurred on Epiphany Eve with all manner of noisemaking, drinking, gunfire, brawling, and music. By 1840 the festival included "guizers" (slang, men in disguises) who pulled sledges with burning tar barrels through town and then visited the homes of friends. Torchlight processions replaced the tar barrels when Lerwick banned the latter in the early 1870s. Guizers dressed as Vikings, who burned a replica of a Viking galley (the ritual commemorated 600 years of Viking domination ending in 1472), topped the festivities in the late 1880s. The festival gradually shifted to January 29 (24 nights after "Christmas Old Style"), then again to its present day in the twentieth century. Today a "Guizer Jarl" or chief guizer initiates Up-Helly-Aa by posting "the Bill," a farcical proclamation containing a year's worth of gossip and local humor, in the town square. A torchlight procession of some 900 guizers then march through the streets to the harbor in the evening to burn the 30-foot galley, after which, amid a night of revelry and imbibing, they perform skits in entertainment halls instead of homes. "Merry Christmas" in Scots Gaelic is *Nollaig Chridheil*.

• WALES. The most traditional of Welsh customs include *Eisteddfod*, *Plygain*, *Calenigg*, and *Mari Lwyd*, all of which involve some form of carol singing.

Lord Rhys (Rhys ap Gruffydd, prince of Deheubarth) is reputed to have first instituted the *Eisteddfod* ("A Sitting of Learned Men") in 1176 at Castle Cardigan, an event which sought the best works of musicians and poets around the country. Numerous Eisteddfodau have been held throughout Wales since that time, and in 1880 the National Eisteddfod Association was formed to sponsor an annual festival, the location of which alternated between North and South Wales. With the exception of the years 1914 and 1940, the festivals have been held in July or August thereafter. Although they broadly encompass arts and crafts with special emphasis on music and poetry, they are a lasting source for original Welsh Christmas carols, one of which is hailed as the most outstanding for the year. An International Eisteddfod, established in 1947, is held annually in the city of Llangollen.

Following the Protestant Reformation, *Plygain* ("daybreak" or "cockcrow") replaced the Roman Catholic Early Dawn Mass held on Christmas morning. Originally, it commenced between 3 and 6 A.M. and consisted of candlelight processions and Christmas services with unaccompanied carol singing, which only men attended. Women remained at home with their children and attended to the baking and preparation of treacle coffee. Following the quite lengthy service, the Christmas feasting began with toasted bread and cheese ("Welsh rabbit"), ale, and perhaps a fowl. Although women and children joined the services during the nineteenth century, *Plygain* had begun to decline by that time because of increasing drunkenness among those in attendance. With its revival in the twentieth century, Plygain now retains the custom of carol singing but at more reasonable hours and only in a few locales. No longer confined to Christmas morning, it may be held anytime during December or early January, usually without religious services.

The *Calenigg* ("small gift") evolved from the Roman Calends; it had been a Roman custom to exchange olive branches as peace offerings for the new year. On January 1, Welsh children armed with water and evergreen branches toured their neighborhoods singing carols and anointing their friends' faces with the water. In exchange for these good luck wishes, they received a few coins or *Caleniggs*. In some areas the children also dispensed good-luck charms, also known as *Caleniggs*, which consisted of apples set on three sticks and decorated with almonds, raisins, greenery, colored ribbons,

and one candle wedged on top. It was said that only those charms given between dawn and noon would bring luck, and that this luck would remain for the life of the *Calenigg*. The custom survives in a few locales.

In pre-Christian times, the Teutonic and some Asian pagans sacrificed horses to their gods, then placed the heads or skulls upon poles (spite-stakes or nithing-posts) and propped open the jaws as talismans against their enemies. During the Middle Ages, such devices were believed to ward off werewolves, witches, illnesses, robbers, and other bogies, and it was commonplace to see carved, wooden images of horses' heads on house gables or horseshoes over thresholds as good-luck charms. Because it was believed that the powers of darkness were especially prevalent at Christmastime, horse skulls played a significant role in the British holidays. Known as the *Mari Lwyd* ("Grey Mare"), this Welsh equivalent consisted of a horse's skull, the jaws of which opened and shut by means of a wooden pulley. Bedecked with false eyes, ears, and ribbons, the Mare was operated by a man hidden under a white sheet. Together, the Mare and its entourage of black-faced men went from house to house, at each of which arose a series of competitive verses in song, known as *pwnco*, between the occupants and the Mare, who sought entrance. At some point the occupants usually failed to counter with an appropriate verse (by reputation, the Mare's repertoire was prodigious), whereupon the revelers invaded the house and committed all forms of mischief, then received food and drink as "rewards." Although the Mare had declined into the twentieth century because of its frequent association with drunkenness and acts of vandalism, it has been revived in some regions such as Llantrisant, where it is a feature of New Year as well as Christmas festivities.

"Merry Christmas" in Wales is *Nadolig Lawen.*

The Greatest Gift
See It's a Wonderful Life

The Greatest Story Ever Told
See **Nativity** (Film and Television Depictions)

Greece

A number of Christ's apostles introduced Christianity into Greece during the first century. By the sixth century, Greece was incorporated into the Byzantine Empire, from which evolved the Orthodox Church, and it is to this church that the vast majority of Greek Christians adhere. Although a number of countries following this faith cling to the old Julian calendar for ecclesiastical events, Greece now observes Christmas on the Gregorian calendar. To the Greeks, however, Easter is a holiday of far greater importance than Christmas (*see* **Christmas Old Style, Christmas New Style**).

To commemorate the 40 days of temptations that Christ suffered in the wilderness following His baptism, the Greek Orthodox Church observes a 40-day fast or Lenten season prior to Christmas Eve, commencing on November 14. Such a fast prohibits the consumption of any animal products, olive oil, or liquor. During this period, St. Nicholas, the patron saint of sailors, among others, is commemorated on December 6, but with much less ado than is found in central Europe (*see* **St. Nicholas's Day**).

The Christmas season extends from Christmas Eve until Epiphany (January 6). It was once believed that specters roamed the earth during this 12-day period, a throwback to pre-Christian times, when winter solstice celebrations throughout Europe devised rituals to dispel the supernatural forces believed to lurk in the winter darkness. To the Greeks at this time, the *kallikantzari*, mythical gremlins from the underworld, temporarily ceased their year-long attempts to destroy the roots of the Tree of Life, which held up the physical world, and came to the surface to wreak havoc and mischief. While they were topside, the roots recovered. Initially appearing at the first Christmas, they have returned annually ever since and remain popular in Greek Christmas folklore. Because *kallikantzari* gain access to the home through the chimney, a fire must burn throughout the 12 days of Christmas to keep them at bay, and all visitors to the home must stir the fire. Additional charms to thwart them include hanging the lower jaw of a pig behind the door, burning old shoes in the fireplace, throwing salt into the flames, and throwing a

cake up the chimney for the gremlins to eat. Children born during these 12 days (or only on Christmas Day in some variations of the folklore) may also become *kallikantzari*, and mothers may counter the spell by binding their newborns in garlic or straw, or by singeing their Toenails. The "Blessing of the Waters" on Epiphany (see below) drives the gremlins back to their abode for another year.

The principal Christmas observances occur on December 24. Groups of children travel from house to house singing *kalanda* (Christmas carols), the lyrics of which traditionally not only relate the Nativity story, but also offer good wishes and effusive praise to the household regarding the social and financial status of the occupants therein (regardless of their actual station in life). Along with drums, triangles, and other simple instruments, the carolers often bear small, intricately carved ships that are illuminated from within and decorated with colored ribbons. These ships are vestiges of the *Panathenaea*, the oldest and most famous festival of ancient Athens, which honored the goddess Athena. As part of this festival, processions of young girls carried small, wooded ships, symbols of mythical vessels that supposedly brought wondrous gifts from the ends of the world. Today, carolers receive rewards of money, fruits, nuts, and sweets, which are tossed into the ships.

Christmas trees decorated with candles and sweets, first introduced to Greece by King Otto I of Bavaria (who ascended the throne in 1832), did not become fashionable until the 1930s. In recent years, the Society of the Friends of the Trees, an organization in Athens devoted to conserving fir trees, has begun a campaign to substitute the lighted ship, described above, for the foreign Christmas tree as Greece's chief Christmas symbol. The Society organizes displays that feature miniature replicas of not only historic Greek ships but also those depicting pure fantasy.

The long fast is broken on Christmas Eve with the family dinner, which always features *Christopsomo* ("Christ bread"). This is a sweet loaf with nuts and dried fruit, the surface of which is usually carved with images of the family's trade. This bread often forms the table centerpiece, along with representations of the bounty of the earth, such as nuts, figs, dates, and fruits. Such a centerpiece is said to derive from pre-Christian thanksgiving oblations to Demeter, goddess of agriculture. As the meal begins, the host makes the sign of the cross over the bread, then slices it and distributes the pieces according to family rank, with the first piece reserved for the first beggar who passes by. Hidden within the bread is a coin, and the person finding it in his slice will receive luck in the coming year. The meal may also include pork, turkey, chicken, lamb, *kourabiedes* (small cakes covered with powdered sugar), *melomacarona* (similar, but soaked in diluted honey), and *loukoumades* (fried dough puffs with honey). Other Christmas Eve customs include pouring drops of oil or wine over the hearth, which derives from libations once offered to Hestia, goddess of the home, and feeding small cakes to the livestock at this time and at the New Year.

Christmas Day begins with Orthodox Mass, which extends from 4 A.M. until dawn, at which time worshippers take communion. Some families wait until after this Mass to break their long fast with the Christmas meal.

Children formerly received holiday gifts only on St. Basil's Day (January 1), which commemorates the death of St. Basil (329–379), one of the Patriarchs of the Orthodox Church. Because of Western influences, *Agios Vassilis* (St. Basil) now brings the gifts at Christmastime, and his appearance closely resembles that of Santa Claus in the United States. At midnight on St. Basil's Eve, families often ritually slice and distribute a *Vasilopita* ("St. Basil Cake"), which also contains a hidden coin. The recipient of the first slice varies among sources, some noting St. Basil, others Christ and the Virgin Mary. Family members receive slices as with the Christ bread, and slices are reserved for the poor and any absent family members. Children again make their rounds to present *kalanda*, and card games traditionally determine one's fate for the new year. On New Year's (St. Basil's) Day, the first person to enter the home is also a portent for the new year. A strong person entering predicts health; a person carrying a religious icon predicts blessing; a wealthy person, riches; and so forth. The more bountiful the table, the more plentiful will be the year.

The Christmas season is closed by Epiphany, the principal ritual of which includes the Blessing of the Waters. After a priest dips a cross with a sprig of basil into basins of water, the worshippers take samples of the blessed water home to be used as medicinals. In cities near rivers and the sea, the priest throws the cross into the water, after which young men compete to retrieve the cross by diving into the water. In the United States, the best-known sites for this latter ritual include Tarpon Springs, Florida, and Asbury Park, New Jersey. The priest also personally blesses the homes of his parish. Both rituals supposedly drive the *kallikantzari* back underground.

"Merry Christmas" in Greece is *Kala Christougenna*.

See also **Epiphany**.

Greenland

A Danish province since 1721, Greenland is the largest island in the world. Because it is the nearest land mass to the North Pole, children from the United States often write letters addressed to Santa Claus in Greenland, and these are forwarded to Copenhagen, Denmark. There, members of the Department of Tourism provide an appropriate response in the guise of the jolly gentleman.

Christmas traditions in Greenland center around the cultures of the two principal societies inhabiting the island, the Inuit (Eskimo) and the Europeans of Danish-Norwegian descent. Danish and Norwegian customs are discussed under entries for those individual countries, and Inuit customs are found primarily in the entry for Canada.

In addition to decorating imported Christmas trees, caroling, dancing, and giving gifts, the Greenland Inuit enjoy such holiday cuisine as *mattak* (whale skin with blubber) and *kiviak* (young auks buried in seal skins for several months and "aged" to an advanced level of decomposition). Christmas night is the only time of year when Inuit men will attend to their women, such as serving them coffee and stirring it for them. A popular game consists of passing a revolting object (usually round, clammy, and rough) from hand to hand under the table.

"Merry Christmas" may be said in Inuit,

Jutdlime pivdluarit ukiortame pivdluaritlo; in Danish, *Glædelig Jul*; or in Norwegian, *God Jul*. *See also* **Canada**; **Denmark**; **Norway**.

Grenada
See **West Indies**

The Grift of the Magi
See **The Simpsons**

Guatemala
See **Central America**

Gunsmoke
Popular, Emmy Award–winning, American Western drama series set in Dodge City, Kansas. It ran for nine years on radio (1952–1961) and 20 years on CBS television (1955–1975). Principal cast members for the radio series included William Conrad as U.S. Marshall Matt Dillon, Georgia Ellis as Miss Kitty Russell, Howard McNear as Dr. Charles Addams, and Parley Baer as townsman Chester Proudfoot. Principals for the television series included James Arness as Matt, Dennis Weaver as sidekick Chester Goode (1955–1964), Amanda Blake as Long Branch Saloon proprietor Miss Kitty (1955–1974), Milburn Stone as Dr. Galen ("Doc") Adams, Ken Curtis as Deputy Festus Haggen (1964–1975), Roger Ewing as sometime-deputy Thaddeus Greenwood (1965–1967), Burt Reynolds as blacksmith Quint Asper (1962–1965), and Buck Taylor as gunsmith and sometime-deputy Newly O'Brien (1967–1975).

• RADIO CHRISTMAS EPISODE. Of the 413 radio episodes, only one centered around Christmas, titled simply "Christmas Story" (December 20, 1952). Matt is out on the trail 40 miles from Dodge when his horse breaks a leg. Forced to walk back, Matt meets a stranger who at first invites him to ride double on his poor specimen of a horse; then, lest Matt arrive late in Dodge for Christmas Eve festivities, the stranger freely bids him to take the horse and ride out. Matt declines, however, and when they make camp for the night, the stranger recounts a most tragic story. Guest stars: Larry Dobkin, Harry Bartell, and John Dehner. Written by Antony Ellis.

• TELEVISION CHRISTMAS EPISODES. Of the

635 television episodes (233 half-hour, 402 one-hour), only two had Christmas themes:

"Magnus" (December 24, 1955). The story was adapted with a holiday twist from a previous radio episode of the same title, which aired December 18, 1954. In both, Robert Easton stars as Magnus, Chester's estranged, uncivilized brother. When Magnus arrives in Dodge just in time for Christmas dance festivities at the Long Branch Saloon, Chester, embarrassed and fearing that his brother will make a complete fool of himself, attempts to "civilize" Magnus by teaching him how to gamble, drink, and socialize with women. In reality, it is Chester who receives the shock, for Magnus handles himself quite well with cards, liquor, and Miss Kitty. Chester really discovers what kind of man his brother is when religious fanatic Lucifer Jones (James Anderson) disrupts the Christmas party by tearing up the saloon and threatening to kill that "wicked woman" Miss Kitty. Guest stars: Than Wyenn, Tim Graham, and Dorothy Schuyler. Written by John Meston. Produced and directed by Charles Marquis Warren. B & W. Video N/A. 30 min.

"P.S. Murry Christmas" (December 27, 1971). When Emma Grundy (Jeanette Nolan), iron-fisted matron of a Kansas orphanage, fires her grizzled caretaker Titus Spangler (Jack Elam) for impropriety at Christmastime, seven of her charges run away and accompany Titus to Dodge City. There, Festus jails him for stealing food. Arriving soon thereafter to reclaim the orphans and bring kidnapping charges against Titus, Ms. Grundy quickly reveals herself as a Scrooge-surrogate, who makes clear the fact that she has never allowed the children to celebrate Christmas. The town rallies around the children nonetheless, and Kitty plans a huge Christmas party for them at the Long Branch. But when Ms. Grundy bars the children from attending, Kitty reasons that a little liquor will soften the hard matron. To Kitty's regret, Ms. Grundy becomes quite inebriated and reveals her personal reasons for shunning Christmas, yet the dark circumstances work eventually toward a happy holiday for all concerned.

This is the only *Gunsmoke* television episode in which Kitty gives Matt a kiss, and on the cheek at that, in the Long Branch while they hold cups of eggnog. All of the seven children appearing as orphans later became screen celebrities: Patti Cohoon, Jodie Foster, Erin Moran, Josh Albee, Brian Morrison, Willie Aames, and Todd Lookinland. Written by William Kelley. Produced by Leonard Katzman. Directed by Herb Wallerstein. Video N/A. 60 min.

Guyana
See **South America**

Hail the Blest Morn
See **Brightest and Best of the Sons of the Morning**

Hamlet
(c. 1601). Play in five acts by English playwright William Shakespeare (1564–1616). *Hamlet* is the only one of Shakespeare's plays that makes any significant reference to Christmas, and that quite briefly. Near the end of Act I, scene one, the officers Marcellus and Bernardo, together with Hamlet's friend Horatio, behold the ghost of Hamlet's father, which vanishes as the cock crows at daybreak. Then Marcellus remarks,

Some say that ever 'gainst that season comes
Wherein our Saviour's birth is celebrated,
The bird of dawning singeth all night long:
And then, they say, no spirit can walk abroad;
The nights are wholesome; then no planets strike,
No fairy takes, nor witch hath power to charm;
So hallow'd and so gracious is the time.
[I.i. 158–164]

Marcellus implies that, according to tradition, the cock, ordinarily crowing with the dawn, also proclaimed the birth of Christ by crowing at midnight, the traditional hour of His birth. British legends also held that evil spirits were powerless during the 12 holy days of Christmas. This was in marked contrast to folklore in some parts of Europe, particularly Germany and Poland, where it was believed that children born during the 12 nights of Christmas could become werewolves. According to a similar, Greek superstition, newborn babies during this period could become *kalli-*

kantzari, evil, half-human monsters. These beliefs undoubtedly carried over from pre-Christian times, when, in the minds of many, spirits populated the darkness of long winter months.

See also **Greece**; **The Twelve Days of Christmas** (time period); **Winter Solstice**; **Yule**.

Hanna-Barbera Christmas Cartoons
Animators William Hanna (1910–2001) and Joseph Barbera (1911–) formed Hanna-Barbera Productions in 1944 while working at Metro-Goldwyn-Mayer Studios, then opened their own studio in 1957 after MGM shut down its animation department. The first studio to produce animated cartoons specifically and successfully for television, Hanna-Barbera created thousands of cartoons in scores of popular series for more than 30 years and revolutionized the animation industry through low-cost, "limited animation" techniques. A series of mergers after 1991 united the studio with Warner Bros., and following Hanna's death in 2001, the name Hanna-Barbera was retired, with production continuing through the Cartoon Network Studios.

Hanna-Barbera's Christmas contributions appeared primarily through television specials, although several theatrical shorts and episodes of series carried the theme. The following list briefly summarizes the Hanna-Barbera holiday titles in alphabetical order of their creation; unless otherwise indicated, each is a television special, discussed as a separate entry:

Baby's First Christmas (1983), series episode (*see* **The Smurfs**).

Casper's First Christmas (1979).

Christmas Comes to Pac-Land (1982).

A Christmas Story (1972).

A Dickens of a Christmas (1983), series episode of *The Dukes* (see **A Christmas Carol** [Film and Television Versions]).

The Elves and the Shoemaker (1990, see **The Elves and the Shoemaker** [Film and Animated Adaptations]).

A Flintstone Christmas (1977, see **The Flintstones**).

A Flintstone Family Christmas (1993, see **The Flintstones**).

A Flintstones Christmas Carol (1994, see **The Flintstones**).

Good Will to Men (1955), theatrical short (*see* **MGM Cartoon Christmas**).

How the Flintstones Saved Christmas (1964), series episode (*see* **The Flintstones**).

A Jetsons Christmas Carol (1985), series episode of *The Jetsons* (*see* **A Christmas Carol** [Film and Television Versions]).

The Nativity (1984, see **Nativity** [Film and Television Depictions]).

The Night before Christmas (1941), theatrical short starring Tom Cat and Jerry Mouse (*see* **Tom and Jerry's Night before Christmas**).

The Smurfs' Christmas Special (1982, see **The Smurfs**).

'Tis the Season to Be Smurfy (1987, see **The Smurfs**).

The Town That Santa Forgot (1993).

Yogi Bear's All-Star Comedy Christmas Caper (1982).

Yogi's First Christmas (1980).

Hanukkah

(Hebrew, "Dedication"). A Jewish celebration of eight days commencing on the twenty-fifth day of Kislev, the third month on the Jewish calendar, which corresponds approximately to the month of December on the Gregorian calendar. It commemorates the victory of Judah Maccabee and his Jewish army over the Hellenist Syrians in 165 B.C., the miraculous burning of a cruse of oil for eight days, and the purification and rededication of the Temple in Jerusalem, which the Greeks had desecrated.

Hanukkah, also known as Chanukah, Festival of Lights, and Feast of Dedication, bears no historical relationship to Christmas, yet because its observance frequently falls at Christmastime, Hanukkah is one of three principal year-end festivals in the United States, along with Christmas and the seven-day African American holiday, Kwanzaa.

• HISTORY OF HANUKKAH. Upon the death of Alexander the Great (356–323 B.C.), who had conquered the Near East including Palestine, his empire split into smaller kingdoms collectively termed the Seleucid Dynasty, which perpetuated the dominion until the first century B.C. In 167 B.C., Antiochus IV Epiphanes (c. 215–164 B.C.), king of Syria and overlord of Palestine, captured Jerusalem. Determined to hellenize the Jews, Antiochus introduced Greek gods, desecrated the Temple with an altar erected to Zeus (upon which pigs were sacrificed), and abolished all Jewish rituals (an event predicted by the Old Testament prophet Daniel, 11:31). Individuals who resisted died as martyrs.

The Jewish priest Mattathias with his five sons initiated a guerrilla war against the Greek invaders. At Mattathias's death, his son Judah Maccabee assumed command and led his army to defeat Antiochus, thus reclaiming Jerusalem and the Temple for the Jews in 165 B.C. (by 160 B.C., Jewish forces had completely expelled Antiochus from Palestine). In purging the Temple, the Maccabees recovered only one cruse of sealed, undefiled olive oil, which ordinarily would have supplied fuel to light the Temple menorah for one day. Instead, this cruse miraculously fueled the menorah for eight days, during which time the Jews rededicated the Temple with festivities.

The accounts of Hanukkah, as recorded in several historical sources, reflect the holiday's changing role with the Jews over time. For example, the earliest versions, found in the First and Second Books of Maccabees (included in the Apocrypha) and the writings of Josephus, a first century A.D. Jewish historian (who referred to the holiday as "Light"), stress the martyrs and military victory of the Maccabees but omit the miracle of the oil. The later rabbinic material (Gemara) of the Talmud, while briefly mentioning the victory, focuses primarily on the miracle, and a medieval work, *Megillat Antiochus* (*Scroll of Antiochus*), also speaks of victory and miracle.

At one time, the importance of the Maccabees' victory diminished in favor of the miracle, possibly because the independence gained by the Maccabees lasted for less than 100 years. Yet with the establishment of the State of Israel in the twentieth century, nationalist and military aspects of the festival have returned to play key roles.

- CUSTOMS AND TRADITIONS. Whatever the emphasis placed on Hanukkah, the menorah remains the chief symbol of the festival, representing the light of religious, national, and cultural freedom, and lighting the menorah remains the chief activity. The *Hanukkiah* (Hanukkah menorah) is a candelabrum consisting of nine candles or oil lamps, one of which is more prominent and is located either centrally or to one side. Called the *Shamash* ("servant light"), this special lamp is used to light the others successively from right to left, one for each night of Hanukkah. Following this ritual, which includes the recitations of blessings and traditional songs, the *Hanukkiah* is usually displayed in a window. Custom also dictates the eating of certain foods made with oil, such as *latkes* (potato pancakes) and *sufganiyot* (doughnuts without holes).

As a result of the influence of Christmas, many American Jewish children now receive gifts, especially *gelt* (money) or chocolate candy wrapped to simulate shekels. Festivities also include games, the most common of which is *dreidel* (or *dreidl*: "rotate, turn"). In this game of chance, children spin a four-sided top, also known as a *dreidel*, the sides of which each contain one of the following Hebrew letters: *Nun*, *Gimel*, *Heh*, and *Shin*. These are the first letters to the words in the Hebrew phrase, "*Nes Gadol Haya Sham*" ("A great miracle happened there").

Although Hanukkah is the only major Jewish festival not recorded in the Hebrew Bible, the Gospel of John (10:22) in the New Testament makes brief mention of it: "And it was at Jerusalem the feast of the dedication, and it was winter."

Since 1979 in the United States, annual ceremonies lighting a National Hanukkah Menorah have taken place, first in Lafayette Park, and subsequently on the Ellipse across from the White House. The president, members of Congress, Jewish leaders, and other dignitaries have participated in the event. Erected by the American Friends of Lubavitch, the 30-foot aluminum National Hanukkah Menorah is reputed to be one of the tallest in the world. Other phenomenal symbols of Hanukkah have included a more than 60-foot tall menorah, built of metal pipes by the Chabad Movement in 1997 in Latrun, Israel; a 32-foot steel menorah designed by artist Yaakov Agam in New York City; a 12-foot pile of 6,400 *sufganiyot* erected near Afula, Israel, in 1997; and a 16-foot *dreidel* built by students at Rutgers University.

On December 21, 1984, President Ronald Reagan delivered the first official "Message on the Observance of Hanukkah" to the United States, and since 1987, these messages have been an annual tradition.

Happy Holiday
See **Holiday Inn**

Happy New Year, Charlie Brown

(1986). Made-for-television animated cartoon, based on characters in the *Peanuts* comic strip, created by Charles M. Schulz.

Compelled to read Tolstoy's *War and Peace* as a school assignment over the holidays, Charlie Brown lugs the tome wherever he goes, including the New Year's Eve party thrown by Marcie and Peppermint Patty. He had invited Heather, the "little red-haired girl," but she never responded. Isolating himself, Charlie Brown falls asleep while reading at the party. While he sleeps, Heather arrives and dances with Linus instead. By the time Charlie Brown awakens, the midnight revel is past, and Heather has departed. He finishes his book-report assignment a few hours before school resumes, receiving a D-minus for his efforts. Upon receiving the next assignment, to read Dostoyevski's *Crime and Punishment*, Charlie Brown falls into a swoon.

In 1987, this picture won a Young Artist Award for Exceptional Young Actress in Animation (Kristi Baker); it was nominated for a Young Artist Award for Exceptional Young Actor in Animation (Chad Allen).

Voices: Chad Allen, Kristi Baker, Melissa Guzzi, Jeremy Miller, Elizabeth Lyn Fraser,

Aron Mandelbaum, Jason Mendelson, and Bill Melendez. Vocalists: Sean Collins, Tiffany Billings, and Desirée Goyette. Written by Charles M. Schulz. Produced by Bill Melendez. Directed by Bill Melendez and Sam Jaimes. A Lee Mendelson–Bill Melendez Production in association with Charles M. Schulz Creative Enterprises and United Feature Syndicate. VHS: Paramount Studios. 24 min.

See also **A Charlie Brown Christmas; Charlie Brown's Christmas Tales; I Want a Dog for Christmas, Charlie Brown; It's Christmastime Again, Charlie Brown**.

Hark! The Herald Angels Sing

Highly popular English carol, the lyrics of which were written by Charles Wesley (1707–1788), a founder of Methodism and author of some 9,000 hymn poems including "Christ the Lord Is Risen Today" and "O for a Thousand Tongues to Sing." Inspired by the pealing of London church bells on Christmas morning, Wesley first published the poem as "Hymn for Christmas Day" in his *Hymns and Sacred Poems* (1739). The poem has undergone various revisions over the years. Originally consisting of ten four-line verses, it began as "Hark, how all the welkin [heaven] rings / 'Glory to the King of Kings.'" The wording of this first couplet was too archaic for George Whitefield, a Calvinist and Wesley's associate, who revised the couplet to "Hark! The herald angels sing: / 'Glory to the new-born King!'" Likewise, verse five, beginning as "Hail the heav'nly Prince of Peace" was altered to "Hail the heaven-born Prince of Peace." These changes, together with omitting verses eight and ten entirely, Whitefield published in his *Hymns for Social Worship* (1753). In 1760 the Rev. Martin Maldan revised the second couplet of verse two, from "Universal nature say / 'Christ the Lord is born today'" to "With the angelic hosts proclaim, / 'Christ is born in Bethlehem!'" The repeat of the opening couplet as a refrain first appeared when the poem was included in an Anglican publication, the Supplement to *New Version of the Psalms* (1782). And the final alteration appeared in *Hymns Ancient and Modern* (1861), in which "Pleased as man with men to appear / Jesus, our Immanuel here" in verse four was replaced with "Pleased as man with

men to dwell, / Jesus, our Immanuel." By this time, the established printing had paired the four-line verses together, creating three eight-line verses with refrain.

For more than 100 years, Wesley's poem was sung to a number of tunes, including that for "Christ the Lord Is Risen Today" and "Take My Life, and Let It Be." None of these musical settings seemed suitable, however. Finally, William Cummings, organist for Waltham Abbey, Essex, discovered an obscure work, *Festgesang*, a cantata in four movements for two male choirs and brass, written by German composer Felix Mendelssohn (1809–1847). Commissioned in 1840 for a celebration in Leipzig that commemorated the 400th anniversary of the Johann Gutenberg printing press, *Festgesang* featured a spirited second chorus, "Gott ist Licht" ("God Is Light"). Cummings adapted this melody to Wesley's poem and published the two together in 1856. Cummings's arrangement has become the carol version most often sung today.

Of *Festgesang*, Mendelssohn had ironically remarked from the outset that only lyrics expressing something gay and popular, and not sacred words, best suited the music.

The Haunted Man and the Ghost's Bargain

See **Dickens, Charles, Christmas stories of**

Have Yourself a Merry Little Christmas

Popular American song written for the 1944 MGM motion picture *Meet Me in St. Louis* by Oklahoma native Ralph Blane Hunsecker (lyrics), better known as Ralph Blane, and Alabama native Hugh Martin (music), both of whom also wrote the picture's musical score. The movie, which can hardly be classified as a Christmas film in the strictest sense of the term, featured such other numbers as "The Trolley Song" (nominated for an Academy Award), "The Boy Next Door," and "Skip to My Lou." Judy Garland, playing a much older sister to young Margaret O'Brien (recipient of the Juvenile Award for Most Outstanding Child Actress of 1944), was supposed to make their imminent move from St. Louis to New York

City seem less distressing by singing "Have Yourself a Merry Little Christmas." When Garland found the original lyrics too depressing to sing to a child and requested something more optimistic, actor Tom Drake convinced producer Arthur Freed to have the composers alter the lyrics accordingly rather than abandon the number altogether. Though the lyrics anticipate celebrating Christmas in new surroundings, the music is quite nostalgic and sentimental. Garland recorded the song on the Decca label in 1944 and 1954, but neither recording made the pop charts.

Of the 25 most frequently performed Christmas songs of the twentieth century listed by the American Society of Composers, Authors and Publishers (ASCAP), "Have Yourself a Merry Little Christmas" ranked number seven. By December 2004, it ranked number two.

See also **ASCAP List of Christmas Songs.**

The Hawaiian Christmas Song
See **Mele Kalikimaka**

He Is Born, the Divine Christ Child
See **He Is Born, the Holy Child**

He Is Born, the Holy Child
("Il est né, le divin Enfant"). French traditional carol thought to date from the eighteenth century. It is also known as "Christ Is Born a Child on Earth" and "He Is Born, the Divine Christ Child." As with many traditional carols, text and music were first published separately, and how or by whom they were paired is not known. The text was first published in a collection by Dom Georges Legeay, *Noëls anciens* (Paris, 1875–1876), the music in *Airs des noëls lorrain* (1862) by an R. Grosjean. In the latter, the tune appears as a hunting song. Although the lyrics appear in various English translations, basically the mood of the verses is joyful praise and adoration of the Child Who has come to earth.

He Is Sleeping in a Manger
See **Infant Holy, Infant Lowly**

He Smiles within His Cradle
("Ein Kindlein in der Wiegen"). Austrian traditional carol, the text of which is thought

to date from the fourteenth century. Although it appeared with an altogether different tune in a publication of 1590, the more familiar tune with text appeared in a Viennese hymn collection published in 1649 by the theologian David Gregor Corner (1585–1648). Whereas a number of hymn texts in that collection bear Corner's initials, supporting his authorship, "He Smiles" does not, yet Corner has on occasion received credit for its tune. It is generally felt, however, that the tune is of folk origin. The best-known English translation was made by English poet and novelist Robert Graves (1895–1985), better known for his novel *I, Claudius*. The carol is also known as "A Baby Lies in the Cradle" and "A Baby in the Cradle."

The text pictures the joy and peace of viewing the Babe being gently rocked in a cradle, a brilliant halo surrounding Him. It is believed that the repertoire of Christmas songs used in German medieval cradle-rocking services included this carol.

See also **Rocking.**

Heap on More Wood
One of several titles assigned to a Christmas verse written by the Scottish novelist and poet Sir Walter Scott (1771–1832). Other titles include "Christmas in Olden Times" and "Old Christmas." Scott's poem beginning with the lines, "Heap on more wood!— the wind is chill; / But let it whistle as it will, / We'll keep our Christmas merry still," lies within his work *Marmion* (1808), a romantic, narrative poem built around the fictitious character Lord Marmion, amid a setting of knighthood and chivalry. This expansive poem consists of six cantos, each preceded by its own introduction, and the 85-line "Heap on More Wood" composes approximately the first half of the "Introduction to Canto Sixth."

"Heap on More Wood" first recalls the pre-Christian, winter solstice festivals (*Iol* or Yule) of Scotland's ancestors from Scandinavia, who celebrated with unrestrained revelry by feasting, drinking, pelting each other with bones, fighting, and dancing around pine-tree fires (according to Scott's notes, any reveler accidentally falling into the fire, if rescued, was required to drink a measure of ale for spoiling the king's fire). The poem next reviews the merrymaking of medieval Christmases, in which the nobility opened their manor halls, bedecked with holly and mistletoe, for purposes of sharing the spirit of the holiday with peers and commoners alike. Christmas dinner featured a boar's head served with pomp, along with wassail, plum pudding, goose, sirloin, and Christmas pie. Entertainment included dancing, caroling, mumming, stories, and card games, all sufficient to brighten "The poor man's heart through half the year."

Marmion is also the source of the familiar proverb, "Oh what a tangled web we weave / When first we practice to deceive," as found in "Canto Sixth."

One of the foremost authors in English romanticism and considered to be the first significant historical novelist, Sir Walter Scott portrayed Great Britain and particularly his native Scotland from the Middle Ages to the eighteenth century. Among his best-known works are the poem *The Lady of the Lake* (1810) and the novel *Ivanhoe* (1820).

See also **The Boar's Head Carol; Christmas Drama; Christmas Pie; The Holly and the Ivy; Mistletoe; Wassail; Winter Solstice; Yule.**

Hear What Great News We Bring
See **Angels and Shepherds**

Heidi

(1937). Motion picture drama, based on the classic children's book of the same title by Johanna Spyri. A key scene takes place on Christmas Eve.

In the nineteenth century Swiss Alpine setting of the little village of Dorfli, seven-year-old Heidi (Shirley Temple), orphaned since infancy and reluctantly raised by her Aunt Dete (Mady Christians), is now cast upon her grandfather, Adolph Kramer (Jean Hersholt). A recluse of the mountains, Adolph holds only bitterness for his kin and humanity because of a family dispute years ago. But Heidi's winsome ways eventually touch Adolph's heart, and the old man is soon humming the same little tune favored by his granddaughter. At first rebuffing a personal invitation from Pastor Schultz (Thomas Beck) to return to church and society, if only for Heidi's sake, Adolph, after reflecting on having given Heidi her first Sun-

day school lesson, "The Prodigal Son," repents and becomes a respected member of the community.

While Adolph is away, Aunt Dete, having made financial arrangements to provide a companion for Klara Sesemann (Marcia Mae Jones), the crippled daughter of a wealthy widower in Frankfurt, returns to steal Heidi. Though circumstances are unfavorable, Heidi still brings joy to this new household, including Andrews the butler (Arthur Treacher), but not to Fraulein Rottenmeier (Mary Nash), Klara's no-nonsense governess. To Rottenmeier, as long as Klara remains an invalid, her position as governess remains secure. Heidi's presence jeopardizes that position, for Klara grows stronger each day through Heidi's influence.

On Christmas Eve, Herr Sesemann (Sidney Blackmer), previously away on business, arrives home to a formal holiday reception with his family and staff, where the song of the evening is "Silent Night." Klara receives a lovely porcelain doll, and her gift to Heidi is a snow globe, precious because its figures of a cabin and an old man remind Heidi of her grandfather. The climax of the evening is Klara's gift to her father, the best he has ever received: Klara steps from her wheelchair and haltingly walks unaided, falling into his arms with, "Merry Christmas, Papa!" Weeks prior to Christmas, Klara had learned to walk again with Heidi's faithful assistance, and the two had kept the secret until now.

Rottenmeier, enraged, causes a scene and is discharged. That night, she seeks revenge by attempting to sell Heidi to gypsies. Heidi escapes into the street, where she is reunited with Adolph, who has walked 100 miles from Dorfli to find her. The two flee in a sleigh but are apprehended, Adolph is jailed on Rottenmeier's charges of child abduction, and a hysterical Heidi begs to law to interview Herr Sesemann to clarify all points.

The final scene cuts to springtime, where a fully recovered Klara and her father visit Heidi and Adolph back on the mountain.

With Helen Westley, Pauline Moore, Delmar Watson, Egon Brecher, Christian Rub, and George Humbert. Written by Walter Ferris and Julien Josephson. Produced by Darryl F.

Zanuck. Directed by Allan Dwan. Twenteith Century Fox Film Corporation. DVD: Twentieth Century Fox Video. B & W. 88 min.

Here Comes Santa Claus

(Film, 1984). English title for a French motion picture comedy, titled *J'ai rencontré le Père Noël*, with English dialogue. This film bears no relationship to the popular Christmas song of the same title.

Touring an airport at Christmastime, little Simon (Emeric Chapuis) and his friend Elodie (Little Alexia) mistakenly board a plane bound for Rovaniemi in Lapland, where they seek out Santa (Armand Meffre) to help locate the boy's parents, who are political prisoners in Africa. With the help of a good fairy (Karen Chéryl), Santa journeys to the Dark Continent, while the two children suffer hardships at the hands of a forest ogre (Dominique Hulin) living near Santa's workshop.

With Jeanne Herviale, Hélène Ruby, Jean-Louis Foulquier, and Baye Fall. Written by Didier Kaminka. Produced and directed by Christian Gion. Lanaca Productions. VHS: Star Maker Video. 78 min.

Here Comes Santa Claus

(Song). Popular American children's song written in 1946 by cowboy singing star and Texas native Gene Autry and California native Oakley Haldeman.

Serving as the grand marshal for the Hollywood Christmas parade of 1946, Autry was riding his horse Champion when the procession came to that section of Hollywood Boulevard locally known to merchants as "Santa Claus Lane." Some distance ahead of Santa's float, Autry heard throngs of children screaming, "Here comes Santa Claus!" The scene inspired Autry to write "Here Comes Santa Claus," which he outlined to Haldeman, manager of his music publishing firms at the time. Haldeman and another colleague, Art Satherly, created a lead sheet and prepared a demonstration tape for Autry, with lyrics sung by guitarist Johnny Bonds. It is said that, during this informal recording, the clinking of ice cubes in a drink which Satherly held prompted the use of sleigh bells in Autry's recording of 1947 on the Columbia label. That recording sold over 2.5 million copies and made the pop charts for the remainder of the 1940s and into the 1950s. Autry re-recorded the song in 1957 on the Challenge label and again in 1969 on the Republic label, but neither recording made the charts.

"Here Comes Santa Claus" was Autry's first Christmas release. He was also the first to record two other holiday standards, "Rudolph, the Red-Nosed Reindeer" (1949) and "Frosty the Snow Man" (1950).

Of the 25 most frequently performed Christmas songs of the twentieth century listed by the American Society of Composers, Authors and Publishers (ASCAP), "Here Comes Santa Claus" ranked number 17. By December 2004, it ranked number 21.

See also **ASCAP List of Christmas Songs**; **Frosty the Snow Man** (song); **Rudolph, the Red-Nosed Reindeer** (song).

Here We Come A-Caroling

English traditional carol, thought by some to date from the sixteenth century in the Yorkshire region. Also known as "Wassail Song," "Here We Come A-Wassailing," and "Here We Go A-Caroling," the carol was one of many sung by the Waits who went from door to door wishing everyone "wassail" (good health), their reward often being a cup of hot wassail.

Although a medieval origin has been suggested, the earliest known written sources include a Manchester pamphlet and a Bradford, Yorkshire, broadside dating c. 1850. This prompted William Husk in his *Songs of the Nativity* (London, 1864) to surmise that the carol was a more recent composition by northern carolers. In Husk's collection, the tune is the familiar one for "God Rest Ye Merry, Gentlemen," with the refrain patterned after a tune known as "Brigg Fair." Although variant tunes and refrains have appeared over the years (the verses remaining fairly constant), the tune and refrain most frequently sung today are derived from the collection by Henry Bramley and John Stainer, *Christmas Carols, New and Old* (London, 1871), the tune again originating in Yorkshire.

Another carol, possibly a variant of "Here We Come A-Caroling," is "We've Been a While A-Wandering" ("The Yorkshire Wassail Song"), which contains very similar lyrics but is also

Some Yorkshire children singing carols on Christmas morning. In the nineteenth century, carolers went out on Christmas Eve as well as Christmas day, but popular opinion was beginning to think that the Eve was a more appropriate time to go around and sing. This may have been because the adult carolers were often given money, which they saved and spent on the merry-making on Twelfth Day. From Robert Chambers, ed., The Book of Days *(London and Edinburgh: Chambers, 1879).*

sung to a variant tune for "God Rest Ye Merry, Gentlemen."

See also **God Rest Ye Merry, Gentlemen; Gloucestershire Wassail; Waits; Wassail.**

Here We Come A-Wassailing
See **Here We Come A-Caroling**

Here We Go A-Caroling
See **Here We Come A-Caroling**

Holiday Affair

(1949). Motion picture romance.

Christmastime in New York City presents two marriage proposals for Connie Ennis (Janet Leigh), a "comparison shopper" (otherwise known as a commercial spy) and young widow with a six-year-old son, Timmy (Gordon Gebert). Her faithful boyfriend, attorney Carl Davis (Wendell Corey), practically lives at her apartment and has popped the question too many times to count, yet Connie, seemingly satisfied with the status quo, refuses to take the leap. Carl's competition arrives in the form of Steve Mason (Robert Mitchum), a toy sales-man with a keen eye for sizing people up, whom Connie meets at Crowley's Department Store. Pegging Connie as a spy for the competition when she pretends to return the same electric train set that she had "purchased" from him, soft-hearted Steve is fired for failing to blow the whistle on her.

Steve pursues Connie, despite the fact that she has suddenly decided to marry Carl on New Year's Day, and rapidly becomes friends with Timmy, something Carl has not achieved. Learning that Timmy wants an electric train for Christmas but that Connie cannot afford it, Steve, now broke, somehow provides the surprise gift, after which Connie attempts to refund his money. Instead, he proposes after knowing her only four days, frankly arguing that she would be marrying Carl strictly for security and not love. Torn by this thought, Connie receives another shock when Timmy, realizing Steve's financial need, walks alone to Crowley's and sacrifices his train for a refund, and from Mr. Crowley (Henry O'Neill) at that. When Connie asks Carl to deliver Steve's refund in her place, Carl realizes that she is truly in love with Steve and, citing the evidence, bows out.

On New Year's Eve, Steve, believing that Connie still desires Carl, boards a train bound for the West Coast, where he plans to establish himself in building boats. Amid the evening's festivities, however, he receives a message, at which he suddenly rushes through the cars and sweeps Connie and Timmy into his arms. Letting go of the past, Connie has made her choice, and with the new year, a new way of life commences.

With Griff Barnett, Esther Dale, Henry Morgan, Larry Blake, and Helen Brown. Written by Isobel Lennart. Based on a story by John D. Weaver. Produced and directed by Don Hartman. RKO Radio Pictures. VHS: Turner Home Video. B & W. 87 min.

In 1996, the picture was remade for television under the same title, starring David James Elliott, Cynthia Gibb, and Tom Irwin. Produced by Vicky Herman. Directed by Alan Myerson. VHS: Ghadar and Associates. 93 min.

A Holiday for Love
See **Christmas in My Hometown**

Holiday in Your Heart: A Novel

Inspirational novel, written by fourteen-year-old country music artist LeAnn Rimes and Tom Carter, published in 1997. An epigraph implies that the story, though almost entirely fictional, delivers a message of truth.

Fourteen-year-old Anna Lee, the newest country music singing sensation, has always been loyal and devoted to her family, especially to her Grandma Teeden and Grandpa Luther. She has always followed her grandmother's advice, that one only truly lives life when one loves God, and that keeping God in your soul keeps a holiday in your heart. But when Grandma Teeden falls gravely ill with cancer a few weeks before Christmas, Anna Lee is reluctant to return home to Mississippi because of pressing business engagements.

To save Anna Lee from becoming a high-handed "victim" of show business, a visitor arrives in the form of her father's favorite female country singer, a legend in the industry decades ago but who has now faded into obscurity. The Legend, whose identity is never revealed to the reader, escorts Anna Lee on a tour of Nashville, "Music City, USA," then spins a tale that changes Anna Lee's life forever:

The Legend's father had disowned her for becoming a country artist, and the two had been alienated for many years, until he had sought to visit her in Nashville at Thanksgiving. But she had turned him away unseen, believing that he only sought money. Within hours, the Legend had boarded a bus that became snowbound in a ditch, and for two days, the passengers had valiantly struggled against freezing temperatures and starvation. The Legend, a diabetic, would have perished, had not an old man on board, himself a diabetic and blind, provided her with his own insulin. Unknown to her at the time, however, the man had willfully donated his entire supply. In so doing, he had given his life for the Legend and died in her arms before their rescue. Only later did the Legend discover to her bitter grief that the man had been her own father.

The Legend concludes the adventure by leading Anna Lee to a magnificent, ten-foot cross, a memorial she and her husband Carl had erected near Wrigley, Tennessee, the site of the bus accident. Then answering a question that Anna Lee had posed earlier, the Legend recommends the only suitable Christmas gift that any child could give her parents—the same gift that Jesus had given to God His Father—loyalty. In the ultimate example, Jesus had obeyed His Father, even unto the cross. And if you have family, so says the Legend, you have everything. Deeply moved and repenting of her disloyalty, Anna Lee rushes to be with her grandmother during her hospitalization.

When it is later revealed that photographs taken earlier do not show the Legend beside Anna Lee and that the former had died a year earlier while attempting to erect a giant cross in a field, the reader is left to ponder whether Anna Lee's visitor had been a supernatural entity.

In 1997, the novel was adapted for television under the title *Holiday in Your Heart*, starring LeAnn Rimes as herself, Bernadette Peters as the Legend, Faith Shawn, Rebecca Schull as Grandma Teeden, Harlan Jordan as Grandpa Luther, Rance Howard as the blind man, and Mark Walters as Carl. In 1998, the picture won the Golden Reel Award for Best Sound Editing. Teleplay by Ellen Weston. Produced by Stephanie Germain and Randy Sutter. Directed by Michael Switzer. Stephanie Germain Productions and Von Zerneck Sertner Films. Video N/A.

Holiday Inn

(1942). Motion picture musical, the idea for which originated with American songwriter Irving Berlin. The songs were not composed to suit the film; instead, the picture was designed to revolve around a series of original Berlin songs that depict the most important American holidays: "Happy Holiday" and "Let's Start the New Year Right" (New Year's Day); "Abraham" (Lincoln's Birthday); "Be Careful, It's My Heart" (Valentine's Day); "I Can't Tell a Lie" (Washington's Birthday); "Easter Parade," composed in 1933 (Easter); "Say It with Firecrackers" and "Song of Freedom" (Independence Day); "I've Got Plenty to Be Thankful

For" (Thanksgiving Day); and "White Christmas," composed in 1940 (Christmas). No songs commemorate Armistice Day (now Veterans' Day) or Memorial Day. Other songs include "I'll Capture Her Heart," "Lazy," and "You're Easy to Dance With." Despite the many holidays honored, *Holiday Inn* is now regarded as a Christmas classic.

A loosely constructed plot ties Berlin's songs together. The Pierre Club in New York City features the song-and-dance act of crooner Jim Hardy (Bing Crosby) and dancer Ted Hanover (Fred Astaire), with Lila Dixon (Virginia Dale) as Ted's dancing partner. Jim, leaving the show for the "easy life" on a farm in Connecticut, returns after a year and decides to convert the farm into an inn that is open only on holidays, "Holiday Inn," which features an appropriate floor show for each occasion. While recruiting Ted and Lila for the inn, Jim meets Linda Mason (Marjorie Reynolds), who aspires to enter show business, and he convinces her to become his vocal partner for the show.

In New York, when Lila throws her fiancé Ted over for a Texas millionaire, a drunken Ted retreats to Holiday Inn on New Year's Eve and dances with Linda by accident. They are a perfect match choreographically, and the next few holidays at the inn find Ted resolved to have Linda romantically and professionally, though she and Jim are already engaged. But when Hollywood plans a film based on the Holiday Inn concept, Ted and Linda head to the West Coast, while Jim remains in Connecticut to write the musical numbers.

By Thanksgiving, when a dejected Jim closes the inn, a pep talk from Mamie the housekeeper (Louise Beavers) puts him out in Hollywood on Christmas Eve, as the movie studio is about to shoot the Christmas finale. Also sick at heart, Linda falters while singing "White Christmas" on the set, at which Jim steps on stage, carries the tune, and rekindles their love. Reopening the inn on New Year's Eve, the foursome (Lila returns because her "millionaire" *owed* millions) sing a happy ending.

In 1943, this picture captured the following honors: Academy Award for Best Original Song ("White Christmas"); Academy nominations for Best Scoring of a Musical Picture and Best Original Story.

This film also promoted one of the most popular Christmas songs ever written, "White Christmas," which Bing Crosby had first introduced on his Kraft Music Hall radio show on Christmas Day, 1941. He sang the song twice in *Holiday Inn*, accompanied both times by Marjorie Reynolds. A blackface musical number performed by Crosby is usually cut from television prints, and the film was remade as *White Christmas* (1954).

Story by Irving Berlin. Adapted by Claude Binyon and Elmer Rice. Produced and directed by Mark Sandrich. Paramount Pictures. DVD: Universal Studios.

B & W. 101 min. Disk also includes *Going My Way*.

See also **White Christmas** (motion picture); **White Christmas** (song).

A Holiday to Remember

(1995). Made-for-television romance, based on the 1993 novel *A Christmas Love* by Kathleen Creighton.

Newly divorced at Christmastime, Dr. Carolyn Giblin (Connie Sellecca) closes her clinical psychology practice in Los Angeles and returns with her teenage daughter Jordi (Asia Vieira) to Mayville, South Carolina, the small community of her childhood. Carolyn's holidays are anything but peaceful: her neighbor is none other than Clay Traynor (Randy Travis), the town policeman and former fiancé whom she jilted at the altar years ago; Jordi, horrified that there is neither a mall nor cable television, trumpets her displeasure; and William (Kyle Fairlie), a ten-year-old suspected runaway, is discovered hiding in Carolyn's basement.

Clay and William care little for Christmas, principally because neither had strong family backgrounds. That changes however, after Clay's aunt, "Miz" Leona (Rue McClanahan), drafts William and Jordi into rehearsals at the church Nativity pageant, and Clay finds more time to assist Carolyn in making her late grandmother's old house habitable with holiday decorations.

Enter the villain, Eve Stevens (Brenda Bazinet), a social worker and Clay's present girlfriend, who overrules Carolyn's desire that William remain with her and hustles William off to a shelter while Clay searches for the boy's parents. As he has in times past, William escapes and becomes a hit at the Christmas Eve pageant where, costumed as a Wise Man, he improvises his lines with a personal, contemporary thought: the Savior has been born to protect children from irresponsible parents and thoughtless adults. Later Clay discovers that William is truly an orphan, and although Eve places him in a foster home on Christmas Eve night, William again escapes, whereupon Clay finds him early on Christmas morning asleep with his dog at the church's life-size Nativity scene outdoors.

On Christmas Night, rather than see William lost to foster care, Clay proposes to Carolyn, both having slowly realized that time had not extinguished their love; Jordi concludes that life in a small town has its own rewards; and William is more than ready to accept them all as his new family.

Teleplay by Darrah Cloud. Produced by Marilyn Stonehouse. Directed by Jud Taylor. Fremantle Media North America and Jaffe/Braunstein Films, Ltd. DVD: Fremantle Video. 90 min.

Holland

See **The Low Countries** (The Netherlands)

Holly

See **The Holly and the Ivy**

The Holly and the Ivy

English traditional, allegorical carol, probably the best-known of the so-called medieval "holly and ivy" carols, which draw analogies between Christmas and the pagan symbols of holly and ivy. Although the exact date for this carol is unknown, Joshua Sylvester (believed to be the pseudonym of English carol collectors William Sandys and William H. Husk) first published the lyrics in *A Garland of Christmas Carols* (London, 1861), based on a broadside from Birmingham dating to 1710. But it is believed that the carol was written at a much earlier date. English folk song collector Cecil Sharp first published the lyrics with the tune in his *English Folk-Carols* (London, 1911), which has become the standard version.

Holly and ivy were pre-Christian symbols

A botanical engraving of the 1850s shows the holly leaves and its berries. Holly and other evergreens were used to decorate English churches, and remained until the end of January. The ecclesiastical canons decreed that they must be gone by Candlemas Day, February 2, probably in part because of local superstitions that if the holly were left up, goblins would proliferate.

of rival entities, predominantly male versus female, respectively, but also good versus evil, and they were popular decorations for homes and public places during winter solstice festivals and other holidays. It has been established that in the British Isles, holly was the "man's plant" and clinging ivy the "woman's plant," these two evergreen plants symbolizing the sexes vying for dominance over each other; yet the precise connections of these plants to such contention remain obscure.

Ivy was used primarily as a fertility charm (girls believed that wearing three ivy leaves would enable them to dream of their future husbands, and ewes fed a few leaves supposedly bore twin lambs more often) and as a protective for dairy products and flocks. In Greek mythology, Dionysus, a fertility god of wine and vegetation, placed the spirit of the dancing girl Ivy into the plant that bears her name after she had expired at his feet. Thereafter, Ivy clung to and embraced all with whom she came in contact.

According to English folk custom, holly was symbolically superior to ivy, a concept tauntingly suggested in a number of fifteenth century "holly and ivy" carols. One of these depicts the fair "Holly and his merry men" reveling in a gala winter event, while "Ivy and her maidens" must stand and weep outside in the cold, and a recurrent refrain calls for Holly to

Punch hands Queen Victoria a bouquet of holly. Punch, *December 1847.*

have the mastery over Ivy. Holly was also the subject of superstition in that it repelled witches, its presence encouraged pleasant dreams, and arguments could be settled more quickly under a holly tree.

When Christianized as Christmas symbols, holly initially came to represent the masculine features of Christ's birth and ivy the feminine, that is, the Virgin Mary, and the latter theme was emphasized in various medieval carols. In time, holly further symbolized not only the attributes of Christ but those of the Virgin as well, to the neglect of ivy, the latter's loss of popularity in song and as a Christmas decoration stemming primarily from its association with mistletoe as a pagan fertility symbol.

As suggested in the lyrics to "The Holly and the Ivy," the white blossoms of holly represent the purity of Virgin and Babe; the red berries, Christ's blood; the sharp thorns, Mary's travail in childbirth and Christ's crown of thorns; the bitter bark, Christ's agony at the Crucifixion.

With ivy now ostracized from Christmas, so-called "prickly" and "smooth" varieties of holly, respectively, acquired the competitive male and female symbolism, particularly regarding superstitions about which sex would rule the household in the coming year. If prickly holly was brought into the home first on Christmas Day, the man would rule; if smooth holly, the woman. The folk belief of

masculine dominance at Christmas also carried over into the custom of "firstfooting," once widely observed throughout Europe. In Great Britain, for example, this quaint tradition still holds that a woman as the first person to enter a home on Christmas Day or New Year's Day brings bad luck. In years past, on Christmas and New Year's Days, a holly sprig would be placed outside the door to ensure that only a man would be the first to enter.

See also **Great Britain; Mistletoe; Winter Solstice.**

A Holly Jolly Christmas

Popular American song written in 1962 by composer John D. (Johnny) Marks, best known for his classic hit of 1949, "Rudolph, the Red-Nosed Reindeer." Encouraging all to have the merriest Christmas ever, the bubbly "A Holly Jolly Christmas" achieved public attention when it became one of several of Marks's creations featured in the 1964 television animated special *Rudolph, the Red-Nosed Reindeer*, with vocals rendered by Burl Ives. Ives's Decca recording of the song ranked thirteenth on the *Billboard Special Christmas Singles* chart in 1964 and twenty-ninth in 1968.

Of the 25 most frequently performed Christmas songs of the twentieth century as listed by the American Society of Composers, Authors and Publishers (ASCAP), "A Holly Jolly Christmas" ranked number 25. By December 2004, it ranked number 18.

See also **ASCAP List of Christmas Songs; Rudolph, the Red-Nosed Reindeer** (television special).

The Holy Baby

See **Children, Go Where I Send Thee**

Holy Innocents Day

Also known as Day of the Innocents or Feast of the Holy Innocents in the Roman Catholic and affiliated churches, and as Childermas (Children's Mass) in England. Traditionally observed on December 28, it is a memorial to those children two years old and under whom King Herod the Great massacred in Bethlehem following the Wise Men's visit to the Christ Child, as described in the Gospel of Matthew 2:1–18. In the Armenian tradition, because the Innocents died 15 weeks after Christ was born, that church observes the Monday following the second Sunday following Pentecost. The official color for the Catholic Mass is purple, symbolic of mourning; if the date falls on Sunday, the Church prescribes red, symbolic of the young martyrs' blood.

Exactly when the Roman Church instituted this feast is not known. The earliest records of its observance date from the end of the fifth century, but its first celebrations could have occurred by the end of the fourth century. During those early feasts, abstinence from meat and from foods cooked in fat was mandatory. During the Middle Ages, Holy Innocents Day was considered unlucky, because the Bethlehem children supposedly had not been baptized prior to their deaths. On the other hand, because these children were regarded as martyrs for Christ, children were venerated and given places of honor in homes and religious orders; in some locales, the youngest member of the community, regardless of his or her age, was fed baby food. Holy Innocents Day was also the final day of reign for the "Boy-Bishop," a young boy who had been elected on St. Nicholas's Day (December 6) to act as bishop from then until December 28.

Parents symbolically whipped their children as a reenactment of Herod's slaughter and to drive out evil spirits, a carryover from year-end fertility rites of ancient pagans. Children in turn would seek out women and girls, brush them with twigs, and chant fertility verses. Related customs whereby children tap elders and contemporaries with sticks occur today in many areas of Europe. In France, children who overslept on this day were punished with whippings.

By the eleventh century, Holy Innocents Day had also become a riotous feast for students and choirboys, which recalled those revels of the pre-Christian Roman Saturnalia, and was one of four degenerate post-Christmas holidays collectively termed the Feast of Fools.

A number of churches now claim to enshrine the remains of several of the Holy Innocents, including the Church of St. Justina at Padua and the cathedrals of Lisbon and Milan, among others.

See also **Boy-Bishop**; **Feast of Fools**; **Nativity**; **Saturnalia**.

Home Alone

(1990). Motion picture comedy that spawned two motion picture sequels and one television sequel.

The family of eight-year-old Kevin McAllister (Macaulay Culkin) accidentally leaves him behind in Chicago while they travel to France for Christmas vacation. Initially, the situation is a dream come true for Kevin, who is often at odds with his family and had even wished that they would disappear. Now with the house at his command, he learns self-reliance amid self-indulgence (such as reading his older brother's *Playboy* magazines, eating junk food, and watching videos with titles like *Angels with Filthy Souls*).

As Kevin prepares for Christmas alone, burglars Harry (Joe Pesci) and Marv (Daniel Stern) have targeted Kevin's seemingly empty, well-to-do home as the next one to hit. When Kevin spots them outside and overhears that they plan to strike at 9 P.M. on Christmas Eve, he booby-traps the entire house from top to bottom.

By now, Kevin misses his family. Feeling pensive while out on a walk early on Christmas Eve, he stops by a church, where a children's choir is singing "O Holy Night." Inside, he is joined by Mr. Marley (Roberts Blossom), the next-door neighbor wildly rumored to have murdered his own family years ago, and the two become friends after sharing some personal problems. Marley, a crusty but kindly old man, has actually been estranged from his son for years and is reluctant to call him, for fear that the son still bears ill will. Kevin encourages the call anyway, and Marley lifts Kevin's spirits about his family (who, unbeknownst to Kevin, are desperately searching for a way to get home to him).

On schedule, inept crooks Marv and Harry find that evading Kevin's 12 challenges is virtually impossible, for they are seared, stuck, gouged, struck, and bashed by a hot coil, sticky tar, sharp ornaments, an iron, a spike, a trip wire, and paint cans-turned-wrecking balls. Calling 911, Kevin steers the police to a house across the street, then lures the crooks there.

Although the crooks initially nab Kevin, Marley appears and bashes the two with a shovel, and the police arrive shortly for the arrest.

On Christmas morning, Kevin's family returns, having at last found a flight home. Gazing outside, Kevin observes Marley embracing his son and family, a sight that gladdens his heart as much as having his own family back again.

In 1991, this picture captured the following honors: Academy Award nominations for Best Original Score and Best Original Song ("Somewhere in My Dreams" by Leslie Bricusse and John Williams); American Comedy Award for Funniest Leading Actor in a Motion Picture (Macaulay Culkin); BMI Film Music Award (John Williams); British Comedy Award for Best Comedy Film; Casting Society of America Award for Best Casting for Feature Comedy Film; Chicago Film Critics Association Award for Most Promising Actor (Culkin); Golden Globe nominations for Best Motion Picture Comedy and Best Performance by an Actor in a Motion Picture Comedy (Culkin); Golden Screen Awards from Germany; Young Artist Awards for Best Young Actor (Culkin) and Most Entertaining Family Youth Motion Picture Comedy; Young Artist nomination for Best Supporting Young Actress (Angela Goethals).

With John Heard, Catherine O'Hara, Angela Goethals, Gerry Bamman, Hillary Wolf, Larry Hankin, John Candy, and Kieran Culkin. Written and produced by John Hughes. Directed by Chris Columbus. A John Hughes Production with Twentieth Century Fox Pictures. DVD: Twentieth Century Fox Video. 103 min.

Home Alone 2: Lost in New York (1992) reunites the principal cast in another holiday comedy that should be classified as a remake of the 1990 film rather than a sequel, for although the location has changed, the characters, plot, and sometime-seasonal sentiment are virtually identical. Boarding the wrong aircraft, Kevin finds himself in the Big Apple at Christmas, while his family jets to Florida, and robbers Marv and Harry, now escaped prisoners seeking revenge, fall victims to Kevin's ingenious booby traps once more. With a cameo appearance by multimillionaire Donald Trump in the

Plaza Hotel, owned by Trump. In 1993, the film won the BMI Film Music Award (John Williams); a Golden Screen Award from Germany; a People's Choice Award for Favorite Comedy Motion Picture; in 1994, a Young Artist nomination for Best Leading Young Actress (Senta Moses). Production credits identical to *Home Alone*. DVD: Twentieth Century Fox Video. 120 min.

Home Alone 3 (1997), again written by John Hughes, presents a similar plot but with a new family and cast of characters featuring eight-year-old Alex D. Linz. In 1998, the film received a Razzie Award nomination for Worst Remake or Sequel; Young Artist nomination for Best Young Actor Age Ten or Under (Linz); Young Star nomination for Best Young Actor in a Comedy Film (Linz). Produced by Hilton A. Green and John Hughes. Directed by Raja Gosnell. Twentieth Century Fox Film Corporation. DVD: Twentieth Century Fox Video. 102 min.

Home Alone 4: Taking Back the House (2002), made-for-television sequel. Kevin McAllister and family are back, but played by different actors. With Mike Weinberg, French Stewart, Jason Beghe, Joanna Going, and Clare Carey. Written by Debra Frank and Steve L. Hayes. Based on characters by John Hughes. Produced by Mitch Engel. Directed by Rod Daniel. Twentieth Century Fox Television. DVD: Fox Home Entertainment. 84 min.

Home Alone 2: Lost in New York
See **Home Alone**

Home Alone 3
See **Home Alone**

Home Alone 4: Taking Back the House
See **Home Alone**

Home for the Holidays
Popular American song written by the New York–born songwriting team of Al Stillman (lyrics) and Robert Allen (music) in 1954. Often listed as "(There's No Place Like) Home for the Holidays," the song recalls the all-American sentiments and pleasures of being at home for the holidays, including homemade pumpkin pie. Because Christmas is never actu-

ally mentioned in the lyrics, the song might also be appropriate for Thanksgiving. Yet it remains inexorably linked with Christmas, popularized by Perry Como's 1954 recording on the RCA Victor label, which became the top Christmas song that year.

Of the 25 most frequently performed Christmas songs of the twentieth century listed by the American Society of Composers, Authors and Publishers (ASCAP), "Home for the Holidays" ranked number 18. In December 2003, it ranked number 21 and fell from the list in December 2004.

Stillman and Allen also contributed such titles as "It's Not for Me to Say" (1956), "No, Not Much" (1956), and "Chances Are" (1957).

See also **ASCAP List of Christmas Songs.**

The Homecoming: A Christmas Story

See **The Waltons**

Honduras

See **Central America**

The Honeymooners

Highly popular, Emmy Award–winning television situation comedy series that initially aired on the DuMont Network in 1950 and went on to become a popular show on CBS. Starring Jackie Gleason as New York City bus driver Ralph Kramden and Art Carney as sewer-working friend Ed Norton, the series, Gleason's creation, featured the domestic, argumentative lives of loud-mouthed Kramden and his nerves-of-steel wife Alice, along with Ed Norton's wife, Trixie. In various incarnations, the show lasted until 1970.

The episodes from *The Honeymooners'* DuMont Network years are lost, but the existing *Honeymooners* Christmas episodes consist of the following:

"Santa and the Bookies" (December 12, 1953). Needing fast cash because he believes that Alice (Audrey Meadows) is pregnant, Ralph answers a newspaper ad for a sidewalk Santa Claus who will supposedly solicit funds for charity. Unknown to Ralph and Ed (dressed as an elf), the operation is a front for bookies. The two initially land in jail but eventually assist the police in capturing the real culprits.

"Honeymooners Christmas Party" (December 19, 1953). This episode is a remake of a now-lost DuMont sketch. Alice is decorating the apartment on Christmas Eve and sends Ralph on a grocery errand. After Trixie (Joyce Randolph) arrives and describes to Alice what Ed gave her for Christmas (a juice squeezer in the image of Napoleon that squirts juice out of its ear), a series of "guests" drop by that are characters played by Gleason, including Fenwick Babbit, the beer-and-ice man; Joe the Bartender; the Poor Soul; Rudy the Repairman; and Reginald Van Gleason III. Other stars visiting the Kramdens are Frances Langford, who sings "Great Day" and "I Love Paris"; child star Eddie Hodges, who sings "Walking My Baby Back Home"; and the June Taylor Dancers, regulars on the Gleason variety shows. With the exist of the final guest, Ralph returns, and he and Alice exchange gifts, a pair of gloves for him and a Napoleon juice squeezer for her.

"New Year's Eve Party" (December 26, 1953). Not wishing to go out on New Year's Eve but anticipating that Alice will, Ralph attempts to dissuade her by being overly obnoxious. His attitude changes when bandleaders Jimmy and Tommy Dorsey, arriving to retrieve a stack of their sheet music that Alice had found in a telephone booth, invite the Kramdens and Nortons to be their New Year's Eve guests at the Statler Hotel. To avoid having to work on New Year's Eve, Ralph feigns illness to his boss, who in turn has lied to his mother-in-law about spending the evening with her, and heads for the Statler instead. On seeing Ralph there, the boss fires Ralph for lying but reconsiders when his wife reminds him about his own lie. With all forgiven, everyone enjoys dancing to the Dorsey band.

"'Twas the Night before Christmas" (December 24, 1955). One of the "Classic 39" episodes from the 1955–56 season, this is a remake of an earlier episode, "The Anniversary Gift" (February 21, 1953), with a Christmas theme substituted. It's Christmas Eve, and Ralph has bought Alice a supposedly one-of-a-kind hairpin box made of 2,000 matches, which, according to the salesman, once belonged to the emperor of Japan. Before Ralph can present his gift, a neighbor drops by with a gift for Alice, another hairpin box exactly like the one Ralph bought. Chagrined, tricked, and without additional funds for another gift, Ralph almost finds a way out when Uncle Leo arrives with his present for the Kramdens, a gift certificate for $25 to a local department store. Alice, however, is aware of this present, which precludes Ralph from using it to buy her a more practical gift, so he hocks his prized bowling ball instead. On Christmas morning, Alice gives Ralph a bag for his bowling ball, and when she insists on seeing if it fits, Ralph confesses all. Instead of the hairpin box, Ralph's gift to Alice is a Napoleon orange juice squeezer, just like the one Ed gave to Trixie (an idea borrowed from the 1953 "Honeymooners Christmas Party"). The sentiment is not unlike that presented in "The Gift of the Magi," a short story by O. Henry (*see* **The Gift of the Magi**).

After 1970, the Kramdens and Nortons returned for several *Honeymooners* specials, none of which are currently aired on television. In *The Honeymooners Christmas Special* (November 26, 1977), Ralph stages a presentation of Dickens's *A Christmas Carol* for the Gotham Bus Company, with Ralph and Ed playing multiple characters. In *Jackie Gleason Honeymooners Christmas* (December 10, 1978), Ralph persuades people to buy hundreds of lottery tickets.

Series written by Marvin Marx, Walter Stone, Syd Zelinka, Leonard Stern, Andy Russell, and Herb Finn. Executive producer, Jack Philbin. Produced by Jack Hurdle. Directed by Frank Satenstein.

The Honeymooners episodes appear in the following video collections: *The Honeymooners Classic 39 Episodes* (DVD: Boxed set of five discs, Paramount Home Video. B & W. 999 min.); *The Honeymooners — The Lost Episodes* (DVD: six boxed sets totaling 24 discs. MPI Video. B & W. 2,400 min.).

Honeymooners Christmas Party
See **The Honeymooners**

The House without a Christmas Tree

(1972). Made-for-television drama, based on a story by Gail Rock, later published as a book in 1974.

The setting is Nebraska, 1946. Each year Addie Mills (Lisa Lucas) begs her father James (Jason Robards) for a Christmas tree; each year he refuses. Embittered over losing his beloved wife after Addie's birth ten years ago, James has put Christmas aside, for its symbols remind him too much of Helen, who had cherished the season. Undaunted, Addie persists in dropping hints about her wish, even singing the carol "O Christmas Tree" with her friends before her father.

A severe altercation erupts after Addie brings home the tree from her class that she "won" at school. Spewing brimstone, James orders the tree out of his house, as expected, after which Addie attaches a note "From Santa" and anonymously gives it to a school chum who has no tree. Shortly thereafter, James recognizes Addie's former tree in a neighbor's home. Hearing how it arrived through Addie's unselfishness more than melts James's stony heart, whereupon he brings home a Christmas tree and shares memories with Addie about the mother she never knew. And from the attic, he retrieves the precious, hand-made star that Helen had intended for Addie's first Christmas tree. Their house has Christmas trees from then on.

In 1973, this picture was nominated for a Directors' Guild of America Award for Outstanding Directorial Achievement in Specials.

With Mildred Natwick, Alexia Kenin, Kathryn Walker, Gail Dunsome, Maya Ryan, and Brady MacNamara. Written by Eleanor Perry. Produced by Alan Shayne. Directed by Paul Bogart. CBS Television. VHS: Paramount Studios. 90 min.

How Brightly Beams the Morning Star
See **How Brightly Shines the Morning Star**

How Brightly Shines the Morning Star

("Wie schön leuchtet der Morgenstern"). German chorale written in 1598 by Philipp Nicolai (1556–1608), Lutheran pastor of Unna in Westphalia. Nicolai wrote only four chorales, of which this and "Wachet auf! Ruft uns die Stimme" ("Sleepers, Awake! A Voice Is Calling") are the best known, the two having achieved the distinctions as the queen and king of chorales, respectively. All four were written following a six-month outbreak of bubonic plague in Unna between July 1597 and January 1598 and were published in Frankfurt in 1599.

The text is founded on Psalm 45, which consists of songs from a royal wedding party. From this, Nicolai developed the variant theme of a spiritually royal bridal song between the Christian soul (bride) and Christ (Bridegroom). References to Christmas appear in the first two of seven verses, in which Christ, symbolized as the "Morning Star" (not the Star of Bethlehem), is the Light born to save a lost world from the darkness of sin (Malachi 4:2 and Luke 1:78). Verse one also refers to Christ as the Branch from Jesse, King David's father, as found in the Messianic prophecy of Isaiah 11:1. And verse two refers to Christ as Mary's son Who has come down to earth as the pearl and crown. In the remainder of the chorale, the soul expresses undying love for Christ.

The Unna plague claimed the life of one of Nicolai's former students, fifteen-year-old Wilhelm Ernst, count of Waldech. According to *The New Oxford Book of Carols*, Nicolai memorialized him in "Morning Star" by using the first letter of each of the seven verses as an acrostic, creating the initials "W.E.G.U.H.Z.W.," which stand for "Wilhelm Ernst, Graf und Herr zu Waldech" ("Wilhelm Ernst, Count and Lord of Waldech").

"Morning Star" has appeared in other settings, such as the accompaniment for "Die Könige" ("The Kings"), an Epiphany carol written in 1859 by the German composer Peter Cornelius (1824–1874) and published in 1871. J.S. Bach's Cantata *Wie schön leuchtet der Morgenstern* (BWV 1, 1725) is also based on the Nicolai chorale.

The best-known English translations have been provided by Great Britain's Catherine Winkworth (1827–1878), a translation specialist who has rendered the title as "O Morning Star, How Fair and Bright" and "How Brightly Beams the Morning Star."

See also **Sleepers, Awake! A Voice Is Calling**.

How Great My Joy
See **While by My Sheep**

How the Flintstones Saved Christmas
See **The Flintstones**

How the Grinch Stole Christmas
Classic children's book by Dr. Seuss (Theodore Seuss Geisel) with animated cartoon and live-action motion picture adaptations.

The book, published in 1957, features the Grinch, a nasty creature who hates Christmas because his heart is two sizes too small. Hearing the little Whos preparing gaily for Christmas in the nearby town of Whoville only irritates him that much more. Determined to keep Christmas from coming, the Grinch, disguised as Santa, steals into Whoville on Christmas Eve with his dog Max disguised as a reindeer and, while the Whos sleep, strips the town of every Christmas item, including the Who-pudding, the roast beast, and the last can of Who-hash. When tiny Cindy-Lou Who discovers him stealing her Christmas tree, the lying Grinch claims that he's merely taking the tree away to replace a broken light bulb and will return it shortly.

On Christmas morning, instead of witnessing a scene of despair, the Grinch hears joyful singing as the Whos welcome Christmas despite the absence of gifts and decorations. Learning that the true meaning of Christmas doesn't come from a store, he restores the Whos' possessions and joins in the festivities.

Geisel also coproduced the animated cartoon *Dr. Seuss's How the Grinch Stole Christmas* for television (1966). Narrated by actor Boris Karloff and featuring a green Grinch, it became a favorite annual telecast. Original songs "Welcome Christmas" and "You're a Mean One, Mr. Grinch" by Dr. Seuss and Albert Hague. Voices: Boris Karloff, June Foray, and Thurl Ravenscroft (vocals). Written by Dr. Seuss, Bob Ogle, and Irv Spector. Coproduced and directed by Chuck Jones. A Chuck Jones Enterprises Production in association with the Cat in the Hat Productions and Metro-Goldwyn-Mayer Television. DVD: Warner Studios. 26 min.

A live-action, motion picture comedy adaptation (2000) starred Jim Carrey, Christine Baranski, Molly Shannon, Josh Ryan Evans, Jeffrey Tambor, and Frankie Ray. In 2001 and 2002, the picture either won or was nominated for more than 40 awards. Notable among them were an Academy Award for Best Makeup; Academy nominations for Best Art Direction/Set Decoration and Best Costume Design; and a Razzie Award nomination for Worst Remake or Sequel. Written by Peter S. Seaman and Jeffrey Price. Produced by Brian Grazer and Ron Howard. Directed by Ron Howard. Imagine Entertainment with LUNI Productions GmbH and Company KG. DVD: Universal Studios. 104 min.

How the Toys Saved Christmas

(1996). English-language title for *La Freccia Azzurra* (literally *The Blue Arrow*), an Italian/Swiss/Luxembourgian animated cartoon, based on a story of the same title by Gianni Rodari. Also known as *The Toys Who Saved Christmas*, this film was one of Italy's first principal productions to employ digital animation.

The original story, set in the 1930s, incorporates a figure from Italian folklore, the old woman *La Befana*, who rides about on her broom and delivers gifts to deserving children on the night of January 5, the eve of Epiphany. When illness prevents *La Befana* (voice of Lella Costa) from making her rounds, her evil assistant, Scarafoni (voice of Dario Fo), would accommodate only those willing to pay exorbitant sums for their children's toys. The toys, believing that they should match themselves with children to whom they would bring the greatest joy, escape and comb the city in search of appropriate recipients while riding on a model train designated as *The Blue Arrow*. Despite Scarafoni's numerous attempts to recapture them, the toys persevere, and intervention from *La Befana* herself ultimately succeeds in defeating the villain.

The English-language version alters the story in several respects: the holiday setting is Christmas instead of Epiphany; *La Befana* becomes Granny Rose (voice of Mary Tyler Moore), who assists Santa Claus in dispensing gifts; and Scarafoni becomes Mr. Grimm (voice of Tony Randall).

In 1997, *La Freccia Azzurra* won the David di Donatello Award for Best Music as well as the Silver Ribbon and the Special Silver Ribbon from the Italian National Syndicate of Film Journalists, respectively, for Best Score and for an Animated Film Produced in Italy.

La Freccia Azzurra screenplay by Enzo d'Alò and Umberto Marino. Produced by Maria Fares, Rolf Schmid, Vreni Trabor, and Paul Thiltges. Directed by Enzo d'Alò. La Lanterna Magica (Italy), Fama Film (Switzerland), Monipoly Productions (Luxembourg). English-language version, *The Toys Who Saved Christmas* (c) 1997, Miramax Film Corp. Script by Shelly Altman. Produced by Eve Chilton. VHS: Walt Disney Studios. 93 min.

See also **Epiphany**; **Italy**.

Humbug Not to Be Spoken Here
See **Bewitched**

Hunting the Wren

Also known as "Going on the Wren." Archaic custom once prevalent in the British Isles and France, a modified version of which survives in Ireland. Dating at least from the eighteenth century and possibly earlier, the custom originally took place on Christmas Eve or Christmas Day but, for unclear reasons, shifted to December 26 (Boxing Day or St. Stephen's Day). Groups of "Wren Boys," attired in outlandish costumes that included masks and women's clothing, would hunt and kill a wren, and, after fastening it to a decorative pole, placing it in a cage, or attaching it to a cluster of holly ("wren bush"), would carry this token while serenading homes in the village with a repertoire of wren songs for the purposes of soliciting food, drink, and money. To those who complied, the Wren Boys bestowed a wren feather for good luck; otherwise, they offered songs of derision and sometimes buried the wren in the yard of an offender as a sign of bad luck. The collected cash then supported a Wren Dance in the village either that night or the night after, to which the public was invited. Rarely, as in one region in Wales, the wren was captured for the ritual but not slain. The ritual was virtually nonexistent in Scotland, except for that on New Year's Day, when a wren occasionally would be captured, decorated, then released with no further ceremony.

Although these wren hunts essentially vanished by the turn of the twentieth century, the Irish custom incorporates either a wren effigy or a caged live wren. The songs and costumes remain, the singers now include women who often appear as transvestites as do men, and the money collected now benefits charities or sponsors traditional Wren Dances.

Precise origins for the hunting of wrens at Christmastime are lacking, and proposed theories are paradoxical, especially when coupled with wren legends and folklore. According to legends, as Jesus and St. Stephen fled from persecution, the wren betrayed them by directing their captors to them (one possible explanation for hunting wrens on St. Stephen's Day). Another holds that as the Irish army secretly approached the camp of invading Vikings, the wren's pecking on a drum alerted the sleeping enemy, who successfully routed the Irish. The Celts particularly regarded the wren as the "Druid's bird," that is, a bird of ill omen. Elsewhere, it was a bird favored of God along with the robin, and the harming of either would bring bad luck. The wren was the "king of birds" in wren verses and folklore. The latter stems from a tale in which the bird that flew the highest would be crowned king. To deceive its competitors, the wren, hiding on the back of an eagle, suddenly appeared above all other birds in flight and won the title.

While some theories have proposed that hunting wrens was an act of vengeance for the birds' alleged betrayals and deceptions, the most plausible theory holds that the custom derived from those pagan New Year's festivals which offered a mock king as a sacrifice following a period of revelry. Examples are found in the ancient Mesopotamian festivals of Akitu and Zagmuk (discussed in the entry for **Saturnalia**). Because some Victorian Christmas cards, for reasons unknown, cast the wren as a symbol of the old year, it is possible that killing wrens also symbolized the death of the old year.

See also **Boxing Day**; **Ireland**; **Saturnalia**.

The Huron Christmas Carol

(Huron, "Jesous ahatonhia," "Jesus Is Born"). First Canadian carol, written in 1641 by French Jesuit missionary Father Jean de Brébeuf (1593–1649). Having resided at a mission set among the Huron Indians of Georgia Bay, Ontario, since 1626, Father Brébeuf created "Jesous ahatonhia," a poem in the Huron language, which adapted the biblical Nativity story to an equivalent concept in the Huron culture. For a musical setting, Father Brébeuf chose a sixteenth century folk tune, "Une jeune pucelle" ("A Young Virgin").

Thus, angel choirs sent from Gitchi Manitou (God) appear to a throng of hunters (shepherds) with the news that Jesus is born. As the hunters approach a lodge of "broken bark" (stable), they find the Babe within wrapped in ragged rabbit skins (swaddling clothes), and three chiefs (Wise Men) present gifts of fur skins (gold, frankincense, and myrrh).

The Hurons kept the carol in their oral tradition until 1649, when a band of Iroquois Indians destroyed the mission, killed Father Brébeuf, and drove the Hurons out, with many escaping into Quebec. There, a century after its composition, another Jesuit priest, a Father Villenueve, committed the carol to paper after hearing it sung by Huron descendants. Attorney and Huron member Paul Picard subsequently produced a French translation of the carol. The popular English version known today, beginning with the words "'Twas in the moon of wintertime," was translated by J.E. Middleton and was first published in 1942 by the *Canadian Messenger of the Sacred Heart*.

See also **Miracle in the Wilderness: A Christmas Story of Colonial America**, which includes another adaptation of the Nativity story to Native American culture.

I

I Heard the Bells on Christmas Day

American carol, the lyrics of which were written by the celebrated poet Henry Wadsworth Longfellow (1807–1882) during Christmas of 1863 and published in 1867 under the title "Christmas Bells." A pacifist, Longfellow, whose son Charles was wounded in 1862 during the American Civil War, wrote the poem as a lament over the war and as an expression of grief over the loss of his wife in 1861 during a fire. According to the lyrics, at first the joyous pealing of church bells on Christmas Day seem to mock the concept of "peace on earth, goodwill to men" in a time of war. But, listening more closely, the bells assure that God is neither dead nor asleep, and eventually that "the wrong shall fail, the right prevail."

The lyrics have been sung to two principal melodies, one by the English organist John Baptiste Calkin (1827–1905), the other by composer Johnny Marks (1909–1985) of "Rudolph, the Red-Nosed Reindeer" fame. Calkin's tune of 1872, "Waltham," was originally paired with an older missionary hymn written in 1848, "Fling Out the Banner! Let It Float!" Further details regarding the match between "Waltham" and "I Heard the Bells" remain obscure. Whereas Johnny Marks composed both lyrics and music for his multitude of Christmas songs, he simply supplied a popular tune for "I Heard the Bells" in 1956, a version that has received wide exposure by numerous recording artists.

See also **The Three Kings**, a poem by Longfellow.

I Know a Rose Tree Springing
See **Lo, How a Rose E'er Blooming**

I Love Lucy

Probably the best-known situation comedy in the history of television, running on the CBS network from 1951 to 1960 and first sponsored by Philip Morris cigarettes. Its weekly episodes featured the domestic antics of zany Lucy Ricardo (Lucille Ball), often to the dismay of her Cuban bandleader-husband, Ricky (real-life husband and bandleader Desi Arnaz), and their older neighbors, Fred and Ethel Mertz (William Frawley and Vivian Vance).

Although none of the 179 regular episodes of the Emmy Award–winning *I Love Lucy* centered around Christmas, the series did feature one Christmas special that was not numbered with the other episodes. Titled "*I Love Lucy* Christmas Show," it aired on Christmas Eve, 1956. In this special, Lucy and Ricky have a five-year-old son, Little Ricky (Keith Thibodeaux, who first came to the series in May 1956), whose Christmas Eve curiosity about Santa's arrival is satisfied with appropriate, quickly improvised tales; for example, Santa slides down the chimney like a fireman and brings the North Pole with him. With the child in bed, Fred and Ethel arrive bearing a five-dollar Christmas tree, which, at Lucy's suggestion, Fred begins to shape by cutting off branches. As Ricky reminisces, the scene flashes back to an earlier episode, "Lucy is *Enceinte*" (December 1952). There, during his act at the Tropicana Club, Ricky received an anonymous note requesting that he sing "We're Having a Baby," because a couple in the audience were expecting a baby. Of course, when he saw Lucy sitting nearby, Ricky quickly deduced that his wife was pregnant. Listening so intently to the tale, Fred hacks the tree to shreds and departs for a replacement.

As the other three strike up "Jingle Bells," Lucy's off-key singing prompts a second flashback to another episode, "Lucy's Show Biz Swan Song" (also December 1952), in which Lucy, the fourth member of a barbershop quartet, sang "Sweet Adeline" as miserably as ever.

Decorating Fred's second tree (purchased for 50 cents) yields the final flashback to "Lucy Goes to the Hospital" (January 1953), in which Ricky and the Mertzes rehearsed their plan to get pregnant Lucy to the hospital as quickly as possible. When the real moment arrived, as expected, pandemonium reigned.

Christmas morning now finds the Ricardos and Mertzes all dressed as Santas, who hide in the kitchen as Little Ricky races to his gifts. The presence of a fifth Santa (Cameron Grant) among them prompts a systematic pulling of beards as the true Santa suddenly vanishes before their eyes. Shaken, the others manage to close with a "Merry Christmas" for the audience. This five-Santa routine originated as a four-minute seasonal "tag" to the episode "Drafted" (aired Christmas Eve, 1951), in which a fifth Santa (Vernon Dent) magically joined the four Santa-clad stars as they frolicked around the Ricardos' Christmas tree. Stunned, the principals again provided a similar closing.

Written by Bob Carroll, Jr., Madelyn Pugh, Bob Schiller, and Bob Weiskopf. Produced by Desi Arnaz. Directed by James V. Kern. Desilu Productions. VHS: Twentieth Century Fox Video. B & W. 26 min.

I Saw Mommy Kissing Santa Claus

(Film, 2002). American/German motion picture comedy, loosely based on the popular 1952 song of the same title by Tommie Connor.

When he unwittingly witnesses "Santa" kissing his mother Stephanie (Connie Sellecca), eight-year-old Justin Carver (twins Cole and Dylan Sprouse) believes his costumed father David (Corbin Bernsen) is the jolly old elf himself and concludes that hanky-panky is afoot. His friend Bobby (Eric Jacobs) reasons that if Justin should suddenly become quite naughty, Santa, the "fat rat," will lose interest in his mother and thus prevent a divorce. On the other hand, Bobby's parents plan to divorce, which prompts Bobby to believe that, should he become a model child, Santa will intervene on their behalf. Thus, to save their families, both boys adopt behaviors alien to their natural personalities.

From here on the picture provides copious scenes of a rebellious Justin, an angelic Bobby, and bewildered parents and school authorities. Aside from schoolyard pranks, Justin targets for persecution Santas on the street, in the mall, and the one who visits his class, all of whom happen to be the same ill-fated person (Sonny Carl Davis).

Only when Stephanie discovers the Polaroid snapshot that Justin had taken of her "affair" with Santa does she finally understand Justin's behavior, but not before he rigs a series of sophisticated booby traps in the yard. Coming home from a business trip late on Christmas Eve and wishing to surprise Justin, Dave dons the same Santa suit and falls prey to his son's remarkable ingenuity.

Despite darts arranged in the fireplace, a somewhat sore albeit real Santa (Duane Stephens) works a little magic of his own by supplying the coveted toy that Justin had desired but that his parents could never find and by granting Bobby's wish for reconciled parents.

Written by Steve Jankowski, John Shepphird, Mike Sorrentino, and Randy Vampotic. Produced by James Rosenthal, Jeffrey Schenck, Shawn Levy, and Steve Jankowski. Directed by John Shepphird. Regent Entertainment in association with ACH GmbH and Medien Capital Treuhand GmbH and Company 1.KG. DVD: Parade Video. 100 min.

See also **I Saw Mommy Kissing Santa Claus** (song).

I Saw Mommy Kissing Santa Claus

(Song). American novelty song written in 1952 by British songwriter Tommie Connor, the only song of note from that composer. Recorded by 12-year-old Jimmy Boyd on the Columbia label, it sold over 2.5 million copies and was the top Christmas song for 1952. As the title suggests, the lyrics feature a young child's account of witnessing his mother kissing "Santa" beneath the mistletoe and tickling the old gent under his white beard. As part of its naïve flavor, the song does not specify whether Mommy's interest lies in the real Santa, Daddy dressed up as Santa, or a third party bent on Yuletide hanky-panky, about which the child would probably not have been aware, at least not in 1952. In the closing segment, though, the youngster believes that it would have been amusing if Daddy could have seen Mommy's actions.

Of the 25 most frequently performed

Christmas songs of the twentieth century listed by the American Society of Composers, Authors and Publishers (ASCAP), "I Saw Mommy Kissing Santa Claus" ranked number 20. By December 2004, it ranked number 19.

See also **ASCAP List of Christmas Songs; I Saw Mommy Kissing Santa Claus** (film).

I Saw Three Ships

English traditional carol believed to have arisen during the fifteenth century. The carol is based on a legend claiming that relics of the three Wise Men eventually came to rest in Germany's Cologne Cathedral in 1162, having been transported up the Rhine River in three ships. Many variant lyrics and tunes exist, the earliest of which was published in John Forbes's second edition of *Cantus, Songs and Fancies* (Aberdeen, 1666).

The earlier versions presented more graphic accounts of the ships' contents, that is, three skulls being transported to Cologne. Later versions softened the lyrics, describing that the ships carried "Our Savior Christ and His lady [the Virgin Mary]," as found in William Sandys's *Christmas Carols, Ancient and Modern* (London, 1833), with no mention of Cologne. However, in virtually all versions, three ships sail either into or from landlocked Bethlehem. Explanations for this physical impossibility have included suppositions that early Britons, knowing virtually nothing about the geography of Bethlehem, pictured it as a coastal town. Alternatively, the ships have been conceived as allegorical media for Father, Son, and Holy Spirit; Jesus, Mary, and Joseph; or Faith, Hope, and Charity.

A remarkably similar English traditional carol, "As I Sat on a Sunny Bank," again mentions three ships sailing by on Christmas Day and that "Joseph and his fair lady [Virgin Mary]" are with them, but specifies neither the ships' destination nor whence they have come. Therefore, although the titles are different, "I Saw Three Ships" and "As I Sat on a Sunny Bank" must be considered as variants of each other.

See also **Nativity; Wise Men.**

I Want a Dog for Christmas, Charlie Brown

(2003). Made-for-television animated cartoon, based on the *Peanuts* comic strip characters created by Charles M. Schulz (1922–2000).

The story consists of a series of loosely connected sketches revolving around Rerun Van Pelt, the little brother of Linus and Lucy. Rerun wants his own dog for Christmas and casts a covetous eye upon Snoopy. But when Charlie Brown refuses to sell his beloved pet for anything less than ten million dollars (Rerun has only 16 cents), Rerun turns to Snoopy for holiday amusement. Annoyed with Rerun's excessive demands for play, Snoopy eventually responds with form-letter rejections. Rerun's hopes rise again, however, when Snoopy receives a letter from his brother Spike, announcing his plans for a visit, and Rerun surmises that he can adopt Spike for Christmas. But Charlie Brown recalls a previous time when Snoopy's doghouse was trashed after a similar visit from a spirited canine relative and wonders if mayhem is on the horizon.

Scattered among this theme are incidental scenes such as Lucy's never-ending attempts to attract Schroder as he practices Beethoven at the piano; Snoopy dressing as Santa and unwittingly shocking a little girl who spies him eating from a dog dish; and Rerun's suspension from school on charges of "sexual harassment" after telling a little classmate that he would like to take her to Paris.

Voices: Jimmy Bennett, Adam Taylor Gordon, Ashley Rose Orr, Corey Padnos, Hannah Leigh Dworkin, Nick Price, Jake Miner, Kaitlyn Maggio, and Bill Melendez. Music by Vince Guaraldi and David Benoit. Produced by Bill Melendez. Directed by Larry Leichliter and Bill Melendez. A Lee Mendelson–Bill Melendez Production in association with Charles M. Schulz Creative Associates. DVD: Paramount Home Video. 75 min.

See also **A Charlie Brown Christmas; Charlie Brown's Christmas Tales; Happy New Year, Charlie Brown; It's Christmastime Again, Charlie Brown.**

I Wonder As I Wander

American carol attributed to John Jacob Niles (1892–1980). A native of Kentucky, a folk singer and composer, Niles began collecting American folk tunes at an early age. Although he had studied classical music in Paris and Cincinnati following World War I, he journeyed to New York during the Depression to pursue a folk music career. There he met and became a guide for famed photographer Doris Ullman, who was undertaking a project in the southern Appalachian Mountains. Niles stated that in July of 1933, while he was touring North Carolina, he came upon the homeless Morgans, a revivalist family in the town of Murphy, who were camped on the town square. Facing eviction and in need of ready cash, Preacher Morgan held a revival meeting, at which time a family member, a young girl named Annie, sang three lines of a most haunting tune for 25 cents a performance. Apparently there was more to the song, but Niles was only able to glean those three lines. By writing additional verses of his own and developing the original melodic material, Niles produced "I Wonder As I Wander," which he published in his collection *Songs for the Hill-Folk: Twelve Ballads from Kentucky, Virginia, and North Carolina, Collected and Simply Arranged with Accompaniment for Piano* (New York, 1934). Since Niles once remarked that his involvement with folk material ranged anywhere from simple arrangement to original composition, it is apparent that "I Wonder As I Wander" is not entirely an original work. Niles sang it for five years in his concerts before it acquired popularity.

The provocatively plaintive tune suggests a spiritual, while the lyrics ponder the mystery that Christ would be born, only to die for "poor on'ry (ornery) people like you and like I."

Iceland

Although Irish monks are believed to have first arrived in Iceland in the ninth century, the island was settled principally by Nordic tribes, who accepted Christianity and Christmas around the year 1000. Christmas customs blended with those of pagan *Jól* (Yule), a midwinter festival honoring the return of the sun at the winter solstice.

In the holidays of yesteryear, villagers helping to process the autumn wool before Christmas received as reward an article of new clothing. Exchanging Christmas presents as such did not become common until the nineteenth century. Because of the scarcity of grain,

the poor stretched their supply of bread by creating *laufabraud* (leaf bread), fried, flat cakes of flour and water rolled into extremely thin sheets and cut into shapes of leaves or other objects. Christmas was also a time for taking annual baths and washing clothes. The principal cuisine for the wealthy consisted of *hangikjöt* (smoked lamb), whereas the less fortunate feasted on wild grouse.

Since evergreen trees were not native to Iceland, Christmas trees originally consisted of twigs nailed onto a pole and decorated with native foliage, sweets, and candles. The first Christmas tree imported to Iceland is said to have arrived in 1862 from Germany, and decorating homes was not common until the arrival of U.S. servicemen during World War II.

Today the majority of Icelanders belong to the Evangelical Lutheran Church and follow typical Advent traditions. Children enjoy two to three weeks of vacation from school, which commences after "Little Christmas," a day devoted to lighting candles at school, singing carols, and reading holiday stories. Families prepare by cleaning their homes and baking spiced cookies for guests, and many traditionally make their own leaf bread. Because of the limited supply of evergreen Christmas trees grown locally, most families purchase imported trees and decorate them on December 23, a day which commemorates the death of a native saint, Thorlakur Thorhallson, bishop of Skalholt (d. 1193). Tree decorations vary, but almost always include miniature Icelandic flags and a star or crown for a tree topper. Families do not light their trees until 6 P.M. on *Adfangadagur* (Christmas Eve), for at that time the national broadcast of the ringing of the bells at the Lutheran Cathedral in Reykjavik officially heralds Christmas.

Family members strive to return to their native homeplace for the holidays and the Christmas Eve supper, the table of which usually features smoked lamb, along with perhaps pork, beef, chicken, grouse, and porridge. Another traditional dish is rice pudding containing one almond in the batch, and the person who receives this almond in his serving will have a successful year. Fish is conspicuously absent, as is any form of liquor. (Although social standards permit full alcoholic consumption on New Year's Eve, drinking in moderation is acceptable on December 26, the Second Day of Christmas.) Afterwards, children, may open their gifts, brought by the 13 *Jólasveinarnir* ("Christmas Lads," see below). A new article of clothing remains a traditional gift, as is a book or other useful item. Earlier on Christmas Eve, families honor their dead by decorating graves with pine or fir branches and by leaving lighted candles, which burn through the night.

Jóladagur (Christmas Day) and *Annar Jóladagur* (Second Day of Christmas) are spent in feasting and fellowship with family, the menu remaining virtually the same as on Christmas Eve. The new year is greeted with fireworks and parties. According to native folklore, animals acquire speech at this time, seals assume human forms, the dead rise, elves move their homes, and one may receive gold from elves on New Year's Eve by waiting at crossroads as they pass by.

• JÓLASVEINARNIR ("CHRISTMAS LADS"). These creatures plus the *Jólakkotur* ("Christmas Cat"), discussed below, constitute the most significant of Icelandic Christmas folklore. The Lads first appeared in the seventeenth century as the sons of two thirteenth century trolls, Gryla and her husband Leppaludi, both of whom stole and ate naughty children at Christmastime. Over the centuries, the sons, having assumed the Yuletide role of their parents, now deliver the Christmas gifts. Yet they are still notorious pranksters and thieves and appear in red suits similar to the Western Santa Claus. Although some 70 names exist for the Lads, 13 are most commonly accepted, each name reflecting a particular preference for mischief, often the pilfering of food: "Gimpy," "Gully Imp," "Most Tiny," "Pot Scraper Licker," "Pot Licker," "Bowl Licker," "Door Slammer," "Yogurt Eater," "Sausage Grabber," "Window Peeper," "Doorway Sniffer," "Meat Hooker," and "Candle Beggar." Residing in the mountains, the Lads appear 13 days before Christmas, one new Lad arriving each day with a Christmas gift. Children prepare for their arrival by hanging up a sock or by placing their shoes on the windowsill on each night up to Christmas Eve. If they have been good, the Lads fill their shoes with treats, whereas naughty children receive either some undesirable object or nothing at all. The Lads begin their sequential departure on Christmas Day and have returned to their mountain abode by Epiphany (January 6), at which time the Christmas season ends.

• JÓLAKKOTUR ("CHRISTMAS CAT"). A pet monster of the parent trolls mentioned above, the gigantic Christmas Cat devours those who have received no new Christmas clothes. In former days when the only Christmas gift consisted of a bonus of new clothing for processing the autumn wool, the Cat was used to threaten those less-productive villagers who would not have received such a bonus. Although the oldest written sources about the Cat date to the nineteenth century, a twentieth century Icelandic poet, Johannes Ur Kotlum, immortalized the beast in a poem, which Vignir Jonsson translated into English as "The Christmas Cat." According to the poem, the Cat stalks about on Christmas Eve and peers into windows in search of poor children, the least likely recipients of new garments. At its conclusion, the poem makes an appeal for all to help children in dire need at Christmastime, not because of a mythical beast, but for the sake of their happiness and well-being.

"Merry Christmas" in Iceland is *Gledileg Jól.*

See also **Advent; Epiphany; Yule.**

I'll Be Home for Christmas

(Motion picture comedy, 1998). Initially refusing to return home to New York for Christmas because he disapproves of his father's remarriage, California college student Jake Wilkinson (Jonathan Taylor Thomas) receives an offer he cannot refuse. If he returns home by 6 P. M. on Christmas Eve, Jake's father David (Gary Cole) promises the gift of a Porsche. Jake and his girlfriend Allie (Jessica Biel) prepare for the cross-country road trek, but Eddie (Adam LaVorgna), Jake's archrival, alters their plans by foiling Jake's scheme to sell answers for an examination to the school's football team. Now seeking revenge, the team waylays Jake and deposits him in the California desert with nothing but a Santa Claus suit and a white beard glued to his face.

Stranded and alone, Jake, drawing upon his prowess as a con artist, hitchhikes and freeloads his way East, befriending a number of eccentric characters along the way, including petty thief Nolan Briggs (Andrew Lauer), and all the while tracking down Allie, who is traveling with Eddie instead. Predictably, Jake accomplishes his goal, gains the Porsche, wins back Allie, and enjoys a Christmas reunion with his family in the Big Apple.

With Sean O'Bryan, Lesley Boone, and Eve Gordon. Written by Michael Allin, Harris Goldberg, and Tom Nursall. Produced by David Hoberman and Tracey Trench. Directed by Arlene Sanford. Leo Productions, Mandeville Films, and Walt Disney Productions. DVD: Walt Disney Home Video. 86 min.

I'll Be Home for Christmas

(Song). Popular American song written by James Kimball (Kim) Gannon, Walter Kent, and Buck Ram in 1943.

Created during the height of American involvement in World War II, "I'll Be Home for Christmas" was especially endearing because it brought visions of home to the thousands of men and women serving in the Armed Forces who were unable to be with their loved ones for the holidays. The song is a wish for snow, mistletoe, presents, and all the secular ideals that make Christmas what it is. But, even if the one wishing cannot be present in body, he or she will still revel in a family Christmas "if only in my dreams."

Bing Crosby, who had enjoyed overwhelming success with his recording of "White Christmas" a year earlier, also recorded "I'll Be Home for Christmas" on the Decca label in 1943, backed by the John Scott Trotter Orchestra. In position three on the pop charts, it became the top Christmas song that year, sold over a million copies (producing Crosby's fifth gold record), and was back on the charts in 1944. To illustrate the lasting popularity of the song, Gemini Seven astronauts James Lovell and Frank Borman, having completed 206 orbits, requested to hear the Crosby recording as they returned to earth on December 17, 1965.

Of the 25 most frequently performed Christmas songs of the twentieth century listed by the American Society of Composers, and Publishers (ASCAP), "I'll Be Home for Christmas" ranked number 12. By December 2004, it ranked number seven.

See also **ASCAP List of Christmas Songs.**

I'll Be Home for Christmas

(Television drama, 1988). The Bundy family of New England experiences a bittersweet wartime Christmas of 1944. Returning home for the holidays are son Terrell (Jason Oliver), who has completed military basic training, and daughter Leah (Nancy Travis), who works away at a steel plant. While Terrell and his father Joseph (Hal Holbrook) must mend a years-long rift in their relationship, Leah, coping with the loss of her boyfriend abroad, invites a lonely G.I., Aaron Kaplan (Peter Gallagher), to spend Christmas with her family. On Christmas Eve, after attending a USO party, expectant mother and daughter-in-law Nora (Courteney Cox) receives news that her decorated pilot-husband Michael has perished in a plane crash en route home from overseas. Amid the tragedies, Nora gives birth to a son on Christmas Day.

As the servicemen depart, youngest son Davey remarks about the irony of Christmas songs that impart messages of "peace on earth" when there is no peace. To that, Joseph replies that those songs still give us hope.

In 1989, this picture won an Emmy Award for Outstanding Art Direction and was nominated for a Young Artist Award for Best Young Actor (Jason Oliver).

With Eva Marie Saint, David Moscow, Whip Hubley, Kieran Mulroney, Charles R. Nelson, Drew Pillsbury, Tarrish Potter, John Shepherd, Charles Tyner, and Harvey Vernon. Written by Blanche Hanalis. Produced and directed by Marvin J. Chomsky. VHS: Goodtimes Home Video. 96 min.

I'll Be Home for Christmas

(Television drama, 1997). Filled with guilt because he could not save his wife's life four years ago, Minneapolis surgeon Dr. Mike Greiser (Robert Hays) suffers a breakdown before the holidays and retreats to his small hometown of St. Nicholas, Iowa, for a vacation. The citizens welcome their favorite son by electing him as the "Grand Electrician," who will light the community Christmas tree on Christmas Eve, and Mike also rekindles a romance with his high school sweetheart, Dr. Sarah Gladestone (Ann Jillian), now St. Nicholas's mayor and veterinarian. The town, lacking a medical doctor, offers Mike the position, but Mike quickly returns to Minneapolis, where he abandons his practice and assumes an administrative role instead. He attains the courage to continue in medicine, however, when his father Bob (Jack Palance), having returned with him rather than spend Christmas in St. Nicholas alone, suffers a heart attack and requires immediate coronary bypass surgery. Further inspired when his young daughter Jilly (Ashley Gorrell) begs him to save her grandfather's life, Mike throws off his fears and performs the surgery successfully.

The news that St. Nicholas's hospital will close without a doctor prompts Mike to make his final career move, for he and Jilly relocate to St. Nicholas on Christmas Eve to start a new life together with Sarah.

With Linda Sorenson, Eric Peterson, Bernard Behrens, and Tom Harvey. Written by Darrah Cloud. Produced by Susan Murdoch. Directed by Jerry London. Jaffe/Braunstein Productions. Available on DVD. 94 min.

The IMAX Nutcracker
See **The Nutcracker**

In the Bleak Mid-Winter

English carol, the text for which was written in 1872 by poet Christina Rossetti (1830–1894). Consisting of five verses, each with eight lines, its first verse, filled with stark imagery of a bitter winter at Christmastime, contrasts with the remaining four verses, which describe the Nativity on a more positive note. The final verse crowns the poem with an admonition for us to give Christ our best gift, our heart.

Two musical settings for this carol remain foremost. That by Gustav Holst (1874–1934), an English composer of Swedish descent, was written for the first edition of *The English Hymnal* (1906), which retained Ms. Rossetti's then-shocking phrase "breastful of milk" in verse three (censored in other hymnals of the period). The other setting (1911) by Harold Darke (1888–1976), organist at London's

Church of St. Michael for 50 years, also included the controversial phrase.

Christina Rossetti is one of England's best-known female poets. Two of her most noted works are *Sing-Song: A Nursery Rhyme Book* and a collection of children's stories, *Speaking Likeness* (both 1872). She also penned the poem "Christmastide," destined to become the famous carol known as "Love Came Down at Christmas."

See also **Love Came Down at Christmas.**

India
See **Asia and the South Pacific**

Indonesia
See **Asia and the South Pacific**

Infant Holy, Infant Lowly

("W zlobie lezy"). Polish traditional carol, considered to be the best-known and earliest significant carol from that country. Thought to date from the thirteenth or fourteenth century, its title has also been translated as "Jesus Holy, Born So Lowly," "Baby Jesus, in a Manger," and "He Is Sleeping in a Manger." The most often-sung English version today, beginning with "Infant Holy," is an adaptation of the translated text that was first published in *Music and Youth* (1921), an English journal founded and edited by Edith M.G. Reed (1885–1933). Consisting of two verses, the lyrics recall the manger, the oxen lowing nearby, the shepherds keeping watch over their flocks, and the angelic message that the Babe has been born.

Iran
See **Middle East**

Iraq
See **Middle East**

Ireland

Although St. Patrick (?389–?461) is credited with introducing Christianity to Ireland in the fifth century, the Irish became acquainted with the British Christmas through King Henry II of England, who initiated the Norman conquest of Ireland (1171–72). Today, Roman Catholicism predominates in the southern five-sixths of the island, known as the

Republic of Ireland, while the smaller Northern Ireland remains a constituent of Protestant Great Britain. For the sake of simplicity, this entry discusses Irish Christmas customs as a whole.

The holiday season extends from Advent until Epiphany, and preparations include baking Christmas cakes a month or two in advance. Fortified with brandy and enveloped in a marzipan coating, these fruitcakes, which also double as Irish wedding cakes, improve with age and are frosted only a few days before Christmas. Roman Catholics may voluntarily fast for periods during Advent, and their homes and churches feature Nativity scenes, often with Celtic figures. While it is customary to pray the rosary each night before the manger, a figure of Baby Jesus is not placed therein until Christmas Eve, and those of the Wise Men are not added until Epiphany. Families thoroughly clean their homes, often whitewashing the exteriors in rural regions, and send Christmas cards only to those friends and relatives whom they will most likely not see during the holidays because of distance or illness. Charitable organizations, schools, and churches stage Nativity plays and mummers' plays during Advent, and Christmas markets peak on the Saturday before Christmas, with their patrons said to "bring home the Christmas." Christmas trees are usually firs decorated with strings of electric lights and homemade garlands of paper and tinsel. These together with evergreens are usually put in place on Christmas Eve or a few days beforehand. At noon on Christmas Eve, most commerce ceases and will remain in abeyance until January 2; the usual exceptions are pubs and taverns, which offer free drinks on Christmas Eve.

Christmas in Ireland centers around family, and all unmarried members are expected to return to their parents' home by Christmas Eve if at all possible, regardless of whether they reside locally or abroad. Married children celebrate Christmas in their own homes, not those of their parents. Families place candles in their windows on Christmas, beginning with a large "principal candle" two feet tall that is set in the central window. Depending on the region, this candle is either red, green, blue, yellow, or pink and may be the only candle that is displayed;

should smaller candles adorn other windows, they are lighted only from the principal candle, and custom dictates that either the youngest daughter or one named Mary light all candles. Then families often walk about, admiring the candle glow from neighbors' windows. Origins for the custom are surrounded in legend. According to one, it was believed that, on Christmas Eve, Mary and Joseph annually retraced their steps to Bethlehem, and that lighted candles in windows offered them shelter. Another dates to the Protestant Reformation, holding that the custom secretly alerted passing priests that the occupants therein were Catholics who desired to receive Mass on Christmas Eve. A fable about the Holy Family's wanderings then supposedly evolved to quell the suspicions of Protestant authorities.

The Church no longer requires fasting all day on Christmas Eve, yet some still prefer this tradition, breaking the fast with a simple, meatless meal of fish and potato soup. Going to confession on Christmas Eve is no longer universal, as was once the custom. Whereas Catholics in other countries attend Midnight Mass, this is a relatively new innovation for the Irish, whose Christmas Masses were formerly held at dawn on Christmas morning, the so-called "First Light Masses."

Before retiring for the evening, children hang up their stockings in anticipation of a visit from Santa Claus, who may also leave gifts in a pillowcase at the foot of the bed. Some families cater to old superstitions by setting out food on the table, unlocking the doors, and keeping at least one candle lit in a window all night. These latter acts not only serve to bid the Holy Family welcome, but they also welcome the spirits of deceased ancestors, who are believed to return home at Christmastime. Other favorite Christmas Eve superstitions once held that Satan had perished at midnight when Jesus was born, for which church bells annually tolled the "Devil's Knell" (the tradition survives locally in Great Britain); further, those who died on this night would never suffer Purgatory, for the Gates of Heaven mercifully remained open to receive all souls.

Families spend Christmas Day quietly together at home. Noted traditions among them include simple gift exchanges that are limited to members living under the same roof, and the distribution of meals and other necessities to those in need, prior to assembling for Christmas dinner. The latter usually features turkey or goose with stuffing, vegetables, plum pudding, bread pudding, mincemeat pie, Christmas cake, and Irish whiskey. Afterwards, families amuse themselves with assorted games and the telling of yarns and stories.

The remainder of the holidays center around St. Stephen's Day (December 26), New Year's Day, and Epiphany. On St. Stephen's Day, the Irish engage in an old custom known as "Hunting the Wren" (discussed as a separate entry), attend mummers' plays (notably in Wexford, Dublin, and Ulster) and sporting events such as horse racing and fox hunting, and visit friends and relatives. Parties, fireworks, bonfires, and parades greet the new year, along with a few superstitions that may still be observed in rural regions. For instance, to thwart hunger and assure plenty in the coming year, consume a heavy meal on New Year's Eve, dash a New Year's cake against the principal door of the house, or strike the door thrice while holding the cake. To protect livestock against hunger, throw the cake against the barn door. Although girls are less likely today to induce dreams of future husbands by placing holly or ivy leaves beneath their pillows, the custom of "firstfooting" on New Year's Day survives as in Great Britain. Three candles often decorate windows to honor the Wise Men on Epiphany, also known as "Women's Christmas," so named because it was once commonplace to serve a meal more delicate than the goose and potent whiskey of Christmas. Some families may still practice an old superstition on this last day of Christmas: Each member is assigned a candle, which is placed atop a cake and lit. The order in which the flames extinguish predicts the eventual order of each person's death.

"Merry Christmas" in Irish Gaelic is *Nollaig Shona Dhuit*.

See also **Advent; Boxing Day; Epiphany; Great Britain; Hunting the Wren.**

Irving, Washington, Christmas Sketches of

Series of five consecutive, interrelated tales by this American author of wit (1783–1859), published in his collection *The Sketch Book of Geoffrey Crayon, Gent* (1819–20), the title also reflecting Irving's pseudonym. This collection is probably best known for two classics, "The Legend of Sleepy Hollow" and "Rip Van Winkle."

A romantic historian fond of antiquated customs, Irving developed a keen interest in English Christmases as celebrated in the days of yore and the customs that had been largely neglected since the decline of the Puritan regime in the late 1600s. Although England once again observed Christmas with the ascent of Charles II in 1660, it was with much less fervor than in times past, the Puritan influence having stamped out Christmas observances altogether during their era.

Living in England for some years since 1815 and fearing that England's rich holiday traditions were in jeopardy of falling into oblivion, Irving created a series of nostalgic tales that served to remind the British of their Yuletide heritage. His *Sketch Book* won wide acclaim on both sides of the Atlantic, and the Christmas stories especially moved British author Charles Dickens to express like sentiments by letter in 1841. Influenced by Irving, Dickens greatly contributed to the resurrection of his country's centuries-old holiday customs through his own Christmas stories, most notably in *A Christmas Carol*.

The following paragraphs briefly summarize Irving's five Christmas sketches:

Christmas. In this sketch, which is more of an essay than a tale, Irving recalls the specifics of the bygone Christmas era and yearns to return to those days. At that time, friends and families, in addition to observing the religious rites of Christmas, joined together in merry fellowship around blazing fires in evergreen-bedecked homes and halls with one purpose: to celebrate "peace on earth" with traditional carols, feasts, and games.

The Stage Coach. A stranger in England, Irving initially plans to spend Christmas at a Yorkshire inn, where he will be more likely to witness the surviving holiday customs, and whiles away a portion of Christmas Eve with a coach tour of the county. His excursion paints a scene of holiday bustle and happiness that has seized the countryside, including the butchers' and merchants' displays of trappings for the traditional feast, the much-anticipated deliveries of packages from the coachman, and the exuberance of schoolboys just released for their vacation. Arriving at the inn, he meets an old traveling companion, Frank Bracebridge, who persuades Irving to spend Christmas at his father's manor hall.

Christmas Eve. Well into the evening, the two friends arrive at Bracebridge Hall, where Squire Bracebridge is hosting a gala affair amid a large company of family and relatives. The squire is a strict proponent of the old customs, and his holiday agenda consists of music and dancing; caroling; and games such as "Hoodman Blind," "Shoe the Wild Mare," "Hot Cockles," "Steal the White Loaf," "Bob Apple," and "Snap Dragon." The Yule log, Christmas candles, mistletoe, mince pie, spiced beverages, and romance add much flavor to the festivities. The younger set particularly enjoy the wit and mischief of the elderly bachelor Simon Bracebridge, and Robert Herrick's (1591–1674) poems are the favored texts for songs of the evening. As Irving retires, a band of Waits (carolers of the time) serenade the Hall outdoors.

Christmas Day. Christmas commences with early morning religious services, first in the chapel at Bracebridge Hall, then in the village church. There, the parson, also clinging to the past, exhorts all to make merry at this time and supports this seemingly novel opinion with innumerable quotes from ancient church authorities. Following a brief historical account of the Puritan banishment of Christmas, restored with Charles II, the squire, keeping ancient custom, throws open the Hall to the poor and peasantry, who partake of beef, bread, and ale, the products of the squire's Christmas charity, as the rustics make merry among the gentry.

The Christmas Dinner. In this most popular of Irving's Christmas sketches, Squire Bracebridge's family and guests assemble at the table to participate in a series of ancient customs, which include the ceremony of the boar's

Washington Irving (1783–1859), American author of The Sketch Book *and the satirical* History of New York, *two works that especially influenced the British and American Christmas. Portrait by M.B. Brady, New York, 1861. Courtesy Library of Congress.*

head, brought in on a silver platter to the tune of "The Boar's Head Carol" (a ceremony annually observed at Queen's College, Oxford, since the Middle Ages); a pheasant pie decorated with peacock feathers (patterned after the peacock pie served at court during the Middle Ages, in which the peacock's head protruded from one end, the tail feathers from the other); and drinking from the wassail bowl. Afterwards, the children play at games such as Blind Man's Buff, the parson spins tales of superstitions and ghost stories, and the children round out the day by performing a Christmas masque or mummery for their elders.

In neither this nor any of the previous four sketches is special mention made of Father Christmas's visit to children or the giving of gifts; instead, the bestowing of charity and the pure happiness of being together with family and other loved ones is considered the essence of Christmas.

Since 1927, the Ahwahnee Hotel in Yosemite National Park in the United States has hosted an annual, modern-day Bracebridge Dinner in December, patterned after that in this latter sketch. The program includes a seven-course dinner, which may include dishes like Parma ham torta with fig and melon crisp, black pepper bread sticks, sweet potato puree garnished with cranberry oil, wassail, and plum pudding; period decorations and sets; Old English carols and Renaissance rituals; and over 100 costumed players who create the roles of the squire and his family, servants, wandering minstrels, the Lord of Misrule, and other characters.

Washington Irving's contributions to the concepts of Santa Claus are discussed under the entry **Saint Nicholas.**

See also **A Christmas Carol; Waits; Wassail; Yule.**

Israel
See **Middle East**

It Came upon the Midnight Clear

(Song). America's first prominent carol, the lyrics of which were written in 1849 by the Rev. Edmund Hamilton Sears (1810–1876), pastor of First Church Unitarian in rural Wayland, Massachusetts, from 1848 to 1865. His poem of five verses was first published in Boston in the *Christian Register* on December 29, 1849. The editor for Boston's *Monthly Religious Magazine* (1859–1871), Sears was a strong opponent of slavery.

The principal musical setting is that by Richard Storrs Willis (1819–1900), who studied music in Germany with Felix Mendelssohn and later became a music critic for the *New York Tribune.* In 1850, Willis published his *Church Chorals and Choir Studies,* of which "Organ Study No. 23" was adapted as the setting for "It Came upon the Midnight Clear" in the United States. It is not precisely certain who made the adaptation; Willis has been credited as well as a Uzziah Christopher Burnap. It is known that by 1860, Willis also adapted the same tune as one setting for the carol "While Shepherds Watched Their Flocks by Night," and it has sometimes been matched with a lesser-known carol by Sears, "Calm on the Listening Ear of Night" (1834).

The Rev. Edmund Hamilton Sears (1810–1876), American Unitarian minister who wrote the lyrics to "It Came upon the Midnight Clear," America's first prominent carol. Courtesy Andover-Harvard Theological Library of Harvard Divinity School, Harvard University, Cambridge, Massachusetts.

"Midnight Clear" reached Great Britain in 1870, when the Sears-Willis version was published in London in Edward Bickerseth's *Hymnal Companion to the Book of Common Prayer.* The setting most commonly applied in Great Britain, however, is an English traditional melody adapted by Arthur Sullivan, which was first published in *Church Hymns with Tunes* (London, 1874), edited by Sullivan.

Ironically, although the religiously conservative Sears frequently wrote about his belief in the divinity of Christ (as opposed to more liberal Unitarians), the lyrics to "Midnight Clear" do not once mention Jesus Christ, Savior, or Christ Child. With indirect references to the Nativity, the lyrics primarily provide a commentary on the angelic host, who arrived at the traditional midnight hour with their "glorious song of old," which would bring "peace on earth, goodwill to men." Two thousand years of wrongs and wars have resulted because mankind failed to heed the angels' message, so imply the lyrics, yet their song brings hope of a future, golden age of world-wide peace.

See also **While Shepherds Watched Their Flocks.**

It Came upon the Midnight Clear

(Television movie, 1984). Retired from the Manhattan police force and now living in California, Mike Halligan (Mickey Rooney) promises to take his grandson, Robbie Westin (Scott Grimes), who has never seen snow, to New York City to experience a truly white Christmas. But before the trip comes to pass, Mike suffers a fatal heart attack. In heaven, he strikes a deal with the archangel (George Gaynes), who allows him to return to Earth as an angel for one week to fulfill his promise. In so doing, Mike brings the spirit of Christmas to the Big Apple.

In 1986, the picture was nominated for a Young Artist Award for Exceptional Performance by a Young Actor in a Television Special (Grimes).

Written by Frank Cardea and George Schenk. Produced by George Schenk. Directed by Peter H. Hunt. An HGV Production with Columbia Pictures Television. Available on VHS. 97 min.

It Happened One Christmas
See **It's a Wonderful Life**

It Nearly Wasn't Christmas

(1989). Made-for-television fantasy/drama.

Disheartened over the rank commercialism surrounding Christmas, Santa (Charles Durning) decides to cancel Christmas, until he receives a letter from little Jennifer Baxter (Risa Schiffman). A business opportunity in Los Angeles has kept her musician-father Jeff (Wayne Osmond) away from her and her mother Laura (Annette Marin) for nearly a year, and now Jennifer only wants her family to be together again for Christmas. Therefore, Santa sets out on a quest, not only to grant Jennifer's wish, but to determine once and for all if people still believe in him and are basically good at heart.

Set on luring her mother to Los Angeles, Jennifer covertly boards a bus in Chicago and joins a portly passenger, whom she quickly deduces to be none other than Santa himself in street dress. Thus the two begin a series of cross-country adventures, which include Santa's brief arrest as the unwitting accomplice of Napoleon (Ted Lange), a black con artist, and a stint in a hot-air balloon, which crashes in a rural town out West. There, Jennifer and Santa enjoy the hospitality of Clyde Jessup (J. Omar Hansen), a poor farmer in need of $5,000 by Christmas Eve to pay his mortgage. Santa easily solves this problem by winning the town's annual sleigh race and its $5,000 prize. Following a train excursion, the two pilgrims next reform Mr. Woodford (Marvin Payne), a workaholic executive, who would have forced his employees to work on Christmas or be fired, then they travel by company jet to Los Angeles, courtesy of Woodford.

All the while, Laura has pursued Santa and her daughter to Los Angeles, together with Napoleon, whom she bailed from jail, and the whole troupe finally discovers Jeff employed as a pianist at a shopping mall. Hardly the record mogul he had billed himself to be, Jeff had delayed joining his family until he could secure a more impressive position. Santa still remains skeptical over mankind's basic goodness, however, until he suffers a near-fatal injury while preventing Napoleon from escaping with illicit raffle funds. His only hope for survival lies in people's faith and belief in him, which Jennifer successfully accomplishes through a passionate plea, and Christmas is saved.

Song "It Nearly Wasn't Christmas" sung by Wayne Osmond. Story by Stanley Isaacs, Golda David, and Alan Jay Glueckman. Teleplay by Golda David and Alan Jay Glueckman. Produced by Mark Burdge and Jon Ackelson. Directed by Burt Brinckerhoff. Ventura Entertainment Group, Ltd., in association with LBS Communications. Video N/A. 100 min.

Italy

This nation has officially celebrated Christmas since the middle of the fourth century, when the Church in Rome selected December 25 as the date to celebrate the birth of Christ. Since the first century A.D., Roman legions had embraced the cult of the Persian sun god Mithra and had observed his birthday on December 25 with ceremonies titled *Natalis Solis Invicti* ("Birth of the Unconquered Sun"). The Church, seeking an alternative to this and other pagan practices held in mid- to late December (Saturnalia and the January Calends), replaced December 25 with celebrations honoring the birth of Christ. From the example of the Roman Catholic Church, much of the world now celebrates Christmas on this date.

Commencing four weeks before Christmas, the Advent season includes festivals on December 6 that commemorate the death of St. Nicholas, the fourth century archbishop of Asia Minor. Men dressed as the saint deliver gifts to children, and processions and parades abound, especially in cities along the coast of the Adriatic Sea. According to legend, mariners enshrined the remains of St. Nicholas in the city of Bari in the eleventh century (*see* **St. Nicholas's Day**). The **Feast of the Immaculate Conception** (discussed as a separate entry) is observed on December 8. St. Lucia, a young girl martyred in Sicily for her Christian faith in the fourth century, is honored on December 13. Riding a donkey, a woman attired in a blue cloak portrays the saint in processions. On the night before, Sicilian children place their shoes outside their doors in expectation of gifts from St. Lucia. The period of nine consecutive days before Christmas Eve constitutes a Novena, during which time worshippers attend a series of Masses that climax with the Midnight Mass on Christmas Eve. The season terminates on Epiphany, January 6; in the Roman Catholic Church, the Christmas season ends with the Feast of the Baptism of the Lord, observed on the first Sunday after Epiphany.

Early in December, virtually every city sponsors a Christmas market, wherein may be found all manner of foods, decorations, sweets, gifts, toys, and other paraphernalia pertinent to the season. Around mid-December, the *zampognari*, rustic shepherds from the mountains arrive in Rome and other villages, as they have for centuries, to play their bagpipes at churches, markets, and before shrines of the Virgin. Legend states that their droning music eased the Virgin Mary's travail of labor. To honor Joseph the carpenter as well, they customarily serenade carpenters' shops. Less often than in the past, the *zampognari* present their repertoire from door to door, as would carolers, and receive rewards of food or cash.

The *presepio* ("manger") or Nativity scene ranks as the most popular of Christmas symbols. St. Francis of Assisi is credited with having created not only the first Nativity scene, but also the first "live" Nativity scene in 1223 in a cave near Greccio, Italy. Desiring to make the Nativity story of the Bible more meaningful to his parishioners (most people of the time could not understand the Latin of the Church liturgy and relied upon the priests to interpret the Scriptures for them), St. Francis had live people portray Mary, Joseph, the shepherds, angels, and Wise Men, along with a traditional ox and ass. After saying the Mass, St. Francis placed a wax figure of Baby Jesus in the manger. Over the centuries, artisans produced likenesses of these characters, and today *presepi* appear in a large variety of sizes, from miniatures with a few figures to those occupying several rooms. Residing in places of honor in homes, churches, and other public places, *presepi* often depict elaborate Italian landscapes rather than those of Bethlehem, and include such items as trees, waterfalls, rivers, mountains, mills, and characters from all walks of Italian life. By custom, the Christ Child figure is placed in the manger only on Christmas Eve, and the figures of the Wise Men are advanced a few paces each day until their "arrival" on Epiphany.

Historic *presepi* may be found throughout the country. One of the oldest resides in the Church of Santa Maria Maggiore in Rome and dates to the end of the thirteenth century. A *presepio* constructed by Charles IV, king of the Two Sicilies (ruled 1754–59), boasts 1,200 carved pieces and resides in the Royal Palace of Caserta, and Rome's Basilica of Saints Cosmos and Damian houses a gigantic, 200-year-old Neapolitan *presepio* that measures 45 x 21 x 27 feet. Living *presepi* remain popular and may attain elaborate proportions, such as that of Rivisondoli, held in its mountain setting on Epiphany Eve with a cast of some 600 characters.

During World War II, American soldiers in Italy popularized Santa Claus and Christmas trees, the latter especially in the North;

Christmas trees still rank second to *presepi* in the southern regions. An alternative decoration and vestige of the Yule log is the *ceppo* ("log"), a pyramid-shaped wooden or cardboard structure with several shelves on which can be placed gifts, ornaments, and a *presepio*.

Vestiges of the "Boy-Bishop," a custom that honored St. Nicholas during the Middle Ages, lie in traditions surrounding the *Santo Bambino* ("Holy Child"), a jewel-studded Nativity figure of the Christ Child in Rome's Church of Santa Maria Ara Coeli. After the figure is placed in the manger on Christmas Eve, children stand before it and deliver sermons or some other form of holiday address. The figure is believed to possess healing powers.

On Christmas Eve, a number of cities across Italy hold fire festivals, deriving from ancient, pagan winter solstice celebrations based on the belief that large bonfires dispelled evil spirits and assisted the return of the sun. One noted celebration is that of Agnone, termed the "Nocturnal Procession of the 'Ndòcciata" (torches). Bearing large, burning torches or torch fans of fir and broomwood up to 12 feet long, men congregate outside the city and march to the town square, where the procession terminates in a gigantic "Bonfire of the Brotherhood," which symbolizes the burning of negative influences over the past year. Other examples of torchlight festivals include the "Lighting of the Log," the traditional lighting of the Christmas log in Calatabiano; "Tree's Burning," a traditional burning of evergreen branches in Camporgiano; "The Shepherdess' Torchlight Procession," featuring folk songs derived from shepherds' lore in Canneto Sull'Oglio; and "Nocturnal Torchlight Parade," a fire procession through the streets of Castelletto D'Orba that terminates at the square with a feast of roasted chestnuts and mulled wine. Formerly, such torchlight processions were associated with fertility rites and courtship. Each man would fashion his most elaborate torch and would stand beneath the window of his intended mate. If the woman opened her window, it signified that she accepted him; if not, the torch was extinguished.

At sundown in Rome on Christmas Eve, cannonfire from the Castle of St. Angelo announces the arrival of Christmas. Whereas the season generally is spent among friends and relatives, Christmas Eve and Christmas Day are reserved for the immediate family. Catholics observe a strict 24-hour fast that terminates with the Christmas Eve dinner, a meatless affair extending for several hours before Midnight Mass. Typical cuisine includes *capitone* (eel), *calamari* (squid), *vongoli* (clams), *baccalà* (codfish), picked or fried vegetables, beans, salads, breads, pasta, various sweets including *pizzele* (lacy cookies), *caffé espresso*, wines, and champagne. In Rome, the Pope celebrates Midnight Mass at 11 P. M., and this Mass is televised worldwide from St. Peter's Basilica (for other papal observances, *see* **The Vatican**).

On Christmas Day, children customarily write letters to their parents requesting forgiveness for having committed any misdeeds during the year with promises to improve, and they hide these letters under the parents' plates or somewhere else on the dinner table. The menu for Christmas Day features meat, such as turkey or ham, *tortellini* (meat pasta), lentils with sausage (for prosperity), and *panettone* (glazed yeast cake with currants and candied fruit). Many other desserts contain nuts and honey, which stems from ancient superstitions regarding the former's role in fertility and the latter's magical properties. Visitations resume on St. Stephen's Day (December 26).

While Epiphany is the principal gift-giving day, children commonly receive gifts at Christmas as well from the so-called "Urn of Fate." Here, wrapped boxes containing either gifts or nothing at all are placed in an urn, and family members take turns drawing out the boxes to see what surprises "fate" has in store for them.

Noise, clamor, and parties fill New Year's Eve. People may throw objects from windows or fire guns, activities that stem from ancient beliefs that loud noises dispelled evil spirits lurking in the winter darkness. Some still believe that whatever happens at this time determines the fate of the year, and girls may observe quaint rituals to determine whether they will marry soon. In one of these, a girl tosses her shoe overhead toward the door. If the toe points to the door, she will wed, but not if it points away. The first person one meets on New Year's Day is predictive: a strong man, a healthy year; a priest, a funeral; a woman, bad luck.

Children traditionally receive gifts on Epiphany from *La Befana* (or simply *Befana*, derived from *Epiphania*, Epiphany), a mythical witch whose legend otherwise is virtually identical with Russia's *Baboushka* (*see* **Russia**). According to the legend, an old woman was sweeping her house when the three Magi passed by en route to Bethlehem. When they invited her to accompany them, she refused, claiming that her housework precluded a long journey. Later, she repented and, after collecting a few toys for the Christ Child, set out to overtake the Magi. Because she found neither them nor the Christ Child, she returns annually via her broomstick and descends into chimneys on Epiphany Eve to examine each sleeping child, hoping to find Jesus. She then fills the stockings or pockets of deserving youngsters with gifts. For the naughty, she leaves a piece of coal. Children write letters to her, describing what gifts they desire, and they hang effigies of the witch as decorations. In some regions, *Babbo Natale* ("Father Christmas," Santa Claus), has replaced *Befana*.

It is believed that *Befana* derives from a winter goddess and fertility figure of Germanic-speaking tribes who protected the home, hearth, motherhood, children, and fields. Dispensing rewards and punishments to deserving adults and children at the winter solstice, this goddess was variously known as Berchta, Bertha, Hertha, Holda, Holde, Holle, and Perchta. In the Christian age, she appeared during the 12 days of Christmas, especially on Epiphany or Twelfth Night, considered to be magical times by the superstitious. How *Befana* became a witch is open to speculation. Germanic folklore depicts Berchta as an old, disheveled woman; and the name of Holde, and perhaps others, became synonymous with witchcraft upon the advent of Christianity. Thus, *Befana* is also known as *La Strega* ("witch") and *La Vecchia* ("old woman").

"Merry Christmas" in Italy is *Buon Natale*.

See also **Advent; Boy-Bishop; Christmas Day; Epiphany; Nativity Scene; Yule.**

It's a Very Merry Muppet Christmas Movie

(2002). Made-for-television comedy and parody of the motion picture *It's a Wonderful Life.*

Holding a mortgage on the Muppets' theater, Rachel Bitterman (Joan Cusack), the villainous CEO of Bitterman Building and Development, schemes to foreclose on the theater and build a trendy nightclub in its place. At first she requires payment in full by midnight on Christmas Eve, but when the Muppets would successfully raise the cash through their Christmas concert, she changes the deadline to 6:00 P. M., because only she, not the Muppets, possesses a copy of the contract. The situation seems hopeless, until Heaven intervenes by sending Daniel (David Arquette), a well-meaning but misfit angel, to their aid. With Whoopi Goldberg as Daniel's "Boss."

In 2003, the show received an Emmy nomination for Outstanding Music and Lyrics (for the song "Everyone Matters," composed by Desmond Child and Davitt Sigerson).

Principal voices: Steve Whitmire, Dave Goelz, Bill Barretta, Eric Jacobson, Robert Smigel, Mel Brooks, Brian Henson, Jerry Nelson, and Kevin Clash. Written by Tom Martin and Jim Lewis. Produced by Martin G. Baker and Warren Carr. Directed by Kirk R. Thatcher. Jim Henson Productions. DVD: MGM Studios. 100 min.

See also **It's a Wonderful Life; A Muppet Family Christmas.**

It's a Wonderful Life

(1946). Highly popular motion picture drama based on "The Greatest Gift," a short story by New York writer Philip Van Doren Stern. Unsuccessful at selling his story to a magazine, Van Doren Stern ordered 200 copies printed at his own expense and sent them out to his friends as 24-page Christmas "cards." His Hollywood agent was one of those recipients and pitched the story to various movie studios. At actor Cary Grant's suggestion, it initially became the property of RKO Radio Pictures, but when this company failed to produce a workable script, RKO sold the story for $10,000 to a new studio, Liberty Pictures, formed in 1945 by director Frank Capra, also known for directing *Mr. Smith Goes to Washington* and *Meet John Doe*. From "The Greatest Gift" evolved *It's a Wonderful Life*, Liberty's first motion picture and the favorite film of Frank Capra, who watched it every Christmas Eve thereafter.

• THE SHORT STORY. George Pratt, a small-town bank clerk who has grown weary of his dead-end job and a life seemingly without meaning, wishes that he had never been born. As he contemplates suicide on Christmas Eve, he encounters an angel posing as a brush salesman, who grants his wish. Seeing the tragedies in the world that would have come to pass had he not been present to prevent them, George realizes that his life has truly been a blessing to all around him, and that people really need him. He renounces his wish, life resumes as before, and George has learned that the greatest gift to humanity is always one's self.

• THE MOTION PICTURE. The film adaptation changes the principal character to George Bailey (Jimmy Stewart), a man filled with creative ideas and a thirst for adventure that is never fulfilled. Stewart was Capra's sole choice for George from the beginning. When Stewart, having recently completed his military service, did not feel prepared to make pictures so soon after World War II, actor Lionel Barrymore convinced him to take the role.

As the film opens, it's Christmas Eve in the little town of Bedford Falls, New York, where numerous prayers rise from house to house on behalf of George, who is in trouble. Heaven decides to investigate George further by sending to earth the former clockmaker Clarence Oddbody (Henry Travers), a simple-witted angel possessing childlike faith and in need of earning his wings (presently Clarence's standing is AS2, "angel second class"). Before sending him, Heaven briefs Clarence on George's life of unwitting self-denial and goodwill as the picture turns to an earlier point in time.

As a boy, George saves his younger brother Harry from drowning and prevents the druggist Mr. Gower (H.B. Warner) from unwittingly filling a prescription with poison. When his father dies, George, instead of going to college, assumes control of the Bailey Building and Loan Company, which otherwise would have

fallen into the hands of the unscrupulous banker, Henry Potter (Lionel Barrymore), and provides for Harry's (Todd Karns) college education. After George's wedding to childhood friend Mary Hatch (Donna Reed), a run on the bank threatens to close the Building and Loan, which George saves with $2,000 of his own cash that was intended for the honeymoon. Ordinary people like cabbie Ernie Bishop (Frank Faylen) receive loans through the Building and Loan to build homes, which Potter's bank would have never financed, and George spares pocket cash for financially strapped "fast girl" Violet Bick (Gloria Grahame) to begin a new life out of town.

This brings the story line back to the Christmas Eve that began the film. On that day, George's Uncle Billy (Thomas Mitchell) misplaces $8,000 that belongs to the Building and Loan. Suddenly facing Potter's charges of embezzlement and misappropriation of funds, George transforms from a gregarious family man into a hunted animal. Returning home, he suddenly despises his surroundings, including the old house that he, Mary, and their four children occupy, a house that now seems to be falling apart with George's life. He argues severely with Mary, upbraids daughter Janie (Carol Coombs) for practicing "Hark! The Herald Angels Sing" interminably on the piano, and delivers telephone insults to the school teacher of little daughter Zuzu (Karolyn Grimes). An altercation with the teacher's husband at Martini's bar leaves George with a bleeding lip, and after running his car into a tree, George is about to jump into an icy river when Clarence dives in, forcing George to save him instead.

Bewailing his life, George wishes that he had never been born, whereupon Clarence grants the wish and allows George to see what Bedford Falls would have been like had he never entered the picture. Several signs herald the transformation: the Christmas Eve snowfall suddenly ceases; George's deaf ear (present since childhood) and bleeding lip are healed; and Zuzu's wilted flower petals, which George had placed in his pocket moments earlier, have vanished, as has his demolished car. As George walks through what should be Bedford Falls, he finds that it has become "Pottersville," corrupted with saloons and burlesque halls. He learns that Uncle Billy lost his business and suffered insanity. Gower served a prison term for poisoning a child and became a drunken bum. "Bailey Park," a neighborhood of homes financed by the Building and Loan, is a cemetery; in that cemetery is the grave of George's younger brother Harry, who drowned. And because Harry did not live to adulthood, he did not perform his act of heroism during the war that saved the lives of many men; instead, all these men are also dead. George's mother (Beulah Bondi), now cynical and heartless, runs a second-rate boarding house, and Violet is arrested for prostitution. George's home is an abandoned building, and Mary wastes away as an old-maid librarian. A dime-a-dance dive has replaced the Building and Loan; Nick the bartender (Sheldon Leonard), now cold and callous, has replaced the jovial Mr. Martini (Bill Edmunds) as proprietor of the Italian restaurant and bar; and Ernie, his wife and child having deserted him, now lives in a shack in "Potter's Field."

Facing such ghastly alternatives, George repents of his wish and begs to return to his former life, at which the signs are reversed (the snow falls, his lip bleeds, and so on). Gladly willing to face prison as long as no one else suffers, he races through town screaming, "Merry Christmas!" and arrives home just as Mary returns from alerting the town about his predicament. It seems a miracle: Scores of citizens come forth with ready cash to pay the debt, many saying that they never would have had homes had it not been for George. In the collection basket, George notes a copy of Mark Twain's *The Adventures of Tom Sawyer*, which Clarence had carried around with him. Inside, an inscription reminds George that no man is a failure who has friends, and thanks him for the wings. At that moment, a little bell on the family's Christmas tree rings, at which Zuzu remarks that, according to her teacher, every time a bell rings, an angel gets his wings. Serviceman Harry, having won the Congressional Medal of Honor for saving a transport plane, arrives to toast his big brother as "the richest man in town," and the film concludes with everyone singing "Auld Lang Syne." Originally the closing song was to have been "Ode to Joy"

from Beethoven's ninth symphony, but "Auld Lang Syne" seemed more appropriate.

In 1947, this picture received five Academy Award nominations: Best Actor (Stewart), Best Director (Capra), Best Film Editing, Best Picture, and Best Sound Recording. It won a Golden Globe Award that year for Best Motion Picture Director; a Cinema Writers' Circle Award from Spain in 1949; an award from the National Film Preservation Board (USA) in 1990; and a Young Artist Award in 1994 — Former Child Star Lifetime Achievement Award (Jimmy Hawkins).

With Ward Bond, Samuel S. Hinds, Larry Simms, Harry Holman, and Jimmy Hawkins. Written by Frances Goodrich, Albert Hackett, Jo Swerling, and Frank Capra. Produced and directed by Frank Capra. Liberty Films. DVD: Republic Studios. B & W. 132 min.

Over the years, attention has focused on several incidental scenes that have especially contributed to the picture's lasting popularity. A high school graduation dance scene with the swimming pool beneath the floor took place on location at Beverly Hills High School, the gymnasium of which sported such a pool. At that time, such a device was considered a high-tech innovation. Mary's date in these scenes, Freddie, is played by Carl Switzer, better known as "Alfalfa" in *The Little Rascals* and *Our Gang* comedies. In another scene, George saves the Building and Loan patrons with his $2,000 by pleading that they withdraw only what is essential for the moment. When a young woman (Ellen Corby, who later portrayed Grandma Walton in the television series *The Waltons*) requests the odd and incredibly low sum of $17.50 (unscripted, Capra having secretly prompted Corby with the line), George leans over and gives Corby a big, unscripted kiss, which blends perfectly. A third popular scene has the inebriated Uncle Billy leaving Harry's wedding reception. When he steps off camera, a loud crash leaves the impression that Uncle Billy has fallen into some trash cans, and he calls out that he is not injured. Actually, a technician backstage had dropped some equipment at that moment, and Capra worked the "blooper" into the final print. Finally, during the scene in which a devastated George prays for deliverance in Martini's bar before meeting

Clarence, Stewart was so moved that he began weeping. Capra had originally filmed Stewart from a distance and wanted to get a closer retake. When Stewart could not reproduce the authentic emotion, Capra enlarged that segment frame by frame.

- ANOTHER VERSION. Frank Capra co-wrote a version for television with Lionel Chetwynd, titled *It Happened One Christmas* (1977). There, Marlo Thomas starred as the principal character, Mary Bailey Hatch, along with Richard Dysart, Christopher Guest, C. Thomas Howell, Cloris Leachman, Wayne Rogers, and Orson Welles. In 1978, the program received two Emmy nominations: Outstanding Supporting Actress (Leachman) and Outstanding Art Direction. Produced by Carole Hart and Marlo Thomas. Directed by Donald Wrye. Daisy Productions with Universal Television. Video N/A. 100 min.

It's Beginning to Look a Lot Like Christmas

Popular American song written in 1951 by Meredith Willson. With its descriptive theme of Christmas symbols (Christmas trees, candy canes, holly) appearing all over town as the season approaches, the song concludes with the philosophy that the best holiday music is the carol that is sung within your own heart.

The public became aware of this piece principally through two means. Perry Como with the Fontane Sisters first recorded it that same year on the RCA Victor label, hitting the pop charts at position 19. Then, Willson incorporated it as the theme song for his 1963 Broadway musical *Here's Love*, which was based on the 1947 motion picture *Miracle on 34th Street*.

Of the 25 most frequently performed Christmas songs of the twentieth century listed by the American Society of Composers, Authors and Publishers (ASCAP), "It's Beginning to Look a Lot Like Christmas" ranked number 16. By December 2004, it ranked number 20.

See also **ASCAP List of Christmas Songs.**

It's Christmastime Again, Charlie Brown

(1992). Made-for-television animated cartoon sequel to *A Charlie Brown Christmas,* based on characters from Charles M. Schulz's comic strip, *Peanuts.*

The gang returns in a loosely connected spoof about Christmas commercialism. Charlie Brown unsuccessfully attempts to sell Christmas wreaths before Thanksgiving; Linus waxes philosophic over the Nativity story as Sally complains about the cost of giving gifts; and Charlie Brown sells his entire comic book collection to buy his girlfriend a pair of expensive gloves, only to find that her mother has already bought them for her. Peppermint Patty must play a sheep in the school Christmas pageant and is appalled that Marcie, who wears *glasses,* is selected to play Mary. And Sally, after having interminably rehearsed her single-word line of "Hark!" as the angel, breaks up the pageant with "Hockey sticks!" instead.

In 1993, this picture was nominated for a Young Artist Award for Outstanding Young Voice-Over in an Animated Special (John Christian Graas).

Voices: Mindy Ann Martin, John Christian Graas, Phillip Lucier, Lindsay Benmisk, Brittany M. Thornton, Jamie E. Smith, Marne Patterson, Matthew Slowik, Dianna Tello, Sean Mendelson, Jodie Sweetin, and Bill Melendez. Written by Charles M. Schulz. Produced and directed by Bill Melendez. A Lee Mendelson–Bill Melendez Production in association with Charles M. Schulz Creative Associates and United Media Productions. VHS: Paramount Studios. 22 min.

See also **A Charlie Brown Christmas; Charlie Brown's Christmas Tales; Happy New Year, Charlie Brown; I Want a Dog for Christmas, Charlie Brown.**

It's the Most Wonderful Time of the Year

Popular American song written by Eddie Pola and George Wyle explicitly for pop singer Andy Williams, who first introduced it in 1962 on his NBC television special, *The Andy Williams Christmas Show.* Williams featured it on each of his subsequent television Christmas specials such that it has now become his holiday signature song and a Christmas standard.

Williams first included "It's the Most Wonderful Time of the Year" in his 1963 Columbia release, *The Andy Williams Christ-*

mas Album, which was ranked as the number-one pop album on the *Billboard* charts that year. At the close of the twentieth century, although the song was not among the 25 most frequently performed Christmas songs of that century as listed by the American Society of Composers, Authors and Publishers (ASCAP), that organization had ranked the song as number 14 by December 2004.

The ebullient lyrics, set to a lilting waltz tempo, laud the secular pleasures of the season with such catchy phrases as "kids jingle-belling" and "hap-happiest season of all." A reference to "scary ghost stories" recalls the British custom of telling ghost stories at this time, which further derives from the ancient belief that at the winter solstice, spirits roamed the earth. (*See* **Great Britain; Winter Solstice**).

Another holiday song that may be confused with "It's the Most Wonderful Time of the Year" is "The Most Wonderful Day of the Year." This latter title applies to separate lyrics written by Johnny Marks that were featured in the 1964 television animated special *Rudolph, the Red-Nosed Reindeer*. Like "Wonderful Time," "Wonderful Day" is set to the same Pola/Wyle tune.

Eddie Pola (1907–1995) divided his time between Great Britain and the United States as a writer, producer, composer, close harmony vocalist, pianist, dancer, and actor. George Wyle (1916–2003) served as music director for many television variety shows, including those by Dinah Shore and Andy Williams. He collaborated chiefly with Eddie Pola from 1948. Together, their works included, among others, "I Said My Pajamas and Put on My Pray'rs" (1950) and "I Love the Way You Say Goodnight" (from *Lullaby of Broadway*, 1951).

See also **The Andy Williams Christmas Show; ASCAP List of Christmas Songs.**

Ivy

See **The Holly and the Ivy**

J

Jack Frost

(1979). Made-for-television animated story using stop-motion puppets (Animagic).

Pardon-Me-Pete the groundhog narrates this tale about Jack Frost, an invisible entity who lives in Father Winter's Kingdom of the Winter Clouds. Because Jack is in love with Elisa, a lovely peasant girl living in January Junction, Father Winter grants his request to become human until spring. Posing as the tailor Jack Snip, Jack discovers that Kubla Kraus the Cossack has taxed January Junction so heavily that Christmas gifts can only be imaginary "dream" presents. Attempting to rescue Elisa from Kraus's clutches, Jack assumes his icy form and blows a blizzard that buries Kraus. But it is Elisa's other suitor, Sir Ravinoe Rightflow the knight, who saves her and marries her. According to the bargain that he had made with Father Winter, Jack would achieve permanent human status if, in addition to win-ning Kraus's castle, his horse, and his gold, Jack took a wife by spring. Although Jack meets the first three conditions, his failure to wed transforms him back to his original, icy self.

Narrated and sung by Buddy Hackett. Principal voices: Robert Morse, Debra Clinger, Larry Storch, Dee Stratton, Paul Frees, Don Messick, Dina Lynn, Dave Garroway, and Sonny Melendez. Written by Romeo Muller. Produced and directed by Arthur Rankin, Jr., and Jules Bass. A Rankin/Bass Production. DVD: Delta Music Video. 48 min.

This television special is further detailed in Rick Goldschmidt's book, *The Enchanted World of Rankin/Bass.*

See also **Rankin/Bass Christmas Cartoons.**

Jacob's Gift

Inspirational children's picture book written by American author Max Lucado, published in 1998.

In Rabbi Simeon's shop for apprenticed carpenters in Bethlehem, the boy that builds the best project will work with the rabbi on the new synagogue. With diligence, young Jacob sets forth to build a manger with a new innovation — wheels. But he must divide his time between the shop and helping his father, who is an innkeeper, for the Roman census is bringing throngs of people to town. On the night before the projects are due, an exhausted Jacob returns to the shop to continue working but soon falls asleep. During the night, he is awakened by the brilliance of a star overhead, shining on the stable behind his father's inn. Within the stable is a young baby lying on the ground and a man and woman in attendance. Now Jacob faces a dilemma: Should he provide the child with the comfort of his unfinished manger, or should he return to the shop, add the wheels, and submit his project for the competition? In the morning, Rabbi Simeon arrives to judge the competition with his carpenter-nephew Joseph, who has recently come from Nazareth. Joseph and Jacob need no introduction, for they had met the night before, when Jacob had given the child Jesus His first gift. When asked what motivated him, Jacob quotes the wisdom of his rabbi: "When you give a gift to one of God's children, you give a gift to God."

In 1999, the book was adapted for live-action video under the same title, starring Ben Israeli as Jacob, Barry Cutler as Rabbi Simeon, Marc Alexander Stern as Joseph, and Rena Strober as Mary. Screenplay by Steve Gottry. Produced and directed by John Schmidt. A John Schmidt Production in association with Tommy Nelson Publishers. DVD: Tommy Nelson Publishers. 25 min. This DVD also includes an animated cartoon adaptation of Lucado's Christmas book *Alabaster's Song* as a bonus disc.

Max Lucado is a minister and the daily speaker for the radio program *UpWords*. His other Christmas books include *Alabaster's Song* (1996), *The Christmas Cross* (1998), *The Crippled Lamb* (1994), and *Cosmic Christmas* (1997), all of which are discussed as separate entries.

Japan
See **Asia and the South Pacific**

Jesse Tree

Through medieval art, a Jesse tree originally depicted Christ's progenitors as the branches of a tree rooted from Jesse, King David' father, the topmost branches of which were crowned with Christ. This concept derived from the Messianic prophecy in Isaiah 11:1, which stated that a Branch (Christ) would spring from the roots of Jesse. Today, the Jesse tree offers a way of converting a Christmas tree into a more religious symbol. A contemporary Jesse tree utilizes ornaments that not only symbolize Christ's ancestors (such as Abraham, Isaac, Jacob, David), but also Messianic prophecies or other noted biblical characters. For instance, a Star of David would symbolize King David; stone tablets, Moses; a whale figure, Jonah.

See also **Chrismons Tree; Christmas Tree.**

Jest 'Fore Christmas

("Just Before Christmas"). Humorous poem written by the American poet and journalist Eugene Field (1850–1895). With words spelled so as to convey a rural dialect, the poem's five verses feature "Bill," a mischievous little boy, who in the first four verses details his typical variety of pranks and antics committed throughout the year. But knowing that Santa would disapprove of anyone getting a ride by hitching a sled to a horse-drawn grocery cart, for example, Bill suddenly curbs his foolishness "jest 'fore Christmas," when he's as good as he can be. In the fifth verse, Bill's sage advice improves any wayward child's chances of having a happy Christmas: wash your face, brush your hair, keep your shoes in good condition, say "Yessum" and "Yessur," and never ask for a second serving of dessert.

Missouri native Eugene Field is best known for his children's poems, such as "Little Boy Blue," "Wynken, Blynken, and Nod," and "The Gingham Dog and the Calico Cat."

Jesu, Jesu, Baby Dear
See **Rocking**

Jesu Parvule
See **Alfred Burt Carols**

Jesus (motion picture)

See **Nativity** (Film and Television Depictions)

Jesus Christ

See **Nativity**

Jesus Holy, Born So Lowly

See **Infant Holy, Infant Lowly**

Jesus of Nazareth (motion picture)

See **Nativity** (Film and Television Depictions)

A Jetsons Christmas Carol

See **A Christmas Carol** (Film and Television Versions)

Jiminy Cricket's Christmas

(1986). Jiminy Cricket (voice of Hal Smith for opening sequence, Cliff Edwards for archival footage) hosts this video collection of excerpts from classic Disney theatrical, animated cartoons. Included are scenes from four feature films, which Jiminy introduces as Christmas "cards": *Snow White and the Seven Dwarfs* (1937); *Pinocchio* (1940); *Cinderella* (1950), and *Peter Pan* (1953). Also included are three holiday "shorts":

Mickey's Good Deed (1932, B & W). In this rarely seen short, street musician Mickey temporarily sells his dog Pluto to a spoiled rich child in order to obtain presents for, and play Santa to, a group of poor, fatherless children who otherwise would have no Christmas. Playing most roughly with Pluto, the rich child turns his house into a shambles to the point that his father casts Pluto out, gives his youngster a well-deserved spanking, and Pluto is reunited with Mickey for Christmas. Voiced by Walt Disney. Produced by Walt Disney and John Sutherland. Directed by Burt Gillett.

The Art of Skiing (1941). Goofy attempts to demonstrate the basics of downhill skiing in typical madcap, slapstick fashion. Narrated by John McLeish. Voiced by George Johnson. Produced by Walt Disney. Directed by Jack Kinney.

Toy Tinkers (1949). Donald Duck battles chipmunks Chip and Dale, who desire the nuts under Donald's Christmas tree. They wage war with antique toys, and after a booby-trapped toy telephone explodes in Donald's face, he sur-renders, and the chipmunks gain a booty of nuts. Nominated in 1950 for an Academy Award for Best Short Subject Cartoon. Voiced by Clarence Nash. Written by Milt Banta and Harry Reeves. Produced by Walt Disney. Directed by Jack Hannah.

An interlude features "Waltz of the Flowers" from Tchaikovsky's *Nutcracker Suite*, during which the animation sequence depicts a gradual transformation of the seasons from falling leaves to shimmering snowflakes. Jiminy Cricket closes with his signature song, "When You Wish upon a Star," as a host of Disney characters gather around in appreciation of the rendition. Walt Disney Productions. VHS: Walt Disney Home Video. 47 min.

See also: **A Disney Christmas Gift**; **A Walt Disney Christmas**.

Jingle All the Way

(1996). Motion picture adventure-comedy.

Neglecting his wife Liz (Rita Wilson) and young son Jamie (Jake Lloyd), workaholic Howard Langston (future governor of California Arnold Schwarzenegger) has also forgotten that Jamie wants a TurboMan action figure, the hottest-selling toy that Christmas. It's now Christmas Eve, and Howard vainly dashes through a myriad of toy stores and packed crowds, creating havoc while racing against Myron Larabee (Sinbad), a mail carrier who needs the same toy. Their numerous escapades include a fight for TurboMan lottery numbers in the mall; Howard's failed deal with a black-market Santa (James Belushi) and his escape from a police raid; their assault on a radio station that offers a TurboMan to the first caller who can name Santa's reindeer; Myron's attempt to stall police with two allegedly fake bomb threats, the second of which actually explodes after they both escape; and Howard's failed attempt to steal the TurboMan from his neighbor, Ted Maltin (Phil Hartman), whose angry pet reindeer prevents the robbery. Ted, divorced and nosy, in the meantime has taken every opportunity to flirt with and be "helpful" to gorgeous Liz while Howard has been away.

Totally disgraced, Howard can only watch as Liz, Jamie, and Ted leave together for the Christmas parade, which features TurboMan as the main attraction instead of Santa Claus.

Drafted at the last minute to replace the parade's TurboMan, Howard must select a child from the crowd to accompany him on the float and receive a coveted TurboMan toy. Howard, certain that this role will atone for his past neglect, summons Jamie, when suddenly a crazed Myron, dressed as TurboMan's arch enemy Dementor, arrives to resume the battle for the toy that Jamie now possesses, and ultimately Myron chases Jamie to a high pinnacle. Forced to use the jet pack and other weapons built into his costume, Howard rockets into the air and saves Jamie just as the boy tumbles from a building. With his boy safe, Howard reveals his identity to an ecstatic Jamie and Liz and vows to be a more attentive husband and father. Content to have his dad as the real TurboMan, Jamie unselfishly gives his action figure to Myron.

In 1997, this picture won a Blockbuster Entertainment Award for Favorite Supporting Actor (Sinbad). It received a Razzie Award nomination for Worst Director.

With Robert Conrad, Harvey Korman, and Martin Mull. Written by Randy Kornfield. Produced by Chris Columbus, Mark Radcliffe, and Michael Barnathan. Directed by Brian Levant. Twentieth Century Fox Film Corporation and 1492 Pictures. DVD: Twentieth Century Fox Video. 88 min.

Jingle Bell Rock

Popular American song, the only significant collaboration of Joseph Beal from Massachusetts and James Boothe from Texas, who otherwise were engaged in public relations and advertising, respectively. Written in 1957 on the centennial anniversary of the publication of the perennial favorite "Jingle Bells," "Jingle Bell Rock" was the first song of the rock-and-roll era to blend that musical style with Christmas. Despite the fact that the lyrics follow no particular train of thought, consisting merely of meaningless, rhyming phrases about such items as "Jingle Bell Square" and "jingle bell time," this song of easy rhythm became a real hit after rocker Bobby Helms recorded it that same year on the Decca label. The top Christmas song for 1957 (position six on the pop charts), it sold some ten million copies and continued to make the pop charts into the 1980s.

Of the 25 most frequently performed Christmas songs of the twentieth century listed by the American Society of Composers, Authors and Publishers (ASCAP), "Jingle Bell Rock" ranked number 11. By December 2004, it ranked number ten.

See also **ASCAP List of Christmas Songs; Jingle Bells; Rockin' around the Christmas Tree.**

Jingle Bells

Highly popular American song written by James Lord Pierpont (1822–1893), a composer, music teacher, the son of a Unitarian minister and abolitionist, uncle to financier John Pierpont Morgan, and native of Medford, Massachusetts. Arguably the most popular of all American secular Christmas songs, "Jingle Bells" was first published by Oliver Ditson and Company of Boston in 1857 under the title "One-Horse Open Sleigh" but was reissued as "Jingle Bells, or the One-Horse Open Sleigh" in 1859. The song is known today as simply "Jingle Bells."

It is widely accepted that Pierpont took inspiration for writing "Jingle Bells" from the sleigh races that were annually held in Medford, yet much uncertainty and debate still surround its origin. Exactly where and when Pierpont wrote "Jingle Bells" remain unknown. According to one popular account, Pierpont is said to have composed his lively winter piece for a 40-member choir of Sunday school children, who first performed it at his father's church in Boston in the early 1840s. The occasion was a Thanksgiving pageant, and the song was so well received, so goes the story, that the performance was repeated at Christmastime, after which the song became a holiday standard.

Another account holds that Pierpont composed "One-Horse Open Sleigh" around 1850 in Medford at a boarding house owned by Mrs. Mary Gleason Waterman, the only person in town at the time with a piano in her establishment. After hearing the tune, the story continues, Mrs. Waterman commented that it certainly was "a merry little jingle," which supposedly inspired Pierpont to include the words "Jingle Bells" in the title when the song was reissued in 1859.

In 1969, research conducted by Milton Rahn, a historian from Savannah, Georgia, discovered that Pierpont was living in Savannah in 1857 at the time that "Jingle Bells" was first published. According to Rahn's research, Pierpont's brother, the Rev. John Pierpont, Jr., became pastor of the Unitarian church in Savannah in 1853. After a short stint in the California gold fields, James left Massachusetts to join his brother as organist and music director for the Savannah church. At the outbreak of the Civil War, brother John returned to Boston, but James remained in Savannah, having married Eliza Jane Purse there in 1857 following the death of his first wife, Millicent Cowee, whom he had married in Massachusetts. Thus Savannah has claimed that Pierpont composed "Jingle Bells" while residing there as a nostalgic memorial to New England Christmases, a claim that has fueled an ongoing debate between Savannah and Medford.

Contrary to a multitude of Christmas song books, which list the composer of "Jingle Bells" as J. Pierpont or even James S. Pierpont, Rahn discovered that Pierpont's correct full name was James Lord Pierpont.

Regardless of its city of origin, "Jingle Bells" has become a Christmas classic through popular association, despite the fact that the lyrics mention absolutely nothing about Christmas as such. They simply reflect the joy of young men and women "dashing through the snow in a one-horse open sleigh" with implications of courtship and betting. From such implications, one argument poses that, because of the strict church etiquette of the 1800s, it is highly unlikely that "Jingle Bells" would have ever appeared on any church program.

Over the decades, the lyrics to "Jingle Bells" have acquired minor changes from the original. In verse one, "Through the fields we go" is now "O'er the fields we go," and "What joy it is to ride and sing" has become "What fun it is to ride and sing." In verse four, "Take the girls along" has evolved to "Take the girls tonight." The identity of "Miss Fanny Bright" in verse two, if she was indeed a real person, remains a mystery, although speculations would link her with the lady mentioned in another of Pierpont's songs, "Ring the Bell,

James Lord Pierpont (1822–1893), American composer of "Jingle Bells," arguably the most popular of all American secular Christmas carols. Photograph c. 1860. Courtesy the Georgia Historical Society, Savannah, Georgia.

Fanny" (1854). The melody to "Jingle Bells," particularly the chorus, has undergone more extensive changes, such that little resemblance remains between the original chorus and that sung today. A rendition of the original melody may be heard in *The Life and Music of James Lord Pierpont* (1994), a VHS video recording produced by the Georgia Historical Society.

Some people have difficulty with one phrase in the first verse: "Bells on bobtail ring." Although this obviously refers to the bells on the horse that pulls the sleigh, some have wondered if "Bobtail" is really the horse's name. An examination of the lyrics shows that "bobtail" is not capitalized; hence the lyrics imply only a bobtailed horse.

Sympathetic with the Confederacy, James Pierpont served in the First Georgia Cavalry during the Civil War, where he wrote battle songs, such as "Our Battle Flag," "Strike for the South," and "We Conquer or Die." Samples of his civilian songs include "Know Nothing

Polka" (1854) and "Geraldine" (1854), yet his memory survives only through "Jingle Bells." He rests in Laurel Grove Cemetery in Savannah.

John Grin's Christmas

See **A Christmas Carol** (Film and Television Versions)

Jolly Old St. Nicholas

American children's song, possibly composed in the latter nineteenth century. Aside from African American spirituals, "Jolly Old St. Nicholas" ("Ole" in some printings) is the only American Christmas standard that is completely anonymous. It has been suggested that Benjamin R. Hanby, composer of another American holiday standard, "Up on the Housetop" (published in 1866), also wrote "Jolly Old St. Nicholas," but the evidence is only superficial: both songs mention a child named Nell or Nellie, and some music scholars believe that the two songs are written in a virtually identical style. If Hanby is the composer, the "Nellie" mentioned in "Jolly Old St. Nicholas" could have referred to a runaway slave named Nellie, whom Hanby's father had sheltered in pre–Civil War days and about whom Hanby wrote in his song "Darling Nellie Gray."

See also **Up on the Housetop.**

Joseph and Mary

See **The Cherry Tree Carol**

Joseph and the Angel

See **The Cherry Tree Carol**

Joseph, Dearest Joseph Mine

("Joseph, lieber Joseph mein"). Anonymous, late-medieval German carol. Leipzig University holds the earliest known manuscript of the text, which dates c. 1400. Incorporated into various church dramas or mystery plays, "Joseph" centers around the tradition of cradle rocking, which prevailed in Germany at Christmastime during the Middle Ages. Its eight verses include parts for Mary, Joseph, and four attendants. Mary opens the carol by bidding Joseph to help her rock Jesus in His cradle and promises that God will reward him for this service. Joseph, gladly responding in the affirmative, voices his faith that he and Mary

will see paradise, after which each attendant pronounces a blessing or summarizes a prophecy fulfilled concerning Jesus' birth. In the remaining two verses, the attendants join together in praise. Then follows a lengthy refrain, which proclaims that Emmanuel is born in Israel. The last two lines of this refrain consist of Latin text derived from a fourteenth century Latin hymn, "Magnum nomen Domini Emanuel" ("Great Is the Name of the Lord Emmanuel").

Predating "Joseph" is another cradle-rocking carol with Latin lyrics, "Resonet in laudibus" ("Let Our Praises Resound"), the tune of which is identical with that for "Joseph." The text is a series of praises for the birth of Jesus. The earliest source is the Moosburg Gradual, a manuscript dating to the mid–fourteenth century, which resides in the University Library of Munich. Similar to "Joseph," "Resonet" likewise includes a refrain drawn from "Magnum nomen Domini Emanuel." "Resonet" was especially associated with the building of a model of the *Krippe* (German, "crib," Nativity scene) in medieval churches, around which boys would leap and dance in time to the music as an expression of the carol's praise.

"Joseph" and "Resonet" are two prime examples of the *Wechselgesang* (antiphonal singing) tradition, which originated in pre-Reformation Bohemia and from there migrated to Lutheran Germany, where it supplanted the Roman Catholic Christmas Masses. According to the tradition, different groups of singers or instrumentalists, placed at different stations around the church, performed certain sections of carols for more dramatic effect. Because "Joseph" and "Resonet" contained extensive passages of vernacular German along with separate sections of Latin lyrics, they often were sung together, with one group performing the vernacular and another the Latin.

The tune has received other vocal settings, notably among them "Geistliches Wiegenlied" ("Spiritual Cradle Song") by Johannes Brahms (1833–1897). W.A. Mozart (1756–1791) also incorporated the tune in the original second movement of his Symphony No. 19 in E flat (K132, 1772).

See also **Rocking.**

Joseph Was an Old Man
See **The Cherry Tree Carol**

Joy to the World!

Highly popular English carol, the words for which were contributed by Isaac Watts (1674–1748). A clergyman who penned some 700 hymns, among them "When I Survey the Wondrous Cross" and "O God, Our Help in Ages Past," Watts reworked the biblical Psalms, paraphrasing and even discarding some, and published his *Psalms of David Imitated in the Language of the New Testament* (London, 1719). "Joy to the World!" is derived from the latter half of Watts's paraphrase of Psalm 98, which he titled "To Our Almighty Maker, God." The lyrics initially began with "Joy to the earth," but "world" in time replaced "earth."

While the origins for the lyrics are clear, the composer of the melody (now known as "Antioch") remains unidentified, although G.F. Handel and Lowell Mason have been named without definitive proof. John Wilson (*Bulletin of the Hymn Society of Great Britain and Ireland*, June 1986) traced the origin of "Antioch" initially (and presumably) to a tune titled "Comfort," which anonymously appeared in two volumes, *Collection of Tunes* (1833) by the Methodist Thomas Hawkes and the nondenominational *Congregational Harmonist* (1835) by Thomas Clark. A revised tune also appeared in William Holford's *Voce di Melodia* (1834). Holford attributed the melody to Handel because it resembled the opening measures of "Glory to God" and "Lift Up Your Heads," two choruses from Handel's oratorio *Messiah*. Musicologists have since considered the brief similarity, among other complex reasons, as merely coincidental.

Lowell Mason (1792–1872), the noted American Presbyterian composer who supplied the music for such hymns as "My Faith Looks Up to Thee" and "Nearer My God to Thee," perpetuated the Handel myth. Mason made further arrangements of the "Comfort" tune, changed its name to "Antioch," and published it together with Watts's lyrics for the first time in his collection *Occasional Psalm and Hymn Tunes, Selected and Original* (Boston, 1836). Deeply devoted to Handel's works and undoubtedly influenced by Holford's premise, Mason included the phrase "from Handel," which appeared in Mason's subsequent collections of 1839, 1841, and 1848. Mason's arrangement has enjoyed widespread popularity in the United States, but it has never attained quite the same appeal in Great Britain, which seems to prefer the original "Comfort" version.

Joys Seven
See **The Seven Joys of Mary**

The Judy Garland Christmas Show

Video recording of episode 15 of the television series *The Judy Garland Show* (CBS network, 1963–1964). Originally recorded on December 6, 1963, it aired on December 22, 1963.

A legend in American entertainment, Judy Garland presents a variety of seasonal and nonseasonal tunes in a home-style setting, together with her children: daughter Lorna Luft, 11; son Joey Luft, eight; and daughter Liza Minnelli, 17. Other guest performers include dancer Tracy Everitt, billed as Liza's "beau"; pop stars Jack Jones and Mel Tormé; and the Peter Gennaro Dancers dressed as "nutritionally deficient" Santas. Mel Tormé also brings along a 12-member group of carolers who join in the festivities.

Ironically, of the 25 selections presented, over one-third are nonseasonal. Judy opens by serenading Lorna and Joey with "Have Yourself a Merry Little Christmas," which she made popular in the 1944 motion picture, *Meet Me in St. Louis*. The remaining numbers and performers appear in the following order: "Consider Yourself" (Judy with her children); "Where Is Love?" (Joey, who sits atop a piano while Judy mouths the words with him); "Steam Heat" (song-and-dance routine by Liza and Tracy); "Little Drops of Rain" (Judy); "Wouldn't It Be Loverly" and "Lollipops and Roses" (both sung by Jack Jones); "Santa Claus Is Coming to Town" (Lorna, while sitting on Jack's lap); "Alice Blue Gown" (Liza); "Jingle Bells," "Sleigh Ride," and "It Happened in Sun Valley" (medley by Judy, Liza, and Jack); "Winter Wonderland" (Judy); "Rudolph, the Red-Nosed Reindeer" (instrumental with dance routine by the Peter Gennaro Dancers); "Here We Come A-Caroling" (carolers); "The Christmas Song" (duet by Judy and Mel Tormé at the piano); "Caroling, Caroling" (carolers); "What Child Is This?" (Judy); "God Rest Ye Merry, Gentlemen" (carolers); "Hark! The Herald Angels Sing" (duet by Mel and Jack); "Good King Wenceslas" (carolers); "It Came Upon the Midnight Clear" (duet by Liza and Tracy); "Silent Night" (duet by Lorna and Joey); "Deck the Halls" (everyone). After the visitors depart, Judy dims the lights, and as Lorna and Joey prepare for bed, Judy sings to them her signature song, "Over the Rainbow," which closes the show.

A few "bloopers" add to the show's spontaneity. During "The Christmas Song," when Judy botches the lyrics in *two* places, Mel Tormé responds with "Close!" after the first error, but ignores the second. And Liza momentarily forgets the lyrics to "It Came upon the Midnight Clear," leaving Tracy to carry the song.

Written by Frank Peppiatt, John Aylesworth, and Johnny Bradford. Produced by Gary Smith. Directed by Dean Whitmore. A Kingsrow Enterprises Production in association with the CBS Television Network in association with H.G. Associates, Inc. DVD: Pioneer Video. B & W. 50 min.

Karroll's Christmas
See **A Christmas Carol** (Film and Television Versions)

Kenya
See **Africa**

The Kid Who Loved Christmas
(1990). Made-for-television drama, featuring an almost exclusively African American cast.

Christmas in Chicago promises to be very special this year for little Reggie Miller (Trent Cameron), for he is about to be adopted by the most loving couple, Tony and Lynette Parks (Michael Warren and Vanessa Williams). Yet when Lynette perishes in an automobile accident shortly before Christmas, the adoption agency shuffles Reggie to other foster homes, because it now views Tony, a traveling jazz musician, as an unstable parent. It's obvious that Tony and Reggie deeply love and need each other, but despite fervent pleadings from Tony's band members and even intimidation from Tony himself, Mrs. Clayton (Esther Rolle), the agency supervisor, remains obstinate.

While Tony fights bureaucracy, Reggie persistently escapes the confines of his foster homes and finally asks a department store Santa to reunite him with Tony. This Santa only calls the authorities, whereupon Reggie bolts and briefly becomes a child of the streets as a raging blizzard descends upon Chicago. He finds refuge in a nearby church and in the stillness communes with the Almighty. Shortly thereafter by coincidence, Mrs. Clayton appears in the same church to escape the weather and discovers Reggie in prayer. His plea so touches her that she repents and, weeping, confesses why she had kept Reggie and Tony apart: Mrs. Clayton had been a foster child herself, raised in environments without love, and she had always felt alone. If she could overcome such adversity, she had reasoned, so could other foster children.

Perhaps Santa had a hand in reuniting man and boy after all. Waiting outside the church is a taxi, the driver of which strikingly resembles the department store Santa, who rushes Reggie and Mrs. Clayton to the Blue Note Jazz Club. Finding that a dejected Tony has given up hope and departed alone for New Orleans via train, the entire troupe dashes to intercept him at the station, and Tony and Reggie are reunited not only for Christmas, but forever as father and son.

With Cicely Tyson as Etta, the social

worker; Della Reese as Alicia, the band's vocal soloist; and Sammy Davis, Jr., as the band's friend, "Side Man" Frank. This was Mr. Davis's last feature film appearance before his death on May 16, 1990.

Story by W. Mark McClafferty, Clint Smith, Mark E. Corry, and Lynn Marlin. Teleplay by and produced by Sam Egan. Directed by Arthur Allan Seidelman. Eddie Murphy Productions and Paramount Television. VHS: Paramount Studios. 118 min.

King of Kings
See **Nativity** (Film and Television Depictions)

Kissing Bough
See **Mistletoe**

Kris Kringle
See **United States**

Kwanzaa

A secular, seven-day African American celebration that commences on December 26 and bears no historical relationship to Christmas. The name is derived from the Swahili phrase "matunda ya kwanza" ("first fruits"). Its roots lie in ancient African first-fruit harvest celebrations, and the present concept of Kwanzaa strives to assist African Americans in relating to their cultural past. It is thought that by so doing, they will be better equipped to understand the present and cope with the future. Kwanzaa is one of three principal year-end festivals in the United States, the other two being Christmas and Hanukkah. .

Conceived by Dr. Maulana Karenga, professor and chairman of the Department of Black Studies at California State University at Long Beach, Kwanzaa originated in 1966 following the Watts riots in Los Angeles. Believing that social revolutionary change for African Americans could be achieved by exposing them to their heritage of African culture (Kawaida Theory), Dr. Karenga created Kwanzaa as an alternative to Christmas, a holiday many blacks have otherwise viewed as "white" and Eurocentric.

Kwanzaa is organized around five fundamental activities and seven cardinal principles, the latter of which Dr. Karenga emphasized by duplicating the final "a" in "Kwanza" to form the seven-letter "Kwanzaa." The five fundamental activities are the gathering together of family, friends, and community; reverence for the Creator and creation; remembering the past by honoring ancestors and learning from African achievements; adherence to the highest cultural ideals; and celebrating the "Good of Life." The seven principles, termed *Nguzo Saba*, focus on family and community and include *umoja* (unity), *kujichagulia* (self-determination), *ujima* (collective work and responsibility), *ujamaa* (cooperative economics), *nia* (purpose), *kuumba* (creativity), and *imani* (faith).

Kwanzaa celebrations include rituals, dialogue, narratives, poetry, dancing, singing, music, and feasting. A major ritual, somewhat similar to that of Hanukkah, is the lighting of a *kinura*, a candelabrum with seven candles (*mishumaa*) in colors of the Black Liberation Flag: three red, three green, and one black. One candle is lit on each of the seven days of Kwanzaa to commemorate the seven principles, after which celebrants, drinking from a *kikombe cha umoja* (unity cup), toast their ancestors by exclaiming, "Harambee!" ("Let us pull together!"). January 1 features a final feast (*karumu*), the table of which must include symbols of the seven principles, beginning with a straw placemat (*mkeka*), on which lie the remaining symbols: candelabrum, candles, assorted fruits (*mazao*), one ear of corn for each child present (*vibunzi*), the unity cup, and gifts (*zawadi*) for the children. These gifts traditionally include a book highlighting black achievement, a heritage symbol, and a toy.

On December 11, 1996, President William Clinton delivered the first official message in celebration of Kwanzaa to the United States; since that time, the messages have become an annual tradition. Over 20 million blacks now celebrate Kwanzaa in North America, the Caribbean, and Africa.

L

Lamb's Wool
See **Wassail**

Latvia
See **Baltic States**

Laurel
See **Christmas Plants**

Laurel and Hardy in Toyland
See **Babes in Toyland**

Lavender
See **Christmas Plants**

Lebanon
See **Middle East**

The Legend of the Candy Cane
See **Candy Canes**

The Legend of the Christmas Rose

Inspirational children's picture book written by American author William H. Hooks, published in 1999. It is based on one of several legends that surround the Eurasian perennial evergreen, *Helleborus niger*, also known as the Christmas Rose.

Having received news from the heavenly host that a Savior is born, shepherd brothers Micah, Joab, and Jonathan set off to Bethlehem with a prized lamb for the Christ Child. Their little nine-year-old sister Dorothy is not permitted to accompany them on such a journey, yet the girl is determined to see the Babe for herself. Alone, she follows her brothers from afar until nightfall, when she suddenly realizes that, unlike her brothers, she has brought no gift for the Babe. Distressed with shame, she weeps bitterly, whereupon an angel suddenly appears with a flower of purest white and causes the ground before Dorothy to yield similar flowers. She gathers as many of them as she can hold and rushes to present her gift. Passing over the Wise Men's costly gifts and her brothers' prized lamb, the Child in the manger chooses one of Dorothy's white blossoms, which is immediately infused with a hue of palest pink. On returning home with her brothers, Dorothy notes that only one white rose remains at the site where the angel had previously appeared. She carries the flower home, where it blooms annually at Christmastime and becomes a source of healing for the sick.

William H. Hooks is the author of numerous children's books, including *The Ballad of Belle Dorcas* (1990) and *Freedom's Fruit* (1996).

See *also* **Christmas Plants** (Christmas Rose); **The Legend of the Christmas Rose** (by Selma Lagerlöf).

The Legend of the Christmas Rose

("Legenden om julrosorna"). Short story by Swedish author Selma Lagerlöf, originally published in December 1907 in *Good Housekeeping*. It was then published in 1908 in a Swedish collection of stories, *En saga om en saga och andra sagor*, and in English as *The Girl from the Marsh Croft* (1910). The story, set in the twelfth century in Skåne, a then-Danish (now Swedish) province, is based on one of several legends that surround the Eurasian perennial evergreen, *Helleborus niger*, also known as the Christmas Rose.

Though they live as outlaws in a cave in the Göinge Forest, the Robber Family is privileged to witness their forest miraculously dressed in summer bloom each Christmas Eve to commemorate the hour of Christ's birth. By chance, Mother Robber encounters the aged Abbot Hans in Övid Cloister and declares that his prize herb garden could never compare to that appearing on Christmas Eve. Desiring to see this vision, the abbot secures Mother Robber's permission to visit Göinge Forest next Christmas unharmed. Meanwhile, the abbot relates the story to Archbishop Abaslon, who promises to pardon the Robber Family if the abbot returns with a blossom as proof.

At Yuletide, the abbot travels to the forest

with a skeptical lay brother, and as church bells signal the hour of Christmas, the vision unfolds in breathtaking glory. As angels playing celestial music approach, the lay brother believes that it is a demonic trick, a work of Satan, and shouts a curse, which immediately cancels the miracle. Mortified, the abbot perishes on the spot while clutching a pair of white root bulbs, and these the lay brother plants in the late abbot's garden. The forest miracle never returns, but on each succeeding Christmas Eve, the planted bulbs sprout into gorgeous white flowers, the Christmas Rose. Presenting these to the archbishop, the lay brother secures the promised pardon for the Robber Family, and to atone for his hard-heartedness, the lay brother voluntarily takes up residence in Robber Cave after the Robber Family returns to decent society.

Selma Lagerlöf (1858–1940) became the first female recipient of the Nobel Prize for Literature in 1909. She is noted for such children's books as *The Wonderful Adventures of Nils* and *The Further Adventures of Nils*, in which she combined the history, geography, and folklore of Sweden.

See also **Christmas Plants** (Christmas Rose); **The Legend of the Christmas Rose** (by William H. Hooks).

The Lemon Drop Kid

(1951). Motion picture comedy-musical based on a short story of the same title by American short-story writer and humorist Damon Runyon (1884–1946), who gained fame with his tales of the gambling, racing, and criminal worlds. Paramount Pictures originally released a film adaptation of the story in 1934, starring Lee Tracy as the Lemon Drop Kid (an alias after his preference for that candy), then followed with a remake in 1951, starring comedian Bob Hope in the title role with singer Marilyn Maxwell. This latter production features the film debut of the now-classic Christmas song "Silver Bells," by Jay Livingston and Ray Evans.

When the girlfriend of gangster Moose Moran (Fred Clark) loses $10,000 at the race track on a hot tip from con man Sidney Melbourne (the Lemon Drop Kid), the Kid must make full restitution by Christmas Eve, lest Moose's goon, "Sam the Surgeon" (Harry Bellaver) "open" him on Christmas morning. To raise the cash, the Kid persuades several comrades to pose as sidewalk Santas around New York, collecting donations for a home for female senior citizens. The Kid even utilizes Moose's old gambling casino and places several homeless, elderly women there, yet neither they, nor his cohorts, nor his nightclub singer–girlfriend, Brainey Baxter (Marilyn Maxwell) realize that the whole setup is nothing but a scam and believe instead that the Kid suddenly has developed a charitable heart.

Seeing the donations roll in, on Christmas Eve Brainey's employer, racketeer Oxford Charley (Lloyd Nolan), attempts to move in on the scam by kidnapping all the women, holding them prisoner at his residence, and stealing the Kid's cash, which had been stashed in a statue outdoors. The Kid gains entrance by posing as a little old lady in drag, and through a series of twists and turns, overpowers Charley, recovers the cash, and hurries back to the casino to meet Moose, who has just returned from Florida. The shenanigans continue as Charley arrives to retrieve the cash, when suddenly the walls open and out spring a horde of merry "gamblers" soon followed by the police, courtesy of the Kid. Moose and Charley are arrested for operating an illegal gambling joint. The Kid goes straight after all, and the accumulated donations sponsor a legitimate home for senior ladies.

Bob Hope and Marilyn Maxwell sing two duets in the picture: "It Doesn't Cost a Dime to Dream," while tending to the ladies at the casino, and "Silver Bells," while strolling down the snowy sidewalks of New York.

In 1990, the picture won the ASCAP Film and Television Music Award for Most Performed Feature Film Standard ("Silver Bells").

With Jane Darwell, Andrea King, J.C. Flippen, William Frawley, and Sid Melton. Story by Edmund Beloin. Screenplay by Edmund Hartmann, Robert O'Brien, and Frank Tashlin. Additional dialogue by Irving Elinson. Produced by Robert L. Welch. Directed by Sidney Lanfield. Paramount Pictures. DVD: Brentwood Communications. B & W. 91 min.

See also **Silver Bells**.

The Leprechaun's Christmas Gold

(1981). Made-for-television animated story using stop-motion puppets (Animagic).

En route home to Ireland on the *Belle of Erin*, a sea captain bids young cabin boy Dinty Doyle to fetch a Christmas tree from a nearby uncharted island. In so doing, Dinty unwittingly releases Old Mag the Hag, a screaming banshee, who had been imprisoned for ages beneath the tree by the leprechauns, inhabitants of the Phantom Island of Tralee. Finding gold at the end of a rainbow, Dinty meets Blarney Killakillarney, guardian of the gold, who relates the history of banshees and the leprechauns:

For centuries, banshees had sought gold from leprechauns before Christmas Day, lest they turn into salty tears and wash away. Yet because the gold must only be given to them willingly, banshees had often transformed themselves into beautiful creatures with great powers of persuasion, their sole identifying marks being tears. With such a ruse, Old Mag had captured all but Blarney's gold on the island. With the help of the lord of leprechauns, Blarney had tricked Old Mag and had trapped her beneath a pine cone, which had grown into a beautiful tree.

Now free, Old Mag spikes Blarney's tea with a potion of persuasion, but he grants his gold to Dinty instead. Undaunted, Old Mag next appears to Dinty as Colleen, a beautiful shipwrecked girl, and he falls prey to her wiles. Now granted Dinty's gold, Old Mag curses Dinty with the sleep of 100 Christmases, then rushes to her claim, but not before the dawn of Christmas Day signals that time has run out, and Old Mag is washed away. As the lord of leprechauns revives Dinty, the *Belle of Erin* appears with the rainbow, and Dinty and all the leprechauns happily return to Ireland.

Featuring the song "Christmas in Killarney." Narrated and sung by Art Carney. Principal voices: Peggy Cass, Robert McFadden, Ken Jennings, Gerry Matthews, Christine Mitchell, Glynis Rieg, and Frankie Moronski. Written by Romeo Muller. Produced and directed by Arthur Rankin, Jr., and Jules Bass. A Rankin/Bass Production. VHS: Warner Studios. 25 min.

This television special is further detailed in Rick Goldschmidt's book *The Enchanted World of Rankin/Bass*.

See also **Christmas in Killarney; Rankin/Bass Christmas Cartoons.**

Let It Snow! Let It Snow! Let It Snow!

Popular American song written in 1945 by New York–born lyricist Sammy Cahn and London-born composer Jule Styne. While suffering through a California heat wave, the two "cooled" themselves by writing this generic winter song. The picturesque lyrics suggest a romantic fireside interlude as cares are left to the wind or, better, to the blizzard outside. No holiday is mentioned, yet the song has become firmly linked with Christmas, a trend noted with a number of other popular, nonspecific winter songs, such as "Jingle Bells," "Frosty the Snow Man," "Winter Wonderland," and others. "Let It Snow!" became an instant hit with Vaughn Monroe's 1945 recording on the RCA Victor label, which was also the top Christmas song for that year.

Of the 25 most frequently performed Christmas songs of the twentieth century listed by the American Society of Composers, Authors and Publishers (ASCAP), "Let It Snow!" ranked number nine. By December 2004, it ranked number six.

Another Cahn-Styne holiday collaboration resulted in "The Christmas Waltz" (1954).

See also **ASCAP List of Christmas Songs; The Christmas Waltz.**

The Life and Adventures of Santa Claus

Classic children's novel, published in 1902 by L. Frank Baum, author of *The Wizard of Oz*. It is a biographical fantasy that outlines the life of Santa Claus with no ties whatsoever to St. Nicholas, the fourth century bishop of Myra in Asia Minor.

Discovering an abandoned baby boy near the enchanted Forest of Burzee, the wood nymph Necile raises him as her son among the other Immortals of Burzee. Named "Claus" (meaning "little one"), the boy grows to manhood among his friends, the Fairies, Knooks, Ryls, and Nymphs. The great Ak, Master

Woodsman of the World, guides Claus on a journey around the world, where he studies mankind and their sufferings. It is the poor little children who capture Claus's heart the most, and he vows to spend his life making them happy.

Leaving Burzee, Claus settles in the Laughing Valley of Ho Ha Ho as the beloved friend of children. Fashioning a wooden cat in the image of his pet Blinkie, Claus launches his career as a toymaker and gradually provides toys to neighboring children at their will, regardless of their status. When Claus's enemies, the fiendish Agwas, repeatedly thwart his efforts by kidnapping him (whom the Fairies and Knooks rescue) or by stealing and hiding his toys, an army of Immortals, led by Ak, annihilates them.

To speed his deliveries, Claus eventually acquires ten reindeer, Flossie, Glossie, Racer, Pacer, Reckless, Speckless, Fearless, Peerless, Ready, and Steady, to pull his gigantic sledge of toys. The Knooks, the reindeer's masters, allow them to work for Claus only one night a year, Christmas Eve, with the stipulation that they be back in Burzee by daybreak.

Finding doors locked, Claus gains entrance to homes through chimneys and leaves toys sometimes in stockings hung by the chimney or sometimes on fir trees that he brings along for the children (the origin of the Christmas tree). Parents, believing that only a saint could bestow such gifts, lay upon Claus the title of Santa Claus. Contrary to the traditional Santa Claus, who leaves coal or sticks for naughty children, Baum's Santa Claus delivers gifts to the naughty as well as the nice.

As Santa Claus ages and the Spirit of Death seeks him, Ak convinces the Immortals that Claus, having done so much good for the world, deserves to wear the Mantle of Immortality, which they gladly confer. According to Baum, that is why Santa still lives today.

In 1985, the story was adapted as an animated television special under the same title and featured stop-motion puppets (Animagic). It was the last Animagic holiday special that Rankin/Bass Productions ever made for network television. In 1987 it received a Young Artist Award nomination for Exceptional Family Television Special. Principal voices: Alfred Drake, Earl Hammond, Earle Hyman, Larry Kenney, Lynne Lipton, Robert McFadden, Lesley Miller, Peter Newman, Joey Grasso, and J.D. Roth. Chorus: Al Dana, Margaret Dorn, Arlene Martel, Marty Nelson, David Ragaini, Robert Ragaini, and Annette Sanders. Written by Julian P. Gardner. Produced and directed by Arthur Rankin, Jr., and Jules Bass. A Rankin/Bass Production. VHS: Warner Studios. 50 min. This television special is further detailed in Rick Goldschmidt's book, *The Enchanted World of Rankin/Bass. See also* **Rankin/Bass Christmas Cartoons.**

In 2000, a made-for-video cel-animated version featured the voices of Hal Holbrook with Robbie Benson and Dixie Carter. Written by Hank Saroyan. Produced and directed by Glen Hill. Mike Young Productions. VHS: Universal Studios. 80 min.

The Light of Christmas

Children's book published in 2002 by American author Richard Paul Evans, illustrated by Daniel Craig. The exquisite paintings suggest a setting of medieval Europe, and the story line pairs Christmas with the thread of the biblical parable of the Good Samaritan.

On the morning of Christmas Eve, young Alexander sets off for the Christmas town of Noel nestled high in the mountains. He is one of many who gather for the annual ceremony at this time, wherein the Keeper of the Flame lights the great Christmas torch to bring the light and warmth of Christmas to the world. This year is even more special, for the Keeper of the Flame will bestow upon the one person who has given the truest gift of Christmas the honor of lighting the great torch.

Late in the day as Alexander approaches Noel, he spies lying nearly frozen in the snow an old man, to whom he ministers basic aid, then dashes into Noel for help. But no citizen will come, lest the city gates close upon them and bar them from the ceremony. With no thought for himself, Alexander hurries back to the old stranger, only to find no trace of him. Yet there's hope, for the gates open a crack, and Alexander, regretting that he bears no gift, hurries in to the ceremony nonetheless.

At last, the Keeper of the Flame appears, a lavishly dressed, white-bearded patriarch with evergreen wreath and small, flaming torch, who surveys the citizens' equally lavish gifts. Declaring that only one has truly given well, the Keeper further declares to the others that, in their haste to keep Christmas, they had forgotten Christmas, for all save one had ignored the Keeper disguised as a poor stranger by the wayside. With that, the Keeper of the Flame bestows upon a most surprised Alexander the coveted honor of the evening.

Richard Paul Evans is best known for his novel *The Christmas Box* (1995). All proceeds from his children's books, including *The Light of Christmas*, are donated to the Christmas Box House International, a one-stop shelter and assessment facility for abused and neglected children.

See also **The Christmas Box; The Christmas Candle; The First Gift of Christmas.**

Like Father, Like Santa

(1998). Made-for-television fantasy.

Tyler Madison (Harry Hamlin), the son of Santa Claus (William Hootkins), couldn't care less about Christmas. Bitterly perceiving that Santa had always been too preoccupied with holiday commitments for a close, father-son relationship, Madison has grown into a workaholic, ruthless toy magnate in competition with his father. Destined for the same fate, he's become a virtual stranger to his young son Danny (Curtis Blanck) and his wife Elyse (Megan Gallagher), who know nothing of his real identity. Also feeling that Santa has taken them for granted, the overworked postal division of the North Pole attempts to overthrow the jolly man and his elves by incarcerating them and crowning chief postal worker Ambrose Booth (Roy Dotrice) as Snow King.

Madison has remained estranged from his father for years but experiences a bittersweet reunion when, upon traveling to the North Pole on Christmas Eve to steal the classified "Naughty or Nice" list for purposes of blackmailing other toy enterprises, he is apprehended and thrown into the same cell as Santa. In exchange for his freedom, Madison would supply the new regime with all of Santa's magical secrets for delivering toys, until he discovers a heartrending e-mail addressed to Santa from Danny. The boy desperately needs the

love of his father, and asks if Santa would please find him and send him home for Christmas. Now Madison realizes his own faults as a father and forgives Santa for his unwitting neglect.

With Madison's help, Santa and the elves recover the North Pole by blasting the disgruntled postal workers with rockets containing heavy doses of Christmas spirit, after which father and son speed away on the Christmas rounds in a high-tech sleigh propelled not by traditional reindeer but by rockets. Their first stop is Madison's home in Los Angeles, where Santa has the pleasure of meeting his grandson and daughter-in-law for the first time, and where a changed Madison decides that the time has come for him to return to the "family business."

With Gary Coleman as Ignatius, Stuart Pankin as Snipes, Jimmy Briscoe as Fitzroy, and Gary Frank as Smitty. Written by Mark Valenti. Produced by Melissa Barrett. Directed by Michael Scott. ABC Family Channel in association with Carroll Newman Productions. Video N/A. 105 min.

Lithuania
See **Baltic States**

Little Bitty Baby
See **Children, Go Where I Send Thee**

Little Christmas
See **Epiphany**

The Little Drummer Boy

(Song). American carol composed by Katherine Davis, Henry Onorati, and Harry Simeone in 1958. Originally published in 1941 as "Carol of the Drum" solely by Davis, it remained obscure until Onorati and Simeone became collaborators. Changing the title to "The Little Drummer Boy" added that tender touch for personal appeal. Simeone, a former choral conductor for Fred Waring (of Fred Waring and the Pennsylvanians), directed the Harry Simeone Chorale for its definitive 1958 recording on the Twentieth Century Fox label, which attained position 13 on the *Billboard Hot 100* chart that year. It sold over six million copies, continued to make the pop charts into the early 1980s, and was also the top Christmas song for 1959, 1964, 1965, and 1966. The drummer boy character was the subject of two television animated specials, *The Little Drummer Boy* (1968) and *The Little Drummer Boy, Book II* (1976).

Similar to the much older carol "Pat-a-Pan," "The Little Drummer Boy" focuses on the age-old desire to give gifts to the Christ Child. With musical imagery of a drum softly beating in the background ("rum-pum-pum-pum"), a little boy speaks of his approaching the manger with nothing to offer but the simple gift of music on his drum. As Mary nods and the animals keep time, the Babe smiles in acceptance.

Of the 25 most frequently performed Christmas songs of the twentieth century listed by the American Society of Composers, Authors and Publishers (ASCAP), "The Little Drummer Boy" ranked number ten. By December 2004, it ranked number nine.

See also **ASCAP List of Christmas Songs; The Little Drummer Boy** (television special); **The Little Drummer Boy, Book II; Pat-a-Pan.**

The Little Drummer Boy

(Television special, 1968). Animated story using stop-motion puppets (Animagic), based on the carol of the same title by Katherine Davis, Henry Onorati, and Harry Simeone.

Hating all people because bandits killed his parents, six-year-old Aaron, a shepherd boy, is captured by the greedy Ben Haramed and taken to Jerusalem. There, together with his three dancing pets, Joshua the camel, Sampson the donkey, and Bim Baa Baa the lamb, Aaron must entertain the populace by playing his drum. Aaron is released when Haramed sells Joshua to the Wise Men who are en route to Bethlehem, and Aaron pursues their caravan. Although he finds Joshua at the stable with the Holy Family, a chariot runs Bim Baa Baa down at their reunion. Only the Babe in the manger can save him, say the Wise Men, whereupon Aaron produces his only gift, a song on his drum. Because Aaron gives out of the simple desperation of pure love, the lamb is healed, and Aaron learns the meaning of joy again.

Narrated by Greer Garson. Title song sung by the Vienna Boys Choir. Principal voices:

Teddy Eccles, José Ferrer, Paul Frees, and June Foray. Written by Romeo Muller. Produced and directed by Arthur Rankin, Jr., and Jules Bass. A Videocraft International, Ltd. Production (forerunner of Rankin/Bass Productions) in association with NBC Television. DVD: Sony Music Video. 22 min.

This television special is detailed further in Rick Goldschmidt's book, *The Enchanted World of Rankin/Bass.*

See also **The Little Drummer Boy** (song); **The Little Drummer Boy, Book II; Rankin/ Bass Christmas Cartoons.**

The Little Drummer Boy, Book II

(1976). Made-for-television animated story using stop-motion puppets (Animagic), a sequel to *The Little Drummer Boy.*

The story continues with drummer boy Aaron having finished his performance for the Christ Child at the stable. He and his dancing pets then accompany wise man Melchior to tell Simeon the bell maker that Christ is born, for Simeon has cast a series of silver bells to be rung at the blessed event. Before they arrive, however, a troupe of tax-collecting Roman soldiers raid Simeon's home and carry away his bells, because he cannot pay the tax. Melchior, Simeon, and Aaron pursue the soldiers to their camp, where Aaron offers to entertain them as a ruse. But the soldiers, bent on melting the bells into silver bricks, sacrifice Aaron's drum and sticks to start a fire instead. While the Romans harass Aaron, his pets slip away with the bells, and the three humans hide them in the desert until the soldiers tire of searching for them. Safe in Bethlehem, the bells peal forth the joy of the Nativity, after which Simeon presents Aaron with a new drum and bids him to return to the stable for an encore performance.

In 1977, this picture was nominated for an Emmy Award for Outstanding Children's Special.

Narrated by Greer Garson. Instead of delivering a vocal rendition of "I Heard the Bells on Christmas Day," Garson simply reads the lyrics. Other featured songs are "The Little Drummer Boy" and "Do You Hear What I Hear?" Principal voices: Zero Mostel, David Jay, Robert McFadden, Ray Owens, and Alan Swift. Written by Julian P. Gardner. Produced and directed by Arthur Rankin, Jr., and Jules Bass. A Rankin/Bass Production. VHS: Warner Home Video. 24 min.

This television special is further detailed in Rick Goldschmidt's book, *The Enchanted World of Rankin/Bass*.

See also **Do You Hear What I Hear?; I Heard the Bells on Christmas Day; The Little Drummer Boy** (song); **The Little Drummer Boy** (television special); **Rankin/Bass Christmas Cartoons.**

Little House Books

Historical fiction, a popular series of nine children's novels by American author Laura Ingalls Wilder (1867–1957). Based in part upon Ms. Wilder's childhood and young adult years, the books chronicle the great hardships that she, her parents, Charles and Caroline Ingalls ("Pa" and "Ma"), and sisters Mary, Carrie, and Grace, endured as pioneers in the great American Midwest during the years following the Civil War. These books were the basis for the television series *Little House on the Prairie* (1974–1983), created by Michael Landon.

All of the books contain either entire chapters or short anecdotes devoted to Christmas, which are summarized here chronologically:

Little House in the Big Woods (1932)— Chapter entitled "Christmas." Four-year-old Laura and her family celebrate the holiday most simply yet very happily in their little cabin in the Big Woods of Wisconsin. Joining them on Christmas Eve are Aunt Eliza, Uncle Peter, and cousins Peter, Alice, and Ella. After a day of frolicking in the deep snow, the children retire, and as they drift into sleep, Laura listens while Uncle Peter recalls how his dog Prince had recently saved Eliza from a panther. Christmas Day brings gifts of hand-made mittens and peppermint stick candy for the children, but since Laura is the youngest to appreciate Christmas, she also receives a rag doll. There is no Christmas tree, and no carols are sung, yet it is still indeed a wonderful Christmas.

Farmer Boy (1933)—Chapter entitled "Christmas." Laura's future husband, Almanzo Wilder, grows up on a farm in Malone, New York. Of more substantial means, he and his siblings, Royal, Alice, and Eliza Jane, also enjoy the pleasures of a large family Christmas and awaken at 3:30 A.M. on Christmas morning to open their gifts. Aunts, uncles, and cousins galore later arrive to share a truly sumptuous Christmas dinner, reputed to be the best meal of the whole year, even though Almanzo and the other children must wait impatiently until the adults are served first. Afterwards, he, Royal, and the male cousins scuffle in the barn, erect a snow fort, then square off for a rigorous snowball fight.

Little House on the Prairie (1935)— Chapter entitled "Mr. Edwards Meets Santa Claus." Now six, Laura and her family have moved to the lonely prairie in what is known as Indian Territory. Instead of snow for Christmas, this part of the country brings only cold, drenching rain that causes the creek nearby to swell, and Laura and Mary fear that the adverse conditions will hinder Santa from visiting them. Christmas Day brings not Santa but the family's good friend, Mr. Edwards, who spins a tale about the jolly old elf. Mr. Edwards had walked 40 miles to the town of Independence (in what is now the state of Kansas), where Santa found him and commissioned him to deliver Mary's and Laura's gifts. After all, Santa's pack-mule and horse could never manage the raging creek. Then kind Mr. Edwards had trudged the 40 miles back to the Ingalls' home and had crossed the creek at great peril, just to bring Christmas to two little girls. In their stockings, they each find a new tin cup, a stick of peppermint candy, little heart-shaped cakes, and the greatest treasure of all, a shiny new penny. With Mr. Edwards joining them for a dinner of roast turkey and trimmings, it is a Christmas to remember.

On the Banks of Plum Creek (1937)— Chapters entitled "The Christmas Horses," "A Merry Christmas," "Surprise," "The Fourth Day," and "Christmas Eve." Two years have passed, and the Ingalls family has moved to a sod dugout on the banks of Plum Creek near Walnut Grove, Minnesota. As Mary and Laura look forward to Christmas, eight-year-old Laura again worries that Santa might pass them by, because their dugout has no chimney. Emphasizing that Christmas is a time for selflessness and making others happy, Ma reveals a bit of truth about Santa, then hints that her girls should wish for nothing but a much-needed team of horses for Pa instead of gifts for themselves. Their disappointment vanishes, however, when given the opportunity to make Baby Carrie's present — a string of buttons. At their parents' suggestion, the girls hang their stockings on Christmas Eve and are more than delightfully surprised to find that not only has "Santa" delivered a pair of beautiful horses the next morning, but that their stockings are filled with assorted candy.

The Ingalls girls' introduction to a Christmas tree comes in another year on Plum Creek, when the family assembles together with other families one night at the local church, pastored by the Reverend Alden, a circuit-riding preacher. Before them, the tree is decked with all manner of colorful streamers and little gifts, with larger gifts placed beneath. Adults and children alike receive gifts, which have been donated by Rev. Alden's more affluent congregation back east. The lovely vision is almost beyond the children's belief, and Laura's most treasured gift of the moment is a little fur cape and muff, which rival those of snobbish Nellie Oleson, Laura's own childhood rival.

Four days before their third Christmas on Plum Creek, Pa sets out for town, but on his return, a howling blizzard overtakes him, and he falls through a snow bank. Sheltered there, he weathers the blizzard for three days and nights, sustained only by snow for water and the oyster crackers and Christmas candy that he had bought for his girls. When the blizzard abates on the fourth day, Christmas Eve, Pa climbs out to find that he had been within 100 yards of his home all along. But all is not lost, for he produces a tin of frozen oysters for Christmas dinner. There are no presents and no candy, but the family has a far better gift — Pa is home safe.

By the Shores of Silver Lake (1939) — Chapters entitled "Christmas Eve," "The Night before Christmas," and "Merry Christmas." The Ingalls family now occupies the surveyor's house by the lake for the winter in Dakota Territory. Mary (now blind from scarlet fever) and Laura are young teenagers, Carrie is growing fast, and there is a new addition, Baby Grace. The three oldest girls have fashioned handmade

Christmas gifts for their parents and Grace, and on Christmas Eve, the family reminisces about their past Christmases, each one seemingly better than the last. As Pa entertains with his fiddle, they receive unexpected houseguests in the form of their friends Robert and Ellie Boast, who are traveling west to put down a homestead claim. Christmas Day brings a round of gift-giving surprises and roasted jack rabbit with stuffing for dinner. And the surprises continue when Mrs. Boast produces popcorn, a true holiday treat.

The Long Winter (1940) — Chapters entitled "Merry Christmas," "The Christmas Barrel," and "Christmas in May." The Ingalls family, now living in De Smet in Dakota Territory (presently South Dakota), are expecting a barrel of Christmas surprises that Rev. Alden has shipped from the East, but fierce blizzards prevent the arrival of any supply trains. Although their cupboard is almost bare, the Ingallses manage to have a merry Christmas just by being together with a few handmade gifts, some recently acquired reading material, and a little Christmas candy. Ma and the girls pool their ready cash, 25 cents, which is just enough to purchase a pair of handsome suspenders for Pa. At last the supply trains arrive in May, and the Ingalls family receives their long-awaited Christmas barrel, which contains, among many items, a frozen turkey and cranberries. So they celebrate spring with a fine Christmas dinner, shared with their friends, the Boasts.

Little Town on the Prairie (1941). Although this book does not contain a chapter specifically devoted to Christmas, Laura, now 15, is granted a third-grade teaching certificate in De Smet on Christmas Eve, 1882, which fulfills her long-awaited dream. Mary is now away at a blind school in Iowa, and with her income as a teacher, Laura is able to assist with Mary's tuition.

These Happy Golden Years (1943) — Chapter entitled "The Night before Christmas." Laura is now engaged to Almanzo Wilder, who has been away for the winter on business with his brother Royal. On Christmas Eve, as the Ingalls family makes preparations and as Pa entertains with his fiddle, Laura allows herself to believe for a moment that Almanzo might forget about her during his long absence.

Laura's ache vanishes, however, when she receives a most special gift in the arrival of her beloved, who could not bear to be away from her for so long. His gift to her is a gold bar pin etched with a little house, before which lie a tiny lake and a spray of grasses and leaves. The family spends the evening listening to Almanzo's adventures, until midnight chimes the arrival of Christmas and the promise of festivities in the morning.

The First Four Years (1971, posthumously). The last of the *Little House* series, this book chronicles the first four years of Laura's marriage to Almanzo Wilder in De Smet, beginning in August 1885. For their first Christmas together, the Wilders purchase a set of glassware, one piece of which is a large oval bread plate. Raised on the plate are heads of wheat and the familiar quotation, "Give us this day our daily bread," from the Lord's Prayer (Matthew 6:9–13).

In 1889, a fire destroyed the Wilders' home in De Smet, yet this plate survived and was later found among the possessions of their child, Rose Wilder Lane (1886–1968), following her death. The plate is on display at the Laura Ingalls Wilder Home Association in Mansfield, Missouri.

See also **Little House on the Prairie**.

Little House on the Prairie

Highly popular, Emmy Award–winning television series of 203 episodes that aired on the NBC network from 1974 to 1983. The final season aired under the title of *Little House: A New Beginning*. Created by Michael Landon and developed for television by Blanche Hanalis, the series was loosely based on the nine *Little House* books by American author Laura Ingalls Wilder. The principal performers included Michael Landon and Karen Grassle as Charles and Caroline Ingalls, Melissa Gilbert as Laura Ingalls (Wilder), Melissa Sue Anderson as Mary Ingalls (Kendall), twins Lindsay and Sidney Greenbush as Carrie Ingalls, and twins Brenda and Wendi Turnbaugh as Grace Ingalls.

Only two episodes were devoted entirely to Christmas, which are summarized in the following paragraphs.

Christmas at Plum Creek (aired December 25, 1974). As the Ingallses prepare for their first Christmas at Plum Creek near Walnut Grove, Minnesota, family members covertly use their own ingenuity to provide Christmas gifts for each other, despite a lack of ready cash. Knowing that Caroline wishes for a new stove, Charles restores a set of wagon wheels for Nels Oleson (Richard Bull) and would trade these for a stove at Oleson's Mercantile, but the only stove in stock has already been sold. Therefore, Charles must order another. On Christmas Eve, Nels delivers a large crate, and Charles is sure that it contains his gift to Caroline. Christmas Morning brings an exchange of homemade articles of clothing among the family, then Charles presents his gift to Laura — a gorgeous saddle for her pony, Bunny. After an emotional exchange between father and daughter, Caroline at last opens the crate and is shocked to find that her stove is a gift from Laura, not Charles. Shortly thereafter, Nels arrives with daughter Nellie (Alison Arngrim) to claim Bunny, for Laura had lovingly traded her pony for the stove, and the touching, bittersweet moment brings to mind the sacrifices made in love in O. Henry's short story "The Gift of the Magi." Lastly, Charles opens Carrie's gift, a silver star to top the family's Christmas tree, which is her gift to Baby Jesus.

With Katherine MacGregor as Harriet Oleson. Written by Arthur Heinemann. Produced by John Hawkins. Directed by William F. Claxton. (*See also* **The Gift of the Magi.**)

A Christmas They Never Forgot (aired December 21, 1981). Snowbound on Christmas Eve at the Ingalls farm, Mary and Adam Kendall (Linwood Boomer), Laura and Almanzo Wilder (Dean Butler), and Hester-Sue Terhune (Ketty Lester) join their hosts in exchanging memorable anecdotes of past Christmases. Beforehand, Charles and Almanzo entertain everyone with duet renditions of carols played respectively on the fiddle and guitar, and Hester-Sue sings a verse of "Sweet Little Jesus Boy." Of interest is the fact that, while the program is set in the late 1800s, this song, a modern spiritual composed by Robert MacGimsey, was not published until 1934. As the stories commence, a background of traditional carols sung quietly by an *a cappella* choir lends a most reverent, ethereal atmosphere to the program.

Caroline recalls that first Christmas Eve following her father's death when she was a girl. Her mother had remarried, and although her stepfather had been most kind, Caroline had initially rejected him until that Yuletide, when he presented her with a keepsake that her father had given to him in friendship — an ivory watch fob etched with a Nativity scene. Deeply moved, Caroline thenceforth had begun the tradition of wearing the little fob at Christmastime in memory of her loving stepfather.

Almanzo next remembers the Christmas when he was six and his older brother Royal had discovered Christmas gifts hidden in the barn. This proved that Santa did not exist, according to Royal, and the revelation had greatly upset Almanzo. But his father had explained that because Santa's sleigh could never hold all the gifts of the world, many gifts must be hidden. That answer was sufficient, and Royal had received no gifts that year because of his skepticism.

Laura remembers when she was eight and Mr. Edwards (Victor French) had walked a round trip of many miles in a raging blizzard to Independence, Kansas, and back, just to bring Christmas gifts to her family. This segment consists of a clip taken from the two-hour *Little House on the Prairie* television movie pilot, which had premiered in 1974.

Hester-Sue concludes the stories with her memory of the Christmas when she was a ten-year-old slave child living on a plantation. Because Santa had always been portrayed as white, she became despondent when other black children had told her that Santa would ignore her, because of her race. That Christmas was memorable, for she had awakened during the night to see a black Santa placing a lovely angel doll on her tree. Only many years later did Hester-Sue learn that this Santa had been her own father, who, aware of her concern, had borrowed a Santa suit from the plantation owner.

With Matthew Laborteaux as Albert Ingalls, Jason Bateman as James Cooper, Missy Francis as Cassandra Cooper, Sheri Strahl as young Caroline, Jerry Supiran as young Almanzo, and Alene Wilson as young Hester-Sue. Written by Don Balluck. Produced by Kent McCray. Directed by Michael Landon.

Little House on the Prairie is an NBC production in association with Ed Friendly. Both Christmas episodes are available together on one VHS tape from Time Life Video/Goodtimes Home Video. 90 min.

See also **Little House Books.**

Little Jesus, Sweetly Sleep
See **Rocking**

The Little Match Girl

A tragic yet unspeakably tender fairy tale by the celebrated Danish author Hans Christian Andersen (1805–1875). On New Year's Eve, a poorly clad little girl is forced to roam bitterly cold streets and sell matches in the snow. She cannot return home empty-handed or her wretched father will beat her. Starving at the end of the fruitless day, she crouches in a corner and begins to strike one match after another, desperately trying to keep warm. With each match, glorious visions appear before her: first a large, polished stove with a roaring fire; next a splendid dinner of roast goose stuffed with apples and plums; then a gorgeous Christmas tree trimmed with candles and colored pictures. Gazing into the night sky, she notes a falling star and recalls what her late grandmother once said about such a sign, that a soul was going to God. Striking another match brings the grandmother smiling before her, whereupon the girl, clinging to the image, strikes all the remaining matches and begs to be taken away. As the light swells brilliantly, the grandmother folds the little girl into her arms and, rising high and joyfully into New Year's Day, carries her granddaughter forever into the presence of God.

Several motion picture and animated versions introduce a more positive or romantic element into the otherwise somber tale:

La petite marchande d'allumettes (1928). Silent French film starring Catherine Hessling, Manuel Raaby, Jean Storm, Amy Wells and Ann Wells. Written by Jean Renoir. Directed by Jean Renoir and Jean Tédesco. B & W. Video N/A. 40 min.

Little Match Girl (1937). Animated cartoon "short" from the Color Rhapsodies series of Screen Gems/Columbia Pictures. Academy Award nomination in 1938 for Best Short Sub-

ject, Cartoons. Produced by Charles Mintz. Directed by Arthur Davis. Video N/A. 8 min.

The Little Match Girl (1983). Motion picture version starring Nancy Duncan, Dan Hays, Matt McKim, and Monica McSwain. Directed by Wally Broodbent and Mark Hoeger. Video N/A. 54 min.

The Little Match Girl (1987). British musical, in which a young girl learns that true beauty lies in friendship and love. Starring Twiggy Lawson, Roger Daltrey, Natalie Morse, Paul Daneman, Nicola Dawn, Jennie Linden, and Jemma Price. Written by Jeremy Paul and Leslie Stewart. Produced by Peter Jefferies. Directed by Michael Custance. Harlech Television and Picture Base International Productions. VHS: East Texas Distributor. 90 min.

The Little Match Girl (1987). Television special in which a woman attempts to reconcile her husband and estranged son at Christmastime, while a match girl's matches create positive outcomes. Starring Maryedith Burrell, Keshia Knight Pulliam, Rue McClanahan, John Rhys-Davies, and William Daniels. Written by Maryedith Burrell. Produced by Robert Hargrove. Directed by Michael Lindsay-Hogg. Video N/A. 96 min.

The Little Match Girl (1991). Made-for-video animated cartoon in which homeless match girl Angela experiences an adventure that promises new beginnings on New Year's Eve, 1999. Narrated by F. Murray Abraham. Other voices: Theresa Smythe, Perry Kiefer, and Heidi Stallings. Written by Maxine Fisher. Produced and directed by Michael Sporn. VHS: Family Home Entertainment. 30 min.

Such Is Life (1924). Silent film comedy starry Baby Peggy, Joe Bonner, Thomas Wonder, Jack Henderson, Arnold MacDonald, and Paul Stanhope. Directed by Alfred J. Goulding. Century Film Corporation. B & W. Video N/A.

Sungnyangpali sonyeoui jaerim (*Resurrection of the Little Match Girl*, 2002). Bizarre South Korean science fiction production in which the delivery boy of a Chinese restaurant reincarnates the little match girl through a computer video game and is drawn into an interchanging world of virtual reality and cyberspace. Although his mission is to lead her to a peaceful death, many obstacles stand in his way. Starring Eun-Kyeong Lim as the match girl. Written by Jin-Mi In and Sun-Woo Jang. Produced by In-Taek Yoo. Directed by Sun-Woo Jang. Kihwik Cine. Video N/A. 123 min.

Hans Christian Andersen wrote a number of tales with winter settings, such as "The Snow Queen," yet only two, "The Little Match Girl" and "The Fir Tree," are set amid the holidays.

See also **The Fir Tree**.

Little Women

Autobiographical novel by American author Louisa May Alcott (1832–1888), published in 1868–69. Based on her childhood experiences in New England, it features the closely knit March family with daughters Meg, Jo, Beth, Amy, and "Marmee," their mother. Initially set during the American Civil War, the first two chapters depict a holiday scene amid the anxiety over their father, who has volunteered as a chaplain in the Union army, and who will not be home for Christmas. Because money is scarce, the girls, renouncing gifts for themselves, prepare a few treasures for Marmee instead. For her girls, Mrs. March places a New Testament under each of their pillows early Christmas morning, then departs on an errand of mercy to the Hummel home before daybreak. There lies a sick mother with a newborn and six other children freezing and starving. With love, the girls sacrifice their meager meal and provide for the wretched family. Then follows an original, melodramatic play, *The Witch's Curse, an Operatic Tragedy*, written by Jo and performed by the girls for their childhood friends. Afterwards, the children are delighted to find special treats of ice cream, fruit, and candy awaiting them. Rich old Mr. Laurence, their reclusive next-door neighbor, upon hearing of their good deed earlier that morning, had sent over the repast. Indeed, despite the times, it is "A Merry Christmas."

The remainder of the novel follows the girls' lives as they grow.

The Littlest Angel

Classic children's book written in 1939 by American author Charles Tazewell, with television and animated versions.

A little boy, between four and five years old and known simply as "the Littlest Angel," finds that living in heaven requires much painful adjustment. His innocent mischievousness, his off-key singing in the celestial choir, his chasing his halo, and his swinging on the heavenly gates prompt a conference with the Understanding Angel. Homesick for earth, the Littlest Angel is allowed to keep his most prized possession: a rough little wooden box that contains a butterfly, a bird's egg, two stones from a river, and his mongrel dog's collar.

When Jesus is born, all the angels lay gifts before the throne of God to honor the birth. With no other gift to offer, the Littlest Angel presents his little box, a seemingly blasphemous gift to the heavenly host. Yet to God, this simplest of gifts is the most pleasing of all, because it represents unselfishness and sacrifice. At this blessing, the little box soars into the heavens, where it transforms into the shining Star of Bethlehem.

The Children's Press of Chicago first published the story as a book in 1946, and actor Helen Hayes narrated it on the Christmas radio show *Manhattan at Midnight. Coronet* magazine also published the story three years later.

In 1969, the *Hallmark Hall of Fame* sponsored an adaptation for television, starring Johnny Whitaker ("Jodie Davis" of the 1970s television series *Family Affair*) as Michael, the Littlest Angel. With James Coco, Fred Gwynne, E. G. Marshall, Tony Randall, George Rose, Connie Stevens, and Cab Calloway. Teleplay by Patricia Gray and Lan O'Kun. Directed by Joe Layton. Osterman/O'Kun Productions. DVD: Diamond Ent. Corp.

A 1997 animated cartoon version features the voices of Maxine Miller, Blu Mankuma, L. Harvey Gold, William Samples, Walter Marsh, Peter DeLuise, and Paulina Gillis. Written by Kayte Kuch and Sheryl Scarborough. Produced by Chris Delaney and Arnie Zipursky. Directed by John Delaney and Don Boone. Delaney and Friends Productions and Littlest Productions. VHS: Family Home Entertainment. 24 min.

Sound recordings include those narrated by Loretta Young (Decca, 1940s) and Dame Judith Anderson (Caedmon, 1973).

Charles Tazewell (1900–1972), a scriptwriter and author of children's books, performed on Broadway during the 1930s. His books include *The Small One, The Littlest Tree,* and *The Littlest Snowman*, the latter of which won the Thomas A. Edison Prize for the best children's story of 1956. He wrote *The Littlest Angel* in just three days, and at the time of his death, it was in its thirty-eighth printing. It has sold over five million copies.

See also **The Littlest Snowman; The Littlest Tree; The Small One.**

The Littlest Snowman

Children's book written by American author Charles Tazewell (1900–1972). The story initially appeared in the December 1955 issue of *Coronet* magazine and won the Thomas A. Edison Prize for the best children's story of 1956.

Each December a little boy on Winter Avenue creates the Littlest Snowman, who comes to life when clad with a candy heart inscribed with "I Love You Truly." When rising temperatures threaten to obliterate any chance for snow on Christmas Eve, the Littlest Snowman, thin from partial melting, devises a counterplan. Consuming great quantities of colored ice cream on Christmas Eve, the now-obese Snowman climbs to the top of the community Christmas tree, where a fierce north wind blows him into multicolored snowflakes all over town. On Christmas Day, the villagers collect all the white flakes and return them to the boy on Winter Avenue, who restores the Littlest Snowman. Thereafter, his heart beats "I Love You Truly" throughout the Christmas season as another way of saying "Merry Christmas."

See also **The Littlest Angel; The Littlest Tree; The Small One.**

The Littlest Tree

Children's book written by American author Charles Tazewell (1900–1972), published posthumously in 1997.

Whenever people on earth select and decorate their Christmas trees, exact replicas of the trees grow in the Forest of the Nativity in Heaven. Saint Isadore, the forest gatekeeper, maintains a meticulous record of each tree's history, for on Christmas Eve, the Son of God annually selects the best-loved of those trees in the forest to be His birthday tree.

All Heaven looks to Solomon, a celestial

sage and former king on earth, to predict the Son's choice, and his accuracy has been flawless each year, with one exception: the year of the Littlest Tree. A mere scrub of a branch, decorated with lipstick, green ink, blueing, yellow twine, a military general's silver insignia, shards of glass, gearshift knobs, and tin foil, the Littlest Tree was a loving Christmas gift from a pack of war-ravaged, homeless orphan boys to a little girl, Laus, their newest member, who had never experienced a Christmas tree of her own, much less seen one. Though this Christmas symbol reflected the waste of war, to Laus, the Littlest Tree radiated breathless beauty, which brought tears of joy to her eyes. And to the Son of God, it was the perfect birthday tree.

See also **The Littlest Angel**; **The Littlest Snowman**; **The Small One**.

Lo, How a Rose E'er Blooming

("Es ist ein Ros' entsprungen"). German traditional carol that originated around the fifteenth century. The basis for the carol lies in the Messianic prophecy of Isaiah 11:1, "And there shall come forth a rod out of the stem of Jesse, and a Branch shall grow out of his roots." The modern interpretation of this scripture is that Jesus (the "rod" or "Branch") was descended from King David, whose father was Jesse. According to medieval interpretation at the time, however, the rod-Branch of Jesse was pictured allegorically as the Virgin Mary, further symbolized as a rose in bloom, with the Christ Child as her young flower.

The text, which centers on this flowering rose concept, exists in numerous versions, with variable numbers of verses ranging from two to 23. The more lengthy versions elaborate on the entire Nativity and include all events from the Annunciation to the Magi. Such variability is thought to have originated from a simple Annunciation carol, to which shorter verses centering on the remaining details of the story were added at different times.

Because the carol contained Roman Catholic themes, it was not printed until 1599 in Cologne, Germany, for the Protestant Reformation had succeeded in preventing such material from reaching the presses until that time. The carol gained further recognition when, in 1609, the German composer Michael Praetorius (1571–1621) published a well-received musical arrangement in his *Musae Sioniae*, which is the setting in use today. In 1896, another German composer, Johannes Brahms (1833–1897), based an organ chorale prelude around the carol (Opus 122, Book II).

The best-known English translation, "Lo, How a Rose E'er Blooming," is by the American music scholar Theodore Baker (1851–1934), who in 1900 published his *Biographical Dictionary of Musicians*. Alternate translations have included such titles as "I Know a Rose Tree Springing," "Behold a Branch Is Growing," "The Noble Stem of Jesse," and "Of Jesse's Line Descended," among others.

Love Came Down at Christmas

English carol, the text for which was written by Christina Rossetti (1830–1894), considered to be England's foremost female poet. A simple poem consisting of three verses of four lines each, "Love Came Down" proclaims that God's gift of love to the world was Jesus; that God, being Love, was born at Christmas. The poem originally appeared with the title "Christmastide" in Rossetti's collection *Time Flies: A Reading Diary* (1855), a book of daily devotions and meditations for the year, in which "Christmastide" was intended for December 29. This collection, together with two other volumes, *Called to Be Saints* (1881) and *The Face of the Deep* (1892), were all combined to form a larger volume, *Verses* (1893). There, the final line of "Christmastide," which originally read "Love the universal sign," was altered to "Love for plea and gift and sign."

The poem was first published as a carol in *Church Praise* (1907), an English Presbyterian hymnal (Rossetti was Anglican), and in *Songs of Praise* (1925). These and several other musical settings never gained widespread popularity. Two additional tunes, one known as "Hermitage," by the Englishman Reginald O. Morris (1886–1948), and another, an Irish traditional melody known as "Gartan," are the two leading settings, though neither shows particular dominance. Despite lacking a suitable tune, "Love Came Down at Christmas" remains a favorite carol. Another of Ms. Rossetti's poems,

"In the Bleak Mid-Winter," has also become a carol of note.

See also **In the Bleak Mid-Winter**.

Lovefeast, Christmas Eve
See **Moravian Church**

The Low Countries
Comprised of Belgium, Luxembourg, and the Netherlands (Holland). Christmas customs of Belgium are varied and are patterned after its three principal cultures, French, German, and Dutch. The predominantly Roman Catholic Luxembourg observes the feast days of the Church, as does Belgium, and customs in the Netherlands are a roughly equal mix of Catholic and Protestant observances.

Common to these countries are the Christmas markets, which are set up early in December in cities throughout and consist of Christmas arts and crafts, toys, floral arrangements, decorations, cuisine, music, exhibits, and spirits (for example, mulled wines and schnapps known as *Drepp*). The Christmas tree and *crèche* or Nativity scene are the principal Christmas symbols, and it is traditional to leave a gift for the poor when passing an outdoor *crèche*. St. Nicholas brings gifts on the eve of his feast day, December 6, the principal gift-giving holiday of the season, and church services are held on Christmas Eve and Christmas Day. December 25 and 26 (Second Christmas Day) are minor holidays compared to St. Nicholas's Day. The following paragraphs summarize other customs peculiar to these countries:

• BELGIUM. Children set out their shoes for St. Nicholas. Favorite pastries include *cougnou* (sweet bread shaped like the Christ Child), *speculoos* (spiced cookies shaped like St. Nicholas), marzipan, and *klaasjes* (flat, hard cakes). Churches in Flanders traditionally present Nativity plays in sixteenth century fashion with period costumes, and characters must resemble those found in the works of Flemish painter Jan Brueghel (1568–1625). Villages usually appoint three men to portray the three Magi. Dressed in regal attire, they parade from door to door collecting for charities and singing carols, especially the Flemish version of "O Tannenbaum" ("O Christmas Tree"). Because the three are offered food and beverage, which

are consumed immediately at each house, the Wise Men are chosen for their gastronomic prowess. In Belgium, one may hear "Merry Christmas" as *Joyeux Noël* (French), *Fröhliche Weihnachten* (German), or *Zalig Kerstfeest* (Flemish).

• LUXEMBOURG. The St. Nicholas ("Kleeschen") and Black Peter ("Hoùseker") customs are similar to those of the Netherlands. In addition, children set out plates as well as their shoes to receive gifts from St. Nicholas. At Christmas, it is the Christ Child who brings the gifts. Traditional foods include *Stollen* (candied fruit loaf), *bûche de Noël* (Christmas cake in the shape of a Yule log), black pudding, hare, venison, and turkey. Fireworks and *Bals* (dance parties organized by university students) usher in the new year. "Merry Christmas" is *Schéi Chrèschtdeeg* (Letzebuergesch).

• NETHERLANDS. A custom deriving from pagan Yule practices of creating loud noises to drive away evil spirits is Midwinter Horn Blowing. From the first Advent Sunday through Christmas Eve, farmers primarily in the rural eastern sections of the country daily blow horns over wells, producing sounds like foghorns. These horns are made from hollowed limbs of elder trees and range from three to four feet in length.

Since Dutch tradition holds that St. Nicholas, *Sinterklaas*, was born in Spain, on the last Saturday in November he arrives in Amsterdam and other harbor cities by boat from Spain along with his antithesis, *Zwarte Piet* (Black Peter), a sixteenth century Moorish personification of the devil. Dressed in full bishop's attire, the person portraying the saint rides a white horse and, with Peter walking behind, is the center of a parade to the city square; the queen welcomes him in Amsterdam. On the eve of St. Nicholas's Day, the saint and Peter visit a number of public establishments as well as private homes to determine whether children are deserving of gifts. It is Peter, black-faced from jumping down chimneys, who actually distributes the gifts, and he also carries a sack in which to stuff naughty children and a rod for beating them. Often Peter knocks at doors and tosses in *peppernøtter* (hard spice cookies). Other seasonal sweets are *letterbanket* (cakes made into shapes of letters) and *speculaas* (gingerbread pastry). During the evening, elaborately wrapped gifts are hidden around the house. Recipients find them through a series of clues, and each gift contains a poem which satirizes the recipient. Then the children set out their shoes filled with hay and carrots for St. Nicholas's horse, and overnight the fodder is replaced with treats; naughty children receive switches.

Although schools may be closed for two to three weeks, the adult holidays consist of First Christmas Day (December 25), Second Christmas Day (December 26), and New Year's Day. The Christmas tree, sporting real candles, is lit on Christmas Eve, and the Christmas dinner often consists of rabbit, venison, goose, and turkey with flaming or cold pudding. Families remain at home at this time and engage in carol singing or reading aloud by the Christmas tree. Second Christmas Day is reserved for activities away from home, such as attending concerts and plays. The Dutch again remain at home on New Year's Eve and play parlor games, then toast the new year as fireworks, pealing of church bells, and the blowing of boat whistles herald the midnight hour. "Merry Christmas" is *Vrolijk Kerstfeest.*

See also **France; Germany; Saint Nicholas; Saint Nicholas's Day.**

Lullaby
See **Rocking**

Lullay, Thou Tiny Little Child
See **The Coventry Carol**

Luminarias
See **Farolitos and Luminarias**

Luxembourg
See **The Low Countries**

Madeline at the North Pole

(2000). Video collection of two Christmas episodes from *The New Adventures of Madeline*, an animated television series that aired on the ABC network from 1995 to 1996. The series was based on characters from the *Madeline* children's books by Ludwig Bemelmans. Madeline is one of 12 little girls attending a boarding school in Paris.

Madeline at the North Pole (1995). When warm weather promises no snow for Christmas, the little girls at Miss Clavel's school are so disappointed that Lord Cucuface takes them via ship to visit Santa's workshop at the North Pole. Trouble strikes when the elves all contract the flu, so it's up to the girls to finish making the toys in their stead; by Christmas Eve, however, even Miss Clavel, Lord Cucuface, and all the other girls except Madeline are sick as well. Madeline heroically completes the tasks and is rewarded by a personal visit from Santa, who presents her with his cap as a gift.

Madeline and Santa (1995). The story continues as Madeline bakes traditional *bûche de Noël* (Yule log cakes) for her sick comrades. But when Santa swipes them and gains too much weight to fit into chimneys, Madeline saves Christmas by accompanying Santa on his rounds and jumping down the chimneys to deliver the gifts.

Narrated by Christopher Plummer. Principal voices: Andrea Libman, Stephanie Louise Vallance, Brittney Irvin, Chantal Strand, Veronika Sztopa, Michael Heyward, and French Tickner. Story by Judy Rothman Rofé. Teleplay by Betty G. Birney and Judy Rothman Rofé. Produced by Stan Phillips. Directed by Judy Reilly. DIC Entertainment. DVD: Vidmark/Trimark. 45 min.

See also **Madeline's Christmas.**

Madeline's Christmas

Classic children's picture book, the last in a series of six *Madeline* books written by the Austrian-American author Ludwig Bemelmans. Told in simple verse with illustrations by the author, the books feature the adventures of Madeline, one of 12 little girls attending a boarding school in Paris. *Madeline's Christmas* was originally published as a book insert in the 1956 Christmas edition of *McCall's* magazine.

It's Christmas Eve, and everyone at the boarding school is sick in bed with colds, except Madeline, who ministers to her schoolmates and Miss Clavel, the headmistress. A mysterious rug merchant seeking shelter from the winter storm appears and magically dispatches Madeline's household chores in short order, then whisks away the girls on 12 flying carpets to their parents' homes for Christmas.

In 1990 the story was adapted for television as an animated cartoon, in which a magic-wielding Madam Marie replaced the rug merchant. Narrated by Christopher Plummer. Other voices: Marsha Moreau, Judith Orban, Sonja Ball, Liz Macrae, Anik Matern, and Mark Hellman. Written by Stephan Martiniere and Peter Landecker. Produced by Ronald A. Weinberg. Directed by Stephan Martiniere. A Cinar Films and France Animation production. DVD: Sony Music Video. 25 min.

Ludwig Bemelmans (1898–1962), a world traveler, painter, and illustrator as well as a writer, sustained injuries in a car accident on an island off the coast of France. As he lay in an island hospital, a little girl recovering there provided inspiration for the *Madeline* books.

See also **Madeline at the North Pole.**

Magi

See **Nativity; Wise Men**

The Man in the Santa Claus Suit

(1979). Made-for-television comedy.

Besides delivering toys to children on Christmas Eve, Santa (Fred Astaire) finds time to help three troubled men out of sticky situations in New York City: a milksop math teacher fearful of proposing to his fashion-model neighbor, a street bum dodging the mob, and a senator's aide estranged from his wife and little boy. Posing out of "uniform" as the owner of a costume shop that ordinarily does not exist, Santa rents Santa suits to each man. Wearing the suits enables each to work through his problems just in time for Christ-

mas. Santa also poses as a chauffeur, a policeman, a taxi cab driver, a floor walker at Macy's, a street food vendor, and a song leader, all in connection with his three "charges."

With Gary Burghoff, John Byner, Bert Convy, Tara Buckman, Brooke Bundy, Eddie Barth, Ron Feinberg, Nanette Fabray, and Harold Gould. Written by George Kirgo. Story by Leonard Gershe. Produced by Lee Miller. Directed by Corey Allen. Dick Clark Cinematic Productions. VHS: Anchor Bay Entertainment. 104 min.

The Man Who Saved Christmas

(2002). Canadian made-for-television biographical drama, based on the career of Dr. Alfred Carlton ("A.C.") Gilbert (1884–1961), a highly respected American toy manufacturer who popularized the Erector Set and other educational toys. Having successfully built Erector Sets along with munitions during World War I, Dr. Gilbert was acclaimed as "The Man Who Saved Christmas" in 1918.

A graduate of Yale Medical School, A.C. Gilbert (Jason Alexander) performs as a magician to support his family rather than practice medicine. Five years after founding the highly successful A.C. Gilbert Company in New Haven, Connecticut, Gilbert reluctantly accedes to a request from the National Defense Council and retools his factory in order to produce munitions instead of toys. The long hours required to meet production demands, coupled with the fact that his products are now the complete antithesis of what his factory once represented, all contribute to low employee morale and strained relations at home.

Gilbert initially tolerates these lamentable conditions as well as the Defense Council's abominable proposal of a national campaign to have the entire country give up Christmas for the war effort. Seizing on an earlier statement that Gilbert had made to them to the effect that not producing toys would be like giving up Christmas, the Defense Council now promotes such slogans as "Santa Claus wants you to give up Christmas," "Buy bonds, not toys," and "All we want for Christmas is our boys back home." In addition, Gilbert is expected to sell America's children on the idea with the slogan "A.C. Gilbert says, 'It's no time for toys, boys!'" The campaign promises to be successful when newspapers hail Gilbert, America's number-one toy manufacturer at the time, as the man responsible for canceling Christmas, for which his young son, Albert Jr. (Jake Brockman), receives a beating from angry classmates. Burdened with this incident, the knowledge that his brother Frank (Ari Cohen) is missing in action, and the sudden news that a valued employee's son has been killed in action, Gilbert rebels against the national no-Christmas campaign.

With wife Mary (Kelly Rowan), son Albert, and his banker-father Charles (Edward Asner), Gilbert marches to Washington, D.C., armed with a host of his educational toys to display before the National Defense Committee. There he successfully delivers a passionate plea that Christmas not be cancelled, for doing so would allow the enemy to rob Americans of hope for a brighter future. The Council also agrees that Gilbert should resume manufacturing his toys, which have the ability to stimulate children's imaginations toward creative goals. But in order to manufacture toys *and* fulfill outstanding munitions contracts, Gilbert conducts the former enterprise from his home.

Shortly thereafter, Germany signs the armistice on November 11, 1918, ending the Great War. That Christmas is one of the happiest for Americans, but even more for the Gilbert family with the return home of brother Frank, injured but safe.

In 2003, this picture was nominated for a Visual Effects Award for Best Matte Painting in a Televised Program, Music Video, or Commercial.

Teleplay by Joe Maurer, Debra Frank, and Steve Hayes. Produced by Randi Richmond. Directed by Sturla Gunnarsson. Alliance Atlantis Communications. Video N/A. 100 min.

For some 40 years after the war, A.C. Gilbert continued to make toys, which included Erector Sets, microscope and chemistry sets, American Flyer electric trains, Mysto Magic Exhibition Sets, and many others. At the time of his death, he held patents on more than 150 inventions. The first artificial heart pump was designed with Erector Set parts.

March of the Kings

("La marche des Rois Mages"). Provençal carol for Epiphany. The traditional melody is believed to date to the seventeenth century, although the thirteenth has also been proposed. It was the basis for a march entitled "Marche de Turenne," which honored the military feats of Henri de la Tour d'Auvergne (1611–1675), vicomte de Turenne, as well as a tune to which the French army marched. Credited with the text is one J.F. Domergue of Amaron, whose name appears on the manuscript of a poem dated 1742 in the Avignon Library and headed "sur l'air de la Marche de Turenne." The poem later was published in *Recueil de cantiques spirituels provençaux et françois* (Paris, 1759).

Domergue's poem describes a traveler on the highway who notes a large, splendid troupe of three kings and their entourage approaching him. They are richly arrayed, and their warrior guards with shields protect a treasure of gold, but frankincense and myrrh are not mentioned. As the kings sing praises to God with most beautiful voices, they follow a star that ever remains before them, and the traveler, most impressed with the pleasing spectacle, follows as well. Their journey ends when the star halts before the Christ Child. Various English translations take some liberties with the text by incorporating petitions to be made perfect for spiritual warfare.

The carol, beginning as "*De matin ai rescontra lou trin*" ("This morning I met a procession"), became a signature song for spectacular Three Kings parades that wound through Provençal towns on the eve of Epiphany as throngs of onlookers cheered from the sidelines. Citizens dressed lavishly as the Three Kings with others as their pages and servants; and together with camels, horses, banners, flags, and other folk trappings of their own era, the troupe marched to the church to bestow their gifts to the Christ Child in the crèche.

The tune to "March of the Kings" acquired further popularity through French composer Georges Bizet (1838–1875), who in 1872 arranged it as incidental music for *L'Arlésienne* (*The Girl from Arles*), a play of rustic passion by Alphonse Daudet that has nothing to do with Christmas.

See also **Epiphany**.

March of the Wooden Soldiers
See **Babes in Toyland**

Marge Be Not Proud
See **The Simpsons**

Marks, John D. (Johnny)
See **Rudolph, the Red-Nosed Reindeer** (song)

A Marshmallow World

Popular American song written in 1949, the only collaboration of New York natives Carl Sigman (lyrics) and Peter DeRose (music). A generic song about winter that does not mention Christmas, its gimmick, besides a catchy tune, lies in likening snow to white confections, primarily marshmallows and whipped cream. According to the lyrics, winter is a "yummy" time for sweethearts. The song was not completed in time to be recorded for the 1949 season, but 1950 saw recordings by Bing Crosby on the Decca label, Vic Damone on Mercury Records, Arthur Godfrey on Columbia Records, and Vaughn Monroe on RCA Victor. Of these, only Crosby's recording was charted.

Separately, Sigman is known for his contributions to other popular pieces, such as "Pennsylvania 6–5000" (1939), "Enjoy Yourself, It's Later Than You Think" (1948), and "Ebb Tide" (1953). DeRose is perhaps better known for "Deep Purple" (1934), originally a piano instrumental.

Mary and Jesus
See **The Cherry Tree Carol**

Mary Christmas

(2002). Made-for-television drama.

A letter written to Santa conveys only one heartfelt Christmas wish from nine-year-old Felice Wallace (Jenna Boyd): a mother who will love her and her good daddy. Since her mother's death two years ago, Felice and her father Joel (John Schneider) have led a lonely existence and do not wish to face a similar Christmas this year. When a local television station receives the letter instead, program director Mac Reeves (Daniel Roebuck) sees a chance to boost ratings through a series of special Christmas stories and assigns reporter Mary Maloney (Cynthia Gibb) the task of recording the Wallace family as they prepare for Christmas. But to cynical Mary, who must forego her annual Christmas vacation trip to snowy Vermont and remain in sunny California, such assignments are "all hype and no heart."

Far from poverty-stricken, as Mary had expected of single-parent families, the Wallaces are not only quite affluent (Joel is a successful broker) but profoundly close as well. At first Joel, seeing the project as too intrusive, declines; but he soon yields to Felice's enthusiastic pleas (she subconsciously believes that through television, she will attract a mother), then decides that Felice must have a nanny. The person who fills the position ever so promptly, however, is none other than Santa himself in the guise of grandfatherly "governor" Les Turner (Tom Bosley), whose little sprinkling of Christmas magic not only draws Mary, Joel and Felice into a tight bond of tender love but also discloses a precious secret that leaves them reeling.

In 2003, this picture received a Young Artist Award nomination for Best Supporting Young Actress (Jenna Boyd).

With Renee Ridgeley. Written by Betty G. Birney. Produced by Timothy J. Warenz. Directed by John Schneider. Heartland Entertainment in association with Once upon a Time Films, Ltd. DVD: New Concorde Home Entertainment. 89 min.

Mary, Did You Know?

American Southern Gospel carol, the lyrics of which were written in 1984 by professional comedian-singer-songwriter Mark Alan Lowry. When his local church in Houston, Texas, commissioned him to write a program for their living Christmas tree presentation, Lowry found himself pondering over the life of Christ from the maternal perspective of the Virgin Mary and created lyrics as if he had actually conducted an interview with her about Jesus. Lowry sought appropriate musical settings from several composers, but when none satisfied him, he shelved the lyrics for six years. Then in 1990 while he was a singer with the Bill Gaither Vocal Band, Lowry received an ideal setting for "Mary, Did You Know?" from musician-songwriter Lee Rufus (Buddy)

Greene III, who had recently joined the group. Greene, described as having produced a most beautiful marriage of music with Lowry's lyrics, is said to have created the setting in only ten minutes. Christian artist Michael English, who had been with the Gaither Band from 1984–1991, first recorded the song for his album *Michael English* (Warner Bros., 1991), after which the song received numerous renditions by artists from other genres, including Kathy Mattea, Natalie Cole, and Kenny Rogers. It has been the favorite Christmas song of President William Clinton.

The lyrics ask Mary if she truly realized that her baby boy was God Incarnate, the Savior of the world. Specifically, did she know that not only would He walk on water, heal the sick, and calm storms, but that He would also raise the dead and rule the nations? And did she know that each time she kissed the face of her little one, she kissed the face of God?

Mark Lowry and Buddy Greene have individually written numerous gospel songs, but "Mary, Did You Know?" is the only one of note on which they collaborated.

Mary Had a Baby

African American spiritual of anonymous authorship, thought to have originated in South Carolina during the nineteenth century. Its verses each consist of one line that is repeated three times, with the seemingly spontaneous phrases of "Oh, Lord!" or "Oh, my Lord!" interrupting the repetitions. Variations in the number of verses exist, with a longer version as follows: 1. "Mary had a baby." 2. "What did she name Him?" 3. "She named Him Jesus" 4. "Named Him King Jesus." 5. "Now where was He born?" 6. "Born in a stable." 7. "And where did she lay Him?" 8. "Laid Him in a manger." 9. "Who heard the singing?" 10. "Shepherds heard the singing." 11. "Who came to see Him?" 12. "Shepherds came to see Him." 13. "Star keep a-shining." 14. "The Wise Men kneeled before Him." 15. "King Herod tried to find Him." 16. "Moving in the elements." 17. "They went away to Egypt." 18. "Traveled on a donkey." 19. "Angels watching over Him." Each verse then concludes with the same, seemingly incongruous statement, "Oh, Lord! The people keep a-coming and the train done gone."

Mary, Mother of Jesus

See **Nativity** (Film and Television Depictions)

Mary's Little Boy Child

Popular American song written in 1956 by the African American composer Jester Hairston. Friend and singer Harry Belafonte popularized this lively, West Indies calypso-style narrative of the Nativity with his 1956 recording on the RCA label. It became the top Christmas song that year, ranking number 12 on the *Billboard Hot 100* chart. As the lyrics summarize, the human race may now achieve immortality because of what transpired on Christmas Day 2,000 years ago.

A Pennsylvania native, classically trained musician, and actor, Jester Hairston (1901–2000) was a musician for the Eva Jessye Choir, a conductor for the Hall Johnson Choir, and a collector of spirituals. He arranged choral music for more than 40 motion pictures and appeared in such films as *In the Heat of the Night* (1967) and *I'm Gonna Git You Sucka* (1988). He is best known for his choral work *Amen*, a spiritual based on the life of Christ.

Mary's Question

See **The Cherry Tree Carol**

Masque

See **Christmas Drama**

Mass of the Divine Word

See **Christmas Masses**

Mass of the Rooster

(*Misa del Gallo*). The Spanish term applied to the Midnight Mass held in Spain and Latin American countries. The term derives from a legend holding that the only time in history when a rooster crowed at midnight was to herald the birth of Jesus at that alleged hour. The legend is certainly of European origin, Shakespeare also having made reference to it in Act I of his play *Hamlet*.

According to one medieval legend, the rooster crowed in Latin, *"Christus natus est"* ("Christ is born"), to which other stable animals witnessing the Nativity took up a series of responses: The raven asked, *"Quando?"* ("When?"); the crow, *"Haec nocte"* ("This night"); the ox, *"Ubi?"* ("Where?"); the lamb, "Bethlehem"; the ass, *"Eamus"* ("Let us go").

See also **Christmas Masses; The Friendly Beasts; Hamlet.**

Mele Kalikimaka (The Hawaiian Christmas Song)

Novelty song written in 1949 by Hawaiian businessman R. Alex Anderson, an amateur songwriter who created such other island pieces as "The Cockeyed Mayor of Kaunakakai," "Lovely Hula Hands," "White Ginger Blossoms," and "Lei of Stars." Translated into English, *"Mele Kalikimaka"* means "Merry Christmas." As opposed to most secular Christmas songs that focus on snow and sleighing, Anderson's simple lyrics state the obvious: that Christmas in Hawaii will be green and bright, and that palm trees will sway on Christmas Day. Bing Crosby and the Andrews Sisters first recorded the song on the Decca label in 1950.

Merry Christmas, Darling

Popular American song written in 1970 by Richard Carpenter and Frank Pooler. Carpenter and his sister Karen, originally from New Haven, Connecticut, at that time were students at the Long Beach campus of California State University, where Pooler was director of choral studies. With Karen's melancholy solo in the lead, the Carpenters first recorded the song as a single in 1970 on the A & M label. It charted # 1 in 1970, 1971, and 1973, then charted # 4 in 1972 and #5 in 1983, all on the *Billboard Special Christmas Singles* chart. Karen reportedly was never satisfied with her track for this recording and rerecorded "Merry Christmas, Darling" in 1978. The new recording appeared in the Carpenters' album *Christmas Portrait*, which charted as the #1 Christmas album for 1978.

Like another popular Christmas standard, "I'll Be Home for Christmas" (1943), "Merry Christmas, Darling" centers around loved ones who cannot be together for the holidays. Sitting alone by the fire and the glittering tree on Christmas Eve, the singer sends a mental wish of "Merry Christmas" to her absent lover. Yet while they are physically apart, they will still be together for Christmas in their dreams.

The Carpenters enjoyed a number of hit tunes, including "Close to You" (1970), "We've Only Just Begun" (1970), "For All We Know" (1971), and many others.

See also **I'll Be Home for Christmas** (song).

Messiah

Oratorio in three parts, the best-known work of George Frideric Handel (1685–1759), composed in 1741 to a libretto by Charles Jennens. Whereas the work is often erroneously designated *The Messiah*, the title is simply *Messiah*.

German by birth, Handel had relocated by 1711 to London, where his opera *Rinaldo* significantly helped to further the Italian style of opera. Other notable operas from that point included *Radamisto* (1720), *Giulio Cesare* (1724), *Tamarlano* (1724), and *Rodelinda* (1725). Except in the most elite circles, however, public taste eventually wearied of operas written in Italian (the only accepted language for opera at that time) and demanded something more English. With the premiere of John Gay's *Beggar's Opera* (1728), a highly popular English satire on the Italian opera, together with the folding of two of Handel's opera companies by 1737 and the failure of two other operas by 1741, Handel chose to pursue the oratorio as a principal alternative. Similar to an opera in having parts for soloists, chorus, and orchestra, but without elaborate scenery or costumes, the oratorio, frequently based on a religious subject, could employ English. Ironically, because oratorios were often performed in theaters, the form was not considered to be church music in the strictest sense.

Handel had written some 15 oratorios prior to 1741, among them *Israel in Egypt* (1739), *Saul* (1739), and *L'Allegro–Il Penseroso–Il Moderato* (1740), the latter two librettos having been supplied by an eccentric friend, Charles Jennens. Aspiring to raise Handel's spirits, in 1741 Jennens presented the libretto for *Messiah*, a compilation of scriptures from the King James Bible and the Anglican Burial Service about the life of Christ. Jennens expected that Handel would complete the oratorio within a year. Instead, Handel set to work on August 21, 1741, and completed *Messiah* on September 14, 24 days later. During this time, the power and majesty of the subject consumed Handel such that he rarely ate or slept. Upon completing the "Hallelujah Chorus," he was found weeping over his work. Handel told the servant who so found him that he thought he had seen all heaven before him and God Himself.

Having received an invitation from William Cavendish, lord lieutenant of Ireland, to give a series of benefit concerts in Dublin, Handel first presented *Messiah* at Dublin's New Music Hall in Fishamble Street on April 13, 1742. The hall, ordinarily seating 600, on that date accommodated 700, for men left their bulky swords behind, as did women their hoop skirts. Although the world premiere of *Messiah* was much applauded, the use of a theater and theatrical singers to perform scriptural texts created mixed emotions after the first London performance at Covent Garden Theatre in March 1743.

At a later performance that same season in London, King George II rose to his feet during the "Hallelujah Chorus." While popular trend holds that the king, overcome with emotion, rose in reverence to this monumental chorus, critics believe that he merely rose to stretch his legs during the oratorio's hours-long performance. Regardless of the reason, when a monarch rose, custom dictated that all present follow suit. Thus King George's act not only established the custom of rising during any performance of the "Hallelujah Chorus" today, but served to boost London's acceptance of *Messiah* overall.

Handel began closing his annual Lent season at Covent Garden with *Messiah* in 1750, which coincided with annual benefit performances at London's Foundling Hospital. The first performance on the Continent was in Hamburg, Germany, in 1772, and, although excerpts had been played in New York City in 1770, the first full American performance was in Boston on Christmas Day, 1818, the same Christmas when "Silent Night" was introduced in Austria.

Yielding to Jennens' criticisms and influenced by the availability of vocalists, instruments, and players' musical abilities, Handel often revised *Messiah*. As a result, no definitive version exists today. Shortly after Handel's death, a movement arose to enlarge the chorus and orchestra from their initial numbers of 40 members each. Originally no part had been written for organ or harpsichord, yet Handel, while improvising, had often conducted performances from the latter instrument. In 1789, Baron van Swieten commissioned Austrian composer W.A. Mozart to update the sparse orchestration, which had consisted primarily of strings, with selected numbers employing trumpets and tympani. Even though the chorus grew into the thousands by the late nineteenth and early twentieth centuries, an increased appreciation of Baroque instrumentation in recent times has prompted a return to a more "original" setting.

Messiah was originally intended as an Easter oratorio, as the dates of its early performances suggested, but popular usage has since brought it into the realm of Christmas music. The three principal parts comprise 53 numbers, but most Christmas performances utilize only part one, which emphasizes the Old Testament prophecies of the coming of Christ and a few passages from New Testament accounts of the Nativity. Favorite choruses include "For unto Us a Child Is Born" and "Glory to God." Often the "Hallelujah Chorus," which concludes part two, is used as a finale to the Christmas section. Part two portrays Christ's passion, resurrection, and the spreading of the Gospel; and part three, an epilogue, depicts the promise of redemption through Christ at the final Judgment.

Whereas in most of Handel's other oratorios the soloists represent specific characters, no characters exist in *Messiah*. Instead, soloists and chorus alike describe the life of Christ indirectly and almost completely through Old Testament prophets, the New Testament being used primarily in part three for the thanksgiving when Christ conquers death. Music scholars cite two reasons for this. First, in the eighteenth century, the general was more often favored over the particular, the abstract preferred over the concrete. Second, an indirect approach often (though not always) circumvented the puritanical objection that sinful entertainers defiled holy writ in theaters.

Mexico

Local customs may vary from region to region, but a number of traditions prevail throughout the country. As in most Latin American countries, the Advent season includes the Feast of the Immaculate Conception (December 8, discussed as a separate entry) and the Feast of Our Lady of Guadalupe (December 12). This latter event commemorates the appearance of the Virgin Mary to the Indian Juan Diego, believed to have occurred in 1531 in the city of Guadalupe Hidalgo (now known as Gustavo A. Madero) in Mexico. The event consists of processions, prayers, songs, dances, and fireworks to honor *La Reina de México* ("The Queen of Mexico"; that is, the Virgin). Celebrations continue with the nine days' fiesta of *Las Posadas* ("The Lodgings," discussed as a separate entry), celebrated from December 16 to 24. A Novena also commences at this time with special *Misas del Aguinaldo* ("Masses of the Gift") during the nine days before Christmas. (The subjects of the Novena are discussed in the introductions to **Central America** and **South America**.) Following the *Misa del Gallo* ("Mass of the Rooster," Midnight Mass), on *Noche Buena* (literally "Good Night," Christmas Eve), families return to their homes for a traditional Christmas dinner of roast turkey, ham, suckling pig, steak, fish, regional dishes, doughnuts, *rompope* (eggnog with cinnamon and rum or grain alcohol), *ponche* (hot fruit punch), and *sidra* (cider); for the thrifty reveler, *tamales* with *atole* (corn gruel) and *tortillas*. Festivities, which extend into the early hours of Christmas morning, include gifts for the children from *El Niño Dios* ("The Christ Child"), a piñata (discussed under **Las Posadas**), and *luces de Belen* ("lights of Bethlehem," sparklers). *Navidad* (Christmas Day) itself is a day of rest.

Los Santos Inocentes (Holy Innocents Day), observed on December 28, is a memorial to those children whom King Herod the Great slaughtered in Bethlehem in his attempt to exterminate the infant Jesus. A day for foolishness and pranks similar to the American April Fools' Day, its activities are vestiges of the European medieval Feast of Fools. Victims of practical jokes receive mock gifts and are branded "Fool Saints" or *inocentes*.

Día de los Reyes (Day of the Kings), Epiphany, January 6, commemorates the Three Kings' visit to the manger and is the principal gift-giving day of the season. On the night before, children fill their shoes with hay for the Magi's camels and set these out on window sills for the *Reyes Magos* (Magi) to fill with gifts. A special event is the cutting of a *Rosca de Reyes* (Kings' Cake), a round, sweet bread with a small, ceramic *muñeco* (doll) symbolizing the Christ Child baked inside. Whoever receives the doll in his slice must host a party for the others present on *Día de Candelaria* (Candlemas), February 2, a day which formerly ended the Christmas season in the Roman Catholic Church.

Santa Claus and Christmas trees play minor roles if any, and only through American influence. The principal holiday display in each home consists of the *Nacimiento* (Nativity scene) or the *Pesebre*, a more elaborate version with miniature reconstructions of pastoral scenes along with the traditional stable, *misterios* (figures of the Holy Family), animals, angels, shepherds, and Wise Men. Custom dictates that the manger receives the Christ Child figure only on Christmas Eve, and the Magi are moved forward each day, "arriving" only on Epiphany. A tiny, decorated Christmas tree, often a local shrub, may accompany the scene. Other typical decorations include poinsettias.

"Merry Christmas" is in Spanish, *Feliz Navidad*.

See also **Candlemas; Epiphany; Farolitos and Luminarias; Feast of Fools; Holy Innocents Day; Mass of the Rooster; Nativity Scene; Poinsettia; Las Posadas.**

MGM Cartoon Christmas

(1993). Video collection of four classic, theatrical animated cartoon "shorts" from the animation department of Metro-Goldwyn-Mayer Studios:

Alias St. Nick (1935). A cat dresses as Santa in an attempt to catch a family of mice who have just read "A Visit from St. Nicholas." Produced by Hugh Harman and Rudolf Ising. Directed by Rudolf Ising.

The Pups' Christmas (1936). Two puppies and their children-masters create havoc among the gifts early Christmas morning. By the time the parents arise, virtually all the toys are broken. Produced by Hugh Harman and Rudolf Ising. Directed by Rudolf Ising.

Peace on Earth (1939). Upon hearing his elder sing "Peace on Earth," a young squirrel wonders what has become of all humans on earth, then learns that the ravages of war eliminated them. The surviving animals soon begin a new society based on biblical principles, which the humans ignored. The imminent involvement of the United States in World War II prompted this cartoon as a declaration on the futility of war. In 1950, it received an Academy Award nomination for Best Short Subject Cartoons. Voice: Mel Blanc. Produced by Fred Quimby. Directed by Hugh Harman.

In 1955, this cartoon was remade under the title *Good Will to Men* with the theme of nuclear disaster. It also received a similar Academy Award nomination in 1956. Produced by Fred Quimby. Produced and directed by William Hanna and Joseph Barbera.

The Peachy Cobbler (1950). Based on the fairy tale "The Elves and the Shoemaker." When a poor cobbler shares his last crust of bread with birds, they reward his generosity by transforming themselves into elves and finishing his work as he sleeps. Narrated by Daws Butler. Written by Rich Hogan. Produced by Fred Quimby. Directed by Tex Avery. *See* **The Elves and the Shoemaker.**

VHS: Warner Home Video. 35 min.

See also **Hanna-Barbera Christmas Cartoons; Tom and Jerry's Night before Christmas.**

Mickey's Christmas Carol

See **A Christmas Carol** (Film and Television Versions)

Mickey's Magical Christmas: Snowed In at the House of Mouse

(2001). Made-for-video animated cartoon, a spin-off of the Disney television series *The House of Mouse* that aired weekly on the ABC network from 2001 to 2002. *The House of Mouse*, about a cartoon nightclub run by Mickey Mouse and his friends, continues in syndication.

When a blizzard traps everyone at the House of Mouse on Christmas Eve, Mickey provides holiday entertainment designed to boost their Christmas spirits. All the Disney-character patrons are certainly lively, except for dispirited Donald Duck, who quacks "Humbug!" To cheer up Donald, Mickey provides a variety of merry songs, skits, and cartoons. The latter include *Donald on Ice* with his three nephews, Huey, Dewey, and Louie; and *The Nutcracker*, a brief, comical retelling of the classic fairy tale narrated by John Cleese, with Minnie Mouse as Maria, Mickey as the Nutcracker, Professor Ludwig von Drake doubling as Drosselmeyer and the King of the Sugar-Plum Fairies, Donald as the Mouse King wearing Mickey Mouse ears, and Goofy as a magical snow fairy. Also featured is the classic cartoon short, *Pluto's Christmas Tree* (1952), with Pluto, Mickey, and chipmunks Chip and Dale. Rounding out the last half of the program is the feature film short, *Mickey's Christmas Carol* (1983), shown in its entirety. As the program closes, the patrons, including a now-jolly Donald, all join together and sing "The Best Christmas of All," which showcases virtually the entire repertoire of Disney characters.

Featured voices: Wayne Allwine (Mickey Mouse), Russi Taylor (Minnie Mouse), Tony Anselmo (Donald Duck), Tress MacNeille (Daisy Duck), and Bill Farmer (Goofy). Words and music to "The Best Christmas of All" by Randy Petersen and Kevin Quinn. *The House of Mouse* written by Thomas Hart; produced by Melinda Rediger; directed by Tony Craig and Roberts Gannaway. *Donald on Ice* written by Jess Winfield. *The Nutcracker* written by Thomas Hart. *Pluto's Christmas Tree* written by Bill Berg and Milt Schaffer. Walt Disney Productions. DVD: Disney Studios. 65 min.

See also **Mickey's Christmas Carol** under **A Christmas Carol** (Film and Television Versions).

Mickey's Once upon a Christmas

(1999). Made-for-video animated cartoon, featuring Disney characters in three Christmas tales:

Donald: Stuck on Christmas. This story is a parody of William Dean Howells's classic short story, "Christmas Every Day." Each day of the year becomes Christmas when Donald's nephews make a wish upon a star on Christmas night. After a few days of the same presents, Christmas dinner, and family visits, their Christmas spirits wear thin, and pandemonium reigns when Huey, Dewey, and Louie seek respite from boredom. Screenplay by Charlie Cohen. Directed by Bradley Raymond.

A Very Goofy Christmas. Goofy's son Max had doubts about Santa after listening to his next-door-neighbor Pete, but Max's spirits really tumble when he discovers Goofy impersonating the gift-giving icon. A true believer, Goofy sets a proper example as the two surprise less fortunate neighbors with a feast and gifts, then Goofy sets out to prove that Santa is real. On Christmas Eve, after many chilly hours in vigil atop his roof with no sign of Santa, Goofy's faith falters, and now it is Max's turn to impersonate Santa. As father and son take comfort in the fact that they only tried to give each other happiness, they are ultimately rewarded by a visit from the real McCoy. Screenplay by Scott Gorden, Tom Nance, and Carter Crocker. Directed by Jun Falkenstein and Bill Speers.

Mickey and Minnie's Gift of the Magi. A contemporary version of O. Henry's classic short story "The Gift of the Magi." Short on cash for Christmas gifts, Mickey sells his beloved harmonica to buy Minnie a beautiful necklace for her heirloom watch, and Minnie sells her watch to purchase a special case for Mickey's harmonica. Screenplay by Richard Cray and Temple Mathews. Directed by Toby Shelton.

Following the stories, the cast gathers to sing a final round of familiar, secular Christmas carols.

In 2000, this picture was nominated for two awards: an Annie Award for Outstanding Achievement in an Animated Home Video Production and a Golden Reel Award for Best Sound Editing.

Narrated by Kelsey Grammer. Narration written by Thomas Hart and Eddie Guzelian. Principal voices: Wayne Allwine, Russi Taylor, Tony Anselmo, Diane Michelle, Tress MacNeille, Alan Young, Bill Farmer, Corey Burton, Shaun Fleming, and Jim Cummings. Walt Disney Productions. DVD: Disney Studios. 70 min.

See also **Christmas Every Day; The Gift of the Magi; Mickey's Twice upon a Christmas.**

Mickey's Twice upon a Christmas

(2004). Made-for-video, computer-generated, animated cartoon. Preoccupation with the hustle and bustle, glitter, and materialism of Christmas preparations leaves Disney characters with anything but "peace on earth" in five holiday tales. The production thus emphasizes the virtues of selflessness, giving, and goodwill over greed and commercialism during the holidays.

Belles on Ice. Though they are good friends, at the holiday ice show, skaters Minnie Mouse and Daisy Duck each believe that they are the stars and attempt increasingly more difficult moves to outdo the other, until one of them is injured. Then they realize that it would have been better to share the limelight rather than to steal it. Champion skater Michelle Kwan was a model for the animators.

Christmas Impossible. Undeserving of Santa's attention this year, Donald Duck's nephews Huey, Dewie, and Louie feel that their only recourse is to break into Santa's abode and add their names to his "Nice List." But unforgettable lessons are in store for the little delinquents.

Christmas Maximus. When Max brings girlfriend Mona home for the holidays to meat his father Goofy, Max, fearing that Goofy will embarrass him, urges his father to be on his very best behavior. But though Goofy's naturally goofy behavior is abominable to Max, Mona respects Goofy for just being himself.

Donald's Gift. Against his wish to forego the hassle of Christmas, Donald Duck reluctantly accompanies Daisy and his nephews to the mall. If the Christmas mob wasn't enough, everywhere Donald goes, he hears the same carol over and over, until he becomes crazed with desire to escape. Eventually, the spirit of Christmas overtakes him.

Mickey's Dog-Gone Christmas. When Mickey severely scolds Pluto for accidentally ruining the Christmas decorations, Pluto runs away and finds himself on a train bound for the North Pole. Basking in the cheery atmosphere there with reindeer for companions, Pluto soon becomes homesick for Mickey; the latter, in turn, has run himself ragged searching for Pluto. Predictably, they are reunited, yet each has learned the importance of friends and family at Christmas.

Principal voices: Wayne Allwine, Tony Anselmo, Jeff Bennett, Jim Cummings, Michelle Kwan, and Russi Taylor. Written by Chad Fiveash, Peggy Holmes, Bill Motz, Matthew O'Callaghan, and James Patrick Stoteraux. Produced by Pam Marsden-Siragusa. Directed by Matthew O'Callaghan. Disney Studios. DVD: Walt Disney Home Entertainment. 68 min.

See also **Mickey's Once upon a Christmas**.

Middle East

Christmas is observed in only a few countries of the Middle East because Islam and Judaism are the prevailing religions in this part of the world. Because Armenia is predominantly Christian, Christmas in that country is discussed as a separate entry.

A favorite bit of folklore among the Christians in this part of the world holds that, at midnight on Epiphany Eve (January 5), all the trees of the world pay homage to the Christ Child by bowing their trunks and branches. According to another legend, when Christ was born, all the trees of the world bloomed in midwinter to celebrate His glory.

• IRAN. Most of the Christian minority celebrate Christmas according to the traditions of the Eastern Church and follow the Julian calendar. As opposed to Easter, known as the "Big Feast," Christmas is known as the "Little Feast." The first 25 days of December are spent in fasting ("Little Fast" as opposed to Easter, "Big Fast," which commences with Lent), with abstinence from animal or dairy products. The fast is broken after the early morning Mass on Christmas Day, when the traditional *harasa* (chicken stew) is served. Formerly Santa Claus was unknown and gift exchanges were not traditional, though children usually received a new outfit of clothes. Western influences in the twentieth century brought the Christmas tree and gifts for children from *Baba Noel* (Santa Claus). "Merry Christmas" is spoken in Farsi: "*Cristmas-e-shoma mobarak bashad.*"

• IRAQ. Five percent of the population is Christian. Of the six major Christian denominations in Iraq, the largest is the Chaldean Church of the East, which follows the Julian calendar for ecclesiastical observances. Thus Christmas is observed on January 7. On Christmas Eve, the family, carrying lighted candles, gathers outdoors around a bonfire of thorns for a reading of the Gospel. The complete burning of the thorns to ashes predicts good luck. Afterwards, each family member makes a wish and jumps over the ashes three times. A similar fire burns in the churchyard on Christmas Day as the priest, holding an effigy of the Christ Child, leads a procession. At the conclusion of the service, the priest initiates the Touch of Peace by touching the person next to him, who in turn touches his neighbor, and so forth, until the Touch has fallen on all the congregation. Again, Western influences brought Christmas trees and *Baba Noel* (Santa) in the late twentieth century. "Merry Christmas" is said in Arabic: "*Idah Saidan Wa Sanah Jadidah.*" *See also* **Christmas Old Style, Christmas New Style**.

• ISRAEL. Christmas celebrations are observed principally in Bethlehem by the Eastern Orthodox, Roman Catholic, and Armenian faiths, the chief Christian denominations. On the eastern fringes of the city are a series of open plains, where tradition holds that the shepherds keeping watch over their flocks by night received the "good tidings of great joy" from the angelic host. Thus, these plains are known as the Shepherds' Fields; one is controlled by the Orthodox Church, one by the Catholics, and a third by the YMCA, the latter featuring a Christmas Eve carol singing service in the early evening.

Also on Christmas Eve, the Latin (Roman Catholic) Patriarch of Jerusalem and his procession travel the five miles to Bethlehem, and, passing through Manger Square, arrive at the Church of St. Catherine, where Midnight Mass is held. During the ceremony, the procession crosses a courtyard to the Church of the Nativity, a medieval structure built over the cave traditionally revered as the place of Christ's birth. There, the patriarch descends to the Grotto of the Nativity and places a life-size statue of the Infant Jesus in a crib. The service is telecast on large screens to thousands congregating in Manger Square. The only Protestant service is

A view of Bethlehem (also called Beit Lahm in some older sources) in the 1850s. From William M. Thomson, The Land and the Book *(New York: Harper & Bros., 1859[?]).*

Anglican, and is held in a Greek monastery near the Church of the Nativity.

Because the Armenians of Jerusalem and the Orthodox Church subscribe to the Julian calendar for ecclesiastical services, their Christmas observances are held on January 19 and January 7, respectively.

"Merry Christmas" might be heard in Hebrew: *Mo'adim Lesimkha*; or in Arabic: *Idah Saidan Wa Sanah Jadidah. See also* **Armenia; Christmas Old Style, Christmas New Style; Church of the Nativity.**

• LEBANON. Some 25 percent of the population is Christian, belonging to the Maronite (branch of the Roman Catholic Church), Orthodox, Armenian, and Protestant churches. The Orthodox and Armenian faiths particularly adhere to the Julian calendar for ecclesiastical observances.

The Christmas season opens on St. Barbara's Day, December 4 (*see* **Advent**), with feasting, charitable acts, and masked children soliciting goodies from homes. At the family feast, someone portrays St. Barbara, dressed in white with

a crown. Muslims in Lebanon often participate in secular Christmas Eve celebrations including dinner and presents, particularly when the Muslim holy month of Ramadan coincides with the Christmas season.

During the weeks prior to Christmas, shops are decorated with Western paraphernalia, and Christmas trees, consisting of plastic varieties or of cypress branches, are decorated with shooting stars, colored balls, tinsel, or homemade ornaments. Tradition once held that children received holiday gifts only on New Year's Day, but now Christmas brings *Papa Noel* (Santa Claus) and gifts as well, and the Social Affairs Ministry in Beruit may sponsor gift parties for those children and orphans who have suffered from the ravages of war.

Christmas Eve is spent strictly as a religious holiday, and total fasting commences at sundown in preparation for the Midnight Mass and communion. Immediately prior to the Mass, young men demonstrate their skill in ringing an array of church bells, heralding the service. During the service, which extends nearly until dawn, it is customary to have a young infant brought forward to the altar. There as the priest rests the Holy Book on its head, he reads the Gospel account of the Nativity. As the service closes, the priest initiates the *Salaam* (Touch of Peace) by touching the person to his right, who touches the one next to him, and so forth, until the Touch has fallen on all the congregation. Afterwards, families retire to social gatherings and visitations, where the traditional offering is sugar-coated almonds, and the Christmas menu features roast turkey.

Christians and Muslims celebrate New Year's Day alike with social gatherings and games of chance that predict the future. Children traditionally receive a monetary token from their father at this time. "Merry Christmas" is said in Arabic: *Idah Saidan Wa Sanah Jadidah.*

• SAUDI ARABIA. The country is entirely Muslim, and public celebrations of Christmas are not tolerated in any form. However, Europeans and other foreign Christian settlements, such as those housing personnel working with various oil companies, are permitted to hold private holiday observances according to the customs of their parent countries.

• SYRIA. The Christian minority primarily

belongs to the Orthodox and Armenian churches. Families gather outdoors on Christmas Eve with lighted candles and ignite a bonfire. While singing carols, the family observes the fire, for its pattern of burning predicts the type of luck in store for the new year. After the fire dies out, each person makes a wish and jumps over the embers. Christmas Eve services also include a bonfire of vines to honor the Magi. Christmas Day is spent quietly with a predawn Church service, and the dinner may consist of chicken, oranges, nuts, and pastries.

On Epiphany eve, the Gentle camel of Jesus or Youngest Camel brings gifts to children. According to legend, the youngest camel in the Magi's caravan en route to Bethlehem nearly expired from exhaustion. Determined to see the Christ Child, the camel's faith and resolve brought great reward, for the Babe granted the little camel immortality. He now returns each year as the bearer of Syrian Christmas gifts. Before retiring for bed, children often prepare bowls of water and wheat for the camel, who rewards the good with gifts and the naughty with a black mark on the wrist. "Merry Christmas" is said in Arabic: *Idah Saidan Wa Sanah Jadidah.*

• TURKEY. Islam predominates, Turkey's Christians numbering less than one percent of the population. Following the Orthodox faith, they observe Christmas on the Julian calendar, January 7. Christmas is a three-day festival with feasting and entertaining. Typical cuisine includes coffee, sweetmeats, fruit, *lebban* (sour milk), *baklava* (honey cake), *etli fasulye* (broth with beans and lamb), *ic pilar* (rice with pine nuts), *labmacun dolmasi* (stuffed cabbage leaves), *borek* (fried pastry stuffed with meat or cheese), tomato-and-cucumber salad with olive oil and vinegar, and *kadayif* (fruit pastry). "Merry Christmas" in Turkish is *Noeliniz Ve Yeni Yiliniz Kutlu Olsun. See also* **Christmas Old Style, Christmas New Style; Epiphany.**

A Midnight Clear: Stories for the Christmas Season

Collection of 12 contemporary short stories with inspirational messages of hope and peace, written by American author Katherine Paterson, published in 1995. She wrote these stories over a number of years for her husband, the Rev. John B. Paterson, to read to his congregation each Christmas Eve. The following paragraphs briefly summarize these stories:

"A Midnight Clear." Ever since his mother's divorce, Christmas has had little meaning for teenager Jeff Pitman. As far as he is concerned, carols, decorations, and even Santa are just "fake." But when he befriends Rosie Dodson, an elderly, homeless bag lady, he gains a new perspective on the holiday.

"Merit Badges." Kate Hensen, a 12-year-old Girl Scout, initially dreads making the required visit to a local nursing home at Christmastime. But when she finds a lonely resident who had lost her husband and daughter years before, child and senior citizen lay aside their stereotypical images of each other's generation and form a genuine friendship, instead of one contrived to gain a merit badge.

"Watchman, Tell Us of the Night." The title of this story derives from the carol of the same name. Passing the long hours on Christmas Eve as a department store night watchman, Gary considers himself a failure for having lost his family's farm. He has prayed for a miracle, but God has never answered, so he thinks, until he discovers a little baby boy abandoned in a crate behind the store. This is a different kind of miracle, one not unlike that which occurred two millennia ago. At that time, the world needed a miracle, and God also gave a baby. (*See also* **Watchman, Tell Us of the Night.**)

"A Stubborn Sweetness." Although the message of Christ is often "swallowed up quickly in the cry of anger or the clack of greed," it sweetly and stubbornly persists, never waning. It could have provided a father with strength when his son perished in Vietnam; instead, the father became bitter and lost his faith. It can steer a 14-year-old, now pregnant, a runaway, and a would-be robber, in the right direction, if she will yield to its call.

"No Room in the Inn." With his parents away for the holidays, Ben looks forward to time alone in "the Inn," his mother's expression for their bed-and-breakfast home in Vermont. The establishment is closed for Christmas, yet on one snowy night an impoverished drifter with his wife and three small children seek shelter there from the freezing weather. At first, Ben is most reluctant to accommodate them, but when the message found in "Silent Night" and "Away in a Manger" haunt him, he makes other arrangements.

"Poor Little Innocent Lamb." Old Lettie has remained a bitter recluse for years, preferring her account books over society. When her eight-year-old grandniece Travis arrives to live with her, it is old Isaiah, Lettie's black farm hand, who becomes a surrogate father, for Lettie simply ignores the child in every respect, except to scold. To make Travis's lonely days more enjoyable and to give her some responsibility, Isaiah assigns her the task of caring for a newborn lamb abandoned by its mother, a pet Travis names "Orphan Annie." On Christmas Eve, after the frisky lamb makes a shambles of the dinner table, throwing Lettie into storms of rage with threats of slaughterhouses, Travis bolts with Annie and would run away. Instead, Isaiah carries them both to see the Christmas play at his church, where Annie steals the show as the only live lamb "abiding in the fields" with the shepherds. Inspired, Travis brings the entire troupe back to sing carols and reprise the play for Lettie. And despite her protests, as the cast sings the spiritual "Rise Up, Shepherd, and Follow," wise Isaiah places "Baby Jesus" (his little grandnephew) into Lettie's arms, for she was never in greater need of such a moment as now. (*See also* **Rise Up, Shepherd, and Follow.**)

In 2002, this story was adapted for television under the title *Miss Lettie and Me*, starring Mary Tyler Moore as Miss Lettie, Holliston Coleman as Travis, and Charles Robinson as Isaiah. In 2003, the picture was nominated for three awards: the American Society of Cinematographers' Award for Outstanding Achievement in Cinematography in Movies of the Week/Mini-Series/Pilot for Cable or Pay TV; a Young Artist Award for Best Family Television Movie or Special; and a Young Artist Award for Best Supporting Young Actress in a Television Movie (Holliston Coleman). Teleplay by Dalene Young. Produced by Jim Westman. Directed by Ian Barry. Magnus Global Entertainment, the Polson Company, Turner Network Television, and Viacom Productions. DVD: Paramount Home Video. 90 min.

"In the Desert, a Highway." The title of this story derives from the command in Isaiah 40:3 to "make straight in the desert a highway for our God." Comrade Wong, a college teacher in Communist China, is introduced to Christianity when Old Lee, an illiterate Christian and night watchman, covertly asks her to read the Bible to him. To reward her kindness at Christmastime, Old Lee repairs her shoes. Eventually, both are exiled to a prison camp deep in the interior, where inmates are building a highway to an unknown destination. As another Christmas approaches, Comrade Wong discovers that the lining of her badly worn shoes had been constructed from pages of Old Lee's Bible. The good man, who now lies at the point of death, had wanted her to have part of his Bible as a Christmas gift, in case circumstances later prevented their reading together. The last words that he hears are those of true comfort, read from the lining itself, beginning with Isaiah 40:1, which prophesizes the coming of Christ: "Comfort ye, comfort ye my people, saith your God."

"Star Lady." Desiring to win a Christmas star in Sunday school for visiting those who are allegedly destitute, eight-year-old Buddy Collins targets Rosamund McCormick, a proud, lonely widow. Although Buddy means well, Rosamund tolerates his persistence and childish sympathy, until a rumor arises that she is penniless and about to be evicted. Hardly anything could be further from the truth, for Rosamund, a lady of considerable means, is merely selling her house and moving to Florida. But rather than see Buddy suffer embarrassment and lose his star because he targeted the wrong person, and because she really does need a friend, Rosamund swallows her pride and attends the Christmas Eve service at Buddy's church as his "Star Lady."

"Amazing Grace." While traveling to visit family late on Christmas Eve, Paul and his pregnant wife Margaret become stranded in the Appalachian foothills. They find shelter from the inclement weather in an old cabin just in time, for Margaret soon delivers her firstborn son. Though the couple are atheists, they receive aid from the religious residents, the oldest of whom believes that the baby is a miraculous sign from heaven at this season.

"Exultate Jubilate" (Latin: "Rejoice, Be

Glad"). A cynical man, seeing the world filled with greed, self-destruction, and cruelty, cannot fathom the immeasurable joy that his wife and two young children experience at Christmastime. Ironically, it is not his family's holiday ebullience that provides the cynic with a sense of inner peace, but that of a young man selling evergreens door-to-door late on Christmas Eve. The man's innocence, his willingness to help assemble a Christmas toy, and his passion for the sacred music of Mozart are such that the cynic wonders whether his visitor had not indeed been an angel.

"The Handmaid of the Lord." For the past two years, Rachel Thompson's performances in the children's Christmas play at church have brought laughter to the congregation but embarrassment to the directors. Because she takes her parts quite seriously and can be over-dramatic, this year Rachel will be the "understudy" for the entire cast, a position equivalent to being cast out. There's hope when Carrie Wilson, "Mary," breaks both arms a few days before the play, but Carrie's appearance at the last moment dashes Rachel's dream of that coveted role. Worse, because her little brother is playing Baby Jesus, Rachel feels that only a relative — herself — should play Mary. The performance goes well, until Baby Jesus begins to bawl, paralyzing Carrie with fright. Rachel then jumps onstage to pacify her brother, assumes the role of Mary, and delivers inspirational yet unscripted lines. This time, no one laughs.

"My Name Is Joseph." This story draws a rough parallel between the journey of Joseph and Mary to Bethlehem and a young family's escape to freedom. Fleeing their war-torn village in Central America, the Indian Joseph, his pregnant wife Elena Maria, and their small boys suffer much hardship on their journey north. Their goal is to reach the freedom of the United States through Mexico, and with Elena at term, it's a race against time. But with the help of convents and mission houses along the way, the family is successfully, albeit illegally, smuggled into Texas by Christmas, when Elena gives birth to a little girl, Esperanza. Translated into English, her name symbolizes all that remains for her people — Hope.

Katherine Paterson has won multiple awards for her children's books, including the Newbery Medal and the National Book Award. Another collection of her Christmas stories is entitled *Angels and Other Strangers: Family Christmas Stories* (1979), discussed as a separate entry.

Midnight Mass
See **Christmas Masses**

Milk Grotto
Shrine in Bethlehem, Israel, located a short distance southeast of the Church of the Nativity. It is an irregular grotto hollowed out of soft, white rock. According to legend, before they fled to Egypt, the Holy Family hid at this site to escape King Herod the Great's Slaughter of the Innocents, the latter of whom were supposedly buried on this site following the massacre. As Mary nursed the Infant Jesus, a drop of her milk allegedly fell to the stone floor, which instantly became chalky white. Franciscans erected a chapel in this grotto in the fifteenth century, and the present structure, decorated with mother-of-pearl carvings, dates to 1872. Because the white rock is believed to aid in lactation, nursing mothers make pilgrimages to the shrine to obtain bits of the white rock, which are ground, mixed with liquids, and consumed while nursing. Other women place a fragment of rock under their mattresses to achieve the same results.

See also **Church of the Nativity; Holy Innocents Day; Nativity.**

Miracle Down Under
See **The Christmas Visitor**

Miracle in the Wilderness: A Christmas Story of Colonial America
Inspirational novella by American author Paul Gallico, published in 1955.

The setting is Christmas Eve, 1755, in the British colonies of North America. In league with the French, who are determined to stop English settlers from spreading into the Ohio Valley, a raiding party of Algonquin Indians pushes northward with three prisoners — the frontiersman Jasper Adams, his wife Dorcas, and their eight-month-old infant son, Asher. Recently captured and their cabin burned, the man and woman have been severely beaten, yet lead warrior Quanta-wa-neh demands that they keep pace, lest they suffer immediate execution rather than inevitably later.

As the party approaches a clearing, the moonlight shines upon three white-tailed deer — a buck, doe, and fawn — facing the east and kneeling as if in worship. The Indians have never seen the like, especially a fawn born out of season, and reason that a magical moment is at hand. Even Adams, whether in truth or from a delusion brought on by his agony, witnesses the Holy Child lying in a cradle before him, while the beasts, empowered with speech, give thanks and praise to God. Realizing that the hour is midnight, the traditional hour of Christ's birth, Adams and Dorcas fall to their knees, the deer rise and depart, and Quanta-wa-neh would know the meaning of this "magic." As if inspired by God, Adams gains strength and presents the simple story of the birth of Christ from the Gospels of Matthew and Luke and adds a legend that three animals knelt and made contributions to the Christ Child: the ox provided his straw for a bed, the ass provided her milk, and the sheep provided the warmth of his wool. Adams continues with a summary of the life of Christ, then concludes with His death, burial, and resurrection. Even though the Indians cannot fathom parts of the story, they easily comprehend the concepts of a star, shepherds, wise men, kings, spirits, and the inhumanity of those who turned Mary and Joseph away. And the animals' speech, according to Adams, was a prayer for God to protect them from hunger, thirst, and predators, and that they all live together in peace with love for one another.

At that moment, news arrives that a band of English and Iroquois are not far behind, and Quanta-wa-neh must press onward. But because Adams' story weighs heavily upon him and Adams' God should not be offended at this time of His Son's birth, the warrior spares the lives of his prisoners and leaves them on their own. On Christmas Day, they are rescued by the English party.

In 1992, the novella was adapted for television under the title *Miracle in the Wilderness*, starring Kris Kristofferson as Jericho Adams, Kim Cattrall as wife Dora, Peter Morris as Asher, and Sheldon Peters Wolfchild as Blackfoot Chief Many Horses. The setting is moved to the American Northwest, where Dora relates the Christmas story, while Adams converts the narration into characters more familiar to the Blackfoot.

In this version, Mary, a 14-year-old Indian maiden, is to be wed to the brave Joseph, a mighty hunter. An eagle ("winged messenger") brings the Annunciation to Mary, while the Great Spirit, appearing as a white stallion, encourages Joseph in a dream to take Mary as his wife, regardless of her pregnancy. The two journey across the plains to the annual Sun Dance, where many different tribes convene, such as the Sioux, Cheyenne, Cherokee, and Cree. At Jesus' birth, the ox kneels and, empowered with speech, asks that the animals be protected from hunger and thirst, and that everyone live together in peace. Three Wise Men come bearing gifts: a Sioux with a peace pipe, a Mandan with a medicine bag and beaver skins, and a Plains Cree with a bow and quiver of arrows.

The picture concludes by showing a portion of a statement made in 1896 by Mountain Chief, last war chief of the Blackfoot Nation. He asked, regarding the time of winter feasting, was it because of the cold that everyone sat around honoring each other, or was it because that was the time when the white man's God was born a baby boy?

Teleplay by Michael Michaelian and Jim Byrnes. Produced by Wayne Morris. Directed by Kevin James Dobson. A Ruddy and Morgan Production with Turner Network Television. VHS: Warner Home Video. 88 min.

Paul Gallico (1897–1976) was a freelance writer of fiction and sports articles. His best-known works include *The Snow Goose* (1941) and *The Poseidon Adventure* (1969).

Miracle on Evergreen Terrace
See **The Simpsons**

Miracle on 34th Street

Highly popular motion picture drama of 1947 with two principal remakes, among others. Based on a story by screenwriter Valentine Davies about a man convinced that he is Santa Claus. Having annually enjoyed Macy's Thanksgiving Day parade from his New York City apartment, Davies, concerned over Christmas commercialism, is said to have conceived the idea for *Miracle* while waiting in line at a department store.

Motion pictures are often based on a previously published book or story, but with *Miracle on 34th Street*, the film came first. Davies pitched the idea to his friend George Seaton, who not only wrote the screenplay for the 1947 picture and the 1994 remake, but directed the original picture as well. Only after the 1947 film's release did Davies receive any invitation to publish his story as a little novel. Compared to the film versions, though, the novel pales in popularity.

• 1947 MOTION PICTURE VERSION. When a jolly old gentleman named Kris Kringle (Edmund Gwenn) replaces a drunken Santa in Macy's Thanksgiving Day parade, store representative Doris Walker (Maureen O'Hara) hires him to play Santa in their toy department. Kris forms a close relationship with Doris and her six-year-old daughter, Susan (nine-year-old Natalie Wood), but finds that personal problems have made them skeptics toward fantasy, Santa Claus, and love.

Realizing that Susan has lead a much too serious life, devoid of simple childhood pleasures, Kris introduces her to the world of imagination by teaching her how to pretend to be a monkey. Kris's kind manner, real beard, and ability to converse with a little Dutch girl in her native language at Macy's almost convince Susan that Kris is truly Santa. To test him, she requests a real house for her mother and herself, instead of a New York apartment.

Because Kris insists that he is Santa Claus, he states on Macy's employment card that he was born at the North Pole, that the eight reindeer are his next of kin, and that he is "as old as my tongue and a little bit older than my teeth." At this, Doris arranges for Kris to undergo a mental status examination from Macy's psychologist, where an altercation with the latter lands Kris in a mental hospital, and a court mental competency hearing follows on Christmas Eve. Defended by Doris's friend, attorney Fred Gailey (John Payne), Kris is declared to be Santa Claus when the U.S. Postal Service delivers thousands of letters to Kris at the courthouse.

On Christmas morning, Fred, Doris, and Susan attend a social at the Brooks Memorial Home for the Aged, where Kris is resident and host, but Susan's failure to find some evidence of her dream house under the Christmas tree shatters her newly acquired faith in Kris. On the way back to the apartment, however, a beaming Susan discovers a particular house for sale and insists that it's *her* house, that Kris meant for her to have it. Doris and Fred only humor her whim, until they spy Kris's cane standing by the fireplace and become total believers.

Instead of a Christmastime release, *Miracle* premiered in May 1947, because Darryl F. Zanuck, then-head of Twentieth Century Fox Studios, believed that more people went to the movies in the summer. Therefore the studio launched a most attractive publicity campaign yet deliberately kept secret the fact that this new release sported a holiday theme.

In 1948, this picture won three Academy Awards: Best Supporting Actor (Edmund Gwenn), Best Original Story, and Best Screenplay; and received an Academy nomination for Best Picture. It won two Golden Globe Awards for Best Screenplay and Best Supporting Actor and won the Locarno International Film Festival Prize for Best Adapted Screenplay. On receiving his award, Gwenn remarked, "Now I know there's a Santa Claus!"

With Gene Lockhart, Porter Hall, William Frawley, Jerome Cowan, and Philip Tonge. Written and directed by George Seaton. Produced by William Perlberg. Twentieth Century Fox Film Corporation. DVD: Twentieth Century Fox. B & W. 96 min.

• 1973 MADE-FOR-TELEVISION VERSION. This remake closely follows the original picture, with the following minor differences: Doris Walker becomes Karen Walker (Jane Alexander), and attorney Fred Gailey becomes Bill Schaffner (David Hartman). The characters of Susan Walker (Suzanne Davidson) and Kris Kringle (Sebastian Cabot) remain as before. Kris converses with a little girl in Spanish instead of Dutch; Dr. Pierce at the Brooks Memorial Home for the Aged receives an emphysema machine instead of an x-ray machine; and in Kris's game of pretending, Susan is a clam instead of a monkey.

With Roddy McDowall, Jim Backus, Tom

Bosley, and David Doyle. Written by Jeb Rose-brook. Produced by Norman Rosemont. Directed by Fielder Cook. Twentieth Century Fox Television and Norman Rosemont Productions. Video N/A. 100 min.

• 1994 MOTION PICTURE VERSION. Because Macy's and Gimble's department stores denied the use of their names for this film (though both allowed them for the previous two versions), Macy's becomes C.F. Cole's, and the competition is Shopper's Express. This time Kriss (spelled with a double "s" — Richard Attenborough) resides at the Mt. Carmel Senior Center, wears glasses, sports a shorter beard, communicates with a deaf child by sign language, and falls victim to a plot by Shopper's Express to remove him legally as their competition. Dorey Walker (Elizabeth Perkins) and her daughter Susan (Mara Wilson) remain skeptical as before, and Dorey's friend, attorney Bryan Bedford (Dylan McDermott), defends Kriss without the help of the U.S. Postal Service. Dorey and Bryan wed (in the previous two versions, the couple only contemplate marriage), and Susan wishes for a dream house as well as a baby brother.

Two particular scenes reflect a 1990s sensibility: Bryan does not invoke the name of any specific deity while saying grace before a meal with Dorey and Susan, and the name on the newlyweds' mailbox reads "Walker-Bedford."

With J.T. Walsh, James Remar, Jane Leeves, Simon Jones, William Windom, and Robert Prosky. Written by George Seaton and John Hughes. Produced by John Hughes. Directed by Les Mayfield. Twentieth Century Fox Film Corporation and Hughes Entertainment. DVD: Twentieth Century Fox Home Video. 114 min.

• OTHER VERSIONS. Obscure television adaptations include those for 1955, 1956 (*Meet Mr. Kringle*), and 1959. The 1947 *Miracle* was also the basis for Meredith Willson's 1963 Broadway musical *Here's Love*.

Mr. Magoo's Christmas Carol

See **A Christmas Carol** (Film and Television Versions)

Mr. St. Nick

(2002). American/Canadian made-for-television comedy/fantasy.

Having reigned as the Santa Claus of the twentieth century, King Nicholas XX (Charles Durning) must now pass the role to his son, Prince Nicholas St. Nicholas von Claus (Kelsey Grammer), who prefers the name Nick St. Nick. Yet Nick's fast, playboy lifestyle in Miami Beach and his high-tech, nontraditional attitude toward Christmas so offend the North Pole that King Nicholas would defy tradition and continue as Santa Claus into the twenty-first century. Notwithstanding the rift between father and son, forces more powerful than they dictate that tradition *will* be upheld, lest there be no Christmas. Therefore, as the magic power and jovial spirit slowly depart from King Nicholas, those same attributes fall upon Nick, who eventually and predictably yields to his fate.

As Nick evolves, he naïvely plans Christmas Eve nuptials with Heidi Gardelle (Elaine Hendrix), a local television-personality-turned-con-artist, who persuades an unwitting Nick to endorse a Web site for a phony Christmas charity called "Mr. St. Nick.com," then sets him up to be arrested on charges of embezzlement. After using Santa magic to escape from jail and seeing that villains Heidi and her accomplice receive their just rewards, Nick has little time remaining before returning to the North Pole, where assuming his father's role will complete the transformation to King Nicholas XXI. Yet Nick has not chosen his queen. He finds her at the eleventh hour, so to speak, in Lorena Braga (Ana Ortiz), his attractive yet headstrong Hispanic cook and housekeeper, the epitome of love and unquestioning faith.

Story by Maryedith Burrell and Matthew Jacobs. Teleplay by Maryedith Burrell, Debra Frank, and Steven Hayes. Produced by Camille Grammer, Tom Rowe, and Mary Anne Waterhouse. Directed by Craig Zisk. Hallmark Entertainment (USA) and Mr. St. Nick, Inc. (Canada). DVD: Lionsgate/Fox. 100 min.

Mistletoe

Common name for a variety of small, parasitic, evergreen shrubs with small, green flowers and white, sticky berries, native to the United States (*Phoradendron flavescens*) and Europe (*Viscum album*). They infest trees such

Punch with a woodland sprite in the mistletoe. Punch, *December 1849.*

as apple, pine, fir, juniper, and (rarely) oak; the leafless, flowering, dwarf variety (*Arceuthobium pusillum*) is an exceptionally lethal parasite.

The holiday custom of kissing under sprigs of mistletoe derives in part from the pre-Christian Celtic Druids of Gaul and the British Isles, who held oak trees and mistletoe as highly sacred, probably because they rarely found the latter growing on oaks. In ceremonies to gather the mistletoe from oak trees during the sixth day of the moon, Druid priests wearing long white robes cut the shrub with golden sickles, after which worshippers below caught the mistletoe in white sheets, taking care that the holy plant never touched the ground. Two white bulls were then sacrificed to consecrate the event.

With a name that means "all-heal" in the Celtic language, mistletoe was sought as a medicinal, an antidote for poisons (mistletoe itself is quite toxic), an aphrodisiac, a fertility agent for animals and humans (symbolized by a kiss), and a talisman against evil. Homes usually sported sprigs fastened over doorways for

good luck and as an emblem of goodwill, and guests who passed beneath received kisses of friendship. Along the same line, two enemies meeting under trees bearing mistletoe traditionally observed a truce for a day.

A tale from Scandinavian mythology lends further support for kissing under the mistletoe. The tale concerns Balder, god of light and son of Odin (Woden) and Frigga, king and queen of the Norse gods, respectively. When Balder foresaw his own death in a dream, Frigga exacted a promise from all creatures, elements, and everything that existed on the earth and under it that no harm would befall her son. But in her haste, Frigga overlooked the mistletoe, an error used to the advantage of Balder's enemy, the evil god Loki. As the other gods hurled spears and arrows at the now seemingly invincible Balder, Loki armed an arrow with mistletoe and gave it to Balder's brother, the blind god Hoder, who delivered the fatal shot. Weeping bitter tears that were transformed into the white berries of mistletoe, Frigga ultimately succeeded in reviving her son with acts of love and kindness. In

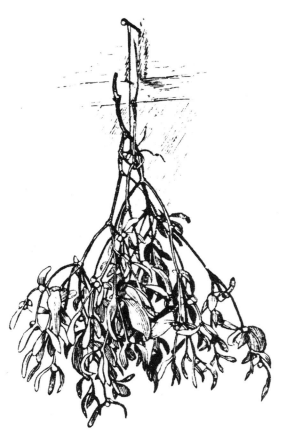

A branch of mistletoe, hung by a cord from a rafter. Illustration by Randolph Caldecott from The Sketch Book of Washington Irving.

her joy, she vowed that nevermore would mistletoe cause harm to anyone, but would symbolize love and goodwill. As a token of those symbols, Frigga kissed all who passed beneath any tree which bore mistletoe and decreed that her subjects would forever do likewise.

Whereas kissing is well associated with mistletoe, the precise origins of its association with Christmas remain unknown. Unlike most pagan winter holiday symbols, which have received Christian analogies, no Christian substitute definitively exists for mistletoe. Some have preferred to interpret the biblical admonition to salute one another with a holy kiss (the kiss of peace, Romans 16:16) as a free license for kissing under the mistletoe.

Until Christmas trees became fashionable in England in the mid-1800s, mistletoe in that country had gained considerable popularity in decorative devices variously termed "kissing boughs," "kissing rings," "kissing balls," and "kissing bunches." These consisted of hoops overlaid with evergreen garland and with streamers extending upward to a central point. Added features may have included apples, nuts, oranges, lighted candles, three small dolls representing the Holy Family, and a sprig of mistletoe hung from the center. Mounted from conspicuous points overhead, kissing boughs encouraged holiday romance, especially during the Victorian era. Traditionally, ladies caught under the bough were to allow themselves to be kissed by a gentleman, and for each kiss bestowed, the gentleman plucked one berry and gave it to the lady; when no berries remained, the kissing bough lost its romantic spell. Another superstition held that a maiden not kissed under the mistletoe at Christmastime would not marry during the coming year.

Banning mistletoe from churches was common during the nineteenth century, the reasons cited ranging from its association with the fertility rites of Druids to an abuse of the kiss of peace as mentioned above. Mistletoe was not altogether banned from medieval churches, however, for at York Minster the clergy often placed a bough of it on the altar at Christmas as a prelude to the traditional pardoning of criminals and other malefactors for the season. The ban was unknown in eighteenth century England, as attested by the dramatist and poet John Gay (1685–1732), who wrote of contemporary "temples" (churches) bedecked with holly, laurel, and mistletoe.

In England and the United States, kissing under the mistletoe has survived as a popular Christmas custom. In Austria, a related custom on New Year's Eve (St. Sylvester's Day) involves the grotesque creature "Sylvester." An old, ugly, pagan entity who wears a wreath of mistletoe and was renamed for the fourth century Pope St. Sylvester I, Sylvester lies in wait for maidens to pass beneath evergreen boughs hanging from the ceiling, when he seizes and kisses them. But at midnight, as a representative of the old year, he is symbolically driven out with the dawning new year.

See also **Christmas Plants**.

The centerpiece of any Moravian Putz is the Nativity scene. Shown here is the manger portion of an elaborate Nativity Putz, with the traditional figures of Mary, Joseph, Infant Jesus, ox, donkey, and lambs. Although not shown, this particular Putz also includes the town of Bethlehem, shepherds in the fields, the announcing angel and heavenly host, larger scale scenes of the shepherds and Wise Men, as well as a scale model of the village of Salem, North Carolina, as it might have appeared in the early 1900s. Used by permission of Gil Frank and the Candle Tea, Women's Fellowship, Home Moravian Church, Winston-Salem, North Carolina, (c) 2001.

Moore, Clement Clarke

See **A Visit from St. Nicholas**

Moravian Church

An evangelical Protestant denomination with historical beginnings in 1457 in what is now the Czech Republic. In the early 1720s, persecuted descendants of that early church sought refuge on the estate of Count Nicholas Ludwig von Zinzendorf in Saxony, Germany, where they completed the renewal of what is now known as the Moravian Church by the end of the 1720s.

Moravians (officially the *Unitas Fratrum* or Unity of the Brethren) arrived in America in 1735, establishing a temporary settlement in Savannah, Georgia, and then permanent settlements in Pennsylvania (e.g., Bethlehem and Lititz) in 1740 and in Salem (now Winston-Salem), North Carolina, in 1753. Today, the Moravians number about 750,000 worldwide, the Moravian Church in America comprising over 54,000 members.

Moravian Christmas customs commence with Advent, its four Sundays presenting in various combinations the themes of Christ's coming: His initial Incarnation on earth in the past, as recorded in the Gospels; His spiritual coming in the present into the hearts of His believers; and His future coming at the final

Judgment. The Moravian Church utilizes two Advent liturgies, one of which is titled "Advent and Palm Sunday," since it is utilized for both occasions. A service of hosannas, it includes the hymn "Hail to the Lord's Anointed," written in 1821 by James Montgomery (1771–1854), an English Moravian who also wrote the familiar carol "Angels, from the Realms of Glory." Petitions of joy, contrition, and praise comprise the second liturgy.

Christmas decorations include those commonly present in respective countries or locales, including the Advent wreath and its candles, yet two remain traditionally Moravian: the Advent Star and the *Putz*.

Large, three-dimensional, multipointed, and illuminated, the Advent Star is hung on the first Sunday of Advent and is taken down on Epiphany, January 6. The Advent Star originated around 1850 at a Moravian school in Niesky, Germany. Subsequently such stars were produced by a former student, Pieter Verbeek, with son Harry at their star factory in Herrnhut (meaning "Lord's safekeeping"), Germany; today the stars are still manufactured and sold in Herrnhut. Hanging in the church or home, the Advent Star serves as a reminder of the stars of Heaven, the Star that guided the Wise Men, and Christ as the Star that arose from Jacob (Numbers 24:17).

The second decoration, the *Putz* (German, "finery"), presents the biblical accounts of the birth of Christ in miniature. Central to the *Putz* are figures of the Holy Family in a stable setting. Around these key elements are often found figures of shepherds and sheep, Wise Men and angels. More elaborate creations may include depictions of Messianic, Old Testament prophecies about the coming of Christ, the Roman census, the meeting of the Wise Men with King Herod, the flight into Egypt, and so forth. There may be realistic landscapes that feature miniature figures of other people in all walks of life in period costume, buildings, streams, assorted animals, moss, trees and other flora, and whatever else the imagination may invent. The figures may be centuries-old heirlooms or purchased elsewhere. A *Putz* may be arranged on a table in the home, adorn the floor beneath the Christmas tree, or consume an entire room, and communities may sponsor a large *Putz*, such as that created annually in Bethlehem, Pennsylvania. Perhaps it was not the first *Putz* to arrive in America, but one of the earliest on record was that erected in Bethabara, North Carolina, in 1760.

Sometime during Advent, many churches host a Candle Tea, sponsored by the Moravian Women's Fellowships. Originally, Candle Teas were work sessions in which colonial Moravian women made beeswax candles for Christmas Eve lovefeasts (discussed below). Today, the agenda for these occasions is quite variable from church to church. Attired in period Moravian dress, members of the church are present to provide explanations of events. Attendees have opportunities to sing carols, hear stories, receive instruction in making the beeswax candles, hear the story of the birth of Christ presented while viewing the *Putz*, and enjoy traditional refreshments of sugar cake and coffee. The sugar cake is a rich, yeast-raised coffee cake of German origin. Other Candle Teas take on the flavor of arts and crafts fairs. The proceeds from Candle Teas support various needs locally and worldwide.

The Moravian Church is the originator of the Christmas Eve lovefeast, a service that has become popular in other denominations. Observed not only at this time of the year but also during other church festivals, the lovefeast itself, patterned after the *agape* fellowships of the early Apostolic Church, was first introduced into the Moravian Church in 1727. The lovefeast is primarily a song service, and usually there is no formal sermon. During the service, the congregation also partakes of a simple, symbolic meal, which often consists of slightly sweetened buns and a beverage such as coffee, tea, or lemonade. Those who serve at lovefeasts are termed *dieners* (servants). Women in white dress and *haube* (lace cap) customarily serve the buns, while men and women together serve the beverage. After a blessing, the congregation eats the lovefeast meal together while special instrumental or choral music is presented. The lovefeast is a service of love and quiet fellowship among members of the congregation and has no sacramental significance.

During the Christmas Eve lovefeast, the church is darkened, and each member of the congregation also receives a lighted, beeswax candle, the Moravian Christmas Candle, trimmed with a nonflammable red, paper frill. At some point in the service, it is customary for a child to sing two lines of the Moravian hymn "Morning Star," whereupon the congregation antiphonally repeats these lines, and all sing the final line in unison. The lyrics to "Morning Star" were composed in 1657 by Dr. John Scheffler, a physician of Silesia, and the tune in 1836 by Francis F. Hagen, a Moravian minister born in Salem, North Carolina. The use of lighted wax tapers at the Christmas Eve love-feast originated in 1747 at a children's Christmas Eve service in Marienborn, Wetteravia, during which Bishop Johannes von Watteville provided instruction by singing lines of hymns in the form of questions, and the children would respond with the next lines in song as well. Then, to impress the Nativity message upon the children more fully, the bishop distributed lighted tapers trimmed with red ribbons as respective symbols of Christ's burning love and His sacrificial blood. Herrnhut adopted the practice a year later, and the custom spread to Bethlehem, Pennsylvania, in 1756, then to the communities of Bethabara and Bethania, North Carolina, in 1762.

A variant of the Christmas Eve candle service is the "Christingle," a device in British Moravian churches and Labrador that teaches children symbolisms about Jesus. Each child receives a Christingle, which consists of an orange (an apple in Labrador) garnished with various candies and topped by a lighted candle trimmed with red and white paper. The orange (or apple) is the world; the burning candle is Jesus, the Light of the world; the red and white paper, respectively the blood of the Lamb and His purity; the candies, the sweetness of being a Christian.

The liturgy for the Sunday closest to Christmas Day focuses on the Magnificat of Mary as presented in Luke 1:47–55 as well as biblical passages emphasizing the Incarnation. It is customary to close with "Christ the Lord, the Lord Most Glorious," a hymn written by John Miller (lyrics) and Edward Leinbach (music), published in 1789.

For those congregations that still adhere to the waning custom of a New Year's Eve "Watchnight service," church musicians abruptly terminate the sermon, which often remains unfinished, at the stroke of midnight. The interruption symbolizes that Christ could return unexpectedly at any time. Then to herald the new year, the congregation sings the German chorale "Now Thank We All Our God."

The liturgy for Epiphany is self-explanatory, for it is titled "Epiphany and World Mission."

See also **Advent**; **Angels, from the Realms of Glory**; **Epiphany**.

Mrs. Santa Claus

(1996). Made-for-television musical starring Angela Lansbury in the title role.

The year is 1910. Feeling neglected by her husband Santa (Charles Durning) each year during the Christmas rush, Mrs. Anna Claus yields to a whim and takes the reindeer sleigh out for a spin around the world six days before Christmas. She becomes trapped in the Big Apple after making an emergency landing in Manhattan's Lower East Side because of inclement weather, and Cupid is injured in the process. While Cupid recuperates, Anna, posing as a revolutionary Mrs. North, participates in a women's suffrage march and fights for better child labor laws after observing intolerable working conditions at the Tavish Toy Company, which employs children. Outraged by Tavish's cheap toys and its motto, "It only has to last till Christmas," she succeeds in staging a citywide boycott of Tavish Toys.

Augustus Tavish (Terrence Mann), seeking revenge, discovers Anna's true identity and captures her reindeer on Christmas Eve. But Tavish's desire to ruin Christmas stems from his having lost a prized Christmas teddy bear as a child. Discerning this, Anna replaces the bear, Tavish reforms, and Anna returns to a more appreciative Santa just in time for Christmas Eve rounds.

In 1997, this picture won an Emmy Award for Outstanding Hairstyling. Emmy nominations: Outstanding Art Direction, Choreography, Costume Design, and Outstanding Music/Lyrics (Jerry Herman, for the song "Mrs. Santa Claus"). It was nominated for an Art Directors'

Guild Award for Excellence in Television Production Design.

With Michael Jeter, Lynsey Bartilson, Bryan Murray, David Norona, and Debra Wiseman. Music and lyrics by Jerry Herman. Choreography by Rob Marshall. Written by Mark Saltzman. Produced by J. Boyce Harman, Jr. Directed by Terry Hughes. Corymore Productions and Hallmark Entertainment. DVD: Lionsgate/Fox. 91 min.

Ms. Scrooge

See **A Christmas Carol** (Film and Television Versions)

Mumming

See **Christmas Drama**

The Munsters' Scary Little Christmas

(1996). Made-for-television comedy, based on characters featured in *The Munsters*, a television situation comedy of 70 episodes that aired from 1964 to 1966.

Those lovable, neighborhood monsters, the Munsters, find that Christmas in southern California just isn't the same as those back in Transylvania, which sported gloom and snow. Realizing that little Eddie Munster (Bug Hall) has the Christmas blues, the Munster family rallies to get him back into the Christmas spirit and plans a Christmas bash with monster friends from all over the world. Herman Munster (Sam McMurray), short on holiday cash, seeks additional employment, while his wife Lily (Ann Magnuson) and Eddie enter the neighborhood home decorating contest. As Marilyn Munster (Elaine Hendrix) mails invitations, Grandpa (Sandy Baron) unwittingly conjures up Santa Claus (Mark Mitchell) and two elves while attempting to make snow. Unable to transport Santa back to the North Pole in time for Christmas Eve, the Munsters save the holiday by converting their home into a toy factory, but not before Santa's brief transformation into a portly fruitcake at the hands of the two elves, who had desired to cancel Christmas.

In 1997, the show received a Young Star Award nomination for Best Performance by a Young Actor in a Made-for-Television Movie (Bug Hall).

Written by Ed Farrara and Kevin Murphy. Based on characters created by Norm Liebman and Ed Haas. Executive producers Leslie Belzberg and John Landis. Directed by Ian Emes. Michael R. Joyce Productions and St. Clare Entertainment. Video N/A.

The Muppet Christmas Carol

See **A Christmas Carol** (Film and Television Versions)

A Muppet Family Christmas

(1987). Made-for-television children's comedy, featuring Jim Henson's Muppets as well as characters from the *Sesame Street* and *Fraggle Rock* television series.

Fozzie Bear brings Yuletide joy and chaos to the country when he arrives unexpectedly at his mother's farm on a snowy Christmas Eve with a host of Muppet friends in tow. Unbeknownst to Fozzie, his arrival dashes Mrs. Bear's plans for a holiday in sunny Malibu, California, and "Doc" (Gerry Parks), an elderly gentleman to whom Mrs. Bear had rented her house for the season, must now share "peace on earth" with a menagerie of fuzzy, colorful critters.

As the crowd awaits the arrival of Miss Piggy, more guests pile in, including the Swedish Chef, who will prepare the Christmas turkey, followed soon by the unwitting Turkey himself in sunglasses, and a throng of carolers from *Sesame Street*, led by Big Bird. When the Chef would nab Turkey, the latter proposes Big Bird (Caroll Spinney) as a more enticing entrée, who in turn thwarts being measured for the roasting pan by presenting Chef with a Christmas gift of chocolate-covered birdseed. The evening's merriment further includes home movies of the first Christmas that the Muppets spent together and a *Sesame Street* parody of "'Twas the Night before Christmas," with the Two-Headed Monster as Santa, little monsters as reindeer, and narration by Burt and Ernie.

A sudden weather bulletin announcing that a major blizzard is at hand alarms Kermit the Frog, whose friend Miss Piggy has still not appeared, and Doc braves the storm to search for her. Meanwhile, Kermit and his nephew Robin discover a Fraggle Hole in the cellar and enter the world of Fraggle Rock with Christmas greetings. At last, Doc returns via a dog sled with Miss Piggy, after which all the gang gathers for a session of traditional and contemporary carols. The program closes with an entrance from Santa, a cameo appearance of Jim Henson cleaning the kitchen, and Kermit and Miss Piggy exchanging smooches under the mistletoe.

Songs: "Jingle Bells," "Jingle Bell Rock," "Here We Come A-Caroling," "Deck the Halls," "The Christmas Song," "Pass It On," "Happy Holiday," "Ding Dong! Merrily on High," "I Saw Three Ships," "Good King Wenceslas," "The Holly and the Ivy," "I'll Be Home for Christmas," "Caroling, Caroling," and "We Wish You a Merry Christmas."

In 1988, this program received an Emmy nomination for Outstanding Children's Program. It won a Writers' Guild Award in 1989 (Jerry Juhl).

Principal voices: Frank Oz, Dave Goelz, Richard Hunt, Kathryn Mullen, Jerry Nelson, Karen Prell, Steve Whitmire, David Rudman, and Jim Henson. Written by Jerry Juhl. Produced by Diana Birkenfield and Martin G. Baker. Directed by Peter Harris. Jim Henson Productions. DVD: Columbia/Tristar. 47 min.

See also **It's a Very Merry Muppet Christmas Movie.**

Must Be Santa

(1999). Canadian made-for-television fantasy.

Instead of employing elves, the North Pole operates on a heavenly, high-tech system of angelic assistants, with the militaristic Tuttle (Dabney Coleman) serving as chief operations officer. Realizing that Santa (Gerard Parkes), whom Tuttle supervises, has become crippled and ill with age, Tuttle must find a replacement, lest the Christmas spirit be lost. Two days before Christmas, Tuttle selects Floyd Court (Arnold Pinnock), a black, deadbeat father and petty criminal, to fill the position. Although Floyd finds living up to Santa's reputation challenging enough, given his previous lifestyle, he faces a seemingly greater challenge in resuming his role as father to his ten-year-old daughter, Heather (Keenan MacWilliam).

In 2000, this picture was nominated for a Gemini Award for Best Performance by an Actress in a Leading Role in a Dramatic Program or Mini-Series (Deanna Milligan). In 2000, it won a Gemini Award for Best Visual Effects.

Written by Douglas Bowie. Produced by Robert Sherrin. Directed by Brad Turner. Canadian Broadcasting Corporation. VHS: Universal Studios. 120 min.

N

The National Christmas Tree

See **United States** (The National Christmas Tree and the Christmas Pageant of Peace)

The Nation's Christmas Tree

See **United States** (The Nation's Christmas Tree)

National Lampoon's Christmas Vacation

(1989). Motion picture comedy, also known as *Christmas Vacation*. It is the third in a series of five *Vacation* films, the other four

being *National Lampoon's Vacation* (1983), *National Lampoon's European Vacation* (1985), *National Lampoon's Vegas Vacation* (1997), and *National Lampoon's Christmas Vacation 2* (2003). In all but the last one, Chevy Chase stars as the well-meaning but wacky Clark Griswold, Jr., to whom life seems bent on dealing a consistently bad hand. Despite his slapstick antics, misadventures, and nearly-completed-but-never-finished projects, his lovely wife Ellen (Beverly D'Angelo) remains patiently supportive. The actors for their two children, teenager Audrey and younger Rusty, vary from film to film. These and the host of other films in the *National Lampoon* collection are based on the satire and humor rampant in *National Lampoon* magazine.

Sporting a loose plot, *National Lampoon's Christmas Vacation* satirizes all of the traditional family values of the holiday. At Clark's invitation, obnoxious, argumentative parents and in-laws crowd into the Griswold home, the most disgusting of whom is Eddie (Randy Quaid), a lazy, hillbilly cousin. Chaos commences as Clark wrestles to decorate his house with 25,000 twinkling lights and battles poorly wired circuits. Aunt Bethany (Mae Questel), a senile lady bearing boxed, wrapped gifts of a live cat and lime Jell-O, arrives on Christmas Eve along with Uncle Lewis (William Hickey), whose cigar promptly flash-incinerates the Griswold's dried-out Christmas tree. Although the tree is replaced, the cat, having escaped from its prison, settles down to gnawing on a string of Christmas lights and succeeds in vaporizing itself through electrocution. Aunt Bethany deems the "Pledge of Allegiance" as an appropriate grace before dinner, and the family sits down to eat. Later, pandemonium erupts when a squirrel residing in the Christmas tree springs out at Clark and attracts Cousin Eddie's dog. The two varmints run amok, making a shambles of the house.

Topping off the evening, Clark's much-anticipated Christmas "bonus" arrives: a one-year membership in the "Jelly-of-the-Month Club," for which an irate Clark delivers a litany of nonseasonal adjectives against his employer. Suddenly Eddie the vigilante appears with Clark's boss in tow, and soon thereafter, a police squad arrives and prepares to arrest the hillbilly on charges of kidnapping. After realizing, however, that cutting Christmas cash bonuses has seriously damaged not just Clark's morale but that of his other employees, the boss reconsiders, reinstates the gift, and drops all charges.

As the family gathers outdoors for a final scene, Clark waxes sentimental over what appears to be the Christmas Star in the heavens. Uncle Lewis, tossing his lit cigar into the storm drain, shatters the illusion with a terse reminder that it's just the beacon atop the sewage treatment plant. Just then, exploding sewer gas shatters the heavens and sends the Griswolds' reindeer display rocketing into space. Inspired, Aunt Bethany closes the film with a chorus of "The Star-Spangled Banner."

With Diane Ladd, John Randolph, E.G. Marshall, Doris Roberts, Juliette Lewis, and Johnny Galecki. Written by John Hughes. Produced by John Hughes and Tom Jacobson. Directed by Jeremiah Chechik. Hughes Entertainment in association with Warner Bros. Pictures. DVD: Warner Studios (also contains *National Lampoon's Christmas Vacation 2*). 97 min.

See also **National Lampoon's Christmas Vacation 2**.

National Lampoon's Christmas Vacation 2: Cousin Eddie's Island Adventure

(2003). Made-for-television comedy sequel to *National Lampoon's Christmas Vacation*. Departing from the other *Vacation* films, the barely discernable plot revolves around Clark Griswold, Jr.'s unsophisticated hillbilly cousin, Eddie Johnson (Randy Quaid).

Found to have less intelligence than his coworker, Roy the chimpanzee, Eddie manages to lose his job as a nuclear waste test subject at Christmastime. In an altercation, Roy bites Eddie's derriere, whereupon the Atomic Testing Agency, to avoid a lawsuit, provides an all-expenses-paid Christmas vacation at the company's resort on the South Pacific island of Maluka. Joining Eddie are wife Catherine (Miriam Flynn); preteen son Clark (Jake Thomas), nicknamed "Third"; and the foul-smelling family dog, infamous for its chronic flatulence. In addition, two down-and-out family members arrive unexpectedly for the holidays: Cousin Audrey Griswold (Dana Barron), who just broke up with her married boyfriend Dan, and Uncle Nick (Ed Asner), a lecherous old coot, whose wife, Aunt Jessica (Beverly Garland), has left him for a man half her age.

Slapstick comedy, courtesy of accident-prone Eddie, prevails from the time the family leaves snowbound Chicago until they leave balmy Maluka, where their guide is the voluptuous Muka Laka Miki (Sung Hi Lee), who must repel Uncle Nick's advances at every turn. Following a gluttonous luau and Eddie's near-disastrous round of deep-sea fishing, Uncle Nick takes charge of their boat and runs aground on a deserted island. Now the family must pull together to survive. While the women fashion a Christmas tree from local fauna, Eddie, Clark, and Uncle Nick, armed with makeshift spears, search for game. By chance alone, Eddie spears a wild boar (which first trees him), assuring a Christmas dinner of roast pork. Through this experience and by helping Eddie construct a shelter, "Third" gains renewed respect for his father, whom he had formerly branded as a lazy failure.

Christmas Day dawns with Uncle Nick dressed as an island Santa. After simple gift exchanges and a few carols, the family enters their shelter, christened with a mixture of coconut milk and liquor, where, predictably, it promptly collapses around them. But all is not lost, for later that day, Melbourne Jack (Julian Stone), a friend whom they had met on Maluka, arrives via pontoon plane to rescue them. En route back, Jack, having previously suffered a tumble, courtesy of Eddie, passes out from a concussion, leaving a terrified Eddie as pilot. Amid aerial acrobatics, true confessions now fill the air. "Third" pleads love for Muka, who in turn vows to return to her husband, who turns out to be *Dan*, leaving Audrey the shocked third member of the sordid triangle. Landing safely in Maluka nonetheless, Eddie, his island exploits having preceded him, declines Atomic Testing's offer to rehire him and teams up instead with Roy the chimp as an island air tour guide.

With Eric Idle and Fred Willard. Written by Matty Simmons. Produced by Elliot Friedgen. Directed by Nick Marck. Elliot Friedgen and Company, National Lampoon Productions, and Warner Bros. Television. DVD: Warner Home Video (also contains *National Lampoon's Christmas Vacation*). 120 min.

See also **National Lampoon's Christmas Vacation.**

Nativity

Derived from the Latin *nativus* (birth). The capitalized form implies not only the birth of Jesus Christ, but also the account of His

Mary, Joseph, and the Baby Jesus are depicted in an embossed, chromolithograph scrap. The scrap was made in Germany in the 1870s or 1880s.

birth as described in the New Testament narratives. Of the four Gospels (Matthew, Mark, Luke, and John), which detail the life of Christ, only Matthew and Luke present the familiar Nativity or Christmas story, and the two versions differ in some respects.

Luke's version begins with the angel Gabriel's appearance to the Virgin Mary in Nazareth of Galilee with the news that she, being blessed among women, will bear Jesus; that He will be called the "Son of the Highest"; and that His kingdom will be everlasting (1:26–38). This announcement is known as the Annunciation. As the story continues (2:1–7), the Roman emperor, Augustus Caesar, has levied a tax or census on all Roman provinces. Because each man must report to his city of birth, the carpenter Joseph, also presently of Nazareth, journeys with Mary, his "espoused" wife, down to Bethlehem of Judea. Pregnant and at term, Mary delivers a son in Bethlehem, wraps Him in swaddling clothes (cloth strips for warmth and immobilization), and places Him in a manger, "because there was no room

A fifteenth century woodcut shows Mary and the Baby Jesus on a donkey, followed by Joseph on their flight to Egypt. The popular imagination often pictures Mary riding a donkey on the journey to Bethlehem and the flight into Egypt, but there is no mention of a donkey in the scriptural story. From Henry Poulaille, La Grande et belle Bible des noëls anciens *(Paris: Michel, 1941).*

for them in the inn." The only other group of people who receive news of this special birth are shepherds, to whom an angelic host pays a nocturnal visit, declaring that a Savior is born in Bethlehem (2:8–11).

The angels give the shepherds a sign for recognizing the Child: "Ye shall find the babe wrapped in swaddling clothes, lying in a manger" (2:12). The shepherds decide to go to Bethlehem, where indeed they find "Mary, and Joseph, and the Babe lying in a manger" (2:15–16). When they depart, they spread the news of the Child's birth (2:17–18).

Although Matthew's account first centers on Joseph's doubts about Mary's pregnancy (which he supposes to be illegitimate) and the reassurance bestowed through God in a dream (1:18–25), Matthew primarily focuses upon the "wise men from the east" (2:1–18). Guided by a star, they first visit King Herod the Great in Jerusalem, looking for the Child who is "born King of the Jews." Fearing that his throne is in jeopardy, Herod feigns a desire to worship the Child and orders the Wise Men to find Him and report His whereabouts. The Wise Men find the Child and present gifts of gold, frankincense, and myrrh. But instead of reporting back to Herod, they depart, after which an irate

Herod, hoping to destroy the Child, orders the massacre of (presumably) all male children in Bethlehem who are two years old and under, "according to the time which he had diligently enquired of the wise men." Because ancient manuscripts of this account do not specify the gender of the victims, however, Matthew 2:16 states that *all children* in this age range were slaughtered, which would imply females as well. Warned by God in a dream, the Holy Family flees beforehand into Egypt to escape Herod's wrath.

Speculations vary widely concerning the number of children that were killed in the massacre (which has come to be known as the Slaughter of the Innocents). According to Greek, Syrian, and medieval sources, the victims totaled 14,000, 64,000, and 144,000 respectively. Because the Bethlehem of 2,000 years ago was quite small, modern writers are more realistic, estimating six to 20 casualties. Oddly, the Jewish historian Flavius Josephus (ca. 37–101) makes no mention of the event, yet he describes other atrocities that Herod the Great committed in his final years. It is thought that the number dying in Bethlehem paled in comparison with the numbers of others whom the king had executed. (*See also* **Star of Bethlehem; Wise Men.**)

• TIME OF THE NATIVITY. Neither the specific year nor time of year when Christ was born is definitively known, although the year is estimated to be between 1 and 4 B.C., the time range corresponding to the death of Herod the Great. Some have attempted to calculate the time of year based on the birth of John the Baptist. According to Luke's Gospel, John's father Zacharias was an aged Temple priest of the order of Abia (known as Abijah in the Old Testament). The ancient Jewish priesthood consisted of 24 orders, the eighth of which was Abijah (First Chronicles 24:7–18), and each order rotated in service for one week or, roughly, twice a year. Because the cycle began each year in the first month, Nisan (approximately March–April on the Gregorian calendar), Zacharias' service corresponded to one week each in the third month, Sivan (May–June), and six months later in the ninth month, Kislev (November–December). During one of his weeks (Luke does not specify which),

Zacharias received word from the angel Gabriel that his aged wife Elizabeth would bear John (Luke 1:5–20). Some contend that, because Elizabeth supposedly conceived in the fourth month of Tammuz (June–July) *after* her husband's service (Luke 1:23–25), John was born the following year on the fourteenth of Nisan at *Pesach* (Passover), after which Christ, six months younger than John (Luke 1:26), would have been born some time between the Feast of Trumpets, the Day of Atonement, and the Feast of Tabernacles, all of which were celebrated in Tishri, the seventh month (September–October) (*see* Leviticus 23:23–36). Of course, if Elizabeth conceived six months later in the tenth month of Tevet (December–January), she would have delivered John in Tishri, and Christ would have been born in Nisan in the spring (see **Popular Assumptions** below).

• POPULAR ASSUMPTIONS. From the Nativity Story, several other popular notions have arisen, for which no definitive biblical evidence exists:

1. *Mary rode a donkey to Bethlehem and during the flight to Egypt.* Because Mary was either pregnant or holding the infant Jesus, it is assumed that she rode on some beast of burden, such as a donkey; however, this is only an assumption.

2. *Jesus was born at midnight.* That shepherds were "keeping watch over their flocks by night" when herald angels appeared is fuel for the assumption of a midnight birth.

3. *Jesus was born in a stable.* That Jesus' cradle was a manger evokes the image of a conventional stable. At that time and in that part of the world, however, inns and other establishments often housed their livestock close by in sections of the same building, for stables as we know them did not exist. Instead, Jesus could have been born in one of several caves around Bethlehem which sometimes doubled as stables. We find this evidence from the early Christian writer Justin Martyr (ca. 100–ca.165), who spoke of Jesus' birth in one such cave. Lending further support, the theologian Origen of Alexandria, Egypt (ca. 185–ca. 254) reported that even the pagans had known of the cave where Jesus was born.

4. *Jesus was born in the spring.* Aside from the biblical calculation based on the birth of John the Baptist, many believe that shepherds

An eighteenth-century woodcut of the Angel Gabriel announcing to Mary the news that she is to give birth to the Son of God. This woodcut shows Mary interrupted while reading the Scriptures, a common theme. From Henry Poulaille, La Grande et belle Bible des noëls anciens *(Paris: Michel, 1941).*

attending flocks in fields implies the spring of the year, especially the lambing season. Some have suggested that Caesar would have demanded a census only during the convenience of spring, but this suggestion is unreliable, for Rome took little note of its subjects' lifestyles. With no definitive evidence either for or against a springtime birth, by the fourth century the Church had established December 25 as the date for marking Christ's birth. By the eighth century, the Church was observing the Feast of the Annunciation in the spring on March 25, a logical date nine months prior to Christmas. (*See* **Christmas Day**.)

5. *Three Wise Men or Kings visited the manger.* This assumption is fully discussed under the entry **Wise Men**.

The Annunciation in a late nineteenth century, highly romanticized version, showing all the common elements: the stem of lillies that Gabriel holds, the dove, and a pious Mary reading Scriptures (here in a very modern-looking book). From John Fleetwood, The Light in the East *(National Publishing Co. and Jones Brothers, 1874).*

6. *Shepherds and Wise Men visited the manger on the same night.* Although Nativity scenes traditionally show shepherds and Wise Men or Kings together around the manger, Matthew's Gospel suggests otherwise. Whereas Luke clearly states that the shepherds "came with haste" to the manger after learning of Jesus' birth, there may have been a two-year hiatus until the Wise Men came on the scene, which is implied in Matthew's story. King Herod ordered the slaughter of Bethlehem children up to two years old after learning specifically when the Wise Men first saw the star. It has also been suggested that, if the Wise Men or Magi visited Jesus at some time after His birth, the visit would have taken place in the home of his mother and Joseph, not in a cave or stable. Indeed, Matthew's account states that the Wise Men found the Child in a "house" in Bethlehem.

7. *An ox and an ass stood by the manger and watched over the Babe.* Since the Middle Ages, Nativity scenes and other depictions of the Nativity have included at least these two ani-

mals. They first appeared as beasts adoring the Christ Child in the Gospel of Pseudo-Matthew from the New Testament Apocrypha, which derived from Isaiah 1:3: "The ox knoweth his owner, and the ass his master's crib."

• WORKS OF ART. Artistic portrayals of the Nativity originated in the early Church principally after the Roman emperor Constantine the Great (ca. 274–337) embraced Christianity. In the West, the Church initially used paintings and mosaics to teach biblical scenes and stories to a largely illiterate laity, for only the clergy and a handful of scholars understood the Latin liturgy and Latin translations of the Scriptures at the time. One of the earliest subjects was the Madonna or Virgin Mary herself; legend, but only legend, claims that St. Luke the Evangelist created some of the oldest extant pencil sketches of her. Some of the earliest mosaics of Madonna and Child appear on the walls of Roman catacombs. Those of St. Priscilla depict the prophet Isaiah pointing to a star above their heads. Another shows shepherds and the Three Kings visiting the Child in His crib, while in a similar scene from a fourth century sarcophagus, the Magi are kneeling. The Virgin rarely appeared on Christian sarcophagi, however. Early depictions of Madonna and Child within a church also include those found on fifth century medallions of the triumphal arch in Rome's Church of Santa Maria Maggiore. Because the Church especially favored the subject of Madonna and Child, artists rendered them not only in portraits but in scenes from the early life of Christ. Therefore, religious Christmas art in the West depicts the following principal subjects: the Annunciation, the Nativity, the shepherds, the Magi, and the flight into Egypt.

The Annunciation. One of the most frequent scenes of Renaissance art, the Annunciation is usually rendered in a home setting with Mary and the angel Gabriel elegantly dressed. An open text nearby implies her piety in reading the Scriptures. Positions of the angel and Mary vary, the angel kneeling with Mary standing or vice versa, while Giotto (Italian, 1267?–1337) has both kneeling (Padua). Gabriel, usually winged, generally bears a spray of lilies, symbolic of purity, or these flowers may appear in a vase nearby. There may be a banner somewhere on the work with the words "Ecce Ancilla Domini" ("Behold the handmaid of the Lord"), for Mary's reaction is most often that of quiet submission. The work of Fra Angelico (Italian, 1400?–1455) in the Prado Museum, Madrid, conveys the medieval notion regarding Mary's divine conception: Rays of light from heaven beam toward her through which a dove emerges, symbolic of the Holy Spirit. Robert Campin (Flemish, 1378?–1444) replaces the dove with a minute figure of the infant Christ bearing a cross as a futuristic emblem (Metropolitan Museum of Art). Other works may depict the dove hovering nearby. Whereas most renderings feature one angel, Andrea del Sarto (Florentine, 1486–1530), Tintoretto (Venetian, ca. 1518–1594), and Fra Bartolommeo (Florentine, 1472?–1517) present an angelic choir. Later renderings such as those of the nineteenth century incorporate a greater sense of realism. For instance, in a painting by Dante Gabriel Rossetti (English, 1828–1882) titled *Ecce Ancilla Domini* (a portrait of his younger sister Christina, Tate Gallery, London), Mary is frankly terrified at the presence of a wingless Gabriel, and in a rendering by James Tissot (French, 1836–1902), the ghostly specter of Gabriel hovers above Mary slumped on the floor (Brooklyn Museum). Other noted artists include Leonardo da Vinci (Florentine, 1452–1519), Simone Martini (Sienese, ca. 1280–1344), Domenico Veneziano (Florentine, 1405?–1461), Fra Filippo Lippi (Florentine, ca. 1406–1469), Sandro Botticelli (Florentine, 1445–1510), and Jan van Eyck (Flemish, 1390?–1441), the latter of whom presents the Annunciation outdoors, a most unusual setting (Metropolitan Museum of Art).

The Nativity. Set at the mouth of a cave (Fra Angelico's school) or in a traditional stable (Giotto's school), in daylight or at night, renderings of the Nativity may feature Jesus in a manger and Mary, with or without Joseph, kneeling or sitting in adoration beside Him. Joseph, seemingly of secondary importance, often occupies a place behind Mary and Jesus, as in works by followers of Jan Joest (Flemish, active ca. 1515, Metropolitan Museum of Art) and Hugo van der Goes (Flemish, 1440?–1482, Uffizi Gallery, Florence). Many Nativities feature angels hovering above or beside the manger (in contrast to Luke's Gospel, where

The three Wise Men "saw the young child with Mary his mother, and fell down, and worshiped him; and when they had opened their treasures, they presented unto him gifts, gold, and frankincense, and myrrh" (Matthew 2:11). From John Fleetwood, The Light in the East *(National Publishing Co. and Jones Brothers, 1874).*

they return to heaven after appearing to the shepherds); others include shepherds near the manger (called the *Adoration of the Shepherds*), and still others set the shepherds in the background to receive the message from the heavenly host. Examples include works by Hugo van der Goes (Uffizi Gallery, Florence), in which Jesus lies on the ground with adoring angels and shepherds nearby; a work by Piero Della Francesca (Italian, 1420?–1492) also shows Jesus lying on the ground, with Mary kneeling and with angels playing lutes and singing (National Gallery, London). Botticelli (National Gallery) combines stable roof with entrance to a cave in which angels not only hover above, but also freely embrace those in attendance around the manger, a scene symbolizing the union of heaven with mankind through Christ's birth. Virtually all Nativities include the traditional ox and ass (see above), and Jesus, to symbolize the Light of the World, is frequently the principal source of light. Other noted artists who painted Nativity scenes include William Blake (English, 1757–1827), Philippe de Champaigne (French, 1602–1674), Jacopo Bassano (Venetian, ca. 1510–1592), Francisco de Zurbarán (Spanish, 1598–1664), Luca Signorelli (Italian, ca. 1445–1523), Carlo Crivelli (Italian, 1430?–1494?), and Andrea Mantegna (Italian, 1431–1506).

The Magi. A favorite subject among catacomb dwellers was the Magi, featured in some 20 mosaics. Numbering from three to six, the Magi appear before Mary, who is enthroned with Jesus lying in her arms. The great masters portrayed the traditional three Magi from two perspectives. In works titled *Journey of the Magi*, the Magi, riding on horses (more familiar to the artists than camels), either lead, or are surrounded by, long processions that wind through the countryside. This treatment stems from the *Compagnia de'Magi*, Epiphany processions that were popular in Florence during the Middle Ages, the members of which dressed as the Magi and paraded on horses. In one such fresco by Benozzo Gozzoli (Florentine, 1420–1497), the three Magi are likenesses of Lorenzo de' Medici, his grandfather Cosimo, and his father Piero, all of whom were influential Florentine bankers and patrons of the arts during the Renaissance (Medici Chapel, Florence). In *Journey* by Sasseta (Sienese, ca. 1400–1450), the Magi appear as scholars (Metropolitan Museum of Art). On the other hand, works titled *Adoration of the Magi* again incorporate either a cave setting (Fra Angelico, National Gallery) or a stable (Giotto, Padua) with the traditional ox and ass present. The Infant Jesus is now somewhat older, for He often is shown sitting naked in Mary's lap with one hand raised in benediction. His nakedness symbolizes His identity with the poor. Usually a large company again has accompanied the three Magi, who appear as lavishly dressed kings. Most often the eldest is shown kneeling before the Babe and kissing His feet in humility while the other two stand or kneel. Whereas their southern colleagues usually featured white-skinned Magi, painters of northern Europe followed the tradition of portraying one Magus as black. Examples of such *Adorations* include those by Albrecht Dürer (German, 1471–1528, in the Uffizi Gallery, Florence) and Quentin Massys (Flemish, 1466?–1530, in the Metropolitan Museum). Yet in these, the eldest white Magus still remains in closest proximity to the Babe. Besides ox and ass, animals such as monkeys and peacocks also have appeared and respectively symbolize sin in the world and the resurrection. Other noted artists include Peter Paul Reubens (Flemish, 1577–1640),

Giorgione (Venetian, 1478?–1510), Gentile da Fabriano (Italian, 1370?–1427), Fra Filippo Lippi, Rogier van der Weyden (Flemish, 1399?–1464), and Giovanni di Paolo (Sienese, 1403?–1482?).

The Flight into Egypt. The escape from Bethlehem sometimes features Mary riding a donkey and holding the Babe as Joseph or an angel leads the beast. Examples include those by Giotto (Padua), Fra Angelico (Uffizi), and Hans Memling (Flemish, 1435?–1494, in the *Alte Pinakothek*, Munich). Many of the masters preferred a scene in which the Holy Family, now exhausted from a flight through the desert, rests in some fertile locale, hence the title *Rest on the Flight*. To this repose, artists sometimes added a depiction of miracles that the Infant Jesus allegedly performed on this flight, as detailed in the eighth or ninth century apocryphal book, the Gospel of Pseudo-Matthew. The *Rest* painting in the Prado Museum, Madrid, by Dutch artist Joachim Patenier (active 1515–1524), depicts a group of King Herod's soldiers in the background questioning laborers cutting grain. This scene is based upon the legend that as the Holy Family journeyed, the Infant Jesus obtained some seed from a farmer sowing grain and threw it onto the ground, which instantly yielded fully mature sheaves. Later, in reply to the soldiers' interrogations, the farmer stated that he had seen a woman and child pass by while he was sowing. Seeing the tall sheaves and inferring that months had passed since the sighting, the soldiers abandoned their pursuit. The repose setting was especially favored by German and Flemish masters.

In virtually all Western frescoes and paintings, the Virgin wears a blue robe, the color traditionally associated with her, and Joseph is depicted as considerably older than Mary, a tradition that coincides with the theme set forth in carols such as "The Cherry Tree Carol." (*See also* **The Vatican** [Works of Art]).

• FILM AND TELEVISION DEPICTIONS. While several motion pictures dramatize the entire life of Christ, few are centered entirely around the Nativity story alone. The following is a brief summary of notable productions that devote some footage to the Nativity.

The Greatest Story Ever Told (1965), based on

a novel of the same title by Fulton Oursler, opens with a brief, anonymous narration from the first chapter of John's Gospel, "In the beginning was the Word …" The scene pauses in a darkened stable, in which the only evidence of humanity lies in the close-up of an infant's hand. Because John does not present an account of the Nativity, the story takes up Matthew's version as the Wise Men seek Jesus through King Herod (Claude Rains). Their individual identities are revealed neither to Herod nor to Joseph (Robert Loggia) nor to Mary (Dorothy McGuire). Each states the significance of the gift he has brought: gold, for the sovereignty of a King; frankincense, to worship God; myrrh, for preservation until time everlasting. The shepherds (from Luke's Gospel) are only incidental characters observing the preceding scenario from a distance, and there are no herald angels. As the Wise Men depart, Joseph hears a Voice (not in a dream) telling him to flee. An irate Herod quotes the prophet Jeremiah (31:15): "A voice was heard in Ramah, lamentation, *and* bitter weeping …" He decides to fulfill this prophecy by killing all newborn babies in Bethlehem (Matthew 2 indicates all children two years old and under). As the raid commences, the camera pans to an empty manger draped with swaddling clothes. This film was nominated for five Academy Awards: Best Color Cinematography, Art Direction, Costume Design, Special Effects, and Best Original Musical Score. With Max von Sydow. Screenplay by James Lee Barrett, Henry Denker, and George Stevens. Produced by George Stevens. Directed by George Stevens, David Lean, and Jean Negulesco. United Artists. DVD: MGM/UA Video. 199 min.

Jesus (1979), a motion picture filmed on location in the Holy Land, is reputed to be the most accurate chronicle of the life of Christ, based entirely on Luke's Gospel. With Eli Cohen, Brian Deacon, Peter Frye, Niko Nitai, Joseph Shiloach, and Rivka Neuman. Written by Barnet Fishbein. Produced by Richard F. Dalton and John Heyman. Directed by John Krish and Peter Sykes. Inspiration Films and the Genesis Project. DVD: Madacy Entertainment. 117 min.

Jesus of Nazareth (1977), a British-Italian television miniseries based on all four Gospels, is the most complete portrayal of the life of Christ, although it does not always follow the Scriptures to the letter. Opening with the betrothal of Joseph (Yorgo Voyagis) and Mary (Olivia Hussey) in Nazareth, the movie depicts key pre-Nativity events as outlined in Luke 1: the angel's Annunciation to Mary (she converses with a brilliant light flooding through her window; the viewer neither sees nor hears the angel); Mary's meeting with her cousin Elizabeth (Marina Berti), the expectant mother of John the Baptist (whereas the film makes Elizabeth a widow, Luke states that her husband Zacharias is alive and serves as a priest); Joseph's anguish over Mary's unexpected pregnancy; and Joseph's dream from God about the coming of Jesus. After their wedding comes the journey to Bethlehem, where Joseph settles Mary into a cave that doubles as a stable. As the Star shines over the cave, shepherds arrive following the Birth, saying that a "man" told them to come because a Savior had been born (again, no herald angels). Eight days pass, after which Jesus is circumcised in the local synagogue, where the devout Simeon (Ralph Richardson) delivers his prophecy of Jesus as a light unto the Gentiles (according to Luke 2:25–35, Simeon delivers his soliloquy when Jesus is presented in the Temple in Jerusalem 40 days after His birth). Returning to the cave, Mary and Joseph find the three Wise Men waiting. Balthazar (James Earl Jones) presents frankincense to perfume the halls of the Mighty; Gaspar (Fernando Rey) presents gold for Kingly rule; and Melchior (Donald Pleasence) presents myrrh, the most precious herb of the Orient as well as the most bitter. It is they who give the warning to flee into Egypt until Herod is dead (Luke writes that Joseph receives the warning from God). The viewer never sees the Wise Men's meeting with Herod (Peter Ustinov), only Herod's rage on their departure from Bethlehem. In the aftermath of the massacre in Bethlehem, Simeon laments over the children by quoting Jeremiah 31:15. This miniseries devotes over one hour to the Nativity. In 1978, the production received Emmy nominations for Outstanding Supporting Actor (James Farentino) and Outstanding Drama Special. It won Silver Ribbon awards from the Italian National Syndicate of Film Journalists for Best Cinematography, Best Costume Design, and Best Production Design. With Robert Powell. Written by Anthony Burgess, Suso Cecchi D'Amico, and Franco Zeffirelli. Produced by Vincenzo Labella. Directed by Franco Zeffirelli. RAI-ITC Entertainment Productions with Sir Lew Grade. DVD: Lionsgate/Fox. 382 min.

King of Kings (1961) is a motion picture that bases its Nativity scenes on the Gospel of Matthew. The film opens in 63 B.C. during the Roman conquest of Jerusalem, and after some 50 years, according to narrator Orson Welles, Emperor Caesar Augustus appoints an Arab, Herod the Great (Gregoire Aslan), as king of Judea. Following a brief scene in which Joseph (Gerard Tichy) leads Mary (Siobhan McKenna) riding a donkey into Bethlehem, the three Wise Men present their treasures. Instead of the Wise Men revealing their names through character dialogue during their visit, the narrator identifies the Wise Men as Melchior, Caspar, and Balthazar of Mesopotamia, Persia, and Ethiopia, respectively. They are not shown meeting with Herod beforehand; neither are there shepherds nor an angelic host. Joseph, warned in a dream about Herod's imminent raid on Bethlehem, awakens and flees into Egypt with his family as the soldiers arrive. The film devotes about as much time to the death of Herod alone as it does to the preceding Nativity events. With Jeff Hunter, Edric Connor, Jose Nieto, Adriano Rimoldi, Hurd Hatfield, and Ron Randell. Written by Philip Yordon and Ray Bradbury. Produced by Samuel Bronston. Directed by Nicholas Ray. A Metro-Goldwyn-Mayer and Samuel Bronston production. DVD: Warner Home Video. 171 min.

Mary, Mother of Jesus (1999) is a television movie that focuses on the relationship between Mary and Jesus and is based on the Gospels of Matthew and Luke. The film opens in Nazareth as the Romans declare that a tax will be due in nine months. Mary (Melinda Kinnaman) receives the Annunciation from the white-robed angel Gabriel (John Light) beside a road where she is working, after which she visits her elder cousin Elizabeth (Geraldine Chaplin), who has been pregnant six months with John the Baptist (Luke 1:5–25). Her husband-priest Zacharias (Edward Hardwicke), previously struck dumb when he doubted Gabriel, recov-

ers his speech at John's birth. After Joseph's (David Threlfall) turmoil over Mary's pregnancy and his dream, the scene turns to Bethlehem, where Jesus has been born in a conventional stable. The shepherds are the first to arrive and relate their experience with the heavenly host (not shown). At the court of King Herod (Hywell Bennett), the Star of Bethlehem is quite visible (contrary to Matthew's account), and Herod receives the three Magi, whose identities otherwise are not revealed. On the following day, the Magi visit the manger, after which Herod orders the slaughter of all male children born in Bethlehem within the last six months (also contrary to Matthew). Instead of receiving a warning from God, the Holy Family escapes during the raid. Written by Albert Ross. Produced by Howard Ellis. Directed by Kevin Connor. Hallmark Entertainment and the Shriver Family Film Company. DVD: Lionsgate/Fox. 94 min.

The Nativity (1978), a made-for-television movie, is primarily a romantic, fictional account of the meeting between Joseph (John Shea) and Mary (Madeleine Stowe) prior to the Nativity. Written by Morton S. Fine and Millard Kaufman. Produced by William P. D'Angelo. Directed by Bernard L. Kowalski. Twentieth Century Fox Television. VHS: Fox Video. 120 min.

The Nativity (1984), made-for-video animated cartoon from the Hanna-Barbera series *The Greatest Adventure: Stories from the Bible*, is the story of three young, modern-day archaeologists who stumble into a time portal. They are carried into the Holy Land, back to the time of the Roman tax in Bethlehem, where the events of the Nativity most reverently unfold before them. The production received the following honors: Golden Eagle Award (1988), National Religious Broadcasters' Distinguished Service Award, Religion in Media's Gold Angel Award, and the Film Advisory Board's Award of Excellence. Featuring a host of familiar *a cappella* carols sung by the Southern California Mormon Choir. Voices: David Ackroyd, Roscoe Lee Browne, Darleen Carr, Dick Erdmans, Scott Grimes, Gregory Harrison, Helen Hunt, Richard Libertini, Terence McGovern, Alan Oppenheimer, Rob Paulsen, Vincent Price, Michael Rye, Jeffrey Tambor, and Frank Welker. Teleplay by Dennis Marks. Adapted by Bruce D. Johnson and Harvey Bullock. Produced by Kay Wright. Directed by Ray Patterson. Hanna-Barbera Productions in association with Wang Film Productions Co., Ltd. and Cuckoo's Nest Studios. VHS: Hanna-Barbera Studios. 32 min.

See also **Epiphany; Hanna-Barbera Christmas Cartoons; Holy Innocents Day.**

The Nativity (television specials)
See **Nativity** (Film and Television Depictions)

Nativity Play
See **Christmas Drama**

Nativity Scene
Also known as "manger scene" and "crib." A three-dimensional replica of those characters and events surrounding the birth of Christ as outlined in the Gospels of Matthew and Luke. Traditional Nativity scenes include figures of the Infant Jesus, manger or crib, Mary, Joseph, three Wise Men or Kings, shepherds, sheep, and perhaps one or more angels, all of which are usually arranged before or within a rustic, conventional stable or the entrance to a cave. Also traditionally included are the ox and ass, two animals not specifically mentioned in the Gospels (*see* **Nativity** [Popular Assumptions]). Although they are known worldwide, Nativity scenes reign as the principal physical symbols of Christmas primarily in southern Europe, Latin America, and in other Spanish-speaking locales. Nativity scenes range from the miniature to life-size.

The earliest Nativity scenes featured a simple replica of the manger. At the Grotto of the Nativity in Bethlehem, St. Helena, mother of Emperor Constantine the Great, is said to have replaced Christ's original manger of clay with one of silver in the fourth century and thus established a shrine at the traditional site of Christ's birth. Rome's Church of Santa Maria Maggiore, completed around 440, housed a shrine patterned after that in Bethlehem, to which were added in the seventh century six pieces of wooden boards believed to have served as supports for the original manger (*see* **Church of the Nativity**). During the Mid-

dle Ages, Christmas vespers often included so-called "crib rocking" ceremonies that recalled the earliest Nativity scenes. In this custom, especially in Germany, the priest would place a figure of the Christ Child in a crib and rock it before the altar during the Mass and sing appropriate *Wiegenlieder* (cradle songs). Children in the congregation often rocked a second crib.

Commencing in the tenth century, medieval liturgical dramas first incorporated simple statues of the Virgin with Child lying in a crib (*see* **Christmas Drama** [Nativity Play]), yet the popularity of the Nativity scene as we know it today is attributed to St. Francis of Assisi, Italy (ca. 1181–1226), a Roman Catholic priest who spent most of his clerical life as missionary and evangelist among the poor. Always believing that people should understand the Gospel in their own language, St. Francis preached in the vernacular rather than in Latin, which only clerics and scholars understood at the time. In 1223, he laid before Pope Honorius III a novel project designed to bring the Nativity story closer to the minds and hearts of the populace. With Church approval, on Christmas Eve of that same year, St. Francis recreated the stable setting in a cave near Greccio, Italy, using live people and animals. One account states that as he sang the Gospel story of the Nativity, the Christ Child radiating brilliant light suddenly appeared in his arms; another version holds that St. Francis simply placed a wax figure of the Christ Child in the crib. Many also believe that his musical Nativity served as a foundation for the first Christmas carols (*see* **Christmas Carols**).

The realism that St. Francis brought to the Nativity so profoundly impressed the masses that multiple variations on this theme appeared throughout Christendom. Figures of traditional Nativity characters crafted by professional artisans became popular additions to the crib scene in churches during the sixteenth century, and by the seventeenth century, families were erecting simple Nativity scenes in their homes and either making or collecting figurines as heirlooms. Throughout Europe the eighteenth century brought considerable expansion to the Nativity scene as depictions of local countrysides and characters joined those

A 1939 catalog offered this Nativity scene; also avilable for half the price was a smaller 14-piece crib set that didn't include the Star of Bethlehem. From the Shure Winner Catalog, *no. 132 (Chicago: N. Shure, 1939).*

of Bethlehem. Probably designed to create an even greater sense of familiarity with the subject, such Nativity scenes featured vast landscapes in miniature with trees and forests constructed from twigs or branches, along with moss, grass, flowers, mountains, working waterfalls, rivers with water, and perhaps volcanoes. Contemporary villages included buildings such as baker's, blacksmith's, and butcher's shops; a mill; police force; a town hall; fashionable residences; and appropriately costumed figures. In the midst of these remarkable settings stood the simple stable or cave with the Holy Family, shepherds, Three Kings, ox, ass, and angels.

Elaborate Nativity scenes are still constructed today, especially in Roman Catholic countries such as France, Italy, Mexico, Spain, and in those respective communities in the United States, as well as in the Moravian Church, where the display is termed a *Putz* (German, "finery"). Their dimensions range from those fitting under the Christmas tree to table models to those that fill one or more rooms. In addition to static Nativity scenes that adorn churches and homes, living tableaux are popular, and those in France and Italy often include stately processions through city streets.

Although static Nativity scenes may be erected a few days to several weeks prior to Christmas, a custom prevailing throughout all Roman Catholic regions of the world keeps the crib or manger symbolically empty until Christmas Eve, at which time churches and homes usually participate in ceremonies adding the Christ Child figure. Figures for the Three Kings are either added only on Epiphany (January 6), or, to symbolize their journey, they may be placed some distance away and moved forward each day to "arrive" at the manger on Epiphany. In Protestant Nativity scenes, all figures usually remain in place from initial setup. Information on specific Nativity scenes and further discussion may be found in the entries for individual countries.

Up to the mid–twentieth century, Nativity scenes sponsored by city officials or private enterprises often graced public property in the United States. Following controversies over the separation of church and state that erupted in the 1960s, many cities across the nation abolished governmental religious displays, including Nativity scenes, and the trend continues to the present.

Nestor, the Long-Eared Christmas Donkey

(1977). Made-for-television animated story using stop-motion puppets (Animagic), based on a song of the same title written in 1975 by Gene Autry, Don Pfrimmer, and Dave Burgess. They had hoped that their donkey

A variety of buildings from what the cataloger called "Christmas Villages," to be spread out under the tree, or with an electric train set-up. They were cardboard with colored cellophane windows like stained glass. The colored sides and roofs were sprinkled with colored glitter, and each building could be electrified by inserting one Christmas tree light bulb in the back. From the Shure Winner Catalog, *no. 132 (Chicago: N. Shure, 1939).*

character would gain as much popularity through recordings as had Rudolph with his red nose, but that popularity never materialized. Instead, the animated version has become a holiday favorite.

Raised on Olaf's donkey farm in northern Europe during the Roman Empire, young Nestor receives nothing but taunts and abuse from all the other donkeys because of his long, floppy ears. Olaf wrongly accuses him of ruining a potentially lucrative deal with a Roman soldier and banishes him from the farm during a hard blizzard. Determined to protect her little colt, Nestor's mother follows, covers him with her body, and sacrifices herself to the elements. Moving southward on his own, Nestor meets Tilly, a little cherub sent to guide him toward Bethlehem, his destiny. Tilly instead leaves him in the care of a desert merchant. In time Joseph, seeking a donkey to carry Mary to Bethlehem, tries to buy Nestor, but the merchant, seeing a halo around Mary, releases him as a gift. When a sudden sandstorm hinders their journey, the spirit of Nestor's mother appears, urging him to listen to the angels and follow them. Guided by their sweet song, which only his long ears can appreciate, Nestor safely arrives in Bethlehem and takes Mary to a stable of his own choosing. After the Nativity, Nestor returns to Olaf's farm, where he receives a hero's welcome.

Narrated and sung by Roger Miller. Principal voices: Eric Stern, Linda Gary, Brenda Vaccaro, Paul Frees, Iris Rainer, Shelly Hines, and Don Messick. Written by Romeo Muller. Produced and directed by Arthur Rankin, Jr., and Jules Bass. Rankin/Bass Productions. DVD: Warner Studios. 25 min.

This television special is further detailed in Rick Goldschmidt's book, *The Enchanted World of Rankin/Bass.*

See also **Rankin/Bass Christmas Cartoons.**

The Netherlands
See **The Low Countries**

New Christmas
See **Christmas Old Style, Christmas New Style**

Father Time holding a baby Punch. Punch, *December 1847.*

New Style Christmas
See **Christmas Old Style, Christmas New Style**

New Year's Day
First day of the new year, January 1 on the present Gregorian calendar. In the Roman Catholic Church, the day marks the "Solemnity of Mary," known prior to 1969 as the "Feast of the Circumcision"; in the Orthodox Church, it is the "Feast of the Circumcision of Our Lord"; in the Episcopal Church, "Feast of the Holy Name of Our Lord Jesus Christ"; in the Lutheran Church, "Feast of the Circumcision and the Name of Jesus." The new year is customarily viewed as a period of ending and of new beginning, respectively symbolized by Father Time, a wizened, white-bearded old gentleman carrying a scythe, and Baby New Year, a toddler in diapers.

• CALENDAR DATES. The date for New Year's Day has varied over the centuries between different civilizations. For example, to the ancient Greeks, the year commenced with the new moon after the summer solstice (June 21 on the Gregorian calendar); the Chinese new year begins on the second new moon after the sunset of the winter solstice, and is now cele-

This wood engraving from about 1890 shows not a Christmas party, but a typical nineteenth century New Year's Day reception. A New York woman festoons her gas chandelier with holly and greens while another brings in a fancy layered cake.

brated sometime between January 10 and February 19 on the Gregorian calendar; and the Jews celebrate *Rosh Hashanah* on the first and second days of the month of Tishri (principally in September on the Gregorian calendar). Although the new year in the Roman Empire originally began on March 1, Julius Caesar (100–44 B.C.) changed it to January 1 in 46 B.C. with a revision of the calendar now known as the Julian calendar. Prior to the Norman Conquest (1066), the English new year coincided with Christmas Day. Incorporating the Julian calendar during the Middle Ages, however, most of Europe observed the new year on March 25, a day exactly nine months prior to Christmas Day and traditionally held as the day that the Virgin Mary received the angel's message that she was to be the mother of Christ. The institution of the Gregorian calendar in 1582 again set New Year's Day on January 1, which Roman Catholic countries readily adopted. Although Scotland converted to the new calendar in 1600, the Puritans in England, objecting to the association of January with its namesake Janus, the pagan two-faced god, succeeded in delaying England's adoption of the Gregorian calendar until 1752, a delay that also

extended to the British colonies in America (*see* **Christmas Old Style, Christmas New Style**).

• ASSOCIATED TRADITIONS. One principal tradition, regardless of the date, included the giving of gifts. This custom preceded Christmastime exchanges in Europe and derived principally from similar customs that the Romans observed during the Saturnalia and the January calends (*see* **Saturnalia**). During the Middle Ages, courtiers and royalty also exchanged gifts, and England's Queen Elizabeth I was especially noted for taking advantage of the custom by requesting special gifts. King Henry VIII's gifts of expensive gold lapel pins to ladies became so popular that they were commercially reproduced; the expression "pin money" supposedly arose as gentlemen set aside cash over periods of time to purchase the cherished items. New year gift-giving at court faded during the eighteenth century, but the citizenry, who had taken up the custom in the seventeenth century, carried it into the nineteenth. It was during that latter century that holiday gift-giving became more associated with Christmas than with the new year. The reasons for this shift are not clear but probably centered around the "Christmas renaissance" that followed the Puritan ban on Christmas. Christmas gift-giving had been recorded in Germany since the early seventeenth century, which date also corresponded to the first records of home-decorated Christmas trees (1605) (*see* **Christmas Tree**).

Whereas the Christmas Day of history was spent quietly at home with the immediate family, for centuries people have greeted the new year with revelry in the form of parties, imbibing, fireworks, and all manner of noisemaking, the latter two stemming from pagan winter solstice festivals that attempted to frighten away the spirits of darkness. Custom dictated calling upon and receiving one's friends and acquaintances on New Year's Day, and in mid–nineteenth century America, it was fashionable for bachelors to call upon unmarried ladies, the latter of whom reserved visitations for themselves for January 2.

According to Old World customs, New Year's Day was the time to consult auguries regarding the weather for the new year, the likelihood of a good crop, the prospects for marriage, and the chance of death during the year. Many countries held to the superstition that whatever transpired on New Year's Day predicted what was in store for the new year. Therefore, families made every effort to be pleasant, clean, well, debt-free, and to have a bountiful feast at this time. The present custom of making New Year's resolutions undoubtedly stems from this superstition.

• CHURCH FEASTS. After the Roman Catholic Church had established December 25 as Christmas Day in the fourth century, January 1 took on significance as "Octave of the Birth of Our Lord" ("octave" signifying any holy day and the seven days that follow). This was also the day to commemorate Christ's circumcision, which occurred eight days after His birth in compliance with the covenant with Abraham and the Mosaic Law (Genesis 17:9–14; Leviticus 12:3; Luke 2:21). With circumcision He also received the name Jesus. The early Church did not universally observe January 1, however, because the pagan revelry and abandon associated with the January calends significantly overshadowed the date. Nevertheless the Council of Tours, France (567), first instituted the Feast of the Circumcision on January 1 as an effort to offset pagan practices. Spain adopted the feast sometime during the life of St. Isidore of Seville (ca. 560–636), and Rome, having first established the Octave of the Birth of Our Lord in the seventh century, combined this feast with the Feast of the Circumcision in the ninth century. Since the eighth century, the Orthodox Church has observed January 1 as the Circumcision as well as the anniversary of the death of St. Basil (ca. 329–379), one of the Orthodox patriarchs. Many regard the January feast as the earliest in the Roman Catholic Church dedicated to the Virgin Mary, for in the Mass are prayers that specifically make reference to her virtues. In 1969, following the Second Vatican Council, the Solemnity of Mary, which celebrates her divine maternity, replaced the Circumcision on January 1.

• NEW YEAR'S DAY IN THE UNITED STATES. Broadcast nationwide is the New Year's Eve celebration from New York City's Times Square, where at least one million people annually crowd together to revel and to watch a large,

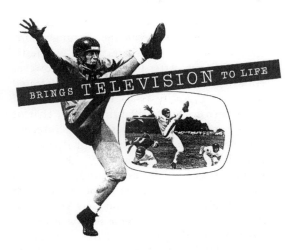

This December 1949 magazine ad for Capehart televisions capitalized on the draw of New Year's Day football to attract buyers.

illuminated ball atop the Times Square Building descend from its pinnacle at 11:59 P. M. Eastern Standard Time. At the stroke of midnight, a large "Happy New Year" sign beneath the ball flashes as cheers and "Auld Lang Syne," the theme song for the new year, fill the air (*see* **Auld Lang Syne**).

New Year's Day is devoted to parades and nationally televised college football games or "bowl" games. One of the foremost parades, the annual Tournament of Roses Parade in Pasadena, California, dates to January 1, 1890, as the highlight of a festival that originated with members of the Pasadena Valley Hunt Club. Designed to display California's roses and other native flora, the first parade included horse-drawn carriages covered with flowers. In 1895, the Tournament of Roses Association relieved the Valley Hunt Club and took charge of the festival. Today, complex floats built by professional companies are appropriately decorated with thousands of flowers according the annual theme selected for the event. In addition to these floral floats, which pass down Colorado Boulevard, the two-hour parade includes marching bands, equestrians, and the float for the reigning Rose Queen and her royal court of six Rose princesses. The latter, selected in September during a month-long competition of poise, personality, public speaking, and scholastic achievement, also reign over the Rose Bowl Game.

Added to the festival in 1902, a college football game served to revive the seemingly waning interest in the Tournament of Roses festival at the time. After this first game, however (in which the University of Michigan defeated Stanford University 49–0), football games did not return to the festival until 1916, chariot races having temporarily filled the interim. Football resumed in Tournament Park, then moved to the Rose Bowl, a new 57,000-seat stadium (subsequently enlarged to 92,542), which hosted the first Rose Bowl Game and the first formal college bowl game on New Year's Day, 1923. The Rose Bowl Game has been played from this stadium since that time, except for 1942 following the Japanese attack on Pearl Harbor on December 7, 1941, when it was played at Duke University Stadium in Durham, North Carolina. Dubbed "The Granddaddy of Them All" in 1947, the Rose Bowl Game has featured the championship teams of the Big Ten and the Pacific Ten conferences. Since the 1998 season, the Rose Bowl has participated in the Bowl Championship Series, which schedules a championship game between the two highest ranked teams in the country. Once the pair is determined, this and other bowls are free to invite the teams of their choice.

Other principal college bowl games that are played on or about New Year's Day include the following:

Orange Bowl, first played in 1933 as a feature of the Palm Festival in Miami, Florida. From 1935 to 1995, it was played in the Orange Bowl Stadium, but from 1996 it has been played in Ft. Lauderdale's Pro Player Stadium (seating 75,000). Since 1998, it has participated in the Bowl Championship Series and usually hosts a Big East or Atlantic Coast Conference champion vs. an at-large opponent.

Sugar Bowl, played from 1935 to 1974 at Tulane Stadium in New Orleans, Louisiana. Since 1975, it has played at the Superdome (seating just over 72,000) in New Orleans and is the first and only bowl to be played indoors. The Sugar Bowl has participated in the Bowl Championship Series since 1998.

Cotton Bowl, played in Dallas, Texas. The first Cotton Bowl matched two high school teams on New Year's Day, 1936, and college teams followed in the years thereafter. This bowl was played in the Fair Park Stadium in 1937 and has been played in the Cotton Bowl Stadium (seating 68,252) since 1938. From 1942 through 1994, the Cotton Bowl matched the Southwestern Conference champion against an at-large opponent. Currently, the Cotton Bowl features teams from the Big 12 and the Southeastern Conference.

Fiesta Bowl, played in Arizona State University's Sun Devil Stadium (seating 73,656) in Tempe since December 27, 1971. The Fiesta Bowl first matched Arizona State against an at-large opponent. The game moved to January 1 after the 1981 season and has been played on that day or thereabouts since then. The Fiesta Bowl has participated in the Bowl Championship Series since 1998.

Another annual New Year's Day parade is the Philadelphia Mummer's Parade (*see* **Christmas Drama** [Mumming]).

New Year's Eve Party
See **The Honeymooners**

Nicaragua
See **Central America**

Nigh Bethlehem
See **Alfred Burt Carols**

The Night Before Christmas
See **A Visit from St. Nicholas**

The Night They Saved Christmas
(1984). Made-for-television adventure.

Santa (Art Carney) and his workshop at North Pole City face annihilation when an oil company drilling in the Arctic Circle plans a blasting project on Christmas Eve, not knowing that the project is near Santa's hidden abode. After geologist Michael Baldwin (Paul LeMat) dismisses Santa's emissary and chief elf Ed (Paul Williams) as a practical joke, Ed convinces Michael's wife Claudia (Jaclyn Smith) to meet with Santa about the problem. Skeptical, Claudia accompanies Ed in a "reindeer zephyr," a self-propelled sleigh, to North Pole City, along with her children, David (Scott Grimes), Maryanne (Laura Jacoby), and C.B. (R.J. Williams). Not only do they become instant believers in awe of Santa's high-tech domain, which boasts a time decelerator device that allows Santa to get around the world in one night and a worldwide language communicator/translator, but Santa also reveals the location of an abundant oil site farther away. Then it's a race against time to inform the oil company before it carries out the scheduled detonation, and Christmas is saved after all.

In 1986, this picture won a Young Artist Award for Best Young Actress Starring in a Television Special or Miniseries (Laura Jacoby).

With June Lockhart as Mrs. Martha Claus. Written by Jim Moloney and David Niven, Jr. Produced by David Kappes and Robert Halmi, Jr. Directed by Jackie Cooper. RHI Entertainment. VHS: Hallmark Home Entertainment Video. 95 min.

The Nightmare before Christmas

(1993). Animated motion picture musical using three-dimensional, stop-motion action, based on a poem by director, producer, writer, and actor Tim Burton. Burton conceived *The Nightmare before Christmas* while working as an animator for Disney Studios in 1983. A dual celebration of Halloween and Christmas (Burton's two favorite holidays), this is the story of Jack Skellington, the skeleton king of Halloween Town, whose inhabitants—ghouls, vampires, and other typically frightful creatures—plan each Halloween celebration a year in advance.

Weary of creating the same screams and nightmares each year, Jack longs for something more meaningful. Wandering through a forest, he comes upon several trees with doors fashioned in various holiday symbols that are alien to him: an Easter egg, a Thanksgiving turkey, and a Christmas tree. He opens the latter door and plummets into a magical world of snow, toys, and Santa Claus—in short, Christmas Town. Anxious to share Christmas with Halloween Town, he returns with simple toys and commissions everyone in his domain to duplicate them as well as create a Santa suit, reindeer, and sleigh. Their efforts are anything but Christmasy, for their limited imaginations are capable of producing only fiendish toys with fangs and a coffin sleigh with skeleton reindeer.

Overcome with the desire to participate in Christmas, Jack decides to assume Santa's role on Christmas Eve. To get Santa temporarily out of the way, Jack orders three mischievous creatures, Luck, Chuck, and Beryl, to kidnap the jolly old elf. These creatures deliver Santa to Oogie Boogie, the Bogey Man. Sally, a female version of the Frankenstein monster created by Dr. Finkelstein, senses that Jack is completely out of his element and conjures up a fog that almost puts a halt to Jack's midnight ride, until Zero, his red-nosed ghost dog, leads the skeleton team skyward in the spirit of Rudolph, the Red-Nosed Reindeer. As Jack disperses his toys, they wreak havoc by chasing and attacking children while Jack, spotted as an impostor, is shot from the sky by ground artillery. With Christmas nearly a disaster, Jack realizes that attempting to venture beyond his realm was a serious error. Just as Oogie Boogie is about to dispatch Santa, Jack returns to his role as skeleton king and saves Christmas.

In 1994, this picture won Saturn awards for Best Fantasy Film and Best Music. It received the following award nominations: an Academy Award for Best Visual Effects; a Golden Globe Award for Best Original Score for a Motion Picture; a Hugo Award for Best Dramatic Presentation; a Young Artist Award for Outstanding Family Motion Picture in Action/Adventure; and a Grammy Award for Best Album for Children.

Principal voices: Danny Elfman (also provided the musical score, songs, lyrics, and lead vocals), Chris Sarandon, Catherine O'Hara, William Hickey, Glenn Shadix, Paul Reubens, and Ken Page. Written by Caroline Thompson. Adapted by Michael McDowell. Produced by Tim Burton and Denise DiNovi. Directed by Henry Selick. Skellington Productions and Touchstone Pictures. DVD: Disney Studios. 76 min.

The Noble Stem of Jesse

See **Lo, How a Rose E'er Blooming**

Noel

See **The First Nowell**

Noel! A New Noel

See **Sing We Now of Christmas**

North Pole

See **Saint Nicholas**

Norway

A succession of Norwegian kings gradually introduced Christianity into Norway starting in the mid–tenth century. The first was King Håkon I (914?–961), a son of the Norwegian king Harold I, who had been raised in the Christian faith by King Athelstan of England. Håkon first decreed that the long-established winter solstice festival of *Jul* (Yule) would coincide with that for the birth of Christ on December 25, a change that initially alienated many of his subjects and hindered their conversion. Norway completely converted during the subsequent, iron-fisted rules of Harold's descendants, kings Olaf I (968–1000) and Olaf II (995–1030), the latter of whom was canonized as the patron saint of Norway. Following the Protestant Reformation in the sixteenth century, the Evangelical Lutheran Church emerged in Norway as the principal Christian faith. Norway continues to celebrate Christmas with customs that blend the spiritual with remnants of pagan Yule.

The Advent season includes Advent candles, calendars, and wreaths. For the latter decoration it is still customary for many families to make their own candles (a related superstition in some regions holds that if someone's candle is extinguished on Christmas night, death lingers nearby). Employers customarily host Christmas buffets for their employees and customers during the weeks of Advent, and a favorite dish served at these occasions is half-fermented trout.

The Christmas season, formerly beginning on St. Thomas's Day (December 21) in Norway's Roman Catholic past, now begins on St. Lucia Day (December 13) with customs akin to those of Sweden, which has become the prototypical country for observing St. Lucia Day. This night was termed *Lussinatten* (Lussi Night) in Norway after Lussi, a vengeful spirit who punished those who did any work at this time. It was also believed that gnomes and trolls were given free rein from this day until Christmas.

Other Advent customs include thoroughly cleaning the house and decorating with fir boughs, erecting a sheaf of grain on a pole outdoors for the birds ("Birds' Christmas Tree"), providing the livestock with extra fodder, withdrawing of hunting traps and snares, sending Christmas cards, and baking traditional Christmas cookies. Consisting of at least seven varieties, Christmas cookies include *peppernøtter* (pepper nuts), *sirupssnipper* (syrup snaps), *berlinerkranser* (Berlin wreaths), *sandkaker* (sand tarts), *krumkaker* (curled cookies), *strull* (sour cream cookies), and *fløtekaker* (cream cakes). For special events, it is customary to serve *kranskake* (almond wreath cake) stacked in the shape of a pyramid, and gingerbread "houses" frequently take intricate shapes of castles, perhaps even entire village scenes.

Christmas trees, a custom adopted from Germany in the early nineteenth century, decorate many public places. The public trees are lighted on the first Advent Sunday, whereas families usually light those trees in their homes only on Christmas Eve. Family tree decorations usually include a combination of homemade and commercially manufactured ornaments. The homemade ornaments often consist of small candles, strands of small Norwegian flags, hearts of red felt, and heart-shaped baskets filled with candies. As a gesture of her appreciation to England for granting political asylum to King Håkon during the German occupation of World War II (1940–1945), Norway has, since 1947, shipped one of her best Christmas trees annually to England, where the tree decorates London's Trafalgar Square.

Although Norwegians are quite familiar with Santa Claus through other European influences, it is not he who brings the Christmas gifts but the *Julenissen*, a composite of St. Nicholas and the *nisse*, a small, mischievous elf or gnome of Norwegian folklore. Attired in a red stocking cap, knee breeches, stockings and fur, and sporting a long, white beard, the *nisse* ordinarily protects the homestead and its inhabitants during the year, and any mishaps occurring thereabouts are said to result from his pranks. Assuming the name *Julenissen* at Christmastime, he requires an annual bowl of rice porridge on Christmas Eve to control his antics. Children not only in Norway but throughout the world may mail their Christmas wish lists to *Julenissen* at his special post office in Drøbak, a small village south of Oslo, and for each letter received, *Julenissen* sends a reply. Decorative versions of the *Julenissen* are known as *smånisser* ("small Santas").

Christmas Eve officially commences at 5 P.M., when church bells throughout all cities ring in Christmas, for most churches hold services at this hour. Families usually place lighted candles and wreaths on the graves of loved ones and then retire to their homes for the traditional Christmas Eve feast, the menu of which will vary from region to region. In general, coastal and northern regions feature *lutefisk* (codfish); eastern regions, pork ribs, sausages, and cabbage; western regions, mutton and pork. Dishes widely found include *lefse* (flat bread), cloudberry cream, caramel pudding, rice, and fruit. A most traditional Scandinavian dish is rice porridge, which contains one almond in the batch. Whoever finds the almond in his serving will receive good luck in the new year. In those households that follow the old customs, the food remains on the table overnight for the spirits of deceased family members, who are believed to return at this time of year to partake of the Christmas feast.

Following the meal, families may read from the Bible or join hands to walk around the Christmas tree while singing carols. Sometime after the meal, someone dressed as the *Julenissen* and toting a sack of gifts knocks on the door, then asks the traditional question before distributing gifts to children: "Are there any good children here?" Some regions may still observe the archaic custom of "Shooting in Christmas," in which marksmen fire a number of rounds on Christmas Eve to greet Christmas. The custom derives from ancient Yule festivals that made much commotion and loud noise at the winter solstice in order to ward off evil spirits.

After church on Christmas Day, families enjoy a large buffet of hot and cold dishes similar to those of Christmas Eve, including fish and pork, cheese and fruit, *lefse*, beer, and a liquor, Norwegian *aquavit*. Activities include various competitive games along with a popular tradition, *Julebukk* ("Christmas Goat"). Resembling the American custom of trick-or-treating at Halloween, *Julebukk* involves bands of costumed children traveling through neighborhoods while leading a billy goat and singing carols in return for treats. Instead of a goat, a man dressed in goat skins and wearing a goat mask may accompany the children for the purpose of imitating a goat's unruly behavior and frightening the children into maintaining proper deportment. The *Julebukk* derives from pre-Christian Yule festivals, which paid homage to the gods. At the winter solstice, it was believed that, as he rode through the skies in a chariot pulled by two billy goats named Gnasher and Cracker, the god Thor distributed gifts to the Vikings while his father Odin, riding his white, eight-legged steed Sleipner, escorted the souls of slain heroes into Valhalla. Men costumed as goats portrayed this belief by making surprise entrances at Yule parties, and after dancing about, "died," then returned to life. During the Middle Ages, the goat figure symbolized the Devil in Scandinavian Christmas folk revels, and men costumed in goat skins and masks frolicked about, much to the dismay of the Church. Although the Church banned such behavior in the sixteenth century, today's *Julebukk* is a relatively tame vestige.

Celebrations after Christmas include St. Stephen's Day (December 26), on which people visit friends and relatives, and costumed men in villages render folk songs about the saint; New Year's Eve, which allows for another round of merrymaking, noise, and parties; and Epiphany (January 6), marked by parades of "Star Boys" (dressed in white with tall, pointed hats bedecked with stars), who provide carols.

The Christmas season terminates 20 days after Christmas Day on St. Knut's Day (January 13), a day named in honor of the Danish king Knut IV (also known as Canute, Cnut, Knud), who was assassinated in 1086. A strong supporter of the Church through acts of piety and charity, he was canonized in 1100. The exact origin of the 20-day feast is uncertain. Some believe that Knut himself decreed it; others hold that, because the Vikings feasted and offered human sacrifices on this day, the Church sought to stamp out such practices by extending Christmas through that day. In festivals today, home parties on St. Knut's Day light the Christmas tree one last time, then remove all decorations and dismantle the tree.

Children retrieve the decorative sweets, and trees are often burned in communal bonfires.

"Merry Christmas" in Norwegian is "*God Jul.*"

See also **Advent; Epiphany; Sweden; Winter Solstice; Yule.**

Now Come, Savior of the Heathen
See **Savior of the Nations, Come**

Nowell, Sing Nowell
See **Sing We Now of Christmas**

The Nutcracker

Ballet in two acts, the last of three ballets for which the Russian composer Peter I. Tchaikovsky (1840–1893) provided the music, the other two being *Swan Lake* (1876) and *The Sleeping Beauty* (1889). The only major Christmas ballet currently performed, *The Nutcracker* is loosely based on a fantastic fairy tale, *The Nutcracker and the Mouse King*, written in 1816 by the German author E.T.A. Hoffmann. A synopsis of this story is essential to appreciate the significant alteration of the story that subsequently emerged in the ballet.

• THE ORIGINAL STORY. Christmas Eve provides unusual festivities for Dr. Stahlbaum's children, seven-year-old Marie and her older brother, Fritz. Their mysterious and eccentric clockmaker-godfather, Judge Drosselmeier, has fashioned a series of ingenious toys, one of which is an ugly yet fascinating nutcracker doll dressed as a prince. Fritz damages the nutcracker in a childish scuffle, and Marie, most attached to the doll, remains with it long after everyone has retired. At midnight, she witnesses a strange battle between an army of Fritz's toy soldiers, led by the nutcracker, and an army of mice, led by a seven-headed mouse king. When the tide turns against nutcracker, Marie saves him by throwing her slipper at the mouse king, but her arm is lacerated by broken glass in the process. Fainting, she is found in the morning lying in her own blood, having almost perished from exsanguination. During her recovery, her family scoffs at her wild story about the Christmas Eve battle, and Drosselmeier, who has repaired the nutcracker, entertains Marie with the intriguing tale about how the doll became so ugly.

Here begins a complex subplot, "The Story of the Hard Nut." Madam Mouserinks, a mouse witch, vows revenge on a king's baby daughter, Princess Pirlipat, because the king ordered the execution of the witch's seven-headed son and other relatives when the witch ruined the king's feast. She transforms baby Pirlipat into a monstrosity, after which Drosselmeier, the court wizard, determines that eating the rare and exceedingly hard Krakatuk nut will reverse the spell. The king promises his daughter to the man who can crack such a nut, and Drosselmeier sets off to find both man and nut. Finding the nut in Nuremberg after a 15-year search, Drosselmeier also discovers that his young nephew from the same locale, who cracks the hardest nuts with his teeth, is most suited to perform the vital nut-cracking ritual. Restored as a beautiful young lady, Pirlipat scorns the nephew, who, having taken the spell upon himself, is transformed into an ugly nutcracker and is banished from the kingdom. In the commotion, the nutcracker accidentally crushes the mouse witch to death. To break this new spell, nutcracker must kill the mouse witch's second, seven-headed son who now reigns as the new mouse king.

Marie now realizes that the battle of Christmas Eve was her beloved nutcracker's initial attempt to break the spell and that he is actually the bewitched nephew of Godfather Drosselmeier. At a magical moment, the nutcracker begs a sword from Marie and ultimately slays the mouse king. In gratitude, he escorts Marie into an incredible fairyland of sweets, beauty, and pleasure, where he is the prince of Marzipan Castle. Awakening as from a dream, Marie vows that, if nutcracker had been human, she would never have spurned him for his ugliness. Her confession of love erases the spell, for Godfather Drosselmeier immediately appears with his handsome, quite-human nephew in tow, who, as the new king of Marzipan Castle, secures Marie's hand in marriage.

• ORIGINS OF THE BALLET. The two-act ballet is a considerably reduced adaptation of a French translation of Hoffmann's tale titled *The Nutcracker of Nuremberg*, made in 1845 by Alexandre Dumas (the elder, author of *The Three Musketeers*). The adaptation originated with Ivan Vsevolozhsky, director of Imperial Theaters in St. Petersburg, the imperial choreographer Marius Petipa, and Petipa's assistant, Lev Ivanov (who completed the choreography when Petipa fell ill). The former two had collaborated with Tchaikovsky on *The Sleeping Beauty*, and they persuaded the composer to provide the musical score for *The Nutcracker*. This was a hard sell, for their adaptation (which changed the character of Marie Stahlbaum to Clara Silberhaus) reduced Hoffmann's complex, often violent, and erotically weird plot to a bland children's Christmas party (first half of Act I) and a little girl's fanciful dream (latter half of Act I and all of Act II) that retained only the initial Christmas Eve scene and a series of dances in the contrived "Kingdom of Sweets." Tchaikovsky, feeling that this abbreviated version suffered from a complete lack of drama and emotional appeal, reluctantly commenced work on it in early 1891.

The Nutcracker Suite and the Ballet. By March of 1892, Tchaikovsky, dividing his time between conducting tours in Europe and America and working on *The Nutcracker*, faced a series of concerts previously booked for St. Petersburg, about which he had forgotten and for which he was unprepared. In desperation, he threw together eight selections from his unfinished *Nutcracker* ballet and presented them at the Maryinsky Theater in St. Petersburg on March 19, 1892, as *The Nutcracker Suite*. This best-known collection from the ballet consists of the "Miniature Overture," "March" (which accompanies the children's entrance in Act I), "Dance of the Sugar-Plum Fairy" (whom Tchaikovsky characterizes with a celesta, an instrument he had discovered in Paris in June 1891), "Russian Trepak," "Arabian Dance" (which personifies coffee), "Chinese Dance" (which personifies tea), "Dance of the Reed-Pipes" (also known as "Dance of the Flutes" and "Dance of the Shepherds"), and "Waltz of the Flowers" (which concludes the entertainment divertissement in the Kingdom of Sweets). The latter six numbers appear in Act II, and the latter five represent a portion of the entertainment that Clara enjoys during her magical visit to the Kingdom of Sweets. The "Spanish Dance," which personifies chocolate in Act II, is not included in the *Suite*.

Peter I. Tchaikovsky (1840–1893), Russian composer of the music to The Nutcracker. *Photograph by Vezenberg and Company, St. Petersburg, Russia, c. 1880–1886. Courtesy Library of Congress.*

The *Suite* was an instant success, not only in St. Petersburg, but abroad as well. It debuted in the United States in Chicago on October 22, 1892, and in London on October 17, 1896.

Tchaikovsky completed *The Nutcracker* ballet in April 1892, but in keeping with its theme, deliberately delayed its premiere until Christmastime. Performed by the eminent Kirov Ballet on December 18, 1892, in St. Petersburg, the ballet generated surprisingly mixed emotions. The chief complaint voiced was that romping children dominated the entire first act, leaving the heart of the ballet for the second act. Today, of course, it is the children, the fantasy, and the opportunity to create spectacular visual effects such as flying sleighs and dancing snowflakes that make *The Nutcracker* a popular holiday attraction.

The Nutcracker ballet was performed only within Russia for over 40 years. Nicholas Sergeyev staged the first complete performance of the ballet abroad in London in 1934. A shortened version followed in the United States in

A shelf of nutcrackers of carved, painted wood flank a tiny Christmas tree in this illustration from a German children's periodical, Deutscher Kinderfreund, *1909.*

1940, performed by Ballet Russe de Monte Carlo, and a complete performance debuted in the United States in 1954, staged by Kirov-trained George Balanchine. It is this latter staging on which many modern American productions are based.

• NOTABLE FILM AND TELEVISION VERSIONS. Numerous motion picture, television, or animated versions exist, most of them titled *Nutcracker* or *The Nutcracker*. The following list summarizes noteworthy performances:

Barbie in "The Nutcracker" (2001). Computer-generated animation made for video. Modern, politically correct adaptation starring Mattel Toys' all-American doll Barbie, with choreography by Peter Martins of the New York City Ballet and music by the London Symphony Orchestra. Honors: 2001, won Video Premiere Award for Best Animated Video Premiere Movie; Video Premiere Award nominations for Best Animated Character Performance (voices of Peter Kelamis and Kelly Sheridan). Other principal voices: Kirby Morrow, Tim Curry, Christopher Gaze, Ian James Corlett, French Tickner, and Kathleen Barr. Written by Linda Engelsiepen, Ruth Handler, Hilary Hinkle, and Rob Hudnut. Produced by Jesyca C. Durchin and Jennifer T. McCarron. Directed by Owen Hurley. Family Home Entertainment, Mainframe Entertainment, and Mattel, Inc. DVD: Artisan Entertainment. 78 min.

The Enchanted Nutcracker (1961). Television adaptation choreographed by Carol Haney. Featuring Robert Goulet, Linda Canby, Carol Lawrence, Charlotte Lawrence, and Pierre Olaf.

Teleplay by Bella Spewack and Sam Spewack. Directed by Jack Smight. Video N/A. 60 min.

George Balanchine's "The Nutcracker" (1993). Performance featuring Macaulay Culkin. Narrated by Kevin Kline. Choreography by George Balanchine. With Bart Robinson Cook, Jessica Lynn Cohen, Darci Kistler, Peter Reznick, Robert LaFosse, Heather Watts, and Robert W. Lyon. Written by Susan Cooper. Produced by Robert Hurwitz and Robert A. Krasnow. Directed by Emile Ardolino. Elektra Entertainment Group, Embassy International Pictures, and Regency Enterprises. DVD: Warner Studios. 92 min.

The IMAX Nutcracker (1997). Starring Miriam Margolyes, Heathcote Williams, Lotte Johnson, and Benjamin Hall. Set in London, the production is IMAX's first venture into classic stories. Written and directed by Christine Edzard. Produced by Lorne Orleans and Olivier Stockman. IMAX Corporation and Sands Films. Video N/A. 40 min.

The Nutcracker (1965). Television production featuring Edward Villella, Melissa Hayden, and Patricia McBride, with the New York City Ballet. Narrated by Eddie Albert. CBS Television. Video N/A. 60 min.

The Nutcracker (1968). Performance featuring Rudolph Nureyev and Merle Park with the Royal Ballet at London's Covent Garden. DVD: Kultur Video. 100 min.

The Nutcracker (1977). Television performance featuring Mikhail Baryshnikov, Gelsey Kirkland, and Alexander Minz with the American Ballet Theatre. Emmy Award nominations in 1978 for Outstanding Classical Program in the Performing Arts and Special Classification of Outstanding Individual Achievement (Baryshnikov). Choreographed by Baryshnikov. Produced by Yanna Kroyt Brandt. Directed by Tony Charmoli. CBS Television. DVD: MGM/UA Home Video. 79 min.

The Nutcracker (1978). Russian production featuring Yekatarina Maksimova, Vladimir Vasilyev and Nadiya Pavlova of the Bolshoi Ballet. Directed by Yelena Macheret. DVD: Kultur Video. 100 min.

The Nutcracker (1985). Featuring principals Lesley Collier and Anthony Dowell with the Royal Ballet, performed at London's Covent Garden. Attempts to revive the original Ivanov/Sergeyev staging. Choreography by Peter Wright and Roland John Wiley. DVD: Kultur Video. 102 min.

The Nutcracker (1989). Principals Miyako Yoshida and Irek Mukhamedov. The Birmingham Royal Ballet. Choreographed by Peter Wright. VHS: Kultur Video. 98 min.

The Nutcracker (1994). Performance by the Kirov Ballet at the Maryinsky Theater in St. Petersburg, Russia, featuring Larissa Lezhnina and Viktor Baranov. Choreographed by Vassili Vainonen. DVD: UNI/Philips. 95 min.

The Nutcracker (1999). Performance by the Deutsche Staatsoper Ballet Company of Berlin, Germany, choreographed by Patrice Bart. Featuring Nadja Saidakova, Oliver Matz, and Vladimir Malakhov. The traditional plot is altered such that Marie is abducted by Russian revolutionaries. Music conducted by Daniel Barenboim. Produced by Francois Duplat. Directed by Alexandre Tarta. DVD: Arthaus Musik.

The Nutcracker (2000). French production, live recording of performance by the Théâtre Musical de Paris Châtelet ballet company, choreographed by Maurice Béjart. The storyline radically departs from the original and depicts Béjart's own life story. Featuring Damaas Thijs, Elisabet Ros, Gil Roman, Juichi Kobayashi, and Yvette Horner. DVD: Image Entertainment. 103 min.

The Nutcracker (2001). Performance by the Royal Ballet of Covent Garden, London. Featuring Shirly Laub, Evgenii Svetlanov, and Sir Anthony Dowell. VHS: Naxos of America.

The Nutcracker: A Fantasy on Ice (1983).

Television performance featuring champion figure skater Dorothy Hamill with Robin Cousins. Narrated by Lorne Greene. Produced by Roy Krost. Directed by Ron Meraska. Eskimo Productions. VHS: Vidmark/Trimark. 85 min.

The Nutcracker and the Mouseking (2004). American-German made-for-video animated cartoon. Principal voices: Leslie Nielsen, Robert Hays, Fred Willard, and Eric Idle. Written by Ross Helford and Andy Hurst. Produced by Sven Ebeling. Directed by Bob Buchholz, Tatjana Ilyina, and Michael Johnson. Media Cooperation One GmbH. DVD: Anchor Bay Entertainment. 82 min.

Nutcracker Fantasy (1979). Japanese production featuring animated puppets, dubbed in English. Honors: 1980, won Young Artist Award for Best Musical Entertainment Featuring Youth and nominated for Best Motion Picture Featuring Youth; Saturn Award nomination for Best Fantasy Film. Narrated by Michelle Lee. Principal voices: Christopher Lee, Eva Gabor, Melissa Gilbert, Roddy McDowall, Dick Van Patten, and Jo Anne Worley. Music adapted and arranged by Akihito Wakatsuki. Written by Eugene A. Fournier and Thomas Joachim. Produced by Mark L. Rosen. Directed by Takeo Nakamura. Sanrio Communications. Video N/A. 82 min.

Nutcracker on Ice (1994). Made-for-video performance featuring champion figure skaters Oksana Baiul, Viktor Petrenko and Vladimir Petrenko. Choreographed and directed by Minnie Madden. VHS: Fox Video. 110 min.

Nutcracker on Ice (1995). Television performance featuring champion figure skater Peggy Fleming, with Nicole Bobek, Todd Eldredge, and Brian Orser. Directed by Richard Wells. Video N/A.

The Nutcracker Prince (1990). Canadian animated cartoon feature, in which the nutcracker is named Hans. Nominated in 1991 for Young Artist Award for Most Entertaining Family Youth Motion Picture in Animation. Music arranged by Victor Davies and performed by the London Symphony Orchestra. Principal voices: Kiefer Sutherland, Megan Follows, Mike MacDonald, Peter Boretski, Phyllis Diller, and Peter O'Toole. Written by Patricia Watson. Produced by Kevin Gillis. Directed by

Paul Schibli. Lacewood Productions. VHS: Warner Home Video. 74 min.

Nutcracker: The Motion Picture (1986). Performance by the Pacific Northwest Ballet Company with sets and costumes by Maurice Sendak. Featuring Hugh Bigney, Vanessa Sharp, Patricia Barker, Wade Walthall, and Russell Burnett. Nominated in 1988 for Young Artist Award for Best Family Motion Picture Drama. Produced by Willard Carroll, Donald Kushner, Peter Locke, and Thomas L. Wilhite. Directed by Carroll Ballard. Hyperion Films. VHS: Polygram Video.

Nutcracker: The Story of Clara (1994). Performance by the Australian Ballet, choreographed by Graeme Murphy. Departing from the original, the storyline chronicles the nomadic life of principal character Clara, a famous Russian ballerina, who comes to Australia in the 1940s. Featuring Vicki Attard, Steven Heathcote, and Dame Margaret Scott. VHS: Kultur Video. 113 min.

The Nuttiest Nutcracker (1999). Made-for-video cartoon comedy with computer-generated animation. Teenage heroine Marie is engaged in a quest to return the Christmas star to her tree, lest the spirit of Christmas fade. Principal voices: James Belushi, Phyllis Diller, Cheech Marin, Cam Clarke, Debi Derryberry, Desiree Goyette, Tress MacNeille, Jeff Bennett, Jim Cummings, and Kevin Schon. Directed by Harold Harris. Dan Krech Productions. DVD: Columbia/Tristar Home Video. 48 min.

The Swinging Nutcracker (2001). Canadian production for television, featuring Paul Becker, Jeff Hyslop, and Debbie Timuss. Blends traditional ballet with jazz and "swing" rhythms of the 1930s and 1940s. Choreographed by Lisa Stevens. Story by Ross Powell. Written and directed by Shel Piercy. Produced by Pat O'Brien. Infinity Films. Video N/A. 60 min.

The Nutcracker: A Fantasy on Ice
See **The Nutcracker**

The Nutcracker and the Mouseking
See **The Nutcracker**

Nutcracker Fantasy
See **The Nutcracker**

Nutcracker on Ice
See **The Nutcracker**

The Nutcracker Prince
See **The Nutcracker**

Nutcracker: The Motion Picture
See **The Nutcracker**

Nutcracker: The Story of Clara
See **The Nutcracker**

The Nuttiest Nutcracker
See **The Nutcracker**

Nuttin' for Christmas
American novelty song written in 1955 by the New York–born songwriting team of Sid Tepper and Roy Bennett. Inspired by an occasion when Bennett's daughter Claire spilled some ink, the lyrics are an actual compilation of childish pranks pulled by Tepper's and Bennett's own children at various times and presented as though a mischievous little boy is the sole culprit. The misdeeds include head-bashing with a baseball bat, hiding a frog, eating bugs, using metal slugs in gum machines, placing tacks in chairs, tying knots in hair, trampling plants, tearing clothes, and adding ants to the sugar bowl. Having been a bad boy all year, the child anticipates getting "nuttin' [nothing] for Christmas." Five-year-old Barry Gordon introduced the song on television's *The Milton Berle Show*, and his recording with Art Mooney and His Orchestra on the MGM label was the top Christmas song for 1955 (position six on the *Billboard Hot 100* chart), selling over one million copies.

Tepper and Bennett collaborated on a number of other hits, such as "Red Roses for a Blue Lady" (1948), the holiday favorite "Suzy Snowflake" (1951), and "The Naughty Lady of Shady Lane" (1954).

See also **Suzy Snowflake**.

"O" Antiphons

Also known as "Christmas Antiphons," "Great Antiphons," and "The Seven O's," these are a group of seven Latin prayers for Advent in the Roman Catholic Church that are consecutively chanted during Vespers on each of the seven nights leading up to the Vigil of Christmas. Originally, the interval extended from December 16 to December 23 (omitting St. Thomas's Day, formerly observed on December 21), but began on December 17 following the Protestant Reformation. Each antiphon petitions Christ in praise and addresses Him with one of seven biblical titles. Collectively, they are termed "'O' Antiphons" because each prayer begins with the interjection "O."

Although the antiphons are believed to date to the time of Charlemagne (742–814), they may have been in usage much earlier, for it is said that the Roman statesman, philosopher, and Christian martyr (by tradition) Anicius Boethius (480–?524) made brief mention of them. It is further believed that, by the twelfth or thirteenth century, five of the antiphons had been arranged to form a single hymn with an added refrain that was not a part of the original antiphons: "*Gaude! gaude! Emanuel / Nascetur pro te, Israel*" ("Rejoice! Rejoice! Emmanuel / Shall come to thee, O Israel"). The earliest known written source for these seven antiphons is an appendix in *Psalteriolum Cantionum Catholicarum* (Cologne, Germany, 1710), a collection from the Tridentine rite. They are the basis for the Advent hymn "O Come, O Come, Emmanuel."

The order of the antiphons is significant: disregarding the "O," the initial letters, when spelled in reverse, reveal the Latin acrostic "ERO CRAS"—"I shall be [with you] tomorrow," which implies the coming of Christ and Christmas. Below are descriptions of the antiphons and examples of their biblical significance:

December 17: "*O Sapientia, quae ex ore Altissimi prodiisti ...*" ("O Wisdom, Who came from the mouth of the Most High ..."). God governs all creation through His wisdom. The antiphon bids Christ to come and teach the way of prudence. Biblical basis: Isaiah 11:2; First Corinthians 1:30.

December 18: "*O Adonai, et dux domus Israel ...*" ("O Lord, and Ruler of the house of Israel ..."). This recalls God's appearance to Moses through the burning bush and the giving of the first Law on Mt. Sinai. The antiphon bids Christ to come and redeem mankind with a mighty hand. Biblical basis: Exodus 3; Micah 5:2.

December 19: "*O Radix Jesse ...*" ("O Root of Jesse ..."). Before Christ, descended from the line of Jesse's son, King David, all nations will make supplication. The antiphon bids Christ to come and deliver mankind. Biblical basis: Isaiah 11:1, 10.

December 20: "*O Clavis David ...*" ("O Key of David ..."). Christ, descended from King David, has the keys to heaven and hell. The antiphon bids Christ to come and free those imprisoned by the darkness of sin. Biblical basis: Isaiah 22:22; Revelation 3:7.

December 21: "*O Oriens ...*" ("O Dawn of the East [Dayspring] ..."). Christ is eternal Light. The antiphon bids Christ to come and enlighten those who dwell in pagan darkness and the shadow of death. Biblical basis: Isaiah 9:2; Malachi 4:2; Luke 1:78.

December 22: "*O Rex gentium ...*" ("O King of the Gentiles [Nations] ..."). Christ is the Cornerstone Who unites mankind with Himself. The antiphon bids Christ to come and save those whom He created from dust. Biblical basis: Isaiah 2:4; Isaiah 9:6; First Peter 2:6.

December 23: "*O Emmanuel, Rex et legifer noster ...*" ("O Emmanuel, our King and Lawgiver ..."). Christ is Emmanuel (meaning "God with us"). The antiphon bids Christ to come and save mankind. Biblical basis: Isaiah 7:14; Matthew 1:23.

See also **O Come, O Come, Emmanuel.**

O Christmas Tree

("O Tannenbaum," literally translated as "O Fir Tree"). Traditional carol of Germany, one of the most popular holiday songs in that country. The tune is believed to have arisen in the sixteenth or seventeenth century, although it did not appear in print until 1799, paired with lyrics unrelated to Christmas. Prior to that time, it had also been the setting for Latin lyrics often sung by students, "Lauriger Horatius." Verse one of the carol known today is of folk origin as well and first appeared with the same tune in a book of folk songs for elementary schools published by August Zarnack (1820). The German poet Ernst Anschütz (1800–1861) contributed verses two and three around 1824. A number of English translations exist, no one superior to the others. Because translators report difficulty in producing a faithful yet sensible set of lyrics from the original words, rather free interpretations of the German are made.

The American James R. Randall, a native of Maryland, adapted the tune in 1861 to his poem about the state's involvement in the Civil War, "Maryland, My Maryland." The melody has been matched with other songs about states, such as "Delaware, My Delaware," and "Kentucky, O Kentucky."

O Come, All Ye Faithful

("Adeste Fideles"). Highly popular Latin carol generally attributed to John F. Wade (1711–1786) between the years 1740 and 1743. During this time Wade, having fled his native England because of his Roman Catholic faith, was working at an English college in Douai, France, as a music teacher and music copyist. In his work he dealt frequently with Latin lyrics. When Wade produced a Christmas hymn of four Latin stanzas titled "Adeste Fideles," the general assumption was that he had merely stumbled upon another song and copied it.

For some 200 years, "Adeste Fideles" was attributed to various sources, including an adaptation of an aria in Handel's *Ottone* (1723), a parody of a tune from a Parisian vaudeville play *Le Comte d'Acajou* (1744), and the seventeenth century English organist John Reading. The lyrics were first printed anonymously in *Evening Offices of the Church* (Paris, 1760), and the modern version (Wade had originally used several different tempo settings) was first published anonymously in *An Essay on the Church Plain Chant* (London, 1782). It is believed that Wade and a colleague, Samuel Webbe, organist for the Portuguese embassy chapel in London, were responsible for this essay. In 1795 Webbe played "Adeste Fideles" at the Portuguese embassy, and the Duke of Leeds was so impressed with the carol that it was introduced at a series of concerts in 1797 that he patronized. Through these concerts, it was assumed that the carol had arisen in Portugal, which led to its sobriquet, the "Portuguese Hymn."

In 1947, research published by Dom John Stéphan, OSB, of Buckfast Abbey, Devon, England, revealed a newly discovered manuscript in Wade's handwriting that dated between 1740 and 1743 (the earliest known copy of the carol); this further supported Wade as the composer, an opinion with which carol authority William Studwell concurs in *The Christmas Carol Reader*. *The New Oxford Book of Carols*, however, does not completely concur with Stéphan's conclusions; among other points, *Oxford* suggests that Wade's setting and the remarkably similar tune in the Paris vaudeville (see above) both probably originated from another source as yet unidentified. Therefore, *Oxford* lists the composer as anonymous.

The complete "Adeste Fideles" as we know it today consists of a hybrid of eight stanzas, although most modern publications include only Wade's original four. According to *The New Oxford Book of Carols*, the French clergyman Abbé Étienne Jean F. Borderies (1764–1832) contributed three additional Latin stanzas during his exile in England in 1793 and published the then-seven-verse carol in the *Office de St. Omer* (1822). An anonymous eighth, Latin verse dealing with the Magi, thought to be of Gallic origin, was subsequently added and published together with Wade's original four and Borderies's three in Belgium in 1850. Wade's Latin text was first published in the United States as a broadside in 1795.

Although there have been some 50 English-language translations of the Latin lyrics, the second of two translations by English

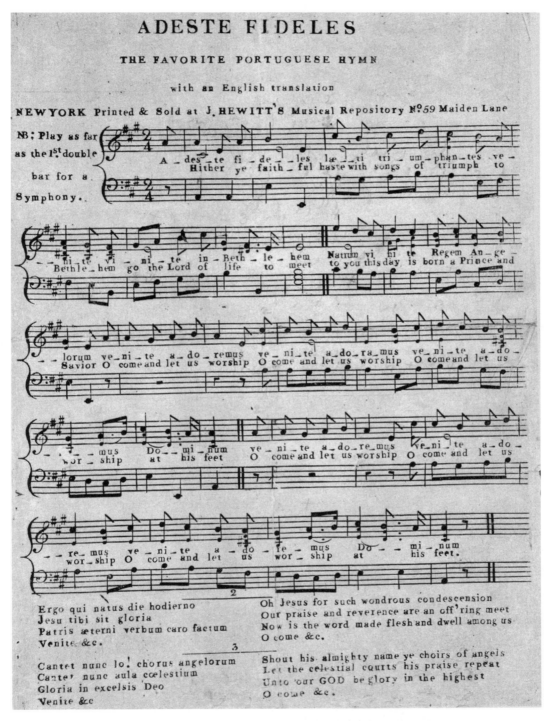

One of the earliest printings of "Adeste Fideles" in the United States, by the James Hewitt Musical Repository in New York, 1804. At that time, John Wade was unknown as the composer, and it was believed that the carol originated in Portugal, as indicated here by the subtitle "The Favorite Portuguese Hymn." This printing includes three of Wade's four original Latin verses. The English translation provided is obscure. Courtesy the Newberry Library, Chicago.

clergyman Frederick Oakeley (1802–1880) remains the most-accepted version. As canon of London's Westminster Abbey, Oakeley's initial translation in 1841 of Wade's original text opened with "Ye faithful, approach ye." When he later converted to Catholicism, he published a second translation of only three verses in 1852, the opening line of which read, "O come, all ye faithful," by which the carol is better known. British hymnologist William Brooke (1848–1917) translated the remaining four verses and combined them with Oakeley's in the *Altar Hymnal* (London, 1884).

O Come, Little Children

("Ihr Kinderlein, kommet"). German carol, the lyrics of which were written around 1850 by Christoph von Schmidt (1768–1854) and the music by Johann Abraham Peter Schulz (1747–1800). A Roman Catholic priest, Schmidt was known for publishing religious literature for children, and Schulz, an organist and conductor, had studied in Berlin with Johann Philipp Kernberger, a former student of J.S. Bach. Although it is not known exactly when Schulz composed the melody for this carol, it is thought to have originated during his tenure (1787–1795) as court musician to the king of Denmark. The lyrics bid first the little children, then "one and all" to hasten to see the Child Jesus, Whose bed is a manger, Whose pillow is hay, now wrapped in swaddling clothes, and more lovely than all the angels together.

O Come, O Come, Emmanuel

("Veni, Veni, Emanuel"). Latin Advent carol. The lyrics derive from a series of seven "O" Antiphons dating at least to the time of Charlemagne (742–814) or possibly earlier, which were sung in monasteries at vespers for seven nights, from December 17 to December 23. Disregarding the letter "O," the initial letter of each antiphon, when read from last to first, spelled the Latin acrostic "ERO CRAS" (freely translated "I shall be [with you] tomorrow"), which implied the imminent coming of Christ and Christmas. The lyrics sung today, originally beginning as "Veni, Veni, Emanuel" and comprising five verses, are thought to date from the thirteenth century, yet the country of origin remains unknown. In 1851, the Anglican

priest John Mason Neale (1818–1866) translated five of the seven antiphons into English with verses initially beginning as "Draw nigh, Draw nigh, Emmanuel" and published them in the third edition of his *Medieval Hymns and Sequences* but revised them in 1853 to "O come, O come, Emmanuel." Neale based his translation on the Latin text as found in *Psalteriolum Cantionum Catholicarum* (Cologne, 1710), the earliest known written source for the "'O' Antiphons. Other English translations include those by Henry Sloane Coffin (1877–1954), John Henry Newman (1801–1890), and Thomas Alexander Lacey (1853–1931); Lacey's seven-verse translation first appeared in *The English Hymnal* (1906).

The lyrics are filled with metaphors and allusions to biblical prophesies about the coming Messiah.

Thomas Helmore adapted Neale's revised translation to a plainsong tune, and the two were first published together with harmony in *The Hymnal Noted*, second edition (London, 1854), edited by Neale and Helmore. Although it is not known exactly where Helmore found the tune, it is now believed to be of French origin, for in 1966 in the French National Library in Paris, the melody was discovered in a fifteenth century French funeral processional that had been used by Franciscan nuns living in Lisbon, Portugal. It is also believed that the refrain, "Rejoice! Rejoice! Emmanuel…," which was not a part of the original verses, was added by the twelfth or thirteenth century to balance them. Indeed, the plainsong manuscript in the French National Library includes this refrain.

See also "O" Antiphons.

O Come, Redeemer of Mankind
See Savior of the Nations, Come

O Hearken Ye
See Alfred Burt Carols

O Holy Night

("Cantique de Noël"). French carol, the lyrics of which were written in 1847 by Placide Cappeau (1808–1877), a wine merchant, amateur poet, and mayor of the village of Roquemaure in the Rhone Valley. Having received a commission from the local priest to write a Christmas poem, Cappeau produced some verses beginning with "Minuit, Chrétiens, c'est l'heure solennele" ("Midnight, Christians, it is the solemn hour"). The priest desired the poem for a vocalist from his congregation, Madame Laurey, who subsequently sought the popular Parisian composer Adolphe Adam (1803–1856) for a musical setting. A prolific composer primarily of light opera and ballet, Adam is best known for his ballet *Giselle* (1841).

Titled "Cantique de Noël" ("Song of Christmas"), Cappeau's and Adam's new carol debuted at the Christmas Eve Midnight Mass of 1847 in Roquemaure, with Madame Laurey performing the solo. The song was first published as an organ arrangement in 1855 and later was translated into many languages, the best-known English version being that by the American John Sullivan Dwight (1818–1893), a music critic and journalist. Compared with the original French, Dwight's translation incorporated a rather free interpretation, beginning as "O holy night, the stars are brightly shining."

Although "O Holy Night" is now one of the world's most beloved Christmas carols, church officials at the time, especially the bishop of Paris, initially condemned it as lacking in musical taste with total absence of religious spirit. It is believed that such undue criticism stemmed from prejudices formed against Cappeau's and Adam's personal backgrounds: neither man embraced Christianity; Adam composed for theaters, areas of sin and abomination in the eyes of the Church; and Cappeau was viewed as a radical socialist.

"O Holy Night" would have an impact on the Franco-Prussian War (1870–1871) to some extent. It is said that on Christmas Eve, 1870, as French and German troops fought in trenches outside of Paris, a French soldier suddenly sprang from his position and began singing "Cantique de Noël" amid the din of gunfire, which soon ceased, at least for a time. Instead of raining bullets on the French soldier, at least one German, perhaps more, responded with "Vom Himmel hoch, da komm' ich her" ("From Heaven Above to Earth I Come"), one of Germany's favorite carols by Martin Luther.

See also **From Heaven Above to Earth I Come.**

O How Joyfully
See **O Sanctissima**

O Little Town of Bethlehem

Arguably the best-known of America's sacred carols, written in 1868 by the Rev. Phillips Brooks (1835–1893) and Lewis Redner (1831–1908). Brooks, who was pastor of the Holy Trinity Episcopal Church in Philadelphia and would become the Episcopal bishop of Massachusetts in 1891, took inspiration from his sojourn in the Holy Land three years earlier, when on horseback he had ridden from Jerusalem to Bethlehem on Christmas Eve. Having paused by the Shepherds' Field, a plain outside the city traditionally held as the site where herald angels brought the "good tidings of great joy," he had attended services at the Church of the Nativity, built over the traditional site of Christ's birth. Later producing a

The Rev. Phillips Brooks (1835–1893), American Episcopal minister who wrote the lyrics to the carol "O Little Town of Bethlehem." In 1891, Brooks became the Episcopal bishop of Massachusetts. Photograph c. 1890. Courtesy Boston Public Library, Print Department.

The small town of Bethlehem, on a hilly rise, as depicted in Reverend John Fleetwood's The Light in the East *(National Publishing Co. and Jones Brothers, 1874). Fleetwood was a missionary for 40 years in the Middle East.*

poem of five stanzas, which the Sunday school children of his church were to sing at the annual Christmas program, Brooks sought a musical setting from Redner, the church organist. A successful real estate broker and director of Holy Trinity's Sunday school, Redner composed nothing suitable until the night before the program when, it is said, he awoke to an "angel strain," "a gift from heaven," which he quickly transcribed. Holy Trinity's Sunday school children first presented "O Little Town of Bethlehem" on December 27, 1868. It was first published as early as 1874 and also appeared in *The Church Hymnal* (1892) of the American Episcopal Church.

In place of Redner's tune, the English composer Ralph Vaughan Williams substituted his arrangement of the folk ballad "The Ploughboy's Dream" in a setting which he titled "Forest Green." This alternate tune for "O Little Town of Bethlehem," now the best-known in Great Britain, was first published in *The English Hymnal* (1906). A melody by Henry Walford Davies (1869–1941), organist of London's Temple Church for 20 years, is sometimes used.

Brooks and Redner collaborated on another carol, "Everywhere, Everywhere Christmas Tonight," composed sometime between 1862 and 1868, which never gained the immense popularity as did "O Little Town of Bethlehem."

See also **Church of the Nativity.**

O magnum mysterium

("O Great Mystery"). Latin responsory sung after the fourth reading during the Roman Catholic Matins service early on Christmas morning. The text is based on an account in the Gospel of Pseudo-Matthew in the New Testament Apocrypha, which depicts an ox and an ass standing by the manger and watching over the newborn Christ Child (*see* **Nativity** [Popular Assumptions]).

The Latin lyrics read:

O magnum mysterium,
et admirabile sacramentum,
ut animalia viderent Dominum natum
iacentem in praesepio.
O beata Virgo, cuius viscera meruerunt
portare Dominum Iesum Christum. Alleluia!

Translated into English:

O great mystery,
And wonderful sacrament,
That animals should see the newborn Lord
Lying in a manger.
O blessed Virgin, in whose unblemished womb
Was carried the Lord Jesus Christ. Alleluia!

"O magnum mysterium" has been the subject of many musical settings, a popular example of which is the sublime *a cappella* motet by the Spanish Renaissance composer and ordained priest Tomás Luis de Victoria (1548–1611). This motet further served as the basis for his *Missa (Mass)* of the same title, published in Rome in 1592. A noted, contemporary setting is the carol cycle *O magnum mysterium*, written for secondary-school children in 1960 by the English composer Sir Peter Maxwell Davies (1934–), who at that time was music master for the Cirencester Grammar School in Cirencester, Gloucestershire. Maxwell Davies's setting for chorus, orchestra, and organ consists of nine movements: three carol variations of "O magnum mysterium"; three carols entitled "Haylle, comly and clene" ("Hail, Comely and Clean"), "Alleluia, pro Virgine Maria" ("Alleluia, to the Virgin Mary"), and "The Fader of Heven" ("The Father of Heaven"); two sonatas entitled "Puer natus" ("A Boy Is Born") and "Lux fulgebit" ("A Light

Shall Shine"); and the finale, a solo "Organ Fantasia" on "O magnum mysterium." In 2004, Queen Elizabeth II appointed Maxwell Davies to the position of Master of the Queen's Music.

Other notable settings include those by Thomas Tallis (English, 1505–1585); Giovanni Gabrielli (Italian, 1554–1612); Franz Schubert (Austrian, 1797–1828); Sergei Rachmaninoff (Russian, 1873–1943); Francis Poulenc (French, 1899–1963); and Morten Lauridsen (American, 1943–).

O Morning Star, How Fair and Bright

See **How Brightly Shines the Morning Star**

O Sanctissima

("O Thou Most Holy"). Anonymous sixteenth century Latin hymn to the Virgin Mary, which originally bore no relationship to Christmas. Since that time its text has been the source for a series of Christmas adaptations variously known as "O Thou Joyful Day," "O How Joyfully," and "O Most Wonderful." Although the earliest known Christmas versions were published anonymously in London in 1792 and 1794, probably the best-known version is that composed in 1819 by Johannes Falk (1768–1826). Superintendent of an orphanage in Weimar, Germany, Falk adapted the first verse of "O Sanctissima" for a children's Christmas play that he titled *Dr. Martin Luther und die Reformation in Volksliedern* (*Dr. Martin Luther and the Reformation in Folk Songs*), published in 1830. A colleague, Heinrich Holzschuher, added two additional verses for the event, and the carol appeared in this drama as "O du fröliche" ("O Most Wonderful").

Other lesser known text variations, titled "O Thou Joyful Day," have appeared in the United States in the twentieth century. While most are anonymous, one bears the name of William Glass. The German composer Ludwig van Beethoven also published an arrangement of "O Sanctissima" for three voices, piano, violin, and cello (1814–15).

A factor common to all of these text variations is the musical setting itself, known as "The Sicilian Mariners' Hymn," a traditional tune believed to have arisen during the eighteenth century. Despite the title of this tune, no direct relationship between the hymn text, Sicily, or mariners has ever been documented.

O Thou Joyful Day

See **O Sanctissima**

O Thou Most Holy

See **O Sanctissima**

Of Jesse's Line Descended

See **Lo, How a Rose E'er Blooming**

Of the Father's Heart Begotten

See **Of the Father's Love Begotten**

Of the Father's Love Begotten

("Corde natus ex Parentis"). Latin carol, also translated "Of the Father's Heart Begotten." The text derives from "Hymnus omnis horae" ("Hymn for Every Hour"), a poem of 37 stanzas by Aurelius Clemens Prudentius (348–ca. 410), a Spanish attorney who, in his latter years, retired to a monastery to write religious poetry. Prudentius included "Hymnus" in his *Cathemerinon*, a collection of daily hymns. The best-known English translation was provided by the Anglican clergyman John Mason Neale (1816–1866), who, together with colleague Thomas Helmore, matched the translation with an anonymous, thirteenth century tune found in *Piae Cantiones*, a Swedish carol collection published in 1582. Neale and Helmore published text and music together in their *Carols for Christmas-Tide* (London, 1853–54), and Sir Henry Williams Baker (1821–1877) revised the piece for *Hymns Ancient and Modern* (London, 1861), edited by William Clowes.

Instead of a conventional narrative of the Nativity, Neale's translation first outlines the creation of the earth by the Trinity, declares that the Father is Alpha and Omega, then recalls that Christ was made incarnate to redeem mankind from the sentence of death by the Mosaic Law. The latter half of the carol is an elaborate exhortation for all creation to praise God.

Oh, Joseph Took Mary Up on His Right Knee

See **The Cherry Tree Carol**

Old Christmas

See **Christmas Old Style, Christmas New Style**

Old Christmas (poem)

See **Heap on More Wood**

Old Lad's Passing Bell

See **Great Britain**

Old Scrooge

See **A Christmas Carol** (Film and Television Versions)

Old Style Christmas

See **Christmas Old Style, Christmas New Style**

Olive, the Other Reindeer

Popular children's book written by American authors J. Otto Seibold and Vivian Walsh, published in 1997. It is a loose parody of the song "Rudolph, the Red-Nosed Reindeer" by Johnny Marks.

Hearing "Rudolph" sung on the radio, the little dog Olive mistakes the phrase "All of the other reindeer ..." as "Olive, the other reindeer ..." and believes that she must be a reindeer instead of a dog. Christmas Eve is at hand, so Olive hurries to the North Pole via *buses* to take her place with Santa's reindeer team. Secured in place by Comet, the largest reindeer, Olive proves quite a valuable addition, for she bails the team out of several mishaps along the way. And to parallel Rudolph, whose bright red nose guided Santa through a foggy Christmas Eve, Olive's keen sense of smell detects Mrs. Claus's cookies and guides the team home safely through the North Pole fog.

In 1999, the book was adapted for television as a computer-generated animated cartoon via *The Simpsons* creator Matt Groening. With Drew Barrymore as the voice of Olive, the production was the first animated Christmas special from the Fox Television Network. The parody on mistaken lyrics is further noted in two characters: the name of character Richard Stands (voice by Tim Meadows) is based on the phrase "which it stands" from the United States Pledge of Allegiance; and Round John Virgin (voice by Mitch Rouse) is based on the phrase "round yon virgin" from "Silent Night." Ironi-cally, Santa's North Pole home sports a menorah. Other principal voices: Dan Castellaneta, Joe Pantoliano, Edward Asner, Peter MacNicol, Michael Stipe (of *REM*), Tress MacNeille, Billy West, and Matt Groening. In 2000, the cartoon won two Annie Awards: Outstanding Individual Achievement for Voice Acting by a Male Performer in an Animated Television Production (Dan Castellaneta) and Outstanding Individual Achievement for Writing in an Animated Television Production (Steve Young). That same year, the show received an Emmy nomination for Outstanding Animated Program (for Programming More Than One Hour). Adapted by Steve Young. Produced by Keith Alcorn, Alex Johns, and Michael Stipe. Directed by Oscar Moore. Twentieth Century Fox Television, Curiosity Company, DNA Productions, and Flower Films. DVD: Fox Home Entertainment. 45 min.

J. Otto Seibold and Vivian Walsh have written and illustrated many children's books together, including *Mr. Lunch Takes a Plane Ride* (1993), *Mr. Lunch Borrows a Canoe* (1994), and *Going to the Getty* (1997).

See also **Rudolph, the Red-Nosed Reindeer** (song).

On Christmas Night

See **The First Nowell**

On That Most Blessed Night

See **Carol of the Bagpipers**

On the 2nd Day of Christmas

(1997). Made-for-television comedy.

When Trish Tracy (Mary Stuart Masterson) and her six-year-old niece/ward Patsy (Lauren Suzanne Pratt) are caught shoplifting at Limber's Department Store on Christmas Eve, they face delayed prosecution. Rather than send them to jail over the holiday, Mr. Limber (Lawrence Dane) places them in the custody of Bert Sanders (Mark Ruffalo), a member of Limber's security department, with strict orders that he return them for prosecution on December 26, a day historically known as the second day of Christmas. The ensuing interval promises romance between Trish and Bert, with much-needed intervention by Santa's legal representative.

Written by Brian Hohlfeld. Produced by John Ryan. Directed by James Frawley. Goldenring Productions in association with ABC Pictures Corporation. Video N/A.

On the Morning of Christ's Nativity

Ode written during the Christmas of 1629 by the English poet John Milton (1608–1674), who placed this work first in his *Poems* (1645). Milton's first great English poem, written shortly after his twenty-first birthday, *Christ's Nativity* begins with a short prelude of six stanzas, which ponders the paradox between the Babe's divine power and His mortality. Then follows *The Hymn*, the principal work consisting of 27 stanzas. Rather than elaborate directly upon the Gospel texts of Matthew and Luke, Milton views the Nativity as an event that creates a closer harmony between heaven and earth (Nature), which the music of the angels and the planets heralds. But compared with the Advent of the Creator, Nature regards herself as most inconsequential. Peering into the future, the poem's latter stanzas emphasize the Incarnate's redemption of mankind through the recovery of righteousness and the overthrow of idolatry, followed by the Day of Judgment. The final stanza returns quietly to the manger and the sleeping Babe, with angels and the Star in attendance nearby.

Regarded as the greatest English poet since Shakespeare, Milton is especially known for his epic poem *Paradise Lost* (completed in 1667), along with its companion *Paradise Regained* (1671).

Once, in Royal David's City

Irish carol, the lyrics of which first appeared in *Hymns for Little Children* (London, 1848), a collection of poems by Mrs. Cecil Frances Alexander (1823–1895). The wife of the bishop of Ireland, Mrs. Alexander created the collection for her godsons to facilitate their appreciation and understanding of the catechism. Thus, "Once, in Royal David's City" serves not only as a simple narrative of the Nativity, but also as an elementary treatise on the divinity of Christ as both man and the Son of God. The designation "Royal David's City" implies Bethlehem, as mentioned in the second chapter of Luke's Gospel. Mrs. Alexander's collection also featured another well-known hymn, "All Things Bright and Beautiful."

The music for "Once, in Royal David's City" was written by Henry J. Gauntlett (1805–1876), an Englishman who published the tune as "Irby" in his *Christmas Carols: Four Numbers* (London, 1849). When Mrs. Alexander issued a second edition of her hymns in 1858, all of them included musical settings for piano by Gauntlett, including his 1849 setting of the present carol.

Traditionally, "Once, in Royal David's City" opens the *Festival of Nine Lessons and Carols*, a world-broadcast, annual musical presentation held on Christmas Eve in the chapel of King's College, Cambridge, England.

See also **A Festival of Nine Lessons and Carols.**

Once upon a Christmas

(2000). Canadian motion picture fantasy.

Disheartened over the mounting greed and materialism that surrounds Christmas each year, Santa Claus (Douglas Campbell) would cancel the holiday. Yet for the sake of his younger daughter, sugar-tempered Kristin (glamorous model Kathy Ireland), he will withdraw the order if she can reform one "naughty" family by Christmas Eve. Working against Kristin is her wicked older sister and rival, Rudolfa (Mary Donnelly Haskell), who would convert the holiday into a prank-filled "Christmas Fool's Day."

Kristin selects the Morgans, a dysfunctional family composed of Bill (John Dye); his two children, Kyle (James Kirk) and Brittany (Kristen Prout); and Johnny (Wayne Thomas Yorke), his dead beat brother-in-law. Posing as the children's *au pair*, Kristen discovers that they had truly celebrated Christmas as a family until the death of Bill's wife shattered their lives. Now, Bill has little time for his children, Johnny is a worthless guardian, and Kyle and Brittany have become cynical, lazy, and irresponsible. The task is almost beyond Kristin's abilities, until a business trip on Christmas Eve compels Bill to take his family and Kristin along. En route, they become stranded in a remote area, thanks to Rudolfa, and find shelter in an abandoned house, where the only

Christmas presents they have are the comfort of each other and working together selflessly to survive. The setting works wonders on Brittany and provides romance between Bill and Kristin, yet Kyle remains obstinate, until he attempts to rescue Bill during an outbreak of fire. Although Kyle is fatally wounded, Kristin trades her immortality for Kyle's life, and Christmas is saved. The story continues in the television sequel, *Twice upon a Christmas*.

Written by Steven Berman. Produced by Deboragh Gabler, Jon Carrasco, and Stephen Roseberry. Directed by Tibor Takács. Ardent Productions, Legacy Filmworks, Lincoln Field Productions, Sterling/Winters Company Studios, and Viacom Productions. Video N/A. 90 min.

See also **Twice upon a Christmas**.

One Christmas

Autobiographical short story written by American author Truman Capote (1924–1984).

When his parents divorce after a year of marriage, young Capote is placed with his mother's family in rural Alabama, where he will live until the age of ten. His mother essentially abandons him for a career in New York, while his father returns to his native New Orleans. Capote develops a lasting friendship with one elderly cousin, Miss Sook Faulk, who instills spiritual values, teaches him about Santa Claus, and nicknames him "Buddy." When Buddy is seven years old, his father arranges a Christmas visit with him in his luxurious home in New Orleans. Life in a large city is overwhelming with cumbersome new clothes, disagreeable Creole food, and a man who is more a stranger than a father. Two additional rude awakenings are in store for the boy. One: his 35-year-old father chases rich, elderly widows, marries one for her cash, then finds another when she passes away. Two: Santa Claus is not real, or so it seems, when Buddy discovers his father placing presents under the tree on Christmas Eve.

In the morning, when his father asks if he is pleased with Santa's gifts, Buddy turns the question around and asks what his father will give him. Stunned, the father grants Buddy's wish for a rather expensive model airplane he had seen earlier in town.

Inebriated, raving, and agonizing over Buddy's imminent departure for Alabama, his father, denying God and Santa Claus, wishes that he and Buddy's mother had committed suicide. He begs to hear Buddy say, "I love you, Daddy," but the boy is not prepared to commit.

Back home, Sook supplies the "straight" story about Santa: He exists in all of us, as the Lord would have it, for no single person could do all that Santa must do. And knowing that he must complete a task, also as the Lord would have it, Buddy sends a simple message via postcard to his father that concludes with "...yes I love you Buddy [sic]."

In 1994, a television dramatization of this story starred Katharine Hepburn, T.J. Lowther, Henry Winkler, Swoozie Kurtz, Tonea Stewart, Pat Hingle, and Julie Harris. For her performance, Hepburn was nominated in 1995 for a Screen Actors' Guild Award for Outstanding Performance by a Female Actor in a Television Movie or Miniseries. Written and produced by Duane Poole. Directed by Tony Bill. Davis Entertainment. DVD: Pioneer Video. 91 min.

See also **A Christmas Memory**.

One-Horse Open Sleigh

See **Jingle Bells**

One-Hundred-One Dalmatians Christmas

See **A Christmas Carol** (Film and Television Versions)

One Magic Christmas

(1985). American/Canadian motion picture fantasy.

Each year Santa Claus (Jan Rubes) sends the Christmas angel Gideon (Harry Dean Stanton), a gentle and rather shabby figure dressed in black with a broad-brimmed hat, on a mission to restore the Christmas spirit to one dispirited individual. This year his assignment is Ginnie Grainger (Mary Steenburgen), a grocery store cashier, wife, and mother, whose husband Jack (Gary Basaraba) has lost his job. Despite this and the fact that, as tenants in a company home, his family must vacate the premises by January 1, optimistic Jack retains the Christmas spirit and dreams of opening his own bicycle shop someday. When Jack suggests taking $200 of their $5,000 savings to buy presents for their two young children, six-year-old Abbie (Elisabeth Harnois) and Cal (Robbie Magwood), Ginnie strongly objects, fearing for their savings and scoffing at the notions of Christmas, Santa, and fantasy at a time when they all should be packing.

Appearing to Abbie one night, Gideon reveals his mission and the fact that she will be involved in its fulfillment. As Ginnie reluctantly mails Abbie's letter to Santa on the night of December 23, Gideon exhorts her to find the Christmas spirit, at which all the neighborhood Christmas lights suddenly go out.

Tragedy strikes Ginnie's life from that point, for on Christmas Eve, Ginnie, pulling a double shift, is fired from the store. Worse, Harry Dickens (Wayne Robson), also down on his luck, robs the bank, kills Jack in the attempt, and escapes in Ginnie's car, kidnapping her children. When Harry loses control, crashes through a roadblock, and plunges into a river, Gideon rescues the children while Harry perishes.

Learning of her dad's death, Abbie searches for Gideon at the city's community Christmas tree as he had instructed her and pleads for him to bring her dad back. Instead, Gideon magically transports Abbie to the North Pole, where Santa retrieves a letter that a young Ginnie had written to him on December 21, 1959. Since only Ginnie's faith can return Jack, according to Santa, she must see this old letter, for then she will remember, and her faith in Christmas will be restored.

The scene now returns to the night of December 23, before Ginnie mailed Abbie's letter to Santa. Ginnie refuses to believe Abbie's tale of an angel having taken her to the North Pole until she examines the old letter that Abbie had brought back. Now convinced, she gladly mails Abbie's own letter and, as the neighborhood Christmas lights suddenly flash back on, Jack returns from a stroll up the street. With a chance of seeing how sad her life would be had she continued without the Christmas spirit, Ginnie spends Christmas Eve with her family, her Scrooge-like manager Herbie (Timothy Webber) demanding that she be at work all the earlier on the day after Christmas. She buys a camp stove from Harry Dickens for $50,

which prevents the bank robbery and its consequences, and writes Jack a check for $5,000, the capital he needs to open a bicycle shop. She has learned the spirit of Christmas, the spirit of giving.

This film won Genie Awards in 1986 for Best Overall Sound and Best Sound Editing; Genie nominations for Best Achievement in Art Direction, Cinematography, Costume Design, Best Motion Picture, and Best Performance by an Actress in a Leading Role (Mary Steenburgen); 1987 nominations for Young Artist Awards for Exceptional Feature Film in Family Entertainment Drama and for Exceptional Performance by a Young Actress Starring in a Feature Film Comedy or Drama (Elisabeth Harnois).

With Arthur Hill, Elias Koteas, Michelle Meyrick, and Sarah Polley. Written by Thomas Meehan. Produced by Peter O'Brian. Directed by Phillip Borsos. Walt Disney Pictures in association with Peter O'Brian Productions, Fred Roos, Silver Screen Partners II, and Téléfilm Canada. DVD: Anchor Bay Entertainment. 88 min.

Orange Bowl
See **New Year's Day**

The Other Wise Man

Classic short story written in 1896 by the American clergyman and author Henry Van Dyke.

Artaban, of the Persian priesthood of the Magi, summons eight of his order together and reveals that, by his astrological calculations, the time is at hand when the Anointed One, the Prince, is to be born as King in Israel. He has sold all of his possessions to purchase a sapphire, a ruby, and a pearl as tribute for the new King. Believing that Artaban is chasing a dream, the others refuse to accompany him to Jerusalem when the astronomical sign appears, the convergence of the planets Jupiter and Saturn.

Setting off to rendezvous with three other Magi bound for Jerusalem — Melchior, Caspar, and Balthazar — Artaban delays his arrival to minister as physician to a critically ill Hebrew exile found near Babylon. Rescued from death, the Hebrew, learning of Artaban's mission, directs him to Bethlehem to find the Messiah, for so say the prophets. But when Artaban's companions leave without him, he returns to Babylon and acquires a caravan with the sapphire.

He arrives in Bethlehem three days after the other Magi have departed and learns from a young mother that they had visited Joseph of Nazareth, whose wife had borne a son. Strangely, she says, Joseph fled with his family to Egypt. As Herod's soldiers raid Bethlehem and begin the "Slaughter of the Innocents," Artaban saves the mother's child by bribing the captain with the ruby, declaring that he is alone.

With only the pearl remaining, Artaban spends years searching for the Messiah in Egypt, to no avail. A Jewish rabbi in Alexandria advises him that the Messiah will be found among the poor and suffering, for so say the prophets. Walking thus among the wretched, Artaban delays his search further in order to feed the hungry, clothe the naked, heal the sick, and comfort the captive.

His search of 33 years finally brings him much aged to Jerusalem, where he ransoms a young girl from slavery with the pearl. Receiving a mortal wound during a sudden earthquake, he hears a Voice gently and faintly addressing him. Artaban replies by denying that he had ever fed, clothed, or visited his Lord and King. The Voice replies, "Verily I say unto thee, inasmuch as thou hast done it unto one of the least of these my brethren, thou has done it unto me" (the story directly quotes the Gospel of Matthew 25:40). Artaban, his gifts accepted, has found the King, for it is the day that Christ is crucified.

Dramatized for television, *The Fourth Wise Man* (1985) starred Martin Sheen as Artaban, with Alan Arkin, Eileen Brennan, Ralph Bellamy, Richard Libertini, Lance Kerwin, and Harold Gould. Written by Tom Fontana. Produced by Michael Ray Rhodes and Lewis Abel. Directed by Michael Ray Rhodes. Paulist Productions. Available on DVD. 72 min.

Henry Van Dyke (1852–1933), a Presbyterian minister, first delivered "The Other Wise Man" as a sermon to his congregation, the Brick Presbyterian Church in New York City, in 1896. In the foreword to a later edition of the story, Van Dyke replied to the many queries that he had received regarding why the noble Artaban had lied to save the child in Bethlehem. He stated that lying, hardly justifiable, is sometimes inevitable, and that Artaban could more easily be forgiven a lie than for the betrayal of innocent blood. Van Dyke is also the author of "The First Christmas Tree: A Story of the Forest."

See also **The First Christmas Tree: A Story of the Forest.**

Over the River and through the Woods

American song, the lyrics of which originated as a poem written in 1844 by Lydia Maria Child (1802–1880), a novelist, journalist, and radical abolitionist from Medford, Massachusetts. Originally titled "A Boy's Thanksgiving Day," the poem was based on Child's pleasant experiences of traveling to her grandfather's house for Thanksgiving. Her original opening lines read, "Over the river and through the woods / To Grandfather's house we go," but "Grandmother" subsequently replaced "Grandfather," and the lyrics, otherwise lauding the sights and delights of winter holidays, have become associated with Christmas as often as with Thanksgiving. Indeed, "Christmas Day" may substitute for "Thanksgiving Day" in the lyrics. Ms. Child first published her poem in *Flowers for Children*, Volume 2 (New York, 1844). The composer of the musical setting remains anonymous.

With the exception of "Over the River," Ms. Child's literary works remain virtually obscure. Her first novel, *Hobomok: A Tale of Early Times* (1824) was the first historical novel to be published in the United States.

The Oxen

Short poem by English novelist and poet Thomas Hardy (1840–1928), penned in 1915.

While sitting by the fireside on Christmas Eve, the poet muses over the ancient legend that, since the first Christmas, oxen have always knelt in reverence at the stroke of midnight on Christmas Eve. Certain that they are kneeling at that very moment, he admits that such a "fancy" would not be accepted today if it was a newly created idea. Yet if someone chall lenged him to see it all for himself, he would still go, truly hoping that he would witness the miracle.

Not mentioned in the poem is the related legend that animals are also empowered with speech at this magical hour. Neither does Hardy speak of the caveat which applies, that those daring souls intent on witnessing such miracles endanger their lives.

Hardy's best-known novels include *The Mayor of Casterbridge* (1886) and *Tess of the D'Urbervilles* (1891).

See also **The Friendly Beasts; Mass of the Rooster; Superstitions.**

P

Pageant of Peace

See **United States** (The National Christmas Tree and the Christmas Pageant of Peace)

Pakistan

See **Asia and the South Pacific**

Panama

See **Central America**

Pantomime

See **Christmas Drama**

Paraguay

See **South America**

Los Pastorelas

See **Las Posadas**

Pat-a-Pan

Carol from the Burgundy region of France, written by poet Bernard de la Monnoye (1641–1728), who published a carol collection of his poems set to folk tunes of the region in 1701. The lyrics encourage the drum-and-flute team of boys Willie and Robin to celebrate Christmas with joy and praise through their music. The title "Pat-a-Pan" is derived from a portion of the lyrics which imitates the beating of a drum, "pat-a-pat-a-pan," as well as the basic, underlying droning rhythm, the latter also identified in a contemporary drum carol of the twentieth century, "The Little Drummer Boy." Above this, a light melody brings to mind the trilling of a flute, written as "tu-re-lu-re-lu." The carol was first published in English in 1907.

See also **The Little Drummer Boy** (song).

The Peace Carol

American song written in 1965 by Bob Beers of the Beers Family, a folk-singing troupe from upstate New York. Beers wrote the carol in honor of the Rev. Edith Craig Reynolds, a Baptist minister, whose gentle demeanor and wisdom were a source of inspiration to the composer. The Beers Family recorded this piece on two albums, *Christmas with the Beers Family* (Columbia) and *Seasons of Peace: A Great Family Sings* (Biograph), both released in the 1970s. Consisting of three verses, "The Peace Carol" assures that the peace inherent in Christmas Day will abolish all worldly cares and woes. Following each verse, a refrain simply lists some key symbols of that peace: a holly branch, a dove, and the light that is Christmas.

Pennyroyal

See **Christmas Plants**

Peru

See **South America**

Philippines

The only Asian nation where Christianity predominates, the Philippines has enjoyed Christmas since the sixteenth century, when it initially became a Spanish colony. Although the culture and, hence, Christmas customs largely reflect those of Spain and the Roman Catholic Church, traditions are quite diverse from region to region and include those of British, Indian, Chinese, Japanese, and American origin. This discussion will center on the Spanish influence.

The holiday season begins with the Feast of the Immaculate Conception on December 8, followed by the nine-day Novena of *Misas del Gallo* (Masses of the Rooster), a series of predawn Masses beginning on December 16. In the Tagalog language, the Masses are known as *Simbang Gabi* (Night Mass). Originally a post-harvest Mass of thanksgiving, *Simbang Gabi* eventually blended with Christmas. Firecrackers, bands, and carols sung over church public address systems summon villagers to these morning Masses; alternatively, the parish priests make rounds awakening their parishioners by knocking on their doors. Afterwards, food booths set up in the church courtyards offer rice cakes with coconut, ginger tea, and hot chocolate. Other traditions during *Simbang Gabi* include groups of carolers parading through the neighborhoods from 6 P.M. until midnight, and the performance of *Pastores* ("Shepherds"), Nativity plays.

Although Santa Claus, Christmas trees, wreaths, candles, colored lights, and Christmas cards are quite familiar through Western influences, the principal Christmas decoration is the *parol*, a five-pointed star symbolic of the Star of Bethlehem. Bedecked with tassels at each point and affixed to bamboo poles, typical *parols* are covered with colored rice paper and may be lit with candles or electric light bulbs within the structures. They actually are variants of the Latin American *piñata* but replace the *piñata*'s candies and trinkets with a source of light. Families traditionally fashion their own *parols* and may interlace them together to form Christmas trees. Alternatively, because pine trees are quite expensive, people may construct Christmas trees from cardboard or decorate palm branches with tiny *parols*, fruit, small wooden or bamboo carvings, tiny baskets, rice paper ornaments, tinsel, and icicles. Another favorite decoration is the Nativity scene, known as the *belén* (Bethlehem).

During the days before Christmas, villages sponsor lantern festivals, the most famous and elaborate of which is that in San Fernando, capital of Pampanga province. These festivals originated from the *parol* parades of the nineteenth century, which preceded the predawn Masses of *Simbang Gabi*. With incentives of cash prizes, entrants vie to construct the largest and most spectacular lanterns of the most complex shapes, illuminated by thousands of colored electric lights and paraded through the streets as floats. The winning float from San Fernando is then taken to Rizal Park in the nation's capital city of Manila and displayed as a feature attraction.

Other holiday activities in Manila include various cultural events at public parks and museums; children's events during the week before Christmas at the Malacanang Palace, once the presidential palace and now a museum; the collection and distribution of gifts for needy children by government-sponsored organizations; and the *Fiesta Intramuros*, a month-long festival within the old, original walls of the city.

Prior to the Christmas Eve Midnight Mass, known here as the *Misa del Aguinaldo* (Mass of the Gift), villages often sponsor a *panunuluyan*, a pastoral street play reenacting the search by Mary and Joseph for shelter in Bethlehem. The performance, which ends at the local church around midnight, features either live players or statues with citizens supplying the dialogue. As crowds and brass bands follow along, the scene closely resembles *Las Posadas* ("the lodgings") processions of Latin America.

Following the Christmas Eve Midnight Mass, families return home for a sumptuous meal, known as the *Noche Buena* (Good Night). This may consist of stuffed chicken or fish, stuffed rolls, noodles, rice pudding with ground coconut, ginger tea, rice cakes, and fruit. Although children may traditionally hang up their stockings for Santa Claus, the principal gift giver is the family's *lola* (grandmother), who distributes presents either during *Noche Buena* or on Christmas Day.

Children visit their godparents on Christmas Day and receive gifts after performing a ritual of respect by kissing the godparents' hands, then touching the hands to their own foreheads. For Christmas dinner, there may be roast suckling pig with caramel custard.

Holy Innocents Day, December 28, is filled with pranks. Those who are successful in their endeavors are absolved of all wrongdoing, and debts need not be repaid. People in costumes may roam the streets portraying King Herod's soldiers in search of the Christ Child.

Noise, fireworks, and superstitions usher in the new year, and the noisier the merriment, the more prosperous will be the outlook. At midnight repasts on New Year's Eve, because round objects are symbols of good luck at this time, revelers customarily follow Spanish tradition by eating 12 grapes at the stroke of 12. House lights are turned on to ensure a bright year, and the first animal heard at midnight predicts the quality of the coming year. For example, a cow portends abundance; a chicken, poverty. Similarly, a sunny New Year's Day forecasts a good year; rain, a miserable year. Families also must remain at home on New Year's Day to guard against being called away from home during the year.

Epiphany, Three Kings Day, originally observed on January 6, is now celebrated on the first Sunday in January with a Mass and pageants about the Magi. On Epiphany eve, villagers adorned as the Magi hold street processions, and children place their shoes on window sills to receive gifts overnight from the royal trio.

"Merry Christmas" in Tagalog is *Maligayang Pasko.*

See also **Epiphany; Feast of the Immaculate Conception; Holy Innocents Day; Las Posadas; Mass of the Rooster; Spain.**

Pinocchio's Christmas

(1980). Made-for-television animated story using stop-motion puppets (Animagic), loosely based on the classic children's book *The Adventures of Pinocchio* (1883) by Italian author Carlo Collodi (pseudonym for Carlo Lorenzini).

Pinocchio, a talking marionette fashioned by the old wood-carver Geppetto, joins Maestro Fire Eater's side show to earn money to buy Papa Geppetto a Christmas gift. He falls in love with Julietta, a plain marionette, and carries her away when Fire Eater plans to change her into a Wise Man. Pinocchio escapes into the Forest of Enchantment, pursued by Sly Fox and Slick Cat, who pose as friends but secretly plan to sell him to a duke who wants an unusual Christmas gift for his son. The forest spirit Lady Azura rescues the two marionettes and teaches Pinocchio that the best Christmas gifts that he can bestow upon Papa Geppetto are simply his love and obedience, neither of which can be purchased with money.

Eventually kidnapped and taken to the duke's castle on Christmas Eve, Pinocchio imparts the lesson he learned, that Christmas means much more than presents. Upon his release, Pinocchio hitches a ride with Santa and returns to a joyful Papa Geppetto just in time for Christmas. Pinocchio receives the best gift of all, a living Julietta, thanks to Lady Azura.

Principal voices: Todd Porter, Alan King, George S. Irving, Robert McFadden, Pat Bright, Allen Swift, Diane Leslie, Gerry Matthews, Ray Owens, Tiffany Blake, Carl Tramon, and Alice Gayle. Written by Romeo Muller. Produced and directed by Arthur Rankin, Jr., and Jules Bass. A Rankin/Bass Production. VHS: Warner Studios. 44 min.

This television special is further detailed in Rick Goldschmidt's book *The Enchanted World of Rankin/Bass.*

See also **Rankin/Bass Christmas Cartoons.**

Plum Pudding

See **Great Britain**

Poinsettia

(*Euphorbia pulcherrima*). Popular decorative plant native to Central America and tropical Mexico. Regarded as symbols of purity, poinsettias originally grew to heights of ten feet. Below inconspicuous floral whorls are large, colored leaves, or bracts, which serve the function of petals. The poinsettia's white sap is known as latex.

Prior to the Spanish conquest of the Americas in the sixteenth century, the Aztecs had used this plant, which they called *cuetlaxochitl* ("false flower"), as a textile and cosmetic dye and its sap as an antipyretic.

As Christmas decorations, poinsettias date from the seventeenth century, when Franciscan priests of Taxo del Alarcon in southern Mexico first incorporated them to add color and festivity to holiday processions. They became the subject of a legend, several variations of which explained their significance to Christmas. According to a composite legend, Pepita, a poor Mexican girl, despaired because she had no gift to lay before the altar at Christmas Eve Midnight Mass. Comforted by her cousin Pedro, who believed that any gift, no matter how small or unsightly, would be accepted if given in love, Pepita plucked a few weeds and placed them before the *Pesebre* (Nativity scene). Miraculously, the weeds were transformed into large, brilliantly red leaves, which led to their Spanish designation, *Flores de la Noche Buena* (Flowers of the Holy Night).

Poinsettias were named for Dr. Joel R. Poinsett (1779–1851), a botanist from Greenville, South Carolina, who took a keen interest in the plant while serving as the first U.S. ambassador to Mexico from 1824 to 1829. In 1828, Poinsett first dispatched a number of the Mexican specimens to his home, where they were cultivated and circulated to other botanical gardens, and by 1836, the plants had acquired their common name, poinsettias. From 1923 on, selective breeding by horticulturists in southern California, such as the Paul Ecke family, produced a shorter variety of poinsettia with more branches and with bracts of green, yellow, white, or pink. In 1963 came the cultivars that grew best as potted plants. Contrary to popular belief, poinsettias are non-toxic.

National Poinsettia Day, December 12, commemorates the death of Dr. Poinsett.

See also **Christmas Plants**.

Poland

This nation has enjoyed *Gwiazdka* ("Little Star"), Christmas, since the late tenth century, when Mieszko, son of the legendary King Piast, introduced Christianity to his land. The holiday traditions are firmly rooted in ancient folklore and superstitions, which center primarily around seeking a mate, repelling evil, and forecasting the future. Roman Catholicism is the predominant Christian faith, its members observing typical Advent customs, including the *Roraty*, a Mass held early each morning during the four weeks of Advent. Homes and churches display the traditional *szopka* (Nativity scene or *crèche*), and the city of Kraków annually hosts a national *crèche* competition at its Historical Museum, where the entries are displayed from early December until February.

Also during Advent are observed *Andrzejki* (St. Andrew's Day, November 30), *Baborka* (St. Barbara's Day, December 4), and *Mikolaj* (St. Nicholas's Day, December 6). Amid the

social gatherings of *Andrzejki*, groups of single girls place their left shoes in a row from a wall to a door. The first girl whose shoe crosses the threshold is soon to wed. The direction in which a needle points when thrown into water indicates the direction in which a boy should seek his mate, and melted wax poured though the eye of a door key into cool water forms shapes, the shadows of which are believed to predict forthcoming events. Festive gatherings also celebrate St. Barbara, patron saint of lightning, artillery, and miners. *Swiety Mikolaj* (St. Nicholas) arrives on his feast day to examine children in their catechism and to leave them treats such as apples, nuts, and cookies, which are placed under their pillows on the evening prior. A small rod of chastisement accompanies these gifts as a reminder that youngsters should maintain proper deportment.

With the preliminary cooking, baking, and traditional house cleaning accomplished, festivities climax on *Wigilia*, Christmas Eve (from the Latin *vigilare*, "watch on the eve of a feast"), commencing with the *Polaznik*, a custom similar to "firstfooting" of Great Britain (*see* **Great Britain**). Because it is believed that a man first visiting a home on this day portends good luck (the opposite if the visitor is a woman), families customarily arrange for the appropriate visitor. Upon his arrival at dawn, the man tosses wheat over the family for luck. After feasting with them and receiving a gift, he departs at evening. It is also believed that events transpiring on this day will affect the coming year. Thus, family members and friends strive to resolve quarrels and disputes, lest these precipitate a troublesome year. The *choinka* (Christmas tree) is decorated at this time with an assortment of items, often handmade, including stars, painted eggshells, nuts, candy, apples, oranges, glass ornaments, candles, "angel hair" (strips of clear paper), and paper chains. Mistletoe hung above the front door serves as a talisman against evil.

Sighting the first star of *Wigilia* (thought to be the Star of Bethlehem) heralds Christmas and the Christmas Eve supper, which breaks a fast observed throughout the day. The table is set with a white tablecloth, under which is placed straw to commemorate Christ's manger. An extra place is also set for any unexpected guest, commemorative of Mary and Joseph who sought shelter, for no one is turned away on this night.

The meal begins with the solemn ceremony of breaking the *Oplatek* (communion wafer, now commercially available but formerly baked by church organists, who distributed them about the parish during Advent). The father or eldest family member breaks the wafer in half and gives half to the mother with wishes for love, prosperity, and happiness for the coming year. After he breaks and eats a portion of her half, the mother reciprocates, after which the ceremony is repeated between the father, children, and other relatives present. Then follows the meatless meal, which traditionally must consist of an odd number of courses (at least 12 in memory of the Twelve Apostles) and an even number of diners for good luck. The menu often includes cooked or dried carp; herring; an assortment of soups such as red beet, fermented rye, fish, and *barszcz* (mushroom soup); sauerkraut with beans; dried fruit compote; *pierogi* (dumplings stuffed with mushrooms, cabbage, or fruit); *makowiec* (baked poppy seed bread); strudel; and *kutia* (poppy seed and wheat pasta with honey, raisins, almonds, and spices). To assure fertility, livestock are fed the *Oplatek*, and fruit trees are beaten with branches. In some rural areas, a fertility ritual involves a man throwing dried fruit upon fruit trees with threats to cut them down. His wife intercedes and ties a straw rope around them, which assures a bountiful harvest.

After the meal, children receive gifts from the Star Man, who symbolizes the Star of Bethlehem. Similar to St. Nicholas, he arrives to quiz youngsters in their catechism and is accompanied by a host of Star Boys dressed as Wise Men, shepherds, or other personae from the Nativity. The latter sing *kolady* (Christmas carols) and receive some remuneration for their efforts. *Wigilia* concludes with the *Pasterka* (Mass of the Shepherds), the term for Midnight Mass.

Christmas Day is spent at home, while visitations are reserved for St. Stephen's Day (December 26). *Herody* ("Herod carolers"), consisting of troupes of 12 boys, wander from house to house with a repertoire of carols and, upon admission, reenact scenes from the life of King Herod. On Epiphany, January 6, the final day of the season, the Star Boys once again travel from door to door, marking a cross over doorways with the letters "C.M.B.," the initials of the traditional names of the three Wise Men: Caspar, Melchior, and Balthazar.

• OTHER *WIGILIA* FORECASTS

Girls grinding poppy seeds will wed soon.

The direction of the first barking dog heard after dinner points the direction from which a girl's future husband will come.

En route to the *Pasterka*, if a blindfolded girl touches a smooth picket fence, her future husband will be resourceful; a rough fence portends a clumsy spouse.

The first object pulled from a river reveals the profession of a girl's future spouse: wood, a carpenter; iron, a blacksmith, and so forth.

If Christmas sees no snow, Easter will see snow.

A sunny Christmas Eve brings fair weather all year round.

A green straw drawn from beneath the tablecloth foretells of marriage; a withered straw, a period of waiting; a yellow straw, spinsterhood; a short straw, an early grave.

If smoke from extinguished candles moves toward a window, the harvest will be bountiful; toward a door, a family member will die soon; toward the stove, a marriage.

"Merry Christmas" in Polish is *Wesolych Swiat*.

See also **Advent; Czech Republic; Epiphany; Slovak Republic.**

The Polar Express

Popular children's book written and illustrated in 1985 by American author Chris Van Allsburg, who won a Caldecott Medal for its illustrations.

Late one Christmas Eve, a little boy boards a mysterious train waiting at his house. The Polar Express, says the conductor, is bound for the North Pole, where Santa will give the first gift of Christmas to one of the many children on board. After a meal of candies and hot cocoa, the children arrive at Santa's toy factories and see hundreds of elves cheering Santa.

When asked what he wants for Christmas, the same little boy requests only one silver bell from Santa's sleigh, which becomes the first gift of Christmas. But when the boy loses the bell through a hole in his pocket, he finds it wrapped in a little box under his Christmas tree back home. Although he and his little sister Sara enjoy the bell's sweet ring, their parents are unable to hear the bell and think that it is broken. Over time the bell falls silent for Sara, but never for the boy, now grown, because the bell is audible only to those who truly believe in Santa Claus.

Boston composer Robert Kapilow adapted the story as a musical setting entitled *Chris Van Allsburg's Polar Express* for baritone solo, children's chorus, and chamber orchestra (New York: G. Schirmer, 1997).

In 2004, the story was adapted as a motion picture utilizing computer animation based on live-action, motion-capture actors. Also released to IMAX theaters in 3-D format. Featured voices: Tom Hanks, Chris Coppola, Eddie Deezen, Ed Gale, Nona Gaye, Ashly Holloway, Josh Hutcherson, Michael Jeter, Connor Matheus, and Peter Scolari. Screenplay by Robert Zemeckis and William Broyles, Jr. Produced by Steve Bing, Gary Goetzman, Steve Starkey, William Teitler, and Robert Zemeckis. Directed by Robert Zemeckis. Castle Rock Entertainment, Playtone, ImageMovers, Golden Mean, Universal CGI, and Warner Bros. Video N/A.

Children's book author Chris Van Allsburg (1949–) also won a Caldecott Medal for *Jumanji* (1981). Other works include *Ben's Dream* (1982), *The Wreck of the Zephyr* (1983), and *The Sweetest Fig* (1993). He also illustrated Mark Helprin's adaptation of *Swan Lake* (1989), based on the Tchaikovsky ballet.

Portugal

Contiguous with Spain, Portugal shares much of its neighbor's holiday traditions. A principal decoration is the *présepio* (Nativity scene), although Christmas trees are not uncommon, and most children send their Christmas wish lists to the Infant Jesus rather than Santa Claus. If a household burns a *fogueira da consoada* (Yule log), the ashes are kept and burned with pine cones in the stormy season, for, according to legend, where smoke drifts, no thunderbolt will strike.

After the *Missa do Galo* (Mass of the Rooster) on *Vespera de Natal* (Christmas Eve), families return for the traditional *Consoada* (Christmas Supper), which may consist of *bacalhau* (cod fish) with boiled potatoes and cabbage. Traditional fried desserts include *filhós* (made from pumpkin dough), *rabanadas* (akin to French toast), *azevias* (round cakes filled with chick peas, sugar, and orange peel), and *aletria* (a vermicelli sweet made with eggs). Remembering their deceased relatives, families set empty places at the table for the *alminhas a penar* (souls of the dead) and leave crumbs for them on the hearth. Formerly, the offering consisted of seeds in the belief that the souls would ensure a bountiful harvest next year. Children open gifts either at this time or on Christmas Day. Instead of hanging up stockings, many families place one *sapatinho* (shoe) of each child beside the fireplace or chimney. The menu for *Dia Natal* (Christmas Day) may feature roast turkey, pastries, fruit, and wine.

During the week before *Dia de Reis* (Day of the Kings, Epiphany, January 6), groups of children travel from door to door singing *janeiros* (Epiphany carols) and are rewarded with coins or treats. Epiphany marks the end of the Christmas season with the cutting of the traditional *Bolo Rei* (Kings' Cake), a fruit cake stuffed with small trinkets and one bean. Whoever receives the bean in his slice must furnish the cake for the festivities next year.

"Merry Christmas" in Portuguese is *Boas Festas.*

See also **Epiphany; Mass of the Rooster; Spain.**

Las Posadas

(Spanish, "The Lodgings"). An important fiesta commemorating the difficulties that Mary and Joseph encountered in finding lodging in Bethlehem. Because, by tradition, their journey from Nazareth to Bethlehem required nine days, this fiesta is observed from December 16 through December 24 in a number of Latin American countries, most prominently in Mexico, and in Spanish-speaking communities of the United States. *Las Posadas* dates from the colonial period, from the Spanish conquest of the Americas in the early sixteenth century. In Mexico, to induce the native Aztec people to accept Christianity more readily, Franciscan friars introduced *Las Posadas* in order to Christianize a portion of the Aztec winter solstice festival, observed from December 7 to December 26, which commemorated the annual rebirth of the Aztec sun god Huitzilopochtli.

Within neighborhoods, those homes determined beforehand to represent the *posadas* are colorfully decorated with such items as Spanish moss, evergreens, and colored paper lanterns. Regardless of whether they are chosen as *posadas*, most homes typically display *Pesebres*, Nativity scenes erected on a special altar in one or more rooms, often completely landscaped with little trees, ponds, a stable or cave with figures of Mary and Joseph, livestock, shepherds, and an empty cradle. Wise Men figures traditionally do not "arrive" until Epiphany. The presence of evil in the world is also represented by a serpent or devil statue.

On each of the nine nights, families form a procession, led by a child dressed as an angel. Two other children dress as Mary (who may ride a burro) and Joseph, while the others, singing *villancicos* (Christmas carols), follow with lighted candles and *faroles* (paper lanterns). Some may be dressed as the three Wise Men or as shepherds carrying decorated *baculos* (walking staffs). In one version, as the procession arrives at the *posada* for the evening, it splits into two groups, the Holy Pilgrims and the Cruel Innkeepers. Marching through the house, the Pilgrims sing a ritual dialogue, asking for shelter, while the Innkeepers respond in the negative. The Pilgrims then identify Mary and Joseph as the expectant parents of Jesus, whereupon the Innkeepers grant lodging. In another version, as the procession travels from house to house requesting lodging in like manner, the occupants (Innkeepers) turn them away, until they reach one designated house, at which the procession enters. Lodging having been granted, the participants gather around the candlelit *Pesebre* for prayers and special blessings.

On Christmas Eve, a statue of Baby Jesus is laid in the crib, followed by the traditional singing of the lullaby "El Rorro" (translated as "The Babe" but also known as "Rocking the Child" and "O, Ru-Ru-Ru, My Little Jesus"), a folk carol thought to date from the eighteenth or nineteenth century.

Following the ceremonies of each evening come festivities with fireworks, singing and dancing, *buñuelos* (thin, fried pastries), *colacion* (assorted candies), fruit, *ponche* (hot fruit punch laced with rum or tequila for the adults or sweetened with brown sugar, cinnamon, and vanilla for the children), *tamales*, *atole* (corn gruel), and a *piñata* (particularly in Mexico). The latter consists of a decorative earthenware jar in the shape of an animal, doll, or other attractive figure, suspended overhead and filled with all manner of treats, nuts, and sweets. Blindfolded children try, one by one, to break the *piñata* with a long stick, and when it is broken, there is a happy scramble for the prizes.

Morality plays, *Los Pastorelas* (Shepherds Plays), also depict the journey to Bethlehem during these nine days, but from the shepherds' point of view. Like *Las Posadas*, these plays date from the Spanish conquest of Mexico and Central and South America. Roman Catholic missionaries, seeking converts, took Native American dramatizations, which those nations had built around historic events in their own culture, and adapted them to key biblical events. Although such plays originally mirrored the strictly religious plots from the mystery plays of medieval Europe, they, like their European counterparts, eventually fell into the hands of folk performers, where they evolved into comedies in which the principal characters, the shepherds, were depicted as lazy oafs and buffoons, along with less-than-spiritual dialogue. But whereas the Shepherds Plays and other mystery plays of Europe declined with the Protestant Reformation, these plays have survived in the Americas, despite their less formal evolutions, and frequently appear as popular public performances during the holidays. As this traditional story of good versus evil now stands, the shepherds, having received the annunciation of Christ's birth from an angel, reluctantly set out for Bethlehem. En route, Satan and his legions attempt to thwart their progress through a series of mishaps; yet the shepherds, whom angels and an old hermit shield from harm, persevere and arrive to worship the Christ Child.

See also **Mexico.**

Prancer

(1989). Motion picture drama.

Rebecca Harrell stars as nine-year-old Jessica Riggs, who claims that one of Santa's reindeer, Prancer, is wounded and loose in the woods around Three Oaks, Michigan. She developed this notion from two sources: First, a reindeer figure that she identified as Prancer fell from the city's overhead Christmas display and crashed to the street. Second, she saw a reindeer in the woods and noticed that it had markings identical to a magazine's rendering of the mythical reindeer. Jessica's father, an impoverished, no-nonsense apple farmer and widower (Sam Elliott), pays little attention to her except to scold and dismisses her story as mere childishness.

Discovering Prancer lying in their barn, Jessica hides him in a remote shed, feeds him Christmas cookies, engages a veterinarian (Abe Vigoda) to treat his wound, and, to buy fodder, works on the sly for a cantankerous old recluse (Cloris Leachman), whose life Jessica also brightens by adorning her roof with Christmas lights discovered in her attic.

Jessica entrusts a photograph and a letter outlining Prancer's condition to a local shopping mall Santa (Michael Constantine), with faith that he will forward these on to the *real* Santa. Instead, he delivers them to the editor at the city newspaper with an idea for a heartwarming, human interest story. By next morning, an editorial titled "Yes, Santa, There Are Still Virginias" (a slant on the famed Francis Church editorial "Yes, Virginia, There Is a Santa Claus") extols the virtues of Jessica's belief in Santa, and curiosity seekers storm Riggs's farm to see Prancer.

When Riggs, irate over Jessica's actions, sells Prancer to a local merchant as an advertising gimmick, Jessica runs away. Feeling that, without Prancer, there is nothing left for her in Three Oaks, Jessica attempts to free him in time for Christmas but falls from a tree and sustains minor injuries. The accident softens Riggs's heart, and on Christmas Eve, the two release Prancer in the woods and follow him to the edge of Antler Ridge, where his tracks end. They never see Prancer again, but the viewer sees a white streak mounting to the sky that meets Santa's team flying in the distance.

In 1990 the picture received Young Artist Award nominations for Best Young Actress Starring in a Motion Picture (Rebecca Harrell) and Best Supporting Young Actress (Ariana Richards).

With Rutanya Alda, John Joseph Duda, Mark Rolston, Walter Charles, and Michael Luciano. Greg Taylor, who wrote the script, created the story for his own seven-year-old daughter. Produced by Raffaella DeLaurentiis. Directed by John Hancock. Cineplex-Odeon Films, Nelson Entertainment, and Raffaella Productions. DVD: MGM/UA Video. 103 min.

See also **Prancer Returns**; **Yes, Virginia, There Is a Santa Claus**.

Prancer Returns

(2001). American/Canadian made-for-video drama/fantasy, a sequel to the 1989 motion picture *Prancer*.

Ten years have passed since the wounded reindeer Prancer first appeared in rural Three Oaks, Michigan. As Christmas Eve approaches, the town prepares for its annual "Prancer Ceremony," a popular ritual that returns a missing figure of Prancer to its proper place among Santa's reindeer in a display suspended over Main Street. Having recently learned of the Prancer story, eight-year-old Charlie Holton (Gavin Fink), a lonely newcomer to Three Oaks, encounters a mysterious little buck, which leads him to a reindeer that has expired in the forest. Suddenly and miraculously the deceased animal vanishes from sight in a burst of snow, which convinces Charlie not only that this reindeer had been Prancer himself, but that he had sired the little buck as his replacement.

Charlie reasons that he must return little Prancer to Antler Ridge on Christmas Eve, so that he can join Santa's team, just as the late Prancer had done years before. In the meantime, Charlie hides Prancer in his room at home and attempts to contact the North Pole via the Internet to alert Santa about Prancer's predicament. Caring for his houseguest is far more than Charlie can handle, for not only does Prancer nearly expose himself through delightfully comical incidents, such as sleeping in Charlie's bed and climbing into the bathtub, spilling shampoo, and creating an enormous bubble bath, but Charlie must provide a proper diet of milk instead of breakfast cereal. Therefore, Charlie coaxes milk from an old cow that belongs to Old Man Richards (Jack Palance), a cantankerous, reclusive neighbor. Although the cow had been dry for ages, after Charlie delivers a pep talk about doing good deeds for Santa, the cow accommodates him accordingly.

The tide turns against Prancer after he escapes, wanders into Charlie's elementary school, and bites Vice-Principal Klock (Michael O'Keefe). But rather than see Prancer destroyed as a public menace, Charlie eludes the authorities and quickly whisks Prancer away into the safety of the forest, where Charlie falls from a ledge while attempting to teach Prancer how to fly. Instinctively, Prancer locates Charlie's mother Denise (Stacy Edwards) with handyman/friend Tom Sullivan (John Corbett), who had been combing the woods with a search party.

Although Charlie is rescued, having escaped serious injury, Prancer's fate would have been sealed had not a local television interview with Charlie sparked public interest in Prancer's return. The participants in a town meeting being reluctant to take any action on Christmas Eve, Charlie, together with the help of Old Man Richards and others, manages to smuggle Prancer out of town before the Prancer Ceremony concludes with a reading of the perennial poem, "A Visit from St. Nicholas." Then at the moment when Richards sets the Prancer figure in place, Prancer, racing toward Antler Ridge, is transformed into a great buck with a full set of antlers. As he springs skyward in his father's footsteps to join Santa's team overhead, Three Oaks witnesses the miracle as a brilliant, awe-inspiring flash.

In 2001, this video won Video Premiere awards for Best Original Score, Best Original Song ("If You Believe"), and Best Supporting Actor (Jack Palance); VPA nominations for Best Actress (Stacy Edwards), Best Cinematography, Best Director, and Best Live-Action Video Premiere Movie. In 2002, it won Young Artist awards for Best Family Television Movie or Special, Best Supporting Young Actor (Robert Clark), and Best Young Actor and Actress Age Ten or Under (Gavin Fink and Hayley Lochner); and was nominated for an ASC Award for Outstanding Achievement in Cinematography.

Written by Greg Taylor. Produced by Oscar Luis Costo. Directed by Joshua Butler. Gypsy Films International, Raffaella Productions, USA Network, and Via Genesis Productions. DVD: UMVD. 90 min.

See also **Prancer.**

The Preacher's Wife
See **The Bishop's Wife**

Pretty Paper

American song written in 1963 by country singer-songwriter Willie Nelson. The lyrics are a reminder that, amid the sparkle, bustle, and dazzle of the holiday, others such as the lonely, the despondent, and the homeless must not be forgotten, for it is at Christmastime that they suffer want more than ever. Nelson's friend, singer Roy Orbison, brought "Pretty Paper" to the forefront, for Orbison's recording on the Monument label placed number 15 on the *Billboard Hot 100* chart in 1963.

Willie Nelson is one of country music's biggest stars. Among many other songs, he wrote the Grammy Award winner "Always on My Mind" (1982) as well as "Crazy" (1961).

Puerto Rico
See **West Indies.**

R

Rankin/Bass Christmas Cartoons

A former art director and graphic designer for ABC, Arthur Rankin, Jr., established Videocraft International in 1955 with partner Jules Bass, a former director of radio and television production for the Gardner

Advertising Agency in New York. Known as Rankin/Bass Productions from 1961, the company produced commercials, animated entertainment programs for television, and theatrical motion pictures for 35 years, beginning with the syndicated television series *The New Adventures of Pinocchio* (1960–61). During this time, the company was a leading producer of animated television specials, many based on classic holiday themes, such that Rankin/Bass became known as "Mr. Christmas," "Mr. Easter," "Mr. Thanksgiving," and so on. Animation was chiefly carried out in Japan, using stop-motion puppets (a technique Rankin/Bass termed "Animagic") as well as cel animation (conventional drawings). Together with composer/conductor Maury Laws, Bass wrote most of the tunes associated with Rankin/Bass Productions, and the company almost always used the voices of well-established actors and other celebrities in order to introduce them to younger audiences. Although Rankin and Bass went their separate ways in 1990, Rankin has led the company into the twenty-first century.

The repertoire of Rankin/Bass Christmas cartoons includes 18 television specials, one theatrical motion picture, and one episode from a television series as listed alphabetically below. Unless otherwise specified, each cartoon is discussed further as a separate entry:

A Christmas Tree (1972), episode from television series *Festival of Family Classics*, starring Carl Banas.

The Cricket on the Hearth (1967), television special starring Marlo and Danny Thomas. See **Dickens, Charles, Christmas Stories of.**

The First Christmas: The Story of the First Christmas Snow (1975), television special starring Angela Lansbury.

Frosty the Snowman (1969), television special starring Jimmy Durante.

Frosty's Winter Wonderland (1976), television special starring Andy Griffith.

Jack Frost (1979), television special starring Buddy Hackett.

The Leprechaun's Christmas Gold (1981), television special starring Art Carney.

The Life and Adventures of Santa Claus (1985), television special that featured no big-name celebrities.

The Little Drummer Boy (1968), television special starring Greer Garson.

The Little Drummer Boy, Book II (1976), television special starring Greer Garson.

Nestor, the Long-Eared Christmas Donkey (1977), television special starring Roger Miller.

Pinocchio's Christmas (1980), television special starring Alan King.

Rudolph and Frosty: Christmas in July (1979), motion picture starring Red Buttons.

Rudolph, the Red-Nosed Reindeer (1964), television special starring Burl Ives.

Rudolph's Shiny New Year (1976), television special starring Red Skelton.

Santa, Baby! (2001), television special starring Eartha Kitt.

Santa Claus Is Comin' to Town (1970), television special starring Fred Astaire.

The Stingiest Man in Town (1978), television special starring Tom Bosley. See **A Christmas Carol** (Film and Television Versions).

'Twas the Night before Christmas (1974), television special starring Joel Grey.

The Year without a Santa Claus (1974), television special starring Shirley Booth.

Redeemer of the Nations, Come
See **Savior of the Nations, Come**

Reindeer
See **Saint Nicholas**

Remember the Night

(1940). Motion picture comedy/romance.
Assistant New York City district attorney John Sargent (Fred MacMurray) takes compassion on Lee Leander (Barbara Stanwyck), a beautiful larcenist arrested just before Christmas. With the trial postponed until after the holidays, John bails her out of jail and, because she has nowhere to turn, invites her to spend the holidays at his mother's farm in Indiana. John's family, simple, wholesome, down-home folks, quickly accept Lee as one of the family, despite her past, and shower her with warmth and love.

The holidays, the most memorably touching moments that Lee has ever experienced, pass all too quickly, and as the hour approaches when they must return to New York, Lee and John realize that they are desperately in love with each other. John, wishing to have Lee acquitted, attempts to throw the case, but Lee, unwilling to compromise John's position, breaks down with a full confession of her guilt in court. Although a few years must separate them, John and Lee vow to be married upon her release.

With Beulah Bondi, Elizabeth Patterson, and Sterling Holloway. Written by Preston Sturges. Produced and directed by Mitchell Leisen. Paramount Pictures. VHS: Universal Studios. B & W. 94 min.

Republic of South Africa
See **Africa**

Resonet in laudibus
See **Joseph, Dearest Joseph Mine**

Revenge Is Sweet
See **Babes in Toyland**

Rich Little's Christmas Carol
See **A Christmas Carol** (Film and Television Versions)

Richie Rich's Christmas Wish
(1998). Made-for-video comedy/fantasy, based on the character Richie Rich, the richest kid in the world, of Harvey Comics.

It's Christmas Eve, and Richie (David Gallagher), a most benevolent and affable 12-year-old, sets forth on his annual mission to deliver presents to the children at the Richville Orphanage. His vehicle is a decorative, motorized sleigh, which his greedy cousin, Reggie Van Dough (Jake Richardson), has secretly sabotaged, so that the sleigh plunges into a ravine. Despite Richie's spotless reputation, the town erroneously blames him for ruining the orphans' Christmas, and Richie wishes that he had never been born. His wish is granted through a washing-machine-turned-wishing-machine, a wacky invention of Professor Keenbean (Eugene Levy), the Rich family's eccentric scientist-in-residence.

Here the picture takes on the ambiance of the film classics *It's a Wonderful Life* and *Back to the Future*. Without Richie's positive influence, the insufferable Reggie now dominates the town, which he renames Reggieville, and its citizens are reduced to utter poverty.

Therefore, Richie must find Professor Keenbean and the wishing machine to set things right. But time is of the essence, for the wishing machine works only on Christmas Eve, and its power will cease at midnight.

Richie soon becomes a fugitive from the law after breaking into his family's mansion, which Reggie now occupies, and is further charged with "dognapping" his pet, Dollar, which now belongs to Reggie. Following a madcap series of chases, twists, and turns, Riche initially skirts the authorities and locates the professor, who requires the large wishbone from a particular species of dinosaur to fix Reggie's malfunctioning wishing machine. Such a wishbone happens to reside in the local museum, and Richie rushes to seize it with the help of friends Gloria (Michelle Trachtenberg), Freckles (Blake Jeremy Collins), Pee Wee (Austin Stout), and his former personal valet, Cadbury (Keene Curtis). They are apprehended in the act, however, and are whisked away to jail, only to be bailed out by Root Canal, a group of punk-rock musicians for whom Cadbury now serves as valet.

As midnight rapidly approaches, Reggie threatens to cancel Christmas and cut off all city utilities unless Richie is captured by midnight. This is the last straw, for when Richie's troupe returns to Reggie's residence, the authorities, appalled that someone would dare to cancel Christmas, interfere no further, and the professor installs the wishbone. With seconds to spare, Richie reverses his wish and returns to his own world of Christmas cheer. Richie's benevolence truly shines after Reggie confesses his evil deed, for Richie bestows gifts on him as well as on his entire household.

Story by Rob Kerchner and Jason Teffer. Screenplay by Mark Turey. Produced by Mike Elliott. Directed by John Murlowski. Saban Entertainment in association with the Harvey Company. DVD: Warner Home Video. 84 min.

The Right to Be Happy
See **A Christmas Carol** (Film and Television Versions)

Ring Out, Wild Bells
Carol for the New Year, the lyrics to which were written by English poet Alfred, Lord Ten-

nyson (1809–1892). The lyrics are taken from the 106th canto of the elegy *In Memoriam*, Tennyson's tribute to a close friend and his sister's fiancé, Arthur Henry Hallam, who died in 1833 at the age of 22. Plunged into deep, spiritual depression, Tennyson composed the elegy over 16 years (1833–1849) and published it in 1850, the same year that he was appointed poet laureate of England. *In Memoriam* consists of 131 cantos, each a separate poem with independent thought. Together, they celebrate Hallam's life, lament Tennyson's loss, express his search to find a way to cope with his feelings of abandonment and depression, and find justification for human immortality by working through the loss of faith that plagued English society at that time (the scientific revolution and secularization had begun to challenge Christian principles, thus creating a spiritual crisis).

With the old year waning quickly, "Ring Out, Wild Bells" is an appeal to ring out false pride, slandering, and spite, and ring in that which is new, the common love of good, truth, and right, and the Christ that is to be. Although the musical setting remains anonymous (as does the one who joined words and music together), it was once attributed to Mozart. It has also been attributed to a Carl Zulehner and to a Wenzel Müller, both of whom are obscure.

Alfred, Lord Tennyson was one of the foremost English poets of the Victorian era. His best-known works include the poems "Morte d'Arthur" and "The Charge of the Light Brigade."

Rise Up, Shepherd, and Follow

Anonymous, African American spiritual collected during the American Civil War and first published in *Slave Songs of the United States*, edited by William Allen, Charles Ware, and Lucy Garrison (New York, 1867). The song received its title from the repetitive phrase traditionally sung by a choir in response to a soloist's rendering of the verses. Urging the shepherds to forsake their flocks, the text bids them to "take good heed to the angel's words" and follow the star in the East to Bethlehem (which takes liberties with the biblical account of the Wise Men and the star as recorded in the second chapter of Matthew's Gospel). The African American soprano Dorothy Maynor

(1910–1996), who recorded with Serge Koussevitsky and the Boston Symphony and who founded New York City's Harlem School of the Arts in 1963, popularized this spiritual in the United States.

Rockin' around the Christmas Tree

Popular American song written by Johnny Marks in 1958. A writer of numerous Christmas songs and known especially for his hit of 1949, "Rudolph, the Red-Nosed Reindeer," Marks entered the rock-and-roll era by contributing "Rockin,'" which was the second major rock Christmas song, the first being "Jingle Bell Rock" (1957) by Joseph Beal and James Boothe. The lyrics center around the Christmas "hop" (1950s teenage term for a dance gathering), where the boys and girls are dancing the "new old-fashioned way."

Thirteen-year-old Brenda Lee (nicknamed "Little Miss Dynamite"), a most promising recording artist since age 11, recorded "Rockin'" on the Decca label in 1958. It did not attract radio disc jockeys for two years, until Lee had accumulated a number of other big-time hits, after which radio stations across the country were more than willing to play "Rockin.'" When the song finally became a hit in 1960 as the top Christmas song that year (position 14 on the *Billboard Hot 100* chart), it sold some 6.5 million copies. Subsequently it was charted each year during the 1960s.

Of the 25 most frequently performed Christmas songs of the twentieth century listed by the American Society of Composers, Authors and Publishers (ASCAP), "Rockin' around the Christmas Tree" ranked number 19. By December 2004, the rank had risen to number 16.

See also **ASCAP List of Christmas Songs; Jingle Bell Rock; Rudolph, the Red-Nosed Reindeer** (song).

Rocking

("Hajej, nynej"). Czech traditional lullaby with variant titles of "Rocking Carol," "Lullaby," "Little Jesus, Sweetly Sleep," "Shepherd's Rocking Carol," and "Jesu, Jesu, Baby Dear." Thought perhaps to be the oldest of carol lullabies, it originated sometime between the fourteenth and fifteenth centuries. The carol's verses mimic gentle cradle rocking, particularly through the repetitive phrase of "We will rock you, rock you, rock you" found in line three of the verses. A number of English translations exist, some of which repeat the entire "We will rock you" phrase for line four as well. In others, line four reads "Gently slumber as we rock you." The melody is somewhat reminiscent of that for the children's tune "Twinkle, Twinkle, Little Star."

Because "Rocking" arose during the Middle Ages, it is believed to have been included in a repertoire of cradle songs used for Christmas cradle-rocking ceremonies of the time. Originating in Germany and thence to all Europe, cradle rocking was once a feature of Christmas Vespers, wherein the priest rocked a cradle containing an image of the Christ Child to an appropriate cradle song. Groups of children rocking cradles would also parade through the streets while singing a lullaby.

Rocking Carol
See **Rocking**

Romania

Having received Christianity from Bulgaria of the Byzantine Empire (of which it was once a subject), Romania has enjoyed Christmas since the ninth century. The principal Christian faiths include the Eastern Orthodox Church and Roman Catholicism. The Orthodox Church in Romania, once following the older Julian calendar for ecclesiastical purposes, adopted the current Gregorian calendar in 1919.

The Christmas season extends from Christmas Eve until Epiphany, 13 days later. A preliminary event, St. Nicholas's Day, is observed on December 6, when children place their boots near an entrance on the eve before, so that *Mos Nicolae* (Old Nicholas) can fill them with candy and treats; naughty children receive sticks.

On December 20, an unusual ritual honors St. Ignatius, third bishop of Antioch (ca. 50–ca. 117), who suffered martyrdom by being thrown to lions on this day. Termed "Ignat," the ritual involves slaughtering a pig, singeing off its bristles with burning straws, then washing it. The head of the household makes the sign of the cross on its head, after which the pig is roasted and eaten, with family and friends in attendance. The custom is reminiscent of pre-Christian Scandinavian winter solstice festivals, which sacrificed a boar to Freya, Norse goddess of fertility.

Colindatul (caroling) on Christmas Eve constitutes the most important tradition of the season and involves community-wide participation. Large groups of *colindatori* (carolers) organize and travel from door to door singing a mixture of sacred and secular *colinde* (carols). The texts of secular folk carols widely vary and include fairy tales and themes of romance and marriage. Other folk carols center around legends of God and the saints, placing them in fictitious situations. Those carols most inspired by the Scriptures are known as *cantece de stea* (star songs) and are usually sung by children, who carry icons of Jesus and painted or illuminated paper stars, *steaua*, on poles. For their participation, the children receive fruit, nuts, pastries, bread, or money. Accompanied by flute and drum in many areas, the carolers call upon the names of each person in the house, beginning with the head and including members deceased during that year, and offer a specific carol of blessing with good wishes for each of them, based upon their marital state, profession, and so forth; hence, the repertoire of carols is quite extensive. Traditional dances always accompany the carols, after which the host offers the troupe food, drink, and gifts.

Christmas Eve customs also include decorating the home with fir branches and the Christmas tree with multicolored ornaments and candles. The evening meal may feature roast pork, cabbage, breads, and *turta*, a pastry of thin, rolled dough that represents the swaddling clothes of the Christ Child. The holiday gift-bringer is *Mos Craciun*, a figure similar to Santa Claus. In Hunedoara of Transylvania, *pizarai*, groups of children bearing a *pizara* (lance) on which is tied a head kerchief, travel from house to house with recitations for health, happiness, and good fortune during the holidays. As they recite, they touch members of the household with the lance as a means of transferring the wishes. This tradition closely resembles *Sorcova* of New Year's Day (see below). The region of Moldavia features the unique

Two children set off with their sorcova, *a branch decorated with fruit and ribbons on New Year's Day. From the journal* Cesky Lid *(published in Prague), 1910.*

Umblatul cu ursul (Bear Custom), in which a man portrays a bear by wearing a bear mask and animal skins adorned with red tassels. The man growls and imitates the grotesque steps of a dancing bear, while throngs of people, especially children and musicians, accompany him. Christmas Eve concludes with Midnight Mass, and Christmas Day traditions mirror those in the United States.

Throughout the season, Nativity plays and masked dances are popular. Best known among the latter is the *Umblatul cu capra* (Goat Tradition), which is performed from Christmas until New Year's Day. In Wallachia and Oltenia, this dance is termed *Brezaia* because the masks feature a host of colors; in other regions, the custom is known as "Stag." The masks are

fashioned after goats, oxen, or deer with movable jaws that champ together as the performers, clad in animal skins, dance and cavort in a comical routine, accompanied by clamoring children and men shouting *strigaturi* (humorous remarks). While the goat once symbolized fertility at the winter solstice, it is said that this goat custom most likely derives from ancient Jewish rituals once performed on the Day of Atonement (Yom Kippur). As detailed in Leviticus 16, one of two goats became a sacrificial sin offering, and the other became a scapegoat that was released into the wilderness, bearing away the sins of the congregation (the scapegoat concept of transferring disease or bad luck onto an animal or human to be sacrificed also was known to the Assyrians, Babylonians, and Greeks). This ritual foreshadowed Christ, Who would become the ultimate scapegoat for the sins of all humanity through His crucifixion, and the Romanian goat custom recalls this theme during celebrations of His birth. Some performances include an Old Man mask, representative of the man who led the scapegoat into the wilderness.

Parties, fireworks, and clamor greet the new year as in the West, and the fertility tradition of *Plugusorul* (Little Plow) brings wishes for a bountiful crop and success in the new year. Bearing a plow adorned with colored paper or embroidered cloth, teenagers travel from house to house and deliver an elaborate, poetic recitation that petitions the spirit of the plowman to bless the crops. The text, delivered amid the din of bells, cracking whips, and a bellowing *buhai* (bagpipe), makes special mention of the foundation of Romania in the days of the Roman emperor Trajan, who conquered the land formerly known as Dacia about the year A.D. 106. In another fertility tradition known as *Sorcova* (from the Slavic *soroku,* "forty"), groups of children wish their parents, friends, and neighbors a long and prosperous life through the *sorcova,* a fruit-tree branch decorated with colored paper and artificial flowers. While reciting a traditional poem of 40 lines, the children, all of whom bear a *sorcova,* touch their elders 40 times with the branch as a symbolic means of transferring the wishes. For their participation, the children receive rewards of sweets and coins.

Forecasting the future remains a favorite New Year's pastime. *Obiceiul mesei* (Table Custom) involves hiding either a coin, corn, mirror, or lump of coal at each of the four corners of a table under a tablecloth. Then four children randomly arrange themselves at the corners and uncover the objects before them. The coin forecasts wealth; the corn, abundant food; the mirror, beauty and nobility of soul; the coal, bad luck. For *Obiceiul puntilor* (Bridge Custom), children take a forked branch and place a stick at the junction of the fork, which symbolizes a bridge between the old and new years. With such a bridge, a child may dream of his destiny on New Year's night.

On Epiphany, the priest, using a branch of basil to sprinkle holy water about, blesses the homes of his parishioners.

"Merry Christmas" is *Sarbatori Vesele*.

See also **Epiphany; Saint Nicholas's Day.**

Rose Bowl
See **New Year's Day**

Rosemary
See **Christmas Plants**

Rudolph and Frosty: Christmas in July

(1979). Motion picture animated story using stop-motion puppets (Animagic), released in July of that year as a sequel to the television specials *Rudolph, the Red-Nosed Reindeer* (1964) and *Frosty the Snowman* (1969). It was the last Animagic theatrical film from Rankin/Bass Productions, the last time that company animated the Rudolph and Frosty characters, and the first time Frosty appeared in Animagic.

In order to help the foundering "Circus by the Sea," Rudolph, Frosty, and Frosty's wife and two children head south to become the circus's star attractions in its "Christmas in July" show over the Fourth of July weekend. The evil Winterbolt, King of the North, forms an elaborate plot to eliminate Rudolph and Santa, so that he will be sole ruler of the North. This involves framing Rudolph for a circus robbery through the evil reindeer Scratcher, whom Winterbolt has commissioned for the task. This extinguishes the magic behind Rudolph's bright, red nose, and Rudolph promises to

keep silent about the truth of the robbery in exchange for the lives of Frosty's family, who wear Winterbolt's amulets to prevent their melting. To silence Frosty, Winterbolt tricks him into relinquishing his hat, his source of life. Rudolph pursues Winterbolt and recovers the hat, the wearing of which also restores Rudolph's bright nose. He returns to the circus, recovers the stolen money, and names the perpetrator, a crooked showman named Sam Spangles, who desired to take over the circus.

The shattering of his ice scepter defeats Winterbolt, but his amulets also fail, and the Frosty family melts. Only the icy winds of Jack Frost, wintering in South America in July, can restore the Frostys. Brought in by Clockwork Big Ben (a whale introduced in an earlier sequel, *Rudolph's Shiny New Year*), Jack accomplishes a happy ending as Santa, delayed by Winterbolt's storm, arrives to return everyone to the North Pole.

Featuring the song classics "Rudolph, the Red-Nosed Reindeer," "Frosty the Snow Man," "Rockin' around the Christmas Tree," and "I Heard the Bells on Christmas Day." Principal voices: Red Buttons, Ethel Merman, Mickey Rooney, Alan Sues, Jackie Vernon, Shelley Winters, Paul Frees, Billie Richards, Hal Peary, Shelby Flint, and Don Messick. Written by Romeo Muller. Produced and directed by Arthur Rankin, Jr., and Jules Bass. Rankin/Bass Productions. VHS: Warner Studios. 97 min.

This film is further detailed in Rick Goldschmidt's book *The Enchanted World of Rankin/Bass*.

See also **Frosty Returns; Frosty the Snowman** (television special); **Frosty's Winter Wonderland; Rankin/Bass Christmas Cartoons; Rudolph, the Red-Nosed Reindeer** (television special); **Rudolph, the Red-Nosed Reindeer and the Island of Misfit Toys; Rudolph's Shiny New Year.**

Rudolph Shines Again
See **Rudolph, the Red-Nosed Reindeer** (character)

Rudolph, the Red-Nosed Reindeer

(Character). Highly popular character created in 1939 by Robert Lewis May (1905–1976), an advertising copywriter born in New Rochelle,

New York, and immortalized in "Rudolph, the Red-Nosed Reindeer," a song written by May's brother-in-law, New York City songwriter John D. (Johnny) Marks (1909–1985). The song was released in 1949.

• BACKGROUND WITH ROBERT MAY. May created Rudolph as a Christmas promotional gimmick for the Montgomery Ward Company, a retail department store chain based in Chicago. Instead of buying coloring books to give away to holiday shoppers as it had done in years past, Ward assigned May, who worked in the Chicago office, the task of producing a give-away booklet of its own, to save money. Small, frail, and ostracized from school teams as a youngster, May used his own childhood experiences to create a story about a little reindeer whom other reindeer taunted for his physical abnormality — a big, shiny red nose. But the reindeer's "deformity" became an asset in guiding Santa's sleigh through heavy fog on Christmas Eve.

Tossing around such names as "Rollo" and "Reginald," May hit on an alliterative name, "Rudolph, the Red-Nosed Reindeer," in keeping with the style of cartoon names in the 1930s, then wrote the story as a poem consisting of rhyming couplets with his four-year-old daughter Barbara as critic. But Montgomery Ward, fearing that parents would associate a red-nosed character with drunkenness, initially rejected Rudolph, until Denver Gillen, May's coworker, provided adorable illustrations based on sketches he had made of reindeer at Chicago's Lincoln Park Zoo. Satisfied, Ward next shortened May's original title from "The Day before Christmas, or Rudolph, the Red-Nosed Reindeer" to its now-famous version.

Montgomery Ward distributed some 2.4 million copies of May's 32-page creation in 1939 alone but ceased distribution when the United States entered World War II. When the booklet was reprinted in 1946, another 3.6 million copies were given away.

In 1944, Max Fleischer produced an eight-minute animated cartoon "short" version of the story for theaters, backed by the Detroit-based Jim Handy Company. Narration by Paul Wing. Written by Robert L. May, Paul Wing, and Joseph Stultz. Original music by Johnny Marks. Theme by George Kleinsinger.

Although Montgomery Ward initially owned the copyright, in 1947 the company generously assigned the rights to May, who temporarily left the company in 1951 to establish Rudolph, the Red-Nosed Enterprises, Inc. A large host of Rudolph products followed, including clothing, jewelry, and toys. An RCA Victor record album consisting of two discs about Rudolph had previously appeared on the market in 1947, narrated by Paul Wing with music by George Kleinsinger. DC Comics also published stories of Rudolph's adventures with new issues each December from 1950 to 1962, illustrated by Rube Grossman. The DC version briefly reappeared in 1972, written and illustrated by Sheldon Mayer. The revenues thus generated provided financial security for Robert May and offset debts he had incurred while caring for his terminally ill wife, who had died during Rudolph's inception. To May, Rudolph was "my generous son."

For more than 25 years, May displayed a nine-foot, papier-mâché figure of Rudolph with a red light bulb nose on the front lawn of his home in Evanston, Illinois. In 1958, he donated the original manuscript and other Rudolph memorabilia to his alma mater, Dartmouth College. That same year, May returned to Montgomery Ward and remained there until he retired in 1970.

Rudolph is considered to be the only original addition to the Santa Claus folklore in the twentieth century.

• MAY'S ORIGINAL STORY. In the reindeer community, far removed from the North Pole, the reindeer are at play on Christmas Eve, except red-nosed Rudolph. Although he is a good little buck, he is jeered at by his peers and barred from their games because of his nose. That night, thick fog hinders Santa's trip, and his blind, low flying results in several mishaps, until he drops by Rudolph's house. Impressed by the red nose, Santa, worried that he will not finish his rounds before morning, persuades Rudolph to bail him out by leading the team. After a successful night, the other reindeer treat Rudolph as a celebrity, and Santa promises to call on him again, should foul weather threaten future Christmas Eves.

• RUDOLPH BOOK SEQUELS. Robert May created other stories about Rudolph. *Rudolph's*

Second Christmas was originally drafted in 1947 but did not surface until 1991, when one of May's daughters discovered the manuscript in a box among his personal effects. It was published posthumously in 1992 with illustrations by Michael Emberley. This sequel is written in prose, except for Rudolph, who speaks in rhyming couplets. As Rudolph and Santa read post-Christmas letters from grateful children, Rudolph notes one letter from a brother and sister whom Santa had inadvertently overlooked. Rudolph investigates the problem and learns that the children are from a traveling circus, the acts of which are so pitiful that no town can tolerate them for more than one day at a time. Thus Santa could never locate the children, because the circus was constantly on the move. En route back to the North Pole, Rudolph discovers the solution in a group of lonely, misfit animals seeking acceptance: a dog that meows, a cat that barks, a fast-running turtle, a slow-walking rabbit, a singing parrot, and a talking canary. Their unusual attributes bring the circus phenomenal success, the children travel about much less frequently, and their next Christmas is much happier, thanks to Rudolph.

Rudolph, the Red-Nosed Reindeer, Shines Again was published in 1954 as a poem of rhyming couplets with illustrations by Marion Guild. It was reprinted in 1981 as *Rudolph Shines Again* with illustrations by Diana Magnuson. With heavy snow forecast for Christmas Eve, Santa bids Rudolph to come to the North Pole and lead his team. The other reindeer once again ostracize Rudolph and make his life difficult, not because he is different but because they are most jealous of his prime status with Santa. When Rudolph wallows in self-pity, the light of his beacon nose fades, after which he runs far away into the forest, where he discovers a large family of rabbits that is missing two young bunnies named Donnie and Doris. With no concern for himself and armed only with his senses of smell and hearing, Rudolph searches alone for them and finally rescues them from the jaws of hungry wolves. Repenting for having left Santa and believing that he can still be of some use to his former master, if not as a guide, Rudolph returns to the North Pole on Christmas Eve. He arrives just in time

to help Santa navigate through the snow and fog that plague the scene, for by now, Rudolph's nose is as bright as ever, restored through his act of heroism and selflessness.

See also **Rudolph, the Red-Nosed Reindeer** (song).

Rudolph, the Red-Nosed Reindeer

(Song). Highly popular song written by New York City songwriter John D. (Johnny) Marks, based on a story of the same title by his brother-in-law, Robert L. May. Although Marks composed his song about Rudolph in 1947, numerous music publishers rejected it on the notion that a song about a misfit reindeer couldn't possibly sell. Eventually a determined Marks established his own publishing house in New York City, appropriately named St. Nicholas Music, Inc., to issue the sheet music, and then he sought a recording artist. Again, Marks met resistance when celebrities such as Bing Crosby, Dinah Shore, and Perry Como declined. Having recorded a most successful "Here Comes Santa Claus" in 1947, cowboy singing star Gene Autry also would have declined had not his wife, Ina, moved by the ugly duckling sentiment in "Rudolph," convinced her husband otherwise.

Autry introduced "Rudolph" during his rodeo show at Madison Square Garden in the fall of 1949, and his recording on the Columbia label became the top Christmas song on the pop charts for three consecutive years, selling two million copies in 1949 alone and over 25 million copies through the years. These figures rank Autry's "Rudolph, the Red-Nosed Reindeer" as the second-largest-selling Christmas single in the world, behind Bing Crosby's version of "White Christmas." Autry also achieved a hit with his remake of "Rudolph" in 1957 on the Challenge label.

Marks's song inspired *Rudolph, the Red-Nosed Reindeer*, a 1964 animated television special with Burl Ives that also launched several animated sequels for television and video.

Of the 25 most frequently performed Christmas songs of the twentieth century listed by the American Society of Composers, Authors and Publishers (ASCAP), "Rudolph" ranked number five. By December 2004, however, it had fallen to number eight. (*See* **ASCAP List of Christmas Songs.**)

Johnny Marks (1909–1985) studied music in Paris and produced shows for the army overseas during World War II. Working primarily as a radio producer, he published some 175 songs, most of which contained Christmas themes, and he was probably the most prolific writer of popular Christmas music in the twentieth century. Although he is best known for "Rudolph," some of Marks's other holiday treasures include "When Santa Claus Gets Your Letter" (1950), "'Twas the Night Before Christmas Song" (1952), "Everyone's a Child at Christmas" (1956), "I Heard the Bells on Christmas Day" (1956), "A Merry, Merry Christmas to You" (1958), "Rockin' around the Christmas Tree" (1958), "Run Rudolph Run" (1958), "A Holly Jolly Christmas" (1962), "Jingle, Jingle, Jingle" (1964), "Silver and Gold" (1964), "The Most Wonderful Day of the Year" (1964, alternate lyrics set to the Pola/Wyle tune for "It's the Most Wonderful Time of the Year"), "We Are Santa's Elves" (1964), and "A Caroling We Go" (1966).

See also **A Holly Jolly Christmas; I Heard the Bells on Christmas Day; It's the Most Wonderful Time of the Year; Rockin' around the Christmas Tree; Rudolph and Frosty: Christmas in July; Rudolph, the Red-Nosed Reindeer** (character); **Rudolph, the Red-Nosed Reindeer** (television special); **Rudolph, the Red-Nosed Reindeer and the Island of Misfit Toys; Rudolph's Shiny New Year.**

Rudolph, the Red-Nosed Reindeer

(Television special, 1964). Animated story using stop-motion puppets (Animagic), loosely based on the 1949 hit tune of the same title by Johnny Marks; also remade for video in 1998 as *Rudolph, the Red-Nosed Reindeer: The Movie.* The television special premiered on the *General Electric Fantasy Hour* in December 1964 and has since become the longest-running television animated special. It was also the first major animated feature for Rankin/Bass Productions.

Unpopular because of his glowing red nose, young Rudolph runs away from Christmas Town with a misfit elf, Hermey, who aspires to be a dentist. Yukon Cornelius, a prospector, joins them in adventures that lead them to the Island of Misfit Toys, populated by toys rejected by their owners. Such toys include a white elephant with red spots, a train caboose with square wheels, and a water pistol that squirts jelly instead of water.

Convinced that Santa could find homes for these toys, Rudolph returns to Christmas Town, where he learns that the Abominable Snow Monster has captured Clarice, his doe friend, and his parents, who had been out looking for him. Rudolph tracks down the Monster, Cornelius incapacitates him, and Hermey pulls his teeth, which renders him docile.

Only when foggy weather sets in and Santa is about to cancel Christmas does Rudolph realize the true value of his red nose. Leading Santa's team, Rudolph proves that even misfits can lead useful lives.

A copyright "blooper" seen during the opening credits reads "MCLXIV" (1164) instead of "MCMLXIV" (1964).

Narrated and sung by Burl Ives. Featuring songs by Johnny Marks: "Rudolph, the Red-Nosed Reindeer" (1949), "A Holly Jolly Christmas" (1962), "Silver and Gold" (1964), "Jingle, Jingle, Jingle" (1964), "We Are Santa's Elves" (1964), "We're a Couple of Misfits" (1964), "There's Always Tomorrow" (1964), and "The Most Wonderful Day of the Year" (1964, alternative lyrics to "It's the Most Wonderful Time of the Year" by Pola and Wyle). Principal voices: Billie Richards, Paul Soles, Larry Mann, Stan Francis, Janet Orenstein, Corine Conley, Peg Dixon, Paul Kligman, and Alfie Scopp. Written by Romeo Muller. Produced by Arthur Rankin, Jr., and Jules Bass. Directed by Larry Roemer. A Videocraft International, Ltd. Production. DVD: Sony Music Video. 47 min.

The 1964 television special is further detailed in Rick Goldschmidt's book *The Enchanted World of Rankin/Bass.*

The 1998 animated cartoon remake follows essentially the same plot as its predecessor, with Stormella, the evil Ice Queen, brewing a blizzard that threatens to bury the North Pole. It received a Golden Reel Award nomination in 1999 for Best Sound Editing in an Animated Feature and a Young Artist Award nomination for Best Animated Family Feature. Principal voices: John Goodman, Eric Idle, Bob Newhart, Debbie Reynolds, Richard Simmons, Whoopi Goldberg, Eric Pospisil, Kathleen

Barr, Alec Willows, Garry Chalk, Vanessa Morley, and Myriam Sirois. Written by Michael Aschner. Produced and directed by Bill Kowalchuk. Cayre Brothers Productions, Goodtimes Entertainment, Rudolph Productions, and Tundra Productions. DVD: Goodtimes Home Video. 90 min.

See also **It's the Most Wonderful Time of the Year; Rankin/Bass Christmas Cartoons; Rudolph and Frosty: Christmas in July; Rudolph, the Red-Nosed Reindeer** (song); **Rudolph, the Red-Nosed Reindeer and the Island of Misfit Toys; Rudolph's Shiny New Year.**

Rudolph, the Red-Nosed Reindeer and the Island of Misfit Toys

(2001). Made-for-video animated cartoon musical and sequel to the animated television special *Rudolph, the Red-Nosed Reindeer* (1964). The sequel utilizes computers to simulate the stop-motion puppets (Animagic) that were used in the original production.

Rudolph with companions Clarice, his doe friend; Hermey, the misfit elf-turned-dentist; Yukon Cornelius, the prospector; and Bumbles, the Abominable Snow Monster, all reprise their roles to save Christmas from another bogey. This time, it's the mysterious Toy Taker, who hypnotizes toys the world over with tunes played on his magic flute, then transports them to his blimp flying overhead. Unaware of the situation, as the citizens of Christmas Town enjoy festivities at Santa's castle, word arrives that King Moonracer requires a dentist, and Hermey departs for the Island of Misfit Toys, together with Rudolph. As before, the island remains populated with odd toys, such as a kite that fears heights, a piggy bank without a slot, a plane that cannot fly, and a boomerang that will not return when thrown.

En route home, Rudolph and Hermey encounter a storm that blows them to Castaway Cove, a region ruled by Queen Camilla, where broken toys are mended. After Rudolph's red nose convinces the queen that neither he nor Hermey are toy thieves, Rudolph ponders whether he should allow Camilla to make his nose normal.

When the two return to Christmas Town and learn that the Toy Taker has robbed not only Santa's warehouse but Castaway Cove as well, Rudolph and companions disguise themselves as toys and wait on the Island of Misfit Toys for the Toy Taker's next strike. It comes in due course, and everyone except the enormous Bumbles is sucked into the Toy Taker's transport tube, so he must remain behind. On the blimp, Toy Taker, after several twists and turns, evades Rudolph's troupe, bails out, and dashes into Cornelius's Peppermint Mine, with Rudolph and Clarice (whom Rudolph has taught to fly) in hot pursuit. After an extended chase in mine carts (reminiscent of the scene in *Indiana Jones and the Temple of Doom*), Toy Taker is cornered, just as Santa and Mrs. Claus, Hermey, Cornelius, and Bumbles arrive to unmask the villain.

Instead of a fiend, the Toy Taker in reality is a benign and somewhat ragged teddy bear named Mr. Cuddles, who walks on stilts. A Christmas gift to a little boy many years ago, Mr. Cuddles became disheartened when the boy grew to manhood and seemingly lost interest in him. Therefore, Mr. Cuddles had set out to ensure that other toys would never suffer as he did. But Santa has good news: the same man wishes that he could find Mr. Cuddles so that he could give him to his little daughter for Christmas. After a makeover from Queen Camilla, Mr. Cuddles returns all of Santa's toys and is delivered forthwith to his proper destination on Christmas Eve, while Rudolph decides that no one will ever change his nose.

In 2001, this picture was nominated for four Video Premiere awards: Best Animated Character Performance (Jamie Lee Curtis and Bill Kowalchuk), Best Animated Video Premiere Movie, Best Original Score, and Best Original Song ("Beyond the Stars" and "Beautiful Like Me").

Narrated by Scoop T. Snowman (voice of Richard Dreyfuss). Other principal voices: Rick Moranis, Jamie Lee Curtis, Kathleen Barr, Scott McNeil, and Garry Chalk. Theme song "Rudolph, the Red-Nosed Reindeer" sung by Tony Bennett. Original songs by Bruce Roberts and Diana B. (*sic*). Story written by Michael Aschner. Produced and directed by Bill Kowalchuk. A Cayre Brothers Presentation, Goodtimes Entertainment, Golden Books Family Entertainment, and Tundra Productions. DVD: Goodtimes Home Video. 74 min.

See also **Rudolph and Frosty: Christmas in July; Rudolph, the Red-Nosed Reindeer (song); Rudolph, the Red-Nosed Reindeer (television special); Rudolph's Shiny New Year**.

Rudolph, the Red-Nosed Reindeer, Shines Again

See **Rudolph, the Red-Nosed Reindeer** (character)

Rudolph's Second Christmas

See **Rudolph, the Red-Nosed Reindeer** (character)

Rudolph's Shiny New Year

(1976). Made-for-television animated sequel to *Rudolph, the Red-Nosed Reindeer* (1964), using stop-motion puppets (Animagic).

Ashamed of his large ears, Happy, the Baby New Year, has run away from Father Time's castle on Christmas Night. Unless Happy is found, time will stop on December 31. Embarking with companions Clockwork Big Ben, a whale; One Million B.C., a caveman; Quarter-Past-Five, a camel; and Sir Ten-To-Three, a knight, Rudolph traces Happy to the Island of No Name, home of Aeon, the evil buzzard, who is Happy's captor. With half an hour remaining before midnight on December 31, Rudolph and friends foil Aeon and, with Santa's help in the (St.) Nick of time, return Happy to Father Time with a fraction of a second to spare.

Narrated and sung by Red Skelton. Featuring an original musical score by Johnny Marks. Principal voices: Frank Gorshin, Morey Amsterdam, Hal Peary, Paul Frees, Billie Richards, Don Messick, and Iris Rainer. Written by Romeo Muller. Produced and directed by Arthur Rankin, Jr., and Jules Bass. Rankin/Bass Productions. DVD: Warner Studios. 47 min.

This television special is further detailed in Rick Goldschmidt's book *The Enchanted World of Rankin/Bass.*

See also **Rankin/Bass Christmas Cartoons; Rudolph and Frosty: Christmas in July; Rudolph, the Red-Nosed Reindeer (song); Rudolph, the Red-Nosed Reindeer (television special); Rudolph, the Red-Nosed Reindeer and the Island of Misfit Toys**.

Russia

In 988, Vladimir I (956–1015), grand prince of Kiev, also known as Saint Vladimir and Vladimir the Great, accepted Orthodox Christianity from the Byzantine Empire and thence introduced Byzantine culture to Russia. For nearly 1,000 years, the Russian Orthodox Church, adhering to the Julian calendar, celebrated Christmas with customs that blended Orthodoxy with Slavic agrarian customs and superstitions. In 1917, however, the Bolshevik Revolution in St. Petersburg ended czarist rule and set the stage for the rise of the Communist Party and the creation of the Soviet Union. Upon implementing its atheistic political platform, the new regime forbade most religious practices, closed many (but not all) churches, and replaced the Christmas season with a secular "Winter Festival." Despite the government's adopting the present Gregorian calendar during this period, the Orthodox Church rejected the change and retained its ecclesiastical days on the Julian calendar as before, which meant that Christmas was observed on January 7 on the Gregorian calendar (*see* **Christmas Old Style, Christmas New Style**). With the collapse of the Soviet empire in 1991, Russia now struggles to regain its Christmas heritage and other religious traditions, large portions of which were lost, possibly forever, during the Communist era.

Prior to the Revolution, a 39-day fast preceded the 12-day Christmas season and prohibited the consumption of any animal products. This conditional fast continued into Christmas Eve with the traditional holiday meal for the immediate family, which commenced upon sighting the first star of the evening, believed to be the Star of Bethlehem. Then followed 12 meatless courses honoring the 12 months of the year and Christ's Twelve Apostles. Typical cuisine included, among other dishes, *borscht* (cabbage soup), assorted fish, *kissel* (oatmeal with honey), and *kutya* (wheat porridge with honey and poppy seeds). Some of the *kutya* would be tossed up to the ceiling, and the amount that stuck predicted the fate of the next harvest. This and a host of other superstitions, now abandoned, embellished the holidays (they derived from ancient winter solstice folklore holding that danger and evil lurked in the winter darkness). Rituals foretold the weather for each of the following year's months, predicted whether a girl would marry in the new year, dispelled evil spirits, assured good health and fortune for the coming year, and so forth. Following Christmas Eve Midnight Mass, which frequently extended until dawn, it was permissible to serve meat as families with friends gathered for Christmas dinner.

Other customs included groups of people traveling about their villages singing *kolyadki* (Christmas carols). Originally commemorating the renewal of the year and other folk themes, these carols later incorporated the message of the Nativity. The carolers customarily expected rewards of confections, but if these were not forthcoming, the subsequent carols bestowed curses upon the household. Other groups, "mummers," donned outlandish costumes as clowns, spirits, and especially as wild animals and entertained at homes and public places. (The Russian author Leo Tolstoy provides a vivid description of Christmas mumming practices among Russian aristocrats in a passage from his novel *War and Peace* [1865–1869].) Christmas trees became popular in the 1800s, and their decorations included fruits, candy dolls and animals, walnuts, wooden figures, paper lanterns and chains, and a star tree topper.

Russian folklore holds that two spirits have brought holiday gifts. One possibly derived from the "Frost," an entity of rural society encompassing all that was bitterly cold. To prevent this unseen menace from harming the crops, it was customary to "invite the Frost to supper" by setting out food for it. In the nineteenth century, the Frost took on human qualities as urban regions concocted the legend of *D'yed Moroz* ("Grandfather Frost"). Residing in the Russian forests, Grandfather Frost arrived at Christmastime with gifts for children in a *troika* (sleigh pulled by three horses abreast). His long, red, fur-trimmed suit with hat and long, white beard somewhat resembled the St. Nicholas of Europe. In Europe, whereas naughty children were threatened with punishment by St. Nicholas's demon antithesis, Grandfather Frost merely ignored them.

The second spirit, *Baboushka* ("Grandmother"), brought gifts on Epiphany Eve. According to legend, *Baboushka* was sweeping her house when the three Magi passed by en route to Bethlehem. When they invited her to accompany them, she refused, claiming that her housework precluded a long journey. Later, she repented and, upon collecting a few toys for the Christ Child, set out to overtake the Magi. Because she found neither them nor the Christ Child, she returned annually on Epiphany Eve to examine each sleeping child, hoping to find Jesus, then left a small gift behind. In variations of the story, all with the same conclusion, *Baboushka* either deceived the Magi or refused them lodging, or she denied asylum to the Holy Family in their flight from King Herod's soldiers.

In 1699, Czar Peter the Great established January 1 as New Year's Day in Russia. At the czar's command, celebrations included the lighting of bonfires on New Year's Eve. Homes were decked with evergreen garlands, and feasting abounded for seven additional days.

Seeking to eradicate Christmas, the Communists established a secular Winter Festival during the last half of December as a period devoted to feasting, fantasy, fireworks, and parades. During his rule (1929–1953), dictator Joseph Stalin declared New Year's Day as a national family holiday instead of Christmas and replaced the Christmas tree with the New Year's tree in 1935. Grandfather Frost, now appearing in either blue or red, was retained to bring gifts on New Year's Eve instead of Christmas Eve, and two more figures were added to complement him. One of these, *Snegurochka* ("Snow Maiden"), was based on a secular legend about a childless, elderly couple who, desiring a child of their own, fashioned a little girl out of snow. Although she achieved mortality and became their daughter during the winter, she melted as spring approached but returned annually with the winter snows. Snow Maiden, portrayed as a beautiful young girl with blond braids, white fur hat, blue robe or short fur coat, and knee boots, became Grandfather Frost's granddaughter who assisted him on his rounds. A youth portrayed the other figure, New Year's Boy, who depicted the freshness of the new year, and his costume bore the numerals of that year. Secular equivalents to Mary, Joseph, and the Christ Child, groups comprising Grandfather Frost, Snow Maiden, and New Year's Boy made public appearances throughout the country, the most notable of which was at the annual New Year's children's festival held at the Palace of Congresses in the Kremlin. Adults imbibed vodka on New Year's Eve, champagne on New Year's Day, and feasted on suckling pig, *karavay* (round bread), and *baba* (round coffeecake). Few could afford such luxuries as caviar, smoked fish, and other roast meats. For many older Russians, the holidays extended until January 14, New Year's Day on the Julian calendar.

Since the collapse of the Soviet Union, although New Year's celebrations have continued to dominate the holidays, Russians have incorporated the "Catholic Christmas" into the season. Thus the holidays begin on December 24 (Gregorian calendar), with Christmas observed on January 7 (Julian calendar), and extend through January 14, New Year's Day (Julian calendar). Still popular are the children's festival in the Kremlin and other parties; Grandfather Frost and Snow Maiden; and

gift exchanges, which may occur at Christmas as well as the new year. The Museum of Folk and National Arts in Moscow sponsors "The Christmas Gift," an exhibit of traditional toys and gifts that were commonly found prior to the Revolution. Typical cuisine is returning to that of former centuries, such as *borscht*, *blini* (small pancakes served with sour cream, caviar, and smoked salmon), fish, *baba*, *kissel*, and *piroshki* (turnovers stuffed with meat, fish, chicken, eggs, and vegetables). Thus *Sviatki* (Christmas season) is resurfacing and changing, as manifested by the appearance of Christmas trees, Nativity scenes (novelties to Russia), the adoption of Western traditions such as Santa Claus decorations and American and English carols (*kolyadki* only occasionally appear in stage performances), and the increasing attendance at Christmas Eve Midnight Mass. The latter is a service of many hours that compels the worshippers to stand during its entirety, with peripheral benches reserved only for the aged and infirm. Then follows *Krestny Khod* ("Walking with the Cross"), a candlelight procession that forms outside around the church as the congregation bears religious symbols.

"Merry Christmas" is *S Rozhdestvom Khristovym*.

See also **Epiphany; Ukraine.**

Saint Andrew's Day
See **Advent**

Saint Barbara's Day
See **Advent**

Saint John's Day
See **The Twelve Days of Christmas** (time period)

Saint Kitts and Nevis
See **West Indies**

Saint Lucy's Day
See **Advent**

Saint Nicholas
(?304–?345). Archbishop of Myra in Asia Minor (now Demre, Turkey) and popularly accepted as the personage on whom the mythical Santa Claus is based.

With the exception of a few fairly certain facts, virtually everything written about St. Nicholas is based on legends. He is known to have lived during the fourth century and was present at the Council of Nicea in the year 325.

Tradition states that St. Nicholas was a native of Patara, a city in the district of Lycia. After serving as a monk in the monastery of Sion near Myra, he rapidly advanced to the office of bishop at a rather early age (for which he was dubbed the "Boy-Bishop") and finally achieved the rank of archbishop of Myra. He is said to have been quite wealthy, and his acts of secret charity and munificence became legendary to the point that, following his death, any gift received under mysterious circumstances was automatically attributed to the spirit of St. Nicholas.

Tradition also held that his death occurred on December 6, which subsequently became St. Nicholas's Day, and that his remains initially rested at the Church of St. Nicholas in Myra, with the exception that in the year 1000, that church transferred some of the relics to Kiev in Russia. In 1087, however, when Muslim occupation of Turkey allegedly threatened to desecrate Nicholas's tomb, sailors from Bari in southern Italy relocated the remains to the Church of St. Stephen in Bari. Today St. Nicholas's relics lie not only in Bari but at the Greek Orthodox Church in New York City, where some were transferred in 1972. This latter church subsequently transferred most of the relics to the Shrine of St. Nicholas in Flushing, New York.

St. Nicholas's various legendary miracles and acts of charity led a number of people and places to adopt him as their patron saint. After he supposedly compelled a group of thieves to return their stolen goods, thieves in general earned the title of "clerks of St. Nicholas" during the Middle Ages. In another story, St. Nicholas miraculously restored life back to three young boys whom an innkeeper in Myra had murdered, dismembered, and stuffed in a salting tub. (Later portraits of St. Nicholas depicted him as a stern, ascetic archbishop standing beside three boys who were sitting in a tub.) Another legend holds that on making a voyage to the Holy Land, St. Nicholas quieted a violent storm and later saved some sailors when they invoked his name. Finally, when his remains came to rest in Bari, it is said that 30 people were cured of distemper after calling upon his name. Thus, St. Nicholas has not only become the patron saint of thieves, children,

St. Nicholas, according to the book from which this picture is taken, was "a saint of great virtue, and disposed so early in life to conform to ecclesiastical rule, that when an infant at the breast he fasted on Wednesday and Friday, and sucked but once on each of those days, and that towards night." This illustration depicts the legend of St. Nicholas miraculously restoring three dismembered boys to life. From William Hone, Ancient Mysteries Described *(London: 1823).*

and sailors, but also of Russia, Greece, Sicily, Liege, Lucerne, Freiburg, Laplanders, scholars, lawyers, and travelers.

The legend that firmly linked St. Nicholas with hanging up stockings and the spirit of giving at Christmastime centered around three dowerless maidens. A father in Myra was unable to give his three daughters in marriage because they lacked sufficient dowries. The desperate father was about to give his daughters up to lives of slavery or prostitution when Nicholas heard about their plight. On each of three successive nights, Nicholas secretly tossed a purse of gold through the father's window and supplied the dowries (in another version, Nicholas climbed onto the roof and tossed the purses down the chimney). Instead of landing on the hearth, where he had aimed them, the

A sheet of embossed, diecut, chromolithographed Santas, some with blue and red hats, ready to be trimmed and pasted into scrapbooks or homemade Christmas cards. These Santas still bespeak their St. Nicholas heritage, with their rather thin faces and long beards. Printed in Germany, about 1900.

purses landed in stockings hanging by the chimney to dry. Because of this legend, some portraits depict St. Nicholas holding three gold balls, which symbolize the purses of gold. When the Medici family of Florentine bankers adopted the three gold balls on their coat of arms in honor of St. Nicholas, the symbol eventually became that of lenders, especially pawnbrokers. From this, pawnbrokers also adopted Nicholas as their patron saint, as did virgins, in recognition of his act of compassion for the three young women.

• SAINT NICHOLAS AND SANTA CLAUS. The European conception of St. Nicholas had always centered around a sternly pious, ascetic elder dressed in crimson robes. He was often pictured with a long, white beard and tall mitre, carrying a crosier (the staff that symbolizes the bishop's office), and riding a white horse. Saint Nicholas often traveled with a demon antithesis known by a host of aliases such as Black Peter, Grampus, Knecht Ruprecht, and others, and the two annually brought joy and terror to villages as they entered homes on St. Nicholas's Day (December 6) for purposes of quizzing young children in their catechism. Those successful in their recitations received gifts from the saint, but should the recitations prove wanting, the hideous demon, fur-clad with blackened face, would growl, rattle chains, brandish a rod with

which to beat the youngsters, and then (so ran the threat) stuff them into a large sack to be whisked away to oblivion. Thus the saint and demon personified good and evil, heaven and hell. Although St. Nicholas always interceded for naughty children at this point, he customarily left them with a lump of coal or a switch instead of goodies.

Popular notion holds that Protestant Dutch settlers founding New Amsterdam (now New York City and the Hudson Valley) were responsible for bringing the St. Nicholas customs to the North American continent and ultimately to Christmas itself. There, the saint's demeanor and physiognomy radically transformed from that of austere archbishop into that of a stereotypical "Dutchman"; that is, a short, plump, jolly fellow with a broad hat and short breeches, who smoked a long-stemmed pipe. Over time, the story goes, American children slurred the saint's formal Dutch name of *Sint Nikolaas* into the vernacular *Sinterklaas*, thence into the immortal "Santa Claus," and a new Christmas personage was born.

On the other hand, Phyllis Siefker's book *Santa Claus, Last of the Wild Men* contends that the phenomenal popularity of the novel *History of New York* (1809) by American author Washington Irving was ultimately responsible for creating a mythical association between the Roman Catholic St. Nicholas and Protestant Dutch immigrants. Author of such memorable tales as "The Legend of Sleepy Hollow" and "Rip Van Winkle," Irving published his *History* as a satire on Dutch life in New Amsterdam; there, St. Nicholas flew across the skies in a wagon as he brought children their gifts and gained access to homes by descending into chimneys.

Irving supposedly modeled his St. Nicholas after the ideas of the St. Nicholas Society of New York, a political society founded by John Pintard after the Revolutionary War, which adopted St. Nicholas as an anti-British symbol. Other accounts note that Irving's saint bore a remote similarity to Thor, the wild Scandinavian god of war and thunder, who was pictured as clothed in red fur and who commanded a golden, airborne chariot pulled by two white goats, Gnasher and Cracker. According to popular belief, Irving's story further inspired the writing of the poem "A Visit from St. Nicholas" ("'Twas the Night before Christmas"), first published anonymously in 1823, which featured a flying sleigh pulled by reindeer instead of goats and which clad a small, elfish but portly St. Nicholas in sooty fur, not in archbishop's robes. The poem, in turn, inspired the German-American political illustrator Thomas Nast (1840–1902) to portray "Santa Claus" and all of his now-familiar trappings (red suit trimmed with white fur, buckled shoes, wide belt, pointed stocking cap, reindeer sleigh) in a series of cartoons that appeared annually in the magazine *Harper's Weekly* from 1863 until 1886, when Nast left *Harper's*. Nast's earliest published cartoon of Santa, entitled "Santa Claus in Camp," appeared on the cover of *Harper's* on January 3, 1863. The political implications were most striking, for Santa sat in his sleigh passing out gifts to Union soldiers while holding a dancing puppet of Jefferson Davis, the president of the Confederacy.

Interestingly, it was also Nast who first depicted Santa as living at the North Pole, for an 1885 sketch depicted two children gazing at a map and tracing Santa's route from the North Pole to the United States. Although Nast never stated why he specifically chose the North Pole, no doubt Santa's furry costume and reindeer sleigh influenced Nast to pick the polar region. In 1886, American writer George P. Webster went further, stating that Santa's polar abode was ordinarily hidden in the ice during summer months.

Siefker asserts that not only the fur-clad, American Santa Claus but also the host of antithetical demons that have accompanied the European St. Nicholas can be traced to a formidable, dark, hairy beast-god of primordial civilizations. Virtually omnipotent, this god commanded all elements of nature, including the cycles of reproduction and death, planting and harvesting; thus to renew the earth, at year's end he "recycled" himself by dying and was resurrected in the following spring. Ancient civilizations reenacted this death, which included sacrifices of people or animals in the god's name. A seer, healer, and god of fertility as well as storm and destruction, he became known as the so-called "Wild Man" of

Thomas Nast (1840–1902), German-American illustrator, whose cartoons in Harper's Weekly *greatly popularized the image of Santa Claus. Photograph 1896. Courtesy Library of Congress.*

the Middle Ages. Because his pagan popularity vied with conversions to Christianity, the Church branded him as evil and, in the seventh century, declared him to be the personification of Satan. Traces of the Wild Man figure are still seen in year-end celebrations throughout Europe and elsewhere, which almost always feature people dressed variously as masked animals or devils.

Siefker concludes that Santa Claus is actually a more recent derivative of the Teutonic being "Pelz Nicholas" ("Furry Nicholas") and not St. Nicholas. Another alias for the Wild Man, Pelz Nicholas (also with numerous spellings such as Pelznickel, Pelznichol, Belznickel, Belsnichol, Bellsniggle) migrated to America with German immigrants, the so-called Pennsylvania Dutch, as the one who brought not only Christmas gifts but punishment to naughty children. In the perennial favorite poem "A Visit from St. Nicholas," Siefker sees a number of characteristics that link Santa to the Wild

A typical engraving of Santa Claus by Thomas Nast. Its caption reads "Christmas Eve.— Santa Claus waiting for the children to get to sleep." Here, Santa sits atop a snow-covered chimney awaiting the magical moment for his descent. Nast included this and many other cartoons of Santa in his book Thomas Nast's Christmas Drawings for the Human Race *(New York: Harper and Brothers, 1890). Courtesy Library of Congress.*

Man–turned–Pelz Nicholas: dressing completely in sooty fur, shouting to reindeer whose names reflect those of the elements or mythical beings ("Dasher" resembling Thor's "Gnasher," "Vixen" the fox, the astronomical "Comet," the god "Cupid," the respective German-American "Donder" and "Blitzen" for "thunder" and "lightning"), erratic behavior such as disturbing the peace with a clatter on the lawn, and toting a sack of toys (the sack originally symbolized the article with which to kidnap children). And Santa's trademark phrase of "Ho Ho Ho" is identical to that of the "devil's bluster" of medieval mystery plays, the literary and folk prankster Robin Goodfellow (a god of vegetation), and those spirits who participated in the "Wild Hunt" during the 12 days of Christmas (*see* **Austria; Christmas Drama; Winter Solstice**).

Santa now lived at the North Pole, and new traditions would add elves as his assistants in making Christmas toys for children. Although mythical elves originated in the rich Viking folklore of Scandinavia and northern Europe, which long predated St. Nicholas and Santa Claus, they seemed to be ideal polar assistants. Denmark's *julnisse* and Sweden's *jultomten*, prototypical elves, are mischievous little beings who live in the attic, under floorboards, or out in the barn. Guardians of the home and livestock, these elves must receive a bowl of rice pudding on Christmas Eve; otherwise, the homeowner falls victim to their pranks, and harvests will be poor.

Another Scandinavian myth contributed to the concept of Santa's personal descent into chimneys on Christmas Eve to deliver gifts. During pre-Christian Germanic feasts at the winter solstice, families prepared altars of flat stones in their homes and laid fires of fir boughs. It was believed that these fires would invite Hertha, Norse goddess of the home, to descend through the fire and smoke to bring health and good fortune to all. Not only was Hertha another forerunner of Santa, but the flat stone altars became the modern hearths of today.

Santa's appearance changed somewhat again in the early twentieth century. Beginning in 1931, the Coca-Cola Company ran a series of commercial ads that featured a full-sized Santa as pitchman for the beverage. We find Santa's second evolution from small elf back to robust human size in the art of Haddon Sundblom, who enlarged the "standardized" Santa image for Coca-Cola.

Popular all through America, Santa Claus has not only crossed the Atlantic to a warm reception in Europe, but he has also influenced the celebration of Christmas the world over.

See also **Boy-Bishop; Saint Nicholas's Day; United States; A Visit from St. Nicholas.**

Saint Nicholas's Day

December 6 on the Roman Catholic Church calendar, this day honors the legendary and charitable fourth century archbishop of Myra (now Demre, Turkey) in Asia Minor. Posthumously canonizing Nicholas to sainthood, the Church declared December 6 (traditionally held as the day of his death) as St. Nicholas's Day by the twelfth century. During pre-Christian times, December 6 was a feast day to the Greek god Poseidon and the Roman god Neptune, both of whom were regarded as the "givers of good things." When the Church began Christianizing pagan feast days, St. Nicholas, also a giver of good things, proved an ideal replacement for the pagan gods for a December 6 celebration.

Celebrations of St. Nicholas's Day prevailed in the Low Countries and Rhine provinces of Europe as early as the tenth century with Church-sponsored dramas, which further fostered legends about the saint. Imitating Nicholas's charity, parents secretly placed small gifts in their little ones' shoes or stockings on St. Nicholas's Eve; French nuns anonymously left small gifts of fruit or nuts on the doorsteps of the poor. Awakening on St. Nicholas's Day, the children learned that their delightful surprises had come from the good St. Nicholas. Because of the proximity of December 6 to Christmas Day (the latter having been established in the fourth century), the customs of the St. Nicholas holiday gradually merged with those of the increasingly important Christmas, with St. Nicholas as the principal gift-giver.

Today, a number of European countries still observe St. Nicholas's Day with gifts and festivities. In the Netherlands, for example, Amsterdam holds an annual pageant in which the white-bearded St. Nicholas, dressed in red clerical robes, carrying a gold crosier, and riding a white horse, makes his first appearance of the season on the last Saturday in November. His horse derives from Sleipner, the mythical eight-legged steed of the wild Scandinavian god Odin. St. Nicholas arrives by boat from Spain for, according to Dutch folklore, that was the country of his birth, not Asia Minor. Accompanying St. Nicholas to the Netherlands is *Zwarte Piet* (Black Peter), the Moorish personification of Satan, whose task is to walk behind St. Nicholas while toting a black bag of gifts. On St. Nicholas's Eve, tradition holds, the austere saint and Peter visit every home to determine if the children deserve gifts or punishment. It is not St. Nicholas who delivers the gifts but Peter, who enters homes by jumping down chimneys; hence, Peter's appearance is black and sooty. Peter carries another bag into which he is said to stuff particularly naughty children and carry them off to Spain to be imprisoned for a year. Commonly on St. Nicholas's Eve, someone playing the part of Peter thrusts a black-gloved hand just inside the door and tosses spice cookies known as *peppernøtter* for the children. Just as commonly, someone dressed like St. Nicholas rides about town on a white horse while dispensing presents.

Children throughout Europe prepare for St. Nicholas's visit by setting out gift receptacles, usually shoes or stockings, into which they stuff carrots or hay for the saint's horse. On St. Nicholas's morning, those children judged to have been good are delighted to see that the animal fodder has been replaced with little gifts and sweets. For naughty children, though, Peter leaves a bundle of sticks and ignores the fodder. Other countries observing St. Nicholas's Day have related customs suited to their culture.

The Netherlands is not the only country having folklore in which a demon antithesis accompanies St. Nicholas on his feast day. In the Czech and Slovak Republics, *Svaty Mikulas* (St. Nicholas) descends from heaven on a golden cord along with an angel, who bestows the gifts, and a representation of the devil, sometimes called "Cert." Dressed in black, the devil carries a whip and rattles chains, at which good children must say their prayers or receive a lashing. The demon is known by many names throughout Germany and Austria: "Knecht Ruprecht" ("Servant Rupert"), "Ru-Klas" ("Rough Nicholas"), "Krampus" or "Grampus," "Klaubauf," "Hans Muff," "Hans Trapp," "Pelz Nicholas" ("Furry Nicholas"), "Bartel," "Butz," "Bullerklas," "Pulterklas," "Aschenklas" ("Ash Nicholas"), and others. By whatever name it is known, this demon, often portrayed as a dark, hideous, furry creature with horns, is thought by some to derive from Odin, the wild king of the Norse gods, or Thor, Norse god of war and thunder; and by others from the so-called "Wild Man," a hairy beast-god of primordial civilizations (*see* **Saint Nicholas**). Similar to Black Peter, it carries a sack of gifts and a rod of chastisement.

See also **Austria; Germany; The Low Countries** (The Netherlands).

Saint Stephen's Day
See **Boxing Day**

Saint Thomas's Day
See **Advent**

Salvation Army

International Christian and charitable organization, initially founded as the Christian Mission in London in 1865 by Methodist minister William Booth. Dedicated to spreading the Gospel and rendering material aid to such destitutes as thieves, gamblers, prostitutes, and alcoholics, Booth worked among the slums and gained a number of converts, who, calling themselves the "Hallelujah Army," preached, marched, and sang hymns in the streets of not only London but other cities as well. In 1878, the organization acquired its present name after Booth corrected a printed statement that had described his organization as a "volunteer army"; Booth substituted "Salvation Army" instead. He adopted a military structure and served as general superintendent (his followers called him "General"), while his uniformed officers held appropriate ranks commensurate with their duties. From the outset, Booth placed iron cooking kettles around London as a novel means of attracting donations for the poor, and the response to this appeal was most significant during the Christmas season. The Salvation Army thus maximized its efforts to relieve the poor during the weeks prior to Christmas, and the kettle became its symbol.

Lieutenant Eliza Shirley, an English immigrant, introduced the Salvation Army into the United States by holding the first meeting in Philadelphia in 1879. A year later, George Scott Railton and seven other Salvationists arrived from England to begin work in New York City and beyond. The concept in the United States of the red Christmas kettle with its accompanying bell ringer originated in San Francisco in December 1891, with Salvation Army Captain Joseph McFee, a former sailor who recalled seeing such kettles at the docks in Liverpool, England. By 1895, the kettles had spread along the West Coast, and Army officers William A. McIntyre and N.J. Lewis brought the idea to the East Coast. McIntyre's kettle efforts in Boston in 1897 alone provided for 150,000 Christmas dinners to those in need. Through kettle contributions in New York City, the first large-scale dinner for the poor was held at Madison Square Garden in 1901 and became an annual tradition that persisted for years. Today, the homeless poor may share holiday dinners and festivities at hundreds of Salvation Army centers.

Following the first presidential endorsement by Grover Cleveland in 1891, the Army expanded throughout the world and now serves in 109 countries. In the Unites States, the Salvation Army aids more than seven million people annually at Thanksgiving and at Christmastime, receives assistance from more than 1.5 million volunteers, and collects more than 65 million dollars in change dropped into its red kettles.

See also **Angel Tree; Toys for Tots.**

Santa and the Bookies
See **The Honeymooners**

Santa and the Three Bears

(1970). Motion picture animated cartoon.

The picture opens in live-action with a grandfather (Hal Smith) telling a story to his two grandchildren, Beth (Beth Goldfarb) and Brian (Brian Hobbs). Merging into animation, the story continues in Yellowstone National Park, where elderly and portly Mr. Ranger settles Momma Bear Nana and her two cubs, Nikomi and Chinook, into their cave for hibernation. Curious about seeing the ranger bringing a Christmas tree back to park headquarters, the cubs follow and are beside themselves with delight over the brilliantly decorated tree. When they press the ranger to tell them all about Christmas, he presents an abbreviated version of the biblical Christmas story, then expounds on the legend of Santa Claus and all his trappings.

The excited cubs hurry back and, waking their mother, persuade her to get them a Christmas tree. But when their frolicking and singing keep her awake, Nana seeks out the ranger for a chat. The ranger, upon learning that the cubs expect a visit from Santa on

Christmas Eve, decides to humor them by playing the part himself, which will satisfy all parties concerned, and the bears can finally return to hibernation. A howling blizzard hinders the costumed ranger from reaching Nana's cave, however, and forces him to take shelter in a park bus depot.

As Christmas Eve wanes, Nana must tell her disappointed cubs the truth about Santa and the ranger's plan to surprise them. But just as the little ones settle down to sleep, Santa, whom the cubs now believe is the ranger, arrives with two gift-filled stockings and hurries away. Shortly before daybreak, the storm abates, and the cubs, seeing the ranger-Santa, are now convinced that the real Santa had visited earlier. A booming "Ho Ho Ho" from the sky signals Santa's departure as the cubs revel in their first Christmas.

Although the original picture is more than an hour in length, often the live-action scenes are cut when it is rerun on television in one-hour time slots with commercials.

Principal voices: Hal Smith, Jean Vander Pyl, Annette Ferra, Bobby Riha, and Joyce Taylor. Written, produced, and directed by Tony Benedict. Live-action direction by Barry Mahon. Ellman Enterprises, Key Industries Ltd., and Tony Benedict Productions. DVD: Delta Music Video. 76 min.

Santa Baby

(Song). Popular American song written by Joan Javits, Philip Springer, and Tony Springer in 1953. First recorded by the African American pop singer Eartha Kitt on the RCA Victor label, it was the top Christmas song that same year. Another noted recording was that by Madonna in 1989, which appeared on the first of a four-album series entitled *A Very Special Christmas* (A & M Records). Proceeds from that series benefited the Special Olympics.

Intended for a seductive, female singer, the blatantly materialistic lyrics detail the mind-boggling Christmas list of a kept woman in exchange for her sole affections, with a reminder to her benefactor that she has been "an angel all year." Clearly, her "Santa" is not at all the jolly old elf, but a sugar daddy, whom she teasingly bids to "hurry down the chimney tonight." Her desired gifts include a sable; a

light blue, 1954 convertible; a yacht; the deed to a platinum mine; a duplex home; blank checks; Tiffany Christmas tree decorations; and jewelry.

"Santa Baby" was not among the 25 most frequently performed Christmas songs of the twentieth century as listed by the American Society of Composers, Authors and Publishers (ASCAP). By December 2004, however, the song's increasing popularity had merited position 24 on the ASCAP list.

The song was also the basis for an animated television special in 2001.

Joan Javits, niece of the late New York senator Jacob Javits, collaborated with Philip Springer on a number of other tunes, including "Broken Hearted," "Don't Play That Song Again," and "Flight 93"; the latter ballad, composed shortly after the tragic events of September 11, 2001, commemorated the heroes of United Airlines Flight 93.

See also **ASCAP List of Christmas Songs; Santa, Baby!** (television special).

Santa, Baby!

(Television special, 2001). Animated cartoon loosely based on the 1953 song "Santa Baby" by Joan Javits, Philip Springer, and Tony Springer. This was the first Rankin/Bass holiday special to feature an all–African American cast.

When little Dakota rescues the nearly frozen Melody Birdsong, a magical Christmas partridge, she receives one wish. But rather than use it on herself, Dakota bestows it upon her father Noel, a songwriter who needs a hit song to overcome his creative slump. As the wish unfolds, Noel and Dakota make Christmas Eve rounds for Santa (who broke his leg while skiing), find Christmas homes for animals from a local shelter, and bring the spirit of a soulful Christmas to their otherwise economically depressed neighborhood.

In 2003, this cartoon was nominated for an award from the Writers' Guild of America for Best Television Animation.

Principal voices: Gregory Hines, Eartha Kitt, Patti Labelle, Kianna Underwood, Vanessa Williams, and Tom Joyner. Written by Peter Bakalian and Suzanne Collins. Produced by Peter Bakalian. Directed by Lee Dannacher.

A Rankin/Bass Production. DVD: Hart Sharp Video. 45 min.

See also **Rankin/Bass Christmas Cartoons; Santa Baby** (song).

Santa Claus (mythical figure)
See **Saint Nicholas**

Santa Claus

(Motion picture, 1985). American/British fantasy, also known as *Santa Claus: The Movie.*

Perishing in a blizzard while delivering Christmas toys to children in their village, wood-carver Claus (David Huddleston) and his wife Anya (Judy Cornwell) find themselves the expected immortals in a magical, polar world of toymaking elves. According to the Ancient Elf (Burgess Meredith), Claus, thereafter dubbed "Santa Claus," has fulfilled the prophecy of a childless "Chosen One," an artisan sent to deliver the elves' gifts of toys to children throughout the world on Christmas Eve.

As time passes and Santa enters the twentieth century, he chooses an assistant, Patch (Dudley Moore), an elf bent on modernizing the workshop with automated technology. But when Patch loses his position because his assembly lines produce inferior toys, he journeys out into the world and unwittingly falls into the hands of a greedy New York City toy magnate, "B.Z." (John Lithgow), whom a Senate subcommittee has investigated for marketing cheap, dangerous toys. Desiring to create something special that will restore Santa's faith in him, Patch produces the "Puce Pop," a lollipop that, when eaten, allows the consumer to walk on air. That Christmas, the Puce Pop takes the world by storm, Patch having distributed the candy via his jet sleigh, and Santa, seemingly outdone, questions whether children will ever need him anymore.

Richer beyond measure, B.Z. demands that Patch alter his invention to enable people to fly, then confides to this assistant, Dr. Towzer (Jeffrey Kramer), his plan to take financial control of Christmas. His young step-niece Cornelia (Carrie Kei Heim) and a homeless street urchin named Joe (Christian Fitzpatrick), whom Cornelia and Santa have befriended, overhear the plan, but B.Z. discovers Joe and kidnaps him.

When Cornelia learns that the new candy will explode if overheated, she writes to Santa for help, the letter magically disappearing up the chimney in British fashion and reappearing on Santa's hearth, as do all letters addressed to Santa. Meanwhile Patch finds Joe bound in his basement, and the two, unaware of the danger, head up to the North Pole with a jet sleigh full of explosive candy. En route, the sleigh overheats and the candy explodes, but Santa and Cornelia, executing the "super-dooper-looper" maneuver with the reindeer, overtake and rescue the other two.

Joe finds a new home with Santa, and Cornelia remains until the following Christmas. B.Z., attempting to escape from the law by eating a mouthful of new candy, floats away into outer space and oblivion.

With John Barrard and Anthony O'Donnell. Written by David Newman and Leslie Newman. Produced by Ilya Salkind and Pierre Spengler. Directed by Jeannot Szwarc. Calash Corporation, GGG, Santa Claus Ltd., and Tri-Star Pictures. DVD: Anchor Bay Entertainment. 107 min.

Santa Claus (song)
See **Up on the Housetop**

Santa Claus Conquers the Martians

(1964). Motion picture science fiction fantasy, also known as *Santa Claus Defeats the Aliens.*

When Martian children Bomar (Chris Month) and Girmar (Pia Zadora) become mesmerized with video shows from earth about Santa Claus, their father, Martian chief Kirmar (Leonard Hicks), is convinced that Santa will have a positive influence on all Martian children. He abducts the jolly old elf (John Call) along with two earth children, Billy and Betty Foster (Victor Stiles and Donna Conforti), after which Santa establishes a toy factory on Mars as if nothing had ever happened. Officer Voldar (Vincent Beck) attempts to foil Santa's mechanized setup, but Santa remains ever jovial, despite the circumstances, and succeeds in spreading Christmas cheer to the Red Planet. Its inhabitants, however, manifest a deep shade of green.

According to the noted film reviewer Leonard Maltin, this film is "absurd."

With Bill McCutcheon, Leila Martin, Charles Renn, and James Cahill. Written by Glenville Mareth. Produced by Paul L. Jacobson. Directed by Nicholas Webster. An AVCO Embassy Pictures and Jalor Production. DVD: Delta Music Video. 81 min.

Santa Claus Defeats the Aliens

See **Santa Claus Conquers the Martians**

Santa Claus Express

Generic name applied to a number of holiday railroad excursions throughout the United States. Often sponsored by railroad museums and incorporating appropriately decorated vintage locomotives and cars, the Santa Claus Express may offer scenic tours beginning in late November and continuing through December. In other cases, the Express stops at towns and villages along the line, at which time professional or amateur performers aboard provide a Yuletide concert or show for citizens awaiting outside.

The Santa Claus Express also is a vehicle for delivering toys and gifts to underprivileged children, an example of which can be found in Appalachia. Since 1943, on one Saturday in late November (the day has varied from the Saturday before Thanksgiving or the Saturday after), officials of CSX Transportation and the Kingsport, Tennessee, Chamber of Commerce have furnished a locomotive and cars so that the Santa Claus Express (better known in this region as the "Santa Special" and "Santa Train") can wind its 110-mile route from Pikeville, Kentucky, across Virginia, and into Kingsport, Tennessee. All along the tracks, children and their families gather, many having camped overnight to secure strategic positions. When the train slows at each whistle-stop, children run behind as Santa and his assistants (local businessmen and celebrities) toss candy, small toys, and other gifts from a platform on the last car into eager hands. Examples of Santa's celebrity helpers have included Patty Loveless and Travis Tritt. Local merchants, some of whom were once among those children chasing behind the train, donate gifts, which become the only Christmas pre-

sents that many children in this region will receive each year. In recent years, the Kingsport Chamber of Commerce has annually selected one or two graduating high school seniors living along the train route as the recipients of a four-year, $5,000 college scholarship.

Santa Claus Is Comin' to Town

(Television special, 1970). Animated story incorporating stop-motion puppets (Animagic), loosely based on the hit song by J. Fred Coots and Haven Gillespie.

A biographical fantasy narrated by Special Delivery Kluger, the North Pole mailman, the story traces the life of Santa from his adoption as an orphan by the Kringle elf brothers, Dingle, Wingle, Tingle, Zingo, and Bingo, toymakers whose mother Tanta names the boy Kris. It is Kris Kringle's destiny to overcome two foes, who would prevent him from delivering toys to the children of Sombertown: Winter Warlock, an evil hermit who bars the path through the Mountain of the Whispering Wind, and Sombertown's Burgermeister who, having slipped on a toy and broken his funny bone, has outlawed all toys in his domain. With the help of Jessica, Sombertown's schoolteacher and his future wife, Kris ultimately discovers that placing toys in children's stockings effectively hides them from the Burgermeister. Kris and Jessica wed on Christmas Eve, but to escape persecution from the Burgermeister, they migrate to the North Pole, where they build a castle for their toymaking enterprise and limit toy-giving expeditions to once a year on Christmas Eve.

Narrated and sung by Fred Astaire. Principal voices: Mickey Rooney, Keenan Wynn, Paul Frees, Joan Gardner, Robie Lester, Dina Lynn, Greg Thomas, Andrea Sacino, Gary White, and the Westminster Children's Choir. Written by Romeo Muller. Produced and directed by Arthur Rankin, Jr., and Jules Bass. A Rankin/Bass Production. DVD: Sony Music Video. 48 min.

This television special is further detailed in Rick Goldschmidt's book *The Enchanted World of Rankin/Bass.*

See also **Rankin/Bass Christmas Cartoons; Santa Claus Is Coming to Town** (song).

Santa Claus Is Coming to Town

(Song). Popular American children's song written in 1932 by Haven Gillespie of Kentucky and J. Fred Coots of Brooklyn.

The song did not debut until 1934, when the wife of singer-comedian Eddie Cantor persuaded Cantor to perform it on his radio show just before Thanksgiving and during the Macy's Thanksgiving Day parade that same year. The song, the lyrics of which cautioned children to be on their best behavior for Santa, had been a hard sell, for numerous publishers initially had rejected it as another unimportant kiddie tune — as had Cantor himself until his wife intervened.

George Hall first recorded the song in 1934, placing number 12 on the *Billboard* charts. The 1943 Decca recording by Bing Crosby with the Andrews Sisters sold over six million copies and has probably become the most popular rendition of this classic tune. It is the best-known work by either Gillespie or Coots, although in the 1950s singer Pat Boone popularized Coots's 1931 tune, "Love Letters in the Sand."

Of the 25 most frequently performed Christmas songs of the twentieth century listed by the American Society of Composers, Authors and Publishers (ASCAP), "Santa Claus Is Coming to Town" ranked number two. By December 2004, it ranked number four.

See also **ASCAP List of Christmas Songs; Santa Claus Is Comin' to Town** (television special).

The Santa Clause

(1994). Motion picture comedy.

Divorced father Scott Calvin (Tim Allen) discovers that Santa has taken a fatal tumble off his roof on Christmas Eve. As he watches, the body of Santa vanishes, leaving only the red-and-white suit behind. A card inside requests that the finder don the suit and mount the reindeer sleigh on the roof. Complying, Scott and his son Charlie (Eric Lloyd) resume Christmas Eve rounds, where Scott finds that the suit enables him to change his shape to enter any home magically through any sort of entrance.

Returning with the reindeer sleigh back to the North Pole, Scott learns from chief elf Bernard (David Krumholtz) that, by wearing the late Santa's suit, he has now become Santa Claus, according to a microscopic clause written on the card, known as the "Santa Clause."

Through the following year, Scott assumes Santa's physical qualities by rapidly gaining weight and developing a full, white beard that instantly reappears despite repeated shavings. Scott's evolving appearance and Charlie's frequent, bizarre tales about the North Pole cause Charlie's mother and his psychiatrist-stepfather, Laura and Dr. Neal Miller (Wendy Crewson and Judge Reinhold), to revoke Scott's visitation privileges with Charlie.

Despite this restriction, the boy again accompanies Scott on Christmas Eve rounds, which forces Laura, who mistakenly believes that Scott has kidnapped her son, to summon the law. Although Scott is arrested while performing Santa duties, Charlie and a squad of elves with "attitude" liberate him from jail.

Returning Charlie to his mother, Scott-Santa, true to character, also returns good for evil, so to speak, by providing gifts that Laura and Neal had always wanted as children but never received: a "Mystery Date" game for Laura and an Oscar Meyer Wiener whistle for Neal. In return, Laura arranges unlimited visitation privileges between Santa and Charlie.

For his work on this film, in 1995 Tim Allen received MTV Movie Award nominations for Best Breakthrough Performance and Best Comedic Performance. The film also won a BMI Film Music Award and a People's Choice Award for Favorite Comedy Motion Picture; also Young Artist Award nominations for Best Family Motion Picture Comedy and Best Performance by a Young Actor Co-Star (Eric Lloyd).

With Larry Brandenburg, Mary Gross, Paige Tamada, and Peter Boyle. Written by Leo Benvenuti and Steve Rudnick. Produced by Brian Reilly, Jeffrey Silver, and Robert Newmyer. Directed by John Pasquin. Hollywood Pictures, Outlaw Productions, and Walt Disney Productions. DVD: Walt Disney Home Video. 97 min.

See also **The Santa Clause 2**

The Santa Clause 2

(2002). Motion picture comedy/fantasy, a sequel to *The Santa Clause* (1994). Principal cast members in the original movie reprise their roles.

This year, two factors plague Santa/Scott Calvin (Tim Allen). First, Curtis (Spencer Breslin), the elf in charge of experimental design, discovers a second, exceedingly minute clause written into the "Santa Clause," which requires that Santa take a wife by Christmas Eve or forfeit his position; hence, the new clause is termed the "Mrs. Clause." Time is precious, for the "desantafication" process has already begun: Santa's broad waistline is shrinking, his magical powers are waning, and his full, white beard soon disappears. Second, Santa's teenage son Charlie (Eric Lloyd) has been placed on the "Naughty List," and Santa must re-enter human society to investigate the problem. Before Santa departs, Curtis duplicates him in the form of a Toy Santa action figure (Tim Allen) to oversee the toy production.

Charlie's frustrations over not having a normal father and having to keep his father's true identity a secret prompt acts of delinquency and put him at constant odds with his school principal, Carol Newman (Elizabeth Mitchell). A cold and cynical yet beautiful woman, Carol has no time for Christmas frivolities and will not tolerate the spirit of the holiday among the student body.

Santa/Scott's initial meetings with Carol about Charlie are little more than civil, yet predictably, Scott pursues a relationship with her that blossoms on the night of the faculty Christmas party. Though it dangerously drains his magic, Scott covertly transforms his car into an open, horse-drawn sleigh. As they travel through snowy streets, the cozy atmosphere prompts Carol to confess that her aversion to Christmas stemmed from childhood, when her parents told her the devastating news that Santa was a myth. Scott further saves the party from total apathy by distributing gifts that the faculty members had individually cherished as children. This consumes all of Scott's magic, yet Carol is overwhelmed and in love.

Back at the North Pole, Toy Santa concludes that too many children have been naughty and orders that they all will receive lumps of coal instead of toys. When Toy Santa produces an army of giant toy soldiers to enforce his edict, Curtis flees and reports the news to Scott/Santa, who must find a way back. By chance, Charlie's little half-sister, Lucy Miller (Liliana Mumy), loses a tooth, which summons the Tooth Fairy (Art LeFleur), who gladly transports Santa and Curtis to the North Pole on Christmas Eve. The toy soldiers quickly apprehend them, but they are freed after Charlie (who sacrifices one tooth) and Carol arrive, courtesy of the Tooth Fairy again. Now Scott/Santa must overtake Toy Santa, who has taken the reindeer team with intent to deliver gifts of coal. Mounting Chet, an inexperienced little buck with lots of "crash time," Santa zooms wildly ahead as the elves battle the toy soldiers below. With victory in hand, with minutes to spare, and with Mother Nature (Aisha Tyler) officiating, Santa and Carol are married, whereupon Santa promptly regains his weight and beard.

In the final scenes, Santa returns Charlie to his home and reveals himself to little Lucy, who has always suspected that her "Uncle Scott" was indeed Santa. As the team speeds away, reindeer Comet, having stuffed himself with too much Christmas candy, lounges in the sleigh while Chet, giggling hysterically through the night, takes his place.

With Wendy Crewson as Charlie's mother, Laura Miller, and Judge Reinhold as Charlie's stepfather, Dr. Neil Miller.

Honors for 2003: Saturn Award nomination for Best Fantasy Film; BMI Film Music Award; Young Artist Award nomination for Best Supporting Young Actor (Eric Lloyd).

Story by Leo Benvenuti and Steve Rudnick. Screenplay by Don Rhymer, Cineo Paul, Ken Daurio, Ed Decter, and John J. Strauss. Produced by Brian Reilly, Bobby Newmyer, and Jeffrey Silver. Directed by Michael Lembeck. Boxing Cat Films, Outlaw Productions, and Walt Disney Pictures. DVD: Walt Disney Home Video. 105 min.

See also **The Santa Clause.**

Santa Comes to Visit and Stays and Stays
See **Bewitched**

Santa Special
See **Santa Claus Express**

Santa Train

See **Santa Claus Express**

The Santa Trap

(2002). Made-for-television comedy/drama.

The hot climate of the American Southwest and lack of snow may not deter little Judy Emerson's (Sierra Abel) Christmas spirit, but when brother Mike (Brandon DePaul) declares that Santa Claus is a myth, she draws the line. To prove that Santa is real to skeptics like Mike and her parents, Bill and Molly (Robert Hays and Shelley Long), Judy constructs an elaborate trap on Christmas Eve, which involves an electric train, golf balls, a bowling ball, the family's cat, a Hula-Hoop, and a ceiling fan. Although she successfully captures Santa (Dick Van Patten), Bill has the jolly old gent arrested as an intruder in disguise. Later that night, when strange noises lead Bill to discover a team of reindeer waiting on the roof, his doubts vanish, and he rushes to free Santa from jail. Instead, bumbling deputies release Max Hurst (Stacy Keach), a rough-and-tumble biker, who has persuaded Santa to exchange clothes with him. Santa escapes with the assistance of little Brian Spivak (Paul Butcher), son of the police chief (Corbin Bernsen).

The police soon find Max at the Emersons, where he is holding the entire family hostage, including Santa. With Christmas hanging in the balance, Santa temporarily foils the law, allowing Max time to visit his mother in the hospital, while Mike and Judy gladly deliver to hospitalized children those gifts that Santa had marked for the Emersons. Santa again dodges incarceration, this time with the assistance of Elf Ranger One (Martin Klebba), a specialist sent from the North Pole. As Santa and his sleigh speed skyward, the magical moment makes believers of all witnesses, and Molly receives a most unusual gift to make her holiday more "Christmasy"—snow.

Written by Steve Jankowski and John Shepphird. Produced by Steve Jankowski. Directed by John Shepphird. Tag Entertainment, a Steve Austin/Jonathan Bogner Production. DVD: Sterling Entertainment. 92 min.

Santa Who?

(2000). Made-for-television comedy.

Out on a pleasure ride with the reindeer, Santa (Leslie Nielsen) falls from his sleigh and suffers complete amnesia a few days before Christmas. On the scene is Peter Albright (Steven Eckholdt), an ambitious, television news reporter in desperate need of a catchy holiday story. By coincidence, Peter's girlfriend Claire Dreyer (Robyn Lively) needs a Santa for her department store, and "Nick" gets the job, at which he is most profoundly adept. Peter then seizes the opportunity to run a series of ads that bid viewers to identify the kind old gent and reunite him with his family for Christmas.

Orphaned as a child, Peter now scorns Christmas, yet he finds himself teaching Nick all he knows about the holiday on professional advice that, by recalling familiar items, Nick may regain his memory. Together Peter and Claire's little boy Zack (Max Morrow) review stories, carols, and classic Christmas movies with Nick, but nothing rings a bell until Peter discovers a letter in Nick's coat that he had written to Santa 25 years ago while at the orphanage. Whereas the discovery does the trick with Nick's memory and makes a true believer of Peter, Zack had never doubted Nick for one moment.

This picture illustrates the tradition of sending letters to Santa by burning them. Most prevalent in England, letters written to Father Christmas are believed to receive favor if they burn quickly; otherwise, they must be rewritten. In *Santa Who?*, Sister Greta (Laura DeCarteret) at the orphanage had "mailed" Peter's letter by fire, yet Peter, feeling betrayed, had misunderstood the significance and had hated Christmas ever since. Santa had received the letter, nonetheless. (*See* **Great Britain** [England].)

Honors for 2001: Saturn Award nomination for Best Single Genre Television Presentation; Young Artist Award nominations for Best Family Television Movie and Best Supporting Young Actor (Max Morrow).

Based on an unpublished story by Chad Hoffman and Robert Schwartz. Teleplay by Debra Frank and Steve L. Hayes. Produced by Frank Siracusa. Directed by William Dear. ABC

Television, Gleneagle Productions, and Hearst Entertainment Productions. DVD: Walt Disney Studios. 92 min.

Santabear

Series of collectible bear dolls and related products manufactured since 1985 by the Dayton-Hudson Corporation, America's fourth largest general merchandise retailer, based in Minneapolis, Minnesota. Santabear prompted the production of two stories, both of which have appeared on video, with subsequent adaptations into children's books.

Santabear's First Christmas (1986). Made-for-television story consisting of static drawings. Separated from his family when the Arctic ice cracks, a little polar bear is swept out to sea on an ice pack and lands in a region of forests previously unknown to him. Marie, a young girl who lives in a cottage with her grandfather, adopts him as her pet, and over time, the three become quite close. As Christmas approaches, Marie introduces the bear to stories of Santa Claus, reindeer, and gifts.

On Christmas Eve, the grandfather falls into an icy pond and lies at home nearly frozen. Desperately needing firewood, the bear hurries into the forest but cannot acquire a sufficient supply. Then he meets Santa on his rounds, who grants the bear any wish for Christmas. Instead of wishing to return to his family in the Arctic, the bear requests firewood for the grandfather.

With Santa felling a few trees and the bear sawing logs, Marie builds a large fire, which soon revives her grandfather. Santa, touched by the bear's unselfishness but now behind on his rounds, commissions the bear to help him by delivering gifts to the forest creatures in his stead, and it is done so efficiently that Santa offers the bear an annual job as his assistant. Dubbing him thereafter as "Santabear," Santa presents the bear with a festive cap and scarf and personally returns him back up north to his family.

Narrated by Kelly McGillis. Illustrations by Howard B. Lewis. Principal voices: John Malkovich and Bobby McFerrin. Written by Barbara Read. Produced by Mark Sottnick and Joel Tuber. Directed by Mark Sottnick. Rabbit Ears Productions, Children's Video Library

Productions, and Family Home Entertainment. VHS: Vestron Video. 25 min.

Santabear's High Flying Adventure (1987). Made-for-video sequel in which Santa asks Santabear to deliver Christmas toys to children at the South Pole, for they have never experienced a Christmas. Bullybear jeopardizes the mission by stealing the toys and impersonating Santabear.

Narrated by Kelly McGillis. Principal voices: John Malkovich, Bobby McFerrin, and Dennis Hopper. Written by Lenore Kletter. Produced by Mark Sottnick, Michael Sporn, and Joel Tuber. Directed by Michael Sporn. Rabbit Ears Productions and Family Home Entertainment. VHS: Vestron Video. 23 min.

Santabear's First Christmas
See **Santabear**

Santabear's High Flying Adventure
See **Santabear**

Saturnalia

A pre-Christian harvest and winter solstice celebration held throughout the Roman Empire in honor of Saturn or Saturnus (from the Latin *satus*, "to sow"), god of agriculture, who reigned during the so-called Golden Age of Rome, a time of peace and prosperity. Under the Caesars, the festival was lengthened from one day (December 17) to seven (through December 24), in which the spirit of gaiety and frolic prevailed, recalling that Golden Age. All work, businesses, schools, and matters of court were suspended, criminals received reprieves from punishment, war was not waged, and no humans were sacrificed to Saturn; the lighting of numerous candles in his temple symbolized such mercies.

Instead, festivities began with the sacrifice of a young pig in the temple. Each community selected a *Magister Ludi* (Master of the Games) or a *Saturnalicus Princeps* (Chief of the Saturnalia), a mock king, who supervised the feasting, revelry, singing, and dancing. He was chosen by lots, sometimes as the one who found the coin hidden in servings of pudding. Masters and slaves traded places, with masters serving their slaves, who could bid the former to perform any task and could exact ludicrous

An imagined scene of a winter solstice Saturnalia celebration in pre–Christian Rome. Harper's New Monthly Magazine, *December 1889.*

punishments should they fail to execute them. Class distinctions were suspended as well, as a spirit of humanity compelled everyone to do good unto his neighbor, including dispensing money to the poor. Transvestism was common and, in keeping with the tradition of masquerades, in northern provinces, Germanic tribes often donned masks in the likenesses of horned beasts and hideous creatures, symbolic of spirits which were believed to inhabit the winter darkness.

Statues of Saturn, as well as homes, were decorated with holly, sacred to this god; with evergreen wreaths, symbolic of the sun; and with evergreen garlands, symbolic of the renewal of life at the approaching winter solstice, December 25 on the Roman or Julian calendar. (In the Christian era, these evergreens would come to symbolize eternal life through Christ.)

At the conclusion of the week came the exchanging of gifts: *signillaria* (clay dolls) for the children and *strenge* (olive branches honoring the woodland goddess Strenia) or *cerei* (wax tapers or candles) for the adults.

The festivities were essentially repeated for three days at the January Calends, beginning on the first day of the new year (January 1). This was especially the time when the populace presented the emperor with *votae* (gifts).

Although the Saturnalia was not the sole winter solstice festival of the Roman Empire (among other festivals, a feast on December 15 honored Consus, god of the storeroom; one on the seventeenth honored his consort, Ops, a mother goddess), it was by far the most important in terms of its traditions and symbols, many of which the early Christian Church adopted into the Christmas season. The lighting of candles, decorating with holly and evergreens, giving of gifts (the Wise Men that visited the manger had no monopoly on gift-giving), holiday charity, and the unrestrained merrymaking all were most recently derived from the Saturnalia.

The basis for these traditions actually originated some 4,000 years before the birth of Christ in the land of Mesopotamia, which included Sumer, later corresponding to Babylonia; through northern and western routes, the customs reached Greece, Rome, and other parts of Europe. The equivalent Sumerian and Babylonian celebrations, respectively, were the *Zagmuk* ("Beginning of the Year") and *Akitu* ("New Year's Festival"). The Sumerian festival was semiannual, held in the fall (month of Tishri) and in the spring (month of Nisan), commemorating the two principal solar points of the year (winter and summer). *Akitu*, however, occurred only at the first new moon after the spring equinox.

The mythology surrounding these festivals held that as the year drew to a close, the world, created by the supreme god Marduk, lay dying. During the festivals, it was traditional for the king to perform rituals to atone for any sins of man against Marduk and to assist him in battling the monsters of chaos in the underworld, acts that would restore the world of the living for another year. To begin the rituals, the king entered the temple of Marduk. There, he suffered humiliation by being stripped of his regal vestments; then he swore annual allegiance to Marduk, after which he was reinstated as king. It is likely that the king then symbolically sacrificed himself by allowing the appointment of a mock king in his stead from the ranks of criminals (his mock counterpart is seen in the Master of the Games of the Saturnalia and Archbishop of Fools of the Feast of Fools). This criminal was then arrayed in regal raiment and sacrificed sometime during a 12-day celebration, which consisted of feasting, socializing, and gift-giving (a parallel is seen in the 12 days of Christmas). Wooden images depicting the monsters of chaos were burned to assist Marduk in his battle for life, and such images are believed to be the earliest precursors of the Yule log.

These, then, were some of the world's earliest known plans for year-end festivals, which most modern civilizations have since adapted to their own cultures.

See also **Christmas Day; Feast of Fools; New Year's Day; The Twelve Days of Christmas** (time period); **Winter Solstice; Yule.**

Saudi Arabia
See **Middle East**

Savior of the Heathen, Known
See **Savior of the Nations, Come**

Savior of the Nations, Come

("Veni, Redemptor gentium"). Latin carol for Advent and believed to be the oldest significant carol, written by St. Ambrose (c. 340–397), bishop of Milan.

Consisting of eight stanzas, the carol implores Christ to manifest Himself in both flesh and spirit as the Virgin-born Redeemer of mankind. The eighth stanza concludes with a doxology to the Father, Son, and Holy Ghost.

"Savior" has received numerous translations, the first German translation of which was "Kum har, Erlöser Volkes Schar" ("Come, Redeemer of the Nations") by Henrik von Laufenberg (d. 1445), a clergyman from Freiburg. The translation made in 1524 by Martin Luther (1483–1546), "Nun komm, der Heiden Heiland" ("Now Come, Savior of the Heathen"), is noteworthy, having appeared in the first Lutheran hymnal, *Etlich cristlich Lider Lobgesang und Psalm* (Wittenberg, 1523–24). The musical setting most frequently used today with Luther's rendering was first printed in *Enchiridion oder eyn Handbüchlein* (Erfurt, 1524). J.S. Bach (1685–1750) further harmonized the latter setting and incorporated some of Luther's verses into several of his Advent cantatas: verse one into *Nun komm, der Heiden Heiland* (1714, BWV 61); variations of the verses into *Nun komm, der Heiden Heiland* (1724, BWV 62); and verses one, six, and eight into *Schwingt freudig euch empor* (*Soar Joyfully Aloft*, 1731, BWV 36). As an organ chorale prelude, "Nun komm" (BWV 599) is the lead number in Bach's *Orgelbüchlein*, and it is the title of seven chorale variations for organ (BWV 659, 659a, 660, 660a, 660b, 661, 661a).

The latter constitute a portion of Bach's "Great Eighteen Chorales," written between 1739 and 1747.

Although the carol's awkward meter has precluded a definitive English translation, many versions have arisen in the attempt. Some of these include "Come, Thou Redeemer of the Earth" (John Mason Neale, 1851); "Come, Thou Savior of Our Race" (William Morton Reynolds, 1850); "O Come, Redeemer of Mankind" (David Thomas Morgan, 1880, with musical setting "Redemptor Mundi" by Arthur Henry Brown); "Redeemer of the Nations, Come" (Catherine Winkworth, 1855); "Savior of the Heathen, Known" (Richard Massie, c. 1854); and "Savior of the Nations, Come" (William Morton Reynolds, 1851).

Scotland
See **Great Britain**

Scrooge
See **A Christmas Carol** (Film and Television Versions)

Scrooge: A Christmas Carol
See **A Christmas Carol** (Film and Television Versions)

Scrooged
See **A Christmas Carol** (Film and Television Versions)

Scrooge's Rock 'n' Roll Christmas
See **A Christmas Carol** (Film and Television Versions)

Seals
See **Christmas Seals**

Second Christmas Day
See **Boxing Day**

Secret Santa

(2003). Made-for-television drama, based on the 2003 novel of the same title by television producer Beth Polson and television writer Robert Tate Miller.

Each Christmas Eve in the peaceful little town of Hamden, Indiana, an anonymous benefactor bestows a much-needed gift on an unfortunate resident, and each year, the *Indianapolis Sentinel* features a story about Hamden's "Secret

Santa." But this year, Rebecca Chandler (Jennie Garth), a young, cynical reporter anxious to rid herself of fluff stories and expand into investigative assignments, is determined to unmask this "bleeding heart do-gooder."

Upon entering Hamden, Rebecca steps into a town that not only turns out *en masse* for the annual Christmas pageant, complete with a live, public Nativity scene, but one that promotes the Christmas spirit of "goodwill toward men" all year long. From Russell (Charles Robinson), an orderly at the rest home where she must lodge (no room in the local inn); from Miss Ruthie (Barbara Billingsley), a grandmotherly resident at the home; from George Gibson (Sam Anderson), the local newspaper editor; and from John Martin Carter (Steven Eckholdt), a wealthy young attorney whom she erroneously assumes is Secret Santa, Rebecca learns that, if exposed, Secret Santa could never again exist in the public eye.

Who is Secret Santa? On Christmas Eve, he again fulfills his role, and Rebecca indeed unmasks him, but not by any investigative skill. He need not fear, however, for the only revelation her story imparts is this simple truth: "giving in its purest form expects nothing in return."

Story by Beth Polson. Teleplay by Robert Tate Miller. Directed by Ian Barry. Madison Avenue Productions and the Polson Company. Video N/A. 120 min.

The Seven Good Joys
See **The Seven Joys of Mary**

The Seven Joys of Mary
Best-known generic title given to a number of English folk songs based on the "Joys of Mary," a series of devotions and petitions to the Virgin Mary which arose in the medieval Church. Whereas the Church on the European continent traditionally incorporated seven or 15 Joys with some variation, which reflected the medieval interest in number symbolism and enumeration rituals, Great Britain observed only five until the fifteenth century, when the number increased to seven. These often included examples of miracles in the life of Christ, in addition to other references to Christ's divinity as well as the Nativity.

Although the Protestant Reformation essentially obliterated all traces of the Joys as Roman Catholic devotional elements, their sentiment survived in British folk carols, which crossed into North America during the eighteenth and nineteenth centuries. In the "Joys of Mary" carols found in both regions, the number of Joys is again most frequently seven. Not surprising are the many variant titles befitting these carols: In addition to "The Seven Joys of Mary," there are "The Seven Rejoices of Mary," "Joys Seven," "The Seven Good Joys," and the Appalachian folk carol "The Blessings of Mary," seven- and ten-Joy versions of which have been sung throughout the eastern United States.

Obviously, the subjects of the seven Joys demonstrate some variation and overlapping from carol to carol, with the following as typical examples: first Joy, Mary first sees Jesus as her infant son; second Joy, Jesus heals the lame; third Joy, Jesus restores sight to the blind; fourth Joy, Jesus reads the "Bible o'er" (this refers to Jesus discussing the Scriptures with learned men in the Temple); fifth Joy, Jesus raises the dead; sixth Joy, Jesus "bears the Crucifix" (hangs on the cross); seventh Joy, Jesus ascends into heaven. A refrain usually follows each Joy, partially repeating the last phrase of the Joy and then praising the Holy Trinity.

"The Seven Joys of Mary" has been sung to various tunes, one of which was that for "God Rest Ye Merry, Gentlemen," once popular with the London Waits. Richard Terry, in his collection *Two Hundred Folk Carols* (London, 1933), provided an arrangement of a traditional tune that has come to be the most frequently used, whereas English churches prefer the variation as published in Henry Bramley and John Stainer's *Christmas Carols New and Old* (London, 1871).

See also **Waits**.

The Seven O's
See **"O" Antiphons**

The Seven Rejoices of Mary
See **The Seven Joys of Mary**

Shepherd, Shake Off Your Drowsy Sleep

("Berger, secoue ton sommeil profound!"). French traditional carol, thought to have arisen during the seventeenth or eighteenth century in the Besançon region. Sometimes the first word in the title is pluralized. The carol urges the shepherd(s) to rouse from slumber and forsake tending mere sheep, for a far greater task is at hand in seeking the Babe, about whom angels are spreading glad tidings. The anonymous English translation appeared in the collection *Christmas Carols New and Old* (London, 1871), edited by Henry Bramley and John Stainer, the latter also having provided a popular musical arrangement of the tune.

Shepherds

See **Nativity**

Shepherds' Mass

See **Christmas Masses**

Shepherd's Rocking Carol

See **Rocking**

Shepherds, What Fragrance All-Perfuming?

See **Whence Is That Goodly Fragrance?**

The Shoemaker and the Elves

See **The Elves and the Shoemaker**

Sierra Leone

See **Africa**

Silent Night

("Stille Nacht"). Austrian Christmas carol, reputed to be the world's most popular, composed by Father Josef Mohr (1792–1848) and Franz Xaver Gruber (1787–1863).

In 1818, Father Mohr served as assistant priest of the Church of St. Nicholas in the then-obscure village of Oberndorf near Salzburg, while Gruber, a school teacher from Arnsdorf, doubled as organist for St. Nicholas. According to one popular myth, frequent floods by the nearby Salzach River had created sufficient rust to incapacitate the church organ by Christmas Eve of that same year; another myth holds that mice had destroyed the organ bellows. Facing Midnight Mass with no music, the myth con-

Postcard with portrait of Franz Xaver Gruber (1787–1863), Austrian composer of the music to the carol "Silent Night." Translated, the German caption reads "Silent Night, Holy Night. Composer teacher Franz Xaver Gruber." Courtesy Tourist Association of Oberndorf, Austria.

tinues, Mohr quickly composed a provocatively simple poem of six stanzas and asked Gruber to furnish a musical setting, whereupon Gruber composed an equally simple tune for two voices, choir, and guitar. The resulting carol beginning with the words "Stille Nacht, heilige Nacht" ("Silent night, holy night") was presented to the St. Nicholas congregation as Mohr sang tenor and played the guitar while Gruber sang bass. The choir joined in only for the two-line refrain which followed each stanza.

In 1995, the discovery of an authentic, autographed copy of "Silent Night" in Mohr's own hand by the Carolino Augusteum Museum in Salzburg dispelled some of the myths regarding the carol's origin. Titled simply "Weihnachtslied" ("Christmas Song") with lyrics arranged for guitar, this manuscript also bore the inscription "Melodie von Fr. Xav. Gruber" ("Melody by Fr. Xav. Gruber"), confirming Gruber as the musical composer, along with the date of 1816 next to Mohr's name. At that time, Mohr was serving as curate in his first parish, a pilgrimage church in Mariapfarr in southern Austria. Authorities dated the manuscript itself to 1820, a year after Father Mohr had left Oberndorf. This manuscript is now believed to be the oldest surviving copy and probably approximates the version first performed on Christmas Eve, 1818.

While it is now certain that Father Mohr first wrote the lyrics to "Silent Night" in 1816 and requested Gruber's musical setting on Christmas Eve two years later, the exact reasons for presenting a new carol with guitar accompaniment during a traditional Roman Catholic Christmas Mass remain unknown. While the church organ could have been inoperable, it remains equally likely that Father Mohr, an avid guitar aficionado, chose to present a folk carol in keeping with a common practice of churches in Austria and Germany at that time.

Conducting the carol at Masses and Christmas programs after its 1818 debut, Gruber freely distributed copies to friends but apparently affixed neither his nor Father Mohr's name nor a specific title. Thus the carol spread through Europe in true folk fashion, popularized particularly by Josef Strasser and his touring family of folk singers from Zillertal in the Tyrol region of Austria. Strasser may have obtained a copy through Karl Mauracher, an organ builder from Zillertal, who had serviced the St. Nicholas instrument around 1824 (tradition states that Mauracher found a discarded copy of the carol in the organ loft at St. Nicholas). The Strassers performed the carol at a concert in Leipzig in December 1832, and A.R. Friese published an arrangement of the carol in his collection of Tyrolean songs, *Vier ächte Tyroler Lieder* (Dresden, c. 1833). The 1838 edition of the *Leipziger Gesangbuch* also included an arrangement. In a concert presented on Christmas Day, 1839, at the Alexander Hamilton Monument outside Trinity Church in New York City, the Rainers, another Austrian family, introduced the carol to a most receptive United States under the title "Song from Heaven."

Father Mohr, a chronically ill priest who was frequently transferred from parish to parish, left Oberndorf in 1819 and died in 1848, never having witnessed the international appeal of his carol. Franz Gruber, who had assumed a new position in Hallein in 1835, also remained ignorant of his carol's success until 1854, when Frederick William IV, King of Prussia, having heard a Strasser rendition of "Silent Night" in 1834, instituted a search for its source. Although Gruber complied by dispatching an explanatory letter and a carol arrangement to the Royal Chapel in Berlin, the world initially refused to credit Father Mohr and Gruber as the songwriters, countering that such a work could only have been the product of a musical genius such as Beethoven, Mozart, or Michael Haydn, the brother of Franz Joseph Haydn.

By mid–nineteenth century, English translations of Father Mohr's poem appeared in print, and the translation of verses one, two, and six in 1863 by the Reverend John F. Young, future Episcopal bishop of Florida, has remained the most familiar. Now known by the title of "Silent Night," the carol depicts a scene of holy calm around the sleeping Babe and the gentle Virgin.

A number of Gruber's later orchestral arrangements for his carol still survive, notably those of 1836 and 1845, which remain in the archives of Hallein. The original manuscript of 1818 has long since disappeared, and the Church of St. Nicholas, which first heard "Silent Night" in Oberndorf, no longer stands today. Over the original site stands the Silent Night Memorial Chapel and Museum, where an annual Christmas Eve service traditionally concludes with a rendering of "Silent Night" in its original format. Visitors to Austria may also tour Franz Gruber's schoolhouse-home in Arnsdorf and the Franz Xaver Gruber Museum and grave at his later home in Hallein. Father Mohr rests in Wagrain, an Alpine ski resort, which hosts the Josef Mohr School. Annually on Christmas Eve, candlelight ceremonies are held at Father Mohr's grave in the churchyard in Wagrain.

In addition to German and English, "Silent Night" has been sung in virtually every other language of the world, and renditions have sometimes occurred under the most trying of circumstances. The carol has been heard along the battlefronts of two world wars during Christmas truces and in prison camps. One account tells how Korean citizens from the bush during the Korean War provided an American soldier on guard duty with a version of "Silent Night" in their native language. One reason the carol has become so popular, particularly during wartime, is because it seems to instill in its singers a yearning for universal peace.

Austria now considers "Silent Night" one of its national treasures, a sentiment reflected in that country's strict protection of the carol against commercialism. For that reason, by tradition, "Silent Night" is neither played, broadcast, nor sung in any form until Christmas Eve.

Silver Bells

Popular American song written by New York State native Ray Evans (lyrics) and Pennsylvania native Jay Livingston (music), both of whom, together with Victor Young, provided the musical score for the Paramount film comedy *The Lemon Drop Kid* (1951), which featured "Silver Bells." Although the song received its screen debut there in a duet performance by Bob Hope and Marilyn Maxwell, Bing Crosby and Carol Richards had first introduced the song in their 1950 duet recording for Decca Records, which became a bestseller. That recording reached position 78 on the *Billboard Hot 100* chart in 1957 and position 22 on the *Billboard Special Christmas Singles* chart in 1966.

According to Evans, he and Livingston, in seeking a popular yet different Christmas theme apart from the usual scenario of snow and sleigh riding, chose to fashion a tune about bells. He remarked that, at the time, "Silver Bells" was the only song that centered on the atmosphere of a big-city Christmas with its hustle and bustle of holiday shoppers, decorated window displays in department stores, and colorful lights. Evans and Livingston had originally titled their creation "Tinkle Bell," but that name apparently reduced Livingston's wife to such giggles that the title was wisely changed to "Silver Bells."

Of the 25 most frequently performed Christmas songs of the twentieth century listed by the American Society of Composers, Authors and Publishers (ASCAP), "Silver Bells" ranked number eight. By December 2004, it ranked number 11.

Together Evans and Livingston produced other notable works for motion pictures, including "Buttons and Bows" for *The Paleface* (1948), "Mona Lisa" for *Captain Carey, U.S.A.* (1950), and "Whatever Will Be, Will Be" ("Que Sera, Sera") for *The Man Who Knew Too Much* (1956), all three of which won Academy Awards for Best Song.

See also **ASCAP List of Christmas Songs; The Lemon Drop Kid.**

The Simpsons

The longest-running prime-time television animated cartoon series, created by Matt Groening, who also created the popular comic *Life in Hell*. Winner of numerous awards, including the Peabody Award and multiple Emmys, *The Simpsons* originated as a group of 15- to 20-second "shorts" for *The Tracey Ullman Show* in April 1987. The regular cast included Homer Simpson, a nuclear safety technician; wife Marge, who sported a blue beehive hairdo; and their three children: ten-year-old Bart, a hell-raising fourth grader; eight-year-old Lisa, a second grader who played the saxophone; and Margaret, the one-year-old baby. Their success led to a series, the first episode of which was titled "The Simpsons Roasting on an Open Fire," which premiered in December 1989.

"The Simpsons Roasting on an Open Fire" features the Simpsons of Springfield short on cash for the holidays: Bart's acquisition of a tattoo forces Marge to exhaust her savings on laser surgery to have it removed, and Homer's employer decides to forego any Christmas bonuses. Unable to afford even the cheapest of Christmas trees, Homer steals onto private property by night and swipes a tree, barely escaping guard dogs and flying buckshot. Homer's desperation for cash next motivates him to moonlight as a department store Santa, where a net gain of only 13 dollars after deductions prompts a quick trip to the dog track. There, Homer just as promptly squanders his meager earnings on the entry "Santa's Little Helper." Rejected by its master for losing, the dog retreats to Homer, who brings it home instead of Christmas presents. Marge, however, interprets the dog as the best gift of all, something with which to share their love and frighten away prowlers. This episode introduces Marge's two sisters, twins Patty and Selma; Ned and Todd Flanders, the neighbors next door (all of whom Homer despises); and their pet, "Santa's Little Helper."

In 1990, this picture received Emmy Award nominations for Outstanding Animated Program (One Hour or Less) and Outstanding Editing for a Special.

Principal voices: Dan Castellaneta, Julie Kavner, Nancy Cartwright, Yeardly Smith, Harry Shearer, Hank Azaria, Jo Ann Harris, and Pamela Hayden. Written by Mimi Pond. Produced by Richard Sakai. Directed by David Silverman. Twentieth Century Fox Television, Gracie Films, and Klasky-Csupo Productions. Episode on DVD collection *Christmas with the Simpsons* from Fox Home Entertainment. 30 min.

• Other *Simpsons* Christmas Episodes

"Marge Be Not Proud" (1995). When Marge denies Bart a violent "Bonestorm" video game for Christmas, he swipes a copy at the local Try-N-Save store but is apprehended. He is released with a warning, but his family learns of the incident only when they return to the store for a family Christmas portrait. Bart's act hurts Marge so deeply that he finds a way to make his mother proud of him once more. Guest voices: Phil Hartman and Lawrence Tierney. Principal voices: Dan Castellaneta, Julie Kavner, Nancy Cartwright, Yeardley Smith, Harry Shearer, Hank Azaria, Pamela Hayden, Tress MacNeille, and Maggie Roswell. Written by Mike Scully. Directed by Steven Dean Moore. 30 min.

"Miracle on Evergreen Terrace" (1997). When Bart accidentally burns the Christmas tree and presents, he buries the remains under the snow, then claims that their house was robbed. The incident soon becomes public knowledge, whereupon friends and neighbors (even some orphans) gather at the Simpson home with donations of more than $15,000, which the Simpsons readily spend. But when a follow-up news crew discovers the buried Christmas tree, the truth is out, and the Simp-

sons become the town pariahs. Guest voice: Alex Trebek. Principal voices: Dan Castellaneta, Julie Kavner, Nancy Cartwright, Yeardley Smith, Harry Shearer, Hank Azaria, Pamela Hayden, Tress MacNeille, Marcia Wallace, and Maggie Roswell. Written by Ron Hauge. Directed by Bob Anderson. 30 min.

"Grift of the Magi" (1999). When a financial crisis temporarily closes the doors of Springfield Elementary School, Kid First Industries comes to the rescue. In reality, the latter is a sinister toy company that has tricked the children into designing "Funzo," a most successful Christmas toy because it destroys other toys. After they discover the truth, Bart and Lisa scheme to thwart such radical Christmas commercialization. Guest voices: Clarence Clemmons, Gary Coleman, Joe Mantegna, and Tim Robbins. Principal voices: Dan Castellaneta, Julie Kavner, Nancy Cartwright, Yeardley Smith, Harry Shearer, Hank Azaria, Pamela Hayden, Tress MacNeille, and Russi Taylor. Written by Tom Martin. Directed by Matthew Nastuk. 30 min.

"Skinner's Sense of Snow" (2000). When a major snowstorm hits on the day before Christmas break, all schools except Springfield Elementary are closed, and the students become trapped. The teachers are absent, however, so Principal Skinner entertains the students with the film *The Christmas That Almost Wasn't but Was*, instead of the *Grinch*, as they had hoped. Fearing that they will miss Christmas, the students revolt at Skinner's restrictions and wreak havoc throughout, while Homer and Flanders battle the elements to rescue the children. Principal voices: Dan Castellaneta, Julie Kavner, Nancy Cartwright, Yeardley Smith, Harry Shearer, Hank Azaria, Pamela Hayden, Tress Mac-Neille, Russi Taylor, Marcia Wallace, and Karl Wiedergott. Written by Tim Long. Directed by Lance Kramer. 30 min.

"'Tis the Fifteenth Season" (2003). When Homer sells a Joe DiMaggio rookie card and spends most of the cash on himself, he regrets his greedy ways after viewing *A Christmas Carol* on television. Homer becomes the envy of do-gooder Flanders when he turns over a new leaf by becoming as helpful a person as he can to all concerned. This prompts a "nice-off" competition between Homer and Flanders. Guest voice: Joe Mantegna. Principal voices: Dan Castellaneta, Julie Kavner, Nancy Cartwright, Yeardley Smith, Harry Shearer, and Hank Azaria. 30 min.

"Miracle on Evergreen Terrace" and "Grift of the Magi" are available on the DVD collection *Christmas with the Simpsons*, along with other nonholiday episodes.

The Simpsons Roasting on an Open Fire
See **The Simpsons**

Sing We Now of Christmas

("Noël nouvelet!"). French traditional carol, also known as "Noel! A New Noel!," "Christmas Comes Anew," and "Nowell, Sing Nowell." The lyrics are believed to date from the late fifteenth century, the oldest known source being a manuscript from that era that resides in the French National Library in Paris. No definitive version of the lyrics seems to exist, however, for they have varied with subsequent printings over the centuries.

Although no tune accompanied the text in that early manuscript, it is believed that the tune with which the lyrics are now associated was well known at the time and was passed down orally, appearing in written form around the seventeenth century. The tune has been adapted to various hymns, and the celebrated French composer Marcel Dupré (1886–1971) incorporated it in a work for organ, "Variations sur un vieux noël" ("Variations on an Old Carol"). Because the French title "Noël nouvelet!" literally means "New Christmas Song," this carol was also a favorite for the New Year celebration (falling in the midst of the 12 days of Christmas) and signified a new carol for the newborn King in a new year.

In addition to a narrative on the Nativity, one lengthy version (13 verses) of "Sing We Now of Christmas," published in Troyes, France (1721), recalls two events not often considered with the traditional Christmas story: Mary's purification forty days after giving birth to Jesus and Simeon's prophecies about Him in the Temple (Gospel of Luke 2:22–35).

See also **The Twelve Days of Christmas** (time period).

Sinner's Holiday
See **Christmas Eve** (1947)

Sisters at Heart
See **Bewitched**

Skinflint
See **A Christmas Carol** (Film and Television Versions)

Skinner's Sense of Snow
See **The Simpsons**

Skipping Christmas

Humorous novel, a satire against neighborhood conformity, written by American author John Grisham, published in 2001.

When their only child Blair leaves after Thanksgiving for a stint in Peru in the Peace Corps, Luther and Nora Krank decide to skip Christmas entirely and plan a ten-day cruise in the Caribbean, to commence on Christmas Day. They'll avoid the suffocating crowds, snow, and commercialism; potential ladder accidents from decorating the tree, house, and the entire property; drunken office parties; useless cards and gifts that no one wants; their annual Christmas Eve bash for friends; and especially the $6,100 spent the previous year on the whole mess. Theirs will be the only house on Hemlock Street without a ridiculous "Frosty" snowman figure stuck on the roof. Their idea is certainly radical and significantly breaks with neighborhood tradition; pulling it off will become a veritable nightmare.

The snowball effects of the Kranks' decision commence when Luther refuses to purchase the usual Christmas tree, calendars, and fruitcakes that the neighborhood Boy Scouts, policemen, and firemen/paramedics respectively peddle each year. As word about the Kranks (alias Scrooges) spreads, neighborhood boss Vic Frohmeyer launches a plan to coerce them into the Christmas spirit and especially to put Frosty on their roof. Without it, Hemlock Street could lose the neighborhood decorating contest. Therefore, in the ensuing weeks before Christmas, protest signs with "Free Frosty" appear in the Kranks' yard, assorted groups of carolers stand on the street howling forth "Frosty the Snow Man" and chanting "Free

Frosty! Free Frosty!" (from his basement prison), and no less than 30 anonymous Frosty Christmas cards arrive by mail. As expected, Hemlock Street loses the contest, at which the neighbors take revenge by setting up outdoor speakers near the Krank property and playing recorded carols to annoy them, while the local newspaper runs an uncomplimentary article that showcases the Kranks' undecorated home. The Frosty cards continue to arrive, yet Luther stands his ground. .

Although Nora has had reservations about Luther's wild scheme, she has supported it nonetheless, despite all the harassment. But with a fateful telephone call early on Christmas Eve, Luther kisses the cruise goodbye, and bedlam reigns: Blair will be coming home that evening after all and on the arm of Enrique, her doctor-fiancé, whom she recently met in Peru. Nora demands a full holiday welcome for darling daughter with decorated tree and home, the Christmas Eve party, and of course, *Frosty*—all to be in readiness before nightfall. Thoroughly beaten, Luther desperately pays $75 for a miserably scrubby tree from the Boy Scouts, which loses all its remaining needles in short order. Next, he "borrows" a decorated tree from a neighbor who is going out of town and is almost arrested by the same calendar-pushing cops for stealing when the other neighbors mistake Luther's intentions. Although Nora frantically gathers party items amid the snow and suffocating crowds, none of their usual guests are free on such short notice to attend the makeshift celebration.

The tide turns when Luther, attempting to hoist Frosty aloft, slips on his icy roof, hangs by his feet tangled in a rope, and is rescued by the same paramedics who peddled the fruit-cakes, as curious neighbors watch with a touch of glee. Learning that the reason for Luther's sudden change of heart is Blair's homecoming, Vic Frohmeyer assumes command and organizes the entire evening's festivities, complete with the neighbors substituting as the Kranks' guests, who donate the cuisine, gifts, decorations, and even a borrowed Frosty. Later, Luther slips away from the revelry for a moment to deliver the cruise tickets to neighbors Walt and Bev Scheel, who did not attend. It's a last-minute gift, but Bev has a terminal

illness with six months to live. She and Walt had been considerably depressed, but now the cruise offer suddenly brightens their spirits beyond measure. Afterwards, Luther counts his blessings and ponders that perhaps he and Nora will skip Christmas the next year instead.

In 2004, the novel was adapted as a motion picture comedy under the title *Christmas with the Kranks*, starring Tim Allen and Jamie Lee Curtis as Luther and Nora Krank, Julie Gonzalo as Blair, René Lavan as Enrique, Dan Aykroyd as Vic Frohmeyer, and M. Emmet Walsh and Elizabeth Franz as Walt and Bev Scheel. Screenplay by Chris Columbus. Produced by Michael Barnathan, Chris Columbus, and Mark Radcliffe. Directed by Joe Roth. Skipping Christmas Productions, 1492 Pictures, and Revolution Studios. DVD: Columbia Tristar Home Video. 98 min.

John Grisham is the author of the novels *A Time to Kill*, *The Pelican Brief*, and *The Firm*, among others.

Sleep, Baby Mine
See **Alfred Burt Carols**

Sleepers, Awake! A Voice Is Calling

("Wachet auf! Ruft uns die Stimme"). German chorale applied to Advent, written in 1598 by Philipp Nicolai (1556–1608), Lutheran pastor of Unna in Westphalia. Nicolai wrote only four chorales, of which this and "How Brightly Shines the Morning Star" are the best known. All four were written following a six-month outbreak of bubonic plague in Unna between July 1597 and January 1598. They were published in Frankfurt in 1599.

The text of "Sleepers, Awake!" is based on Jesus' parable of the five wise and five foolish virgins awaiting the return of the bridegroom, as found in Matthew 25:1–13. The allegorical implications here and in the chorale are concerned with the second coming of Christ (the bridegroom). Because He will someday return at an unknown hour (midnight is suggested, not only as an hour of surprise but as the traditional hour of His birth) to claim His brides (the Church, the faithful) and proceed to the marriage feast (heaven), mankind should watch and be prepared to meet Him and not be left behind, as were the five foolish, unprepared virgins. Thus the carol is considered appropriate for Advent, when Christianity not only celebrates the first coming of Christ, but looks forward to His second coming.

The Unna plague claimed the life of one of Nicolai's former students, 15-year-old Wilhelm Ernst, count of Waldech. According to *The New Oxford Book of Carols*, Nicolai memorialized him in "Sleepers, Awake!" by using the first letter of each of the three verses as a reverse acrostic, creating the initials "G.Z.W.," which stand for *Graf zu Waldech* (Count of Waldech).

The German composer J.S. Bach (1685–1750) based two works on Nicolai's chorale: sacred cantata *Wachet auf!* (BWV 140) and an organ chorale prelude of the same title (BWV 645).

The best-known English translation was provided by Great Britain's Catherine Winkworth (1827–1878), a translation specialist.

See also **Advent; How Brightly Shines the Morning Star.**

Sleigh Ride

Popular American song, the music for which was written in 1948 by Massachusetts-born Leroy Anderson (1908–1975) during an August heat wave. Anderson was an orchestrator for Arthur Fiedler and the Boston Pops Orchestra beginning in 1935. He originally scored "Sleigh Ride" as a purely instrumental work, which clearly conveyed the merriment of gliding over the snow in a horse-drawn sleigh. The Boston Pops first introduced live audiences to the lively piece, which featured a number of colorful sound effects, such as sleigh bells, clip-clops, whip cracks, and even the horse's whinny at the conclusion, imitated by a trumpet. Much like "Jingle Bells," it was an instant success and was quickly absorbed into the Christmas season. Although Mitchell Parish (1900–1993), a lyricist from Shreveport, Louisiana, added a vocal setting in 1950, performances still frequently feature the orchestral version only. Arthur Fiedler and the Boston Pops first recorded "Sleigh Ride" in 1949 on the RCA Victor Red Seal label, and the recording received chart status.

Of the 25 most frequently performed Christmas songs of the twentieth century listed by the American Society of Composers, Authors and Publishers (ASCAP), "Sleigh Ride" ranked number six. By December 2004, it ranked number 12.

Respected as a popular and a classical composer, Leroy Anderson contributed other classics, such as "Fiddle Faddle" (1948), "The Syncopated Clock" (1950), "Blue Tango" (1952), "The Typewriter" (1953), and "Bugler's Holiday" (1954). Mitchell Parish also provided lyrics for "Stardust" (1929), "Deep Purple" (1939), and "Moonlight Serenade" (1939), among others.

See also **ASCAP List of Christmas Songs.**

Slovak Republic

Czechs and Slovaks united in 1918 after World War I to form Czechoslovakia, which Soviet Communists dominated from the end of World War II until 1991, after which Soviet troops withdrew. During the approximately 50 years of Communism's atheistic regime, Christmas was repudiated, the midwinter holiday was moved to New Year's Day with a secular agenda, and St. Nicholas or Baby Jesus, who had brought children's gifts, was replaced by a Soviet "Santa" known as "Grandfather Frost" (*see* **Russia**).

Following the cessation of Soviet occupation, Czechoslovakia split into two independent nations, the Czech Republic and the Slovak Republic, on January 1, 1993. By then, Communism had nearly extinguished the old holiday customs, yet a number of them still survive, primarily in rural areas. These customs revolve around agrarian rituals, romantic matchmaking, the repelling of evil, and forecasting the future.

The principal Christian faith in the Slovak Republic now is Roman Catholicism. Christmas customs are closely similar to those of the Czech Republic, and minor differences or variations are outlined here.

The Advent season includes observing the feast days of several saints: St. Andrew the Apostle (November 30), St. Barbara (December 4), St. Nicholas (December 6), and St. Lucia (December 13). On the more popular St. Nicholas's Day, personages dressed as *Svätý Mikuláš* (St. Nicholas), an angel, and a devil parade about, distributing treats to children and visiting homes to quiz youngsters about

Painted Slovakian ceramic manger scene, with a wooden X-form manger. Late nineteenth or early twentieth century. From the journal Český Lid *(published in Prague), 1908.*

Early twentieth century Slovakian silhouette of a child and the gift-giver messenger of the Little Jesus holding a small fir tree. From Berta Wegner-Bell, Herzblättchens Beitvertreib *(Berlin: Fleming, 1910).*

their catechism. The devil, in some places known as "Cert," carries a whip and chains and threatens to whisk away naughty children. Children usually set out their shoes by the windowsill on St. Nicholas's Eve to receive treats. Superstitions once associated with each feast day, particularly concerning romantic forecasts, are now usually held for Christmas Eve

and New Year's Day (see below). During Advent, the entire house and property are thoroughly cleaned, personal disputes and debts are resolved, objects borrowed are returned, and children write letters to Baby Jesus. The Christmas tree is decorated on Christmas eve with gilded walnuts, candy, fruit, candles, electric lights, colored balls, and gingerbread. All must be in readiness for "Bountiful Evening," Christmas Eve, also known as *Vigilia* (Latin, "watch on the eve of a feast"), the most important and eventful night of the season.

Central to Christmas Eve is Holy Supper, at which all family members gather after having fasted all day. The table is covered with a white tablecloth, under which lies a layer of straw, symbolic of the manger, and straw may be spread on the floor beneath. The table centerpiece often consists of a small *crèche* or a plate of straw containing *oplatky*, unleavened communion wafers stamped with Nativity scenes. The meal commences upon sighting the first star of the evening, believed to be the Star of Bethlehem, after which the host and hostess bring honey and holy water to the table with ritual greetings. The hostess anoints the table and home with holy water, grace is said, then the host, taking honey, traces the sign of the cross upon the foreheads of all present. At this point, no one may leave the table (superstition holds that violators will perish in the coming year), for the host now distributes the sacred *oplatky* with honey (considered to be a medicinal) to each person present, along with blessings and wishes for health and happiness. Variations of the ritual include spreading honey in the shape of a cross within a circle on each wafer prior to dispensing it and eating the wafer together with garlic (a talisman against evil and sickness) and honey.

Although the menu prepared for Holy Supper may vary somewhat from region to region and house to house, it traditionally consists of 12 meatless dishes, symbolic of Christ's Twelve Apostles. Along with the obligatory *oplatky* and honey, there may be porridge, *bobalky* (small, baked biscuits with a topping of milk, honey, and poppy seeds), Christmas cake, fruit compote, mushroom soup, sauerkraut soup, *pirohy* (boiled pastries filled with mashed potatoes, cheeses, dried fruit, or sauerkraut), beans, peas, fish (the scales of which are placed under the plates or tablecloth for luck), breads, rolls, and nuts. Mushrooms and fish also symbolize prosperity. Following Holy Supper, the children are escorted out and return only after a bell signals that Baby Jesus has deposited presents beneath the Christmas tree. Children traditionally present their parents with holiday greetings in the form of a song or poem. After livestock receive portions of the meal, the leftovers remain on the table overnight as an oblation to the spirits of family ancestors, who are believed to arrive at midnight. Christmas Eve concludes with Midnight Mass.

From Christmas Day to Epiphany, families visit and feast together, while caroling dramatists present traditional Christmas dramas from house to house. This latter tradition, adopted from Germany in the eleventh century, features four shepherds plus an angel character adorned in white with a golden crown. The angel bears a wooden *crèche* or "Bethlehem," the shepherds perform an *odzemok*, a traditional folk dance, and the household rewards the troupe with food and drink. The cuisine for the remainder of the holidays includes most meats except for New Year's Day, wherein poultry and rabbit are omitted to guarantee lasting happiness and prosperity. The menu on that day includes pork, lentils, and pasta, all symbols of abundance and prosperity.

On Epiphany or *Tri Krále* (Three Kings' Day), which concludes the holiday season, the clergy travel about, blessing the homes and chalking above the entrances the initials of names of the three traditional Wise Men: Caspar, Melchior, and Balthazar, plus the current year. The numerals are evenly divided before and after the letters; thus, the year 2005 would read: "20+C+M+B+05." Groups of "Star Boys" parade about, dressed as the Three Kings (one of whom is blackfaced as Balthazar, the traditional king of Ethiopia). A boy costumed as an angel in white leads them and carries a large paper star on a pole.

• SUPERSTITIONS. A large number of superstitions, now of historical interest, once surrounded the entire Christmas season, and a few popular ones are detailed here. By making a three-legged stool between St. Lucia's Day and Christmas Eve and then sitting on that stool during Midnight Mass, one would encounter witches. To escape their clutches while traveling home from church, a person would cast either needles or poppy seeds behind him; the witches were compelled either to pass through the needles' eyes or pick up every poppy seed, acts which slowed their pace. Another charm against evil was to rub door hinges with garlic. Following Holy Supper, family members each cracked a nut and sliced an apple. A rotten nut portended bad luck for the new year, as did a cross pattern in the sliced apple; a star pattern predicted good luck. The burning candle wick at the supper table would incline toward any person doomed to die in the coming year. On Christmas Eve, farmers sought predictions about the new year's weather by preparing either 12 nut shells filled with water or 12 onion slices moistened with water. All were labeled for the months of the year and were exposed to air overnight. On Christmas morning, those items remaining wet predicted rain for the corresponding months; for dry items, fair weather or drought. Binding fruit trees with straw, shaking them, or spreading poppy seeds around them on Christmas Eve would yield better crops, and the number of times a rooster crowed on Christmas morning indicated the number of weeks remaining before spring plowing would commence.

Predictions of romance and marriage were favorite pastimes among young girls on Christmas Eve or New Year's Day. The direction of the first star sighted or the first dog bark heard after supper indicated the direction from which a future spouse would come. In one variation, a girl swept the floor after supper, took the refuse to a crossroads, then listened for the first dog bark. If a girl poured hot lead into water, the shape of the congealed mass provided some hint to a future spouse's occupation. Before retiring for the night, a girl placed a ring in one small bag and a piece of bread in another. She put these plus a third, empty bag either under her pillow or at her bedside. If she awoke during the night, she blindly chose one bag but examined it the next morning. The ring predicted an ultimately happy marriage; the bread, a life of hardship to acquire bread; the empty bag, spinsterhood.

"Merry Christmas" in the Slovak Republic is *Vesele Vianoce*.

See also **Advent; Croatia; Czech Republic; Epiphany; Poland.**

The Small One: A Story for Those Who Like Christmas and Small Donkeys

Classic children's book written by American author Charles Tazewell (1900–1972), published in 1947. The setting is Old Mexico a few days before Christmas.

When little Pablo scolds Cupido, his seemingly stubborn donkey, an old and gentle Padre explains that, because of a great honor bestowed upon one donkey many years ago, what appears as laziness or a stubborn streak in all donkey descendants is actually pride. Then the Padre tells Pablo the story of Small One.

At his father's bidding, a boy must sell his beloved pet, 14-year-old Small One, the oldest and smallest of the family's donkeys, because the animal is no longer useful. Instead of selling him to a tanner for slaughter, as his father had ordered, the boy wanders through the city all day, pleading for someone to buy Small One for one piece of silver. All reject the offer with disdain and deem the donkey as worthless. Yet the boy defends Small One, asserting that his pet is fine enough for a king's stable.

When night falls and Small One has not been sold, the boy is about to resort to the tanner, when Joseph, needing a gentle animal to carry Mary to Bethlehem, purchases him for the piece of silver.

The Padre concludes the story by explaining that Small One, who indeed witnessed the birth of a King in a King's stable along with those who paid homage to his "small Master," fulfilled the destiny of donkeys for all time. And that is why all donkeys, especially at Christmastime, stand and dream of the Small One of Bethlehem.

Bing Crosby provided a narrative recording of the story for Decca Records in 1947.

The Walt Disney Company adapted the story as an animated cartoon short, *The Small One* (1978), which centered only around the Judean boy and Small One. Principal voices: Sean Marshall, William Woodson, Olan Soule, Hal Smith, Joe Higgins, and Gordon Jump. Written by Vance Gerry and Pete Young. Produced and directed by Don Bluth. Walt Disney Productions. VHS: Walt Disney Home Video. 25 min.

Disney subsequently published a book version of the cartoon under the same title in 1995, written by Alex Walsh with a foreword by television celebrity Kathie Lee Gifford.

See also **The Littlest Angel; The Littlest Snowman; The Littlest Tree.**

A Smoky Mountain Christmas

(1986). Made-for-television drama loosely based on the Grimms' fairy tale "Snow White and the Seven Dwarfs," starring country singer Dolly Parton in her first television movie venture.

As the holidays approach, singing celebrity Lorna Davis (Parton), needing a welcome break from the pressures of Hollywood, retreats to an old friend's remote cabin in the Great Smoky Mountains of Tennessee. There, she discovers that seven runaway orphans have set up residence in the cabin and have become a makeshift family led by an older boy, Jake (Chad Sheets). Not wishing to take any action until after Christmas, Lorna allows the children to remain and soon wins their hearts while acting as their loving foster mother.

In keeping with the "Snow White" scenario, Lorna meets her "prince" in Mountain Dan (Lee Majors), who saves her from Jezebel (Anita Morris), a beautiful mountain witch bent on destroying her (Jezebel believes that Lorna is a "white" witch who intends to usurp her domain). Jezebel strikes again after the law, having traced the orphans to the cabin, places them in a local children's home and throws Lorna in jail for obstruction of justice. Baking a spell into an apple pie, Jezebel transforms herself into a sweet-appearing old lady and carries the pie to the jail, where Lorna samples it and falls into a deep sleep. Dan and Jake stage a jailbreak, but instead of Dan's princely kiss, Jake's tears falling on Lorna's cheek break the spell, and she awakens. When Jezebel appears for another coup, Lorna tricks her into tasting the pie, thereby dispatching Jezebel.

Now they must rescue the other orphans, who otherwise will be split up on Christmas Eve. Posing as Santa and Mrs. Claus, Dan and Lorna create a diversion at the children's home while Jake rounds up his comrades. As they all are about to escape in a one-horse sleigh, the law apprehends them and hauls them into court early on Christmas morning, where a soft-hearted judge (John Ritter) drops all charges and grants Lorna custody of the children.

With Danny Cooksey, Gennie James, Marc D. Robinson, Daryl Bartley, Ashley Bank, Micah Rowe, David Ackroyd, Rene Auberjonois, Douglas Seale, Dan Hedaya, and Bo Hopkins. Written by William Bleich. Produced by Robert Lovenheim. Directed by Henry Winkler. A Sandollar Production. VHS: Fox Home Entertainment. 94 min.

The Smurfs

Popular animated cartoon series from Hanna-Barbera Productions and SEPP International, S.A., that aired on the NBC television network from 1981 to 1990. The creation of Belgian cartoonist Pierre "Peyo" Culliford, the Smurfs were tiny blue, elfin characters "three apples high" that first appeared in *Le Journal de Spirou* on October 23, 1958. A number of Smurf dolls followed, which prompted the television series after Fred Silverman, then-president of NBC, saw the pleasure that such a doll brought to his little daughter. Led by Papa Smurf, the citizens of the sylvan Smurf Village bore names commensurate with personal characteristics: Brainy, Hefty, Handy, Grouchy, etc., with two female characters, Smurfette and tomboy Sassette. Serving as their nemeses were the evil wizard Gargamel, his assistant Scruple, and the diabolical cat Azriel.

Of the series' 427 episodes, only three featured Christmas themes:

The Smurfs' Christmas Special (December 12, 1982). Gargamel interrupts the Smurfs' happy Christmas celebrations by striking a bargain with a malevolent, cloaked stranger. Kidnapping and delivering two human children whom the Smurfs rescued from a sleighing accident, Gargamel receives from the stranger a magic scroll as the means of destroying Smurf Village. The Smurfs launch a search for their charges, whereupon Gargamel, en route to destroy the village, meets the children's uncle, who offers a large reward for their return. With the village dispatched, although Gargamel then plots to double-cross the stranger and collect the reward, the stranger, anticipating a betrayal, captures Gargamel and is about to sacrifice him along with the children in a ring of fire, when the Smurfs arrive. The only spell that will cancel the stranger's powerful magic is a Smurf chorus of "Goodness Makes the Badness Go Away," which everyone sings, including Gargamel. The stranger vanishes in a fit of rage, the children return home with their uncle, and the Smurfs return to a leveled village. Undaunted, the Smurfs proceed with their holiday celebrations, for the blowing of a Smurf trumpet miraculously restores their village directly. Written by Creighton Barnes, John Bates, John Bonnaccorsi, et al. Produced by Gerald Baldwin. Directed by George Gordon, Bob Hathcock, Carl Urbano, and Rudy Zamora. Video N/A. 30 min.

Baby's First Christmas (1983). When Chlorhydris poisons Santa with hate by kissing him under the mistletoe, only Baby Smurf can cure him in time for Christmas Eve rounds. Written by Creighton Barnes, John Bates, John Bonnaccorsi, et al. Produced by Gerald Baldwin. Directed by Oscar Dufau, George Gordon, Carl Urbano, John Walker, and Rudy Zamora. Available on VHS. 15 min.

'Tis the Season to Be Smurfy (December 13, 1987). When Grandpa Smurf and Sassette visit an outside village to learn how humans celebrate Christmas, they befriend an elderly couple by filling their lives with Christmas cheer. In the meantime, a Yuletide thief must be caught. Written by Creighton Barnes, John Bates, John Bonnaccorsi, et al. Produced by Bob Hathcock. Directed by Don Lusk, Jay Sarbry, Carl Urbano, and Rudy Zamora. Video N/A. 30 min.

Principal voices for the series: Don Messick, William Callaway, Linda Gary, Paul Winchell, Michael Bell, Hamilton Camp, June Foray, Lucille Bliss, Alan Oppenheimer, and Paul Kirby.

See also **Hanna-Barbera Christmas Cartoons.**

The Smurfs' Christmas Special
See **The Smurfs**

Snow Maiden
See **Russia**

A Snow White Christmas

(1980). Made-for-television animated cartoon, loosely based on the fairy tale by the Brothers Grimm. This version introduces a second Snow White, the teenage daughter of Queen Snow White and King Charming, who rule the kingdom of Noel.

With Christmas drawing nigh, Queen Snow White's stepmother, the Wicked Queen, returns and casts a spell that engulfs all of Noel in ice. Young Snow White and friend Grunyon escape and are befriended by seven giants, cousins to the seven dwarfs: Thinker, Finicky, Corny, Brawny, Tiny, Hicker, and Weeper.

Failing to eliminate Snow White through fire and flood, the Wicked Queen poses as the giants' aged sister and induces Snow White to fall into a deep sleep by means of poisoned flowers (not an apple). The giants seek revenge, but it is the Wicked Queen's own magic mirror that revolts and destroys her and her castle forever. All spells are broken, except that on Snow White. Only her mother's and father's kisses (not those from a prince) restore her, just in time for Christmas Eve.

Principal voices: Erika Scheimer, Arte Johnson, Melendy Britt, Diane Pershing, Charlie Bell, Larry Mann, and Clinton Sundberg. Written by Marc Richards. Produced by Don Christensen. Directed by Kay Wright. Filmation Associates. VHS: Hallmark Home Entertainment. 46 min.

The Snowman

(1982). British motion picture animated cartoon short, based on a wordless picture book written and illustrated by British author Raymond Briggs published in 1978. The original book does not feature the subject of Christmas, but its motion picture adaptation alters the story slightly to include holiday sentiment and incorporates only mime and music with a single vocal selection, "Walking in the Air," sung by Peter Auty.

Coming to life at midnight on Christmas Eve, a little English boy's snowman frolics with his creator indoors while the household sleeps. After a nocturnal joyride on a motorcycle around the countryside, the snowman lifts the boy, and together they fly to the North Pole, where they join Father Christmas and a host of other snow people (not elves) who are making merry. While touring Father Christmas's domain, the boy visits the reindeer and receives his Christmas gift, a new scarf wrapped in a package labeled with his name, James Brighton.

When James awakens on Christmas morning, nothing is left of the snowman except his old hat, scarf, and pieces of coal, all left in a pile in the front yard. The previous night could have been a dream, yet James's new scarf is proof to the contrary.

In 1983, this picture received an Academy Award nomination for Best Short Animated Film and won the Grand Prix Award in 1984 from the Tampere International Short Film Festival.

Written by Raymond Briggs. Produced by John Coates. Directed by Dianne Jackson. A Snowman Enterprises Production. DVD: Columbia/Tristar Home Video. 26 min. The video release includes an introduction by David Bowie with "Walking in the Air" sung by Aled Jones.

Raymond Briggs (1934–) began a career in advertising but soon switched to illustrating children's books and teaching. Two of his earlier books, *The Mother Goose Treasury* (1966) and *Father Christmas* (1973), each won Great Britain's Kate Greenaway Medal, equivalent to the Caldecott Medal in the United States. Among other honors, *The Snowman* received the Boston Globe-Horn Book Award and the International Reading Association's Children's Choice Award.

See also **Father Christmas** (book).

Some Children See Him
See **Alfred Burt Carols**

Song of the Bagpipers
See **Carol of the Bagpipers**

South America

Overwhelmingly Roman Catholic because the countries on this continent were former

Spanish colonies dating to the sixteenth century, Christmas traditions derive from Spain in every country but Brazil, a former Portuguese colony. Therefore, the principal customs common to South American countries include *Nacimientos* or *Pesebres* (respectively, simple or more elaborate Nativity scenes, known in Brazil as *Presépios*); the Feast of the Immaculate Conception (December 8); the Midnight Mass, termed "Mass of the Rooster" (*Misa del Gallo*, Spanish; *Missa do Galo*, Portuguese), celebrated on Christmas Eve; a large Christmas Eve dinner for family and friends held either before or just after the Midnight Mass; Holy Innocents Day (December 28); New Year's Day (January 1); and Day of the Kings (Epiphany, January 6).

Through foreign influences, predominantly from the United States, Santa Claus and Christmas trees are well known, but the Nativity scene remains the most important holiday symbol. It is customary for families to visit Nativity scenes of friends and relatives, as well as the scene erected in the local cathedral. Traditionally, the crib or manger within each Nativity scene remains empty until midnight on Christmas Eve, at which time each family or church adds a figure of the Christ Child to symbolize that Christ is born.

Nativity scenes are usually handmade and occupy a large space in the principal room of the home. Consisting of ornate landscapes with perhaps hills and waterfalls, they include figures of the Holy Family, animals, angels, shepherds, the Three Kings, and figures of local familiarity, such as the mayor, police officer, butcher, carpenter, and so forth, the latter figures bonding the past with the present.

Formerly, children received gifts only on Epiphany from the Three Kings, but it has become customary for children to receive gifts on Christmas Eve as well, brought either by Santa Claus or the Christ Child. More commonly on Epiphany Eve, children place their shoes upon a window sill, and the Three Kings fill them with treats by morning.

Religious processions and festive parades with fireworks, music, singing, and dancing abound. Employers in some regions are compelled by law to provide employees with a Christmas bonus.

The period from December 16 to 24 constitutes a Novena, on each day of which a special Mass is held. The first Mass is dedicated to the Annunciation; the second, the visit between Mary and her cousin Elizabeth; the third, the journey to Bethlehem; the fourth, the Nativity; the fifth, the shepherds; the sixth, the Magi; the seventh, the flight into Egypt; the eighth, the boy Jesus in the Temple with the scholars; the ninth, the boy Jesus' return to Nazareth. The Christmas season generally ends on Epiphany.

The following paragraphs summarize additional customs found in the individual countries. "Merry Christmas" in Spanish is *Feliz Navidad*; in Portuguese, *Feliz Natal*.

• ARGENTINA. Home decorations often consist of red and white garlands, with Father Christmas's boots placed at the door. Following Midnight Mass, the Christmas dinner may consist of roast *lechon* (suckling pig), *niños envueltos* ("children wrapped up," pieces of steak rolled and seasoned with minced meat, hard-boiled eggs, and spices), *sidra* (apple juice with liquor), *pan dulce* (sweet Christmas bread with dried fruit), and *turron de mani* (Christmas candy). Another drink consisting of different fruits mixed with juice and cider is quaffed for a midnight Christmas toast. Because the holiday falls during the summer, beach activities are common with fireworks on Christmas evening.

• BOLIVIA. Because Christmas is more of a religious celebration here, Christmas decorations and gifts are few, and Christmas trees are absent. Villagers congregate for communal meals, which may feature pork, beef, fresh vegetables, *locotos* (chili), and soup with beef stock and vegetables. Amid the folk dancing and regional music, children attired in assorted costumes also participate in street dancing to the music of drums, whistles, and cymbals. More colorful festivities are reserved for New Year's Eve.

• BRAZIL. Because it is a former colony of Portugal, Brazil's customs derive from that country, and celebrations vary considerably between urban and rural areas. Generally, the more urban, the more elaborate are the festivities. As in other Latin American countries, the *Presépio* (Nativity scene) remains the chief

Christmas symbol, which the Jesuits first introduced in 1583 in Rio de Janeiro. The Christmas Eve dinner often features turkey with *farofa* (stuffing made from manihot meal, butter, hard-boiled eggs, olives, and raisins), suckling pig, assorted fish in northern regions, fresh fruits, nuts, *rabanada* (a dessert resembling French toast, made with cinnamon, eggs, sugar, and milk or wine), fruit punch, and liquor. Christmas trees generally consist of artificial pines or equivalents, and Santa Claus, termed *Papai Noel,* has supplanted a native equivalent, Grandpa Indian. Christmas Day includes a meal with invited guests, followed by distribution of food and gifts to the needy in public squares, at which the first lady of Brazil and governors' ladies traditionally participate in their respective states.

Traditions are more authentic in rural areas, particularly in the Northeast. In addition to singing and dancing, rural celebrations often feature pageants and traditional Portuguese folk dramas performed on the local church square. These dramas begin around Christmas Day and extend until Epiphany. Considered to be the most interesting of these is *Bumba-Meu-Boi* ("Whoa, My Ox"), a satire about the death and resurrection of an ox, which is again killed. Its theme reflects elements of black African culture (black slaves were imported to Brazil in the sixteenth century), which are also found in other dramas now in decline. *Pastoris* or *Pastorinhas*, originally sacred Nativity plays with performers attired as shepherds, eventually evolved into burlesques, the final acts of which burned the *Presépio* on stage; today, *Pastoris* assume a purely carnival atmosphere. The name *Pastoris* also refers to Christmas carols sung around Nativity scenes to the accompaniment of tambourines, guitars, and wind instruments. Similar dramas include the *Reisado*, which centers around the Three Kings and which may terminate with a scene from *Bumba-Meu-Boi*, and the related *Folia dos Reis* ("Frolic of the Kings"). Dance festivals at this time include the *Fandango* and the *Chegança* or *Changaca*, both based on maritime plays. A relatively new drama that arose around 1930 is *Guerreiro* ("Warrior"), performed in the State of Alagoas, which features the death and resurrection of a lyre bird and a dancing ox, akin

to the *Bumba*. Epiphany features poetry contests, in which participants improvise verses and sing them to instrumental accompaniment. A custom instituted by Protestant missionaries is the "white gift" Christmas collection for the poor. Though many live in poverty, it is customary for those who can to bring gifts to their church. These gifts, often food, are wrapped in white packages and distributed to those who are most destitute. *See also* **Portugal.**

• CHILE. Christmas is more of a secular holiday; while the country remains predominantly Roman Catholic, only some ten percent of the population practice the faith. The principal gift-bringer is *Viejo Pascuero* ("Christmas Old Man"), who closely resembles Santa Claus and even rides in a reindeer sleigh, despite the summer weather below the equator in December. Children place their shoes in window sills or in corridors on Christmas Eve for Christmas Old Man to fill with treats. Families congregate on Christmas Eve for gift exchanges and a large dinner, which may consist of turkey, seafood, a variety of salads, *azuela de ave* (chicken soup with potatoes and onions), *pan de pasqua* (Christmas bread filled with candied fruit), fruits, cakes, *rompon* (an alcoholic beverage similar to eggnog), *cola de mono* (milk and coffee flavored with liquor and cinnamon), and Chilean wine. The Christmas Day dinner itself consists of leftovers plus *choclo* (corn cake) and *chirimoya alegre* (a sweet fruit dish). Citywide fiestas are common, and one in particular is that in Andacollo, which honors the Virgin. According to legend, an Indian wood cutter named Collo, obedient to a divine vision, discovered a three-foot statue of the Virgin in the area. Termed the *Virgin del Rosario* ("Virgin of the Rosary"), the venerated statue is always displayed at the fiesta on a platform of roses. Epiphany is called *La Pascua de Los Negros* ("Holiday of the Black Ones"), paying special tribute to one of the Three Kings who tradition says came from Ethiopia.

• COLOMBIA. Unique to Colombia is the Christmas Eve *Aguinaldos* ("gifts"), a costume ball held in many cities that resembles an American Halloween party. Clad in elaborate disguises, thousands of merry people flock the streets during the evening and attempt to recognize their friends. If they are successful, they are entitled to claim an *aguinaldo* from the one recognized. The Christmas dinner may include *lechona* (stuffed pork), fowls, salads, vegetables, *tamales*, *ajiaco* (soup with potatoes), *natilla* (corn-based dessert), *buñuelos* (deep-fried pastries served with powdered sugar, cinnamon, and honey), and liquor. In addition to attending Mass, families exchange gifts and shoot fireworks at midnight. Those in the north may place gifts under the children's beds early on Christmas morning. From December 26 until New Year's Day, most villages host a Sugar Cane Festival, which sports a carnival atmosphere.

• ECUADOR. The Christmas meal may include *pernil* (baked pork), chicken, *pristiños* (molasses pastries), *canelazo* (spiced, hot liquor with cloves, cinnamon, and sugar), and *anizado* (anise-flavored brandy). Gifts are opened on Christmas Eve, and families often personally donate toys and candy to needy children. The city of Cuenca hosts the most popular of the country's Christmas Eve processions, termed *Pase del Niño Viajero* ("Steps of the Little Traveler"), in which people display their stock of wealth and plenty as they ride in vehicles or on burros.

While the Church observes Holy Innocents Day with religious ritual, the day in Ecuador has become a children's festival akin to the American Halloween, for children dress in costumes and pull pranks and practical jokes. The custom is based on a legend that mothers in Bethlehem saved some children from the Slaughter of the Innocents by disguising them. On New Year's Eve, most people create representations of the "Old Year" by fashioning effigies of objectionable persons or items, which are burned at midnight in a custom known as *La Quema de los Años Viejos* ("Burning of the Old Years"). Shortly into the new year, families remove their images of the Christ Child from their *pesebres* and carry them to church for a Mass, which is termed *El Paso del Niño* ("The Step of the Child").

• GUYANA (formerly British Guiana). The majority of the population consists of descendants of slaves from India (50 percent) and black Africa (30 percent). Some 42 percent of the population is Christian, divided between Anglican and Roman Catholic faiths. From the second week of December until Christmas Day, masquerade street bands clad in colorfully ornate costumes dominate festivities with street dancers and dancers on stilts, all of whom perform for profit. Central to the merriment is "Mother Sally" or "Long Lady," a figure costumed as a large doll, which descendants of West African slaves adapted from a protective matriarchal goddess. Typical musical instruments, vestiges of the British influence, include the fife, kittle, boom, and steel drums (oil drums with indented heads). Guyanese spend Christmas Day with close family, and Boxing Day, December 26, is also a national holiday devoted to a broader range of fellowship. "Merry Christmas" is said in English, the official language.

• PARAGUAY. The Christmas season begins with the Feast of the Immaculate Conception, and he who brings children their Christmas gifts is a figure similar to Santa Claus, known as *Papa Noel* (Father Christmas). Christmas dinner often features duck, lamb, chicken, and turkey, along with salads, a soup resembling a soufflé, beer, and cider. Paraguay is bilingual, with some 90 percent of the population speaking the Guarani Indian dialect in addition to Spanish. A Guarani "Merry Christmas" is *V'ya pave mita tupara-pe*.

• PERU. This country's Quechua Indian artisans, Inca descendants, are noted for their Nativity figures carved from wood using techniques dating from the sixteenth century. Open-air markets in this summertime holiday feature all manner of these and other crafts, toys and delicacies. Such crafts may include the *retablo,* a personal, portable shrine that aids the bearer in giving thanks for spiritual blessings. While *retablos* are known throughout Latin America as principally religious paintings on tin, the Peruvian version consists of a three-dimensional box with triangular top and one or two doors that open outwardly. Overlaid with gesso and brightly painted, *retablos* range from matchbook size to several feet. They are usually divided in half, the top symbolizing heaven, the bottom, earth. At this time of year, figures within the shrine are based on the Nativity. These figures are molded from a potato-based paste, painted, and varnished. The triangle and doors often sport floral patterns.

Children carol from house to house while playing on whistles, small harps, flutes, and bells; their repertoire also features songs dedicated to the *pesebres* passed along their route. Children open gifts on Christmas Eve, and afterwards the family congregates for dinner, which features turkey and stuffing, *panetón* (bread with raisins and glazed fruit), *biblia con pisco* (eggnog made with pomace brandy), hot chocolate, and champagne. On Christmas Day, particularly in Lima, citizens attend a grand bullfight. Then follows an elaborate procession to honor the Virgin, symbolized by a statue held on high. Epiphany is not particularly emphasized, but some families partake of *rosca*, a bread containing a coin or other figure baked inside, similar to the European "Kings' Cakes" of Epiphany.

• URUGUAY. The large majority of the population is of European descent, primarily from Spain, Italy, and France, with Christmas customs reflecting those of the parent countries. Santa Claus is known as *Papa Noel*.

• VENEZUELA. The Christmas season begins with the Novena as described above, called *Misa del Aguinaldo* ("Mass of the Gift"), which is held each morning around 5 A.M. Church bells pealing and children setting off firecrackers alert villages that the hour of Mass has arrived. Holiday music, also called *aguinaldo*, is lively and rich; the specific rhythm is known as the *gaita* ("bagpipe"). Arising in the Zulia State, *gaita* has no relationship to a literal bagpipe; instead, typical instruments include a *cuatro* (ukulele), *furruco* and *tambora* (two kinds of drums), *maracas* (rattles), and electronic organs and guitars.

Virtually everyone in Caracas traditionally roller skates to all Masses, including the Christmas Eve Midnight Mass. Then follows the Christmas dinner, which usually includes *hallacas* (cornmeal pie stuffed with pork, chicken, olives, raisins, wrapped in banana leaves and boiled), *pan de jamón* (long bread filled with ham and raisins), *pavo* (turkey), *pernil de cochino* (pork dish), *dulce de lechoza* (cold dessert of green papaya and brown sugar), and *ponche crema* (cream punch with or without liquor). Children receive Christmas gifts from *El Niño Jesus* (the Christ Child), Who leaves them under their beds.

Holy Innocents Day is spent in performing mischievous pranks, and bands of costumed musicians and singers provide entertainment as they roam about. One notable Innocents Day festival, termed "On the Loose," is that in Agua Blanca. Attired with swords, ornamental hats, and colored ribbons, the bands first meet in Bolivar Square amid a din of firecrackers. Following Mass, they disperse into the neighborhoods with music and dancing.

In some locales on New Year's Eve, children create a life-size effigy of the apostle Judas and solicit money for the poor. At midnight, they burn Judas with fireworks as a sign of burning away the old year and bringing in the new. Another New Year's custom, decidedly Spanish, is to eat 12 grapes for luck within the final minute before midnight.

Between New Year's Day and February 2 (Candlemas, which formerly ended the Christmas season in the Catholic Church), Andean cities, especially Mérida, Tachira, and Trujillo, observe the custom of *La Paradura del Niño* ("The Standing Up of the Christ Child"). The custom centers around the young Jesus, Whom tradition holds stood upright after the first week of His life. Family and friends congregate at the home of the selected manger for each observance, where *padrinos* (godparents) are chosen. The figure of the Christ Child is then removed from the *pesebre* and placed in a large handkerchief, the four corners of which the godparents hold, and the entourage, carrying lighted candles and singing traditional carols, parades around the neighborhood. At the conclusion, the ceremony ritually stands the Christ Child figure upright, prayers are offered for those who participated, and refreshments with festivities follow. The figure then remains upright until Candlemas. In a variation of the ceremony, the figure is secretly stolen from the *pesebre*, which precipitates a formal procession to search for the statue and return it to its original place. Such a gala affair includes fireworks, music, traditional carols, and youths dressed as Mary, Joseph, and shepherds.

Epiphany is not widely commemorated today as in previous eras, yet some villages still present pageants about the Three Kings. For example, in the Andean village of San Miguel de Boconó, people clad in extraordinary costumes dance in the streets until the Kings dressed in appropriate regal attire ride into town. House parties then continue well into the night. By the end of the twentieth century, gift-giving on this date was no longer customary.

See also **Epiphany; Feast of the Immaculate Conception; Holy Innocents Day; Las Posadas; Mass of the Rooster; Nativity Scene; Spain.**

Spain

As in most Spanish-speaking countries, the Christmas season in Spain begins with the Feast of the Immaculate Conception, traditionally celebrated on December 8, when choirboys costumed in pale blue satin trimmed in lace and with plumed, wide-brimmed hats perform a ritualistic dance called *Los Seises* (Dance of Sixes) before the altar of the cathedral in Seville. The dancers, whose costumes reflect the attire of seventeenth century page-boys, originally numbered six but have increased to ten. As the boys dance, they sing an Advent hymn invoking the presence of Jesus. From December 16 through 24, villages observe a Novena, a devotional period of nine days, in which the Nativity scene, known either as *Nacimiento* ("Birth") or *Belén* ("Bethlehem") is the central figure, although the Christmas tree and Santa Claus are becoming more popular. *Belenistas* are clubs or organizations that sponsor competitions and displays of Nativity scenes. Homes and businesses light small oil lamps that illuminate statues of the Virgin, and the Christmas markets are filled with all manner of fruits, decorations, flowers, sweets, and handmade gifts. Pageantry, dancing, and Nativity plays abound, as do *tuna*, groups of university students in traditional garb who provide entertainment by singing and playing *villancicos* (traditional carols). Folk instruments commonly providing accompaniment include the tambourine, *sonaja* (a round percussion instrument), *zambomba* (a hollow, drum-like instrument that produces a rhythmic wail), castanets in the southern regions, and bagpipes in the northwest regions.

Before the *Noche Buena* (literally "Good Night," Christmas Eve) Midnight Mass, known as the *Misa del Gallo* (Mass of the Rooster), the immediate and extended family gathers for a Christmas Eve dinner of multiple courses, the dishes of which vary from region to region. Fairly universal courses, however, include *escudella* (soup with meatballs and grated cheese); turkey stuffed with bacon, sausage, or ham; pork; *paella* (saffron-flavored rice); *flan* (caramel custard); *besugo* (Mediterranean sea bream) or flounder; roasted chestnuts; marzipan; fruit; *turrón* (nougat candy); and assorted wines. In the region of Galicia, the principal courses consist of *bacalao* (codfish) and suckling pig or meat pie; in Aragon, lamb or chicken; in Madrid, turkey with red cabbage. Festivities include dancing and singing traditional carols around the Nativity scene (which receives the figure of the Christ Child only on Christmas Eve), with the merry-making continuing until Epiphany, January 6. Although children may receive gifts on Christmas morning, the traditional gift-giving day is Epiphany (see below).

On Christmas night, citizens gather at the village square to draw from the "Urn of Fate," which contains all participants' names individually written on slips of paper. As the names are drawn out by twos, according to custom, each pair will be friends for the coming year. If an unmarried man and woman pair, fate may precipitate their marriage.

In Basque folklore, the ancient pagan figure Olentzero, a mountain-dwelling coal miner, descends into villages on Christmas Eve with the good news that Christ is born. Abandoned at birth, Olentzero was raised by a woodland couple after a fairy brought him to them. He grew up a favorite of children and made toys for them, giving his life to save them in a time of calamity. The fairy bestowed immortality on Olentzero, and he returns each year during the time of the winter solstice with gifts for children. Over time, his annual mission acquired a Christmas theme. He is depicted as a plump, straw- or herb-stuffed doll wearing a regional *boine* (cap), woolen socks and goatskin vest, and carrying a wine flask and a frying pan. In Olentzero parades, men dress the part and are carried about on the shoulders of their comrades.

Children in Cádiz often participate in "Swinging in the Sun" and compete to swing the highest in conventional swings. The purpose, derived from ancient winter solstice festivals, is to lead the sun back north and encourage the coming of spring. Another solstice custom, common in Granada and Jaén, is *Hogueras* (bonfires); it is believed that jumping over fires will provide protection against illness. Although *piñatas* are not commonly seen in Spain as in Mexico, an equivalent activity for Christmas Day exists in the Catalonian "Lucky Strike Game." A *tío* (hollow Yule log) is decorated and filled with small gifts or other treats, and when it is suspended overhead, children hit the log with sticks until the gifts tumble from the trunk. Catalonian boys beat Yule logs with sticks on Christmas Day to bring luck for the new year and drag them from door to door in anticipation of treats.

December 28, Holy Innocents Day or Fools Festival, recalls the Feast of Fools of medieval Europe. Masked men choose a mayor to supervise ludicrous activities. Dressed as clowns or women, the men search out businesses against which mock charges and fines are levied if their commands are not obeyed. In the evening, citizens convene to hear a litany of "crimes" that were committed. The fines received are used to fund the festivities.

Just before midnight on New Year's Eve, one must swallow 12 grapes to ensure good health and fortune for the coming year. The event is most popularly celebrated at the *Puerta del Sol* (Gate of the Sun) in Madrid, along with festive parties with revelers in costumes and masks. To ensure luck for the new year, Spaniards consume pork, for the pig roots in a forward direction; likewise, fowls are not consumed on New Year's Eve, because they scratch backward for food, a sign of bad luck.

The Christmas season ends on Epiphany, January 6. Tradition holds that the three Wise Men passed through Spain on their journey to Bethlehem, arriving there on Epiphany. Therefore the day is known as *Día de los Tres Reyes* ("Day of the Three Kings"). In the weeks prior to Epiphany, children write letters to the Magi with requests for gifts and visit them in department stores, much like children do in the United states with Santa Claus. Magi parades, known as *cabalgatas*, along with figures of the Magi and people costumed as the Kings prevail

throughout and are usually held on Epiphany eve. Also on this eve, children fill their shoes with barley or straw for the royal camels and set them on window sills, balconies, or doorsteps as receptacles to be filled with gifts by the Three Kings, particularly by the black king Balthazar; the Kings reject the camel fodder from naughty children and leave either a lump of coal or nothing at all. Some parents may mark their children's cheeks with coal or dark ash while they sleep, so that, upon awakening, the children will believe that Balthazar kissed them during the night.

A favorite Epiphany treat is *roscón*, a fruitcake that contains a small toy. Whoever finds the toy in his slice will receive good luck in the new year.

"Merry Christmas" in the Spanish language of Spain is *Felices Pascuas de Navidad*; in the Basque language, *Zorionak eta Urte Berri On*; in Catalan, *Bon Nadal*.

See also **Epiphany; Feast of Fools; Feast of the Immaculate Conception; Holy Innocents Day; Mass of the Rooster; Nativity Scene.**

The Spirit
See **The Waltons**

The Spirit of Christmas
See **A Christmas Carol** (Film and Television Versions)

Sri Lanka
See **Asia and the South Pacific**

The Star Carol
See **Alfred Burt Carols**

Star in the East
See **Brightest and Best of the Sons of the Morning; Nativity; Star of Bethlehem**

Star of Bethlehem
Term applied to the celestial phenomenon that appeared to the Wise Men or Magi and guided their journey from the East to the Christ Child in Bethlehem, as outlined in the Gospel of Matthew 2:1–12. This phenomenon has been the subject of much speculation, with modern explanations ranging from the purely supernatural to actual astronomical events. Concerning the former, Matthew's Gospel describes

the Star as moving ahead of the Wise Men and eventually standing over the site where the Child resided, implying that it had a will of its own. To that end, various Gnostic texts, works originating in the second and third centuries and considered heretical by the Roman Catholic Church, further state that not only did the Star first appear two years prior to Jesus' birth (as does Matthew), but that it was a "secret power" that appeared like a star, the actions of which behaved contrary to those of other heavenly bodies. Whereas the paths of the latter normally appeared to move from east to west (due to the earth's rotation), the Star coursed "north to south" (Bethlehem lies southwest of Persia, whence the Wise Men are believed to have begun their journey), was visible during the day as well as the night, and varied its height in the heavens relative to the other stars. Thus the Gnostic texts imply a supernatural force behind the Star.

On the other hand, the most popular astronomical theory, first proposed by the German astronomer Johannes Kepler (1571–1630), is a conjunction of planets, which would have appeared as a very bright "star." Indeed, by modern calculations, three different conjunctions of Mars, Jupiter, and Saturn occurred in 7 B.C. Other conjunctions include those of Venus and Jupiter in 3 B.C. and in 2 B.C.; and of Jupiter with Regulus, a star of the first magnitude in the constellation Leo, once in 3 B.C. and twice in 2 B.C. These dates all correspond to two time frames proposed for Jesus' birth: between 7 and 4 B.C. (based on scholarly claims that King Herod the Great of the Nativity story died in 4 B.C. shortly after Jesus was born) and about 3–2 B.C. (based on other claims that Herod died in 1 B.C.).

See also **Nativity; Wise Men.**

Stealing Christmas

(2003). Made-for-television drama.

When his attempted robbery of a Chicago department store goes awry, Jack Clayton (Tony Danza) hops a bus out of town disguised as Santa and lands in the peaceful, rural town of Evergreen three weeks before Christmas. Mistaken as the Santa whom the young widow Sarah Gibson (Lea Thompson) has hired to promote her Christmas tree farm, Jack, alias

Shepherds are awed by the angel announcing the birth of Christ in Bethlehem, over which the brilliant star is shining. From John Fleetwood, The Light in the East *(National Publishing Co. and Jones Brothers, 1874).*

Oscar Burton, plays along while plotting to rob the local bank on Christmas Eve.

First, a most personable "Santa" easily wins the trust of Evergreen's naïve citizens, including Sarah's rebellious teenage daughter Noelle (Angela Goethals) and Emily Sutton (Betty White), whose year-round Christmas shop lies adjacent to the bank. Next, to boost Evergreen's failing economy (and stuff the bank vault), Jack convinces the citizens to hold a lottery. Third, to gain access to the bank, Jack plants accomplice Harry Zordich (David Parker) as an elf in Emily's store.

By Christmas Eve, however, Jack has a change of heart, won over by Evergreen's down-home family values, friendships, and the strong love that he, Sarah, and Noelle now share; all positive experiences that Jack has lacked in his life. Bounding from the Christmas Eve candlelight service after a muffled explosion signals that Harry has blown the vault, Jack subdues Harry but is arrested on the scene.

He serves one year in prison, yet despite having betrayed their trust, Jack receives forgiveness and a second chance from his friends in Evergreen, especially from Sarah and Noelle, who need "Santa" back on their farm.

Story by Greg Taylor. Screenplay by Lucky Gold. Produced by Oscar Luis Costo. Directed by Gregg Champion. Raffaella Productions. DVD: UMVD. 90 min.

The Stingiest Man in Town

See **A Christmas Carol** (Film and Television Versions)

Stockings

See **Saint Nicholas; Saint Nicholas's Day**

The Story of Holly and Ivy

Classic children's book by British author Margaret Rumer Godden (professional name Rumer Godden), the text for which was first published in *Ladies' Home Journal* in 1958.

For six-year-old Ivy, a runaway child from St. Agnes Orphanage, having a doll and finding a real grandmother are her fondest Christmas wishes. Holly, a beautiful doll adorned in red in Mr. Blossom's toy shop, wishes not only to find "my Christmas girl," that is, a little girl who would want her as a Christmas gift, but also to be free of the cantankerous owl, another doll that berates her and all the other toys in the shop. And for Albert Jones and his wife, a middle-aged, childless couple, their wish is to share the love of Christmas with a child. In this wishing story, the magic of Christmas unites Holly, Ivy, and the Joneses together in a special bond of love.

A made-for-television animated cartoon version, titled *The Wish That Changed Christmas* (1991), included only minor alterations from the printed original and featured the voices of Paul Winfield and Jonathan Winters. Written by Romeo Muller. Produced by Nicole Paradis Grindle. Directed by Catherine Margerin. Children's Television Workshop. VHS: Republic Pictures Home Video. 23 min.

Author and translator Rumer Godden (1907–1998) centered her fiction principally around foreigners in exotic lands, particularly in India, where she wrote novels for adults and children. Her children's books, which often featured dolls in worlds of their own, included *A Doll's House*, *The Rocking Horse Secret*, and *The Mousewife*.

Sugar Bowl

See **New Year's Day**

Sugarplums

Now-archaic term, synonymous with "bonbons," describing rich, chocolate confections usually filled with fruit preserves or cream fillings. Hence, the name is a misnomer (implying sugar-coated plums), unless the filling consists of plum preserves. Actually, "plum" is an obscure, generic term for "fruit," as the "plum" in plum pudding (also a misnomer because it contains no plums) is known to imply the raisins and other fruits that may be present.

The term "sugarplums" has remained a traditional element of Christmas, at least in concept, and has been perpetuated primarily through two sources: the classic poem "A Visit from St. Nicholas" ("'Twas the Night before Christmas"), in which the children's Christmas Eve dreams include "visions of sugarplums," and Tchaikovsky's ballet *The Nutcracker* with its "Dance of the Sugar-Plum Fairy," featuring a central character in the Kingdom of Sweets.

Superstitions

Christmas is associated with numerous superstitions derived from pagan European folklore, which has blended with Christian beliefs over two millennia. The sources for many are quite obscure but a few can be traced to specific countries. In the following illustrative compilation — by no means exhaustive — countries or regions of origin, where known, are indicated in parentheses. Other superstitions pertinent to specific countries are listed in the entries for those countries.

The number of happy months a person can expect in the coming year is determined by the number of different homes in which mince pie is eaten during the holidays.

On Christmas Eve, pour melted lead into cold water. The pattern of hardened metal in the water enables an unmarried woman to determine her future husband's initials, appearance, or profession. To predict the future in general, Germans carry out this practice, *Bleigiessen*, on New Year's Eve.

Water turns to wine at midnight on Christmas Eve.

Place a branch of a cherry tree in water indoors on the first day of Advent (or on St. Barbara's Day, December 4, or on St. Lucia's Day, December 13). If it blooms by Christmas, good luck is in store. An alternative version states that a branch blooming for a maiden portends marriage in the coming new year.

A child born on Christmas Eve or Christmas Day will have good fortune.

A child born during the 12 nights of Christmas may become a *kallikantzari*, an evil, half-human monster (Greece); or a werewolf (Germany and Poland).

If an unmarried woman allows a bowl of water to freeze overnight on Christmas Eve, the ice patterns seen on Christmas morning will disclose her heart's desire.

If an unmarried woman lies on the floor on New Year's Eve and tosses her shoe backward over her head, the toe points in the direction from which her future husband will come.

Eating an apple on Christmas Eve brings good health for the coming year.

Refusing mince pie at Christmas dinner brings bad luck for a year.

Buried treasure reveals itself during the reading of Christ's genealogy at Midnight Mass.

The woman accepting edelweiss at Christmas also accepts the man who presents it (Switzerland).

On Christmas Eve, if an unmarried woman peels an apple, making sure it remains as a single ribbon, and if she throws it on the floor from above her head, the pattern of the peeling on the floor will disclose her future husband's initials.

Burning old shoes during the Christmas season prevents misfortune in the coming year (Greece).

A windy Christmas day brings good luck.

The weather on each of the 12 days of Christmas will determine the weather for the corresponding month in the coming year.

During the 12 days of Christmas, place a blindfolded goose in a circle of unwed girls. The first girl that the goose touches will be the first to wed.

At midnight on Christmas Eve, animals are empowered with speech, cattle kneel facing east, and bees hum Psalm 100.

A fire (Yule log) burning all through the 12 days of Christmas brings good luck. Likewise, bad luck is in store should the fire go out.

The gates of paradise are always open on Christmas Eve; those who die at this time may avoid purgatory (Ireland).

He whose appetite fails first at Christmas will be the first to die.

On Christmas Eve, if a girl knocks on the henhouse door and a rooster crows, she will marry within the year.

Place shoes side-by-side on Christmas Eve to prevent family quarrels (Scandinavia).

The spouse who first brings holly into the home for Christmas will rule the home in the coming year. Alternative: Prickly holly signifies that the husband will rule; smooth holly, the wife will rule.

Bread baked on Christmas day never molds.

Leaving a loaf of bread on the table after Christmas Eve dinner assures bread for the coming year.

A clear sky on Christmas Eve promises good crops for the following summer.

From cockcrow until dawn on Christmas Day, trolls roam the land (Sweden).

Washing an item of clothing before it is given as a Christmas gift spoils the good luck of the gift.

On Christmas Eve, tie a plum cake to a cow's horn and throw cider into her face. If the cake falls off, the harvest will be plentiful (England).

Wearing new shoes on Christmas Day brings bad luck (England).

Eating a raw egg before eating anything else on Christmas morning enables one to carry heavy weights.

A cat meowing on Christmas Day predicts bad luck (American Appalachia).

Any dreams experienced during the 12 nights of Christmas will come true (Germany).

Discarding evergreen decorations without burning them brings bad luck.

Discarding ashes on Christmas Day is equivalent to throwing them into the face of Christ.

Ashes from the Yule log will protect a household all year from natural disasters; if soaked in water, they form a cure for all manner of illnesses.

Eating plum pudding on Christmas Day assures having a friend for the coming year (England).

On Christmas Eve, the former priest of a parish conducts Midnight Mass for the dead, who are believed to rise and kneel at the cemetery cross; afterwards, these souls return to their graves (French Canada).

If a man lies in a coffin during the 12 nights of Christmas, someone from his community will die each month in the coming year (Germany).

A girl may see an image of her future husband if she approaches a pear tree backwards and walks around it three times on Christmas Eve.

During the 12 days of Christmas, a girl wishing to wed the man of her dreams throws her shoe into a pear tree up to 12 times. If the shoe remains in the tree at least once, her wish will come true (Germany).

Suzy Snowflake

Popular American song written in 1951 by New York natives Sid Tepper and Roy Bennett, dedicated to Tepper's baby daughter Susan. A light, generic winter song, its lyrics mirthfully personify a snowflake as a little girl dressed in a white gown who is eager to frolic with anyone in her medium, particularly if one is interested in building a snowman or in taking a sleigh ride. Rosemary Clooney first recorded the song in 1951 on the Columbia label, and it received chart status. Although the song never mentions Christmas, it has found its way into the season through popular association.

Tepper and Bennett also collaborated on a number of other hits, such as "Red Roses for a Blue Lady (1948), "The Naughty Lady of Shady Lane" (1954), and the novelty tune "Nuttin' for Christmas" (1955).

See also **Nuttin' for Christmas.**

Sweden

This nation has enjoyed Christmas since the ninth and tenth centuries, when Frankish missionaries brought Christianity to Swedish Vikings, and Olaf Skotkonung became the first Swedish king to convert to the new faith. As the Protestant Reformation swept northward from Germany during the sixteenth century, Sweden embraced Lutheranism as its principal faith, which now exists as the Evangelical Lutheran Church of Sweden. Christmas customs blend some traditions of the ancient winter solstice festival of *Jul* (Yule) with Christian beliefs.

The Advent season features Advent candles; Advent stars fashioned from paper, wood, straw, or metal; and Advent calendars, the latter two decorations having been introduced in the early twentieth century from Germany. During the season, friends gather informally to partake of a custom hosted by virtually every restaurant in the nation during the early weeks of December, the "Christmas Dinner Table." A holiday buffet or *smörgåsbord*, the menu often features pickled herring, liver pâté, hot and cold pork products of every kind, cabbage, "Jansson's Temptation" (creamed potatoes seasoned with onions and anchovies), fried meatballs, rye bread, and schnapps. A custom common in rural areas is to erect a sheaf of wheat on a pole for birds, the so-called Birds' Christmas Tree.

The Christmas season officially opens on *Luciadagen* (Lucia or Lucy Day, December 13). The name is coincident with that of an Italian (Sicilian) saint martyred around A.D. 304, about whom many legends have circulated but with whom Sweden shares nothing else in common, except for the Italian folk song "Santa Lucia" (see below). The term "Saint" is not used in reference to Lucia in Sweden. Although some legends hold that Christianized Vikings instituted the celebration after hearing tales that St. Lucia brought gifts of food and light to starving Sicilians, with similar events allegedly transpiring later in Sweden, some scholars contend that Sweden's Lucia derived as a Protestant replacement for St. Nicholas instead. Because the Protestant Reformation forbade the adoration of saints, St. Nicholas was replaced as the bearer of gifts with *Christkindlein* ("Little Christ Child," or more specifically His messenger), who brought gifts on Christmas Day instead of December 6, St. Nicholas's Day. In Germany, this messenger appeared as a young girl clothed in white with wings and a golden crown and who carried a small fir tree, symbolic of eternal life. Sweden also adopted this figure in the seventeenth and eighteenth centuries but transferred her to December 13 (the date of the winter solstice prior to the adoption of the Gregorian calendar), where she presided over the tradition of a large, early morning breakfast served in wealthy establishments. A Christmas fast, a tradition dating to the Middle Ages, immediately followed this meal and extended until Christmas. This female figure assumed the name "Lucia" based on *lux* (Latin, "light") and the winter solstice. She kept the white gown, added a red sash, shed the wings and fir tree, and replaced the golden crown with a wreath of lingonberry sprigs containing lighted candles.

By the nineteenth century, Lucia had evolved into a simple household tradition. The youngest daughter would rise at dawn and, attired as Lucia, serve coffee and *lussekatt* ("Lucia cats," saffron buns) to her family. Any sisters or young female friends would follow, attired in white with halos of tinsel, and each would carry a lighted candle. Any brothers present would assume roles as *stjärn gossar* ("star boys") by donning tall, white, pointed hats adorned with stars, while someone dressed as a *tomten* (elf) formed the last of the procession, and together the entire group would parade through the house singing the Italian folk song "Santa Lucia" as well as Swedish carols.

Today, in addition to the family ritual described above, Sweden celebrates Lucia at the public level with Lucia parades, which date to the 1920s. Virtually all institutions, schools, and offices crown their own Lucia "Queen of Light," as does each city through a series of beauty competitions. Lastly, the winner of the Nobel Prize in Literature crowns a national Lucia in Stockholm, and together she and Lucias from other regions participate in an evening parade, first held in Stockholm in 1927.

Advent continues as homes sport decorations of winter greenery, Nativity scenes, and Christmas trees adorned with candles and sweets. Sweden adopted Christmas trees from Germany during the mid-1800s, while Nativity scenes, initially resisted as Roman Catholic

A little girl flying over the world on a little pig on Christmas Eve. Perhaps the Julgrisen *(Christmas pig) relates not only to the suckling pigs and boar's heads of Christmas feasts, but also to the Norse goddess Freya and her golden boar. Scattered throughout the secular Christmas world history are gift bearers riding unusual steeds, high above the earth, from Odin on his eight-legged horse Sleipner, to Odin's son Thor riding on a chariot pulled by two billy goats, Gnasher and Cracker, to Santa and all his reindeer. From* Harper's Young People, *December 26, 1882.*

symbols, found their way into Lutheran homes and churches by the early twentieth century.

On *Julafton* (Christmas Eve), families congregate for the traditional midday meal. Prior to this, some families may observe an old custom, "Dipping in the Kettle," commemorative of a long-past famine, by eating pieces of dark bread dipped into a pot that contains the drippings of pork and corned beef. Then dinner is served, which consists of the *smörgåsbord* with its numerous varieties of pork products, along with *lutefisk* (codfish treated with lye and served with a white sauce and seasonings), *pepparkakor* ("pepper cakes," actually gingersnaps), and rice pudding. It is a typically Scandinavian custom to hide one almond in the batch of pudding, and the one finding it in his serving is said to receive luck. In Sweden, the recipient must also compose a "porridge rhyme."

Rhymes continue after the meal with the distribution of *Julklapp* ("Christmas knocks"), the term for Christmas presents. This term derives from bygone days when it was customary on Christmas night to knock loudly on doors, then quickly toss in gifts and depart before those inside could identify the giver, who provided a mischievous flare by attaching comical or satirical rhymes about the gifts' contents, the recipient, or the giver. Sometimes the recipient found that he must open a series of empty boxes, each stuffed within another, before finding the gift in the smallest, innermost box. At the extreme, a giver sent the recipient scrambling on a treasure hunt by inserting clues within several boxes strategically hidden about the property. Today, poems still accompany Christmas gifts.

Also on Christmas Eve, Swedish television broadcasts a special service from Turku, Finland. This service formally declares the "Peace of Christmas" in Scandinavia (*see* **Finland**).

While St. Nicholas has traditionally remained the principal bearer of Christmas gifts in Europe, the gift-bringer in Sweden has varied over the centuries. The oldest of these, *Julbock* ("Christmas goat"), derives from pre-Christian Yule festivals, which paid homage to the gods. At the winter solstice, it was believed that, as he rode through the skies in a chariot pulled by two billy goats named Gnasher and Cracker, Thor distributed gifts to the Vikings, while his father Odin, riding the white, eight-legged steed Sleipner, escorted the souls of slain heroes into Valhalla. Men costumed as goats portrayed this belief by making surprise entrances at Yule parties, and after dancing about, "died," and returned to life. During the Middle Ages, the goat figure symbolized the Devil in Scandinavian Christmas folk revels, and men costumed in goatskins and masks frolicked about, much to the dismay of the Church, which banned such behavior in the sixteenth century. By the eighteenth century, this masked *Julbock* had evolved into the holiday gift-bringer, and the figure, now often fashioned from straw, remains as Sweden's oldest Christmas symbol.

In the 1880s, Swedish artist Jenny Nyström created a large series of Christmas cards that combined the traditional physical features of St. Nicholas with those of the *tomten*, a small, aged, mischievous elf who, according to rural folklore, guarded the home and farm throughout the year. Any mishaps occurring around the house were attributed to his pranks, and he required an annual bowl of rice porridge on Christmas Eve to appease him. Thus emerged the *Jultomten* ("Christmas elf"), who replaced the *Julbock* as the principal gift-bringer. Today on Christmas Eve, someone in each household, disguised as the *Jultomten* with white beard, pointed red cap, and toting a sack of gifts, raps loudly on the door and cries, "Are there any good children here?"

Christmas Day is spent with family, who perhaps attend the 7 A.M. *Julottan* (Christmas church service), but people celebrate *Nyårsafton* (New Year's Eve) with friends at parties amid noise and fireworks. In former days, noisemaking at this time supposedly kept evil out of the new year, and one may still find those who attempt to peer into the future through such devices as interpreting the shape formed when hot lead is poured into water (*see* **Superstitions**). Formerly, "star boys" dressed as the Wise Men or other Nativity characters performed dramas among households and collected donations on Epiphany, a custom that became obscure after the nineteenth century. Today, star boys primarily accompany Lucia processions.

The Christmas season terminates 20 days after Christmas Day on *tjugondedag Knut* ("twentieth day Knut," January 13), a day named in honor of the Danish king Knut IV (also spelled Canute, Cnut, and Knud), who was assassinated in 1086. A strong supporter of the Church through acts of piety and charity, he was canonized in 1100. The exact origin of this 20-day feast is not known. According to some, Knut is said to have made such a decree; others claim that, because the Vikings feasted and offered human sacrifices on this day, the Church sought to stamp out such practices by extending Christmas through that date. In festivals today, home parties light the Christmas tree one last time, then the decorations are removed, the tree is dismantled and children retrieve its decorative sweets, and trees are often burned in communal bonfires.

"Merry Christmas" is *God Jul.*

See also **Advent.**

The Swinging Nutcracker
See **The Nutcracker**

Switzerland

Known as Helvetia to the ancient Romans, the region of Switzerland was conquered through a series of invasions by Germanic tribes from the fourth to the sixth century. The Frankish Empire principally brought Christianity and Christmas to Switzerland by the eighth century, although the Irish monk St. Gall had established a monastery in this land around 613.

Lying in proximity to France, Germany, and Italy, Switzerland's 23 states or cantons (three of which are divided into half-cantons) reflect considerable cultural diversity, especially during the holiday season. The majority of cantons, those in the northern, eastern, and central regions, speak Swiss-German, a German dialect; the western cantons of Fribourg, Geneva, Jura, Neuchâtel, Valais, and Vaud reflect the French language and customs; and the southern canton of Ticino is predominantly Italian. These cantons mirror those customs of the three bordering countries, the entries for which provide further discussion. The remainder of this entry is concerned with customs unique to several Swiss cities and cantons.

During the Advent season, Christmas markets and bazaars flourish throughout the country, and cities such as Zurich, Bern, and Basel feature decorated *Weihnachtstramer* (Christmas trolleys) operated by conductors in the guise of Santa. Swiss-German cantons are noted for their *Weihnachtsguetzli* (Christmas cookies), especially *Tirggel* from Zurich, flat cookies of flour and honey that take origin from pagan Germanic sacrificial cakes served in the days before sugar was known in Europe. Once fashioned in animal shapes, *Tirggel* now bear religious scenes and figures. Also favored by many are *Leckerli* from Basel, spiced almond cookies that date to medieval times.

In most cities, carolers parade through the streets. Noted among these are the *Sternsinger* (star singers) of Swiss-German cantons, who bear illuminated stars and are accompanied by people dressed as the Wise Men and the Holy Family. Theaters usually feature a production of *D'Zaller Weihnacht* (*A Swiss Nativity*), a play by Swiss composer Paul Burkhard (1911–1977), and those who most appreciate Nativity scenes will enjoy the Bethlehem Diorama in Einsiedeln, Schwyz canton. Consisting of some 500 carved wooden images, the diorama stands adjacent to the city's Benedictine monastery, founded in the ninth century.

Citizens of Graubünden, the largest and most diverse canton (the languages of Swiss-German, Italian, and Romansh are all spoken here) decorate their homes with evergreens and cover the exteriors with *sgraffito* etchings of the season. After applying whitewash to the dark stucco walls, homeowners create drawings by etching through the dried coating. To Catholic citizens of Graubünden, the Christmas gift-bringer remains St. Nicholas; to the Protestants, however, it is *Sontgaclau*, a composite of the saint and a mean-spirited being who bears switches. Christmas trees and *Purseppen* (Nativity scenes) remain the chief holiday symbols, and the Christmas meal is likely to feature *Bündnerfleisch* (dried beef). This canton is famous for its *Churer Zimmetstern* (star-shaped, cinnamon cookies).

To dispel any evil spirits lurking about, loud noises—for example, ringing cowbells, cracking whips, and blowing horns— greet St. Nicholas's Day celebrations and parades throughout Switzerland on December 6. Attired in traditional bishop's robes with mitre and staff, a man portraying St. Nicholas parades about on a horse or donkey while distributing treats to children. Accompanying him especially in Swiss-German cantons is an antithetical demon, *Schmutzli*, who carries switches and a sack in which to stuff naughty youngsters. On St. Nicholas's Eve, children put out their shoes to be filled with small gifts. The city of Küssnacht in Schwyz canton hosts the *Klausjagen* ("Pursuit of St. Nicholas") on St. Nicholas's Eve, in which citizens dress as St. Nicholas and wear *Iffele*, gigantic, elaborately decorated mitres illuminated with candles. In a related custom, Hallwil in Aargau canton hosts the *Chlauswettchloöpfe* (St. Nicholas's

Day whip-cracking competition), which selects six young teenage boys to participate in its *Chlausjage* on the following day. There, the six champions portray mischievous spirits who visit homes and distribute gifts or warnings to children as their past behavior warrants. In festivities elsewhere, citizens frequently mimic St. Nicholas in his clerical attire.

Processions also dominate Christmas Eve. Young teenage girls of Hallwil form groups of seven, one of whom, veiled in white, poses as the *Wienechtchind* ("Christmas Child"), the other six as her attendants. As they travel from house to house, the Child greets each family with a silent handshake and distributes treats to any children present; then she and her attendants depart after the attendants have sung a carol. Men in the cities of Rheinfelden and Ziefen don black attire including "stovepipe" hats of great height in preparation for, respectively, *Brunnensingen* ("Fountain Singing") and *Nünichlinger* ("Ringing of Bells at 9 P.M."). In the former, kept as a memorial to the bubonic plague epidemic of 1348, 12 from the Brotherhood of St. Sebastian proceed to seven different city fountains, at which they sing a carol, removing their hats when the lyrics mention the deity. In the latter, groups of men parade through the streets ringing large bells at the appointed hour and are led by a white-bearded man carrying a sooty rag on a pole. A personification of *Samichlaus* (St. Nicholas), this leader once anointed people with the soot to expel evil spirits.

Noise, commotion, and masquerades continue on New Year's Eve, also known as St. Sylvester's Day (Sylvester I was the first pope to hold office after Constantine the Great accepted Christianity in the fourth century). The most intricate of these celebrations is the *Silvesterkläuse* of Appenzell canton, especially in the city of Urnäsch. Only males participate, donning one of three bizarre costumes known as *Chläuse*: *Schöne* ("pretty," depicting either a man or woman with a large, ornate headdress), *Wüeschti* ("ugly," depicting a demon clad in assorted forest vegetation), or *Schö-Wüeschti* ("less ugly"). All *Chläuse* travel through the streets yodeling and ringing large bells affixed to their costumes. A related custom is the *Achetringele* ("Ring Bells Downhill") of Laupen, Bern canton. Groups of boys carrying either large bells, brooms, or pigs' bladders inflated with air, call out New Year's wishes as they parade from the hills into town, then hurl the bladders toward young girls in fulfillment of a fertility rite now completely obscure. At 6 P.M. children carrying homemade lanterns parade through the city of Wil and sing carols to the beat of drums, a custom known as the *Silvesterumzug*. By 11:50 P.M., the villagers of Hallwil have assembled around a bonfire on the hill above town, at which time eight men commence rhythmic beating on a threshing board. Moments before midnight they cease, but as the New Year arrives, they resume with greater zeal, thus "beating" away evil spirits.

Another pagan ritual most likely derived from an obscure festival anticipating spring forms the theme of *Bärzelitag* (Berthold's Day), January 2. Notably observed in Hallwil, the day is filled with pranks and mischief, committed by 15 young, unmarried people. Five of them must masquerade as the "Green" (symbols of spring and life), and five as the "Parched Brown" (symbols of winter and death). According to *Christmas in Switzerland*, the other five portray a camel and its drivers.

Epiphany, with its Three Kings pageants and Kings' cakes, concludes the Christmas season.

"Merry Christmas" may be said in any one of several languages: *Schöne Weihnachten* (Swiss-German); *Joyeux Noël* (French); *Buone Feste Natalizie* (Italian); *Legreivlas Fiastas da Nadal* (Romansh).

See also **Advent**; **Epiphany**; **France**; **Germany**; **Italy**; **Saint Nicholas's Day**.

Syria
See **Middle East**

T

There Is No Rose of Such Virtue

English traditional carol dating to an early fifteenth century manuscript, which resides at Trinity College, Cambridge. Incorporating a typically medieval concept, this anonymous, macaronic carol (a mixture of English and Latin) metaphorically depicts the Virgin Mary as a flowering Rose, whose younger flower is the Infant Jesus. This is also the theme of another popular carol, "Lo, How a Rose E'er Blooming."

Each of the five verses in English terminates with Latin phrases. The first two verses introduce the Rose concept, ending respectively with "*Alleluia*" and "*Res miranda*" ("A wonderful thing"). Verse three declares that through the Rose will mankind see God as the Trinity "*Pari forma*" ("Of the same form"). Verse four recalls the angelic chorus to the shepherds and urges, "*Gaudeamus*" ("Let us rejoice"). Verse five urges all to put away earthly pleasure and seek Him Who is born, with the admonition "*Transeamus*" ("Let us go").

The carol has enjoyed two other noteworthy musical settings, one by the English composer Benjamin Britten (1913–1976), included in his *A Ceremony of Carols* (1942) for treble voices and harp. The other is by the South African composer John Joubert (1927–) for unaccompanied voices (1954).

See also **A Ceremony of Carols; Lo, How a Rose E'er Blooming.**

This Christmas

American song written by Chicago-born soul artist Donny Hathaway with Nadine McKinnor. A staple on radio play lists and soul Christmas compilations, it was featured on *Soulful Christmas*, a 1968 compilation album now available on compact disc from Time Life. The song has been recorded by a host of artists in the soul and rhythm-and-blues genres, including Gladys Knight, the Temptations, Peabo Bryson, Usher, Ashanti, and Ruben Studdard. It also appeared on the soundtrack for the 2002 motion picture *Friday after Next*.

The secular lyrics suggest that trimming the Christmas tree with that special someone in a fireside setting and with mistletoe nearby will provide a most romantic, holiday experience.

"This Christmas" was not among the 25 most frequently performed Christmas songs of the twentieth century as listed by the American Society of Composers, Authors and Publishers (ASCAP). By December 2004, however, the song's increasing popularity had merited position 25 on the ASCAP list.

Hathaway and McKinnor also collaborated on "Sands of Time and Changes" and "Take a Love Song."

See also **ASCAP List of Christmas Songs.**

This Is Christmas

See **Alfred Burt Carols**

Thou Didst Leave Thy Throne

English carol, the lyrics of which comprise the only poem of note written in 1864 by hymnist Emily E.S. Elliott (1836–1897) of Brighton.

The lyrics are a brief narrative of significant scriptural events in the life of Christ, beginning with the Nativity in the first two verses and concluding with His crucifixion and the hope of redemption at His second coming. Ms. Elliott's approach to the Nativity is unusual in that she elaborates on what Christ left behind in heaven when He came to earth in human form. Matched with an 1876 tune by Anglican clergyman and organist Timothy R. Matthews (1826–1910), this carol often appears in contemporary hymnals.

Three Days

(2001). Made-for-television drama.

Beth Farmer (Kristin Davis) simply radiates the Christmas spirit, yet her husband Andrew (Reed Diamond), an ambitious Boston literary agent, hardly notices the holidays, much less her. Three days before Christmas,

Andrew departs on a business trip along with his voluptuous assistant, and Beth fears that her troubled marriage of ten years has ended. When Andrew returns late on Christmas Eve, Beth bitterly accuses him of infidelity and storms outdoors, only to be struck and killed by a passing car while attempting to rescue a neighbor's dog. More than grief-stricken, Andrew deeply regrets that Beth perished with the mistaken belief that he had betrayed her and prays for a second chance. The answer to his prayer is Lionel (Tim Meadows), an angel posing as a black locksmith. Andrew may relive the past three days with Beth in any way that he chooses, but Lionel advises that he use that time to prove his love for her. Nevertheless, on Christmas Eve at 11:58 P.M., Beth must meet her fate which, *with rare exception*, neither Lionel nor Andrew may alter.

A reincarnated Beth surprises Andrew with a desire to visit Mahone Bay, the quaint little town of their childhood that provides an idyllic, snowy Christmas setting of community carol singing and coziness. But when Andrew, now excessively solicitous, fails by conventional means to prove what he had always taken for granted, Lionel suggests that he consider a most special gift as a worthy and final present to his wife. And as a reminder that time is short, after Beth revives a little girl who was trapped in a children's snow fort, the child, recalling her near-death experience, describes the presence of angels who are waiting for Beth.

Complicating Andrew's task are Beth's desire to have children and her ulterior motive for bringing Andrew to Mahone Bay — to make peace with his estranged father, a widower now in ill health who, like Andrew, had neglected his family to make a buck. Andrew initially finds both options objectionable, yet after Beth angrily returns to Boston alone upon hearing more rumors of her husband's alleged out-of-town affair, Andrew has no choice but to become reconciled with his father at Lionel's insistence.

Dashing home on Christmas Eve to protect Beth, Andrew, fearing that she has left him, finds her musing in a nearby ice skating rink and fervently assures her of his loving fidelity and desire for a family, whereupon she reveals that she is pregnant. Andrew hopes this child is the gift that Lionel requires, but that is not the case. As midnight approaches, Beth steps into the street to rescue her neighbor's dog with Andrew on her heels. Lionel allows him to follow, for Andrew has vowed to give *anything* to save her. Shoving her from the path of the oncoming vehicle, Andrew lovingly takes her place in death — the ultimate gift and that rare exception about which Lionel had earlier referred. Having proven his love, Andrew receives the Christmas gift of life. The final scene cuts to a year later, as Andrew and Beth happily celebrate their first Christmas with their infant son, named Lionel, of course.

Written by Robert Tate Miller and Eric Tuchman. Produced by Randy Sutter. Directed by Michael Switzer. Von Zerneck–Sertner Films. Video N/A. 120 min.

Three Kings
See **Nativity; Wise Men**

The Three Kings
Poem by American poet Henry Wadsworth Longfellow (1807–1882). A narrative based on the Gospel account of the Wise Men in Matthew 2, its 14 verses follow the trek of the three traditional Magi, Melchior, Caspar, and Balthazar, on their search for the Child born "King of the Jews." Their gifts, according to Longfellow, are symbolic portents for Christ in later years: the gold is their tribute to a King, the frankincense is for the Priest and Paraclete (Holy Spirit), and the myrrh is to anoint His body for burial.

Longfellow's other works include such narrative poems as *Evangeline* (1847), *The Song of Hiawatha* (1855), and *The Courtship of Miles Standish* (1858).

Three Kings of Orient
See **We Three Kings of Orient Are**

Three Wise Men
See **Nativity; Wise Men**

Thyme
See **Christmas Plants**

'Tis the Fifteenth Season
See **The Simpsons**

'Tis the Season Christmas Trivia

Quiz game distributed by Debco, a division of Anton Publications of Downers Grove, Illinois. Designed for playing on *Trivial Pursuit* game boards, *'Tis the Season* consists of 1,800 holiday-oriented, short-answer questions printed on 300, 3½" × 2⅜" cards, each with questions in six categories on one side, the answers on the opposite. The categories are represented by symbols and include "History, Facts, and Figures" (star); "Traditions around the World" (candy cane); "Cartoons, Animation, Made-for-Television Movies, Specials" (Christmas tree); "Carols and Songs" (Yule log); "Movies on the Silver Screen" (candle); and "Literature and the Performing Arts" (tree ornament). Also included are instructions and score sheets for playing an alternate game, in which individuals or teams receive a successive letter in the word "Christmas" for each correct answer. The winner is the first to spell "Christmas" completely.

'Tis the Season to Be Smurfy

See **The Smurfs**

To Grandmother's House We Go

(1992). Made-for-television comedy featuring the Olsen twins, Ashley and Mary-Kate.

Believing that they are a burden to their single mom, Rhonda Thompson (Cynthia Geary), five-year-old twins Julie and Sarah plan to run away to their great-grandmother Mimi (Florence Patterson) for Christmas. Thinking that their mom's friend, parcel truck driver Eddie Popko (J. Eddie Peck), could take them, the twins stow away in Eddie's vehicle. Sarah's full bladder betrays their presence and forces a shocked Eddie to search for a truck stop, where the twins outline their mission.

A cowboy "wannabe" who is far more interested in playing the lottery than in looking after children, Eddie nevertheless treats the girls to lunch and later ice cream, for they must remain with him until his deliveries are completed. Seeing the adorable little girls with Eddie, customers are inspired to give generous tips. By evening, the three have become such good friends that, en route home, the twins are quite satisfied to listen to Eddie's passion: music on the radio by cowboy star Roy Rogers.

Just outside the twins' apartment, husband-and-wife bandits Shirley and dim-witted Harvey (Rhea Perlman and Jerry Van Dyke) overpower Eddie, steal his truck, kidnap the twins, and head for their motor home already laden with stolen Christmas gifts. The bandits, suggesting a $10,000 "reward" for "finding" the twins, set up a meeting with Rhonda to return the girls on Christmas Eve in Edgemont, their great-grandma's town. Because Eddie's ulterior motive for finding the twins lies in their holding his winning lottery ticket, which will allow him to spin for a million-dollar jackpot on television's "Win-O-Lotto," he hocks all the recovered Christmas gifts that were aboard his truck to raise the ransom.

At the Christmas Carnival in Edgemont, the twins escape in a horse-drawn wagon, which rapidly becomes a runaway. It's Eddie's big chance to redeem himself and fulfill the role of his dreams—a cowboy rescuing ladies (in this case little girls) in distress. Racing on a pony, he springs onto the team just as Roy Rogers would have done, and prevents the wagon from plunging off a cliff. With wills of their own, the horses return Eddie and the twins to great-grandma Mimi's house for a joyous reunion with Rhonda. The police, believing that Rhonda and Eddie robbed the parcel truck, arrive for the arrest, but soft-hearted Harvey confesses all.

Arriving back home at the television station with moments to spare, the twins spin and win the lottery for Eddie, who replaces the hocked gifts, and together the four make house deliveries late on Christmas Eve to satisfied customers.

With Stuart Margolin, Rick Poltaruk, and Venus Terzo. Written by Jeff Franklin and Boyd Hale. Produced by Mark Bacino. Directed by Jeff Franklin. Jeff Franklin Productions in association with Green/Epstein Productions in association with Warner Bros. Television. VHS: Warner Studios. 89 min.

Tobago

See **West Indies**

Tom and Jerry's Night before Christmas

(1991). Video collection of four classic,

theatrical animated cartoon "shorts" from the animation department of Metro-Goldwyn-Mayer Studios.

The Captain's Christmas (1938). This cartoon was part of the *Captain and the Kids* series, based on the United Features Syndicate comic strip *Katzenjammer Kids* by Rudolf Dirks. A crusty pirate and three henchmen usurp Santa's role to bring Christmas and mayhem to the Captain's family. Voice: Billy Bletcher. Produced by Fred Quimby. Directed by Friz Freleng.

One Ham's Family (1943). The Big Bad Wolf impersonates Santa while attempting to make Mama, Papa, and Junior Pig his Christmas dinner. However, he is no match for little Junior. Written by Rich Hogan. Produced by Fred Quimby. Directed by Tex Avery.

Toyland Broadcast (1934). Toys broadcast a musical revue over the radio from a toyshop. This cartoon was one of the first in the *Happy Harmonies* series, a group of musical cartoons created by former Disney animators Hugh Harman and Rudolf Ising, the series' producers. Directed by Rudolf Ising.

The Night before Christmas (1941). This features the Academy Award–winning team of Tom Cat and Jerry Mouse in their first holiday cartoon, as madcap antics reign under the tree on Christmas Eve. In 1942, this cartoon received an Academy nomination for Best Short Subjects Cartoons. Produced by Fred Quimby. Directed by William Hanna and Joseph Barbera.

VHS: Warner Home Video. 45 min.

See also **MGM Cartoon Christmas.**

Tomorrow Shall Be My Dancing Day

English traditional carol, believed to have arisen in the West Country during the fifteenth or sixteenth century. Consisting of eleven verses written in the first person singular, the carol poses Christ as presenting a complete narrative of His life, with verse 1 calling for " . . . my true love . . . / To see the legend of my play / To call my true love to the dance." Verses 2 and 3 describe His Nativity; verse 4, His baptism; verse 5, His temptation; verse 6, His interactions with Jewish leaders; verse 7, His betrayal; verse 8, His trial before Pilate; verse

9, His crucifixion; verse 10, His descent into hell and His resurrection; and verse 11, His ascension. The last line of each verse makes reference to Christ leading or bringing others to His dance, and a refrain addresses " . . . my love, / This have I done for my true love."

Whereas the seemingly romantic passages have been interpreted to represent Christ's expressions of love for His Church, the references to dancing and a "play" are believed to place the carol among those written for religious dramas of considerable length. Such dramas often included text that instructed the local musicians to strike up a dance tune either before or after certain segments of the play. In the case of "Tomorrow Shall Be My Dancing Day," the role of Christ in the first verse probably serves to call spectators' attention to the drama at hand. The references to "the dance" or "my dance" in the last line of each verse may signify a life with Christ, filled with joy and dancing.

The text for the carol first appeared in William Sandys's *Christmas Carols, Ancient and Modern* (London, 1833). The musical setting shares opening passages with two other traditional carols, one from Dorset in the West Country, "Rejoice and Be Merry"; the other from Wales, "Wel, dyma'r borau gorau i gyd" ("Behold! The Best of Mornings Is Here"). Russian-American composer Igor Stravinsky (1882–1971) also provided a musical setting in his *Cantata* (1951–52).

Tournament of Roses

See **New Year's Day**

The Town That Santa Forgot

(1993). Made-for-television animated cartoon that utilizes rhyming dialogue to present the moral that giving is truly better than receiving.

The epitome of the spoiled brat, little Jeremy Creek has a seemingly insatiable lust for toys and more toys. But instead of politely asking for them, he acquires each new toy by throwing tantrums that can be heard for miles until his parents and relatives fulfill his wishes. He has far more toys than other children, yet Jeremy refuses to share them, and eventually his parents decide that he will have no more toys. Undaunted, Jeremy then turns to Santa, but instead of waiting until Christmas to submit his list, Jeremy begins in June. Upon completion, his list is half a mile long.

When Jeremy's bulky list reaches the North Pole, 12 elves are required to unfurl it, and a bewildered Santa surmises that such a list naming virtually every toy imaginable could only have come from an entire town — not one person. Searching the map, Santa not only discovers a town by the name of Jeremy Creek, but it is a town that he has never previously visited. Thus on Christmas Eve, Santa delivers all the toys on the list to delighted little boys and girls in the town of Jeremy Creek, while little boy Jeremy Creek throws another tantrum for having received no Christmas toys. On Christmas morning, a television news broadcast carries an interview with a grateful little girl from Jeremy Creek, who expresses appreciation to the unknown person who wrote Santa on their behalf and thus brought untold happiness to all the children of her impoverished town. When Jeremy realizes that his greed had unwittingly been turned into good, his heart melts to the core, and the experience molds him into a generous person.

In 1994, this cartoon received an Emmy nomination for Outstanding Animated Programming (One Hour or Less).

Principal voices: Dick Van Dyke, Miko Hughes, Hal Smith, Haven Hartman, and Troy Davidson. Produced and directed by William Hanna and Joseph Barbera. Hanna-Barbera Productions. VHS: Hanna-Barbera Studios. 20 min.

See also **Hanna-Barbera Christmas Cartoons.**

A Town without Christmas

(2001). Made-for-television drama, the first in a series of Daniel H. Blatt productions to feature Peter Falk as Max, the mischievous angel.

Feeling alone, alienated, and fearing that her parents are planning a divorce, nine-year-old Megan McBride (Isabella Fink), under the pseudonym of "Chris," writes a passionate letter asking Santa to intervene. The letter, which suggests that she may commit suicide on Christmas Eve, receives national attention as representatives of the media storm the community of Seacliff, Washington, in search of the child. Among them is M.J. Jensen (Patricia Heaton), a television reporter whose past emotional trauma has left her hard-nosed and cynical of love. Believing that the letter is a hoax, she reluctantly collaborates with David Reynolds (Rick Roberts), a struggling writer, who has returned to his hometown to investigate a set of mysterious paintings that he received from an anonymous artist.

Supernatural forces are at work, for the paintings portray scenes of events that will shortly transpire in Seacliff and that ultimately lead M.J. and David to identify Megan as "Chris." Megan claims that her friend Max prompted her to send the letter, and that it is he who is the artist. Her story reminds David of having felt alienated when he himself was a boy. As a foster child, he had run away at Christmastime, had fallen asleep in the snowy woods, and would have succumbed to the elements, had a mysterious lumberjack not rescued him. By a series of deductions, David concludes that Max was also that "lumberjack."

In reality, Max is an unconventional angel who has been sent to bring peace to Megan's troubled household, to initiate romance between David and a love-starved M.J., and to instill the Christmas spirit in the people of Seacliff (the town being on the brink of bankruptcy because a new dam has ruined the salmon fishing industry there).

David is indispensable in reviving Seacliff's holiday spirit, for when a power failure threatens to cancel the annual Christmas Eve pageant, he arrives with 2,000 candles, which Max has conveniently supplied. And by Christmas Eve, M.J. is a changed woman. After learning Megan's plight and seeing the hope and joy of Christmas in Seacliff's citizens despite their difficulties, M.J. refuses to exploit the "Chris" hoax to boost news ratings and instead turns a live broadcast of the pageant into a heartwarming human-interest story.

Written by Michael J. Murray. Produced by Ken Gross, Stephanie Gaines, and Michael Mahoney. Directed by Andy Wolk. A Daniel H. Blatt Production in association with Viacom Productions. Video N/A. 93 min.

See also **Finding John Christmas; When Angels Come to Town.**

Toys for Tots

Charitable organization operated by the United States Marine Corps Reserve, founded by retired Marine Corps colonel Bill Hendricks in 1947 in Los Angeles. That year, Hendricks's wife Diane had fashioned a handmade Raggedy Ann doll and had desired that an underprivileged child should receive it for Christmas. When Hendricks discovered that no programs existed that distributed toys to needy children, he created Toys for Tots to fill the void. In the first year, 5,000 toys were collected and distributed throughout Los Angeles. The program rapidly evolved into an annual, nationwide project and sported the familiar train logo designed in 1948 by Walt Disney, who also created the first Toys for Tots Christmas poster. In 1956, Sammy Fain and Paul Webster composed a Toys for Tots theme song, which was recorded by Nat "King" Cole, Peggy Lee, and Vic Damone. From 1947 through 1979, Marines collected and distributed new and used toys, but in 1980 the organization implemented the policy of distributing only new toys because of public health concerns and to foster self-esteem in the recipients. National spokespersons have included such celebrities as First Lady Nancy Reagan (1983), First Lady Barbara Bush (1992), and country-western singer Billy Ray Cyrus (2003). Since 1991, the Marine Toys for Tots Foundation has served as the fund-raising and support organization for the Toys for Tots Program.

Since its inception, Toys for Tots has brought Christmas joy to more than 100 million children. Public awareness has been achieved through the work of motion picture and television celebrities, professional athletes, entertainers, and thousands of volunteers at the local level who have donated their time to the cause. Many communities across the United States also sponsor local drives, in addition to those by the Marine Corps Reserve. Toys for Tots is the largest nationwide drive dedicated to collecting new toys for children.

In 2003, United States Marines distributed 15 million new toys to 6.6 million needy children, with campaigns conducted in more than 450 communities throughout the United States.

See also **Angel Tree; Salvation Army.**

The Toys Who Saved Christmas
See **How the Toys Saved Christmas**

The Trail to Christmas
See **A Christmas Carol** (Film and Television Versions)

Trinidad
See **West Indies**

Turkey
See **Middle East**

'Twas in the Moon of Wintertime
See **The Huron Christmas Carol**

'Twas the Night before Christmas (poem and song)
See **A Visit from St. Nicholas**

'Twas the Night before Christmas (television episode)
See **The Honeymooners**

'Twas the Night Before Christmas

(Television special, 1974). Cel-animated cartoon loosely based on the poem "A Visit from St. Nicholas."

When Santa rejects letters from Junctionville because its newspaper published a slanderous letter about him, clockmaker Joshua Trundle builds a clock with magic chimes that will lure Santa to town on Christmas Eve. But a trial run finds the clock inoperative, broken by inquisitive Albert Mouse, who tinkered with its mechanism. Father Mouse also discovers that it was his own son who anonymously wrote the letter against Santa, because he doesn't believe in anything he cannot see.

After learning the degree of sadness there will be if Santa continues to ignore Junctionville, Albert fixes the clock with the aid of a book by Copernicus, and Santa arrives to everyone's happiness.

Narrated and sung by Joel Grey. Principal voices: George Gobel, Tammy Grimes, John McGiver, Patricia Bright, Scott Firestone,

Robert McFadden, Allen Swift, Christine Winter, and the Wee Winter Singers. Written by Jerome Coppersmith. Produced and directed by Arthur Rankin, Jr., and Jules Bass. A Rankin /Bass Production. VHS: Warner Studios. 25 min.

This television special is further detailed in Rick Goldschmidt's book *The Enchanted World of Rankin/Bass.*

See also **Rankin/Bass Christmas Cartoons; A Visit from St. Nicholas.**

Twelfth Day
See **Epiphany**

Twelfth Night
See **Epiphany**

The Twelve Days of Christmas

(Song). Traditional carol, the origins of which are uncertain and controversial. Some contend that English Roman Catholics, whom the Church of England prohibited from openly practicing their faith from the mid–sixteenth century until the nineteenth century, created this carol, probably during the sixteenth century, as an underground memory device for teaching children their catechism. Supposedly it was patterned after the so-called counting songs that were most popular during the Middle Ages, as well as a popular game during that period that was often played on the last night of the 12-day Christmas season, Twelfth Night (Epiphany eve, January 5, or Epiphany night, January 6, depending on the local reckoning). The game consisted of players in turn reciting a list of objects from memory while adding a new one each time. Failure to recite the growing list correctly resulted in a forfeit or a player's elimination from the game. The additional custom among the nobility of exchanging gifts on each of those 12 days is thought to have influenced the secular gift theme of the carol's lyrics. Other views hold that the carol is of French origin; that the concept of hidden symbolisms in the secular gifts is without foundation; or that, because the religious symbolisms assigned to the gifts are not restricted exclusively to Roman Catholic doctrine, the carol was not devised to teach catechism.

The following paragraphs discuss the symbolic meanings of the gifts along with variations and any pagan counterparts:

First Day. "On the first day of Christmas, my true love gave to me a partridge in a pear tree." The number "one" represents one God in Jesus Christ, the "true love" of all Christians. "Partridge in a pear tree" has acquired multiple symbols. In one sense, the phrase further likens Jesus to a mother partridge which lures predators away from her young by feigning injury; in another sense, it recalls Jesus' lamentation over Jerusalem (Matthew 23:37). An opposing view likens the partridge to Satan, who, according to legend, told King Herod where the Virgin Mary had hidden herself from his soldiers, who sought to kill the Babe. The pear tree represents the cross, the metonymic "tree" upon which Christ was crucified. In this sense, the partridge and pear tree represent the battle between good and evil. In a secular sense, it has been suggested that, because the gifts come from "my true love," the carol incorporates a pagan superstition regarding pear trees, namely that a girl may see an image of her future husband if she approaches a pear tree backwards and walks around it three times on Christmas Eve (*see* **Superstitions**).

Second Day. "Two turtle doves" symbolize the Old and New Testaments of the Bible as well as the sacrifice of two turtle doves made when the infant Jesus was presented in the Temple (Leviticus 12:8 and Luke 2:24).

Third Day. "Three French hens" represent the theological virtues of Faith, Hope, and Charity (First Corinthians 13:13); the gifts of the Nativity: gold, frankincense, and myrrh (Matthew 2:11); and the Holy Trinity of Father, Son, and Holy Ghost (First John 5:7).

Fourth Day. "Four calling birds" represent the four Gospels and Evangelists (Matthew, Mark, Luke, and John); the four major Old Testament prophets (Isaiah, Ezekiel, Jeremiah, and Daniel); and the four horsemen of the Apocalypse (Revelation 6:1–8).

Fifth Day. "Five gold rings" symbolize the first five books of the Old Testament, also known as the Pentateuch, the Books of Moses, and the Law of Moses (Genesis, Exodus, Leviticus, Numbers, and Deuteronomy). In a secular sense, the gold rings are thought to imply either the rings of ringed pheasants or a corruption of the Scottish words "goldspinks" (goldfinches) or "gulderer" (turkeys). A Roman Catholic variation includes the five "decades" (prayer divisions) of the rosary.

Sixth Day. "Six geese a-laying" represent the six days of creation.

Seventh Day. "Seven swans a-swimming" symbolize the seven gifts of the Holy Spirit: prophecy, ministry, teaching, exhorting, ruling, giving, and mercy (Romans 12:6–8). Roman Catholics would include their seven sacraments: baptism, confirmation, Eucharist, penance and reconciliation, anointing the sick, holy orders, and matrimony. Also note that birds comprise the first seven secular gifts.

Eighth Day. "Eight maids a-milking" represent the eight beatitudes: "Blessed are the poor in spirit . . . they that mourn . . . the meek . . . hunger and thirst after righteousness . . . the merciful . . . the pure in heart . . . peacemakers . . . persecuted for righteousness' sake" (Matthew 5:3–10).

Ninth Day. "Nine ladies dancing" symbolize the nine fruits of the Holy Spirit: love, joy, peace, long suffering, gentleness, goodness, faith, meekness, and temperance (Galatians 5:22–23).

Tenth Day. "Ten lords a-leaping" represent the Ten Commandments.

Eleventh Day. "Eleven pipers piping" represent the 11 faithful apostles who did not betray Jesus, as did Judas.

Twelfth Day. "Twelve drummers drumming" symbolize the 12 points of doctrine in the Apostles' Creed, which clearly bears some Catholic doctrine:

(1) I believe in God the Father, maker of heaven and earth. (2) I believe in Jesus Christ, His only Son, our Lord, (3) Who was conceived of the Holy Spirit, born of the Virgin Mary. (4) He suffered under Pontius Pilate, was crucified, died, and was buried. (5) He descended into hell; the third day He rose from the dead. (6) He ascended into heaven and sits at the right hand of God, the Father Almighty. (7) He shall return to judge the living and the dead. (8) I believe in the Holy Spirit, (9) the Holy Catholic Church, the communion of saints, (10) the forgiveness of sins, (11) the resurrection of the body, (12) and life everlasting.

Other versions of the lyrics in Great Britain include four colly or cally birds (blackbirds), four canary birds, eight deers (sic) a-running, nine lads a-leaping, ten ladies skipping, 11 bears a-baiting, and 12 parsons preaching. Theoretically, any type of gift could be substituted, but those listed in the previous paragraphs constitute the carol as sung in the United States.

Another English traditional carol that openly assigns similar, religious meanings to each of the 12 days of Christmas (but with a different tune) is "In Those Twelve Days," believed to date to 1625. Incorporating a question-and-answer format but hardly intended as a catechism song, this carol appeared in William Sandys's *Christmas Carols, Ancient and Modern* (London, 1833), along with variant versions titled "A New Dyall [Dial]" (referring to a clock face or sundial) and "Man's Duty, or, Meditation for the Twelve Hours of the Day." The symbolisms are as follows: one God; two Testaments; three persons in the Trinity; four Gospels or Evangelists; five senses; six days of creation or six ages of the world; seven days of the week or the seven liberal arts; eight beatitudes; nine degrees of angels or nine muses; Ten Commandments; 11,000 virgins (hyperbole that refers to several virgins supposedly martyred in Cologne, Germany, with St. Ursula in the fifth century); and 12 apostles. Therefore, some have further surmised that, over the centuries, the religious symbolisms of "In Those Twelve Days" blended in variant forms with the secular gifts in "The Twelve Days of Christmas."

See also **The Twelve Days of Christmas** (time period).

The Twelve Days of Christmas

(Time period). The designation "Twelve Days of Christmas" as the time period from Christmas Day, December 25 (Day 0), to Epiphany, January 6 (Day 12), derives from a decree issued in 567 by the Second Council of Tours, France, which proclaimed the sanctity of those 12 days, preceded by fasting during the Advent season. Alfred the Great (849–899), king of the West Saxons and king of England from 866 until his death, issued a similar decree for England, but instead of sanctity, he proclaimed a time for "righteous pleasure"

A Twelfth-Day scene outside a London Confectioner, early 1800s. "From the taking down of the shutters in the morning, the pastry-cook and his men ... are fully occupied" decorating the window with pastries, baking, taking orders, and at dusk "the gas is turned on ... to illuminate countless cakes of all prices and dimensions, that stand in rows and piles on the counters and in the windows ... Stars, castles, kings, cottages, dragons, trees, fish, palaces, cats, dogs, churches, lions, milkmaids, knights, serpents, and innumerable other forms in snow-white confectionary, painted with variegated colours, glitter by 'excess of light' from mirrors against the walls." From William Hone, Every-Day Book, *Vol. 1 (London: 1825–1826).*

The Lord of Misrule, masked and done up like a fool, with his small boy page, derived from Saturnalian festivals. Re-enactments of Medieval festivals always include a lord of Misrule. From Robert Chambers, ed., A Book of Days *(London and Edinburgh: Chambers, 1879).*

during those 12 days. Thus, Christmas during the Middle Ages evolved from a time of reverence to a time of revelry and licentiousness akin to the pagan Roman Saturnalia, which Christmas particularly Christianized. This was the period not only for the Feast of Fools with its Lord of Misrule, mumming, gaming, gambling, court tournaments with jousting matches, and Twelfth Night — to name but a few of the celebrations observed — but also a time when landowners of large estates opened their manor halls to the peasantry with feasts, merriment, and reprieve from labor. In return, the peasants and workers were to bestow gifts upon their masters in the form of fruits and other produce from the fields. In some locales, landowners provided their tenants with holiday meals only as long as the Yule log burned.

During those 12 days, the nobility sought to gain favor with the monarchy through lav-

ish Christmas gifts. King Henry III of England (1207–1272), displeased with the parsimonious merchant class, was once said to have closed their shops for two weeks until they collectively presented him with the expected "gift" of £2,000. Those desiring a more quiet holiday could engage in gambling, which was quite popular among the upper classes. During his reign, King Edward IV of England (1442–1483) permitted gambling only during the 12 days of Christmas, and Queen Elizabeth I (1533–1603) gambled with loaded dice.

Pagans once believed that at the winter solstice, the gates between the physical and spirit worlds stood ajar, enabling communication with and appearances of spirits. This belief carried over into the 12 days of Christmas during the Middle Ages and generated numerous superstitions to counter the presence of evil or to predict the future (*see* **Superstitions**). Belief in the supernatural also spawned the tradition of telling ghost stories at this time, a tradition still practiced in some parts of Europe and the United States.

Within the 12 days of Christmas are found six additional observances. Five of these are discussed as separate entries: **Boxing Day** (also known as St. Stephen's Day, December 26), **Holy Innocents Day** (December 28), **Feast of the Holy Family** (first Sunday after Christmas), **New Year's Day** (January 1), and **Epiphany** (January 6). The sixth, St. John's Day, is discussed below.

• St. John's Day. Falling on December 27, St. John's Day is devoted to St. John the Evangelist (or the Divine), one of Christ's apostles, whom early Christian tradition credits as the author of the Gospel of John. According to St. Irenaeus (140?–202?), John suffered persecution under the Roman emperor Domitian (ruled 81–96), who, around the year 93, sentenced him to exile for life on the island of Patmos in the Aegean Sea. There John, receiving a vision from Christ, wrote the Book of Revelation. The Church established the Feast of St. John by the fifth century, and the consumption of blessed wine punctuated the observance by the sixteenth century. According to legend, St. John suffered no ill effects from having unwittingly consumed tainted or poisoned wine, which led to the belief that blessed wine imbibed on this day would stimulate health.

The feasts of St. Stephen, St. John, and the Holy Innocents, falling consecutively, honor some of the earliest people persecuted for the sake of Christ.

See also **Christmas Drama** (Mumming); **Feast of Fools**; **Saturnalia**; **Yule**.

Twelve Tales of Christmas

Collection of inspirational short stories written by American author Richard Siddoway, published in 1992. Based on actual people and events that influenced the author's life, the stories, utilizing some literary license, begin with childhood Christmas memories dominated by Santa Claus and gifts received, then progress to Christmases of mature, later years dominated

by Jesus Christ and gifts given. The following paragraphs briefly summarize the stories:

"I'm a Believer." The author recalls the sounds, sights, and scents of Christmas and childhood memories of his family working in concert to make every Christmas Eve a memorable, magical time.

"The White Snows of Winter." Bumps and spills of sledding and skiing adventures with a cousin fill a snowy Christmas Day in Salt Lake City.

"Roses Are Red." At the third-grade Christmas party, children draw names for anonymous gift exchanges. For an unkempt little girl with a most unpleasant odor, the author provides a bottle of cheap cologne with a cruel note attached in reference to her aroma (for which the author has remained remorseful), and the girl bursts into tears. But she weeps not because of the words — she cannot read — she weeps because she could not even afford 25 cents to buy a gift.

"Pins and Needles." The author and his cousin find that buying Christmas gifts for the family can be quite taxing, when only a dollar exists between them.

"Let Us Have Christmas the Whole Year Round." Now a college student, the author meets Lily the Tie Lady, an elderly, disheveled peddler of neckties. Yet appearances are truly deceiving, for no one could image the real gift that she has bestowed upon her patrons, not only at Christmastime, but throughout the year.

"A Christmas Found." A young college student returns a lost wallet to the local police station on Christmas Eve, then refuses to accept any reward. Unable to go home for the holidays, the young man becomes a Christmas gift to the elderly couple who claim the wallet.

"The Least of These." While standing in a drug store checkout line, the author is drawn to an elderly man who has all but four dollars to purchase vital medication for his wife. The author has little cash of his own for Christmas gifts, yet he supplies the man's need. Later, the author receives a mysterious envelope simply inscribed with "Matthew 25:40." Inside, his generosity has been rewarded 25-fold.

"Harold Angel." The author befriends Harold, a lonely widower and handyman at a summer camp. Then later, promising to keep Harold's secret, the author experiences unmeasured joy when he assists in delivering Harold's handmade gifts anonymously to less fortunate families on Christmas Eve.

"Blessed Be the Poor." Now a high school teacher, the author and two teenage students work through their school's "Sub-for-Santa" program to bring Christmas magic and aid to an injured, destitute widow and her five children, who live on the brink of starvation and exposure to the elements.

"Angela Ann." When a family's home becomes flooded at Christmastime, neighbors unite to assist them and make their holidays brighter. As donated gifts arrive, little Angela Ann, a child with Down's syndrome, contributes a gift that, much the worse for wear, is far greater than all of the others combined. Whereas the others give from their abundance, Angela Ann's gift can be likened to the "widow's mite" (see Luke 21:1–4).

"Have Faith, My Son." Through faith and prayer, the author, now a Mormon bishop, seemingly receives divine assistance in raising Christmas funds for an underprivileged family who is otherwise too proud to ask for help.

"Amy's Song." Born "crippled in body if not in spirit," Amy would never have auditioned again for her high school's annual Christmas pageant, had not Mr. Simons, the new choral director, suggested that she do so. The previous director, repulsed by Amy's twisted spine, had summarily dismissed her, yet Mr. Simons overlooks appearances and judges Amy's vocal abilities to be worthy of the part of the angel's solo. Shortly after the pageant, Amy loses her battle against her lifelong infirmities and is finally laid to rest on Christmas Eve. Inspired by a physically challenged choral director, Amy had discarded her negative self-image, had looked far beyond the audience, and had sung for the Christ Child Himself.

A former bishop in the Church of Jesus Christ of Latter-Day Saints, Richard Siddoway is a Utah State legislator and an educator in the Utah public school system.

See also **Christmas of the Cherry Snow; The Christmas Quest; The Christmas Wish.**

Twice upon a Christmas

(2001). Made-for-television fantasy, a sequel to the motion picture *Once upon a Christmas* (2000).

Virtually the same principals return as the story resumes at Christmastime a year later. Kristin Claus (Kathy Ireland) and Bill Morgan (John Dye) plan Christmas Day nuptials, yet Kristin is ambivalent. Now a mortal, she has lost all memory of her identity and heritage, save anything relating to Christmas itself. Although Bill and his children, Kyle (James Kirk) and Brittany (Kristin Prout), together with Uncle Johnny (Wayne Thomas Yorke), earnestly set out to discover Kristin's past, they uncover nothing, until Brittany presents Kristin with an antique doll as an early Christmas gift. Attached is a tag inscribed to Kristin from her father with the admonition that those who believe are always rewarded with the truth. Suddenly, Kristin's memory returns like a flood, for the doll was a childhood gift from Santa, her father (Matthew Walker). At that moment, Kristin spots her wicked sister Rudolfa (Mary Donnelly Haskell) on television selling authentic artifacts of the North Pole as souvenirs—whence came the doll—and she realizes that her former home is in serious trouble.

With the Morgans, Kristin zaps to the North Pole and learns of Rudolfa's scheme to sell Santa's establishment piece by piece, including her father's personal effects, and replace it with a gambling resort. With Christmas Eve at hand, Kristen overtakes the Pole's television studio, and her worldwide plea for faith in and loyalty to this Christmas icon successfully restores the North Pole in time for Santa's rounds.

Written by Steven Berman. Produced by Deboragh Gabler, Jon Carrasco, and Stephen Roseberry. Directed by Tibor Takács. Ardent Productions, Legacy Filmworks, Lincoln Field Productions, Sterling/Winters Company Studios, and Viacom Productions. Video N/A. 90 min.

See also **Once upon a Christmas.**

The Twilight Zone

Popular, Emmy Award–winning, science-fiction television series that aired weekly on the

CBS network from 1959 to 1964. Created and narrated by Rod Serling, the series also had television incarnations in the 1980s and briefly in 2002–03. Of the 156 episodes in the original series, only two featured Christmas themes:

"Night of the Meek" (December 23, 1960). After losing his job as a department-store Santa Claus because of drunkenness on Christmas Eve, Henry Corwin (Art Carney) discovers a magical bag that produces any item desired. Thus Henry continues unofficially as Santa and freely distributes gifts, until a police officer, believing that the merchandise is stolen, takes him into custody. Upon finding only a stray cat and garbage in the bag, however, the officer releases Henry, who resumes his gift-giving rounds until the bag seemingly yields no further treasures. Burt (Burt Mustin), a bum who has witnessed the evening's "miracles," remarks that Henry has not claimed a gift for himself, whereupon Henry replies that his only wish would be to repeat this joyous gift-giving feat each year. Soon, Henry wanders into an alley, where an elf and reindeer sleigh await to whisk him to the North Pole in fulfillment of his wish.

To cut costs, this was one of six episodes originally shot on videotape and transferred to 16-mm. film for broadcast. With John Fiedler and Robert Lieb. Written by Rod Serling. Produced by Buck Houghton. Directed by Jack Smight. CBS Television and Cayuga Productions. This episode is included in volume one of the *Twilight Zone* DVD collection from Image Entertainment. B & W. 30 min. The episode was remade in color under the same title in a later incarnation of the series (CBS/syndi-

cation, 1985–89). Airing on December 20, 1985, it starred Richard Mulligan, William Atherton, Bill Henderson, and Teddy Wilson. Teleplay by Rockne S. O'Bannon. Directed by Martha Coolidge.

"Five Characters in Search of an Exit" (December 22, 1961). Five characters—a major in the army (William Windom), a clown (Murray Matheson), a ballerina (Susan Harrison), a tramp (Kelton Garwood), and a bagpipe player (Clark Allen)—find themselves trapped in a large cylinder without knowing how they arrived there. After considering plans of escape, the group follows the major's idea and forms a human ladder, by which the major climbs to the top of the mysterious prison. There, he loses his balance and drops over the side onto the snow-covered ground below, where he immediately discovers that not only is the cylinder a barrel designated for donations of Christmas toys, but that he and his companions in reality are those toys. Spying the major on the ground, a little girl returns him to the barrel, where he and the other dolls, though riddled now with fear and loneliness, may take comfort that soon they will fall into the arms of loving children.

With Mona Houghton and Carol Hill. Written by Rod Serling. Based on "The Depository," a short story by Marvin Petal. Produced by Buck Houghton. Directed by Lamont Johnson. CBS Television and Cayuga Productions. This episode is included in volume 21 of the *Twilight Zone* DVD collection from Image Entertainment. B & W. 30 min.

U

Uganda
See **Africa**

Ukraine
This nation has enjoyed *Rizdvo* (Christmas) since the tenth century, when Prince Volodymyr accepted Christianity from the

Byzantine Empire in the year 988. Following the Eastern Orthodox Church, which bases its ecclesiastical (but not secular) events upon the older Julian calendar, Ukraine observes *Rizdvo* on January 7 by the Gregorian calendar. Traditions are highly symbolic and blend former pagan agrarian beliefs and harvest symbols from *Koliada*, an ancient, winter solstice festival, with those of Christianity. Soviet domination (1922–1991) once suppressed Christmas celebrations, replaced St. Nicholas with *Died Moroz* (Grandfather Frost), and sponsored a secular, year-end festival on New Year's Day. Today, Ukraine has rapidly returned to her centuries-old holiday customs.

Preparations for Christmas begin 40 days in advance with a meatless and milkless fast, which not only commemorates Christ's fasting in the wilderness for 40 days after His baptism, but also honors livestock, since no animals are slaughtered for food during this season. Prior to this cleansing of mind, body, and soul comes the ritual cleaning of homes and property, the resolution of debts, the return of items borrowed, and the settlement of arguments and disputes, all of which must be completed prior to the days of fasting. During the holy days, marriages and dancing are forbidden, and everyone strives to speak only words of peace.

The Orthodox Church observes six feast days during these holy days prior to Christmas, which are usually accompanied by folk customs and auguries. The Feast of the Presentation (December 4) opens the holy days and commemorates the presentation of the young Virgin Mary in the Temple. On St. Catherine's Day (December 7), girls traditionally place cherry tree branches in water in anticipation that these will bloom by New Year's Eve, a sign of good luck. Mischief and pranks reign on St. Andrew the Apostle's Day (December 13), and girls seek predictions about future mates. December 17 honors St. Barbara, and on December 18, the eve of St. Nicholas's Day, children set out plates or shoes to be filled with treats by *Sviatyj Mykloaj* (St. Nicholas). Three traditional gifts on this day include an article of clothing, a toy, and a "gift of wonder." Traveling about in the company of an angel and the Devil, St. Nicholas makes appearances in public places and at homes to quiz youngsters about their religion, while the Devil leaves switches for the naughty. On December 21, the Feast of the Immaculate Conception honors the Virgin Mary as having been born without original sin.

The principal Christmas celebration centers around *Sviata Vecheria* (Christmas Eve and Holy Supper), observed on January 6. The day begins with a total fast, and preparatory rituals include opening the doors of one's home early that morning to receive the blessing of the sun; using blessed logs to light the oven; leading the farm animals past an ax to disperse any evil; and introducing the *didukh* ("Grandfather spirit"), a sheaf of wheat that the head of the household sets in a place of honor after carrying it around the interior of the home three times. The spirits of all family members, living and dead, are believed to reside in the *didukh*, which also symbolizes eternal life through Christ, the fertility of the land, and bread as the staff of life.

After the table is first prepared with a layer of hay on top and beneath to symbolize the earth and the manger, two tablecloths are laid. The first is white, symbolic of deceased family members; the topmost is highly embroidered and symbolizes those living in the present. A band of string or length of chain, symbolic of family ties, binds the table legs, and scattered in the hay on the floor are little treats for the children to discover after dinner. Cloves of garlic placed at each corner of the table ward off illness, and an extra place is set to honor deceased family members as well as any stranger. The centerpiece consists of three loaves of *kolach* (circular, braided Christmas bread) stacked on top of each other, representing the Holy Trinity, and a single white candle in the top loaf represents the sun and Christ as the Light of the world. After these preparations, children search the eastern sky for the first star of the evening, believed to be the Star of Bethlehem, for when the first star appears, *Sviata Vecheria* begins. No family member must ever be late; a violation predicts that someone in the family will die in the next year.

As Holy Supper commences, the host ritually beckons the ancestral spirits and forces of nature to partake of the bounty, followed by a prayer and a *koliadky* (Christmas carol). The menu traditionally consists of 12 meatless dishes, symbolic of Christ's Twelve Apostles and the moon's 12 phases around the earth. The first and most indispensable dish is *kutia* (believed to have been offered to the sun god Dazhboh at pagan winter solstice festivals), which consists of boiled wheat, poppy seeds, and honey (wheat symbolizes property, poppy seeds the beauty of the earth, and honey the family unity). Holding the bowl of *kutia* in a *rushnyk* (embroidered religious cloth), the host serves this dish to each family member while reciting the greeting "Khrystos Rodyvsya" ("Christ is born"). Upon receiving the *kutia*, each person responds, "Slavim Yoho" ("Let us glorify Him"). Alternatively, the greeting and response may be said in unison before the meal. Next, the host tosses a small portion of *kutia* toward the ceiling; the amount that sticks is believed to predict the degree of prosperity in store for the new year. Then follows a toast to the dead, after which the host may, in some regions, offer a piece of bread dipped in honey with garlic to each member at the table (the act symbolizes that life is filled with the sweet as well as the bitter). Although the 11 remaining dishes will vary from region to region, the following are typical examples: *borsch* (beets), baked or fried fish, *osyletsi* (picked fish), *holubtsi* (stuffed cabbage), *varenyky* (small pies with potato, sauerkraut, or prune fillings), *pyrohy* (dumplings with fruit fillings), beans, *kapusta* (sauerkraut) with peas, fruit compote, and *pompushky* (fried fruit pies). Following the meal, families usually engage in a period of singing carols, portions of food are served to the farm animals, and the remaining food stands on the table overnight in order that family spirits may partake of the feast. Christmas Eve concludes with Midnight Mass, which may extend until dawn.

The week between *Rizdvo* and New Year's Day is filled with visitations, feasting, and *koliadnyky* (carolers), the latter of whom tour neighborhoods attired as shepherds, angels, and Wise Men. Grouped behind an illuminated, eight- or ten-pointed star on a pole, the carolers provide a vast repertoire of ancient songs centering around nature, the Nativity, and matchmaking, for example, which they customize for each person at the homes visited. The carolers may also carry a *vertep* (three-dimensional Nativity scene), and among them a boy may be costumed as a *koza* (goat, a pagan symbol of prosperity and fertility), who dances for everyone's amusement. As rewards, the carolers receive food, drink, and donations for charity.

Two additional feast days fall within this week: the Syntaxis of the Blessed Virgin, which commemorates Mary and Joseph as Jesus' earthly parents, and St. Stephen's Day, which honors the first Christian martyr.

Shchedryi Vechir (New Year's Eve) is observed either on January 13 (eve of the Feast of St. Basil, an Orthodox patriarch) or on January 18 (eve of the Feast of Jordan, see below), depending on the locale. The customs resemble those of Christmas Eve as families again congregate for a large meal (meat is now permissible), auguries are read, and carolers present a completely different set of tunes, *shchedrivky*, filled with wishes for health and prosperity. Named for a girl in Ukrainian folklore, the popular New Year's Eve tradition of *Malanka* derives from pagan rites that banished evil from the new year. A man dressed as Malanka leads a procession of villagers costumed either as good or evil spirits, who sing carols, present plays, and offer good wishes to households.

New Year's Day brings groups of touring boys who throw wheat and seeds into homes for luck, and many families still observe this day as the principal time for gift-giving and erecting a *yalynka* (Christmas tree). Others prefer St. Nicholas's Day or Christmas Day. Favorite ornaments include spider figures and webs of straw, which derive from legends holding that a spider decorated a poor widow's Christmas tree with its web and that, while lying in the manger, the Baby Jesus first played with a spider's web. Other ornaments may include apples, candy, cookies, foil, and homemade items such as paper chains.

The Christmas season ends with the Feast of Jordan (January 19), which commemorates Christ's baptism in the River Jordan and is comparable to the Feast of Epiphany in Western (Roman) churches on January 6. People traditionally mark their homes with crosses above windows and doorways. The principal event here is the Blessing of the Waters, in which a priest blesses containers of water by dipping a cross into them. Believers then take samples of the blessed water to sanctify their homes and to repel illness. Priests may also throw a small cross into rivers, lakes, or other bodies of water, after which men dive for the cross as a display of strength, and the one retrieving it is hailed as a hero. On this day, the *didukh* is either burned to release the indwelling spirits, or it is saved and burned in the spring to strengthen orchards. Children customarily leap through the flames, believing that if they do so, their ancestors will not harm them in the new year. The less superstitious merely retain their *didukh* from year to year.

"Merry Christmas" is *Veseleoho Vam Rizdva*.

See also **Carol of the Bells; Epiphany; Russia**.

The Ukraine Carol
See **Carol of the Bells**

United Kingdom
See **Great Britain; Ireland**

United States

Europeans settling in North America brought a diversity of holiday customs, which mirrored those of their parent countries and religious faiths. Indeed, Christopher Columbus is credited with first observing Christmas in the New World when, on Christmas Eve, 1492, his flagship *Santa Maria* ran aground off the Caribbean island of Hispaniola, whereupon he erected a fort named *Villa de Navidad* ("Village of the Nativity").

The first real Christmas celebration in what would become the United States took place in Spanish Florida. Gulevich credits Hernando De Soto's party, which in the fall of 1539 set up a camp of five months' duration near the site of present-day Tallahassee, as probably the first to hold Christmas services. The Spanish conquistador Francisco Coronado, whose party explored the American Southwest in 1540 and wintered near present-day Santa Fe, may also have observed Christmas, although definitive records are lacking. The first recorded Christmas service was held in 1565 in the city of St. Augustine, Florida, conducted by a Father Francisco Lopez de Mendoza Grajales.

Through Coronado's exploration, Spanish missionaries spread Christianity and Christmas to the native peoples of the American Southwest and instituted the customs of *Las Posadas* and the related *Los Pastorelas* as tools

for conveying the Christmas story, as they had earlier to the natives of New Spain (Mexico) (*see* **Las Posadas**).

Although the Spanish Catholics freely celebrated Christmas, differing attitudes prevailed among the English colonists, primarily Protestants settling along the East Coast. The first Christmas in the first permanent English settlement of Jamestown, Virginia (1607), consisted of hardly more than a simple prayer service, as fewer than 40 Anglicans struggled against cold and privation. The Pilgrims, Puritans who founded Plymouth Colony, Massachusetts (1620), not only ignored the season completely but ultimately imposed fines of five shillings in 1659 against those acknowledging Christmas in any form; the fine was repealed in 1681 (*see* **Great Britain** for further discussion about Puritans). Other Protestant colonists who denied Christmas for lack of a biblical precedent included Quakers, Presbyterians, and Congregationalists of New England, and Mennonites and Amish of New York and Pennsylvania.

On the other hand, Anglicans, Lutherans, English Catholics, members of the Dutch Reformed Church, and the Moravians brought traditional, Old-World customs to their respective settlements. German immigrants of Pennsylvania, the Dutch of New Amsterdam (New York), and especially the English plantation owners of Virginia and other Southern colonies were noted for creating a most festive atmosphere, which included feasting on roasted game birds with stuffing, smoked hams, assorted vegetable dishes, elaborate confections, and liquors (George Washington was particularly noted for concocting a highly potent eggnog spiked with whiskey, brandy, sherry, and rum); elegant balls; gaming; costumed mummers known as "fantasticals"; sporting events; noise-making with fireworks and shooting of firearms; and open houses among the affluent to which numerous guests flocked without invitation. New Yorkers, who once advertised the hours at which they would receive guests on Christmas Day or New Year's Day, eventually ceased this practice because of the throngs of strangers who arrived in expectation of a free meal. Decorations were simple, consisting of a Yule log, evergreens, flowers, and fruits. Christ-

A lithographed trade card from Lissauer & Sondheim Jewelers shows a young wife, ca. 1880, having "A Christmas Dream" while her pets play and the tabletop tree displays rings, bracelets, and other fine baubles.

A handful of headlines from 1949 pre–Christmas magazine ads shows that everyone had the perfect gift for sale. The most telling of the group is for an aluminum table cooker which "looks many times what it costs"— a valuable asset if you were going to give presents to a lot of people!

mas trees and gift-giving to family and friends did not become popular until the mid–nineteenth century (*see* **Christmas Tree**), although the well-off gave obligatory gifts to their inferiors, servants, and slaves. A custom among a number of plantation owners was to grant their slaves freedom from work during the holidays as long as the Yule log burned. Therefore, to increase the burning time, slaves commonly chose the greenest logs and soaked them first in water. The custom "Christmas gif'" was a favorite among the slaves of the Old South. Upon meeting anyone, especially a white person, on Christmas Day, the slave would call out "Christmas gif'!" whereupon the one addressed was to supply some coins or other token. Children in the American Southwest continued this practice into the nineteenth century.

With Dutch immigrants came customs that centered around *Sinterklaas* (St. Nicholas), who initially brought gifts to children on December 5, the eve of St. Nicholas's Day, and who eventually became known as "Santa Claus" through repeated slurring of his Dutch name (*see* **Saint Nicholas** and **Saint Nicholas's Day**). Likewise, German immigrants settling in Pennsylvania (known as "Pennsylvania Dutch") brought the concept of the *Christkindlein* ("little Christ Child"), shortened to *Christkindl*, a heavenly messenger who brought Christmas gifts in place of the Infant Jesus (*see* **Germany**). Further corruptions of this name led to "Krish-kinkle" and thence to "Kris (or Kriss) Kringle," who merged as an alternate identity with Santa Claus in the nine-

teenth century (classically portrayed in the 1947 motion picture *Miracle on 34th Street*). A similar corruption changed "Pelz Nicholas" ("Furry Nicholas"), a combined gift-bringer and holiday bogey to the Pennsylvania Dutch, to "Pelsnickel" and "Belsnickel." Originally on St. Nicholas's Day, Pennsylvania youths dressed in ragged furs, blackened faces, or masks paraded from house to house with bells and whips, creating comedy and commotion with expectations of food and drink as rewards. This custom, "belsnickeling," incorporated English mumming practices during the eighteenth and nineteenth centuries, then shifted to the 12 days of Christmas and finally to New Year's Day by the turn of the twentieth century, when Philadelphia instituted the annual Mummers Day Parade (*see* **Christmas Drama** [Mumming]).

Another practice, common not only in Pennsylvania but in the South, was known as "barring out the schoolmaster." Derived from a sixteenth century British custom, this practice was designed to acquire a few days' vacation from the despotic, often harsh methods (including floggings) that British schoolmas-

Thomas Nast, a German-born American artist, was noted for the wonderfully tubby, grandfatherly Santas he drew for over 20 years for Harper's Weekly *and* Harper's Young People. *Here he has fun with two sky-borne children's idols: Mother Goose, spilling books, and Santa, whose sack is leaking toys above the world.* Harper's Young People, *December, ca. 1882.*

This complex wood engraving from Peterson's Magazine, *December 1866, shows a group of children gazing devoutly at a small tabletop tree, decorated with the Stars and Stripes (the flag of the Union, which had just won the Civil War), while a society ball takes place in the medallions above, and a loving child feeds hungry birds in the snow below.*

ters frequently employed to maintain discipline. School boys would collect provisions and barricade themselves in their classrooms just prior to Christmas or other holidays. The masters either forced the issue, resulting in violence, bloodshed, and even death, or they relented and granted a few days' reprieve. The practice in America consisted more of mock battles between students and teachers and declined in the nineteenth century as public schools published schedules for vacation days.

John Adams (1735–1826), second president of the United States (1797–1801), became the first chief executive to occupy the White House upon its completion in 1800. The first presidential Christmas celebration there consisted of a party for Adams's four-year-old granddaughter Suzanna and her friends. Held in the grand ballroom, the event sported a small orchestra, cake, punch, greenery, carols, and games. Popular tradition holds that Christmas trees did not grace the White House until President Franklin Pierce first erected one there in 1856. Rosenbaum's *A White House Christmas* implies, however, that this is nothing more than an urban legend, which supposedly originated with Pierce's grandnieces. According to Rosenbaum, President Benjamin Harrison (served 1889–93), an Episcopalian, erected the first White House Christmas tree. Theretofore presidents of the post–Civil War era had either been primarily Westerners (the concept of the Christmas tree was not well known west of the Allegheny Mountains until the latter nineteenth century) or Protestants (many denominations of whom were disinclined to observe Christmas), two factors which Rosenbaum cited to explain the former absence of White House Christmas trees (*see* **The White House**).

As pioneers pushed farther west across America, Christmas observances continued to

An American card from 1879 with a seasonal design and a secular greeting with catch-phrases still in use: "cheery glow," "many pleasures bring," and "'Tis the happy time of the year." From "The Story of the Christmas Card," House and Garden, December 1921.

be rather simple, communal affairs consisting of prayer services, socials, dances, and noise-making. French descendants living in Louisiana, Missouri, and the Great Lakes regions hosted the Christmas Eve *le réveillon* (*see* **France**) after Midnight Mass, and their children customarily received gifts on New Year's Day. Native Americans, observing the white man's Christmas, termed it either the "Big Eating" or "Kissing Day," the latter term deriving from French fur trappers who exchanged gifts with a kiss.

While different cultural and religious communities continued to observe Christmas in unique ways, some researchers believe that the mass immigrations of Europeans, accelerated lifestyles, and the cultural and industrial revolutions of the mid–nineteenth century produced a kind of Christmas melting pot, with the assimilation of various cultures into a more uniform and widely celebrated holiday in the home with family. This change, most pronounced following the Civil War, has been attributed to the popularity of three principal traditions: Santa Claus, Christmas trees, and giving of gifts, all of which created a commercial and secular synergy, despite the original religious significance of the holiday.

Through the poem "A Visit from St. Nicholas" (published 1823) and magazine illustrations by political cartoonist Thomas Nast

(1840–1902), St. Nicholas-turned-Santa Claus became a sensation as a "jolly old elf" from the North Pole who stuffed gifts into children's stockings on Christmas Eve (*see* **Saint Nicholas** and **A Visit from St. Nicholas**). Francis Church's editorial titled "Is There a Santa Claus?" published in the *New York Sun* (1897) in response to an eight-year-old girl's inquiry, masterfully portrayed this personification of Christmas festivities as a spirit who would "continue to make glad the heart of childhood" (*see* **Yes, Virginia, There Is a Santa Claus**). And where else was the center of childhood than home and family? The German custom of the Christmas tree also swept through America in the late nineteenth century and joined the stocking not only as a decoration but as a family medium upon which small gifts were hung, until the acquisition of larger gifts required their placement beneath the tree.

Through consumer demand, the 1870s and 1880s saw an increase in commercially produced items which, ironically, shoppers appreciated but initially regarded as too impersonal as Christmas gifts compared with more simple, handmade presents. Retail dealers countered with colorful wrapping paper and ribbons, which concealed the gifts (wrapped gifts were previously unknown), thereby making commercial items more attractive for Christmas. When consumers readily accepted this innovation, retailers saw a means of promoting even the most mundane of items as gifts through newspaper advertisements, fanciful window displays, and Santa himself, who appeared in person prior to Christmas to promote sales. By the end of the nineteenth century, Americans had begun to place more emphasis on giving presents at Christmastime rather than on New Year's Day as had been the tradition in previous eras.

A heightened urge toward giving to the poor and other charitable causes was especially manifested at Christmastime. As Penne Restad noted, while gift-giving to family members and friends served as a private means of reinforcing attachments and communal bonds, giving to the needy became more of a "cathartic exercise" in unselfishness: in other words, a symbolic escape for the guilt-ridden (*see* **Angel Tree**, **Salvation Army**, and **Toys for Tots**).

Printed Christmas cards, popular from the post–Civil War era onward, served as substitutes for the former tradition of writing a multitude of Christmas letters or making numerous personal Christmas visits. Cards also conveniently replaced the seemingly obligatory, cheap trinkets which families had bestowed upon distant friends and relatives (*see* **Christmas Cards**).

By 1870, 33 states had passed legislation establishing Christmas Day as a legal holiday. The remainder of what would become the 48 contiguous states would also legally recognize Christmas by the end of the nineteenth century. According to Rosenbaum's *A White House Christmas*, the first federal recognition of a Christmas holiday came in 1870, when employees of the District of Columbia were given this day as a paid holiday. Full federal recognition of Christmas as a legal holiday nationwide came with a Congressional Act on January 5, 1885.

The following provides an alphabetical listing of the 48 contiguous states and the years in which Christmas became a legal holiday therein: Alabama 1836, Arizona 1881, Arkansas 1838, California 1851, Colorado 1861, Connecticut 1845, Delaware 1855, Florida 1881, Georgia 1850, Idaho 1863, Illinois 1861, Indiana 1875, Iowa 1862, Kansas 1868, Kentucky 1864, Louisiana 1838, Maine 1858, Maryland 1862, Massachusetts 1855, Michigan 1865, Minnesota 1856, Mississippi 1880, Missouri 1877, Montana 1865, Nebraska 1873, Nevada 1861, New Hampshire 1861, New Jersey 1854, New Mexico 1876, New York 1849, North Carolina 1881, North Dakota 1863, Ohio 1857, Oklahoma 1890, Oregon 1862, Pennsylvania 1848, Rhode Island 1852, South Carolina 1875, South Dakota 1877, Tennessee 1857, Texas 1879, Utah 1882, Vermont 1850, Virginia 1849, Washington 1888, West Virginia 1870, Wisconsin 1861, and Wyoming 1886. Thus Alabama and Oklahoma were the first and last of the original 48 states, respectively, to legalize Christmas.

American Christmas music came to the forefront in the nineteenth century as church-affiliated men produced lyrics to the now-familiar carols of "O Little Town of Bethlehem" by Episcopal minister Phillips Brooks, "It Came upon the Midnight Clear" by Unitarian minister Edmund Hamilton Sears, "We Three Kings of Orient Are" by Episcopal minister John Henry Hopkins, Jr., and "Jingle Bells" by composer James Lord Pierpont. Whereas the former three carols were reverent Nativity narratives, the latter, completely secular with no mention of Christmas, seemed to pave the way for a large collection of popular, primarily secular songs that extolled the pleasures of a twentieth century Christmas. Many became bestsellers in the recording industry, and the American Society of Composers, Authors and Publishers (ASCAP) hailed 25 of them as the most frequently performed in the twentieth century, with "White Christmas" ranked as number one (*see* **ASCAP List of Christmas Songs**).

As commercialism soared into the twentieth century, large department stores such as Gimble's and Macy's in principal Northern cities began sponsoring Thanksgiving Day parades that included Santa Claus as the feature attraction. This grandest of advertising gimmicks, which began in the early 1920s, served to launch the Christmas shopping season from that point. Furthermore, Federated Department Stores of Ohio, seeking to expand the season, convinced President Franklin Roosevelt in 1939 to change Thanksgiving Day from the last Thursday in November to one week earlier, a date that Congress re-established on the fourth Thursday of November in 1941, which ultimately provided four weeks for Christmas shopping. Other mid-century gimmicks featured Santa landing at shopping centers via helicopter.

According to the National Retail Federation, holiday sales continue to increase from year to year. For example, holiday sales totaled about 160 billion dollars in 1997, over 205 billion dollars in 2002, and over 216 billion dollars in 2003, with sales in 2004 expected to rise by another five percent. Figures published by the American Express Retail Index reflected an average household Christmas gift budget of $1,042 in 2001, $1,073 in 2002, and $1,086 in 2003. To finance such expenses, many Americans partially relied upon Christmas bonuses (more prevalent in the late nineteenth and early twentieth centuries) or "Christmas clubs," which arose in the early twentieth century and consisted of savings accounts into which cash could be deposited and held through the year for Christmas expenses. Otherwise, credit card users required about four months on the average to pay off Christmas debts.

During the latter half of the twentieth century, a materialistic emphasis on Christmas presents and Santa Claus as secular lord of Christmas dominated numerous motion pictures, television specials, and animated cartoons, the majority of which repetitively presented the following generic plot: When a disaster or other bogey threatened to prevent Santa from delivering gifts on Christmas Eve, a quick solution was in order, lest Christmas be "canceled." While such pictures were occasionally peppered with holiday sentiment, they still lifted up Santa as the centerpiece of Christmas. Other story lines combining reality with fantasy frequently centered around children of broken homes and dysfunctional families who

Calvin Coolidge (right), the first president to light the National Community Christmas Tree on the Ellipse in Washington, D.C., holds his hat as he presides at ceremonies on Christmas Eve, 1923. Courtesy Library of Congress.

besought Santa to use his magic power as a means of bringing their divorced or separated parents back together for Christmas. An offbeat third thread spawned productions that, for the sake of innovation and diversity, significantly altered traditional holiday personae and the story lines of established literary works. They were balanced in part by such classics as *It's a Wonderful Life, The Homecoming,* and *Miracle on 34th Street,* all of which, though not particularly religious, interjected home and family values as vital components of a traditional Christmas; and Dr. Seuss's *How the Grinch Stole Christmas,* which clearly sent the message that the joy of Christmas "doesn't come from a store."

• THE NATIONAL CHRISTMAS TREE AND THE CHRISTMAS PAGEANT OF PEACE. In 1913, President Woodrow Wilson, at the request of many citizens from Washington, D.C., gave his support for a National Community Christmas Tree lighting ceremony, first held that Christmas Eve on the East Plaza of the United States Capitol; Wilson, however, was unable to attend the event. The 1914 ceremony was fraught with financial difficulties, and no ceremonies were held in 1915 or 1916. They were further suspended during American involvement in World War I but were held again in November 1918 on the East Plaza following the Armistice.

Responding to a suggestion from Lucretia Hardy, an official from the District of Columbia Public Schools, President Calvin Coolidge moved the ceremonies to President's Park (the Ellipse) near the White House in 1923, at which time he became the first president to light the National Community Christmas Tree. The tree, a 48-foot cut balsam fir adorned with 2,500 red, white and green bulbs that were provided by the Electric League of Washington, D.C., was donated by Middlebury College from Coolidge's native state of Vermont. Coolidge's speech opposing cut trees, made in 1924 to the American Forestry Association, would have abolished the ceremony from then on, had a 35-foot Norwegian spruce not been planted in Sherman Plaza, where the ceremonies continued from 1924 to 1933. Subsequent locations included Lafayette Park (1934–1938), the Ellipse (1939–1940), and the South Lawn of the

White House (1941–1953). The ceremony was first broadcast by radio in 1925 (Coolidge) and by NBC television in 1946 (Truman). Prime Minister Winston Churchill of England attended the 1941 ceremonies with President Franklin Roosevelt, after which the National Community Christmas Tree remained unlighted from 1942 to 1944 because of blackouts imposed during World War II.

On December 17, 1954 (theretofore, the tree lighting ceremonies had been held on Christmas Eve), President Dwight Eisenhower officiated at ceremonies on the Ellipse that expanded the National Community Christmas Tree lighting ceremony by advocating worldwide peace through Christmas. This program, conceived by the Washington Board of Trade and the Washington Citizen's Committee, established the annual "Christmas Pageant of Peace," a three-week winter festival, the first of which that year hosted 27 foreign embassies that presented music, dances, and tableaux interpreting Christmas traditions in their respective countries. The first pageant also inaugurated "The Pathway of Peace," an annual display of 57 smaller, decorated trees that by 1990 would come to represent all 50 states, the District of Columbia, and U.S. territories. In addition, the first pageant included a Nativity scene, which appeared annually until 1973 when a U.S. Court of Appeals decision forced its removal. A private group, the American Christian Heritage Association, then erected its own *crèche* just outside pageant grounds. In 1984, the pageant reinstated the Nativity scene following a U.S. Supreme Court decision that such a display was historically and legally appropriate. Around 1972, the National Community Christmas Tree was renamed the National Christmas Tree to emphasize the national nature of the pageant.

Since 1954, the Ellipse has been the traditional site for the pageant. Pageants from 1954 through 1972 brought in a cut tree each year from a different state, the tallest being 99 feet in 1965, but in 1973 a live, 42-foot Colorado blue spruce was planted on the Ellipse. When that tree and another after it did not survive, both ultimately were replaced with a 40-foot Colorado blue spruce planted in 1978 on the

Ellipse. This tree currently serves as the National Christmas Tree.

In 1963, the National Christmas Tree was not lit until December 22, which ended 30 days of mourning following the assassination of President John F. Kennedy. In 1979 and 1980, President Jimmy Carter ordered only the top ornament lit in support of the American hostages held in Iran. Although the tree was fully lit in 1980 for only 417 seconds to commemorate the 417 days the hostages had been held up to that point, it was fully lit again following the hostages' release on President Ronald Reagan's inauguration day, January 20, 1981. On Christmas Eve, 1985, Reagan ordered the lights dimmed momentarily in support for Americans held hostage in Lebanon; the thousands of red, white, and blue lights on the 1989 tree symbolized President George H.W. Bush's "thousand points of light" speech made during his 1988 election campaign; and on New Year's Eve, 1999, the multicolored lights on the tree all turned white to celebrate the new millennium.

Since 1994, a large model train display running around its base has complemented the National Christmas Tree and the Pageant of Peace. The annual project originated with Bill Frank, then–Customer Service Manager for Aristo Craft Trains of Irvington, New Jersey, who felt that the National Christmas Tree looked "unfinished" without a model train running beneath it.

Following the tragic events of September 11, 2001, the National Tree's traditional, seasonal color scheme that year of red, green, and gold was changed to patriotic colors with red garland, 100,000 white (clear) and blue lights, and 100 large, white star ornaments.

• THE NATION'S CHRISTMAS TREE. Different from the National Christmas Tree described above, this 267-foot giant Sequoia resides in Kings Canyon National Park near Sanger, California. About 4,000 years old with a circumference of 107 feet, this tree, known since 1867 as the "General Grant," has been the site of an annual Christmas ceremony at its base since 1925. Charles Lee and R.J. Senior, members of the Sanger Chamber of Commerce, urged President Calvin Coolidge to endorse the General Grant as the "Nation's Christmas Tree," but when he declined, Congress did so in 1926.

President Dwight Eisenhower subsequently proclaimed the tree a national shrine in 1956 as a living memorial to all United States veterans who gave their lives for their country. Because its lowest branch is some 130 feet from the ground, the General Grant is not decorated for Christmas. Instead, members of the National Park Service place a large wreath at its base during the Christmas ceremonies.

• CHRISTMAS IN THE TWENTY-FIRST CENTURY. At present, the American Christmas of the early twenty-first century varies little from that of the late twentieth. Groups of carolers tour neighborhoods soliciting donations for charities, though perhaps not as frequently as before. Shopping malls play traditional and contemporary carols as crowds swarm the aisles on the day after Thanksgiving, dubbed "Black Friday" by the retail industry. Because of ongoing controversies over the separation of church and state arising in the 1960s, public Nativity scenes and other religious displays are generally absent, as are Nativity pageants in public schools. Sometime during the four weeks before Christmas, most offices will hold one or more parties, where the chief traditions include secular music, dancing, eating, and drinking.

As Thanksgiving has gradually lost its standing as a separate holiday and become more widely regarded as the opening of the Christmas season (though Christmas decorations often appear in retail stores immediately after Halloween), more families have begun setting up Christmas trees and decorating their homes on the weekend following Thanksgiving. Some families still prefer to wait until the last week or two before Christmas, especially if they are using real trees. Trees are usually decorated with commercially produced ornaments, garlands, tinsel, and electric "minilights," though some families cling to old-fashioned popcorn and cranberry strings, colored paper chains, and strings of electric lights.

Schools usually declare a holiday vacation approximately one week prior to Christmas and remain closed until shortly after New Year's Day. Most businesses grant only Christmas Day and New Year's Day as holidays during the season.

Christmas Eve to many remains a special family night, on which parents may read Christmas stories to their children, and the family may attend a midnight or candlelight church service. Young children generally awaken early on Christmas morning to open gifts, and families may attend another church service on Christmas morning. In most American homes, a family dinner is served sometime during Christmas Day. Traditional fare includes roast turkey with stuffing or dressing, ham, chicken or goose, cranberry sauce, sweet potatoes, green beans, squash, beets, assorted cakes and pies, coffee, tea, wassail, and eggnog. In the afternoon or evening, families may visit relatives and friends.

Some churches in the United States still observe special celebrations of Epiphany, but the final celebration of the predominantly secular American Christmas season is usually the New Year's Eve party. Traditions at this time include fireworks displays at parks and fairgrounds, noisemaking, and, at the stroke of midnight, kisses, embraces, and the singing of "Auld Lang Syne." The season ends with New Year's Day.

See also **Auld Lang Syne; Moravian Church; New Year's Day; The White House.**

Unlikely Angel

(1996). Made-for-television comedy/fantasy.

Dolly Parton stars as Ruby Diamond, a brassy lounge singer who has led a less-than-virtuous life. Shortly before Christmas, she is killed in an automobile accident and finds that the gates of paradise in heaven are closed to her. Yet St. Peter (Roddy McDowall) has hope for her redemption and sends her back to earth to help a dysfunctional family. Ruby has the week before Christmas in which to turn the family around, with midnight on Christmas Eve as the deadline. Two other stipulations: she must tell no one the purpose of her mission, and she must have no romantic affairs (at which she had been rather proficient in life). If she is successful, she will earn her wings. Failure is not an option.

Ruby literally drops from the sky and finds herself assigned as a nanny to the family of Ben Bartilson (Brian Kerwin), a widower who, following the loss of his wife a few years ago, has buried himself in his job, ignored his 14-year-old daughter Sarah (Allison Mack) and eight-year-old son Matt (Eli Marienthal), and shunned Christmas celebrations altogether. With such depression hanging over them, the family is adrift without purpose or direction, and Ruby must not only help them find the Christmas spirit but each other again.

With Maria Del Mar and Gary Sandy. Story by Katherine Ann Jones. Teleplay by Liz Coe and Robert L. Freedman. Produced by Jonathan Bernstein. Directed by Michael Switzer. Image Entertainment. DVD: Image Entertainment. 92 min.

Up on the Housetop

American children's song written by Benjamin R. Hanby (1833–1867). A relatively obscure figure and an abolitionist, Hanby also pursued teaching, the ministry, and musical composition. Living in Westerville, Ohio, at least during the latter half of his short life, Hanby wrote some 80 songs, two of which remain familiar today: "Darling Nellie Gray" (based on the story of a runaway slave whom his father had sheltered in the Underground Railroad) and "Up on the Housetop." According to the Ohio Historical Society, this latter carol was first published in October of 1866 under the simple title of "Santa Claus," but it has since come to be known by the first four words of its lyrics. Prior to Hanby, the poem "A Visit from St. Nicholas" ("'Twas the Night before Christmas"), first published anonymously in 1823, had depicted Santa and his reindeer landing on rooftops; surely this poem inspired Hanby's Christmas tune. That Hanby also wrote another children's Christmas standard, "Jolly Old St. Nicholas," has been suggested but not documented.

See also **Jolly Old St. Nicholas; A Visit from St. Nicholas.**

Uruguay
See **South America**

The Vatican

An independent city-state within Rome, Italy, the site of the Holy See, the seat of government for the Roman Catholic Church and the residence of the Pope. Possessing a long and complex history, the Vatican originated as a simple memorial chapel erected over the traditional burial site of St. Peter the Apostle (reputed to be the first Pope) and other first century Christians martyred at the hands of Emperor Nero. Constantine the Great replaced this chapel with a large basilica in the fourth century, and the building of adjacent papal palaces commenced in earnest in the early sixth century. The present Saint Peter's Basilica replaced that of Constantine during the Renaissance, and in the fifteenth century, following the return of the popes from their exile in Avignon, France (1309–1377), and the Great Schism (1378–1417), the Vatican became the permanent papal residence.

The following paragraphs summarize the principal Christmas celebrations as observed within the Vatican and in Rome by the reigning pontiff at the time of this writing, Pope John Paul II (Karol Wojtyla), who became the 264th successor to St. Peter in 1978. A detailed presentation of the specific liturgies may be found on the Vatican's official Web site at www.vatican.va.

The Pope presides at Mass for each of the four Advent Sundays; along with the *Angelus* (a thrice-daily recitation commemorating the Annunciation to the Virgin), on these Sundays the Pope usually delivers a message calling the faithful to prepare their hearts with spiritual penance for the coming of Christ. The Advent liturgy not only echoes the precursors of Christ, the prophets who foretold of His coming (the last of whom was John the Baptist), but also emphasizes the Virgin Mary as spiritual model and guide. The liturgy for the third

Advent Sunday, termed "*Gaudete* Sunday" (*see* **Advent**), changes to expressions of joy in expectation of the coming Christ. Following an annual tradition since 1968, on *Gaudete* Sunday the youngest child of each family brings the Nativity figure of the Christ Child to be blessed by the Pope.

On December 8, the Pope holds Mass to celebrate the Feast of the Immaculate Conception, then visits the *Piazza di Spagna* ("Spanish Square") in Rome, where he pays homage to the Virgin by placing a bouquet of flowers at the foot of her statue that sits atop the *Colonna dell'Immacolata* ("Column of the Immaculate Conception"). Next, the Pope venerates a fifteenth century Byzantine icon of the Madonna and Child, known as the *Salus Populi Romani* ("Protectress of the Roman People"), which is located above the altar in the *Cappella Paolina* ("Lady Chapel") of the Church of Santa Maria Maggiore (St. Mary Major) in Rome. There the Pope places a bouquet of roses and papal colors on the altar. On December 8, 1996, citizens from the region of Molise, Italy, honored the fiftieth anniversary of the priesthood of Pope John Paul II with a spectacular *'ndòcciata* torchlight procession, an ancient tradition with pagan roots (now Christianized) and peculiar to their region, in which some 2,000 people carrying *'ndòccia* (tall, lighted torches of fir and broomwood) marched down the *Via della Conciliazione* ("Road of Conciliation") to St. Peter's Square. The event terminated in a gigantic "Bonfire of the Brotherhood" (*see* **Feast of the Immaculate Conception; Italy**).

Other Advent traditions: The Pope conducts a Mass for the students of the Roman state universities, and shortly before Christmas, he summarizes significant events that have transpired in the Church during the year in an address made to the cardinals, papal household, and the Roman Curia with expressions of thanks for their faithful service. A recent tradition requested by the Pope has been the life-size Nativity scene and Christmas tree that have annually graced St. Peter's Square since 1982. Each year a different region of Europe presents the Pope with a Christmas tree, which is lighted in ceremonies attended by the donors of the tree and the governor of the Vatican City State.

Since 1992, the Vatican has sponsored the *Natale in Vaticano* ("Christmas in the Vatican"), an annual benefit concert filmed early in December at the Vatican's Aula Paolo VI Theater and broadcast via television on Christmas Eve. With cardinals, Italian nobles, members of Italian society, and American dignitaries in attendance, these concerts benefit the Vatican project "Fifty Churches for Rome, Third Millennium," which raises funds to finance the social activities of the Catholic Church and to build 50 new churches in underprivileged Roman suburbs. Each concert features a diverse program of traditional and contemporary Christmas music, performed by noted entertainers from around the world, such as Tom Jones, Jewel, Dionne Warwick, Manhattan Transfer, and Sarah Brightman. The tradition includes a private audience with the Pope for all participants. The 2002 concert is available on DVD as *A Musical Christmas from the Vatican* (Delta Entertainment, 102 min.).

Advent terminates in Midnight Mass, termed the Angels' Mass, held on Christmas Eve in either St. Peter's Basilica or St. Peter's Square, where children from all over the world place flowers and gifts before an image of the Christ Child lying below the altar, on which lies a copy of the Gospel open to Luke's account of the Nativity. The Pope delivers a homily at this time and on Christmas Day presents his annual holiday message and blessing, known as *Urbi et Orbi* ("To the City and to the World"), at noon from the central balcony of St. Peter's Basilica to an audience of many thousands. The themes of these holiday messages often center on spirituality and world peace with the condemnation of consumerism, commercialism, and world violence. On Christmas Eve, 2003, the Pope touched on the war in Iraq and other conflicts by stating, "Too much blood is still being shed on the earth! Too much violence and too many conflicts trouble the peaceful existence of nations!" Midnight Mass has been televised since 1948; this and the *Urbi et Orbi* message have been broadcast worldwide via satellite since 1974, co-produced by the Vatican Television Center (CTV) and RAI, Italy's state television network. The other two Christmas Day Masses, those at dawn (Shepherds' Mass) and later in the day (Mass of the Divine Word), are not usually televised (*see* **Christmas Masses**).

Between Christmas and New Year's Day, other Masses include those for the Feasts of St. Stephen (December 26), St. John the Evangelist (December 27), the Holy Innocents (December 28), the Holy Family (first Sunday after Christmas), and the *Te Deum Laudamus* (hymn, "We Praise Thee, O God") and First Vespers of the Solemnity of Mary (December 31). The latter is an evening celebration of thanksgiving for God's blessings for the year.

In 1969 following the Second Vatican Council (1962–65), the Solemnity of Mary, which celebrates her divine maternity, replaced the former Feast of the Circumcision on New Year's Day. Observed with the Solemnity of Mary on January 1 is the World Day of Peace, instituted by Pope Paul VI in 1968 as a day of world prayer for peace. Thus throughout his Pontificate, Pope John Paul II has stressed the theme "To reach peace, teach peace."

Wrapping up Christmastide are Masses for the First Sunday of the New Year; Solemnity of the Epiphany (January 6), in which new bishops are ordained; and the Feast of the Baptism of the Lord (first Sunday after Epiphany), at which time children are baptized, and the Christmas season ends. Originally the Baptism was celebrated on Epiphany, together with the miracle at Cana (when Jesus first turned water into wine) and the adoration of the Magi, but the Baptism was assigned to January 13 in 1960. Then following the Second Vatican Council, the Baptism was reassigned to its present date. If Epiphany falls on a Sunday, however, the Baptism is celebrated on the following Monday.

• HOLY YEAR OF JUBILEE. According to Leviticus 25:10, each fiftieth year, the "Year of Jubilee," was one of remission and universal pardon. Since the year 1300 and the Pontificate of Pope Boniface VIII, at designated intervals the Roman Catholic Church has observed a Holy Year of Jubilee, commencing on Christmas Eve and usually terminating on Epiphany more than a full year later. Originally, Jubilee was observed at 100-year intervals, but these were gradually reduced to the present interval of 25 years in 1450. During the Jubilee year, the faithful receive indulgences for sins (a remission of the penalty, not of the guilt) upon making confession, taking Communion, and performing other acts of piety and charity as stipulated by the Pope. Early Jubilees also required pilgrimages to each of the four patriarchal basilicas in Rome: St. Peter's, St. John Lateran, St. Paul's Outside the Walls, and St. Mary Major. To symbolize Christ as the door to salvation (John 10:9), each of these basilicas was assigned a special "Holy Door" which was ritually opened during Christmas and through which pilgrims passed to gain the Jubilee; ritual closing of the doors terminated the Jubilee. The first documented opening of a Holy Door in the history of Jubilee was of that to the Basilica of St. John Lateran in 1423; the first documented closing was of that to St. Peter's Basilica on Epiphany, 1501.

In preparation for the most recent "Great Jubilee of the Year 2000," on the first Sunday of Advent in 1998, Pope John Paul II read the Bull of Indiction, *Incarnationis Mysterium*, which presented the rite of consignment and stipulations for gaining the Jubilee. Whereas in past eras the Pope traditionally opened the Holy Door to St. Peter's and cardinal legates opened those to the other three Roman basilicas, Pope John Paul II became the first pope in history to open all the Holy Doors to the four basilicas for Jubilee 2000, which began in 1999: Christmas Eve, that to St. Peter's; Christmas Day, that to St. John Lateran; January 1, 2000, that to St. Mary Major; and January 18, that to St. Paul's. On Epiphany Eve, 2001, cardinal legates closed all the basilica doors except that to St. Peter's, which the Pope closed on Epiphany, thus ending Jubilee 2000. The complete rituals for the opening and closing of the Holy Doors may be found at the Vatican's official Web site.

• WORKS OF ART. Within the *Pinacoteca*, the fine arts collection in the Vatican Museum, are examples of Christmas art, primarily by fifteenth century Italian painters: *Annunciation* by Giovanni di Paolo (c. 1403–c. 1483); *Nativity and the Announcement to the Shepherds* and *Flight into Egypt* by Sano di Pietro (1406–1481); *Annunciation* by Marco Palmezzano (c. 1460–1539); *Crowning of the Virgin, Natività,* and *Adoration of the Magi* (Rospigliosi Triptych) by Bartolomeo di Tommaso da Foligno; *Nativity and Arrival of the Magi* (*Madonna of the Spineta*) by the Spaniard Giovanni di Pietro (also known as Lo Spagna, d. 1528); *Annunciation* and *Rest during the Flight into Egypt* by Barocci (Federico Fiori, also called Fiori Da Urbino, c. 1528–1612); *Adoration of the Magi* (icon) by Vittore di Bartolomeo; *Annunciation, Adoration of the Magi, Presentation in the Temple*, the predella of the *Crowning of the* Virgin (Oddi Chapel altarpiece) by Raffaello Sanzio (1483–1520); *Rest during the Flight into Egypt* by Francesco Mancini (1679–1758); *Stories of St. Nicholas of Bari* by Gentile da Fabriano (1370?–1427). This latter, one of the side panels in the predella of a polyptych commissioned by the Quaratesi family, is a series of four paintings depicting legendary events in the life of St. Nicholas: his birth, the gift to the three dowerless maidens, reviving three youths in brine, and saving a ship from sinking.

See also **Christmas Day; Epiphany; Feast of the Holy Family; Holy Innocents Day; Nativity** [Works of Art]; **New Year's Day** [Church Feasts]; **"O" Antiphons; St. Nicholas.**

Venezuela
See **South America**

A Very Brady Christmas
See **The Brady Bunch**

A Very Merry Cricket
(1973). Made-for television animated cartoon sequel to *The Cricket in Times Square* (1973), an earlier cartoon that was based on a children's book of the same title by George Selden, published in 1960. In the book, Chester C. Cricket, a most unusual insect from rural Connecticut with the ability to play mesmerizing, violin-like music on his wings, was unwittingly transported via a picnic basket to New York City, where he met friends Tucker Mouse and Harry Cat. There, Chester's music had brought peace and harmony to the harsh environment of the Big Apple.

With the holidays nigh at hand in the sequel, Chester returns to New York, not by accident this time, but as a favor to Tucker and Harry, who desire to bring the true meaning of Christmas back into Manhattan through the cricket's talents. The roar of the streets obliterates Chester's initial strains, however, and the endeavor seems futile, until a massive power outage silences the city. Then from the silence emerge "Silent Night" and other carols, which work their magic of "peace on earth."

Voices: Les Tremayne and Mel Blanc. Written, produced, and directed by Chuck Jones. A Chuck Jones Enterprises Production. VHS: Family Home Entertainment. 30 min.

A Virgin Most Pure
See **A Virgin Unspotted**

A Virgin Unspotted
English traditional carol, thought to have arisen in the Gloucestershire region during the sixteenth century. The text first appeared in *New Carolls for This Merry Time of Christmas* (London, 1661), the sole copy of which currently resides in the Bodleian Library, Oxford. Originally, the carol consisted of 13 verses with refrains before and after each verse exhorting all to rejoice and be merry. The first verse of this Nativity narrative initially began as "In Bethlehem city, in Jewry it was." By the eighteenth century, however, the now-familiar first verse, commencing with "A virgin unspotted, the prophet foretold," had been added. Variations of text exist; notable examples include those published by Davies Gilbert in *Some Ancient Christmas Carols* (London, 1822) and William Sandys in *Christmas Carols, Ancient and Modern* (London, 1833). These versions are believed to derive from West Country broadsides; they begin with the phrase "A virgin most pure," which serves as an alternate title. Modern printings of the text feature only one "rejoice and be merry" refrain, which appears after the verses.

The carol has known countless musical settings, the first of which appeared in John Arnold's *The Compleat Psalmodist* (London, 1741). An original setting surfaced in America by the New England composer William Billings (1746–1800), which he published in his *The Singing Master's Assistant* (Boston, 1778).

A Vision of Sugar Plums
See **Bewitched**

A Visit from St. Nicholas
Highly popular American poem, also known as "'Twas the Night before Christmas"

and "The Night before Christmas." Its authorship is controversial. Popular accounts attribute the poem to Clement Clarke Moore (1779–1863), a poet and professor of Greek and Oriental literature at the Episcopal General Theological Seminary in New York City from 1821 to 1850, who supposedly composed his legendary poem during Christmas 1822 to entertain his children. It is said that Harriet Butler, a family friend and daughter of the rector of St. Paul's Episcopal Church in Troy, New York, was visiting the Moore home at the time and copied the poem as Moore first recited it to his children. A year later, Orville Holley, editor for Troy's newspaper, the *Sentinel*, received a copy of the then-anonymous poem from an unnamed woman (possibly Ms. Butler) and published it on December 23 under the heading "Account of a Visit from St. Nicholas" (later printings shortened the title to "A Visit from St. Nicholas"). The poem was an instant success and became a featured item in the *Sentinel* for several Christmases. In time, children came to know the poem, not by its original title, but by its opening phrase, "'Twas the Night before Christmas," or simply "The Night before Christmas."

Although the popularity of the poem spread widely, the author remained anonymous until 1837, when the poem appeared in *The New York Book of Poetry*. This book was the first to credit Clement Moore as the author, apparently at the suggestion of his friend Charles Fenno Hoffman. A sober, religious pedant not inclined to frivolous verse, Moore ultimately claimed authorship when he included "A Visit from St. Nicholas" in his own *Poems*, published in 1844. He later attributed his long silence to embarrassment over his "trifle."

According to descendants of Henry Livingston, Jr. (1748–1828), however, their ancestor is the poem's true author. Livingston, a painter, cartographer, and amateur poet of Dutch descent from Poughkeepsie, New York, supposedly read his poem to his family and a "guest," after which the latter requested a copy. This guest subsequently became a governess for Moore's children, and it is conceivable that it was she who first delivered the poem to the Troy *Sentinel*. Livingston knew nothing of the dispute, having died long before Moore ever claimed authorship.

Since the latter 1800s, the Livingston family has continued to maintain their claim upon "A Visit from St. Nicholas" based upon circumstantial evidence. According to a *New York Times* article by David D. Kirkpatrick, research published in 2000 by Don Foster, an English professor at Vassar College, supports Livingston as the author. Among the many facts that Foster cites as evidence: Moore's other poems are generally stern, pious, and moralistic, mimicking those of other pious poets, and rarely featuring anapestic meter (the meter of "A Visit from St. Nicholas"); Livingston's poems are light, fanciful, and mimic the style of William King and Christopher Anstey, two eighteenth century poets who also wrote popular poems in anapestic meter. Livingston annually wrote anapestic Christmas verses for his family; he preferred the seasonal salutation "Happy Christmas" to "Merry Christmas" (the last line of "A Visit from St. Nicholas" begins "Happy Christmas to all . . ."); and his favorite expression was "Dunder and Blixem" (Dutch-American words for "thunder and lightning"), which supposedly became the basis for the names of St. Nicholas's last two reindeer, currently known by the German-American equivalents of "Donder" and "Blitzen" (see below). Moore, on the other hand, was conversant in German, not Dutch. In Foster's opinion, Moore simply plagiarized Livingston's poem.

Further controversy surrounds Donder and Blitzen. Popular accounts claiming Moore as author hold that, because of a printer's error, the 1823 publication produced "Dunder and Blixem" and not "Donder and Blitzen" as Moore supposedly intended. Foster contends that the *Sentinel* originally printed "Donder and Blitzen" in error and that Moore perpetuated the error in the four copies of the poem that he produced by hand late in his life. Unfortunately, no original manuscript of "Account of a Visit from St. Nicholas" has ever surfaced to lay the matter to rest.

The name "Donner" (German for "thunder") has sometimes replaced "Donder" in reproductions of the poem in twentieth century collections. According to some accounts, "Donner" did not appear in print prior to 1950, the substitution allegedly originating with songwriter John D. (Johnny) Marks, who created the hit tune "Rudolph, the Red-Nosed Reindeer," recorded by cowboy singing star Gene Autry in 1949. Marks's "Rudolph" lyrics included the names of all of the now-famous reindeer and, possibly to improve the flow of the lyrics, supposedly used "Donner" instead. After "Rudolph" became a hit song, the story continues, "Donner" appeared more frequently in printings of "A Visit from St. Nicholas." While Marks may have nurtured the error, he certainly was not responsible for creating it. Basing his song on Rudolph, a reindeer in a story that his brother-in-law, Robert May, had written in 1939 for the Montgomery Ward Company, Marks was probably influenced by the reindeer names listed therein, which also included "Donner." But one only needs to note "Donner" written in a 1932 Walt Disney animated cartoon short, *Santa's Workshop*, for confirmation that "Donner" existed before the birth of Rudolph, long before 1950. Although the exact origin for the substitution remains obscure, it likely stems from publishers' confusion over two sound-alike words from two foreign languages, both of which mean "thunder."

Ken Darby, a composer noted for having devised the Munchkin voices for *The Wizard of Oz* in 1939, is credited with providing the first musical setting, titled "'Twas the Night before Christmas" and published in 1942. Recorded by Fred Waring and the Pennsylvanians on the Decca label that same year, it sold over a million copies. Although similar contributions shortly appeared from other composers such as Frank Klickmann in 1951 and Johnny Marks in 1952, Darby's is considered the definitive version. Nevertheless, neither Darby's tune nor any of the others appeared in the 1974 made-for-television animated cartoon *'Twas the Night before Christmas.*

Films based on the poem include four silent versions, three titled *The Night before Christmas* (1906, animation by the Edison Company; 1912; and 1926) and *'Twas the Night before Christmas* (1914, the Edison Company). Sound versions titled *The Night before Christmas* include animated cartoon "shorts" (Walt Disney, 1933; MGM featuring Tom and Jerry, 1941, nominated for an Academy Award, Best Short Subjects Cartoons) and an animated television special with host Art Linkletter and the Norman Luboff Choir (1968).

New York City has held an annual tribute to Clement Clarke Moore's memory since 1911. Late in December, the Clement Clarke Moore Commemoration convenes in Manhattan's Church of the Intercession for a candlelight service. After hearing a reading of "A Visit from St. Nicholas," a solemn procession proceeds to Moore's grave in the cemetery at Trinity Church nearby.

Phyllis Siefker's book *Santa Claus, Last of the Wild Men* further contends that the American Santa Claus and the St. Nicholas of "A Visit from St. Nicholas" both derive from "Pelz Nicholas" ("Furry Nicholas"), a mythical being that migrated with the "Pennsylvania Dutch" to America. The subject is more fully discussed in the entry **Saint Nicholas.**

See also **Rudolph, the Red-Nosed Reindeer** (song); **Saint Nicholas's Day; Tom and Jerry's Night before Christmas; 'Twas the Night before Christmas** (television special); **A Walt Disney Christmas.**

The Voice of Christmas
See **The Brady Bunch**

Waits

Groups of street minstrels in Great Britain principally noted for providing nocturnal Christmas music. During the eighteenth and nineteenth centuries, waits would go caroling from door to door, soliciting donations from their hosts.

A word with several applications, "waits"

first denoted medieval minstrel-pages at court, whose nightly task it was to guard the streets and call out the hours. Their duty was akin to the night watchman's; hence, the possible derivation from the German *Wacht* (guard) or even from the Scottish *waith* (roaming about). A company of waits was first known to have been established at Exeter in 1400.

During the seventeenth century, "waits" or "wayghtes" indicated not only hoboys or oboes but also those groups who played wind instruments (other accounts also mention violins) while roaming about at night. By this time, waits were either employed and licensed by cities as watchmen and town criers, or they worked as freelance minstrels. In the latter case, it became commonplace for men to hire waits to serenade their ladies, sometimes well into the night.

By the eighteenth and nineteenth centuries, the waits' activities included only nocturnal performances of seasonal music for a few weeks prior to Christmas, terminating on Christmas Eve. In Scotland, performances focused on the new year. The waits are believed to have performed some of the best-known of English traditional carols, such as "God Rest Ye Merry, Gentlemen," "The Wassail Song," and "We Wish You a Merry Christmas."

"Authorized" waits under municipal employment apparently had no monopoly on the profession, for an 1820 dispute that arose in Westminster regarding the legality of itinerant minstrels performing the same functions as waits came to naught.

The late nineteenth century saw a decline not only in the waits but all other British holiday customs that solicited money, such as Boxing Day.

See also **Boxing Day.**

Wales

See **Great Britain**

A Walt Disney Christmas

(1981). Video collection of six classic, animated cartoon "shorts":

Once upon a Wintertime (1952). A December valentine featuring the memories of a romantic couple in their courting days. Vocals by Frances Langford. Produced by Walt Disney. Directed by Hamilton Luske.

Santa's Workshop (1932). A cartoon from the *Silly Symphonies* musical series showing Santa in his workshop with toys being made and prepared for delivery on Christmas Eve. One reindeer's name appears as "Donner," instead of the "Donder" as found in the poem "A Visit from St. Nicholas." Produced by Walt Disney. Directed by Wilfred Jackson.

The Night before Christmas (1933). Based on the poem "A Visit from St. Nicholas," the story depicts Santa delivering gifts at one house and the merriment that the toys enjoy as they arrange themselves under the tree. From the *Silly Symphonies* musical series. Vocals by Donald Novis. Produced by Walt Disney. Directed by Wilfred Jackson.

Pluto's Christmas Tree (1952). When Mickey Mouse and Pluto bring in their Christmas tree, chipmunks Chip and Dale are hidden inside. In vain, Pluto attempts to rid the house of them. With Minnie, Donald Duck, and Goofy. Voices: Dessie Flynn, Clarence Nash, Pinto Colvig, Ruth Clifford, and James MacDonald. Written by Bill Berg and Milt Schaffer. Produced by Walt Disney and John Sutherland. Directed by Jack Hannah.

On Ice (1935). Ice-skating antics with Mickey and Minnie Mouse, Goofy, Donald Duck, and Pluto. Voices: Pinto Colvig, Walt Disney, Marcellite Garner, and Clarence Nash. Produced by Walt Disney and John Sutherland. Directed by Ben Sharpsteen.

Donald's Snow Fight (1942). When Donald Duck deliberately runs his sled into a snowman built by his three nephews, the latter declare a snow war on their uncle. Voice: Clarence Nash. Written by Carl Barks. Produced by Walt Disney. Directed by Jack King.

Walt Disney Company. VHS: Walt Disney Home Video. 46 min.

See also **A Disney Christmas Gift; Jiminy Cricket's Christmas; A Visit from St. Nicholas.**

The Waltons

Emmy Award–winning family television series of 210 episodes that ran from 1972 to 1981 on the CBS network, with six specials appearing after that time. Created by novelist and co–executive producer Earl Hamner, Jr., the series depicted the life and adventures of a large, closely knit family living in the Blue Ridge Mountains of Virginia during the Depression years. The regular cast of characters included John and Olivia Walton (Ralph Waite and Ms. Michael Learned); their children, John-Boy (Richard Thomas, who left the series in 1977), Mary-Ellen (Judy Norton-Taylor), Jason (Jon Walmsley), Erin (Mary McDonough), Ben (Eric Scott), Jim-Bob (David Harper), and Elizabeth (Kami Cotler); and the Walton grandparents, Zebulon (Will Geer, who died in 1978) and Esther (Ellen Corby, who died in 1999). The series began on a Christmas note, inspired by Hamner's short, autobiographical novel *The Homecoming: A Novel about Spencer's Mountain*. Hamner, who grew up in Schuyler, Virginia, based this story on that Christmas Eve of 1933 when his father was late coming home from work.

- THE NOVEL. Clay and Olivia Spencer, together with their eight children, Clay-Boy, Becky, Shirley, Matt, Mark, Luke, John, and Pattie-Cake, struggle to make ends meet during lean years. Jobs are scarce, and Clay works all week in a machine shop 40 miles away, coming home only on Friday evenings.

Late one Christmas Eve when Clay has not returned, Olivia sends Clay-Boy out on a search. His trek takes him to an African American church, where Clay has been known to gamble at odd hours with his white friends. Instead, a Christmas Eve service is in progress with no sign of his father. Next comes a visit to the home of Emma and Etta Staples, two eccentric, old-maid sisters whose avocation is making bootleg whiskey ("The Recipe"). This visit results in Clay-Boy's near-inebriation from spiked eggnog. The situation looks grim until 1 A.M., when Clay, having missed his bus, finally returns loaded down with gifts. So that his younger children will keep faith in Santa Claus, he explains that he "wrassled" an old burglar dressed in a red suit outside and grabbed an armload of presents before the stranger took off in a reindeer sleigh.

- THE TELEVISION SPECIAL. The next evolutionary step was Hamner's 1971 adaptation of the novel into a two-hour television special, titled *The Homecoming: A Christmas Story*, which introduced the Walton family. The special starred Andrew Duggan as John, Patricia Neal as Olivia, Edgar Bergen as the grandfather, and Ellen Corby as the grandmother. These roles were all recast for the television series, except for Corby, who remained. The Walton children in this special also remained for the series. Although there was no change in "The Recipe," the Staples Sisters (played by Dorothy Stickney and Josephine Hutchinson in the special) became the Baldwin Sisters (Mary Jackson and Helen Kleeb) in the series. Cleavon Little wrapped up the principal cast as the Reverend Hawthorne Dooley. Originally not intended as a pilot for any series, *The Homecoming* nevertheless launched one of the most beloved shows on television.

Memorable scenes from *The Homecoming* include six-year-old Elizabeth's encounter with the overly pious missionary lady who distributes charity gifts on Christmas Eve at Ike Godsey's store in exchange for Bible quotes. As Mary-Ellen prompts them with whispered verses, several children, including Elizabeth, receive presents. But to her horror, the unwrapped doll stares at her through a hideously cracked face; as far as Elizabeth is concerned, someone had "killed" it.

Back at home, Olivia presents John-Boy with his Christmas gift, one of her handmade knit scarves, then sends him out to search for his father. John-Boy's trek takes in the children's Christmas Eve pageant at Rev. Dooley's church, after which he and the minister make inquiry at the Baldwin sisters' home. Though John-Boy's efforts prove fruitless, he returns home with a jar. Olivia, of the Baptist persuasion, initially believes this to be "The Recipe" and prepares to rain damnation on all, until she realizes that it is merely plain eggnog.

About midnight, as the children worry over their father's return and Olivia quietly despairs, John-Boy gathers the family together and tells them about the miracle of cattle kneeling and talking at that time of year. Shortly after, John's safe return brings gifts for all and draws the special to a most happy ending as each family member bids the others good night. But just beforehand, Olivia, seeing that John has exhausted his paycheck on presents, wonders what they will live on in the coming week. John's reply: "Love."

In 1972, *The Homecoming* captured the following honors: American Cinema Editors Award nomination for Best Edited Television Program; Emmy nominations for Outstanding Directorial Achievement (Fielder Cook) and Outstanding Leading Actress (Patricia Neal); Golden Globe Award for Best Television Actress (Neal); Golden Globe nomination for Best Television Movie.

With William Windom. Narrated and written by Earl Hamner, Jr. Produced by Robert Jacks. Directed by Fielder Cook. Lorimar Productions and CBS Television. DVD: Paramount Home Video. 98 min.

• THE SERIES. Christmas was the subject of only four *Waltons* episodes:

"The Best Christmas" (December 9, 1976). Olivia believes that this will be the last Christmas with everyone together before World War II calls her boys into military service. A blizzard on Walton's Mountain, however, creates a series of emergencies that keep the family apart until the last moment, Christmas Day. With Joe Conley, Ronnie Claire Edwards, Tom Bower, John Ritter, Lynn Hamilton, and Robert Donner. Written by John McGreevey. Directed by Lawrence Dobkin.

"Day of Infamy" (December 7, 1978). As Mary-Ellen prepares to spend Christmas with her physician-husband, Dr. Curtis Willard (Tom Bower), who is stationed at Pearl Harbor, John and Olivia plan to surprise her with an early Christmas by chopping down a Christmas tree that Grandpa Walton had planted. A radio broadcast announcing the Japanese attack on Pearl Harbor shatters the holiday spirit, and the Walton boys ponder military service, while Mary-Ellen reminisces about the peaks and valleys of her marriage to Curtis. In the ensuing days, after the family learns that Curtis perished while attending the wounded, Grandma presents Mary-Ellen with a letter of fatherly love which Curtis had previously addressed to their infant son, John-Curtis (twins Michael and Marshall Reed). With Joe Conley, Ronnie Claire Edwards, Lynn Hamilton, and Robin Eisenmann. Written by Paul Savage. Directed by Harry Harris.

"The Spirit" (December 20, 1979). The Waltons on Christmas Eve share the spirit of the season with Paul (Ned Bellamy), an escaped German POW, who had been hiding out on Walton's Mountain. With Joe Conley, Ronnie Claire Edwards, Peggy Rae, Martha Nix, and Keith Mitchell. Written by Kathleen Hite. Directed by Herbert Hirschman.

"The Children's Carol" (December 5, 1977). This two-hour episode could be listed as a Christmas special, though it was never billed as such. Set during World War II, the episode features Tess and Pip Wrayburn (Sally Boyden and Jeff Cotler, Kami Cotler's brother), two English children orphaned during the London *Blitzkrieg*, who come to stay with the Waltons. Their adjustment appears impossible until Allison, an English girl overseas with whom Jim-Bob has been communicating via shortwave radio, locates the children's mother and broadcasts a Christmas reunion with them across the Atlantic. Richard Thomas and Ellen Corby were absent from this telecast, Thomas having left the series earlier in 1977 and Corby having suffered a stroke in 1976, because of which she missed 18 months of the series. With Joe Conley, Ronnie Claire Edwards, Lynn Hamilton, and Tom Bower. Narrated by Earl Hamner, Jr. Written by John McGreevey. Produced by Andy White. Directed by Lawrence Dobkin. Lorimar Productions and CBS Television. VHS: Warner Home Video. 97 min.

Wassail

Hot beverage generally consisting of wine, cider, ale, or other liquor with spices such as cloves, ginger, cinnamon, and nutmeg. Other ingredients have included eggs, milk, sugar, molasses, lemon, roasted apples, and thin slices of toast (which yielded the term "toast," a ritualistic salutation of honor). The name "wassail" derives from slurring an old Anglo-Saxon expression, "wes hael" ("be well," "be hale," or "your health"). Wassail was also known as "lamb's wool," so named for the appearance of fleece which the floating, soggy toast or roasted apples imparted to the beverage.

Wassail's association with the drinking or "toasting" of one's health stemmed from a legend surrounding the fifth century British king, Vortigern. During a feast honoring Vortigern, a group of Saxons offered a bowl of ale to the king, saying, "Louerd king, wes hael" ("Lord king, your health"). They explained the Saxon custom of offering ale to a friend, who, upon receiving the ale, was to respond with, "Drinc hael" ("I drink your health"). Then the latter would reciprocate. By the sixteenth century, the liquor as well as the toast itself had acquired the name "wassail," the act of toasting had become "wassailing," and the bowl containing the liquor had become the "wassail bowl." If the toasting became excessive, "wassail" also described a drinking binge.

Toasting became a popular social pastime that eventually played a prominent role during the revelry of holiday feasts, especially at Christmastime. Although guests originally saluted their host by drinking from a single wassail bowl passed from person to person, in due course the wassail was served in individual vessels. In another custom, drawing upon a pagan superstition that toasting orchard trees in midwinter would increase the fruit yield, people ceremoniously congregated during the 12 days of Christmas to pour wassail from the wassail bowl over tree roots and trunks. That custom of "wassailing the fruit trees" further evolved into bands of carolers wassailing through the streets and singing from door to door, wishing everyone good health during the holidays. A number of popular wassailing songs subsequently emerged, and some of them have survived into the present, such as "We Wish You a Merry Christmas," "Here We Come A-Caroling (Wassail Song)," and "God Rest Ye Merry, Gentlemen." Households almost always rewarded the wassailers with a taste of wassail from the wassail bowl, and the modern party punch bowl is a descendant of that bowl.

A Scandinavian variation of wassail employed slices of a spiced loaf, Yule cake, which floated to the top of the wassail bowl.

See also **God Rest Ye Merry, Gentlemen; Here We Come A-Caroling; The Twelve Days of Christmas** (time period); **We Wish You a Merry Christmas; Yule.**

Wassail Song
See **Here We Come A-Caroling; Wassail**

Wassail, Wassail All Over the Town
See **Gloucestershire Wassail**

Watchman, Tell Us of the Night
English Advent carol, the lyrics of which were published in 1825 by Sir John Bowring

(1792–1872). An author, editor for the *Westminster Review*, member of Parliament, and governor of Hong Kong, Bowring based his carol's lyrics on Isaiah 21:11–12. This otherwise metaphorically grim passage predicts that Dumah, a key oasis in Northern Arabia, which had fallen to Assyria, will pass through the "morning" or light of relief from this menace, only to fall victim to the "night" or darkness of Babylonian captivity.

Bowring chose to turn the passage around by creating a carol with lyrics promising hope of salvation in Christ, Who eradicates the darkness of sin (night) with the glory of eternal life (dawn). Consisting of three verses, the lines alternate between questions from a "Traveler" in anxious expectation and replies from the "Watchman," who, having seen the Eastern Star, heralds the coming joy that the world will experience through the birth of Christ.

No single musical setting for "Watchman" has ever gained general popularity, despite matches with several melodies from Germany, Wales, England, and the United States. The settings most often used include those by Jakob Hintze (1622–1702), a German composer and music editor, and by Welsh music professor Joseph Parry (1841–1903), whose tune has also been used as a setting for the Charles Wesley hymn "Jesus, Lover of My Soul."

We Need a Little Christmas
Song from the 1966 Broadway hit musical *Mame*, written by composer and lyricist Jerry Herman. In this musical, Mame (played in the original production by Angela Lansbury), an eccentric lady with a youthful approach to life, strives to impart her philosophy to nephew Patrick Dennis (Frank Michaels) and husband Beauregard Burnside (Charles Braswell). When Mame and Patrick find themselves destitute in the Great Depression, only Christmas festivities can restore their spirits. Therefore, despite the fact that it's not Yuletide by the calendar, they deck the halls, light the candles, and lift their voices to the tune of "We Need a Little Christmas."

The show has had numerous touring versions, and a 1974 film version starred Lucille Ball and Robert Preston.

Of the 25 most frequently performed

Christmas songs of the twentieth century listed by the American Society of Composers, Authors and Publishers (ASCAP), "We Need a Little Christmas" ranked number 21. By December 2004, however, it had fallen from the list.

Although *Mame* is considered to be Jerry Herman's best score, that for *Hello, Dolly!* (1964) was also a smash hit, including its Grammy-winning title number. Herman has been inducted into the Theatre Hall of Fame and the Songwriters Hall of Fame.

See also **ASCAP List of Christmas Songs.**

We Three Kings of Orient Are

American carol written in 1857 by the Rev. John Henry Hopkins, Jr. (1820–1891). Founder and editor of the *Church Journal* (1853–1868) and an instructor of church music at the Episcopal General Theological Seminary in New York City, Hopkins composed "We Three Kings" as part of an elaborate Nativity drama he created for the seminary. Other sources state that Hopkins, a bachelor, also wrote the carol as a Christmas drama for his nieces and nephews who lived in Burlington, Vermont, for which he was subsequently dubbed "Vermont's Father Christmas."

The carol first appeared in print under a variant title, "Three Kings of Orient," in Hopkins's collection, *Carols, Hymns, and Songs* (New York, 1865). At the time of its publication, Hopkins was rector of Christ's Church in Williamsport, Pennsylvania. The carol became popular in England and was included in the prestigious collection *Christmas Carols New and Old*, edited by Henry Bramley and John Stainer (London, 1871).

Hopkins originally scored the carol for three male voices with parts for each of the traditional Three Kings, Melchior, Gaspar, and Balthazar, who brought gifts to the manger. The trio were to sing verse 1 together, followed by Gaspar, who sang of bringing gold for a King in verse 2; Melchior, frankincense to worship God in verse 3; and Balthazar, myrrh for Christ's future passion and death in verse 4. The trio together concluded with verse 5. Today, the carol is generally sung without regard for individual solos.

Hopkins contributed the lyrics and music

The Rev. John Henry Hopkins, Jr. (1820–1891), American Episcopal minister and composer of the carol "We Three Kings of Orient Are." Hopkins was also known as "Vermont's Father Christmas." Courtesy Vermont Historical Society, Barre, Vermont.

for another, lesser-known carol, "Gather around the Christmas Tree."

We Wish You a Merry Christmas

Traditional carol thought to have originated in the West Country of England during the sixteenth or seventeenth century. Although it remains today as one of the most popular of the secular carols, little else is known of its history, other than that the waits included this carol in their repertoire of holiday melodies. The lyrics are preoccupied with "figgy pudding" (plum pudding), demanding that the dish be brought to the carolers awaiting outside as a reward for their musical efforts. This is in keeping with the older wassailing carols as opposed to those of the eighteenth and nineteenth centuries, the lyrics of which often clearly expect the master of the house to invite the troupe indoors for some refreshment.

See also **Waits; Wassail.**

We'll Dress the House

See **Alfred Burt Carols**

West Indies

Following Christopher Columbus's landing in the Bahamas at San Salvador in 1492, a number of European nations laid claim to various islands in the West Indies, including Portugal, the Netherlands, France, and Great Britain. During the seventeenth and eighteenth centuries, black slaves from West Africa were imported to work on sugar plantations, and in the nineteenth century, following the abolition of slavery, Muslims and Hindus replaced the blacks on some of the islands. Descendants of these workers now largely occupy the islands, along with people of mixed African-European heritage. Roman Catholicism is prominent, with a number of traditions reflecting that faith. Also evident are influences from the colonial period as well as the United States, such as Christmas trees, Santa Claus, and traditional carols known well in the United States.

• JONKONNU. African slaves introduced this unique tradition into the West Indies, as well as the Bermuda Islands, the southern United States, and portions of Central America such as Belize and Honduras. The tradition is perpetuated in the West Indies by their descendants, the black Caribs or Garifuna. Consisting of masked dances, the tradition is thought to have originated early during the eighteenth century as a memorial to John Conny, a celebrated chief on the Guinea coast. Whereas some believe that the word "Jonkonnu" derived from Conny's name, with multiple variations such as "Johnkankus," "John Kooner," "John Kuner," "Junkanoo," "Jonkanoo," and "John Canoe," others hold that these names corrupted the French term *gens inconnu* ("unknown people"), a name bestowed because the masks, often skin-covered and imitative of horned beasts, shielded the dancers' identities. The costumes featured colorful strips of paper or cloth attached to the headdresses as well as outfits of dark gunnysack material. To the lively music of gumbay drums, fifes, and triangles (a musical form known as *Wanaragua*), parades of mostly male dancers sang humorous and often satirical verses. Originally these parades were held on Boxing Day, December 26, and New Year's Day, two days on which slaves were permitted to rest from their work. The dancers often solicited donations of money or liquor, and

their repertoire reflected an African-European blend of dance steps and mumming. With the abolition of slavery in the mid-1800s, Jonkonnu essentially vanished in many regions of the Caribbean; it now survives primarily, though not exclusively, in Jamaica, where dancers still perform in public on December 26.

The following paragraphs summarize additional customs in several of the sovereign islands as well as Puerto Rico.

• BAHAMAS. The Christmas season in this former British colony extends from Christmas Eve until New Year's Day. The Christmas dinner often features a variety of seafood, turkey, ham, pigeon peas, rice, and a soup containing ox tails or pigs' feet. The Garifuna celebrate their festival of Jonkanoo between December 26 and New Year's Day. "Merry Christmas" is said in English.

• BARBADOS. Traditions combine those from more than 300 years of former British rule and those from descendants of black African slaves. General revelry dominates the weeks prior to Christmas. Decorations are often fashioned from local shrubs, particularly the casuarina tree. Rural districts sponsor house-to-house caroling events, and churches hold concerts. There are midnight services on Christmas Eve, and many gather in Queen's Park in Bridgetown on Christmas Day for the annual concert performed by the Royal Barbados Police Band.

Family and friends gather together for Christmas dinner, which often consists of turkey and stuffing, ham, pork, spicy sauces, fruitcake, mince pie, plum pudding, rum, and *sorrel*, a traditional drink. The latter is made from the red or white, fleshy portion of *sorrel* (*Hibiscus sabdariffa*), a shrubby annual originating in the Sudan, and sweetened with sugar or fermented.

"Scrubbers," obsolete since the mid–twentieth century, once consisted of bands of four or five men who traveled about each district, singing carols and delivering poetic speeches at homes early on Christmas morning. In such often humorous and sarcastic poems, the scrubbers clearly made known their desire for a handout, especially liquor. Most households willingly complied, but when some refused, the scrubbers scrawled messages of complaint on the houses. This gave rise to the term "scribes," which evolved into "scrubbers." "Merry Christmas" is said in English.

• CUBA. Prior to Cuba's Communist era, Christmas celebrations were Roman Catholic and typically Latin American: Christmas trees, Nativity scenes, and processions honoring the Virgin Mary; a large family meal on *Nochebuena* ("Good Night," Christmas Eve) featuring *lechón asado* (roast pork), black beans and rice, *tostones* (fried plantain), *yuca* (tapioca), breads and pastries, *turrón* (nougat candy), ciders and liquors; *Misa del Gallo* ("Mass of the Rooster," Midnight Mass) on Christmas Eve; eating 12 grapes for luck, parties, fireworks, and burning the *Año Viejo* ("Old Year," a scarecrow representing the evils of the old year) on New Year's Eve; gifts for children and parades honoring *Los Reyes Magos* (the Wise Men) on Epiphany.

After dictator Fidel Castro declared his Communist government atheistic in 1962, Christmas remained an official holiday until 1969, when the government's ban claimed that the holiday interfered with the sugar cane harvest. Although decorating a Christmas tree at that time would probably bring disfavor from local officials, many churches continued to hold Midnight Mass on Christmas Eve with participants attending incognito to avoid arrest. Children did not receive gifts on Epiphany but on July 26, which commemorated the "July 26 Movement," an uprising in 1953 against former President Fulgencio Batista Zaldivar. In 1976, the government granted freedom of religion and in 1992 declared itself a secular rather than an atheistic state. Christmas officially returned to Cuba in 1997, when Castro initially sanctioned the holiday as a then-one-time gesture to honor the imminent visit of Pope John Paul II in January of 1998. Thousands packed parish churches for services, choir members at the Havana cathedral wore yellow T-shirts sporting a portrait of the pope and sang carols to drums, and plastic Christmas trees and other decorations had sold out weeks in advance. Responding to a request from the pope and claiming that mechanization had now reduced the need for manpower at the sugar cane harvest, the government reinstated Christmas as a permanent holiday in

1998 and authorized Cuban Catholic leader Cardinal Jamie Ortega to broadcast a national holiday greeting over government-controlled radio. Time will determine the extent to which past holiday traditions will be resumed. "Merry Christmas" is said in Spanish, *Feliz Navidad*. *See also* **Mass of the Rooster**.

• DOMINICAN REPUBLIC. Roman Catholicism predominates in this former Spanish colony, with the population primarily of mixed Spanish and black African descent. A summary of general Latin American Christmas customs is found in the introductions to the entries for **Central America** and **South America**.

The holidays are quite noisy with fireworks. In addition, Dominican Republic observes a period of caroling during the first 25 days of December, in which bands of people arrive at church before dawn to sing. Afterwards, they divide into groups to sing in various homes, where they are usually rewarded with refreshments such as ginger beer and confections. Christmas decorations are similar to those in the United States, along with those fashioned from dried fruits and palm leaves. Employers usually grant an *aguinaldo* ("gift," Christmas bonus) in the form on one month's salary to employees, who also engage in gift exchanges known as *angelitos* ("little angels"). Christmas Eve dinner usually features roast pork, turkey, *tamales*, *pan de huevo* (bread), rice pudding, and fruitcakes. Children generally receive gifts from the Three Kings on Epiphany rather than on Christmas Day, and, since the Kings may have forgotten some poor children, tradition holds that these latter children receive gifts from the *Vieja Belén* ("Old Woman of Bethlehem"). "Merry Christmas" is said in Spanish, *Feliz Navidad*.

• GRENADA. Roman Catholicism predominates in this former British colony, about 85 percent of the population being descendants of black Africans. Christmas customs include caroling groups traveling from house to house during the weeks prior to Christmas; decorations of Nativity scenes, poinsettias, streamers, and stars; and community Christmas trees. The Christmas dinner often features turkey, pork, pigeon peas, yams, ginger beer, and *sorrel*, a drink discussed under **Barbados**, above. The season ends on Epiphany, January 6, when all decorations are removed. "Merry Christmas" is said in English.

• JAMAICA. Today the best-known Christmas tradition in Jamaica is Jonkonnu, discussed above.

• PUERTO RICO. A former Spanish colony, this commonwealth of the United States is primarily Roman Catholic. Santa Claus and Christmas trees are well known, but the principal symbol remains the *Belenes* (Nativity scene), known as the *Pesebre* in many other parts of Latin America. Each of the early morning Masses held during the Novena prior to Christmas is known as *Misa de Aguinaldo* ("Mass of the Gift"). During the weeks of Advent, families and friends hold *Parrandas* ("Sprees," all-night Christmas parties) in different homes, at which groups of carolers known as *Asaltos* ("Assault") traditionally make surprise visits. Each of these groups carries a figure of the Christ Child, which is left at the home of the final *Parranda*, and that family then brings the figure to Midnight Mass.

The Christmas Eve dinner often features baked chicken, turkey, pork, Spanish rice, pigeon peas, cooked greens, yams, *pasteles* (mashed plantains with meat and vegetables wrapped in plantain leaves and boiled), *arroz con dulce* (rice cooked with spices and coconut milk), *tembleque* (custard of cornstarch, sugar, and coconut milk), *turrón* (nougat), nuts, and *coquito* (eggnog made with coconut milk and rum). All festivities include much music and dancing throughout the season.

December 28, *Día de los Inocentes* (Holy Innocents Day), is a time for practical jokes. On this day in Hatillo, citizens engage in comic reenactments of the Slaughter of the Innocents. Men dressed as the evil soldiers of King Herod parade from house to house and "kidnap" the firstborn boys found therein. The families redeem their children by bribing the soldiers with gifts, and when these "lost boys" have all been returned, the village hosts a gala event in celebration. Among the festivities of *Año Viejo* ("Old Year," New Year's Eve) are social gatherings where everyone attempts to swallow 12 grapes for luck during the final minute before midnight.

Although children receive gifts on Christmas Day, the traditional, Spanish gift-giving day is Epiphany, January 6, better known as *Día de los Tres Reyes* (Three Kings Day), on which the Three Kings deliver the gifts. On the night before, children prepare for the Kings' visit by placing shoe boxes filled with grass and grain under their beds. The Kings in turn feed the fodder to their camels and replace it with gifts in the boxes. Bethlehem Day, January 12, is closely related, in that children parade through the streets, led by three of their peers dressed as the Three Kings riding horses and bearing gifts for the Christ Child. Also following are those portraying angels and shepherds, along with musicians.

A custom not often practiced today is *Octavas*, observed eight days after Epiphany. In that custom, a person who receives a visit from a friend on Epiphany must return the favor in eight days, amid festivities. The day is now largely observed as a time for putting away decorations and closing the Christmas season. "Merry Christmas" is said in Spanish, *Feliz Navidad*.

• SAINT KITTS AND NEVIS. Landing on the islands in 1493, Christopher Columbus named St. Kitts after his patron, St. Christopher. The islands are former British colonies, and their population now consists primarily of descendants of Europeans and West Africans. Aside from Eurocentric customs, the African Christmas traditions date to the days of slavery, when "Christmas Sports," a synergism of African, European, and American Indian elements, appeared throughout these islands from Christmas Eve to New Year's Day, the time period when work on the plantations ceased.

Christmas Sports were conducted by lay street dancers in tribal costumes, who performed to the music of the drum, fife, triangle, *quatros* (banjo), *baha* (long, metal pipe that is blown), and *shack-shack* (tin can containing beans). Their routines usually revolved around various plays based on biblical stories, everyday situations, classic drama, and sketches that often satirized their white overlords, something permissible (to a degree) only at Christmastime. Because of these sketches, it was mandatory that the first performance of the season be held at the local police station for appropriate censorship.

Emigration, players' deaths, the lack of an

organized program, and white oppression have been cited as causes for a decline in Christmas Sports. Only six of numerous, original varieties primarily remain: "Masquerades," six dances performed by a chief with twelve to fifteen dancers wearing multicolored shirts, pants, ribbons, handkerchiefs, mirrors, beads, and headpieces of peacock feathers; "Bull," a humorous play exaggerating a plantation event of 1917, which revolves around the revival of a wounded bull; "Mocko-Jumbies," stilt dancers wearing long gowns and conical hats; "Mummies" (variation of "Mummers"), depicting characters from European legends such as St. George and the Dragon, with players wearing colorful short jackets, long white pants, mirrors, and handkerchiefs; "Actors," acrobats from St. Peter's parish performing dangerous feats such as somersaulting over upturned garden forks and having large rocks broken on their chests; and "Clowns," usually fifty players performing whip-swinging dances in loose, two-colored costumes decorated with numerous small bells. These sports usually carry over into the pre-Lenten Carnival Season. Examples of Christmas Sports now virtually extinct include "Niega Business," "Sagwa," "Soldiers," "Cowboys and Indians," "Selassie," "Japanese," and "Millionaires."

Other Christmas customs include caroling by church or civic groups who solicit donations; bands of laborers who serenade comrades all night on Christmas Eve in return for liquor; and street parades of scratch or string bands with throngs of dancing adults and children who are led by a few attired in rags or sack cloth.

"Merry Christmas" is said in English, the official language.

• TRINIDAD AND TOBAGO. These islands are former Spanish, French, Dutch, and British colonies. The people are chiefly of African and East Indian descent (about 40 percent each), the remainder consisting of Chinese, West Europeans, and those from the Middle East. Roman Catholicism constitutes the largest single Christian faith. Preparations for Christmas include making plantain wine and *sorrel* (*see* **Barbados** above) as well as black rum cakes, dark fruitcakes soaked in rum. People customarily paint their homes and clean them

thoroughly, and performers playing lively *Parang* music on *quatros* (banjos) serenade their neighbors in the early hours of the morning. The Christmas menu features ham, cakes, yams, pigeon peas, crab, macaroni, rice, and *souse* (broth with pigs' feet). Artificial Christmas trees are the general rule, and Santa Claus brings the Christmas gifts, which children open on Christmas morning. "Merry Christmas" is said in English, the principal language.

See also **Advent; Christmas Drama; Epiphany; Holy Innocents Day; Mass of the Rooster.**

Western Australian Christmas Tree
See **Christmas Plants**

We've Been a While A-Wandering
See **Here We Come A-Caroling**

What Are the Signs?
See **Alfred Burt Carols**

What Child Is This?
English carol, the verses of which were taken directly from a larger poem, "The Manger Throne," published around 1865 by William Chatterton Dix (1837–1898). The verses were paired with the well-known English folk tune "Greensleeves" and published as "What Child Is This?" in *Christmas Carols New and Old* (London, 1871), edited by Henry Bramley and John Stainer. Although the person who matched the verses with "Greensleeves" remains unknown, it may have been Stainer, for he also harmonized the musical setting. Dix was manager of a marine insurance company in Bristol; his avocation was poetry and hymn writing, and he wrote the carol "As with Gladness Men of Old "(1859).

"Greensleeves" is thought to have arisen during the latter half of the sixteenth century, although it could be older. One of the first references to the tune came from a Richard Jones, who registered it in 1580 with a set of somewhat vulgar lyrics. His authorship remains unsubstantiated, however, as is that of King Henry VIII, who has also been suggested as the song's composer. Queen Elizabeth I, daughter of Henry VIII, danced to it, and by 1600 it had become a well-established piece. The tune has enjoyed extensive utilization. It has been the setting for numerous ballads, an accompaniment for executions, a segment of John Gay's *The Beggar's Opera* (1728), and a Cavalier party song during the British Civil War (1642–1648). It is twice mentioned in William Shakespeare's *The Merry Wives of Windsor*.

Verse 1 asks a rhetorical question: What Child is this Who sleeps on Mary's lap, about Whom angels sing while shepherds keep watch? The answer: This is Christ the King, come and praise Him! Verse 2 asks why He lies in base surroundings, then answers that, even as a silent Babe, He pleads for sinners, then predicts His death on the cross. Verse 3 calls for all people, poor and rich, to accept Christ. All verses end with "The Babe, the Son of Mary!"

See also **As with Gladness Men of Old**.

What Is This Fragrance?
See **Whence Is That Goodly Fragrance?**

What Is This Perfume So Appealing?
See **Whence Is That Goodly Fragrance?**

What Perfume This? Oh Shepherds Say
See **Whence Is That Goodly Fragrance?**

When Angels Come to Town
(2004). Made-for-television drama/fantasy, the third in a series of Daniel H. Blatt Productions to feature Peter Falk as Max, the mischievous angel.

Max once again appears at Christmastime to assist those in need, but when his heavenly supervisor Jo (Katey Sagal) discovers that Max has supposedly contacted the wrong family in the little town of Moonstone Bay, Maine, she comes to earth to discipline him. Instead of visiting Karl Hoffman (Seann Gallagher), who intends to automate his family's Christmas ornament factory and lay off its skilled artisans, Max has visited Sally Reid (Tammy Blanchard) in the same town. Sally has been unable to gain custody of her twelve-year-old brother Jimmy (Alexander Conti), who has been in foster care since their parents' deaths seven years ago, because she cannot meet the county's income

requirement. Alas, the Beehive, the small department store where Sally works, is too financially strapped to accommodate her; worse, following the holidays, Jimmy is scheduled to be placed in another home out of town, which would further separate them.

Although Jo has no "field" experience, she initially fires Max, orders him to turn in his wings, and attempts to take control. Instead, she bungles the case and pleads for Max's assistance. Through a host of disguises, Max works his own kind of magic to interconnect Sally's and Karl's families through a mysterious box containing a necklace, and even Jo learns that, for the sake of humanity, efficiency and regulations must often give way to joy and grace.

With Vlasta Vrana. Written by Michael J. Murray. Produced by Ken Gross and Irene Litinsky. Directed by Andy Wolk. A Daniel H. Blatt Production in association with Viacom Productions. Video N/A.

See also **Finding John Christmas; A Town without Christmas**.

When Christ, the Son of Mary
See **Carol of the Bagpipers**

When Joseph Was an Old Man
See **The Cherry Tree Carol**

Whence Comes This Rush of Wings Afar?
See **Carol of the Birds**

Whence Is That Goodly Fragrance?
("Quelle est cette odeur agreable?"). French traditional carol, the text of which is believed to have originated in Lorraine during the seventeenth century. Other translations include "What Is This Perfume So Appealing?" "What Is This Fragrance?" "Shepherds, What Fragrance, All-Perfuming?" and "What Perfume This? Oh Shepherds Say."

Based on the annunciation to the shepherds in Luke 2, the first three verses are cast in dialogue between three different shepherds regarding a marvelous fragrance, brilliant light, and soul-stirring singing that herald the coming of the heavenly host. The remaining three verses depict the angels' command to heed their message, Gabriel's tidings of good joy, and the final chorus of "Glory to God in the highest." Although no reference to perfume exists in Luke's account of the Nativity, it is possible that the carol draws upon a legend that when Christ was born, every tree in the world bloomed and perfumed the earth to welcome Him.

Ironically, the musical setting, also traditional and dating to the eighteenth century, has been used in a number of drinking songs, such as that included in John Gay's *The Beggar's Opera* (1728).

While by My Sheep

("Als ich bei meinen Schafen wacht'"). German traditional carol, believed to date approximately to 1500. Because phrases in the verses and refrain are repeated, it is also known as the "Echo Carol." Another alternative title is "How Great My Joy."

This echo format suggests that the carol may have been used as an antiphonal song for two or more groups of singers placed in separate locations in the church. It may also have been composed for a Nativity or shepherd folk drama, a traditional art form that was prevalent in Germany and other parts of Europe during the Middle Ages.

The carol first appeared in a Cologne hymnal in 1623 with a Latin echo, "Benedicamus Domino" ("May we bless the Lord"), tacked onto the German refrain. A later setting published in Trier, Germany, in 1871, which became more popular in the United States, eliminated the Latin, limited the echoes to the refrain, and rephrased the refrain as well: "How great my joy! (great my joy!) Joy, joy, joy! (Joy, joy, joy!)," etc. The American music scholar Theodore Baker (1851–1934) provided the best-known English-language translation.

While Shepherds Watched Their Flocks

English carol with lyrics by Nahum Tate (1652–1715), the Irish-born poet laureate of England (1692). The lyrics were constructed as a paraphrase of the Nativity story as found in Luke 2:8–14. In 1700 Tate first published this text in his supplement to the *New Version of the Psalms of David* (London, 1696), co-edited by Nicholas Brady. At that time, Tate's text was one of only six hymns legally authorized by the Church of England as suitable for congregational singing (congregational hymns as such in England were remarkably uncommon before the eighteenth century, for the usual music theretofore had comprised the regulation canticles).

Of the scores of musical settings that have been paired with "While Shepherds Watched," two have gained the most popularity. In the United States, this carol is usually sung to a tune adapted from an aria found in G.F. Handel's opera of 1728, *Cyrus, King of Persia*. Although the person specifically creating the adaptation is not known, speculation includes two Americans, Richard S. Willis (1819–1900), who supplied the musical setting for "It Came upon the Midnight Clear" (that setting also has been paired with "While Shepherds Watched" on occasion), and hymnist Lowell Mason (1792–1872). The other principal setting is "Winchester Old," an anonymous, sixteenth century English tune, which a George Kirbye arranged and published in 1592. The Kirbye setting did not appear together with Tate's text, however, until their inclusion in *Hymns Ancient and Modern* (London, 1861), edited by William Clowes.

White Christmas

(Motion picture, 1954). A remake of *Holiday Inn* (1942) and Paramount Pictures' first film photographed in VistaVision, the answer to CinemaScope.

Bob Wallace and Phil Davis (Bing Crosby and Danny Kaye), buddies during World War II, team up after the war to form a musical revue. After auditioning Betty and Judy, the Haynes Sisters (Rosemary Clooney and Vera-Ellen), the enamored lads follow them to the Columbia Inn in Pine Tree, Vermont, where the ladies are booked for a series of holiday performances.

The inn is owned by retired General Tom Waverly (Dean Jaggar), Bob's and Phil's former commanding officer. The boys learn that the inn is foundering, and to rescue their beloved superior, they transfer their New York show to the inn. Further discovering that the general misses his command, Bob makes a television plea for all members of his former regiment to join him at the inn for a tribute to the general on Christmas Eve. Betty, initially misunderstanding Bob's motives, temporarily leaves the show for a job in New York but returns after Bob's telecast to resume their budding romance. To Waverly's surprise, hundreds of his former troops salute him during an elaborate show, at which the general, with renewed spirits, takes "command" of his division. Of course, the two leading couples conclude the show and the picture with a memorable rendition of Irving Berlin's "White Christmas."

Fred Astaire, who starred in *Holiday Inn* with Bing Crosby, was Paramount Pictures' first choice for the character Phil Davis in *White Christmas*, but he rejected that role, which then went to Danny Kaye. As in *Holiday Inn*, Crosby sang "White Christmas" twice in this remake, as a solo at the beginning and as a Crosby/Clooney duet at the finale. Most of the cast actually performed the finale twice, the second time for the benefit of the king and queen of Greece, who visited the *White Christmas* set after the finale's filming was complete. Crosby, however, choosing not to yield to the whims of royalty, refused to return. Crosby also met his future second wife, Kathryn Grant, on this set. Thirty years his junior, Grant had auditioned for the part of Susan, Waverly's granddaughter, but was unsuccessful.

White Christmas boasted a number of memorable songs by Irving Berlin in addition to "White Christmas": "We'll Follow the Old Man," "Blue Skies," "Sisters," "Snow," "Count Your Blessings Instead of Sheep" (for which the picture received its only Academy Award nomination for Best Original Song), "Choreography," "The Best Things Happen While You're Dancing," "Love, You Didn't Do Right By Me," "What Can You Do with a General?" and "Gee, I Wish I Was Back in the Army."

With Mary Wickes, John Brascia, and Anne Whitfield. Written by Norman Krasna, Norman Panama, and Melvin Frank. Produced by Robert Emmett Dolan. Directed by Michael Curtiz. Paramount Pictures. DVD: Paramount Home Video. 120 min.

See also **Holiday Inn; White Christmas** (song).

White Christmas

(Song). Highly popular American song written in 1940 by Irving Berlin (1888–1989) and arguably the most popular of American secular Christmas songs. The number was included in the Paramount motion picture *Holiday Inn* (1942), which not only paid tribute in song to the major holidays of the year and boasted Berlin's musical score, but also featured the singing talents of legendary crooner Bing Crosby. Crosby had first introduced the public to "White Christmas" through his *Kraft Music Hall* radio program on Christmas Day, 1941 (which followed the Japanese attack on Pearl Harbor), and the song achieved even greater fame on film.

It is said that, while he experienced little difficulty in composing songs for most of the other holidays, Berlin, of Jewish heritage, felt that writing a piece about Christmas was a more challenging task and was not sure how "White Christmas" would be received. Crosby, after studying the lyrics, eased Berlin's fears with confidence that his masterpiece would certainly become a hit.

"White Christmas" indeed won Berlin an Academy Award for Best Song in 1943, and Crosby's Decca recording in May of 1942 (backed by the John Scott Trotter Orchestra) sold over 30 million copies alone, making it the largest-selling single Christmas record in the world. By March 1947, because millions of pressings had worn the original master disk, Crosby had to re-record "White Christmas," and it is that version which is most frequently heard today. The Crosby recording was the top Christmas song not only for 1942, but also for 1944, 1946, and 1947; it was number 1 on the *Billboard Christmas Singles* chart for 1963 (36 weeks), 1969, and 1983; and it continued to be charted for more than thirty years following its initial release. Andy Williams's recording on the Columbia label in 1963 also became a number one hit on the *Billboard Christmas Singles* chart (7 weeks).

Although Berlin's lyrics originally included an introductory passage that expressed a preference for spending Christmas up north rather than in sunny Los Angeles, that passage is rarely sung today, and Crosby also omitted it from the film versions as well as his recordings.

Over the decades, "White Christmas" has been recorded by virtually every recording artist in the music industry, surviving a host of genres and styles. Not every style pleased Berlin, however, for when he learned that rock-and-roll king Elvis Presley would include "White Christmas" on his 1957 *Elvis' Christmas Album* (RCA Victor), Berlin launched a campaign that petitioned radio stations not to play the Presley recording. After all, Berlin, not known for modesty, thought highly of his piece and boasted, "Not only is it the best song I ever wrote, it's the best song *anybody* ever wrote!"

Of the 25 most frequently performed Christmas songs of the twentieth century listed by the American Society of Composers, Authors and Publishers (ASCAP), "White Christmas" ranked number 1. By December 2004, however, it ranked number 5.

During World War II as Crosby toured the world entertaining American troops, hardly a show closed without a request for "White Christmas." Its home-filled sentiment touched the troops deeply, often bringing tears to their eyes. The effect, far greater than either Berlin or Crosby had ever anticipated, prompted a remake of *Holiday Inn* by Paramount, this time appropriately titled *White Christmas* (1954).

Bing Crosby recorded over 70 sacred and secular Christmas songs during his illustrious career. After he signed with Decca Records in 1934, company president Jack Kapp requested that Crosby record "Silent Night" and "Adeste Fideles." Feeling uncomfortable about recording sacred songs for profit, Crosby arranged for charities to receive all proceeds from those recordings, a policy that remained in force for the duration of his career.

See also **ASCAP List of Christmas Songs; Holiday Inn; White Christmas** (motion picture).

The White House

The executive mansion, the official residence for the president of the United States and first family in Washington, D.C. Plans for a presidential residence were first drawn in 1791 by artist and engineer Pierre Charles L'Enfant, who envisioned a structure four times its present size. Architect James Hoban reduced the scale, and together with President George Washington, supervised the construction of the residence, which was completed in 1800, after Washington's tenure as president. The first chief executive to occupy the new residence was President John Adams on November 1, 1800. Originally made white with lime-based whitewash in 1798 and subsequently painted white, the executive mansion acquired the nickname "White House" in the early nineteenth century. In September 1901, President Theodore Roosevelt made the name official.

For the first 100 years, Christmas celebrations in the White House were quiet affairs that centered around family, friends, and worship and were often eclipsed by the City of Washington's series of winter social events, which traditionally commenced in early December. A White House Christmas was merely an aside that provided a brief moment of peace, comfort, and good cheer among the affairs of state. In the twentieth century, White House Christmas events evolved into a grand, public celebration with spectacular decorations and magnificent entertainments, including individual festive events for the diplomats and politicians on Capitol Hill, the White House staff, and their children.

The following paragraphs provide a chronological summary of noteworthy holiday events and traditions in the White House by president.

• JOHN ADAMS (TENURE 1797–1801). Adams's one White House Christmas was marked by a party given for his four-year-old daughter Suzanna and children of diplomats. Held in the grand ballroom, the event sported a small orchestra, cake, punch, greenery, carols, and games. On January 1, 1801, Adams initiated the annual custom of a New Year's Day reception that was open to the public; at the first of these, the president personally greeted some 135 visitors. The tradition was discontinued during Herbert Hoover's presidency in the 1930s.

• THOMAS JEFFERSON (1801–09). De-emphasizing the spiritual aspects of religion, Jefferson saw Christmas merely as a time for reckoning, not celebration. He did, however, grant Christmas as a holiday to his slaves. At the Christmas party that Jefferson gave for his grandchildren and 100 of their friends in 1805, he provided the entertainment by playing his fiddle.

• JAMES MADISON (1809–17). British troops burned the White House in 1814 (War of 1812), preventing most Christmas observances during a three-year period of restoration. The Treaty of Ghent, Belgium, ending the war, was signed on Christmas Eve, 1814.

• JAMES MONROE (1817–25). The White House reopened on New Year's Day, 1818, to receive visitors after its reconstruction.

• JOHN QUINCY ADAMS (1825–29). Adams appointed Dr. Joel R. Poinsett, a botanist, as ambassador to Mexico in 1825. While there, Poinsett developed an interest in a plant locally known as *Flor de la Noche Buena* (Flower of the Good Night [Christmas Eve]), which would become a holiday decoration known as the poinsettia (*see* **Poinsettia**).

• ANDREW JACKSON (1829–37). Jackson held a "frolic" on Christmas Day, 1835, for his family's children and those of diplomats. Entertainment consisted of games such as blind man's bluff and hide and seek, as well as forfeit games. The dinner table was decorated with a pyramid of cotton snowballs and ice sculptures in the shapes of fruits and vegetables. Afterwards, the children staged a snowball fight in the East Room using cotton snowballs.

• MARTIN VAN BUREN (1837–41). Christmases were uneventful.

• WILLIAM HENRY HARRISON (1841). Died of pneumonia 31 days after taking office.

• JOHN TYLER (1841–45). Following the death of his first wife, Letitia, Tyler courted Julia Gardiner, the daughter of a New York Senator, during Christmas 1842. Vying for her hand was Tyler's son, John, Jr., who was already married but separated from his own wife. The president and Julia were married the following year. Between Christmas Day, 1844, and New Year's Day, 1845, Texas became the twenty-eighth state.

• JAMES K. POLK (1845–49). As a Presbyterian, Polk forbade hard liquor and dancing at White House social functions, including Christmas. Though he did not regularly attend church, he received official visitors on Christmas Day but never on Sunday. During Christmas 1848, a bill was introduced into Congress outlawing slavery in the District of Columbia.

• ZACHARY TAYLOR (1849–50). Died in office.

• MILLARD FILLMORE (1850–53). On Christ-

mas Eve, 1851, a fire at the Library of Congress destroyed much of the collection acquired from Thomas Jefferson. During the 1852 holidays, Fillmore dedicated in Lafayette Park a bronze, equestrian statue of Andrew Jackson, sculpted by Clark Mills.

• FRANKLIN PIERCE (1853–57). Popular tradition holds that Pierce was the first president to erect a Christmas tree in the White House in 1856. According to Rosenbaum, this was an urban legend begun by Pierce's grandnieces. The Pierces were not only Presbyterians, a denomination that denounced Christmas celebrations at the time, but were grieving over the loss of their third child, who died shortly before Pierce's inauguration.

• JAMES BUCHANAN (1857–61). Buchanan removed the egalitarianism of the White House prevalent since the days of Andrew Jackson and reinstated the formal rules of protocol for admission to the New Year's Day receptions; that is, by rank and station. On December 20, 1860, South Carolina became the first state to secede from the Union.

• ABRAHAM LINCOLN (1861–65). During Christmas 1861, Mrs. Lincoln helped to care for wounded Union soldiers, raised money for Christmas dinners, and donated all White House liquor to hospitals for medicinal purposes. On New Year's Day, 1863, the Emancipation Proclamation became law. During Christmas of that same year, young son Tad sent a box containing books, blankets, and food to troops and successfully obtained a "pardon" from his father for "Jack," a pet turkey that had been fattened for Christmas dinner.

• ANDREW JOHNSON (1865–69). Johnson's grandchildren honored him on his sixtieth birthday with a "Juvenile Soirée" on December 29, 1868.

• ULYSSES S. GRANT (1869–77). As regular contributors to local orphanages, at Christmastime President and Mrs. Grant sent gift barrels of confections and fruit, and Mrs. Grant often took groups of the children to shops for holiday surprises. In 1870, federal employees of the District of Columbia were first granted Christmas Day as a paid holiday. On December 22, 1874, Grant hosted the first dinner for a foreign head of state in White House history, David Kalakaua, king of the Sandwich Islands (later Hawaii). On New Year's Day, 1875, Grant announced the engagement of his daughter Nellie to Algernon Satoris, a British diplomat.

• RUTHERFORD B. HAYES (1877–81). Hayes and his wife Lucy celebrated their twenty-fifth wedding anniversary in 1877 with festivities beginning on December 30, followed by a New Year's Eve party and a grand reception on New Year's Day, 1878. During these events, the press described scarlet Christmas plants in full bloom throughout the residence. This is thought to be the first reference to White House Christmas decorations—possibly poinsettias. In 1880, Hayes saw that everyone in the White House received as a Christmas gift nothing less than a five-dollar gold piece. No hard liquor was served at any White House function, for Mrs. Hayes encouraged a dry presidency.

• JAMES GARFIELD (1881). Assassinated in office.

• CHESTER A. ARTHUR (1881–85). Arthur declared December 22, 1881, a national day of mourning for President Garfield. The Congressional Act of January 5, 1885, established Christmas Day as a federal holiday nationwide.

• GROVER CLEVELAND (1885–89). Christmases were uneventful.

• BENJAMIN HARRISON (1889–93). On Christmas Eve, 1889, Harrison erected a Christmas tree in the Blue Room of the White House for his two grandchildren (later it was moved to the Yellow Oval Room on the second floor). Illuminated by lighted candles, it was the first Christmas tree in White House history. The residence was bedecked with greenery, wreaths, and stockings, and the president, dressed as Santa Claus, distributed gifts beneath the tree on Christmas morning. He presented turkeys and gloves to his staff and received a silver-dollar-shaped picture holder from his daughter, Mame Harrison McKee. Christmas trees in the White House would follow sporadically until First Lady Lou Hoover would establish them as an annual tradition. In 1891, noted businessman Andrew Carnegie initiated a holiday tradition of sending each sitting president a ten-gallon keg of Scotch whiskey; the practice ended with President Woodrow Wilson in 1913.

• GROVER CLEVELAND (1893–97). In his sec-

ond term, Cleveland erected the second White House Christmas tree in 1895 for his children. The first tree to sport electric lights, its ornaments included gold angels, gold and silver sleds, toy tops, and tinsel. First Lady Frances Cleveland was quite active in Christmas Club charities in Washington.

• WILLIAM MCKINLEY (1897–1901). Assassinated in office.

• THEODORE ROOSEVELT (1901–1909). Roosevelt stressed a family Christmas. His Christmases in New York as a boy were so delightful that he vowed to reproduce them for his own children, with the exception of Christmas trees. Never having had one in his childhood, he initially denied his own children the decoration, citing reasons of conservation. After concluding that, by 1900, the demand for Christmas trees had decimated about 50 percent of all timber in the United States, Roosevelt officially barred Christmas trees from the White House during his administration, beginning in 1901. In 1902, his two younger sons, Archie and Quentin, however, secretly erected a small tree of their own with electric lights in a closet in their room. Upon consultation with Gifford Pinchot, a cabinet member and founder of the Yale School of Forestry, who assured the president that proper cuttings would thin the timberland, Roosevelt permitted his children to have an "unofficial" tree each year. The Roosevelt children hung their stockings on the mantel in their parents' bedroom in anticipation of gifts, and they received larger gifts on tables set up in the library. On December 26, 1903, the White House hosted an elaborate party for 550 children, consisting of vaudeville and theatrical acts; classical, folk, and patriotic music; traditional carols; dinner with party favors; a table-size Christmas tree; and dancing. Through such events, the Roosevelt Christmas popularized the holiday more as a national celebration rather than a religious observance.

• WILLIAM HOWARD TAFT (1909–13). In addition to enjoying Christmases with decorated trees, dances, dinners, and gifts, the Tafts presented their daughter Helen to society with a tea given on December 14, 1910. Her debutante dance followed in the East Room shortly after Christmas that same year.

• WOODROW WILSON (1913–21). In 1913, Wilson supported a National Community Christmas Tree lighting ceremony on the Capitol, though he personally did not attend (*see* **United States** [The National Christmas Tree and the Christmas Pageant of Peace]). Having lost his first wife Ellen in 1914, Wilson married Edith Galt at her home on December 18, 1915, and the First Couple took a honeymoon during Christmas in Hot Springs, Virginia. It was the first time that a president had been away from the White House at Christmas since fire forced James Madison from the White House in 1814. On Christmas Eve, 1916, the Wilsons attended a program of carols and patriotic music performed by children from local public schools and Girl Scout troops; a featured soloist was the Wilsons' daughter, Margaret. In early December 1918, the Wilsons departed on a ten-week trip to spend Christmas with the troops in Europe, where they visited Buckingham Palace and other points.

• WARREN G. HARDING (1921–23). On Christmas Day, 1921, Harding pardoned the socialist labor leader Eugene Debs and 24 other political prisoners whom President Wilson had considered as traitors to the war effort. Responding to a series of anonymous letters warning that an assassination attempt would be made on Christmas Day, 1922, the President and First Lady Florence Harding sought refuge for the day at a friend's home nearby. Harding subsequently died in office of natural causes.

• CALVIN COOLIDGE (1923–29). On December 6, 1923, Coolidge became the first president to have his message to a joint session of Congress broadcast via radio. That season, a spruce Christmas tree was set up in the Blue Room, and First Lady Grace Coolidge held a dance for her two boys, Butch and Cal, and 60 of their friends; Mrs. Coolidge danced with each boy. She also distributed gifts at the Salvation Army and brought Christmas cheer to patients at Walter Reed Hospital. On Christmas Eve, 1923, Coolidge became the first president to light the National Community Christmas Tree, which would become an annual tradition (*see* **United States** [The National Christmas Tree and the Christmas Pageant of Peace]), and in 1927, he also initiated the first annual Christmas message to the nation from the White House. Writ-

ten by his own hand on White House stationery and printed in major newspapers on Christmas Day, his short message included the thought that "to cherish peace and goodwill, to be plenteous in mercy, is to have the real spirit of Christmas." Thereafter, it became customary for the president to deliver an annual Christmas message to the nation.

• HERBERT HOOVER (1929–33). In 1929, First Lady Lou Hoover began the as yet unbroken tradition of trimming an official White House Christmas tree. On Christmas Eve of that year, a fire damaged the executive office during a presidential dinner party, and the Hoovers utilized the wood that was removed in the restoration process to have assorted Christmas gifts made for their staff in 1930. As a memento of that fire, in 1930 the Hoovers presented holiday gifts of toy fire trucks to the children of presidential secretary George Ackerson, whose family had dined with the president when the fire was discovered. The Hoovers also drew from their collection of old prints of Washington and the White House to provide other Christmas gifts. Until 1932, the annual New Year's Day receptions were elaborate social events anticipated by diplomats, government officials, military personnel, and the public. Citing the excessive numbers of visitors (which by then numbered more than 9,000 for each event) and concerns over security, Hoover ended the tradition with the reception of 1932. Hoover spent his last Christmas in office cruising aboard the USS *Sequoia*.

• FRANKLIN D. ROOSEVELT (1933–45). Like the Theodore Roosevelts, the Franklin Roosevelts also stressed family Christmases, which were three-day affairs comprising Christmas Eve, Christmas Day, and a children's party on December 26. Mrs. Roosevelt not only shopped for Christmas gift treasures throughout the year (which she kept in a "Christmas Closet"), for forty years she kept a detailed list of all recipients of her gifts and was engaged in many philanthropic and charitable works of the season. To create Depression-era jobs and train men in metal craft, Mrs. Roosevelt founded the Forge, pewter creations from which served as sources for Christmas gifts, until World War II forced its closure. Other traditions: the children's and grandchildren's stockings were hung in the president's bedroom; the president annually read Dickens's *A Christmas Carol* to his family on Christmas Eve and recited portions from memory; the official White House tree was customarily trimmed in silver and white with electric lights (another tree in the family's quarters sported burning candles at the president's insistence); and the president, though he enjoyed giving gifts, rarely opened his own during the holidays. To protest the Gridiron Club Dinner, an annual, Christmastime roast given by the press for political celebrities since the 1890s but which excluded all women, Mrs. Roosevelt in 1933 initiated the Gridiron "Widows" Dinner exclusively for women. The event was held at the White House on the same evening as the Gridiron. During the war years with her sons away in various branches of the Armed Forces, Mrs. Roosevelt recalled that White House Christmases were not as cheerful. Prime Minister Winston Churchill of England visited Roosevelt in December 1941 and attended the National Community Christmas Tree lighting ceremony on Christmas Eve, where both leaders delivered messages of courage and hope. On New Year's Day, 1942, Roosevelt and Churchill traveled to Mt. Vernon, where Churchill laid a red-white-and-blue wreath at the tomb of George Washington. On his estate in Hyde Park, New York, the president maintained a Christmas tree farm of some 30,000 trees, which included Norwegian spruces, balsam firs, Canadian white spruces, and Douglas firs. As a gift to his ally in 1943 during the war, Roosevelt shipped a Christmas tree from his tree farm to Churchill in Chequers, England. The president's final Christmas gifts to his family, friends, cabinet, members of Congress, and the executive and administrative office staff were copies of his D-Day Prayer Scroll from June 6, 1944.

• HARRY S. TRUMAN (1945–53). For the first Christmas following the end of World War II, the White House was fully decorated in evergreens and poinsettias, and Truman presented his staff with gift copies of his V-E Day Proclamation from May 8. The Trumans often had their Christmas greetings embossed or printed on various utilitarian gift items and photographs to their staff, making greeting cards

unnecessary. White House Christmases became more formal observances (contrary to the Trumans' modest, down-home private lives) with official receptions, dinners, teas, and lavish decorations on the State floor. Yet Truman annually requested that one local, poverty-stricken white family and a similar black family receive cooked turkeys and gifts for the holidays on his behalf. After the annual staff party on Christmas Eve at the White House, Truman almost always went home to Independence, Missouri, for the holidays; at those times when he left earlier, the president lit the National Community Christmas Tree in Washington by remote control from Missouri. In 1946, NBC television first aired this ceremony from Washington. From 1948 to 1952, the Trumans lived in Blair House, while the White House underwent a complete renovation.

• DWIGHT D. EISENHOWER (1953–61). Although the Eisenhowers divided their holidays between the White House, a cottage at the National Golf Club in Augusta, Georgia, and the family farm in Gettysburg, Pennsylvania, Mrs. Eisenhower thoroughly prepared the White House for Christmas. Virtually every room sported a decorated Christmas tree, the number of trees totaling 27 in 1958. Additional decorations included ribbons, garlands, mistletoe, red carnations, and red and white poinsettias in each room. On December 17, 1954, Eisenhower officiated at the first annual Christmas Pageant of Peace, which expanded the National Community Christmas Tree lighting ceremony (*see* **United States** [The National Christmas Tree and the Christmas Pageant of Peace]). Whereas Hoover, F.D. Roosevelt, and Truman had sent presidential Christmas cards to their personal relatives, friends, and immediate staff, in 1953 Eisenhower significantly expanded the list of recipients by sending 1,100 cards to American ambassadors, foreign heads of state, government officials, and members of his cabinet and Congress. Thereafter, these greetings became the official White House Christmas cards. The principal Eisenhower card motif each year included an embossed presidential seal with "Season's Greetings" engraved in gold below. Colors and borders varied. Each card bore the year, except those for

1953, and the enclosed sentiment extended best wishes for Christmas and the New Year. In 1959, the stars on the embossed seal were increased from 48 to 50, reflecting the addition of Alaska and Hawaii as new states. With no formal training in painting, Eisenhower frequently gave gift prints of his own original works of art, which included portraits of Washington and Lincoln and landscape scenes. Hallmark Cards produced 38 different cards and gift prints for the Eisenhowers, the largest variety of greetings ever sent from the White House.

• JOHN F. KENNEDY (1961–63). In addition to the quickened pace of entertaining, redecorating in period furnishings, and virtual doubling of the White House staff in this administration, the Kennedys hosted three annual parties specifically related to Christmas: one for the staff, one for the children of diplomats, and one for underprivileged children. To enhance the East Room, Mrs. Kennedy borrowed an antique *crèche* from New York. Called to his ailing father's bedside in Palm Beach, Florida, during the 1961 holiday, the president was able to attend only the 1962 Pageant of Peace, and the First Family otherwise spent their two Christmases at a friend's home in Palm Beach. Gifts to staff consisted of a photograph of the White House and prints of State Rooms rendered by professional artist Edward Lehman.

Kennedy White House Tree Themes. With her first Christmas as first lady, Mrs. Kennedy established the tradition of decorating each official White House Christmas tree according to a specific theme, which also became the decorative theme for the entire mansion. That for 1961 was Tchaikovsky's *The Nutcracker* ballet, featuring a host of ornamental toys. These same ornaments adorned the 1962 "Children's Tree," along with brightly wrapped packages, candy canes, gingerbread cookies, and straw ornaments fashioned by senior or disabled craftspeople.

Kennedy Official Greeting Cards. 1961: white, green, and gold card with presidential seal, "Season's Greetings 1961," and sentiments varying according to religions of recipients. 1962: black-and-white photograph of Mrs. Kennedy, Caroline, and John, Jr., taking a sleigh ride on a snowy White House South Lawn. 1963: color

photograph titled *Crèche in the East Room, The White House* (never sent out, and less than 30 were autographed by the president and Mrs. Kennedy).

• LYNDON B. JOHNSON (1963–69). The First Family spent most of their Christmases at the L.B.J. Ranch in Johnson City, Texas. One of Johnson's first duties as president was to attend the candlelight memorial service for President Kennedy on December 22, 1963, at the Lincoln Memorial, which ended the 30 days of mourning and which preceded the Pageant of Peace on that same date. In 1966, the National Christmas Tree Association, the trade group for the Christmas tree–growing industry in the United States, established the tradition of presenting a Christmas tree to the president and First Family. The Grand Champion winner of the Association's annual pageant in August was awarded the honor of selecting the tree, which has been displayed in the Blue Room of the White House as the official White House Christmas Tree for each season. In 1967, philanthropists Jane and Charles Engelhard donated an antique *crèche* to the White House to replace that which Mrs. Kennedy had borrowed. Obtained from Naples, Italy, and displayed in the East Room, it consisted of 30 eighteenth century carved, wooden figures, each between 12 and 18 inches high. Mrs. Engelhard contributed another ten figures to the set in 1978. The Johnsons' daughter, Lynda Bird, married Captain Charles Robb at a White House wedding on December 9, 1967. Gift prints consisted of a Johnson family photo in 1963, a Robert Laessig springtime watercolor in 1968, and art identical to that on the official greeting cards in the remaining years.

Johnson White House Tree Themes. Early American décor with traditional ornaments, nuts, dried seedpods, gingerbread cookies, fruit, popcorn strings, Hawaiian wood roses, silver balls and stars, small round mirrors, and papier-mâché angel tree toppers. 1966: balsam fir from Wisconsin, 1967: blue spruce from Ohio, 1968: white pine from Indiana.

Johnson Official Greeting Cards. Except for the 1963 card, the art for the Johnsons' official greeting cards was also rendered by Robert Laessig. Printed sentiments varied. 1963 (undated): blank embossed presidential seal with red border, 1964: black-and-white reproduction of a southwestern willow tree against a backdrop of the White House, 1965: *Winter at the White House*, featuring tree-covered mounds on the South Lawn, 1966: a night view of the White House North Portico, featuring the American elm planted by Woodrow Wilson in 1913, 1967: Blue Room Christmas tree, 1968: winter scene depicting the South Portico.

• RICHARD M. NIXON (1969–74). Evening candlelight tours for the public highlighted the Nixon White House Christmases, a tradition begun by Mrs. Nixon in her first year as first lady. Visitors viewed the furnishings in the State Rooms and splendid decorations as the Marine Band provided music; increasing popularity necessitated expanding the tours to several evenings by 1974. Television specials such as *Christmas at the White House* (1969) featured scenes of the First Family in their private quarters explaining traditions and the history of White House Christmases. The 1969 season also initiated a tradition of creating an elaborate gingerbread house for display in the State Dining Room; the first house stood three feet tall and weighed 45 pounds. At the Pageant of Peace in 1969, jeers and chants of, "Peace now, stop the war!" from hecklers protesting the Vietnam War competed with Nixon's remarks at the ceremony. Nixon also established the tradition of a Christmas worship service in the White House for the administrative staff and their families, first held in the East Room on December 20, 1970. The services included special music with noted clergymen such as the Rev. Billy Graham and others. Concern for energy conservation in 1973 prompted only the lighting of the star atop the National Christmas Tree with additional illumination by four spotlights on the ground. Gift prints to staff consisted of portraits of American presidents: Washington, Jefferson, Lincoln, T. Roosevelt, and Monroe.

Nixon White House Tree Themes. 1969 (blue spruce, Ohio): "American Flower" tree adorned with velvet and satin balls featuring the flower of each state, fashioned by disabled citizens in Florida, 1970 (white spruce, Wisconsin): same decorations plus fans patterned after the James Monroe era, made by disabled citizens from New York, 1971 (Fraser fir, North Carolina):

same with addition of gold foil angels, 1972 (noble fir, Washington): "Still Life" tree with ornaments based on paintings by Severin Roesen, represented by 3,000 pastel satin-finish balls, the state flower balls, and 150 gold federal stars, 1973 (Fraser fir, North Carolina): "Gold" tree featuring gold bead strings and gold balls.

Nixon Official Greeting Cards. 1969: blank embossed engraving of south view of the White House, 1970: gold embossed representation of the North Portico within a green embossed foil wreath on green background, 1971: reproduction of *Building the First White House*, a 1930 painting by N.C. Wyeth, 1972: reproduction of *View from the Tiber*, an 1839 etching of the White House by English artist William Henry Bartlett, 1973: reproduction of *President's House*, a nineteenth century painting by German artist August Kollner.

• GERALD R. FORD (1974–77). The Fords annually spent the holidays skiing at their condominium in Vail, Colorado, and brought an informality to White House Christmases that was warm, simple, and low key. For her first Christmas as first lady, Betty Ford encouraged all Americans to make patchwork Christmas ornaments from scraps and thus save money. To introduce the nation's upcoming Bicentennial at the Pageant of Peace in 1975, a green-and-gold, four-foot replica of the Liberty Bell sat atop the red-white-and-blue-bedecked National Christmas Tree. Gifts to staff consisted of prints of winter scenes by artist George Durrie (1974–75) and for the Bicentennial, a print of *Philadelphia in 1858* by Danish artist Ferdinand Richardt.

Ford White House Tree Themes. 1974 (concolor fir, Michigan): "Crafts" tree featured handcrafted ornaments made by Appalachian women and senior citizens' groups in New York and Maryland, 1975 (Douglas fir, New York): "Old-Fashioned Children's Christmas" tree featured ornaments of paper snowflakes, acorns, dried fruits, pine cones, vegetables, straw, cookies, and yarn, 1976 (balsam fir, Wisconsin): "Love That Is the Spirit of Christmas," the Bicentennial Tree, was decorated with 2,500 handmade flowers, including the flowers of all 50 states (fashioned by garden clubs, art schools, and senior citizens), along with small baskets of flowers, baby's breath, and small white lights.

Ford Official Greeting Cards. 1974: reproduction of *The President's House, Washington*, an 1831 engraving by English artist H. Brown, 1975: reproduction of *Farmyard in Winter*, a Connecticut snow painting by George Durrie, 1976: reproduction of *Going to Church*, a Connecticut snow painting by George Durrie.

• JIMMY CARTER (1977–81). During the first two years in office, the Carters spent the holidays at home in Plains, Georgia, but remained at the White House during the Iran Hostage Crisis. At the Pageant of Peace in 1979, only the star atop the National Christmas Tree remained lit to honor the hostages, and in 1980, the tree was lit for 417 seconds—one second for each day the hostages had been in captivity up to that point. In 1979, Carter lit the *Shamash* candle at ceremonies lighting the first National Hanukkah Menorah, located at that time in Lafayette Park. Figure skater Peggy Fleming provided an outdoor performance on ice at the 1980 staff Christmas party.

Carter White House Tree Themes. 1977 (noble fir, Washington): homemade ornaments such as painted milkweed pods, nutshells, and eggshells, and those constructed from foil, contributed by 1,500 members of the National Association for Retarded Citizens, 1978 (Veitch fir, New York): "Antique Toys" tree bedecked with Victorian dolls and miniature furniture on loan from the Strong Museum in Rochester, New York, 1979 (Douglas fir, West Virginia): "Colonial American Folk Art" tree with ornaments constructed from wood, fabric, and dried flowers by students of the Corcoran School of Art in Washington, 1980 (Douglas fir, Indiana): "Victorian Christmas" tree with dolls, hats, fans, tapestries, and laces of the period.

Carter Official Greeting Cards (also served as gift prints). 1977: *The White House: Christmas 1977*, a pen-and-ink drawing of the South Portico by Harvey Moriarty, 1978: reproduction of an 1877 hand-colored engraving of carriages at the North Portico by L.E. Walker, 1979: reproduction of *The President's House, Washington*, an 1860 watercolor by Lefevre J. Cranstone, 1980: reproduction of *The President's House*, a nineteenth century, anonymous painting after a drawing by William H. Bartlett.

• RONALD W. REAGAN (1981–89). Moments after Reagan took the oath of office on January 20, 1981, the hostages in Iran were released, and the National Christmas Tree was hastily redecorated and relit just as the aircraft carrying the former hostages cleared Iranian airspace. Because of an assassination attempt on Reagan's life that year, the Secret Service prevented him from attending any of the Pageants of Peace during his administration. Instead, he lit the National Christmas Tree and delivered his remarks for the ceremonies from the White House. The 1982 season launched the first annual *Christmas in Washington*, a musical extravaganza that aired on NBC television, in which Reagan used the essay "One Solitary Life," by Dr. James Allan Francis, as a means to tell a group of children about the life of Christ. In 1983, Reagan attended Hanukkah ceremonies and made an address at the Jewish Community Center of Greater Washington in Rockville, Maryland, and on December 21, 1984, he delivered the first official "Message on the Observance of Hanukkah" to the nation. A similar message followed in 1985, and since 1987, the messages have been an annual tradition. In 1986, representatives from American Friends of Lubavitch (an office of the Chabad-Lubavitch movement, the largest network of Jewish educational and social service institutions in the world) presented Reagan with a Hanukkah menorah in the Oval Office. On Christmas Eve, 1985, Reagan ordered the lights on the National Tree to be dimmed momentarily in support for Americans held hostage in Lebanon.

Reagan White House Tree Themes. 1981 (Douglas fir, Pennsylvania): "Old-Fashioned American Christmas" tree with animal ornaments fashioned from wood, tin, and fabric, on loan from the American Folk Art Museum in New York. From 1982 to 1988, young people from Second Genesis, a regional drug rehabilitation center, assisted in decorating the trees and made a number of the ornaments. 1982 (Fraser fir, North Carolina): 2,000 silver and gold metallic ornaments, 1983 (noble fir, Washington): same from previous year with antique toys on loan from the Strong Museum, 1984 (Fraser fir, North Carolina): ornaments from plant material along with natural pieces made at Pennsylvania's Brandywine Museum, 1985 (blue spruce, Michigan): 1,500 ornaments from Christmas cards that Reagan had received in 1984, 1986 (Fraser fir, Washington): "Mother Goose" tree featuring nursery rhyme characters and goose ornaments, 1987 (Fraser fir, West Virginia): "Music" tree with miniature instruments, notes, and sheet music, 1988 (balsam fir, Wisconsin): wooden candles by White House carpenters, glass ornaments from the Eisenhower collection, and the state flower balls from 1969.

Reagan Official Greeting Cards. The Reagans commissioned young artists to produce paintings of the White House, which served as art for the official greeting cards as well as gift prints. 1981: *Christmas Eve at the White House* (Jamie Wyeth), 1982: *The Red Room* (James Steinmeyer), 1983: *Green Room at the White House* (Mark Hampton), 1984: *Christmas Morning at the White House* (Jamie Wyeth). Thomas William Jones produced the four remaining paintings: *The Blue Room at Christmas, The White House* (1985); *The East Room at Christmas, The White House* (1986); *The State Dining Room at Christmas, The White House* (1987); and *North Entry Hall at Christmas, The White House* (1988).

President Ronald Reagan and First Lady Nancy Reagan pose before the official White House Christmas tree in the Blue Room in 1986. This Fraser fir from Washington, decorated with a "Mother Goose" theme, featured a host of nursery rhyme characters and goose ornaments. Each year since 1966, members of the National Christmas Tree Association have provided the White House with its official Christmas tree for display in the Blue Room. Courtesy Ronald Reagan Presidential Library.

Historical Association Ornaments. Since 1981, the White House Historical Association has annually issued a holiday keepsake ornament depicting an element of White House or American history. 1981: replica of 1840 angel weathervane atop the Universalist Church in Newburyport, Massachusetts, 1982: replica of Dove of Peace weathervane atop Mt. Vernon, 1983: north façade of White House during John Adams's presidency, without the Portico or Wings, 1984: replica of 1801 Jefferson Peace Medal with sentiment "Peace and Friendship." 1985: silhouettes of James and Dolley Madison, 1986: replica of south façade of White House with Portico during Monroe's presidency, 1987: replica of White House double mahogany doors during J.Q. Adams's presidency, 1988: commemoration of Andrew Jackson's 1835 White House Christmas party for children.

• GEORGE H.W. BUSH (1989–93). Christ-

The official White House Christmas tree for 1992 was this grand fir from Oregon, decorated with a "gift-givers" theme. Eighty-eight figures depicted various gift-givers from around the world, such as St. Nicholas, Santa Claus, Father Christmas, the Christkindl, Père Noël, and others. Courtesy George Bush Presidential Library.

mases were mixed with goodwill, political unrest, and celebration. In 1989, St. Martin's Episcopal Church in Houston bestowed upon the First Family a 50-piece needlepoint *crèche*, which was displayed in the family's quarters. As First Lady Barbara Bush brought holiday cheer to children at a local homeless shelter, American troops were deployed in December 1989 on a peacekeeping mission to Panama. That year, the thousands of red, white, and blue lights on the 1989 National Christmas Tree symbolized Bush's "thousand points of light" speech made during his 1988 election campaign. In 1989, Bush received a Hanukkah menorah from the Synagogue Council of America, which was displayed at the White House, and in 1991 he participated in Hanukkah ceremonies for White House staff at the Eisen-

hower Executive Office Building. As the Soviet Union crumbled, troops were in place by Christmas 1990 for Operation Desert Storm in the Persian Gulf. 1991 saw the release of Terry Anderson, an Associated Press correspondent held hostage in Lebanon for six years; that year he and four other former American hostages in Lebanon stood with President Bush to light the National Christmas Tree. As wife of the vice-president and then as first lady, Mrs. Bush set a record by riding the "cherry picker" for 12 seasons (1981–1992) to place the top ornament on the National Christmas Tree. For her support of the Pageant of Peace, Mrs. Bush received a plaque from National Park Service Director James Ridenour.

Bush White House Tree Themes. 1989 (Fraser fir, Pennsylvania): "Storybook" tree emphasized family literacy and featured sculptures of storybook characters and miniature books, 1990 (Fraser fir, North Carolina): "The Nutcracker" tree with 45 porcelain dancers, 50 pairs of ballet slippers, numerous ornaments from the Eisenhower collection, and a Kingdom of Sweets castle, 1991 (noble fir, Oregon): "Needlepoint" tree with 1,200 needlepoint ornaments, an 82-piece needlepoint village beneath the tree with electric train, and a wooden Noah's ark with 92 needlepoint figures, 1992 (grand fir, Oregon): "Gift-Givers" tree featured the evolution of holiday gift-givers through 88 characters designed by White House florists.

Bush Official Greeting Cards (also served as gift prints). 1989: *Celebrating Christmas at the White House* painting by William Gemmell, then–White House director of graphics, was the first card designed by a White House staff member, 1990: *The Oval Office, The White House* painting by Mark Hampton was the first card to feature the Oval Office, 1991: *The Family Tree, Upstairs at the White House* by Kamil Kubik was the first card to feature the First Family's living quarters, 1992: *The National Christmas Tree*, also by Kubik, was the first presidential card to feature the National Christmas Tree.

Historical Association Ornaments. 1989: replica of the presidential seal to commemorate the Bicentennial of the American presidency, 1990: replica of the Blue Room, 1991: commemorated President Harrison riding a white charger, 1992: reproduction of 1848 lithograph of White House north face.

• WILLIAM J. CLINTON (1993–2001). First president to serve in the twenty-first century and the third millennium. The Clintons brought a contemporary décor to White House Christmases (see below). Like Eleanor Roosevelt, First Lady Hillary Clinton shopped for gifts all year, as opposed to the president, who was known for last-minute shopping on Christmas Eve in person at local malls. Notable gingerbread houses that traditionally graced the State Dining Room included a replica of Ms. Clinton's childhood home in Park Ridge, Illinois, a creation of five months' work in 1995; and that of the 2000 season, which depicted the State Dining Room, Blue Room, and East Room all decorated with themes of the Clintons' past seven holiday seasons. This latter work weighed 250 pounds and was one of the largest created by Executive Pastry Chef Roland Mesnier. Just as Clinton had read "The Night before Christmas" to daughter Chelsea all of her life, he maintained a holiday tradition of inviting local children into the White House for a reading of the classic poem. At the lighting of the National Christmas Tree in 1997, heavy rain forced Clinton's remarks to 140 words, the shortest in the history of the ceremony since Herbert Hoover's 23-word address in 1929 (the record went to Calvin Coolidge's two-word address in 1927: "Fellow Americans"). In December 1997, Clinton hosted 14 children in the Oval Office at a ceremony to light a Hanukkah menorah, and in 1998, he joined Israel's President Ezer Weizman in Jerusalem for Hanukkah ceremonies. On December 19, 1998, the House of Representatives voted to impeach Clinton on charges of perjury to a federal grand jury and obstruction of justice in a sexual harassment case; the Senate later acquitted him. Clinton's last holiday as president coincided with the Bicentennial of the White House; for the occasion, all former living presidents and first ladies (except the Reagans, who could not attend) were honored at the White House in November 2000.

Clinton White House Tree Themes. 1993 (Fraser fir, North Carolina): "Angels" tree with 7,000 craft-style angel ornaments constructed of fiber, ceramic, glass, metal, and wood, 1994 (blue spruce, Missouri): "The Twelve Days of Christmas" tree with ornaments made by art students, 1995 (Fraser fir, North Carolina): "The Night before Christmas" tree with ornaments fashioned by culinary schools and members of the American Institute of Architects, and stockings made by the American Needlepoint Guild and the Embroiderers' Guild of America, 1996 (blue spruce, Ohio): "The Nutcracker" tree adorned in woodcraft, 1997 (Fraser fir, North Carolina): "Santa's Workshop" tree sported needlework crafted by the National Needlework Association and the Council of Fashion Designers of America as well as glass ornaments, 1998 (balsam fir, Wisconsin): "Winter Wonderland" tree with ornaments of fabric snowmen, knitted mittens, and hats by individual fabric crafters from each state and the Knitting Guild of America, along with painted wooden ornaments from the Society of Decorative Painters, 1999 (noble fir, Washington): "Holiday Treasures at the White House" tree featured dolls of historical American figures (for example, Benjamin Franklin, Amelia Earhart, Rosa Parks) and hand-forged tin ornaments of colonial trade, 2000 (Douglas fir, Pennsylvania): "Holiday Reflections" tree with assorted ornaments representing themes from the previous seven years.

Clinton Official Greeting Cards (also served as gift prints). 1993: *The White House, State Dining Room, 1993* (photograph of Mr. and Ms. Clinton), 1994: *The White House, The Red Room, 1994,* painting by Thomas McKnight, 1995 (300,000 cards printed): *The White House, The Blue Room, 1995,* painting by McKnight, 1996: *The White House, The Green Room, 1996,* painting by McKnight, 1997: *White House Nocturne, South Lawn 1997,* painting by Kay Jackson, the first woman to create the art for an official White House Christmas card, 1998: *The White House, The State Dining Room, 1998,* painting by Ray Ellis, 1999: *The White House, an American Treasure, North Portico, 1999,* painting by Ellis, 2000 (over 400,000 cards printed): *The Yellow Oval Room, First Family Residence, The White House, 2000,* painting by Ellis. The word "Christmas" never appeared in any of the Clintons' official card sentiments, as opposed to those of previous administrations.

Historical Association Ornaments. 1993: reproduction of portrait of Julia Gardiner Tyler, 1994: reproduction of 1846 daguerreotype of the White House Marine Band, 1995: flags and eagle from a Zachary Taylor window shade, 1996: presidential seal of Millard Fillmore, 1997: reproduction of 1857 engraving of White House South Grounds, 1998: American eagle in wreath of camellias and magnolia blossoms reminiscent of decorations from James Buchanan's presidency, 1999: reproduction of portrait of Lincoln in State Dining Room, 2000: commemorative of the 200th anniversary of the White House.

• GEORGE W. BUSH (2001–). First president to serve a full term in the twenty-first century and the third millennium A.D. Following terrorist attacks on the World Trade Center in New York City and the Pentagon on September 11, 2001, the White House was closed to all but invited guests that holiday season, and the annual candlelight Christmas tours were cancelled. However, the Bushes hosted over twenty holiday parties and receptions for Congress, White House staff, the Secret Service, and various government officials. Holiday seasons were ecumenical, for President Bush and First Lady Laura Bush not only read Christmas stories to children at the White House and made charitable visits, for example, to distribute gifts to Angel Tree children (*see* **Angel Tree**), they hosted annual Hanukkah receptions to light candles on menorahs. In 2001, the president celebrated Eid al-Fitr, the Islamic holiday ending Ramadan (which fell during Advent that year), and presented gifts to Muslim children. Under tightened security, the 2001 Christmas Pageant of Peace proceeded as usual; assisting the president and first lady in lighting the National Christmas Tree were five-year-old Leon Patterson and six-year-old Faith Elseth, whose fathers were victims in the attack on the Pentagon. That year the National Tree's original color scheme of red, green, and gold was changed to patriotic colors with red garlands, 100,000 white and blue lights, 100 large, white star ornaments, and a star tree-topper. This and succeeding Pageants of Peace during the Bush administration stressed a hope for peace during a time of war on terrorism as American troops were deployed to Afghanistan in search

of *Al Qaeda* terrorist leader Osama bin Laden and then to Iraq to depose dictator Saddam Hussein. On December 13, 2003, Hussein was captured alive, yet by Christmastime 2004 and the close of Bush's first term, the United States was still at war with Iraq.

Bush White House Tree Themes. 2001 (concolor fir, Pennsylvania): "Home for the Holidays" tree with miniature replicas of historic homes and houses of worship, contributed by artisans from all 50 states, 2002 (noble fir, Washington): "All Creatures Great and Small" tree with miniature replicas of birds indigenous to each of the 50 states, contributed by artisans from each state, 2003 (Fraser fir, Wisconsin): "A Season of Stories" tree featuring 675 balls and 80 literary figures which Barbara Bush had used in 1989, on loan from the George H.W. Bush Library. 2004 (noble fir, Washington): "A Season of Merriment and Melody" tree featuring 390 balls and 350 musical instrument ornaments hand-painted by members of the Society of Decorative Painters from all 50 states.

Bush Official Greeting Cards (also served as gift prints). 2001: *The White House Second Floor Corridor with Mary Cassatt's 1908 Painting "Young Woman and Two Children,"* a painting by Adrian Martinez, with a passage from Psalm 27:8, 13 (this was the first official card to contain a passage of Scripture, which Mrs. Bush selected following the events of 9/11), 2002: *1938 Steinway Piano in the Grand Foyer*, a painting by Zhen-Huan Lu, with a passage from Psalm 100:5, 2003 (over 1.5 million cards): painting of the White House Diplomatic Reception Room decorated for the holidays by Barbara Ernst Prey with a passage from Job 10:12, 2004 (over two million cards): painting of the White House Red Room decorated for the holidays by Cindi Holt with a passage from Psalm 95:2. The word "Christmas" never appeared in any of the Bushes' official card sentiments during their first four years.

Historical Association Ornaments. 2001: red-and-gold, horse-drawn carriage recalling Andrew Jackson's presidency, 2002: oval, gilded leaf motif topped by American Eagle with blue-and-white silhouette of White House, commemorating the 1902 Roosevelt restoration, 2003: boy on rocking horse with toy train below, commemorating President Grant's philanthropy to children, 2004: snowy scene of sleigh on White House South Lawn, commemorating President Hayes.

Winnie the Pooh and Christmas Too

(1998). Video collection of two made-for-television animated cartoons from the Disney series *The New Adventures of Winnie the Pooh*, which aired on the ABC network from 1988 to 1991. The series was based on characters found in the *Winnie the Pooh* books, first published in 1926 by British author Alan Alexander Milne (1882–1956). The principal characters were Winnie the Pooh, a small, gentle yet rather witless bear with a passion for honey; Tigger, the bouncing tiger; Eeyore, the moping, ever-complaining donkey; Rabbit; Piglet; Owl; Gopher; and Christopher Robin, a young boy modeled after Milne's own son of the same name. All the animals lived in the 100-Acre Wood.

Winnie the Pooh and Christmas Too (1991). Television special. As the animals discuss their Christmas wishes, Christopher Robin compiles them in a letter to Santa, then tosses the letter to the wind, which should blow it to the North Pole. But when Piglet realizes that Pooh never listed his wish, the two set out in a makeshift balloon to intercept the letter before it reaches Santa. They discover the letter trapped in a branch and return it to their comrades who, caught up in the spirit of giving, increase the list many times over on behalf of each other. Again, the wind receives the letter, only to blow it back to Pooh's house. Pooh's attempt to bring Christmas to his friends by dressing as Santa also fails, as does his mission to deliver the letter to Santa personally on Christmas Eve, for with a final blast, the wind whips the letter out of sight. Now, Pooh believes, all is lost, and he returns dejectedly on Christmas morning to his awaiting friends. Soon, Christopher Robin arrives on the very sled that he had requested, and laden thereon are the others' gift wishes all fulfilled. The wandering letter had found its proper destination after all.

In 1992, this program received an Emmy nomination for Outstanding Children's Program.

Voices: Peter Cullen, John Fiedler, Michael Gough, Edan Gross, Tim Hoskins, Nicholas Melody, Patty Parris, Ken Sansom, and Hal Smith. Written by Karl Geurs and Mark Zaslove. Producer/supervising director: Ken Kessel. Produced and directed by Jamie Mitchell. 26 min.

Magic Earmuffs (1988). Series episode. When the gang desires a game of "ice cookie" on the frozen river (using an oatmeal cookie for a hockey puck), Piglet declines, because he cannot ice skate. To build Piglet's confidence, Christopher Robin loans his earmuffs, claiming that Piglet will now be able to skate, because the earmuffs are magical. After goalie Eeyore eats the "puck," the gang continues with a honey jar for a puck, which they leave on the ice. Pooh and the others return without their skates to retrieve the jar, when suddenly the ice cracks, sending them on ice floes down river toward a waterfall. Piglet, practicing in a tub of ice on shore, now dons the earmuffs to rescue his friends. Despite losing the earmuffs, Piglet overcomes his fear and saves the day.

Voices as above. Story by Terrie Collins and Mark Zaslove. Teleplay by Carter Crocker. Produced and directed by Karl Geurs. 15 min.

VHS: Walt Disney Home Video.

Winter Solstice

In the Northern Hemisphere, that astronomical point in the apparent great-circle annual path of the sun (the ecliptic) at which the sun seemingly achieves its lowest position south of the celestial equator. If the heavens are imagined as a great sphere (the celestial sphere), the celestial equator is the great circle produced where the equatorial plane of the earth intersects the celestial sphere. Because the earth is tilted on its axis, the plane of the ecliptic intersects the celestial equator at an angle of 23° 27,' resulting in four seasons with two annual solstices and two annual equinoxes. The winter solstice in the Northern Hemisphere occurs around December 21 or 22 and produces the shortest day of the year with the longest night, while the opposite is true for the summer solstice, occurring around June 21 or 22, in which the sun seemingly achieves its highest position north of the celestial equator.

For several days around a solstice, the sun

appears to rise from the same position on the horizon, then begins slowly returning in the opposite direction. This apparent solar pause gives rise to the term "solstice," meaning "sun standing still." Twice in the year the ecliptic intersects the celestial equator to produce the vernal and autumnal equinoxes (meaning "equal nights"), respectively occurring around March 21 and September 21, in which the days and nights are of approximately equal length. All seasons, solstices, and equinoxes are simply reversed in the Southern Hemisphere.

For countless generations prior to the Christian age, the sun's annual declination at the winter solstice had been the source for numerous myths among ancient civilizations regarding the natural cycle of death and rebirth, such as the death of some solar or fertility deities at this time of year and their subsequent rebirth in the spring. Examples include Tammuz, originally a Babylonian sun god who died in winter but revived in the spring, and who later evolved into a god of animal and plant fertility; and Attis, originally a Syrian deity, who in Greek mythology was the son of Cybele, a mother goddess, and whose myth symbolized the death of vegetation in winter with revival in the spring. A similar cycle was known for Dionysus, Greek god of wine and vegetation.

Egyptians, on the other hand, celebrated the winter solstice birth of the sun god Ra at Heliopolis, the chief center for sun worship prior to the Christian age, although by their calendar, the winter solstice fell on January 6. Other Egyptian gods said to have been born on the winter solstice included Osiris, the male productive force in nature, who was murdered by his brother Set, after which Isis, the female productive force and sister-consort to Osiris, resurrected him so that Osiris became ruler of the underworld and a source for renewed life; and Aeon, patron god of Alexandria, born of the virgin goddess Kore (see **Epiphany**).

The Persians also observed the birthday of their sun god, Mithra, on the day that coincided with the winter solstice on the Roman or Julian calendar, December 25. Roman soldiers, introduced to the cult of Mithra during their campaigns in the eastern portions of the Roman Empire, popularized this new god in the West during the first century A.D. By the third century, this cult, which the Roman emperor Aurelian endorsed as *Sol Invictus* ("the Unconquered Sun"), along with the Saturnalia and a host of other pagan Roman holidays lying in proximity to the winter solstice, became a principal factor in eventually motivating the Church in the fourth century to adopt December 25 as the birthday of Christ (see **Christmas Day; Saturnalia**).

Ancient civilizations greeted the winter solstice with pomp and circumstance, with feasting, drinking, and considerable merriment. Rituals included the lighting of bonfires (especially in northern regions) to assist the sun in its return, the performance of fertility rites, sacrifices to gods, and the veneration of evergreen vegetation, which was believed to hold magical powers because it apparently remained alive through the dead of winter. At the winter solstice, because the barrier between the physical and spirit worlds was said almost to vanish, myths regarding the dead and the supernatural came to the forefront. Divination practices predicted the future, and various talismans, such as the bonfires and the creation of as much noise as possible, warded off evil that supposedly lurked just beyond the long darkness. In Norse mythology, the chief god Odin (or Woden) descended on Sleipner, his white, eight-legged steed, during the midwinter festival of Yule and transported the souls of warriors who had been slain that year to eternal life in Valhalla, his palace in Asgard, the home of the gods. The spirits of deceased ancestors and family members were also believed to visit their families and former abodes at this time, and food was set aside for their benefit.

Belief in the return of the spirits at the winter solstice probably contributed to the concept of the "Wild Hunt," "Furious Hunt," "Furious Host," and other terms for groups of spirits prevalent in northern Europe during the Middle Ages. Appearing most commonly during the 12 days of Christmas, these spirits raced across nocturnal skies to increase the fertility of fields or as messengers of death. Odin's gleaning of warriors' souls was one example of the Wild Hunt, which was also termed "Asgard's Ride." Among the Teutons, Berchta (also known as Bertha, Perchta, Holde, Hertha, and other names), goddess of the home and protector of fields, led children's souls on agrarian fertility missions at this time.

Christianized vestiges of many of these ancient winter solstice customs survive in Christmas celebrations today throughout the world: December 25 as Christmas Day, the Christmas dinner, the Christmas tree, the lighting of candles, the adorning of homes with winter greenery, noisemaking, auguries, and the telling of ghost stories, among others.

See also **Christmas Tree; The Holly and the Ivy; Mistletoe; Yule.**

Winter Wonderland

Popular American song written in 1934 by lyricist Richard Smith of Pennsylvania and composer Felix Bernard of New York. First introduced that same year with a recording by Guy Lombardo and His Royal Canadians that achieved the number 2 position on the *Hit Parade*, the simple lyrics and bubbly tune outline a couple's romantic interlude of walking through a wonderland of snow, building a snowman, then dreaming cozily by a fire together. The lyrics never mention any specific holiday, yet by popular association, the song has become a pleasant fixture in the repertoire of Christmas music.

Two recordings of "Winter Wonderland" became bestsellers in 1946. Lombardo's band provided the backup for the Andrews Sisters' recording on the Decca label which, despite the fact that it never achieved chart status, sold over a million copies. Perry Como's recording on the RCA Victor label was among that year's Top Ten.

Of the 25 most frequently performed Christmas songs of the twentieth century listed by the American Society of Composers, Authors and Publishers (ASCAP), "Winter Wonderland" ranked number 4. By December 2004, it ranked number 3.

Bernard also co-wrote the music for "Dardanella," a hit of 1919, recorded by Ben Selvin's Novelty Orchestra. It is believed that this was the first record to sell one million copies in the industry's history.

See also **ASCAP List of Christmas Songs.**

The three Wise Men, or Magi, are shown in an old engraving of a silver disk, chased in high relief and gilded, said to have formed the center of a large brooch used to fasten the decorated cope of a fourteenth century churchman.

Wise Men

Mysterious troupe of gentile sages who, guided by a Star, journeyed from the East to pay homage to the Christ Child in Bethlehem, as recorded in the Gospel of Matthew (2:1–12). Aside from this brief account, in which they presented gifts of gold, frankincense, and myrrh, everything written about the Wise Men stems principally from legend. In some stories, the Wise Men's journey to Bethlehem required two years, during which time they miraculously never lacked provisions; in others, they traveled only 12 days, in which they required neither rest nor provisions. In another, Mary gave away the Wise Men's gold, either to the poor or as a Temple offering, and the gold later filtered down to Judas Iscariot for betraying Jesus into the hands of the chief priests (although Matthew 26:14–16 states that, for his act, Judas received "thirty pieces of silver," not gold). Many years after the death of Christ, the Wise Men allegedly converted to Christianity in India through the evangelism of St. Thomas the Apostle and suffered martyrdom there for their faith. About 300 years after their deaths, the legend continues, Empress Helena, mother of Constantine the Great, supposedly carried

Herod's audience with the three Magi when he learns of the birth of the Messiah. This interview may have taken place as long as two years after Jesus' birth. From Sunday Reading for the Young *(New York: Young & Co., 1903).*

their remains from the East to Constantinople, and from there they rested at the Church of St. Eustorgius in Milan. Then around 1164, the German emperor Frederick Barbarossa enshrined their relics in jeweled caskets at the cathedral in Cologne, where it was believed that anything that touched their skulls was empowered to prevent accidents. In 1903, Cologne returned a portion of the relics to Milan.

Popular tradition during the third century held that the Wise Men were kings, in fulfillment of Psalm 72:10–11: "The kings of Sheba and Seba shall offer gifts. Yea, all kings shall fall down before him: all nations shall serve him." Sheba and Seba were once located in what is now the Republic of Yemen, in "the East." The theologian Origen of Alexandria (c. 185–c. 254) numbered them at three because of the three gifts named in Matthew, and this number has become traditional. Although no one has ever determined the identities of the Wise Men with any degree of certainty, the now-familiar names of Caspar (Gaspar or Kaspar), Melchior, and Balthazar (or Balthasar) first surfaced in the sixth century. These names appeared in a Greek manuscript of the same period as well as above

a Byzantine mosaic of three Wise Men adoring the Infant Jesus, extant in the nave of the Church of Sant'Apollinare Nuovo (c. 560) in Ravenna, Italy. St. Bede the Venerable (673?–735), the English Benedictine monk and scholar, also mentioned these names. According to the thirteenth century journals of Marco Polo, the Italian explorer claimed to have viewed in the city of Sewa, in what is now Iran, the tombs of three alleged kings with names of Caspar, Melchior, and Balthazar.

Even more confusion and uncertainty arise over their ages, their ethnic backgrounds, and the specific gift which each brought, because of variability among different sources. Their proposed countries of origin include Ethiopia, Arabia, Tarsus (in Turkey), Egypt, Mesopotamia, and Persia, and their ages have ranged from 60 to 20. Despite this diversity, the most common of legends assigns the following identities: Melchior, king of Arabia, fair-skinned, white-bearded, and elderly, brought gold; Caspar, king of Tarsus, ruddy, young, and beardless, brought frankincense; and Balthazar, king of Ethiopia, middle-aged and black, brought myrrh. The Wise Men portrayed in the Ravenna mosaic mentioned above are also of three distinct ages, but an African is not represented. The nearest to Mary is white-bearded and elderly, the second is young and beardless, and the third is middle-aged with dark beard. If the names above the mosaic respectively identify each man, then the eldest is Gaspar, the youngest Melchior, and the third "Balthassar" (sic). Nothing regarding their specific gifts can be ascertained from the mosaic.

As John and Caitlin Matthews discuss in *The Winter Solstice: The Sacred Traditions of Christmas,* so-called Gnostic texts, originating during the second and third centuries and considered heretical by the Roman Catholic Church, further contribute to the enigma. Works such as *The Book of Adam, The Book of the Cave of Treasures,* and *The Book of the Bee* number the Wise Men from three to 12. Additional identities for the traditional three include Hor, king of Persia; Basantar, king of Saba; and Karsundas, king of the East. According to Matthews and Matthews, these books also cite the names of 12 other Persian Wise Men who represented the 12 months of the year and the signs of the zodiac. Four of these allegedly presented gold, the second four myrrh, and the remaining four frankincense.

Another clue about the Wise Men lies in Matthew's Gospel. The phrase "wise men from the east" (2:1) implies the various philosophers, astrologers, and other practitioners of the occult arts at that time. That one or more of the Wise Men came from Persia (presently Iran) is very likely, for the priests, known as Magi (from the Greek *magos*, whence comes our word "magic"), who belonged to the order of the Persian prophet Zoroaster, dwelt there as master soothsayers and demonologists. By the first century, indeed, the Wise Men of Matthew's Gospel were equated with the Magi.

The three gifts that the Wise Men bestowed have been interpreted to be the earliest symbolic portents for the Infant Jesus. Gold, a precious metal, has always symbolized royalty; thus gold represented Jesus as King of Kings and Lord of Lords. Prayers have arisen to heaven with the burning of sweet incense in ceremonies ancient and modern; thus the frankincense symbolized Jesus as the ultimate High Priest. The ointment myrrh has been used not only as a medicinal balm, but also as an agent in ancient times with which to anoint the deceased prior to burial; thus the myrrh symbolized Jesus as both the Great Physician and as one Who would be crucified.

See also **Nativity**; **Star of Bethlehem**.

A contrarian depiction of Caspar, supposedly the young, beardless King of Tarsus. This fictionalized image, complete with fourteenth century knight's armored footwear, is described as "Caspar, impersonated by a wealthy merchant prince of Rouen" in a miracle play of the Middle Ages. From Harper's New Monthly Magazine, *December 1889.*

The Wish That Changed Christmas
See **The Story of Holly and Ivy**

Wonderful Christmastime

Popular song written in 1979 by British rock star Paul McCartney (1942–) of Beatles fame. McCartney recorded it as a single that same year on the British label Parlophone (released simultaneously in the United States on the Columbia label) with his now-late wife Linda providing background vocals. On the record's B-side was "Rudolph, the Red-Nosed Reggae," McCartney's parody of the immortal tune by Johnny Marks. Both songs were released as bonus tracks on the remastered version of McCartney's album, *Back to the Egg* (1979). The light lyrics to "Wonderful Christmastime" make nonspecific references to the secular pleasures of the holiday. In 1984, the song charted number ten on the *Billboard Special Christmas Singles* chart.

"Wonderful Christmastime" was not among the 25 most frequently performed Christmas songs of the twentieth century as listed by the American Society of Composers, Authors and Publishers (ASCAP). By December 2004, however, the song's increasing popularity had merited position 22 on the ASCAP list.

Although the Beatles' albums are legendary, by the 1990s, solo artist Paul McCartney was creating classical works, such as *The Liverpool Oratorio* (1991), *A Leaf* for solo piano (1995), and the symphonic poem *Standing Stone* (1997). In 1996, Queen Elizabeth II knighted him for his contributions to music.

See also **ASCAP List of Christmas Songs.**

Wooden Soldiers

See **Babes in Toyland**

Works of Art

See **Nativity** (Works of Art); **The Vatican** (Works of Art)

Wreaths

See **Saturnalia**

Wren Hunt

See **Hunting the Wren**

X

Xmas

Abbreviation for "Christmas," derived by combining the Greek letter "X" (Chi) and a contracted form of "Mass" in the Roman Catholic usage. "Chi" is the first letter in the Greek word for Christ, "ΧΡΙΣΤΟΣ" (transliterated *Christos*). Although this abbreviation for Christmas has been in common usage since the twelfth century, over hundreds of years the significance of the letter Chi has been lost among the general public. As a result, people have often protested that using "Xmas" instead of "Christmas" cheapens the season by eliminating Christ or crossing out Christ. This was never the intent of the early Christians who originally developed the abbreviation.

See also **Christmas Day.**

Now old XMAS has come once more,
And boys bring holly to the door.
Now let me hope you'll always find,
Christmas bring gifts of choicest kind.

From an alphabet in American Chatterbox *(New York: Worthington, 1884).*

The Year without a Santa Claus

Classic children's book (actually a narrative poem) published in 1956 by Phyllis McGinley, adapted for television as an animated cartoon special.

In the book, Santa suffers from a cold and other ailments and announces that he will take a vacation from the hassle of delivering Christmas gifts. At first the news is devastating to children around the world, but six-year-old Ignatius Thistlewhite argues that it is time for Santa to have his own Christmas holiday for a change. Rallying behind Ignatius, children forward millions of gifts to the North Pole, an act that touches Santa beyond measure. With gifts filling his abode, there's no place for the toys except in his sleigh. Seeing his sleigh packed with gifts, Santa declares that he doesn't need a holiday after all. Not only does he make his usual rounds on Christmas Eve, he also leaves a special gift and a note of thanks for Ignatius.

The 1974 television special features stop-motion puppets (Animagic). When Santa believes that the world no longer cares anything about Christmas, Mrs. Claus sends two elves, Jingle and Jangle Bells, out into the world to find some remnant of the Christmas spirit. They find it in Ignatius, and together the three experience a whirlwind of adventure with Snow Miser, Heat Miser, Mother Nature, and the mayor of Southtown, U.S.A. Featured songs: "Blue Christmas," "Here Comes Santa Claus," and "Sleigh Ride." Narrated and sung by Shirley Booth. Principal voices: Mickey Rooney, Dick Shawn, George S. Irving, Robert McFadden, Rhoda Mann, Bradley Bolke, Ron Marshall, Colin Duffy, Christine Winter, and the Wee Winter Singers. Written by William Keenan. Produced and directed by Arthur Rankin, Jr., and Jules Bass. A Rankin/Bass Production. DVD: Warner Studios. 51 min.

The television special is further detailed in Rick Goldschmidt's book *The Enchanted World of Rankin/Bass.*

See also **Rankin/Bass Christmas Cartoons.**

Yes, Virginia, There Is a Santa Claus

Title now applied to an editorial by Francis P. Church that appeared in the *New York Sun* on September 21, 1897. Originally headed "Is There a Santa Claus?" the editorial was published in response to a letter written by eight-year-old Virginia O'Hanlon of 115 West 95th Street. Virginia had always believed in Santa but began to have doubts when her friends scoffed at her notions. Well acquainted with the *Sun* because her family often submitted queries to its question-and-answer column regarding matters of historical fact, Virginia wrote, "Papa says, 'If you see it in the *Sun,* it's so.' Please tell me the truth, is there a Santa Claus?" Church's editorial, a masterful and sensitive appeal for Virginia to have faith in what she could not always see, answered with an emphatic, "Yes, Virginia, there is a Santa Claus." It became an instant success and was published annually thereafter in the *Sun* until 1949, when the newspaper folded.

Virginia O'Hanlon received numerous inquiries about her letter, to which she always replied with an attractive, printed copy of Church's editorial. Receiving her education at Hunter College and Columbia University, she taught in the New York City school system and also became a principal, retiring after 47 years of service. Virginia O'Hanlon Douglas died in 1971 at the age of 81.

Francis P. Church covered the Civil War for the *New York Times* and spent 20 years as an editorial writer for the *Sun.* His literary interests included controversial issues, especially theology.

Two television versions of the story remain holiday favorites. The animated cartoon *Yes, Virginia, There Is a Santa Claus* (1974), featuring actual photographs of Virginia, Church, and Virginia's father, Dr. Philip

O'Hanlon, won an Emmy Award for Outstanding Children's Special for the 1974–75 season. Narrated by Jim Backus. Vocalist: Jimmy Osmond. Voices: Courtney Lemmon, Susan Silo, Billie Green, Sean Manning, Tracy Belland, Christopher Wong, Vickey Ricketts, Jennifer Green, Herb Armstrong, and Arnold Ross. Written by Mort Green. Produced by Bill Melendez and Mort Green. Directed by Bill Melendez. A Burt Rosen Company Production in association with Wolper Productions and Bill Melendez Productions. VHS: Paramount Home Video. 25 min.

The live-action drama *Yes, Virginia, There Is a Santa Claus* (1991) is a more fictionalized account of the lives of Virginia (Katherine Isobel), her poverty-stricken father (Richard Thomas), Church (Charles Bronson), and Church's editor (Ed Asner). There, a cynical Church, broken by his wife's death, battles alcoholism amid the holidays. Written by Val DeCrowl and Andrew J. Fenady. Produced by Duke Fenady. Directed by Charles Jarrott. American Broadcasting Company. Video N/A. 95 min.

Yogi Bear's All-Star Comedy Christmas Caper

(1982). Made-for-television animated cartoon, featuring an all-star cast of Hanna-Barbera characters.

With Christmastime at hand, Huckleberry Hound, Super Snooper the Cat, Blabber Mouse, Snagglepuss, Quick Draw McGraw, Auggie Doggie, Doggie Daddy, and Hokey Wolf all arrive at Jellystone Park to visit pals Yogi Bear and Boo Boo for the holidays. Instead, the troupe and Mr. Ranger discover that the two bears have escaped and are en route to the city on a similar visitation mission. Seeing bears loose, the police chase them into Gacy's Department Store, where, disguised as Santas, they meet Judy Jones, a little seven-year-old who has run away because her billionaire father has no time to spend Christmas with her. As Yogi and Boo Boo commiserate with Judy in a nearby park, Huckleberry Hound and the gang catch up with them and, when the child refuses to provide her address, launch a search for her residence. This endeavor involves inquiries with other Hanna-Barbera characters, who

make cameo appearances: Fred Flintstone, Barney Rubble, Jinx the Cat, mice Pixie and Dixie, Magilla Gorilla, Yakky Doodle Duck, and Wally Alligator. Soon, J. Wellington Jones, Judy's father, arrives with the police, who would arrest the bears, but after Yogi explains the reason for Judy's disappearance, the man realizes his error and is reconciled with his daughter.

Voices: Daws Butler, Mel Blanc, Henry Corden, Georgi Irene, Allan Melvin, Don Messick, Hal Smith, John Stephenson, Janet Waldo, and Jimmy Weldon. Written by Mark Evanier. Produced by Art Scott. Directed by Steve Lumley. Hanna-Barbera Productions. VHS: Turner Home Video. 30 min.

See also **Hanna-Barbera Christmas Cartoons; Yogi's First Christmas.**

Yogi's First Christmas

(1980). Made-for television animated cartoon, based on characters from *The Yogi Bear Show*, a series of 97 episodes from Hanna-Barbera Studios that aired in syndication from 1961 to 1962. In addition to Yogi, that series included cartoons devoted to Snagglepuss the Lion and Yakky Doodle Duck. Additional *Yogi* series followed over the decades.

Ordinarily hibernating in Jellystone National Park at Christmastime, Yogi Bear and pal Boo Boo are awakened by the revelry of other Hanna-Barbera cartoon characters, Huckleberry Hound, Snagglepuss, Augie Doggie, and Doggie Daddy, who are attending Christmas Carnival Week at Jellystone Lodge. The week is fraught with a series of mishaps created by Herman the Hermit in an attempt to get Mrs. Throckmorton, the owner, to sell the lodge. Collaborating with Herman is Snively, Mrs. Throckmorton's young brat of a nephew, who despises Christmas as much as Herman does. Barred from the Christmas Eve tree-trimming party because of his attitude, Snively finds Herman poor company compared to the gaiety at the lodge.

At the party, Mrs. Throckmorton also hosts a group of orphans, to whom Yogi and Boo Boo (respectively disguised as Santa and elf) distribute gifts. Eventually she takes pity on the two culprits outside and shares Christmas cheer with them as well. When they both receive unexpected and undeserved gifts,

Christmas means something more to them than before. Mrs. Throckmorton donates the lodge as a year-round vacation spot for the orphans, and Santa himself arrives with the ideal gift for Yogi, a picnic basket.

Voices: Sue Allen, John Borks, Daws Butler, Paul DeKorte, Darlene Lawrence, Edie Lehmann, Ida Sue McCune, Don Messick, Marilyn Powell, Michael Redman, Andrea Robinson, Marilyn Schreffier, Hal Smith, John Stephenson, and Janet Waldo. Written by Willie Gilbert. Produced by Lewis Marshall. Directed by Ray Patterson. Hanna-Barbera Productions. VHS: Turner Home Entertainment. 98 min.

See also **Hanna-Barbera Christmas Cartoons; Yogi Bear's All-Star Comedy Christmas Caper.**

Yule

Midwinter celebration observed by pre-Christian Celtic and Germanic tribes of northern Europe. Whereas some believe that Yule extended from mid-November until the end of January, others hold that it originally commenced in November but switched to the time of the winter solstice through contact with, and influence from, the Roman Empire. Another view is that the festival originally centered around the winter solstice.

"Yule" derives from *Jul,* which in turn is thought to derive from several sources, including the Germanic *Giul* and the Saxon *hweol* (both meaning "wheel"); the Germanic *Geola* ("feast"); and "Jolnir," an alternative name for Odin or Woden, king of the Norse gods, to whom sacrifices of boars were made at this time (a boar symbolized Freya, Norse fertility goddess, who rode in a chariot pulled by a boar). Yule celebrated fertility and the rebirth of life and the sun, the latter visualized as a return of the "burning wheel" at the winter solstice.

Yule was a time for bonfires, a symbol of the returning sun in the heavens and the promise of spring, and for revelry and clamor to repel evil spirits which were believed to inhabit the winter darkness. It was a time for divination and magic; a time when Odin, riding upon his white, eight-legged steed Sleipner, descended to collect the souls of Viking warriors slain in battle to his palace, Valhalla;

A relatively short Yule log is being dragged to the fire in an Elizabethan-era scene in Harper's New Monthly Magazine, *December 1884.*

a time when Odin's son Thor rode through the skies in a chariot pulled by two billy goats, Gnasher and Cracker; and a time for feasting. Because heavy November snows barred livestock from grazing, large numbers of cattle were slaughtered for feasts and for sacrifices to Odin. Hence, St. Bede the Venerable (673?–735), the English Benedictine monk and historian, referred to November as *Blotmonath* ("Blood Month"), and the entire season paralleled the abandon of the Roman Saturnalia.

From the fifth century onward, the Christianization of northern Europe gradually witnessed local Yule customs merging with those of Christmas, and by the eleventh century, Yule and Christmas had become synonymous holidays. The formerly venerated gods had fallen away, but other vestiges of Yule remained, including boisterous revelry and the Yule log with its associated superstitions.

The Yule log is thought to have evolved from the Zagmuk, a New Year festival of ancient Sumer. According to Sumerian mythology, the supreme god, Marduk, annually saved the world from dying at year's end by defeating the monsters of chaos in the underworld. The burning of wooden effigies of those monsters was believed to assist Marduk in his task; hence, primitive Yule logs.

Recalling those midwinter bonfires of past ages, the Yule log of the Middle Ages slowly burned all during the 12 days of Christmas, lest evil befall the house or hall wherein the flame prematurely died. To burn a log for this duration generally required an entire tree trunk,

A Victorian Yule scene, with a very big Yule log (obviously the bottom of a pollarded tree like those still standing). From Robert Chambers, ed., A Book of Days *(London and Edinburgh: Chambers, 1879).*

which was placed headlong into the fireplace and advanced as needed, with the remainder occupying a large portion of the room. Traditionally, each family selected their own Yule log for the following season on Candlemas, February 2, a day that, until the Second Vatican Council (1962–1965), had officially ended the Christmas season in the Roman Catholic Church. Logs often were of ash wood in memory of a legend holding that the Christ Child was first washed and dressed by an ash wood fire; alternatively, logs cut from fruit trees became tokens of the fertility of the land. Logs could also be of oak, olive, or birch wood. The log was never bought. It was laid up to dry during the spring, and a piece of the previous year's log was saved to light the new log, the latter act symbolically cycling the light of life from one year to the next.

Because of the belief that spirits of family ancestors became manifest in the glowing embers, a libation of wine poured over the log beforehand honored their memories, and all who touched the log first purified themselves by washing their hands. A ceremony invoking blessings for Christmas and the coming new year customarily preceded the lighting, the tra-

dition in some locales requiring that the log first be dragged around the exterior of the house or hall a specified number of times to dispel any evil.

In medieval England, tenants often presented Yule logs to their landlords, who in turn furnished their meals for as long as the log burned. On the same note, slaves in the antebellum United States were granted rest from their work for this duration; to prolong the burning, slaves first soaked the log in water.

A number of other customs and superstitions surrounded the Yule log, including the following:

A person casting a headless shadow from the light of the fire would die within one year.

In certain parts of England, the log was banded or hooped with strips of the same tree. As each band snapped, the master of the house was expected to furnish his guests with a fresh bowl of cider or liquor. The bands were often associated with pairs of lovers, and the order of the snapping bands predicted the sequence of their weddings.

Upon beating the log, one could see evil spirits departing in a shower of sparks.

A barefoot person, squinting person, or a flat-footed woman approaching the log brought bad luck.

Ashes from the log, if placed in fruit trees, improved the crop yield, and if placed under the bed, prevented lightning from striking the house.

Today, the custom of burning a Yule log still exists in Europe and the United States, albeit on a much smaller scale than in earlier days. Instead of continuously burning a log for 12 days, the trend is to burn the log only during Christmas Eve and Christmas Day; alternatively, some prefer to burn their log for a brief period on each of those 12 days. In France, the Yule log survives only as a log-shaped cake, the *bûche de Noël* ("Christmas log").

See also **Saturnalia; Superstitions; The Twelve Days of Christmas** (time period); **Winter Solstice.**

Yule Log
See **Yule**

Z

Ziggy's Gift

(1982). Made-for-television animated cartoon based on the popular comic strip *Ziggy*, created by Tom Wilson.

Responding to an ad recruiting street Santas for charity, Ziggy unwittingly peddles for a fraudulent ring run by the Fly-by-Nite Loan Company. Dogged by a petty thief as well as a policeman intent on arresting Ziggy as one of the ring, Ziggy still manages to perform good deeds, such as miraculously pulling cash from his empty kettle for donations, liberating live Christmas turkeys, and befriending a homeless man. Ziggy's greatest gift is to the children at Mrs. Ostblom's Foster Home, in which the thief and cop also become unsuspecting instruments of Christmas magic for the little ones.

This program, Ziggy's first prime-time special, won an Emmy Award for Outstanding Animated Program.

Voices: Richard Williams, Tom McGreevey, Tony Giorgio, John Gibbons, Harry Nillson, David Arias, Perry Botkin, Katrina Fried, Natasha Fried, Jack Hanrahan, Linda Harmon, Anna Ostblom, Latoya Prescod, Gloria Prosper, Andy Raub, Terry Stillwell-Harriton, Lena Tabori, Holly Williams, Tim Williams, Tom Wilson, and Tom Wilson, Jr. Written by Tom Wilson. Produced by Tom Wilson, Richard Williams, and Lena Tabori. Directed by Richard Williams. A Welcome Production in association with Universal Press Syndicate. VHS: Vestron Video. 24 min.

Zimbabwe
See **Africa**

References

Abate, Frank R., ed. *Omni Gazetteer of the United States of America*. 9 vols. Detroit: Omnigraphics, 1991.

Albright, Ann Lane. *Samuel Sparrow and the Tree of Light*. Danville, Virginia: Ascension Lutheran Church, 2003.

Alcott, Louisa May. *Little Women*. New York: Pocket Books, 1994.

Alfred Burt Carols Web Site: www.alfredburtcarols.com

Alston, G. Cyprian. "Boy-Bishop." In *The Catholic Encyclopedia*. Vol. II. Online Edition, 2003. New Advent, Inc. Web Site: www.newadvent.org/cathen/02725a.htm

_____. "Gaudete Sunday." In *The Catholic Encyclopedia*. Vol. VI. Online Edition, 2003. New Advent, Inc. Web Site: www.newadvent.org/cathen/06394b.htm

"Amazing Hanukkah Feats." From the History Channel. Web Site: www.historychannel.com/exhibits/holidays/hanukkah/feats.html

"American Express Consumer Survey Suggests Modest Increase in Holiday Spending This Year Despite the Soft Economy." American Express Retail Index. Web Site: newsroom.mbooth.com/amex/RetailIndex/Holiday2002Release.html

"American Express Retail Index Finds Holiday Budgets Dip Slightly." American Express Retail Index. Web Site: home3.americanexpress.com/corp/latestnews/holiday-retail01.asp

American Society of Composers, Authors and Publishers. Web Site: www.ascap.org

"Americans Plan Another Frenzied Black Friday..." American Express Retail Index. Web Site: newsroom.mbooth.com/amex/RetailIndex/BlackFriday2003Release.html

Andersen, Hans Christian. *The Complete Illustrated Stories of Hans Christian Andersen*. Translated from the Danish by H.W. Dulcken. Illustrations by A.W. Bayes. London: Chancellor Press, 1982.

Andrews, Bart. *The "I Love Lucy" Book*. New York: Doubleday, 1985.

"Andy Williams Biography." Andy Williams: The Official Web Site: www.andywilliams.com

"Andy Williams Discography, Lyrics, MP3s, CDs, Pictures." All Music Guide. Web Site: www.lyrics-discography-mp3.com/discography/andy_williams-cds.html

"The Andy Williams Show." Lisa's Nostalgia Café. Web Site: www.anzwers.org/free/retrolisa/andywilliams.html

"Angel Tree Newsroom." Web Site: www.demossnewspond.com/at/

Arbelbide, C.L. "Christmas Pageant of Peace History." President's Park. Web Site: www.nps.gov/whho/pageant/cpophistory/index.htm

Ashe, Geoffrey. "Magical Glastonbury." Britannia, America's Gateway to the British Isles. Web Site: www.britannia.com/history/glaston1.html

"Auld Lang Syne." In *The Burns Encyclopedia*. The Official Robert Burns Site: www.robertburns.org/encyclopedia/index.shtml

Auld, William Muir. *Christmas Traditions*. New York: Macmillan, 1931.

"Australian Christmas Plants." Australian National Botanic Gardens. Web Site: www.anbg.gov.au/christmas/christmas.html

Autry, Gene. *Back in the Saddle Again*. Garden City, New York: Doubleday, 1978.

"*Babes in Toyland*: The 1934 Classic Film Starring Stan Laurel and Oliver Hardy." Way Out West Tent. Web Site: www.wayoutwest.org/toyland/

Baggelaar, Kristin, and Donald Milton. "John Jacob Niles." In *Folk Music: More Than a Song*. New York: Thomas Y. Crowell, 1976.

Barabas, SuzAnne, and Gabor Barabas. *Gunsmoke: A Complete History and Analysis of the Legendary Broadcast Series with a Complete Episode-by-Episode Guide to Both the Radio and Television Programs*. Jefferson, North Carolina: McFarland, 1990.

Barrett, John. *The Bear Who Slept Through Christmas*. Illustrations by Rick Reinert Productions. Developed by the LeFave Company. Chicago: Children's Press, 1980.

Barth, Edna. *Holly, Reindeer, and Colored Lights: The Story of the Christmas Symbols*. New York: Seabury Press, 1971.

Bartlett, Clifford. Program notes for George Frideric Handel, *Messiah*. Bavarian Radio Symphony Orchestra and Chorus. Sir Colin Davis. Philips compact disc set 412 538–2, 1985.

Basinger, Jeanine. *The "It's a Wonderful Life" Book*. New York: Alfred A. Knopf, 1986.

Baum, L. Frank. *The Life and Adventures of Santa Claus*. Illustrated edition with pictures by Mary Cowles Clark. New York: Greenwich House, 1983.

Baumgarten, Paul Maria. "Basilica of St. Peter." In *The Catholic Encyclopedia*. Vol. XIII. Online Edition, 2003. New Advent, Inc. Web Site: www.newadvent.org/cathen/13369b.htm

_____. "The Vatican." In *The Catholic Encyclopedia*. Vol.

XV. Online Edition, 2003. New Advent, Inc. Web Site: www.newadvent.org/cathen/15276b.htm

Baxter, Batsell Barrett, and Harold Hazelip. *A Devotional Guide to Bible Lands*. Grand Rapids: Baker Book House, 1979.

"Bells on Bob-tails Ring." Best Read Guide Savannah. Web Site: www.bestreadguide.com/savannah/shopping/jinglebells.shtml

Bemelmans, Ludwig. *Madeline's Christmas*. New York: Viking Kestrel, 1985.

Bendazzi, Giannalberto. "La Freccia Azzurra (The Blue Arrow)." Web Site: www.awn.com/mag/issue1.10/articles/bendazziblue1.10.html

Berenstain, Stan, and Jan Berenstain. *The Bears' Christmas*. New York: Beginner Books, 1970.

_____. *The Berenstain Bears' Christmas Tree*. New York: Random House, 1980.

_____. *The Berenstain Bears Meet Santa Bear*. New York: Random House, 1984.

_____. *The Berenstain Bears Save Christmas*. Illustrated by Mike Berenstain. New York: HarperCollins, 2003.

Bertrin, Georges, and Arthur F.J. Remy. "Miracle Plays and Mysteries." In *The Catholic Encyclopedia*. Vol. X. Online Edition, 2003. New Advent, Inc. Web Site: www.newadvent.org/cathen/10348a.htm

Bindokiene, Danute Brazyte. *Lithuanian Customs and Traditions*. Translated from the Lithuanian by Vita Matusaitis. Chicago: Lithuanian World Community, 1989.

Black, Naomi, Nancy Kalish, and Loretta Mowat, eds. *The Whole Christmas Catalogue: The Complete Compendium of Christmas Traditions, Recipes, Crafts, Carols, Lore, and More*. Philadelphia: Running Press, 1994.

Blue Ridge Mountain Holiday: The Breaking Up Christmas Story. County Records compact disc CO-CD-2722, 1997.

Bob Hope Official Web Site: www.bobhope.com/

Bogle, Lara Suziedelis. "Scots Mark New Year with Fiery Ancient Rites." National Geographic News. Web Site: news.nationalgeographic.com/news/2002/12/1230_021231_hogmanay.html

Boudreaux, Jonathan. "Happy Holidays with Bing and Frank." Web Site: www.tvdvdreviews.com/bingfrank.html

Briggs, Raymond. *Father Christmas*. New York: Coward, McCann, and Geoghegan, 1973.

_____. *The Snowman*. New York: Random House, 1978.

Brown, Les. *Les Brown's Encyclopedia of Television*. 3rd edition. Detroit: Gale Research, 1992.

Brunhoff, Jean De. *Babar and Father Christmas*. Translated from the French by Merle Haas. New York: Random House, 1940.

Bull, George. *Inside the Vatican*. New York: St. Martin's Press, 1982.

Bynum, Russ. "Dashing Through the Sun? North–South Debate Rages Over Roots of 'Jingle Bells.'" Associated Press article published December 21, 2003. Web Site: cnews.canoe.ca/CNEWS/WeirdNews/2003/12/21/294160-ap.html

Capote, Truman. *A Christmas Memory*. New York: Random House, 1956.

_____. *One Christmas*. New York: Random House, 1983.

"Card Purchases a High Priority During the Holidays." Retail Industry. Web Site: retailindustry.about.com/cs/stats_consumers/a/blh_gca111803.htm

"Cardigan Castle." Castles of Wales. Web Site: www.castle-wales.com/cardigan.html

Carpenter, Humphrey. *Benjamin Britten: A Biography*. New York: Charles Scribner's Sons, 1992.

Cathcart, Rex. "Festive Capers? Barring Out the Schoolmaster." *History Today* (December 1988).

Chalmers, Irena. *The Great American Christmas Almanac*. New York: Viking Penguin, 1988.

Chambers, E.K. *The English Folk-Play*. 1933. Reprint, New York: Haskell House, 1966.

"Chanukah on the Ellipse: National Menorah Council." From American Friends of Lubavitch, Washington Office. Web Site: www.afl.us/NMC.php

"Children Light Candle with Clinton." Cable News Network article published December 23, 1997. Web Site: www.cnn.com/SPECIALS/1997/hanukkah/washington. menorah/

"Chrismons." Ascension Lutheran Church. Danville, Virginia. Web Site: chrismon.org/site/chrismon.htm

"Christmas and New Year's Eve in Denmark." The Royal Danish Embassy, Washington, D.C. Web Site: www.denmarkemb.org/christmas.html

"Christmas Around the World." From Christmas.com, Inc. Web Site: christmas.com/worldview

"Christmas Customs in Estonia." Estonia Ministry of Foreign Affairs. Web Site: www.mfa.ee/estonia/kat_459/pea_174/1191.html

Christmas in Australia. Chicago: World Book, 1998.

"Christmas in Austria." Austrian Press and Information Service, Washington, D.C. Web Site: www.austria.org/oldsite/dec98/ausmas.html

Christmas in Brazil. Chicago: World Book, 1991.

Christmas in Britain. Chicago: World Book, 1996.

Christmas in Canada. Chicago: World Book, 1994.

Christmas in Colonial and Early America. Chicago: World Book, 1996.

Christmas in Denmark. Chicago: World Book, 1986.

Christmas in France. Chicago: World Book, 1996.

Christmas in Ireland. Chicago: World Book, 1996.

Christmas in Italy. Chicago: World Book, 1996.

"Christmas in Luxembourg." Luxembourg Tourist Office, London. Web Site: www.luxembourg.co.uk/xmas.html

Christmas in Mexico. Chicago: World Book, 1996.

"Christmas in Norway." The Royal Norwegian Ministry of Foreign Affairs, Washington, D.C. Web Site: odin.dep.no/odin/engelsk/norway/history/032005–993721/dok-bn.html

Christmas in Poland. Chicago: World Book, 1989.

Christmas in Russia. Chicago: World Book, 1997.

Christmas in Spain. Chicago: World Book, 1996.

Christmas in Switzerland. Chicago: World Book, 1995.

Christmas in the American Southwest. Chicago: World Book, 1996.

"Christmas in the City of Turku, Finland." From Christmascity of Finland. Web Site: www.christmascity.com/dynamic/eng/index.php?page=joulukaupunki

Christmas in the Holy Land. Chicago: World Book, 1987.

Christmas in the Philippines. Chicago: World Book, 1990.

Christmas in Today's Germany. Chicago: World Book, 1993.

Christmas in Ukraine. Chicago: World Book, 1997.

The Christmas Mood: Original Recording of the Alfred Burt Carols. Program Notes. Collegium USA. Compact disc sound recording, 2000.

"Christmas Pageant of Peace." From Christmas Pageant of Peace, Inc. Web Site: www.pageantofpeace.org

"The Christmas Pageant of Peace and National Christmas Tree." The National Park Service. Web Site: www.nps.gov/ncro/PublicAffairs/NationalChristmasTree.htm

"The Christmas Story of Rudolph, the Red-Nosed Reindeer." Business Library: Montgomery Ward (1872–2000). The University of Western Ontario. Web Site: http://www.lib.uwo.ca/business/wards-ourpage.html

The Christmas Story Told Through Paintings. Commentary by Richard Mühlberger. New York: The Metropolitan Museum of Art and GulliverBooks/Harcourt Brace Jovanovich, 1990.

"Christmas Traditions in France and in Canada." French Ministry of Culture and Canadian Heritage. Web Site: www.culture.gouv.fr/culture/noel/angl/noel.htm

Collins, Ace. *Stories Behind the Best-Loved Songs of Christmas.* Illustrations by Clint Hansen. Grand Rapids: Zondervan, 2001.

Crowley, T.J. "Feast of Asses." In *The Catholic Encyclopedia.* Vol. I. Online Edition, 2003. New Advent, Inc. Web Site: www.newadvent.org/cathen/01798b.htm

Curtis, Jack. *Christmas in Calico: An American Fable.* Monterey, California: Monterey Publications, 1996. Re-issued as *Christmas in Calico.* New York: Daybreak Books, 1998.

The Cyber Hymnal. Web Site: http://www.cyberhymnal.org.

"Czech Christmas." From Radio Prague. Web Site: archiv. radio.cz/christmas/

Davies, Valentine. *Miracle on 34th Street.* Text, Twentieth Century Fox Film Corporation, 1947. Illustrated edition, with an introduction by Elizabeth Davies and paintings by Tomie de Paola. New York: Harcourt Brace Jovanovich, 1984.

Dearmer, Percy R., Vaughn Williams, and Martin Shaw. *The Oxford Book of Carols.* New York: Oxford University Press, 1964.

"December 24, 25, 26." In *The Book of Days,* edited by Robert Chambers. Vol. 2, 1862–1864. Reprint, Detroit: Gale Research, 1967.

Del Re, Gerard, and Patricia Del Re. *The Christmas Almanac.* Garden City, New York: Doubleday, 1979.

Dickens, Charles. *A Christmas Carol and Other Christmas Books.* Everyman's Library. New York: E.P. Dutton, 1961.

_____. *Christmas Stories.* The Oxford Illustrated Dickens. New York: Oxford University Press, 1956.

_____. "A Good-Humored Christmas Chapter" and "The Story of the Goblins Who Stole a Sexton." Chaps. 28 and 29 in *The Pickwick Papers.* New York: Penguin Books United States, 1964.

Dinneen, Mark. *Culture and Customs of Venezuela.* Westport, Connecticut: Greenwood Press, 2001.

"Do This in Memory of Me": The Christmas and Easter Liturgies Celebrated by Pope John Paul II. Narrated by James Fox. Centro Televisio Vaticano, Eurovideo Service Pool. VHS: HBO Home Video, 1996. Videocassette recording.

"Dr. Elmo Celebrates 25 Years of 'Grandma Got Run Over by a Reindeer.'" Dr. Elmo's Official Web Site: www. drelmo.com/BioNews.htm

Dr. Seuss. *How the Grinch Stole Christmas.* New York: Random House, 1957.

Donovan, Stephen M. "Crib." In *The Catholic Encyclopedia.* Vol. IV. Online Edition, 2003. New Advent, Inc. Web Site: www.newadvent.org/cathen/04488c.htm

Drum, Walter. "Magi." In *The Catholic Encyclopedia.* Vol. IX. Online Edition, 2003. New Advent, Inc. Web Site: www.newadvent.org/cathen/09527a.htm

Dumitru, Petru, and students. "Romanian Winter Festivals and Traditions." Duiliu Zamfirescu School, Focsani, Romania. Web Site: http://www.european-schoolprojects. net/festivals/Romania/winterindex.html

Dumois, Luis. "Posadas, Pastorelas and Nacimientos." Inside Mexico–The Series. From Mexico Connect. Web Site: http://www.mexconnect.com/mex_/travel/ldumois/ ldcposadas.html

Duris, Joseph, ed. *Slovak Christmas: A Symposium of Songs,* *Customs and Plays.* Cleveland, Ohio: Slovak Institute, 1960.

Edelstein, Andrew J., and Frank Lovece. *"The Brady Bunch" Book.* New York: Warner Books, 1990.

Egan, Bill. "Oldest Known 'Silent Night' Manuscript Discovered." From *Austrian Information.* Austrian Press and Information Service, Washington, D.C. Web Site: www. austria.org/dec96/silent.html

_____. "The Song Heard 'Round the World." From *Austrian Information.* Austrian Press and Information Service, Washington, D.C. Web Site: http://www.austria. org/oldsite/dec99/silentnight.html

Elliott, Sara. *Italian Renaissance Painting.* London: Phaidon Press, 1993.

Evans, Richard Paul. *The Christmas Box.* New York: Simon and Schuster, 1995.

_____. *The Christmas Candle.* Paintings by Jacob Collins. New York: Simon and Schuster, 1998.

_____. *The First Gift of Christmas.* Salt Lake City: Gibbs Smith, 1996.

_____. *The Light of Christmas.* Illustrated by Daniel Craig. New York: Simon and Schuster, 2002.

"Feast of the Holy Family." Web Site: filebox.vt.edu/ users/rcade/holyfam.html

"A Festival of Nine Lessons and Carols." King's College, Cambridge, England. Web Site: www.kings.cam.ac.uk/ chapel/ninelessons/

Foster, Don. *Author Unknown: On the Trail of Anonymous.* New York: Henry Holt, 2000.

Frankel, Stanley A. "The Story Behind 'Rudolph, the Red-Nosed Reindeer.'" *Good Housekeeping* (December 1989).

Fries, Adelaide L. *Customs and Practices of the Moravian Church.* 4th edition. Bethlehem, Pennsylvania: Moravian Church in North America, 2003.

Frisk, M. Jean. "*Salus Populi Romani*: Protectress of the Roman People." The Marian Library, International Marian Research Institute, Dayton, Ohio. Web Site: www. udayton.edu/mary/meditations/saluspr.html

Frost, Robert. *Christmas Trees.* Text, New York: Holt, Rinehart and Winston, 1916. Illustrated edition by Ted Rand, New York: Henry Holt and Company, 1990.

Gallico, Paul. *Miracle in the Wilderness: A Christmas Story of Colonial America.* New York: Delacorte, 1955.

Gardner, Martin, ed. *The Annotated Night Before Christmas: A Collection of Sequels, Parodies, and Imitations of Clement Moore's Immortal Ballad About Santa Claus.* New York: Summit Books, 1991.

"The Garifuna History, Language and Culture." *San Pedro Sun.* Web Site: www.sanpedrosun.net/old/98–453.html

Garrison, Webb. *Treasury of Christmas Stories.* Nashville: Rutledge Hill Press, 1990.

Gascoigne, Mike. "Birth of Yeshua." Web Site: www.write-on. co.uk/birth.htm

"George Wyle." American Society of Music Arrangers and Composers. Web Site: www.asmac.org/frameshome. html

Godden, Rumer. *The Story of Holly and Ivy.* 1957. Illustrated edition by Barbara Cooney, New York: Viking Penguin, 1985.

Goldschmidt, Rick. *The Enchanted World of Rankin/Bass.* Bridgeview, Illinois: Miser Bros. Press, 1997.

Goodwin, Joan. "Lydia Maria Child." Unitarian Universalist Biographical Dictionary. Web Site: www.uua.org/ uuhs/duub/articles/lydiamariachild.html

Greene, Richard Leighton, ed. *The Early English Carols.* 2nd edition. Oxford, England: Clarendon Press, 1977.

"Greeting Card Industry General Facts and Trends." Greeting Card Association. Web Site: www.greetingcard.org/gcindustry_generalfacts.html

Griffith, Alison B. "Mithraism." The ECOLE Initiative. A service of the University of Evansville, Evansville, Indiana. Web Site: www2.evansville.edu/ecoleweb/articles/mithraism.html

Grisham, John. *Skipping Christmas.* New York: Doubleday, 2001.

Grubb, Nancy. *Angels in Art.* New York: Artabras, 1995.

Guida, Fred. *"A Christmas Carol" and Its Adaptations: A Critical Examination of Dickens's Story and Its Productions on Screen and Television.* Foreword by Edward Wagenknecht. Jefferson, North Carolina: McFarland, 2000.

Guinn, Jeff. *The Autobiography of Santa Claus: As Told to Jeff Guinn.* Illustrated by Dorit Rabinovitch. New York: Jeremy P. Tarcher/Penguin, 2003.

Gulevich, Tanya. *Encyclopedia of Christmas.* Illustrated by Mary Ann Stavros-Lanning. Detroit: Omnigraphics, 2000.

Hamilton, James. "Paintings." In *Christmas,* edited by Jacqueline Ridley. Poole, Dorset, Great Britain: Blandford Press, 1978.

Hamner, Earl, Jr. *The Homecoming: A Novel About Spencer's Mountain.* New York: Random House, 1970.

"Hanby House" (regarding Benjamin R. Hanby). Ohio Historical Society. Web Site: www.ohiohistory.org/places/hanby/

Hardy, Thomas. "The Oxen." In *The Complete Poems of Thomas Hardy,* edited by James Gibson. New York: Macmillan, 1976.

Harper, Donna Akiba Sullivan. "Langston Hughes." From Thomson Gale Database. Web Site: www.galegroup.com/free_resources/bhm/bio/hughes_l.htm

Harrison, Jim. *American Christmas.* Atlanta: Longstreet Press, 1994.

Hartman, Leda. "'Breaking Up Christmas': An American Mountain-Music Tradition." Cedar Ridge, North Carolina. From ClassBrain.com. www.classbrain.com/artholiday/publish/article_253.shtml

Hartman, Tom, ed. *Guinness Book of Christmas.* Enfield, Middlesex, England: Guinness Books, 1984.

"*Helleborus niger*— Christmas Rose." Cornell University: Poisonous Plants Informational Database. Web Site: http://www.ansci.cornell.edu/plants/christmasrose/christmasrose.html#medicine

Henry, H.T. "O Antiphons." In *The Catholic Encyclopedia.* Vol. XI. Online Edition, 2003. New Advent, Inc. Web Site: www.newadvent.org/cathen/11173b.htm

Henry, O. *The Gift of the Magi.* 1905. Reprint, Mankato, Minnesota: Creative Education, 1984.

Hicks, Anthony. Program notes for George Frideric Handel, *Messiah: A Sacred Oratorio.* Choir of Christ Church Cathedral, Oxford, and the Academy of Ancient Music. Christopher Hogwood. Decca Records *Editions de L'oiseau-Lyre* box set SD189D 3, 1980. Long-playing records.

Hill, Richard S. "Not So Far Away in a Manger: Forty-One Settings of an American Carol." *Notes,* vol. 3 (December 1945).

"History of the Cracker." From Absolutely Crackers. Web Site: www.absolutelycrackers.com/historynew.html

"History of the 'King Cake.'" Mardi Gras Digest. Web Site: www.mardigrasdigest.com/html/history_of/history_of_the_king_cake.htm

"The History of the Poinsettia." Paul Ecke Ranch. Web Site: www.ecke.com/html/h_corp/corp_joelp.html

Hoffmann, E.T.A. *Nutcracker.* Translation of *Nussknacker und Mausekönig* from the German by Ralph Manheim. Pictures by Maurice Sendak. New York: Crown, 1984.

Holweck, Frederick G. "Candlemas." In *The Catholic Encyclopedia.* Vol. III. Online Edition, 2003. New Advent, Inc. Web Site: www.newadvent.org/cathen/03245b.htm

_____. "Holy Innocents." In *The Catholic Encyclopedia.* Vol. VII. Online Edition, 2003. New Advent, Inc. Web Site: www.newadvent.org/cathen/07419a.htm

_____. "Immaculate Conception." In *The Catholic Encyclopedia.* Vol. VII. Online Edition, 2003. New Advent, Inc. Web Site: www.newadvent.org/cathen/07674d.htm

The Holy See. Official Web Site: www.vatican.va

Hooks, William H. *The Legend of the Christmas Rose.* Paintings by Richard A. Williams. New York: HarperCollins, 1999.

Hottes, Alfred Carl. *1001 Christmas Facts and Fancies.* New York: Dodd, Mead, 1944.

Howells, W.D. "Christmas Every Day." In *Christmas Every Day and Other Stories Told for Children.* New York: Harper and Brothers, 1892.

Hubert, Maria. "The Great British Christmas." In *The Christmas Archives.* Web Site: www.christmasarchives.com/gbx.html

Hughes, Langston. *Carol of the Brown King: Nativity Poems.* Illustrated by Ashley Bryan. New York: Atheneum, 1998.

Humphrey, Mark. "What Is Old-Time Music?" The Old-Time Music Home Page, sponsored by David Lynch. Web Site: www.oldtimemusic.com/otdef.html

Irby, Rebecca LeeAnne, and Phil Greetham. "Laura Ingalls Wilder: Frontier Girl." Huntington, West Virginia: Marshall University. Web Site: webpages.marshall.edu/~irby1/laura/index.html

Irving, Washington. *History, Tales, and Sketches.* Edited by James W. Tuttleton. The Library of America. New York: Literary Classics of the United States, 1983.

_____. *The Sketch Book of Geoffrey Crayon, Gent.* Everyman's Library. New York: Dutton, 1963.

"James Lord Pierpont." The Hymns and Carols of Christmas. Web Site: www.hymnsandcarolsofchristmas.com

The Japan of Today. 3rd edition. Tokyo: The International Society for Educational Information, 1996.

"Jean Shepherd Web Site." Provided by Jim Sadur. Web Site: www.keyflux.com/shep/

Jesko, Mark. "Christmas in Eastern Slovakia." The Baltimore Czech and Slovak Heritage Association. Web Site: www.iarelative.com/xmas/jesko.htm

"Jewish Calendar." From *Judaism 101.* Web Site: www.jewfaq.org/calendar.htm

"John Jacob Niles Sings American Folk Songs." Produced and hosted by Azoth Interactive. Web Site: www.john-jacob-niles.com/media.htm

Jones, Nick. Program Notes for *Handel: Messiah.* Atlanta Symphony Orchestra and Chamber Chorus. Robert Shaw. Telarc compact disc set CD-80093, 1984.

Jonson, Ben. *Christmas His Masque.* In *Ben Jonson: The Complete Masques,* edited by Stephen Orgel. The Yale Ben Jonson, vol. 4. New Haven, Connecticut: Yale University Press, 1969.

Kaufman, Joanne. "Life in Hell's Matt Groening Goes Overboard to Make *The Simpsons* the First Family of TV 'Toons." *People Weekly* (December 18, 1989).

Kaye, Andrew L. Liner notes for *Southern Journey, Volume 2: Ballads and Breakdowns.* Rounder Records compact disc 1702, 1997.

Keyte, Hugh, and Andrew Parrott, eds. *The New Oxford Book of Carols.* New York: Oxford University Press, 1992.

Kiesewetter, John. "'Grandma' Novelty Song Keeps Dr. Elmo in the Christmas Green." *The Tennessean* (December 10, 1997).

Kightly, Charles. *The Customs and Ceremonies of Britain: An Encyclopedia of Living Traditions.* New York: Thames and Hudson, 1986.

Kirkpatrick, David D. "Whose Jolly Old Elf Is That, Anyway?" *The New York Times* (October 26, 2000).

Kletter, Lenore. *Santabear's High Flying Adventure.* Minneapolis: Santabear Books, 1987.

Lagerlöf, Selma. "The Legend of the Christmas Rose." In *The Girl from the Marsh Croft.* Translated from the Swedish by Velma Swanston Howard. Boston: Little, Brown, and Company, 1910.

Lamb, Peter. Program Notes for Benjamin Britten, *A Ceremony of Carols.* Westminster Cathedral Choir. David Hill. Hyperion compact disc CDA66220, 1986.

Lawrence, Robert Means. "Horses' Heads As Talismans." In *The Magic of the Horse-Shoe* (1898). Web Site: www.sacred-texts.com/etc/mhs/index.htm

Lenburg, Jeff. *The Encyclopedia of Animated Cartoons.* 2nd edition. New York: Checkmark Books, 1999.

Lewis, Jone Johnson. "Over the River and Through the Woods: The Woman Who Wrote the Winter Favorite." Women's History Guide. Web Site: womenshistory. about.com/library/weekly/aa110800a.htm

Lewis, Steven. Bing Crosby Internet Museum. Web Site: www.kcmetro.cc.mo.us/pennvalley/biology/lewis/crosby /bing.htm

The Life and Music of James Lord Pierpont. Georgia Historical Society. VHS video recording, 1994.

Linder, Vladimir. "Slovak Christmas Traditions." From Slovak Heritage Live. Web Site: www.slovakheritage.org/ Folkcustoms/christmas_trad.htm

Lishtar. "Akitu: The Babylonian New Year's Festival." From Gateways to Babylon. Web Site: www.gatewaystobaby-lon.com/

"Llangollen International Eisteddfod: How It Started." Llangollen International Musical Eisteddfod. Web Site: www.llangollen.com/eist3.html

Longfellow, Henry Wadsworth. "The Three Kings." In *The Complete Poetical Works of Henry Wadsworth Longfellow,* edited by Horace E. Scudder. Student's Cambridge Edition. Boston: Houghton Mifflin, 1922.

Lucado, Max. *Alabaster's Song: Christmas through the Eyes of an Angel.* Illustrated by Michael Garland. Dallas: Word Publishing, 1996.

_____. *An Angel's Story.* Nashville: W Publishing Group, 2002.

_____. *The Christmas Child: A Story of Coming Home.* Nashville: W Publishing Group, 2003.

_____. *The Christmas Cross: A Story about Finding Your Way Home for the Holidays.* Nashville: Word Publishing, 1998.

_____. *Cosmic Christmas.* Nashville: Word Publishing, 1997.

_____, Jenna Lucado, Andrea Lucado, and Sara Lucado. *The Crippled Lamb.* Illustrated by Liz Bonham. Dallas: Word Publishing, 1994.

_____. *Jacob's Gift.* Illustrated by Robert Hunt. Nashville: Tommy Nelson, 1998.

Magnier, J. "Archconfraternity of the Holy Family." In *The Catholic Encyclopedia.* Vol. VII. Online Edition, 2003. New Advent, Inc. Web Site: www.newadvent.org/cathen /07407b.htm

Mallory, Michael. *Hanna-Barbera Cartoons.* Westport, Connecticut: Hugh Lauter Levin Associates, 1998.

Margetson, Stella. "Medieval Nativity Plays." *History Today* (December 1972).

"Mari Lwyd." Internet movie from World Wide Wales. Web Site: www.worldwidewales.tv/index2.php?mid=162

"Mark Lowry Biography." Today's Christian Music. Web Site: www.todayschristianmusic.com/Profile-MarkLowry. htm

Markstein, Donald D. "Rudolph, the Red-Nosed Reindeer." Toonopedia. Web Site: www.toonopedia.com/ rudolph.htm

Marston, Elsa. *Lebanon: A New Light in an Ancient Land.* New York: Macmillan, 1994.

Martindale, Cyril. "Christmas." In *The Catholic Encyclopedia.* Vol. III. Online Edition, 2003. New Advent, Inc. Web Site: www.newadvent.org/cathen/03724b.htm

_____. "Epiphany." In *The Catholic Encyclopedia.* Vol. V. Online Edition, 2003. New Advent, Inc. Web Site: www.newadvent.org/cathen/05504c.htm

"Masque." In *The Cambridge Guide to Theatre,* edited by Martin Banham. Revised edition. Cambridge, England: Cambridge University Press, 1995.

"Masque." In *The Oxford Companion to the Theatre,* edited by Phyllis Hartnoll. 3rd edition. New York: Oxford University Press, 1967.

Mastrantonis, the Rev. George. "The Feast of Epiphany: The Feast of Lights." The Greek Orthodox Archdiocese of America. Web Site: www.goarch.org/en/ourfaith/ articles/article8383.asp

Matthews, John, and Caitlin Matthews. *The Winter Solstice: The Sacred Traditions of Christmas.* Wheaton, Illinois: Quest Books, 1998.

Mattingly, Terry. "A Christmas Mystery: 12 Days' Worth." From Terry Mattingly on Religion. Web Site: tmatt. gospelcom.net/column/1999/12/22/

May, Robert L. *Rudolph, the Red-Nosed Reindeer.* Illustrated by Denver Gillen. Chicago: Montgomery Ward, 1939.

_____. *Rudolph, the Red-Nosed Reindeer, Shines Again.* Illustrated by Marion Guild. Chicago: Follett, 1954. Reprinted as *Rudolph Shines Again.* Illustrated by Diana Magnuson. Chicago: Follett, 1981.

_____. *Rudolph's Second Christmas.* Illustrated by Michael Emberley. Bedford, Massachusetts: Applewood Books, 1992.

McCloud, Barry, et al. *Definitive Country: The Ultimate Encyclopedia of Country Music and Its Performers.* New York: Berkley, 1995.

McCrohan, Donna, and Peter Crescenti. *The Honeymooners' Lost Episodes.* New York: Workman, 1986.

McGinley, Phyllis. *The Year Without a Santa Claus.* Pictures by Kurt Werth. New York: J.B. Lippincott, 1957.

"Medieval Drama in Europe." In *The Cambridge Guide to Theatre,* edited by Martin Banham. Revised edition. Cambridge, England: Cambridge University Press, 1995.

Menendez, Albert J., and Shirley C. Menendez. *Christmas Songs Made in America: Favorite Holiday Melodies and the Stories of Their Origins.* Nashville: Cumberland House, 1999.

Menotti, Gian Carlo. *Amahl and the Night Visitors.* New York: G. Schirmer, 1951. Adaptation, New York: William Morrow, 1986.

_____. *Amahl and the Night Visitors: Original Cast of the NBC Telecast, Christmas Eve, 1951.* RCA Gold Seal compact disc 6485–2-RG, 1987.

Mershman, Francis. "Advent." In *The Catholic Encyclopedia.* Vol. I. Online Edition, 2003. New Advent, Inc. Web Site: www.newadvent.org/cathen/01165a.htm

"Michael English Biography." Christian Music.com. Web Site: www.christianmusic.com/michaelenglish/bio.html

Mikkelson, Barbara. "Candy Cane." Urban Legends Reference Pages. Web Site: www.snopes.com/holidays/christmas/candycane.asp

_____, and David P. Mikkelson. "The Twelve Days of Christmas." Urban Legends Reference Pages. Web Site: www.snopes.com/holidays/christmas/12days.asp

Milton, John. "On the Morning of Christ's Nativity." In *The Complete Poetical Works of John Milton*, edited by Douglas Bush. Cambridge Edition. Boston: Houghton Mifflin, 1965.

"Mummers' Play." In *Cassell Companion to Theatre*. Revised edition. London: Market House Books, 1997.

"Mumming Play." In *The Oxford Companion to the Theatre*, edited by Phyllis Hartnoll. 3rd edition. New York: Oxford University Press, 1967.

National Christmas Tree Association. Web Site: http://www.realchristmastrees.org/

"The *'Ndòcce* of Agnone and the Sacred Days of the Solstice." From the City of Agnone, Italy (Italian language). Web Site: http://www.comune.agnone.is.it/ndocciata.htm

"New Year's Eve: Hogmanay." From RampantScotland.com www.rampantscotland.com/know/blknow12.htm

Nosal, Salomea. "The Polish Christmas Tradition." *Polish American Journal*. Web Site: www.polamjournal.com/Library/Holidays/xmasindex/xmas-nosal/xmas-nosal.html

Nowlan, Michael O. "How the First Christmas Stamp Came to Be." Professional Stamp Experts. Web Site: http://www.psestamp.com/articles/article1087.chtml

"NRF Reports Holiday Sales Increased 5.2% Over Last Year." National Retail Federation. Web Site: www.nrf.com/content/press/release2004/retailsales0104.htm

"O Come, O Come, Emmanuel." The Hymns and Carols of Christmas. Web Site: www.hymnsandcarolsofchristmas.com

"O magnum mysterium." Los Angeles Philharmonic Association. Web Site: www.laphil.org/resources/piece_detail.cfm?id=1339

Ola, Per, and Emily D'Aulaire. "Glorious Gift from Christmas Past." *Reader's Digest* (December 1993).

"'One Solitary Life' Authorship." San Joaquin Valley Library System. Web Site: www.sjvls.org/bens/bf007sl.htm

"Our Nation's Christmas Tree." The National Park Service. Web Site: www.nps.gov/seki/xmastree.htm

Palfrey, Dale Hoyt. "Feliz Navidad: Making Merry in Mexico." From Mexico Connect. Web Site: www.mexconnect.com/mex_/christmas.html

"Pantomime, English." In *The Cambridge Guide to Theatre*, edited by Martin Banham. Revised edition. Cambridge, England: Cambridge University Press, 1995.

"Pantomime." In *The Oxford Companion to the Theatre*, edited by Phyllis Hartnoll. 3rd edition. New York: Oxford University Press, 1967.

"La Paradura del Niño." From *Estado Mérida: Tierra de Mágicas Montañas*. Web Site: www.venezuela.8m.com/trad_15.htm

Pasadena Tournament of Roses Web Site: www.tournamentofroses.com/index.html

Paterson, Katherine. *Angels and Other Strangers: Family Christmas Stories*. New York: Thomas Crowell, 1979.

_____. A *Midnight Clear: Stories for the Christmas Season*. New York: Lodestar, 1995.

Patsavos, Lewis. "The Calendar of the Orthodox Church." From the Greek Archdiocese of America. Web Site: www.goarch.org/en/ourfaith/articles/article7070.asp

"Patsy Trigg (of Elmo & Patsy)." *Chicago Tribune* (December 16, 1990).

Pattillo, Craig W. *Christmas on Record: Best Selling Xmas Singles and Albums of the Past 40 Years*. Portland, Oregon: Braemer Books, 1983.

Penkala, Gary. "The Feast of the Holy Family." Cantica Nova Publications. Web Site: www.canticanova.com/articles/xmas/art331.htm

Perry, Leonard. "Herbs with a Holiday History." The University of Vermont Extension, Department of Plant and Soil Science. Web Site: pss.uvm.edu/ppp/articles/xmasherb.html

Peter Maxwell Davies Web Site: http://www.maxopus.com/

"The Philadelphia Mummers New Year's Day Parade." The Philadelphia Mummers Parade Web Site. www.mummers.com/

Pilato, Herbie J. *Bewitched Forever: The Immortal Companion to Television's Most Magical Supernatural Situation Comedy*. Arlington, Texas: Summit, 1996.

The Postal Service Guide to U.S. Stamps. 32nd edition. New York: HarperCollins, 2005.

Prescott, Dorothy. "Saints." In *Christmas*, edited by Jacqueline Ridley. Poole, Dorset, Great Britain: Blandford Press, 1978.

"Rankin/Bass Productions." The Big Cartoon Database. Web Site: http://www.bcdb.com/cartoons/Other_Studios/R/Rankin_Bass_Productions/

Read, Barbara. *Santabear's First Christmas*. Minneapolis: Santabear Books, 1986.

Restad, Penne L. *Christmas in America*. New York: Oxford University Press, 1995.

_____. "Christmas in Nineteenth-Century America." *History Today* (December 1995).

Rice, John. "Cuba Declares Christmas a Holiday." Associated Press article published December 1, 1998. Web Site: www.fiu.edu/~fcf/cubadeclaresxmas.html

Ridley, Michael. "Cards." In *Christmas*, edited by Jacqueline Ridley. Poole, Dorset, Great Britain: Blandford Press, 1978.

Rihtman-Auguštin, Dunja. *Christmas in Croatia*. Translated from the Croatian by Nina H. Antoljak. Zagreb, Croatia: Golden Marketing, 1997.

Rimes, LeAnn, and Tom Carter. *Holiday in Your Heart: A Novel*. New York: Doubleday, 1997.

Robinson, Barbara. *The Best Christmas Pageant Ever*. Pictures by Judith Gwyn Brown. New York: HarperCollins, 1972.

Robinson, Dale, and David Fernandes. *The Definitive "Andy Griffith Show" Reference: Episode-by-Episode, with Cast and Production Biographies and a Guide to Collectibles*. Jefferson, North Carolina: McFarland, 1996.

Robinson, James Harvey, ed. "Willibald's Life of Boniface." In *Readings in European History*. Vol. I. Boston: Ginn, 1904.

Robinson, Paschal. "St. Francis of Assisi." In *The Catholic Encyclopedia*. Vol. VI. Online Edition, 2003. New Advent, Inc. Web Site: www.newadvent.org/cathen/06221a.htm

Rock, Gail. *The House Without a Christmas Tree*. New York: Alfred A. Knopf, 1974.

Rognvaldardottir, Nanna. "History and Legends of Favorite Foods: Eggnog." From What's Cooking America web site, maintained by Linda Stradley. Web Site: whatscookingamerica.net/Eggnog.htm

Rosen, Jody. "I'm Dreaming of a White Christmas: How an Obscure Tune from a So-So Film Became the Greatest Hit of All Time." *Reader's Digest* (December 2002).

Rosenbaum, Alvin. *A White House Christmas*. Washington: The Preservation Press National Trust for Historic Preservation, 1992.

Salokorpi, Sinikka. "Christmas in Finland." Virtual Finland. Web Site: virtual.finland.fi/finfo/english/joulueng.html

The Salvation Army International Heritage Center. Web Site: www1.salvationarmy.org/heritage.nsf?Open

Sammon, Paul. *The "Christmas Carol" Trivia Book: Everything You Ever Wanted to Know About Every Version of the Dickens Classic*. New York: Citadel Press, 1994.

Sansom, William. *A Book of Christmas*. New York: McGraw-Hill, 1968.

Saunders, Father William. "What Are the 'O Antiphons'?" Catholic Educator's Resource Center. Web Site: www.catholiceducation.org/articles/religion/re0374.html

Sawyer, Edwin A. *All About the Moravians: History, Beliefs, and Practices of a Worldwide Church*. Bethlehem, Pennsylvania: Moravian Church in North America, 2000.

Schug-Willie, Christa. *Art of the Byzantine World*. Translated from the German by E.M. Hatt. Panorama of World Art. New York: Harry N. Abrams, 1969.

Scott, Sir Walter. *Marmion*. In *Poetical Works: With the Author's Introduction and Notes*, edited by J. Logie Robertson. London: Oxford University Press, 1904.

Seeley, Mary Evans. *Season's Greetings from the White House: The Collection of Presidential Christmas Cards, Messages and Gifts*. 4th edition. Tampa, Florida: A Presidential Christmas, 2002.

Seibold, J. Otto, and Vivian Walsh. *Olive, the Other Reindeer*. Illustrated by J. Otto Seibold. San Francisco: Chronicle Books, 1997.

Shakespeare, William. *Hamlet*. In *The Complete Works of William Shakespeare with Themes of the Plays*. New York: Walter J. Black, 1937.

Sheppard, Donald E. "Brief Biography of Doctor A.C. Gilbert: Erector Set Inventor, Athlete and Promoter." Web Site: erectorset.net/gilbert-biography-brief.html

"Shetland Islanders Norse a Hangover and Torch a Longship, Too." Cable News Network. Web Site: www.cnn.com/WORLD/9801/29/norse.festival/

Siddoway, Richard. *Christmas of the Cherry Snow*. Salt Lake City: Eagle Gate, 2001.

_____. *The Christmas Quest*. Salt Lake City: Eagle Gate, 2002.

_____. *The Christmas Wish*. Salt Lake City: Bookcraft, 1995. Reissued New York: Harmony Books, 1998.

_____. *Twelve Tales of Christmas*. Salt Lake City: Bookcraft, 1992.

Siefker, Phyllis. *Santa Claus, Last of the Wild Men*. Jefferson, North Carolina: McFarland, 1997.

Silent Night Association (*Stille Nacht Gesellschaft*). Oberndorf bei Salzburg, Austria. Official Web Site: http://www.stillenacht.at/

Simon, William L., ed. *The Reader's Digest Merry Christmas Songbook*. Pleasantville, New York: The Reader's Digest Association, 1981.

"Sir Paul McCartney Biography." EMI Classics. Web Site: www.emiclassics.com/artists/biogs/paulmc.html

"Slovak Christmas Traditions." From Slovakia — Heart of Europe. Web Site: http://www.heartofeurope.co.uk/history_traditional4.htm

Smalls, Irene. "Johnkankus: Roots of an African-American Christmas." Web Site: www.melanet.com/johnkankus/roots.html

Smith, Brian. "A History of Up-Helly-Aa." *The Shetland Times Ltd*. Web Site: http://www.up-helly-aa.org.uk/history.htm

Smith, Jon Guyot. "Track-by-Track Notes" for *Gene Autry, Sing, Cowboy, Sing! The Gene Autry Collection*. Rhino Records. http://www.rhino.com/features/liners/72630lin.html

Snodgrass, Denise. "The Zagmuk" and "Saturnalia." In *Heathen Holidays: The Xmas Story Part 2*. Web Site: www.prime.org/holiday/xmas2.html

Snow, Anita. "Cuba Broadcasts Christmas Message." Associated Press article published December 25, 1998. Web Site: www.fiu.edu/~fcf/xmasmessageortega.html

Snyder, Phillip V. *The Christmas Tree Book: The History of the Christmas Tree and Antique Christmas Ornaments*. New York: Viking, 1976.

Spencer, Michael. "Life of Jim Bishop." Friedsam Memorial Library. St. Bonaventure University, New York. Web Site: web.sbu.edu/friedsam/jimbishop/jbbiography.htm

Spieler, Gerhard. "A Savannah Church, a Christmas Song, a Beaufort Minister." *The Beaufort Gazette* (November 27, 2001).

"Sports History: Major Events, Champions, Awards, Medalists, Statistics and Records." Web site maintained by Ralph Hickok with information about the New Year's Day bowl games and all other sports events. Web Site: www.hickoksports.com/history.shtml

Stéphan, Dom John. *The Adeste Fideles: A Study of Its Origin and Development*. Devon, England: Buckfast Abbey Publications, 1947.

Stockert, Father Hal. "Origin of 'The Twelve Days of Christmas': An Underground Catechism." Catholic Information Network. Web Site: www.cin.org/twelvday.html

"The Story of Christmas Seals." American Lung Association. Web Site: www.christmasseals.org/history_00.html#first

Stradley, Linda. "History and Legends of Favorite Foods: Plum Pudding." From What's Cooking America web site: whatscookingamerica.net/Cake/plumpuddingTips.htm

Strassfeld, Michael. *The Jewish Holidays: A Guide and Commentary*. New York: HarperCollins, 1985.

Studwell, William. *The Christmas Carol Reader*. Binghamton, New York: Harrington Park Press, 1995.

_____. *Christmas Carols: A Reference Guide*. New York: Garland, 1985.

Sullivan, Robert. *Flight of the Reindeer: The True Story of Santa Claus and His Christmas Mission*. Drawings by Glenn Wolff. Art direction by J. Porter. New York: Macmillan, 1996.

Swahn, Jan-Öjvind. *Maypoles, Crayfish and Lucia: Swedish Holidays and Traditions*. Stockholm: The Swedish Institute, 1999.

Swiney, Cathleen. "Grandma's Hit." *The Tennessean Magazine* (December 1995).

Tazewell, Charles. *The Littlest Angel*. Chicago: Children's Press, 1946. Illustrated edition by Paul Micich. Nashville: Ideals, 1991.

_____. *The Littlest Snowman*. Pictures by George De Santis. New York: Grosset and Dunlap, 1958.

_____. *The Littlest Tree*. Illustrated by Karen A. Jerome. Nashville: Ideals, 1997.

_____. *The Small One: A Story for Those Who Like Christmas and Small Donkeys*. Illustrated by Franklin Whitman. Philadelphia: John C. Winston Company, 1947.

Thomas, Dylan. *A Child's Christmas in Wales*. Text, New Directions, 1954. Illustrated edition by Trina Schart Hyman. New York: Holiday House, 1985.

Thompson, Charles. *Bing: The Authorized Biography*. New York: David McKay, 1975.

Thompson, Sue Ellen. *Holiday Symbols and Customs*. 3rd edition. Detroit: Omnigraphics, 2003.

Thurston, Herbert. "Feast of Fools." In *The Catholic Encyclopedia*. Vol. VI. Online Edition, 2003. New Advent, Inc. Web Site: www.newadvent.org/cathen/06132a.htm

_____. "Holy Year of Jubilee." In *The Catholic Encyclopedia*. Vol. VIII. Online Edition, 2003. New Advent, Inc. Web Site: www.newadvent.org/cathen/08531c.htm

Tierney, John J. "Feast of the Circumcision." In *The Catholic Encyclopedia*. Vol. III. Online Edition, 2003. New Advent, Inc. Web Site: www.newadvent.org/cathen/03779a.htm

_____. "New Year's Day." In *The Catholic Encyclopedia*. Vol. XI. Online Edition, 2003. New Advent, Inc. Web Site: www.newadvent.org/cathen/11019a.htm

"Tomás Luis de Victoria." BBC Music/Artist Biography. Web Site: http://www.bbc.co.uk/music/profiles/victoria.shtml

Toys for Tots. Web Site: www.toysfortots.org

The Twilight Zone. From TV Tome. Web Site: www.tvtome.com/TwilightZone/

The Twilight Zone: 1985. From TV Tome. Web Site: www.tvtome.com/TwilightZone_1985/

Van Allsburg, Chris. *The Polar Express*. Boston: Houghton Mifflin, 1985.

Van Ausdall, Clair W. Program notes for *Joy to the World*. Reader's Digest compact disc set RC7–103, 1994.

Van Dyke, Henry. *The First Christmas Tree: A Story of the Forest*. Marietta, Georgia: The Larlin Corporation, 1987.

_____. *The Other Wise Man*. Fort Worth, Texas: Brownlow, 1989.

VanLiere, Donna. *The Christmas Blessing*. New York: St. Martin's Press, 2003.

_____. *The Christmas Shoes*. New York: St. Martin's Press, 2001.

Wakefield, Charito Calvachi. *Navidad Latinoamericana: Latin American Christmas*. 2nd edition. Introduction and Novena prayers by Marco Vinicio Rueda, S.J. English translation by Grace Catalina Wintemute. Illustrated by Fernando Reinoso. Lancaster, Pennsylvania: Latin American Creations, 1999.

Walburg, Lori. *The Legend of the Candy Cane*. Illustrated by James Bernardin. Grand Rapids, Michigan: Zondervan, 1997.

Waldron, Vince. *The Official "Dick Van Dyke Show" Book*. New York: Hyperion, 1994.

Walkup, Nancy. *The Retablo and Beyond: A Cross-Cultural View of Personal Shrines*. North Texas Institute for Educators on the Visual Arts. Web Site: http://www.art.unt.edu/offlinentieva/artcurr/latino/retablo.htm

Wallace, Lew. *Ben-Hur: A Tale of the Christ*. New York: Harper and Row, 1880.

Walsh, Alex. *Disney's "The Small One."* Illustrated by Jesse Clay. New York: Disney, 1995.

The Waltons Web Site. From Blue Ridge Publications. Web Site: http://www.the-waltons.com/

"Welsh Culture and Traditions: Y Nadolig (Christmas)." From Go Britannia! Web Site: www.britannia.com/wales/culture2.html

Wernecke, Herbert H. *Christmas Customs Around the World*. Philadelphia: Westminster Press, 1959.

West, Ewan. Program notes for Peter Ilyich Tchaikovsky, *The Nutcracker*. Royal Philharmonic Orchestra. André Previn. EMI compact disc set CDS 7472678, 1986.

Whitburn, Joel. *The Billboard Book of Top 40 Hits*. 8th edition. New York: Billboard Books, 2004.

_____. Program Notes for *Billboard Greatest Christmas Hits: 1935–1954*. Rhino compact disc DPC1 0884, 1989.

_____. Program Notes for *Billboard Greatest Christmas Hits: 1955–Present*. Rhino compact disc DPC1 0885, 1989.

"White Christmas." Sold on Song. Web Site: www.bbc.co.uk/radio2/soldonsong/songlibrary/indepth/whitechristmas.shtml

The White House Official Web Site: http://www.whitehouse.gov/

The White House Historical Association Official Web Site: www.whitehousehistory.org

Widemark, Sue. "'Twelve Days of Christmas': All You Wanted to Know and More Than That." Web Site: suewidemark.netfirms.com/12days.htm

Wiggin, Kate Douglas. *The Birds' Christmas Carol*. New York: Houghton Mifflin, 1888.

Wilder, Laura Ingalls. *By the Shores of Silver Lake*. New York: Harper, 1939.

_____. *Farmer Boy*. Illustrated by Helen Sewell. New York: Harper, 1933.

_____. *The First Four Years*. Illustrated by Garth Williams. New York: Harper and Row, 1971.

_____. *Little House in the Big Woods*. Illustrated by Helen Sewell. New York: Harper, 1932.

_____. *Little House on the Prairie*. New York: Harper, 1935.

_____. *Little Town on the Prairie*. Illustrated by Helen Sewell and Mildred Boyle. New York: Harper, 1941.

_____. *The Long Winter*. Illustrated by Helen Sewell and Mildred Boyle. New York: Harper, 1940.

_____. *On the Banks of Plum Creek*. New York: Harper, 1937.

_____. *These Happy Golden Years*. Illustrated by Helen Sewell and Mildred Boyle. New York: Harper, 1943.

Wilkins, Doug. "Eddie Pola — Another Jack of All Trades." Web Site: http://www.memorylane.org.uk/previous_articles.htm

Wilkins, Edward. *The 10 Greatest Christmas Movies Ever Made: Fun Facts, Quizzes, and Behind-the-Scenes Trivia About Your Holiday Favorites*. Downers Grove, Illinois: Anton Enterprises, 1994.

Wilson, John. "The Origins of the Tune 'Antioch.'" *Bulletin of the Hymn Society of Great Britain and Ireland*, no. 166 (June 1986).

Wojciechowski, Susan. *The Christmas Miracle of Jonathan Toomey*. Illustrated by P.J. Lynch. Cambridge, Massachusetts: Candlewick Press, 1995.

Wolfe, Charles K., and Neil V. Rosenberg. Program notes for Bill Monroe, *Bluegrass: 1950–1958*. Vollersode, Germany: Bear Family Records box set BFB 10013, 1989. Long-playing records.

Wolff, Christoph. *Johann Sebastian Bach: The Learned Musician*. New York: W.W. Norton, 2000.

"The Yankee Transplant Who Gave the World 'Jingle Bells.'" History, Valdosta–Lowndes County, Georgia, Conference Center and Tourism Authority. Web Site: http://www.valdostatourism.com/history_jingle.htm

"Yes, Virginia, There Is a Santa Claus." Ascension Research Center. Web Site: www.ascension-research.org/yes.html

"Yule *Jól* in Iceland." Hosted by Simnet. Web Site: www.simnet.is/gardarj/

Index

Aames, Willie 199
Abbott, Norman 162
Abbot of Unreason 162, 189
Abel, Sierra 352
Abraham, F. Murray 255
Achetringele 382
Adam, Adolphe 311
"Adam Lay I-Bounden" 63
Adams, John 94, 399, 423
Adams, John Quincy 424
"Adeste Fideles" 33, 181, 308–310
Adler, David 9
Advent 1–3; calendars 2; candles 1, 2; colors of 1; comings of Christ 1; houses 2; star 280; wreaths 1, 2; *see also* specific countries
advocaat 154
Aeon, patron god of Alexandria, Egypt 157, 436
Africa 3–5; Aksum, Kingdom of 3; Egypt 3; Ethiopia 3–4; Ethiopian Orthodox Church 3; Ghana 4; Kenya 4; River Jordan (gorge in Ethiopia) 4; Sierra Leone 4; South Africa, Republic of 4; Uganda 4–5; Zimbabwe 5
aguinaldo 60, 61, 62, 370
"Ah, Bleak and Chill the Wintry Wind" 6
Ahrens, Lynn 81
Ahwahnee Hotel, Yosemite National Park 227
Aiken, David 8
Airs des noêls lorrain 203
A.J. Showalter Company 32
Akitu 217, 354
Aksum, Kingdom of 3
Alabaster's Song: Christmas Through the Eyes of an Angel 5
Alan, Devon 106
Albee, Josh 199
Albert, Eddie 304
Albert, prince consort to Queen Victoria of England 130
Albrecht, Hermann 131
Albright, Ann Lane 68

The Alcoa Hour 87
Alcott, Louisa May 255
aletria 324
Alexander, Cecil Frances 315
Alexander, Jane 275
Alexander, Jason 81, 260
Alexander the Great 200
Alexander VII, Pope 164
Alfred Burt Carols 6–7
Alfred the Great 92, 390
Alias St. Nick 266
Alix, Stephen 104
An All Dogs Christmas Carol 76
All I Want for Christmas (motion picture) 7
"All I Want for Christmas Is My Two Front Teeth" 7–8
"All My Heart This Night Rejoices" 8
"All on a Christmas Morning" 6
Allen, Chet 8
Allen, Clark 394
Allen, Corey 260
Allen, Karen 86
Allen, Rae 81
Allen, Robert (Bob) 18, 212
Allen, Tim 350, 351, 362
Allen, William 330
Allwine, Wayne 84, 267, 268, 269
alminhas a penar 324
Alpert, Herb 121
"Als ich bei meinen Schafen wacht'" 421
Altbömische Gesänge 14
Altieri, Ann 64
Altschul, David 139
Alvarez, José María 83
Alvin and the Chipmunks 67, 76
The Alvin Show 67
Alvino Rey Orchestra 7
Alvin's Christmas Carol 76
Amahl and the Night Visitors 8, 95
American Ballet Theatre 304
An American Christmas Carol 76
American Conservatory Theatre (San Francisco) 79

American Society of Composers, Authors and Publishers (ASCAP) 18, 42, 58, 67, 121, 134, 164, 175, 203, 205, 210, 213, 220, 223, 235, 236, 239, 247, 250, 330, 335, 347, 350, 359, 363, 383, 401, 415, 437, 440
Amsterdam, Morey 84, 150, 338
Amundsen, Tom 77
Anaya, Yano 126
Ancient Mysteries Described 65
Anders, William 96
Andersen, Hans Christian 167, 254, 255
Anderson, Bob 360
Anderson, Bobby 41
Anderson, James 198
Anderson, Dame Judith 256
Anderson, Leroy 18, 363
Anderson, Loni 45
Anderson, Lynn 86
Anderson, Maxwell 79
Anderson, Melissa Sue 253
Anderson, R. Alex 264
Anderson, Sam 356
André, Billie 91
Andrée, Salomon 120
Andrews Sisters 264, 350, 437
Andrzejki 322
The Andy Griffith Show 8–9
Andy Williams and the NBC Kids Search for Santa 10
The Andy Williams Christmas Show 9–11, 235
The Andy Williams Christmas Show (Live from Branson) 11
Andy Williams' Early New England Christmas 10
"angel hair" (Christmas tree decoration) 132
The Angel of Pennsylvania Avenue 11–12
Angel Tree 12
Angels and Other Strangers: Family Christmas Stories 12–14
"Angels and Shepherds" 14

"Angels, from the Realms of Glory" 14–15, 280
Angels' Mass 108, 406
An Angel's Story 140
The Angel's Sweater 161
"Angels We Have Heard on High" 11, 14, 15, 138, 153
"Les anges dans nos compagnes" 14, 15
Anglican Church 1, 3, 92, 157, 188
The Anglo-Saxon Chronicle 92
"The Animal carol" 174
Annabelle's Wish 15–16
Annunciation 285
Anschütz, Ernst 308
Anselmo, Tony 267, 268, 269
Ansley, Zachary 91
"Antioch" (tune) 242
Antiochus IV Epiphanes 200
aquavit 301
Arbeau, Thoinot 153
Archbishop of Fools 162, 189, 354
Archer, Beverly 136
Arden, Eve 84
Ardolino, Emile 304
Arens, Peter 81
"Aren't You Glad You're You?" 33
Argentina 369
"Arise, Sir Knight!" 11
Ark of the Covenant 4
Arkin, Alan 318
Armenia 16–17
Armenian Orthodox Church 16, 55, 92, 111, 269
Armstrong, Bess 103
Armstrong, Moira 79, 81
Armstrong, Neil 44
Arnaz, Desi 218
Arness, James 198
Arngrim, Alison 253
Arnold, Danny 36
Arnold, Eddy 69
Arnold, John 408
Arquette, David 232
Arquette, Lewis 48
The Arraignment, Conviction, and Imprisonment of Christmas 190
arroz con pollo 62
Art Mooney and His Orchestra 306
The Art of Skiing (cartoon) 238
Arthur, Chester A. 425
Arthur, Jean 41
Arthur Fiedler and the Boston Pops Orchestra 363
artists *see* Nativity [works of art]; The Vatican [works of art]
Artzi, Ami 112
"As Dew in Aprille" 63
"As I Sat on a Sunny Bank" 220
"As Joseph Was A-Walking" 64
"As with Gladness Men of Old" 17–18, 419
Asaltos 418
ASCAP *see* American Society of Composers, Authors and Publishers
ASCAP list of Christmas songs 18
Ascension Lutheran Church 67, 68

Aschenklas (mythical being) 345
Aschner, Michael 337
Asgard's Ride (mythical group) 436
Ashe, Martin 36
Asher, William 36, 37
Ashton, Joseph 28
Asia and the South Pacific 18–21; China 19; Fiji Islands 19; India 19; Indonesia, Republic of 20–21; Japan 19–20; Pakistan 20; Sri Lanka 21
Aslan, Gregoire 292
Asner, Ed 80, 155, 177, 261, 284, 314, 442
The Association (rock group) 86
Astaire, Fred 38, 39, 208, 260, 328, 349, 422
Athelstan, king of England 300
Atkinson, Rowan 76
Attenborough, Richard 276
Auberjonois, Rene 367
Audlay, John 88
Auer, Mischa 127
Augustus Caesar, Roman emperor 285
"Auld Kyndnes Foryett" 21
"Auld Lang Syne" 21, 234, 297, 404
Aurelian, Roman emperor 92, 436
Australia 21–23
Australian Ballet 306
Austria 23–24
The Autobiography of Santa Claus 24–25
Autry, Gene 18, 42, 175, 205, 294, 335, 409
Auty, Peter 368
"Ave Maria" 10, 25, 185
Avedon, Barbara 37
Avery, Tex 267, 386
"Away in a Manger" 25–26
Axelrod, David 81
Axton, Hoyt 86, 91
Ayers Rock 22
Aykroyd, Dan 362
Ayton, Sir Robert 21
Azaria, Hank 360, 361
azevias 324

B., Diana 337
baba 340
Baba Noel 269
babalki 146
Babar and Father Christmas 26–27
Babbin, Jacqueline 33
Babbo Natale 232
Babes in Toyland 27–28
Baborka 322
Baboushka 174, 232, 339
"A Baby in the cradle" 203
"Baby Jesus, in a Manger" 224
"A Baby Lies in the Cradle" 203
Baby's First Christmas 199, 367
bacalhau 324
Bacall, Lauren 7
baccalà 231
Bach, Catherine 82
Bach, C.P.E. 186
Bach, Johann Michael 186

Bach, Johann Sebastian 25, 47, 49, 111, 112, 174, 186, 215, 310, 355, 363
Backus, Jim 84, 182, 275, 442
baculos 325
Badnjak 142
Badnje jelo 142
Baer, Parley 37, 198
Bagdasarian, Ross, Jr. 66, 76
Bagdasarian, Ross, Sr. 18, 67
"Bagpipers' Carol" 57–58
Bah, Humbug! The Story of Charles Dickens' "A Christmas Carol" 76
Bailey, Derek 76
Baiul, Oksana 305
Baker, Carrol 44
Baker, Sir Henry Williams 313
Baker, Martin G. 84
Baker, Theodore 257, 421
baksheesh 19
Balanchine, George 304
Balder (god) 277
Balding, Rebecca 177
Baldwin, Peter 49
Balk, Fairuza 35
Ball, Lucille 45, 218, 414
Ballard, Carroll 306
Ballet, William 42
ballet de cour 97
Bals 258
Baltic States 29–31
Balthasar or Balthazar (Wise Man) *see* Wise Men
"Balulalow" 63
Banas, Carl 127, 128, 328
banisa 52
Bank Holiday Act 95
Banks, Norman 22
Bantock, Leedham 85
Bara Din 20
Baranov, Viktor 305
Barbados 416–417
Barbara branches 23
Barbarossa, Frederick 438
Barbera, Joseph 125, 170, 199, 267, 386, 387
Barbie in "The Nutcracker" 304
"Barley Toys" (candy) 54
Barnes, Peter 80
Barnett, C.Z. 75
Baron, Sandy 282
Barrett, Brendon Ryan 60
Barrett, John 31
barring out the schoolmaster (custom) 398–399
Barron, Dana 284
Barry, Ian 120, 136, 272, 356
Barrymore, Drew 28, 314
Barrymore, Lionel 77, 95, 233
barszcz 323
Bart, Patrice 305
Bartel (mythical being) 23, 345
Bartel-Lauf 23
Bartholomew the Apostle 16
Baryshnikov, Mikhail 304, 305
Bärzelitag 382
Basaraba, Gary 316

Basilica of Saint John Lateran (Rome) 407
Basilica of Saint Mary Major (Rome) *see* Church of Santa Maria Maggiore
Basilica of Saint Paul Outside the Walls (Rome) 407
Basilica of Saint Peter (Rome) *see* Saint Peter's Basilica
Basilica of Saints Cosmos and Damian (Rome) 230
Bass, Jules 87, 128, 152, 168, 176, 236, 247, 248, 250, 251, 295, 321, 327, 328, 333, 336, 338, 349, 389, 441
Bate, Philip 81
Baum, L. Frank 247
Bavier, Frances 8
Baxter, Stanley 39
Bazinet, Brenda 208
B.C.: A Special Christmas 26
Beal, Joseph Carleton 18, 239, 330
The Bear Who Slept Through Christmas 31–32
Beard, Mary Kay 12
Beasley Sisters 42
"Beating to Wellness and Good Health" (custom) 24
Beautiful Praise 32
"Beautiful Star of Bethlehem" 32
Beavers, Louise 208
Beban, Richard 136
Beck, Thomas 204
Beck, Vincent 348
Beckett, Paul 91
Beddoe, Don 36
Beers, Bob 319
Beethoven, Ludwig van 313, 358
Befana 174, 216, 232
Begley, Ed, Jr. 81
"Behold a Branch Is Growing" 257
Beilby, Peter 134
Béjart, Maurice 305
Belafonte, Harry 263
belén see Nativity scene
Belenes see Nativity scene
Belenistas 373
Belgium 258
Belize 60
Bell, Francis 134
Bell, Michael 32
Bellamy, Ned 413
Bellamy, Ralph 318
Bellaver, Harry 246
Belles on Ice 268
Belletable, Henri 163
Bellini, Giovanni 124
The Bells of St. Mary's (film) 32
"The Bells of St. Mary's" (song) 11
Belsnickel (also Belsnichol, Bell-sniggle, Belznickel) 99, 178, 343, 398
belsnickeling 398
Belushi, James 28, 238, 306
Bemelmans, Ludwig 259, 260
Benedict, Tony 51, 347
Benedict XV, Pope 163
Ben-Hur: A Tale of the Christ 33–34

Bennett, Hywell 292
Bennett, Jeff 81, 269, 306
Bennett, Roy 306, 378
Bennett, Tony 337
Benny, Jack 45
Benny Jarrell Band 50
Benny Jarrell: Lady of the Lake 50
Benoit, David 64, 220
Benson, Jay 53
Benson, Robbie 141, 248
Benson, Sally 139
Berchta (goddess) 2, 128, 179, 232, 436
Berchten Runners 179
Bercovici, Leonardo 41
Berenstain, Jan 34
Berenstain, Stan 34
The Berenstain Bears' Christmas Tree 34
The Berenstain Bears Meet Santa Bear 34
The Berenstain Bears Save Christmas 34–35
The Berenstain Bears: The Bears' Christmas 34
Berg, Barry 49
Bergen, Edgar 412
"Berger, secoue ton sommeil profound!" 357
Bergman, Ingrid 33
Berlin, Irving 18, 37, 95, 207, 208, 422, 423
berlinerkranser 300
Berman, Serena 64
Bernard, Felix 18, 437
Bernsen, Corbin 219, 352
Bernstein, Gregory 53
Bernstein, Jaclyn 48
Bernstein, Sara 53
Berquist, Douglas 82
Bertha (goddess) 2, 128, 232, 436
Berti, Marina 291
Bertinelli, Valerie 165
"The Best Christmas" (television episode) 413
Best, James 82
Best, Wayne 103
The Best Christmas Pageant Ever 35–36
The Best of Andy Williams Christmas Shows 10
"Bethlehem" (place name) 114
Bethlehem, Israel *see* Church of the Nativity; Nativity
Betlehem see Nativity scene
Betlem see Nativity scene
Bettis, John 16
Bewitched 36–37
A Bewitched Christmas 36
A Bewitched Christmas II 37
Bicat, Tony 81
Bickerseth, Edward 228
Biel, Jessica 222
Bieri, Raymon 136
Biersuppe 154
Big Feast 269
Bill, Tony 63, 316
Bill Gaither Vocal Band 262, 263

Bill Monroe and the Blue Grass Boys 127
Billings, William 408
Billingsley, Barbara 356
Billingsley, Dick 84
Billingsley, Peter 125
Bing and Carol Together Again for the First Time 38
Bing Crosby and the Sounds of Christmas 38
A Bing Crosby Christmas 39
The Bing Crosby Christmas Show 38
The Bing Crosby Show 38
The Bing Crosby White Christmas Special 39
Bing Crosby's Merrie Olde Christmas 39
Bing Crosby's Sun Valley Christmas Show 38
Birch, Thora 7
Bird, Brian 53
"The Birds" (carol) 58
The Birds' Christmas Carol (novel) 39–40
birds' Christmas tree 149, 166, 300, 378
"The Birthday of a King" 40
Bishop, Jim 11
Bishop, Ron 81
Bishop, Wesley 121
The Bishop's Wife 40–41
Bissell, Emily 118, 119
A Bit o' Heaven 40
Bizet, Georges 261
Black Luca 3
Black Peter 258, 342, 345
Blackadder's Christmas Carol 76–77
Blackmer, Sidney 204
Blackstone, J.C. 75
Blackwell, Ken 16
Blake, Amanda 198
Blanc, Mel 51, 83, 170, 408, 442
Blanchard, Tammy 420
Blanck, Curtis 249
Blane, Ralph 18, 202
Bledsoe, Tempestt 10
Blémont, Émile 51
"Blessed Be That Maid Marie" 41–42
Blessing of the Waters 17, 55, 158, 196, 396
"The Blessings of Mary" 356
Bletcher, Billy 386
Blethyn, Brenda 42
blini 340
Blizzard (film) 42
Blondell, Joan 102
Blossom, Roberts 211
Blotmonath 443
Blowing in the Yule 42, 181
"Blue Christmas" 18, 42, 441
"Blue Danube Waltz" 24
Blue Ridge Mountain Holiday: The Breaking Up Christmas Story 50
Blue Ridge Mountains 49
Bluth, Don 366
Bluth, Toby 28

"The Boar's Head Carol" 15, 43, 89, 193, 227
The Bob Hope Christmas Special: Around the World with the USO 45
Bob Hope Christmas Specials 44–45
Bob Hope's Bag Full of Christmas Memories 45
Bob Hope's Christmas with the Troops 45
bobalky 364
Boden, Richard 77
Boethius, Anicius 307
Bogart, Paul 214
Bogas, Ed 136
Bogeaus, Benedict 102
Bolen, Lin 90
Bolger, Ray 28
Bolivia 369
bollos 60
Bolo Rei 324
Bolshevik Revolution 338
Bolshoi Ballet 305
Bolton, Martha 45
"bonbons" (noisemakers) 22
Bond, Ward 234
Bondi, Beulah 234, 329
bonenkai 20
Bonet, Lisa 10
Bonfire of the Brotherhood 231, 406
Boniface VIII, Pope 407
Bonn, Hermann 47
Booke, Sorrell 82
Boomer, Linwood 253
Boone, Debbie 182
Boone, Don 256
Booth, Shirley 328, 441
Booth, Walter R. 85
Booth, William 346
Boothby, Ian 60
Boothe, James Ross 18, 239, 330
Borden, Marshall 80
Borderies, Abbé Étienne Jean F. 308
Borgnine, Ernest 76
Boris I, kahn of Bulgaria 51
Borman, Frank 96, 223
Borrowed Hearts: A Holiday Romance 45–46
borscht 338
Borsos, Phillip 317
Bosley, Tom 87, 262, 276, 328
Bostron, Zachary 48
Bostwick, Barry 153
Bosustow, Stephen 84
Bottoms, Timothy 182
Bouillon, Godfrey de 119
Bouquet, Michael 80
Bouquet Spirituel 54
bouri 3
Boutron, Pierre 80
Bowden, Richard 79
Bower, Tom 413
Bowie, David 39, 368
Bowker, Peter 81
Bowl Championship Series 298
Bowring, Sir John 414
Boxing Day 4, 19, 23, 46, 54, 55,

95, 186, 193, 216; *see also* Saint Stephen's Day
Boy-Bishop 46–47, 99, 211, 231, 341
"A Boy Is Born in Bethlehem" 47
A Boy Was Born 63
Boyce, Robert Fisher 32
Boyd, Jenna 262
Boyden, Sally 413
"A Boy's Thanksgiving Day" 318
Bracebridge Dinner 228
Bradford, Jim 27
Bradley, Edward 72
Brady, Nicholas 421
The Brady Bunch 47–49
Braham, Lionel 77
Brahms, Johannes 241, 257
Bramley, Henry 89, 169, 184, 205, 356, 357, 415, 419
Brand, Oscar 52
Brandis, Jonathan 186
Brandon, Henry 27
Bransby Williams (telecast of *A Christmas Carol*) 77
Braswell, Charles 414
Bratcher, Nicholas 63
Brazil 369–370
Brazzi, Lilia 127
Brazzi, Lydia 127
Brazzi, Rossano 126, 127
"Break Forth, O Beauteous Heavenly Light" 49, 111
Breaking Up Christmas 49–50
Breaking Up Christmas: A Blue Ridge Mountain Holiday 50
Brébeuf, Father Jean de 217
Brennan, Eileen 28, 318
Brent, George 102
Brer Rabbit's Christmas Carol 77
Breslin, Spencer 351
"Brich an, o schönes Morgenlicht" 49, 111
Bricusse, Leslie 86, 212
Bridges, Beau 119
Briggs, Raymond 160, 161, 368
"Bright, Bright the Holly Berries" 6
"Brightest and Best of the Sons of the Morning" 50
Brinckerhoff, Burt 229
"Bring a Torch, Jeannette, Isabella" 50–51
Bristow, Agnes 42
Bristow, Brittany 42
Bristow, Leif 42
Britten, Benjamin 62, 63, 164, 383
Brockman, Jake 261
Bronson, Charles 442
Broodbent, Wally 255
Brooke, William 310
Brooks, Garth 53
Brooks, Mel 232
Brooks, Phillips 311, 312, 401
Brooks, Randy 187
Brothers Grimm 156
Brothers Ziemassvetki 29
Brough, John 27
Brown, Arthur Henry 355
Brown, Clancy 16
Brown, Evert 175

Brown, Leigh 126
Brown, Les 38
Brown, Melleny 26
Brown, Paul 50
Brownell, Janet 106
Browning, Kirk 81
Brueghel, Jan 258
Brull, Mark 83
brune kager 148
Brunhoff, Jean De 26
Brunhoff, Laurent De 26, 27
Brunnensingen 382
Bryan, Ashley 58
"BubbleLights" 132
Buchanan, James 424
Buchanan, Robert 82
bûche de Noël 54, 173, 258, 259, 444
Buchholz, Bob 305
Bugs Bunny's Christmas Carol 51
Bugs Bunny's Looney Christmas Tales 51
buhai 332
Bulgaria 51–52
Bull, Richard 253
Bullerklas (mythical being) 345
Bumba-Meu-Boi 370
buñuelos 325
Burchinal, Frederick 80
Burgess, Dave 294
Burghoff, Gary 260
"The Burgundian Carol" 52, 174
Burke, Brian 83
Burke, Johnny 33
Burkhard, Paul 381
Burnap, Uzziah Christopher 228
Burnett, Carol 38, 39
Burns, Margaret 79
Burns, Robert 21, 26
Burrell, Maryedith 255, 276
Burt, Alfred S. 6–7
Burt, Anne S. 6
Burt, Bates G. 6
Burt, Frank 87
Burton, Corey 268
Burton, Hal 79
Burton, LeVar 42
Burton, Tim 299
Bush, George H.W. 403, 431, 432, 433
Bush, George W. 434, 435
Bushman, Francis X. 87
The Buskers 38
Butcher, Paul 352
Butler, Daws 59, 83, 125, 442, 443
Butler, Dean 253
Butler, Frank 28
Butler, Hugo 77
Butler, Joshua 327
Buttenmandelhaut 178
Buttons, Red 328, 333
Butz (mythical being) 345
Buxtehude, Dietrich 47, 186
By the Shores of Silver Lake 252
Byner, John 38, 39, 260
Byrd, Phillip 11
Byrom, Dr. John 68, 69

Caan, James 155

cabalgatas 374
Cabot, Sebastian 275
Caesar, Julius 110
caffé espresso 231
Cage, Nicholas 81
Cahn, Sammy 18, 134, 247
cailleach 194
Caine, Michael 84
calamari 231
Caldwell, William 50
Calends (of January) 93, 128, 195, 230, 296, 297, 354
Calenigg 194, 195
Calkin, Jean Baptiste 218
Call, John 348
Call Me Claus 53
Callow, Simon 81
Calloway, Cab 256
"Calm on the Listening Ear of Night" 228
"Camaraderie" 39
Cameron, Trent 243
The Camp Creek Boys (album) 50
Campbell, Douglas 315
Campbell, Glen 38
The Campbell Playhouse 95
Canada 53–55
cañas de azúcar 62
Candle Tea, Moravian 280
Candlemas 55–56, 61, 266, 444
candles 30, 55, 56, 146, 181, 225, 226, 227, 269, 271, 300, 354
Candy, John 212
The Candy Cane Story 57
candy canes 56–57
The Candymaker's Gift: A Legend of the Candy Cane 57
Canning, Effie I. 27
Cannon, Dyan 45, 106
"El cant dels ocells" 58
"Cantique de Noël" 310, 311
Cantiques de Première Advenement de Jésus-Christ 50
Cantor, Eddie 350
Cantus, Songs and Fancies 220
"Canzone d'i Zampognari" 57–58
Capelle, Gerry 27
capitone 231
Capote, Truman 109, 316
Cappeau, Placide 310, 311
Capra, Frank 233, 234, 235
The Captain's Christmas 386
Caribbean Islands *see* West Indies
Carney, Art 213, 247, 298, 328, 394
"Carol, Brothers, Carol" 40
A Carol Christmas 77
Carol for Another Christmas 77
"Carol in War-Time" 6
"Carol of the Bagpipers" 57–58
"Carol of the Bells" 18, 58, 138
"Carol of the Birds" 58
Carol of the Brown King: Nativity Poems 58–59
"Carol of the Drum" 249
"Carol of the Mother" 6
Carol Ship 54
"Caroling, Caroling" 6, 7, 11, 243, 283

"A Caroling We Go" 336
Carolino Augusteum Museum, Salzburg 357
Carols by Candlelight 4, 22
Carols for Christmas-Tide 89, 186, 313
Carols, Hymns, and Songs 415
Carols in the Domain 22
Carpenter, Karen 264
Carpenter, Richard 264
Carr, Gerald P. 96
Carr, Mark 131
Carradine, David 78
Carradine, John 78, 90
Carrey, Jim 216
Carroll, Courtney 27
Carroll, Eddy 84
Carroll, Joan 33
Carroll, Leo G. 77, 78
Carroll, Pat 176
Carson, Jenny Lou 69
Carson, John "Fiddlin'" 127
Carter, Dixie 45, 248
Carter, Jimmy 403, 430
Carter, Nadine 134
Carter, Tom 207
Cartier, Jacques 53
Cartwright, Nancy, 360, 361
Carver, Lynne 77
Caspar (Wise Man) *see* Wise Men
Casper's First Christmas 59, 200
Casper's Haunted Christmas 59–60
Cassidy, Jack 84
Cassidy, Patrick 103
Castel, Nico 8
Castellaneta, Dan 314, 360, 361
Castle Cardigan 194
"Castle in Spain" 27
Cates, Joseph 87
Cathemerinon 313
Cattrall, Kim 274
Cavadini, Catherine 28
Cavanaugh, James 106
Cavendish, William 265
Celsius, Anders 95
ceppo 130, 231
cerei 354
A Ceremony of Carols 62–63, 164, 383
Cert (mythical being) 144, 345, 364
Chabert, Lacy 28
Chadwick, James 15
Chaffey, Don 182
Chain, Barbara 84
Champion, Gregg 376
Champlain, Samuel de 53
A Chance of Snow 63
Chanukah *see* Hanukkah
Chapin, Lauren 161
Chaplin, Geraldine 81, 292
Chapman, Beth Nielson 16
Chapman, Steven Curtis 92
Chapuis, Emeric 205
Charendorff, Tara 81
Charisse, Cyd 38
Charlebois, Amie 27
Charlemagne 307
Charles I, king of England 75, 189

Charles II, king of England 75, 89, 189, 226, 227
Charles IV, king of the Two Sicilies 230
A Charlie Brown Christmas 63–64
Charlie Brown's Christmas Tales 64
The Charlie Drake Show 79
Charlotte, queen consort to King George III of England 94, 130
Charmoli, Tony 305
Charpentier, Marc-Antoine 51
Chase, Chevy 283
Chase, Stanley 76
Chechick, Jeremiah 284
Chelsom, Peter 81
Cherry, John 159
"The Cherry Tree Carol" 64–65
Chéryl, Karen 205
Chester Cycle of mystery plays 100
Chesterfield Show 37
"Chestnuts Roasting on an Open Fire" *see* "The Christmas Song"
Chevalier, Maurice 38
chica 61
"Chicken Bones" (candy) 54
Child, Lydia Maria 318
Childermas *see* Holy Innocents Day
"Children" (song) 39
"Children, Go Where I Send Thee" 65, 108
"The Children's Carol" (television episode) 413
Children's Day 70
The Children's Friend: Number III. A New Year's Present to the Little Ones from Five to Twelve 66
Childs, Geri 27
A Child's Christmas in Wales 66
Chile 370
The Chimes 151
China 19
Chinese New Year 19
A Chipmunk Christmas 66
"The Chipmunk Song (Christmas Don't Be Late)" 18, 67, 76
Chlausjage 382
Chlauswettchloöpfe 381
Choice Collection of Scots Poems 21
choinka 322
Choix de antiques sur des airs nouveaux 15
Chomsky, Marvin J. 223
Chorus of Shepherds and Villagers 8
Chragaloyts 17
Chris Van Allsburg's Polar Express (musical setting) 324
Chrismons (book) 68
Chrismons: Advanced Series (book) 68
Chrismons: Basic Series (book) 68
Chrismons: Christian Year Series (book) 68
Chrismons for Every Day (book) 68
Chrismons tree 67–68
Christ Child (Baby Jesus, Little Jesus), as gift-bringer 23, 60, 61, 62, 128, 258, 266, 364, 365, 372

"Christ in the Stranger's Guise" 6
"Christ Is Born a Child on Earth" 203
"Christ the Lord, the Lord Most Glorious" 281
Christbaum 129
Christian IX, king of Denmark 118
Christian Observer 50
Christian Register 228
Christians, Mady 204
"Christians, Awake, Salute the Happy Morn" 68–69
Christingle 281
Christkindl (or *Christkindlein*) 23, 179, 378, 398
Christkindlmarkt 178
"C-H-R-I-S-T-M-A-S" 69
"Christmas" (place name) 114
Christmas aerogrammes 122
Christmas Antiphons *see* "O" Antiphons
Christmas at Plum Creek 253
"Christmas Auld Lang Syne" 21
Christmas bell (plant) 22, 114
Christmas berry 114
The Christmas Blessing 69–70
The Christmas Box 70–71
Christmas Box Foundation 71
Christmas Box House International 71
Christmas boxes 46
Christmas bush 22, 115
Christmas cactus 115
Christmas cake 19, 20
The Christmas Candle 71
Christmas cards 19, 71–73, 401
A Christmas Carol (novella) 36, 73–87, 90, 95, 105, 126, 184, 190, 214; film and television versions 76–87
"A Christmas Carol" (poem) 87
A Christmas Carol II: The Sequel 81
A Christmas Carol at Ford's Theatre 81
A Christmas Carol: Being a Ghost Story of Christmas 81
A Christmas Carol in Prose: Being a Ghost Story of Christmas (novella) 74
A Christmas Carol in Prose; or, A Ghost Story of Christmas 81
A Christmas Carol; or, Past, Present, and Future 75
A Christmas Carol; or, The Miser's Warning 75
Christmas Carol: The Movie 81
Christmas Carolles 43
Christmas carols 87–90; *see also* individual carols
Christmas Carols, Ancient and Modern 89, 169, 184, 220, 386, 390, 408
Christmas Carols: Four Numbers 315
Christmas Carols New and Old 89, 169, 184, 205, 356, 357, 415, 419
Christmas Cat (mythical beast) 222
Christmas Child (film) 92

The Christmas Child: A Story of Coming Home 91
Christmas clubs 401–402
The Christmas Coal Mine Miracle 90
"Christmas Comes Anew" 361
Christmas Comes to Monster Island 32
Christmas Comes to Pac-Land 90–91, 200
Christmas Comes to Willow Creek 91
"Christmas Cometh Caroling" 6
The Christmas Cross: A Story About Finding Your Way Home for the Holidays 91–92
A Christmas Cruella 81
Christmas Day (December 25) 92–96; births on 96; coronations on 94; deaths on 96; in exploration, medicine, and science 95–96; first Christmas celebrations 93–94; government, military, and political events of 94–95; as legal holiday in the United States 401; in literature, music, and the performing arts 95; *see also* individual countries
Christmas Day Mass 108, 109
Christmas Eve (film titles) 101–103
Christmas Every Day 103–104, 267
Christmas fern 115
Christmas flower 115
"Christmas for Cowboys" 104
A Christmas Ghost Story 74
"Christmas gift'" (custom) 398
The Christmas Gift (film) 104–105
Christmas His Masque 97, 190
Christmas Impossible 268
Christmas in Bedrock 171
Christmas in Calico: An American Fable 105–106
Christmas in Connecticut 106
"Christmas in Killarney" 106, 247
Christmas in My Hometown 106–107
"Christmas in Olden Times" 203
Christmas in Washington 430
Christmas Is (cartoon) 107
"Christmas Is" (song) 107
"Christmas Is Coming" 11
"Christmas Is Here" 11
Christmas Island 95, 96
Christmas Lads (gift bringers) 222
The Christmas Lamb 141
Christmas Lights Across Canada 53
Christmas Lilies of the Field 107–108
The Christmas List 108
A Christmas Love 208
Christmas lunches 149
Christmas Masses 108–109
Christmas Maximus 268
A Christmas Memory 109
Christmas Miracle in Caufield, U. S. A. 90
The Christmas Miracle of Jonathan Toomey 110
The Christmas Mood 6
"Christmas Needs Love to Be Christmas" 11
Christmas Night (film) 81

Christmas of the Cherry Snow 110
Christmas Old Man 19
Christmas Old Style, Christmas New Style 110–111, 183
Christmas Oratorio 49, 95, 111–112, 174
Christmas orchid 115
Christmas pageants 19
Christmas parades 54, 60
The Christmas Path 112–113
Christmas Peace *see* Peace of Christmas
Christmas pie 113
"Christmas pieces" (cards) 72
Christmas pig *see* Julgrisen
Christmas place names 95, 96, 114
Christmas plants 114–117; Christmas bell 22, 114; Christmas berry 114; Christmas bush 22, 115; Christmas cactus 115; Christmas fern 115; Christmas flower 115; Christmas orchid 115; Christmas rose 115–116, 245, 246; desert Christmas cactus 115; laurel 116; lavender 116; pennyroyal 116; rosemary 116; thyme 117; Western Australian Christmas tree 116–117
Christmas plays 19
Christmas Portrait 264
Christmas post office 23
Christmas Present (film) 81
The Christmas Quest 117
A Christmas Romance 117–118
Christmas rose 115–116, 245, 246
Christmas Seals 118–119, 149
The Christmas Secret 119–120
The Christmas Shoes 120–121
A Christmas Sing with Bing 38
"The Christmas Song" 10, 18, 39, 86, 121, 242, 283
Christmas Sports (custom) 418–419
Christmas stamps 121–125
Christmas story (biblical account) *see* Nativity; Star of Bethlehem; Wise Men
A Christmas Story (cartoon) 125, 200
A Christmas Story (film) 125–126
"The Christmas Story" (poem) 59
Christmas Story (television episodes) 8, 161, 198
The Christmas That Almost Wasn't 126–127
A Christmas They Never Forgot 253–254
Christmas Tide 89
"Christmas Time Is Here" 63
"Christmas Time Will Soon Be Over" 127
Christmas Time with the Judds 32
"Christmas Time's A-Coming" 127
Christmas tree 5, 54, 56, 128–133, 400, 404; farms 132, 133; lights and ornaments 131–133; new products and innovations 131–133; origins and history

128–131; varieties of 133; *see also* individual countries
"The Christmas Tree" (short story) 127, 130
"A Christmas Tree" (television episode) 127–128, 328
"Christmas Trees" (poem) 132, 133
The Christmas Visitor 133–134
"The Christmas Waltz" 18, 134
The Christmas Wife 134–135
The Christmas Wish 135–136
Christmas with the Beers Family 319
A Christmas with the Bing Crosbys 38
Christmas with the Kranks 362
A Christmas without Snow 136
"Christmastide" (poem) 257
Christopsomo 196
chugen 20
Church, Francis P. 326, 400, 441
Church Chorals and Choir Studies 228
The Church Hymnal 312
Church Hymns with Tunes 228
Church of Santa Maria Ara Coeli (Rome) 231
Church of Santa Maria Maggiore (Rome) 109, 230, 288, 293, 406, 407
Church of Sant'Apollinare Nuovo (Ravenna, Italy) 438
Church of the Nativity (Bethlehem, Israel) 136–138, 269, 273, 311
Church Praise 257
Churchill, Winston 403
Churer Zimmetstern 381
Circumcision of the Lord 17 *see also* Feast of the Circumcision
Claman, Dolores 84
Clark, Bob 126
Clark, Fred 246
Clark, Oliver 159
Clark, Roy 38, 39
Clark, Thomas 242
Clawson, Elliott J. 85
Claxton, William F. 253
Claymation Christmas Celebration 138–139
Clayton, Alison 27
Clement of Alexandria 92, 157
Clemmons, Clarence 360
Cleveland, Grover 346, 425
Clifton, Verlen 50
Clinch Mountain Gospel 32
Clinger, Debra 87, 236
Clinton, William J. 244, 263, 433, 434
The Clock Watcher (cartoon) 154
Clooney, Rosemary 38, 69, 421
Cloud, Darrah 107, 118
Clowes, William 18, 313, 421
Cockerham, Fred 50
Coco, James 256
Coe, Fred 78, 87
Coffin, Henry Sloane 310
Cohen, Ari 261
Cohn, Mindy 10
Cohoon, Patti 199

colacion 325
Colbert, Claudette 33
Cole, Gary 222
Cole, Sir Henry 72
Cole, Marcus 71
Cole, Nat "King" 121, 388
Coleman, Dabney 283
Coleman, Edwin 79
Coleman, Gary 77, 249, 360
Coleman, Holliston 272
Colindatul 331
Collection of Christmas Carols 89
Collection of Psalm-Tunes, Anthems, Hymns, and Chants 69
Collection of Tunes 242
Collier, Leslie 305
Collins, Blake Jeremy 329
Collins, Coleen 107
Collins, Dorothy 38
Collodi, Carlo 321
Colman, George 101
Colombia 370–371
Colonna dell'Immacolata 164, 406
Colson, Chuck 12
Columbus, Chris (director) 212
Columbus, Christopher (explorer) 94, 397, 416
"Come, All Ye Shepherds" 14
"Come, Dance and Sing" 58
"Come, Dear Children" 6
"Come, Redeemer of the Nations" 355
"Come, Thou Redeemer of the Earth" 355
"Come, Thou Savior of Our Race" 355
Come to the Stable 139
"Come, You Shepherds" 14
"Comfort" (tune) 242
Commandini, Adele 106
commedia dell'arte 101
commercialism 401–402
Communist regime 29
Como, Perry 7, 213, 235, 437
Compagnia de'Magi 290
The Compleat Psalmodist 408
Conforti, Donna 348
congoli 4
Congregational Harmonist 242
Conner, Tim 139
Connor, Kevin 292
Connor, Tommie 18, 219
Conrad, William 198
Conrad, Robert 239
Conried, Hans 107
Constantine, Michael 326
Constantine the Great, Roman emperor 136, 288, 293, 405, 437
Consus (god) 354
Conti, Alexander 420
Cook, Fielder 276, 413
Cook, Joseph S. 186
Cook, Michele 63
Cook, Victor 81
Cookie Bear 10
Cooksey, Danny 367
Coolidge, Calvin 95, 402, 403, 426
Coombs, Carol 233

Cooper, Gladys 40
Cooper, Irving S. 96
Cooper, Jackie 299
Cooper, Stuart 103
Coopersmith, Jerome 76
Coots, J. Fred 18, 349, 350
Copley, John Singleton 123
Coptic Orthodox Church 3
Coral Ridge Ministries 86
Corbeil, Pierre de 174
Corbett, John 327
Corby, Ellen 234, 412, 413
Corcoran, Kevin 28
"Corde natus ex Parentis" 313
Corey, Wendell 206
Corley, Pat 104
Corner, David Gregor 203
Corning Glass 132
Cornish, William 63
Cornwell, Judy 348
Coronado, Francisco 397
Las Corridas 61
Corrigan, D'Arcy 77
Corti, Jesse 141
"cosaques" 193
Cosby, Bill 10, 82
The Cosby Show 10
Cosgrove, John 83
Cosmic Christmas 140
Costa, Lorenzo 125
Costa, Mary 38
Costa Rica 61
Cotler, Jeff 413
Cotler, Kami 412
Cotton, Donald 83
Cotton Bowl 298
Couch, John 16
cougnou 258
Council of Basle 47
Council of Braga 128
Council of Nicea 340
Council of Tours 1, 297, 390
Counsil, Noel 27
Counterfit, Johnny 139
Cousins, Margaret 87
"The Coventry Carol" 140–141
Coventry Cycle of mystery plays 65, 100, 140
"The Coventry Shepherds' Carol" 141
Cowan, Jerome 275
The Cowley Carol Book 42, 153
Cox, Courteney 223
Cox, Ronny 106
Cox, Wally 28
Cracker (mythical goat) 167, 301, 342, 380, 443
"crackers" (noisemakers) 22, 192–193
cradle rocking 241, 293
Craig, Tony 267
Crain, Jeanne 182
Crane, Bob 38
Cranny, Jon 80
crèche *see* Nativity scene
Cree, customs of 55
Creed, Kyle 50
Creighton, Kathleen 208

Crewson, Wendy 82, 350
crib *see* manger; Nativity scene
crib rocking *see* cradle rocking
Crick, Richard 35
The Cricket on the Hearth 151–152, 328
Crimean War 138
The Crippled Lamb 141
Croatia 142–144
Croise, Hugh 85
Cromwell, James 136
Cromwell, Oliver 75, 113, 189
Cronin, Charlie 16
Croo, Robert 141
Crosby, Bing 32, 33, 37–39, 78, 95, 154, 184, 185, 186, 208, 223, 262, 264, 335, 350, 359, 366, 421, 422
Crosby, Dennis, 37
Crosby, Gary 37
Crosby, George E. 81
Crosby, Harry (son of Bing) 38, 39
Crosby, Harry Lillis *see* Crosby, Bing
Crosby, Kathryn 38, 39, 45
Crosby, Lindsay 37
Crosby, Mary Frances 38
Crosby, Nathaniel 38
Crosby, Phillip 37
The Crosby–Clooney Show 38
The Crown of Jesus Music 15
Cuba 417
Cubitt, David 165
Cukor, George 95
Culkin, Kieran 212
Culkin, Macaulay 45, 211, 304
Culliford, Pierre "Peyo" 367
Cummings, Brian 16
Cummings, Jim 268, 269, 306
Cummings, William 202
Cunningham, Allan 40
Currier and Ives 123
Curry, Tim 80
Curtin, Valerie 136
Curtis, Jack 105
Curtis, Jamie Lee 337, 362
Curtis, John "Whit" 32
Curtis, Keene 329
Curtis, Ken 198
Curtis, Mann 21
Curtis, Richard 76
Curtis, Tony 106
Curtiz, Michael 422
Curzon, Aria Noelle 16
Cusack, Joan 232
Custance, Michael 255
Cutler, Barry 237
Czech Midnight Mass 146
Czech Republic 144–147

da Conegliano, Giovanni Battista Cima 124
Dailey, Bill 36
Dainty Songs for Little Lads and Lasses, for Use in the Kindergarten, School and Home 25
Dale, J. Miles 42
Dale, Virginia 208
d'Alò, Enzo 216

Damone, Vic 87, 262, 388
Danch, Bill 82
Dane, Lawrence 314
D'Angelo, Beverly 283
Daniel, Rod 212
Daniels, Marc 87, 182
Daniels, William 255
Dannacher, Lee 347
Danny Davis and the Nashville Brass 86
Dano, Royal 84
Danza, Tony 375
Darby, Ken 410
Darin, Bobby 21
Darke, Harold 224
Darling, Jennifer 16
da Todi, Jacopone 88
Daudet, Alphonse 173, 261
Davenport, Nigel 80
David, Gerard 123
David, king of the Jews 17, 165, 237, 257
Davidson, Alice Joyce 57
Davidson, Suzanne 275
Davidson, Troy 387
Davies, Henry Walford 312
Davies, Sir Peter Maxwell 312, 313
Davies, Valentine 87, 274, 275
Davis, Ann B. 48
Davis, Arthur 255
Davis, Carl 80
Davis, Don S. 12
Davis, Jefferson 343
Davis, Jim 176, 177
Davis, Jimmie 32
Davis, Katherine K. 18, 249, 250
Davis, Kristin 383
Davis, Mac 38
Davis, Maggie 117
Davis, Sammy, Jr. 244
Davis, Sonny Carl 219
Davison, Bruce 177
Dawn Mass 108, 109
Day, Dennis 87, 106, 176
Day, Doris 44
Day, John 101
Day of Atonement 93, 287, 332
"Day of Infamy" (television episode) 413
Day of the Kings *see* Epiphany
Dayton, John Philip 109
Dayton–Hudson Corporation 353
Daywalt, Drew 83
Dazhboh (god) 395
Deacon, Richard 150
Dear, William 352
DeCarteret, Laura 352
December 25 *see* Christmas Day
"Deck the Halls with Boughs of Holly" 11, 148, 243, 283
DeGuzman, Michael 12
Dehner, John 198
DeKorte, Paul 59, 125, 443
Delaney, John 256
Delaney, Kim 91
Delgado, Julie 107
della Robbia, Andrea 123
della Robbia, Luca 123

Del Mar, Maria 121, 405
DeLuise, Dom 76
de Matteis, Paolo 124
Denmark 148–150
Dennison, Michael 22, 94
Denny, Reginald 101
Denoff, Sam 150
Dent, Vernon 219
Denver, John 104
DePaul, Brandon 352
Depositio Martyrum 93
Dern, Jonathan 28, 76
DeRose, Peter 262
desert Christmas cactus 116
Desmond, Johnny 87
Desmond-Hurst, Brian 78
De Soto, Hernando 94, 397
Deters, Timmy 64
Detten, Eric von 103
Deutsche Staatsoper Ballet Company (Berlin) 77
Devil's Knell 191, 225
Devine, Loretta 41
DeWolfe, Billy 175
DeWolff, Francis 78
Día de Candelaria 266
Día de los Reyes 60, 266
Día de los Tres Reyes 374
Dia de Reis 324
Diamond, Reed 383
The Dick Van Dyke Show 150–151
Dickens, Charles John Huffam 73–76, 87, 90, 105, 127, 130, 151, 152, 184, 190, 214, 226
Dickens' Christmas Carol (television special) 81–82
A Dickens of a Christmas 82, 200
Dickerson, Albert T. III 77
didukh 395, 397
Diego, Juan 61, 266
diener 280
Dievo pyragai 30
A Different Kind of Christmas 153
Diller, Phyllis 45, 305, 306
Dillon, Melinda 125
Dinehart, Alan 84
"Ding Dong! Merrily on High" 153, 283
Dionysus (god) 209, 436
Diorio, Derek 27
Dipping in the Kettle (custom) 379
Disney, Walt 95, 154, 238, 388, 411
A Disney Christmas Gift 154
A Diva's Christmas Carol 82
Dix, William Chatterton 17, 419
Dixon, Dianne 76
"Do You Hear What I Hear?" 39, 86, 154, 250
Dobkin, Lawrence 413
Dobson, Kevin James 274
Dobson, W.A. 72
Dr. Elmo *see* Shropshire, Elmo
Dr. Elmo's Twisted Christmas 187
Dr. Martin Luther und die Reformation in Volksliedern 313
Dr. Seuss's How the Grinch Stole Christmas 215
"Doin' the Bing" 39

Domergue, J.F. 261
Dominican Republic 417
Donahue, Elinor 9, 161
Donald on Ice 267
Donald: Stuck on Christmas 267–268
Donald's Gift 268
Donald's Snow Fight 411
"Donkey Carol" 174
Donner, Clive 28, 80
Donner, Richard 86
Donohue, Jack 28
Donovan, Tom 33
"Don't Make Me Play That 'Grandma' Song Again" 187
Doodletown Pipers 38
Doran, Chris 64
Dorff, Steve 16
dorowat 4
Dorsey, Jimmy 213
Dorsey, Tommy 213
Dotrice, Roy 249
Douglas, Melvyn 87
Dowell, Anthony 305
Downey, Roma 45
Downs, Johnny 28
Drake, Charlie 79
Drake, Tom 203
The Dream of Old Scrooge 82
dreidel 201
Drepp 258
Dreyfuss, Richard 337
Drum Dance 55
Dryer-Barker, Sally 64
Dubin, Charles S. 177
Duff, Gordon 78
Dugan, Dennis 83
Duggan, Andrew 412
Duke, Patty 109
The Dukes of Hazzard 82
Dumas, Alexandre 302
Dun Che Lao Ren 19
Dunbar, Helen 87
Dunn, John 51
Dunn, Teresa 27
Dunn-Leonard, Barbara 16
Dupont, René 126
Dupré, Marcel 361
Durante, Jimmy 176, 328
Durning, Charles 156, 229, 276, 281
Dwan, Allan 205
Dwight, John Sullivan 311
Dye, John 315, 393
D'yed (or *Died*) *Moroz see* Grandfather Frost
Dysart, Richard 235
D'Zaller Weihnacht 381

Earley, Mark 12
Earth, Sky and Air in Song 40
Easter Bear 32
Eastern Orthodox Church 1, 51, 92, 100, 111, 138, 157, 196, 269, 295, 297, 331, 338, 395
Easton, Robert 198
Easton, Sheena 76
Ebbie 82
Ebeling, Johann 8
Ebenezer 82

Eberhardt, Thom 7
Ebert, Bernard 78
Eccles, Teddy 250
"Echo Carol" 421
Eckardt, Max 132
Ecke, Paul 322
Eckholdt, Steven 352, 356
Eckhouse, James 134
Ecuador 371
Eden, Barbara 45
Edgar Bergen and Charlie McCarthy 38
Edison Electric Company 132
Edmund, Justin Pierre 41
Edmunds, Bill 234
Edward II, king of England 158
Edward IV, king of England 391
Edwards, Cliff 238
Edwards, Henry 85
Edwards, Kemp 27
Edwards, Sam 9, 87
Edwards, Stacy 327
Edzard, Christine 304
eggedosis 155
eggnog 155, 397
Egley, William 72
Egypt 3
Eisenhower, Dwight D. 95, 403, 404, 427, 428
Eistedfodd 95, 194
Ekberg, Anita 44
Ekland, Brit 77
El Salvador 61
Elam, Jack 86, 198
Elf (film) 155–156
Elfman, Danny 86, 299
Elias, Jeannie 141
Elie, Tom 82
Elizabeth I, queen of England 47, 189, 296, 391, 419
Elizabeth II, queen of England 45, 95, 313
Elizondo, Hector 45, 46
Elliott, Bob 26
Elliott, David James 206
Elliott, Denholm 66
Elliott, Emily E.S. 383
Elliott, Sam 326
Ellis, Georgia 198
Ellis, Howard 81
Ellis, Robert 12
Ellison, Casey 10
Elmo Saves Christmas 156
Elton, Ben 77
elves 148, 166, 300, 344
The Elves and the Shoemaker (cartoons) 156, 157, 200
"The Elves and the Shoemaker" (fairy tale) 156
Emancipation Proclamation 424
Emes, Ian 282
The Enchanted Nutcracker 304
Enchiridion oder eyn Handbüchlein 355
Enders, Ruth 127
Engel, Samuel G. 139
England 188, 191–193; *see also* Great Britain

English, Michael 263
English Folk-Carols 209
The English Hymnal 41, 153, 224, 310, 312
Engstad, Kai 27
Epiphanius, Greek church patriarch 157, 158
Epiphany 16, 24, 47, 49, 55, 93, 143, 157–159, 162, 261, 321, 407; *see also* individual countries
Episcopal Church 1, 92, 295
Erdölpfarre 23
"Ermuntre dich, mein schwacher Geist" 49
Ernest Saves Christmas 159
Ernst, Wilhelm 215, 363
"Es ist ein Ros' entsprungen" 257
escabeche 61
Esmond, Henry V. 85
An Essay on the Church Plain Chant 308
Estonia 29
Ethiopia 3–4
Ethiopian Orthodox Church 3
Etlich cristlich Lider Lobgesang und Psalm 355
étrennes 173
Evangelical Lutheran Church of North America, General Council of 25
Evans, Dame Edith 85
Evans, Sir Geraint 79
Evans, Ray 18, 246, 359
Evans, Richard Paul 70, 71, 168, 169, 248, 249
Evans, Trevor 85
Evening Offices of the Church 308
evergreens 354, 397
Everitt, Tracy 242, 243
Ever-Ready Company 132
"Everyone's a Child at Christmas" 336
"Everywhere, Everywhere Christmas Tonight" 312
Ewing, Roger 198
Ewing, William 92
The Examination and Tryal of Old Father Christmas 190
"The Exeter Boar's Head Carol" 43
Eye on New York 79

Fabray, Nanette 260
The Facts of Life 10
Fain, Sammy 388
The Fair God 34
Fairlie, Kyle 208
Faith, Percy 107
Falana, Lola 44
Falk, Johannes 313
Falk, Peter 165, 387, 420
Falkenburg, Jinx 44
Falkenstein, Jun 268
A Family Circus Christmas 160
Famous History of the Seven Champions of Christendom 98
Fantasia on Christmas Carols 169
"fantasticals" 397
Farentino, James 291

Farmer, Bill 267, 268
Farmer Boy 251
farofa 370
faroles 325
farolitos 160
Farrar, David 80
Fat Albert and the Cosby Kids 82
The Fat Albert Christmas Special 82
Father Andrew 6
Father Christmas (book) 160
Father Christmas (gift giver) 4, 5, 22, 30, 75, 98, 189–190, 191, 227
Father Knows Best 161–162
Father Knows Best: Home for Christmas 162
Faulk, Sook 109
Faust 25
Favorite Radio Songs 32
Favreau, Jon 155
Fawcett, Eric 78
Faylen, Carol 38
Faylen, Frank 233
Feast of Adam and Eve 30, 128
Feast of Asses 162, 174
Feast of Corpus Christi 99, 140
Feast of Dedication *see* Hanukkah
Feast of Epiphany *see* Epiphany
Feast of Fools 47, 99, 161–163, 189, 211, 354, 374, 391
Feast of Jordan 55, 157, 396; *see also* Epiphany
Feast of Lights *see* Epiphany
Feast of Our Lady of Guadalupe 61, 266
Feast of Saint John the Evangelist *see* Saint John's Day
Feast of Saint Stephen *see* Saint Stephen's Day
Feast of Tabernacles 287
Feast of the Annunciation 287
Feast of the Baptism of the Lord 230, 407
Feast of the Circumcision 162, 295, 297, 407
Feast of the Holy Family 163, 407
Feast of the Holy Innocents *see* Holy Innocents Day
Feast of the Holy Name of Our Lord Jesus Christ 295
Feast of the Immaculate Conception 2, 60, 61, 163–164, 230, 266, 320, 369, 371, 373, 395, 406
Feast of the Presentation 395
Feast of Theophany 16, 17; *see also* Epiphany
Feast of Trumpets 287
Februa 55
Feldon, Barbara 32
Feliciano, José 18, 164
"Feliz Navidad" (song) 18, 164
Ferdinand III, emperor of Germany 49
feres gugs 4
Ferguson, Andrew 134
Ferrell, Will 155
Ferrer José 38, 250
Festgesang 202

Festival of Lights *see* Hanukkah
A Festival of Nine Lessons and Carols 164–165, 191, 315
"festoons" (lights in series) 132
Field, Barbara 80
Field, Eugene 237
Fiesta Bowl 298
Fiesta Intramuros 320
figgy pudding *see* plum pudding
Fiji Islands 19
filhós 324
Fillmore, Millard 424
Finding John Christmas 165
Fink, Gavin 326
Fink, Isabella 387
Finland 29, 166–167
Finlay, Frank 80
Finney, Albert 85
"The Fir Tree" 167–168
Fireside Theatre 78
fireworks 19, 22, 60, 61, 62, 181, 226, 258, 266, 296, 320, 321, 332, 339, 372, 380, 397, 404
The First Christmas: The Story of the First Christmas Snow 168, 328
The First Christmas Tree: A Story of the Forest 168
The First Four Years 253
The First Gift of Christmas 168
First Light Masses 225
First Nations 54, 55
The First Nowell (play) 169
"The First Nowell" (song) 39, 169
firstfooting 54, 190–191, 194, 226, 322
Fitzgerald, Barry 184, 185
Fitzpatrick, Christian 348
"Five Characters in Search of an Exit" (television episode) 394
Die Fledermaus 24
Fleischer, Max 334
Fleming, Peggy 305, 430
Fleming, Shaun 268
Fleming, Victor 95
Flight of the Reindeer 119
A Flintstone Christmas 170, 200
A Flintstone Family Christmas 170–171, 200
The Flintstones 169–171
A Flintstones Christmas Carol 171, 200
Flores de la Noche Buena 322, 424
Flores de Pastor 62
fløtekaker 300
"Flow Gently, Sweet Afton" 26
Flowers, Tennyson 11
Flowers for Children 318
Flynn, Miriam 284
fogueira da consoada 324
Folia dos Reis 370
Folksong Festival 52
Follen, Charles 130
Follows, Megan 92, 305
Fonda, Henry 182
Fontaine, Joan 186
Fool Saints 266
football bowl games 298
"For the Beauty of the Earth" 18

Foray, June 51, 107, 176, 215, 250, 367
Forbes, John 220
Ford, Gerald R. 429, 430
Ford, Paul 28
Ford, "Tennessee" Ernie 6, 7
Ford, Tony 28
Ford, Wallace 161
Ford's Theater (Washington, D.C.) 81
"Forest Green" (tune) 312
Forsythe, John 86
The Fort Worth Star-Telegram 24, 25
Foss, Hubert 81
Foster, Ami 10
Foster, Jodie 199
Foster, Penelope 92
The Four Lads 87
The Fourth King 171
The Fourth Wise Man 318
Fox, Bernard 37
Fox, Erica 71, 136
Fox, Sonny 127
Foxx, Red 44, 45
France 171–174
Franchini, Bob 86
Francis, James Allan 11, 39, 430
Francks, Don 135
Frank, Bill 403
The Frank Sinatra Show 38
frankincense (gift) 286, 384, 437, 439
Franklin, Jeff 385
Franklin, John 119
The Franklin Square Song Collection 148
Franz, Elizabeth 362
Frawley, James 315
Frawley, William 218, 246, 275
La Freccia Azzurra 216
Fred Waring and His Pennsylvanians 38, 249, 410
Frederick William IV, king of Prussia 358
Fredericks, Roger 60
Frees, Paul 84, 87, 176, 236, 250, 295, 333, 338, 349
Freeze Frame 51
Freleng, Friz 51, 386
French, Victor 254
Freya (goddess) 43, 145, 331, 379, 443
Friendly, Ed 254
"The Friendly Beasts" 174
Friese, A.R. 358
Frigga (goddess) 277, 278
Fright Before Christmas 51
Frish- und G'Sundschlagen 24
Frislev, Michael 82
"The Frivolous Four Plus One" 10
"Frölich soll mein Herze springen" 8
"From Bethl'em's City" 14
"From Greenland's Icy Mountains" 50
"From Heaven Above to Earth I Come" 111, 174–175, 311

"From Heaven Came the Angel Host" 174
"From Out of the Forest a Cuckoo Flew" 58
"Frost" (mythical being) 339
Frost, Robert 132, 133
Frosty Returns 175
"Frosty the Snow Man" (song) 18, 175, 176, 205, 333
Frosty the Snowman (television special) 175–176, 328
Frosty's Winter Wonderland 176, 328
Fruitman, Sarah Rosen 46
Frye, Soleil Moon 10
Frye, William 87
fufu 4
"Fum, Fum, Fum" 176
Funicello, Annette 28
Furious Host (mythical group) 436
Furious Hunt (mythical group) 436
F.W. Woolworth Company 132, 133

Gable, Christopher 80
Gabor, Eva 305
Gabriel, Charles H. 25
Gabrielli, Giovanni 313
Gabriel's Vineyard Songs 25
Gallagher, David 329
Gallagher, Megan 249
Gallagher, Peter 223
Gallagher, Seann 420
gallette des rois 173
Gallico, Paul 273, 274
gallina de patio 62
Galway, James 10
Ganjitsu 20
Gannaway, Roberts 267
Gannon, James Kimball (Kim) 18, 223
Gardiner, Reginald 106
Gardner, Don 7, 8
Gardner, Joan 84, 349
Gardner, Julian P. 168, 248, 250
Garfield, James 425
A Garfield Christmas 176–177
Garland, Beverly 38, 284
Garland, Judy 202, 203, 242, 243
A Garland of Christmas Carols 209
Garret, Lila 36
Garrison, Lucy 330
Garroway, Dave 28, 236
Garson, Greer 250, 328
"Gartan" (tune) 257
Garth, Jennie 356
Garwood, Kelton 394
Gaspar (Wise Man) *see* Wise Men
"Gather Around the Christmas Tree" 415
The Gathering 102, 177
The Gathering, Part II 177
Gatlin, Larry 86
Gaudete Sunday 1, 406
Gauntlett, Henry J. 315
Gazzara, Ben 77
Geary, Cynthia 385
Gebert, Gordon 206
Geer, Will 412
Geisel, Theodore Seuss 215

Geistliche Lieder 174
"Geistliches Wiegenlied" 241
General Electric Company 132
The General Electric Fantasy Hour 336
The General Electric Theatre 87
"General Grant" tree 403, 404
The Genius of Nonsense 101
Genna 3
Gentle Camel of Jesus 271
"Gentle Mary Laid Her Child" 186
George Balanchine's "The Nutcracker" 304
George Burns Comedy Week 81
George II, king of England 265
George V, king of England 95, 193
Gerhardt, Paul 8, 111
Germany 177–181
Gerstein, Mordicai 34
"Gesu Bambino" 181–182
Geurs, Karl 435
Ghana 4
Ghirlandaio, Domenico 123
Ghostley, Alice 36
Gibb, Cynthia 206, 262
Gibson, Edward C. 96
gift bringers: *Agios Vassilis* 197; *Baba Noel* 269; *Babbo Natale* 232; *Baboushka* 339; *Befana* 232; Black Peter 258, 342, 345; Christ Child (Baby Jesus, Little Jesus) 23, 60, 61, 62, 143, 146, 258, 266, 364, 365, 369, 372; *Christkindl* (or *Christkindlein*) 23, 179, 378, 398; Christmas Lads 222; Christmas Old Man 19; *Dun Che Lao Ren* 19; Father Christmas 4, 5, 22, 30, 189–190, 191; Gentle Camel of Jesus 271; Grandfather *Boûicnjak* 143; Grandfather Christmas 31; Grandfather Frost 29, 142, 143, 339, 340, 363, 395; Grandpa Indian 370; *Hoteiosho* 20; *Jezisek* 144; *Jólasveinarnir* 222; *Joulupukki* 166; *Julbock* 380; *Julemand* 149, 150; *Julenissen* 300, 301; *Jultomten* 380; *Kalédu Senelis* 31; Kris Kringle 130, 398; *Lan Khoong-Khoong* 19; *lola* 320; *Mos Craciun* 331; *Mos Nicolae* 331; Nice Old Father 19; *El Niño Dios* 266; Olentzero 373; *Papa Noel* 270, 371, 372; *Papai Noel* 370; Pelz Nicholas 99, 343, 345, 398; *Père Noël* 173; *Le Petit Jésus* 173; St. Basil 17, 197, 297; St. Lucia 142; St. Nicholas 23, 55, 142, 178, 258, 340–344, 381; Santa Claus 19, 20, 22, 23, 29, 60, 61, 225, 342–344, 369, 402; *Santa Kurosu* 20; *Sinterklaas* 20, 398; *Sontgaclau* 381; Star Man 323; *Svaty Mikulas* 144, 345, 363; *Sviatyj Mykloaj* 395; Swag Man 22; *Swiety Mikolaj* 322; Three Kings 60, 62, 266, 321, 369, 374; *Vieja Belén* 417; *Viejo Pascuero* 370; Wainamoinen 167; *Weihnachts-*

mann 179; Youngest Camel 271; *Zwarte Piet* 258, 345
gift giving 227, 296, 340–344, 354, 398, 400
The Gift of Love 182
"The Gift of the Animals" 174
"The Gift of the Magi" 182, 214, 253, 268
La Gigantona 62
Gilbert, A.C. 260, 261
Gilbert, Davies 89, 169, 408
Gilbert, Ella 40
Gilbert, Melissa 90, 107, 253, 305
Gilbert, Ronnie 52
Gillen, Denver 334
Gillen, Jeff 125
Gillespie, Haven 18, 349, 350
Gillett, Burt 238
Gilley, William 66
Gimme a Break! 10
Gion, Christian 205
The Girl from the Marsh Croft 245
Glascoe, Jon 66
Glass, William 313
Glastonbury Thorn 94, 111, 182–183, 193
Glazer, Mitch 86
Gleason, Jackie 38, 213
Gleason, James 40
Glöckler 24
glögg 149
"Gloucestershire Wassail" 183
Glover, John 86
Gnasher (mythical goat) 167, 301, 342, 344, 389, 443
"Go Tell It on the Mountain" 90, 183–184
"Go to Sleep, Slumber Deep" 27
Gobel, George 388
"God Rest Ye Merry, Gentlemen" 184, 205, 243, 356, 411, 414
Godal, Edward 85
Godden, Rumer 376
Godey's Lady's Book 131
Godfrey, Arthur 262
Godfrey, Peter 106
Goelz, Dave 84, 157, 232, 283
Goethals, Angela 212, 375
Goetzelman, Vlad 26
gogoli 4
Going My Way 32, 184–185
going on the wren *see* hunting the wren
gold (gift) 286, 384, 437, 439
Gold, Louise 84
Goldberg, Whoopi 42, 53, 64, 80, 336
Golddiggers 44
Goldfarb, Beth 346
Goldsboro, Bobby 86
Goldthwait, Bobcat 86
Goldwyn, Samuel 41
Gombert, Ed 84
Gomez, Thomas 139
Gone with the Wind 95
Gonzalo, Julie 362
"Good Christian Men, Rejoice" 89, 185–186

"Good King Wenceslas" (song) 89, 186, 243, 283
Good King Wenceslas (television specials) 186–187
Good Will to Men 200, 267
Goodman, Dody 76
Goodman, Gary M. 104
Goodman, John 336
Gorbachev, Mikhail 95
Gordon, Barry 90, 306
Gordon, Gale 85
Gordon, Mack 139
Gorrell, Ashley 224
Gorshin, Frank 338
Gosnel, Raja 212
The Gospel According to Scrooge 82–83
Gospel accounts of the Nativity *see* Nativity
Gossaert, Jan 125
Gottlieb, Carl 81
Gould, Harold 318
Goulding, Alfred J. 255
Goulding, Ray 26
Goulet, Robert 38, 304
Gounod, Charles 25
Graas, John Christian 235
Grabenstein, Christopher 105
Graff, Todd 41
Graham, Bruce 120
Graham, Eddy 80
Grahame, Gloria 233
Grajales, Francisco Lopez de Mendoza 94, 397
Grammer, Kelsey 81, 268, 276
Grampus (mythical being) 178, 342, 345
Grandfather Christmas 31
Grandfather Frost 29, 142, 339, 340, 363
"Grandma Got Run Over by a Reindeer" (song) 187, 188
Grandma Got Run Over by a Reindeer (television special) 187–188
Grandma Luca 3
"Grandma's Killer Fruitcake" 187, 188
"Grandma's Spending Christmas with the Superstars" 187, 188
Grandpa Indian 370
"Grandpa's Gonna Sue the Pants Off of Santa" 187, 188
Granger, Farley 182
Grant, Cameron 219
Grant, Cary 40, 41, 232
Grant, Kathryn 422
Grant, Ulysses S. 424, 425
Grassle, Karen 253
Graves, Peter 182
Graves, Robert 203
Graves, Teresa 44
Graves, Warren 86
graves, adorning of 29, 145, 166, 181, 301
Gray, Billy 161
Great Antiphons *see* "O" Antiphons
The Great Bear Scare 32

Great Britain 89, 188–195
"Great Mystery" 17
"The Greatest Gift" 232, 233
The Greatest Story Ever Told 290–291
Gréban, Arnoul 100
Greece 196–197
Green, Martyn 86
Green, Sidney 38
Green, Whitney 136
Greenbush, Lindsay and Sidney (twins) 253
Greene, Lee Rufus (Buddy) III 262, 263
Greene, Lorne 305
Greenland 197–198
"Greensleeves" 419–420
Greenstreet, Sydney 106
Greenwood, Edwin 85
Gregorian calendar 2, 92, 94, 110, 111, 193, 196, 295, 338, 340, 394
Gregory I, Pope 188
Gregory IV, Pope 46
Gregory VII, Pope Saint 1
Gregory the Great, Pope Saint 1
Grenada 417–418
Grey, Joel 328, 388
Griffith, Andy 8, 176, 328
Griffith, Don 84
Griffith, Hugh 83
"Grift of the Magi" (television episode) 360
Grimaldi, Joseph 101
Grimes, Karolyn 40, 41, 233
Grimes, Scott 229, 292, 298
Grimes, Tammy 182, 388
Grinde, Nick 28
Grisham, John 361, 362
Groening, Matt 314, 359
Grossman, David 157
Grossman, Rube 334
Grosvenor, Charles 28
Grotto of the Nativity 108, 137, 269, 293
Groundhog Day 55
Groves, Herman 36
Gruber, Franz Xaver 357, 358
Guaraldi, Vince 63, 64, 220
guaro 62
Guatemala 61–62
Guest, Al 77
Guillaume, Kevin 83
Guillaume, Robert 83
Guinn, Jeff 24, 25
Guinness, Alec 85
The Guinness Book of Records 45
Gunnarsson, Sturla 261
Gunsmoke 198–199
Guthrie Theater 80
Gutteridge, Lucy 80
Guy Lombardo and His Royal Canadians 21, 437
Guyana 371
Gwenn, Edmund 275
Gwiazdka 322
Gwynne, Fred 256

Habersack (mythical being) 178
Hackett, Buddy 86, 236, 328

Hagen, Francis F. 281
Hagen, Julius 85
Hagen, Kevin 87
Haidle, David 57
Haidle, Helen 57
"Hail the Blest Morn!" 50
"Hail to the Lord's Anointed" 280
Hairston, Jester 263
"Hajej, nynej" 330
Håkon I, king of Norway 300
Haldeman, Oakley 18, 205
Hall, Bug 282
Hall, George 350
Hall, Porter 275
Hall, Tom T. 86
hallacas 372
Hallam, Arthur Henry 330
Halley's comet 96
Hallmark Hall of Fame 8, 256
Hallmark Keepsake Ornaments 133
Hamel, Veronica 177
Hamill, Dorothy 10, 305
Hamill, Mark 141
Hamilton, Aileen 106
Hamilton, Barbara 26
Hamlet (play) 199, 263
Hamlin, Harry 249
Hamner, Earl, Jr. 411, 412, 413
Hampshire, Keith 26
Hanalis, Blanche 103, 223, 253
Hanby, Benjamin R. 241, 405
Hancock, John 326
Handel, George Frideric 57, 242, 264, 265, 308, 421
handsels 194
hanetsuki 20
Haney, Carol 304
hangikjöt 221
Hanks, Tom 324
Hanna, William 125, 170, 199, 267, 386, 387
Hannah, Jack 154, 238, 411
Hans Muff (mythical being) 178, 345
Hans Trapp (mythical being) 178, 345
Hansel and Gretel 95
Hansen, J. Omar 229
Hanson, Barry 81
Hanukkah 200–201
Hanukkiah 201
"Happy Holiday" 10, 11, 207, 283
Happy Holidays: The Best of the Andy Williams Christmas Shows 10–11
Happy Holidays with Bing and Frank 38
Happy New Year, Charlie Brown 201–202
harasa 269
Harbord, Carl 102
Harding, Ann 101
Harding, James P. 50
Harding, Warren G. 426
Hardwicke, Edward 292
Hardy, Lucretia 402
Hardy, Oliver 27
Hardy, Thomas 318, 319

"Hark! The Herald Angels Sing" 39, 202, 233, 243
Harlequin Executed 101
harlequinade 101
Harman, Hugh 267, 386
Harnois, Elisabeth 317
Harold I, king of Norway 300
Harper, David 412
Harper's Weekly 343
Harrell, Rebecca 326
Harrington, Pat, Jr. 176
Harris, Emmylou 32
Harris, Harold 306
Harris, Harry 413
Harris, Jo Ann 360
Harris, Jonathan 79
Harris, Julie 135, 316
Harris, Neil Patrick 136
Harris, Peter 283
Harris, Rossie 90
Harrison, Benjamin 94, 399, 425
Harrison, Gregory 117, 177, 292
Harrison, Kathleen, 78
Harrison, Rex 85
Harrison, Susan 394
Harrison, William Henry 424
Harry Simeone Chorale 159, 249
Hart, John 84
Hart, Johnny 26
Hartford-Davis, Robert 79
Hartman, David 38, 275
Hartman, Don 206
Hartman, Haven 387
Hartman, Phil 238, 360
harukoma mai 20
Harvey, Iain 81
Harvey, Megan Taylor 64
Haskell, Mary Donnelly 315, 393
Hathaway, Donny 18, 383
Hathcock, Bob 83
hatsumode 20
haube 280
The Haunted Man and the Ghost's Bargain 152
Hausner, Jerry 107
Hautau, Mathew 136
"Have Yourself a Merry Little Christmas" 18, 39, 45, 86, 202–203, 242
Hawes, Steve 80
Hawkes, Thomas 242
Hawkins, Jimmy 234
Hawley, Lowell S. 28
Hawthorne, Nigel 53
Hayden, Pamela 360
Haydn, Franz Joseph 358
Haydn, Michael 358
Hayes, Billy 18, 42
Hayes, Helen 256
Hayes, Melvyn 79
Hayes, Michael 79
Hayes, Rutherford B. 425
Hays, Lee 52
Hays, Robert 103, 223, 305, 352
Hayter, John 79
"He Is Born, the Divine Christ Child" 203
"He Is Born, the Holy Child" 203

"He Is Sleeping in a Manger" 224
"He Smiles Within His Cradle" 203
"Heap on More Wood" 203–204
"Hear What Great News We Bring" 14
Heather, David 80
Heather, Jean 185
Heaton, Patricia 387
Heaton, Tom 11
Heber, Reginald 50
Hecht, Lawrence 79
Hedaya, Dan 367
Heidi 204–205
"Heigh-Ho" 10
Heim, Carrie Kei 348
Die Heinzelmännchen 156
Heironymus, Eusebius 138
Helene, princess of Mecklenburg 172
Hellerman, Fred 52
Helmore, Thomas 89, 186, 310, 313
Helms, Bobby 239
Hémy, Henri 15
Henderson, Dan 15
Henderson, Florence 48
Hendricks, Bill 388
Hendrix, Elaine 276, 282
Henrici, Christian Friedrich 112
Henry, Charlotte 27
Henry, O. 182, 214, 253, 268
Henry II, king of England 224
Henry III, king of England 391
Henry IV, king of England 98
Henry VIII, king of England 97, 98, 113, 114, 183, 296, 419
Henson, Brian 84, 157, 232
Henson, Jim 84, 283
Hepburn, Katharine 316
Herbergsuchen 23, 100, 181
Herbert, Victor 27
Here Comes Santa Claus (film) 205
"Here Comes Santa Claus" (song) 18, 42, 205, 335, 441
"Here We Come A-Caroling" 11, 205–206, 242, 283, 414
"Here We Come A-Wassailing" 138, 205
"Here We Go A-Caroling" 205
The Hereford Breviary 47
Herman, Jerry 18, 281, 282, 414, 415
"Hermitage" (tune) 257
Herod the Great, king of the Jews 47, 99, 140, 141, 210, 266, 273, 323, 375; *see also* Nativity; Star of Bethlehem
Herody 323
Herrick, Robert 227
Herrmann, Bernard 79
Hersholt, Jean 204
Hertha (goddess) 2, 128, 179, 232, 344, 436
Hetzenbrot 24
Hewitt, Frankie 81
Hewitt, Henry 74
Hewitt, Jennifer Love 81
Hickey, William 284, 299
Hicks, Kevin 46
Hicks, Leonard 348

Hicks, Seymour 75, 85
Highway to Heaven (album) 32
Hilger, Richard 80
Hill, Arthur 102
Hill, Glen 248
Hill, Richard S. 25
Hill, Tom 77
Hill-Guillaume, Melissa 83
Himmlische Lieder 49
Hines, Gregory 347
Hingle, Pat 77, 316
Hintz, Jakob 414
Hirschman, Herbert 413
Hirson, Roger O. 80
Hisnak 17
History of New York 227, 342
Hobbs, Brian 346
Hobley, MacDonald 78
Hod Bozi Vanocni 147
hodening 193
Hoder (god) 277
Hodges, Eddie 213
"Hodie Christus natus est" 62
Hoeger, Mark 255
Hoffmann, E.T.A. 302
Hogmanay 193–194
Hogueras 374
Holbøll, Einar 118, 119, 149
Holbrook, Hal 223, 248
Holda (or Holde, goddess) 2, 232, 436
Holden, William 44
Holford, William 242
Holiday Affair 206
A Holiday for Love 106
Holiday in Your Heart (novel and television special) 207
Holiday Inn 207–208, 421, 422
A Holiday to Remember 208–209
Holland 258–259
Holland, Anthony 35
Holle (goddess) 232
holly 190, 210, 226, 354
"The Holly and the Ivy" 209–210, 283
"A Holly Jolly Christmas" 18, 210, 336
The Hollywood Palace 38
Holm, Celeste 139
Holman, M.L. 58
Holmes, Fred 86
Holmes, Taylor 78
Holst, Gustav 224
Holt, Robert 32
"The Holy Baby" 65
Holy Birth Festival 19
The Holy Family Hymns 15
"Holy, Holy, Holy" 50
Holy Innocents Day 24, 47, 60, 143, 162, 210–211, 266, 320, 369, 372, 374, 407; *see also* individual countries
Holzschuher, Heinrich 313
Home Alone (film and television productions) 211–212
"Home for the Holidays" 18, 86, 212
The Homecoming: A Christmas Story 402, 412

The Homecoming: A Novel about Spencer's Mountain 412
Honduras 62
Hone, William 65
Honeyman, Paul 79
The Honeymooners 213–214
"Honeymooners Christmas Party" (television episode) 213
The Honeymooners Christmas Special 214
Honorius III, Pope 293
Hooks, William H. 245
Hootkins, William 249
Hoover, Herbert 426
Hope, Bob 38, 44, 45, 185, 246, 359
Hope, Dolores 45
Hope, Leslie Townes *see* Hope, Bob
Hope, Linda 45
Hopkins, Bo 367
Hopkins, John Henry, Jr. 401, 415
Hopper, Dennis 353
Hordern, Michael 78, 79, 83
Horner, Thomas 113
Horsley, John C. 72
The House Without a Christmas Tree 214
Household Words 130
Houseman, John 86, 136
Houser, Jerry 16, 48
Houser, Lionel 106
Houston, Whitney 41
"How Brightly Shines the Morning Star" 214–215, 362
"How Great My Joy" 421
How the Flintstones Saved Christmas 170, 200
How the Grinch Stole Christmas 59, 215–216, 402
How the Toys Saved Christmas 216–217
Howard, Rance 207
Howard, Ron 8, 216
Howard, Trevor 102
Howells, William Dean 103, 104, 267
Howes, Sally Ann 182
Hubley, John 84
Hubley, Season 103
Hucker, Walter J. 79
Huddleston, David 348
Hughes, Bernard 78
Hughes, John 212, 284
Hughes, Langston 58, 59
Hughes, Miko 387
Hughes, Terry 282
Hugo, Victor 163
Hugo Winterhalter and His Orchestra 42
Huitzilopochtli (god) 325
Hulin, Dominique 205
Humbug Not to Be Spoken Here 36
Humperdinck, Engelbert 95
Humphreys, Alfred 11
Hunt, Helen 292
Hunt, Peter H. 229
Hunter, Jeff 292
hunting the wren 46, 216–217, 226
Hurley, Owen 60, 304

Hurn, Douglas 83
"The Huron Christmas Carol" 217
Husk, William H. 89, 205, 209
Hussarenkraperl 24
Hussey, Olivia 291
Huston, Carol 48
Hutchinson, Josephine 412
Hutson, Wihla 6
Hutterites 54–55
Hymn to St. Cecilia 62
Hymnal Companion to the Book of Common Prayer 228
The Hymnal Noted 310
Hymns Ancient and Modern 18, 202, 313, 421
Hymns and Sacred Poems 202
Hymns for Little Children 315
Hymns for Social Worship 202
Hymns from the Cross 32
"Hymnus omnis horae" 313

"I Heard the Bells on Christmas Day" 218, 250, 333, 336
"I Know a Rose Tree Springing" 257
"*I Love Lucy* Christmas Show" 218–219
I Saw Mommy Kissing Santa Claus (film) 219
"I Saw Mommy Kissing Santa Claus" (song) 11, 18, 219–220
"I Saw Three Ships" 220, 283
I Want a Dog for Christmas, Charlie Brown 220
"I Wonder As I Wander" 141, 220–221
Iceland 221–222
"icicles" (Christmas tree decorations) 131, 132
Iekatas 30
"Ignat" (custom) 331
"Ihr Kinderlein, kommet" 310
"Il est né, le divin Enfant" 203
Ildefonsus, bishop of Spain 108
I'll Be Home for Christmas (film) 222–223
"I'll Be Home for Christmas" (song) 9, 10, 18, 223, 264, 283
I'll Be Home for Christmas (television specials) 223–224
Ilyina, Tatjana 305
The IMAX Nutcracker 304
Imgard, August 56
"In dulci jubilo" 185, 186
"In Freezing Winter Night" 63
"In the Bleak Mid-Winter" 224, 258
"In the Land of Beginning Again" 33
"In Those Twelve Days" 390
India 19
Inditos 61
Indonesia, Republic of 20–21
Ineffabilis Deus 164
"Infant Holy, Infant Lowly" 224
injera 4
inocentes 266
Inuit, customs of 55, 197
Iran 269
Iraq 269
"Irby" (tune) 315

Ireland 188, 216, 224–226
Ireland, Kathy 315, 393
Irmas, Matthew 77
Iroquois, customs of 55
Irvin, Brittney 11
Irving, Washington 84, 226, 342; Christmas sketches of 226–228
Irwin, Tom 206
Ising, Rudolf 266, 267, 386
Isobel, Katherine 442
Israel 269–270
Israeli, Ben 237
"It Came upon the Midnight Clear" (song) 90, 228–229, 243, 401
It Came upon the Midnight Clear (television special) 229
It Happened One Christmas 235
It Nearly Wasn't Christmas 229
An Italian Carol Book 42, 153
Italy 229–232
It's a Very Merry Muppet Christmas Movie 232
It's a Wonderful Life 33, 41, 126, 232–235, 402
"It's Beginning to Look a Lot Like Christmas" 18, 235
"It's Christmas" 10
It's Christmastime Again, Charlie Brown 235
"It's the Holiday Season" 10, 11
"It's the Most Wonderful Time of the Year" 10, 18, 235–236
Ivanov, Lev 303
Ives, Burl 210, 328, 335, 336
ivy 209, 210, 226

The "J" Is for Jesus 57
The Jack Benny Show 106
Jack Frost 236, 328
Jackie Gleason Honeymooners Christmas 214
Jackson, Andrew 424
Jackson, Dianne 368
Jackson, Mary 412
Jackson, Wilfred 154, 411
Jacobs, Eric 219
Jacobs, William 106
Jacob's Gift 236–237
Jacoby, Laura 298, 299
Jaggar, Dean 421
J'ai rencontré le Père Noël (film) 205
Jaimes, Sam 202
Jamaica 418
James, Gennie 104, 367
James, William Garnet 58
James I, king of England 97
James D. Vaughan Publishing Company 32
janeiros 324
Janjic, Zoran 79
Japan 19–20
Jarrell, Tommy 50
Jarrott, Charles 108, 442
Jarvis, Bob 84
Javits, Joan Ellen 18, 347
Jefferson, Thomas 423
Jeffreys, Anne 78
Jennens, Charles 264, 265

Jeruzalem see Nativity scene
"Jesous ahatonhia" 217
Jesse tree 237
"Jest 'Fore Christmas" 237
"Jesu, Jesu, Baby Dear" 330
"Jesu Parvule" 6
Jesus (film) 291
Jesus Christ 16, 55, 92, 93, 99, 108, 138, 140, 146, 157, 179, 182, 196, 207, 210, 220, 228, 237, 257, 262, 263, 279, 280, 281, 375, 383, 386
"Jesus Holy, Born So Lowly" 224
Jesus of Nazareth (film) 291–292
Jetsons Christmas Carol 83, 200
Jillian, Ann 224
Jiminy Cricket's Christmas 238
"Jing, Jing, Jing of the Jingle Bells" 39
Jingle All the Way 238–239
"Jingle Bell Rock" 18, 86, 239, 283, 330
"Jingle Bells" 10, 39, 86, 239–241, 242, 283, 401
"Jingle, Jingle, Jingle" 336
Jinnah, Quaid-I-Azam Mohammed Ali 20
jobai 4
Jobe, Andrea 92
Joffre, Dan 83
Johansen, David 86
John Canoe (custom) *see* Jonkonnu
John Daniel Quartet 32
John Grin's Christmas 83
John Paul II, Pope *see* The Vatican
John Scott Trotter Orchestra 223, 422
John the Baptist 2, 93, 286, 287, 405
Johns, Mervyn 78
Johnson, Andrew 424
Johnson, Arte 32, 368
Johnson, Charles Eric 83
Johnson, Cherie 10
Johnson, Christopher Ryan 64
Johnson, Edward 132
Johnson, Gerry 36, 170
Johnson, James 21
Johnson, Jay 16
Johnson, Jay W. 18, 42
Johnson, Lamont 394
Johnson, Lyndon B. 428, 429
Johnson, Michael 305
Johnson, Richard 98
Jólakkötur 222
Jólasveinarnir 222
"Jolly Old St. Nicholas" 241, 405
Jones, Aled 368
Jones, Chuck 51, 215, 408
Jones, David 80
Jones, David Hugh 135
Jones, Dean 82, 86
Jones, Inigo 97
Jones, Jack 242, 243
Jones, James Earl 76, 291
Jones, Katherine Ann 135
Jones, Marcia Mae 204
Jones, Richard 419
Jones, Rick 27
Jones, Shirley 45

Jonkonnu (custom) 60, 62, 416
Jonson, Ben 97, 190
Jonsson, Vignir 222
Jordan, Glenn 109
Jordan, Harlan 207
"Joseph and Mary" (carol) 64
"Joseph and the Angel" 64
"Joseph, Dearest Joseph Mine" 241
"Joseph, lieber Joseph mein" 241
Joseph of Arimathea 182
"Joseph Was an Old Man" 64
Joubert, John 383
Joulupukki 166
Joulutonttuja 166
jour de rois 173
Le Journal de Spirou 367
"Joy to the World!" 11, 39, 89, 138, 242
joya no kane 20
Joyner, Tom 347
"Joys Seven" 356
Jubenvill, Ken 82
Jubilee Singers 184
The Judds 32, 45
The Judy Garland Christmas Show 242–243
Juhl, Jerry 84, 283
Jul 148, 300, 378, 443
Julbock 380
Julebukk 301
Julemand 149, 150
Juleneg 149
Julenissen 300, 301
Julgrisen 379
Julian, Rupert 85
Julian calendar 3, 92, 94, 110, 111, 196, 269, 271, 296, 338, 340, 354, 394
Julian the Apostate 157
Julius I, Pope 93, 94
Julklapp 380
Julnisse 148, 149, 344
Jultomten 344, 380
June Apple (album) 50
June Taylor Dancers 213
Jurist, Ed 37
Justinian I, Byzantine emperor 55, 137

Kaczender, George 82
Kaczmarek, Jane 104
kadomatsu 20
kagamimochi 20
Kaghand 17
kahk 3
Kahn, Bernie 36
Kahn, Mary 46
kaladnieces 30
kalanda 196, 197
Kalédu Senelis 31
Kalends *see* Calends
Kalevala 167
kallikantzari 196, 197, 199
kalpaci 52
Kane, Carol 86
Kapilow, Robert 324
karavay 340
Karenga, Dr. Maulana 244

Karloff, Boris 215
Karlsen, John 127
Karman, Janice 66, 76
Karns, Todd 233
Karns, Virginia 27
Karroll's Christmas 83
karuta 20
Kasem, Casey 32
Kaspar (Wise Man) *see* Wise Men
Kavner, Julie 360, 361
Kay, Norman 79
Kaye, Danny 421, 422
Keach, Stacy 352
Kean, Jane 84
Keane, Bill 160
Keene, Malcom 78
kekatnieki 29
Kellaway, Cecil 36
Kelly, Gene 39
Kelman, Alfred R. 80
Kemner, Randy 125
Kemp, Ross 81
Kendall, Edward C. 96
Kennedy, Craig 27
Kennedy, D. James 86
Kennedy, John F. 403, 428
Kent, Walter 18, 223
Kenya 4
Kepler, Johannes 375
Kern, James V. 219
Kernberger, Johann Philipp 310
Kerr, Bill 134
Kerridge, Jeremy 80
Kerry, Margaret 9
Kerwin, Brian 404
Kerwin, Lance 318
Khiahk 3
The Kid Who Loved Christmas 243–244
Kilburn, Terry 77
Kimball, Ward 28
"Ein Kindlein in der Wiegen" 203
King, Alan 321, 328
King, Cathy 86
King, Dennis 78
King, Henry 182
King, Jack 154, 411
King Family 38
King of Kings 292
King of the Bean 158, 181
Kings' Cake 54, 158, 173, 192, 194, 266, 372, 382
King's College, Cambridge, England 164, 191, 315
Kinnaman, Melinda 292
Kinney, Jack 238
Kirby, Bruce 153
Kirbye, George 421
Kirk, James 315, 393
Kirk, Tommy 28
Kirkland, Gelsey 304
Kirkpatrick, William J. 26
Kirov Ballet 305
kisielius 30
kissel 338
"kissing balls" 278
"kissing boughs" 278
"kissing bunches" 278

"kissing rings" 278
Kitt, Eartha 328, 347
kiviak 197
klaasjes 258
Klane, Jon 83
Klapparbock 150
Klaubauf (mythical being) 23, 345
Klaubaufgehen 23
Klausjagen 381
Klebba, Martin 352
Kleeb, Helen 412
Kleinbach, Henry 27
Kleinsinger, George 334
Kleiser, Randal 177
klejner 149
Kletter, Lenore 353
Klickmann, Frank 410
Kline, Kevin 304
Klopfelnachten 179
Knecht Ruprecht (mythical being) 23, 178, 179, 342, 345
Knell, David 77, 136
Knight, Christopher 48
Knight, Felix 27
Knotts, Don 8
Knut IV, king of Denmark 301, 380
Kobler, Erich 156
Kocher, Conrad 18
Kohler, Dennis 87
Kokobusserl 24
kolach 395
kolady 146, 323
Kolb, Clarence 102
koledari 52, 143
Koledars 52
Kolede 143
koledni gevreci 52
Koleduvane 51
Koliada 395
koliadky 395
kolyadki 339
"Kommet, ihr Hirten" 14
"Die Könige" 215
Koonce, Ken 81
Korchinska, Maria 62
Korman, Harvey 170, 239
Korty, John 84, 136
Koster, Henry 41, 139
Kotcheff, Ted 46
Kotlum, Johannes Ur 222
kourabiedes 197
Koussevitsky, Serge 330
Kouzel, Al 160
Kowalchuk, Bill 337
Kowalski, Bernard L. 292
Kozak, Harley Jane 7
Kraft Music Hall 37, 95, 422
Kraft Television Theatre 78
Kramer, Jeffrey 348
Kramer, Lance 360
Kramer, Richard 7
Krampus (mythical being) 23, 142, 178, 345
kranskake 300
Kraus, Alison 16
kravai 52
Krestny Khod 340
Kreutzer, Peter 66

kringle (pastry) 149
Krippe see Nativity scene
Kris Kringle (mythical being) 130, 398
Kris Kringle Tree 130
Krish, John 291
Kriss Kringle's Christmas Tree 131
Kristofferson, Kris 106, 274
Kroon, Piet 81
Krumholtz, David 350
krumkaker 300
kuba 146
kucia 30
Kucios 30
Kuhlman, Ron 48
Kuhlman, Rosemary 8
Kurisumasu Keiki 19
Kurtz, Swoozie 316
Kuter, Kaye E. 16
kutia 146, 323, 395, 396
kutya 338
Kwan, Michelle 269
Kwanzaa 244

Labelle, Patti 347
LaBeouf, Shia 112
Lacey, Thomas Alexander 310
Lachman, Mort 45
"The Lady of the Lake" 25
Lafferty, James 16
LaFortune, Roc 27
Lagerlöf, Selma 245, 246
Lageson, Lincoln 77
lait de poule 154
Lalibela, king of Ethiopia 4
Lambillotte, Louis 15
Lamm, Karen 90
Lan Khoong-Khoong 19
Lanchester, Elsa 41, 139
Landau, Richard H. 102
Lander, David 81
Landon, Michael 38, 39, 253, 254
Landres, Paul 78
Lane, Charles 36
Lanfield, Sidney 246
Lang, Richard 91
Lange, Kelly 32
Lange, Ted 229
Langford, Frances 154, 213, 411
Langley, Noel 78
Lansbury, Angela 168, 281, 328, 414
lantern festival 22, 320
L'Arlésienne 261
Larry, Sheldon 118
latkes 201
La Tour, Georges de 51
Lattanzi, Chloe 117
Latvia 20–30
Laub, Shirley 305
Lauer, Andrew 223
laufabraud 221
Laufenberg, Henrik von 355
laurel 116
Laurel, Stan 27
Laurel and Hardy in Toyland 27
Lauridsen, Morten 313
Lavan, René 362
lavender 116

LaVorgna, Adam 222
Lawrence, Carol 304
Lawrence, Joey 10
Lawrence, Matthew 10
Lawrence, Nathan 153
Lawrence, Steve 77
Laws, Maury 328
Layton, Joe 256
Lea, Ron 82
Leachman, Cloris 16, 235, 326
Leaf, David 11
Lean, David 291
Learned, Michael 136, 412
Lebanon 270
Lebkuchen 24, 179
lechonitos 62
Lee, Brenda 330
Lee, Charles 403
Lee, Christopher 305
Lee, Dixie 37
Lee, G.W. 48
Lee, Michelle 305
Lee, Peggy 388
Lee, Richard Egan 74
Lee, Sung Hi 284
Leech, John 74
LeFleur, Art 351
lefse 301
Legeay, Dom Georges 203
The Legend of Christmas 83
The Legend of the Candy Cane 57
The Legend of the Christmas Rose 245–246
legends: animals 174, 263, 264, 319, 389, 396; Ark of the Covenant 4; bells 58; candles 225; candy cane 57; Christmas rose 116; Christmas Lads 222; Christmas tree 128; Glastonbury Thorn 183; John the Baptist 2; Lalibela, king of Ethiopia 4; lavender 116; pennyroyal 116; poinsettia 321–322; rosemary 116; St. Anastasia 109; St. Barbara 2, 23; St. George 98; St. Lucia 2; St. Nicholas 341, 342; St. Thomas 3; thyme 117; Vortigern, king of the Britons 413–414; werewolves 199; Wise Men 437; wren 217; *zampognari* 230
Leibman, Ron 102
Leichliter, Larry 220
Leigh, Janet 206
Leigh, Vivian 95
Leinbach, Edward 281
Leipziger Gesangbuch 358
Leisen, Mitchell 329
LeMat, Paul 298
Lembeck, Michael 351
The Lemon Drop Kid 45, 246, 359
Lennon Sisters 10, 38
Leo I, Pope Saint 93
Leo XIII, Pope 163
Leonard, Bill 79
Leonard, Jack E. 28
Leonard, Sheldon 234
Leonardis, Tom 53
Leontovich, Mykola 18, 58

The Leprechaun's Christmas Gold 247, 328
Leslie, Noel 78
Lester, Ketty 253
"Let It Be Me" 21
"Let It Snow! Let It Snow! Let It Snow!" 18, 39, 134, 247
LeTet, Robert 134
letterbanket 258
Levant, Brian 239
Levels, Calvin 136
Levinson, Robert Wells *see* Wells, Robert
Levitow, Abe 84
Levy, Barbara 83
Levy, Eugene 329
Levy, Ralph 79
Lewis, Emmanuel 45
Lewis, Jennifer 41
Lewis, N.J. 346
Leyenda de Navidad 83
Lezhnina, Larissa 305
Liberius I, Pope 93, 108
Libertini, Richard 318
Lichtstock 130
Liddle, Ralph 139
Lieberman, Robert 7
The Life and Adventures of Santa Claus 247–248, 328
Light, John 292
The Light of Christmas 248–249
Light of the Stable 32
"Light's Abode, Celestial Salem" 15
Like Father, Like Santa 249
Lincoln, Abraham 424
Lindsay, Robert Howard 78
Lindsay-Hogg, Michael 255
Lineberry, Audine 50
Linson, Art 86
"Linus and Lucy" (song) 63
Linz, Alex D. 212
lion dance 20
Lishner, Leon 8
Litel, John 102
Lithgow, John 348
Lithuania 30–31
Little, Cleavon 412
Little, Rich 85
"Little Alexia" (actor) 205
"Little Bitty Baby" 65
Little Children's Book for Schools and Families 25
Little Christmas 29, 143, 157, 166, 221
"Little Drummer Boy" (song) 18, 39, 150, 249–250, 319
The Little Drummer Boy (television special) 250, 328
The Little Drummer Boy, Book II 250–251, 328
Little Feast 269
Little Folks' Song Book 40
Little House in the Big Woods 251
Little House on the Prairie (book) 251
Little House on the Prairie (television series) 253–254
"Little Jesus, Sweetly Sleep" 330

The Little Match Girl (fairy tale with animated and live-action adaptations) 254–255
"Little Snow Girl" 11
Little Town on the Prairie 252
Little Women 255
The Littlest Angel 255–256
The Littlest Snowman 256
The Littlest Tree 256–257
Lively, Robyn 352
Livingston, Henry, Jr. 409
Livingston, Jay 18, 246, 359
Llewellyn, Robert 81
Lloyd, Eric 109, 350, 351
Lloyd, Jake 238
Lloyd, John 77
"Lo, How a Rose E'er Blooming" 257, 383
Locke, Philip 79
Lockhart, Gene 77, 185, 275
Lockhart, June 77, 299
Lockhart, Kathleen 77
Logan, Tex 127
Loggia, Robert 291
Loki (god) 277
lola 320
London, Jerry 107, 224
Long, Ronald 37
Long, Shelley 153, 352
The Long Winter 252
Longet, Claudine 9
Longfellow, Henry Wadsworth 218, 384
Lookinland, Mike 48
Lookinland, Todd 198
Loos, Rob 141
Lord of Misrule 97, 158, 162, 189, 228, 391
Loring, Gloria 45
Lotto, Lorenzo 122
Louise, Mary 40
loukoumades 197
Love, Mike 86
"Love Came Down at Christmas" 257–258
lovefeast, Moravian 280, 281
Lovell, Dyson 80
Lovell, James 96, 223
Loveton, John W. 78
lovo 19
Lovy, Alex 59
Low Countries 258–259
Lowe, Charlie 50
Lowe, Rob 121
Lowry, Mark Alan 262, 263
Lowther, George 77
Lowther, T.J. 316
Loy, John 28
Luca the Hag 142
Lucado, Max 5, 91, 92, 140, 141, 236, 237
Lucas, Lisa 214
Lucci, Susan 82
Luce, Clare Booth 139
luces de Belen 266
Luciadagen 378
Lucking, Bill 112
Lucky Strike Game 374

Luft, Joey 242, 243
Luft, Lorna 242, 243
"Lullay, Thou Tiny Little Child" 141
luminarias 160
Lumley, Steve 442
Lundigan, William 78
Luske, Hamilton 154, 411
lussekatt 379
Lussinatten 300
lutefisk 301
Luther, Martin 1, 25, 47, 111, 123, 129, 174, 179, 311, 313, 355
Lutheran Church 1, 25, 29, 166, 221, 295
Lutzelfrau 3
Luxembourg 258
Lye, Les 27
Lynn, Dina 168, 236, 349

Macay, Barry 77
Maccabee, Judah 200
MacDonough, Glen 27, 28
MacGimsey, Robert 253
MacGregor, Katherine 253
MacGregor, Mary 86
Macheret, Yelena 305
Mack, Allison 405
MacMurray, Fred 328
Macnee, Patrick 78, 86
MacNeil, Robert 76
MacNeille, Tress 267, 268, 306, 314, 360
MacNicol, Peter 314
MacRae, Gordon 182
MacWilliam, Keenan 283
Madden, Minnie 305
Madeline and Santa 259
Madeline at the North Pole 259
Madeline's Christmas 259–260
Madison, James 424
Madonna (pop star) 347
Maffeo, Neil T. 28
Magi 99, 113, 137, 157, 158, 257, 271, 374, 375, 439; *see also* Three Kings; Wise Men
Magic Earmuffs 435
Magister Ludi 353
"Magnum nomen Domini Emanuel" (hymn) 241
"Magnus" (television episode) 198
Magnuson, Ann 282
Magon, Jymn 76, 80
Magwood, Robbie 317
Mahoney, Michael 121
Majors, Lee 86, 366
Make-a-Wish Foundation 16
The Making of "A Charlie Brown Christmas" 64
The Making of Mickey's Christmas Carol 84
makowiec 323
Maksimova, Yekatarina 305
Malakhov, Vladimir 305
Malanka (tradition) 396
Maldan, Martin 202
Malkovich, John 353
Malleson, Miles 78

Mame 414
The Man in the Santa Claus Suit 260
The Man Who Saved Christmas 260–261
Manchester Mercury and General Advertiser 69
Mandel, Mel 86
Mandrell, Barbara 86
manger 30, 51, 108, 142, 146, 285, 322, 364, 395
manger scene *see* Nativity scene
Manger Square 269
"The Manger Throne" 419
Mankiewicz, Joseph L. 77
Mann, Terrence 281
Manoff, Dinah 77
Mansfield, Jayne 45
Mantegna, Joe 360, 361
Manton, Stephen 79
Maples, Marla 108
Marcel Marceau Presents A Christmas Carol 83
Marcellinus, Ammianus 157
March, Fredric 78, 79
"March of the Kings" 261
"March of the Toys" 27
March of the Wooden Soldiers 27
"La marche des Rois Mages" 261
Marck, Nick 285
Marcus Ward and Company 72
Marduk (god) 354, 443
"Marge Be Not Proud" (television episode) 360
Margerin, Catherine 376
Mari Lwyd 193, 194, 195
Marie, Rose 150
Marienthal, Eli 405
Marin, Annette 229
Marin, Cheech 306
Marin, Edwin L. 77, 102
Marino, Tony L. 84
Marks, John D. (Johnny) 18, 210, 218, 236, 314, 330, 334, 335, 336, 338, 409, 410
Marks, Julian 84
Marlowe, Hugh 139
Marmion 203, 204
Marquis, Charles 198
Marsh, Ronald 79
Marshall, Don 37
Marshall, E.G. 256, 284
Marshall, Penny 41
"A Marshmallow World" 262
Martin, David 42
Martin, Dean 21
Martin, Donald 82
Martin, Hugh 18, 202
Martin, Mary 38, 39
Martin, Toby 108
Martiniere, Stephan 260
Martyr, Justin 287
Marvin, Lee 45
"Mary and Jesus" (carol) 64
Mary Christmas 262
"Mary, Did You Know?" 262–263
"Mary Had a Baby" 263
Mary, mother of Jesus *see* Virgin Mary

Mary, Mother of Jesus (film) 292
"Mary's Boy Child" *see* "Mary's Little Boy Child"
"Mary's Little Boy Child" 10, 263
"Mary's Question" 64
marzipan 149, 258
Mason, Lowell 242
masque 97, 227
Masque of Blackness 97
Mass of the Divine Word 108, 406
Mass of the Rooster 60, 263–264, 369, 373; *see also* individual countries
Massie, Richard 355
Masterson, Mary Stuart 314
Matheson, Murray 394
Matheson, Tim 106
Mathews, Larry 150
Mathieson, Jean 77
matoke 5
mattak 197
Matthau, Charles 87
Matthau, Walter 87
Matthews, Marie 84
Matthews, Timothy R. 383
Mattinson, Burny 84
Matz, Oliver 305
matzebaum 130
Mauldin, Nat 41
Mauracher, Karl 358
Mawdycke, Thomas 141
Maxwell, Marilyn 246, 359
Maxwell, Spence 107
May, Robert Lewis 333, 334, 335, 410
"May Each Day" 10
Mayer, Sheldon 334
Mayfield, Les 276
Maynor, Dorothy 330
Mayor's Christmas Cheer Fund 5
McAndrew, Stephen 125
McBrearty, Don 66
McCarey, Leo 33, 185
McCartney, Paul 18, 440
McCaskey, J.P. 148
McClanahan, Rue 16, 208, 255
McCormack, Eric 45
McCormick, Maureen 48
McCune, Ida Sue 59, 443
McCune, Susie 125
McDermott, Dylan 276
McDermott, Marc 77
McDonough, Mary 412
McDowall, Roddy 81, 275, 305, 404
McDowell, Rider 12
McEntire, Reba 45, 106
McFadden, Robert 171, 247, 248, 250, 321, 389, 441
McFarland, John T. 25
McFee, Joseph 346
McFerrin, Bobby 353
McGalliard, W.V. 132
McGavin, Darren 126
McGillis, Kelly 353
McGinley, Phyllis 441
McGinnis, Michael 16
McGreevey, John 84, 108, 413
McGuire, Biff 79

McGuire, Dorothy 291
McHugh, Bart H. 99
McHugh, Frank 38
McIntire, John 87
McIntyre, Lizzie 131
McIntyre, William A. 346
McIver, Bill 8
McKeen, Michael 81
McKenna, Siobhan 292
McKinley, Andrew 8
McKinley, William 425
McKinnor, Nadine 18, 383
McLean, Seaton 66
McLoughlin, Tom 153
McMurray, Sam 282
McNear, Howard 198
McRae, Murray 42
McWhirter, Julie 59
Meadows, Audrey 213
Meadows, Tim 314, 384
Mear, H. Fowler 85
Medieval Hymns and Sequences 310
"Meditation on the First Prelude of S. Bach" 25
Meek, John L. 11
Meet Me in St. Louis 202, 242
Meffre, Armand 205
Megillat Antiochus 200
Meins, Gus 28
Melchior (Wise Man) *see* Wise Men
"Mele Kalikimaka (The Hawaiian Christmas Song)" 264
Melendez, Bill 64, 175, 202, 220, 235, 442
Melendez, Sonny 236
melomacarona 197
Melton, Sid 246
Melvin, Donnie 109
Memling, Hans 122
Mendelson, Jason 64, 202
Mendelson, Karen 64
Mendelson, Lee 64
Mendelssohn, Felix 202
Menken, Alan 81
Mennonites 54
menorah 201
Menotti, Gian Carlo 8, 95
Meraska, Ron 305
Mercator, Gerhardus 121
Mercer, Johnny 38
Meredith, Burgess 348
Merman, Ethel 333
Merrill, Bob 84
The Merry Christmas 83
"Merry Christmas, Darling" 264
Merry Christmas, Fred, from the Crosbys 38
Merry Christmas from London (album) 11
"A Merry, Merry Christmas to You" 336
Merton, Michael 81
Messiah (oratorio) 57, 95, 136, 242, 264–265
Messick, Don 59, 83, 107, 125, 168, 170, 171, 236, 295, 333, 338, 367, 442, 443

Métis, customs of 55
Michael III, Byzantine emperor 51
Michaels, Frank 414
Michaels, Richard 37
Michelle, Diane 268
Michelle, Janee 37
Mickey and Minnie's Gift of the Magi 268
Mickey's Christmas Carol 83–84, 267
Mickey's Dog-Gone Christmas 268–269
Mickey's Good Deed 238
Mickey's Magical Christmas: Snowed In at the House of Mouse 267
Mickey's Once Upon a Christmas 267–268
Mickey's Twice Upon a Christmas 268–269
Middleton, J.E. 217
A Midnight Clear: Stories for the Christmas Season 271–272
Midnight Mass 3, 24, 54, 60, 62, 108, 146, 149, 173, 181, 225, 230, 231, 269, 270, 323, 340, 365, 369, 372, 396, 406; *see also* specific countries
Midwinter Horn Blowing 258
Mieszko, king of Poland 322
Mikolaj 322
Mikulas 144
Military, Frank 21
Milk Grotto 273
Millard, Oscar 139
Miller, George 134
Miller, John 281
Miller, Larry 83
Miller, Paul 79
Miller, Robert Tate 355
Miller, Roger 295, 328
"The Miller's Daughter" 21
"The Miller's Wedding" 21
Mills, Donna 45
Milne-Buckley, Kenneth 77
Milton, John 33, 315
The Milton Berle Show 306
mince pie 22, 227
Minnelli, Liza 242, 243
Minz, Alexander 304
Miracle Down Under 133
Miracle in the Wilderness: A Christmas Story of Colonial America 273–274
"Miracle on Evergreen Terrace" (television episode) 360
Miracle on 34th Street 112, 235, 274–276, 398, 402
Misa del Aguinaldo 62, 266, 320, 372, 418
Misa del Gallo 60, 263, 266, 320, 369, 373
Miss Lettie and Me 272
Missa do Galo 324, 369
Mr. Magoo's Christmas Carol 84
Mr. Scrooge 84
Mr. St. Nick 276
Misterio 61, 266
mistletoe 227, 276–278

Mitchell, Camille 12
Mitchell, Elizabeth 351
Mitchell, Mark 282
Mitchell, Thomas 233
Mitchell Boys' Choir 38, 41, 78
Mitchum, Robert 86, 206
Mithra (god) 92, 157, 229, 436
Mitternachtsmette 24, 181
mochi 20
mochitsuki 20
Mohr, Josef 357, 358
Monachino, Frank 8
Monaco, Lorenzo 125
Monk, William H. 18
Monnoye, Bernard de la 52, 319
Monroe, Bill 127
Monroe, James 424
Monroe, Phil 66
Monroe, Vaughn 247, 262
Montgomery, Elizabeth 36, 37
Montgomery, James 14, 15, 280
Montgomery Ward Company 334
Month, Chris 348
Monts, Sieur de 53
Moody, Ron 39
Mooney, Paul 53
"Moonlight in Vermont" 10
Moore, Benjamin 79
Moore, Clement Clarke 25, 409, 410
Moore, Dudley 348
Moore, Karen 120
Moore, Mary Tyler 150, 216, 272
Moore, Melba 38, 39
Moore, Oscar 314
Moore, Steven Dean 360
Moore, Tedde 125
Moran, Dolores 102
Moran, Erin 199
Moravian Church 130, 279–281
Morgan, Al 69
Morgan, David Thomas 355
Morgan, Dennis 106
Morgan, Elaine 79
Morgan, John 79
Morgan, Kewpie 27
Morgan, Lorrie 11
Morgan, Ray 78
Morgan, Russ 42
Moricone, Massimo 80
Morita, Pat 28
Mormon Tabernacle Choir 38
"Morning Star" 281
Moroni, Giovanni Battista, 124
Morris, Anita 366
Morris, Peter 274
Morris, Reginald O. 257
Morris, Richard 84
Morrison, Brian 199
Morriston Boys' Choir 62
Morrow, Max 121, 352
Morse, Robert 87, 236
Morshead, Catherine 81
Mos Craciun 331
Mos Nicolae 331
Moses, William R. 92
Moss, Tegan 11
"The Most Wonderful Day of the Year" 236, 336

Mostel, Zero 250
Mott, Abram 131
"Mottram" 69
Mozart, W.A. 241, 265, 330, 358
Mrs. Santa Claus 281–282
Ms. Scrooge 84
Mubarak, Hosni 3
Mueller, Carl 25
muérdagos 62
Muhlenberg, William Augustus 40
Mukhamedov, Irek 305
Mull, Martin 239
Muller, Romeo 87, 152, 176, 236, 247, 250, 295, 321, 333, 336, 349, 376
Mulligan, Richard 28
Mulrooney, Kelsey 71
mummer's plays, mumming 54, 97–99, 190, 227, 339
Mumy, Billy 36
Mumy, Liliana 351
Munsel, Patrice 87
The Munsters' Scary Little Christmas 282
The Muppet Christmas Carol 84
A Muppet Family Christmas 282–283
Murakami, Jimmy T. 81
Murdoch, Susan 107
Murlowski, John 329
Murphy, Erin 36, 37
Murphy, Graeme 306
Murray, Bill 86
Murray, Brian Doyle 86
Murray, James R. 25, 26
Murray, Joel 86
Murray, John 86
Murray, Stephen 83
Musae Sioniae 47, 186, 257
Musgrave, Thea 80
Music, Lorenzo 176
Music Revue 84–85
Must Be Santa 283
Mustin, Burt 394
"My Ain Countree" 40
"My Favorite Things" 10, 11
Myerson, Alan 206
Mynors, William 95
Myron, bishop of Crete 17
myrrh (gift) 286, 384, 437, 439
Mystère de la Passion 100
mystery play 100, 128

N. Town Cycle of mystery plays 100
nacatamal 62
Nacimiento 60, 266
Nakamura, Takeo 305
Nall, Joy Merchant 57
Nall, Thomas, Jr. 57
Napier, Alan 78
Nash, Clarence 84, 154, 238, 411
Nash, Mary 204
Nast, Thomas 25, 343, 400
Nastuk, Matthew 360
Natale in Vaticano 406
Natalis Solis Invicti 92, 93, 230
Nathan, Robert 40
National Baptist Young People's Union Convention 11

The National Christmas Tree and the Christmas Pageant of Peace 402–403, 427
National Hanukkah Menorah 201, 430
National Lampoon's Christmas Vacation 283–284
National Lampoon's Christmas Vacation 2: Cousin Eddie's Island Adventure 284–285
The Nation's Christmas Tree 403–404
Nativity 92, 285–293; biblical account 285–286; film and television depictions 290–293; popular assumptions 287–288; time of 286–287; works of art 288–290
The Nativity (animated and live-action depictions) 200, 292–293
Nativity play 23, 62, 99–101
Nativity scene 60, 293–294, 403; *belén* 320, 373; *Belenes* 418; "Bethlehem" 365; *Betlehem* 142; *Betlem* 144; *crèche* 172, 364, 365; *Jeruzalem* 23, 178, 241; *Krippe* 23, 178, 241; *Nacimiento* 60, 266, 369, 373; *Pesebre* 60, 61, 62, 266, 325, 369; *portal* 61; *presepio* 230, 231, 324, 369; *Purseppen* 381; *Putz* 280, 294; *szopka* 322; *vertep* 396
Natwick, Mildred 214
'Ndòcciata 231, 406
Neal, Patricia 412
Neale, John Mason 89, 186, 310, 313, 355
Nealon, Kevin 7
Neame, Ronald 86
Near, Timothy 81
Negulesco, Jean 291
Neidlinger, William Harold 40
Nelson, Jerry 84, 157, 232, 283
Nelson, Ralph 108
Nelson, Steve 18, 175
Nelson, Willie 327
nengajo 20
Neptune (god) 345
Nero, Roman emperor 405
Nestor, the Long-Eared Christmas Donkey 294–295, 328
Netherlands 258–259
Neuwirth, Bebe 76
New Carolls for This Merry Time of Christmas 408
New Version of the Psalms 202, 421
New Year's Boy 340
New Year's Day 20, 29, 99, 143, 295–298, 339, 340; associated traditions 296–297; calendar dates 295–296; church feasts 297; in the United States 297–298; *see also* specific countries
"New Year's Eve Party" (television episode) 213
New York City Ballet 304
New York Sun 441
Newhart, Bob 38, 155, 336
Newman, Alfred 139
Newman, Eric 92

Newman, John Henry 310
Newman, Tom 92
Newton-John, Olivia 45, 117, 118, 156
Nicaragua 62
Nice Old Father 19
Nicholas plays 23
Nichols, Charles A. 170
Nichols, Dudley 33
Nicolai, Philipp 214, 362, 363
Nielsen, Judith 136
Nielsen, Leslie 7, 305, 353
"Nigh Bethlehem" 6
The Night Before Christmas (cartoons) 154, 200, 386, 410, 411
"The Night Before Christmas" (poem) *see* "A Visit from St. Nicholas"
"Night of the Meek" (television episode) 394
The Night They Saved Christmas 298–299
The Nightmare before Christmas 299
Niles, John Jacob 58, 141, 221
niños envueltos 369
Niven, Barbara 77
Niven, David 40, 1
Nixon, Richard M. 12, 44, 429
"The Noble Stem of Jesse" 257
La Noche de Griteria 62
Nochebuena (or *Noche Buena*) 60, 266, 320, 373
"Noël des ausels" 58
"Le Noël des oiseaux" 58
"Noël nouvelet!" 361
Noëls anciens 203
Noëls français 51
Nolan, Jeanette 198
Nolan, Lloyd 246
NOMA Lights 132
Norell, Michael 91
Norman Luboff Choir 38
Norris, Helen 134
North, Steven 81
North Pole 343, 344, 400
Northern Ballet Theatre (troupe) 80
Norton-Taylor, Judy 412
Norway 300–302
Novena, Masses during 60
"Now Come, Savior of the Heathen" 355
"Now Thank We All Our God" 281
"Nowell, Sing Nowell" 361
"Nun komm, der Heiden Heiland" 355
Nünichlinger 382
Nunn, Edward Cuthbert 51
Nureyev, Rudolph 304
The Nutcracker 267, 302–306, 376; film and television versions 304–306; *Nutcracker Suite* and the ballet 303; original story 302; origins of the ballet 302–303
The Nutcracker and the Mouse King 302, 305
Nutcracker Fantasy 305
The Nutcracker: A Fantasy on Ice 305
The Nutcracker of Nuremberg 302

Nutcracker on Ice 305
The Nutcracker Prince 305–306
The Nutcracker Suite 238, 303
Nutcracker: The Motion Picture 306
Nutcracker: The Story of Clara 306
The Nuttiest Nutcracker 306
"Nuttin' for Christmas" 306
nyama choma 4
Nye, Louis 38
Nyström, Jenny 380

"O" Antiphons 307, 310
"O Christmas Tree" 138, 258, 308
"O Come, All Ye Faithful" 11, 39, 48, 308–310
"O Come, Little Children" 310
"O Come, O Come, Emmanuel" 307, 310
"O Come, Redeemer of Mankind" 355
"O du fröliche" 313
"O Hearken Ye" 6–7
"O Holy Night" 10, 11, 39, 310–311
"O How Joyfully" 313
"O Little Town of Bethlehem" 184, 311–312, 401
"O magnum mysterium" 312–313
"O Most Wonderful" 313
"O, Ru-Ru-Ru, My Little Jesus" 325
"O Sanctissima" 33, 313
"O Tannenbaum" 258, 308
"O Thou Joyful Day" 313
"O Thou Most Holy" 313
Oakeley, Frederick 310
Oberer, Amy 7
Oberon, the Fairy Prince 97
Obiceiul mesei 333
Obiceiul puntilor 333
O'Brien, Margaret 202
O'Callaghan, Matthew 269
Occasional Psalm and Hymn Tunes, Selected and Original 242
Ockrent, Mike 81
O'Connor, Matthew 118
O'Connor, Una 33, 106
Octave of the Birth of Our Lord 297
Odin (god) 167, 277, 301, 345, 380, 436, 443
O'Donoghue, Michael 86
odzemok 365
Ogle, Bob 59
"Oh, Joseph Took Mary Up on His Right Knee" 64
O'Hanlon, George 83
O'Hanlon, Virginia 441, 442
O'Hara, Maureen 71, 275
O'Keefe, Michael 327
Okuma, Enuka 108
Olaf I and II, kings of Norway 300
Oland, Pamela Phillips 42
"Old Christmas" (poem) 203
Old Christmas (time period) 49,

183; *see also* Christmas Old Style, Christmas New Style
Old Lad's Passing Bell 191
Old Scrooge; or, The Miser's Dream 75
Old Yeller 95
Olentzero (mythical being) 373
Olive, the Other Reindeer 314
Oliver, Jason 223
Olsen, Ashley and Mary-Kate (twins) 385
Olsen, Susan 48
Olsher, Laura 84
Omisoka 20
"On a Christmas Night" 59
"On a Pallet of Straw" 59
On Christmas Night 169
On Ice 411
"On That Most Blessed Night" 57–58
On the Banks of Plum Creek 251–252
On the Morning of Christ's Nativity 33, 315
On the 2nd Day of Christmas 314–315
"Once, in Royal David's City" 164, 165, 315
Once Upon a Christmas 315–316
Once Upon a Wintertime 154, 411
One Christmas 316
One Ham's Family 386
"One-Horse Open Sleigh" 239
101 Dalmatians Christmas 81
One Magic Christmas 316–317
"One Solitary Life" (essay) 11, 39, 430
O'Neil, F.J. 48
O'Neill, Henry 206
Onorati, Henry V. 18, 249, 250
Ontkean, Michael 63
Operation Desert Storm 44
Oplatek 323
oplatky 364
Oppenheimer, George 78
Ops (goddess) 354
Orange Bowl 298
Orbison, Roy 327
Orgel, Lee 84
Orgelbüchlein 47, 175, 186, 355
"Orientis partibus" 174
Origen of Alexandria 92, 287, 438
Original Scotch Tunes 21
Orthodox Church *see* Eastern Orthodox Church
Ortiz, Ana 286
Osmond, Donnie 10
Osmond, Jimmy 442
Osmond, Marie 45, 182
Osmond, Wayne 229
Osmond Brothers 9, 10, 11
The Other Wise Man 317–318
Otis, Carl 132
O'Toole, Annette 71
O'Toole, Peter 305
otoshidama 20
Otto I, king of Bavaria 196
Our Gang comedies 27
Our Miss Brooks 84

"Over the River and through the Woods" 318
Overstake, Lucille 69
Owen, Reginald 77
"The Oxen" 318–319
Oz, Frank 84, 157, 283
Oziol, Hari 16

Pace, Adger M. 32
Pacific Northwest Ballet Company 306
Padnos, Corey 64
Page, Geraldine 109
Paine, George 83
painters *see* Nativity [works of art]; The Vatican [works of art]
Pakistan 20
Palance, Jack 82, 224, 327
pallaq 55
pan dulce 369
Panama 62
Panathenaea 196
panettone 231
Pantoliano, Joe 314
pantomime 4, 101
panunuluyan 320
Papa Noel 270, 371, 372
Papai Noel 370
Paper Novelty Products Company 132
Paperny, Caryn 32
paplotelis 30
Paradise Tree 128
La Paradura del Niño 372
Paraguay 371
Parish, Mitchell 18, 363
Parker, David 375
Parker, Horatio 8
Parker, Noelle 159
Parkes, Gerard 283
Parkinson, H.B. 85
Parks, Gerry 282
Parley's Illustrated Library 74
parol 320
Parranda 418
Parris, Patricia 84
Parry, Joseph 414
Parton, Dolly 366, 404
La Pascua de Los Negros 370
Pase del Niño Viajero 371
Paso 61
Pasquin, John 350
Passover 287
Pasterka 323
pastorales 172
Los Pastorelas 62, 325, 397
Pastores 99, 320
pastorinhas 370
"Pat-a-Pan" 250, 319
pâté a la rapure 54
Paterson, John B. 12
Paterson, Katherine 12, 271, 273
Paterson, William 79
Patterson, Bobby 50
Patterson, Florence 385
Patterson, Ray 82, 83, 90, 171, 293, 443
Paul Revere and the Raiders 86

Paul VI, Pope 407
Paul Weston and His Orchestra 38
pavlova 22
Pavlova, Nadiya 305
Paykuss, Marc 83
Payne, John 275
Payne, Marvin 229
"The Peace Carol" 39, 319
Peace of Christmas 29, 166, 380
Peace on Earth 267
The Peachy Cobbler 267
Peacocke, Thomas 12
Pearce, Alice 36
Pearsall, Robert 186
Peary, Hal 333, 338
Pease, R.H. 73
pebernødder 149
Peck, J. Eddie 385
Peck, Jeff 134
Peerce, Larry 104
Pellegrini, Norman 77
Pelz Nicholas (mythical being) 99, 343, 345, 398
Pelznickel (mythical being) (also Pelznickel, Pelznichol) 23, 99, 178, 343, 398
Pennsylvania Dutch 99, 398
pennyroyal 116
pepparkakor 379
peppernøtter 258, 300, 345
Perchta (goddess) 2, 24, 128, 232, 436
Perchten 24
Père Fouettard 172
Père Noël 173
Perkins, Elizabeth 276
Perlman, Rhea 385
Perlove, Paul 81
Perrin, Vic 107
Persky, Bill 150
Peru 371–372
Pesci, Joe 211
Pesebre *see* Nativity scene
Peter the Great, Russian czar 339
Peters, Bernadette 39, 207
Peters, Sheldon 274
Petipa, Marius 303
Le Petit Jésus 173
La petite marchande d'allumettes 254
Petrella, Ian 126
Petrenko, Viktor 305
Petrenko, Vladimir 305
Petrie, Daniel 87
Pfrimmer, Don 294
Philadelphia Mummers' Parade 99, 398
Philco Television Playhouse 38, 78
Philippines 319–321
Phillip, Arthur 21, 94
Phillips, Stan 80
Philocalus, Furius Dionisius 92
Piae Cantiones 47, 89, 186, 313
Piazza di Spagna (Rome) 164, 406
Picard (pseudonym) 112
Picard, Paul 217
The Pickwick Papers 74, 87
Piemeneliu Misos 31

Pierce, Franklin 399, 424
Piercy, Shel 306
pierogi 323
Pierpont, James Lord 239, 240, 401
Pierpont, John, Jr. 240
Pierpont Morgan Library 76
Pierson, Arthur 78
pifferari 57
pikkujoulu 166
Pillsbury, Sam 106
pin money 296
Pinacoteca 407
piñata 320, 325, 374
Pinchot, Bronson 28
Pinnock, Arnold 283
Pinocchio's Christmas 321, 328
Pinsett, Gordon 107
Pintard, John 342
Pintoff, Ernest 84
piragi 30
Piro, Grant 134
pirohy 364
piroshki 340
Pisana, Jennifer 42
Pitillo, Maria 120
Pius, IX, Pope 164
pizarai 331
pizzele 231
Plager, Joseph 118
"The Play of St. George" 98
Pleasence, Angela 80
Pleasence, Donald 291
Pleasure Reconciled to Virtue 97
plokstainelis 30
plotkeles 30
"The Ploughboy's Dream" (ballad) 312
Plowright, Joan 86
Plugusorul 332
plum pudding 22, 192, 415
Plumb, Eve 48
Plummer, Christopher 28, 42, 259, 260
Pluto's Christmas Tree (cartoon) 154, 267, 411
Plygain 194, 195
Podmore, William 77
Pogue, William R. 96
Poinsett, Joel R. 322, 424
poinsettia 61, 62, 321–322, 424
Poitier, Sidney 107
Pola, Edward 18, 235, 236
Poland 322–323
The Polar Express 323–324
polaznik 143, 322
Polk, James K. 424
Pollak, Kevin 42
Pollard, Michael J. 86
Pollock, Alexander 11
Polo, Marco 438
Polson, Beth 136, 355
ponche 61, 62, 266, 325
pony dance 20
Poole, Duane 109
Pooler, Frank 264
"Poor Little Innocent Lamb" (story) 272
Pope, Randy 77

"poppers" (noisemakers) 22
portal see Nativity scene
Porter, Don 90
Porter, J. 119
Porter, William Sydney 182
Portugal 324
"Portuguese Hymn" 308
Las Posadas 23, 60, 61, 181, 266, 320, 324–325, 397
Posant Christkindl 23
Poseidon (god) 345
Potamkin, Buzz 34
potlatch 55
Poulenc, Francis 313
Powell, Jonathan 79
Powell, Marykay 7
Powell, Robert 292
Powell, Tristram 83
Powers, Dennis 79
Powers, Stefanie 186
Praetorius, Michael 47, 186, 257
Prancer 326
Prancer Returns 326–327
Prang, Louis 73, 123
Pratt, Lauren Suzanne 314
Prayer of the Rosary of the Holy Child 61
The Preacher's Wife 41
Prendes, Luis 83
Prescott, Norm 82
presepio see Nativity scene
Presley, Elvis 42, 423
Pressman, Lawrence 177
Preston, Robert 33, 414
"Pretty Paper" 327
Previn, Andrè 38
Price, Vincent 78, 292
The Prince of India 34
Prison Fellowship 12
Prohaska, Janos 10
The Promise 38
Protestant Reformation 1, 25, 89, 100, 179, 188, 191, 225, 257, 300, 325, 356, 378
Protevangelium of James 65
Prout, Kristen 315, 393
Prowse, Juliet 38
Prudentius, Aurelius Clemens 313
Pryce-Jones, John 80
"P.S. Murry Christmas" 198–199
Psalms and Hymns for Divine Worship 14
Psalms of David Imitated in the Language of the New Testament 242
Psalteriolum Cantionum Catholicarum 310
Pseudo-Matthew, Gospel of 65
"Puer natus in Bethlehem" 47
Puerto Rico 418
Pulliam, Keshia Knight 10, 255
Pulterklas (mythical being) 345
Punky Brewster 10
The Pups' Christmas 266–267
Puritans 75, 89, 97, 113, 189. 190, 226, 227, 296, 397
Purse, Eliza Jane 240
Purseppen 381
Putz see Nativity scene

Pyle, Denver 82
pyrohy 396

Quaid, Randy 284, 285
"Quando noctis medium" (song) 108
Queen Victoria Shopping Center 22
Queen's College, Oxford 43, 193, 227
"Quelle est cette odeur agreable?" 420
La Quema de los Años Viejos 62, 371
La Quema del Mal 61
queque Navideno 61
Questel, Mae 284
Quinn, Aileen 10

Rabagliati, Alberto 126
rabanada 324, 370
Rachmaninoff, Sergei 313
Rae, Charlotte 81
Rafkin, Alan 36
Raft, George 102
ragout de boulettes 54
Rahn, Milton 240
Railton, George Scott 346
Raine, Gypsy 78
Rains, Claude 291
rakia 52
Ralph Stanley and the Clinch Mountain Boys 32
Ram, Buck 18, 223
Ramer, Henry 26
Ramsay, Allan 21
Randall, Ethan 7
Randall, James R. 308
Randall, Tony 216, 256
Randolph, John 177
Rankin, Arthur, Jr. 87, 128, 152, 168, 176, 236, 247, 248, 250, 251, 295, 321, 327, 328, 333, 336, 338, 349, 389, 441
Randolph, Joyce 213
Rashad, Phylicia 45
Rathbone, Basil 78, 79, 87
Ravenscroft, Thurl 215
Rawls, Lou 176
Ray, Nicholas 292
Raye, Martha 86
Raymond, Bradley 268
Read, Barbara 353
Read, Merilyn 27
Reading, John 308
Reagan, Ronald W. 87, 201, 403, 430, 431
"Real Estate Venture" (television episode) 38
Recueil de cantiques spirituels provençaux et françois 261
Recueil de noëls provençaux 50
Reddish, Jack 108
"Redeemer of the Nations, Come" 355
Redford, Paul 82
Redgrave, Sir Michael 79
Redlich, Ed 82
Redman, Michael 59

Redmond, John 106
Redner, Lewis 184, 311, 312
Reed, Donna 233
Reed, Edith M.G. 224
Reed, Marshall and Michael (twins) 413
Reed, Robert 48
Rees, Roger 80
Reese, Della 244
Reeves, Keanu 28
Reeves, Mathonwy 66
"Regent Square" 14
Regney, Noel 154
Reid, Kate 103
Reid, Taylor-Anne 120
Reilly, Charles Nelson 28, 76
Reilly, Judy 259
Reiner, Carl 150
Reinhold, Judge 350
Reisado 370
"Rejoice and Be Merry" 386
Remember the Night 328–329
Renoir, Jean 254
"Resonet in laudibus" 241
Resurrection of the Little Match Girl 255
retablo 371
Retton, Mary Lou 86
le réveillon 54, 173, 400
Revenge Is Sweet 27
Rey, Fernando 291
Reyes Magos 266
Reynolds, Burt 198
Reynolds, Debbie 136, 336
Reynolds, Edith Craig 319
Reynolds, Marjorie 208
Reynolds, William Morton 355
Rhodes, Grandon 87
Rhodes, Michael Ray 318
Rhys ap Gruffydd, prince of Deheubarth 95, 194
Rhys-Davies, John 255
rice cake pounding 20
Rich, John 101
Rich Little's Christmas Carol 85
Richards, Ariana 326
Richards, Billie 128, 333, 336, 338
Richards, Carol 359
Richards, Judi 125
Richardson, Gillian 66
Richardson, Jake 329
Richardson, Ralph 78, 291
Richie Rich's Christmas Wish 329
Richman, Caryn 48
Richmond, Randi 106
Ricketts, Thomas 77
Riedel, Karl 14
Riedesel, Major General Friedrich von 53
The Right to Be Happy 85
Riis, Jacob 118
Rimes, LeAnn 207
Rinaldi, Joe 28
"Ring, Christmas Bells" 58
"Ring Out, Wild Bells" 329–330
"Rise Up, Shepherd, and Follow" 330
risengrød 149
Rist, Johann 49, 111

Ritchard, Cyril 84, 168
Ritchie, Jean 65
Ritter, John 367
River Jordan (gorge in Ethiopia) 4
Roach, Hal 27, 28
Robards, Jason 134, 214
Robb, R.D. 126
Robbins, Peter 64
Robbins, Tim 360
Roberts, Bruce 337
Roberts, Florence 27
Roberts, Rick 387
Robin Goodfellow (mythical being) 344
Robinson, Barbara 35, 36
Robinson, Bridgitte 27
Robinson, Charles 272, 356
Robinson, Michael 79
Robson, Wayne 317
Roche, Dominic 78
Rock, Charles 77
Rock, Gail 214
Rock, George 7
"Rock-a-Bye Baby" 27
"Rockin' Around the Christmas Tree" 18, 86, 330, 333, 336
"Rocking" (or "Rocking Carol") 330–331
Rocky Mountain Christmas 104
Rodari, Gianni 216
Rodriguez, Percy 77
Roebuck, Daniel 262
Roemer, Larry 336
Roger Wagner Chorale 78
Rogers, Charles 28
Rogers, Mimi 108
Rogers, Venetta 37
Rogers, Wayne 235
Rolle, Esther 243
Rollins, Walter E. 18, 175
rom ponche 62
Roman, Phil 177, 188
Roman, Ruth 38
Roman Catholic Church 1, 2, 3, 29, 46, 51, 55, 92, 100, 108, 113, 138, 157, 230, 269, 295, 307, 331, 444; *see also* The Vatican
Romania 331–333
Romano, Antoniazzo 124
Romeo and Juliet 25
Romersa, Joanna 171
rompope 60, 62, 266
Rooney, Mickey 229, 333, 349, 441
Roosevelt, Franklin D. 109, 401, 402, 426, 427
Roosevelt, Theodore 119, 423, 425
Roraty 322
"El Rorro" 325
Rosca de Reyes 266
Rose, George 256
Rose Bowl 297, 298
rosemary 116
Rosemont, David A. 105
Rosen, Barry 104
Rosen, Stu 16
Ross, Vicki Taylor 92
Rossetti, Christina 224, 257
Roswell, Maggie 360

Roth, Joe 362
Rouse, Mitch 314
Rowan, Kelly 261
Rowden, W. Courtney 85
Rowe, Tom 12
Roxburghe Ballads 184
Royal Ballet (Birmingham) 305
Royal Ballet (London) 304, 305
Rubes, Jan 316
Ruby, Joe 125
Rudman, David 84, 283
Rudolph and Frosty: Christmas in July 328, 333
"Rudolph, the Red-Nosed Reggae" 440
Rudolph, the Red-Nosed Reindeer (character) 333–335; background 334; book sequels 334–335; original story 334
"Rudolph, the Red-Nosed Reindeer" (song) 205, 210, 218, 242, 314, 330, 333, 334, 335–336, 409
Rudolph, the Red-Nosed Reindeer (television special) 210, 236, 328, 335, 336–337, 338
Rudolph, the Red-Nosed Reindeer and the Island of Misfit Toys 337–338
Rudolph, the Red-Nosed Reindeer, Shines Again 335
Rudolph, the Red-Nosed Reindeer: The Movie 336–337
Rudolph's Second Christmas 334–335
Rudolph's Shiny New Year 328, 338
Ruffalo, Mark 314
Rufus Rose Marionettes 82
Ru-klas (mythical being) 178, 345
"Run Rudolph Run" 336
Runyon, Damon 246
Runyon, Jennifer 48
Rush, Merrilee 86
rushnyk 396
Rusmanis, Kriss 80
Russ, William 165
Russell, Kurt 90
Russell, William D. 161
Russia 338–340
Rutherford, Ann 77
Ruysdael, Basil 139
Ryan, Jim 82
Ryan, Marion 38
Ryan, Mitch 90
Ryan, Will 84
Ryba, Jakub Jan 146

Sabella, Paul 28, 76
Saboly, Nicholas 51
sabots 173
Sachs, Norman 86
"Safe in His Love" 32
Sagal, Katey 420
Saidakova, Nadja 305
saint (bread) 52
Saint, Eva Marie 77, 78, 223
Saint Aidan 188
Saint Ambrose 88, 164, 355
St. Anastasia's Church (Rome) 109

Saint Andrew's cross 2
Saint Andrew's Day 1, 2, 144, 322, 363, 395
Saint Athanasius 157
Saint Augustine 93, 188
Saint Barbara's Day 2, 23, 142, 143, 144, 270, 322, 363, 395
Saint Basil 17, 197, 297
Saint Bede the Venerable 438, 443
Saint Bernard of Clairvaux 164
Saint Boniface 128, 168, 177
Saint Caesarius 1
Saint Catherine's Day 395
Saint Columba 188
Saint Elizabeth of Hungary 109
Saint Ephrem the Syrian 17, 164
Saint Francis of Assisi 88, 94, 172, 230, 293
Saint Frumentius 3
St. Galler Kindheit Jesu 100
Saint Gregory of Nazianzus 93
Saint Gregory of Nyssa 17, 93
Saint Gregory the Illuminator 16, 17
Saint Gregory the Wonderworker 17
Saint Helena 137, 293, 437
Saint Ignatius 331
St. Ignatius Boys' Choir 78
Saint Irenaeus 92, 164
Saint Isidore of Seville 297
Saint James, brother of Jesus 17
Saint James of Nisibis 17
Saint James the Apostle 17
Saint Jerome 138
Saint John Chrysostom 93
Saint John the Evangelist 17, 392; *see also* Saint John's Day
Saint John's Day 143, 162, 392, 407
St. Johnston, Joshua 81
Saint Joseph 57, 138, 230; *see also* Nativity
Saint Kitts and Nevis 418–419
Saint Knut's Day 301
St. Louis Carol Association 38
Saint Lucia 2, 142, 230, 378; *see also* Saint Lucia's Day
Saint Lucia's Day 2, 3, 142, 144, 166, 230, 300, 363
Saint Margaret 98
Saint Mary *see* Virgin Mary
Saint Mary of Zion Church (Aksum, Ethiopia) 4
Saint Maximus 1
St. Michael's Choir 38
Saint Nicholas 17, 23, 24, 47, 54, 66, 99, 142, 172, 178, 196, 230, 258, 322, 340–344; *see also* Saint Nicholas's Day
"St. Nicholas" (place name) 114
St. Nicholas Society of New York 342
Saint Nicholas's Day 2, 20, 23, 47, 70, 142, 144, 178, 179, 211, 230, 258, 322, 331, 342, 344–346, 363, 381, 395, 398; *see also* individual countries
Saint Patrick 224
Saint Peter the Apostle 1, 17, 405

Saint Peter's Basilica (Rome) 109, 405, 406, 407
Saint Stephen 17, 46; *see also* Saint Stephen's Day
Saint Stephen's Day 24, 46, 143, 162, 181, 186, 193, 216, 301, 323, 396, 407; *see also* individual countries
Saint Sylvester's Day 24, 181, 278, 382
Saint Thomas Aquinas 164
Saint Thomas the Apostle 3, 437
Saint Thomas's Day 3, 300
Saintsbury, Kathleen 77
Sakall, S.Z. 106
sake 20
Salmon, Scott 86
Salus Populi Romani (icon) 406
Salvation Army 346
Salway, John 79
Salzman, Bernard 112
Samichlaus 382
Samuel Sparrow and the Tree of Light 68
sandkaker 300
Sandrich, Mark 208
Sands, Tommy 28
Sandy, Gary 405
Sandys, William 89, 169, 184, 209, 220, 386, 390, 408
Sanford, Arlene 223
"Santa and the Bookies" 213
Santa and the Three Bears 346–347
"Santa Baby" (song) 18, 347
Santa, Baby! (television special) 328, 347–348
Santa Claus (film) 348
Santa Claus (mythical being) 19, 20, 22, 24, 29, 60, 61, 166, 189, 197, 225, 230, 342–344, 398, 400, 402
"Santa Claus" or "Santa" (place names) 114
"Santa Claus" (song) 405
Santa Claus Conquers the Martians 348–349
Santa Claus Defeats the Aliens see Santa Claus Conquers the Martians
Santa Claus Express 349
Santa Claus Is Comin' to Town (cartoon) 328, 349
"Santa Claus Is Coming to Town" (song) 11, 18, 242, 350
The Santa Clause 350
The Santa Clause 2 350–351
Santa Comes to Visit and Stays and Stays 36–37
Santa Kurosu 20
Santa Maria ad Praesepe (Rome) 108
Santa Ship 54
Santa Special *see* Santa Claus Express
Santa Train *see* Santa Claus Express
The Santa Trap 352
Santa Who? 352–353
Santabear's First Christmas 353

Santabear's High Flying Adventure 353
Santa's Workshop (cartoon) 410, 411
Santo Bambino 231
santon 173
Los Santos Inocentes 266
sapins 172
Sapolsky, Robert 8
Sarandon, Chris 299
Sargent, Dick 36, 37
Sarson, Christopher 81
Satenstein, Frank 214
"The Satisfiers" (singing group) 7
Saturnalia 92, 98, 128, 158, 189, 211, 230, 296, 353–354, 391, 436, 443
Saturnalicus Princeps 353
Saudi Arabia 270
sauna 29, 166
Saunders, Marcella 37
"Savior of the Heathen, Known" 355
"Savior of the Nations, Come" 88, 355
Sawyer, Stephanie 117
Sbarge, Raphael 28
Scarpa, Romano 171
Scarwid, Diana 11
Schaefer, George 35
Schaffel, Lauren 64
Scheffier, Dr. John 281
Scheimer, Lou 82
Schell, Maria 107
Schibli, Paul 306
Schiffman, Risa 229
Schindler's List 95
Schippers, Thomas 8
Schmidt, Christoph von 310
Schmidt, John 237
Schmutzli 381
Schnebly, Lindsay 28
Schneider, David 83
Schneider, John 82, 91, 262
schnitz 130
Schop, Johann 49, 111
Schroder, Aaron 86
Schroder, Rick 82
Schubert, Franz 25, 313
Schull, Rebecca 207
Schulz, Charles M. 63, 64, 201, 202, 220, 235
Schulz, Johann Abraham Peter 310
Schumacher, James P. 82
Schwan, Henry 131
Schwartz, Lloyd J. 48
Schwartz, Scott 126
Schwartz, Sherwood 49
Schwarzenegger, Arnold 106, 238
Schwingt freudig euch empor 355
Scoble, Keith 187
Scopp, Alfie 128
Scotland 188, 189, 193–194, 203, 216, 296; *see also* Great Britain
The Scots Musical Museum 21
Scots Reels 21
Scott, Allan 41
Scott, Eric 412
Scott, George C. 80

Scott, Michael 249
Scott, Randolph 102
Scott, Tom Everett 83
Scott, Sir Walter 25, 203, 204
Scotus, John Duns 164
Scrooge (film titles) 78, 85, 86
Scrooge (play) 75
Scrooge: A Christmas Carol 86
Scrooge and Marley 86
Scrooge, or Marley's Ghost 85
Scrooge: The Musical 86
Scrooged 86
Scrooge's Rock 'n' Roll Christmas 86
Seale, Douglas 159
Sears, Edmund Hamilton 90, 228, 401
Seasons of Peace: A Great Family Sings 319
Seaton, George 275
Second Christmas Day 24, 46, 143, 167, 181, 222, 259, 314
Second Vatican Council 55, 407, 444
Secret of Giving 106
Secret Santa (film) 355–356
Sedawie, Gale Gibson 85
Sedawie, Norman 85
Seegar, Sara 36
Seeger, Pete 52
seibo 20
Seibold, J. Otto 314
Seidelman, Arthur Allan 81, 244
Los Seises 373
Seiter, William 41
Selden, George 408
Select Scottish Airs 21
Selick, Henry 299
Sellecca, Connie 208, 219
Sellers, Peter 77
Sendak, Maurice 306
Senior, R.J. 403
Sergeyev, Nicholas 303
Sergius I, Pope 55
Serling, Rod 77, 394
"The Seven Good Joys" 356
"The Seven Joys of Mary" 356
The Seven O's *see* "O" Antiphons
"The Seven Rejoices of Mary" 356
Seville, David (pseudonym) 18, 67, 76
Shakespeare, William 199, 420
Sharp, Cecil 169, 209
Sharpsteen, Ben 411
Shatner, William 77
Shavick, James 108
Shaw, Harold 77
Shaw, Robert 77
Shawn, Wallace 83
Shayne, Gloria 154
Shayne, Konstantin 102
shchedrivka 58
shchedrivky 396
Shchedryi Vechir 396
Shchedryk (choral work) 58
Shea, Christopher 64
Shea, John 292
Shearer, Harry 360, 361
Sheen, Martin 76, 318
Sheets, Chad 366

Sheffield Iris 14
Sheffield Register 14
Shelton, Toby 268
Sheng Dan Jieh 19
Shepherd, Jean 125, 126
"Shepherd, Shake Off Your Drowsy Sleep" 357
shepherds *see* Nativity
Shepherds' Fields 269, 311
Shepherds' Mass 108, 406
"Shepherd's Rocking Carol" 330
"Shepherd's Song at Christmas" 59
"Shepherds, What Fragrance, All-Perfuming?" 420
Shepphird, John 219, 352
Sheridan, Jamie 7
Sherry, Diane 38
Sherwood, Robert E. 41
shide 20
Shields, Brooke 45
Shigeta, James 77
shimenawa 20
Shiney Brite Company 132
Shirley, Eliza 346
shishi mai 20
Shoemaker and the Elves (cartoon) 156
Shogatsu 20
shooting in Christmas 143, 179, 301
shooting in the New Year 98, 143
Shower of Stars 78
"showing the Christ Child" (custom) 23
Shropshire, Dr. Elmo 187, 188
"The Sicilian Mariners' Hymn," 313
"Side by Side" 10
Siddoway, Richard 110, 117, 135, 136, 392, 393
Sie werden aus Saba alle kommen 47
Siegel, Andy 91
Siegler, Bill 80
Sierra Leone 4
Sigman, Carl 262
signillaria 354
"Silent Night" 10, 11, 38, 39, 45, 78, 95, 185, 204, 243, 265, 357–359
Silo, Susan 28, 90
"Silver and Gold" 336
"Silver Bells" 9, 10, 18, 39, 45, 246, 358
Silverman, David 360
Silvers, Nancy 104
Silvers, Phil 45
Silvesterkläuse 382
Silvesterumzug 382
Sim, Alastair 78, 79, 86
Simbang Gabi 320
Simeone, Harry 18, 154, 249, 250
Simmons, Richard 336
"The Simpsons Roasting on an Open Fire" (television episode) 359–360
Sinatra, Frank 21, 38, 134
Sinatra, Nancy 38
Sinbad (actor) 238
Sinclair, Ronald 77
"Sing We Now of Christmas" 361

Singerman, Wesley 64
The Singing Master's Assistant 408
Singleton, Penny 83
Sinner's Holiday 101
Sinterklaas 20, 258, 342, 398
Sirani, Elisabetta 124
sirupssnipper 300
Sisters at Heart 37
Sixtus III, Pope 108
"Skater's Waltz" 10
Skelton, Red 45, 328, 338
The Sketch Book of Geoffrey Crayon, Gent. 226
Skinflint: A Country Christmas Carol 86–87
"Skinner's Sense of Snow" (television episode) 360
Skipping Christmas 361–362
Skotkonung, Olaf 378
Slan, Jon 76
Slaughter of the Innocents 99, 140, 273, 286; *see also* Holy Innocents Day
Slave Songs of the United States 330
slaves 49, 398
"Sleep, Baby Mine" 6
"Sleepers, Awake! A Voice Is Calling" 214, 362–363
"Sleigh Ride" 10, 18, 39, 86, 242, 363, 441
Sleipner (mythical steed) 167, 301, 345, 380, 436, 443
slizikai 30
Slovak Republic 363–366
The Small One: A Story for Those Who Like Christmas and Small Donkeys 366
Small Songs for Small Singers 40
smånisser 301
Smart, Henry 14
Smert, Richard 44
Smight, Jack 304, 394
Smith, Christopher 77
Smith, Hal 48, 59, 84, 125, 170, 238, 346, 347, 366, 387, 435, 442, 443
Smith, Jaclyn 298
Smith, Kate 38
Smith, Kurtwood 104
Smith, O. 75
Smith, Richard B. 18, 437
Smith, Sid 45
Smith, Thorne 78
Smith, Tom 192, 193
Smith, Yeardley 360, 361
A Smoky Mountain Christmas 366–367
smörgåsbord 378, 379
Smothers, Tom 32
The Smurfs' Christmas Special 200, 367
snapdragon 190, 227
Snegurochka 339, 340
A Snow White Christmas 368
The Snowman 368
Society of the Friends of the Nativity 23

Society of the Friends of the Trees 196
Il Sogno dell' usuraio 82
Sol (god) 92
Sole, Richard 103
Solemnity of Mary 297, 407
Solo, Robert H. 86
Some Ancient Christmas Carols 169, 408
"Some Children *see* Him" 6, 7, 10, 86
Somerset-Ward, Richard 76
"The Somerset Wassail" 183
"Song of the Ass" 174
"Song of the Bagpipers" 57–58
"Song of the Three Kings" 24
Songs and Carols 89
Songs for the Hill-Folk 221
Songs of Praise 257
Songs of Syon 42, 153
Songs of the Nativity 89, 205
Sontgaclau 381
Sorcova 331, 332
Sottnick, Mark 353
Soucie, Kath 16, 81, 170
Soulful Christmas (album) 383
Sousa, John Philip 95
South Africa, Republic of 4
South America 368–373
Souther, John 87
The Southern Harmony 50
Southwell, Robert 63
Spain 373–374
Spano, Vincent 112
Sparger, Rex 86
Spears, Ken 125
Spector, Joel 87
speculaas 259
speculoos 258
Speers, Bill 268
Spelling, Tori 77
Spencer, Frances Kipps 67, 68
Spielman, Fred 87
Spike Jones and His City Slickers 7
Spilman, Jonathan E. 26
Spinney, Caroll 282
"The Spirit" (television episode) 413
Sporn, Michael 255, 353
"Spring Carol" 63
Spring Festival 19
Springer, Philip 18, 347
Springer, Tony 18, 347
Sprouse, Cole 219
Sprouse, Dylan 219
Spyri, Johanna 204
Squires, Emily 156
Sri Lanka 21
Stafford, Jo 38
Stainer, John 89, 169, 184, 205, 356, 357, 415, 419
"Staines Morris" (tune) 42
Stalin, Joseph 339
Stallings, Laurence 102
stanenik 52
Stanley Brothers 32
Stannard, Eliot 85
Stansbury, Arthur 66
Stanton, Harry Dean 316

Stanwyck, Barbara 106, 328
Stapleton, Maureen 177
Star Boys 301, 365, 379
The Star Carol (album) 7
"The Star Carol" (song) 6–7
"Star in the East" (song) 50
Star Man 323
Star of Bethlehem 30, 51, 146, 322, 338, 364, 374–375, 395
Statler Brothers 86
Stealing Christmas 375–376
steaua 331
Stedry Vecer 144
Steenburgen, Mary 155, 316
Steinbeck, John 182
Steinberg, Cathy 64
Steinman, Leonard 82
Stéphan, Dom John 308
Stephenson, John 59, 125, 170, 171, 442, 443
Sterling, Robert 78
Stern, Daniel 211
Stern, Mark Alexander 237
Sternsinger 24, 381
Stevens, Connie 38, 39, 44, 256
Stevens, George 291
Stevens, Lisa 306
Stevens, Risë 185
Stevens, Stella 108
Stewart, Jimmy 87, 233
Stewart, Patrick 80
Stewart, Tonea 316
Stickney, Dorothy 412
Stiles, Victor 348
"Stille Nacht" 357
Stillman, Al 18, 212
The Stingiest Man in Town 87, 328
Stipe, Michael 314
Stir-Up Sunday 192
Stirling, Edward 75
stjärn gossar 379
Stocker, John 26
stockings 4, 5
"Stockport" 69
Stokey, Mike 78
Stollen 258
Stone, Jack 285
Stone, Milburn 198
Storch, Larry 236
Storke, William F. 80
Storm, Gale 45
"The Story of a Starry Night" (song) 21
The Story of Babar 26
The Story of Holly and Ivy 376
"The Story of the Goblins Who Stole a Sexton" 74
Stossel, Ludwig 161
Stout, Austin 329
Stowe, Madeleine 292
The Strange Christmas Dinner 87
Strasser, Josef 358
Stratas, Teresa 8
Stratford, Tracy 64
Strathspey Reels 21
Stratton, Dee 236
Strauss, Johann 24
Stravinsky, Igor 386

straw 30, 51, 142, 143, 146, 322, 364, 395
La Strega 232
strenae 354
Strenia (goddess) 354
Strickland, Gail 177
strigaturi 332
Strober, Rena 237
strull 300
Struthers, Sally 38
Studwell, William 6
Styne, Jule 18, 84, 134, 247
Such Is Life 255
sufganiyot 201
Sugar Bowl 298
sugar tree 129
sugarplums 376
sugoroku 20
Sullivan, Arthur 228
Sullivan, Robert 119
Sundblom, Haddon 344
superstitions 145, 323, 364, 365, 366, 376–378; Candlemas 55; candles 300; holly and ivy 210; New Year's Day 296–297; nuts and honey 231; St. Lucia's Day 3; twelve days of Christmas 391, 392; Yule log 443, 444; *see also* individual countries
survakam 52
survaknitsa 52
Susceno, Richard 107
Suso, Heinrich 185
Sutherland, Hal 82
Sutherland, Kiefer 305
Sutphin, Paul 50
"Suzy Snowflake" 306, 378
Svateho Stepana 147
Svaty Mikulas 144, 345, 363
Svetlanov, Evgenii 305
Sviata Vecheria 395
Sviatyj Mykloaj 395
swaddling clothes 285
Swag Man 22
Swanton, Scott 106
Sweden 378–381
Sweeney, Bob 9
"Sweet Little Jesus Boy" 253
Sweeten, Madylin 112
Swetland, William 136
Swiety Mikolaj 322
Swift, Allen 160, 250, 321, 389
Swift, David 78
Swinging in the Sun (custom) 373
The Swinging Nutcracker 306
"Swinging on a Star" 185
Swit, Loretta 35, 45
Switzer, Carl "Alfalfa" 185, 234
Switzer, Michael 207, 384, 405
Switzerland 381–382
The Sword in the Stone 95
Sydow, Max von 291
Sykes, Peter 291
Sylvester (mythical being) 24, 278
Sylvester, Joshua 209
Sylvester I, Pope Saint 17, 24, 147, 181, 278, 382; *see also* Saint Sylvester's Day

Symington, Stuart 44
Synchretics 5
Synod of Constantinople 93
Synod of Lerida 1
Synod of Mâcon 1
Synod of Saragossa 1
Synod of Whitby 188
Syntaxis of the Blessed Virgin 396
Syracuse, Sicily 2
Syria 270–271
szopka see Nativity scene
Szwarc, Jeannot 348

Ta Chiu 19
tabot 4
Taft, William Howard 425
Taft High School 77
Takács, Tibor 315, 393
takoage 20
Talbot, Mary 40
Tales from Dickens 79
Tallis, Thomas 313
Talvistepüha 29
Tamayo, Manuel 83
Tarta, Alexandre 305
Tate, Kevin 36
Tate, Nahum 421
Taweel, George 141
Tay, Michael 155
Taylor, Buck 198
Taylor, Greg 71, 136, 326, 327, 376
Taylor, Jud 90, 209
Taylor, Nannie Lou 32
Taylor, Russi 90, 171, 267, 268, 269, 360
Taylor, Samuel 78
Taylor, Zachary 424
Tazewell, Charles 255, 256, 366
Tchaikovsky, Peter I. 302, 303, 376
Tea and Sugar Train 22
Ted E. Bear Rescues Santa Claus 32
Tédesco, Jean 254
Tedesco, Lou 86
Telesphorus, bishop of Rome 15
Temple, Shirley 28, 204
Ten Christmas Carols from the Southern Appalachian Mountains 141
Tennyson, Alfred, Lord 329, 330
Tepper, Sid 306, 378
Terry, Richard 356
Terry-Thomas 38
Tertullian, theologian of Carthage 92, 128
Tetley, Walter 125
Tewksbury, Peter 162
Thaddeus the Apostle 16
Thanksgiving Day 401, 404
"That Yonge Child" 63
Thatcher, Kirk R. 232
Théâtre Musical de Paris Châtelet 305
Theodore, Pope 108
Theodosius I, Roman emperor of the East 93, 94
"There Is No Rose of Such Virtue" 62, 383
These Happy Golden Years 252–253

Thibodeaux, Keith 218
"This Christmas" 18, 393
This Is Christmas (album) 6
"This Is Christmas" (song) 6–7
"This Little Babe" 63
Thomas, Danny 152, 328
Thomas, Dylan 66
Thomas, Jake 284
Thomas, Jonathan Taylor 222
Thomas, Marlo 152, 235, 328
Thomas, Richard 71, 119, 412, 413, 442
Thomas Jefferson High School 37
"Thomasing" (custom) 3
Thomasnikolo 23
Thompson, Hugh 121
Thompson, Lea 375
Thomson, George 21
Thor (god) 167, 301, 342, 344, 345, 380, 443
Thorhallson, Thorlakur, Saint 221
Thorndike, Russell 85
"Thou Didst Leave Thy Throne" 383
Three Days 383–384
Three Dog Night 86
Three Kings (characters) 24, 60, 143, 372; *see also* Wise Men
"The Three Kings" (poem) 384
Three Kings Day *see* Epiphany
"Three Kings of Orient" *see* "We Three Kings of Orient Are"
Three Wise Men *see* Wise Men
Threlfall, David 292
throat singing 55
thyme 117
Tichenor, Harold 82
Tichy, Gerard 292
Tierney, Lawrence 360
Tiersot, Julien 51
Till, Eric 76
Tillis, Mel 86
Time Flies: A Reading Diary 257
"A Time to Shine" 10
Times Square, New York 297
Timkat 3, 4
Tingwell, Charles 134
"tinsel" (Christmas tree decoration) 132
Tirggel 381
"'Tis So Sweet to Trust in Jesus" 26
"'Tis the Fifteenth Season" (television episode) 360–361
'Tis the Season Christmas Trivia 385
'Tis the Season to Be Smurfy 200, 367
tjugondedag Knut 380
To Grandmother's House We Go 385
toasting (custom) 413, 414
Tobias, George 36, 37
Toddman, David R. 82
Tom and Jerry's Night Before Christmas 385–386
Tom Nicholas (mythical being) 23
"Tomorrow Shall Be My Dancing Day" 386
Tonge, Philip 275
El Tope 61
Topper 78

Tordesillas, Jesús 83
Tormé, Mel 18, 121, 242, 243
Torre, Janice 87
Torrence, Dean 86
tortellini 231
toshidana 20
toshigami 20
toshikoshi soba 20
toso 20
Touch of Peace 269, 270
Tournament of Roses 297, 298
tourtières 54
Towers, Harry Alan 79
Towers, Lisa 12
The Town That Santa Forgot 200, 386–387
A Town Without Christmas 387–388
Towneley Cycle of mystery plays 100
Toy Tinkers 238
"Toyland" (song) 27
Toyland Broadcast 386
Toys for Tots 388
The Toys Who Saved Christmas 216
Tozzi, Giorgio 8
Trachtenberg, Michelle 107, 329
Tracy, Lee 246
The Trail to Christmas 87
The Travailes of the Three English Brothers 101
Travers, Henry 32, 233
Travis, Nancy 223
Travis, Randy 16, 60, 208
Treacher, Arthur 78, 204
Treaty of Dresden 95
Treaty of Ghent 95, 424
Trebek, Alex 360
Tree of Life 21
Tree of Light 19
Tremayne, Les 84, 408
Tresterer 24
"Treuer Heiland" 17–18
Tri Krále 365
Tri kralu 147
Trigg, Patsy 187
Trinidad and Tobago 419
Trinity Boys' Choir 39, 78
Tripp, David 127
Tripp, Paul 127
Tritt, Travis 107
troika 339
Troyer, Verne 83
Truman, Harry S. 403, 427
Truman Capote's "A Christmas Memory" 109
Trump, Donald 212
Tubb, Ernest 42
Tuchner, Michael 186
Turkey 271
Turmblasen 23, 181
Turnbaugh, Brenda and Wendi (twins) 253
Turner, Brad 283
Turner, Frank 12
turron de mani 369
turta 331

"'Twas in the Moon of Wintertime" 217
"'Twas the Night Before Christmas" (poem) *see* "A Visit from St. Nicholas"
'Twas the Night Before Christmas (television episode) 213–214
'Twas the Night Before Christmas (television special) 328, 388–389, 410
"'Twas the Night Before Christmas Song" 336, 410
Twelfth Night 158–159, 181, 192, 194, 391
"The Twelve Days of Christmas" (song) 389–390
Twelve Days of Christmas (time period) 390–392
Twelve Days of Christmas at Darling Harbor 22
Twelve Tales of Christmas 392–393
Twice Upon a Christmas 393
Twiggy (pop star) 39
The Twilight Zone 77, 393–394
Two Hundred Folk Carols 356
Tych, Jean 80
Tyler, Aisha 351
Tyler, Ginny 77
Tyler, John 424
Tyson, Cicely 84, 243

Ubach, Alanna 83
Uganda 4–5
Ukko (mythical steed) 167
Ukraine 394–397
Ullman, Doris 221
Uluru 22
Umblatul cu capra 332
Umblatul cu ursul 332
"Un flambeau, Jeannette, Isabelle" 50–51
Underwood, Kianna 347
Union Harmony or Family Musician 50
Unitas Fratrum 279
United Nations Children's Choir 38
United States 397–404; Christmas Day as legal holiday 401; commercialism 401–402; National Christmas Tree and Christmas Pageant of Peace 402–403; Nation's Christmas Tree 403–404; New Year's Day in 297–298; twenty-first century 404
Unlikely Angel 404–405
Unwin, Dave 161
Up-Helly-Aa 194
"Up on the Housetop" 241, 405
Up Your Chimney 187
Urban IV, Pope 99, 140
Urbana, Carl 59
Urbi et Orbi papal message 406
Urich, Robert 11
Urn of Fate 158, 231, 373
Uruguay 372
Ustinov, Peter 291

Vaccaro, Brenda 295

Vainonen, Vassili 305
Valentine, Karen 38
Van Allsburg, Chris 323, 324
Van Ark, Joan 45
Van Bork, Bert 182
Van Buren, Martin 424
Vance, Courtney B. 41
Vance, Vivian 218
Vander Pyl, Jean 83, 170, 171, 347
Van Doren Stern, Philip 232
Van Dyke, Dick 150, 151, 387
Van Dyke, Henry 168, 317, 318
Van Dyke, Jerry 16, 385
Van Eyck, Jan 122
Van Heusen, Jimmy 33
Vanillekipferl 24
vanillekranse 149
VanLiere, Donna 69, 70, 120, 121
vanocka 146
Van Patten, Dick 10, 305, 352
"Variations sur un vieux noël" 361
Varney, Jim 16, 159
Vasilopita 197
Vasilyev, Vladimir 305
The Vatican 405–408; Holy Year of Jubilee 407; works of art 407–408
Vaughns, Byron 60
La Vecchia 232
Vegh, Mark S. 83
Venable, David 105
Venable, Ronald 105
"Vénès leou vieira la Pieoucelle" (carol) 50
Venezuela 372–373
"Veni, redemptor gentium" 88, 355
Vera-Ellen 421
Verbeek, Pieter 280
Vergel, Alberto Gonzáles 83
Vernon, Jackie 175, 176, 333
vertep *see* Nativity scene
A Very Brady Christmas 48
A Very Goofy Christmas 268
A Very Merry Cricket 408
A Very Special Christmas (album) 347
Victoria, queen of England 130
Victoria Theatre (Halifax) 80
Victoria, Tomás Luis de 312
Vieira, Asia 208
Vieja Belén 417
Viejo Pascuero 370
Vienna Boys Choir 250
Vienna Philharmonic Orchestra 24
Vier ächte Tyroler Lieder 358
Vigilia 364
Vigoda, Abe 326
Villa de Navidad 397
"Village of St. Bernadette" (song) 10
villancicos 325, 373
Villenueve, Louise 27
Vinton, Will 138, 139
Virgin del Rosario 370
Virgin Mary 2, 25, 55, 61, 63, 100, 108, 140, 141, 162, 164, 165, 210, 220, 257, 262, 273, 293, 296, 297, 356, 383; *see also* Nativity; The Vatican
"A Virgin Unspotted" 408

Virginia Opera Association 80
The Virtue of Rags 87
A Vision of Sugar Plums 36
"A Visit from St. Nicholas" 25, 90, 282, 327, 343, 376, 388, 400, 405, 408–410
Vladimir I, grand prince of Kiev, Russia 338
Voce di Melodia 242
Vogl, Johann Michael 25
"The Voice of Christmas" 48
Voices of Jimmy Joyce 6
Volodymyr, prince of Ukraine 394
"Vom Himmel hoch, da komm' ich her" 111, 174–175, 311
"Vom Himmel kam der Engel Schar" 174
vongoli 231
Vormsi, Island of 29
Vortigern, king of the Britons, 413
votae 354
Voyagis, Yorgo 291
Vsevolozhsky, Ivan 303

"W zlobie lezy" 224
"Wachet auf! Ruft uns die Stimme" 214, 362
Wade, John F. 308, 309, 310
Wainamoinen (mythical being) 167
Wainwright, John 68
"Wait Till the Sun Shines, Nellie" 39
Waite, Ralph 412
Waits 68, 227, 356, 410–411
Wakefield Cycle of mystery plays 100
Walburg, Lori 57
Waldo, Janet 83, 125, 442, 443
Wales 188, 194–195, 216; *see also* Great Britain
Wales, Dr. Joseph 118
"Walk Through Advent" (custom) 23
Walker, Matthew 11, 393
Walker, William 50
Wallace, Earl 46
Wallace, Lewis 33, 34
Wallace, Marcia 360
Wallace, Pamela 46
Wallace-Stone, Dee 112, 134
Wallerstein, Herb 199
Walmsley, Jon 412
Walsh, Alex 366
Walsh, M. Emmet 362
Walsh, Vivian 314
A Walt Disney Christmas 411
Walters, Anthony 80
Walters, Mark 207
Walther, Johann 47, 186
The Waltons 234, 411–413
Ward, Kelly 28
Ward, Zack 126
Ware, Charles 330
Waring, Richard 79
Warini 62
Warner, David 80
Warner, H.B. 233
Warner, Jack 78
Warner, Malcom Jamal 10

Warner, Zoë 42
Warren, Katherine 161
Warren, Michael 243
Warrenton, Lule 40
Washburn, Bryant 87
Washington, Denzel 41
Washington, George 95, 123, 397, 423
wassail 189, 227, 413–414
"Wassail, O Wassail All Over the Town" 183
"Wassail Song" 205, 411
"Wassail, Wassail All Over the Town" 183
wassailing the fruit trees 414
Watch Night service 281
"Watchman, Tell Us of the Night" 414
Waterman, Mary Gleason 239
Waters, John 134
Watkins, Thom 76
Watson, Donald 40
Watteville, Johannes von 281
Watts, Isaac 89, 242
Watts, Naomi 136
Wayne, John 45
"We Are Santa's Elves" 336
"We Have Heard the Joyful Sound" 26
"We Need a Little Christmas" 18, 39, 414–415
"We Three Kings of Orient Are" 39, 138, 401, 415
We Wish You a Merry Christmas (album) 52
"We Wish You a Merry Christmas" (song) 11, 283, 411, 414, 415
Weaver, Dennis 198
Weaver, John 101
The Weavers 52
Webb, Charles 75
Webbe, Samuel 308
Webber, Timothy 317
Weber, Steven 76
Webster, George P. 343
Webster, Nicholas 349
Webster, Paul 388
Wedderburn, James 63
Wedderburn, John 63
Wedderburn, Robert 63
Wee Winter Singers 168, 176, 389, 441
Weihnachtsguetzli 381
Ein Weihnachtslied in Prosa oder Eine Geistergeschichte zum Christfest 81
Weihnachtsmann 179
Ein Weihnachtsmärchen 81
Weihnachtsoratorium 111
Weihnachtspyramide 130
Weihnachtstramer 381
Weisberg, Steve 104
Weiss, Marie 108
"Wel, dyma'r borau gorau i gyd" (song) 386
Weldon, Frank 106
Welker, Frank 80, 81, 83, 90, 171, 293

"We'll Dress the House" 6–7
The Well Tempered Clavier 25
Welles, Orson 235, 292
Wells, Richard 305
Wells, Robert 18, 121
werewolves 199
Wery, Carl 81
Wesley, Charles 202
West, Adam 38
West, Billy 314
West, Dottie 86
West Indies 416–419
Western Australian Christmas tree 116–117
Westminster Children's Choir 349
"We've Been a While A-Wandering" 183, 205
Wharton, Theodore 87
"What Are the Signs" 6
"What Are You Doing New Year's Eve?" 10
"What Child Is This?" 17, 243, 419–420
"What Is This Fragrance?" 420
"What Is This Perfume So Appealing?" 420
"What Perfume This? Oh Shepherds Say" 420
Wheeler, John 58
When Angels Come to Town 420
"When Christ, the Son of Mary" 57–58
"When Joseph Was an Old Man" 64
"When Santa Claus Gets Your Letter" 336
"Whence Comes This Rush of Wings Afar?" 58
"Whence Is That Goodly Fragrance?" 420–421
"While by My Sheep" 421
"While Shepherds Watched Their Flocks" 228, 421
"Whistle While You Work" 10
Whitaker, Johnny 256
White, Betty 375
White, David 36, 37
White, Joshua 79
White, Willard 8
White Christmas (film) 208, 421–422
"White Christmas" (song) 9, 11, 18, 37, 38, 39, 86, 168, 187, 208, 335, 401, 422, 423
The White House 44, 399, 423–435
Whitefield, George 202
Whiting, Richard 113, 114
Whitley, Patrick 135
Whitmire, Steve 84, 157, 232, 283
Whitmore, Dean 243
Whitmore, James 81
"Who's Afraid of the Big Bad Wolf?" 27
Wickes, Mary 104
"Wie schön leuchtet der Morgenstern" 214
Wiedergott, Karl 360
Wiegenlieder 293
Wienechtchind 382

Wierum, Howard 79
Wiggin, Kate Douglas Smith 39
Wigilia 322, 323
Wild, Franz Josef 81
Wild, Jack 38
Wild Hunt (mythical group) 23, 344, 436
Wild Man (god) 343, 345
Wilder, Almanzo 251–253
Wilder, Laura Ingalls 251–253
Wildes Gjaid 23
Wiley, Roland John 305
Wilhousky, Peter J. 18, 58
Williams, Andy 9–11, 154, 235, 422
Williams, Barry 48
Williams, Billy Dee 107
Williams, Bobby 10, 11
Williams, Bransby 75, 77, 78, 85
Williams, JoBeth 63
Williams, Kimberly 121
Williams, Paul 84, 298
Williams, Ralph Vaughan 169, 312
Williams, Richard 79, 445
Williams, R.J. 298
Williams, Vanessa 82, 243, 347
Williams Brothers 9–11
Williamson, Laird 79
Willis, Richard Storrs 90, 228
Willson, Meredith 18, 235
Wilson, Alexandra 136
Wilson, Mara 276
Wilson, Marie 28
Wilson, Rita 238
Wilson, Roy 16
Wilson, Tom 445
Wilson, Woodrow 402, 426
Winchell, April 81
Winchell, Paul 125, 367
"Winchester Old" (tune) 421
Windom, William 276, 394, 413
Winfield, Paul 376
Winfrid (or Winfried), St. Boniface *see* Saint Boniface
Wing, Paul 334
Winkler, Henry 76, 316, 367
Winkworth, Catherine 8, 174, 215, 355, 363
Winnie the Pooh and Christmas Too 435
Winslet, Kate 81
Winter, Edward 104
winter solstice 92, 435–437
"Winter Wonderland" 18, 39, 86, 176, 242, 437
Winters, Jonathan 28, 175, 376
Winters, Shelley 176, 333
Wise Men 141, 181, 210, 220, 280, 354, 374, 375, 437–439; *see also* Magi; Nativity; Star of Bethlehem; Three Kings
The Wish That Changed Christmas 376
witches 210, 232
Woden (god) *see* Odin
Wojciechowski, Susan 110
"Wolcum Yole" 62
Wolff, Glen 119
Wolk, Andy 121, 165, 387, 420

Women's Christmas 226
"Wonderful Christmastime" 18, 440
Wood, Charles 42
Wood, Natalie 275
Wood, Ted 84
Woodard, Alfre 86
Wooden Soldiers 27
Woodson, Bill 87
Woodward, Edward 80
Woodward, George R. 41, 153
Woolley, Monty 41
Wopat, Tom 82, 91
Work, Frederick Jerome 183, 184
Work, John W., III 184
Work, John Wesley, Jr. 183, 184
Workman, Jimmy 106
works of art *see* Nativity [works of art]; The Vatican [works of art]
World Day of Peace 407
Worley, Jo Anne 182, 305
Worre, John 82
Worsley, John 79
wren boys 216
wren bush 216
Wright, Kay 82, 90, 368
Wright, Peter 305
Wright, Teresa 41
Wright, Thomas 89
Wright, Will 9, 87
Wrights, B.J. 53
Wrye, Donald 235
Wyatt, Jane 161
Wyle, George 18, 235, 236
Wynkyn de Worde, Jan van 43, 89
Wynn, Ed 28

Wynn, George 85
Wynn, Keenan 349

Xmas 440
Xmas in the USA 187

yalynka 396
yamurluci 52
Yavheh, Cyrus 106
year-crossing noodles 20
The Year Without a Santa Claus 328, 441
Yellen, Barry B. 127
Yes, Virginia, There Is a Santa Claus 326, 441–442
Yogi Bear's All-Star Comedy Christmas Caper 200, 442
Yogi's First Christmas 200, 442–443
Yon, Pietro A. 181, 182
York, Dick 36
York, Michael 80
York, Susannah 80
York Cycle of mystery plays 100
Yorke, Wayne Thomas 315, 393
"Yorkshire" (tune) 69
"The Yorkshire Wassail Song" 183, 205
Yoshida, Miyako 305
"You Meet the Nicest People" 10
Young, Alan 84, 171, 268
Young, Dalene 90
Young, John F. 358
Young, Loretta 40, 41, 102, 139, 256

Young, Mark 28
Young, Robert 161
Young, Steve 314
Youngest Camel 271
Yule 166, 181, 203, 221, 378, 443–444; *see also* Jul
Yule buck 166
Yule log 49, 55, 227, 354, 391, 397, 443, 444

Zachary, Beulah 78
Zachau, Friedrich Wilhelm 186
Zadora, Pia 348
Zagmuk 217, 354, 443
Zahm, Matthew 130
zalabya 3
zampognari 230
Zarnack, August 308
Zeffirelli, Franco 292
Zemeckis, Robert 324
Ziemassvetki 29
Ziggy's Gift 445
Zimbabwe 5
Zimbalist, Ephrem, Jr. 177
Zimbalist, Stephanie 177
Zimtsterne 24
Zindel, Paul 28
Zinzendorf, Count Nicholas Ludwig von 279
Zisk, Craig 276
zoni 20
Zoroaster, Persian prophet 439
zvjezdari 143
Zwarte Piet 258, 345
Die Zwölf Rauchnächte 181